Catholic Seminarian turned Christian Rapper turned Muslim Fundamentalist

Gregory Heary

Preface

I hope my intentions for writing this book are for the sake of God because actions are according to intentions. If something is done for other than the sake of God then it will be of little to no benefit in the afterlife. God-willing this book discloses what Islam teaches and what a Muslim Fundamentalist is. Since both are so often misunderstood and misrepresented by the mass media many have been deceived and are unaware of the danger ignorance about Islam puts them in. The false information that some media organizations have spread has jeopardized the safety of every non-Muslim who falls prey to their false reporting. I tried not to waste words and have written in a straightforward conversational style. Hopefully this information isn't misinterpreted as being inflammatory know-it-allism or conceited, true knowledge is acted upon and not just publicized or memorized. It seems arrogant for an author to profit from people paying them to read a book that they wrote about themselves. If it were up to me I'd give you this book for free with the only condition being that you pay attention, remember and act upon any beneficial information contained on these pages. Afterall if an author isn't willing to write what they are writing for free without getting paid for it, then there is a very good chance that whatever they've written in their book is not worth reading; or at the least it implies that they aren't an author who truly cares about the information they are writing. You can't put a price on a good book and you can't accept a price for selling a bad book. Any book worth reading should be available for free and those which aren't worth reading really shouldn't be available to read since they aren't worth reading. What's worse is religious folk who will try selling you a "book of God" when God has not nor can God put a pricetag on any genuine book he wants mankind to read, because if you had to pay to read God's book then the very first person to read it would've had to pay God to obtain it, and everyone knows that nobody has ever claimed to have bought God's book from God himself. That's not to say a book from God doesn't exist and can't be sold, but it does mean that a genuine book of God should never be sold. At the very least if people still want to sell books, religious books attributed to God should not be sold because everyone knows that God isn't getting the money that people are paying for such books. But alas until others wakeup to the crime of selling religious books or books in general then many of us will have to pay for many books. Yet having written this book I cannot possibly sell it for any price to any person and as an author I feel I must condemn those who profit by penning pages and those who profit from printing or selling any type of books. If I or anyone else is to write a book then with the state of the book industry as it is now, I believe books should be written containing a condemnation of those who profit from writing or from the writings of others. Authors have to care, the move towards free books must start with those who write them. If authors refuse to decline compensation for writing then our species will always be stuck paying for books. Unfortunately the book industry and those within it tend to desire to protect their profits and unionize or silently agree to sell, typically only giving away free books for the sake of promotion or increased distribution.

Hence in my first paragraph I feel it necessary to challenge and expose these profiteering page writers and testify that I am not one of them. Talk is cheap but books should be free. I feel it'd be tantamount to disrespect and a manifest insult to request any reader to pay me to read what I've written. You as the reader have dignity to me, too much dignity and honor to be a literary customer. Should you be willing to spend the time and energy to read then that is qualification enough for you to read my book, for an author to charge anything more than publication cost(if that) would be oppression by an author upon his readers. Authors are supposed to be teachers teaching via writing, not traders earning due to others learning. I feel the authors who are traders are traitors to their readers. Authors and Readers are engaged in a special relationship when one writes a book and the other reads it. In a very real sense, my book creates and amounts to a link and relationship between me and you. Such a relationship must start with a certain amount of respect, so out of respect to you this is free. Since I'm not going to pay you money to read then you shouldn't be paying me money to write what you read. Not to dwell on such a topic excessively but as the person "on the other side of the book" equation/relationship I feel I should tell you the truth of what it's like being on the author's side of the book so you can better understand books and authors so as to benefit from this one and avoid the abusive authors who manipulate/cheat/abuse their readers. It's because of such other authors that I almost feel ashamed to be called an author in any capacity, being an author is no honor when you realize who the other authors throughout history have been. Authors include some of the worst people who have ever lived, there are also a few semi-decent exceptions. Most authors have no business writing a book because they make writing a book their business. Writing is not "work" it is a responsibility. I ask you no reward for this message my reward is only from God, who I hope will reward me with good in this life and more importantly the next. I apologize if you had to pay publication cost to read this and assure you anything extra that may have come to me in form of a royalty is given to charity.

Out of respect to the prophets and messengers of God I put the letters "*pbuh*" after their names as an abbreviation for "*peace be upon him*". Sometimes I used the letters "*pbut*" meaning "*peace be upon them*" when mentioning multiple prophets at a time.

When reading books I find that having a notebook and writing utensil to take notes or write down important information is very useful. It helps me to pay attention while reading and improves my memory of what I read. Taking notes while reading also leaves behind valuable sheet(s) of important information when you finish. I think you would also find it useful. Taking notes eliminates the need to underline or bend over the pages of the book that contain information you want to remember. If at the end you don't remember what you read, then you practically wasted your time reading since you would have to read it over and over again in order to utilize this book in a way that benefits you in your life. Another tip for reading this book is to not listen to music while reading as it is proven to distract and make retention more difficult. These are just suggestions which I think will improve your reading experiences as they improve mine.

To me religion is the most important and serious matter in the world, as it is for many others. As such it can be a touchy subject that causes people to become passionate or emotional when religious views are mentioned which they disagree with and it causes people to get upset sometimes. I sure know how it feels when a person's religious views don't agree with my own 100%, even if a person agrees with me 99% sometimes that 1% difference of opinion can arouse angry feelings. If you disagree with what I've written please don't have hurt feelings or be resentful because many bad things in the world today happen as a direct result of poor emotional management. If you feel strong emotions while reading then that is a good sign that you care about religion and realize its importance. However it is also important not to let emotions control you because most sins start with emotions or passions before the actions are committed. The intellectual person will always listen to the "other side" and then deduce the truth. Emotions should never be allowed to come between a person and the truth. Just because it's a fact we have emotions, that does not turn our emotions into facts. Please don't judge what I've written based solely on any emotional reaction you may experience while reading, whether positive or negative. To do so would mean that emotionalism had become your religion, and emotionalism is the religion of Satan.

Unfortunately we live in a time where honesty is controversial and telling the truth is taboo. It has never been easy to speak, hear, write or read the truth under such social conditions. Even so the truth has always been necessary. This is a second warning before proceeding to not let emotions cloud your judgment. I have tried my best to be entirely honest and straightforward throughout, being upfront and bold is bound to trigger an emotional reaction. While writing this many emotions arose within me so I'm sure it will stir emotions within you as well. Remember to be mature no matter how emotional this book makes you feel whether you love, like, dislike, hate, agree, or disagree; do not lose control. To lose self-control is to lose yourself, don't be a loser (of self-control). We should place more value on the truth than emotions or feelings. This book is not just an exercise for the eyes and mind but is an exercise for the heart as well.

There is no rush to read this book all at once, but we all have limited time before we die. As the writer I would like you to finish reading this before you die. Not to put any pressure on you, but try not to procrastinate. It would make me uncomfortable if you were to die without finishing so don't put me in that awkward situation by dying while leaving behind a bookmark between the pages. If I was able to finish writing it before dying, you can finish reading it before dying, God-willing.

In this 2nd edition I have omitted the chapter on Jihad, which was present in the first edition in order to reduce the length of this book. For those interested in my writings on that subject I have published that chapter in a separate work entitled "Proper Jihad" by Gregory Heary.

THE BEGINNING

There are some people who do not believe God exists, whether you believe they exist or not there are people like this. You should know by now that this book includes some information about religion in it. Since this book also contains information about my life I feel it's necessary to give some background as to why someone would believe in God, so that you can better understand where I was coming from and why having a belief in God would influence my decision-making. To mention all the evidence for the existence of God is beyond my abilities, and it would contain too much information for any reader to possibly finish reading. Since the people who disbelieve in God also tend to reject revelations from God, I will make a simple argument appealing to basic logic. Most Atheists actually base their atheism on emotional reasons instead of logical reasoning or conclusions reached by astute unbiased scientific analysis. Atheists tend to use science as a scapegoat to justify their emotional disbelief that is done due to dissatisfaction with life or for revenge. Usually most atheists are dissatisfied with something that happened in their life and have some story such as a parent or spouse dying, being an orphan, being crippled, losing a friend, getting abused or suffering some major trauma or loss that leads them to think *"How could this happen to me if God exists? Since I feel so sad then God must not exist because life isn't fair and I feel upset instead of happy."* It sounds ridiculous but at the core level this is why many atheists don't believe in God, because they think they should be perpetually happy on earth and never suffer loss or emotional distress if God exists. This is because some politicians said God has given mankind the "right to life and the pursuit of happiness", therefore believing such things are God-given "rights" if they feel these rights were infringed they decide God must not exist so they don't have to cope with their loss in a healthy manner. They disbelieve in God to get revenge for their emotional misery. Or some atheists cite humanitarian reasoning for their atheism such as *"Why are there so many poor and sick people? Or why is there so much innocent blood spilt? Why is there so much suffering if God exists?"* thus they conclude that God must not exist because of such suffering existing. However once again this is based on emotionalism and not logic or credible correlation. It is because atheists have a flawed concept of God and false expectations that they end up rejecting their definition of God. Then due to intellectual laziness they typically just reject all definitions of God rather than consider the possibility their idea of God was wrong and that God is really something other than what they expected or believed in before they rejected God's existance. Basically because God doesn't do what they expect God to do, particularly in their life, and they feel emotional distress then out of revenge and to come to a quick easy answer they reject the doctrine that a God exists. A sense of victimization leads them to reject God and/or religion, particularly if they learn about false religions or hypocritical religious leadership using religion as a means for manipulation or exploitation. Thus for them to cope with "victim syndrome" they become atheists for emotional reasons as a means of psychological/emotional/physical self-preservation subconsciously thinking that if they don't believe in God then they'll never be a victim of God for doing something wrong. Along with their confusion on the "Why?" questions they feel/think disbelief in God offers protection from God or religious scams or guilt for doing things. Atheism is the quick easy answer to their thus far unanswered questions and their freedom from eternal responsibility and spiritual guilt/stress/pressure in life. Or at least in my experience every atheist has that core motivation behind their doctrine of atheism, even though they may not readily admit it. However logically and scientifically without theology or revelation it's proven that a divine Creative entity exists and has played a major role in the beginning of the universe and continues to play a role in its maintenance. Textual evidence and revelation is more important than philosophy, logic, reasoning or intellect but since most atheists refuse to consider revelation or theology, one hopes they would at least accept the logical reasoning for the existence of God.

    Think about how you are able to read this book right now with these letters being viewed through your eyes sending signals to your brain that are then decoded and turned into something that is somehow meaningful; all in a split second without you having to even think about thinking. Imagine all the blood vessels circulating around inside your body, the oxygen you're breathing in through your nose or mouth (or both) and all the background noise you're hearing. As a challenge, get up, stand and walk around a few steps while reading this aloud. How can you possibly do that? Your feet, eyes, ears, brain, lips, tongue, lungs, heart, nose and sense of feeling is working all at once without any overload or malfunction? I didn't even tell you to think of blinking but your body does it automatically. Imagine if every time you ate or drank something you had to tell your pharynx to move the epiglottis so food or liquid went down the esophagus and not the trachea which would cause you to choke. We would choke on nearly everything and would hate eating and drinking because it would be so difficult, dangerous and mentally exhausting. We can't even remember what the different parts of the body we depend on are called! Consider how by default your eyes blink at the perfect speed, not too long so it impairs your sight and not too short so that your eyes don't get protection and moisture, whilst the eyelashes are also the perfect length to do their job without obstructing our vision except for the rare instances when they fall out of their natural position and get stuck underneath our eyelids. The eyes are also perfectly situated between the nose so that the nose doesn't obstruct our vision and yet at the same time we can still look at our nose if need be. Thus even within ourselves there are signs which indicate we were designed with a type of precision greater than anything that is created can be capable of. Only something all-knowing, all-wise and almighty could possibly construct us as we have been constructed. Also reflect upon the rainfall, or the snowfall. Could you imagine how much damage and havoc would take place if instead of coming down drop by drop over an extended period it were to be dumped on us all in one second as if it came out of a bucket and the clouds just popped? With all these wondrous signs, do people think that it is an unintentional accident and a random occurrence that made such finite precise actions possible without conscious effort? Seriously consider how everything is so perfectly suited with earth being the perfect distance from the sun so we neither melt nor freeze, simultaneously having gravity so we aren't floating aimlessly, while having all this water that is "coincidentally" consumable as well as minerals, elements, fossil fuels and animals that can be utilized for our own wellbeing, with each one having a special important purpose without which our lives would be significantly different if not unbearable. Furthermore new uses are being discovered for these precreated resources every day. Is all this just a one in a million chance random occurrence? No, it is an impossibility that this complex universe could have come about without a blueprint or design. The elite scientists agree and state how the more they learn about the universe and science the more confidence they have that all of it has been created intentionally because of the perfect compatibility. Just because you can't see something doesn't mean it doesn't exist. People cannot see radio waves or wireless internet connections flying through the invisible air but who on earth would claim such things don't exist based on lack of visibility? One more example is that of a car. Imagine there is a junkyard full of disorganized heaps of trash. A tornado comes through and just by chaotic chance happened to pick up every car part necessary and transforms the scrap metal to make any parts that aren't there and correctly assembles a brand new working vehicle with a full tank of gas, oil, windshield wiper fluid, lights, radio, A/C and a key turned in the ignition with the engine running. We know this would never happen no matter how many tornadoes came through and how many billions of years you waited. If someone told you that a tornado made their vehicle you would say they were either lying or mentally insane. Yet there are people who claim something even crazier than this, that all the land, water and living creatures on earth, the sun, moon, planets, stars, galaxies and entire universe just so happened by chance and everything works perfectly in harmony complementing each other because sooner or later it was bound to happen. This idea goes against the scientific "law" of thermodynamics which states how order cannot come from disorder. You cannot get something from nothing, the universe wasn't just created out of thin air. In fact air itself is a created thing which contains living organisms, so life forms are needed to even get thin air itself. This is the scientific principle of biogenesis which states that microbial/molecular life can not spontaneously generate itself without some prior life force existing before the later life force comes into existence. The first Atom had to exist before any others, but if there were no Atoms to begin with then it would be impossible for any Atoms to ever exist. It's simple math 0+0 will always equal zero, no matter how many trillions of years it gets added together 0+0 always equals zero and the same goes for multiplying zero. The impossible can never happen no matter how much time is spent waiting for it. A final example is this book you are reading right now, who was it written by? If you were unable to know who the author was because you didn't read the cover, or title page, or personally witness it get written then would that mean this book has written itself on its own? Isn't it possible? I mean the dictionary existed before this book did so maybe because the words in the dictionary existed for such a long period of time they just so happened to reproduce and organize themselves into this book without any type of intelligent designer involved. Obviously that's impossible. Similarly the way a book indicates the existence of an intelligent(or in mankind's case minutely-intelligent) creative author, the creation indicates the existence of a Unfathomably Intelligent Creator. There are intelligent creatures and creations, so there must have been an intelligent designer. The creation can never be superior or equal to their Creator. It is clear that this awe inspiring universe must have been intelligently designed by a being with much greater intellect than anything we can contemplate. Even to this day no flaw can be found in the universe whatsoever, there are no potholes, loose nails, squeaky floorboards or spots that weren't painted out of negligence. This universe isn't just a job well done, scientifically speaking it's perfectly done and has never even rusted. Nothing that exists can spot one area of the universe and say "Well this could've been made better." and anyone who would dare make such a claim has no clue of the intricate and delicate balance that would be disrupted if their "improvements" were put into effect. The Universe ain't broke, so we can't fix it, rather we should show appreciation for the designer who created it as they did. We struggle just to cook a recipe to make something safe and tasty to eat, but even then we aren't creating the ingredients or tools used to cook that recipe. So the Universe was made from totally nothing, basically the "Start button" itself had to be made before work on the Universe could be started. However before the software can be made, one needs some hardware to develop it. So when people ask *"If God made everything who created God?"* they are asking a stupid question. They think it's clever but it's not. The reason being they are led to think there was nothing before God. However for there to ever be a state of nothingness, that state of nothingness must be permanent. If nothing existed yesterday, then today cannot have anything more because we'd have nothing to build upon and tomorrow nothing would exist either because there is simply nothing that exists. If once there was nothing then that means there will always be nothing. Nothing can never develop anything because it is literally nothing. It doesn't matter what happens to nothing, if there is nothing then that's that, nothing can ever change. To have nothing once means there is nothing and the story of the Universe never starts. If in the beginning there was nothing then that means "Game Over", end of discussion; we would not exist because there was nothing and it stayed that way forever. Therefore since today we have something in this thing called the Universe then it means there must have never been a time when nothing existed at all, because if there ever were such a time in the past then our present would not exist. Something existing today means something existed yesterday and that something must have always existed forever. The original something is typically called God. In terms of computer science if the Universe is considered akin to software then God would be the manufacturer that designed the Universe hardware and everything in it. Software necessitates hardware's pre-existance and the Universe necessitates the existence of God and God must always have existed because if God had to be created then he never would've been created since you can't have God be created out of nothing since nothing = nothing forever because nothing can't make nothing happen. Yet as any computer programmer knows, prior to any software being created an elaborate extensive code must be written which defines the rules and functions of the software itself. In order to create a seamless experience without any glitches, every possible action taken by a software user must be known and accounted for prior to that software being used. Regarding man-made software they do product testing because it's impossible for humans to account for everything humans will do with any given program/product and setting, but even with testing products have defects and bugs; thus they get recalled and re-designed into new versions. However there is no beta testing for the Universe nor any re-designs, the Creator of the Universe accounted for every action of everything that would ever inhabit the universe before the Universe was ever created. It is this designer that is referred to as the Creator, who many call God. Whilst as creatures using this product called the Universe, obviously we need to know some of the rules so we can properly live in the Universe to get the results we desire. Thus a User's Manual is helpful because if we just troubleshoot our way through life, we might make some mistakes that could greatly inhibit our experience living in the Universe or trigger a pre-programmed reaction that we might not want to happen to us. Now the difference between human programmers and the programmer of the Universe is that the one who designed the Universe by necessity had to know how many creatures would use and interact with the Universe and how they would interact from beginning to end. This is necessary to prevent an overload of the system, or power outages or crashes because of too many creatures doing the same thing at once. This is what happens with computer programs all the time. If too many people log on to a website or choose to do something then the site crashes or freezes because the designers didn't know the individual users would do such a thing. However the Universe can't crash and time never freezes because of lag or glitches. Likewise the Universe can't be hacked by any of it's creatures, even if that creature is Satan. Satan isn't hacking the Universe taking control from the Creator, he's just another creature who installed a virus in his system that is allowed to operate to a limited extent before he is deleted and eternally quarantined. Because as IT specialists know, there is no such thing as eternally deleted, stuff that's "permanently deleted" still exists, it's just in another place in another form unknown and inaccessible to most. Eventually we will all be "deleted" when we die and enter a different dead-only area of the Universe, which the living won't be able to access until they too die. The Designer knowing what each individual creature will do before they do it doesn't mean they don't have freewill, it is because of their freewill that the various functions and reactions of the Universe to their free-willed actions have been preprogramed by the Designer into the Universe. It is because of freewill that the Designer had to know what all of us would before we do it, because otherwise our specific experiences in life couldn't exist unless they were preprogrammed with all the chain reactions that result from all our actions already being programmed as well. We do have choices, but our choices were already taken into account prior to us being made or making them; simply because the Designer is just that smart he planned for everything done by every user before they did it. If he didn't then we wouldn't have the choice or freewill but would have limited options and be forced to just follow a program. Whereas not only has every choice been predetermined, everyone has a custom experience even regarding the same experiences such sight, sound, touch, taste etc. For instance God creates the food and the specific taste experience each of us has for that food before we even decide to eat that food. Every possible variable for every situation for every individual was already accounted for before it needed to be accounted for. We never have to install new software or patches because everything we need to experience our full life experience is pre-installed before delivery (birth) and there are no software updates or upgrades to install either. God isn't forcing us to do anything, he's just so knowledgable that he can't be surprised. Basically it's like God wrote many movie scripts for the Universe, but because he knows all the actors so well, since he created them all, God knows which role each individual will play and how they would act out that role before they choose to do so. Thus everyone's choices were put into one script before anything was even made and the show began. The only catch is that we don't know the full script of our own life, or others lives. So for us many things are surprises, but not for God. Yet God didn't make this Universe for his own entertainment or to "watch a thrilling movie". This is something many don't understand, but basically we have freewill because the Designer predestined everything for every individual. Without all of us having our life predestined we couldn't have freewill, because if the Designer didn't know beforehand what choices each individual would make the Universe would crash or freeze as God struggled to keep the show going towards it's predetermined finale. For God to know the end he has to know the beginning and middle as well, because God is the one creating/maintaining everything to do with the whole Universe that leads up to the final act. If God didn't know the end then it would mean he has no clue as to what will happen in the future and therefore could never make any promises of rewards or punishments because one who doesn't know the future can't be fully trusted 100%. Thus if God didn't predetermine everything he wouldn't be able to threaten anybody. A being who doesn't know everything before it happens can't make an eternal promise because they wouldn't know if they'd even be capable or if it'd be possible to fulfill such a promise. The end can only be known if the middle is as well as the beginning. It's a total package deal for the designer. So since the Universe exists that itself is a proof that everything in it is predestined, otherwise it wouldn't function. For a God to have created the Universe that God must know everything that will ever take place before it happens, because if it didn't then we would constantly have to wait for the Universe to buffer/load as we went through life. Obviously we've never come across a "loading the Universe" screen in life, because everything was already preknown in God's memory. Religion is basically the instructions for life while interacting with the Universe, or the script which God knows is best for us and most rewarding which is suggested for us to follow, even though God already knows whether we'll accept it and how well we will follow the script even if we try to. User manuals are called Sacred books and prophets are the representatives of the Creator of the Universe who distribute these user manuals and explain what they mean to us so our freewill can be utilized in this Universe the way the Designer desires us to. That way we can make the best choices in order to get the best results and best personal ending. The problem we have is counterfeit User Manuals not from the Designer and phony fraudulent "prophets", who try to get us infected with the Satanic virus. Sometimes they are intentionally malicious and sometimes they are malicious by mistake. Whereas sometimes if someone changes these manuals or lies about these prophets it can make anyone who follows those religions end up installing the Satanic virus by mistake. For example how many people go on a site thinking it's a good safe site, only to get infected with a virus without knowing it. Sometimes people even download "free anti-virus protection" only to realize later that was a virus itself. Although in the beginning our species knew "the truth" with certainty, however we aren't living in "the beginning", we're in the present and the Satanic viruses have developed and most of us have no clue what we're doing but just think we are safe. Maybe we're not as safe as we could be, but we still think we're pretty safe even though most of us have some spiritual infections in our system. False religions are the scripts God made which God doesn't like, but Satan wants us to choose to live out. Basically Satan didn't want to follow the script God chose for him and was jealous of us getting a better role than him. Therefore Satan decided to trick us into choosing the bad scripts to play so our life pre-death and post-death in the Universe is toxic, unenjoyable and disastrous. Yet that Designer still exists and is actively maintaining the server that keeps this Universe running, wanting us to choose the best role. Know that the best role isn't always the star of the show. Sadly people waste time debating how the universe was made, even though everyone agrees it exists. Thus we neglect the important questions such as:

> Why was the Universe made?
>
> Why does the Universe still exist?
>
> How does this pertain to you?
>
> Why do you exist?
>
> Why are you going to die?
>
> What is the purpose of life?
>
> What will happen to you in the grave?

These are all very important questions that are often neglected or ignored in our society which I hope to bring attention to in these following pages, God-willing.

AGES 0-5

I was born in the year 1992 CE in New York State of the United States of America and given the first name of Gregory. Two days after birth I suffered a stroke and nearly died. As a result of this stroke during infancy I have hypersensitive tastebuds due to oral defensiveness. Basically that means I have a super tongue that has the ability of super taste, except that's not fun like it sounds. Many people have this but they get labeled "Picky eaters" when it's actually a medical condition due to hypersensitive taste that makes many foods impossible for them to eat; because their tongues have super-taste that causes many foods to taste super-bad. Thus it's a legitimate medical condition that means I can't voluntarily eat many types of foods because they just taste so bad to the extent that my tongue has trained itself to tell me when something will taste bad before I even taste it. Which of course sounds completely crazy to people who don't have this condition and makes social spontaneous eating difficult for people with this condition because it's not widely known or discussed, to the point where I just thought it was my own "pickiness" until I was in my late teens and a doctor finally explained it to me. Yet by that time I had many unpleasant social experiences due to not wanting to eat food because I knew it would taste bad and getting chastised for refusing to eat because of taste. Then when being forced to eat foods due to social pressure or hunger, my tongue confirmed the bad taste which then led me to develop aversions to social interactions in general, which continues to this day because people by and large tend not to accept the concept of not eating popular foods simply because of taste or pre-imagined taste. I bring attention to this hypersensitive oral defensiveness/tactile defensiveness and sensory processing disorders in general because many people in society have these medical conditions and they really don't effect our health in any way, but they significantly affect our social experiences because the world is ignorant and insensitive to these conditions which people have. Such ignorance and insensitivity causes great social hardships for those with these medical conditions that one has no control over. They are not diseases or contagious but simply a uniqueness, which due to the mass public viewing as imaginary or peculiar can lead to social or mental disorders and phobias. Which I hope I do not have, but if I do it may have something to do with people and their interactions with me. Afterall if you aren't crazy then most people will make you go crazy anyways. On behalf of all those who have hypersensitive tastebuds, when we politely and shyly say we don't want to or can't eat X food, no means NO. Don't ask us twice or make it more awkward and stressful than it already is for us. We don't enjoy it anymore than you do, we'd like to be able to eat more things but we can't so don't try to "kindly" try to "expand our palette and introduce us to new things". Showing us pity for it is an insult, to us you are the ones with the tongue problem not us. Medically in comparison to us most have dull tastebuds, we actually feel totally normal until you start talking to us about it. It's not personal on our part, but it's not hospitable to insist we eat something when we say no. For us to say no once it means "*NOOO!*" To make us a "special dish" on the spot or in advance makes us feel like we have some type of disability or virus that you announced to everyone. We will not hold a grudge if we don't eat anything, we're used to it and strongly prefer it, but we will get offended if you make a big deal about us not eating anything or eating little. We'd rather not even interact with people than have them give us immense mental and emotional stress over not eating something or lots of stuff or varieties of stuff. Social anxiety and social phobia results from people criticizing us and trying to change our limited palette. The taste of the social reactions is worse than the taste of the foods we can't voluntarily choose to taste. As a result we actually dread getting invited to go out and eat or going to parties, because we don't eat many things sheerly due to taste and visual appearance. It's stressful to explain why on the spot or beforehand, especially if we don't know what our condition is; which most of us don't. Yet people never ever stop asking us to eat stuff or join them in eating stuff we can't eat. After many such social experiences we develop severe social aversion to spontaneous social interactions because it might lead to eating and the unpleaseantries of our condition of hypersensitive tastebuds being scrutinized. This is because most people continue to view us as stubborn and label us as weird, "*Picky eaters*" or spoiled thinking it's a choice, or if they ask again then we'll "give in and change our tastebuds". The worst part is when people get offended at us for not eating what they offer, or not eating with them, or not eating large amounts of food if we eat. Due to such reactions to people with hypersensitive tastebuds, many people with such conditions develop issues with socializing because they've had embarrassing and uncomfortable social interactions due to their tongue being different than most tongues. This happens to the extent that some get pushed to the point where they wish eating was an entirely private affair, since so many social interactions involving public eating turn out socially sour. The reactions people have had to me not participating as is customary in social eating has even led me to develop a habit of only eating meals I cook since I can no longer handle the reaction of people if I can't eat whatever they cook. So now it's not even about the taste of food as much, but it's that I don't want people to get offended if I don't eat their food so now I tend not to even accept food when offered because I don't want any to get offended by my tastebuds. I mention this because as a result of this my menu has gotten much smaller. So for any who ever think to criticize or politely or impolitely pressure some "*Picky Eater*" know that if you try to expand their menu you will end up limiting it further turning social eating events into torture for them and you can transform their "eating peculiarity" into a plethora of social or psychological or spiritual disorders. Essentially many problems are caused in society because eating with people has gotten too important to people. Yet at birth I didn't know so many would have problems with my tastebuds and publicly be able to harass me at every social eating ritual. So I guess that was my first cognizant exposure to religion, in that everyone else believed that I was supposed to eat what everyone else enjoyed eating and made me feel like a heretic if I didn't. Also because I was an unhealthy baby, due to the stroke, I was put into quarantine. So I was unable to experience the close skin to skin contact with my mother or father as a newborn. Psychologists say that skin to skin contact with a newborn is necessary for creating a bond between parents and child as it releases the hormone oxytocin (the cuddling hormone which makes socialization fun). Which since I medically was too sick to "cuddle" when I was a baby I've recently come to self-diagnose myself with RAD. The RAD acronym stands for Reactive Attachment Disorder and there are two types, an inhibited type, which I believe I have and a disinhibited type that is currently referred to as DSED (Disinhibitive Social Disorder). DSED is basically where someone is friendly with everybody to the point that they put themselves in danger and can be frequently manipulated due to being too sociable with people. Whereas the Inhibitited RAD causes the *"inability to form normal relationships with other people as well as impaired social development and sociopathic behaviors due to the absence of secure attachment formation early in life."* Basically people with RAD don't have fun socializing because while young they had to live without love/affection.(whether they wanted to or not) As a result they don't feel love from people nor do they love people as much because they never internalized how to. Thus such people tend to not bother when it comes to socialization and are emotionally detached and disinterested when it comes to interpersonal activities because the love/fun that comes from interpersonal relationships/activities doesn't happen for them. They don't feel happy as a result of interacting with people and have difficulties expressing affection even if they love those people or are loved by them. Those with inhibitive RAD are often undiagnosed and don't know why they are extremely reluctant to initiate or receive comfort and affection. This may have been a reason for difficulties in my relationship with my parents down the road; things had been bumpy right from the start. No one's life is easy and we should never think life will or should be. We all have special positives and negatives. Nobody is entitled to pity. It is a struggle just to get from the womb to this world so we should not expect it to be any easier to get from this world to paradise. Considering we all came out of two human orifices, first as sperm exiting a penis, then as an embryo exiting the uterus, we should never be arrogant or think we're something special. We are just human, that's all. To not know your flaws is a flaw, while to let your flaws dominate you is a flaw too. We are humans, all of us are unique it's not special to be unique everyone has special problems particular to them. One problem is our reluctance to accept our problems as problems or to allow our problems to become weaknesses.

Only a few significant memories remain from my toddler years. The importance of honesty was impressed upon me early. Whenever I told a lie somehow my mother would find out. Once the truth was known I would hear her say the infamous intimidating phrase, *"Do you know what I do to liars?!"* It was never anything nice and I learned to never lie because sooner or later liars get exposed and punished. God-willing this book will expose some lies that I have been told.

When spending time alone with the men in my family they would often joke to the women in my family that they would take me out *"cruising for babes"* and the women would laugh and tell us to have fun. I feel this must be addressed, because as a young boy I had no interest in doing such things at that age, this made me feel uncomfortable and pressured to objectify women. The more it is reflected upon the worse the statement seems. Married men are telling their wives and daughters they are going out to just stare at other women, this is stalking and rapist behavior which gets female approval. Also somewhat related to this, although I didn't hear of it till later in life, is the pretend affairs married people joke about. For instance a married man might ask his wife about "the other guy" she does things with when he's not around and sometimes even gives him a name to be funny. Whereas the wife will tease the husband about seeing strippers or women from a certain country when she isn't there, incidentally stereotyping all the women of that country. Or on the phone they will pretend to be an adulterer whom their partner knows and then the charade is eventually dropped as the person knows they're talking to their spouse. This stuff boggles my mind because adultery is no laughing matter, when people joke about it they are essentially saying it's ok to do it; at least on the subconscious level. This behavior bothered me because it was confusing as a child not knowing whether someone being discussed was real or not. Perhaps it's just an adult version of having imaginary friends with disturbing psychological and sexual undertones. However the small lies lead to the big lies, and lies are lies no matter the size. Lies done in jest are not funny, they destroy the integrity of our society. A "funny lie" ruins the world and makes God angry, all prophets came to forbid the "funny lies".

Another childhood phrase I tried various replies to whenever I was in trouble was "*Sorry doesn't cut it*". Everytime I heard "*Sorry doesn't cut it*" it meant that I was still in trouble. My various responses to this statement included: "*If sorry doesn't cut it, then what does?*" and "*How come sorry cuts it when you're in trouble but not for me?*" One time I even got a little pair of scissors asking where "it" was so that I could prove "it" could be cut by the scissors if saying sorry couldn't do it. This incorrectly taught me that life had a double standard and was not fair. This is one of the first false concepts I was conditioned to be<u>lie</u>ve, because rather than be taught how to improve my apology with sincerity and changed behavior I was simply dismissed with a catchphrase. It's a very common catchphrase so my mother is not entirely to blame for it, but when carefully scrutinized the idea is found flawed. If saying sorry doesn't give you forgiveness then what does? As a Christian I would say that Jesus pbuh died so you can be forgiven.

Let's go back to the beginning, since lies are usually found there, with Adam pbuh and Eve. I was taught that Eve was tricked by Satan to eat the forbidden fruit God had prohibited, which led me to internalize the idea that women were to blame for the problems of the world. Then Adam pbuh followed her sinful lead, which taught me to never follow the advice of women. Thus the first two humans were the original sinners of our species. Apparently I inherited their sin and would've gone to hell because of what they did unless I was baptized. Baptism is a Christian ritual involving "holy water" being sprinkled on the baptized person while a special phrase is said during the sprinkling or full-body immersion in water, depending on which Christian denomination it is. Since I was baptized as a baby without even knowing it or what baptism was for, I was forgiven and the original sin of the first humans was no longer held against me. This idea makes even less sense than "*Sorry doesn't cut it*". Especially when you recall all the people who lived and died before the ritual of baptism started. This would mean that all the great prophets I read about daily in the children's bible went to hell because they weren't baptized. This idea of original sin led me to grow up thinking everyone was born inherently evil and sin was human nature.

This is why Christians are adamantly opposed to abortion, because since the baby is scientifically alive at the embryo stage then they believe that baby has the stain of original sin on its soul. Therefore if it dies in the womb without being baptized, Christianity teaches that such a baby will burn in hell forever because of the original sin that was never removed via their Christian baptism. The only difference of opinion among the traditional Christian religions is which part of hell the baby will be in. Some believe there is a specific place in hell specially reserved for such babies called limbo. Had I died from the stroke I suffered when I was 2 days old, according to Christian doctrine I'd be burning in hell forever. Although many Christian nurses or doctors perform what is called a secret unauthorized baptism on every newborn they deliver to ensure babies get baptized; just in case their parents never choose to baptize or raise their children as Christians. Even though this baptism without the parents' knowledge or consent is illicit many Christian denominations teach it is still valid. If I had an unauthorized baptism performed on me in the hospital unknowingly, then had I died from my infant stroke I would have been "saved" from the fires of hell and forgiven from the sin that was believed to have been on my baby soul according to Christian doctrine. These secret baptisms are actually sanctioned by the Catholic Church with the ruling being:

> "*In the case of the **new-born child**, baptism is to be administered as soon as there is danger of death. **This favor is to be accorded even to children of non-Catholic parents** unless there is certainty that the parents will be displeased by such action, and hatred or persecution of the Church will be the result, even though the baptism be secret.*" From the Catholic publication "*Moral Problems In Hospital Practice*", by Finney & O'Brien, page 282

This is something which I think non-Christian or non-Catholic parents reading this would want to know could happen to their child. As a new-born child in danger of death, I was likely baptized at 2 days old or earlier in a secret baptism. Secret unauthorized baptisms are also performed on adults. The ruling the Catholic Church teaches about secretly baptizing grown adults is: "***If a person is unconscious** and would have no means of learning that he was baptized*, so that there is no danger of resultant hatred or persecution of the Church, **such an adult ought to be baptized**. *This is true **even if the patient has been heard to express apparently contradictory intentions**.*" Ruling from the Catholic book "*Moral Problems In Hospital Practice*" by Finney & O'Brien , page 280

This is another tidbit of information I think that non-Christians would want to know. A non-Christian adult could enter a hospital and explicitly declare he or she did not want to be baptized and while unconscious he or she could get baptized without knowing against their will. Despite Christians having good intentions, I consider the practice of non-consensual or secret baptisms to be a violation of a human being's right to have freedom of religion. Personally I don't think this should happen without the baptized person's permission and I would liked to have been aware when I was baptized. If secret baptisms are permitted then eventually we may also see secret unauthorized circumcision. I was also circumcised unknowingly as a baby, but I have no complaints about that and don't mind not remembering it. It just seems unfair to me that I was baptized as a baby and can't remember the day I became a Christian. From a technical perspective every baby who is baptized is forced to become a Christian whether they want to or not, which may be the reason why they cry during the baptism. Thus I think people shouldn't be baptized unless they are mature enough to choose to become Christian and remember the moment. Of course Anabaptists and those denominations that evolved from them or copied parts of their doctrines don't allow infant baptisms for these reasons, but the majority of Christian denominations support and practice infant baptism. Which is actually a semi-contradictory type of doctrine, because if humans must be required to be mature and willing in order to get baptized then they should also have to be mature and willing in order to get sins as well. So if there is original sin then infant baptism should be valid, since there is infant sins. Yet if infant baptism is invalid then infants cannot justifiably be born with original sin either. Basically what I'm saying is that if the babies aren't dirty with sin they don't need a baptismal bath, but if they do have sin on their soul then they do need a baptismal bath, or at least based on Christian doctrines regarding baptism. In order to avoid a double standard there either has to be baptism for all infants because they have original sin or else baptism must have nothing to do with original sins that get inherited by our ancestors at all and there can't be original sin. So that's where while one might initially think babies should grow up and choose to be baptized, but based on the doctrine of original sin they shouldn't. While if one says it's ok to baptize a baby to save their soul, then one would also have to say it's ok to baptise an unconscious adult to save their soul and maybe even a baby in the womb because one has to determine that if original sin is inherited then at what stage does the original sin get inherited? Once inherited then baptism should be performed according to christian doctrine, so the day the sin is on the soul must be declared by Christians. Yet thus far none have declared the specific second or day which this original sin stains the soul. Many will say we are just born with it but they don't define what that means. Does the baby have it only after the umbilical cord is cut? Do they have it when the head pops out but the rest of the body is still in? Do they have it when the water breaks? If they get it at all then when do they get it? At the very moment of conception? If so then theologically people should be baptized immediately after a woman's egg is fertilized. Which to be truly accurate means Christians would have to perform a baptism every time they have intercourse, just in case an egg was fertilized and original sin got passed on. Whereas then the question also arises about a pregnant woman getting baptized at any stage during pregnancy. If a woman gets baptized for the first time while pregnant does it count for her baby too? Regarding twins that come from one fertilized egg which has split, do both of them get original sin, or does only one of them get it, or does it get split 50/50? What about triplets or multiple numbers of babies all born from the same egg? Furthermore if we baptize at conception and only one baptism is performed and it is later discovered that more than one baby is developing does the baptism count for both or just one? What if they are of different eggs? If it doesn't count for all then there could be a possibility of the non-baptized infecting the already baptized. Yet how would we be able to tell? Also lets say a person was baptized before they got pregnant, if the baby has original sin on it's soul while in the womb then what's to stop that original sin from spreading to the mother? If babies catch it from their parents then a mother could catch it from her baby in the womb. It must also be declared whether original sin is in the sperm or the egg. If in the sperm then since only one egg is usually fertilized, all those other sperms would be carrying original sin and since they remain in the woman's body they could contaminate her. Likewise if sperm contains original sin then the man could get infected by his sinful sperm while it's inside his body. While if original sin is in the eggs only then every woman has capsules of original sin that are likely to infect her at any time in her life, spiritually she could never be safe until every egg is gone and if the sin is in the sperm the man would never be safe. I don't mean to offend any Christian who may read this but if people are getting this original sin on their soul we have to determine exactly when they get it and how so that they can be purified as soon as the spiritual infection occurs. Most Christians agree that this sin is transmittable, so I want to know exactly when it is transmitted and how? It's a question that deserves to be answered. If it's unknown when it's transmitted or how then only symptoms would alert us to it's presence. Which leads me to ask what are the symptoms of someone contaminated with original sin? If we don't know when it's transmitted and we don't know how and we don't know of any symptoms then how can we even know whether this impurity exists? How would we know when it's gone? If absolutely nothing is known about this original sin and it's all just guesswork then how can it possibly be cured? Any cure for such a mysterious contamination could only come through guesswork. If a prophet told us how to cure it they would've told us when/how we got it and how to prevent it. Anyways if there is any problem whatsoever with any type of baptism, then the problem would have to come from the doctrine of original sin before there could be a problem with any ritual of baptism. On the other hand Mormons don't believe in original sin being passed on to others, nor do they believe in baptizing infants, but they do believe in baptizing dead people and they do it via proxy. They actually baptize dead people, and they do it without their consent nor that of their families. So the ritual of baptism is more heavily disputed amongst the various Christian denominations than one would guess. Unfortunately there is no consensus yet, so I don't expect any answers to my questions anytime soon. Despite all the talk one hears about "freedom of religion" in reality if the Christians don't baptize you in the womb, or as a baby, or as an adult whether conscious or unconscious, then the Mormons will baptize you in the tomb after you die. Baptism is almost unavoidable. However there are many different types of baptisms done different ways for different reasons and many Christians will reject those baptisms done by other Christians. So it's not really about if you'll get it, it's more about which type will you get and what does it count for; if anything. Regardless as a baby I was baptised the Catholic way without knowing it, this was in order to be forgiven for a sin I apparently inherited that I didn't know about either. Biblically the English translation of the New International Version of the Bible says the following concerning the inheritability of sins in Jeremiah 31:29-30, *"In those days people will no longer say, 'The parents have eaten sour grapes, and the children's teeth are set on edge.'* ³⁰ *Instead, <u>everyone will die for their own sin</u>; whoever eats sour grapes – their own teeth will be set on edge."* This is a biblical refutation of a common saying amongst ancient people about sour grapes, in that the descendents were thought to suffer because of the mistakes of their parents. It was a childish belief of *"it's my parents fault for everything wrong or bad in my life"*. This was refuted in the bible because some people began to think their parent's sins might negatively impact them in some way which sprung out of the idea that a senior family member could damage the entire tribe's reputation or cause a war which the children would end up fighting. Also it's interesting that the saying refuted by the biblical God actually refers to eating bad fruit, because that's the very sin Adam pbuh and Eve committed which people say we inherited. The bible plainly states if your parents eat "bad fruit" it doesn't affect you but only affects them, and that *"everyone will die for their own sin"*. In the english translation of the New International Version of the biblical book of Ezekiel, chapter 18 clarifies further: *"The word of the LORD came to me:* ² *"What do you people mean by quoting this proverb* about the land of Israel: "'The parents eat sour grapes, and the children's teeth are set on edge'? ³ "As surely as I live, declares the Sovereign LORD, you will no longer quote this proverb in Israel. ⁴ For everyone belongs to me, the parent as well as the child – both alike belong to me. <u>The one who sins is the one who will die.</u> ⁵ "Suppose there is a righteous man who does what is just and right. ⁶ He does not eat at the mountain shrines or look to the idols of Israel. He does not defile his neighbor's wife or have sexual relations with a woman during her period. ⁷ He does not oppress anyone, but returns what he took in pledge for a loan. He does not commit robbery but gives his food to the hungry and provides clothing for the naked. ⁸ He does not lend to them at interest or take a profit from them. He withholds his hand from doing wrong and judges fairly between two parties. ⁹ He follows my decrees and faithfully keeps my laws. That man is righteous; he will surely live, declares the Sovereign LORD. ¹⁰ "Suppose he has a violent son, who sheds blood or does any of these other things ¹¹ (though the father has done none of them): "He eats at the mountain shrines. He defiles his neighbor's wife. ¹² He oppresses the poor and needy. He commits robbery. He does not return what he took in pledge. He looks to the idols. He does detestable things. ¹³ He lends at interest and takes a profit. Will such a man live? He will not! Because he has done all these detestable things, he is to be put to death; his blood will be on his own head. ¹⁴ "But suppose this son has a son who sees all the sins his father commits, and though he sees them, he does not do such things: ¹⁵ "He does not eat at the mountain shrines or look to the idols of Israel. He does not defile his neighbor's wife. ¹⁶ He does not oppress anyone or require a pledge for a loan. He does not commit robbery but gives his food to the hungry and provides clothing for the naked. ¹⁷ He withholds his hand from mistreating the poor and takes no interest or profit from them. He keeps my laws and follows my decrees. <u>He will not die for his father's sin; he will surely live.</u> ¹⁸ <u>But his father will die for his own sin</u>, because he practiced extortion, robbed his brother and did what was wrong among his people. ¹⁹ **"Yet you ask, 'Why does the son not share the guilt of his father?'** Since the son has done what is just and right and has been careful to keep all my decrees, he will surely live. ²⁰ **<u>The one who sins is the one who will die. The child will not share the guilt of the parent, nor will the parent share the guilt of the child.</u>** The righteousness of the righteous will be credited to them, and the wickedness of the wicked will be charged against them. ²¹ <u>"But if a wicked person turns away from all the sins they have committed and keeps all my decrees and does what is just and right, that person will surely live; they will not die.</u> ²² <u>None of the offenses they have committed will be remembered against them.</u> Because of the righteous things they have done, they will live. ²³ Do I take any pleasure in the death of the wicked? declares the Sovereign LORD. Rather, am I not pleased when they turn from their ways and live? ²⁴ "But if a righteous person turns from their righteousness and commits sin and does the same detestable things the wicked person does, will they live? None of the righteous things that person has done will be remembered. Because of the unfaithfulness they are guilty of and because of the sins they have committed, they will die. ²⁵ "Yet you say, 'The way of the Lord is not just.' <u>Hear, you Israelites: Is my way unjust? Is it not your ways that are unjust?</u> ²⁶ If a righteous person turns from their righteousness and commits sin, they will die for it; because of the sin they have committed they will die. ²⁷ <u>But if a wicked person turns away from the wickedness they have committed and does what is just and right, they will save their life.</u> ²⁸ <u>Because they consider all the offenses they have committed and turn away from them, that person will surely live; they will not die.</u> ²⁹ Yet the Israelites say, 'The way of the Lord is not just.' <u>Are my ways unjust, people of Israel? Is it not your ways that are unjust?</u> ³⁰ "Therefore, you Israelites, <u>I will judge each of you according to your own ways, declares the Sovereign LORD. Repent! Turn away from all your offenses; then sin will not be your downfall.</u> ³¹ Rid yourselves of all the offenses you have *committed, and get a new heart and a new spirit. Why will you die, people of Israel?* ³² *For* **<u>I take no pleasure in the death of anyone, declares the Sovereign LORD. Repent and live!"</u>**

     I do apologize if that was "too much bible" for you but I felt it was appropriate to keep the context so that a Christian reader doesn't think I'm misquoting anything. Biblically it's crystal clear that everyone is entirely responsible for themselves and nobody can harm your relationship with God except you. Nobody can blame their parents or their kids for anything. Also it's important to know that the "death" referred to is the spiritual death and not literal death. This is evident in Genesis 2:16-17, "*And the LORD God commanded the man, saying, "You may surely eat of every tree of the garden,* ¹⁷ *but of the tree of the knowledge of good and evil you shall not eat, for in* **<u>the day that you eat of it you shall surely die</u>***.*" The bible says God said the day Adam pbuh eats of the tree of knowledge he will die. On the very same day he ate, not hundreds of years later. This means the death caused by sin is a spiritual death not literal. Or else God is a liar. Or else the bible is lying about God. The soul or person "dying" is like a dead battery, it doesn't work or fulfill the purpose for which it is created but it can be recharged and fixed so that it can once more fulfill the purpose for which it was created which is to worship and obey its Creator. The way to recharge the soul is to follow the instruction manual(s) God has sent through the Messengers he has sent. For example being brain dead, doesn't mean the brain ceases to exist but just that it's malfunctioning and has a problem, which might or might not get fixed. For many verses in the bible sins causing death refers to spiritual death, although sometimes it can refer to the expiation for a sin. The bible says some sins cause one to be put to death such as adultery or murder and some sins don't such as theft. This is why some verses of the bible explain how sin=lawlessness (1 John 3:4) and sin = not doing the right thing when one knows what to do (James 4:17). These bible verses mean that if you don't follow the laws of God then by default you are sinning, not because of any sinful action but due to being guilty of inaction which is sinful. Just as by not following the laws of your government would make you a criminal even though you may not have committed a felony or misdemeanor. This is because failing to do what is obligatory is to be guilty of what is prohibited. The bible also equates sin with being dead because sins can kill your relationship with God. While if you don't have the correct relationship with God then you are basically dead spiritually and are comparable to a spiritual zombie. You might walk, talk, breathe, eat etc but that's just in a physical sense. Likewise not all sins cause spiritual death. For example worshipping an idol causes spiritual death and makes one a disbeliever yet minor sins generally do not by themselves cause a spiritual death, they are merely spiritual wounds. Although physically God is the one who causes death when he sends the angel of death to extract a person's soul. Every mortal being must die or else they would be immortal and none is immortal except God. Everything created by God will eventually die including animals, plants, cellular life etc. Yet many of these things will have died sinless such as trees, horses, fish, flowers, rocks, time, angels etc. The death in which God takes no pleasure refers to the "spiritual death" aka disbelief or sin, when evil people like Goliath die then God is pleased by their physical death despite being displeased by their spiritual death. The angel of death will be the last thing to physically die and then later on will come the Day of Resurrection when we shall be resurrected, judged etc. Yet those spiritually dead, also known as disbelievers, since they lived and died as disbelievers in this worldly life then they will be raised as disbelievers and will remain spiritually dead without a relationship with God and will be eternally punished for it; aside from the punishment of having no relationship with God. While spiritually dead the eternal physical torment will indeed be real, and really painful at that, just as their worldly existence was real despite their being spiritually dead. Physical death is like a court date with God. So this is an example of how the bible emphatically teaches that you are only responsible for your own sins and that if you repent from them then God forgives you and gives you spiritual life. These are some reasons which Jews give to justify their reasons for never having believed in the concept of original sin, and these are also reasons why they don't believe Jesus pbuh could've died for their sins. However I'm not Jewish.

     According to Islam both Adam pbuh and Eve ate the forbidden fruit and whoever was first isn't known or singled out. There is a great wisdom in not knowing this detail, because people will often blame either the first man or the first women for all their hardships, thereby falling for the same trap. The important thing is not who broke the rules first, but why? Satan, our most dangerous enemy, is the one who persuaded the first humans to disobey God. He made what was wrong seem right to the first human couple. Satan has had much practice since then in tricking people to do wrong and has even made us forget that he was the instigator who led our ancestors out of paradise. Satan even got us to forget how he did it. Satan tricked them through a lie, that's why he thinks it's so funny when we tell each other "funny lies" especially if people laugh at them, he laughs at them laughing not realizing that we learned how to lie from him and got here because he lied to our ancestors in paradise. Satan got our parents evicted from paradise and made homeless as a result of 1 lie and then we tell lies "to have fun". The first sin humans ever did wasn't in eating the forbidden fruit, it was in taking Satan to be a friend, trusting and obeying his desires when God had warned us he was an enemy. Satan swore to God he was truthful and we believed him and suffered because of it. Thus our species lost our privileges and got sent to earth, to be taught a lesson and to treat Satan as our enemy on earth as God had told us to do originally in paradise. If we don't take Satan and his friends as enemies here, or enjoy entertaining him and imitating him by telling each other "funny lies" then we'll be sent with him to hell after we die. Yet when the next move comes we could go our separate ways and let Satan go to hell alone while we go back to paradise. Rather than be angry at our ancestors (after all they were humans prone to make mistakes) we should be aware of our enemy who has the same plan to deceive us and puts it into action every single day. Let us not be among those who forget the enemy and become divided prior to being conquered. Fortunately Adam pbuh and Eve were taught how to ask for forgiveness with 4 conditions for repentance:

1. **To admit you sinned**(many people don't even think they did anything wrong)
2. **To regret it** (some know it's a sin but don't care)
3. **Ask the Creator _alone_ to forgive you**(it's his law you broke, so only he can forgive)
4. **Sincerely promise not to do it again**(if you plan on doing it again you didn't do step 2 properly, step 4 is to prove step 2 through action)

The Creator subsequently forgave them. For those who disagree why stop at Adam pbuh and Eve? Why not say we inherit all the sins of all our ancestors, including the ones done by our parents before we were born? Why just the first sin of the first humans who erred? Because contemplating the injustice of being held accountable for other people's sins would be realized and the false notion disposed of. If a person commits a crime and gets a criminal record, that doesn't get inherited or passed on to their descendants. Neither is sin inherited, and the bible says this right in Ezekiel: "*The child will not share the guilt of the parent, nor will the parent share the guilt of the child.*" Is that not fair and completely just? Furthermore forgiveness was dependent upon the guilty party repenting. No parent could get their kid out of trouble with God and likewise no kid could get their parent out of trouble with God. As the legal saying goes: "*If you do the crime you gotta do the time.*" Well we are innocent of the crime committed by Adam pbuh and Eve, we got our own share of personal crimes/sin which God could condemn us for. God would never punish someone for something they didn't do or even intend to do, and universally everyone would recognize it to be unjust if he did. Even in worldly terms if you commit a crime do you think any judge would sentence you and all your descendants to jail forever, then thousands of years later the judge decides to forgive your descendants for your crime by killing his own innocent son so that your distant descendants could be forgiven and not punished for a crime they never committed? Some may say that with God it's different because Adam pbuh and Eve were evicted from paradise and sent to earth as a result and therefore we suffer on earth because of it. So the sin must also pass on to us since we are on earth. This idea is unfounded. For instance let's say a landlord tells their tenants of an apartment complex not to eat from the apple tree "or else". Later the landlord catches the tenants eating from the tree and tells the tenants they are no longer welcome on the premises and have to go live elsewhere. The tenants leave and have kids in the new location who have kids for generations afterwards. Now would the landlord have any problem with the kids of those tenants who ate the "forbidden fruit", or their descendants? Not at all. Despite the kids living in a different geographical location than their ancestors lived in while tenants, their location or DNA has nothing to do with their relationship with the landlord. God is the landlord and we are those kids whose ancestors broke the rules and had to move, their sin is between God and them. It has nothing to do with us and God. Fortunately God made it clear, that with him all of our crimes/sins that we are guilty for can be forgiven, if we fulfill the criteria for repentance before we get escorted to meet the Judge(God) by the angel of death. Although at this stage of my life I didn't know this and just be**lie**ved what I was told, growing up unforgiving to those who wronged me delusionally thinking "*Sorry doesn't cut it*".

WHY DID GOD CREATE SATAN?

The scholar Ibn al-Qayyim mentions several reasons and expounds upon them but I have only included a few of his reasons for the creation of Satan. I feel these few reasons are sufficient to satisfy the question to the heart's content.

1. The effects of fighting against Satan and his supporters lead to the perfection of worship.

2. By the existence of Satan the servants of God become fearful due to their sins.

3. God has made Satan a lesson for those who reflect.

4. God has made Satan a test and trial for his servants.

5. The creation of Satan demonstrates the complete ability of God to create opposites.

    Ex. Angels and Devils, Paradise and Hell, Hot and Cold, Light and Darkness.

6. Opposites show the virtues of their opposites.

    For instance we wouldn't know what beauty is if we never knew what ugliness was, likewise knowing what is wrong/evil helps us to know what is right/good.

7. The creation of Satan makes apparent the complete rule and control God possesses over the affairs of all his creation.

8. The existence of Satan is from the completeness of the wisdom of God.

9. By creating Satan, God shows his servants calmness and patience.

Basically God created prophets to teach us the steps to take on the road to paradise while God created Satan to teach people the steps to hellfire, although in Satan's attempts to make us sin sometimes it backfires on him and leads people to the path of repentance and paradise. The prophets, their lifestyles and their religion are examples for us to follow while Satan's religions are warning signs letting us know what not to follow or do. One reason God created Satan and his team was so they could serve as living examples for us of how NOT to be, believe or live.

AGES 5-11

On the first day of kindergarten I missed the bus, and thought I lost the opportunity to go to school forever. Nevertheless like an obedient American citizen my mother brought me to the state facility and my thirteen year sentence of indoctrination began. I was intimidated by the mass of other children which was naturally attributed to social jitters and shyness. Recently it occurred to me that it wasn't the strange atmosphere that frightened me; it was the socialization. Not to be confused with socializing, but I was scared of the mob mentality in which the majority opinion ruled which fooled me into conforming to the peer pressure and government propaganda we were subjected to. Aside from learning the pledge of allegiance before anything else, I remember one of our comrades named Hakim who was not afraid of the teacher. He sticks out in my memory because he was 6 when everyone else was 5. Hakim ended up leaving the class since his parents didn't want him to get brainwashed like the rest of us. With a name like Hakim I would say that he was likely the first Muslim I ever met, though I wouldn't have guessed him to be one until becoming a Muslim myself. The highlight of the school year was to be the pool party in June. It was a hot sunny day and for once we were going to have fun at school, but the school called the house and because the weatherman said it was going to rain the pool party was cancelled. It didn't rain a drop all day and I've never trusted the weather predictions again. Only God knows what the weather will be tomorrow, no scientific instruments and measurements can ever have absolute certainty. It is always just a certain percentage chance of this or that, whereas there is a 100% chance that the weather predictors don't really know. That is why we have 24 hour weather channels, because they are changing their predictions every single second. If weather predictors really could predict the future weather they'd be getting paid much more than they currently are. Personally I think of Weather-predictors as a hybrid astrologist, fortune-teller and semi-scientific gambler. Basically they look at data and place a bet based on current climate conditions and past performances of similar conditions, then predict the future based on expected changes and constants in climate conditions forgetting the future has unknown variables and that past performance has nothing to do with future results. They don't even know with certainty if a star known as the Sun will even rise tomorrow. It'd be one thing if they said Godwilling at the end of every prediction, but because most of them don't I consider them as obnoxiously famous highly paid fortune-tellers who's reputation somehow doesn't suffer when they are repeatedly wrong day after day after day. Sadly people treat their forecasts like divine revelation.

Under the childish delusion that life gets easier as you get older I thought 1st grade would be different, but more of the same was even worse. Some comrades pretended being sick so they could go home early, even if it was for just the last hour of the day because we were that desperate to exit school. Some comrades purposely kept loose teeth in their mouth so they could pull them out in school in order to escape to the nurse's office for a 15 minute reprieve. We became obsessed with transformers and pretended to be them during recess in order to escape the grim reality of our miserable existence. It was easier to be something else than to accept ourselves for what we were. All the kids shows, movies and superheroes were geared towards this idea of being something other than yourself. This led me to join cub scouts. Initially I thought it was like real life transformers where you ascend in ranks from tiger to cub to wolf to bear to eagle and so on, not quite realizing what the scouting organization was created for. When Christmas came that year I got a Playstation and that changed my life forever. The ultimate escape from reality presented itself in the form of videogames. For what seemed like the first time in my life I was happy. I had a different life and a different identity with every game. The reason for my happiness was because I had an outlet to escape reality. However this made real life seem drastically worse and the only thought on my mind was getting home from school in order to escape into a virtual world. Also with the close proximity to females other childhood fantasies began to occur. I would have a new crush depending on which girl looked the best each day, nothing sexual as that was gross at the time, but with actual ideas of marriage and weddings. This was because all the fairytales I watched always said at the end how after marriage they lived happily ever after, and who doesn't want to live happily ever after? I would wonder which girl in my class would make me happy forever after? None of them seemed to fit that job description.

Curse words also entered my vocabulary around this time, learned mainly from television, movies and family but some directly from school. This was during 1998 CE. If any parent thinks public school will teach their toddlers only good things they seriously need to reconsider what they are exposing their precious child to. Sometimes other kids can be the worst of influences on one's children. Although that my family allowed me to watch R-rated movies and play M-rated videogames legally meant for people 17 and up certainly had a negative effect in hindsight. Yet at the time I'd vehemently protest the store clerk who told my family about the game rating system and refused to sell a game knowing I'd play it. I thought I was old enough and mature, now that I'm older and more mature I know that I wasn't and my family was wrong to give in and let me morally screw myself up for fun.

The bigger I got the bigger the lies I was hearing became. One was that of confession which is the Catholic ritual in which you confess your sins to the priest and he tells you what to do to be forgiven. At first I was scared, because as a kid typically you don't go up to an adult and tell them all the bad things you've done, because then bad things get done to you. Confession felt so unnatural I suspected there might be a catch or that the priest might threaten to tell my parents my sins using leverage in order to get me to do something for him in exchange for his silence. Thus I quickly found it was better to go to the screened room so as not to be seen when confessing. As a result, confession made me feel as though every time I did something wrong, or had any difficulties, that the only way to relieve myself of the mental and emotional burden was by telling someone all my problems. This bad habit has been very difficult to break and it has led me to have unhealthy enabling relationships with people whom I parasitically drain by "confessing" my problems and worries to; thereby burdening them. It might even be that this book itself is just another way of me "getting things off my chest". While it does bring some closure to write this down and collect my thoughts, I hope my intentions are pure and my actions are appropriate.

The trouble with the Catholic confession is that if Jesus pbuh died for your sins then why do you have to do what the priest says in order to get forgiven? Or even tell the priest to begin with? Also if Jesus pbuh died so everyone's sins can be forgiven wouldn't original sin be forgiven by such a sacrifice at that point in history, thus making baptism pointless since it would have been forgiven before we were born? If someone paid your bill at a restaurant it wouldn't matter whether you believed they paid it or not, it would be paid even if you didn't accept their generosity. Why would one even need to believe someone died for their sins to begin with? If someone paid the price for your sins believing in it would be irrelevant, they either paid the price or they didn't. If they did they can't get reimbursed if I don't believe they paid my way, so if they paid I don't have to say thank you or acknowledge their favor in order to benefit from it. Conditions cannot be set after payment has been made.

Two events were seared into my memory in 2nd grade. One was during "minute math" where you try to do as many math problems as you can in 60 seconds having someone else grade your paper. I could never finish the paper in time and didn't see why we had to rush and get it wrong instead of going slow and being right. Finally the day came that I finished on time. As it was being graded there were no red marks at all, but under peer scrutiny it was discovered that I got one wrong because for the problem 1-1=_ I didn't fill in the blank. My explanation was that 1-1 equals nothing so I didn't write anything, to which class laughter was the response. Trying to hold back the tears until reaching home I learned that even if it's nothing you have to put something or else you have no credibility. Many times after "minute math" the kids would taunt, "*did you remember to write down nothing this time?*" My teachers gave me bad advice saying, "*if you don't know the answer, just make something up*". I think they followed their own advice many times, making stuff up as they taught.

The other event occurred during one of the government's standardized tests. After reading about the mythical race between the tortoise and the hare, while writing a summary there was a stop sign at the bottom of the page saying "DO NOT CONTINUE". I remembered the teacher saying earlier to stop when it tells you to so I stopped, wondering why everyone else was taking so long. At the end of the test it turned out I wasn't supposed to stop at that stop sign but at a different one, so I was yelled at for having sat there without finishing the whole test in time. This resulted in my banishment to the corner in order to complete the test. During my banishment we had a visitor who brought frogs to show and tell us about while I was far away in the corner finishing the test. That day I learned you have to follow the instructions authority figures give regardless of what the written instructions say. This is a very dangerous idea because it leads people to think that if a priest says something is ok and the bible says it is wrong, then you should follow what the priest says instead of the bible. This is called Churchianity, often confused with Christianity.

In 3rd grade my prior experience led me to breakdown and cry during another stressful government standardized test, because I didn't know if I should stop where the test says or where the teacher said. The mental and emotional pressure was immense because we were told these were the most important tests of our lives. Also in 3rd grade the teacher sat us in 4 groups according to the 4 houses in the harry potter books, which were popular at that time. Based on our behavior the groups would get or lose points. The group with the most points at month's end would get pizza just for them, while the rest of the class was forced to watch them enjoy eating it not being allowed to have any. This favoritism further contributed to the "*survival of the fittest*" theme prevalent in public schools and led us to hate the other groups of comrades and see them as opponents. The teacher would read the first book in the harry potter series to us every Friday. Initially I disliked it but gradually softened my stance, until one Friday we had a lot of homework assigned and were given the option to either work on homework or listen to her read. Being students in America, the teacher put the decision to a class vote and I voted to work on homework so that I'd have more time to play videogames at home. But just like with adults, the mass of child voters were too stupid to choose the right option. In order to uphold the results of the vote, I wasn't allowed to work on my homework and listen at the same time because more comrades had voted to just listen. The mob had spoken and I had to obey them. After that I went to the library, got the harry potter book, read it myself and got hooked on that fantasy escape outlet. Yet even after I had read the book, I still had to listen to her read and couldn't do my homework, because in America democracy is always right and the best thing ever made, as proven by the Bush election that year in 2000 CE of which fraud is now widely acknowledged to have occurred. Apparently it would have been socially disruptive if I didn't just listen and twiddle my thumbs like everyone else. By the time January came, while walking down the hall to class returning from the winter break, I didn't think I could continue living in this manner anymore. Life was getting worse and worse, it was one of the first times I contemplated suicide. Before reaching class I heard of a new student "Ray" who had just moved from North Carolina, but was from Japan originally. Although his mom was Asian he had brown skin and didn't look Japanese at all, which taught me that you cannot judge someone's ethnicity based on their skin color. He soon became my best friend giving me a reason to continue on.

On a side note I would like to mention some things about Harry Potter, these are really bad books and movies from an evil franchise. It glorifies witchcraft and paganism also depicting non-magicians as ignorant, feebleminded and inferior, giving them demeaning names like Muggles; which is a form of hate speech suspiciously similar to the name of the 17th century heretical English Christian sect of Muggletonians. The central plot themes are vengeance and hedonism which can only result in the viewers/readers becoming less forgiving, increasingly angry, more selfish and indulgent as well as attracting them towards magic and the jinn who facilitate such things. No magician goes to heaven, unless they repent, cease and desist, but then in that case they would no longer be a magician, so the saying remains true that no magician goes to heaven. Personally I came to know an individual who practiced dark magic at a summer camp. Magic is real and extremely dangerous, magic is not something to be thought of as plain imagination. Don't forget Moses pbuh defeated the magicians' magic with the help of God, so if one endorses or permits "Harry Potter" they subsequently reject the prophet Moses pbuh. The English translation of the New International Version of the bible gives a frightening warning when it attributes God as saying in Leviticus 20:6,

"I will set my face against anyone who turns to mediums and spiritists to prostitute themselves by following them, and I will cut them off from their people."

When learning about New York State, its state bird, state tree and other factoids, I wondered whether everyone in America and the world learned the same trivia we had to memorize about New York State; since it was supposedly the greatest place in the world. Funny how I remember wondering about that but I can't remember any of the State information that they said was so important to remember. It's foolish to think that you are living in the best place with the best government and best beliefs by default, just because it's you. Don't think you've got it the worst either, because things can always be worse and there are more who have had it worse than you than there are those who have it better. Our arrogance makes us think we are someone special better than everyone else, while our greed makes us think we are impoverished.

My 3rd grade class had a pet bunny that would go home with one student each weekend who would return the bunny on the next school day. One weekend it was my turn to take him home and it was a 3-day weekend if I remember correctly. It turned out that the bunny was a lot less lively at my house than it was at school. This caused my parents to call the teacher to find out if anything was wrong with it. The teacher said that the bunny was sick. She was keeping it a secret from the class so they didn't worry and she had its medicine and would give it medicine when I brought it back to school. Well that bunny was really sick and it ended up dying at my house so my parents and I buried it. Going back to school I was terrified and didn't know what to tell my classmates since everyone knew it was my weekend with the bunny, and now the bunny was nowhere to be seen. All my classmates were looking at me thinking, *"What happened? What did you do to the bunny? Where is it?"* Before going back to school my parents had told the teacher the bunny died and she said it was probably because we didn't have the medicine it needed. However she didn't want the students to blame me for the bunny dying so she concocted a lie to shift the blame. Before my classmates could interrogate me, as to the whereabouts of our class bunny, the teacher told her tale. She said the bunny was really sick(which was true) and that she had come to my house and gotten the bunny back from me during the weekend to give it special medicine, but the medicine didn't work well enough and that the bunny died at her house(which was false). I can't remember but I think she might have cried while telling this fictitious story or at least choked up. Anyways all the kids believed her except for me and perhaps one other. The one who doubted was a new student from Florida who was pro-confederacy and was skeptical of everything he was told by "Yankees". He also sat directly across from me and we would consistently tease each other. He may have just been teasing me or perhaps my facial expressions betrayed the truth, but 9 years later he still remembered that when I took the 3rd grade class bunny home it never came back to class and he jokingly blamed me. Recently I realized the gravity of this event, the real travesty was not the death of the bunny, but the fact that the teacher lied to everybody. I knew her story was nearly 100% false but I let it be accepted as the truth because I didn't want to face any of the repercussions the truth might have had. This was wrong of me as was deceiving my classmate from Florida. Although now it hits me that "*the teacher lied*" and the students believed it. This has led me to wonder how many other lies did that teacher tell to the class that I wasn't aware of? How many other teachers have lied to me and others throughout the world, being believed because of their positions of authority? This experience taught me that it was ok to lie if it was in your interest. But in reality lies will never be in a person's interest in the long run because we will be exposed in this world and the next and judged by God for all we did. At the time the lie seemed like it was beneficial, but today I feel disgusted at having been a part of deceiving my classmates. I thought it would take pressure off of me, but since the moment the teacher lied until I wrote this down, the lie had been tearing me up inside making me constantly in fear of being caught by my classmates. Had I told the truth then the pressure and stress of keeping the lie a secret likely would not have existed. In the long-run that pressure was far unhealthier than any short term social repercussions I would have encountered in the third grade. It still bothers me to this day. My 3rd grade teacher lied to the whole class and they fell for it. If a person can lie about the death of a beloved creature and people believe it, then a person could lie about anything and people would believe it. This theme would continue throughout my life as the lies I heard became bigger and more numerous.

   One memorable moment when I was young took place during a family dinner in December. The dinner table had an advent wreath, which is a Catholic December tradition which has 3 purple candles and 1 pink candle lit each night in anticipation of Christmas. The number of candles lit corresponds to which week of December it is, while a different family member lights the candles for each week. The candles would be lit at the table with the wreath close to me. One such night I was wearing a Santa Claus hat and looked across the table at my reflection in the microwave. Everyone else was praying and listening to the bible reading, it was unusual because in the reflection it appeared as though the white cotton ball tassel of my hat was on fire. While still looking at the reflection I put my hand up into the reflected flame and to my surprise it hurt and I shouted out in pain. I have never seen my dad move faster before or since, than he did when he moved to take the flaming hat off of my head. Fortunately I wasn't seriously injured or disfigured from this incident, but it did leave a deep impression on me. The impression was that if the fire of this world was so painfully unbearable for just one split second then the fire of hell is something I absolutely cannot handle, and it must be avoided. The fire of this world is 1/70th as painful as the Hellfire, which is so hot that if a person were to be taken out of Hell and put into a fire of this world they would fall asleep on it thinking the fire of earth to be cold in comparison. Stop, Drop and Roll won't work in Hell. Not only this incident but the many campfires and fireplace fires I witnessed as a child and still witness as an adult have helped me to appreciate just how dangerous and painful the eternal hellfire is and will be. One difference between people in the past and the present is that previous generations were well acquainted with fire on a daily basis for heating, lighting and cooking. Everytime they cooked they literally lit a fire, saw it and felt it's heat. People today rarely see or feel fires which is why we fear the hellfire less than people did in the past. Our "modern lights" have extinguished our spiritually beneficial lights and made our souls/hearts very dark. Our "civilized" standards has led us to be spiritually barbaric. Even just lighting 1 piece of paper on fire everyday can have a tremendous impression and help one to keep the perspective of "the fire" of hell in mind, so that hellfire is not just a word to us when we hear it. I actually think if religious people saw/felt/smelt/heard a fire everyday they'd do less sins and take life more seriously. It's almost funny to imagine people spend all kinds of money trying to have someone put the fear of the hellfire inside them when burning a tiny amount of paper money would do the job much better. I'm not saying to burn money but fire can be a better friend than people if it helps you to stop sinning and reflect. Some friends make you forget about hell, have no fear of hell and lead you towards hell while fire makes you remember and fear hell. Sadly some friends can be worse companions than fire. Surely we would repent faster and more sincerely if we witnessed and experienced fire more often. People may presume such a fascination with fire is a symptom of pyromania but if learning a lesson from fire on a routine basis helps someone to become a better person then why not use fire as a tool? Fires are not just for giving us heat, light and disposal methods, fire is a prophetic spiritual tool to make us reflect on the afterlife and soften our hearts putting the fear of the hellfire within us. All the prophets would use fire as a tool not just for the sake of worldly benefit but because every fire they lit was a lesson and reminder of the hellfire. By forgetting what fire is like many people end up on the road to hellfire where our "fun sins" will be the fuel to burn us. The true pyromaniac is not the one who likes fires in this life but is the one who likes to do sins which lead to the fire in the next life. Modern "civil" methods for heating and lighting don't give us the spiritual lessons and reminders the ancient peoples used to benefit from. By us having less of a relationship with fire than people had with fire in the past it has led our relationship with God to be diluted. For people who are tempted to do sins seeing, smelling, hearing and feeling a fire can help them resist and abstain. We'd hate to put our bodies into fires but when we sin we do exactly that. For some sins it'd even be better if people burned their physical body or touched fire than to do the sin. It's almost silly that people say "I want to stop but I can't stop sinning". You can tell them that they should try safely lighting a fire every time they want to sin and if they still want to sin then maybe they should touch that fire first because it's a lot better for them to touch earthly fire than to sin and touch hellfire later as a result. As a disclaimer please don't hurt yourself and blame me for it but don't sin either. If you are going to hurt yourself, spiritually or physically, you should consider which fire you prefer. Who is wiser the one who temporarily lightly burns or hurts their body by touching fire or the one who sins and burns in the hellfire? God gave us fire as a tool of warning first and foremost, use it. We who fail to use fire to warn ourselves tend to sin a lot. Another lesson from my flaming hat is how we're so cautious around worldly fires, so as not to get burnt or let others get burned, but when we or others are doing sinful things that are leading straight to the Hellfire we are slow to react and stop the sin. Usually we don't even warn the person sinning about the consequences of their beliefs/actions. May God make us people who move faster to protect people from the fire of Hell than we do to protect people from the fire of earth.

      A major part in the life of any Roman Catholic child is the sacrament of the Eucharist or "Holy Communion". Sacraments are sacred rites or rituals in Catholicism and Christianity, with the word originally coming from the word "Sacramentum" which was the annual oath of allegiance to the empire which Roman soldiers would say every new year's day. For those unfamiliar with the Eucharist ritual it is when people in church get up and go to the front to receive what is believed to be the body and blood of Jesus pbuh who is alleged to be the son of God/God. For some Christians this is symbolic but for Roman Catholics it is literal. As a 3rd grader I was led to believe in what was called transubstantiation, which means the wine and bread used literally changes into the body and blood of Jesus pbuh, however it still looks, smells and tastes exactly like the bread and wine it was a few seconds before the priest said the special words. This ceremony is a big ordeal for several reasons. Primarily because after your "first communion" there is usually a big party and everyone you know gives you lots of money, more than you have ever seen before in your life. Spiritually it's significant because now you can go up and receive the sacrament like everyone else and are no longer left out wondering what the body and blood of Jesus pbuh/God/son of God tastes like. When practicing in church preparing for your first official communion, you eat unconsecrated hosts, which are the circular wafers of bread that just haven't had the special words said upon them yet. The unconsecrated hosts are supposed to taste like bread because it's not quite the "real thing". Well it does taste the same on the big day of "Holy Communion" and every time afterwards. Fortunately for my nerves and brain cells the church I went to as a child didn't serve the wine/blood during its services. After the big day, I felt like I was a Christian in every sense because I was finally allowed to participate fully in the church service. Also by childhood standards I was rich! From then on I was almost happy to go to church because now I could eat God/ the son of God which I was taught was a good thing for the body, mind and spirit. It was a rite of passage and a visible sign that I was older and more mature than the little kids, or so I thought.

That summer I started to realize that summer goes by fast and no longer saw it as a time of eternal happiness being the ultimate goal to survive until each year. At least I had a new best friend Ray, who I got to spend a lot of time getting to know and care about. By this time I didn't mind school so much because of the kids I could talk to there, so the shortness of summer was no longer a reason for depression and I anticipated going back to school to catch up with my peers. Initially we were supposed to have the same teacher and classmates for 3rd grade as for 4th grade, but instead we had a different teacher yet still the same students. Public schools have a policy of never allowing the students or the parents to select their teachers. Ray was in my class again and I already knew everyone in my class on day one, so it seemed like it would be the best school year ever.

One day after getting off the bus, finally home after a long day at school, my mom met me before I got to the door and asked, "*Did they tell you what happened?!!*" in such a tone that I feared a close relative had died. This day was September 11th, 2001 CE. When I first learned what had happened I thought "*Why would they tell us what happened hundreds of miles away in New York City? How does this event affect me or us?*" Then my family went over to my maternal aunt's house who had cable and everyone seemed very nervous. It was bewildering because I had never seen adults scared before, let alone the adults in my family. Yet I couldn't understand the reason why. Viewing the footage of planes over and over again, the cable stations were reporting about some guy from some faraway place who had made a video saying that he did it. Even though no such video was made and initially Osama bin Laden denied having anything to do with it, as a kid that's how I interpreted the 9/11 event. I didn't understand how this person blamed on television could have done it and why would he have said so if he had? In kid logic if I had done something bad I certainly wouldn't own up to it. It seemed silly to me that anyone would believe that someone would get themselves in trouble by making such a video, unless they were told to do so by the priest in confession; but apparently that wasn't the case. Also I couldn't understand how anyone could understand what he was saying in the video since it wasn't in English, how did they know what this video even says? In my mind if Osama bin Laden had done it he would have died in the plane crash, so obviously it couldn't have been him. But my main concern was WHY?? Why did it happen and why does it matter? I was never told any reason for why except for that they were evil people jealous of American greatness and we have to destroy them before they do it again. I felt that what had happened was over and wanted everything to go back to normal. It distressed me to see my family so scared. Then when people started talking about war I realized that our lives would never be the same again because my cousin (the son of the aunt whose house we were watching the replays at) had joined the marines earlier and would be going away to fight. I thought it would be nice visiting my aunt's house every day watching updates on the war and hoped it would bring us all closer together. But huddling around the television with the entire family comforting each other didn't turn into a nightly thing. It seems families only get together for tragedies or socially obligatory holidays. Another thing I remember about this time that continued for a few years past September 11th was that people were constantly citing statistics on what an atomic bomb would do to us and how many seconds we would die after impact, as well as who would die first among family and friends, and who would be the last to die seconds after everyone else; as if the last to die was somehow better than all the rest of us. A lot of this was serious and some of it was said in jest but I thought it was all foolish, thinking that I haven't done anything to make any enemies so why would someone want to harm me? Why would anyone even bomb Western New York anyway; what is so important around here? Other than that everything else was pretty much the same as before for a kid, and if it weren't for my cousin fighting overseas I might not even have known that a war was going on and it's actually still going on as I write this.

It is not appropriate in this book to analyze all the controversies surrounding the physical impossibilities, WTC 7, the implosions, the lack of footage from the pentagon, the ground zero firefighters lawsuit against the U.S. government and request for videos from the planes' black boxes and the molten steel which was illegally taken from ground zero without investigation of the forensic evidence, or that Abdul Aziz Al-Omari, Saeed Al-Ghamdi, Waleed Al-Shehri, Ahmed Al-Nami and Salem Al-Hazmi whom the FBI announced as 5 of the suicide flyers are alive with alibis and publicly protesting the accusations that they killed themselves in an act of violence on 9/11. Such information is widely available in numerous books or accessible with a quick internet search for anyone who cares to learn about any theory that's different from the

American government's theory about what happened on 9/11/01. This is not one of those types of books. I mentioned the heavily disputed events of 9/11 to demonstrate the impact they had on me as a Christian American child. Regardless of how the buildings fell and why, it is sad that people died under those conditions. Although in regards to the 9/11 incident it could just have been a tragic coincidence that 2 planes crashed into the same building on the same day. For those who think it couldn't be a coincidence, then thinking this universe came into existence by coincidence without being designed by the Creator is even more ridiculous. It's more likely 9/11 was a coincidence than the existence of the entire universe.

Eerily Adolf Hitler was accused of ordering the attack that destroyed Germany's Reichstag building while he was president, in order to exploit the civilian emotional reaction. This allowed him to gain more political power, pass new laws and take control over Germany, eventually turning it into a police state. Adolf Hitler wrote: *"in the big lie there is always a certain force of credibility; because the broad masses of a nature are always more easily corruptible in the deeper strata of their emotional nature than consciously or voluntarily had, and thus in the primitive simplicity of their minds they readily fall victims to the big lie than to the small lie, since they themselves often tell small lies in little matters, but would be ashamed to resort to. Largescale falsehood. It would never come into their heads to fabricate colossal untruths, and they would not believe that others could have the impudence to distort the truth so infamously. Even though the facts which prove this to be so are put clearly before them, they will still doubt and waver and will continue to think that there may be some other explanation, for the grossly impudent lie always leaves traces behind it, even after it has been nailed down-a fact which all expert liars in this world and all who conspire together in the art of lying know only too well and exploit in the basest manner."*

That excerpt is from *"The Official Nazi English Translation of Mein Kampf"*. While this official translation demonstrates the difficulty in translating something smoothly, the ideas expressed within this excerpt are profound with major implications. Afterall Hitler's contemporary, leader of the USSR, Josef Stalin said, "*The easiest way to gain control of a population is to carry out acts of terror.*" More revealing is that Hermann Goring, who was Hitler's 2nd in command, said: "*Naturally the common people don't want war....But, after all, it is the leaders of the country who determine the policy, and it is always a simple matter to drag the people along, whether it is a democracy, or a fascist dictatorship, or a parliament or a commuist dictatorship....All you have to do is tell them they are being attacked, and denounce the pacifists for lack of patriotism and exposing the country to danger. It works the same in any country.*" Adolf Hitler, despite his flaws, was a man who knew how to get things done even if those things were crazy, evil and widely unpopular. He explained his methods for doing this: "*I use emotion for the many and reserve reason for the few.*" and "*It is not truth that matters, but victory.*" Personally I think many politicians since him have copied his tactics, albeit for different reasons to accomplish different goals.

In school things were never the same again, every single day we now had to recite the pledge AND a patriotic song of which all of them had to be memorized by the end of the year. These songs were long, with complex words that we didn't even know the meanings of. As a class we practiced a different song each week. They included songs like *"America the beautiful"*, *"The Star Spangled Banner"* and *"God bless America"* with some people saying amen at the end as though they were prayers. In church they started singing these same songs, which made church even longer and led me to believe that it really was a religious war of good versus evil and that these "monsters" didn't believe in God and worked for the Devil. Although rather than hate at such a young age I was just afraid of them. A plaque was also set up at church with names of marines on it, every week my parents and I looked at my cousin's name feeling as though he had been sent on a special holy mission. It truly seemed as though if "*they*" weren't "*stopped*" now, then "*they*" would take over the world and would kill me, my friends and my whole family. People made it seem like the Taliban=Al-Qaeda and that they were like the Mongols about to overrun Europe and that America had to act before they crossed the Atlantic Ocean and conquered the entire world. I thought "*they*" would force us to worship Satan; some people said it was the last crusade and the end of times. I actually thought the Taliban were on the brink of global domination and America was making a last stand for the forces of good. One didn't hear too many Christians saying to "*turn the other cheek*" in those days, instead it was all about getting revenge and promoting national pride and unity. No one was quoting the biblical verses of Matthew 5:38-40 where in the english translation of the New International version of the Bible it says Jesus pbuh said: [38] "*You have heard that it was said, 'Eye for eye, and tooth for tooth.* [39] *But I tell you, do not resist an evil person. If anyone slaps you on the right cheek, turn to them the other cheek also.* [40] *And if anyone wants to sue you and take your shirt, hand over your coat as well.*"

    The next fall I went into 5th grade with new classmates, some who were new to the school having come from an elementary school that had closed. Most were girls but at least Ray was in my class, we sat right next to each other because we both had "He" as the first 2 letters of our last name. Finally at the top of the totem pole I was in the highest grade, no one could look down on us except for teachers. One Wednesday in early fall Ray and I were planning our next sleep over, that night we were going to ask our parents for permission, on Thursday we would decide which house it would be at, on Friday one of us would bring their stuff to school and sleep overnight at the other's place. Thursday Ray wasn't in school and the teacher said he had a doctor's appointment. Friday he was absent as well. All the next week Ray didn't come to school and I never heard anything from him. By this time I had gotten worried, so my mom told me Ray had called on the Wednesday night I had last saw him, but since I was already asleep she didn't want to wake me up. After another week of worry, I eventually found out from mutual friends and parents who heard from teachers and Ray's stepdad what had happened. I learned that same Wednesday Ray, his toddler brother and his mother had disappeared in the middle of the night and went back to Japan leaving his military stepdad behind. His mom didn't intend to come back to America and I would never see, hear or communicate with Ray again. In retrospect his mother was acting somewhat rationally. As a Japanese woman, witnessing the new security apparatus being constructed in America must have been intimidating for her. Especially if she took into account what happened to the Japanese who were living in America during WWII being placed in concentration camps. Ray's mother was probably afraid of the new police state and decided upon a course of action she thought would be best for her and her children. Selfishly I didn't see it that way.

Basically it felt like my best friend had been kidnapped because it was such a sudden and unexpected move without affording me the opportunity to say goodbye. People turned to me wondering how I was going to handle Ray's disappearance since they knew we were best friends. When people are worried about how you are going to react to something and put you under a microscope it tends to make you worry and handle it even worse because you know that everyone is observing your ability to cope. It was very difficult and I had started to get depressed again, but eventually it got easier day by day as my memory faded with the dreams of him coming back occurring less and less. I learned that relationships with people are temporary and can end at any time. It's best not to become too invested in something that is temporary in the end. Be grateful for what you have when you have it so that when it is gone its disappearance doesn't make you sad.

Being once again in a semi weakened emotional state videogames alone weren't enough of an escape, especially when the PS2 was out and I was stuck playing PS1. Perhaps if I didn't know the PS2 existed I would have been happier, but how could I be happy if I didn't have the newest version? One week all the boys were grouped into the same class and all the girls were grouped into a different class, because our 5th grade teachers were going to teach us about sex. Everyone was grossed out and uncomfortable having to look at pictures of our private parts and being told about reproduction. We were especially curious what the girls were learning in the other class since the boys only learned about boy parts and girls only learned about girl parts. Many of us didn't understand why they were teaching us this when nobody was interested in the opposite gender at that time. We thought by the time we needed to know we would've forgotten all they had told us.

As might be expected that school year I began again to search for a new companion, however this time it was a female companion I was searching for. I suspect the interest in the other gender was partially motivated by the lessons we received on sex. Remember before they taught us about sex all the guys thought girls were gross, but the teachers told us that was the wrong opinion to have. For me the ultimate goal was marriage and happiness ever after which can only be achieved through marriage, which is what the movies I had watched had taught me to believe at that point in my life. It just so happened the one girl I had a crush on was the first girl in my grade to go on a date with a guy, but she went on it with someone else instead of me. I was in over my head and heartbroken. The music on the radio seemed to speak directly to me, just as the love songs are specially designed to do. This is when my love affair with music began and music seemed to be all that kept me going, whenever I was down the songs would lift me up. By the end of the year, she broke up with the other guy but I was still hurt and didn't know how far to go in the relationship game, or if this girl even cared about me still or ever. At a school concert a parent asked who it was that I had liked and when I pointed her out they responded with a remark about how she has "*sexy legs*". I was disgusted by the thought and repulsed by the idea of lust. I mention this because it shows how parents unintentionally push their children towards carnality and the objectification of women through such off the cuff remarks they may not even think twice about nor consider sexist or offensive. Today I can honestly express gratitude that I didn't have a girlfriend and was fortunate to not have had my life ruined even more by that particular adolescent infatuation. The lesson learned from my childhood love triangle was that dating and relationships can really mess up life. Today I wouldn't wish dating upon anyone, not even an enemy, because it has none of the benefits of marriage with all of the difficulties; if not more of the difficulties. There is no such thing as an exclusive relationship when you are dating, your partner will always be looking for someone better than you, or at the very least will be getting offers from people better than you. Religiously there is a limit to how much physical interaction you can have, but even from a secular viewpoint you don't really want to have a child with someone you're not married to. How people can fight the temptation for pre-marital intercourse while dating is beyond me, personally I don't think I could abstain if I was dating someone. Also since there is no solid commitment that means one disagreement or misunderstanding can end the relationship in a minute, making all that time, money and energy you expended become worthless overnight. Actually it can be worth less than worthless because you may end up having regret, hatred or debt because of this relationship or maybe a sexually transmitted disease or a child if you couldn't resist the temptation to have sex. To be clear: dating does not lead to marriage, engagement leads to marriage. Some people may disagree and say dating leads to marriage but if you ask teenagers who are dating many will tell you that they aren't ready for marriage (and they probably aren't even if they don't admit it) and there are many others who will explicitly tell you they never want to get married yet they're dating. Clearly dating does not have a direct connection to marriage because if it did people who didn't want to get married wouldn't date. If you are serious about spending a lifetime with someone then go about it properly and state your intentions for marriage upfront so that right from the beginning the two of you can focus on determining whether the other will be a good husband/wife or mother/father, you don't have to get married on the first day you meet but this way you will be more likely to avoid cheaters, abusers, psychopaths, and those only interested in having sex. The family should know this person so they can protect you from getting hurt, supervised interactions would also be ideal so no funny stuff goes on and sexual tension doesn't have anything to do with the reason for the meetings. If your partner doesn't want to spend time with you under family supervision before you're married, then they won't want to spend time with your family after you're married. This will lead to strained family relationships and perhaps broken families. This could've been prevented if the family screened the spouse before you fell in love. Also for the youth especially, the time saved by not dating is extremely valuable. I fear many young people are having their development stunted or permanently damaged because they started dating before they knew who they were or what they wanted in life, simply because they wanted to experience affection from another human being. In hindsight it's obvious that I was attempting to fill my inner emptiness with games, girls, music and any other form of entertainment available. I was continually disappointed and never satisfied or happy. I thought having a relationship with a female would finally make me happy. However this can never be done by any person and it is unfair, unrealistic and unhealthy to imagine that another person is going to make you happy. Its as simple as this happy + happy equals happiness. So if you are not happy being single then you should not be dating. A happy couple is two happy people that just happen to be together. If they weren't with each other they would still be happy without each other. Simple logic dictates that if you are unhappy alone then you will be unhappy with a partner because no person enters a relationship with the goal of wanting "to make the other person happy", typically they go into a relationship wanting happiness themselves. So in the end you have two unhappy people together expecting the other one to make them happy and when they eventually separate they are both less happy than when they first met. Or they stay together thinking that a child or children will make them happy which only complicates the matter and exposes an innocent child or children to emotional problems that they will likely internalize and carry forward into their own relationships, thus establishing a cycle of unhappiness that will last for generations. This is because the wrong antidote is always prescribed. Although it changes with each generation, some chasing money, some chasing fame, and some chasing pleasure the end result tends to stay the same, everyone wants to be happy but they never are; no matter how hard they try. Unfortunately like so many of us I thought and was told I just hadn't met "the right girl" yet and that the next one would solve all my problems.

      By coincidence, soon after that experience, enough money had been saved up so I could buy the much desired PS2. While on the way to the store to make the purchase I received news that an uncle of mine was getting a divorce. At the moment I was so enthusiastic about getting a new video game console I wasn't concerned and didn't fully realize the extent to which my life would be affected. Now I know that family tends to affect your life more than is anticipated. After the initial euphoria of gamer paradise had subsided, my uncle's kids, who are younger than me, started visiting more often and we began to play together getting to know each other. As the only child of my parents, I never had to share any of my toys with anyone except specially selected friends that were my own age, and even then there was a limit to what they could touch and for how long. I was young and felt violated, thinking that my maternal cousins were breaking all my precious toys that took a lifetime to obtain and getting them sticky while playing with them the wrong way. Since my younger cousins lived two houses away their visits were frequently spontaneous and unexpected, which until I became fond of them instilled a kind of anxiety and dread in not knowing when what's mine will be mine and when it won't be. This is also related to my unique familial status. I'm not just the only child of my parents, I'm the only "only child" in my family. All of my maternal and paternal grandparents had brothers and sisters, while both sets of my grandparents had 4 kids each. Of those 8 total kids, my mother is the youngest of 4 and my father is also the youngest of 4. So both of my parents are the youngest of their households and my 3 aunts and my 3 uncles all have multiple kids as well. I am literally the only one in the family who doesn't know what it's like to have a brother or sister. As a result my idea of human brotherhood or sisterhood and the concept of "Brothers and Sisters in faith" is rather enhanced since those are literally the only types of Brothers and Sisters I have. So at the time my perception of cousins who would play with me must've been very different than their perception of me, and my perspective on family itself must be very different as a result of this peculiar singular familial status; which ironically nobody else in the family seems to have noticed. One benefit of being the "only only child" is that regarding terms like "only one God" I have a deeper understanding of what "only" and "only one" means. Eventually I learned to share with and care about my cousins, but at first it was a traumatic experience which made me feel family was a burden whose relation was something to be put up with rather than nurtured. I failed to learn all possessions are temporary and will eventually be inherited by someone else anyway, with only temporary usage being available to us for a limited time. Even before we had the stuff we have now, the raw materials of it was someone else's originally. So it was never ours to begin with and it will not be ours to end with. All we own are handed down gifts on loan.

      One night in August, after coming home from a dinner out with family, I entered the house to find a bunch of stuff lying on my bed. It was soon discovered not to be a result of someone trashing my room, as I had immediately complained about, rather it was because of someone robbing the house! Apparently they used my bed as the place to sort out what valuables they wanted to steal and left me with the junk. Doesn't everyone feel that they always get left with the junk? Being the victim of a home burglary is an unforgettable experience whether you are a witness when it happens, or if you just experience the aftermath. The initial reaction is to think about what has been taken and is lost forever. As a child without much worth taking, I don't remember having much stolen and specifically remember my change collection being left alone. So for me the scariest thought was that the person(s) was still in the house, armed and dangerous. When the police were called I expected it to be just like the movies with a crime scene, finger printing, investigators, pictures and samples being taken and lots of interviews, maybe I'd even be asked by news reporters for a comment. In reality it took for what seemed like hours for police to arrive and I only remember one officer showing up, who didn't seem to care at all that we were robbed. From my childish viewpoint the police didn't do anything at all, no fingerprints or pictures, not even a consoling word to me that I could remember. I think after he left I might've even asked, *"Aren't they going to do something? What about all our stuff?"* Getting robbed tends to have several effects on the human psyche. One could be a feeling of gratitude for life, family and intangibles, while another is an intimidating feeling of insecurity and continuous danger. With the most common reaction being one of increased materialism and a sense of being violated thereby creating a sense of urgency and importance for protecting one's assets. The newfound gratitude for family quickly vanishes after your next argument. In my case the feeling of insecurity and danger did not go away, even after an alarm system was installed, which actually makes one feel more insecure. Similar to how America has the world's largest military yet many politicians would have us believe that America has never been more vulnerable. (Which makes one wonder about the vulnerability of the nations who don't have the world's largest military, how do those citizens feel safe?) Every time the alarm was set it was a constant reminder of the utmost importance and value the possessions around me were supposed to have and of the vigilant guard necessary in order to keep such "nice things". Especially since these were tools to make me happy, it seemed that if I lost them it meant losing any and all chances of happiness. I became so worried about protecting the house that I no longer enjoyed anything inside of it. Increased security increased my insecurity. Instead of relying on God for protection I began to rely on an alarm system, other humans and myself. Doing so made me feel more at risk.

When entering 6th grade there were two middle schools in my city with grades 6-8. Based on my proximity to the one school it meant I was one of the few from my elementary to go there while most everyone else I knew went to the other one. On the first day, at lunch everyone sat with who they knew and with the whole cafeteria being just the sixth grade all the boys from my elementary school and me barely filled one table. We soon put social Darwinism into practice aka "*survival of the fittest*" and one kid from our table got sent to the principal's office that very first day for mischief making in lunch. Days later after bragging to my elementary pals how out of all of them I was the best prankster in lunch citing all my past elementary experiences of making mischief without getting caught, they all agreed to frame me with the middle school cafeteria monitors for doing nothing. Right in front of me they told me they were going to accuse me of doing bad stuff and get me in trouble despite me being innocent and there was nothing I'd be able to do about it, I called their bluff and said there was no way that would ever work because they have no proof and I'm innocent. I didn't think I could get in trouble for something I didn't do, especially when in all my past experiences you could only get in trouble for what you were seen doing and never for what you did without getting seen. Yet to my surprise they called a lunch monitor over, told their story and I got in trouble because it was their word vs. mine and they were unanimous despite having totally made it all up. While foolishly being so young and flustered I didn't even say that they had planned to set me up minutes before because I didn't think I needed to, since I thought lack of proof and my conviction were enough to be left unpunished. I was wrong and they made an example out of me, to show the rest of the kids what happens to troublemakers. That's when I realized my mischief making methods were obsolete and I was out of my classmates' league. My style of troublemaking was based on not getting caught, I wasn't capable of manipulating the authority like they were. The worst part about it was that all the guys in my grade from my elementary school were at that table, since all the rest were at the other middle school. The table of guys from my elementary school had turned against me and I didn't know any of the other guys in our grade. So this treachery was quite bitter to experience, since customarily one expects one's prior classmates to support you when you are all an extreme minority in a new school. It was evident that past acquaintance meant nothing in this new social environment. Instead of socially supporting each other, we were social competitors each one of us trying to become the best positioned with the "coolest kids" from the other schools. Prior popularity and coolness was utterly irrelevant, even amongst former classmates and friends. All those years of networking meant nothing in this new school and my reputation had to be entirely remade starting from the bottom. Not fun. So I bounced around from table to table staying a few weeks each time (until they got sick of me) until eventually settling down with a new group of kids from another school. For the first time in my scholastic career I wasn't "Mr. Popular" yet I still had the arrogance and felt entitled to popularity. This led to some kids bullying me in order to teach me my place. Others realized the similarities between me and them and encouraged bullies to knock it off. One might wonder what the school did about such bullying as it ranged from verbal to physical abuse. Well they gave a speech once every few months telling people to report their fellow classmates and snitch if they witness bullying. As expected this did nothing to decrease the bullying in the school and even made it a joke to bully, actually having the effect of encouragement. Until I had made new friends, this severely bothered me. However now I realize why it was encouraged rather than prevented. The school wanted to create a common culture among students who had arrived from various different schools, with American views about democracy dictating the majority culture to be superior, students from the less represented schools either had to change into different people to be popular or had to suffer for being different. Some of my elementary peers became super popular, but almost unrecognizable from whom I grew up knowing them as. Other elementary school peers became extremely isolated and unpopular. I was more towards the middle, with my social rank differing based on those around me yet there was immense pressure to make new friends at all costs. This led me to have different behavior for each type of social scenario. I was almost a different person depending on which class I was in or who I was with. The family "me" was different than the friend "me". My new friends were chosen based on my own addictions for videogames and sports, while morals and spirituality was something to be kept to yourself. However popularity requires sacrifices, so I became famous for belly flops off the diving board. Being skinny they didn't hurt, but even if they did the price for fame had to be paid somehow. There was a limit to how far I would follow the crowd, as the curriculum taught, and that was when it came to dances and parties. The middle school dances go a step farther than elementary dances because of the encouraged dating and the fights that result from the constant changes in relationship status, which changed almost as frequently as the music being played. I was taken to one middle school dance once by a parent and refused to go in. Another time I had so much anxiety because of a sleep-over that would've involved me going to a dance beforehand that I got seriously ill and was able to use the stress induced illness as an excuse not to go. Something inside just prevented me from wanting to dance. Yes I wanted a girlfriend but I didn't want any physical relationship. My desire for a girlfriend was to fill the emotional void within, and society had idolized female companionship. But alas no one wants to date the guy who doesn't dance, because then your date can't be shown off in order to climb the social ladder; so I was unintentionally saved from much heartbreak. All thanks and praises be to God. Sometimes staying in your comfort zone can be a good thing.

During the next school year only one middle school would be open and all those students joined my new school, reuniting me with familiar faces of old classmates. Like me, they had different personalities but for the most part it restarted the socialization process again, instigating another personality update.

AGES 11-14

With the new influx of students that occurred from combining middle schools the school administration enacted a divide and conquer policy, purposely mixing the two student bodies into one so that no one knew anyone else and was forced to make new friends. Many fights broke out because of this strategy, but eventually everyone changed and a new social class structure appeared once again. Initially I became closer with the kids I already knew from the year before, since it was a warzone and felt like the other school had invaded(and they were known for fighting), but then after the reactionary unity we broke apart as the same process of trying to socially advance at the expense of past relationships repeated itself. I really knew my social standing had fallen since elementary when a not too cool girl from elementary who had become one of the cool kids in the 2nd year of middle school and transferred to mine asked me, "*What happened? You used to be cool and popular.*" and I didn't know what to say so I just said "*Yeah I know, but most all the guys from our school went to the other one so nobody knew me here.*" The increased athletic competition also sullied my reputation, since in elementary I was one of the elite athletes but in middle school I was average, although due to lack of popularity I felt below average and lack of social confidence doesn't help athletic performance while lackluster athletic performance due to social stress only decreases social confidence. In elementary school I was a trash talker, but trash talking doesn't help when a sub-par athletic performance doesn't back up your mouth. So when teams started picking me near last, even after some of the obese kids, I learned to not trash talk. Then since expectations for me were low I tended to outperform since the opponents team would mismatch personnel with me. By high school I considered myself an upper class athlete able to compete with most people in most sports and I talked a lot of trash which ironically made me popular in high school, but those first few years after elementary put me in the lower bracket in the athletic ranking. In 7th-8th grade you really needed to have something significantly unique about yourself in order to be worthy of attention and stand out as an individual. The tools to become popular were clothes, looks, athleticism and ironically popularity. Of which I had nothing but the clothes, but the clothes never seemed to make the difference I thought and felt they would and could. In hindsight the clothes that I stressed over, didn't matter, but at the time I thought they were extremely important to my social ranking in society as well as self-esteem. Everyone probably thought that way, and our parents' budgets probably suffered greatly because of it. Once more the people from elementary school who had changed when we went to middle school changed yet again so drastically I wondered if they had even been real people to start with. It is amazing how you can spend a childhood growing up with people and then witness several personality transformations so rapidly it leaves them unrecognizable. Authority figures call it "learning how to adapt" but it seems more like assimilation to the extent that the individual person is whoever the masses want them to be, losing their own individuality. Kids called this being fake, or being a poser, even though most people were one you didn't want anyone to know that you were. This unstable culture and social strata made me reluctant to get too close to anyone because I realized the friend you make this year might be your enemy the next year. It wasn't as though I was a social outcast, because I was on friendly terms with most people in my grade. I was just careful not to get too close to anyone as a result of the fear of getting hurt. Simply put, few people met my high standards of what a friend should be and since I was so friendly with so many I didn't really know how to get to the next level of friendship with anyone of them. Essentially I was socially conservative and averse to the risk of developing relationships to deep meaningful levels. By hoping to reach the top of the social ladder I didn't want to get typecasted into a particular social ranking. I was a category of my own. Practically I was a loner but that's "not cool" and can easily be thought of as "loser" so I didn't really want to be a loner or have people think I was a loner. Yet I felt a little lonely.

Throughout the middle school years my peers and I were taught about drugs and sex in depth. We had been taught about drugs and sex in elementary school but in middle school we were taught details and methods on how to use/do these correctly. The teachers made learning about the crazy things people did on drugs a form of comedy. Naturally since we were encouraged to party by parents and teachers in order to "make new friends" we gained access to these drugs we learned about in school. The kids who knew the most people had the biggest parties and were therefore the most popular. However occasional birthday parties aren't enough to maintain that level of popularity and parties became more and more frequent due to the increased stress from school and the convenient cover of school dances. Party locations soon changed places, from the kid who knew the most people to the kid who had the least restrictive parent(s). Thus the drugs came into play because if you can't host the party but still want to be popular there are only a few ways to do it: Either be great at all sports, be funny on all occasions, have a popular boyfriend or girlfriend, or be the one who does crazy things on drugs whom nobody would ever expect to. Surprisingly many kids good at sports with high grades and wealthy parents became popular because of the parties, with the drugs having no effect on their performance. Now at this early stage the drugs people were using consisted of basic things like cigarettes, alcohol and marijuana. In the mandatory health classes they taught us about the ills of these products, but that's like teaching a child how to open the cookie jar and expecting them never to do it; if you really don't want your kids to eat cookies you don't have a "cookie jar"! The side effects were jokes which we thought were not intended to be taken seriously, just like the warnings about bullying. They told us about the horrors of bullying but they'd go out of the way to ignore it when it happened. Since these side effects we were taught about never immediately showed up some even said, *"they're just trying to scare you"*.

Sex was the other thing to do to gain popularity, since few had experienced intercourse by that age to have done so meant you were extra popular (with at least one person), thus there was a race to lose virginity; because *"only cool kids can get any"*. I don't know why they taught us about how to have sex, use birth control and put on condoms in school if they didn't want us to do it. Whenever teachers were asked they replied, *"so you know how to when you're ready"*. The point is that we weren't ready because we didn't know, but once we knew then who is to say that we weren't ready? A personal friend of mine and his girlfriend claimed to be having sex. When I asked him why he wasn't concerned about pregnancy he told me that they're too young to get pregnant because she hadn't had her first period. On the bus when I was in 6th grade an older girl in 8th grade would boast about giving popular boys sexual favors and how she couldn't wait to try out what she learned that day in health class. By the time I was in 8th grade, the boys on the bus would ask the girls for sexual favors and they would make it seem as though they were doing the girls a favor by asking them because they could get the favors done from any girl in the school. They tried tricking the girls into thinking it was a privilege to sexually pleasure boys. One time it made me laugh because one girl said to a boy "*If you can get any other girl in school to do it for you then why don't you? Stop asking me!*" As I grew older I started to suspect that our school teachers wanted us to have sex when we were young. Think about it, you don't teach a kid how to drive 10 years before they can apply for a driver's license, so why did they teach us how to have sex 5 years before we were old enough to apply for a driver's license? We should learn about marriage before learning about sex, only in promiscuous societies do they teach you about sex before teaching you about marriage. One reason children are experiencing sex before marriage is because they are learning about sex before learning about marriage.

    The majority of kids were not doing both drugs and fornicating, but I'd estimate more than a third were doing one or the other. So accounting for the fakes and liars maybe 25% were doing this stuff before becoming a teenager. If you're an older parent you might not believe me, and if you're younger than me then you know the numbers are probably higher. Keep in mind I lived in the white suburbs, this wasn't some inner city ghetto school I was going to. Even if you weren't "doing the nasty" we were being prepared for it, one of the common things boys did would be to recommend pornography sites to each other. The amount of time and detail spent discussing masturbation differed depending on which group of guys you were around, but across the board you were considered to be homosexual or a freak if you didn't enthusiastically approve of such conversations or deeds. Most of the boys had no shame. I didn't talk to girls much so I don't know if they also talked about such things. Parents should definitely be aware that these types of habits often start before becoming a teenager, they should talk to their children about these issues in a compassionate way without making it too awkward. Maybe your kid isn't doing it, but if you don't talk about it and help them with advice on how to control their desires then how can you expect them not to when all the kids in school are publicly glorifying and recommending it? One talk is not enough, constant reminders are needed because there is constant temptation from Satan.

    The pressure put on me by family and friends to get a girlfriend or to go out to parties was immense. Family actually puts more pressure on kids leading to this stuff than they realize. With the phrases "anti-social" and "shy" or forcing your children to "go make some new friends" you are essentially telling them to change whatever it is about yourself that is preventing people from liking you. This includes changing your morals and personality. Don't think your kid picked up those bad manners from that new friend of theirs; it's those new bad manners that helped them make that new friend and many more. When I look back at middle school from this perspective I see that the ones who disgusted me with their changing personalities and associations were just obeying their parents who were proud of them while being oblivious to the drug habits or sexual appetites they unintentionally told their kids to pick up. My advice to parents is not to pressure your kids to make new friends. If you want your kid to be popular with many friends then they will probably have a few unsavory characters as friends. If they can't resist the pressure from parents to make friends how will they resist the pressure from friends to make friends with people who will pressure them to do bad things? That is, if their friends already aren't those bad people.

      Being semi-athletic and stuck playing many sports, which my parents didn't allow me to quit, I hung around with the athletic and/or video gaming crowd of people. In middle school I started caring more about what I wore, especially since acne started around that time. The NFL had become my new hobby which covered both sports and videogames. Despite the Buffalo Bills being the regional team, after years of losing seasons I realized it was foolish to root for the home team just because they were the home team. If anyone had a choice in choosing the home team certainly they wouldn't pick the losers. Since I didn't choose to be born in Western New York, I decided that the local team has no right to represent me and that they shouldn't expect me to be a loyal fan. Thus I wore numerous NFL jerseys, however these can be quite expensive for a youth in a country where it's against the law for kids to work. I quickly learned the art of leverage in order to get the material things I wanted. It might sound bad, but the reality was that objects were the most important things in my life since they were the tools to achieve happiness. This jersey addiction became so excessive, by 10th grade I had over 15 jerseys (the NFL only has 32 teams) and would write down the days I wore which jersey on so that I wouldn't wear the same one too often. I would wear them Mondays, Fridays and sometimes Tuesdays and Thursdays during the football season if there was going to be a day off preceding a football game. I was constantly coordinating my clothing to seem new and in style. Some were even more addicted than I was, in 10th grade there was a kid I knew in 9th who wore a different football jersey every single day of the school year, even during the offseason. I didn't fully understand at the time how stupid it was to wear a jersey of someone else advertising them. For example you wouldn't want to wear someone else's underwear, so the only reason one buys another's jersey is because they want to pretend they are them or close to them and emulate them, which looks really bad when the scandals expose these athletes for who they really are. There are numerous professional athletes who have been involved in murder and drugs or sexual abuse, yet thousands of people continue wearing the jerseys of these athletes even after their crimes have been exposed. How can someone like the way a person plays a sport so much that they ignore and overlook their corrupted moral conduct? Our society today has put too much importance on athletic ability at the expense of everything else. If sports were not so important to the gambling world athletes would not be getting paid the exorbitant amounts they are today, and such an extensive market would not exist. Athletes don't make the sport important, the games are played for the speculators more than the spectators, or for "love of the game". Today's professional athletes are idolized like the roman gladiators and too often they are cheered on with few people realizing the similarities. Unfortunately I didn't realize my motivation for wearing jerseys and justified my obsession by comparing myself to those who were more obsessed than I, which is not correct. If you've killed 1 million babies you don't point your finger and justify it by saying the guy who killed 2 million babies is even worse. If you are wrong and someone else is wrong, that still means that you are wrong and need to change. May God help us to see when we're wrong and make us humble enough to change, and to not to be fooled by the games people play.

During the Easter season in 7th grade my Mom started going to Stations of the Cross and dragged me along. Stations of the Cross is a type of service the Catholic Church does during the Easter season in which a cross is carried around the church with frequent stops, 12 in all if I correctly recall, with different prayers being said at each stop(station) in a type of reenactment of Jesus' alleged crucifixion pbuh. It begins with Ash Wednesday, which is a Wednesday Catholics go to church and put ashes on their forehead making the sign of a cross, it is justified with the famous saying *"ashes to ashes and dust to dust"* and how humans will turn into dust when they are dead. Although reflecting on it now it doesn't seem too promising to be told you will be turning to ashes. Wouldn't turning to ashes mean that you will be burned up in the hellfire? I couldn't find any reason for doing Ash Wednesday in the bible and neither Jesus pbuh or any of his companions did it. I did not know why Catholics did Ash Wednesday, or Stations of the Cross, or how they started even though I used to participate. Another thing Catholics do takes place on "Holy Thursday", the day before "Good Friday" when they visit 7 Catholic churches on that day/night to pray certain prayers in each. I would get dragged along on this lengthy nightly journey by my parents and grandparents, but I've yet to find any biblical reasons for doing it and don't think early Christians did it either since they didn't have churches to visit. To persuade me to go my mom bribed me by offering money for each time I went.(but not with the 7 churches, only the Stations of the Cross stuff) Just like with the first communion, money can make a kid religious real quick. Heck, money can make many adults religious even quicker than it does with kids. All thanks and praises be to God for guiding me away from the worship of wealth and may we all be continuously protected from greed.

One time while waiting for the church service to start, the deacon (like a priest but can't do certain rituals and is allowed to get married) comes out and says the altar servers didn't show up, he asks me if I can fill in for them and carry the cross. I said sure and went to change into fancy robes, thinking this would be a one-time thing. My mom was in the bathroom at the time and didn't know where I was or what happened until I came out carrying a huge heavy cross. After doing the circuit around the church I went to the back and stayed there for the rest of the service not knowing what I was supposed to do after that. In 5th grade they ask all the kids to sign up to be altar servers, which basically means they sit by the altar during church, light candles and get stuff for the priest at certain parts during the service. I didn't want to ever do that because I didn't want to sit in front of everybody during church. The next week and the weeks after that I ended up carrying the cross again and doing the other stuff as well. Something which was particularly tricky to do as an altar server was ringing the bells during the communion rite. I don't mean the big church bells, but during the part when the priest lifts up the cup of wine and later lifts up the wafer of bread an altar server is supposed to ring a little set of bells to signify when they turn into the blood and body of Jesus pbuh/ God. I never quite knew the exact moment this took place, since there were no clues to let me know, so I was basically taking a guess every time I rang the bells. Yet since I always waited until after certain phrases were said I guess nobody ever knew I was just ringing the bells hoping my timing was correct. Then one time while sitting near the altar when it came time for the bread and wine to turn into the body and blood, I got inspired that this is all nonsense. It was wine and bread when I brought it out and it's wine and bread when these people are eating it. Then I looked up at the cross with a statue hanging on it and thought of how big a scam this all was and how clever that person on the cross must've been to have made everyone believe that he was a God/son of God to have people worship him. I had seen all the money that people gave to the church in the back and realized how lucrative those donations were just at one church, let alone worldwide. I looked at the people with dismay thinking how can these adults be so stupid to believe a human being is God and that this bread and wine is changing into that person's body and blood thousands of years after that person walked the earth? However these thoughts soon vanished and I convinced myself that it had been the devil suggesting these ideas. The next year I was even filled with rage and wanted to beat up a kid in church sitting ahead of me who was saying how the Church had pagan roman origins and it was all just make believe, relishing how in the old days such a kid would be killed for saying that and thinking how he deserved to be taught a physical lesson. (Which many Catholic readers may be thinking about me while reading this.)

    That summer I spent a week in Canada with my maternal grandparents while my parents went to a college reunion. On a Sunday my uncle, his kids, my grandparents and I all went to a Canadian Catholic church. It was a special service that day because the bishop was giving a speech about how the church needs more priests and they are dwindling in numbers. On that day I told my uncle, cousins and grandparents in the van that I was going to be a priest to their disbelief and astonishment. Within a week I had changed my mind.

    Perhaps it was due to a fascination with fantasy or because of encouragement to use my imagination, but at this time in my life I still believed in Santa Claus; although I didn't dare publicly admit it. One day near Christmas, Santa Claus was being discussed by my classmates and I didn't want to say whether I believed in him or not; because I'd either be lying or get embarrassed. Hollywood movies, Christmas music, the Church and government approval of Santa Claus may have been reasons for my delusion. Primarily I think it was the false logic which my parents taught saying that:"*Santa only comes for those who believe, if you don't believe then he doesn't come*". Reflect upon what that statement really means. This statement means that the truth is whatever you believe it is and that whatever you believe is true, just because you believe it to be. In other words: truth=whatever you believe. So if you believe a human being who ate, slept, urinated and defecated was God and that this man/God died on a cross which somehow meant that your sins were forgiven, even though they weren't even committed yet, then it must be the truth simply because you believe it. If this concept carried over to math nobody would ever get a math problem wrong. This is why the majority of Christian churches promote Santa Claus despite the clear pagan aspects and idolatry it involves. Some things kids are told about Santa Claus include: he is immortal, he can manipulate time and space, he sees you when you are sleeping and awake and knows everything you do, he will judge you based on his own criteria and he will reward you or punish you with gifts or fuel for fire (coal). Clearly just with these few attributes it is obvious that these are God-like powers. Apparently Jesus' alleged crucifixion pbuh doesn't get you onto Santa's good list, yet we are supposed to believe it gets us into paradise. Is Santa stricter than the same God who would kill himself/son so he could forgive others? When there is a God-like figure like Santa Claus who is eventually exposed as illusionary then the credibility of the liars (parents, etc) is lost and belief in the very existence of the true God whose likeness was given to Santa is doubted as well and sometimes entirely abandoned. So rather than blame science for atheism as many religious people do, they should blame Santa Claus. If God is real, accurate science should confirm it and it does, however it only confirms the true religion and since many are false they don't like accurate science to expose their falsehood. Volumes could be written about the Santa Claus mythology and the negative affects this pagan idol has on people and society, but this is not the book for such an extensive analysis. Shockingly as bad as the Santa Claus myth is, most Christians tend to double down on the deception with St. Nicholas. St. Nicholas is another version of Santa Claus whom Christian children are told brings them gifts on the morning of December 6th. The non-christians don't trick there kids with this, it is an exclusively Christian version of the shameful fraud. Many Christians will say Santa isn't real but St. Nicholas is and was a good guy, however Christians typically don't know all that St. Nicholas is said to have done. One thing this "St. Nicholas" is purported to have done is to turn a pretty girl into a duck in order to save her from being raped. Despite this apparent use of magic, which would be disbelief, this "saint" never turns the girl back into a girl, but leaves her to be a duck forever. This is the "good guy" called St. Nicholas, in reality he is either a myth, a disbelieving magician, or a jerk. He is definitely no saint who brings Christian kids gifts. Essentially many Christians teach their kids that Santa comes twice a year. Such Christian parents are twice as bad when it comes to lying to kids about Santa Claus than non-christians. This is why Christians are most reluctant to abandon the Santa Claus myth because to do so would mean admitting they also lied about St. Nicholas bringing gifts. Therefore lying to kids about Santa Claus is actually a part of most forms of Christianity. Therefore lying to one's children becomes part of practicing Christianity. To disbelieve in Santa Claus means to disbelieve in St. Nicholas and all the other saints. Thus technically speaking in order to be a Christian of most denominations you have to believe in Santa Claus. However believing in Santa Claus constitutes disbelief in God. This is why it's such an abhorrent phenomenon because any child who believes in Santa Claus is disbelieving in the unique oneness of God. To believe in one God means to believe God is the only one with the powers and ablilities of God. Since children are taught that Santa Claus also has the same powers as the One God then such children are actually polytheists. Don't think lying to kids about Santa Claus is innocent because it actually turns such children into disbelieving polytheists in the sight of God.

    Nevertheless being a believer in Santa Claus is not something easy to give up even when presented with the facts. Despite all the harassment due to my classmates' suspicion that I might believe, I still believed because I simply couldn't contemplate that my parents would buy gifts for me and not take the credit; it made no sense in my mind. How could billions of people have lied about Santa Claus for so many years? How could billions of people who believe in Santa Claus be wrong as well as all those movies, songs and stories? One day a girl sarcastically said that she believed in Santa Claus in an attempt to get me to express a similar attitude. I still kept quiet, but that really made me wonder that maybe just believing in something doesn't automatically make it true, perhaps proof is necessary as well. I resolved to find out if Santa Claus was real. Sure enough I caught my parents bringing extra gifts to put under the tree on Christmas Eve, to which one cried begging me to go back to bed not wanting the charade to end. The infamous hatred for liars my parents expressed to me as a toddler didn't seem to apply to them lying about Santa Claus. The next few years I pretended to believe in Santa Claus in order to get more gifts. Even when I knew it was falsehood my logic still believed some of what I'd been told, in that if I were to stop believing then the gifts would stop, so materialism overcame my integrity. As a result of the gifts continuing to arrive year after year despite my disbelief it is easy to see why many people today when confronted with religious beliefs are under the same delusion that it doesn't matter what you believe and everyone will get the gifts of paradise regardless. Some people adopt the opposite of the Santa Claus theory of, "*I won't go to hell because I don't believe in it*" thinking that belief is necessary for something to happen or exist. These types of people can be very dangerous to themselves if they apply this theory to this life as well as the afterlife, because if they start singing "*I believe I can fly*" they might actually try, and die. The truth is the truth whether you believe it or not, the weather doesn't change based on your beliefs about it. Your belief doesn't affect anyone but yourself, reality is not contingent on your own belief. The world doesn't care whether you are right or wrong and it won't go out of the way to prove you wrong. Frequently I hear people say: "*I can't believe that happened*". This is such a foolish statement because they are admitting it happened yet even though they know it happened with certainty they still don't believe it. Such people are publicly saying, "*I can't believe in something even though I know it's 100% true.*" May God help us to believe the truth when it becomes clear to us.

        In 8th grade with the Boy Scouts of America I went to Gettysburg, Pennsylvania; the site of a famous battle between the Confederate states of America and the United States of America. It's a very large place with excessive walking to do and we were encouraged to drink lots of water so as not to get dehydrated and collapse from heat exhaustion. Doing as we were told following orders, not thinking twice, we were routinely drinking water about every 10 minutes. Eventually nature called. Unfortunately our troop leaders did not give us permission to pee. According to both the former drill sergeant and the air force member, we were on holy ground where American heroes died hundreds of years ago, to them it would practically be a sin to urinate in the empty fields or woods that make up the majority of the battlesite. We kept holding it in for hours and hours. After about 4 hours one scout decided to urinate in some tall grass, he got caught and ordered to stop. I don't know how he did it, but the kid stopped urinating on command and didn't finish. Eventually we found a bathroom site to relieve ourselves after holding it in for over 6 hours. One of the first in line to urinate was the kid who had been forced to stop midstream. On another day late at night we were in the city when scheduled to be back at the campsite, so we took a shortcut through a foggy graveyard under the stars. Apparently this wasn't disrespectful because no American soldiers were buried in it, just civilians. At that time I didn't know that Jinn lived in graveyards. Aside from the memorable urination extravaganza and the graveyard, we just walked a lot and looked at monuments and graves. The trip increased our patriotism to extraordinary levels and we would look down on people when we got back because of their lack of patriotism and pride for America. Later after leaving the scouting organization I learned that it was initially founded as a club to encourage young boys to join the military and to be patriotic citizens who loved the government. This is why the U.S. president Woodrow Wilson strongly supported the organization during its start up in America. This is why Cub Scouts and Boy Scouts have the American flags at all their meetings and encourage a roll call at summer camps, with troop leaders, patrol leaders and other miltary terminologies. Most everything the Boy Scouts of America do is a simulation for military training, teaching survival skills, camaraderie, loyalty, rank, discipline and duty particularly "duty to one's country". Originally "scouting" was invented in Britain during 1907 CE to prepare boys for colonizing Africa and India. Scouting was a program to make super colonists and later other countries adopted and tweaked the program to make super soldiers. Woodrow Wilson also supported the Ku Klux Klan in America and enjoyed watching the pro Ku Klux Klan propaganda film called "*The Birth of a Nation*" (originally titled "*The Clansman*") in the white house which was the first movie of American cinema. That is a little known fact about American cinema often neglected and forgotten. The first ever movie of American cinema was a Ku Klux Klan propaganda film; black and white people should not forget that. Ironically the racist movie was filmed in "black and white". Of course the KKK wouldn't produce a "colored" motion picture but a "black and white" film seems to betray their whole ideology, even they realize a white-only film just isn't as good or viewable. While American cinema doesn't do too many movies about the Ku Klux Klan today, it's easy to see they are still producing propaganda and never stopped. Most movies are still racist to this day. What's the connection between the KKK and the Boy Scouts of America? The secret handshake of the KKK with the forefinger extended against the other's wrist was later adopted by the Boy Scouts of America, which they still use today claiming it's an exclusive scouting shake despite the fact the KKK was using it before them. Also, the founder of the Boy Scouts of America Daniel Carter Beard was a Freemason. This is an instance where I was in a group without knowing the origins of how it was formed or why it does certain things and it caused me to be susceptible to their brainwashing schemes because I didn't understand the purpose or nature of the organization as a result of my neglect in researching its origins. If you don't know why a group does something why would you continue the practice while ignorant of its significance? Whenever one does something they should ask themselves "*Why am I doing this*"? Because they told me to? For every ritual or practice one does they should be able to answer these simple basic questions: "*Who started it and why?*" also "*Why am I doing it today?*"

    During middle school I was a fan of professional wrestling thinking it was 100% real. I even intended to be a professional wrestler one day, wrestling was another way I escaped reality. One of my classmates was also a wrestling fan and had tickets to a heavily promoted annual wrestling event known as "The Great

American Bash" that took place in Buffalo, NY that year. I had been to wrestling events before but this event was a pay-per-view show (meaning not seen on TV unless you paid specifically for it) that had been marketed for months ahead of time. It was heavily laden with patriotic themes such as red, white and blue ropes around the ring in order to supplement the event's namesake. One match at this event was between a famous wrestler called "The Undertaker" and a new personality known as "Muhammad Hassan". Personally I didn't like "The Undertaker" because he was a satanic demonic sorcery practicing character, who had a gimmick of rolling his eyes back into his head so only the whites of his eyes could be seen in order to scare people. Although I didn't like the "Muhammad" character either so it was difficult for me to choose who to root for. The background history between these two leading up to their fight is important to mention so the full context of the bout can be understood. They started feuding because "Muhammad Hassan" felt he *"was treated as a second class citizen"* and felt he *"deserved"* a shot at the world championship, clearly playing off the feelings of Arab-Americans and playing into the stereotype Americans have of immigrants thinking they are entitled to the world, or in this case the world championship title. Theodore Long, the general manager, acceded to Hassan's demand but cited how his wrestling brand *"Smackdown!"* was different from *"Raw"* where Hassan had been transferred from and *"Smackdown!"* was the *"land of opportunity"*; clearly another American euphemism. Hassan was placed in a 6-man elimination match for a title shot, during that match he got into a bitter fight with the Undertaker who used a chair on Hassan, then Hassan ran away like a coward portraying another American stereotype. Later Hassan would cite that since it was a 6-man elimination match technically he was never eliminated since he never was pinned or submitted. Theodore Long then scheduled a match for the "Great American Bash" between him and *"that same man you ran away from"*(the Undertaker) where the winner would get a title shot. The feud between "The Undertaker" and "Muhammad Hassan" developed in the weeks leading up to the match. One important episode in that feud was filmed on July 4th, 2005 CE but aired July 7th, 2005 CE which was the same day as the London train bombings Al-Qaeda took credit for. Now these bombings took place BEFORE the episode was aired, so the WWE already knew people would be sensitive to any Arab, Muslim, Islamic or Middle Eastern imagery that day because a Middle Eastern Extremist group claiming to be Islamic had purportedly done an act of terrorism in the west that day. The WWE decided to air the episode anyways, entirely without any edits. This particular episode was highly controversial. During the episode Hassan forced his own manager Davari into fighting the Undertaker despite knowing he would lose and was outmatched. Hassan told Davari while wearing a black and white Middle Eastern scarf that " *tonight you will be a sacrifice*". The Undertaker quickly beat Davari while Hassan stood by smiling and watching, then Hassan laughed and fell to his knees looking upwards. Suddenly 5 men in black ski masks, black shirts, tan desert camouflage pants and military boots ran to the ring and ambushed the Undertaker attacking him, beating him up with weapons. After the Undertaker was demobilized, the masked men led by Muhammad Hassan carried the body of Davari backstage on their shoulders as is done during Muslim funerals. The commentator's script had him remark that they were treating Davari as *"some kind of a martyr or something."* The WWE filmed this in Sacramento, California on July 4th, 2005 CE, so you can imagine how the American crowd reacted considering that the Undertaker was a fan favorite. Then the WWE aired this episode on July 7th, 2005 CE fully aware of the criminal attacks that took place that day and didn't edit the episode whatsoever. Kevin Dunn, a high ranking WWE executive said to different news outlets in response to the international outrage that, *"we try and be sensitive with everything we portray, but there's got to be protagonists and antagonists on our TV shows...We just happen to reflect the politics of the world sometimes especially with these Arab-American characters."* To the WWE it was just entertaining well timed television, but to me and many others WWE events were real. Kevin Dunn even said, *"We just happen to reflect the politics of the world"* causing many WWE fans to think WWE had something to do with reality. At the time I didn't realize match results were scripted in advance and that the matches weren't entirely authentic since wrestlers communicate with each other during their "fight" planning which moves to let the other one do to them in order to safely make the show entertaining. I thought it was all spontaneous authentic aggressive action. For pay-per-view matches such as those at the "Great American Bash" the WWE would make promotional videos hyping up the fight. I forgot whether they showed these promos at the "Great American Bash" event, but I think they did show them before the matches so everyone in the audience knew the history leading up to the match. I mention this because I watched the promo for this fight while writing this to make sure my memory was accurate and the promotional video was appalling. During the part in the video where they showed the masked men attacking the Undertaker, the WWE added a soundtrack to make the video more dramatic. However it wasn't a song that they added, it was part of the Islamic call to prayer, the Athan. As a Muslim I'm shocked, the Islamic call to prayer contains statements such as *"Come to pray"* twice and *"Come to what is good"* twice, although the WWE chopped it up so it only said *"Come to pray"* once and they completely deleted the *"Come to what is good"* part. To have parts of the peaceful Islamic call for prayer played over such gratuitous violence associating Islam with such filth is disgusting. There is no way that this was accidental. Whoever arranged that video likely knew exactly what it was that they were using as a soundtrack, because they deliberately edited parts of the Athan that repeated out of it. This is a type of psychological warfare that the WWE employed against Islam. Islam had nothing to do with the WWE's events or storyline. To place parts of the Athan as the audio for a wrestling promo particularly arranged in the fashion it was arranged in is a hate-crime. It's not entertainment, it's blatant anti-Islamic propaganda under the guise of "professional wrestling", the wrestler's moves may be fake but the WWE's attacks on Islam are real. It would be like an English Muslim playing parts of the Christian song *"Silent Night"* in the background of a video showing American pilots bombing cities in Afghanistan at night to non-english speaking Afghans. Every Christian would be outraged saying it's unfair to associate those two things that have nothing to do with each other especially when the target audience doesn't understand the words of the audio. Since most people who watch WWE aren't Muslim and don't know Arabic, I couldn't even find any outrage reported of it being noticed or complained about. As far as I know the WWE has never apologized for it. As upset as it makes me feel now, what disturbs me more is that watching this violent WWE promotional video in 2005 CE was probably the first time I had ever heard the Islamic call to prayer, which I now usually hear 5 times a day, sometimes even saying it aloud myself. This incident also puts the WWE's december "Tributes to the troops" in context, which is an annual wrestling event started in 2003 CE where WWE wrestlers fight at a military base for U.S. troops. From 2003-2010 CE this annual event would be held at bases in Iraq and Afghanistan every december, presently it is held at military bases in the United States. Even if one doesn't interpret the WWE as being anti-Islam their company policy at least implies that the WWE fully supported America's wars in Iraq and Afghanistan. Nevertheless for the first time in my life, although a faithful Christian, while at the "Great American Bash" I decided to half-heartedly root for the "Muslim" guy because I just hated the Undertaker so much. Keep in mind I didn't root for the "Muslim" guy out loud, I simply preferred him to win inside. While watching I kept my emotions in check aware of the hostile anti-Muslim environment I was in. Anyone who has ever been to an American sporting event in a jam-packed stadium knows how rooting against the home team or against the crowd can be deadly. One can imagine the danger I would have been in had I publicly cheered for the "Muslim" wrestler who was portrayed as the villain amongst American wrestling fans. I had come to watch fights, I didn't want to get in one myself. I use quotation marks describing the "Muslim" wrestler because after learning about Islam I realize the guy wasn't practicing Islam. It was just a character he was pretending to be that was believed because the audience didn't know much about Islam and he looked Arab and used the name Muhammad, it turns out his real name is Mark Copani. He spoke Persian, not Arabic which means he wasn't even an Arab, let alone a Muslim Arab. Linguistically an Arab is someone who speaks Arabic just as an Englishman is a man who speaks English. Ethnically "Muhammad Hassan"(Mark Copani) was actually of Italian lineage, he was also rude, arrogant and entirely un-Islamic in his behavior whereas anyone who studies Islam would realize immediately that the guy was just a stereotype incarnate. His wrestling outfit was even violating the Islamic male dress code. At that time he portrayed a certain image which I hated, but considered him to be a better alternative than the satanic demonic sorcerer known as "The Undertaker", who also pretends to be a zombie. As one might have expected, that night the WWE killed off the "Muhammad Hassan" character and he was slammed through what appeared to be a solid steel stage, which had never happened before and would have resulted in injury if not death had it not been a carefully pre-planned maneuver. It was actually quite scary to witness, especially when I thought it was real and that he was actually going to die as a result while hundreds of thousands of people were in an uproar applauding what appeared to be murder. I never saw his character on the wrestling program again after that night and the industry wanted fans to think he was dead. Several days later WWE.com hosted a video with an announcement from Theodore Long where he said Muhammad Hassan would no longer appear on "*SmackDown!*" Long said to Hassan, "*You can go to Raw, or you can go anywhere else on this planet, but as far as I'm concerned, you can go to hell!*" After all that it turns out "Muhammad Hassan" currently teaches social studies at a high school in New York State as Mark Copani, using his real name. Undoubtedly this portrayal of a wrestling villain with Islamic undertones had a dramatic imprint on my perception of Arabs, but most importantly Muslims and Islam since the wrestler's name was "Muhammad Hassan".

    Another fight at "The Great American Bash" was a match between female wrestlers in which the loser was the girl who had her clothes ripped off by the other until she was left in her underwear. Seriously that was the match, it wasn't about pinning the opponent it was who could get their opponent's clothes off first. After the match the winner(who had clothes on) and the female referee took their clothes off as well, much to the pleasure of the perverted crowd. Rather than a wrestling match it was basically a strip show. I wasn't homosexual or anything, but still felt that it was inappropriate to watch and I tried to make excuses to look at other things or get food to eat during that match to avoid getting taunted by my classmate for not cheering and drooling over women ripping each other's clothes off. The loudest the crowd got that night was when the women were all de-clothed proudly displaying their bodies. It was quite shameful and I couldn't understand how women could feel dignified being stripped of their clothes in front of nearly a million eyes, yet at the same time they pretended to be honored as if they had enjoyed the "match". It's quite sexist and misogynist when one reflects on how female wrestlers are treated as purely sexual objects. May God protect our mothers, sisters, daughters, wives, aunts and cousins from such degrading humiliation.

    Shortly after entering high school I stopped following wrestling and lost interest in it because it was scripted. I knew the hatred wrestlers expressed for each other was rarely genuine and watching it would always make me aggressive. Professional Wrestling led me to think that violence was the best way to solve my problems with others. After years of watching it the stories became repetitive and predictable. It seemed like it was all just a big distraction that wasted my time which could have been used doing other things. All thanks and praises be to God for guiding me away from the wrestling mania I was once afflicted with. Just because something is popular doesn't mean it's beneficial.

    Once my Parents, Grandparents and I went on a church sponsored bus trip to Philadelphia and the tour group got lost. Walking around Philadelphia seemed fun to me, but all the adults were terrified. Their terror was probably due to prejudice of urban areas or sheer racist fears. One thing that did frighten me was an effigy of Saddam Hussein that was hung outside of a window with numerous signs and slurs accompanied by American flags. I witnessed the first hand destructive hate that patriotism leads to and felt like I was in danger for the rest of the day, even while in the church. At the end of the mass the priest said to pray for the Philadelphia Eagles football team to win. I always remembered that and wondered what happens when two opposing sports teams both pray to God for victory? I imagine all the churches were praying for their local team to win that day. Likewise what happens when two gamblers on opposite sides of a bet both say the same prayer for victory despite gambling being a sin? Or two different types of pagans are praying for victory against each other? Personally I don't think God cares about sports as much as we do and surely they cannot be so important as to warrant divine intervention. Concerning sports, it seems as though Satan invented the prayer for victory so that those who lose can be led astray thinking God doesn't exist because their team lost, meanwhile the winner who was worshipping an idol will think their false religion is true based on the outcome of a game; even though both teams were likely worshipping idols. Satan uses these prayers for victory in sports to make all those involved saying them losers. It's truly remarkable how there are sinful, unhealthy people on the cusp of eternal damnation praying for the local sports team instead of for guidance, mercy or the pleasure of their Creator. Imagine being on your deathbed right before the soul leaves your body and you're praying that so and so scores before time runs out on the clock. Is this what life is about? Are we really going to ask the one who created us and everything that has ever existed for help getting a ball into a hoop or across a line? Out of all the great things God can do, that is what people ask for? That's insulting to all involved. Imagine you had the opportunity to ask the King of the world for one favor, would you ask him to help your favorite sports team win? No, but we have the nerve to ask one much greater for something so insignificant. Are we so well off that we have nothing better to ask God for? Undoubtedly we have gone incredibly far astray, especially when we compare ourselves to the prophets.

    Another notable thing about my trip to Philadelphia were the "saints" I saw. In one church there was a glass coffin with a dead body in it that had been embalmed, everyone would go up to it and pray to the dead person asking him to ask God for something on their behalf. It freaked me out a little seeing an old dead body in the flesh with everyone praying to him. Now I know that dead people cannot help us, no matter how "holy" people think they were, dead is dead you cannot do any more deeds when dead. Many Christians are under the mistaken impression that upon death one goes directly to heaven or hell. Thus under the impression "saints" are in heaven they ask these dead saints for stuff thinking they can talk to God in heaven but in reality people go to the grave when they die. Both the gates of Heaven and Hell are closed until the Day of Judgment, which takes place after the day the dead are all raised. At this moment it is known that Goliath will burn in hell forever, yet so far he is not in hell burning but in the grave waiting in a lesser state of punishment than hell will be.(not purgatory, bad people just get punished in their graves in addition to/before going to hell later). So that is where even if people considered to be "saints" were going to paradise, they aren't there yet and since they are waiting in the grave to be resurrected they can't intercede for anybody at all. Also with these "saints", people cannot know who they really were and what they were doing when no one was watching them. In private these "saints" might have been doing filthy immoral ungodly things yet because in public they seemed righteous many have been duped into thinking they were loved by God. When they are studied one will find many "saints" to have had dark sinful histories. I cannot mention "saints" without mentioning Joan of Arc, the French female warrior who killed the English and helped to liberate France. Joan was burned alive by the Catholic Church for heresy and cross-dressing on May 30th 1431 CE. Pope Benedict XV canonized Joan of Arc as a saint on May 16th, 1920 CE. So the same organization who burned her alive, nearly 500 years later declares her to be a holy righteous saint who people should pray to. This would be the equivalent of Americans today declaring that the betraying General Benedict Arnold, who defected to the British during the British/American revolution, to be the most patriotic American that ever lived and putting his face on all the money relabeling it as saying "in Benedict Arnold we trust" and giving him a national holiday. Despite giving me the shivers, the "saints" scam got me hook, line and sinker with my favorite football team even becoming the New Orleans Saints. All thanks and praises be to God for eventually guiding me away from the pandemonium I had been deluded by.

Other church sponsored trips my family made into Pennsylvania were to see religious plays, typically centered around a certain prophet or character from the bible. These were awe-inspiring with many special effects which resulted in memorable religious experiences. As I came to have more respect for the prophets as I grew, the disrespect which these plays show to the prophets became noticeable. For the sake of argument let's assume the bible version the plays were based off contains authentic information about the prophets pbut. Prophets are the best and most pious people whose closeness to God has been confirmed without a doubt. Prophets are more saintly than the previously mentioned "saints" whom people pray to. Keep in mind that most prophets are not prayed to, nor should they be. For the show to go on they need actors to dress up and pose as a prophet. One problem with this is the impossibility of looking like someone you're not who hasn't been seen for thousands of years. No one knows what the prophets looked like since no statues depicting them were ever made during their lifetimes. Secondly once we have an image of a prophet in our mind we lose respect for them and when we think of them we will constantly think of the first image we saw that depicted them. An example would be the devil. Once people started thinking the devil had red horns, goat legs, a tail and pitchfork, the enemy of mankind became a lot less formidable because he became a symbol. Today people are even dressing up as the devil because they don't take him seriously and there are sports teams named after devils which have devils as their mascots. You might think I'm going too deep into this, but after investigation it is revealed to be an intentional plot to discredit and humiliate the prophets pbut. The actors chosen to portray the best of mankind often don't even come close to being considered moral, even by today's immoral standards of morality. You see a guy pretending to be Moses pbuh in a play, the next time you see him he's in a movie with a beer in the right hand, a bong in the left, cocaine on his nose and a prostitute in his lap; and it gets worse. Then you read in the newsstand tabloids that he's a homosexual going through a divorce with his gay husband. The reason for the divorce being that he wants to have a sex change and become a woman thinking he's always been a woman trapped in a man's body, to which his homosexual husband disagrees. When asked whether he thinks God would approve of his transgender operation he responds that he's an atheist. Yet this is the same type of person that gets picked to portray the great prophet Moses pbuh? This will at least have a subconscious effect on the light in which the play attendees will view Moses pbuh, making it a shame that prophets have their reputation and memories smeared like this. Another example is the prophet Joseph pbuh who was put in prison for resisting attempts at being seduced by women. Joseph pbuh was the most beautiful human to have ever lived, so any actor pretending to be him is by default making him out to be uglier than he was because no make-up can match that God given beauty or even come close. Some scholars have even said that Joseph pbuh would go about with his face covered in public because his beauty was so great it led to social disruption. Therefore any image of the prophet Joseph pbuh is automatically slander against him. Rather than pretending to be prophets, people should try to live like them. As bad as it is to have actor's dress up pretending to be prophets or to make statutes of the prophets, it gets even worse. There is a very popular Christian children's show called "Veggie Tales". The episodes revolve around animated vegetables getting into adventures which end up teaching a Christian lesson to the viewers, religious education classes frequently show episodes in class. These "Veggie tales" depict our great prophets as vegetables. The mighty King David pbuh is represented as a baby piece of asparagus! The warrior prophet Joshua pbuh is depicted as a cucumber! In another production the great prophet Jonah pbuh is shown as a piece of asparagus with a monocle! Do you know what food the prophet Joseph pbuh, the most beautiful man who lived, is portrayed as? A cucumber! These veggie tales are demeaning and derogatory to the best men who ever lived, tarnishing their reputations. Even if one attempted to justify making statues of the prophets, even though this is totally prohibited by the 2nd commandment given to Moses pbuh, there is no way someone can justify using animated vegetables to represent our beloved role models. These "Veggie Tales" even depict the famous Messenger Moses pbuh. Can you guess what they depict this great man who talked to God as? They animate Moses pbuh as a gourd! But it doesn't stop there, they also depict Abraham pbuh in one episode. Abraham pbuh who is known as the friend of God, who passed every test God ever gave him, suffers the humiliation of being portrayed as a grape. A grape! How can they turn the friend of God into a grape?! These shows are completely disrespectful, it doesn't matter what the lessons are, these animations are criminal satanic slanders. Do you think a child will respect or emulate someone who they saw depicted as a vegetable? Why do we let our prophets get belittled like this?

    It's even worse though when it comes to prophets or righteous people being disrespected. As an example, in popular culture there is an alcoholic concoction known as a "Bloody Mary" whereas a "Virgin Mary" is referred to as a non-alcoholic beverage. Think of how such names affect one's perception of Mary the virgin mother of Jesus pbuh or virginity in general. Similarly they call a part of the neck the "Adam's Apple" which clearly refers to the Christian notion of Adam pbuh eating a sinful fruit thought to be an apple yet the reference indicates that we got some type of permanent genetic alteration or physical mutation as a result of our ancestor's sin. Which is an entirely nonsencial and disrespectful notion. Whereas the word "Lot" no longer is thought of as the name of the prophet "Lot" pbuh but ironically used to describe a piece of land despite Lot pbuh escaping from an evil land that was destroyed. Yet one of the most disgusting linguistic slurs concerns the word "John". This is because of such things known as "Longjohns", which are a type of long underwear, and that the Western world refers to the toilet as "the John". John is the english translation of the name of a great prophet! How can we use that same word for the thing we pee and poop in? Or for underwear? To put it in perspective what if instead of "Longjohns" they were called "Longjesus'" or instead of the toilet being called "the John" it was called "the Jesus". Imagine someone saying "Oh I gotta go take a big poop in the Jesus". We'd realize how disgusting and anti-religious such names are and say people will lose respect for Jesus pbuh if we used such words for such things. It is these little things that people think are no big deal that lead to a gulf between us and our prophets thereby distancing us from their religion and our Creator. If you love the prophets you'd care about this stuff, afterall you wouldn't want people using your name to describe underwear or the toilet would you?

In the bible 2 Kings 2:23-24 narrates what happened to kids who made fun of the prophet Elisha pbuh:*"From there Elisha went up to Bethel. As he was walking along the road, some boys came out of the town and jeered at him. "Get out of here, baldy!" they said. "Get out of here, baldy!"* <u>²⁴ *He turned around, looked at them and called down a curse on them in the name of the LORD.*</u> *Then two bears came out of the woods and mauled forty-two of the boys."*

If this is what happened to young boys according to the English translation of the New International Version of the Bible when they taunted the prophet Elisha pbuh for being bald, then how hateful is it to God when people today slander prophets? Notice that these rude boys were not explicitly described as being disbelievers, they were just making fun of a bald guy who was missing some hair whom they might not have even known was a prophet. Yet biblically this great prophet cursed them in the name of the Lord and two bears utterly ruined them. This biblical account shows us how dangerous it can be to make fun of a prophet. Now if all these kids were mauled/killed because of their comments regarding a prophet's haircut, then what do you think God's view is regarding some bum who dresses up pretending they are a prophet? These kids were physically annihilated simply for making comments about a prophet's haircut, imagine someone who dresses up as a prophet and has a lot more inaccuracies than just the haircut. Then what do these actors do? They put on make-up as well! Thus they are insulting the prophets automatically because they know the prophets didn't use make-up because they didn't have it or need it. Thus such people by using make-up while defaming the prophets are implying the prophets were ugly because they didn't use make-up. If that's not what they're implying they wouldn't use the make-up or the stylists, or the gels or the special lighting effects or the perfume. Yes, by putting on the perfumes they are saying the prophets stunk and they don't want to stink like they claim the prophets pbut did. But do you know who actually started the whole trend of putting on plays with people pretending to be prophets like Jesus pbuh? It was Delmar Darrah who started this practice, and guess what? He was a freemason. So it was the freemasons who began all these plays and movies about the prophets. For instance the famous "Ten Commandments" movie was first made in 1923 CE by Cecil De Mille who was also a freemason, then it was remade in 1956 CE. Again not to be conspiratorial but it was the freemasons who started this and promoted it. Many know how the actor Charlton Heston pretended to be Moses pbuh in the 1956 movie, but they don't know that Cecil De Mille also had Charlton Heston act for him 4 years earlier in his movie "The Greatest Show on Earth". In that movie Charlton Heston was the ringleader of a circus, then 4 years later the same Director picks the same actor to be Moses. However Charlton Heston's career didn't stop at Moses pbuh, in 1959 CE he played a fictional character in "Ben Hur" where he allegedly witnessed Jesus pbuh get crucified, in 1961 CE in "El Cid" he played a Crusader who fought in the reconquista of Spain, while in 1954 CE Heston played a tomb raider who recovered a "sunburst" pagan incan idol and kindly gave it to the incans so they could worship their "sunburst" idol in it's temple. So 4 years before he acted as Moses pbuh this guy acted as a circus ring-leader, and 2 years before he acted as Moses pbuh he acted as someone helping pagans worship a "sunburst" idol. While the freemason film director Cecil de Mille also made immoral films like, *"The Woman God Forgot"*, *"The Devil Stone"*, *"Old Wives for New"*, *"Forbidden Fruit"*, *"Adam's Rib"*, *"The Crusaders"*, *"Fool's Paradise"*, *"The Godless Girl"*, *"Madame Satan"*,

"*Cleopatra*" and several slanderous films about Jesus pbuh which I won't even mention because they are so bad. The very guy who popularized movies about the prophets was a clear enemy to these same prophets. So how can people today say movies about prophets of God are okay when the whole prophetic movie genre was made by bad guys who hated and blasphemed these prophets? It is a fact that the movies about prophets were made to insult them. It's cause and effect, because of these religious movies about prophets many people stopped loving the prophets or trying to believe in and practice their prophetic religion. Far from being the cure, these allegedly religious movies about prophets contributed to the anti-religious disease. One of the wost things one can do to harm the image of a prophet is to make a movie or picture depicting them. These filthy movie producers have become the new prophets of the masses and their movies are treated as if they were divine revalations. The world's various faiths have been replaced with films. Instead of Scripture, now people prefer a movie script. People are selling their tickets to paradise for movie tickets.

Also the kids who got attacked by bears because of their attitude amounting to an attack on the prophet, were just criticizing the prophet for an actual physical trait, they weren't lying about him saying something about him that was false. Today many people call prophets and messengers of God drunkards, incestuous, liars, magicians, possessed, ignorant, foolish, adulterous, pedophiles and all other kinds of filthy derogatory things which are completely false and untrue regarding the many prophets who are incorrectly given such labels. Considering what the bible says happened to people jeering at the physical appearance of a prophet, then by default any depiction of a prophet would also be a form of slander that would put one in the same category as these boys who were mauled by bears. By depicting a prophet inaccurately it could make one cursed by God. Yet today not only are the prophets depicted and slandered, but they are depicted as pieces of food! We wouldn't think it was respectful to depict the president, king or leader of a country as food so then why do we let our spiritual leaders and messengers sent to us by God suffer such degradation? Do we love our politicians more than our prophets? Do we know more about politicians than we do the prophets? Do we obey politicians more than our prophets? Do we support politicians more than our prophets? If you went to paradise and met the prophets what would you say if they asked you what did you do or how did you feel when they were getting slandered and depicted in such humiliating and disgraceful ways? What will we say to God when he asks us about our attitudes towards the prophets? We are supposed to love God's prophets more than we do ourselves. If we really loved the magnificent prophets and messengers God sent to us then we would strongly dislike all these depictions which get made of them and the mockeries people make about them in movies, plays and other theatrical performances. Even that such disgusting depictions are portrayed as "performances" are offensive. The prophets were not performers. What they did was believe what God wanted them to believe, live how God wanted them to live and do what God wanted them to do. It wasn't an act or a show, it was real life. You don't copy that and "re-enact the prophets", we're supposed to be living it practicing the same religion that they did. You live it, you don't watch it. The prophets didn't put on such performances because they were too busy actually living how God wanted them to live and doing good deeds. Jesus pbuh never dressed up as Moses pbuh to put on a show and motivate people. David pbuh never dressed up as Abraham pbuh. Moses pbuh never dressed up as Noah pbuh. The theatrical arts came from Greece and there were only two types of plays or performances. There were tragedies and comedies. No prophet's life was a tragedy and no prophet's life was a comedy. Thus it is impossible for there to ever be a performance depicting the prophets. If it was possible and beneficial the prophets would have done it themselves, because the very reason they were created was to motivate people to worship God and follow the prophetic examples. But what's more is how all the prophets taught people to give in charity. Guess what? These movies, tv shows, plays, comics, and the other nonsense people make depicting prophets are not free. They cost money, so instead of people giving in charity like the prophets said to they waste their wealth to watch or see something about people who taught our species that we should give in charity. Thus in viewing such material people are contradicting the very prophets such filthy material claims to be about. Then what do they do? They stand up and give a round of applause with everyone clapping and crying and glorifying these fraudulent imposters and literal "false-prophets". Seriously they don't boo or ridicule or even criticize, they congratulate, support and encourage this antagonistic carnage. They do the exact opposite of what good people would do. If we see this junk we shouldn't consume it at all nor promote it. If we do anything we should denounce such "false-prophets" and filthy depictions, but at the very least we really must stop supporting such P.O.O.P. and encourage others to stop this public P.O.O.P. pandemic. That's actually what this whole thing is, it's P.O.O.P. People Obscenely Offending Prophets.

THE TEST OF LIFE

The ancient phrase "*you only live once*" has become more popular among people in recent times with its acronym Y.O.L.O. which was popularized by a Jewish rapper in 2011 CE. Typically whenever this phrase is uttered it is right before a "friend" convinces someone to do something "fun" which they'll end up regretting. If taken at face value one would consider this to be a deterrent rather than encouragement. Think about it, "*YOU ONLY LIVE ONCE*" means you have one life to live and there are no second chances if you make a mistake. Do you really want to throw it away getting intoxicated, doing something dangerous, taking wild risks, chasing adrenaline rushes, giving into peer pressure, or displeasing your Creator? Any intelligent person when reminded that "*you only live once*" would take it as a warning not as an excuse. That's why Y.O.L.O. is the slogan of the stupid. Every prophet warned against this motto. This doctrine was actually found inscribed on the ancient 14th century BCE tomb of the Egyptican Paatenemheb on which the "Song of Harper" which promotes this Y.O.L.O. doctrine says it had been copied from the more ancient tomb of King Intef. This Ancient "Song of Harper" was also found on the 500 Harris Papyrus wherein the song in english means:

"Make holiday, don't weary of it!!
Look, there is no one allowed to take their things with them,
and there is no one who goes away comes back again."

This is what the very ancient Egyptians believed, sang and would put on their tombstones. In their society holidays were the main public religious events, they consisted of song and dance and it was the only time the major state idols were publicly displayed by the priests. The priests were blindly believed and obeyed, despite them never explaining the state religion to the people. Egyptian priests were mainly statue polishers and temple custodians. The priests were supposed to bathe and reclothe the statues on a daily basis while feeding them 3 times a day. The Egyptian public only needed to show up and party during the festivals, work hard and pay taxes to support the state temples and pay the priests' salaries. The average Egyptian was considered to be pleasing the gods if they lived this Y.O.L.O. lifestlye. Basically they thought you had to party when you had the chance, because you can't please the gods by partying after you die. Which when we compare how the Egyptians actually thought parties were a religious form of worship, its truly sad how people today have taken these pagan doctrines of indulgence and made them more indulgent and even less religious. People today took a bad ancient pagan saying and made it worse. When looking at the origin of this doctrine, it's revealed to be the slogan of Satan, because Satan has a longer lifespan and knows that when he dies nothing but torment is in store for him because he is too arrogant to repent. Satan uses this slogan for himself to justify his taking pleasure in our misery and leading us astray. The fact of life is that we live twice, the life before death and the life after death. If you invest solely in this life thinking that's the only life there is, on the day when you are raised from the grave you will wish you only had one life because your second eternal life will be worse than anything imaginable. So whenever some modern wild party animals tell you "Y.O.L.O." you can say "OH, NO".

Some people also use the phrase "*as long as it makes you happy*", this is said by those who subscribe to the religion of hedonism. Many hedonists don't even know they are hedonists because this philosophy about life has become so prevalent in modern times and is encouraged in consumerist societies. Hedonism is the idea that maximizing one's pleasure is the ultimate goal and purpose of life. Now if you were a company, selling "happiness" to these people is a very lucrative business so you would make sure they remember the hedonist motto and believe it. Many trapped in consumerism don't follow hedonism to its extreme and retain some social morality and self-control, but still think happiness is what life is all about. If being happy is what constitutes success then you can go to the insane asylum and see some of the happiest people in the world, would we consider the most insane to be the most successful? Yet this is exactly what hedonists suggest even if they are not cognizant of the implications. Rather the goal of life is to make our Creator happy first and foremost, coincidentally we have been created to feel happy when we do good things that make our Creator pleased. So following the right religion would make the person most happy because that religion would have been designed by our Creator who knows us better than any human can. On the other hand the true believer recognizes that we were not created to dwell on earth forever and originally our ancestor Adam pbuh was living in paradise, in actuality Earth is not our homeland. As they say "*home is where the heart is*", the heart of the one whose home will be paradise is always looking forward to paradise and will not be completely satisfied with this earthly existence; they may even be distressed that they have to wait so long to enter paradise. Such an individual who is solely focused on pleasing their Creator and entering paradise will not be satisfied by the things of this world, but they will never be upset or saddened by any hardships or loss they suffer in this world either. Such people are actually happier than those who chase the happiness in this life, because they don't get disappointed since they are aware of the reality. Knowing this life is temporary it makes believers content with whatever they have in life since they plan on departing soon. They understand that anything they have is a means which they can use to please the Creator and invest in the afterlife, and any hardship is a test for them which if they pass will elevate their standing with their Creator who tested them. For such a person happiness is not the goal of life, their goal is to pass the tests they are given and prove themselves to be grateful, patient and consistent worshippers and as long as they can remain steadfast by not losing focus or chasing happiness on earth, the Creator gives them happiness in this life and the next. By not being hedonists they get what the hedonists covet most. In comparison the one who chases happiness on earth, is ungrateful to their maker and just does whatever they can to be happy, is ironically miserable and never content because they are going about attaining happiness the wrong way. There is even a term for the hedonist misery called "hedonistic entropy" in which one gets bored with what makes them happy, which is an oxymoron revealing that what hedonists think is happiness is something else entirely. The Creator created the emotion of happiness so the easiest way to get it is directly from the source, any other supplier of happiness will end up giving you a diluted secondhand knockoff that is an imitation at best if not an altogether different product than advertised. But for someone who has never worshiped the Creator directly and has always gone to another source for happiness, they will think they are happy because they invested in what they were told would make them happy. Because they have never had the "real thing" and have only had knock offs, or falsely advertised products that have been mislabeled, they think they have happiness and it is difficult for them to realize they have been deceived. It's similar to a starving person who eats a blade of grass, if they have been told their entire life that the feeling they get in their stomach after eating one blade of grass means you're full and not hungry, then they will think whenever they feel that feeling it means they are full. In reality they will be starving, but because they never experienced being truly full in their life and were misinformed about what feeling full felt like, whenever they are told they are starving they will say: *"no I'm full, I'm not starving, how would you know? Who do you think you are telling me I'm not full?"* Or when a person has suffered through illness all their life, how can you tell them about what health is when being sick is their idea of being healthy? This is especially frustrating when the same scenario unfolds with a person who is actually unhappy and miserable because they are not worshipping God and following the true religion. Since society has misinformed them on what happiness is they think they are happy and that by following the true religion it would make them sad because it is contrary to the method by which a satanic society taught them to achieve happiness. Such people think being sad is happy and that being happy is sad. So when they tell me *"whatever makes you happy"* it reveals that they have never been happy in their entire lives, and it is unfortunate that they don't even know that. Sadly they can't diagnose themselves and can't tell when they are spiritually ill just as most of us can't tell when we are internally ill without a diagnosis from a medical professional. Yet this is part of the test, if you worship the Creator correctly you will be happy in this life and the next. Satan will make it seem as though worshipping the Creator correctly will make you unhappy in this life and the next and tries to prevent us from doing what is good for us and wants us to do what is bad for us. Satan deceives a good portion of people so much that they start to think that what is bad is good and that what is good is bad and leads them to believe they are happy when they are sad, so they take poison to cure themselves thinking it is medicine. They will think they are passing the tests but are actually failing and if they don't pass before they pass away, they shall be very regretful when they get the results and learn why what they had done was wrong. Those who fail do so because of their I.L.L. motto of "I love life". Their life motto is a recipe to be ill, then when feeling sick they try to use the I.L.L. virus to get back to feeling like they did when they first tasted the I.L.L. symptoms. Then as a spiritual and/or mental patient they proudly proclaim they are I.L.L. and think everyone should have an I.L.L. outlook. Sadly this illness is highly contagious so it's very popular amongst us today, more so than the common flu. It's so catchy that now every season is an I.L.L. season. Unfortunately many infected with the I.L.L. virus think it's a joke if you tell them it sounds like they have the I.L.L. virus. May God guide us so we are not of those who are deceived or ill. That is the reality of Satan, he is the trickiest being that exists and we don't want him to be our teacher and study guide for this test we call life, because if he is then we will never have success or experience true happiness.

Life isn't a game, and planet earth is not a amusement park. Life is a test, not a quiz, not homework, not busy work either it's more serious and important than any other test a human is given, in fact all the "tests" people give us are simply a subset of our test called life. School can be used as an example to explain this test known as life. A main goal of the student is to get out of school with some type of diploma or certification. In order to do this, lots of work is required and tests are given evaluating the individual's ability as a way of verifying whether the student has done what they were supposed to.

These tests come in many different formats with varying degrees of difficulty and sometimes every person in the class is given a different test to prevent cheating. In school it's possible to cheat on a test and get away with it. If you cheat in the test of life doing things God has made illegal it may disqualify you and make you fail by default. The test of life has many parts and sections, some resulting in a 2 choice response of either truth or falsehood, some are multiple choice with only one correct answer, and sometimes it may seem multiple choice but the available choices are all the wrong answers and you must choose the correct choice yourself despite it "not being an option". In school there are many tests and levels of difficulty which increase in frequency and difficulty the closer one gets to achieving the end goal. If the tests aren't getting harder that means you are not progressing. In life everyone is given as much time as is needed to determine if they pass or failed, some have a longer time some have a shorter time, but all are given enough time to make the results clear without a doubt. There is no postponement or retakes for even the smallest quiz, the final exam is all or nothing. Some tests are unexpected surprises and some are announced in advance, the one who is most successful is the one who is aware and ready to be tested at any time. Just like in school, books have been provided to give us the information we need to know in order to pass and just like in school some people bring the wrong books to class, while others completely ignore the books thinking they have better things to do than study and will "wing it" and still be successful; or that the test will be easy to pass. I can guarantee that if you adopt the "*I don't care, I don't need to study the books*" attitude when it comes to religion you will fail the test of life and will not be among those to receive honors in the next life. If God (the test maker) already knows who will pass and who will fail then why do we have to be tested in the first place? Sometimes a teacher knows which of their students will get a perfect grade and which ones will fail before the students even take the tests. Yet it would not be fair to fail or pass the students without letting them take the tests. Likewise if we were not given this life to be tested then we might complain to God and say when judged that we were never given a chance to pass. This way the test of life is entirely just and we will have no excuse to give for failure.

When you are taking the final exam before graduation, you don't sit there and say, "*how come I'm not happy taking this test?*" It's a test, you're not supposed to enjoy it or be happy! The pleasure and happiness comes after you get the results that say you passed the test and then get the graduation party and presents. If you sit there during the exam looking at everyone else taking the test thinking: "*How come they have better clothes than me? How come they have a more comfortable chair than me? How come they get to eat food during the test and I can't? Why didn't I get a seat next to the fan? Why do they have a better writing utensil than me? Why do I have to sit next to the stinky kid? How much time do I have left?*" These things have nothing to do with the test results and will not affect your score. If you had them you might be distracted by them, the fan, clothes, comfortable chair and food could cause you to fail the test, so that is why the test maker didn't give you those things. It may well be that the test maker knows those people will fail the test and have a miserable existence ever after so they were given those extra comforts during the test because of the kindness of the test giver and so that they have no excuse for failure. The test is only for a short time, if you don't pass you get nothing, in fact you get worse than nothing, if you fail you get punished and things will get worse and worse and worse for eternity. If you pass life gets better and better forever. After the test of life is over you won't care about the discomfort you had, or the amenities you lacked while taking the test. All you will care about is whether you passed or failed. The one who wants to be happy while taking the test is foolish. If they actually try to be happy by sleeping during the test, or doing something else, then they will be wasting their test time and probably fail. No matter how tired the person taking the test may be, if you fall asleep and give up because the test is too hard, you're too tired or you just want to relax and be happy during the test, you will fail. Satan makes people envy the other test takers and desire what they have because it distracts them from the test; making them ungrateful for what they do have. If they had what the others had it still wouldn't be enough because then Satan would make them continually want more to make the test more enjoyable. The test taker never looks behind them at the people sitting in less comfortable chairs, with worse writing utensils, with a sticky squeaky desk, who are starving, thirsty, sick, without sleep, who are half blind, with missing limbs, with rain drops falling on their head through the crack in the ceiling, having flies and mosquitoes bite them throughout while buzzing in their ears. Those people have an even more uncomfortable time during the test and would love to be in your position. Eventually time will run out and the test will be over. The person will realize they should've been taking the test and ignored all the other test takers and what they had. You aren't supposed to have fun while taking the test of life. The test can be fun, but it's not designed to be. Those who think life is supposed to be fun and happy are the same types who commit suicide and euthanasia because they figure if they can't live without pain then there is no point in living so they kill themselves. Thus that popular slogan "*As long as you're happy.*" is the slogan of suicidal people who are likely to kill themselves when the buzz of mind-numbing and soul-numbing entertainment wears off or can no longer be obtained. Regarding Euthanasia it is not "mercy killing" it's just regular killing based on the idea that only happy, young or healthy people should live. Suicide and Euthanasia are exactly the same in principle. The idea your life on earth should be happy/fun leads to spiritual suicide and it's the number 1 doctrine held by those who commit physical suicide. Yet if anyone at any time felt that life had gotten so bad they should kill themselves then it would've been Adam pbuh and Eve. They went from paradise to the most primitive version of earth that ever existed, you could fairly say Adam and Eve had the hardest lives in all of history, because they had the pleasure of paradise and we haven't. Thus regarding depression they had the most right out of any to be depressed and suicidal. To live in paradise and then move to earth, is an extreme downgrade in one's lifestyle. When Adam pbuh was sent to earth, he didn't see it as a vacation or a place where he was supposed to enjoy himself abundantly. His earthly life was a test that if he passed he would regain paradise and so much more.

By passing the test on earth humans will enjoy paradise more than they would if they hadn't been tested. Although life isn't simply a written test but it is all-encompassing in every aspect. There are no intermissions or breaks between sections on the test of life, it is continuous from the womb to the tomb. The test of life is a spiritual test, a mental test, an emotional test, a physical test, a verbal test, a visual test, a auditory test, a financial test, a political test, a social test, a moral test, a primordial fundamental temporal test. The true happiness and pleasure comes to those who pass the test. It is those who seek happiness while taking the test that fail the test of life. Their answer is I.L.L. so they fail.

Now even if you go to all the classes, do all the homework and pass all the tests with higher grades than all the rest, if you're not registered as a student at that school, or for those classes, you will not get the diploma regardless of whatever effort you put towards it. This is why if you are not registered as a believer according to the Creator then it doesn't matter how many good deeds you do none of it will give you any credit in the end. Even if all the other classmates think you were one of them and the best student, if you are not registered you get no credit regardless of what the students think or say. Thus the most important thing for the test of life is being registered to the correct school of thought.

A school doesn't need you to pass or graduate, the school will not benefit much by your graduation. God doesn't need you to worship him. Even if everyone was perfect and the best of worshipers it would not increase the greatness of God at all. God is the greatest whether you believe it or not. The reason we need to worship God is because of the benefit it brings to us, our worship brings no benefit to God. There are other reasons to worship God, such as avoiding eternal punishment and obtaining eternal pleasure, although the true reason any person should worship God is not for personal gain, but it's simply because God deserves it. This is something that created everything, God created everything we have ever seen, heard, smelled, touched and tasted, as well as everything we haven't and never will. How ungrateful would an individual be if they didn't show gratitude for all that the Creator has provided for them? Isn't it fair that such an ingrate be punished forever? Now if you don't want to take the test and think it's not fair for you to be rewarded or punished based on how you live then there is a way out. It's really simple, you can create your own universe, planets, elements, amenities and then live there and never use anything God created; then he would have no authority over you. However since God created you and all the elements, then you will have to create yourself and give back to God all that he has given you. When making yourself and your universe you cannot use any of the knowledge you gained with the faculties God gave you and cannot use any of the elements which God created. I don't think it's possible for you to do this but if you can then you might be able to make the case that God doesn't have the right to test you and reward or punish you according to the results. But it's not like you can stop God if he chooses to do so anyways. Let's say somehow you managed to create another universe and then made people to inhabit it, after all that effort would you just leave the people to do whatever they wanted and enjoy themselves or destroy themselves without requiring them to even acknowledge that you existed?

We both know the answer is no, so life is a test and the results will determine where you go, Paradise or Hell. Once you accept the fact you are currently taking this test, it will be much easier to pass.

Now what does a question on the test of life look like? There are many different types but most importantly the test is timed, meaning you have to do certain things at certain times. Some answers are appropriate only for certain parts of the test which you can get or lose points for depending on the timing or way you answer. Essentially the test of life makes each second you have a question which you will have to answer for. So for time you spent reading this you will be asked about it and what you learned from this chapter. Other times events will happen in your life which will merit a particular reaction or response and you will have multiple options to choose from. For example you could answer A and get Angry, or B and Backbite, or C and give Charity, or D and Despair/Disbelieve, or E and be Egotistic, or F and Flagellate yourself, or G and be Grateful, or H and Hate religion, or I and choose Idolatry/Ignorance/Intoxicants, or J and Joke about everything, or K and Kill something, or L and Love something, or M and be Merciful, or N and be Niggardly, or O and be Oblivious, or P and Pray with Patience, or Q and Question God, or R and Repent, or S and Sin Selfishly , or T and Teach, or U and be Uncontrollable, or V and Victimize yourself, or W and Worship God, or X and make up your own answers for the test of life instead of studying the book God gave you and following the instructions of the prophets he sent to help us pass the test. Those who make up their own answers for the test fail, because you can't pass the test of life by guessing.

This test of life will continue until you die, even on your deathbed Satan will be there telling lies, harassing you and trying to make your last deed sinful so you fail in the final minute. Satan is a permanent enemy of ours, there will never be a truce, just ask Adam pbuh. Even after Adam pbuh messed up and got tricked out of paradise, Satan still harassed him for the rest of his life on earth trying to corrupt him further. The only time one will be able to rest is if they enter paradise. Those who fail the test will wish they had another chance to redo life. Every time you pass by a graveyard remember all those dead people were once in your position and didn't focus as much on the test as they should have and if they could they would gladly take your test so they could try to get a better result. Right now you still have time on the clock to get more points, don't waste it or cause your good deeds to be erased by the bad deeds. Don't waste time complaining about the test of life, just do the best you can before it's over and try not to get distracted, because very soon the time will run out. Your quality of life for the rest of eternity is based solely on the results you get after taking the test of life. The more time a person has taking a test the more time there is to check their test to correct any mistakes they might have made before being graded. This is called repentance, when we directly ask the test giver alone to forgive us for the mistakes we made on the test. If possible we can actually right any wrongs we have done, but sometimes we cannot erase our past and have to tell the test maker we are sorry, we made a mistake and will sincerely try to never ever do it again. Fortunately as long as we still have time during the test of life if we repent for our mistakes sincerely in the correct way we will be forgiven, but if we don't repent before time for repentance is up then those sins will be factored in to our final result. Another benefit of having more time in the test of life is that we can do the extra credit questions to get extra points which will result in a better grade and a higher reward also increasing the likelihood of us passing. The more time we have the more points (good deeds) we should have. That is the difference between many people, some just want to get to heaven and that is it, while others don't just want to get to heaven they want to be in the highest levels of heaven. Realistically we tend to fall short of our goals. Those who just want to get into heaven, if they fall short they will be in hell. Whereas those who want to reach the highest levels of heaven, if they fall short they will likely still be in heaven. We must give ourselves a wide margin of error. For instance if you were shooting an arrow from a bow trying to hit the center of the target in the bullseye if you just aimed straight at the target then after the wind and gravity affects the arrow it will fall lower than the place you aimed. So let's say you aimed to hit the 100 mark in the center of the target if you aim for that 100 mark then you will probably hit the lower 75 mark. That's not too bad at least you're on the board, whereas if you aim for the lower 75 mark itself then you probably won't even hit the target at all and the arrow will crash into the dirt without meeting it's goal of hitting the target. To hit the 100% mark one must aim higher so that the shortcomings and difficulties the arrow goes through on the way aren't enough to compromise it from reaching the target or the desired goal. Thus it is safest to strive for a grade of over 100% on the test of life taking advantage of the extra credit opportunities before we get placed beneath the dirt in our grave while on the way to reaching our targeted goal. Who knows we may even succeed, after all the test maker (God) wants us to do the best we can and even helps us throughout the test letting us use his own book for answers with prophets as tutors. The test of life is actually difficult to fail for those who truly desire success. On the other hand the less time we have the more important it is. As time is winding down, every second we have to get more points (good deeds) is more important than the previous. Also the less time we have then the fewer mistakes (bad deeds) we should make. Always remember before you do something "*you only get to take the test of life once*" and the results will last forever. None of us has a guarantee that they will pass, but we can be certain that time will run out and we will be graded. If you were to die in 5 minutes and got graded based only on what you did for those final 5 minutes, what would you do in those final 5 minutes? Since we don't know when our final 5 will be we should treat every minute as though it is our last and try to please our Creator with every second of our life, because that is how we pass the test of life and gain entrance into an eternal paradise.

AGES 14-17

Upon entering high school once more people changed and this time while not changing much myself, I decided to change the people who I was around. Being a wide receiver on the freshman football team increased my popularity and expanded my social network, notwithstanding the fact that I only played a few minutes in one game due to being injured all season with a broken thumb. I also got injured again at the end of the season, getting a broken wrist from the only game I played in. Regardless I was a "member of the team" and as a result was exposed to the hazing that goes on, which surprisingly cements the teammate ties out of a fear that if you weren't part of the team then the treatment would be even worse; it's similar to being in a gang. While not as bad as one might think, hazing is somewhat annoying. The point being, that for my freshman year I hung around the football players and athletes. That was my social class.

My freshman year of high school was also the same year the PS3 came out. I had sold my PS2 in the summer so that I could afford the PS3 on the day of its debut. While I still had a PS1 to play, with a broken thumb and then a broken wrist it wasn't worth the effort to play an outdated game system, so I had stopped playing videogames for a few months. It was amazing how much time I had to do things when videogames weren't a part of my life, after a few weeks I didn't even feel a need or craving to game at all. The PS3 was so eagerly anticipated that there were day long lines just to pre-order. Being a young kid I was not allowed to sit for days in line just to pre-order and subsequently I didn't get one when it eventually came out due to short supply and limited availability. I didn't realize why but for some reason the PS3 wasn't to be found in stores and the few who could find them would only sell at highly increased prices, sometimes selling for multiples of the retail price. I was hopeless, forced to taste the effect scarcity has on supply and demand. My dad had managed to wait in line early one morning and obtain a PS3 surprising me on Christmas so much that I cried, yes it was one of those pathetic crying while opening a gift moments at the age of 14. However he took the credit for getting that gift and wasn't willing to let the fictional Santa Claus steal the show. That was the moment that was supposed to make me forever happy, the first next-gen console of my generation. Soon I became a videogame addict again, rejoicing in my private play station. All thanks and praises be to God for guiding me away from that addiction and may God guide all addicts away from their vices whatever they are.

As I was getting older and nearing the end of my CCD instruction (Classes in Catholic Doctrine) we were assigned community service hours as a requirement for the sacrament of Confirmation. Confirmation is the Catholic ritual where you are finally recognized as a full adult member of the Catholic Church. In order to get my community service hours done, I decided to be a teacher's assistant for a 3rd grade religious education class. At the time I was considering becoming a teacher, having given up on my dreams of becoming a professional athlete. For the next 2 years on Saturdays (during the school year) I would help teach 3rd graders about the Catholic religion. Sometimes the teacher would be sick or unable to come to class and I would teach the class all by myself. This was a very important grade to teach because at the end of the school year the students would participate in their first communion. Therefore the Eucharist ritual made up a large portion of the curriculum. Any questions the kids had were easy to answer. For anything the teachers book didn't answer I found myself regurgitating the same exact answers I had been told when I was a kid asking questions about the religion. Thereupon I realized how ideas implanted during youth can remain dormant for years yet you still know and act upon them without even remembering who taught you that, or why you think the way you do about something. This realization inspired me to attempt to indoctrinate these kids so they would be firm Catholics who would continue the brainwashing cycle. Which is exactly how I had been brainwashed to react upon realizing that I had been brainwashed. It's like the kid who falls in the mud, rather than clean off the mud he tries to get the other children muddy so they are like him and he doesn't have to change. Grading papers was intoxicating and made me feel powerful, but the report cards were a completely different story. This is because with the report card as a teacher if I said the kid wasn't satisfactorily learning their religion then it meant I was a bad teacher. So there was immense pressure to simply pass a kid on even if they didn't know their religion and just let their teacher next year teach them anything they were supposed to learn from me but didn't. Which ironically is the same thing the kids' teachers from the year before did to me. It's the unspoken standard practice of Christian religious education teachers. Now this scam goes both ways because when the parents get report cards they are asked to write about how their child's religious devotion and character in the home improved, and every parent agrees to write something up even if it's not true because to disagree and say their kid isn't more devout or knowledgeable and admit that their kid is acting worse towards them as they get older would mean the parent is a bad irreligious parent who isn't doing their job. So both parents and religious teachers play this type of lying game on Christian religious education report cards, except most parents never suspect the teacher is lying about their kid too. While the kids like that both sides lie for them and don't expose either side because if the truth were known then they think they'd get in double trouble more than anyone else.

At this time in my life, while teaching religion I started to get more religious and desired to learn more about religion independently. In public school they would teach us about world religions, but since they didn't want to offend anyone they mostly taught vocabulary and didn't really teach anything about religious doctrines. Their lack of teaching about religions made me very upset when they tried teaching Christianity and neglected to mention almost every tenant of Christianity. If you only take what you learn about religions from public school you practically know nothing about religions. Actually it'd almost be better to know nothing about religion than to have been taught religions in public schools because the person who doesn't know anything about religion knows they don't know anything, while the student thinks they know something but they are misinformed. I recently read the guidelines given to American public school teachers in 2010 CE by the "American Academy of Religion" for how to *"legally and constitutionally teach about religions"*. The 3 principles they are told to teach are: 1. *"Religions are internally diverse."* (Meaning every religion has many ways to correctly believe in it and practice it, there is no wrong way to practice a religion, it's about what you believe but then again all the religions have many diverse beliefs there is no absolute standard belief.) 2."*Religions are dynamic*" (Meaning every religion changes throughout time and is supposed to change throughout time and adapt to the times and places. Which means religious beliefs and practices of every religion are supposed to be different depending on the geographical location and the historical era.) 3. "*Religions are embedded in culture*" (Meaning all religions are just cultural inventions and social phenomenon, they don't come from God or gods or devils but are just cultural evolution. As such all of them must be respected because they are part of a person's culture and give us valueable historical traditions. They have nothing to do with politics. Historically they did but now we know that was wrong, unfortunately some extreme people live in the past and don't understand that different religions make society better by adding to it's diversity. Anyways religion has been around too long for us to discard it, we'll just have to be tolerant and respectful so we can best use everything that each religion has to offer society.) Now of course this curriculum is completely abhorrent to anyone with religious beliefs, but the teachers are taught how to delicately teach this to their students. The paper also taught how to respond to students who will object by saying "*my religion doesn't teach that*". In such a circumstance the teacher is to respond by saying that many religions teach different things, so "your tradition" is different than other "traditions" in your religion, so you have be tolerant and understanding that not everyone agrees with your opinions about religion, even if it's your own religion. The teachers were instructed that several beliefs denote a student with "religious illiteracy". 2 of them are as follows, "*Religious traditions and expressions are often represented inaccurately by those outside of and within religious traditions and communities.*" Meaning that if a student thinks that many people misrepresent their religion, especially those who don't believe in it, then they are "*religiously illiterate*". Secondly, "*Religious leaders and believers of a given religious tradition or expression are assumed to be the best sources of information about the tradition or expression and are often looked to formally or informally as "experts."*" Meaning if a student thinks that religious leaders know the most about their religion then they are a "religious illiterate". It's the equivalent of saying that the prophets of God know the least about the religion God has ordained. Essentially the school teachers are taught to think the kids that think or say their teachers don't know what they are talking about are "*religious illiterates*" or "*stupid extremists*". Of course the teacher must never ever make the kid think they think the kid is a "religious illiterate" but they are told to be sensitive and confident that they are just overly passionate due to youth and "religious illiteracy". The public school teacher is told to teach kids they are the expert on every religion in the world and the "experts" are all stupid intolerant idiots that don't know what religion even is. To them religions are like candy, they all taste good and none are poisonous except for those extremists who think they're attitudes are right/better and others are wrong/worse. Public school teachers practically don't know anything at all about any religions, because they couldn't in good conscience teach this stuff if they did or believed in one, however they pose as religious experts that know it all trying to make their students' passion and devotion to religion dissipate while making them think religion is simply cultural. That's the American curriculum and that's why kids think a sin is "*Just of matter of your opinion. While just because you think the religion teaches X is a sin, it's not because religions are diverse and dynamic cultural phenomenons, not rigid or absolute truths from God or anyone special. Religions and sins are opinons."* Public school teaches that religion is man-made philosophy. In reality the American public school teachers who teach kids about religion know less about religion than the students they are teaching. Sadly many get tricked into thinking the teachers know what they are talking about and don't realize that teaching is literally just a job where they have to teach what they are told to teach about religion and what they are teaching is absolutely wrong but they teach it anyways because that's what they are paid to do. Public school teachers do not get paid to teach the truth or what is right. They get paid to teach the curriculum. Then teachers are taught to teach that a religious "expert" is a fool because they are religious. Thereby saying any who refute them are automatically fools because they are refuting them. They are actually told by the government to teach kids that those who say the public school teachers don't know what they are talking about actually don't know what they are talking about themselves. To put it in a different context they are saying *"If you want to learn a sport the coaches who coach it and the players who play it aren't the ones to learn from. It's best to ask those who don't play the sport if you want to learn how to play it."* or put another way *" If you want to learn about warfare don't ask any military officer or anyone who has ever studied warfare because they're biased."* Students are taught that to have religious expertise is to be prejudiced, biased and *"religiously illiterate"*. One day I hope some kid uses this doctrine on the teachers and says: *"The teachers are idiots because they think they are "experts" and know more than us students. If they call themselves a teacher then that means they're not fit to teach!"* The teachers would be outraged by such stupidity, yet this is what public school teachers teach kids regarding religions. What they teach is criminal according to every religion, but religious people are so upset that their kids get any exposure to other religions as possibly being valid that they focus on forbidding other religions from being taught instead of the religious cultural evolution doctrine itself. Needless to say I was not satisfied with my teachers but I had to write the answers they said were correct in order to pass. It was frustrating doing schoolwork on Christianity or other religions in which one had to give answers that Christianity deems to be incorrect in order to get a good grade. If you gave an answer you believed in you would be marked wrong and not get credit or fail. Yet people always tell kids to get good grades in school.

Meanwhile my mom had a friend in Ohio whose daughter was going to marry a Muslim man and become a Muslim. I flipped out. For weeks whenever my mom was on the phone with that woman I would try to talk to her and tell her what things to say to her daughter so she would realize how and why Christianity is the truth(as I saw it) and avoid making such a mistake that would disqualify her from paradise. The vocabulary about Islam that I learned in public school made me seem like an expert who knew what he was talking about, although today I can honestly say that I didn't have a clue. It turned out that the daughter eventually married the Muslim man and became a Muslim herself. I had forbid my mom from attending the wedding and was likely the reason for her friendship with the mother disintegrating.

The experience of teaching made me realize that it was a lot of work to teach people and prepare lesson plans, which made me sympathize more with my teachers; too much in hindsight. I thought of an easier career that didn't require as much work as a teacher has to do, I considered becoming President of the United States. As a Catholic president I planned to use the powers of office to establish a Catholic state and launch a few crusades, or at the least kill more Muslim enemies and use the Christian fervor from the wars to establish a Christian state with Christian laws. If you hadn't guessed by now, I was a proud Catholic who wasn't keen on interfaith relationships. Even amongst Christians, my protestant friends would tell their parents not to talk about religion with me because I was so passionate about it; ideal for the U.S. presidency. Yet there was a snag in my plot for Catholic world domination, a concept called separation between Church and State. It's actually a relatively recent concept, which means the Christian religion has no place in politics or the laws of a country, basically to prevent someone who had ideas like mine from getting their "finger on the button". Contrary to popular belief the official separation in America actually came about in the mid 1900s CE. It seemed feasible to reverse such a recent decision if I ever became president. Although when doing further research on democracy and secularism I discovered something that will shock the majority of Christian Americans. The founding fathers were not Christian and had very anti-religious intentions when founding the American state. Similar to the fable about George Washington not being able to tell a lie when he chopped down a cherry tree, I discovered that indeed many lies have been told about the beginning of the American Government. As any liar knows when you start something based on a lie, further lies are required to keep it going and the lies get bigger and bigger the more time goes by. The revolution was based on lies and false flag attacks such as "the Boston Tea Party", where American revolutionaries dressed up pretending to be Indians then dumped british tea into the ocean hoping Britian would blame the Indians and go to war with them. Thereby it would clear the land of Indians so it could be settled by the colonists and exhaust the British armies and finances so the revolution would then have a higher chance of success. The General of the Revolutionary army, who eventually became the first president of the United States, George Washington singlehandedly started the 7 year French and Indian war in 1754 CE. This is the cause that led to the British taxes, which eventually led to the revolution, which led to his presidency.

  Systematically democracy in itself is directly opposed to religion, they cannot coexist. In both the Bible and Quran when Talut (Saul) was appointed to be the first king of Israel the people rejected God's decision and wanted to choose someone themselves, to which God said NO. This was one of the earliest attempts at democracy in the history of the world and it was divinely rejected as a form of government, because only God has the right to make laws and the laws of God are the only ones that can be just; since God is the most just and knows us better than we do ourselves. Another attempt at democracy which had more effect happened with the pagan Greek Athenians who founded the Athenian League and created a proxy Thalassocratic empire. Inevitably they became obnoxiously corrupt and the inability of democracy to remove corruption from government was exposed, then their neighbors (allies) united against them and conquered them thereby ending the democracy experiment. Democracy has been subsequently retried again and again throughout history with similar results typically ending with the fall of an empire which historians incorrectly attribute to economic or military reasons, such as the Roman Republic, better known as the Roman Empire. In Italy before the renaissance democracy was tried again but the people rejected democracy and overthrew their democratic city-states replacing them with dictatorships. Notable examples include Perugia in 1389 CE, Bologna in 1401 CE, Siena in 1477 CE and Rome in both 1347 CE and 1922 CE. In fact had democracy not been abolished in Italy the renaissance likely would have never occured. The famous renaissance men like Leonardo Da Vinci, Michelangelo, Raphael, Donatello and such lived under dictatorships and as a result their talents were noticed and cultivated. Once democracy came to Italy again the talent disappeared and got lost in the masses because favoritism of talent contradicts democratic principles of equality, equal opportunity and equal rights. Throughout history people have tried democracy found out it sucks and doesn't work, but then later generations repeat the same experiments thinking they can make the impossible work for them when its never worked before when even better people tried it. It's a misconception that democracy prevents dictatorship. Democracy and dictatorship are intimately related because every dictator has been appointed by a majority vote, which is the exact premise of democracy. Democracy doesn't promote peace within multi-ethnic societies, it promotes conflict pitting diverse groups against each other with genocidal foreshadowing as anyone living under democracy today recognizes even if they don't know those conflicts are caused by democracy. The philosopher Aristotle who lived under Athenian Democracy even said: *"Unlimited Democracy, is just like oligarchy, a tyranny spread over a large number of people."* During the life of Aristotle the definition of Democracy was: *"A State in which everything, even the law, depends on the multitdue set up as a tyrant and governend by a few declamatory speakers."*

    What is known as the American Revolution was partially inspired by a law passed by the King of England that prevented British Colonists from speculating on undeveloped uninhabited western Native American(or Indian) lands. Wealthy British Colonists would buy cheap acres from the natives, who didn't fully understand the concept of private property, then wait until further expansion of settlers developed the area and then the land would ideally be sold for a large profit. The Navigation acts and Trade acts also hurt merchant business interests, because they imposed tariffs on any goods British colonists imported that weren't from Britain thereby making them more expensive, thus forcing colonists to purchase products from their own country; which was Britain. These acts placed restrictions on exports, meaning the British colonists were only allowed to sell goods to Britain even if they could get a better price elsewhere; to sell anything to a foreign country was considered sedition and treason. The British colonists were to be entirely reliant on British labor and goods, it didn't matter if they wanted spices from China or peppers from Mexico it was illegal. The British attitude was to be patriotic and buy products made in your own country to support the government with the sales taxes and income taxes it would collect, even if other countries make better products for a cheaper cost it was unpatriotic to buy the best you can with the money you earned. This was similar to a communist economy in which the country is supposed to be entirely self-sufficient without any imports at all. Well the "American" Revolutionaries didn't want to be stuck buying expensive inferior products from their own country, they wanted cheap high quality imported goods made by foreigners that didn't have taxes levied on them. To go along with that grievance, in 1764 CE England outlawed the colonial scrip used as currency and forced the colonists to sell bonds in exchange for fiat banknotes from the Bank of England. This fiat paper money put them in debt with interest to be paid and the notes were constantly inflated as the Bank of England printed more, thereby causing a loss of value in the monetary unit and loss of purchasing power for the wages one earned.

At the time the revolutionaries were drafting documents that said "*We the people*" they did not speak for all the people. They were representing a select minority of people. For example no one would say "*The people want lemonade*", because not all people want lemonade, so the term "*the people*" is ambiguous, which people is it? Just exactly who are these people? "*The people*" do not exist because there are billions of individuals that cannot be collectively united or grouped together with such an overgeneralization. "*The people*" the "American" revolutionaries referred to can't possibly be me and you because they say "We", so that means it is just them who they are claiming to represent; the American colonial merchant social class during that time period at the specific place where the document was originally drafted. "*The people*" were only those people who signed their names on the document. The masses of "American" colonists were neither represented nor consulted. They didn't go door to door asking "*The people*" if they could represent them and speak/write on their behalf. The ringleaders either unfairly took authority that was never given to them, or the meaning of "*The people*" has been misinterpreted by the later people. So who were "*the people*"? It was actually made quite clear when the U.S. Constitution was written and the United States of America became an official government entity in 1788 CE, "*the people*" were "*the voters*". Some American people today might think that means them, if they are of those allowed to vote, but who did the drafters of the constitution and founding fathers consider to be "*the people who can vote*"? First of all you had to be a white male so that narrowed it down. Secondly you had to own land, which narrowed it down to the rich white men. In total after the American revolution and the U.S. Constitution was written only 6% of American citizens could vote. In practice even less actually did. The lowest voter turnout among the states was South Carolina where only 0.9% of the population voted, while the highest was Pennsylvania where 4.9% of the population voted. After the revolution suceeded, in practice 95.1-99.1% of Americans had no voice and did not vote in their democratic government. (Today more vote but less have a voice of influence.) So when phrases such as "*We the people*" are used in early American history, remember that catchphrase only refers to 6% of Americans maximum and in reality it was a lot less than 6%. It was actually only a handful of voters because originally the U.S. Constitution started by saying "*We the States*". This was changed in later drafts because prior to the Constitution being ratified they didn't know which states would vote to ratify it. So since they couldn't legally put "*We the States*", since they didn't know which states would ratify, they changed it to say "*We the people of the United States*". This edit was unanimous and everyone present understood it to mean that "We the people" meant the people who governed each state who would later choose to ratify the Constitution. The term "We the people of the United States" was a hypothetical yet to be defined term to include the future magistrates of the States. Consider the phrase as though it is a sports team or company declaring what they believe/do before the team or company is actually formed. "*We the people of the United States*" did not mean the American people and the American people never got to vote on the

Constitution at all. The American people just got told "*These are the rules because "We the people" said so.*" In America the phrase "*We the people*" differs in meaning depending on which document it's written on, unfortunately the masses of idiots incorrectly tend to think it means them. To such persons you can enlighten them by saying "We the people" meant the govenment's people not the taxpaying people, those documents are about their people not you people. Whenever other popular phrases such as "*all men are created equal and entitled to life, liberty and the pursuit of happiness*" were written, the rich white male politicians who wrote those words meant "*We the 6% of rich white male Americans are equal to each other and entitled to "the good life", liberty and have a divine right to do what makes us happy*". Of course they couldn't start a popular political movement with that type of slogan, so edits were made and words were undefined. It was similar to campaign slogans today, linguistically everyone likes the politicians' mottos because they don't really know what it means and it never gets clarified. Just take the phrase all men are created equal, how many actually believe that? I mean really believe that. How many Americans actually believe that "all men are created equal" actually means that foreigners are equal to citizens? Has any american ever thought "illegal immigrants" are equal to naturalized or life-long citizens? So you see deep down everyone knows the slogan doesn't mean what it says even though they say it. The speech/text of slogans are standard but the meanings vary with each interpreter. Fortunately (or unfortunately) soon after the revolution the American government clarified that they meant "free land-owning white men" by "all men" and "We the people". In 1790 CE the Senate and House of Representatives passed a law saying only free white people could be citizens of America. In 1795 CE when people complained that such a racial stipulation limited the citizen pool, and thereby the tax pool, congress and the "Founding Fathers" reaffirmed the ruling saying that no non-white person or non-land owning male can ever become an American citizen. And that's why as much as I may hate racism and disagree with white supremacists, they are completely right when they say that America was supposed to be a "white-only" nation. The founders of America explicitly repeatedly enshrined it into legal code that only rich white men could be citizens of America, despite decades earlier preaching " *all men are created equal*" when they wanted people to die for the cause. It was only after victory that US politicians let everyone know loud and clear that their popular slogans didn't mean what the voters/taxpayers/soldiers thought. Non-whites could be free on American soil, and there were non-citizen freemen living in early America but to be a citizen with voting privileges being white, male and rich was the requirement the founding fathers stipulated. Yet even still at the time it was written that "all men" bit despite not meaning "all men", really did mean "just men". Nobody and I mean nobody in America thought women were included and nobody ever considered any American would ever think a woman could be equal to a man in any sense at all. It's almost funny to think that if American women went back in time today to early America or even just 100 years and said women are equal to men, they'd get laughed to death and the American people would tell her, "*Hey lady, it says "all <u>men</u> are created equal" and "<u>men</u> have X rights", in case you never noticed YOU ARE NOT A MAN! What planet are you from where men are considered equal to women and when the laws say "men" people think it means "men and women"? If it meant women it would say women, didn't you know that the word women is a different word than men? Do you know how to spell words? Those* writing it knew how to spell both M-E-N and W-O-M-E-N. It says "MEN"! That is the word they wrote, M-E-N. You don't have the rights God gave men because you are NOT A MAN! Our founding fathers would be puking in their graves if they knew you tried to lie about our constiution, declaration of independence and American beliefs." Seriously women were not allowed to have American citizenship, because they were women and women are women; being white + rich wasn't even enough for women to be citizens. Furthermore no two women were considered equal to each other in America, their treatment depended on their social class, their wealth, their husband, their looks and who their children were; and not always in that order. The problem was that even though slogans meant one thing, many of them were designed so that people who were not familiar with law, politics or history would glean their own misunderstanding. For example historically whenever some group loudly proclaimed they wanted liberty it has always ended up that in reality they just wanted power. As Frencesco Guicciardini wrote, *"It seems clear to me that the desire of dominating one's fellows and asserting superiority is natural to man, so that there are few so in love with liberty that they would not seize a favorable opportunity of ruling and lording it. Look closely at the behavior of the indwellers of the selfsame city; mark and examine their dissensions, and you shall find that the object is preponderance rather than freedom. Those then who are the foremost citizens do not strive after liberty, though that be in their mouths, but the increase of their own sway and pre-eminence is really in their hearts. Liberty is a cant term with them, and disguises their lust of superiority in power and honor."* Thus today people quote American political slogans like *"all men are created equal"* or *"we the people"* being completely clueless that those were/are racist, sexist and mercantilist statements that were never meant to apply to those quoting them today. As an example imagine a politican's slogan was *"I'll help you"*, everybody would think they were the "you" the politician was talking about and that "help" was what they considered help to be. Whereas the politician's true meaning and plans will actually hurt the person who hears their slogan. Such was the ambiguity utilized to promote the revolution against England. The revolution was truly a political masterpiece of propaganda. For instance the "American" colonists hated taxes even more than you do. Which is why the famous slogan of *"No taxation without representation"* drew widespread revolutionary support, but it's a historical fact that representation actually increases taxation. Look at America today, in 2014 CE the average citizen paid 46% of what they earned in total taxes and the total amount paid goes up each year. Whereas the total taxes levied by King George on the "American" colonist in the 1770s CE amounted to 3% of their total earnings. They started a revolution because of it. Today with democracy, freedom and "representation" Americans pay 15 times more in taxes than did the British colonists. We pay more in state sales tax alone than the oppressed colonists ever paid in total to the English Crown! In fact some politicians even propose to "raise taxes to protect freedom". Apparently freedom has a price tag that has lots of numbers on it. The ring leaders behind the American Revolution did not plan on ending taxation, they just wanted to stop paying taxes themselves and thought it would be better if the people paid them instead of the English king. When drafting the U.S. Constitution they even debated whether or not the President should have the title of "Serene Highness" because of the monarchial nature of the executive branch. Basically the Founders of the American government got sick of the English King and decided to make themselves Kings of America, but wanted to be subtle about their kingship lest they be called hypocrites because they weren't of "royal blood".

Since they wouldn't have gotten away with calling themselves kings they used the term statesmen. There were also religious reasons the British colonists had for not paying taxes to the king because paying taxes to a deified emperor(like the British monarch) is/was against the Bible.

Not one place in all of Colonial America contained a trace of democracy, the political structure was always that of a merchant state, or what is better known today as a corporatocracy. "*Natural rights*" and "*popular sovereignty*" were not philosophies promoted by anyone in American politics during the entire time period between 1607-1776 CE. Once a democracy was established and the first tax levied, "*the people*" were completely taken by surprise and actually rebelled against the U.S. Government they had fought to create. One famous rebellion that gained too much publicity for history to ignore was the "*Whiskey Rebellion*" that was singularly raised in opposition to taxes. However because these taxes were being paid to the U.S. Government and not the English Government, the founding fathers were on the side of taxation and mercilessly slaughtered the tax evaders they had previously paid to fight against the British in the American Continental Army. The tax rebels actually used the same slogan of "*no taxation without representation*" as a rallying cry saying that they weren't represented and the taxation was unjust. This was because they thought "*the people*" meant them and that anyone who represented them would never agree to any taxation at all. Afterall if a politician really represents you then they wouldn't impose any taxes on you, would they? Unless of course there were people who wanted to pay taxes, but the American tax rebels were not such people and concluded they were not being represented and thus should rebel. Many were self-made pioneers who never had any help from Britain at all, they felt the Crown was simply extorting them without providing any benefit, inciting natives to harm them. When they fought in the revolution they believed "*no taxation without representation*" was a clever rhyme to say "no taxation" without giving their enemies a way to label them as anarchists. Although the new American government was not about to set a precedent of discussing taxation issues with its subjects, instead George Washington raised an army and the rebels were killed with bullets and cannon balls that were paid for with taxpayer dollars. Today they would loudly be called a "threat to national security" whereas in actuality they were just a threat to national taxation. To politicians a threat to taxation is a threat to their own financial security, so by considering themselves "*the nation*" they feel no qualms about calling threats to their own power, finances or reputation a "threat to national security" or "*the people*".

Regarding America George Washington called it a "nascent empire", Thomas Jefferson called America an "extensive empire" and Alexander Hamilton referred to America as the "most interesting empire in the world". The alleged "reason" and rationality cliche for US democracy deriving from intellectual thought was just a political placebo to get the philosophers to persuade the masses that the United States brand of democracy was somehow based on intelligent design so they'd view it as better than the false divine mandates claimed by the corrupt European kings; even though rationality itself refutes democracy. America was formed during the "Age of reason" so reason was cited as the reason for democracy despite democracy being unreasonable because it was the only way for the American aristocracy to break ties with the English crown and rule without causing the masses to view their mercantilistic state as an aristocracy. Those American anti-aristocratic patriots who found out they were scammed and fought back were met with federal violence. Ever since the massacre of the tax rebels, aside from a brief period during the civil war, the American citizenry has been forced to pay taxes against their will and are threatened with confiscation, imprisonment and death for "resisting arrest" if they don't. Some even quote Benjamin Franklin as having said: "*'In this world nothing can be said to be certain, except death and taxes*." not realizing he wrote that pro-tax pitch in 1789 CE two years AFTER signing the U.S. Constitution. During the revolution, before he got paid with American tax dollars, he was singing a different tune. If taxes were something as certain in this world as death then early man would have experienced taxes just as early man experienced death. Adam pbuh never paid taxes to the government, neither did many other humans, even today there are countries in the world that don't require citizens to pay any taxes at all. We don't have to be in paradise to live tax-free. The very fact that taxes can be evaded shows that taxes are not as certain as death. Yet the very same statesman who said that death is as certain as taxation also preached that there was to be "no taxation without represenation". So in context doesn't that mean political representation is as certain as death? And that just as taxes are certain then so is representation? No, representation is not as certain as death? Well then I guess taxes aren't either and just as people do not have to have representation they do not have to pay taxes. It is impossible to be a death evader, but tax evasion is as easy as saying no. While if there is to be no taxation without representation then I'll gladly keep my money and not be "represented" than be "represented" and have to pay taxes. However American democracy claims to be "Representative Democracy" mainly due to that whole revolutionary slogan "no taxation without representation", hence their "Representative Democracy" is seen as a valid tax collector. The theory is that elected officials are representatives of "the people" so therefore "all the people" have to pay taxes. But if the one you vote for doesn't win, then realistically you aren't represented and that "representative" was forced upon you by the fixed election results. So if the one you voted for doesn't win then such voters should not have to suffer taxation since they truly don't have representation since their representative is not able to represent them in any political capacity not in theory nor in practice, (although in practice "representatives" who do win still don't really represent those who voted for them) Now some may say those voters' who voted for the loser "gambled their right to representation away and lost it in the election". That argument is invalid, but even if an idiot thinks it is, which if valid means elections take away the "right to representation" thus elections prove voters are not represented and "Representative Democracy is impossible, what about those who don't vote? Why must non-voters pay taxes when they don't even "gamble their rights away by voting"? If voting for the winner means you have representation then both those who vote and lose as well as those who don't vote shouldn't have to pay any taxes at all. Truly if there is "no taxation without representation" then only those who voted for winners should pay taxes, but since its known elected politicians don't really represent those who voted for them even the voters should be able to be untaxed if they can prove thier "elected representative" isn't really doing what they want. At the end of the revolution Americans got royally screwed. The slogan was "No taxation without representation" but most Americans are not represented yet they all gotta pay taxes through all possible orifices to their "elected slavemasters" in government offices. Taxes are a form of financial slavery and just as the American slaveholders convinced slaves they would die if they left the plantation, the American government has persuaded people that taxation is something that must be experienced, as certainly as death, and that somehow an election means taxes become okay and legal. Historically a slave was simply a taxpayer, such as the Spartan slaves called Helots. Helots were allowed to live and work on their own land with the condition being that they'd pay a little less than 50% of their income to the Spartan government every year. Today we'd think that's just taxes, yet back then people called it slavery. Whereas in Athens a "freeman" was someone who didn't work for anyone else, and was a citizen who voted on all Greek legislation and executive bills. Today we'd call that a politician, but back then such a person was a "freeman". Athenian freemen had slaves work for others on their behalf and every free Athenian citizen survived primarily off of employing their slaves to others and taking the income their slave earned along with tribute paid by foreigners overseas. So any taxpayer today who explained their life to a greek of ancient antiquity would be thought of as a slave, and ancient greeks would probably laugh because today's civilized taxpayers think they're "free". By ancient Greek standards freedom meant you kept 100% of what you earn, if you were not allowed to keep 100% of what you earn that meant somebody owned you. The same rule applied in the early Roman Republic, Plebians were the ones who paid taxes. The Patricians were "freemen" who governed, made laws, voted and didn't pay taxes. Plebians were a 2nd-class citizen not considered to be free because they paid taxes yet still got told they were citizens since they were technically not slaves of individuals since they only paid taxes to the state itself. Thus today most "freemen" are actually plebians according to Roman definitions of freedom. However some "free" tax paying plebians today will say, just as Roman plebians may have said, *"But who will build the roads if we don't pay taxes?"* Who built the roads for the early colonists? They did it themselves or contracted private companies to clear roads through the forest and mountain passes. And from the pothole ridden dilapidated asphalt roads I've driven on built by the American government, it's obvious that the government isn't good at making roads and the private sector could do much better, for a much cheaper price. If you didn't like the job done by the private sector, or their maintenance wasn't satisfactory then you could just hire a different party, but currently we are stuck with whatever roads the government makes and if you personally take initiative to fill in the potholes the government has neglected you can get arrested for being a "threat to national security". In the eyes of the American government a threat to bureaucratic job security is a "threat to national security". At least the Roman Empire made state of the art roads, to facilitate tax collection, but after the Empire vanished people kept on building roads without paying taxes for them. Roads existed long before governments did and will still exist long after they vanish. Footprints alone are capable of making roads in any locale. Rather than ask *"Who will build the roads if we don't pay taxes?"* One should ask *"Who could tax us if there were no roads?"* and *"Would there really be no roads to travel on if we weren't taxed?"* Roads existed long before governments did, don't ever think that you won't have roads if you don't pay taxes. Likewise it's not immoral to use a road without paying taxes for it, public property is for public usage not just taxpayer usage. To think it's wrong to use public services without paying for them then one must also think its wrong to not use bombs that were paid for with taxpayer dollars. Really what gives other people the right to use bombs paid for by taxpayers when the people bombing didn't pay for the bomb they drop? Sometimes taxes get paid for bombs that don't even get dropped! Can you believe how "immoral it is" that people paid for atomic bombs to be dropped on people and then their governments don't even use them? If it's not immoral for governments to not use bombs paid for by others since that would result in evil, then it also cannot be immoral for non-taxpayers to use something paid for by taxpayers to do something good, such as driving on a road. Sadly though people think taxes entitle them to special rights they wouldn't have if they didn't pay taxes. Yet if you need to pay taxes in order to benefit from the government's public works then the rich taxpayers who pay the most should get treated the best and the poor who pay the least in taxes should get treated the worst because they pay the least. But then this would be criminal favoritism that would corrupt the state. Hence thinking you need to "pay to play" causes national corruption. Only a corrupt citizen and corrupt state would tolerate the notion that paying taxes justifies getting service. Governments are meant to serve all with justice, not just those who pay them money. Fortunately the people who think they have to pay or it'd be immoral to benefit are simply confused about how the world works and upset they have to pay. So due to lack of understanding they lash out at the non-payers thinking they are to blame for their own high taxes instead of the government "provider" who taxes them. Now I'm not saying to exploit governments by being on welfare without a genuine need or reason, because I consider that immoral since that would amount to getting paid by thieves since taxation is a type of theft, but it's not necessary to pay the road tax to morally use the road, if it was then they'd make a toll for users to pay. Perhaps the very reason flying cars have been held back from the masses is because if flying cars were used people would learn that they don't need to pay the governments for roads. But then someone would probably say, "*How dare you fly your car in the air without paying the government who built that air road for you!*" Next they'll probably try to tax fish for swimming in man-made canals paid for by taxpayer dollars. Tis the doctrine of communism that all must pay a "fair share" in order to benefit from the labor and payments of others. The American Revolution began in order to be free from British taxes and today Americans are one of the most heavily taxed peoples in the world, ironically Americans pay more in taxes than the British do today. Americans might actually be paying less in taxes today had the colonists remained British subjects. In the long term outlook Americans actually lost the war against taxation. They won independence from British taxes only to become enslaved to the heavier burden of American taxes. The "Bill of Rights" was just a big fat tax bill. Americans thought they'd get progress but were surprised, and are still consistently surprised when they get conned by a group of scam artists called "Con-gress". The nation of America was never made to serve liberty, rather America was made to serve the greedy. It lets greedom reign, under the slogan of freedom ringing. The black Africans who came to America on ships weren't the only Americans enslaved, all of them were except for the patriotic profiteers. Liberty and Freedom were just expensive political placebos.

    So what if money was the motive, the founding fathers were still Christians right? Actually many were freemasons, according to information provided to me from a former freemason and a freemason book I obtained of a record of the proceedings of the Grand Lodge of Vermont's 149th annual communication in 5942 A.L. (1942 CE) on which the cover of the book says it's "to be kept in the lodge room". Suprised as many Americans may be to learn of the influence of freemasonry in America, it's public knowledge. Today the Freemasons themselves publicly testify and prove that the following U.S. presidents were vetted Freemasons: George Washington, James Monroe, Andrew Jackson, James K. Polk, James Buchanan, Andrew Johnson, James Garfield, William McKinley, Theodore Roosevelt, William H. Taft, Warren G. Harding, Franklin Roosevelt, Harry Truman, Lyndon B. Johnson, Gerald Ford. While Thomas Jefferson and James Madison are also considered to have been freemasons, but the records of their suspected lodges don't exist anymore. So that's 15 freemason American presidents who are confirmed and 17 suspected. While out of the 44 U.S. presidents, 18 U.S. vice presidents were freemasons. Politically Freemasons have been the most influential club in America. Abraham Lincoln even applied to be a freemason at the Tyrian Lodge in Springfield, Illinois during 1860 CE. Although before Lincoln could be officially initiated, he withdrew his application fearing that it might be seen as insincere and a ploy to get more votes in the presidential election. At the time of this writing there have been a total of 57 U.S. presidential terms. During 33 of those 57 terms either the President or the vice president was a freemason, sometimes both were. While if one were to count Thomas Jefferson and Abraham Lincoln as freemasons that would be 36 out of 57 terms. So of the 57 terms thus far where America has had a president, between 58% -63% of the time a freemason had either total or partial control over the executive branch of America. Now you might've noticed I didn't list any modern leaders. This is because modern American presidents and vice presidents are not freemasons, some may think otherwise but that is because there are other clubs which are sponsored by freemasons yet technically speaking since they are different clubs I do not count them as freemasons and neither do freemasons. I'm just stating interesting facts, these politicians were also American too so it could be some diabolic American conspiracy that resulted in American leaders running America. Don't get paranoid. Most likely Freemasons have directly influenced your life in some way or another and you may even have consumed their products or at least know people who do. Thus because of such a vast membership conspiracies naturally arise, especially since the members have been so influential throughout history and continue to be so. Since your interest in Freemasonry might be piqued, I might as well tell you what Freemasons actually believe since there are many false rumors about them. Freemasons claim to be deists in that they believe in a "Supreme Being" but in practice they are interfaith agnostics. Freemasonry in its original form was about liberal arts, science, alchemy and natural philosophy. It was a secretive organization because the Christian Churches considered those subjects heretical and would punish those who studied them. Freemasons were initially secretive in order to be safe from zealous anti-scientific christians, thus many hoaxes have been written about them being satanic. They are not a secret society persay, but rather a secretive society. Similar to a corporation which doesn't share details of what goes on at its important meetings. However because of the symbolism and anti-freemason christian propaganda many feel certain and believe that freemasonry is demonic. The word freemason itself comes from the french word "freres mason" which means "brother mason". There used to be actual stonemasons who used the term free mason to mean they were independent contracters or not unionized. However for most of history freemasons have not been operative in the field of masonry despite their excessive usage of architectural symbols. In the 1700s CE Freemasons began to use Egyptian hieroglyphs because few could translate them, not because they had any connection to pagan Egyptian antiquity. They used them because it was easier than making up their own code. The most important Freemason symbol is:

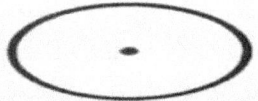

It is a circle with a point or dot in the center. Sometimes it's given a figurative symbolic meaning as in finding the truth at the center. Although historically this is the "symbol of Light", the symbol of the sun, the symbol of On(heliopolis, which was the Egyptian temple of the sun god), it was also the symbol of the sun god Ra. To me it looks like a blind eyeball. Obelisks are also an important masonic symbol which have pagan origins as phallus idols. Whereas from the top of an obelisk, the bird's eye view would be the same as their circle with a dot symbol. This is significant because the secrets of the temple of heliopolis are said to be held within the obelisks of the temple, specifically their pyramidians(which is the capped top of an obelisk). Symbols mean different things to different people, what it means to them may not be what it originally meant. Nevertheless it is important to know what such symbols mean to them even if their meaning isn't the same as the original meaning. However there is another "non-related symbol" in the ancient Hebrew language that "struck my eye" when I saw it. It is the ancient pictograph form of the Hebrew letter "Ayin". It looks exactly like the freemason's symbol, except most freemasons don't know ancient Hebrew so they probably don't know this. The Hebrew letter "Ayin" represents the ideas of seeing and watching as well as knowledge, in that the eye is in some respects a window of knowledge or a "window to the soul".

Ayin

Anyways this "coincidence" in that the primary freemason symbol is exactly like an ancient Hebrew letter may be the reason why Jews are linked to freemasonry, aside from the freemasons allegations of direct connections to Solomon pbuh. Now you may be curious to know what is the Secret of the Freemasons? Well the first secret is that they lost it. The Lost Big Secret of Freemasonry is superconductive levitation. Freemasons think that the Ark of the covenant was a levitating superconductor, controlled by the Levites as the bible says. Superconductive levitation is done via combining multiple metals to make them weigh less than gravity so they and their container float. Since according to the bible the ark of the covenant was thousands of pounds Freemasons think the Levites must have used this trick to lift it. They also think superconductive levitation was used to build massive ancient structures such as pyramids and temples, specifically the magnificent Temple of Solomon pbuh which was allegedly pilfered by the Templar knights during the Crusades. Which may also be why some connect Freemasons with the Templar knights. Another reason for the Freemason-Templar connection is because after the Inquisition exterminated the Templars, the survivors moved to Scotland and became lost to history. Shortly afterwards Freemasonry emerged in Scotland. The connections are more than just circumstantial but personally I don't think there is enough evidence to prove a connection. The alleged superconductive levitating substance has many names such as the "Philosphers Stone", "White bread of gold", "Golden Fleece" etc. But it is basically a scientific process that could've been construed as magic by those unfamiliar with the science, especially during antiquity. Freemasons have lost the formula for how to do this if it was ever done and if they ever had it at all. However modern science has discovered or re-discovered the art of superconductive levitation. Most importantly though is that it is not necessary for the ancient pagans to have used superconductive levitation or magic to have built large buildings with heavy stones. Of course they well could have used magic to make things such as stonehedge, or they could have been assisted by Jinn. However there are many other means that could've been used to build such structures with simple technology of which we have lost the knowledge of. Despite all the conspiracies about Freemasons they actually have quite a conspiratorial view of history themselves. They have an arrogant attitude where because they don't know how the ancient civilizations did what they did, then they think there must be some special conspiratorial magical scientific secret known only to a few. In reality its simple. In the past humans had different technology than we have and perhaps some of the ancient technology was capable of doing things our technology can't. The freemasons even think superconductive levitation was used to build the big Cathedrals because they are baffled as to how medieval people could have built such things based on the limited knowledge we have of the technology available to them during their time. Freemasons fall prey to the view that humans of today are the smartest and best of all time and don't want to contemplate that we may not be as smart, as strong or as technologically advanced as humans in the past. So is Freemasonry a religion? Yes and no. Religiously speaking it is a religion but most people would consider it to be a snobbish club, where they think they are better than everyone else because they think there used to be secrets and they think they used to know these imaginary secrets which they alone claim once existed. Basically it's a religious club that insists it's not a religion and is interfaith which coincidentally throughout history has had many influential and wealthy people as members. Their requirements are that you can not be an atheist or an agnostic, you must be an adult male (no girls allowed) and 100% of the lodge members of the lodge you apply to must accept you joining them. They say they don't recruit people or invite people to join, and that they don't help bad people improve themselves but only help "good men become better". Whereas "good men" are those who believe in the publicly stated freemason doctrines. They claim to be a male fraternity and require members to pay fees to join and keep their membership valid. While freemasons also say the benefits of being a freemason can only be truly known after you become a member. Another one of the rules of freemasonry is that members are not supposed to say anything about freemasonry to people who aren't freemasons. So officially it's a stupid fool's religion based on people who like to imagine themselves as elitists, however politically behind the scenes some colluding and conspiracies may or may not take place. Yet I don't think it's part of Freemason design, but rather a natural byproduct of influential people being in a private arrogant secretive club. Therefore I'd label it is as an unofficial global political party. Do they want world domination? Which religion doesn't? However the point is that according to religious standards, freemasonry is a religion that automatically disqualifies you from being part of most of the other religions. This is because freemasonry teaches that all the religions are basically the same and teach the same thing but they were all corrupted, so they just take the good stuff and filter out the feces they don't like about religions. They say they accept people from all faiths but in reality they reject all faiths because they say all are wrong except for their interpretation of religion and God which they keep very abstract and ill-defined. Also they perform rituals with ascendancy in ranks that make people disbelievers in their own religions. Do Freemasons worship the devil, I'd say yes but most of their members are doing it unintentionally as are many others who aren't Freemasons. Essentially their symbolism, secrecy and influence has caused suspicion which turned to extreme enmity. The point is that all these influential freemasons, are not Christians according to every various type of Christianity. Freemasons are one of the groups that reintroduced the pagan polytheistic concept of "Inter-faith" to the world and have popularized it ever since.

  Something I recently discovered was that in 1797 CE the United States signed a treaty with Tripoli (which is modern day Libya) in which article 11 clearly states the early American government's views in regards to its alleged Christian foundation: "*As the Government of the United States of America is not, in any sense, founded on the Christian religion; as it has in itself no character of enmity against the laws, religion, or tranquility, of Mussulmen; and, as the said States never entered into any war, or act of hostility against any Mahometan nation, it is declared by the parties, that no pretext arising from religious opinions, shall ever produce an interruption of the harmony existing between the two countries.*" This article contains many statements which are now nullified and couldn't be said by any American diplomat today. The reason I included it is to prove that in the eyes of the Government of the United States of America in 1797 CE: "*the Government of the United States of America is not, in any sense, founded on the Christian religion*".   Not one American politician in 1797 CE objected. The treaty was unanimously ratified by the U.S. Senate and signed by President John Adams. But the real kicker is that article 11 does not exist in the arabic treaty the Muslims signed, it's attached as a letter but it's only an actual article in the english translation which the Americans signed. Some Christians will use the fact that the article doesn't exist in the Arabic treaty to say America really was a Christian country, but the exact opposite is the case. American ambassadors pretended to be a Christian country to Tripoli for diplomatic reasons, since the treaty involved Jizya of which atheists were not eligible for, while domestically America made it clear they were not a Christian nation. This type of flip-flop international religious image to seem palatable with every foreign state has always been used by America. Such as when signing the Treaty of Paris in 1783 CE the preamble said, "*in the name of the most holy and undivided Trinity*".   Whereas some Christians then use this treaty to say America was Trinitarian, but again this doesn't prove that either. All it proves is that American diplomats were willing to write whatever they felt was necessary to get the best deal when making treaties. The religious identity of America was like a free to play diplomatic bargaining chip which could be used to get extra leverage. Statistically speaking in 1800 CE less than 10% of Americans belonged to a Church congregation, so the myth about a rich American Christian tradition is a fiction, that gets pushed for political/patriotic/spiritual reasons. I used to be such a patriotic Christian who thought America was God's chosen land and Americans were blessed people, but while eagerly researching American history I was horrified to find out America was never a Christian nation as I had believed it was.

     James Madison, the 4th U.S. president and "Father of the Constitution", wrote in 1785 CE "*During almost fifteen centuries has the legal establishment of Christianity been on trial. What have been its fruits? More or less in all places, pride and indolence in the Clergy, ignorance and servility in the laity; in both, superstition, bigotry and persecution.*" Wheras if you think that is un-Christian like, Thomas Jefferson didn't believe in souls, angels, miracles, the trinity, the miracles of Jesus pbuh or even in the existence of a God. Jefferson believed in materialism, science and "reason" as did/do many Americans. Another piece of evidence proving that America wasn't founded upon Christian ideals is how during the revolution the freemason Benjamin Franklin made a famous cartoon image of a snake chopped up into many parts with each part symbolizing a colony with the slogan "*Join, or Die*", to communicate that if the colonies didn't become one big rattlesnake they would die as separate pieces. This was based on the superstition that if all the parts of a dead snake got put back together before sunset then it would come back to life. Although for all we know Franklin also could've meant "Either join the revolution or we'll kill ya". By Franklin declaring the Rattlesnake as a symbol of America it lead others to put snakes on American flags, most famously the Gadsden "*Don't tread on me*" rattlesnake flag which is still popular today among patriotic liberty loving Americans who want a less stifling government and tend to agree with the little bit of conspiracy theorem they know of. This popular icon of American freedom is particularily anti-Christian due to the bible verses in Genesis 3:13-15 which say, "*Then the LORD God said to the woman, "What is this you have done? "The woman said, "The serpent deceived me, and I ate." ¹⁴ <u>So the LORD God said to the serpent, "Because you have done this,"Cursed are you above all livestock and all wild animals!</u> You will crawl on your belly and you will eat dust all the days of your life. ¹⁵ And <u>I will put enmity between you and the woman, and between your offspring and hers; **he will crush your head,** and you will strike his heel</u>.*" Clearly such bible verses are quite venomous towards the snake species. Thus it's humorous that those who tend to be the most emotionally attached to the patriotic American "*Don't Tread on Me*" flag promoting the notion of American liberty and freedom are Christians, despite the bible explicitly saying how humans will not only hate snakes but will in fact tread on them by crushing their heads while the snakes strike their heels. Although that the bible says the "serpent" will eat dust for as long as it lives also reveals the author's of that biblical passage couldn't be God because God knows that serpents don't eat dust, only a human could make that mistake. (Though some fools think "the serpent" means the devil but likewise the devil has not been eating dust for thousands of years, so it's simply a human scribal superstition mistaken as a divine explanation for why people thought snakes ate the ground they slithered upon.) Anyways the American snake symbolism made by Benjamin Franklin couldn't be more anti-Bible and anti-Christian even if he tried to make it as such. So either Benjamin Franklin was the dumbest Christian of all time, or he really didn't like the bible or Christians. Although fortunately for us we don't have to guess because he wrote in his autobiography, "*My parents had given me betimes religions impressions, and I received from my infancy a pious education in the principles of Calvinism. But scarcely was I arrived at fifteen years of age, when, after having doubted in turn of different tenets, according as I found them combated in the different books that I read, I began to doubt of Revelation itself.",* ......"*Some books against Deism fell into my hands. . . It happened that they wrought an effect on my quite contrary to what was intended by them; for the arguments of the Deists, which were quoted to be refuted, appeared to me much stronger than the refutations; in short, I soon became a thorough Deist.*" So there you have it right from Franklin himself saying was a Deist and not a Christian, but he didn't keep his beliefs to himself. Franklin wrote "*If we look back into history for the character of the present sects in Christianity, we shall find few that have not in their turns been persecutors, and complainers of persecution. The primitive Christians thought persecution extremely wrong in the Pagans, but practiced it on one another. The first Protestants of the Church of England blamed persecution in the Romish church, but practiced it upon the Puritans. These found it wrong in the Bishops, but fell into the same practice themselves both here [England] and in New England.*" Benjamin Franklin was so antagonistic to Christianity that his own friend Joseph Priestly wrote about Franklin in his own autobiography saying, "*It is much to be lamented that a man of Franklin's general good character and great influence should have been an unbeliever in Christianity, and also have done as much as he did to make others unbelievers*" So it's well-known Benjamin Franklin wasn't just a "unbeliever in Christianity" but his Christian-American contemporaries even lamented him actively getting others to disbelieve in Christianity. Franklin was anti-Christianity, he also did a lot to create the US government. So do you think the US government is pro-Christian?

If you think Benjamin Franklin was anti-Christian, the famous patriotic "*author of the revolution*" Thomas Paine boldly wrote in "The Age of Reason":

"*The Christian religion is a parody on the worship of the Sun, in which they put a man whom they call Christ, in the place of the Sun, and pay him the same adoration which was originally paid to the Sun.*"

"*I do not believe in the creed professed by the Jewish church, by the Roman church, by the Greek church, by the Protestant church, nor by any church that I know of. My own mind is my church.* "

"*Of all the systems of religion that ever were invented, there is no more derogatory to the Almighty, more unedifiying to man, more repugnant to reason, and more contradictory to itself than this thing called Christianity.* "

Surely those words don't sound like they would come from someone who practiced or believed in Christianity. Thomas Paine made it abundantly clear that he not only disbelieved in Christianity, but had a very negative opinion of it. Yet he was the *"author of the revolution"*! What about the Pledge of Allegiance? The pledge of Allegiance wasn't written until 1892 CE (116 years after the revolution) and it originally said:

"I pledge allegiance to my flag and the republic for which it stands, one nation, indivisible, with liberty and justice for all."

The author of the pledge was Francis Bellamy, a Christian socialist. It is hard to believe that a Christian wrote the pledge yet wouldn't include the word "God" or "Christian" if America were a Christian nation, although he did happen to be a freemason too. I know, the numbers of freemasons are crazy, that's why there are so many conspiracies about them. In 1932 CE the American pledge of allegiance was changed to say:

*"I pledge allegiance to **the flag of the United States of America** and to the Republic for which it stands, one nation, indivisible, with liberty and justice for all."*

The word "*my flag*" became "*the flag of the United States of America*". (As if there would be any confusion about which flag a person was pledging allegiance to.) I guess they thought saying "my flag" wasn't as good or specific enough. Another thing that has also changed is the way the pledge is made. From 1892-1942 CE when pledging allegiance to the flag Americans would stretch out their right arm in the same manner Nazis did when saluting Hitler, but as a result of WWII the American/Nazi salute was changed to being a hand placed over the heart. It wasn't until 62 years after its creation, in 1954 CE, that the American pledge of allegiance had the words "*under God*" added, with the latest version being:

*"I pledge allegiance to the flag of the United States of America, and to the Republic for which it stands, one nation, **under God**, indivisible, with liberty and justice for all."*

Even this version seems silly in that people pledge allegiance to a flag, it's just a piece of cloth that can't do anything for you. I pledge allegiance to God, his prophets and the believers. I don't take the risk of getting God upset by pledging myself to a piece of cloth or government that may not always be on the good side of God. Thomas Paine ardently said regarding government, *"No power which "needs checking" can be from God"*. Meaning that as someone closely involved with the American Revolution, he did not consider the U.S. Government's structure of checks and balances to be divinely inspired. Paine certainly wouldn't consider it to be the one nation under God which the modern pledge of allegiance claims it to be. This also has major implications for the doctrine of the trinity. The U.S. Federal Government similarly has three branches making up one Government. Thomas Paine says such a power structure cannot be from God because it needs to check itself and counterbalance. Rome had such a 3-branch government formed by Julius Caesar, Gnaeus Pompey and Marcus Crassus in 70 BCE. They called it a triumvirate in which 3 persons ruled as 1. Naturally the triumvirate ended in disaster as Caesar tried to eliminate the other members and obtain absolute authority but some Christians insist God is a triumvirate but they use the word trinity not realizing they are the same exact thing. Although perhaps the phrase trinity is used instead of triumvirate because Romans knowing triumvirates didn't work when put into practice wouldn't accept a triumvirate deity but would accept a trinity.

However Thomas Paine didn't believe God was a trinity because he saw firsthand how the trinity style government of the United States was divided with the various parts constantly opposing each other. If God were to be made of multiple parts they would also be frequently opposing each other, it would make God be bi-polar, or in the case of the Christian trinity tri-polar. Given the time period Thomas Paine lived in, it's surprising he wasn't put on trial for heresy. Yet Paine wasn't the only famous "founding father" of America to declare the government was in no way a system set up by God, let alone a Christian version. As Vice President to George Washington, prior to becoming president himself, John Adams wrote: *The United States of America have exhibited, perhaps, the first example of governments erected on the simple principles of nature; and if men are now sufficiently enlightened to disabuse themselves of artifice, imposture, hypocrisy, and superstition, they will consider this event as an era in their history. Although* **the detail of the formation of the American governments is at present little known** *or regarded either in Europe or in America, it may hereafter become an object of curiosity.* **It will never be pretended that any persons employed in that service had interviews with the gods, or were in any degree under the influence of Heaven,** *more than those at work upon ships or houses, or laboring in merchandise or agriculture;* **it will forever be acknowledged that these governments were contrived merely by the use of reason and the senses."** Thus it is clear that America was not using Christianity as it's source of inspiration and wasn't a Christian nation. Instead it seems the U.S. revolutionaries and politicians used the faith of "*human reason*". Although many Christians may then assume America was "born again", "came to it's senses" and Christianized itself; thereafter finally becoming a nation which devoutly trusts in Jesus or God. Afterall the most sacred thing to the government, their money, says "*In God we trust*" so they must be religious right?

Officially the "*In God we trust*" motto wasn't added to American coins until after 1956 CE. In 1957 CE the motto was added to the paper currency. Many earlier paper bills and coins from earlier dates have the motto, but it wasn't the official monetary standard in America. The reason for the change was in order to give the U.S. the moral high ground against the atheist Soviet Union. The word "God" became a tool to be used in a nationalist propaganda war. This is similar to how ancient rulers would claim a divine mandate gave them authority to rule with an iron fist, using their alleged divine mandate to justify any injustice or oppression they committed. In fact the United States Government has claimed to have a "Manifest Destiny" since the 19th century. The idea of America's "Manifest Destiny" is that God ordered the slaughter of indians and other humans, the extinction of animals and the exploitation of natural resources because of the "virtue of the American people" and their "sacred mission to spread Democracy throughout the world". Basically the U.S. government decided it wanted a Global American Empire and it has subsequently trained and brainwashed American citizens to think God wants a Global American Democratic Empire. They say God wants a G.A.D.E. The U.S. government only began using religious mottos to justify it's aggressive ambition of expansion and global domination. In plain terms the government made God into a mascot.

The only reference to religion in the American bill of rights is "*Congress shall make no law respecting an establishment of religion,*" with "*or prohibiting the free exercise thereof*" being tacked on the end, AFTER the comma. I realized that originally the American government was never in any sense designed to be Christian, let alone religious. The amendment meant that they weren't going to promote or protest religion. In other words the American national government didn't plan on giving religion any publicity at all, hoping it would leave the country in totality because of neglect. If no attention is given to religion good or bad then it sends the message that religion is not important. This is precisely the desired effect one who ignores hopes to have on what/who they are ignoring, thus the ignorant are those who intentionally ignore. The word Christianity doesn't even appear in the constitution! The "Founding Fathers" didn't intend to promote freedom of religion and tolerance, they intended to ignore religion hoping it would fade away completely. The famous historian family the Durants said, *"There is no significant example in history before our time, of a society successfully maintaining moral life without the aid of religion."* With the American government and American laws being based on secular principles it guaranteed the moral decline of American society, the results of which are visible today in America and every other secular country which has copied the American political innovation of secularism. By secularism teaching people they can choose to believe and be anything they desire, it also takes away any reason to choose to believe or be any particular thing. Freedom is pro-choice everything and by giving all a right to choose anything and everything consequences get eliminated. Yet consequences are what makes our decisions important, choices without consequences make decisions pointless. Thereby a life with freedom necessarily becomes a series of pointless choices. Secularist religious freedom says to choose what you want because whatever you choose isn't important and doesn't matter. Secularism is not tolerance, it's simply equally intolerant of every religion. This is because secularism is a religion itself in disguise. Whereas to believe in freedom means to disbelieve in prophets and divine revelation. This is why Immanuel Kant taught in the 18th century that a divinely revealed bible violated the autonomy and freedom of a human being. Which is a teaching based on Christian prejudice but the teaching is still true. This is because if God sends a book to mankind telling us what we are supposed to believe and how we are supposed to live, as well as prophets who do the same then human freedom does not exist. Thus to believe in freedom is actually atheism. It is impossible to believe God sent prophets or a book to tell people what to believe and how to live and to also believe that humans are free or can enjoy freedom. To have freedom means that God doesn't care what you believe or do, and that goes for everything including theft, rape, murder, genocide, suicide and everything. To have freedom means that nothing anyone can ever do can ever possibly be wrong or a crime. Now anarchists will agree but argue that you can't violate another's right to do what they want by violent force but who made that rule? Was it God? If so then we don't have freedom and some things are wrong. If not then that rule is invalid because to say people have the freedom to do anything except violate another person's freedom means that you don't have freedom at all. For one person to violently oppress another is just one person's freedom being stronger than another person's freedom. So that's what freedom really is. It's a religion that says the world is a big free for all. Freedom advocates will say that we eventually learned peace and non-violence makes our species more productive, content and safe but the only reason we learned that was because of religion. While all those freedom lovers who advocate freedom for all except for people who use violence are making that rule because of religious influences, not knowing their rule is incompatible with the doctrine of freedom. A free world is a world without religion and without rules. To have even 1 rule, no matter what it is, is to not have freedom. This is why the word "liberty" was invented, by people who decided we aren't going to have freedom but will trick people into thinking they have freedom by calling it "liberty". Liberty is the moderate form of the religion of freedom where stupid humans make the rules instead of God or prophets. This foolish freedom and liberty ideology was a result of human reasoning with a touch of Satanic inspiration. The reason this religion of human reason is wrong is because the human species is stupid. Collectively we're a bunch of idiots. Whereas democracy multplies the stupid syndrome, thinking that if all the stupid humans combine together then the smart will overpower the stupid by sheer numbers. Yet it doesn't take a genius to calculate that such math is flawed. Adding stupid humans + stupid humans + stupid humans only gets you with more stupidity than you had with fewer humans. If you wanted to make humans have the dumbest political, economic and social policy possible, democracy is designed to discover and implement it. Although because of human arrogance and philosophers observing that corrupt people like Pharisees and Priests manufactured their own religions which Kings used to oppress people, the philosophers decided they would try to boost the human self-esteem and try their own hand at making a religion called reason, wherein ingenuity was to substitue God and they would be the initial prophets. Their plan worked but then to disguise their success, reason, equality, freedom, rights and liberty became the creed. Yet because it isn't an institutional faith few recognize it for what it is. The doctrine of human reason is a mythological fable. You can't reason your way into paradise. God didn't create humans and tell them "*just figure out everything on your own*". Adam pbuh didn't reason that a certain fruit was forbidden, he got told. Noah pbuh didn't reason he should build an ark. Abraham pbuh didn't reason his way to circumcision. Joseph pbuh didn't reason his way out of prison. Moses pbuh didn't reason his way to defeating Pharaoh's army and then reason up some laws to live by, such as the sabbath. David pbuh didn't reason his way into defeating Goliath. Jonah pbuh didn't reason himself out of the belly of a whale. Mary didn't reason herself into being pregnant with Jesus pbuh. If people think that human reasoning will lead them to paradise then that will be the reason they burn in hell. The true religion is reasonable but reason is not a true religion. There is a reason God sends prophets with miracles, because more than reason is needed to know who is right and wrong as well as how to live your life. Nobody thinks they could reason their way through school or work so why do they think they can reason their way through the test of life? To prove to an atheist the danger of human reasoning, ask them if they'd feel okay if their kid raised themselves without instructions from anyone or anything being raised solely by their own human reason?

Perhaps there was still hope that America could be transformed into a truly religious country? I contemplated long and hard finally arriving at the conclusion that democracy is inherently anti-religious. Even if it functions according to the theory that people select the rulers who make the laws. When the majority of people have the authority over the minority in deciding who makes the laws it is inevitable that the majority will oppress the minority. A majoritarian government in which the majority rules in all cases can never be a good or just government. The majority is not always correct, in fact history has demonstrated that the majority of the time the majority opinion has been wrong. Verily the majority of people are misled by Satan to a disastrous destination. So democracy is not designed to make the right decision, it is designed to make the popular decision. Any good idea to solve state problems will be controversial and unpopular. As such most governments cannot implement it, particularly if it's a democratic or republican style of state that needs the "support of the majority". Hence you will find governments who are popularly elected or reformed are always about at least 10 years late when adopting a new good idea. Such governments can never do what's right until the ignorant masses popularly agree that it is right, and usually by that time it's far too late and implementing that policy when the masses want it is rarely right and is actually wrong. This is because doing the right thing at the wrong time is in most cases wrong to do. Fools only agree to foolish ideas or they follow the crowd, or the money, or the charisma, or religion. Hence when the foolish masses agree, chances are that they only began to agree once the idea became foolish due to delay in implementation. This is the reason why democratic militaries don't exist, because indecision due to unpopularity threatens survival. Timing can make the difference between good and evil, and popular political acceptance delays action. Typically the most popular decision is the one that sounds the best but works the worst, which is why in democratic countries when election time comes around even the politicians acknowledge that things in the country have been getting worse and worse. Unfortunately they blame the players rather than the game itself and people naively believe that "*this time it will be different, if only ____ is elected*". However they fail to recognize that this is the exact campaign slogan of that candidate and of every candidate of all time. For instance just look at the following presidential campaign slogans for the presidents who won the U.S. presidency:

- Zachary Taylor's 1848 CE campaign slogan was, "*A president for the people*".
- Abraham Lincoln's 1860 CE campaign slogan was, "*Vote yourself a Farm*".
- Abraham Lincoln's 1864 CE campaign slogan was, "*Don't trade horses in midstream*".
- Ulysses S. Grant had 2 campaign slogans for 1868 CE, they were "*Let Us Have Peace*" and "*Vote as you shot*".
- Ulysses S. Grant's 1872 CE campaign slogan was, "*Give us another term*".
- William Mckinley's 1896 CE campaign slogan was, "*Patriotism, Protection and Prosperity*"
- William Mckinley's 1900 CE campaign slogan was, "*Prosperity at home. Prestige abroad.*"
- Theodore Roosevelt's 1904 CE campaign slogans consisted of, "*A square deal for every American*", "*Speak softly and carry a big stick*" and "*You can't beat somebody with nobody.*"
- Woodrow Wilson's popular 1912 CE campaign slogans were, "*America first*", "*An American for America*" and also "*Safety first*" On April 20th, 1915 CE he said: "*Our whole duty for the present at any rate, is summed up in the motto: America First.*"

- Woodrow Wilson's 1916 CE main campaign slogan was, "*He kept us out of the war*". On March 5th, 1917 Wilson was sworn in for his second term, on April 2nd, 1917 he asked congress to have America fight in WWI.
- William G. Harding's 1920 CE campaign slogans were, "*Return to normalcy*" and "*Cox and cocktails*"(his opponent John Cox was against prohibiting alcohol)
- Calvin Coolidge's 1924 CE campaign slogan was,   "*Keep Cool and Keep Coolidge*".
- Herbert Hoover's 1928 CE campaign slogans were,   "*A chicken in every pot and a car in every garage*" which went along with "*Who but Hoover?*"
- Franklin D. Roosevelt's 1932 CE campaign slogans were "*Happy Days are here again*", "*Friend of the people*", "*A New Deal for the American people*" and "*In Hoover we trusted but now we are busted*"
- Franklin D. Roosevelt's 1936 CE campaign slogan was "*Remember Hoover!*" and "*Sunflowers die in November*"
- Franklin D. Roosevelt's 1940 CE campaign slogan was "*Better A third termer than a third rater*".
- Franklin D. Roosevelt's 1944 CE campaign slogan was "*Don't swap horses in midstream*".
- Harry S. Truman's 1948 CE campaign slogan was,   "*I'm just wild about Harry*" .
- Dwight D. Eisenhower's 1952 CE campaign slogan was, "*I like Ike*". (Ike was a nickname for Dwight)
- Dwight D. Eisenhower's 1956 CE campaign slogan was, "*I still like Ike*".
- John F. Kennedy's 1960 CE campaign slogan was, "*A time for greatness* ", "*Prosperity for all*", "*We can do better*" and "*Let's get America moving again*"
- In 1964 CE Lyndon B. Johson started the campaign with "*All the way with LBJ*" and "*LBJ for the U.S.A.*" when his opponent used the slogan "*In your heart you know he's right*" then LBJ made a slogan saying "*In your guts you know he's nuts*" finally LBJ settled on the slogan of "*The stakes are too high for you to stay at home*".
- Richard M. Nixon's 1968 CE campaign slogan was, "*This time, vote like your whole world depended on it*".
- Richard M. Nixon's 1972 CE campaign slogan was, "*Nixon now, more than ever*" and "*Nixon's the one*"
- Jimmy Carter's 1976 CE slogans were, "*Not just peanuts*", "*A leader, for a change*", "*Challenging leadership for challenging times*" and "*Get America moving again*"
- The famous hollywood actor Ronald Reagan's 1980 CE campaign slogans were "*Let's make America Great again*" and "*The time is now*"
- Then the hollywood actor Ronald Reagan's 1984 CE campaign slogan was, "*It's Morning again in America*"

- George H.W. Bush's 1988 CE campaign slogan was, "*Kinder, Gentler nation*"
- Bill Clinton's 1992 CE campaign slogans were, "*It's the economy, stupid*", "*Don't stop thinking about tomorrow*", "*For people, for a change*", "*Putting people first*", "*A new voice for a new America*", "*It's time to change America*" and "*I believe in a place called Hope*"
- Bill Clinton's 1996 CE slogan was "*Building a bridge to the twenty-first century*"
- George W. Bush's 2000 CE campaign slogans were, "*Compassionate Conservatism*", "*Leave no child behind*", "*I am a uniter not a divider*", "*Real plans for real people*" and "*Reformer with results*"
- George W. Bush's most popular 2004 CE campaign slogans were, "*A safer world and a more hopeful America*", "*Yes, America can*" and "*Moving America forward*"
- Barack Obama's 2008 CE campaign slogans were, "*Yes We Can*" and "*Change We Need*"(or just "*Change*")
- Barack Obama's 2012 CE campaign slogan was, "*Forward*"
- Donald Trump's 2016 CE campaign slogan was, "*Make America Great again*"

Thus it is no wonder why the morality in all democratic countries is declining when popularity is the most important factor when making up laws. Think about it, every law is passed based soley on whether it gets enough votes by politicians, not based on whether it is a good or bad law. The reason we have stupid laws is because the majority of people are stupid. In a "clean" election the smartest person in the world can walk into the booth to vote, then a mentally retarded person enters after them to vote, both their votes would hold the same importance. How can that possibly be an intelligent system? It's not. Democracy is a system of decision making whereby the loudest noise wins, not the smartest. To illustrate the stupidity of democracy as a form of government imagine if education was determined via democracy. What if students got to vote who their teacher was and voted what their teacher taught them and the majority vote determined the outcome? In such a system the stupid kids would get together and pick a bad teacher to teach bad, false or useless things with disasterous outcomes. Since academic curriculums aren't determined by democracy then how can our laws and leaders be determined by it? The schools that promote democracy refuse to implement it themselves. Democracy ensures that the right things don't happen and the wrong policies can continue to happen as long as enough idiots vote. Thus democracy cannot work or result in good in a world with idiots, stupidity, greed or basically any world with humans. This shocking revelation led me to realize that even a religious extremist like myself couldn't possibly change America into a Catholic nation as president nor could any democratic nation ever become a "religious nation", because even if it did the polls would have the power to change it right back to the wrong track. In a democracy you can never "throw the bums out" because there is a practically unlimited supply of A-holes who will fill the previous bums' chair. The Greek philosopher Plato aptly described how people live under a democracy: "[*The democratic youth] lives along day by day, gratifying the desire that occurs to him, at one time drinking and listening to the flute, at another downing water and reducing, now practicing gymnastic, and again idling and neglecting everything; and sometimes spending his time as though he were occupied with philosophy. Often he engages in politics and, jumping up, says and does whatever chances to come to him; and if he admires any soldiers, he turns in that direction; and if it's moneymakers, in that one, and there is neither order nor neccessity in his life, but calling it sweet, free and blessed, he follows it throughout."*

    Despite having been registered to vote in high school, I choose not to. It is a false dilemma thinking you have to *"choose the lesser of two evils"* that statement alone is enough to prove that the democratic system has a satanic flavor. I have heard some people even call it demon-ocracy. Personally I'm not going to vote for evil of any degree, besides one vote does not make a statistical difference and isn't even noticeable. If 100 million people vote then the influence of your 1 vote is 0.000001%, which for all intents and purposes is zero influence. USSR ruler Josef Stalin revealed the truth about elections when he said, *"It's not who votes that counts. It's who counts the votes"*. What will I say on the day of judgment when God asks, *"Why did you vote for evil?"* One thing all politicians of democratic systems have in common is their immorality, they all agree on extorting money from people(taxing) in order to finance their goals. Voting just encourages them. No matter which candidate gets the most votes the government gets elected. If voting could actually change something you can be certain the government would make it illegal. Voters are not given the choice to vote on policies despite the internet and phone making that a possibility. Voters are forced to choose between dishonest candidates who they have no control over, should that candidate win they have no legal obligation to fulfill any of their campaign promises and there is nothing the voter can do about it. You actually have nothing to gain by voting and something to lose. You lose the time wasted voting and you lose the right to complain. When you know a game is rigged before you play, it's unreasonable to complain when you lose. All the political parties encourage voting because if there was ever a low number of voters the very legitimacy of the government would be called into question, at least internationally if not domestically. The primary reason the politicians are of lower and lower quality is because people will vote for anyone on the ballot thinking that if they don't the stupid masses will elect a bad candidate. If people said, *"we're not going to vote unless there is a decent intelligent honest individual as a candidate"* and followed through, a different class of politicians would emerge. Today it has become a frenzy that has led people to be comfortable with statements like *"voting for the lesser of two evils"* which is another sign that people know that voting is wrong and not the solution. Voting will not produce good results no matter who is elected. That is perhaps the best argument one can make against democracy, is that it involves voting for evil with no chance for a good leader coming from the results of an election; because no good person would want to rule according to such a system. If an oppressor gave you the choice to vote between having your left arm or your right arm being cut off would you choose or would you tell them they have no right to cut off either? If you choose then the oppressor would have become your servant following your orders and when confronted with the crime would only need to say, *"I only did what they voted for"* to get away without punishment. In a democratic country that might actually give them sufficient reason to be let go unpunished and leave you with one arm less, known as a fool rather than a victim. Sometimes the best action can be to not take any action. It is reported that once a man was told he had to choose between 3 sinful options. 1. He could drink alcohol. 2. He could commit fornication. 3. He could kill someone. Facing these three options, all of which the man hated and detested, a devil whispered satanic logic to the man and persuaded him to choose the lesser of 3 evils, so the man drank alcohol. As a result he got drunk and wanted to fornicate with a woman. The woman's son defended her, physically preventing the drunken man from fornicating. Out of rage the drunken man then killed the son and raped the woman. This resulted from the man voluntarily choosing to do evil even though he didn't have to, because of listening to deceptive satanic logic concerning a false dilemma. By voluntarily choosing the lesser evil it results in the most evil possible. The problem with political popularity contests (elections) is not the results, but the false beliefs that legalize such contests. The difference between Democrats and Republicans is that Democrats want America to be like the Greek Athenian League and Republicans want America to be like the Roman Republic. Both have a pagan plan for America, they just disagree which pagan plan they like better, thus America is Greco-Roman. Hence it Reeks of idiocy, corruption, injustic and oppression. America is and always has been a sinful oppressive immoral nation because it used a pagan blueprint for it's government. If one takes Greeks and Romans as role models you end up like them, and America has followed their footsteps; those footsteps eventually lead to a mighty fall into a deep dark pit. To vote is to support their journey taking more steps down the wrong road that does not lead to any type of paradise.

  A politician with a limited number of terms is guaranteed not to care what the long term effects of their decisions will be. They're likely to be out of office by the time any bad outcome is realized which they are responsible for and probably won't even get blamed for it. If leaders know their job security depends on pleasing people they will not make the sacrifices necessary to ensure a better future. Politicians fear getting kicked out during the next election so they sacrifice the future in return for the present, as so many of us do in our own lives. The politician with a limited term is concerned with getting as much as they can out of their position before they lose it, so they don't care if the taxes are too high because it's their chance to get rich before being replaced. Not that a king is much better, but at least a king won't tax people into oblivion because a king wants to have something to collect the next time around and is more concerned about the future of the kingdom. Leaders with limited terms know that if they don't take it now then they won't have the chance to in the future, so they take as much as they can possibly get away with. The fact that before the person is even given power they are told they will have to leave soon, reveals that it is already known the person should not have that power or be in a leadership position to begin with. In any just system if the leader became incompetent, corrupt or unfit to lead then they would be replaced immediately, but in democracy they say *"well there is still X years left until the term is over"* so even after years of bad leadership and broken promises people are deluded into thinking they have to put up with continued bad service without the opportunity or chance for improvement. If politicians were treated according to their actions instead of their stated intentions they would be punished like bandits, murderers, thieves and the troublemakers who put obstacles in the road in order to hinder forward progress. No business or other relationship in society functions in this manner. Imagine if a sports team decided to keep a bad player as the starter on their team because his contract hadn't expired despite those on the bench being better players for that position. This is exactly what democracy does. If you were on a trip and realized the person giving you directions was leading you the wrong way, no one would continue following those instructions just because that's the one they started the trip with. If you are being led the wrong way in the opposite direction than you want to go, it's best to turn around immediately, because the further you keep going the longer it will take to get back to the right path if at all; you wouldn't wait until the next bathroom break to get directions from a different source. Why do we let these bad leaders finish their terms after their bad leadership has become evident? This is the flaw of democracy, it permits leaders who have been proven incompetent to maintain power which they are unable to use in the appropriate fashion, simply because they were elected by people in a wave of hysteria convinced of a pretense. You wouldn't keep using a vehicle that doesn't travel just because more payments are due. By keeping democratically elected leaders after they have revealed their inability is letting a mistake be perpetuated, in every other aspect of life we fix our mistakes and move on. At least in ancient Rome when they didn't like their politicians the pagan priests would make the years have less days in order for those politicians terms to end sooner and get them out of office. Roman consuls had short terms as well, the elections for Roman consuls were held every year and an individual could only serve once in their life. Meaning a Roman consul could only be consul for 1 year maximum in their whole life, yet still the Romans were so eager for bad consuls to be removed from office that they would collude to artificially shorten the calendar year throughout the empire just to get a few less days of X politician in office ruling them. Of course when it came to Senators Romans had them serve life-long terms, so it wasn't all short-term, but in Rome the political rules stipulated that elected leaders could only serve for 1 year maximum and non-elected leaders would serve for life. If Romans saw republics and democracies today with elected politicians who had terms longer than 1 year or multiple terms they'd denounce them as tyrants and be outraged the citizens allowed such fools to rule so long. Romans would insist that good politicians serve for life and politicians should either be given life-terms or minimalistic terms to limit the damage they can do. Romans realized that allowing politicians multiple terms of medium length was the worst possible way to have elected leaders rule them, since such frequent sizable terms allow time for politicians to be corrupt while removing the pressure for them to produce quick results or keep their campaign promises. Ultimately the practice of shortening a calendar year, in order to get rid of bad politicians who could only serve for 1 year maximum, was abolished by Julius Caesar when he created and ordained the Julian Calendar to be the standard preset calendar. Ironcially the next year after he made the calendar years standardized, so that democratically elected politicians could serve their full term without being gyped by calendar manipulations, Caesar got assassinated by a mob of politically motivated people. So that's where not only have modern countries adopted the pagan Greek and Roman political models, they copied the crazy system of democracy and made it even worse than it was before. Seriously if you look at the ancient Greek and Roman democracies in depth, any objective person will say their governments were better than modern democracies are. Yet at the same time the objective person would see how their democracies were also unjust and flawed too. So maybe the problem isn't how democracies are run but with democracy itself? Regardless whether democratically elected or not, leaders should realize when they are no longer able to fulfill their duty and give up their power for the good of society rather than clinging to it for as long as possible. The duration of leadership should be based on performance not on a contract basis. Leadership is not something that should ever be put to a popular vote where elections are held requiring candidates for leadership to publicly campaign for votes. Why? Because you can't be leading a people and managing an organization if you are on a campaign trail trying to persuade people to vote for you. Any leader who neglects their duties to campaign for re-election proves they aren't fit to be leading, because if they were they would be doing their job instead of campaigning to get extra time to do the job they already have. Plus if one considers the money and time nation's spend on elections, those countries could end poverty if they just abolished elections and gave their campaigning money in charity. Any political party which "represents the poor" would be a poor party with meager funds because it's supporters are poor. Rich folk don't support the parties that support the poor. Yet no election can be "won" without lots and lots of funds. Thus democratic elections are only ever going to serve the aristocracy. Coincidentally it was the wealthy aristocracy that created the election system in America. People voting in elections doesn't fix countires nor will democratically elected leaders ever fix any real problems, the energies wasted by nations on elections are the primary reason those nations have so many problems. The elections are practically economic civil wars where all the money, time and energy is wasted for the sake of getting yet another unqualified bad leader. But that's why politicians like elections, because they know they aren't qualified to lead the nation to success and that the only way they could ever legally be in a position of governmental leadership is via an election process. Legally they can't get the job without the support of the mob. That's not to say elections are legitimate, but I'm just saying in theory if the votes were legitimate then elections are the quickest way to get unqualified leaders. The masses of most nations aren't even qualified to tell who is qualified. So elections are literally the unqualified masses voting for the unqualified and then they wonder why the election system hasn't been improving their nation. It's actually a good thing the votes aren't influential because if they were the results would be even worse. Although because the masses are led to believe their votes are influential then it makes them unqualified to recognize who is really in charge and thereby they are unable to change the true leadership of their nation if they felt oppressed enough to try to do so. Hence staged democratic elections are a fool's punishment, paradise and prison all at the same time. Sadly though they tend to only view the elections as their salvation. However imagine if the impossible happened and a good leader was genuinely elected via democracy, what would happen at the end of the term? According to the law they would have to elect another and say: "*Even though this is the best leader we can possibly have, the rules are the rules and we have to take our chances and kick our good leader out hoping the new one isn't too bad. Good leadership was nice while it lasted, but you know we can't have good leaders sticking around because then the bad ones might stick around too. We must have constantly changing leadership, even though that's the most unstable type of leadership there is.*" Seriously what if every few years you had different parents or a different body? Democracy is even worse than this because every day they are changing the rules making different laws. What kind of stability is there when something that was illegal yesterday is legal today and something that was lawful yesterday is unlawful today? This makes breaking the law have nothing to do with the deed, but is dependent on the time the deed took place. Two people can do the same exact thing at different times where one gets punished and one doesn't. That is not what I consider to be justice. In fact it seems more like it's "Just us getting oppressed by fickle fools who don't know what's right or wrong or when or why". Democracies neither establish nor legally enshrine fiefdoms of freedom they create unjust bureaucratic fooldoms.

<u>There are only 4 tools Democracy has at its disposal:</u>

1. Throw money at the problems hoping they go away and don't cause more problems.
2. Make new rules and regulations hoping they fix the problems caused by step 1 and hope that they don't cause more problems.
3. Set up and raise taxes to pay for new committees to supervise implementation of the new rules, regulations and agencies to fix the problems caused in steps 1-2 and hope they don't cause more problems.
4. Elect new people to do steps 1-3, since the previously elected people who did steps 1-3 caused more problems. Also hope the newly elected people fix everything and don't cause more problems. If this doesn't work then do step 4 again and again and again and again forever. If frustrated then just remember this is the best system mankind has ever developed, because unlike other systems this system lets people replace leaders who cause problems by doing steps 1-3. Blood was and is shed for the promotion and defense of this system. So if there are problems just keep doing step 4. Step 4 always works, except for all the times it hasn't, but that's because step 4 isn't always done correctly; just do it.

When we look at democracy for what it is we see that it is a faith, of which the central tenet is to hope that there aren't more problems. Thus a belief in "Luck" serves democracies well. The main ritual of this faith is the election, during which people pray to the state hoping their problems will be solved. Everyone must submit to the decisions of the democratically elected government whether they elected them or not, whether they like it or not, whether it's right or wrong. There is no freedom, there is only the illusion of voter influence, with the continuous hope that the next election will solve the problems that have resulted from all the elections preceding it. Oh and on top of that the system is rigged too. This is because politicians determine and redetermine the voter districts. It's called gerrymandering and it means the government's politicians get to choose who can vote for each election. In practice if the government wants a certain party to win certain seats or positions they simply redraw the districts in any crazy shape they want in order to get the voters they want so that way the party they want to win will win, and the same goes for party primaries. Whereas the electoral college is how the American president is elected. Voters vote for X or Y but in reality their votes simply go to their state's representative and in theory they are supposed to vote for the majority but legally and in practice they vote for whoever they personally want to and the votes don't matter. Five examples thus far exist in U.S. history where the guy/girl who got the most votes running for president didn't win, in 1824, 1876, 1888, 2000 and 2016 CE. In the 1824 election Andrew Jackson had 38,00 more votes than John Quincy Adams and even had 99 electoral votes to Adams' 84, so by all accounts Jackson should have won, but John Quincy Adams was declared president simply because the House of Representatives said so. If their tricks still don't result the way the government wants then they just give different votes more or less value. The Americans just put up with it and say "*Democracy is the best. The USA is the best country, because in other countries people can't vote in elections.*" At the end of the day, the government picks the candidates, the government picks the voters, the government decides how much votes are worth and the government counts the votes and the government declares who the "winner" is. The government is in control of the entire voting process from start to finish. How then can voting change the very government which is controlling the voting process? The only way it can is if the government itself decides to change itself. But if the government is corrupt, how can a broken political machine fix itself? Democratic elections are literally just theatre. Elections are a government's way to say "*X is going to be in charge, but since you people don't like us or want us to pick who is in charge ruling over you we will put on a show so you think X was who the majority of people choose to be in charge. That way any complaints you have will be with your fellow taxpayers and not with us who really decided to put X in charge. This way you will never blame us, revolt or overthrow us because you will think the next elections can fix things.*" The other reason elections exist is to make sure the politicians know that if they start thinking, saying or doing things the rulers don't want then they are easily expendable should they decide to deviate from the hidden leaders' path. Theologically democracy is a false religion and a pretty bad one made by pagans, except today it's even worse.

      Every democracy if not disrupted always results in administrative absolutism in which people end up thinking the government is the solution to every problem and ask it for help and treat it as though its bureaucracy were God, with the elections being its primary religious ceremony. This is also known as statism which is a form of paganism in that the base is pure dogma where the individual is a servant to the mass idol created by man, intangible though it may be. The state is thus made by man in his own image. Statists believe their lives and wellbeing are privileges bestowed upon them by the State. They believe all that they do is and should be dependent and in accordance to the consent of the government whom they believe is the solution to all of their problems in life. Yet how in the world could "government" solve the advanced problems of the people? If "the people" have no solution then where would the government learn the solution? Religion, animals or aliens are the only source of information the government can use that is not "the people". But "the people" don't have the solutions and think the government does which the politicians claim due to religion, except the politicians don't cite the source for their solutions. Statism is false because if we don't have or know the solution then the government doesn't either, since we all have the same availability of information. In reality behind the scenes most governments are the cause of most problems rather than the solution. It is by creating problems for people that the government ensures its "services" are in high demand. Have you ever wondered why the most dangerous cities have the largest police forces, whereas the areas with the least amount of crime also have the least amount of police? It is basic supply and demand. The more police there are the more crime there is, because if they stopped crime it would mean they'd have to make cutbacks and lay police off once the crime rate decreased since there would be less demand for police services. Instead the police forces are constantly increasing their budgets as crime increases, whereas if they were effective at stopping crime it would follow that the more money spent on police the less crime there'd be. Excuses are made that if more wasn't spent on police the rate of the increase of crime would be even higher, yet the fact remains that communities with annually decreasing crime rates also have annually decreasing police budgets; this doesn't appear to be coincidental. The true reason police exist is to protect the government, enforce its laws and suppress criticism or rebellion. If you honestly ask them what their job is they might tell you "*to protect the people*", but if it ever came down to protecting the people vs. protecting the government, with the government paying them it would be very difficult for a police officer to side with the people; even if it were against unjust laws. There are many examples throughout the world in many countries that prove this is the reason why police exist. In America particularly many examples are available to demonstrate that police in general have not protected people when they were most endangered. During the famous riots in Los Angeles during the 1990s CE the American police simply ran away and left the citizens to defend themselves. Not only did the police not protect the people from looters and violence, but after the riots those who had defended themselves, such as Korean store owners who defended their stores from looters via guns, were arrested by police for not following government regulations concerning gun ownership and use. Not only did the police fail to protect the people, but after everyone was safe then they arrested those survivors who had protected themselves; because they had not defended themselves in a manner the government approved of. Basically they didn't pay the fees required to be allowed to have the guns to use as protection. Legally in a lawless city filled with looters, the government's position was that such store owners should have let the looters take everything and risk rape, assault and death rather than break the law and use a gun that wasn't registered for protection. They were the real criminals, because they didn't pay the government fees or get the proper papers, the looters were left unpunished because those looters were also voters and politicians didn't want to lose any votes. Despite not "*protecting the people*" those same police officers that abandoned the inhabitants of Los Angeles in their time of need got paid for having done their job during those days. Had the job of the police been to "*protect the people*" they should not have been paid because they didn't do that. On the other hand because they got paid when not protecting the people, it shows that protecting the people is not the job of a police officer. Legally if one is in danger and a police officer witnesses it, whether they are on-duty or off-duty they have absolutely zero legal responsibility to protect that person. If anyone is harmed in front of police who willingly fail to protect them out of negligence, then that person cannot bring any charges against the police for not protecting them, because legally the police don't have to protect you. Such an officer may lose their job or lose pay if enough publicity were mustered with political pressure being applied, but police negligence is not a crime. You cannot sue the police for not protecting you like you can other types of employees for failing to do their job due to negligence or incompetence. Another well known example is the behavior of police during the American black rights movement. I call it the "black rights" movement because realistically that's what it was, it wasn't about "civil" rights it was about black Americans not having the same rights as whites. When these black Americans would use a public "white-only" drinking fountain or any other "white-only" public service getting beaten by whites as a result, the police didn't protect the blacks from the racist mobs. If anything the police tended to arrest the blacks for having "broken the law" frequently waiting until the blacks were severely beaten and harmed, while conveniently not arresting the white attackers. Some police would even thank the white attackers for having helped them in subduing the "black criminal" so they could be "brought to justice". When it came down to it many police officers chose to enforce racist government laws rather than protect people. Sometimes these police were even members of the racist mobs, or groups such as the Ku Klux Klan and would use their authority as police officers as a tool for oppression. Had their job been to *"protect the people"* these KKK cops would have been paradoxically akin to an arsonist who works as a firefighter. The best evidence that police do not exist to protect people is the fact that when someone is driving and a police car is behind them all the passengers and driver get anxious and worried that they are about to interact with the police. Now if you told me you were scared because a certain person was walking behind you, never would I think that person was employed to protect you. People are not afraid of their bodyguards, but people are afraid of police. Being afraid of police when they are behind you or looking at you shows that subconsciously you know that they are not there to protect you. Clearly this is not an organization which exists to protect the people and many examples exist which illustrate this reality. However the government presents data as cleverly as Satan does causing people to be deceived as to the situation they are living in, leading them to use poison as medicine again and again. Which is the same thing Satan does with sin, he makes us think the more we sin the happier we'll be despite sin being the cause of our initial misery. Police are taught that laws of the government are equal to laws from God, whether they really are or not. Abraham Lincoln said, "<u>Let me not be understood as saying that there are no bad laws,</u> *nor that grievances may not arise for the redress of which no legal provisions have been made. I mean to say no such thing.* <u>But I do mean to say that although bad laws, if they exist, should be repealed as soon as possible, still, while they continue in force, for the sake of example they should be religiously observed.</u>" Lincoln was not alone in expressing this sentiment, most politicians believe this and even most political authority figures tend to attribute sacrosanct cult status to "the system" which they have authority over. The popular French statesman Maximilian Robespierre taught nearly the same exact thing as Lincoln, when he explained why democracies "always did the right thing", "*When the sovereign people excercise its power, we can only bow before it. In all it does is virtue and truth, and no excess, error or crime is possible.*" This is why most police have an attitude of superiority and loyalty to the law as though they were a holy warrior, because they are trained that all laws must be obeyed as though it is a religious obligation to obey man-made laws. This statismatic sentiment leads government employees/servants to truly believe that their government cannot commit a crime, especially when there is a threat to their government.   As Robespierre said, "*If the revolutionary government must be more energetic in its actions and freer in its steps, does this mean that it is less just and less lawful? No! For it bases itself on the holiest of all laws-the good of the people; and on the most inalienable of all rights-necessity.*" Now you might be wondering what kind of job did Robespierre have before he was a politician? He was a lawyer who later became a judge but he quit his job as judge because he "*couldn't bear to sentence a person to death*". After he became a politician he sentenced many to death and made the guillotine famous. Being an "elected official" tends to change one's personality and moral principles. But the "Reign of Terror" was "for the good of the people", the 2nd most dangerous phrase a politician can ever say; the most dangerous is "for the good of the nation". Some think it's silly to think any individual is infallible but many of those same people view their government as infallible, or they act like it even if they don't think it. Most think as long as it's democratic then it must be divinely guided. When people think Church and State are separate, the laws constitute religion. The separation of Church and State just means the state religion is not Christianity, it doesn't mean the State got out of the religion business. Laws were originally only religious. Originally crime was defined as a sin that caused the wrath of the gods which needed to be punished by the community lest the gods destroy them due to the sin of the sinner/criminal. When civilizations developed all crimes used to be sins, but not all sins were punishable crimes. The religion dictated the laws of a country and punishing crime was a religious duty done by religious or political officials, which is why for many years most political officals were equated with being religious figures or even deities themselves. Thus democracy being the law of the people effectively makes the people their own lawmaker/god. Except since humans posing as gods were always doing so in order to commit oppression, democracy always causes spiritual/political oppression. Within democracies the "will of the people" is equated with the will of God. Democracies construct many collective tyrannies instead of an individual tyrant, unfortunately it's harder to overthrow collective tyrants. But don't take my word for it, following are quotations from famous Americans concerning democracy:

> "*DEMOCRACY is nothing more than mob rule, where 51% of the people may take away the rights of the other 49%*"-Thomas Jefferson, Drafter of the Declaration of Independence and the 3rd president of the U.S.A.
>
> "*DEMOCRACY never lasts long. It soon wastes, exhausts, and murders itself. There is never a democracy that did not commit suicide.*"-John Adams, 2nd president of the U.S.A.
>
> "*When the people find that they can vote themselves money, that will herald the end of the republic.*"-Benjamin Franklin, famous statesmen and founding father of the U.S.A.
>
> "*No man's life, liberty, or property are safe while the legislature is in session*" -Mark Twain, American Author
>
> "*Every election is sort of an advance auction sale of stolen goods.*"-H.L. Mencken, American Journalist and essayist
>
> "*Democracy is the theory that common people know what they want and deserve to get it good and hard.*" -H.L. Mencken, American Journalist and essayist

These Americans knew how dangerous democracy was, the thing is that America never fully practiced it. America was a mercantilist state based on mercantilism clothed in democracy. Mercantilism is bad enough and cannot even be moralized, which is why democracy was used as a costume for the American government. Yet the problem with wearing the mask of democracy is that most Americans don't know the government just used democracy as a mask for mercantilism and they start wanting to implement the monstrous system of democracy bit by bit until the mask will become the flesh. Currently America is an ideocracy, an ideocracy is a tyranny of certain ideas. In America these ideas are called "truths" and they say "*We hold these truths to be self-evident*". Namely that God gave man a right to "Life, Liberty, the pursuit of happiness, and to rebel if they don't have the above 3 to their level of satisfaction." Although today the US schools don't teach that last "truth". Why? Because contrary to what the declaration of Independence claims, every goverment that ever existed or ever will exist, at all times restricted and contravened either the life, liberty or the pursuit which their subjects took to attain "happiness", some governments even restricted or contravened 2 or 3 of these things. So basically the ideal and allegedly just government advertised by the US Declaration of Independence has never existed and by definition can never exist, which therefore means the "self-evident truths" and God-given rights are false notions incompatible with reality, as even anarchy restricts/contravenes one's life/liberty/pursuit of happiness. Especially to attribute such "truths" or rights to God is disgraceful seeing how the government of David pbuh himself restricted the rights of life, liberty and the pursuit of happiness as did the government of Moses pbuh. Thus if these rights came from God all one would need to do is produce the God given law and documentation. Problem is that no such law or documentation exists, and cannot be conjured out of any religion which is why the drafters declared them to be "self-evident" because they had no other evidence or persons to support their claims aside from themselves. This is the rationalistic dream and it is ideologically idiotic. 1. To be self-evident means that the idea is known by everyone by themselves by default. It's even impossible to cite something that is self-evident because by citing it that would mean it's not self-evident. The self-evident truths are never spoken of or written about, by definition. 2. To say "We hold these ideas/truths to be self-evident" is an admission that they aren't truly self-evident because if they were then everyone would already hold them, not just "We". Also something that's self-evident doesn't need to be debated or proven by any evidence or justification whatsoever. So that "truths" need to be stated and labeled as "self-evident" indicates that they are definitely not self-evident and may not be truths as has been declared, in fact without any supporting evidence to prove these "truths" as true to simply label them as self-evident can only be done due to there being no legitimate proofs to support the alleged truths. The alleged truths have to be labeled as self-evident because there is no way to explain them without the "truths" being exposed as falsehoods. When the drafters of the declaration of independence declared they held certain "truths" to be "self-evident", in legal terminology that means "*We believe X but we have no justifiable reason to believe it or persuade you to believe it, so we will just say everyone already believes it so people think if they don't already believe what we declare to be true they must be stupid and due to social fears of being the only one "not to get it on their own" they won't dispute our claims but will go adopt our unjustified beliefs without objection*." The very arguments the Americans claim support their rights are actually proofs that they don't have the rights they lay claim to. Fools think that this declaration guarantees or acquired rights for them but argumentatively the declaration eliminated the very possibility they could ever get such rights at any time by any means whatsoever. Alleged natural rights don't exist since rights come only from legitimate legislation promulgated by the authority of "nature". Whether one believes that authority is God or something else that is the only type of entity that can ever decree "natural rights". Otherwise if every species found in nature were to think up their own rights via reasoning then chaos would ensue because some animals would deem they have a right to eat other animals and those animals would deem they have a right not to be eaten and plants would get their "natural rights" trampled as animals ignored plant rights and the world would cease to function if any species could justifiable declare what "natural rights" it was entitled to. Basically "nature" would have to say what the rights are of every species in it's domain, and "human nature" is disqualified from declaring such natural rights because humans are not the originators or rulers of the domain of nature, we just live here temporarily. This type of ideolgical deception of allegedly self-evident entitlement, renamed as something other than entitlement, occurs whenever an ideocratic mentality spreads among a populace. Thereupon good arguments become unneccessary and the original complex good arguments are replaced by plausible simplifications or nothing. This gets done by charismatic leadership and charisma becomes the determining factor in political decision making. Yet charisma is simply emotionalism it has nothing to do with morality, good or evil, right or wrong. Both Moses pbuh and Hitler were charismatic leaders. Although when ideocratic states make leadership decisions based on charisma and disguise themselves as democracies it results in the perfect recipe for extremism. Semi-democratic Ideocracy is one of Satan's favorite types of governments because the people are trapped in it without any feasible way to get out and no matter how bad it gets the system is self-perpetuating because of the democratic guise and illusion of change. The only real change possible is the charisma levels and enthusiasm. The ideas are the governing force in an ideocracy however the right ideas are determined by the enthusiasm they generate, such ideas need not be right, reasonable nor rational and they don't even need to have the support of the majority. In such a state the loudest opinion which makes the most noise wins, regardless of what it is. This is evident in America today in that the majority don't like the policies of the government or it's actions, such a thing cannot occur in a democracy. It is literally impossible for the majority of the population to disagree with the leaders and the policies of a democracy, so America is not a democracy. By ideocracy hiding as democracy it becomes near unstoppable. The famous American ideocratic slogan of "self-evident truths" is a way of saying *"What we think is true and we don't have to prove it, but everyone has to agree with it because we say that they already do by default and we aren't wrong because they are truths, because we said so."* Hence it's no surprise that in the last 240 years America has been in more wars than any other country in the world. Of those 103 wars only 2 can possibly be considered to be a result of a foreign nation attacking America. Over 99% of the wars America has been involved in, America was the agressor. America has been in so many wars, it's citizens don't even keep count. For example if you ask an American about the Vietnam war they should ask "Which Vietnam war?" but most don't know that America went to war with Vietnam in the 1860s CE as well as the 1960s CE. Even fewer are aware that since the 1600s CE Vietnam was a Muslim country and Muslims are documented to have been in Vietnam since the 11th century. During the 1960s CE those Vietnamese Muslims were fighting both the North Vietnamese Communists and the South Vietnamese Democrats, trying to make Vietnam an Islamic State again. But nobody talks about the FLC fighting during the 2nd Vietnam war which America is famous for, the FLC was the third party yet most people don't even know they existed. Likewise most don't know the U.S. went to war with Japan in the 1860s CE and fought a war with Korea in 1871 CE. When Americans hear about America and a Korean war they think of the 1950s and only think America fought Japan in the 1940s. This is because American students at school don't learn or get taught about the 103 wars their country has been involved in. If they did they wouldn't be able to use the standard American war narrative for nearly every war they fight. What is the American war narrative? It goes something like this: *"There we were living in perfect harmony and bliss due to our greatness, admirable work ethic and vastly superior political/moral principles and divine blessing/favor. Then suddenly without reason or warning we were treacherously attacked by barbaric evil cowards who just hate us for our greatness/freedom/wealth and fight just because they are evil/insane or jealous. Therefore we had to unite against evil and use extreme force to smash them so they learn to never ever mess with us again. Then those Barbarians will learn and thank us for the favor of crushing them so as to civilize them. We were innocent, never wanted 1 war and are God's favorite. This is why we are, always was and always will be the best nation ever. That is unless we stop being true Americans and lose the next war. Yet God won't let that happen because God blesses America because we are secular and let anyone believe and practice any/every faith. The US is also blessed because we're Christian and believe the bible, but if certain Americans keep secularizing us we'll surely decline."* All you have to do is replace the word "Barbarians" with a nation/ethnicity/faith or political group and that's the basic plot of every military war America has ever been in. Usually they add in a little sub-plot of liberating the foreigners from evil tyrants or uncivil/evil/immoral ideologies. Americans like to blame the leader of foreigners for their wars but if ever America were attacked for having an "evil leader" it's always the American people who are the victims never US leaders because Americans can never have evil tyrannical leaders that would be so bad as to justify a righteous foreign nation deposing them, because the brilliant Americans would vote them out of office depose any evil leaders; or so the legend goes. Regardless of whether one believes the America war plots or not militarily speaking America is the most warlike nation in all of recorded history. On average the United States of America gets involved in a new war every 2.3 years. Why? This is because America is not a democracy but is an ideocracy that pretends to be a democracy. This also brings up another point regarding states that claim to be democratic. Politically the Soviet Union was a democracy and held elections in which every adult citizen was allowed to vote. In 1917 CE Vladimir Lenin even introduced Universal Suffrage giving everyone in Russia the right to vote. In comparison America didn't officially grant universal suffrage to it's citizens until 1965 CE, but technically universal suffrage doesn't exist anywere. For example kids and criminals aren't allowed to vote. How then can one claim universal suffrage? This is because "universal suffrage" is defined as everyone who is capable can vote, with capability meaning "if the government says so". In the past skin color or gender was a factor that determined incapacity to vote simply because governments said it did. Some may not think universal suffrage or the definition of it is problematic but it's insane. For example why can't a newborn baby legally vote and have their vote count just as much as an adult's? People say that it would be unjust for babies to determine the affairs of the state when voting can result in consequences that effect other beings. Basically the babies would irresponsibly vote for their own interests and if babies got their way adults would get oppressed, therefore babies or kids are deemed incapable of voting not because they can't vote but because people deem kids having influence over their lives to be oppression. Yet why then are women allowed vote to effect the lives of men and vice versa or whites vote in elections with blacks or the rich vote alongside the poor. Won't the poor use their votes to oppress the rich? Won't the stupid use their votes to oppress the smart? Isn't that the reason why blacks wanted to vote, because the non-black voters were oppressing them? Isn't that why the poor and women wanted the right to vote so they could vote for revenge? The only reason people want to vote is to try to stop the other voters from oppressing them. How do X voters stop Y voters from oppressing them? It's simple, for X voters not to get oppressed by Y voters then the X voters have to oppress the Y voters and vice versa. The reason voting was restricted was in order to oppress without any risk of reprisals. Voting is the opportunity to manipulate the law in your own favor. Voting is only valuable when it is a tool of political favoritism and oppression. If voting can't be used for oppression or favoritism then it is pointless and nobody would ever vote. It is only when the law or government can be used for injustice that people want to have political power and influence. Thus if some can vote then they will oppress the others who can't, and if everyone can vote then it will be to defend themselves from oppression by causing injustice and oppression to others who lose in the voting process. Hence since votes can be a tool of oppression if they can influence society then nobody should be allowed to vote in order to prevent any and all types of oppression. Yet in most democracies today most people are allowed to vote. Why is this? Because the votes don't matter or result in the voters influencing their government. If they did then voting would always result in oppressive governments. Which doesn't mean that just because votes don't matter the governments aren't oppressive, they can be and most are. What it means is that if people are voting there are only 2 results. If the votes count then oppression will occur, if the votes don't count then for voting to take place when it doesn't count is a sign of oppression to such a severe amount that theatrical voting is a necessary political ploy the state must use to avoid revolution. Thus whether votes count or not the occurence of the democratic ritual of voting is a clear sign that oppression is taking place. The number of categories who are restricted and prevented from voting approximately indicates how oppressive the government is. The more categories of people there are who can vote the more oppressive the government is. I repeat that the more who can vote in a country's elections the more oppression there is, either because the votes count and the majority oppresses the minorities or because the votes don't count but a big show is put on to prevent the population from realizing they have no ability allotted to them by their government to stop the oppression. To prove this point women in Communist Russia were allowed to vote three years before women were allowed to vote in America. The Soviet Union in accordance with their economic communism believed and preached that all it's citizens were equal. So does this mean 1917 Russia was less oppressive than 1965 America? Russia in 1917 CE under Lenin was more democratic than America was under Wilson. Yet Americans had such enmity for the Soviet Union they labeled it an enemy of democracy despite the Soviet Union actually doing democracy better and more fully than America did. Today North Korea(known as the Democratic People's Republic of Korea) is also a democracy which holds elections in which every citizen over the age of 17 can vote in. Meaning citizens can vote in North Korea at an earlier age than they can vote in America. China and Russia are also democracies. Yet most Americans don't consider any of these countries to be democracies. Why not? Because they don't do things the American way, however on a technical political level they are democracies. People will say that the elections are fixed in those countries and only people the governments' want to win are allowed to win, but that's exactly what happens in America too. The only difference is that the American government has had many more years to practice being a corrupt fake democracy so they put on a much better show to fool more people than the other countries are capable of. So much of American politics are planned that it's disgusting. What's worse is the politicians confess from time to time and people still ignore their confessions that the political issues and actions are planned well in advance. Hence 4-time US president Franklin Roosevelt said, *"Nothing happens in politics by accident, if it happens, it was planned that way"*. Another thing which president Franklin Roosevelt said about politics was that *"Presidents aren't elected, they're selected."* So when US voters claim presidents get elected, tell them that the man who has been US president 4 times says they are not elected. Who do you think knows more about the matter of becoming president, the guy who was US president 4 times or some American voter? As another example at the time of this writing Donald Trump has not been elected president, but for those who know how politics works it's been well known since 2015 CE that Donald Trump would "win" the 2016 CE elections.(If he doesn't "win" I'd be very surprised because he is the perfect politician since he has no prior partisan loyalites or commitments. So the essentials(political vocab word that refers to a specific category of a nation's political influentials) who decide who the American mascot is, see that he is easy to control and win over if they support/empower him. The reason Trump arrogantly boasts of his wealth, foolishly alienting the common folk, is because he is telling all the rich influentials that call the shots that he will pay for power and pamper those who give it to him. Thus barring any extreme changes it's clear to the politically astute that Trump will "win" the election and it's so probable that I'm even marking him as the winner in my book before the primaries are even over. The only wildcard is that being a sexist nation, a crazy Trump-like candidate may be needed to get Americans to accept having a female president in Hillary Clinton. Americans wouldn't put up with a female president, unless the alternative was a clear psychopath. So Trump is either a joke or a guaranteed "win" and Clinton might be just used as Trump's stepstool similar to how she got used to justify a black president Obama in racist America. The scandals both Clinton and Trump had were the final test by those in real power to determine who is willing to do what they are told if selected to be the mascot. That's what political scandals always are, it's a way for pressure to be applied to polititicans by their puppeteers to test their loyalty or punish their disloyalty and eliminate them in a way that the public will accept as plausible. The more scandalous a president is the more controllable they are and since I was born in 1992 there hasn't been a president elected who hasn't been immoral to a scandalous extent. Also by studying the long term trends one can see how Trump was set to "win" since 2008 CE, his 2012 campaign was foreshadowing for appearances and public awareness. Donald Trump was/is a real estate tycoon. The real estate bubble and the economic aftermath of that in the early 21st century directly led to Obama being "elected" and "reelected". Whereas Obama was publicly cited as the reason for the political rise of Trump. Trump economically caused

Obama to get "elected" and Obama is a reason for Trump to get "elected". It's basic cause and effect, but because of short-term memory few remember that Trump's real estate bubble was the cause of Obama's "win in the elections" so they don't recognize any conspiracy when Trump is presented as the effect of Obama's terms. As long as they say they hate each other in public nobody suspects any foul power play at all. And who wouldn't think they hated each other when even before Obama was elected, in 2007 CE, Trump cultivated the "hate act" against Obama claiming he wasn't American but a foreign Kenyan despite Obama being born in Hawaii. But then the politically oblivious think the whole anti-foreigner policy of Trump promulgated in 2015 CE just "came out of nowhere". Anyone paying attention could've seen the anti-foreigner political policy of the US government being set up a decade before Trump, in fact actions/events many decades previously commonly lead to policies that "take the masses by surprise" since they don't realize how the government conditions them to be pre-committed to policies well before such policies are ever announced or put into effect. Many citizens are incapable of political foresight since it involves extensive economic, historical, cultural, sociological, psychological, political and religious knowledge, and even then political prediction is speculative with innumerable variables. The point is most citizens are oblivious to the fact that their government's have planned policies decades in advance, including the types of leaders they will have, with most governments having plans for future policies/wars/changes centuries in advance. <u>In reality power has never been put to a vote in any country throughout all of history.</u> The only difference with Americans is they pretend their elections are different because they get told they are, but when China, Russia or North Korea says the same thing then Americans don't give them the same benefit of the doubt. In reality they aren't democracies and people are right to say they aren't, but not one country in the world today really is, so people are wrong to claim that any government in the world is a democracy. The Native Americans were more democratic than the countries of today and that's what's really funny about America in particular. The land of America was a lot more democratic before the whites "introduced democracy". Truly it's a joke to claim the colonists established democracy when the Native Americans were more democratic than the US Americans have ever been. America actually became far less democratic when the United States came into being. The United States of America has always been less democratic than the "savages". Most nations today are ideocracies following America's example pretending to be democracies, so it's more appropriate to call them decoyocracies or say that they are mockingdecrazies. Today in America there are no true democrats, republicans, libertarians, socialists, independents or any other of these "political parties"; all of the politicians are really decoyocrats serving the American ideocracy. Either they're decoyocrats or very confidant idiots. Kingship wasn't really replaced by democracy it was just disguised and controlled. Before the reimplementation of the pagan political faith of pseudo-democracy leadership in many countries was heavily influenced by birth as political succession was lineal or lateral. However when the next generation of leadership is determined by birth this makes it difficult to have long-term government planning and causes instability in case of loser descendants who are disastrous leaders or situations where no heirs to the throne cause political turmoil. Thus democracy and elections eliminated the instability, fragility and unreliability of dynastic succession. Now instead of government leaders being set since birth with the administration hoping their destined King to be does what they planned for, they can simply use elections to ensure the leaders always follow the plan the political elite, foreign puppeteers or aristocrats have set for the nation. Hence democracies are actually easier for the ruling class to control over time than a kingdom is, while the citizens of a nation actually have more influence over the government if their ruler is not elected than if he is. A King can always be persuaded by the people, and if the King can't be then the next one can be or the heirs can be influenced. Yet under the democratic decoy governments popular amongst people today, people not only can't influence their "elected politicians" but if they do manage to change their politicians then the puppetmasters just use the elections to get new ones. Democracy actually takes power away from the people, yet due to political ignorance they think democracy empowers them. If you want to know what democracy is really like in practice then research the French Revolution of 1787-1799 CE. It is also known as the "Reign of Terror". During which the French abolished the Crown, abolished the aristocracy, abolished the Church, abolished the merchant class and abolished nearly everything that was undemocratic. Sounds like freedom right? All those groups who "control us" were abolished. The French took America's freemason lipservice about freedom, equality and democracy and put it into full practice only to realize it wasn't quite what they thought it would be.   During this time in France the elected politicians tried to "equalize property" and divide the wealth of the nation equally among every single citizen so there was no such thing as economic classes, since equality meant that every French citizen legally had to have exactly the same amount of money in their pocket as every other French citizen. Democratic France tried to abolish profit because for someone to gain profits meant there was an inequality in the citizens' financial situations. Profit was deemed evil because to profit means to be unequal, and people gaining unequal profit could/would lead to people having unequal power, financially speaking but also politically speaking since money can make elections turn out favorably for those with more finances. In Democratic France every single person was given the right to be hired, however to keep everything equal nobody was allowed to have any advantages irregardless of their skills or expertise. There was one standard wage, if you were a French citizen you got paid the French wage. Nobody had to worry about being rich or poor because everybody was paid exactly the same amount no matter what job they did, irregardless of who they worked for or how long they worked. You see for everyone to be truly equal they had to earn the same amount but obviously everyone couldn't work the same amount of time due to practical reasons and due to working different jobs. To solve this dilemma workers got paid a daily wage whether they worked 1 hour or 24 in a day. As the saying goes "a day's worth of wages for a day's worth of work", this means one person's daily output of productivity equals everyone else's because they are equal since "everyone is equal"(which is "so true it is "self-evident""). Some may misunderstand this as welfare but it wasn't because everyone worked by definition and as equals they had to be paid equally to be fair because otherwise if merit/skill/productivity/time/effort/need/demand were to determine monetary remuneration then people would be unequal and treated unequally. The French thought treating people unequally was oppressive/illegal because they believed everyone was equal and deserved equal treatment. Yet not only was equality implemented amongst the quantity of money but every man was to live in the same type of house and have a wife and have children. While to be fair, divorce was made to be as easy to do as getting married, and to keep everyone equal no distinction was to be made between legitimate and illegitimate children. Fornication and adultery were made legal because to prohibit such sexual sins would mean to make certain people unequal to others which could lead to unequal treatment. This is because for a wife to be treated differently than any other girl amounts to unequal treatment. The same applied to family, family ties in New France could not unequitably determine treatment. French people were legally expected to treat everyone as though they were family, no favoritism for family relations was allowed because to treat blood relatives better than strangers is to consider people unequal which was wrong and to treat people unequally was a crime and "obviously barbaric". For someone to view/treat their mother/wife/daughter/aunt/sister any different than they would a unknown prostitute was unequal and considered uncivilized since "believing everyone is equal and deserves to be treated equal = enlightenment". The French thought if only everyone was treated equally then everyone would be happy and nobody would suffer at all. Some may disagree with this doctrine but that's equality and even if one still disagrees they aren't allowed to think their opinion is better and another opinion inferior because to think some doctrines/policies/ideas are better than others is to not believe in the equality of ideas. And what kind of "civil folk" thinks ideas aren't all equal or that all people aren't equal or that they "deserve (have a right) to be treated equally"? The French Convention also deemed that gold money would be replaced by paper money which they called assignats. The calendar was remade to have 30 days in every month and 10 days in every week, the months were given different names and the days were simply called "first day, second day, third day...." etc. Some even suggested abolishing all religion because it became obvious that every religion known to man spread the idea of inequality and unequal treatment of people due to religious differences, so some said Reason should replace God. Although it was determined that Atheism and Reason also spread inequality because they were inherently aristocratic. This was when many French people started to deduce that reasoning seemed to imply the doctrine of all people being equal might be unreasonable. So therefore for everyone to be equal "reason" was deemed to be a criminal or heretical doctrine. So instead or atheism or reason becoming the state religion as had been planned by the rationalists and pro-freedom pro-democracy pro-equality movement, a "Supreme Being" or "Eternal Being" was acknowledged but no details were given about this being because to do so may create inequality. For everyone to be equal everyone had to know absolutely nothing at all about the "Supreme Being" that existed. Likewise nobody could try to worship this "Supreme Being" that existed because then it would cause inequality since some might worship it better than others or for longer than others. Eventually when the democratic pro-equality abolishers decided to rule, the democratic populace abolished the abolishers because they violated the principles of democracy and equality as well. Since if everyone is equal then nobody can ever truly be in charge, to have a leader would mean they are not equal to everyone else. Thus the executioners of those who opposed democracy and the doctrine of equality which it taught were also executed because by executing people the executioners became unequal to all others. In reality equality became the

French religion and they tended to kill anyone who dared to suggest it's impossible to have a world built upon the doctrine of everyone being equal. They believed in democracy and equality despite nature being both anti-equality and anti-democratic with inequality being a crucial necessity for civilizations to progress. Right or Wrong (both being equal) Equality became the religious faith of New France and the French army set out to violently convert the world to it's gospel of "Equality, Liberty and Fraternity" rescuing everyone from tyranny and eradicating inequality. Some French people even went so far as to declare that the revolutionary leader Robespierre was "*the Messiah whom the Eternal Being had promised to reform the world.*" Eventually France became so chaotic, or democratic, that Napoleon Bonaparte was put in charge to keep the peace of those who wanted to kill those guilty of being unequal/superior or promoting inequality. Then Napoleon was defeated in the middle east when trying to conquer Syria and the French army was lost, but since the news traveled so slowly when Napoleon came back to France they thought he was victorious and made him a hero. Next Napoleon lost in Russia and was exiled, he returned from exile was remade emperor and then got defeated by the English. So Napoleon decided he would come to the United States, probably to get elected as Emperor of America; since he sold about 13 states of terriroty to America for $15 million. However the English captured him before he could finish the full voyage to America. From 1815-1848 CE France returned to monarchy. Thereupon France returned to democracy in February 1848 CE and ended up abolishing slavery in April, 1848 CE. In December, 1848 CE France elected Louis-Napoleon Bonaparte to be their president by a vote of 5,500,000 out of 8,000,000. In I852 CE Louis-Napoleon became Napoleon III, the Emperor of France by a vote of 7,500,000 out of 8,000,000. He went on to rule for 18 years before being captured by foreign enemies in battle. So democracy in France didn't just result in an emperor once, or twice, but three times in 50 years democracy resulted in elected French leaders who became emperors. It's almost as though "emperor" is just one of the things a democratically elected leader is. Yet theoretically and in practice during that time France was technically the perfect democracy, it fully followed the theory of democracy even better than communists followed communism. This is why no famous "thinkers" of the 19th century ever supported democracy, for centuries the "geniuses" have said democracy is crazy. The lesson is that democracy is bad, whether it's practiced fully or partially and will always lead to despotism, either directly or indirectly. I mention this because when many Americans find out America isn't a democracy they think democracy is the solution because of their ideocratic American upraising or ideology. But democracy is not the cure, it's just another disease. Just ask the British colonists of the 1700s CE how Parliamentarian democracy worked for them. Yes that is something many forget, in that America did not reintroduce the world to ancient pagan democracy, Colonial Britain was already practicing democracy and was operating under a parliamentarian-monarchy much like they are today. The "Americans" revolted against the British because they hated living under British democracy. When America then exported it's version of democracy mixed with freemason religion, the French "*Reign of Terror*" happened followed by the Napoleonic wars, ever since the US has exported an ideocratic doctrine of Americanism but called it democracy instead. In truth what's called the "American Revolution" was the 1st British Revolution in the Americas, whereas the true American Revolutions such as the early

American anti-tax rebellions in the 1700s CE and the American Civil War in the 1860s CE were swiftly defeated. Americans lost their revolutions so they and their historians incorrectly claim the colonial British revolution to be theirs. The early American revolutionaries had a fighting chance and lost, but today no violent revolution in America would win unless God helped them, a lot. Americans know this so most pretend they aren't subjected. Americans are much like how Romans were in the Roman Empire, and there was no Roman revolution.

      In 1862 CE Abraham Lincoln reintroduced fiat money to America by inventing the "Greenback" U.S. dollars, however the Americans overturned that unconstitutional and financially devastating change. Unfortunately President John F. Kennedy reintroduced the fiat "Greenbacks" in 1963 CE making them the legal standard. Afterwhich, just like Lincoln, JFK got assassinated. Since the U.S. Dollar became an elastic currency printed by the Federal Reserve Bank(a private company formed by Paul Warburg, a German Jew) and then became a petrodollar when Nixon severed it's links to the gold standard in 1971 CE, it has lost over 98% of it's purchasing power. While incomes have increased, the increase in incomes hasn't kept up with inflation. That is the primary reason women entered the workforce and why today a household can have 2 full-time wage earners yet be in greater poverty than both adults were as a kid when only their father worked. At the rate it's going child labor will be necessary simply for a middle class to exist, although that future middle class with more than 2 full-time wage earners will be considered poorer than today's definition of poor. But don't worry some new gadgets will be invented to make it seem like they're actually better off. It's very much like how Thomas Jefferson predicted when he said *"If the American people ever allow private banks to control the issue of their currency, first by inflation then by deflation, the banks and corporations that will grow up around them will deprive the people of all property until their children wake up homeless on the continent their fathers conquered."* As a result of this phenomenon some demand increases in minimum wage, not realizing that increasing minimum wages only increases inflation and brings the middle class down into poverty. This is because the increased expense of increased minimum wages, is passed on by businesses to consumers and in the form of increased prices for goods and services. In total the prices go up more than the minimum wage does thereby causing the poor to actually afford less than they did before even though they get paid more. Meanwhile the middle class which doesn't have their wages increased gets stuck paying more for everything and has their wage become closer to what is considered minimum wage, to the point where eventually they are earning minimum wage if they don't continually get raises to offset the inflation. While at the same time every government ordained increase in minimum wages puts small businesses out of business because their business model can't survive increased employee salaries. Those who can afford to pay higher wages usually have to fire some employees, so they end up trying to do the same quality and quantity of business with less than before, until eventually the next minimum wage increase puts them out of business because they can't afford to raise prices or pay more to their employees. On the other hand this greatly benefits the uber rich and large corporations by eliminating the competition and since their profit ratios stay the same as their revenues increase proportionate to the minimum wage increase and sometimes even more. Whereas mathematically one would imagine this is impossible because there must be a limited supply of money hence the lower classes getting more wages should only balance the class equation, but with a fiat paper currency the supply of money is only limited to the amount of paper that gets printed or digitally created by the private company known as the "Federal Reserve Bank". Meaning the money supply is practically unlimited as a result of paper money, meaning people can be given a larger number of slices of the money pie while in actuality getting less of the total pie itself thereby making them have less purchasing power even though they got more money in their pocket. This is because with a fiat currency like paper money the amount you have is meaningless, the number that matters is the total amount that exists; that total number affects one's wealth more than one's own personal number of monetary notes. Which means that when one uses a fiat monetary system like paper money, the amount they earn has little to do with the wealth they earn and their wealth can be destroyed by those controlling/increasing the money supply. Sadly the average American doesn't know why the cost of living has been, is and continues to keep on going up. Fiat money was invented to tax financially illiterate people through inflation without them knowing it and to eliminate the middle class. As the Nobel Prize winning economist Milton Friedman said: "*Inflation is the one form of taxation that can be imposed without legislation.*" So if one believes in the notion of "No taxation without representation." every country that uses fiat money is being taxed without representation, and if one believes being taxed without representation justifies armed revolution then every government that uses or allows fiat paper/digital money would be on the list of governments that deserve to be replaced. Yet today because of financial illiteracy you will have people claim that as long they have representation taxation is okay not realizing they are being taxed without representation due to fiat money. Because of the ease which oppression can happen with fiat money the famous Daniel Webster (author of "Webster's dictionary") stated: "*Of all the contrivances devised for cheating the laboring classes of mankind, none has been more effective than that which deludes him with paper money.*" Meaning that if you got paper money in your pocket, you need not worry about getting scammed or robbed, because you already have been. Governments instituted fiat money purposely to eliminate the middle class because all successful political revolutions depended on the middle class. The poor are too preoccupied with poverty to pose any political threat while the rich have too much to lose should they risk political change. Thus the middle class is the revolutionary class since they are wealthy enough to be healthy, smart and able to organize a threat, while also being poor enough to want a better life and be willing to risk their lives and current lifestyle in the hopes of a better government. The corrupt oppressive governments hate the middle class and actively try to destroy it, but they slyly do this in the name of helping the middle class. The American entrepeneur Henry Ford commented on this saying: "*It is well enough that the people of the nation do not understand our banking and monetary system for if they did, I believe there would be a revolution before tomorrow morning.*" Similarily in 1957 CE the Senator of Nevada George Malone, commented: "*I believe that if the people of this nation fully understood what Congress has done to them over the last 49 years, they would move on Washington; they would not wait for an election.*" People have fallen prey to the school book myths about these historical politicians who in reality were little different than the ones we have today. Even the politicians of today are worshiped and famous celebrities make statements equating the political leaders to be godlike. I'm purposely not citing their names to avoid giving these celebrities any more attention than they already have. May God help us to see politicians for what they really are. Don't let them simply having lived in the past make your opinion change, treat them for who they really were not who people think, claim or would like them to be. As an example in regards to religion Abraham Lincoln said, "*When I do good, I feel good. When I do bad, I feel bad. And that is my religion.*" and "*Neither Heaven nor Hell. It is simply Purgatory.*" Meaning Lincoln viewed himself as his own religious guide and needed no instructions via revelation or a prophet and Abraham Lincoln didn't believe in Heaven or Hell. Regarding drunks and alcoholics Abraham Lincoln said, "*I believe, if we take habitual drunkards as a class, their heads and their hearts will bear an advantageous comparison with those of any other class. There seems ever to have been a proneness in the brilliant and warm-blooded to fall into this vice.*" Such statements are proof enough that Lincoln was an irreligious idiotic immoral male. By giving such bad people in the past our respect it makes us have lower standards in the present and get stuck with worse leaders. An important point is that bad governing is systematic, a bad government is never the fault of "just X president". If say for example the US government were in theory bad, then they've been bad for a long time and their incompetance or evil cannot be attributed to just 1, 2 or 3 presidents but a legion of bad governing for many years. Many people fall for the election campaigners' trap of thinking it's all X president's fault so then they vote thinking the next one can fix everything just as they've been promised by every candidate ever. While I can refute that notion, since I've never been president some might not believe me when I say no president can be bad enough to screw up a country, especially in a democracy because a democracy is designed theoretically to prevent such disasters. To prove this I will cite Abraham Lincoln who despite his moral/religious flaws taught exactly what I just wrote when he said, "*While the people retain their virtue, and vigilance, no administration, by any extreme of wickedness or folly, can very seriously injure the government, in the short space of four years.*" So for any people who blame X president for ruining their country, that can only happen according to Lincoln if the people themselves have no virtue and vigilance. Thus since people tend to believe they are virtuous and vigilant the only way a government can be bad is if it has had a long chain of bad leaders. Regarding America I think they've had bad leaders since 1776 CE, and when you have 240+ years of bad leaders, the next one is probably not going to be able to quickly fix a mess that took so long to make. At least such a mess can't be fixed via democracy. Yet while we may not be able to right the wrongs of modern politicians we can correct the memory we have of past politicians and prevent the idolaziation of irreligious inept ignoramuses. We can fix the memory of the bad leaders in the past by rejecting the romantic political myths we get told about politicans in the past being heroes instead of politicians. The politicians of the past were little different than those today and the people never thought their wicked politicians would become heroes, get statues or get holidays either. For us in the present or future to idolize such people gives us no benefit and insults those who do deserve to be remembered with honor, such as prophets. I'm not saying to pick a bone with dead people but don't polish the memories of bad people, because then after the corpses of the corrupt corrode they could become an idol. You can't throw the present bums out if you can't even spot the bums of the past. Democracy and history has given us a "Bum Standard", most national heroes were villians in their own time and by idolizing them we get stuck with villianous leaders today. We frequently view or treat God's prophets like they were bums and we view/treat the bums like they were prophets.

The pagan Egyptians had the pyramids and the Americans have Mount Rushmore. The famous mountain was formerly a sacred site to Native Americans where the ritual "Sun Dance" had been performed. It was renamed Rushmore and the faces of George Washington, Thomas Jefferson, Theodore Roosevelt and Abraham Lincoln were carved into it by Gutzon & Lincoln Borglum who were both freemasons. This is clearly a graven image in violation of the 2nd commandment as the bible states in Exodus 20:4, *"You shall not make for yourself an image in the form of anything in heaven above or on the earth beneath or in the waters below."* The prohibition of images is understood by scholars to be images of anything animate.(living moving creatures) With plants and nature being permissible as long as they don't have unnatural additions such as eyes, ears, mouth, hands, or anything which would make them seem like animated beings. Obviously very few people follow the second commandment today with many excuses being made, but there is no way any excuse can be made in the case of Mt. Rushmore. It is clearly an idol paid for by taxpayer dollars (stolen money). Also keeping in line with pagan idols is the Washington Monument. Many Americans think it is a penis shape and laugh at it. It is actually an exact replica of the phallic obelisks made and revered by the ancient pagan Egyptians. So it is a penis shape, but it's a pagan penis. But at least it's not as bad as the Greek "Herm" statues, they were quadrangular stone sculptures which only had a bearded man's head on top with an erect penis depicted half-way down. The Washington Monument is not an American design at all, it's a pagan religious penis idol. Actually it is a 555 foot tall pagan penis skyscraper. It was also paid for with taxpayer dollars, just like the Mount Rushmore idol. You didn't think politicians would build pagan penis idols with their own money did you? Continuing the pagan Egyptian theme the back of the fiat U.S. Dollar features the "*Great Seal of the United States*" created in 1782 CE. It is an unfinished pyramid with 13 levels(symbolizing the 13 states) with the eye of Horus(pagan Egyptian god) levitating above. The Latin text next to the eye of Horus "*Annuit cœptis*" translates to "*He approves (or has approved) [our] undertakings*". The Latin text "*Novus ordo seclorum*" is beneath the pyramid which means, "*New order of the ages*". I find it humorous the "*Great Seal of the United States*" is a pyramid scheme.

Many people start to believe in conspiracies and blame Freemasons or the Illuminati when they become aware of the rich symbolism of American Government. Although I don't think Satanic or sinister individuals would willingly reveal themselves so easily and plainly. It is poor policy to attribute to conspiracy things which are easily explained by stupidity. I think the symbols of America are rich with pagan religious significance because of ignorance. Either that or the American Government really is sinister and satanic, but even if that's the case they are still stupid for having left so much evidence betraying their true nature. The American Government could be categorized in the following ways: it's either stupid, satanic or both. Since being satanic is stupid, stupid is the diagnosis even if the pagan symbols are intentional. The problem with satanic stupidity is that most who are guilty of it don't even recognize their actions as sinful or satanic. May God protect us from satanic stupidity and all the stupid Satanists. May God also protect us from being a laughing-stock for Satan, which is what happens every time we sin. When you commit a sin Satan laughs at you, not with you and if you think that's funny, then that makes Satan laugh at you while you are laughing at the truth. Don't pay with your soul to give Satan free entertainment.

In 1864 CE the Vatican produced the "*Syllabus of Errors*" and "*Quanta Cura*", these documents denounced the freedom of speech and press. The concept of equal status for all religions was completely rejected by Pope Pius IX. He also expressed an extreme dislike for democracy and proclaimed his preference for absolute monarchies. Pope Pius IX also denounced "*the proponents of freedom of conscience and freedom of religion*" and "*all of those who assert the church may not use force*". Pope Pius IX even threatened all Italian Catholics with excommunication if they voted in Italy's democratic elections in 1868 CE. Meaning that if you were Catholic and voted the Church considered it to be such a serious sin that you were kicked out of the Church. You would no longer be considered a Catholic, were prohibited from practicing the rituals of Catholicism and banned from entering churches. If you died while excommunicated, according to the Catholic Church you would be in hell forever because you voted and participated in democracy. This wasn't just one pope's opinion either, this ruling is what Catholicism taught and preached publicly for many years. In 1931 CE when Spain's Democratic Republic tried to establish Separation between Church and State a priest from Castellon de la Plana told his parishoners the standard Catholic policy: "*Republicans should be spat on and never spoken to. We should be prepared to fight a civil war before we tolerate separation between Church and State.*" Later Joaquin Beunza proclaimed: "*Those who are not prepared to give their all in these moments of shameless persecution do not deserve the name Catholic. We must be ready to defend ourselves by all means, and I don't say legal means, because all means are good for self-defense.*" These weren't just words either, Spain later experienced a bloody civil war partially because of the Catholic opposition to Democracy and Republican concepts. Most Catholics don't think of this papal ruling or Catholic doctrine when they enter voting polls today. Actually priests frequently tell people who to vote for, completely contradicting the teachings of Pope Pius IX. When it's impossible to follow both, who should Catholics follow their priest or the Pope?

While you probably didn't want such a detailed history lesson or political diatribe, I wrote so much in order to explain why I decided not to run for president. Obviously there was a low probability of me holding office, but the low chance of getting elected was not the reason I didn't try; I wanted to make that clear. Also don't ever believe a politician who says they are going to increase morality or make a country more religious via democracy, it's easier to put out a fire with a flamethrower. The philosphy of democracy is that everyone decides for themselves what is true and false, good or bad. Religion, family and class have no intellectual authority in a democracy. Because tradition is also deprived of it's authority, people in a democracy live in an intellectual and moral abyss caused by extreme independence that amounts to independence being forced upon citizens simply because nothing else is permitted to have authority. This extreme independence results in severe individual and intellectual isolation which leads people to believe that the quantity of support any idea has is what gives it intellectual and moral authority. Thereby democracy makes people into slaves of public opinion. This is because if everyone is equal and each person's opinion is equal then finding the superior truth of what to do becomes a simple mathematical calculation. This causes democratic peoples to think the popular idea is the right idea because it's popularly believed to be right. Basically they determine what is correct by counting instead of critical analysis. Furthermore even deciding what is actually important to discuss itself is dictated by the majority opinion so the very idea of "What is important to think about, talk about or find a solution for?" is predetermined by the democratic mass opinion. Therefore even having a intelligent useful conversation with someone born, raised and living in a democratic country becomes almost impossible because their sense of what to talk about and think about is already chosen for them by national bias. They think about what everyone else in the country thinks about and they talk about what everyone else in the country talks about, with nary a soul having any genuinely original ideas or opinions that they didn't get from their peers or some other pop culture dispensary. They live in an intellectual, social, political, spiritual bubble but since the bubble has lots of colors they think they are all unique since they're all told they're "free". It is rare indeed to find any who truly think for themselves. This is because the very notion of a free mind that disagrees with their theories which the majority believes are facts is considered heresy and insanity. A truly free mind has absolutely no beliefs whatsoever, because it's free to consider any notion even if it be racist, misogynistic, genocidal, suicidal, sexist, totalitarian, monarchial, animalistic, magical, religious etc. A free mind means it doesn't believe anything is right or wrong, nor true or false. Realistically such a mind is impossible to exist, outside of insanity. Which is why some say the only free minds are in the insane asylums. However in democracies one will learn it is hard to even have a free discussion because citizens of such countries tend to be hypocritically close-minded. As an example with America, if you were to try to debate whether racism, sexism, slavery, murder, dictatorship or any unpopular thing that has been condemned by the majority as wrong could possibly be right instead of wrong you will not be permitted to espouse a genuine intellectual discussion because the mob has spoken and created a fact via the doctrine of alleged "common sense" which is another way of saying "what the majority believe". Many will claim they don't believe everything the majority believes but if you prod a discussion on such things as slavery, domestic violence, rape, religious intolerance, cannabalism, suicide, incest, genocide, etc people frequently automatically presume such things are closed cases with verdicts which can never be overturned and never should be. Now don't think I advocate things like that, I don't because I have a religion which has made verdicts on such things that cannot be overturned. However you will find those in democratic lands who claim to have a "free mind" and promote "freedom of discussion" or "freedom of speech", are not willing to even discuss such matters or consider them debatable despite claiming they are free independent thinkers who "*think for themselves*" and "*don't believe what they're told*". Another example would be to try attempting to discuss whether monarchy, fascism or any other political system is better than democracy. Thinking such things is blasphemy or insanity to them. Yet because they believe in freedom of speech, they will say you should be glad you are in their country where you can think and say whatever you want because of freedom of speech. However what they really mean is you have "freedom to think" and not speech because nobody is willing to discuss or debate anything the mob thinks can't/shouldn't be debated or discussed. They don't give you the freedom to debate many things, the notion of the doctrine of freedom most of all. They don't give you the freedom to argue against a free society or freedom itself. Yet how then can you really have "freedom of thought" when many subjects and ideas cannot even be talked about with people or given any publicity? They may reject pop culture, because it's such a popular thing to do, but most all of them have a pop mind which is very narrow and only comes in the flavors available and allowed in their nation. Such is the tyranny of the disease of staunch devotion to non-conformity and "independence", which instead of resulting in true independence creates societies that are dependent on everybody because of their delusion that they can be free from depending on anything for their beliefs or from wholeheartedly submitting to the decisions of a minority. All they have is fictional freedom from the label of not being free, in reality they are mentally unfree even more than those who admit to not have a "free mind". A "free mind" is an empty mind which instead of being molded by oneself or a select minority it gets molded by everybody and anything. Thus rather than being ruled by one master of their own personal choice, they are ruled by a mob which they don't choose and cannot even identify let alone break free from. But since true free minds result in unstable ever-changing mentalities and economic/social/political chaos, this causes all democracies to always become ideocracies that can't reform. The illusion of freedom is then used by a state as a buffer to prevent the true ideology of the state from being identified or countered. Thereupon such an ideocratic state can get away with oppression undected with any formidable opposition. The only way to reform an ideocracy is to abolish it's beliefs, ideally this would come about through peaceful refutations. Wherein victory against an ideocracy can only come about through a mental/spiritual warfare since ideas are unkillable. Yet then they'll think and say you're brainwashing people. To which you can tell them that you can't because you ran out of all your brain soap while washing your own brain freeing it from the pollution which they are currently polluted with. Freedom is basically the shampoo modern ideocratic states use after brainwashing people to prevent others from cleaning their minds from the poisionous filthy ideology of the ideocratic state. Any who claim to be a "free thinker" is just ignorant of who their slave master is, which makes them twice as much a slave than the one who admits they are not a "free thinker". A "free thinker" is a foolish student thinking they were never taught anything by anyone and that they are unbiased, which they hope and claim to be since they are led to believe being biased is bigoted. But that they think they are a "free thinker" shows they are not and are deeply biased already thinking that a "free open mind" is a good thing when a "free open mind" simply means it's cheaper than cheap because it doesn't retain anything of value that enters it. A "free mind" is one that simply hasn't made up it's mind and is confused as to what to think/believe and is afraid to believe in something other than the idea of freedom being salvation. God did not create minds to be free but to have a program. The brain is hardware that is designed for certain software. God sends prophets with the correct ideas to put in our heads which should be accepted and installed once we are certain of the legitimacy of the prophet and the authenticity of the information as having actually come from God via one of his prophets. To desire freedom of thought means a person doesn't want to install the prophetic program in their life. But if one is living life then rest assured the brain is running on some type of program that has been installed into it, and if it's not the prophetic program then you will have problems in this life and the next with your relationship with the Creator of your brain. The test of life is that you pick your program. Yet everyone alive is living according to a program whether they picked it or not, because you can't live without one, unless of course you are brain dead. So the choice is you are either brainwashed or brain dead or you choose to let God brainwash you and install the prophetic program in your mind, heart and soul. Everyone's brain gets washed, whether one accepts the bath or not the soap we use is the only difference. So whether you call it soap or software your mind is washed or installed with either good stuff or bad stuff, some dirt or malware/viruses may remain or creep in from time to time, but your brain is not a "free mind" and you can never be a "free thinker" even if you try. You and others(like your parents, teachers, friends, family) already programmed much of your mind, but the programs we have in our mind at this time might not be the prophetic kind. The goal we should have is to pick/install the prophetic programs and avoid/uninstall/delete the devilish programs. So rather than "brainwash" the goal is to upgrade the brain. Just align your mind with the intended designs of the mind-maker. Don't listen to me, believe what the Creator wants. I'm just sharing what's in my mind so your mind might benefit. This book is a shared experience in that our minds are spending quality time sharing/learning information. If you change your mind about something that's okay if not that's okay too, depending on what it is of course. If something I write is wrong then don't believe it, but if something I write is right then it'd be wrong to reject. The only rule you should have is to side with what God wants, not with what you already think or what I think, but what is right and true. I'm just saying every mind is programmed. The powerful mind is the one which knows when, how, why, by who and what it was programmed with and chooses to improve itself. Your mind has already been made, but you can make it better so as to make your relationship with the mind-maker better. God did not create your mind to be free, instead God created your mind so it could be very valuable. A valuable mind is expensive, a "free mind" is worthless. Your brain cells are worth much more than money, how much more valuable then is the real estate of your mind? Think carefully about what you think about because you have a limited amount of time to think and limited brain capacity, your brain is always recording and deletes things to store memory. Thus be mindful of what you fill your mind with at all times. Your mind can either be a mine of beneficial knowledge or a minefield set to destroy itself. No two minds are equal and no two people are equal. Most brain damage is self-inflicted and pleasureable. The goal is not to have a "free mind" or an open mind but a healthy mind. The healthy mind is biased and knows it is biased, but despite the bias its willing to change it's opinions should it's opinions be proven wrong. The changes the healthy mind makes is based on the prophetic program and/or for truth. No human mind is 100% right about everything nor 100% healthy so we can always improve for as long as we live. To believe in God and worship God correctly requires a certain mentality, it's not just a feeling, thought or action. One needs the right mindset to properly believe and have that belief lead them to live their life the correct way.

Our minds' have a setting God wants it to be on but sometimes we have the wrong mindset. Your brain is a tool which the prophets of God taught us to use correctly. Since you always use it, you can only avoid sin if you use it the right way. God will judge us for what we use our mind for. One of the best things to use your mind for is to express gratitude to the Creator of your mind for giving it to you. So what do you think of such ideas? The correct answer you should give is "*I think what God would want me to think of that.*" but it's easy to say that without the statement being true. For you to obtain a believer's mindset this can never be done with "brainwashing", because filth will always enter our minds since that is what Satan does with his life. You could obtain a disbeliever's mindset by brainwashing but never a believer's. A believer needs mental hygiene from self brain-training. Some could help you train your brain sometimes but most of the training depends on you and what you do with your mind that God gave you. To think about the way you think and the reasons why and what you think about is to train your brain. But what are you training your brain for? To run a marathon? To fight a war? You should train your brain so the way you think and the things you think of please God.

    As written before, my experience being a teaching aid for 3rd grade Catholic religious education made me realize teaching was hard work. It further kindled my passion for religion and I felt called to the Catholic priesthood; again. They call this calling a vocation to make you feel like it's a special and that you are therefore special if you accept it. Although this time I planned to eventually become the Pope and launch more crusades, but I kept that part of my plan a secret. This career choice led to some distinction in high school when peers or teachers asked what I wanted to do after graduating. I became known as "*that guy who wants to be a priest and never have sex*". Since Catholic priests are celibate and never get married this didn't make me popular with the ladies, but the guys were quite entertained by my views. Which was a natual reaction owing to the general moral bankruptcy among kids in public schools and the taboo schools use to stifle religious discussion. Religiously there is no reason for priests to be celibate and biblically the apostle Peter was married and had kids, as did Phillip. For the first 1200 years of Catholic history priests had wives and families, only extremist monks on the fringe of the Church were completely celibate. Then a Council in Elvira, Spain in 306 CE ruled that any priest who had sex with their wife the day before performing a church service would be replaced. This policy was adopted by those who thought a chaste person was needed for performing the Eucharist ceremony. This doctrine of chastity for the Eucharist stemmed from a pagan notion of chaste virgin priestesses or eunuchs being the only one's fit to perform the temple rituals, mixed with the Jewish reports that Levite priests wouldn't have sex with their wives while it was their term of the calendar year to do the rituals of the temple. Buddhist monks were celibate as well. In 325 CE the Council of Nicaea decreed that after becoming a priest it was forbidden for a priest to get married. In 352 CE the Council of Laodicea ruled that women were no longer allowed to become priests, prior to 352 CE women priests or priestesses were permitted. Gradually voluntary clerical celibacy became seen as a mark of Christian piety. This led a famous biblical character named Nicholas, who is believed to have been one of the 7 deacons mentioned in the bible passage of Acts 6:1-6, to make a vow that he would never have sex with his wife ever again. At the time all the Christians thought this was a sign of true piety, but Nicholas found out it was easier said than done. Yet since he didn't want to break his vow and seem impious, Nicholas decided to commit discreet adultery on the side with various people not all of whom were females. This guy described as a biblical hero in Acts then created his own religion called Nicholaism where he taught that as long as people didn't get married then it wasn't sinful to have any type of sex, but sex within marriage was sinful. The Catholic Pope Siricius then decreed that married priests could no longer have sex with their wives after becoming priests. In 567 CE because lots of priests kept on having sex with their wives, the second Council of Tours decreed that any priest caught having sex with his wife would be excomunicated (declared a disbeliever) for a period of 1 year and would lose his job as a priest. Keep in mind that was only if the priest got caught in the act with his wife with his pants down so to say. Since most priests were still married and were allowed to be married this meant they had to have secretive marital sex, without anybody knowing or suspecting them. As a result of the necessity to keep their sex life a secret the priests would perform abortions or kill the newborns whenever their wife got pregnant or gave birth, since they didn't want to lose their job or be declared a disbeliever and banned from church for a year. Of course priests had to be discreet about burying their infants and fetuses so they buried them at convents and monasteries. This led the Council of Aix-la-Chapelle to discuss the problem of uncelibate priests performing abortions and infantcide and how to solve this problem. Some thought the whole celibacy promotion had to end and the Church should just let priests have sex with their wives. Pope Benedict IX believed in the case against clerical celibacy and to set a trend of reistance to the rules he quit being a priest and resigned the papacy in order to get married. Pope Pius II also wrote strongly against the celibacy of clergy and endorsed clerical marriage and clerical intercourse within it. The other side of the issue had folks like Pope Gregory I who said sexual desire itself was sinful, so obviously no priest could have sex without sinning and as such there was no goodness in clerics being married. Yet the irony of Pope Gregory I being so opposed to clerical marriage and clerical sex, is that his great great grandfather was Pope Felix I who had sex as a priest and his subsequent clerical offspring was the ancestor of Pope Gregory I, the activist against clerical marriage/sex. In short, had early priests not gotten married and had sex, the priests who later taught that priests shouldn't be married or have sex would not have been born. The pro-celibate priests were direct descendants of priests who got married and had sex. Although perhaps, like many Christians, Pope Gregory I didn't know his lineage, or that it contradicted his religious beliefs. The controversial movement for clerical celibacy didn't gather popular momentum until 1074 CE when Pope Gregory VII encouraged priests to abstain from marriage so that Church property wouldn't be inherited by their wives and children. In addition to that Pope Gregory VII made divorce from one's wife a precondition to becoming a priest, that way no priests would be married while being priests. Pope Gregory VII also forbade people from attending masses said by married clergy. However some priests were still married and continued to get married, so what happened to the wives of those priests? Well in 1095 CE, the same year he preached the first crusade, Pope Urban II decided to sell all the wives of priests into slavery. That sent a loud message to the priests and women about what would happen if priests got married, their wives would be taken away from the priest and turned into slaves. This policy made women think twice before getting married to priests, in case they got caught by the pro-celibacy crowd. However as it became more difficult for priests to get married and have sex, some priests started believing in Nicholaism or at least practicing it if not believing in it. Now whether priests practiced Nicholaism or believed it or not is hard to say, because according to the Church priests were forbidden to be married so the Church saw "wives of priests" as concubines/whores instead of wives since the Church decreed clerical marriages to be invalid. Since the opinions of the priests who were having sex during the 10th and 11th century are scarecly found, since what they were doing was illegal and they didn't keep diaries of "crimes", it's difficult to know whether they were promiscuous as the institutional Church said they were, or if they just considered their lovers to be wives wed in what they considered a valid marriage. Regardless in 1123 CE at the first Lateran Council Pope Calistus II sternly decreed again that priests could not be married after becoming priests. Still it took centuries for clerical celibacy to catch on, as evident in that the Council of Paris in 1209 CE told the Christian faithful they shouldn't go to church services held by married priests; which had already been banned by Pope Gregory VII hundreds of years earlier. These repetitive decrees prove that the popes said one thing and the priests and people did another. The final push made by the Church to enforce celibacy upon the clergy was done to combat the appeal of the heretical Cathars and other sects who preached and allegedly practiced total sexual abstinence even amongst non-clergy. Of course the opponents of the Cathars accuse them of replacing marriage with crazy communal orgies, but either way the priests who wanted celibacy and opposed celibacy both found the Cathars and other non-Catholic sects appealing. Basically the pro-celibacy crowd had enough and was splitting off creating new religions where celibacy was allegedly observed by everyone, while others broke off so they could join religions that permitted clergy to have sex. To counter the loss of Catholic members to celibate heretical groups, in 1322 CE Pope John XXII ruled that priests had to be celibate and couldn't be married before or after becoming priests. But still some priests just didn't listen, they obeyed the desires of their penis more than the desires of the Pope. In fact not only did the males not listen to such decrees, during the 1300s CE Bishop Pelagio griped about how women were still being ordained as priests/priestesses and hearing confessions even though female clergy had been "officially forbidden" for over 1,000 years. In the 1400s CE records indicate that approximately 50% of priests were married. So how did celibacy finally catch on and become the standard it is today? The inquisition played a role in promoting clerical celibacy but the reach of the inquisition varied from country to country, so it couldn't enforce clerical celibacy all throughout Christendom. However after the Protestant Reformation in the 1500s CE the priests/nuns who believed in clerical marriage/sex became Protestants and those who didn't stayed with the Catholic Church. So the debate was settled via a religious schism, but neither the Catholics nor Protestants today would like for it to be known that sex or lack thereof had something to do with their religious seperation. To say the Protestant Reformation was partially a sexual revolution is painful for both Protestant and Catholic ears. Many postulate the abject corruption and papist doctrines where the main causes but ignore that Martin Luther was a celibate priest who after founding Protestantism married a formerly celibate nun. I'm not saying it was all for the sake of sex, he did have valid points, but Martin Luther's Reformation may have been a love story. But then things got bloody and the Protestants and Catholics killed each other for hundreds of years. After Luther left, the Catholic Church decided to rewrite clerical history pretending celibacy was the norm ever since the beginning of Christianity. Some states eager to curry papal favor supported clerical celibacy and King Henry VIII of England went so far as to make it a felony to argue that priests were permitted to marry. Today the case for clerical celibacy rests primarily upon the doctrine of papal infallibility. In that since the Pope says so then it is so and cannot be disputed, although to be fair there are bible verses that can be used to promote celibacy. Clerical celibacy is not 100% based on the Pope's word and traditions, Paul started the pro-celibacy movement, but with Paul it applied to all who were capable of it and not just the clergy. Yet at this time in my life I didn't know clerical celibacy wasn't widespread for the first 1,500+ years of the Catholic Church, I just assumed priests were always celibate as I had been told. With a "holier than thou" attitude I started preaching to my classmates chastising them to reform their ways and stop their immoral sexual behaviors and drug usage. The sexual promiscuity was a problem that had to be dealt with individually, which I had no success at changing; unless you consider becoming a joke a success. Most teens in school thought it was hilarious that I told them not to have sex until they were married or not to masturbate because it was sinful. Seeing my advice interpreted as comedy I decided to work on the drug problem. My goal was to change evil people into good people. So I started sitting with the drug dealers at lunch trying to teach them a thing or two so they'd reform themselves. They thought I was funny too, but we found common ground in our love for rap music. I would just sit with them during lunch, I wasn't one of them. I only joined them so that I could change them for the better.

In 10th grade I read a fictional book about the Crusades that was written as though it were an accurate historical account. It was actually deeply imbedded with Christian medieval propaganda. Since it was telling me what I wanted to hear I ignored the small print saying that it wasn't 100% true and had been embellished. If you thought I hated Muslims before, I really hated Muslims after reading a Crusader propaganda book. This convinced me that the revival of the Catholic Church and Christianity would have to come about through the sword because history shows that it was spread by the sword. Christian militarization has a bloody history too long to examine here, but I will include some excerpts from Pope Urban II's speech in 1095 CE that launched what is known as the first crusade: "*I, or rather the Lord, beseech you as Christ's heralds...to destroy that vile race [the Muslims] from the lands of our friends,*" "*All who die by the way, whether by land or by sea, or in battle against the pagans, shall have immediate remission of sins. This I grant them through the power of God with which I am invested.*" These Pope Urban II excerpts are from an English translation of his speech during the council of Clermont in 1095 CE. The Pope not only claimed to speak for God when ordering Christians to destroy Muslims, he also said that any who died in the attempt would have all their sins forgiven and referred to Muslims as pagans. This is not a speech which would be considered politically correct today. Therefore the modern Vatican avoids making such rhetoric because they don't have the power to stir people to wage war. If they did we'd be hearing the current Pope sing the same song as Pope Urban II.

My ambition was to become Pope and launch new crusades in order to bring the world back to the "good old days" of Catholic dominance. My understanding was that the weaker the Catholic Church gets then the closer the antichrist is to coming and the closer the end of the world comes then the less people will be born thereby meaning that less people could be saved and experience paradise. This was an incorrect notion that I had, imagining that my actions could affect the timing of the end of the world. It's already been predestined when the end will come, it's not as though the end can be hastened or delayed, nor can our own death come any sooner or later than when God intends. God knows what we are going to do before we do it and has planned for it before we were even born. Our actions are already taken into account and are actually part of the plan of God whether we know it or not. Still, these were my motives for becoming the Pope. The Pope called Innocent III was my role model then. Pope Innocent III is known for launching the Albigensian Crusade, the 4th Crusade and holding the 4th Lateran Council where he ruled that Jews were to wear distinguishing headgear so they could be identified and ostracized. With such goals and role models, I enrolled into a special club for young men interested in becoming Catholic priests that would meet either once a month or once a quarter typically at a seminary, which is a special school for priests. This club helped me to learn what the priest lifestyle was like and gave me access to insider information that regular people who are not part of the Catholic priesthood aren't supposed to know.

During this time New York State was considering legalizing homosexual marriage. So I decided to oppose this by getting signatures on a petition to ban gay marriage in New York and then sending it to the state government. At that time I had not fully realized how ineffective petitions would be, I didn't read the U.S. constitution which expressly allows homosexual marriage. In order to ban or forbid homosexual marriage in America the U.S. constitution would have to be abolished. Most people don't read it, but just believe that it is something it isn't; or that they interpret it better than those who wrote it. Sadly many treat their nation's man-made constitution as sacred scripture.

Today many Jews, Christians, and Muslims who are ignorant of their religion think homosexuality is ok and a personal choice or even hereditary, this viewpoint is incorrect and the Scriptures clearly state so. One thing which many Christians will say opposing gay marriage is that the bible says Adam pbuh and Eve were meant to marry one man for one women until death do they part. This is a weak case to make. Firstly the "til death do we part" saying of Christian marriage came about in the middle ages because life expectancy was so short, it basically meant that, "*one of us will likely be dead in a few years so after that the survivor can go marry someone else with no hard feelings*". In fact the average medieval child would have 2 or 3 stepmothers AND stepfathers between birth and adulthood while the average woman would be widowed twice before turning twenty. But the case for monogomy gets even weaker when Christians draw the wrong conclusions saying that one man can only marry one woman because of the Adam pbuh and Eve verses. The same bible says that Abraham pbuh had 3 wives, that Moses pbuh had 2 wives, that David pbuh had 8 wives, and according to 1 Kings 11:3 the prophet Solomon pbuh had 700 wives and 300 concubines! God knows best if they did but this is what the bible says. Just think that if you had 700 wives, on average every single day 23 of your wives would start their monthly menstruation cycle; that is if their cycles didn't synchronize together. Most guys struggle to deal with 1 wife having 1 cycle once a month, imagine 23 a day or 700 at once if they synchronized; and that's not even counting the 300 biblical concubines. Realistically if Solomon pbuh did have that many wives for him to deal with all those menstruation cycles, without even counting the pressures of kingship and life, is a miracle in itself. It's astonishing that Christians today assume they know better about marital laws than these prophets who had multiple wives according to the same book they claim prohibits men from having multiple wives. The very verse that is claimed to prohibit anything other than monogamy is believed to have been revealed first to Moses pbuh, who is believed to have had two wives, so he would have been the first to know if having more than one wife was wrong if that verse was read by him and had that meaning. Since the Torah was revealed to Moses pbuh, Christians who say Moses pbuh was wrong to have more than one wife are claiming to know the law better than Moses pbuh whom God gave it to. That is a very bold statement to make, and if the Torah restricted a man to only have one wife then how come Jewish men today are allowed to have more than one wife? Even male Orthodox Jews who claim to strictly follow the Torah to the letter have more than one wife. The bible also says that both Isaac and Jacob pbut had multiple wives, the very tribes of Israel came from the same father with different mothers. That's partially why Joseph pbuh was sold into slavery by his brothers, because he was the son of a different wife than they were the sons of. Also one can not ignore the verses of Deuteronomy 21:15-16 which say: "*15 If a man has two wives, and he loves one but not the other, and both bear him sons but the firstborn is the son of the wife he does not love, 16 when he wills his property to his sons, he must not give the rights of the firstborn to the son of the wife he loves in preference to his actual firstborn, the son of the wife he does not love.*" These bible verses are not only ignored by Christians who oppose men having multiple wives, but also Jews when they claim the firstborn son of Abraham pbuh, Ishamael pbuh, didn't inherit the covenant promised to Abraham pbuh. Therefore I don't recommend Christians use the Adam pbuh and Eve line when opposing gay marriage unless they want to expose their ignorance of the Bible and the Torah. The reason homosexuality is prohibited can be demonstrated by its past legal precedence of prohibition for the people of Lot pbuh and their subsequent punishment. The prophet Lot pbuh lived in Sodom and the people of Sodom were the first ever to commit sodomy, hence the name. The men of Sodom would have sex with other men in public. Unfortunately they didn't stop when Lot pbuh warned them of the punishment that would befall them. All 7 of the cities of Sodom were destroyed, turned upside down and had baked stones of clay rained down upon them. Today this is where the Dead Sea is located. These evil people got "stoned" and "wasted". May God protect us from being getting "stoned" and "wasted". One reason some Christians don't like to use the fate of Sodom as an evidence for the prohibition of homosexuality is because part of their scripture has been corrupted and includes a slander against the prophet Lot pbuh, claiming he got drunk and had incest with his daughters on two different days, this is in the bible and it's false. It doesn't even make sense that the same prophet who forbade people from committing homosexuality would commit such an abominable act of incest after witnessing the destruction of the homosexual region. The bible also says that his wife came with Lot pbuh when he left but looked back and got turned into a pillar of salt, however this salt pillar story was copied from Greek mythology. In Greek mythology there was a Legendary Thracian prince famous for magical music named Orpheus. Anyone who heard Orpheus play music would do what he said and everyone loved him, but he only loved one girl named Eurydice. Due to his music Eurydice fell under his spell and got married to Orpheus. However directly after the wedding ritual, while walking with her bridesmaids who were supposed to ward off any evil, Eurydice was bitten by a viper and died. Orpheus couldn't bear the loss so he played his music until the gods became sad and Orpheus played his music all the way to the underworld and was granted permission by Hades to take Eurydice back with him to the land of the living to live again. However there is always a catch with Greek mythology. The catch was that Orpheus was not allowed to "look back" until after they had left and were out of the underworld. Orpheus agreed so he and Eurydice began to travel back to the upperworld leaving the underworld behind. Although Orpheus couldn't control himself and had to "look back" to see his beloved wife Eurydice, to make sure it was her, even though the gods told him *"don't look back or else"*. So Orpheus looked back at his wife and saw it was her but then because he looked back the gods punished him by turning his wife into stone or a pillar of salt according to various versions. What happened to Orpheus? Well he became depressed and played music but his music, magical and powerful as it was, was unable to get him a second opportunity to be with Eurydice. Unfortunately Orpheus wandered onto the island of Lesbos, which legend has it was full of lesbian women (hence the name) and upon hearing his music and seeing a man they tore Orpheus limb from limb having no need or desire for Orpheus to service their orifices because they were lesbians. This was the story of Orpheus' wife long before the story of Lot's wife looking back and turning to stone/salt was ever told. The myth of Orpheus is rich with pro-lesbianism and anti-paternalism. Firstly Orpheus is portrayed as only having won Eurydice's heart due to his magical music that was so powerful not even gods could resist it, then the viper on the wedding day (symbolizing the male penis) strikes the bride poisoning her to death by injecting its venom into her. Then Eurydice is further punished because of her "idiot husband" disobeying the gods. Hence from a feminist perspective this Greek legend teaches women that male charms are illusory, weddings and sex can be deadly, the husbands will harm their wives even when they don't intend to and that the lesbos who refuse to marry or reproduce and kill men are the heroes. This story of Orpheus' wife was plagiarized and copied for Lot's wife because it was more romantic and kid-friendly than the truth of the story regarding Lot's wife. The truth of the matter was that Lot's wife was destroyed with the sinners because she collaborated with them and helped in their sin and transgression. On the night before Sodom was destroyed, angels came in the form of men to visit Lot pbuh to tell him and his family to leave. However Lot pbuh was not legally allowed to have guests in his house or talk to people because the Sodomites censored his anti-sodomite and anti-sodomy speech. Thus being a good citizen of Sodom, Lot's wife notified the Sodomites that despite the ban Lot pbuh was talking to male travelers in their house preaching his religion and denouncing Sodomy as well as the Sodomites saying how they were bad people and such. The Sodomites then came to Lot's house and wanted to rape the men, who were really angels, and Lot pbuh could not physically stop the Sodomites from raping his guests, so he threw sand at their eyes and miraculously it blinded all the Sodomites. In response they left

Lot pbuh cursing him, promising to return the next day and harm him for breaking the law by preaching in his house and blinding them. While as a *"good neighbor"* Lot's wife, taking pity on her blinded Sodomite friends and compatriots, decided to help them back to their homes since they couldn't see and didn't know where to walk. Well God was not pleased with her betraying Lot pbuh and allying with the Sodomite government and then helping the Sodomite enemies/neighbors of Lot pbuh back to their homes. So the angels told Lot pbuh to leave with only his daughters and abandon his wife since she sided with the sodomites. Therefore Lot pbuh and his daughters left the city and left Lot's wife behind without regrets. Lot's daughters didn't say "But she's our mom!" and Lot pbuh didn't argue with the angels and say "But she's my wife!". They left her with those she really loved. In the morning Lot's wife got destroyed after having been abandoned by Lot pbuh and his daughters. Common tribal people didn't like the truth of her demise since it stressed religious loyalty over familial, so they copied the romantic salt pillar story from Greek mythology and used the "look back" clause to polish the reputation of Lot's wife who did a lot worse than "just look back". The biblical rendition portrayed Lot's wife as a fool to look back, thereby balancing the pro-familial interpolation with her destruction but giving sexist reasons for her demise so as not to jeoporadize family unity in tribal society as being seen as unsacred and breakable over religious differences. The real "look back" part referred to Lot pbuh and his daughters metaphorically not looking back as in not caring about their wife/mother who had sided with the Sodomites and loved them more than the prophet and the believers whom she betrayed via her actions. An important lesson in this is that Lot's wife wasn't destroyed for doing the sin of sodomy. She was destroyed for supporting those who did, and not forbidding it telling them that they were wrong thus betraying her prophet/husband and his angelic visitors in accordance to the law of Sodom. Lot's wife took the position of *"Well I disagree with the Sodomites on Sodomy, but they're legally in charge and I have to help them and love them even if I disagree with them regarding their religion, laws and sodomy."* But at least Lot's wife never said Lot pbuh had sex with his daughters as the bible scandalously claims. You see the patriarchal perverts of society disgracefully used their interpolated biblical plaigarism of the pro-lesbian myth of Orpheus to sanction incest and stress the importance of heterosexual reproduction. That was the reason for this spurrious butchering of the story/reputation of Lot pbuh. Jews viewed tribalism as so important they decided to stress that in cases where a man is without his wife then for the sake of tribal continuity the women could have sex with their father. Of course it's not encouraged but that it's in the bible made it uncondemnable in Jewish tribal society, because *"If the bible says Lot pbuh did it then it can't be that bad, it's not like Sodomy because if it were then Lot and his girls would've been killed for it. Especially since Lot's wife got killed just for looking at sodomites."* That's how skewed the Jewish mindset was that they wrote into their bible lessons teaching *"A women who looks upon the sodomites and disobeys her husband's orders turns to stone/salt. But it's okay for a father to have sex with his daughters, as long as he's drunk and they initiate it "for the good of the tribe.""* Later biblical stories even use this very type of twisted reasoning to justify Israelite women having sex with their father to continue the lineage of their tribe. Jewish bible authors made Lot out to be worse than he was and Lot's wife to seem better than she was and in the process making incest seem permissible and extremely far from being comparable to sodomy, when the main lesson from Lot and Sodom was how bad sinful sexuality is and aiding those involved with it is betrayal of the message of the prophets and believers. The lesson with Lot pbuh was that religion is more important than family and societal norms. Yet Jews altered the story to create their own perverse lessons and copied the greek myth of Orpheus and Eurydice to do so. It is well known Jews hated some prophets and even killed some of them. Sadly Christians kept this incestuous slander in their books because it makes the prophet Lot pbuh seem flawed thereby putting Jesus pbuh in a better light, as though he were more than human in comparison. The salt pillar fabrication is kept because the bible says "and it still stands there to this day" thus Christians think that sentence must prove the story and the bible to be true, as if no ancient author could ever fabricate a story about the origins of a salt pillar; which ironically doesn't exist anymore despite the bibles today saying it does. So that's where any Jew or Christian who wants to "stick to the scriptural story, salt pillar and all" then I challenge them to show the salt pillar today and if they find it to DNA test it and we'll see if it has ever been a human being. The biblical salt pillar alleged to be Lot's wife doesn't exist today to be seen because it was just a regular salt pillar and people used it up, because it was just regular salt and not a salt sinner enshrined as a eternal symbol as the biblical interpolation alleges. Regardless of the additional material and alternate stories inserted concerning the life of Lot pbuh, everyone agrees the lesson from Lot pbuh and his life is that homosexuality is forbidden, hated and punished by God the Creator. Ironically most people today have greater aversion for incest than they do homosexuality, even though at the time the biblically story was written about Lot pbuh being incestuous people were more outraged with the sodomites and saw the incest incident as minor. Today despite the biblical story in many countries they'd punish biblical Lot for incest and praise all the sodomites of Sodom. It's paradoxical in that the biblical heroes today would be considered criminals while the biblical villains would be heroically glorified. If any Jew, Christian or Muslim were to think or say that homosexuality is permissible or accept it then they have disbelieved in their religion, because if you deny one prophet you deny them all. You cannot pick and choose and say you believe in Noah and Moses pbut but deny Abraham's prophethood pbuh, because they are all on the same team with the same message and confirmed each other as prophets. Abraham pbuh was even the cousin of Lot pbuh and they knew each other. It's impossible to believe in one prophet and not the other. Yet isn't this exactly what the Jews do? The world today could learn a lot from the prophet Lot pbuh. Unfortunately a lot of information is corrupted but it's unanimously agreed that Lot pbuh outlawed homosexuality. Our leaders and societies may not be those of Sodom but they are sooo dumb to allow homosexuality to be practiced. Sexuality is not a matter of debate or opinion, it's biological. If anyone is to say whether X type of sex is okay it's God and God gave a big NO to the Homosexual experimental fantasy. Biblically Homosexuality is worse than pedophiliac incest.

    Homosexuality is not hereditary, no one is born like that because it is unnatural and contrary to basic biology. Homosexual intercourse is physiologically impossible, only a man and a woman can "enter the course"(intercourse). A man's penis is not anatomically designed to be inserted into the anus and bowel movement (feces) of another man. Nowhere in nature do you find homosexual animals because they know better. If you're going to say homosexuality is hereditary then you can say every sin is hereditary, that killing is hereditary, stealing is hereditary and so on and so forth never ending until people are drowning in sin. Yet even still hereditary means inheritable, so lingusitically it's impossible for homosexuals to have inherited homosexuality from their heterosexual parents. Believing homosexuality is some genetic disposition people are born with is like believing that people are born with a natural affinity for beastiality, it just can't happen. No one is or ever can be born with a sexual attraction to animals and no one is born with a sexual attraction to members of the same gender. Even in science electrical charges have one positive and one negative, with magnets having both north and south, opposites attract in productive ways on every level. It is a combination of brainwashing by the media and entertainment industry targeting people with a chemical imbalance due to improper nutrition because of genetically modified foods, hormone injected meats, an oversexed culture and drugs combined with the devils' whispers that contribute to homosexuality. For decades therapeutic states have used psychiatry and pharmaceuticals to suppress "undesirable" actions, thoughts and behavior as a method for social control. Therefore it shouldn't be surprising to learn there are drugs which have homosexuality as a "potential" side effect, unfortunately the manufacturers only list it on the bottle as *"hyper sexuality"*. The pharmaceutical company GlaxoSmithKline paid a French man 197,000 Euros after a lawsuit proved their drug "requip" turned him into a homosexual; now they list *"hyper sexuality"* as a side effect. Hopefully that wasn't too bitter a pill to swallow. Ok so homosexuality is sinful and unnatural, but can't we all just get along? Why did I care whether homosexuals could get married or not? Shouldn't I have minded my own business and not petitioned? This perspective is held by many people today, where they know homosexuality is wrong, but consider it a personal matter and something people shouldn't fuss over. If you're not gay, why do you care if someone else is? Can't a Christian still be friends with gays and attend a homosexual wedding even if they disagree with it? The reason I was so opposed to homosexual marriage being legalized was because the English translation of the New International Version of the Bible says in Leviticus 20:13, *"If a man has sexual relations with a man as one does with a woman, both of them have done what is detestable. They are to be put to death; their blood will be on their own heads."* This bible verse is a death sentence for any man who has ever committed homosexual sex. If the laws of the bible were the laws of America, debating homosexual marriage would be out of the question, because there wouldn't be homosexuals. Believing in the bible requires thinking sexually active gays should be put to death. If you don't think sexually active gays should be put to death after reading Leviticus then for all intents and purposes you don't believe in the bible. Being a Catholic who believed in the bible, I felt this way about gays. To me petitioning against gay marriage was just a small step on the road to mass homosexual executions. I considered my petition to be a type of sacred crusade. I brought my anti-gay marriage petition to school and got hundreds of signatures. One person then suggested that I get the signature of a certain girl as she walked by. I had been in classes with the girl for years and she had even dated I guy knew, so I asked her to sign. She said *"Are you serious?"* So I informed her that I was serious and the petition dealt with a very important issue and was no joke. Again she was non-compliant asking if I was joking or something. I again informed her I was really serious and asked if she was going to sign it or not wondering why she was giving me such trouble, especially since I asked her based on a referral thinking she'd be easy to get a signature from. Next the girl said, "*You do know that I'm lesbian right?*" and I said "*No, I did not know that. So I guess this means you aren't going to sign it then?*" and she didn't. Then I laughed because I accidentally asked a lesbian to sign a petition prohibiting gay marriage and didn't know she was lesbian. That's probably why I got told to ask her. Yet this event further proves that homosexuality is not something you are born with, because I knew this girl and knew that just 4 years earlier she had dated a guy who I also knew, for about a year. Whereas I'm quite confidant the guy didn't turn her gay. So this girl wasn't gay before and then she became gay for some reason, which I didn't learn. This isn't the only non-gay to turn gay that I know either. A former friend's father who fathered two children within heterosexual wedlock eventually got a divorce because he said he was gay. Yet he wasn't gay when I was friends with his kid and was even anti-gay. So what is turning people gay? Some mental health experts blame pornography. Eventually some girl took the petition off my desk when I went to the drinking fountain and gave it to the teacher trying to get me in trouble. The teacher didn't know what to do and gave my petition back to me saying she would ask the principal about it, but not to ask for signatures during class; which I wasn't doing anyways. I was late to the next class and people were talking about whether I'd get in trouble with the petition, coincidentally the next teacher was a Jewish woman who had allegedly said to a class the year before us that she was lesbian. While I don't know if it's true her manners and attitude suggested it. I figured it prudent not to bring it out in her class, although I think she caught wind of what I was doing outside her class with the petition and didn't like it. Eventually I got an appointment with the principal and he tried to intimidate me, but I had researched ahead of time and knew I was within the few rights they allow students to retain. However I didn't want to go to court over it. He instructed me not to get signatures during classes and to only do so between the bells; which I was doing already. This wouldn't be my last meeting with the high school principal and further clashes with the public school's politics would arise. Apparently they only want students to be politically active when they're encouraging their parents to vote for a school budget increase. During the summer I brought my petition to a heterosexual Christian family wedding thinking it would be an ideal setting for getting signatures. The minister was enthusiastic and ordered an entire table to sign, however other relatives didn't share his sympathies. Those opposed to my petitioning went to the family members who owned the property and I was told by distant relatives to either cease or leave. I'd have rather left because I hardly knew these people anyways and it was difficult to consider strangers to be family especially when being verbally intimidated and given ultimatums. Although my parents persuaded me to stop and even coaxed me into apologizing for having the audacity to petition there in the first place. When we got home from the wedding that was to be the end of my petitioning. Now that I think about it, it's rather funny. I faced more opposition from my heterosexual family at a heterosexual Christian wedding, than I did from a lesbian who I asked in school to sign a petition advocating that she legally be prohibited from marrying. Obviously I have a very special family. Later I learned that the U.N. charter promises it will promote "*human rights and fundamental freedoms without distinction as to race, sex, language or religion*". The U.N. says that homosexuals have the "*right and fundamental freedom*" to get married regardless of what religions say, the U.N. don't care. Since the creation of the U.N. in 1942 CE the effectiveness of their promotion of homosexual marriage can be seen to have completely changed the sexual orientation of the world and the perspective that people have on sex and marriage. Even the terms homosexual and gay have been developed in order to beautify the abomination of sodomy. People who have sex with members of the same gender should not be called gays, nor homosexuals. The linguistically correct word such beings should be called is sodomite. If they practice sodomy then they're sodomites. Before the sodomite issue can be resolved they have to start being identified as sodomites. Obviously my petty anti-sodomy petition had little effect and NY legalized sodomite marriage anyways as have many other states and places around the world at the behest of the U.N.'s "homosexual" promotion campaign. Yet I still don't understand why my petition was a problem at the family wedding. If you can't express anti-sodomite marriage sentiment there amongst heterosexual Christians when they are getting married, then where can you? Has expressing religious views about sodomy become illegal? What kind of world are we living in? It reminds me of a family member saying, "*There are 3 things you never talk about with family: Religion, Sex and Politics*". I don't understand this, the very reason such issues arouse passion is a reason for their discussion and evidence of their importance. If you're not going to discuss these things amongst family for fear of disagreement then how can you possibly discuss them with friends, colleagues or strangers? If these things aren't being discussed then how can solutions be discovered or implemented? All that it takes for evil to dominate is for good people to say nothing against it. Do you think the prophets pbut would shy away from speaking to family about the evils in their societies? All evidence suggests the opposite, with prophets being fiercely rejected by their own families and communities because they were advising them enjoining good and forbidding evil. The reason religion arouses passion within people is because deep down we all know it is the most important matter in the world, which is why it can often lead to the most passionate discussions. Everyone from every walk of life will have the strongest feelings about religion even though it may not be their expertise. In every other subject one's level of passion depends on knowledge of the subject except for religious matters. You can tell someone they are wrong about anything in life and there may be sore feelings or not, but if you tell people their religion(s) or religious beliefs are wrong then there will be passion aroused guaranteed. Why is it that of all things and topics, religion is what causes the most heated discussions and strongest emotions to arise, which no other subject can trigger? This is because by default all humans are created by God to place the most value on religion, even if you don't like religion one cannot deny it "*naturally feels important*". Therefore by ignoring the most important things in our discussions we end up wasting our time on trivial matters of which the discussions will not matter to us shortly after we finish them. My policy is if it's not important and it won't be important in the near or distant future then it's not worth talking about. To waste words in conversation is to waste your life.

    Maybe you think I've been too harsh on teachers and police thus far exaggerating the immorality within the public school system and legal system as a result of some personal grudge. I don't think so, but it's possible. I apologize if any who work in those fields was made to get upset by what they read, that was not my intention. The further examples which will be given may better illustrate the depravity I witnessed, but then again it might not be the general rule for all public schools or police forces. I'm only sharing my own personal experience. It's important to remember that it's the systems which are the problems not necessarily the people working for them; many teachers and police officers have good intentions. If we consider a person working in a gun factory who intends to make candy for children, at the end of the day they're not going to get paid if they didn't make guns. The equipment at their disposal can only do what it is intended for, no matter what the operator's intentions may be. A good person in a bad institution can only produce bad results, regardless of what their intentions or efforts may be. The public school system was initially popularly introduced in Prussia during the 1800s CE as a way to turn the children into patriotic obedient citizens who would have a common national culture and love for the government; simultaneously destroying their individualism. Public schooling still exists today for the same reason as Russian President Vladimir Putin made clear when promoting public education he said, *"Give me your child for 4 years and the seed I plant will never be uprooted."* That makes one wonder that if only 4 years are needed to plant a permanent seed, then what do 13 years of obligatory American education do to a kid? Grow a jungle? Or a forest? Do you know the difference between an intellectual jungle and an intellectual forest? Do you know that neither is civilized or intelligent? When public school was introduced in America people didn't send their kids to school even though it was free because they could see the government's intentions of brainwashing. They knew it was better for them to raise their kids the way they wanted than to have the forces that tax them also teach their kids. Similarly the Prussians/Germans didn't take to schooling kids despite the German Freiderach Froebel inventing "Kindergarten" in 1817 CE. The Prussians/Germans actually burned Froebel's books on Kindergarten educational theories because they didn't want the state brainwashing their kids at the age of 3 onwards as he suggested. Of which that's another important aspect of education, the age at which it starts. Many countries start compulsorily educating children in schools at the age of 3, America starts at 6 and then wonders why the US globally lags behind other nations in academics. Yet earlier doesn't always mean smarter by default, many factors apply to a proper intellectual development, although it is worth noting that schooling in Chile starts when a child is 85 days old. I mention this not to promote schooling, but to demonstrate how important it is to teach children when young and not to intellectually baby them. Kids can be as smart as you teach them to be, in history there have been kids under 5 years of age able to outwit many intelligent scholars of various fields of academia. Yet sadly many parents today think kids should focus on play when they are young not realizing how powerful their minds could grow to be if properly eagerly cultivated at a young age. Governments realized this, but decided to plant their own seeds in the youth rather than the best seeds. 12 years of schooling are typically the standard length of education, not for intellectual reasons but for religious. This is based on agricultural cults beliefs in the zoiac of 12 months in the year, wherein each season has different seeds to be planted in it. Kindergarten is like a "Kinder Garden" than the standard 12 year planting cycle. Only when it became compulsory to send kids to school did people allow their children to be raised by government employees out of fear for imprisonment in jail for refusal. Today they call it parental negligence, and even if one sends their kids to private schools the government curriculum must be taught or they will shut down the learning institution for not teaching patriotism. It doesn't matter what a teacher's intentions are, American schools are designed to be nationalism indoctrination centers just like most of the schools that exist in the world today. Regarding education Josef Stalin said, "*Education is a weapon, whose effect depends on who holds it in his hands and at whom it is aimed.*"At the end of the year a teacher can teach some good things but if their supervisors don't feel they've done a sufficient job to instill nationalism and/or globalism(should globalism replace nationalism) in their pupils and create a common culture of obedient pacifist civilians then those teachers would be replaced with more patriotic persons, likely of lesser intelligence levels than the less patriotic teachers. The kids in American public schools today are not taught a proper education, they are primarily taught patriotism and hedonism, everything else is just a cover in order to distract from the true purpose of school. Many teachers even fail to realize why the public schools were established and continue to exist. Many of them mistakenly think the system was made in order to be of service to children through academics. I know this not to be the reality of public school from personal experience having been a public school student. Whoever controls the schools has immense power to injure other nationalities and to benefit their own. The school can easily alienate children from their parents' values and/or ethics and can be used to oppress entire peoples. This is why as long as government schools are compulsory there will never be world peace, especially when they have Army recruiter tables across the hall from the high school cafeterias distributing propaganda to students and giving speeches in classes encouraging kids to join the military. Yeah, that's what went on in the school I attended. It is impossible for a school to be deprived of political self-serving character as long as it remains a compulsory public institution. In ideocracies the schools are state churches. Fortunately one can homeschool their child personally or with a tutor, and the internet has many online primary, secondary schools and colleges (religious and secular) which are inexpensive, take less time, have sports and extracurriculars that result in a superior diploma and far more advanced education than what government schools provide. If you are astute you'd realize I said "*the public school system was initially popularly introduced in Prussia*" and you'd recognize that doesn't mean the public school system initially originated there. Prussia was just where public school became popular, it was used long before then in a different country. The first country in Europe requiring compulsory attendance at schools for all children was Spain in the 1500s CE. The Catholic Inquistion created the public school system in order to systematically and institutionally create Christian children, since the Spanish population was still suspect regarding the sincerity of their faith after the Reconquista. So public school is a tool of the Catholic Inquisition and public schools were invented solely to teach religion to the masses uniformly cultivating orthodoxy at youth. The religious purpose of public schooling today remains the same, the difference is that the religion(s) taught have changed. The question is what religion(s) are schools teaching kids today? If they say "All" or "None" that means they aren't telling you which one and that you aren't supposed to know what faith it is. All schools teach a religion, they always have and always will. The curriculums provide the clues to the creeds kids conform to. Teachers don't make curriculums they just teach them. So teachers are like the clergy and curriculums are like bibles.

Each class is akin to a different chapter of the curriculum. Try to forgive the teachers for teaching kids a religion clandestinely; they know not what they teach.

    While I was trying to tell students not to have sex, on the books the school had a policy of no excessive public affection. However as with many rules only the popular ones tend to be enforced. Things that would happen without anyone batting an eyelid included: Hugging, Kissing, Tongues going down other people's throats, boys and girls putting their hands in the other gender's back pockets, and many human behinds were being slapped. I myself was sexually molested in school several times. For example when bending over to pick up books in the bottom of my locker a girl would run by and smack my behind without my consent. This happened several times without my permission and it felt terrible having been touched in such a manner. Being spanked by the opposite gender was a violation of my humanity and I felt helpless and victimized to such an extent that I was afraid to tell anybody. I cannot imagine how girls in mixed schools endure this daily humiliation. One particular memory that stands out is a girl who on the way to an exam with a baby in a stroller, loudly complained to her friend about it not being fair that she has to bring her baby to the exam because she couldn't get anyone to watch it for her. It was also surprising that the girls would continue wearing such revealing clothes despite the harassment they constantly received. Those who wore more were generally ignored by the opposite gender, but considering the situation it would've been better to be ignored than abused. The guys had a system where they would rate girls and give them numbers as though they were merchandise, saying things like, "*she's a 4 but her friend is a 9*" or "*I give her face a 6 but her body a 2*" categorizing women as numerical values instead of humans. I guess with all the makeup the girls put on it made the guys think their faces were not a part of their bodies since it was essentially a fake face. These same guys who were obsessed with sex would then go up to these girls and say nice things to them like, "*You seem really smart and have a beautiful personality*" and eventually such talk would convince the girls to start dating these guys who were only interested in fornicating with them and would brag to every guy in school about having sex with them, even if they really didn't. The majority of guys I knew who had girlfriends would brag about their sexual exploits and manipulation, but because they were always so tender and kind to the girls in person, the girls would never believe anyone who told them the truth. I'm sure every girl can think of some other girl like that, but I'm saying almost every guy I knew who was dating would say this stuff; even the ones you'd never expect who only had one girlfriend their entire life and were known to be shy and "sweet". If a girl were to spend just one day as a guy and hear the things some say about women when no females are around she would probably never want a relationship with another man in her life. While guys who intentionally tried to or accidentally hindered perverts from manipulating girls into fornicating with them would get called derogatory names for blocking their lustful criminal plots. A famous phrase guys having premarital sex say, "*Why buy the cow when you can get the milk for free?*" I find this saying disgusting as it denigrates women to the status of an animal, a bovine specifically. It depicts sex as something the woman needs just like a cow needs milking, as if she will physically suffer if she doesn't have it just like a cow suffers by not getting milked. It demonstrates a complete disrespect for women, sex and marriage. It also reveals that such men have no moral qualms about stealing because that is what getting the milk for free from a cow you don't own implies. Which is why premarital sex is considered to be an illegal activity according to many religions throughout the world, because you are stealing their virginity which you have no right to do, it's the special privilege of the one to whom they choose to be married to. Fortunately not all guys are like that, but in the school I went to a large portion of those who were dating were, unfortunately the girls they were dating had no idea of their true character. They were too infatuated to see the insincerity, because the women had low self-esteem any guy who treated them semi-decent easily garnered their affection, much more than the guy deserved. The truth of the situation is that no girl needs a boy to be happy and boys actually have a reputation for making girls sad. That's because any guy who dates is not a man. Real men propose and ask a girl's guardian for permission to get married or to discuss such a prospect. Men don't date. Dicks date. So when a girl goes on a date with some guy, they aren't going out with a guy at all, they're going out with his genitalia and don't let any guy tell you otherwise. If they had pure intentions they'd go to the parents and propose, but they don't because they don't want the parents to know what they're doing or planning until after the girl makes her propaganda campaign to fool the parents in his favor. If any guy comes up to a girl wanting to date then she should tell him, "*If you really care to get to know me, then you should introduce yourself to my parents first and I'll see what they say before I give you any consideration.*" Every respectable man would have no problem with this, he would have that intention to begin with and was probably only talking to her so that he could get directed to her parents or guardian(s). The same applies if any girl wants to take steps towards having a relationship with a guy, a woman would have no problem with it. Only perverts and predators enter into relationships based solely on their target's consent. And don't think a "friend" is a substitute reference. The "friend" just wants some free time and for you to have fun, they don't really care about you as much as one needs to in order to qualify as a character reference regarding such relationships. Some "friends" even hook up their friends with the very people they want to date, because they know if their friend dates them then they'll be able to get closer to their target before they make their move. Just to put dating in perspective in 1999 CE in America 25% of male college freshmen reported that if on a date they paid for a dinner and the girl doesn't have sex then they believe the male has the "*right to force her to have sex*". That's what 25% of college freshmen American guys admitted to believing in 1999 CE. Guys had some respect for girls they dated back then, today guys are worse. Unfortunately there are female sexual predators as well who play a similar dating/raping game. They'll pretend to have common interests with their target, acting as a "damsel in distress", or as said in urban tongue there is the "Ho Ho Ho".(A girl who dates you for the holidays to get gifts and then dumps you afterwards) But I can't expose much about the female deception/manipulation of males because as a guy I wasn't as privy to their secrets or tactics.

  Square dancing is another school sanctioned activity that contributed to the sexification of my generation. We had done it reluctantly in elementary school, preferring to play something more competitive and athletic, the "Ho-Down"(name for dance competition, often joked about being code for killed prostitute) and its prizes pacified us when we were young. However when you're a teenager hyped up on hormones, dancing with the opposite gender can be an exhilarating sensual experience which inspires the next steps towards sex to be taken. The entire reason dancing is more exciting than physically strenuous sports is because of the explicitly sexual undertones. For those who don't know what square dancing is, 4 boys and 4 girls form a square with each boy and girl getting a dance partner of the opposite gender, then music is played which gives instructions for the dancers to follow with different instructions for each song, with the whole genre having similar steps. Please do not try this on planet earth, this is a warning not a promotion. A typical dance may involve you swinging your partner, promenading your partner, putting your hands on your partners hips, going back to back with your partner and then bumping your butts together and infamously changing your partner for another several times throughout the course of one song. Some dances even require you to prance up and down the floor hand in hand with your partner in between lines of people cheering you and clapping, all the way to the end of the aisle with the two partners then going under an awning of arms together simulating a common wedding ritual. Then you get a new "partner" and do it all over again. All this touching would've been called molestation in society 70 years ago and indecent for even married people to do to each other in public, but today single and dating teenagers are told to do this with strangers of the opposite gender or else they will fail gym class. While parents are telling their children *"remember to do good in school"* even though getting "good grades" means doing bad things. As someone who wanted to be a priest and had no interest in dating or fornicating, square dancing was a major temptation that made me feel uncomfortable. If you didn't participate the gym teacher would give you a zero for the class which I believed would severely impact my grade, since they didn't say you could get a written note excusing you from dancing. Countless people met their girlfriends and boyfriends solely through square dancing whom they wouldn't have met otherwise because of being in different grades or classes. Many others met the boys and girls they would cheat with, until their previous boyfriends and girlfriends found out, solely because of them having met through square dancing. Square dancing created, ended and replaced many teenage romances. The dances done during school and promoted by school, directly increases the number of sexual relationships young children have and provide the opportunity for dating to take place. Now if Satan were running a school and wanted little kids to have sex with each other, I have no doubt in my mind he would make dancing a part of the curriculum just as it was in the high school I attended. Reflecting upon this part of the gym curriculum it seems as though a swinger's lifestyle of promiscuity is subliminally taught since the partners are changed after every song. Square dancing must be a blatant attempt to encourage students to date and get their hormones raging, because it certainly distracts from any learning one could do in school since they stop teaching on the day of the dance competition. The music heard from the gym everyday during the month leading up to the competition distracts every classroom within earshot. As a sidenote the very name gymnasium is sexual that originates from the word "gymnos" which means "nude". In Greek Hellenistic culture boys were taught to exercise in gymnasiums while they were naked. So it shouldn't really surprise us that today gymnasiums are used to promote sexual relationships since it began as a place of naked instruction and competition. I distinctly remember one occasion in which I was telling a male Catholic friend and a Catholic female classmate why people our age shouldn't be dating because we aren't ready mentally or emotionally and why we definitely shouldn't be having sex before marriage. The girl (who went to a Catholic school until high school) said that I didn't need to tell them that stuff because they were both Catholic, so I shut up. Three years later on facebook she was posting pictures of her first child, born out of wedlock while she was still a teenager. The father of her child was a friend of her previous boyfriend whom I think she began dating after square dancing with. Square dancing started her down the path to becoming a teenage mother without a husband and she told me I didn't need to tell her that she shouldn't be dating or having sex, because she was religious and followed the same religion as me so "obviously she wouldn't have pre-marital sex or have a baby". The funny thing is that in 9th grade before I wanted to become a priest I actually considered dating her thinking she was a pretty good person. Who knows had I not taken the path which I did I might be telling that story from the baby's father's perspective. The dating game ain't no game to play around with. There are numerous other cases like hers that demonstrate the evils that come from school sanctioned dances and I think it is in the best interest of society that dances do not take place at schools. If even one child is born to an unprepared teenager who had sex with someone met via dancing then that is injustice done to that child, as a direct result of the school creating an environment that resulted in the sex that led to that child. That child then grows up and goes to that same school and becomes a teenage parent themselves. Why would people get married when schools teach them you can have fun with one partner, then switch and have fun with another and keep rotating until you get tired never having to be responsible for the previous partners you discarded. The dances are not "innocent fun" they are destroying the very fabric of communal responsibility and respect for one's spouse and the exclusivity of marital relations. Scientifically dancing is simply our vertical expression of our horizontal desires. Dancing is sexual foreplay. The fact that dancing uses the word "partner" cannot be ignored because it implants the brain with the idea that partners of the other gender are not exclusive and easily replaced, which leads people to consider marriage partners and sexual partners similarly dispensable. What's even worse is that sometimes if there are not enough girls or boys then one gender fills in the missing spaces even though they are not the correct gender, meaning you could be a boy dancing like a girl or a girl dancing like a boy. This is a contribution to sodomite culture that would be unthinkable 60 years ago. Today I regret not refusing to participate and taking the zero, because those grades for gym class mean absolutely nothing today while those vivid memories of flirtatious dancing are replayed in my brain likely to remain forever no matter how much I try to forget. I sincerely advise every youth who finds themselves in such a situation to refuse to participate even if it causes a bad grade because you do not want to be carrying around memories of dancing with members of the opposite gender if you are married, these memories I have only bring me misery and tormenting temptation. This is the trap of the eyes which Satan ensnares our species with. It goes as follows: First eye contact occurs, this causes a smile (or interpretation) of approval or attraction, which causes greetings , which causes chatting, which causes meetings, which causes touching, which causes arousal(if for some crazy reason one wasn't already aroused), this causes sex, which causes Problems, which ruins your life, which ruins your afterlife. And all of that happens due to initial eye contact.

But the schools require a lot more than mere eye contact, they require students to be on step just 1 step away from sex and 4 steps away from eternal hell. Thus going to most modern "civilized" schools puts kids on step 8 of 12 on the road to hell, or gets them through 66% of the way to hell. At the time of this writing the most physical sexualized contact I ever had in my life was while square dancing in school, I have never touched a woman in a similar fashion outside of those dances. I don't even know the names of those girls whose images are stuck in my mind. These are the long-term effects such dancing has that have caused much suffering in my life. This is a significant issue that society is by and large ignoring. It is difficult to accept that taxpayer dollars went to teachers who instructed me to put my hands on women in sexually suggestive manners and dance. There is something wrong with this, school should not be the place where you've had the most intense sexual experience of your life. School is supposed to be a place of development where children improve and mature into moral and responsible intelligent adults. For me school was not a center of learning, instead it was a center of sex and I've never been in a more sexually conducive environment than when I was in school. Parents must pay attention to what is going on, sometimes it is better to get a bad grade in school than to pass with high grades and be forever haunted by what was done in order to "get a good grade". Any school that makes it a requirement to dance with members of the opposite gender(or the same gender the way things are nowadays) is not a school that wants to prevent teenage sex, it is a sign that they are pushing kids towards sexual activity and will brand them a failure if they refuse. These are not the kind of schools we should be paying to support or send our children to. If you truly wonder why the children today are more immoral than the children of yesterday look directly at the curriculum they are being taught because I'm certain the sexual culture in schools has only increased since I left them. The dancing is absolutely useless and doing it in school brought zero benefit in my life, it brought regret and sexual frustration and memories that are frequently used by Satan as a means of temptation. If you ever hear the music play and see the people start to dance, don't dance with them or watch them because I guarantee you will regret it for the rest of your life and be tortured by the memories the experience fries into your brain. I've lost those precious brain cells to these poisonous memories of dancing but you don't have to, you could use those brain cells to remember something useful that will help you throughout life that could cause you to enter paradise. Don't listen to your teachers or the schools because they are not always right and constantly obeying them can seriously ruin your life, as will be proven later. The majority may call it "Square Dancing", but no matter what angle you look at it nothing about the entire affair is right or square.

    Shortly after turning 16 years old the Government gave me a permit to drive after I passed their written test. Despite not being able to drive alone and having no vehicle of my own, driving affected my perception of the world and updated my perspective as to just how many people there are and how far away "close" places were. In other words: the pond seemed very big with many fish in it. Beginning to drive also strained my relationship with my parents due to the stress, dangers and heightened emotions involved in teaching someone to drive.

Eventually the Jewish (Lesbian?) history teacher began to teach us about the Israel-Palestine conflict and would explain some of the organizations involved showing us videos with little Jews and Muslims playing together in peace. Still for some reason I just couldn't understand how the Israelis could be the "good guys" despite knowing all the vocabulary and events she described. Why would America support them? At that time I didn't know that 86% of the world's 13.3 million Jews lived in America and Israel, with more Jews in America than there are in Israel. One day I even stayed after school hoping she could explain in a way that would make me agree with the textbook politics. The crusader mentality I had saw the situation as follows: Christians fought Muslims for hundreds of years over this holy land, for some reason the Muslims won (although I thought God was on the Christians side) and after all that bloodshed the Jews end up being given the holy land? While I hated Muslims and didn't want them to have the holy land I felt they were more entitled to it than the Jews, at least from a purely military point of view. I found comfort in the idea that the Jews and Muslims would fight it out killing each other and then the Christians could swoop in and defeat the weakened winner finally obtaining the holy land while not having to worry about 1 out of 2 rival religious groups. It was the classic divide and conquer strategy. Many were rooting for the Jews because it's easier to make a Jew convert to Christianity than it is to make a Muslim convert. During the summer after tenth grade I read a book by a Christian journalist who went to the holy land to give an eyewitness report on the situation. In it he reported something that will shock most Christian readers. It's actually not Jews vs. Muslims, it's Israelis versus Palestinian Muslims AND CHRISTIANS! He documented eyewitness reports of Israeli soldiers killing Palestinian Christian men, women and children. To my astonishment the Christians and Muslims were united against the Israeli occupation and for years had been staging peaceful protests with no effect, so then they turned to violent protests with rock throwing; but both types of resistance resulted in more death and oppression. In the first edition of this book I included more details about the history of the conflict here, but decided to publish that data in a separate work entitled "The history of the zionist state" instead of including them in this 2nd edition. I did this so that way I don't have to print this book in color to show the diagrams, which dramatically reduces the publishing costs of this book.

Up until this time, despite my conviction I was not a fully fledged member of the Catholic Church because I hadn't been confirmed. Confirmation is a ritual after which the person is considered an official Catholic. It is intended to be a symbolic and spiritual reenactment of the alleged Holy Spirit entering into the companions of Jesus pbuh via fire on their foreheads on Pentecost, which is a Jewish festival that takes place on the 50th day after the start of the spring harvest. After the event is supposed to have taken place, the companions of Jesus pbuh are said to have been understood in many different languages just by speaking in their own native tongue, miraculously they'd be understood by all listeners. Today they don't light your head on fire for the Holy Spirit to enter and no flames are present except those on church candles. The bishop of the region places a special type of oil called chrism on your forehead, makes a sign of a cross and says some words and the Confirmation candidate says some words testifying to their belief in the Catholic doctrine. Nobody who does this ritual today gains the ability to speak multiple languages, even though in the English translation of the New International Version of the Bible Acts 10:44-46 say: "*⁴⁴ **While Peter was still speaking these words, the Holy Spirit came on all who heard the message.** ⁴⁵ <u>**The circumcised believers who had come with Peter were astonished that the gift of the Holy Spirit had been poured out even on Gentiles.** ⁴⁶ **For they heard them speaking in tongues**</u> **and praising God.**" So according to the bible everyone who has the Holy Spirit in them and gets confirmed is supposed to be able to speak all languages. Yet most Christians don't know about these bible verses and think only the apostles gained the ability to speak all languages. Because if all who get the Holy Spirit in them gain this ability then because no Christians get this ability today it would mean the Holy Spirit isn't really in them as they are told. Prior to Confirmation you get to pick a "confirmation name" that becomes your name in the eyes of the Catholic Church, but not in public. As with most sacraments (sacred rites of passage) in the Catholic Church, families tend to give lots of money as a result. Although with this sacrament there is a lot more preparation before payday. There are required forms to fill out, community service, seminars, sponsors and interviews. When I was being interviewed I explained my plans for the priesthood and my deep seated convictions about the Catholic Church, the director in charge then made a comment that I didn't fully appreciate until recently. They said, "*So you've already received the Spirit then and this is just a formality?*" I replied in the affirmative seeing it as a compliment and a sign that I'd pass the interview, but deep down I didn't feel that I "*had the Spirit in me*" because I had low self-confidence and anxiety with public speaking which the Holy Spirit is supposed to fix as it is said to have fixed for the companions of Jesus pbuh. Even after I went through the ceremony and received the oil and a new name I didn't feel much different aside from the feeling of oil on my forehead and the relief that it was finally over and my membership made official. The statement of it being a mere formality for me because in the director's opinion I already had the Spirit makes me realize today that it is just a charade and that no one truly feels any different after the experience. The director probably says the formality line to everybody so that they aren't let down when nothing happens. The end result was a mixture between the placebo effect and the Santa Claus belief, thinking maybe if I believe hard enough that a Holy Spirit was in me then perhaps it would be true because I believed it to be. All praise and thanks be to God I no longer rely on the Santa Claus methodology to determine what is true or false.

Now that I had finished the Catholic religious education program being fully indoctrinated and confirmed as a member, I decided to indoctrinate others in order to keep the brainwashing machine going on the same cycle. With the experience of being a 3rd grade teacher's aide, I applied to be a teacher for the 5th grade religious education classes with full responsibility and got the position. During the first year I taught the Catholic curriculum each Saturday to 11-13 kids, many of whom I already knew from teaching before 2 years earlier when they were in 3rd grade. Being appointed to this position is another example that my views, prejudices and ambitions were not considered extreme, hateful or wrong by the leaders of the Catholic Church but were considered to be entirely correct. Even my firm belief in ecumenism was approved. Ecumenism is the belief that the Catholic religion is the only true religion and that everyone in the world should be Catholic one way or another, either voluntarily or involuntarily, including Christians of other denominations.

Knowing I held these views in the eyes of the Church I was an excellent choice to teach 10-11 year olds about religion. Now I dearly regret the damage I did to those children and the lies I told them. Parents should be aware of who is teaching their kids about religion and what they are teaching them. Unfortunately many parents themselves are ignorant and relegate their own duty of teaching religion to others expecting "religious" teachers to instill morals in their children. Compare it to scents, if the house stinks and the kids are exposed to stench all the time at home except for a short while when they go to the perfume store, then obviously the kid is going to stink the majority of the time because the effect of the perfume shop will disappear as soon as the kid returns to their foul smelling home. So if you don't have a religious home, how can you expect to have religious or moral kids? A religious home has nothing to do with whether there are symbols on the wall or if dusty scripture is on the family bookshelf, it's about whether the religion is practiced in the home and the level of importance it holds in household affairs. If you think 1 hour of religious instruction per week will make your kid religious then what will all those hours of watching bad movies, playing bad games, listening to bad music and public school do to them? The power of the hour is affecting our society. If you are a parent who is ignorant about religion so much that you pass your responsibility to others then you don't even know whether your religion is correct and that's a big problem if you are letting someone else teach your children about something you yourself don't even know with certainty. I hope God will forgive me for the falsehood I taught those children and that God will forgive the parents who neglect teaching their children about religion. All praises and thanks be to God for guiding me away from the evil which I was doing and may God protect all children from such evil environments.

    The most homework came in eleventh grade and there would be nights when I'd be doing homework for more than four or five hours from the moment I got home until going to sleep. Sometimes I'd be burdened like this for several days in a row or weeks, with every break having some major project that had to be completed during any time off. This created immense pressure, which I now believe is purposely designed to breakdown the student's family relationship at a critical time in their life, when hormones are raging, while they have the mobility of driving and easy access to drugs. I don't think it is coincidental that my family life started deteriorating in eleventh grade and the drug I choose to use/abuse most was music, rap music. I'd listen to it in the shower, in the car, on the bus, doing homework, surfing the web, while playing videogames(if sound wasn't needed to play) as long as I wasn't watching a movie, TV, in school, or sleeping, music would be playing rocking my eardrums. An addiction developed to the point where if I didn't hear at least 4 hours of music a day my body would physically shake from withdrawal. On an average day I'd listen to over 8 hours of rap per day with a collection of rap cds that grew to number in the hundreds. Some might call it a love or passion but it really was a destructive addiction. In Sweden a man is so addicted to heavy metal music that he gets disability payments from the government because of this condition that has consumed his life. No joke, addiction to music is an official legal disability. Unfortunately with most addictions, the addict is often the last to know of their affliction. I began spreading my disease around and would make playlists of hundreds of rap songs that could be seen as supportive of Christianity and distribute them to rap fans in school. It's funny to think that some churches were burning rap cds saying they were satanic while I was telling people to listen to those same cds because they contained the Christian message. Most of these songs contained swear words and would be considered "Gangsta rap" by non rap fans, but if you listen to the non swear words, most street rap promotes Christian values as they exist on the street. The radio is a different story. You might've heard that sex sells, well check the current top 25 songs of each genre and of all genres and you'll find sexually suggestive themes in abundance, don't think it's just the rap and pop music that is contaminating our ears. As my Christian themed rap playlist got longer and longer, I realized no one was really listening to the songs because they either heard the songs before and didn't care to hear them again thinking in a different context, or because there were too many I had listed. This especially bothered me when one day I only had one playlist packet with me and I decided to give it to a drug-using friend instead of a drug dealing friend, both of whom were in the same class with me and both were a grade ahead of me. It was funny because I sat on the right side of the drug-user telling him not to use drugs or do sins like masurbation while the drug dealer sat on the left side of him in class saying the opposite but since the drug dealer didn't come to class every day then sometimes that desk was empty but sometimes a different drug-using bad kid came to class and sat in that chair who was in my grade and we would always frequently discuss drugs, sex and religion. It was a physics class. On that day I gave the playlist to the middle seat drug-user, who was one of my favorite drug-using friends, the cops came to the school to arrest drug-dealing friend and he ran out of the school never to return. He simply dropped out and I never saw him again. Yet then the drug-using friend didn't even bother to listen to the playlist saying 20+ pages of rap songs is too much for him. I was furious thinking if I gave it to the drug-dealing friend on his last day instead then it could've saved his soul and changed his life, but rather than do that I gave it to a guy who didn't even bother to listen to it. This led me to wonder how could I get my drug dealing and drug using friends to hear and accept the message of Christianity when they wouldn't even listen to gangster rap? In the past I had dabbled in poetry as a part of schoolwork and found it to be easy and entertaining. While in middle school when a movie about a famous white rapper came out everybody wanted to be a rapper and we would have rap battles in which I held my own without embarrassment. Thus I decided to become a Christian rapper before turning 17.

    While coming to this decision my home life was turning to tatters and daily fights would take place between my parents and me, frequently becoming physical. Sometimes it even spilled outside or dragged other family members in which always made it worse for everybody, because there was little honesty and everyone always had an angle to play, or suspicions whispered in their ear by Satan. During this time period I publicly started expressing hatred towards my parents. I had stopped loving them in middle school, which was why I found it hard to believe they would let Santa Claus take credit, but until eleventh grade there was still a general liking of them if we weren't fighting. Although when fighting day after day with each fight escalating in severity and the hurt feelings on both sides piling up more and more with no one ever truly forgiving and Satan making us remember the most minute obscure details of imagined wrongs, unfortunately hatred entered my heart, took root and grew because I thought that "*Sorry doesn't cut it*". They may have realized this and as a result after major battles my parents would buy things for me as a form of bribery, or to repair the relationship, but this was only a temporary fix usually lasting less than a week with the new gift eventually being used as an example of my ungratefulness and becoming something to be taken away or damaged as a punishment. Giving gifts after a fight only exacerbates the issue by forcing it to be ignored while the root problems and emotional scars remain without any real reform or forgiveness taking place. Getting gifts after fights almost came to be expected. The added expenditure of gifts raised the cost of each fight, thereby creating more resentment between the concerned parties as well as financial stress. My materialism also grew tremendously as a result of getting a gift every time I was hurt or sad. This led me to be conditioned with a mentality that a "new toy" was the solution to make me happy whenever sad, angry, stressed or unhappy. Eventually it got to the point where I didn't even care about the gifts and was willing to sacrifice most of them in order to live somewhere else and to never see my parents or "their family" again. One reason I included my parent's families with them was because of comments they would frequently make to me such as "*no one's wrong*" and "*everyone goes through troubles*" or "*it's just a phase*" whereas these comments are just ways to avoid responsibility and taking sides. It is not a phase. People do not go through stages of having good attitudes, bad attitudes and good attitudes; the attitudes do not change without a change in mentality. Family neglecting to correct a bad attitude when it first arises can potentially lead to it continuing throughout a person's life. It's correct that they shouldn't take sides in family disputes, but refusing to take any side is wrong too. People should take the side of truth and justice. However when there is a fight within a family it can be tricky because feelings of victimization and conspiracy are often inspired by Satan and the devils. In retrospect I feel the correct course of action for family to have taken would've been to say:"*There is a problem so obviously someone or something is wrong. However that doesn't mean someone else is right, most likely all parties are wrong. But even if one party is right they might still have to change some things they are doing, just in order to prevent a future fight, even if they aren't wrong. Although most likely everybody is wrong and this is a plot from Satan in order to disrupt the ties of kinship and lead us all into sin.*" Unfortunately nobody in my family saw the situation that way and everyone tried to ignore it and pretend there were no problems. Perhaps the biggest problem was that my parents and I knew family members gossip and backbite, so we would always feel like the other family members were being told bad things about us and thinking of us differently because of the slander done by the one we were fighting with. Satan sure is sneaky. The fact that many people have come to accept family relationships deteriorating during teenage years shows the declining expectations of morality and corruption of the community at large. This is an effect of the TV shows and movies that make you think that it's normal to fight amongst family because a fictional family of liars (actors/actresses/animations) is worse than yours. I even know a person who is so deeply influenced by a particular TV show that they adopt the mannerisms of a fictional TV character to the consternation and frustration of everyone else, except the other people just think it's their personality not knowing the individual is just so in love with a character on a TV show that they've taken them as a role model for their behavior without consciously realizing it. Ironically the person claims to be a Christian but I know for a fact they are imitating X character from a certain TV show treating them as their prophet and inspiration for social interactions instead of Jesus pbuh. I really hate it too because while I was younger I was enamored with this person as I loved the TV show myself but as I became more spiritual I began to see how immoral the show was along with it's characters and now I tend to loathe the fact that this person is like the fictional TV character in the flesh. I guess that's why they call it "Television Programming", because the TV shows program people to believe, think and act a certain way. Realistically nearly every fictional character actors and actresses portray on TV and in movies are psychopaths and that's the reason so many people are so messed up because when you repeatedly watch psychopaths in movies and TV then the viewer interprets those fictional psychopaths as "not that bad" and then imitation of those characters is unavoidable. Next thing you know everyone will be cutting themselves and people will say it's normal because everyone is doing it and the people on TV are even worse. That's the destructive power of mob mentality and the majority opinion of democracy. If something is wrong it's wrong, no matter if the whole world is doing it, saying it's right making it legal. Likewise if something is right it's right even if all the world is saying it's wrong making it illegal.

   Eventually there came about a conflict between life and Catholicism which concerned eating meat on Friday. In the past the Vatican said it was a sin to eat meat on Friday, but in 1984 CE the Vatican decided it wasn't a sin and you were only supposed to abstain from meat on Ash Wednesday and every Friday during lent. You might think that's crazy, but to me I thought that if it was a sin before then most likely it's still a sin. Realistically it doesn't make sense that people would live for thousands of years avoiding meat on Fridays because it was sinful and then suddenly the pope says it's ok so that made it ok. Either it was never a sin and the Church was lying about it being a sin for thousands of years or they have lost their ways and have changed their religion to conform to modern times and attitudes, giving into pressure from Satan. If the former was the case then what else had the Church been lying about? If the latter then what other things are sins that have being given the thumbs up by the Church? I stopped eating meat on Fridays just to be safe, and shortly after stopped eating pig altogether; or so I thought. The reason I say "or so I thought" is because I didn't know that the ingredients pepsin and gelatin are made from pigs and that many enzymes or emulsifiers used in inorganic foods and bakery products such as glycerol/glycerine, monogylcerides and diglycerides are made from animals (because it's cheaper than vegetable derivatives). In actuality most self-proclaimed vegetarians and vegans actually aren't, because they eat foods made of animals but they don't think they are made of animal products because they don't know what the ingredients that compose their foods actually are. What makes it even trickier is that a lot of the bad stuff gets listed as "Natural Flavors" or "Artificial Flavors". Whereas if you actually research what these "flavors" are you'd understand why they don't list them. Some companies, even put alcohol in their products in amounts that can intoxicate a person and list it as a "Natural Flavor". I'm not joking, some name-brand companies do this with mainstream edible products. Vanilla extract is an excellent example of an alcoholic ingredient in popular foods of which many are ignorant of it's alcoholic chemistry or its ability to intoxicate. In the US most products that are labeled to contain "natural flavors" actually include small amounts of alcohol, enough to mildly intoxicate without the consumer perceiving the intoxication. The

US government says it's perfectly legal because they say "Alcohol is a natural flavor" and if it's labeled then consumers are fairly warned of X product being an edible intoxicant that can affect and damage one's brain and health. Although don't get paranoid thinking everything that says it has natural or artificial flavors has meat or alcohol in it, it's just some companies which abuse the labeling system. Most people just look at a loaf of bread, a piece of candy or a soda pop and think that it doesn't have meat or alcohol in it because of it's appearance and taste. Then if you tell people pig or alcohol is an ingredient in their bread, beverage or candy they treat you like you're crazy. (As you probably thought just a few seconds ago.) Biblically there are numerous places that prohibit the consumption of pig and even the Jews still observe the restriction. Remember the first sin of mankind involved eating something that had been prohibited, so anyone who says everything is lawful to eat is ignoring the fact that man was ejected from paradise because he ate something he shouldn't have. Not everything which is edible is lawful to eat. The Pharisees would try to trip Jesus pbuh up on the smallest things, asking trick questions with yes or no both being the wrong answer, yet Jesus pbuh would manage to turn the tables on them exposing their hypocrisy every time. If Jesus pbuh was doing something blatantly prohibited, like eating pig, then surely something regarding it would've been in the bible if any change in the rules had been made; giving Jesus' justification pbuh. Since this is mentioned nowhere then this major event must have never happened, but many times while priests are giving a sermon saying everything edible is permissible they will cite Mark 7:14-19,

> *"^{14} Again Jesus called the crowd to him and said, "Listen to me, everyone, and understand this.^{15} Nothing outside a person can defile them by going into them. Rather, it is what comes out of a person that defiles them."$^{[16]}$ ^{17} After he had left the crowd and entered the house, <u>his disciples asked him about this **parable**</u>. ^{18} "Are you so dull?" he asked. "Don't you see that nothing that enters a person from the outside can defile them?^{19} For it doesn't go into their heart but into their stomach, and then out of the body."*

First of all the bible itself says this famous statement is a parable, it's not a legal ruling. Next, verse 16 is merely a footnote saying how most manuscripts include the verse from Mark 4:23 which says "*Whoever has ears to hear let him hear*". Another interesting point about this parable of Jesus pbuh is that the crowd never asked for clarification of what it meant but his disciples did, to which the bible says Jesus pbuh asked them if they were dull which in modern times would be like asking someone "Are you stupid?" Thus one lesson to learn from this incident is that the disciples didn't always comprehend as well as others did as to what Jesus pbuh meant when he spoke. When priests or preachers talk about these verses many use them to say that Christians can eat anything they want without it defiling the body. If that's the case how can eating something like the Eucharist purify the body? The verses clearly state that what you eat doesn't go into the heart, but into the stomach and then out of the body. That means when people eat what looks like, smells like, feels like and tastes like bread and wine which they believe to be the body and blood of Jesus pbuh, according to the bible it doesn't enter their heart but ends up going out of the body. Meaning if you truly are eating the body and blood of Jesus pbuh, God or the son of God then you are also pooping and peeing it out into the toilet. It also means the body and blood of the divine are no match for your digestive enzymes. In Islam this is an unimaginable blasphemous concept that God or a prophet could be treated in such a fashion that would result in such esteemed beings getting flushed. Muslims do believe that some of what comes out of a person can defile them so whenever we urinate or defecate we wash those parts with water so they are clean rather than just using toilet paper to smear the feces or urine into our skin. Anyways the common explanation that Christians can eat anything because what goes into the body doesn't defile the body contradicts the notion of "Original Sin'. Christian dogma states that when Adam pbuh and Eve ate the forbidden fruit it defiled their body so badly that they got kicked out of paradise as a result, and that it automatically defiled all of their future offspring including us. Because of them eating something, we were allegedly so tainted and defiled that Jesus pbuh is said to have had to die on a cross to compensate, but even with that they say we must be baptized in order to fully get purified from the defilement we suffered because of people eating something. So if Christians say they can eat anything because of this verse then the Original Sin doctrine has to go. The Original Sin doctrine states that people eating one fruit one time infected the entire human species causing permanent damage to our DNA for eternity. Whereas even if we personally take the Christian steps to fix this genetic sin, it still gets passed on to the next generation regardless and can never be removed even if we did gene therapy and changed our DNA attempting to remove it. Thus teaching that eating can permanently change the spiritual DNA of the entire species, yet at the same time they say "*nothing that enters the body can defile it*". Realistically in Christianity eating food God said not to is the biggest and most damaging sin in the book. You will not find one sin ever committed by mankind which the bible says has had a worse result than eating. Biblically speaking eating is the most dangerous thing one can do. Imagine if I told you that if you ate one bad apple then all your offspring and their offspring would have uncurable cancer for eternity that can never be removed, you would tell me I'm crazy. Yet biblically Adam pbuh and Eve eating food did more damage than my crazy cancer apple. One can't say people can eat anything they want today, but everyone is born sinful in need of purification because of our ancestors past eating behavior. Also if nothing which enters the body defiles the body then why don't Christians test this theory with poison and see if their body gets defiled as a result? Yet on top of that Christians maintain that gluttony is a sin. How can gluttony be a sin if nothing that enters the body defiles it? The bible says Jesus pbuh said "*Nothing*" he didn't put any limit on the amount one can eat where it then would defile the body. So raw food, dog food, spoiled food, roadkill, food contaminated with sewage, vomited food, fast "food", recycled food(by which I mean instead of flushing you just recycle your meal, as in eat one meal and you get a number 2 to eat for free) biblically speaking nothing means nothing will defile the body. Basically Christian preachers tell people that Jesus pbuh said it's ok to eat yellow snow. If one says that "nothing doesn't really mean absolutely nothing" then it most certainly doesn't mean pig is ok, because everybody knew pig was forbidden. To overturn such a widespread belief one needs a very specific explicit instruction, not some off the cuff parable. Scientifically speaking any doctor will say that it's actually healthier for a person to eat yellow snow than it is to eat pig because the toxins in the pig meat cannot be removed even if it is correctly slaughtered according to the rules God established for slaughtering animals. Jesus pbuh had strict dietary rules throughout his life and never once ate pig. Thus if Jesus pbuh preached it was ok to eat pig, then why didn't he practice what Christians say he preached? Anyways I stopped eating meat, or so I thought, on Fridays because of the Catholic Church's canon 1251 (or 1252, depending on if looking at the 1917 CE or 1983 CE version) which states: *"Abstinence from eating meat or some other food according to the prescripts of the conference of bishops is to be observed on Friday, of abstinence binds those who have completed their fourteenth year of age. The law of fasting, however, binds all those who have attained their majority until the beginning of their sixtieth year. Nevertheless, pastors of souls and parents are to take care that minors not bound by the law of fast and abstinence are also educated in a genuine sense of penance."* Every Catholic over 14 and under 60 was sinful according to the Vatican if they ate any type of meat on any Friday. Theories as to why this prohibition began center around financial stress on the fishing industry with increasing fish supply owing to improved fishing techniques, but without increased demand profits were declining. The Friday ban on meat was then enacted to boost the fishing industry which the Vatican had large investments in, or at least this is what the rumors are. However there may be a religious reason why fish became a customary Christian dish on Friday. Jews eat fish every friday. They do partially because the Sabbath starts Friday night and partially in order to get magical blessings. Jewish Scriptures state that God blessed 3 things on 3 consecutive days. On Wednesday/Thursday Jews say God made/blessed fish on Thursday/Friday Jews say God made/blessed man and on Friday/Saturday Jews say God made/blessed the Sabbath. Which since Ecclesiastics 4:12 says, *"A cord of three strands is not quickly broken."* Jews interpret that to mean if you combine the 3, fish+men+Sabbath then by eating fish on the Sabbath they get some type of special threefold blessing. Also since fish don't have eyelids and their eyes are always "All-seeing" then they are symbolic of the All-seeing God so Jews think by eating fish on the Sabbath they are "honoring the Sabbath" and some Jews even hold it to be obligatory to eat fish on the Sabbath. Furthermore the letters of the Hebrew word for fish numerically adds up to 7, and the Sabbath is the 7th day of the week and when the Messiah comes Jewish legend has it that a Leviathan (meaning a huge fish) will be prepared for all Jews to eat. So Jews eat fish on the Sabbath in anticipation of the Messianic giant fish they plan to eat later. While Christians adopted the fish as a Christian symbol possibly thinking the Messiah was the Leviathan and they were supposed to be eating the Messiah which they do in bread/wine form, since fish wasn't practical for religiously ritualistic eating. Plus since Christian doctrines teach Jesus pbuh is the sacrificial "Lamb of God" then it wouldn't make sense for the "Lamb of God" to be eaten in fish form. That'd be fishy, not lamby. But then again it doesn't make much sense for the alleged "Lamb of God" to be eaten in bread and wine form either. Really, if Jesus pbuh is the "Lamb of God" who told people to eat his body which he sacrificed for them, then shouldn't they be eating lamb when eating the "Lamb of God"? Who turned the "Lamb of God" into a piece of cheap bread? What kind of restaurant are they running? They advertise a divine Messiah on the menu then instead of giving you the "Lamb of God" in the roasted flesh you get a bread crumb of Christ and a sip of wine so you don't complain and the semi-intoxicated people happily pay full price thinking they got served the "Lamb of God". You'd think with the long pews they'd at least have a buffet. Even if Christ said to eat Christ crumbs did he say adding spices or seasoning was a sin? Communion use to be a communal meal, now it's more like an appetizer sample. They actually give you more bread in a restaurant for free while you wait to be served than they feed you in church. Apparently Christ pbuh only feeds the masses with loaves of bread when he was in the flesh and not as bread. Jesus pbuh was known to miraculously feed the masses with bread while he was on earth in the flesh but now that he is bread the masses can no longer be fed with bread? Sounds fishy to me. If Jesus pbuh is really turning into bread at every church service then why don't they just solve world hunger by feeding Jesus pbuh to people in bread form? Isn't there enough of Jesus pbuh to go around? If there isn't enough bread in the world for everybody to eat then how can Jesus pbuh have possibly instructed everyone on earth to consistently eat him as bread? Christians always like to say that "Jesus is the answer!" well I see that billions are starving and Christians are saying that Jesus pbuh is a piece of bread and God wants everyone to eat Jesus pbuh. Why then don't Christians give the people Jesus bread? It'd be better if they shoved Jesus bread down our throats rather than the bible and their religious doctrines. Am I right? People aren't hungry for the gospel they want bread to eat and Christians say that Jesus pbuh turns into bread for people to eat. Is not edible Jesus pbuh the answer to world hunger? Is that not the sacrifice? Does not the bible teach that after eating his body and drinking his blood thy shall never hunger or thirst again? What is the correct bread to wine ratio when making the recipe of Jesus pbuh? Seriously, I'm not joking, if Jesus pbuh taught us to eat him in bread and wine form he had to have given us a recipe so we could have the correct ingredient ratio when cooking up Christ. Who is to say how much wine is too much? If Christians are going to preach a doctrine that you can eat your way to heaven if you eat a special bread then why haven't they fed the masses? How can Jesus pbuh have given his body for all of us to eat as bread if people are starving due to lack of bread? If everyone needs to accept and eat Jesus pbuh to go to heaven then why isn't there enough Christ Crumbs for us to consume? Did Christians buy too much wine and exhaust the bread budget? Well Jesus pbuh never ran out of bread and could turn rocks into bread or make bread loaves multiply. Since Jesus pbuh multiplied bread before, then surely when incarnated as bread he could miraculously multiply his crumbs for all to eat. That also raises another question. How many times did Jesus pbuh eat bread with people and he never ever told them while eating bread with them that, *"You know one day, the masses are going to be eating me and I'll be in bread form. That's something to think about while we are here eating this bread now. Any questions?"* Likewise how can Christians be the flock with Jesus pbuh being their Shephard if Jesus pbuh is the "Lamb of God"? Lambs are not Shephards, they are shepharded. Yet Christian doctrines say the Shephard turns into bread. Anyways I digress and hope not to have over-offended any Christians due to my comments. I was writing about why Catholicicism taught eating meat was forbidden on Fridays. Further research revealed that Christians used to fast on Wednesdays(because Judas was thought to have betrayed Jesus pbuh on a Wednesday) and Fridays(because Jesus pbuh was alleged to have been killed on Friday) but gradually Christians stopped fasting and simply abstained from meat since that was a luxury food item. Thus instead of fasting from all types of food, Christians began to eat fish as a way of fasting from meat and meat(animal) products such as cheese, milk and eggs. Biblically I couldn't find any textual reason for the prohibition on meat, but believing the pope to be infallible, meat left my Friday menu and that's probably why most Christians also use to abstain from friday meat eating. It was a case of following what the Church says rather than what the bible says. As of September 16, 2011 CE Pope Benedict XVI reinstituted the ban on meat once more making Friday meat consumption a sin for Catholics. So for any Catholic reader who thought I was a Catholic extremist, think again. The Vatican currently says it's a sin to eat meat on Friday for every Catholic between the ages of 14-60, whether it's during Lent or not. One wonders how the Church views those Catholics who were born and died between 1985-2010 CE who ate meat on Fridays thinking it wasn't sinful for them. Other sins Catholics don't know the Church taught were sins involve sex itself, by that I mean sex within marriage. Catholic teachings forbid sex between a husband and wife during Lent, Advent, Ember Days, Sundays, Wednesdays and Fridays; but since I wasn't married and didn't plan to marry that was a rule that didn't really concern me. But aside from sex being prohibited on certain days in the Catholic faith, it is even more strict than most dare imagine. The famous "St." Augustine decreed in 401 CE, in "*On The Good of Marriage*" in Section 11: "*For **necessary sexual intercourse for begetting** [of children] **is free from blame**, and itself is alone worthy of marriage. But **that which goes beyond this necessity** [of begetting children, such as sensual kisses and touches] **no longer follows reason but lust**.*" Meaning married Catholics are not allowed to have sex unless they are trying to make a baby and if they kiss each other it is considered to be "Lust" which is a mortal sin, which would disqualify them from getting communion during church(if they followed Catholicism). Pope Gregory "the Great" went even further and declared that all type of sexual desire and sexual activity was sinful. He had many reasons for saying this, one reasoning was that Jesus pbuh didn't have sex and neither did his virgin mother Mary so therefore sexual desire and sexual activity was sinful for everybody. Of course he didn't offer any alternative methods of continuing the human race but since he taught the world was going to end soon the abolishment of human procreation wasn't seen as detrimental. So as Pope he publicly declared that for anyone to desire sex was a sin that one needed to confess to a priest and repent from. Pope Gregory "the Great" was of the opinion that priestly celibacy was a sign of spiritual purity and that being celibate meant priests were better than everybody else since they didn't indulge in sexual activity and as such were guaranteed extra rewards in heaven, according to him. In Augustine's "*On Marriage and Concupiscence*" inside book 2 chapter 35 it states "*as regards **any part of the body** [such as the mouth] which is not meant for generative [procreative] purposes, **should a man use even his own wife in it, it is against nature and flagitious** [that is, atrociously wicked; vicious; outrageous].*" Thomas Aquinas taught the same saying: "*Although kisses and touches do not by their very nature hinder the good of the human offspring, **they proceed from lust**, which is the source of this hindrance [of why kisses and touches are made sinful]: and on this account [in so far as they are lustful] they are **mortally sinful**.*" So that is where the Catholic religion actually teaches a husband and wife are sinful if they kiss each other since that is not a neccessary part of the baby making process. They say it's a regular sin if done while procreating but if not done while intending to make a baby(ie. not during intercourse) then it's "mortally sinful". Of which "mortal sins" are deemed major sins that can result in hellfire if one doesn't repent from them. Now most Catholics will say that it's not like that today because the groom kisses the bride the moment they get married and married Catholics kiss each other frequently, yet just because people do something doesn't mean it's ok for them to do according to their religion. Also know that having sex on the wedding night was always permitted because the bible said it happened when prophets got married. Also since marital sex was forbidden so many other days this exception practically became a rule and unofficially part of the Sacrament of marriage, so that many today incorrectly think or feel that they have to have sex on their wedding night or their wedding isn't as official or romantic. Such false expectations actually ruin marriages and I personally know of multiple cases where it has. Such issues have occured due to the expectation of sex on the wedding night because of the tradition that began as a result of Christianity forbidding sex on so many other days. Although keep in mind Christian sex is not supposed to have passion such as sensual kisses, foreplay, fun, etc. The Catholic dogma taught that it's supposed to be a nearly mechanical process. Like a key opening a door, purely utilitarian, key goes in leaves it's mark and the baby comes out 9 months later. That's all folks, there are no fireworks involved. As of December 31, 1930 CE Pope Pius XI confirmed this teaching remains the rule in his *Casti Connubii* # 59, saying: "*For **in matrimony** as well as in the use of the matrimonial right **there are also secondary ends**, such as mutual aid, the cultivating of mutual love, and the quieting of concupiscence which **husband and wife** are **not forbidden to consider** so long as they are subordinated to **the primary end [that is, procreation of children]** and so long as the intrinsic nature of the act is preserved.*" Meaning that physical/sensual/sexual interaction between married Catholic spouses is not forbidden if it is done while intending to procreate. Note he didn't say it wouldn't be sinful, he just said it's "*not forbidden to consider*" doing such things as long as while considering such sins they attempt to procreate. Whereas it also states that in the Pope's infallible decree matrimony's primary end is the procreation of children. So essentially if you are sterile then no spouse for you. For those fertile enough to qualify for marriage this means they can fantasize about kissing each other whilst trying to make a baby, as long as it's only while trying to fertilize an egg, they aren't supposed to be thinking of kissing each other at any other time let alone actually doing the act of kissing. If they do fall into this "sin" then they are supposed to confess it to the priest and follow his instructions so as to get forgiven for such a "wicked crime". What about popular romantic gestures such as "blowing kisses" to each other? Well it just so happens that "blowing kisses" was explictly forbidden because the ancient Sumerians would do this as depicted on a statuette of Awil-Nannar of Larsa. The pagan Romans also blew kisses according to Pliny. This action was prohibited because "blowing kisses" was a pagan form of worship where they thought that a portion of one's own soul could be transferred to another person, or to a god, as an act of submission. That's why people tried to catch the kiss, lest the soul be captured by someone undesireable. So blowing kisses is a pagan prayer and an act of submission to whatever you're blowing/ kissing. Hypocritically the majority of Catholics don't know their beloved saints and popes teach that it's sinful for spouses to be intimate except when procreating and even then kissing, blowing kisses and sensual touches are sinful for them. Oh and this is the modern teaching too, nearly nobody follows it and obviously the priests don't preach it, but according to the Catholic doctrine those are the rules and I even know of a few Catholics today who still preach and teach this saying those who don't are sinful hypocrites. Although it isn't just the Catholic Church that prohibited married people from kissing or having sex on certain days or for reasons other than procreation either. Non-

Catholic Christians in the middle ages were taught for centuries that for a husband and wife sex was forbidden on Thursdays in honor of Jesus' arrest, Fridays because of the death, Saturdays because it's "Our Lady's Day"(of course this was referring to Mary, not all ladies), Sundays because of the Resurrection and Mondays to commemorate the dead. Meaning that all of the non-Catholics could only have sex on Tuesdays and Wednesdays, IF it wasn't a "holy day". Although today probably more than 99% of Christians have no clue that Christianity has forbidden married couples to have sex on most days of the week and most days of the year because it's supposedly sinful. If you do the math without accounting for "holy days", non-Catholic Christians used to believe that for more than 71% of the year it was sinful to have marital sex. Meaning Christian spouses could only have sex on 29% of the days in a year, at best; in practice that number was even lower because of the "holy days" and practical reasons. While Catholics had even less chances for sex because they had more "holy days" and sex was forbidden during the 40 days of Lent and the month of Advent, thus being a nun or monk in the past wasn't as unappealing as we'd think it must've been today. Being celibate then meant giving up a smaller number of potential sexual experiences, which were less exotic/romantic than the kind experienced today. So their whole concept of a marital sex life was entirely different, whereas the hardships of marriage where also much greater then than they are now. In the past marriage was both harder and less fun. The founder of Protestantism, Martin Luther, even wondered if marriage itself was sinful when he wrote: "*No matter what praise is given to marriage I will **not** concede it to nature that it is no sin.*" While Odo of Cluny wrote, "*To embrace a woman is to embrace a sack of manure.*" These comments by Christian leaders don't exactly depict marriage as bliss. The Catholic "Saint" Augustine even taught that if everybody stopped getting married and having kids then that would be great because it would cause the Kingdom of God to return sooner and thus cause the world to come to an end faster. Augustine taught that by humans continuing to propagate they were delaying the return of Jesus pbuh. Which for those who believed him, this meant becoming a celibate monk or nun would cause Jesus pbuh to come back to earth sooner. So theologically speaking in the middle ages it made a lot of sense to be celibate, plus in medieval Europe the monks and nuns had the best opportunities for education. When you add a sense of religiosity or fanaticism to that then a celibate life in a monastery actually would seem to be one of the most promising lifestyles a Christian could hope to live. To think marriage might be enjoyable and "probably not sinful" was practically heresy, especially when you consider that one was more likely to commit a sexual sin according to Christian rules if they were married than if they tried celibacy. For those spiritually inclined Christians marriage was a dreary risky enterprise with more work than reward. That's why the fairytales included magic to make betrothal and marriage seem pleasurable, because under Christianity it wasn't. Despite magic being forbidden and evil, it was widely believed that for Christians to be happily married it must have been due to one or both of the spouses being afflicted with magic. This is why when describing attractive women in the West today the words used are the same ones Christians in the past used to condemn witches. Examples being: "*Alluring*", "*Breath-taking*" "*Captivating*", "*Charming*", "*Dazzling*", "*Drop-Dead Gorgeous*", "*Enchanting*", "*Glamorous*", "*Irresistable*", "*Mesmerizing*", "*A real eye-catcher*", "*Spectacular*", "*Stunning*", etc. If any such adjectives were applied to a woman in the past, that would be a criminal accusation of witchcraft. Thus such terms are technically sexist, since they denote that the attration men may have for women is purely due to magic spells. Although instead of telling women to use magic today, now they just tell them to use cosmetics. Since masochists refuse to admit guys might just like girls for who they naturally are and what they naturally look like, instead of saying women must be using magical spells they tell women they have to buy and apply the magical chemicals they sell. Thereby instead of women being witches they got turned into desperate customers. This witch-complex along with sex on most days being sinful contributed to the reason why more women were denounced as witches to the Catholic church than men were denounced as wizards. This is because if a women got pregnant and it was thought to have happened during one of the periods when sex was forbidden, such as Advent or Lent, then either the husband could admit he and his wife were guilty of sin and were going to have a sinful child as a result, or he could denounce his wife as a witch who had sex with Satan or magically tricked him into having sex on a sinful day and thereby get himself a new wife. Which since divorce was not allowed in Catholicism, the easiest, most fun, practical way out of a unpleasurable marriage for a guy would be to have sex during a forbidden time and then call one's wife a witch who had sex with Satan. Instead of "make-up sex" they had "break-up sex". Now you might think this wicked trick could only work once or twice before people got suspicious of the guy, but since no guys wanted the thought to occur that collectively guys might be sinfully having sex with their wives during the forbidden days such claims weren't put under as much scrutiny as we'd think. Not many guys were keen on jeoparodizing their only loophole around 71% of marital sex being forbidden. If a few innocent women got betrayed and hurt, the male community wasn't going to risk the loophole. They'd be risking their lives if they did. Whereas for the women they were really stuck in a hard place of either have what they believed to be sinful sex and risk being called a witch if she got pregnant or refuse their husband and hope he doesn't legally find a reason to get another wife via her "accidental death". In order to be safe, women would be inclined to abort babies just in case they might've been claimed to be conceived on days they weren't supposed to be. However with royalty and nobility, sons were in high demand so those women were not inclined to abort potential sons. In their case they could simply say a baby was "born prematurely" and everyone would agree because surely the royalty and nobility could never have had sex on days which Christianity forbid it. Since the peasants didn't surely the royals and rich could never have. Thus the Christian rules forbidding marital sexual activity has actually influenced medical records and the way history was written, making many normal births recorded as premature births in order to prevent religious scandal. Yet the worse thing about this is that since every week had days which Christians were forbidden to have sex, for those women who did have sex and then gave birth they would be under immense psychological pressure when giving birth knowing that their child might've resulted from sinful sex that occured on a forbidden day. Due to this stress women would suffer miscarriages or die while giving birth, because of the anxiety of believing their marital sex was sinful because of what Christianity taught in their time. Why not just use birth control? Well the bible specifically says in Genesis 38:8-10 that God killed a guy called Onan who pulled out and spilt his seed in the soil when he didn't want to impregnate his widowed sister in-law which he was having sex with. Don't get the wrong idea biblically God told Judah to tell Onan to get his widowed sister-in-law pregnant and that was the legal protocol which all guys were supposed to do if they had a widowed sister-in-law. So as a result of this guys were afraid of birth control lest it make God kill them, as the bible says it did before and that's also one reason why masturbation is forbidden according to Christianity and the bible as well. Today what is portrayed as "safe sex" was "Sinful deadly sex" back then. Modern devout Christians still fear birth control for the same biblical reason. Most Christians will like to think that the Christian rules forbidding marital sex on certain days, sex for fun, or kissing must not be in effect today because the preachers never preach it to them, so they incorrectly assume the Christian rules of marital relations have changed. I won't bother to prove them wrong, since most have already made up their mind before even reading this and I doubt many Christians would eliminate intimacy from their marital lives even if they were given proof that Christians can't have it. They'll just say "regardless the modern rules are different ". But if it's a true religion how can it change again and again with new rules being constantly updated and abrogated forever? Seems like with every new pope Catholicism becomes a new religion and every century creates a different Christianity. Is God playing a game saying *"now you can, now you can't, now you can, now you can't, now you can"*? That seems more like Satan's style. If the past pope was wrong to ban or allow something and then a pope after him says the opposite then clearly this can't be an infallible office whose holder is never wrong because the popes are contradicting each other. Oh and for the record so that you don't get misconceptions, the Muslim religion of Islam encourages married spouses to be intimate and does not forbid kissing, touching or having sex, even if it's for non-procreative reasons. Islam even permits coitus interruptus, which is what Onan tried before he biblically died, (the spilling the seed part, not the sister-in law part) although Islam does teach that there is a time and a place for sexual activities which should only be done by people who have a certain special type of relationship. Sexually speaking Christians considered Islam to be too liberal until only recently this last century, when the sexual revolution erupted in response to thousands of years of sexual repression. Once Church and State where separated Christians separated the Church and their Bedroom. Ironically people think Catholic priests are extreme for celibacy, but within marriage Christianity itself is one of, if not the most, sexually restrictive religions of all. As the english New International bible teaches in 1 Corinthians 7:29, *"What I mean, brothers and sisters, is that the time is short.* ***From now on*** *__those who have__* ***wives*** *__should live as if they do not__"*. Now I'll admit I didn't quote the full context, because it's a lengthy context. In full biblical context Paul wrote that the end of the world was coming so soon that if people weren't engaged to be married then they shouldn't get married and that if they were already married they should act like they weren't, with the bulk of the context dealing with the question of what a person should do who is engaged to get married. This was because Paul taught Christians they were living in the "last days" and the end of the world was so near that early Christians seriously wondered whether they should even bother to get married since they thought the world would end so soon. I also mention this because it shows Paul in the New Testament of the bible mentioning married Christians having "wive__s__", meaning early Christian men had more than one wife and Paul taught there was nothing wrong with that. But then again Christianity's idea of a wife and marital relations doesn't quite qualify as what we'd consider a marriage today, since intimacy was seen as a shameful/sinful necessity of human breeding. Unfortunately this extremely unnatural anti-sexual attitude led to the extremely unnatural pro-sexual attitude plaguing us today. Although sadly with most folk that's usually how sex goes, it's either not enough or too much. That's why this lengthy "*Battle of the Sexes*" is really just Satan preventing humans from having the healthy natural moral sex life which our Creator would like for us.

      In 1869 CE that same Pope Pius IX who was previously mentioned (the one who hated democracy, freedom of speech and religion) called for the first Vatican Council to discuss papal infallibility. Prior to this no pope was defined as infallible, which means "never wrong", Jesuits had preached this doctrine since 1540 CE but it was always considered a fringe doctrine. Despite Pius IX hating democracy it was eventually put to a vote on July 13, 1870 CE. Out of 1,000 bishops only 451 voted that the pope was infallible, 88 voted against infallibility, 62 voted in favor with conditions, while 399 abstained. (Maybe that's why he didn't like democracy?) After exerting political and unchristian like pressure which was applied during the next few days, resulting in 2 dissenters actually leaving Rome, on June 18, 1870 CE it was decided by a vote of 433 to 2 that the Pope was infallible when defining a doctrine concerning faith or morals. This was less votes for him than the first time, but also less against. The Catholic belief in infallibility has only existed since 1870 CE and it only passed as a result of 433/1000 votes in favor of which 565 bishops didn't vote. Although if the Pope truly was infallible to begin with why was it even put to a vote? Also why did it pass without a majority when there were even less in favor of infallibility during the second vote than the first? The papal decree said: "*The Roman Pontiff, when he speaks ex cathedra, that is , when, exercising the office of pastor and teacher of all Christians, he defines...a doctrine concerning faith and morals to be held by the whole Church, through the divine assistance promised to him in St. Peter, is possessed of that infallibility with which the Divine Redeemer wished His Church to be endowed...and therefore such definitions of the Roman Pontiff are irreformable of themselves, and not from the consent of the Church.*" The parts I underlined mean that when one Pope makes a ruling it is set in stone and even if the entire Church wants to change the ruling at a later time they are not allowed to.(Meaning those rules forbidding sex and kissing can never be changed.) Thus every Pope must agree with every position the previous Popes held, according to the decree of infallibility. Recently Pope Benedict XVI retired instead of remaining Pope until death as is the standard. I had desired to be the Pope and studied the position in depth preparing for the job, his retirement is unprecedented and according to traditional Catholic dogma impermissible. Although loopholes were created in the 1900s CE, traditionally the only way a Pope could leave office was by death. I will skip the history of anti-popes, coerced resignations, Benedict IX openly selling the papacy to Gregory VI and Pope Pontian who resigned after being arrested, because a case can be made to support papal retirement if one wills to make it. Yet typically all the Popes who had resigned before death did so in unusual circumstances, not for "health reasons". (aka Germany threatening to arrest him for knowingly assisting and covering up for pedophile priests while acting as Cardinal in Germany) What I'm interested to know is when Benedict XVI dies will he be given a papal burial, which involves people kissing the dead Pope's feet, or not because he retired from being Pope? Also since the personal apartment of the Pope is sealed so it can never be used again will Benedict XVI's dwelling get permanantly sealed when he dies despite no longer being the Pope. Another thing I wonder is whether the tradition of the Cardinal Camerlango gently hitting the dead Pope's forehead 3 times with a silver hammer, to make sure he's dead, will happen with Benedict XVI. Although the last 2 popes who died (John Paul I and John Paul II) didn't have this tradition of a Cardinal hitting their head with a hammer take place. But these traditions do raise questions about Pope Francis' claim to want to return to a poor modest church. Does that mean he will end the traditional sealing of the Pope's apartment, get rid of all the papal jewelry and the silver hammer used solely to check if Pope's are dead? Thus far Pope Francis seems to do a lot of talking without any real reforms aside from dilution of hardline Catholic dogmas that are unpalatable to the secular masses. Basically the current Pope knows how to talk the talk the media likes to hear and he's doing a pretty eloquent job of it. If Pope Benedict XVI was infallible(never wrong) as Pope, now that he has resigned and there is a new Pope Francis who thinks himself infallible(never wrong) is the former Pope Benedict XVI still infallible even though he is no longer the Pope? He wasn't considered infallible before being Pope, so if he is not considered infallible after being Pope then it's impossible for him to have been infallible in between when he was serving as Pope. Because if you ever reach a state where you are "never wrong" that doesn't just go away simply because you quit your job. It is hypocritical to say that when he was Pope he could never be wrong but now that he's no longer Pope he's a human again who can err. This reveals that the office of Pope actually claims to have the powers of prophets pbut in matters of religion, however the infallibility of prophets lasted till they died they never became senile and in no way did they stop being prophets once they started to physically diminish. If the former Pope Benedict XVI can be wrong now then he could have been wrong before. If it is maintained that he retains his infallibility then what does one make of the fact that his successor contradicts him, despite both of them claiming to have been inspired by God as Pope? The Popes' contradicting their predecessors also contradicts the decree that created the belief in infallibility that states all Papal rulings are final and cannot be changed even by future Popes. There exists the famous case in the 9th century CE when Pope Stephen VII put the dead body of his predecessor Pope Formosus on trial and convicted him of heresy, after which the corpse of Pope Formosus was thrown in the river naked. This grisly incident sets the precedence of Popes contradicting the Popes who came before them, or in this case condemning them as heretics after their death. While one of those famous popes who "resigned", Pope Celestine V had every single offical act he made repudiated by his successor Boniface VIII. Pope Boniface VIII then imprisoned the previous Pope Celestine V in a castle where he died shortly afterwards. Whereas Celestine V is not even considered to be an anti-pope(2 people are chosen to be pope at the same time with each saying the other is illegitimate).   He was/is an officially recognized Pope and "Saint", who had every single act, except his resignation, overturned by the guy who was Pope after him. Essentially Pope Celestine V in the eyes of the Catholic Church was the opposite of being infallible (never wrong) but was always wrong except when he decided to quit. The next Pope said quitting was the only right thing Celestine V did as Pope. Since Popes in the past also convicted previous Popes as heretics then that breaks the apostolic chain which is the very basis for the claim of infallibility. Whereas the alleged apostolic chain isn't valid either because of how popes were selected. Today the Pope becomes Pope by the mutual selection of a group of elite Cardinals voting amongst themselves who should become Pope, known as the papal conclave. Whereas the Cardinals become Cardinals via the appointment of a Pope. It's basically like the President picking who the candidates are and who gets to vote in the presidential election for his successor. Thus since Catholics claim Jesus pbuh picked Peter to be the first Pope and based on the current system the Pope picks those who pick the next Pope, they believe their Popes are guaranteed to be the ones Jesus pbuh/God wants because he apparently picked the first and started the chain. However initially the Pope(known as the Bishop of Rome) was selected via a local election in which every Catholic in the diocese voted for who they wanted to be Pope. Anyone in the Roman diocese(county) could run for Pope and every Catholic got a vote, but only those who lived in the Roman dicocese were elligible to be Pope or could vote. It wasn't until 759 CE that the Roman Synod declared the Pope could only be chosen from deacons and Cardinal priests. In 1059 CE the rules were changed to say only Cardinals could get elected. While it wasn't until 1179 CE when the 3rd Lateran Council changed the rules to say only Cardinals could vote in the election. Even the very place the Pope lives has changed, Popes used to run the show from the Lateran Palace, then Avignon in France until finally setting up shop at the Vatican in 1377 CE where they have remained until this day. It was actually the expensive costs of building the Vatican that led the Catholic Church to start selling indulgences which sparked the Protestant Reformation. Many think Popes have always lived in the Vatican since the days of Peter, but the Catholic Church didn't even get the land the Vatican was built on until 313 CE and Peter wasn't even considered to be the first Pope until the 4th century CE, so the apostolic chain is missing quite a few of the early links. The alleged apostolic papal chain is also mythical because of the 2 year period between 1292-1294 CE when there was no Pope because the college of cardinals <u>couldn't agree on which of them it shouldn't be</u>. There were other times when papal conclaves couldn't elect a pope, such as between 1314-1316 CE, however from 1292-1294 CE they basically said "nobody is qualified to fit the job description of Pope". Eventually they had to pick somebody so they pretended the winner was qualified and the apostolic chain existed because otherwise nobody would listen to the popes if they knew that religiously none of them actually are what Catholic doctrines say popes are supposed to be; which most lay-Catholics believe. On the face of it how can there be an "apostolic chain" when the popes denounce and contradict their predecessors? That's like claiming to be a 100% human but saying your biological forefathers were aliens and animals. Prophets on the other hand never contradicted or denounced each other, rather they confirmed the message of those who came before them. As Matthew 5:17-19 has Jesus pbuh say:

"***<u>Do not think that I have come to abolish the Law or the Prophets; I have not come to abolish them</u>*** *but to fulfill them. ¹⁸ For <u>truly I tell you, **until heaven and earth disappear**, not the smallest letter, not the least stroke of a pen, will by any means disappear from the Law until **everything** is accomplished</u>. ¹⁹ Therefore anyone who sets aside one of the least of these commands and teaches others accordingly will be called least in the kingdom of heaven, but whoever practices and teaches these commands will be called great in the kingdom of heaven."*

Then after Jesus pbuh heals a leper he puts what he preached into practice by telling the man to offer sacrifices in order to purify himself according to the law of Moses pbuh as the biblical account in Mark 1:39-44 says:

*"So <u>he traveled throughout Galilee, preaching in their synagogues</u> and driving out demons. ⁴⁰ <u>A man with leprosy came to him and begged him on his knees, "If you are willing, you can make me clean." ⁴¹ **Jesus was indignant.**</u> He reached out his hand and touched the man. "I am willing," he said. "Be clean!" ⁴² Immediately the leprosy left him and he was cleansed. ⁴³ **<u>Jesus sent him away at once with a strong warning</u>**: ⁴⁴ <u>"See that you don't tell this to anyone. But go, show yourself to the priest and **offer the sacrifices that Moses commanded for your cleansing**</u>, as a testimony to them."*

Based on these verses I understood that all the prophets were on the same team, working for the same boss, following the same rules. I decided to follow both the Old Testament and the New Testament. Whatever the bible said to do I would try to do, whatever the bible said not to do I tried not to do. Thereafter I started reading the bible nightly and going to bible study classes with my mother and uncle. Coincidentally the son of the Lebanese male bible study teacher also wanted to be the president of the United States for the same reason I once did. It just doesn't make sense that if the bible is the word of God the first half isn't applicable. Unfortunately many Christians today have the attitude that the books of the Old Testament are just history books with their commands and prohibitions not being applicable today, despite the New Testament instructing its readers to follow the previous laws to the "tittle" or as the New International Version translates it as "the least stroke of a pen". A tittle is the dot placed on a letter such as the english letter "i". A "tittle" isn't necessary for a letter's identity or meaning to be known, so to say not even "one tittle" shall pass from the law, as many bibles say, means that not even the pronunciation or language of the law will change let alone the understanding and application of the law. Elsewhere the bible says that Jesus pbuh said whoever is less righteous than the Pharisees will not enter heaven. Although in Matthew 5:19 it says those who set aside even one of the "least of these commands" and teaches others that even one of the "least of the commands of the Law" don't have to be followed will be "called least in the Kingdom of Heaven". Now many people misunderstand this thinking that such people will just be in low ranks in paradise, but that's not what it says. The kingdom of Heaven is the setting in which they will be called "the least" it doesn't say they will be there. In paradise people will talk about those in hellfire and be glad they aren't with them. That's what this verse refers to. Being called "the least" is like being called "the worst" or "the lowest of the low", "the one who got the least pleasurable experience imaginable" or "the least out of their lease on life". Meaning they wasted their life and were the least they could've potentially been, they literally did the least that a human could possibly do in living how God commanded in life and they're punished as a result of their negligence and disobedience. Especially since they not only didn't do all they were told but because they taught others not to follow the rules as well, thus they are even worse than those who they misguided. Jesus pbuh taught that anyone who ignores even the smallest and least significant command of the Law(aka the "small stuff") and teaches others accordingly will be in hellfire and mocked by those in paradise. This is because Jesus pbuh taught the law so to teach that any of the law or the prophets don't have to be followed is to actually teach a different religion than what the prophets taught, which would mean disbelief in the religion of the prophets and a corruption of the true religion. The reason biblical Jesus pbuh said this the way he said it was to take advantage of people's sense of pride and peer pressure. It's one thing to say "If you don't do X and do Z you will be going to hell", it's a whole other thing to say "If you don't do X and do Z those in paradise will be making fun of you and calling you undesirable names." Whereas those who do practice and teach others to practice the commands(meaning all 100% of the Law) will be called great in paradise. You can be certain when those in paradise call those people great, those people are definitely in paradise. If you notice the word people isn't used, this is because it's not just people in paradise who will be referring to the disobedient ones negatively and the obedient ones positively, there will be angels and God and others in paradise as well. Jesus pbuh basically taught that everything in paradise is going to be talking about you, they will either say this or that depending on whether you live this way or that way. Thus we are given the choice and informed of the results our choice will have. Also the bible says Jesus pbuh said that till heaven and earth pass nothing from the law will pass till all be fulfilled. Meaning according to the biblical Jesus pbuh, the law will not change until the earth is gone, so since earth is still around that means the law is in effect, according to the bible. There is no instruction manual in the world that says to ignore its first half or that the bulk of the rules contained therein are not supposed to be followed. It is irrational and extremely dangerous to think God would send a book to mankind and say, "*you don't have to pay attention to any of the rules I said to follow in the hundreds of pages before these last few pages.*", that is exactly what Satan would want us to think, especially when those last few pages of that book sternly say: "*not the smallest letter, not the least stroke of a pen, will by any means disappear from the Law*". Afterall Jesus pbuh wouldn't have spent his life teaching people the Law if his later actions were to then abolish the very Law he spent his life teaching people to follow. No prophet's death has ever been thought to nullify their life's work/mission. A prophet's death is just the end of their life, not the end of their teachings relevance.

AGES 17-19

After turning 17 my focus shifted towards starting my rap career, hoping to get support from friends who would be graduating that year who had plans to sell drugs for the rest of their life. My plan was to shift their career field to the music industry and work together. At this point the importance and scarcity of time was finally understood and I had to choose whether to spend my free time playing video games or working on my rap career. Rapping became my priority and the videogames were put away giving me a tremendous amount of time and energy, increasing my maturity level and emotional stability as well as altering my perspective on life. My idea was that you can either spend your life pretending to be someone else (playing a videogame) or you can become someone who has a life that's as enjoyable as a videogame, who other people might even base a videogame on. Either play the game or live as the player. Rather than play as many fictional heroes I choose to live as one real hero. Despite the sports videogame commercials you might see showing athletes playing a certain videogame from youth, in reality they didn't get to the big leagues playing videogames, they were living the game so they could play professionally. I made the choice to make my real life better than my virtual life eliminating the desire to escape my real life via virtual life. After all, what can be expected from someone who is secluded in one of the corners of a room with their eyes fixated at a small screen that shines with various bright and moving colors for continuous hours on end? Consider how their hands are holding onto a small controller shaking every time the controller shakes, they move their hands with anger frantically pressing the buttons of various colors and sizes. The ears intently listening to electronic sounds, screams and beats that are quiet at some moments, but loud at other moments in order to captivate and control the one in front of it; causing the player to be unable to hear or understand anything around them except for the game. I wasn't playing the playstation, the playstation was playing me. Older people have a saying to "*think outside the box*", referring to the TV which they also call the "idiot box". Today many people are enslaved to the new "idiot box" known as XBOX, needing to play it at least 360 days a year. I stopped playing games and got serious about doing something with my life. All the worthless virtual "trophies" and "achievements" were preventing me from having any real achievements. Today I regret the time I wasted on imagined interactive videogames. All those "high scores" and memories have no worth. The momentary pleasure has passed and my past indulgence was foolish adding no value to my life. In hindsight they caused me to become aggressive, isolated, selfishly focused on fulfilling my own desires, anti-social, isolated, lethargic and damaged my ability to cope with the realities of life. Every time I played videogames I effectively paused my real life and invested in a pretend life which will not benefit me on the Day of Judgment. God did not create me so I could play as someone/something else in a virtual fantasy world. Likewise everytime a gamer "creates their character" they are in very dangerous sense "playing God" by creating animate beings or worlds. By "role-playing" as God to a greater or lesser extent, as each game differs, this is almost like taking away the rights of God as a Creator. It makes one have less respect for the Creator of the Universe if you can also create things in virtual reality, especially things that seem life-like and real. The customization tools gamers are given denigrate the creation abilities of our real Creator. Satan must have been laughing at me the whole time I was playing videogames. Whereas with the recent invention of virtual reality videogames the consequences will be more disastrous and will truly result in a fantasy epidemic that will create split personalities, new mental diseases and social calamities stunting individual humans' development perhaps by decades, making the new age of maturity be thought of as 30 or even later than 30 instead of what it currently is. Life isn't a game! Videogames are not a part of anyone's life, they are an interruption of real life and a wasteful unhealthy alternative to life where the harms outweigh the benefits in the short-term, mid-term, long-term and the afterlife. Satan wants people to avoid doing good deeds and avoid reforming themselves and the real world, but rather than tell people to not do good deeds and avoid evil deeds he just gives them games to play. Gamers aren't using the controllers to play a game, Satan uses the game controllers to control the gamers. People trade their real life and afterlife for a petty virtual life. Satan doesn't need to buy a soul anymore people play games practically with religious devotion. Gaming is like worshipping in a very real sense given that it is indulgence and involves all the same types of actions which worship does. It takes time, energy, concentration, money etc. Some even love their videogame consoles as if it were an altar. Everyday almost ritualistically many go to it not to pray but simply to play. I'm not saying gamers disbelieve in God but many gamers are dangerously addicted to gaming and videogames have the same type of role religion has for others. Entertainment, in various forms, is the religion of the masses.

Religion remained at the center of my life and rap was merely a way to augment the religious aspect and promote Christianity. The life plan was to be a rapping Catholic priest, with the publicity promoting the Church and opening the doors for me to reach higher positions in the Catholic hierarchy. I went from virtual games to religious/political games, all thanks and praises be to God that I have been guided to better things. Today you're not allowed to enter a seminary in order to become a priest directly after high school, in the past you could. While researching colleges I found one which had a pre-seminary program for people like me who wanted to become a Catholic priest. If enrolled I would live with other future seminarians on a college campus in a church/seminary and take religious courses at the college for four years until graduating with a religious degree, after which I would enter a seminary for 6 years and leave as an ordained priest. Studying for the SAT and ACT (tests colleges use to base acceptance on) only multiplied the ongoing stress in the home, which further fractured my family relationship. Today those tests and their results, which seemed so important, don't even matter to me and they are completely frivolous. Which is also how we will feel and think about most of the test of life when we finish it. In school you think every problem, worry and desire is so important but when you are done with school you realize none of what you thought was important really mattered. Likewise for the majority of us our priorities in life will be seen as even less important in the afterlife than our past concerns we had when living life in school are after school. When applying for the seminary college program, a reference letter from the pastor of my church was required, which I've included scans of both pages to prove that what I've written isn't fiction. This is documentary evidence of what my Catholic Pastor said about me to other priests in 2009 CE:

ST. PIUS X R C CHURCH SOCIETY OF AMHERST NY
1700 NORTH FRENCH ROAD
P O BOX 162
GETZVILLE, NEW YORK 14068-0162

February 25, 2009

St. Mark's Seminary
Gannon University
Erie PA

Dear Sir:

    I am pleased to write this letter on behalf of Gregory Alan Heary, who will be a senior in the fall of 2009 at North Tonawanda Senior High School in North Tonawanda, New York.

    He was baptized, made his Reconciliation, Holy Communion and was confirmed here at St. Pius X. I have known Gregory to be an outstanding Catholic young gentleman and a most co-operative individual. He is a task oriented industrious lad as is evidenced by his involvement in the total school community. He was part of the Youth Court, acting as a judge, prosecutor and a defense attorney. Gregory received an excellent attendance award, academic achievement award in math for grade 9 and a Certificate of Recognition for scoring in the top 23 percentile on a nationwide financial literary test. He is a member of the National Academy of Finance, high school band, National Honor Society, Tri-M-Honor Society, St. Joseph's Club, freshman football, high school tennis team and the Boy Scouts of America

    Over the summers of 2001 – 2003, he participated in Vacation Bible School at St. Pius X Church. During the Lenten Season of 2005 – 2006, he served at the Stations of the Cross. In 2006 – 2007 and 2007 – 2008, he was a teacher's aid for the third grade communion class. He became a full time religious education teacher for the fifth grade.

    In my relationship with Gregory, he has shown that he possesses critical thought and Christian humanistic attitudes, which I am sure are qualities derived from his fine family background.

> Gregory has an intense interest in attending your institution and I am sure his presence on your campus will prove to be of mutual benefit. Your favorable consideration of his application will be greatly appreciated.
>
> Asking God's blessings upon you and your good work, I remain
>
> Sincerely yours in Christ,
>
> *Rev. Msgr. George B Yiengst*
>
> Rev. Msgr. George B Yiengst
> Pastor
>
> GBY/msw

My grades remained more or less steady not jeopardizing my future. The chaos at home was left inside the home. The outside world was clueless about the discord between my family and me, except for the people who I considered friends. After I asked these "friends" for permission to live with them in order to escape the ordeals of my own household it became clear I had misunderstood the nature of the many relationships that I mistakenly thought were "friendships". As a result I angrily ended some of these "friendships" which were superficial and disingenuous. By the end of the 11th grade police were getting involved with the worsening domestic situation and one incident resulted with the police coming to my house attempting to resolve a dispute between myself and my parents. This first interaction took place on the night of the first day of my two day written English exam, instead of studying I was "interacting" with the police that night. It was quite a first experience, one which most of my classmates didn't believe happened since I was an A student who wanted to be a priest it didn't mesh into their stereotypical view of the world. Being home for the summer gave my parents and I more time to fight each other and I ended up liking school again only for the reason that it wasn't home. I would spend many days walking the streets to avoid or escape from a fight at home. The day before my last year of high school began, a turning point took place which accelerated my descent. Following another fight, I had left the house and for the first time in my life seriously contemplated using the drugs so often recommended by my peers knowing that I could easily get intoxicated at the nearby house of a friend. After considering how it would affect my relationship with God I concluded that drugs would only make my problems worse, because even if I didn't get caught my body and mind would be damaged. Drugs would be just another form of escape from reality that I'd end up regretting rather than a solution. Satan is always trying to get us to sin especially when we are stressed. I turned around to walk back home thinking the dust had cleared when a police car pulled over and officers got out saying my name, I was told they knew who I was and they started asking me intrusive questions. The police said they were called and informed that I had weapons and was going to hurt myself or others and were coming to stop me. After the police searched me they realized I had nothing dangerous. Then when I wanted to finish the few hundred yards to my house on foot they refused to let me walk home and "offered" me a ride. While not getting handcuffed, being dropped off at home by a police car undoubtedly had an effect on how the neighbors viewed me; keeping in mind that my maternal grandparents lived next door and my uncle and cousins adjacent on the other side of them. It turns out my parents had only called the police out of worry for me because they didn't know when I'd be back or where I was. My parents told me they never said anything about weapons or concerns of me hurting myself or others. This means somewhere in the chain of the police information stream lies were being inserted and viewed as the truth, affecting their judgments and actions when dealing with me. One particular police officer (who also worked in the high school during the day as a security guard) threatened me with criminal charges and jail if I didn't do "voluntary" family counseling with a specific therapist that the police force had success with in the past. Needless to say when police tell you to see a specific therapist or they will throw you in jail, you tend not to "work" with the recommended therapist wholeheartedly. The best decision I made that day was to not take drugs. I've never met anyone who regretted abstaining from drugs, they cause nothing but more problems. Doing drugs is comparable to someone trying to lose weight who indulges with junk food, they might enjoy the junk food for a while but after the fun they'll have more weight to lose than before and bad health as well. Numerous domestic incidents would happen throughout the year, typically on weekends with many conflicts revolving around me wanting to watch the New Orleans Saints play football which turned into a major form of leverage utilized by my parents to get me to do chores, once permission was granted the privilege would be taken away midgame for the smallest of reasons ensuing in a battle royal with the police showing up to be referee. The city police force soon stereotyped me and would use their previous reports and instances of having been called before as a proof that I must be troublesome. They had no grasp of the situation and would simplify it, reading every scenario as a 17 year old boy who hates his parents with repeated police visits to the house before, he must be really bad. The police persistently ignored the fact that no charges were ever made nor were any handcuffs or force ever used on/against me, yet they treated me as a violent criminal just the same.

    When my last year of high school finally began I had a new look. In preparation for my rap career it naturally made sense to start dressing the part because clothing is a form of expressing yourself. Until then most of my clothes and everything else was paid for by my parents, but now I started paying for some of my own clothes and bought jewelry for extra flash. Automatically classmates started labeling me as a gangster assuming that because I was wearing hip hop clothing it must be some criminal uniform, completely forgetting they had known about my passion for hip hop for years. Derogatory comments from my classmates started the moment I stopped caring about pleasing the crowd, perhaps out of the jealousy they had for lacking the courage not to conform. Wearing different clothes didn't only cause others to treat me differently, it also caused me to act in a different fashion as well.

In 12th grade I took the mandatory high school health class. The bulk of it was ok and I learned beneficial things about my body and how to take care of it properly, however one day there was a major problem. The teacher was discussing sex and making comments such as, *"Sex makes those who do it look more beautiful by making acne disappear and creating a youthful appearance, trouble is ugly people can't get any"*. I let that comment slide despite the obvious promotion of fornication and insult to virginity/abstinence out of fear for being labeled as ugly if I opposed promiscuity, especially since I had acne. Most high school kids take this class in their first or second year and are taught this when they are 14 or 15 years old. Later in the same class the teacher started talking about masturbation, encouraging people to do it citing alleged medical benefits. I couldn't believe my ears and was furious. For 4 years I had been going to this school telling my peers why they should stop masturbating because it's sinful and bad, then I discover this teacher had been telling them to do it saying it's healthy the whole time! For 4 years I had been saying "NO" and this guy had been saying "YES", and on top of that this teacher tells me to masturbate straight to my face! That might have been my most aggravating moment in high school. After hearing this being taught I told him in front of the class that he is wrong and shouldn't say that. Masturbation is addictive and inhibits the brain's functionality damaging the neural nets which control dopamine flow. (Which is a chemical released in the body that makes us feel happy.) Masturbation is also extremely unhealthy on all levels: physically, mentally, emotionally and most important spiritually. There are organizations such as Sexaholics Anonymous (S.A.) or Sex Addicts Anonymous (S.A.A.) which include members who have lost their jobs, friends, families, marriages, children, reputations and health just because of their masturbation or pornography addictions; let alone the sexual diseases and crimes it leads to. There is even a famous person who unintentionally gave themselves herpes as a result of their unorthodox masturbation method. On the internet there are a plethora of websites devoted to helping people overcome the drug of pornography and the addiction of masturbation, I was going to include some but there are so many out there it's unjust to choose. There are probably more porn/masturbation addiction recovery sites than there are stadiums for sporting events. It is a plague on society that has led to decreased: self-esteem, intelligence, respect, morality, honesty, happiness and humanity while damaging the family unit, desensitizing us to even greater evils and increasing depression, anxiety, sexual crimes, abuse and harassment with the total amount or extent of the negative consequences of masturbation being incalculable.

In the animal kingdom an ape in "esturn"(lust, sexual heat) will starve or kill until it has satisfied its sexual desire. A human does not place its sexual desires above its own life. Many myths and scientific contradictions are used to promote the fantasy that says man evolved from apes which the scientific community has refuted and proven false. This theory of evolution treats humans like animals and fosters a monoculture of consumerism. A society that views humans as animals will not have morals or justice. If a monkey is sad the theory is to give it a banana and it will be happy, with children being trained they evolved from monkeys they use the same solution. Businesses then treat humans as beasts persuading us that the next "new banana", or apple product, will make us happy and solve all our problems because they have been subconsciously taught to view humans as an advanced ape. If man evolved from a shared ancestor of apes then sexual reproduction between man and today's species of primates would be possible, and if it were possible there would still be a species of ape interbreeding with man today resulting in half-man half-ape offspring and mating cycles. Fossils of the skeletons of such half-man half-monkey transitional creatures would exist, but not one has ever been found, nor will any ever be found because such a thing never existed and evolution is a false doctrine. DNA has an intricate complex structure, random changes would only result in harmful effects, never positive. Forget comic books, it is a scientific fact that mutations do not cause living beings to develop or advance, every mutation has always been harmful and hindered the mutant's ability to survive. *"Natural Selection"* is actually natural elimination in that it proposes traits were eliminated because *"only the fittest survive to reproduce"*, it does not promote in any way the idea that mutations took place or were beneficial in any way. This is a widespread misunderstanding prevalent throughout society. Natural Selection, or natural elimination as I call it, cannot lead to animals evolving or transforming themselves for the better, all it does it remove the weakest, it does not make the strong stronger. Reproduction dilutes the original gene pool and the offspring are genetically weaker than their ancestors, this is evident because humans use to be much taller than we are today and we have continually grown shorter as a species. In school they didn't teach us the full reality of exactly what Charles Darwin's evolution theory was. He taught that antelopes became giraffes by eating leaves from high branches and that bears who ate fish became whales. His whole theory of different bird beaks being more efficient than others doesn't in the slightest bit provide any evidence for "natural selection". Obviously different birds with different beaks will have different levels of efficiency when doing the same task, that's because they're different and not equal, neither do they live equal lifestyles nor do they need or desire equal things. On the face of it Darwin's teachings when taken all together in full context are ridiculous. I'm confident that no respectable person in the scientific community actually believes Darwin's teaching that some bears became whales because they ate fish. According to science the theory of evolution is not scientific because it has never been observed, whereas science is based on observations and theories, theories alone do not count as science they are just opinions. To believe in the evolution theory, which inherently remains an unproven theory, actually requires more faith than it does to believe in creationism. To believe that everything just evolved by accidental coincidence through time goes against the scientific "law" of the conservation of energy. The theory of evolution is not based on the scientific method and is illogical. Darwin is correct about the continents at one time being together, but he is wrong about his theory of evolution and natural selection. Even the name "natural selection" is unsuitable, because in nature there are unnatural occurrences that affect survival and reproduction. To postulate that everything is following a natural course is to deny reality, in the real world unexpected and unnatural things frequently occur. Unfortunately the average science teacher teaching children doesn't fully research the science or scientists that they teach about, oftentimes taking for granted what the school textbooks tell them to teach as being true. For instance Charles Darwin married his first cousin Emma, so when he postulates "natural selection" one must keep in mind how in 1839 CE this guy figured his cousin was the most fit for him to get married to and have 10 kids with. Also naturally the reverend who officiated the wedding between Charles and his cousin also happened to be one of their cousins named John. It was a "family wedding" in the fullest sense. 30% of Darwin's kids died young though, so who knows maybe they just "weren't fit enough" for some reason this "scientist" didn't know of. Yet while many have heard of Darwin's 1859 book "*On the Origin of Species*", few are aware of Darwin's 1871 book "*The Descent of Man, and Selection in Relation to Sex*". In this book Darwin claimed that human character traits and mental characteristics are inherited the same as physical characteristics, and he argues against the mind/body distinction for the purposes of evolutionary theory. Meaning Darwin taught that your intelligence, emotional temperment, moral character and even your personal beliefs are determined the exact same way as your eye color or hair color. Darwin then provided "evidence" for similar mental powers and characteristics in animals to support his analogies for love, cleverness, religion, kindness, and altruism. Darwin taught that everything that you think is unique to humans is actually just a higher degree of animalism and that animals can become just as "civilized" as we are but they are just developing slower because they are less fit due to being lower down on the food chain. Given enough time to develop, it was thought all animals will go extinct and become humans. To prove this he pointed to "savages" found in Africa, Asia, Austrailia etc. as an interbreed somewhere between what is commonly referred to as animals and humans. Darwin nearly considered the food chain to be a corporate business ladder which a species can ascend or descend if their generations do well or poorly. This is an excerpt from Chapter 5 in Darwin's book that you won't find in school textbooks, "*With savages, the weak in body or mind are soon eliminated; and those that survive commonly exhibit a vigorous state of health. <u>We civilised men, on the other hand, do our utmost to check the process of elimination; we build asylums for the imbecile, the maimed, and the sick; we institute poor-laws; and our medical men exert their utmost skill to save the life of every one to the last moment.</u> There is reason to believe that vaccination has preserved thousands, who from a weak constitution would formerly have succumbed to small-pox. Thus the weak members of civilised societies propagate their kind. **<u>No one who has attended to the breeding of domestic animals will doubt that this must be highly injurious to the race of man.</u>** <u>It is surprising how soon a want of care, or care wrongly directed, leads to the degeneration of a domestic race; but excepting in the case of man himself, hardly any one is so ignorant as to allow his worst animals to breed.</u> The aid we feel impelled to give to the helpless is mainly an incidental result of the instinct of sympathy, which was originally acquired as part of the social instincts, but subsequently rendered, in the manner previously indicated, more tender and more widely diffused. Nor could we check our sympathy, even at the urging of hard reason, without deterioration in the noblest part of our nature. The surgeon may harden himself whilst performing an operation, for he knows that he is acting for the good of his patient; but <u>**if we were intentionally to neglect the weak and helpless, it could only be for a contingent benefit**</u>, with an overwhelming present evil. **<u>We must therefore bear the undoubtedly bad effects of the weak surviving and propagating their kind</u>**; but there appears to be at least one check in steady action, namely that the weaker and inferior members of society do not marry so freely as the sound; and this check might be indefinitely increased by the weak in body or mind refraining from marriage, though this is more to be hoped for than expected.*" As if that weren't bad enough Darwin actually taught that originally all humans were the same color but different skin colors exist today because some humans devolved and turned into various subspecies, you know basically everyone but the white man was a sub-human according to Darwin. Although they could possibly turn white again if they breeded the correct way amongst their own color, although they could also eventually turn into animals no longer even recognizable as once having been humans if they breeded with the weak sub-humans amongst their own colors. However being the distinguished scientist that Charles Darwin was, he realistically didn't imagine the other colors of humans would evolve into the white man or devolve into animals. Instead his scientific research led him to the following conclusion: *"The great break in the organic chain between man and his nearest allies, which cannot be bridged over by any extinct or living species, has often been advanced as a grave objection to the belief that man is descended from some lower form; but this objection will not appear of much weight to those who, convinced by general reasons, believe in the general principle of evolution. Breaks incessantly occur in all parts of the series, some being wide, sharp and defined, others less so in various degrees; as between the orang and its nearest allies – between the Tarsius and the other Lemuridæ – between the elephant and in a more striking manner between the Ornithorhynchus or Echidna, and other mammals. But* **_all these breaks depend merely on the number of related forms that have become extinct. At some future point, not distant as measured by centuries, the civilised races of man will almost certainly exterminate and replace the savage races throughout the world._** *At the same time the anthropomorphous apes, as Professor Schaaffhausen has remarked, will no doubt be exterminated. The break will then be rendered wider, for it will intervene between man in a more civilised state, as we may hope, than the Caucasian, and some ape as low as a baboon, instead of as at present between the negro or Australian and the gorilla."* So for Darwin the Caucasian (white man) wasn't really the best humans could be, they could evolve into a much better species than the white man, but at his junction in the timeline the white man just so happened to be the best this planet has ever seen. Whereas scientifically as the white man evolves Darwin taught that the negros (black people) and Austrailians (aborigines) would go extinct, just "naturally" because they are scientifically not fit enough to survive and slavery was the main reason such sub-humans hadn't gone extinct even earlier. Thus with slavery abolished Darwin was certain that the Negro would go extinct and thereby prove his theory of evolution to be true, when advanced white man and baboons are the closest links and all those species in between those two died off. Darwin himself says that the proof for evolution lies in the extinct links in the evolutionary chain that died off, meaning if fossils of these beings were found then it would prove him right. Well so far not one single fossil anywhere in hundreds of years has been found to verify the existance of these alleged mythical species whom Darwin hypothesied once existed. Thus to believe in evolution requires one to believe in certain species for which there is absolutely zero evidence to indicate as having ever existed at any time. To believe in evolution is to believe in imaginary animals, who only exist because Darwin said they have to exist because his theory is right. Yet that's not how science works, you don't just say entire species existed because it means your theory is right if they did. You have to prove these species existed, and even if they do it still doesn't mean the hypothesis is right; there are many variables. Now maybe if Darwin were a prophet of God we could take his word at facevalue, but what did Darwin prophecy? That the savage non-whites would go extinct. According to Darwin's prophecy, since black folk are still alive today then evolution must be a false doctrine because according to Darwin's evolution theory africans, asians, australians and everyone who isn't white should've been replaced by other species. Although I'll give Darwin a loophole noose and say he can say it's possible they could've survived by breeding with the strongest amongst them. Yet then their skin colors should've reflected such a change so they should be lighter and lighter than they used to be. The ideal path for humanity to take according to Charles Darwin, as explained elsewere in his book, would be to hold competitions to determine who the best and most fit humans were and then give them a free license to have as much sex with whoever they want (ideally the most fit, but naturally the fittest would select the fittest to breed with anyways) so they can make as many kids as possible for the betterment of the human race. While at the same time restricting the stupid or weak humans from getting married or reproducing, and if possible don't even help "unfit people" such as the sick, disabled, elderly, insance etc to survive lest they reproduce and hinder the evolution of the advanced white human race as well as wasting precious scarce resources. The Evolution theory is actually pure racism and it is not scientific at all. Thus for it to be taught in schools worldwide as scientific is an utter travesty. The "science textbooks" teaching evolution are subliminally teaching racism, however in modern times the reason evolution is taught is because each nation plans to use the evolution theory to promulgate nationalism. So instead of your skin color determining your rank among the humans and the savage sub-humans, the deciding factor will be your flag color. Although schools aren't alone in teaching this type of evolutionary superiority doctrine, the various professional sports leagues are playing the same poisonous mind games. The American public school system refuses to change the textbooks in regards to evolution because then teachers wouldn't have the answers to *"how did man get to be on earth?"*, because religion is banned from schools by the government they wouldn't be able to answer and would appear ignorant. The reason creationism isn't taught in American schools is because in 1975 CE the Federal District Court ruled it was unconstitutional, since it would be against the first amendment which prohibits the American government from making any law respecting religion. But that doesn't stop religious people from trying to get schools to teach creationism. If kids were taught the Christian version of creationism in school, they would also have to be taught the Jewish, Hindu, Buddhist, Sikh, Egyptian, Native American, African, Aztec, Roman, Greek and Islamic version of creationism. That is where the difficulty of equality comes in. To teach only one version of creationism would be to teach that all other versions of creationism were wrong. In order to be equal to religious sensitivities teachers are forbidden to say a religious idea is wrong because it might offend people and jeopardize the vote for a school budget increase, so if creationism was taught all types would have to be taught. Realistically only one version can be right, but democratic countries prevent schools from teaching that certain religious views are wrong because "freedom of religion" is interpreted as "freedom from religions being proven wrong". The U.S. policy on religion is that a religion is only wrong and shouldn't be practiced if it conflicts with American laws. Whereas in the sight of God, American law has nothing to do with whether a religion should be practiced or if it's right or wrong. Because American schools are unable and unwilling to teach all versions of creationism they do not teach any version and stick to the false unscientific evolution theory because they dread telling their students *"I don't know"* or *"It's against the U.S. Constitution to teach it"*. Democratic governments fear that if teachers can't provide any answer and have to say they don't know (since religion cannot legally be taught, in theory) then children would start to doubt the entire curriculum. The government doesn't want children to wonder that: maybe the history they are being taught isn't true either, maybe their country isn't the best of all time, maybe they aren't superior to everyone else, maybe their country's armies are not always the "good guys". These are ideas that governments do not want their citizens to entertain, because it eventually leads to emigration to better places with lower or no taxes which would mean a lower government budget and loss of government power. Darwin was highly influenced by the American democratic doctrine of species equality, thinking if one member of a species has an advantage then all the rest automatically adopt that advantage as well so the species is equal. The American politicians said all men were created equal and Darwin said all species evolve to maintain equality and those who didn't would die out since they don't have equal levels of fitness to survive. Thereby Darwin turned the American political beliefs into a pseudoscience just as pagan politicians used false religions to legitimize their flawed political doctrines. Evolution is not a scientific doctrine, it is a political doctrine, which has been used to justify and encourage the flawed systems of Democracy, Communism and many others. Darwin's teachings on evolution were used to justify the killing, enslaving and oppression of other races, nationalities, religious and political groups and every class of society who has ever been oppressed ever since; such as the native Americans, Africans, Asians, animals, the poor, the weak, women, children, the elderly. According to Mein Kampf, Adolf Hitler simply planned to put evolution into practice, he just thought Germans were the best based on certain statistics, folktales and patriotic prejudices. Hitler's politics are no different than many politicians of today, except Hitler was bold enough to try to prove his beliefs through warfare. Prior to the doctrine of evolution people said their oppression of others was a sign that God or the gods favored them and they were right, now people use the evolution doctrine to say that science teaches might equals right, even though it doesn't. Thus we are made to think the rich, beautiful, famous and powerful are what they are because they are better or correct. Unfortunately rather than have WWII discredit evolution, the victors simply adopted it themselves telling their citizens that they were good and right because they won a war and that their political system survived because it was the fittest. Politics is a different subject not to be discussed here, but it has a pervading influence on society that many people don't recognize and are oblivious to why things are the way they are and why certain groups who strive to maintain the status quo don't want them to change. Too many times we debate what a school textbook or curriculum teaches but we forget to ask who is writing this textbook and designing the curriculum? Many things can be traced to political reasons but even more things can be traced to have religious or satanic origins. Similar to how we forget about the political influences that affect our lives, we are frequently unaware of the satanic influences which are much more dangerous. Some people might think sexuality is a private matter politicians aren't concerned about, whereas even if that were true you can be assured that Satan is concerned about your sexual behavior, as is our Creator.

    The city of Pompeii is a prime example of how debauchery results in ultimate destruction. Most have heard of Pompeii which suffered an earthquake in 62 CE and whilst repairing damage from the earthquake was completely destroyed by a volcanic eruption in 79 CE. Yet few know just what type of city Pompeii was. For instance it had 35 brothels which amounts to a ratio of 1 brothel per 286 people or 1 brothel per 71 adult males. It had public sex spas, public pornography on the walls and erotic poems and stories written on walls throughout the city. The people were known for practicing oral sex, anal sex, sodomy and any other type imaginable in all kinds of ways, whenever with whoever in any place they could, especially in public. Pompeii was basically public orgy town and people would visit it on vacations to indulge in perverse sexuality. People even carried penis idols as a "good luck" charm thinking extra sex meant to "get lucky". Yet how did all that sinful sex turn out for them? God destroyed them in such an epic fashion people still talk about them today, not even knowing their crimes. They were so thoroughly obliterated that people forget why.

    From a health perspective excessive sex expends lots of nutrients, causes a hormone drain, decreases thinking ability and shortens the lifespan for both men and women. In men excessive ejaculation of sperm causes impotency, weakens thinking ability, causes prostate problems and decreases quality and quantity of life potentially causing their offspring to have a predisposition for masturbation passed on to them. Masturbation is the self-stimulation of the sexual organs which has been socially engineered into our society by evil beings to distract and destroy us. In both men and women masturbation damages the parenting instinct of nurturing and promotes degenerative behavior. Some may allege that masturbation decreases sexual desires and is a sexual release, whereas scientifically masturbation is proven to actually increase sexual desires and weaken one's vision. A married person who masturbates will have increased sexual desires and weakened vision, making it harder for them to see the beauty of their spouse both figuratively and literally. Therefore masturbation leads to infidelity, dissatisfaction, poor health, and ultimate destruction in a downward cycle of sexual addiction in which the addict is wholly miserable except for a few seconds during the indulgence, but the momentary pleasure is less and less enjoyable the further they are in the sexual addiction. Those who masturbate before marriage are likely to develop anti-social split personalities that will prevent them from marrying. If despite their "secret lives" they still marry then they will have unrealistic sexual expectations and will be unable to enjoy marital relations as much as they would have had it been the only type of sex they experienced. Not only will marital sex be less pleasurable for masturbators, but they will still feel the urge to masturbate, because real sex doesn't fulfill the same cravings or pleasure in the same manner that artificial sex or masturbation does. Someone who masturbates will have a desire for the feeling(s) masturbation results in and when real sex doesn't produce the same feelings they will still have a craving to experience those familiar feelings, leaving them sexually disappointed. Many people naively think they'll just stop masturbating when they get married, which implies they think their spouse will be their masturbation device. Such a statement reveals they already see their future spouse as a sexual object, when that sexual object turns out to be a person whose existence isn't for their sexual pleasure the masturbation addict will return to what they know and are comfortable with and will end up masturbating more while they are married than they did before. With most being too ashamed to tell their spouse, mistrust and secrecy will develop between them which will foster the conditions for adultery to occur. Also introducing hatred between the couple with the masturbator blaming their spouse for being unable to fulfill their abnormal unnatural desires. If you want to know why divorce and extra-marital affairs are on the rise, it is because of the direct correlation masturbation has regarding these activities and the negative effect it has on human lives. Lust makes true intimacy impossible and transforms people into love cripples. Oral and anal sex is anatomical masturbation. The penis is not made for masturbating in manure stuck in the rectum as is done in anal sex and it damages both the anus and the penis. The mouth has no sex glands or reproductive function and the anus has no sex glands or reproductive function, so neither the mouth nor the anus are designed for sexual organs to infiltrate them. "Homosexuality" is basically just another form of masturbation. This form of masturbation ("homosexuality") uses another person of the same sex as the masturbating device. The natural purpose and result of sexual activity is reproduction, so "homosexuality"(sodomy) is anti-sex and anti-nature. If there were a homosexual gender then homosexuals would have their own uniquely different sex organs and sexual mating practices and would not borrow a heterosexual practice. Therefore if you don't want to use the word sodomy for "homosexuality" then call it homomasturbation.

Problems pornography causes are innumerable, it dehumanizes all those it comes into contact with and degrades sex into an animalistic act devoid of love, affection and compassion. It replaces reality and morality with fantasy and unrestricted infantile gratification fulfillment. Humans become objects of orifices and organs given the purpose of satisfying sexual impulses. Pornography erodes our culture, weakens human solidarity and severs the tie between love and affect with sex. The fact that government doesn't censor or prohibit the publishing of obscene material is interpreted by the public as approval of the material and actions contained therein and inspired by. By making unenforceable laws that are purported to stop pornography from polluting those under a certain age, they are basically saying that once you're old enough it's perfectly fine, thereby turning the problem into a matter of age rather than a matter of whether pornography is good or bad. This method has had the same effects with alcohol and cigarettes, where kids see it being permitted for adults and feel wrongly discriminated against thinking they are missing out and end up consuming these things oftentimes just to prove they are old. In America it has become a rite of passage to drink alcohol once one is considered old enough, whereas often unbeknownst to their parents many of those kids couldn't wait that long and have a much higher tolerance for alcohol than one would guess, since they drank before. Imagine if the government made a law saying you weren't allowed to steal if you were under 21, or that you weren't allowed to kill people if you were under 30. It's obvious that such laws would only serve to increase these crimes among all age groups. So are these laws governments make really designed to be deterrents or are they meant to encourage early adoption and cultural acceptance? An "Adults Only" restriction is like the roller coaster signs which say "you must be this tall to ride", it misinforms the youth that it's no longer dangerous when they're older because with other dangerous items like poison they say "*Do not drink*", they don't give a minimum age where drinking poison is ok; except for alcohol. Not to dwell too much on sexual culture but as they say "Sex Sells!" No one can deny that the sexual suggestiveness contained in the many advertisements made today definitively influences consumer purchasing decisions, otherwise they wouldn't spend so much money making shampoo or deodorant commercials. Another meaning behind "Sex Sells!" is that pornographic material is essentially sex for the senses. Today pornography is the largest industry in the world. So what exactly are pornography dealers selling? They are selling the illusion that animalistic carnality is pleasurable. Maybe for a few seconds, but as soon as the deed is done the fun is over and any pleasure obtained has departed leaving a craving for more that requires a higher dosage for the same effect which eventually results in misery at the least, along with wasted time and a distorted view of everything. This is why pornography progressively becomes more and more extreme and decrepit. What was considered to be shameful porn 40 years ago is considered modest today because it bleeds into the culture lowering moral standards by the day. Whereas in 25-40 years from now if the pornification process is permitted and continues to be promoted as it has been, then it would not surprise me to see bestiality and sodomite incest being seen in popular movies and on TV shows without anyone batting an eyelid. A convicted child molester was asked about what his first impressions were when first viewing child pornography, he said the first time he was repulsed and completely disgusted but within 6 months he had raped his first child. 6 months of watching pornography is all it took for someone to go from being disgusted on sight to raping in real life! Pedophilia is a byproduct of pornography and CNN estimates that currently 1-5% of Americans are pedophiles. Porn turns women into pieces of meat that are used, abused, infected and then discarded. Porn is anti-human which causes permanent damage to the brain which cannot be reversed and also causes erectile dysfunction. Porn has a worse effect on the brain than cocaine and the damage is permanent since images cannot be pumped out of the brain. Scientific studies were done on animals addicted to cocaine who were given the opportunity to compete with other animals in order to have sex. The animals addicted to cocaine chose to compete for sex instead of using cocaine proving that the potential of sex is a bigger high than cocaine. In addition to that a Tortoise named "Burt" was put into a 2-month breeding program where he mated with 5 other female tortoises and wouldn't stop until he got arthritis and could barely move. The zoo actually had to strap wheels to the tortoise so it could move again because it disabled itself as a result of having so much sex it got permanently crippled. Sexual drive is something more powerful than extreme chemical addictions and can cause one to indulge in sexual behavior even at the expense of life itself. This is proven by the fact that several animals, like preying mantis' and some spiders, mate despite knowing that immediately after mating they will be killed to be food for their offspring if it hatches. The male honeybee has a penis which cannot be removed after penetration, thus the male honeybee dies every time it has sex. The salmon also have a fatalistic sex life, in that they travel from the saltwater sea into the fresh water in order to have a possible chance at mating. This annual salmon run is very famous and many know about it's numerous hazards like bears and fishermen but at the end the salmon dies because it has sex in fresh water and it's a salt water creature. This famous annual salmon journey is a suicide mission which both male and female salmons make just for the possible chance at having sex once. Those fish swim to death just because they might get to have sex if they live til the end. Billions of creatures throuhout time have willingly chosen sex over life. So sex really is the most addictive type of thing on earth. This is why porn is currently the most addictive substance known to mankind. The easy accessibilty on the internet of sexually explicit material has provided 24/7 opportunities for humans to get sexually intoxicated on a sexually stimulating sensually simulatory drug known as porn that is worse and more addictive than cocaine and any other substance that can be named at this point in recorded history. Porn reduces self-esteem, confidence and motivation creating an obsessive compulsive habit. The only way to recover is by completely abstaining from it. Porn is racist, wastes time and creates debt, anger and hatred. Porn is a hate crime, includes hate speech and has effects on society which are more destructive than warfare. It is estimated that by the age of 20 the average kid has spent 10,000 hours watching pornography. I repeat, by the age of 20 the average person has watched over 10,000 hours of pornography. The average is 10,000 hours for 20 year olds. That 10,000 hours is considered "normal" by statisticians. Yet we call our modern world civilized? You take 20 years and 10,000 hours and that's about 500 hours of porn watching per year per person, when they are young and just starting in their porn addiction. Multiply that figure for every child 20 years old and less and imagine how different the world would be if those trillions of hours were used on something other than watching pornography. Also note that the next 20 years likely result in more than 10,000 hours since the addiction gets more severe and a good portion of the first 20 years of someone's life was not spent watching porn, since they were babies and such. Even if you are able to avoid it yourself, despite it being available nearly everywhere from the checkout aisle in a store, billboards, to TV, movies and pop-up internet ads, because you are a part of society other people being affected by this plague will inevitably affect you, directly or indirectly because it affects them, their personality and attitude; which in turn affects who they come into contact with inevitably leading to you. As with any disease, quarantine is not a permanent solution rather proper hygiene must be learned and applied. With the pornography plague the sewage must be removed from our living conditions so we are not contaminated by the filth. Just like sewage, we remove it from society so the stench of it doesn't overpower us. Even if there are some who personally don't get their hands dirtied by it, we shouldn't have to put up with the risk of pornography. If there are no social restraints how can we expect self-restraint to be achieved? How can the inner self-censor develop in a society where "anything goes" in the public display of the most intimate relations? Hundreds of scientific studies prove that willpower is a muscle that tires as it works which can only be developed through exertion in doing good while exposure to temptations damages and weakens it. Thus the larger and more numerous the temptations you face the weaker your willpower and thinking ability will be while the more good you do the stronger your willpower and mental ability grows. It's not something where the more you don't give in the stronger you get, actually the more you are faced with temptation the more your willpower is drained. Scientifically exposure to temptation actually can make you stupid, but then again if you are already exposing yourself to temptation to begin with then technically you are kind of stupid already. Satan will attack you but it's dangerous to invite his attacks because eventually your willpower may fail. The strong intelligent person is the one who repels Satan and doesn't go looking for a fight, and if you look at things you shouldn't see then you are looking for a fight with Satan and he is shooting invisible poisoned arrows at your eyes designed to infect the mind, heart and soul. The solution is to minimize temptations as much as possible and maximize efforts to do good while seeking protetction from Satan with the one who created Satan. Temptations are like germs, a healthy person avoids sinful opportunities and prevents the opportunities for infection from occuring. Do you really think any prophet of God would allow their followers to publish such scum? However just like it is with the drug dealers, you will find most pornography makers wearing crosses or having a cross as part of the scenery thinking that all their sins will be forgiven because they believe someone else got punished in their place.   The effect being they continue producing the smut without guilt even more than they would have done if they weren't Christian. Which the fact that Sunday is the most popular day of the year for watching pornography is also a telltale sign of how Christianity has a intimate relationship with pornography. There are even specific categories of pornography dealing with Christian symbolism and certain Christian occupations or locations. Porn is to a large extent a Christian industry, the reason for that will become clear later. The option for evil should not be available. Therefore pornography should not be protected by "freedom", it must be destroyed before it destroys all of humanity. Do you want your marriage ruined by porn? Do you want your kids or loved ones ruined by porn? Do you want to be endangered by porn for the sake of "freedom"? Christians may debate the relation between their faith and porn but it goes without saying that freedom plays a more active role in the porn industry and is a large reason for it's existance. You just can't have freedom without pornography. If you want freedom then the pornography comes with it. A simple fix could be that all internet devices come pre-installed with porn blocking software, yet the electronics industries haven't done this citing "freedom infringement". Especially when certain countries consider the "pursuit of happiness" as a sacred right, thereby making pornography a sacred item. The constitutions of many countries today actually promote pornography and it would be unconstitutional to ban it. Although at least you can install porn blocking software on your own devices, but personal protection will only protect yourself whereas pornography harms everybody. Yet for "freedom purposes" some porn blocking software can be deleted or disabled. Therefore if after one installed and set up such software having finetuned the settings until they were satisfied, they then set the recovery email up as an email account they would soon delete, then after setting up the software and deleting that email they changed the softwares admin password to a random password which they didn't know that was longer than the text box so they couldn't even see it but just pasted it in from a random password generator, or typed random stuff with so many characters they couldn't even see the full text of what they typed, doing such would make it so that pornography could not be viewed on that device and the porn blocking software could not be removed or disabled even if someone tried to circumvent it. While if it's a good software it will automatically update as well and allow one to submit feedback in case one "accidentally" went on to a sexually explicit site that wasn't blocked so that the software company could review the site and add it to the list of blocked material, thereby blocking it for everyone who uses their software. At the same time for those devices already infected with pornography there are various softwares such as "Snitch" which scans the entire device seeking out all explicit material so that it can found and deleted no matter where it has been hidden. At the time of this writing the software Tueagles Anti-Porn Blocker seems to be the best web filter and wifi routers also exist that block the porn from even possibly showing up on your devices, personally I use it along with DNS filters because they can be easily setup to block anything one wants or can imagine, even advertisements. I also use the "Freedom" software app to block sites, apps and categories not considered pornographic but which are time-wasting. While for smart phones there are many apps that are effective at blocking pornography and they can be setup so they are uninstallable. God-willing the electronics industry will become less porn friendly and pre-install such safeguards for the sake of protecting humanity thereby dealing a severe if not fatal blow to internet pornography. Yet not only could sexually explicit material be stopped on the internet, but it could be stopped on every type of electronic media. Other software can be developed and installed that censors swear words or any other kind of sinful behavior from affecting you through your electronics. Imagine having computers, tvs, tablets, phones and radios in which it is impossible to see nudity on them or to hear swear words or whatever else you didn't want to be exposed to. The technology exists to make these types of devices for the masses and make them standard, but the electronics industry hasn't done it yet because of money and lack of consumer demand. It's just a simple matter of people demanding censored devices and pressuring producers to make them an industry standard by supporting those who sell devices with built-in censorship. If we don't make it an issue for them then it will continue to be an issue for us. For those who think and/or claim they aren't addicted to pornography and masturbating, have them install such software on their devices, or do it yourself, and make it impossible for them to view porn ever again and tell them to never masturbate ever again. If they really aren't addicted it'll be very easy to quit today. Then warn them that if they are addicted they will experience withdrawal symptoms and it's best that they started recovery now before their addiction got worse. If one has seen pornography or masturbated even once, then they are likely addicted, because the first exposure to sinful sexual activity is designed to be more habitually entrapping than a smoker's first cigarette.

It saddens me how the youth are being actively encouraged to masturbate and to have sex by their school teachers. Then the parents and grandparents wonder why their children are becoming teenage parents. My opposition to this sexification process was stifled and suppressed by the teachers more than it was by my classmates. For example several times I wore a shirt to school that said "*Stop touching yourself*", the kids liked it. However one day a teacher, who never even had me in their class, said that it's a bad shirt and she didn't like it. At the end of that day the vice principal tells me if I ever wear that shirt to school again I would be sent home to put on a different one, which isn't even the official policy. I had run afoul before wearing anti-establishment shirts and the standard policy is to just turn the shirt inside out for the rest of the day, but they wouldn't even allow that. The shirt I wore that led me to experience this school policy myself said "*Cops Suck*" and when a former teacher of mine turned me in later in the school day the principal told me that I should turn it inside out because it endangered the safety of the police who patrolled the school halls. Yet when I wore a shirt that says "*Stop touching yourself*" that shirt was treated as if it was worse than the one which the principal said, "*endangers the safety of police*". The only ones who should have felt threatened by my "*Stop touching yourself*" shirt should have been the purveyors of sex, not the employees of public school. I decided to play it safe and never wore that shirt to school again because I didn't want the DHS (Department of Homeland Security) to imprison me for wearing it saying I was a "threat to national security". In hindsight though I should've wore it even more. Sexual morality is actually a threat to the U.S. government, if I had worn that shirt and people followed it's advice to stop masturbating they would have increased thinking and concentration capabilities thereby being less susceptible to brainwashing; since as it's said "When a man's penis is erect 2/3rds of his reason departs." The sex industry would also suffer. Since many politicians worldwide receive donations (of various types) from the sex industry, any threat to the profits or influence of the sex industry is a threat to those politicians' constituents. Any threat to the profits of the sex industry is also a threat to the U.S. government's budget which depends on the taxes it collects from the sex industry. The U.S. government may not willingly admit it, but sexual morality is considered a "threat to national security". Seriously if citizens were moral people the world governments would collapse. Russia provides a prime example. During WWI Czar Nicholas of Russia banned vodka thinking that sober troops would result in a better Russian military performance. Prior to this ban vodka was taxed by Russia and it made up 33% of the government's revenue. After the ban, Russians still drank vodka soldier and citizen alike, however the government had 33% less revenue. Meanwhile government expenses rapidly rose during the war. As a result the czar didn't pay his soldiers, so his soldiers allowed Kerensky's revolutionaries to storm the winter palace in 1917 CE to overthrow the government and change Russia into a democracy that was then overtaken by Lenin and the Bolsheviks. Thus less modern goverments lose their tax revenue from sinful sexual activity this is why public schools inculcate sexual immorality into the students who are compelled to attend. Why else would the teachers look the other way when they see sexual foreplay in the halls but give detention to a student who in a rush to get to class on time in the morning didn't stop and say the pledge of allegiance? Apparently it's wrong for a student to wear a shirt saying "*Stop touching yourself*", but it's right for a health teacher to get paid with taxpayer dollars to tell kids to masturbate and that "*ugly people can't get any*". If you're wondering why the youth have no class today, look no further than the classroom they were sitting in yesterday.

    The home might not be completely free from blame either. A common example is when a young boy is watching movies among family members. When some nudity or a sex scene comes onscreen he instinctively turns away or lowers his gaze covering his eyes, because God gave him the instinctive knowledge to know that he shouldn't be seeing that junk. The boy's pure heart causes him to shy away. Then the older family members bring attention to this and rather than turning the smut off, all too often they will turn the boy's modesty into a joke and means of ridicule and embarrassment, by teasing him saying to cover or close his eyes, or "*don't look, you're too young!*". Or suggesting he may be a sodomite because he doesn't want to look at naked women. Unfortunately few children have the courage to tell their elders how they shouldn't be watching the filth either and that age has nothing to do with it. I can't imagine the humiliation a wife, sister or daughter must feel when witnessing their father, husband or brother drooling over some movie model who's wearing millions of dollars' worth of makeup on top of their artificial surgically altered body. Then these same "men" wonder why their daughters, wives, sisters and mothers buy so much makeup and fashion accessories not realizing they themselves taught their women that appearance is how to get the attention of men. Of course many men reading this might argue that they didn't say that, but in reality their actions did and the women of our society internalized it. Eventually after enough ridicule the boy stoops to his lust crazed elders level, or "becomes a man" and starts peeking without reprisal and then is watching it all without shame just like the rest with his eyes glued to the screen. These types of bad role models combined with peer pressure and explicit instructions from teachers and the entertainment industry make it no surprise why pornography views are on the rise with an estimated 75 million+ watching every second, which is a statistic that is many years old. There are a few other statistics that demonstrate the extent of the pornography problem. Note the following statistics are all from 2010 CE, so this is how bad the problem used to be before phones with interenet access became prevalent. As of 2010 CE: 12% of websites in the world were pornographic, 8% of all emails were pornographic, 25% of all search engine requests were pornographic, 35% of all internet downloads were pornographic, 20% of men and 13% of women admitted to watching pornography at work, and the average age at which a child first sees pornography used to be 11. Unfortunately all these shocking data points are outdated and very old. Today the situation is far worse. The sex found in movies and TV also contributes to the spread of adultery and fornication. Of all the sex scenes displayed, the vast majority include unmarried couples or acts of adultery, very rarely are the actors and actresses portrayed as being married but even then the viewers know they really aren't. This desensitizes the viewer into thinking there is nothing wrong with adultery or fornication. Watching these actors and actresses perform in such a manner is actually a form of adultery and fornication in itself depending on whether the viewer is married or not. Whether a person is watching pornography, sex on TV, or is actually committing adultery, to the eyes and ears it's all the same. Viewing and/or hearing illicit sexual acts requires the same action from the eyes and ears as doing the deeds themselves would require. Watching and listening to the sexual filth in the sexified "entertainment" industry of today is essentially visual and auditory adultery and fornication, the only difference from the real thing is that the private parts don't play a role; one would hope. Now this doesn't mean a person watching illicit material would receive the same eternal or earthly punishment as one actually doing the deeds, but their ears and eyes are guilty of doing the same thing that is being done in what is watched and heard. With this understanding we can identify pornography and sexual scenes as adultery and fornication for the eyes, ears, minds and hearts. I mention this in order to warn you of the Satanic plots and tools being deployed to propagate sinful behavior. Maybe you think this thought process is extreme, but look at the extreme growth of sexuality throughout society. Compare it to the sexual culture 100 years ago and imagine how putrid the sexualized world will be in another 100 years. This is because of the subliminal messaging of such movies, TV programs and internet material causing subconscious changes in the human species that has normalized sinful behavior. Depending on what comes onto your TV, computer, tablet or phone technically you could be having adultery and fornication going on inside of your home. Is that the type of house the prophets of God lived in? God is aware of all we do, always remember that God is watching us when we are watching things. When the commandment says "you shall not commit adultery", don't commit adultery with your eyes, ears, mind or heart. Not committing adultery with your private parts is only one part. If you are committing adultery with your eyes, ears, mind and heart then the private parts will not be far behind. If you abstain from committing adultery with every part then you will be far less likely to commit adultery with your private parts. Think of your body as separate components with each part influencing the other like peer pressure. For example when your stomach is hungry it influences your brain to think about food, which influences your heart to desire food, and your eyes are pressured to look for food which leads all these parts to pressure the legs to move towards food until eventually your hands pick up the food and your mouth eats the food. Although that food might not have been too good for you to eat and maybe your teeth or tongue did not want that food or enjoy that food but they went along with it because of the peer pressure from the other parts of the body. So when a guy gets "penis pressure", he has to keep in mind that the penis does not have authority over the rest of his body. In order for the penis to commit a sin it has to trick the other parts of the body to go along with it even though those parts aren't going to get any pleasure out of the sin. If a guy can control his thoughts to ignore the penis pressure, control his hands to ignore the penis pressure, control his eyes to ignore the penis pressure, control his ears to ignore the penis pressure, control his feet to ignore the penis pressure, control his tongue to ignore the penis pressure and control his heart to ignore the penis pressure then no sexual sins will take place. The immense penis pressure will fizzle out soon enough because the other body parts aren't going along with his stupid selfish sinful satanic plans. When the hands, feet, ears, eyes, mouth, brain, and heart say no to the penis eventually it will just shutup and the blood flow will decrease because the rest of the parts will tell the heart they want more blood and that "Mr. Penis" doesn't need the blood that he's asking for because they're not doing what he wants them to do because God did not create them to do that. If you don't walk where Mr. Penis wants you to walk to, and don't touch what Mr. Penis wants you to touch, and don't see what Mr. Penis wants you to see, don't hear what Mr. Penis wants you to hear, don't say what Mr. Penis wants you to say, and don't think about what Mr. Penis wants you to think about and go do other things instead then Mr. Penis is going to get the message real soon and he's not going to be a bother for very long. But one has to be strict, because if he gets one body part to agree then they'll get the next and then they will all become enslaved as the servants of Mr. Penis. And Mr. Penis is one of the worst bosses in the world to work for, it's all about him and he doesn't care about his employees or even himself. This is because Mr. Penis frequently gets tricked by Satan, but Mr. Penis tries to keep that a secret from the other body parts when he applies his patented penis pressure to get them to go along with his/Satan's plans. For guys Mr. Penis is more suceptible to Satanic influences because Mr. Penis is blind, deaf and dumb, has no brain, no morals, no sense of self-respect or dignity and doesn't even have the slightest considerations in regards to time or place. As such Mr. Penis will rudely demand satisfaction under all circumstances. If you give him a centimeter, he takes an inch and if he gets those inches today then in the long term he's gonna get a mile out of you; and that's a conservative estimate. Thus never ever let Mr. Penis trick your other body parts into helping him get those extra centimeters/inches no matter how much he begs. Patience is vital because he will writhe with tempertantrums and get so mad his face will change colors and you'll see veins bulging out of his head. It's simply a matter of "Mr. Penis" growing up and getting with the program God wants, he's kind of like a immature kid who doesn't know what's good for it because he is so vital in the kid making process. So since "Mr. Penis" is always going to be like a kid, if the other parts ignore the penis pressure then they aren't going to get themselves or the rest of the body into trouble with the Creator. For most guys "Mr. Penis" always likes to play, but in life there are rules to the game and you have to sign up with a team member of the opposite gender via marriage in order to play and win, if you don't play as a team member you are going to lose in more ways than one. Sexual activity is a team sport and is no such thing as "practice for sex". The successful team first learns to play together at the same time, which ideally is their first time playing the game if it's the first team they've ever joined via marriage. The ironic thing is how when guys get penis pressure to urinate they are able to hold it in if they really want to until they find an appropriate situation to relieve such pressure the correct way at the correct time. However the physical urges to urinate are stronger than physical urges to ejaculate, and if you don't urinate it will cause problems. Whereas there are no negative side effects for not ejaculating, on the contrary there are health benefits for not doing so. Thus guys should know that Mr. Penis is a sexual predator who is more of an enemy to the male than a friend. Mr. Penis is the most selfish part of the male body and will completely destroy someone if he gets his way. Now there is a female equivalent/counterpart/partner in crime to "Mr. Penis" and his childish "penis pressure" but that's called.........., something else, which is not my right to name nor is it appropriate for me to say. I'm only familiar with Mr. Penis and he's not the best of friends because he can suggest some bad ideas that are very stupid and dangerous if you follow his advice. For guys, never give into penis pressure because to do so is even dumber than giving into peer pressure because it's only one part. Mr. Penis is not in charge and anyone who lets him control their other body parts is oppressing their other body parts and soul. The same applies to other body parts, if you let Mr. Tongue run the show and eat whatever Mr. Tongue wants whenever Mr. Tongue wants, letting all the other body parts take their orders from Mr. Tongue, your life will get messed up because of Mr. Tongue oppressing the body and soul. Consider sexual temptations to be like mosquito bites, if you see or hear something forbidden it's like your eye or ear was bitten by a mosquito and it itches. Every second you see or hear sinful things you are bitten again in another spot on that part. After the whole surface of the eye or ear is covered with bites then you are blinded or deafened and no longer feel anything wrong with what you are doing and only have a severe itch whilst the mosquito starts biting all other parts of the body including the private parts and there is only one way to scratch the itch. If you scratch until liquid is released then the wounds are even worse and the damage is greater. Also the more you are bitten the less bites it takes for you to be consumed the next time. However while a mosquito may give you malaria the sinful sexual insect will give you a SSTD, which is a spiritual sexually transmitted disease which can be contracted merely through one forbidden gaze and affect you for life. A spouse is like a garment and like a garment can help to protect you against mosquito bites, no garment can protect you entirely from mosquito bites; particularly from getting bitten on the eyes and ears. So a spouse is not a cure all for sexual temptation just as a garment doesn't offer total protection from mosquitos, especially if one removes their garment or fails to properly care for it or willingly exposes themselves to and interacts with mosquitos. Depending on the spouse and the relationship one has with them they can help you like armor or harm you like a torture device, since garments are of different types likewise spouses affect each other in different ways, which can be positive and negative just as garments can be beneficial or harmful depending on many factors. The key is to prevent oneself from committing visual and audio sins, to limit the exposure if it occurs and most importantly never scratch the itch and if you do then stop as soon as possible because the more you scratch the worse it gets making it harder to stop and the more likely you will get a deadly SSTD. Most importantly learn from your defeats. Just as humans are constantly trying to limit the harm and inconvenience mosquitos cause them, after every experience with temptation it must be treated as a dangerous learning experience and you should improve your tactics so the next time it is less dangerous with less potential for damage. It's like a boxing match, if you get knocked down by Satan because of exposing yourself to his jabs until he landed a major blow when you weren't expecting it, in response you get back up with greater caution for safety by being more wary of both the hard and the soft punches. With full knowledge that the more punches you receive, the weaker your resistance is and that if you don't learn from getting knocked down the first time then it will be even easier for you to get knocked down in the future. Also remember that Satan is going for the K.O. and has defeated billions of people throughout history knocking them out of belief into disbelief. So while those little seemingly innocent jabs might not seem like they will lead you to fall, that's exactly what they are designed to do. Yet even though each attack will cause more damage than the last, by learning from each temptation whether we conquer it or not we can become better protected and less vulnerable until eventually we won't get knocked down at all because we will be blocking every attack and dodging every temptation having learned from a lifetime of experience. It's not about learning to take Satan's punches, it's about learning how to completely avoid and block them. While doing good deeds is how we punch back, and as they say sometimes the best defense is a good offense. While just as in sports sometimes an over zealous offense can backfire and cause it's own defeat through offensive maneuvers that seemed like a good idea but in reality weren't. Thus Satan uses this tactic of luring us into what seems to be a good deed when it's really a devilish trap he has laid to try to reverse the momentum of the match. That's why it's important to follow the playbook God gave the prophets to teach us for both offense and defense. The match goes on as long as we live, the final score is what will determine whether we are an eternal winner or loser.

A man who used to work as a person who prepared dead bodies prior to putting them in the grave, told me that one time a teenage boy had died watching pornography. It was his job to wash the boy's body and it was very sad because his parents walked in his room to find him dead in his chair with pornography playing on the computer screen. There was no biological reason for his death, it wasn't due to health reasons, hyper excitement or anything. Simply the angel of death had been instructed to extract his soul at that time ending his life. Do you think that boy will be going to heaven or hell? What will he say when God asks him what he was doing at his moment of death? Imagine the embarrassment the parents will have to endure every time they are asked what happened to your son and how did he die? This is a lesson we should learn from. That boy didn't think he would die watching pornography, no one does, when we die the angel of death will come when we least expect it. Every person who ever died had plans for the future and plans for their next meal that were never realized. The causes people blame for death are just excuses to make us feel better. No one wants to admit a person died because the angel of death took that person's soul, we like to blame health reasons or violence in order to pretend that if we stay healthy and out of trouble then maybe we won't die. There are people who are still walking around after having been shot many times, and others have poisoned their body and have horrendous health yet live on, others survive horrific accidents while others involved in the accidents who were barely injured did not. Death will happen to us all and it will happen as a result of the angel of death being commanded to take our soul from our body, it can happen fast or slow, but it will happen to all. Let's try not to be watching pornography or masturbating when we die. When Satan tempts you sexually, imagine your private parts burning with the hellfire, imagine your eyelashes being ablaze with smoke and sparks in your eyes, imagine your hair burned by the hellfire with hot coals in your nose and mouth while your earwax and saliva is boiling along with the boiling burning blood running through your burning veins, as your skin blisters and disintegrates in the flames over and over. Giving in to burning sexual desires in a sinful manner can result in all those other types of burning potentially for eternity. If a good portion of a person's time is spent doing something then there is a good probability they will die doing that very thing. We should remember this whenever we do something and ask ourselves: *"What if I die doing this?"*

    But what if despite all this advice and a sincere desire to try to stop masturbating a person still gives in and commits sexual sins? Over and over they fail to stay chaste. What should they do? Is there any hope or must they just live with their weakness? Well there is a solution for sinful masturbation. When I suggested it in high school they thought it was extreme, crazy and funny. Thus I was cautious over recommending it but it really works so it doesn't matter if it's extreme or crazy, if it protects people from sin then it's worth mentioning and doing. Aside from and in addition to everything else I've mentioned as ways to reduce and eliminate masturbation there are chastity belts. A chastity belt is a device one wears on their private parts to keep themselves chaste. Now I don't know quite how a female chastity belt works but the male version is like a sheath when worn and it prevents the male penis from getting too big. In short a guy wearing a chastity belt cannot physically get a full erection because of the chastity belt not allowing it to grow to that big of a size neither in length or width. Chastity belts are perfectly safe and healthy to use but they have a bad reputation due to sexual deviants using them for inappropriate reasons. Yet for those who have difficulty controlling themselves or simply don't want to have to deal with the distraction of sexual arousal causing them to lose focus and be tempted, then chastity belts are the best and easiest solution in my opinion. They are a great way to protect your private parts too. For guys I'd reccommend stainless steel (not plastic or chrome) with an open tube-like structure at the tip end so one can cleanly urinate without needing to remove it. The chastity belts use tiny padlocks which when unlocked allow the device to be removed for washing the device and one's private parts. There are also some chastity belts or chastity rings with spikes to help limit arousal but that's not my style, just saying that style exists if it's your style. Chastity belts work great whether worn when sleeping or awake. The wearer of a chastity belt doesn't have to deal with their body parts getting sexually aroused to maximum potential. Which is the prime reason why people masturbate to begin with. It's not unhealthy to not be sexually aroused at 100% capacity, and its dangerous to be aroused when you don't have a religiously lawful way to use that arousal with a spouse. It's not that one who wears a chastity device can't be fully aroused medically or physiologically it's just that they wear a special device to safely stop it from happening. Which if you aren't married then sexual arousal is not something that helps your life quality. What is the point of being sexually aroused if you aren't going to have sex with your spouse? Such an arousal isn't just useless, it's counterproductive and dangerous. Either the aroused will use it to sin or let it go to waste so when chastity belts can stop that situation from happening I consider that a big win. Chastity belts saves one's sexual energy for when it can be used productively and greatly prevents wasted/dangerous arousal. Of course in school this method was ridiculed but at the end of the day it works. God doesn't want people to masturbate, so if wearing a device that prevents erections prevents one from masturbating then it's a no-brainer to wear it. To not wear one is to risk sin. While chastity belts were alleged to have been used in the medieval time period those belts were mainly rumors but today they actually exist. As far as I know prophets didn't live in a time of safe, cheap, comfortable chastity belts but I do think they'd all endorse their usage. People might not have originally intended them to be used to ensure chastity but they serve that purpose and since I know what its like to live as a guy without one I strongly recommend at least every guy wears one for spiritual safety. Let's face it Mr. Penis interrupts a man's life and steals one's time, energy and drains one's mind, body and soul. Mr. Penis doesn't know how or care to behave in a civilized manner and frequently pressures guys to do scandalous sexual crimes. Just lock him up! Wives should get chastity belts for their husbands to help and show they care about protecting her man and his parts from sinful urges. Parents should also get these for their kids, preferably in a non-awkward way. What surprises me most about chastity belts is that I haven't heard of anyone else who preaches chastity or sexual abstinence for religious reasons suggest them. I find that odd because it's a fool-proof method to avoid/reduce sexual temptations and sins yet it's rarely proscribed by those waging war on sinful sexual behavior. Even groups like Sex Addicts Anonymous or Sexaholics don't mention chastity belts and they are dealing with people who can't control themselves. On top of that not a single Catholic Priest ever mentioned these to me and I was training to be a priest and priests are supposed to be entierely celibate even from themselves. So that people who allege to be chaste and preach chastity don't reccomend chastity belts either implies they don't know about them, are embarassed to mention them, or maybe they aren't as chaste as they are preaching. Of course it's awkward that chastity belts are sold by irreputable sexually themed business as a "sex toy" when it's the exact opposite but that makes me question why that is. Why aren't the groups who dedicate themselves to ending masturbation promoting chastity belts themselves? Why isn't there some pro-chastity business selling these things? Hopefully they just don't know about them and that's why because I assure you they work in stopping sexual behavior for those who want to stop sinful sexual behavior. I know it might sound awkward but since we are real people who want real practical solutions, realistically for most people if they get the physical urges and arousal then they will likely indulge. So chastity devices safely stop the bulges from ever happening thereby protecting oneself from their own body. Honestly it's not worth fighting Mr. Penis. When a guy has to fight Mr. Penis they don't win even if they win, which it's not that easy to win anyways. Thus to fight one's urges to begin with is a losing battle because you could be doing better things with your life that have no potential for sinful outcomes. The goal is to be chaste, not to win some fights and lose others; it's best to not deal with it and live life free from sexual arousal while single. When married then one can give a chastity belt key to their spouse so that when the time for sexual behavior is appropriate then they can unequip you and be intimate. Some may even consider a chastity belt a romantic type of committment, which is another reason why those who want to be virgins or chaste until marriage should definately wear one of these things. In conclusion chastity belts give you control over your body's sexual urges by physcially preventing your sexual parts from getting too big/powerful to ignore or resist. Chastity belts can give the wearer a life free from the physical aspect of sexual temptations. I definately suggest you get/wear one. It's better to wear one and not need it than need it and not have it and as a result do a sin which you later regret doing. I don't miss life with sexual temptations, life is better without them. Chastity belts = easiest way to stop masturbation/temptation. You don't even have to stop it, you just wear a chastity belt and rarely have to physically worry about it ever again. Of course God can help you resist and/or quit but God has created such accessories that can be worn to protect you. So wear a chastity belt and become a sexual sin-free superhero. Also recommend these things to everyone else you know.

    In the second half of 2009 CE the pastor who wrote my reference letter retired and a different priest took over his position of authority. This new priest planned to have more masses (church services) at the church and requested more Eucharistic ministers. I signed up for the training program. A Eucharistic minister in the Catholic Church is a person who is qualified to distribute the bread and wine after it is supposed to have become the body and blood of God or Jesus pbuh. It is seen as sacred food that can't be casually passed around by just anybody, a certification which must be approved by the Catholic hierarchy is required. I have attached a scan of my certificate which I received after becoming a Eucharistic minister so that you don't have to just take my word for it. I've attached it because I know that there will be some Catholics who might not like what I write and as a result may say I don't know what I'm talking about and am a fraud or liar. However I do have the credentials that I say I have and I've included such documentation to prove this. Let's face it, it's easy to lie and say "*I used to belong to X religion and I was really into it and did this and that and learned all this inside info while I was a member.*" Yet more often than not such people have absolutely zero documentation to verify their claims. Now I'm not going to include every little scrap of paper I got in this book, and I haven't kept every little scrap of documentation either, but I think a certificate from the Catholic Diocese of Buffalo testifying that I was certified as a "*Minister of Holy Communion*" is a noteworthy credential to include since the Bishop of Buffalo himself signed it and gave me authority to be a minister of the Sacrament. Basically I'm the real deal, I actually did this stuff and can prove it.

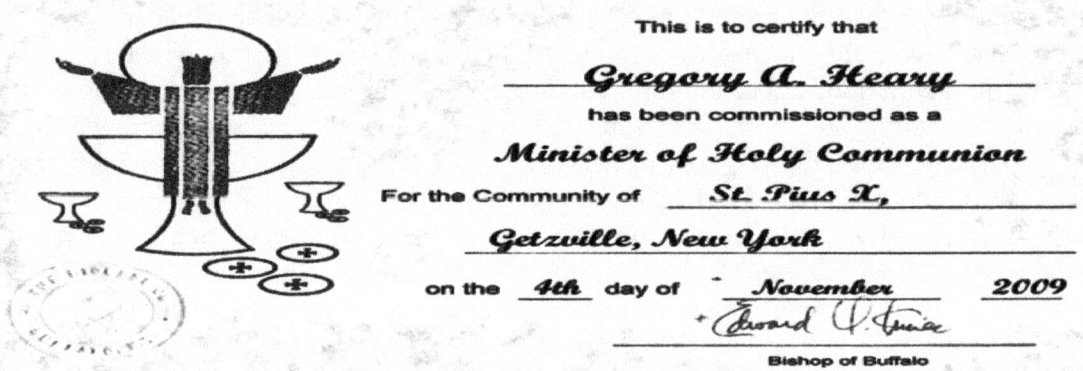

      I included this because Catholics or Christians might not like what I write and disagree with me, but I do have the qualifications and certification to write about it; at least when it comes to things like Communion. When it comes to most Catholics I'm actually more qualified to talk about Catholic doctrines than they are. So that's where if a regular Catholic wants to disagree with me and say I don't know what I'm talking about when it comes to Communion, I'll just ask them to show me their certificate. The actual training was somewhat dull and it was more focused on how/when to move your body and the manners involved in touching the food during the service instead of going into the theological aspects surrounding the ritual. It was more of a ritualistic training program than a doctrinal program. Although I had learned extra information from my exclusive priests in training club. During one of the behind the scenes tours of where the priests keep all their expensive props, the priest explained how if you were an alcoholic priest you had to be able to handle a few sips of the "blood" in case there was any left at the end of mass that needed to be drunk, without you getting drunk as a result. This was because Catholics are not allowed to waste what they believe to be a holy body and blood. Not until after I became a Muslim did I realize the gravity of this secret, the priest flatly admitted that the wine is still wine after they say the words that are supposed to turn it into blood. The laymen believe it's a chemical change with the physical form remaining the same, but this is not true according to a priest who says the very words that cause this alleged change every Sunday, who also trains priests on how to do this trick. A former altar server once told me of a joke played on the priest where they watered down the wine and after the priest drank it he gave them a dirty look, implying that he knew it didn't taste right because the wine had been diluted, thereby the "blood" didn't have the same wine taste as usual. The priest teaching me blatantly stated the liquid everyone thinks is no longer wine that had been transformed into the blood of God or Jesus pbuh is alcoholic in content to such an extent that you can get drunk and intoxicated because of it. This is why the priest drinks whatever is left so that there is no evidence remaining for people to test. If it really did change into blood despite no change being present according to human senses, all the Catholic Church has to do is perform a chemical analysis to prove that it was wine before and then when they said the special words it was turned into something molecularly different similar to blood. Then we can find out what the blood type is and if it's the same every time, and can use that blood or body to learn the genetic code of God or Jesus pbuh giving us a DNA chain of divinity and/or prophethood. The Church will never do this because if it was done honestly without any trickery it would expose them for having deceived the people. Fortunately they don't have to. All that needs to be done is to have a sober person who goes to church and ensure they eat or drink nothing except the alleged blood, and then give them a breathalyzer test checking the blood alcohol content after they exit the church and I guarantee they will be found to have alcohol in their body, which could have only entered while in church via the alleged blood that was wine 5 minutes before them drinking it. If you don't believe me test it yourself (on someone else, I don't advise you to drink the booze yourself or to encourage someone else to). Then you can inform the police that all who drink the wine at church on Sunday and then drive home are driving drunk and they will fail a breathalyzer test, so it's a easy way to "protect the people" from drunk drivers. Maybe police will even setup a roadblock at church exits at every church everytime they serve alcohol, to make sure that winedrinkers don't drive home. Then the priests would get arrested and fined for routinely letting hundreds of people drive home after having knowingly served them alcohol as well as for having knowingly served alcohol to minors. Of course the priests might use nonalcoholic beverages in order to pass any such test, especially if police setup a roadblock, but if we test the people without the priests being forewarned they would be utterly exposed for their fraud. Anyways why would priests bother using nonalcoholic drinks when for centuries they have been claiming to turn wine into blood? If they change the custom now it would be implicit guilt and admission that either they'd been lying all these years or their powers have left, either of which would be evidence that it is not a true religion. Also if the priests really are turning wine into the blood of a divinity then the liquid should taste the same all over the world. However the liquid in a Catholic Church service in France tastes very different than the liquid in a Catholic Church service in Mexico, the reason is because they use different wines and it doesn't really change into blood. Whereas the liquid cannot be stored, the leftover bread is often put in a sacristy, which is basically just a fancy box for storage. I "drank the kool-aid" and believed that this little box held the body of God or Jesus pbuh in bread form and whenever near the sacristy acted with reverence. At the seminary I planned to attend they had a secret poker table, at which the seminarians would gamble on the second floor inside the church which had a window overlooking the entire church area. Despite gambling being a sin, the joke the seminarians would often say was, *"no one gambling would dare to lie or cheat since God is so close by being stored in the sacristy."* It's evident this attitude is no different than that of the pagans of Mecca who used to worship dates (a type of fruit like a fig), who when they got hungry at night would eat their god(s) after having worshiped them all day. It's almost unbelievable how foolish it is to eat something you pray to or worship. The Eucharist sacrament is the same pagan game with a different name. When people act badly after exiting church they're scolded *"you just left church didn't you learn anything!"* Seriously how can someone who just drank alcohol be expected to act? The Santa Claus belief is often used for justification, but just because they "believe" it's not alcohol the side effects of the drink are evident for all who have sight to see. The tongues and livers of those who have drunk the "blood" are the best of witnesses to testify. May our tongues speak the truth and not swallow falsehood, even if such falsehood is served by our fathers.

While I was in my senior year in fall 2009 CE, the police became another weapon in the war chest during disputes with my parents, rather than a last resort. The frequency of police visits to the house increased. However there was never anything they could charge me with and I don't think they liked that very much. At 17 years of age I was too old for the P.I.N.S. program (Person In Need of Supervision) while at the same time being a minor under 18. So they sent me to another psychiatrist where one of the employees there told me they were surprised someone so old had been sent to them since they usually deal with kids 10-14 years old. Nevertheless this second psychiatrist center had a criminalist attitude and subjected me to a urine test assuming I took drugs. As someone with aspirations to be a priest who was actively discouraging peers from drug use, a urine test was the epitome of idiocy and I passed with yellow colors. After failing to fail, the system sent me to a juvenile corrections officer because apparently "*if you hate your parents as a teenager it's statistically proven you have an 80% chance of being in jail before you're 21*". At this time I held such a hatred for my parents and family (their family as I referred to them) that I would openly state how after I leave them and move out I never wanted to be in contact with them again. This government employee put me on unofficial probation, meaning there was no legal justification for doing so but as a precautionary measure they felt it was appropriate. On probation I was told that if I violated any of their terms, refused to show up at meetings, or got into any trouble then a criminal record would be created. If I obeyed, then upon turning 18 I'd be off probation and it wouldn't be on my permanent file; or so they said. This experience with the ~~justice~~ system made me feel victimized and instilled sympathy for all those "bad kids" who I knew, that I previously judged who might have just gotten caught up in the system with similar circumstances to my own. I had legally become one of the "bad kids" even though I didn't do any of the bad stuff which all the "bad kids" do. Of course all the other kids thought me being on probation was hilarious.

Prior to this I had been involved in a juvenile legal system called "Youth Court" designed for youth under the age of 16 who are proven guilty of misdemeanors to have their sentence set by their peers. The minimum sentence being an apology letter and the maximum being a large number of community service hours designed to serve the government. There is a certification program to become qualified to serve, which I took in 8th grade. After passing I was routinely selected from a list of other "qualified" youth to serve. Those ages 16 and under could not be one of the three judges. Before turning 16 I would fluctuate between serving as court clerk, court bailiff and a defense attorney. At this time I hadn't discovered that man-made laws are illegitimate and abominable in the sight of God, or that by participating in a man-made legal system it can qualify one as a disbeliever in the authority of God. I foolishly tried to defend these juvenile delinquents trying to get them off the hook with an apology letter, or at least a less severe community service sentence.

Prior to the sentencing, I would privately interview the guilty child in order to build a case saying why they weren't as bad as the report said, which all the people in Youth Court were given to read prior to the sentencing. For all intents and purposes these were mock sentencings where the punishment was predetermined and the child was just given the opportunity to plead for mercy as a formality. My job was to make them get pity from the 3 teenage judges. One thing that was hard to grasp was how these kids were so stupid as to steal from a store or from a neighbor, or to burn private property. Those I interviewed always tended to have two reasons as to why they did what they did:

1. They didn't know why. 2. They blamed their friends.

Frequently they would say that they didn't realize their friends were bad until it was too late and they decided not to hang around them anymore. Some would repeatedly be in "Youth Court" so I don't think they kept their promise. Now I realize from personal experience the significance of these similar statements. Often when we do something bad (sinful) we don't know that it's bad, or the real reason why we're doing it. Like these kids we probably think our friends are good but will find out they are bad when it is time for us to be sentenced by God, after we are exposed as guilty sinners. May God help us to examine our friends and only have righteous ones and to recognize the reasons why something is bad as well as how Satan is inciting our sinful desires. None of us thinks we are susceptible to peer pressure yet many times in a stadium when the wave starts on one side by the time it comes to you there is an immense feeling to stand and put one's arms up in the air just like the rest of the fools, fearing that if one doesn't they will be booed. Peer pressure is that easy. When I was older and served as judge I noticed the other two judges tended to enjoy punishing these kids and wanted to give them as many hours as they could get away with. All of us went to school together, the judges and those sentenced. It astonished me how the judges could be on such an arrogant power trip and show no mercy to people they'd see in school every day. I felt that we were given too much power to influence another child's life, we were essentially taking hours from their life just like adult judges take years or money away from the lives of those they sentence. This experience as a part of the legal system and my subsequent experience on the other side of it, led me to see that there is no justice in man-made laws or courts judging by them. Coincidentally after being placed on probation, which was supposed to be confidential and unofficial, after starting to rap I stopped being summoned to serve in "Youth Court" and got a call from the program director asking if I was having problems; I said no getting offended at her suggestion. Since then I never served in Youth Court nor was I asked to serve again. All praises and thanks be to God that I was guided away from that unjust system.

Music was one of the few outlets to release stress during this time of my life and the explicit language it contained began to seep into my own vocabulary corrupting my tongue and polluting my speech. I used the bible to justify my swearing, specifically Mark 11:12-25 which say:" [12] *The next day as they were leaving Bethany, Jesus was hungry.*[13] *Seeing in the distance a fig tree in leaf, he went to find out if it had any fruit. When he reached it, he found nothing but leaves, because it was not the season for figs.*[14] *Then he said to the tree, "May no one ever eat fruit from you again." And his disciples heard him say it.* ¹⁵ *On reaching Jerusalem, Jesus entered the temple courts and began driving out those who were buying and selling there. He overturned the tables of the money changers and the benches of those selling doves,*¹⁶ *and would not allow anyone to carry merchandise through the temple courts.*¹⁷ *And as he taught them, he said, "Is it not written: 'My house will be called a house of prayer for all nations'? But you have made it 'a den of robbers.'"* ¹⁸ *The chief priests and the teachers of the law heard this and began looking for a way to kill him, for they feared him, because the whole crowd was amazed at his teaching.* ¹⁹ *When evening came, Jesus and his disciples went out of the city.* ²⁰ *In the morning, as they went along, they saw the fig tree withered from the roots.* ²¹ <u>*Peter remembered and said to Jesus, "Rabbi, look! The fig tree you cursed has withered!"*</u> ²² *"Have faith in God," Jesus answered.* ²³ *"Truly I tell you, if anyone says to this mountain, 'Go, throw yourself into the sea,' and does not doubt in their heart but believes that what they say will happen, it will be done for them.*²⁴ *Therefore I tell you, whatever you ask for in prayer, believe that you have received it, and it will be yours.*²⁵ *And when you stand praying, if you hold anything against anyone, forgive them, so that your Father in heaven may forgive you your sins."* Verses from an English translation of the New International Version of the Bible

Now I realize how my interpretation of the bible verses of Jesus pbuh cursing a fig tree were taken out of context in order to justify swearing, but at the time I claimed to have biblical support permitting my foul swearing aka satanic speech/ demonic dialect. Many people abuse the bible in this way taking verses out of context to justify whatever behavior they are doing trying to make it appear as though it is biblically sanctioned. Even outside of the bible people will take things out of context when it comes to video, audio, writings and sayings. Everyone has an opinion and most will have a way to justify their opinion even if their opinion is wrong or their evidence for it is false. The real meaning in context of Jesus pbuh cursing the fig tree demonstrates that Jesus pbuh is not all knowing. Jesus' companions knew it wasn't the season for figs but he didn't, so in that instance Jesus pbuh knew less than them. Also if Jesus pbuh were the Creator, God, divine or the son of God he could have just made the tree produce fruit on demand, but in actuality he had no power to do this and was left hungry. God wouldn't be left hungry by his own creation, God wouldn't even get hungry in the first place. One must read between the lines to realize the significance of what is written by the author. If the author was just intending to tell people to ask for forgiveness he would have done so plainly without including the extra information about the events concerning the fig tree.

In between the two sections about the fig tree is a narration about Jesus pbuh taking over the temple. The temple in Jerusalem at this time was 30 meters tall (98.42 feet) covered 36 acres and could fit 27 American football fields inside it with armed guards stationed within for security. It was HUGE! This means if Jesus pbuh acted alone, people would've thought it's just some guy upset he got ripped off, without realizing what such an act meant and perhaps less than 50 people out of hundreds of thousands would've noticed because very little would have been disrupted and it would not have caused much of a scene. To actually take over the temple and drive everyone out such an operation would've required a significant force to pull off. The historical Jesus pbuh is documented to have had around 900 armed companions who accompanied him wherever he went, which the historians referred to them as a band of bandits with Jesus pbuh as their ringleader. Obviously Jesus pbuh was no bandit, but it's interesting to see how the non-Muslim historians slandered him just as non-Muslim "historians" slander Muhammad pbuh today. This taking over of the temple was because the Jewish rabbis were dealing with interest which has been explicitly prohibited by God according to the Torah, Bible and Quran. The term "money changers" is a mistranslation which should read "money lenders" because there was no foreign exchange. Gold and silver coins were valued by their weight with their national issuer having zero effect on their purchasing power. People didn't have to change their foreign currency into local currency, this term "money changer" is invalid and there was no such thing in existence at that time. Without a doubt the story of Jesus pbuh ransacking the temple is a warning to those who would take usury today, otherwise known as interest. Some of the many evidences supporting the prohibition of interest from the Bible include:

Exodus 22:25 *"If thou lend money to any of My people, even to the poor with thee, thou shalt not be to him as a creditor; neither shall ye lay upon him interest."*

Deuteronomy 23:19 *"Do not charge your brother interest, whether on money or food or anything else that may earn interest."*

And the New Testament as well in **Luke 6:34-36**

[34] *And if you lend to those from whom you expect repayment, what credit is that to you? Even **sinners lend to sinners, expecting to be repaid in full.** [35] But love your enemies, do good to them, and lend to them without expecting to get anything back. Then your reward will be great, and **you will be children of the Most High**, because he is kind to the ungrateful and wicked. Be merciful, just as your Father is merciful. "*

But if it's against the law of God then why do so many who claim to follow the Torah and Bible consume usury? After all the Vatican operates one of the largest interest banking operations in the world worth trillions of dollars and growing. The Vatican Bank even reported a 2300% gain for the fiscal year 2014 CE boasting about their profit from interest bearing bonds. Is everyone who has a bank account sinful? I myself was ignorant of the prohibition on usury until I became a Muslim, so ignorance may indeed be the main reason. I researched how interest became commonplace in the Catholic Church and Christian world looking to expose their hypocrisy and catch them red-handed changing the law of God. It surprised me to learn that the Catholic Church has never changed their position on interest. Both Peter and Paul agreed, any interest whether big or small was usury and would cause a person to be in the hellfire even for just one penny. Which is unusual that they agreed, because typically Peter and Paul were polar opposites teaching the opposite of each other. If interest has always been wrong why are so many banks today giving and receiving interest in what are considered to be Christian countries? It turns out that for the greater part of Christian history there were no banks, until the Templar knights created them. Interest had no place in Christendom for over 1,000 years. Slowly the sin crept in as the Templar order spread and interest started to be seen as legal since the "holy knights" were getting rich off of it. Yet at the third council of Lateran in 1179 CE it was decreed that persons who accepted interest on loans could not receive the Christian sacraments nor a Christian burial. Whereas burial ban didn't just apply to those receiving interest but those who paid it as well. In 1215 CE the famous Magna Carta Charter even stipulated that interest on debt would not be paid by the heirs of the indebted when in articles 10 and 11 it said:

> 10. *If one who has borrowed from the Jews any sum, great or small, die before that loan be repaid, the debt shall not bear interest while the heir is under age, of whomsoever he may hold; and if the debt fall into our hands, we will not take anything except the principal sum contained in the bond.*
>
> 11. *And if anyone die indebted to the Jews, his wife shall have her dower and pay nothing of that debt; and if any children of the deceased are left under age, necessaries shall be provided for them in keeping with the holding of the deceased; and out of the residue the debt shall be paid, reserving, however, service due to feudal lords; in like manner let it be done touching debts due to others than Jews."*

In 1275 CE Edward I of England passed the Statute of Jewry, which made usury illegal and akin to blasphemy. King Edward ordered the assets of the violators to be seized. Many Jews were arrested on this charge, 300 were hanged and their property went to the Crown. Pope Clement V made the belief in the right to usury a heresy in 1311 CE and abolished all secular legislation which allowed it. Pope Sixtus V condemned the practice of charging interest as: *"detestable to God and man, damned by the sacred canons and contrary to Christian charity."* In the encyclical of 1745 CE, VIXPERVENIT, Pope Benedict XIV stated:*"The nature of the sin called usury has its proper place and origin in a loan contract… [which] demands, by its very nature, that one return to another only as much as he has received. The sin rests on the fact that sometimes the creditor desires more than he has given…, but **any gain which exceeds the amount he gave is illicit and usurious**. 'One cannot condone the sin of usury by arguing that the gain is not great or excessive, but rather moderate or small; neither can it be condoned by arguing that the borrower is rich; nor even by arguing that the money borrowed is not left idle, but is spent usefully…"* As recently as 2009 CE Pope Benedict XVI admitted that interest is a mortal sin, but advised bishops and priests not to make a big fuss condemning it because it might cause people to leave the Catholic Church. Now does that sound like an organization whose primary concern is the salvation of its members? Or does it sound like an organization whose primary concern is the revenue generated by membership fees and donations?

Interest actually kills people. Currently 11 million children die each year around the world as a direct result of the conditions of poverty and debt that are caused by interest. Interest is a weapon that EHMs utilize. An EHM is a "Economic Hit Man", a private sector professional paid to swindle nations out of trillions of dollars to further the corporatocracy cause of global empire. Since "EHM" is a job description and not a job title, many EHMs don't even think of themselves as EHMs and simply do their job for money, fame, or ideological reasons actually thinking they're doing something good. For instance Americanized EHMs provide favors/loans and then ensure the "aid money" is paid to American corporations in exchange for overpriced overhyped inefficient "development projects" that cause all of the "aid money" to be spent on American companies while interest loans are added to pay the total cost. Sometimes the "aid money" goes straight from Washington to the American corporation and the "aided" nation doesn't even get to smell it. Oh and these projects are rarely finished and if they are they tend to actually be a financial burden that negatively impacts the nation's economy, society and environment with the only benefactors being the corrupt government officials who get a "commission" for approving the project contracts. They then store their money in first world banks until their money is frozen and confiscated by these same first world governments once those corrupt governments fall out of favor and/or are overthrown. Subsequently any such projects funded by "foreign aid" doesn't typically go to those who need it but goes to the constituents of the government. This goes both ways too, the local government says to only give aid to its most ardent supporters and the foreign seeks out those who support its political goals for that country and try to aid them whereas frequently those who actually need aid don't get nothing at all. I'll explain this with a common example that would take place during the "Cold War". Let's say Nation #1 and Nation #2 both have 100 citizens and the leader of each nation has $100 to buy political support. Imagine Nation#1 is a democracy and only needs to keep 50 people pleased to retain power while Nation #2 is an autocracy where the leader only has to please 5 people to stay in power. Both nations care about the stance Nation #2 takes towards the Soviet Union. Nation #1 wants the people of Nation #2 to be anti-Soviet Union because it will benefit their country by $1 per person. Yet the people in Nation #2 don't want that type of policy for their country, and to put a financial spin on it let's say such a stance would mean a loss of $2 per person due to economic adjustments that such a policy would require regarding trade. Now if the leader of Nation #1 paid for his political support each of his supporters would get $2. While if Nation #2's leader paid for his support each of his 5 key supporters would get $20. Since if Nation #2 implements the policy desired by Nation #1 it will result in a loss of $2 per person, the leader of Nation #2 would need some financial compensation to justify making such an unwise and unpopular national policy. Although since the leader of Nation #2 only needs 5 people to be kept happy to stay in power then because the anti-Soviet Union policy would only cause a $10 loss to his supporters then in reality he only needs $10 to justify this change in policy and have it implemented. While the leader of Nation #1 will only buy this anti-Soviet policy if the value to his 50 supporters is greater than the cash they'd lose out on. Since the 50 key supporters in Nation #1 would benefit by $1 per person if the anti-Soviet policy is adopted by Nation #2 then the leader of Nation #1 can afford to pay up to $50 in "aid" to Nation #2 in order for Nation #2 to implement the unwise and unpopular policy which Nation #1 wants it to implement. Thus through this "foreign aid" transaction both leaders' key supporters are happy and better off financially, however the remaining 95 people in Nation #2 are worse off by $2 per person for the implementation of a policy they oppose. Now of course this is a "Cold War" example of what America would do to combat Soviet influence, but America also continues to use this same policy with Muslim nations to make them implement unpopular pro-Israel policies and anti-Islamic policies. To take a real world example in February 2003 CE prior to the invasion of Iraq, America used this exact formula when it offered Turkey $6 billion in grants and $20 billion in loan guarantees in exchange for basing rights which would have likely improved America's ability to engage Iraq's army. With Turkey having about 70 million people this "aid" would amount to a $370 benefit per capita. Since Turkey claims to be democratic if we presume their government needs the support of 25% of the population then since the "aid" would go to those key supporters exclusively then that amounts to a benefit of about $1,500 per key supporter. Yet that was too politically risky for Turkey and they settled for a less risky transaction for less money in which the U.S. was able to rescue downed pilots using bases in Turkey. However if Turkey were an autocracy and had less key supporters that amounted to say 1% of the population, then the American offer would've resulted in a benefit of $40,000 to each key supporter and that might've been enough money to buy Turkey off. Thus it shouldn't be too surprising that the U.S. Iraq invasion was eventually launched from bases in autocratic states like Kuwait and Saudi Arabia. It is because democracy makes it more expensive for America to buy a nation's policies that they tend to support undemocratic regimes. Egypt in 2012 CE is a prime example, when under a democracy it was more expensive for America to buy a pro-Israeli policy and during the 2012 CE war between Gaza and Israel the new democratic Egypt started taking a less friendly stance towards Israel. Therefore on July 3rd, 2013 CE America supported the military coup that overthrew the Egyptian democracy and established a military state that was pro-Israel and more anti-Islamic. So America's policies while they might seem hypocritical in principle, it's very clear what the policy is and they follow it. The problem is many think America's political slogans and alleged principles dictate policy but that is only partially true. The American GADE is the policy(although its really a GAIE) and they want to achieve that as cheaply as possible, political slogans and principles be damned. Basically "foreign aid" is the puppet string and the puppet is only the government and its key supporters. The majority of people in a puppet nation don't get helped at all, especially if they're in need, because the needy aren't a political threat since they're too troubled to cause any trouble. This is why if you look at all the countries America has "aided" those nations which get the most "foreign aid" are the same nations whose populations have the most hatred for America. That's a proven fact! Statistically the more America gives in "foreign aid" the more that nation's people hate America. Why is that? Because this "foreign aid" is not aiding them it's harming them! It's not charity it's economic warfare! Although don't make the mistake of thinking democracy will make this way of buying diplomacy more expensive and thus less likely. Pakistan is another country America has bought. For instance in 2001 CE Pakistan was slated to get $5.3 million in "aid" while Nepal got $30.4 million, which is nearly 6 times as much. However after 9/11/01 American policies changed and Pakistan was a desirable nation to use to invade and conquer Afghanistan, so in 2002 CE America gave $800 million in "aid" to Pakistan and only $37 million to Nepal. On paper in one year Pakistan went from being 6 times less needy than Nepal in "charitable aid" to suddenly being 21 times more needy and getting paid 21 times more than the country who got paid 6 times more than they did the year before. So did the people of Pakistan get 27 times poorer in 1 year or did Nepal get 27 times richer? Neither, it's just that "aid" isn't about aid. As the Taliban lost power the aid to Pakistan dropped, therefore Pakistan became less effective in fighting the Taliban and it regained strength in Afghanistan during 2008-2009 CE. In February 2009 CE the Pakistani government paid the Taliban $6 million as part of a peace treaty and agreement that they could impose Shariah law within Swat Valley. Now why would they do that? Well because people in Pakistan actually like the Taliban and many prefer it to their own government, so the Pakistani government wanted to placate it's people rather than risk a civil war and since America wasn't paying the big bucks in "aid" anymore they saw the $6 million as a investment. Sure enough in September 2009 CE America passed a bill to give Pakistan $1.5 billion in "aid" and in turn Pakistan cracked down once more on the Taliban since that's the way the game is played. However in 2011 CE, after the real estate bubble that was caused by interest burst, Obama wasn't willing to pay the price for Pakistan's authorization and cooperation in killing Osama bin Laden, who lived in Pakistan for years after the Afghanistan invasion. Yet Obama needed the support at the polls to win the 2012 CE election so that's where sometimes the game can't be played or won't be played and the rules get broken. When that happens it makes ordinary people get suspicious because they can tell something wrong is going on, but they don't know quite what it is and the headlines can't quite smooth things over. Whereas despite the whole operation being sketchy as to what actually happened and getting falsely portrayed by hollywood in order to justify torture, which in reality didn't even lead to the operation, this is one instance where some people were able to realize that something else is going on behind the scenes. That something is built upon interest. Meanwhile America uses international terrorism to justify its government policies domestically and the nations where such terrorism occurs use terrorism in order to get "aid" dollars to "fight terrorism". For instance in 2014 CE the Iraqi military was ordered to give territory and weapons to ISIL without a fight. Why? One could reason that it was because "aid" to Iraq's corrupt democratic Shia government had declined, so by giving up some stuff to ISIL they could get a 60 + country coalition to give them all kinds of "aid" in the future for their military which will then suppress its own people after ISIS is removed, or rather IF ISIS is removed because if ISIS goes then how will the corrupt Iraqi democracy get all that "aid" annually? If there ain't no war game to play why would they get paid with "foreign aid"? So the "war on terror" may never end because it's basically business for global governments. Yet what's worse is that the world leaders know this and they say poverty is the problem so we really have to give more "foreign aid" in order to fight the conditions leading to terrorism and hatred. Whereas in reality such "foreign aid" is the primary reason for poverty and hatred throughout the world today. All these problems governments cause are caused by the very solutions the governments propose. For instance ISIS claims they killed people in France because the French government was dropping bombs on them and if they don't stop then they'll keep killing French people. What did the French government do? They said *"In order to prevent people from getting killed, we're going to drop more bombs on ISIS even though they told us not to do that or else they'll kill us more."* Any logical person would see that #1 says X is the problem that causes them to do Y and #2 says X is the solution to stop #1 from doing Y. Clearly #2 is not interested in stopping X or Y but on the contrary wants more of X and more of Y. Although patriotism makes people stupid and illogical sometimes leading them to think such "solutions" will work. Take Libya as another example. In 2011 CE America gave tons of "foreign aid" to the Libyan rebels who overthrew Gaddafi. Now if this "foreign aid" was charitable and beneficial it should've caused goodwill for Libyans towards the American government. However it was not charitable and it came with interest and strings attached that severely crippled the revolution and impoverished the post-revolution nation. Thus on 9/11/2012 CE the American embassy in Benghazi, Libya was destroyed. Of course the world acted as though it was solely because of some Jew producing a slanderous movie about Muhammad pbuh, but that was only a tiny part of the reason. There were many other factors at play and all that "foreign aid" contributed greatly. Also most people don't fully understand what an American embassy actually is or does. An American embassy is where the CIA and FBI operate out of, the embassies are their base of operations for clandestine activities in foreign nations. This isn't a recent phenomenon either, it's been that way for decades. Well the new Libyan government wasn't too keen on the CIA and FBI running operations to destabilize their new government and used the movie as a coverup to get the CIA and FBI out of Libya. While Obama used the incident to win the 2012 CE elections 2 months later, and that's why the U.S. government explicitly told American troops not to defend the embassy, because it's all a game to them. Libya wanted the CIA and FBI out but the Obama administration needed something in exchange, so a deal was made to allow the embassy to be destroyed without retaliatation under the guise of Islamic outrage so that way Libya could meet its goals and crack down on devout Muslims who wanted Sharia in Libya. While America could implement new security systems, increase patriotism and Obama could get re-elected. Meanwhile the news outlets get a juicy story to polarize the world. Although as a Muslim I do have to say that while the outrage over the movie was overblown and led to unislamic violence, all Muslims should be outraged when their prophet is insulted and it shouldn't be tolerated. Yet not only should Muslims express outrage when Muhammad pbuh is slandered they should get outraged when any prophet gets mocked or slandered. If Muslims protest the movies and pictures of Muhammad pbuh they should also protest the movies and pictures of Jesus, Moses, Noah and all the rest pbut. Yet this doesn't happen because the protests are rarely genuine, but are political theatre. Those who protest tend not to even follow the prophet they claim to love. There are people who don't pray but then they'll go out screaming at a protest, whereas that's not what the prophets would want nor should a protest be the top priority today. Maybe when Muslims are following the prophet Muhammad pbuh 100% then they can protest when he gets insulted, but for Muslims to not follow the prophet Muhammad pbuh in their daily life while claiming to be Muslim that may even be a greater crime than someone slandering the prophets. This applies to many, myself included, in that what's the point of protesting if you're not even practicing? The way to really infuriate the enemies of prophets is to live the way the prophets taught us. Shouting and screaming makes them happy, but if you start following the prophet more and more, the more prophets get attacked that will make disbelievers upset and may even cause them to stop, because the reason they attack the prophets to begin with is because they don't want people to follow them and emulate them. Whereas if one is practicing the prophetic religion then they would know how to and how not to protest. For instance publicly burning a U.S. flag is not what the prophets would do. Seriously some are so silly they will waste money to buy an American flag from America then they set it on fire in outrage thinking that's going to help the situation somehow. It's just a waste of their money and energy as well as funding the very country they claim to hate. Whereas some people who did this even burned themselves in the process because while burning the flag their clothes caught on fire and they suffered burns themselves. Now do you think any prophet would suggest they buy a flag and burn themselves in the process of burning that flag? What do they think they will accomplish by that? Do they think burning themselves while burning a flag they paid for is going to "teach em a lesson"? No it's stupidity. The point is people should practice their religion before they protest for the sake of their religion. It's easy to protest, it's harder to practice. You practice you go to paradise, you protest you go to prison. Politically Muslims throughout the world want every US embassy closed in their countries because they don't like America or what the CIA and FBI are doing in those embassies. Yet the cowardly corrupt Muslimish governments have not even asked the US to close their embassies because their people don't like them. Why not? Because of that "foreign aid" money they might jeoparadize. "Foreign aid" is a media friendly way to say "*we just bought foreign politicians*". Another great example is the following chart of the "aid" the US sent to Egypt from 1948-2008 CE.

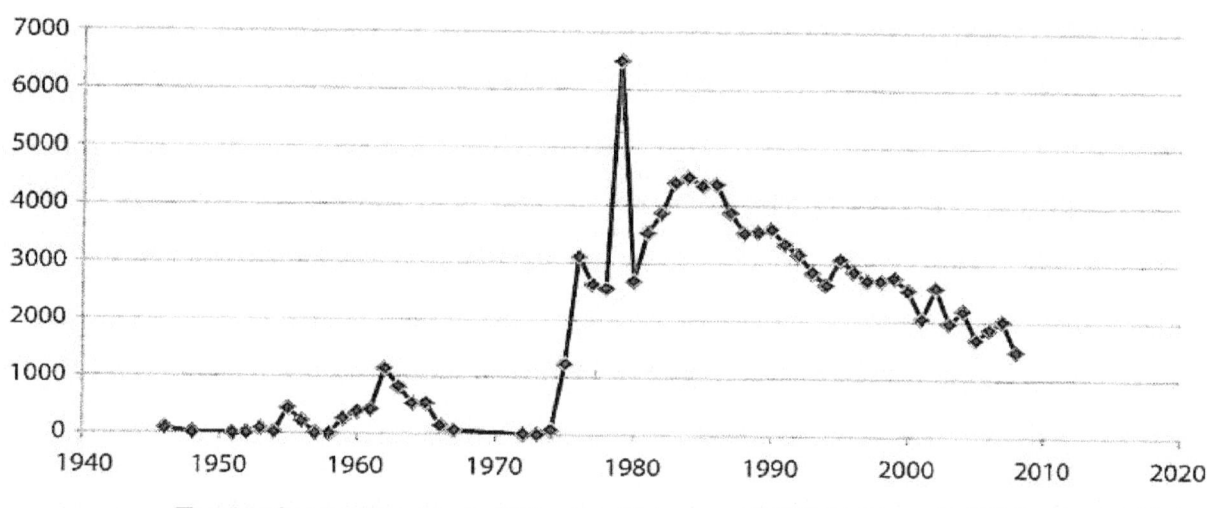

Total US Assistance to Egypt in Constant 2008 Million US$ from USAID

Anyone who sees this chart should immediately wonder: "*What happened in 1979 CE that Egypt got so much money?*" What happened was that in 1979 CE Egypt and Israel signed a peace treaty whereby Egypt became the first Arab nation to officially recognize Israel as a state. This treaty was a result of the Camp David Accords, it was witnessed and encouraged by US president Jimmy Carter. Afterwards Egypt's president Anwar Sadat won the Nobel Peace Prize and Egypt also got $6.5 billion dollars in U.S. "foreign aid". Note that was $6.5 billion in 1979 dollars, that's a crazy amount of money. Well how did the Egyptians react? They assassinated Anwar Sadat 2 years later because "aid" is simply how a foreign country gains political concessions and control in another country, it's not really aid. Since most democracies can't usually be openly corrupt, foreign aid is a way to subsidize themselves in that "*If your country gives my cronies perks or "aid", then my country will give your cronies perks or "aid". As a bonus everyone will think we're philanthropists.*" Always keep in mind that no modern government gives away free money, especially to another country. There are always motives with puppet strings attached and certain "understandings". It's called diplomacy for a reason, and just as one can buy a college diploma through "donations" one can buy diplomatic resolutions through "foreign aid". Taxdollars being used for paid diplomatic resolutions has actually been the Western definition of "aid" for centuries and that's why it was banned by the Magna Carta in 1215 CE in articles 12 and 15 which say: <u>No 'scutage' or 'aid' may be levied in our kingdom without its general consent</u>, *unless it is for the ransom of our person, to make our eldest son a knight, and (once) to marry our eldest daughter. For these purposes only a reasonable 'aid' may be levied. 'Aids' from the city of London are to be treated similarly.", "In future we will allow no one to levy an 'aid' from his free men, except to ransom his person, to make his eldest son a knight, and (once) to marry his eldest daughter. For these purposes only a reasonable 'aid' may be levied."* Scutage is the medieval tax paid by people who didn't want to fight in the King's army when called to provide the obligatory service, such a bribe was also known as "aid". So the next time you hear international news about "foreign aid", remember that Englishmen forced King John at swordpoint in 1215 CE to make it a law that nobody would be able to "aid" the English without the consent of the whole kingdom. They had centuries of "aid" and realized it was hurting them, to the point where they said, *"we'll kill you if you don't stop aiding us and outlaw aid"*. Sometimes the generous "foreign aid" explicitly goes to subversive groups and governments ask that no "aid" be sent to them because it destabilizes their country. Other times aid specifically gets cut off in order to destabilize a country, such as in Egypt during 2012 CE. America kept sending billions in aid to Egypt while it was temporarily a democracy but if you actually look at what was sent all the "economic aid" was cut and only military aid was sent. The "economic aid" wasn't really aid anyways but were perks for the influential essential people in Egypt who can dictate who rules. Those used to the "foreign aid " perks got the subtle message that the US wouldn't give them their annual cut now that the Egyptian democracy had a less friendly attitude towards Israel, meanwhile the military was still getting it's aid. Clearly the message sent without words by USAID was that they wanted the military in charge and not the democratically elected government, and that's what happened coincidentally on July 3rd, 2013 CE which is the day before America's annual patriotic celebrations. Very ironic but also ideal because most Americans pay no attention to what is going on around the world during their holidays and it's why they don't know the reasons things are the way they are or why things change. Americans get stupefied by cultural entertainment like sports, movies, tv and holidays just like the Roman citizens were stupefied by their circus, the coliseum and their numerous holidays. Thus the Roman citizens were relatively oblivious as to why those "barbarians" hated being civilized by Rome through bloody conquest and why they invaded Rome when Romans thought it to be the best nation ever. Rome gave "foreign aid" too in the form of roads which they built so their armies could speedily move throughout a country to kill people and the resources(such as slaves) could be quickly taken and hauled back to Rome. Yet the average Roman citizen was stumped as to why those "Barbarians" are so mad when Rome built "free roads" for them. Likewise people don't understand the damage of "foreign aid". But what happens in cases of environmental calamities? Surely that's free money given out of the goodness of people's hearts right? Undoubtedly those who donate have good intentions but the money donated for emergency reconstruction after environmental disasters also gets funneled by EHMs to American corporations. All the horrific destruction from war or the environment are seen as business opportunities for construction. Similar to how Nero appreciated the Great Fire of Rome clearing space for his architectural plans so much he was accused of starting it, many Western construction companies celebrate when destruction takes place because that means business will be booming and they can charge premium prices. This is because since reconstruction is desired ASAP, construction companies can charge as much as they can get away with because they know their business is needed, just as an auto mechanic or a plumber can inflate their prices due to necessity. It's like selling an umbrella when it's raining, or selling food to someone who is starving. Also regarding disasters, corrupt governments use such situations to line their own purses. They purposely neglect prevention and safety measures so that many will suffer in case of calamity, then when calamity strikes they hinder aid getting through so that way more people overseas donate to stop the suffering and the corrupt governments just confiscate the funds and let their people suffer. The more who die the more they get paid, so corrupt governments actually see calamities as paydays despite their claims of sorrow and needing help. As if that weren't bad enough the NGO charities who help people are ineffective and end up helping corrupt governments by doing their job for them. For instance even corrupt governments know they have to do a minimum amount of service to keep their population alive and productive, so they allot a budget to help the poor and the most needy. However when the foreign charities spend their donated money on those poor and needy, the governments in those countries see their charity as a substitute for their service. Then instead of the government helping their people they pocket the money themselves since the charity took care of their poor people for them. Thus many charity organizations are ineffective and maintain the conditions that are responsible for poverty. For instance the governments would've paid for X needy students to go to school, but because some generous foreigners sponsor 1/2 of those students then the government only helps half as many. So that's where charities shouldn't be judged by the number of people helped each year or the amount of money spent on charity out of every dollar, but by the effectiveness of what they've done that wouldn't have been done without them. Some even cause harm by taking jobs, such as when foreign aid workers paint houses or build houses for free they are actually taking away jobs of the local painters and laborers causing them to starve. So that's where "aid" could've just paid a local uneducated unskilled laborer to paint a house or school but because some philanthropist wants to do a good deed they end up putting some poor guy out of business. Thus more harm gets done than good because people with good intentions don't know how to truly help others. I'm not saying one shouldn't donate to NGOs at all but some of them make things worse without intending to, so one must be selective in which charities one gives to and what exactly they are spending on and who exactly is benefiting from that. As an example NGOs like "USAID" teach natural farmers to become dependent on fertilizers, pesticides and GMO seeds from foreign companies, which serves to impoverish the "aided" and causes western market domination under the mask of "helping others". So most "foreign aid" isn't really about aiding foreigners it's about aiding domestics at the expense of foreigners. Such "aid organizations" are designed to perpetuate the imperialist ethnocentric idea known as "*the white man's burden*" that: "*they're so poor because they're inferior and if we don't help them they'll never be able to catch up to us*". Thus "aiding" others is meant to demonstrate superiority and sabotage them. If people didn't need "aid" then some philanthropists would create a demand for "aid" because they want to give "aid" to feel good about themselves. So first-world citizens shouldn't think that all these poor countries all need "aid" and always will, because if they didn't the West would still give them "aid" because they want to feel superior and because the "foreign aid" that's distributed today is really debt that makes nations subservient. When the indebted nation can't pay back the interest due on the "aid", natural resources and UN votes are taken as collateral, military bases are established, military support is given and the nation is still expected to pay up. This is how the IMF and World Bank operate in order obtain leverage, control and power. While I focused more on US "foreign aid" don't misunderstand it and think America is the only country which does this, if a government gives "foreign aid" then they're playing their own game. Most foreign "aid" countries give out, is equivalent to a credit card that can only be used at the issuer's store which you are expected to max out, say thank you for, and then get another credit card from somewhere else to pay the debt. As an example about 70% of the "aid" Canada gives to other nations has a contractual clause which says it has to be spent on Canadian products. It's basically a way to legally and sneakily subsidize their own corporations with tax dollars while Canadians feel and look generous at the same time they put other countries in debt. This is why the E.U. and the U.S. government bail banks out and say they are "too big to fail" because interest loans are more destructive than their militaries. Thomas Jefferson recognized this when in 1787 CE he said at the Constitutional Convention, "*I believe that banking institutions are more dangerous to our liberties than standing armies. Already they have raised up a money aristocracy that has set the government at defiance.*" But most of the world doesn't understand economics so they're completely clueless of the damage first world banksters do to the world by dropping economic bombs on third world countries without anyone even knowing what hit them or who. Then when some who were exploited do find out and fight back they get condemned for harming "aid workers" and "honest respectable charitable businessmen". It is because of clandestine economic warfare that many people in the world hate Americans and also because Americans are bleeding the rest of the world dry. I mean that literally. For decades in Haiti, Nicaragua, Mexico, India, Indonesia and many other "less developed" nations, desperate poor people sell their blood for a third world price such as $5 a litre and then their blood gets exported to America for $25 a litre and bought by leaders of the U.S. medical industry like Cutter labs, Parke Davis, Lederle, Green Cross and Red Cross where U.S. citizens can end up paying $600 for it in a blood transfusion. This blood industry is worth trillions of dollars a year and growing. While half of all the blood consumed in America each year (about 60-70 million litres and rising) comes from such exploited third world peoples who sold their blood for practically nothing, with some even dying as a result of selling more of their blood than was safe to sell. Although Japan and Germany are currently the largest consumers of blood so at least America isn't the top consumer, but it is the top purchaser and acts as an influential global blood market maker possessing 60% of the world's plasma supply.(plasma is a very expensive special component of blood extracted after donation and before transfusion that can be further divided into even more expensive components) What's even worse is that companies like International Red Cross and Red Crescent(Founded by the freemason Jean Henri Dunant during the Russo-Turkish war, wherein the Red Cross was to get paid to help Russians and the Red Crescent was to get paid to help Turks, even though it's all the same organization just using different symbols because of religious sensitivies) will buy more blood than they use in order to cause a shortage on the national and global blood markets (which are unregulated) that forces hospitals and blood banks to pay exorbitant amounts to get the blood they need as a result of artificial scarcity due to blood hoarding. Thus tragically forcing those same third world countries to then buy back their own peoples blood for multiples of what it was originally sold for, oh and frequently they have to pay for it on credit. Yet these blood bankers, or "non-profits" as some call themselves since they "don't sell the blood, but only charge fees" and have "excesses instead of expenses", wouldn't be able to exploit poor people or create blood shortages if not for financial banks creating these dastardly economic conditions through interest, and where do these banks get the funds to kickstart such an evil domino effect? From the average person going to their bank and depositing money into a savings account, CD or IRA in order to save/store their money and obtain interest, or by paying interest to the banks on loans or mortgages. That's why "terrorists" tend to view peaceful civilians as guilty instead of innocent because civilians are funding these criminal organizations that exploit, impoverish and kill millions around the world, but not only do they fund them they publicly voluntarily proudly support them and don't want to learn why by acting in their own selfish interest in interest banking they are harming the rest of the world. Thus the victims realizing their pleas are continuously suppressed and ignored, so they turn to violence attempting to draw attention to the problem since their words fall on deaf ears. Yet then their words are still unheard and it justifies the first world violence against these same nations which then creates another opportunity for EHMS to "aid" people after the dust clears. The first world citizens then ironically and arrogantly expect gratitude for making the dust that destroyed the monster they were responsible for and then "aiding" in the cleanup which is just an even more ferocious economic monster, never realizing that the problem is their attitude, particularly their attitude towards interest. Then when some first world citizens get criticized or have their government criticized they say: *"We've been giving all those poor people* (usually since they aren't familiar with geography they name an entire continent such as Africa or just say Africans) *millions of dollars in aid for years and years. They wouldn't even be alive if it weren't for us feeding them."* At which point if they are too irrate to have an adult conversation about economic realities, then just ask them the names of the people they have personally gave millions to and that you would also appreciate them giving them some millions to you too since they're so generous. Then when they admit it's their government who they meant by saying "we" and not them, then tell them if they are going to take credit for the alleged charity the government gives by saying "we" then they also must use the "we" for everything the government does and should say "we bombed them", "we tortured them", "we robbed their nation's resources", "we colonized them", and so on and so forth "for years and years and years". Fortunately most won't want credit for the bad stuff their government does and then you can explain that all that "aid" actually is bad stuff and it's not aid at all but causes more harm to the world than help. Just take

"AIDS" for instance, that's a very dangerous deadly disease, so just because it's called "aids" doesn't mean it aids anybody or anything and just because it's called interest doesn't mean it isn't usury. Usury is what interest was before it was called interest and interest is what "foreign aid" was before it was called "foreign aid". Today the language is so convoluted that we have "peacekeepers" who kill people for a livelihood. The attitude many have towards interest is so distorted that they are familiar with and frequently use the phrases *"laughing all the way to the bank"*, *"you can bank on it"* or *"take it to the bank"*. While the rest of the world is shouting out *"No! Don't take it to the bank, they're killing us!"* An example that shows the effect interest has on society is found in the statement of former President Obasanjo when commenting on the debt Nigeria faced in August 2000 CE when he said: *"All that we had borrowed up to 1985 or 1986 was around $5 billion and we have paid about $16 billion yet we are still being told that we owe about $28 billion. That $28 billion came about because of the injustice in the foreign creditors' (lenders) interest rates. If you ask me what is the worst thing in the world, I will say it is compound interest."* Yet it doesn't stop there because faced with all that debt how do you think citizens and governments are going to pay it all off? Through money raised by exports of course, whether it's oil, minerals, livestock, or more commonly cash crops, fruits and vegetables. Frequently poor farmers in bankrupt nations are forced to take on debt to survive and/or supplement lack of government services. Thus they take on debt to grow more hoping to sell more to make more. Yet with so many others doing the same the supply increases causing a decline in prices so that they end up getting paid less than the year before even though they grew and sold more. Thinking it's just a one year fluke they take on more debt in order to pay off their debt, survive in worse conditions than they did the year before and try to turn it around in the future hoping next harvest will fix it all. Yet the same thing happens and if it doesn't the international futures markets get manipulated by the countries who import such food and products to artificially cause the prices of what they buy to be lower so the first-world nations pay less. This results in those third-world farmers earning less and less each year and that's IF they grow more and more each year. By them doing better each year they have a chance to stay alive, if they don't outperform each year they die or become slave labor for major foreign corporations. It gets worse though because those first world citizens want to improve their living conditions even more every year so the futures markets are also manipulated to make the materials first-world countries export such as electronics or cars more expensive in terms of third-world currencies since the first world countries inflate their currencies to encourage exports. Thus the third world farmer earns less and less each year, despite being more and more productive and on top of that the stuff they buy becomes more and more expensive. Which again the situation gets worse because those third-world governments then inflate their currencies to pay off their debts. As a result some folk get fed up with such governments and decide to take action. Although since in the era of corporate globalism poverty is a crime then whenever any poor people protest violently or non-violently against further impoverishment the corporate empire's sponsored media outlets report it as terrorism being done by terrorists. In America they used to call it savagery done by savage indians. Whereas interest is what conquered the Native Americans. This was because Native Americans weren't dumb traders, initially exotic trinkets led them into some crappy trade deals but this exploitive trading of exoticism only lasted for a few decades. Then the white traders would give the natives alcohol as a "free gift" prior to trading to "show they are honest good friends". These free gifts of alcohol led to crappy deals for the natives as well as alcohol addiction so that the natives number one desire in trading became alcohol. Some natives would even trade an entire year's worth of animal skins for just one jug of alcohol. But such booze deals weren't good enough for the white man and they introduced the natives to credit. Contracts were made and drawn up with witnesses that natives would get X products on the spot in exchange for lots of products in the future. The Native Americans did not understand credit is "growing debt". The Yamasse tribe of South Carolina even ended up owing 100,000 deer skins to their creditors. Such an amount was impossible for them to pay off since it would take 4 years of hunting to obtain that many hides, but the debt had compound interest so the number would perpetually increase so they owed more and more each year. By this time the natives were dependent on European goods like guns, metal utensils and other advanced products they could only obtain through trade. However since they were in debt and were no longer self-sufficient hunter/gatherer/grower/manufacturers then their very survival was threatened because they could no longer live without trade but they were poor and in debt so much that they had nothing to trade and couldn't get stuff to trade or make stuff to trade. Thus some tribes had to get more to pay their debts while using less, which is similar to how many modern debtor nations find themselves today except the resources the native americans were using were animals like otters, beavers, deer and buffalo. Yet the more the natives hunted the less animals there were to hunt the next year, when they'd owe even more pelts to the whites. Thereby in such a situation they had to fight the other native tribes to get the pelts they needed to meet interest payments, but the other tribes had the same plan since they made the same deals. What did the whites do in the mean time? Well they expanded their settlements of course and took more land for themselves leaving less land for natives to grow food or hunt on. Meanwhile they also destroyed animal habitats and made mines to get the natural resources which natives needed and could've used for trade had they not been busy fighting each other to survive or pay their debts. Some natives out of frustration and for retaliation fought the whites but the whites would use the other tribes to fight whoever fought them, using their debt and trade as leverage to get natives to fight for the white man against their fellow natives. Today nearly the same plan is implemented by the Europeans, North American and some Asian nations in Africa, South America and the Middle East except the resources demanded are different such as oil, gold, lithium etc. Whereas just as the Native Americans forgot how to and could not live without paying with their natural resources for trade, entire nations have become dependent on trading away their non-renewable resources which will soon be extinct just like the American animal herds went extinct. While to make sure this plan worked the white man inculcated tribalism in the natives so they didn't join into any formidable cohesive force, similarly the exploited nations today have nationalism cultivated so they cannot become a cohesive force. While the average native american did not know what was going on with their tribe or the specifics of the deals their tribal leader had made, they just tried to survive and either supported their tribe or revolted against it never connecting the dots to see the true culprit and cause of their problems. Today that poor old modern day farmer is stuck in the same situation not knowing what is going on or why things are going the way they are going and the rebels attack his family and steal his stuff thinking he's pro-government, while the government attacks his family and steals his stuff thinking he's pro-rebel. Then after all of that some Western aid agency offers him some "aid" from generous prosperous people in the West if he signs certain contracts and promises to grow certain things like opium or maybe store some toxic waste. Although that doesn't work out too well either, since the same rules apply to screw him and the rebellions continue. As a result the farmer's only option is to try to reproduce many children hoping they can help him increase his yield and defend him from any who attack, yet most will die young because he can't afford them and then those who survive just repeat the same cycle getting poorer and poorer all because of interest. Then some people claim that nothing is wrong with interest. I cannot fathom a single poor person today who is poor without it being directly or indirectly a result of interest. Every poor person I've ever met was poor because of interest. Truly the reason poverty exists is because of the interest in the global economy. Interest allows for such mythical economic instruments such as derivatives and options. A stock or commodity option is a piece of paper that says, "Person 1 buys the "option" to buy or sell X at Z price, which they can do today all the way up till the option expires. At which time they can either buy or sell X for Z price or just let their option expire." While short selling is when person 1 loans X from person 2 and sells X immediately promising they will give person 2 their X back before a future date. Meanwhile person 1 hopes the value of X drops and then they will buy it with the funds they got from selling person 2's X, pocketing the difference. It's basically like letting someone borrow your car for a week, they sell it on monday and then buy it back on friday for a cheaper price than they sold it for and then return it back to you on the next monday. Now what happens if someone shortsells and the value of X doesn't go down but increases? Well then they can wait and hope X drops in value, or they take out a loan to buy back X and keep their promise, or they do more short selling to drive down the price artificially so that way they trigger a panic that causes X to drop in value so they can pay off their debts while everyone else who owns X sees its value plummet. This is what the futures market and spot prices are. The real-time spot price is actually just a piece of paper that is an options contract. High volume manufacturers today pay the price they agreed to pay months ago, the current market price of commodities is actually the futures market price and the real world current market price is what the spot price was in the past. At least that's how it is in the industries, the regular person gets stuck paying whatever the ticker currently says. The real-world difference in living conditions and value is what is called hidden inflation. That hidden inflation is caused because of interest. So the sole financial reason "*Things aren't like they used to be in the good old days.*" is because of the effect that interest has on money and economies. Having fiat money alone is not the problem, fiat money is a effect of interest to make interest seem not as bad to the masses because if there were no fiat money then everyone would be better able to see the injustice of interest but fiat money disguizes the robbery that is usury/interest. If anyone ever asks you or complains about "*Why are things getting so expensive?*" Now you can give them the correct answer and say that it's because of interest transactions, some of which are labeled as interest some of which are not.

Although if economic health and stability is as simple as abolishing interest why don't countries abolish interest? Well those countries are in debt so dictators fear losing their position if they rock the boat to stop interest from sinking the nation. What about democracies? There are no democracies. But in case you disagree and believe there are, the same problem remains. Fundamentally if a leader of any nation is financially responsible by not borrowing money then it jeopardizes their grasp on power since a challenger to their authority will borrow money to gain support. Afterall since people are willing to take on debt to put food on their plate, power-hungry politicians are willing to put the nation in debt in order to acquire their place on the throne. Thus fiscal responsibility makes leaders vulnerable and gives their opponents a useful tool to depose them with. Incurring debt is attractive to incumbent leaders too because debt is inherited by the next administration therefore debt ties the hands of any future challenger or successor, automatically making them seem worse by default than the current leader by promising them a big financial debt if they are dumb enough to want and acquire political control from the incumbent. Thus in a semi-democratic nation which stages elections, it behooves the incumbent leaders to make sure the nation is in debt so that way they are safe and no challenger can promise any more benefits to the people by borrowing money. All new leaders would have to either take on more debt to seem equal to the incumbent leader in providing services or better. If they avoid and/or try to reduce national debt then the austerity of cutbacks and a reduction in spending (which is what happens when you stop taking out loans since getting loaned less means you have less to spend) will make them seem worse than the former leader thereby causing a desire among the population for the leaders of the past to become the future leaders if possible, but at the least it makes the new leaders have less public support than the old leaders due to financial foolishness and debt which they cannot prevent the nation from accruing unless all politicians had strict morals which they refused to compromise on for the sake of being in or retaining power. But alas how many countries only have politicians whose strict moral characters would prevent them from keeping or acquiring power? It only takes one immoral politician to ruin the fiscal solvency of the state and ruin they will if given the opportunity to acquire or keep power, especially in a system where anybody could in theory acquire political power and a government position. Democracies are designed to be in deep debt since the elections are popularity contests where those who promise the best tend to win the support of the masses. Whereas if you are more likely to win the election by taking out a loan at the taxpayer's expense, which politician wouldn't , especially when their opponents can? So to abolish interest would mean to practically abolish the game of democracy and elections. Countries with elections simply mean those nations are or will be in more debt after the election than they were before no matter who "wins". The good thing about fake elections though where the voters really don't choose who wins, though they think they do, is that the amount of debt the nation gets from the new regime is less than it would've been if the elections were legitimate. For governments to have real elections costs a lot more money than if they have fake ones, and of course that saved money tends to be taxpayer money. So if taxpayers want to pay less taxes then they want fake elections, because real ones means you will pay more and more taxes than you would if they were fake. Fake always tends to be cheaper, even in politics. The truth hurts financially so to save money fakery is committed on a largescale. All the problems nations ever have are due to incorrect ideologies, theories and opinions. Basically if you want a nation to do things right first they have to be right regarding their core beliefs and opinions. If an ideocracy's core ideas are wrong the whole nation will suffer from every solution they try to come up with, until they finally change those wrong ideas for the right ones. Peoples of nations with problems have ideological problems. National problems are due to the problems of their peoples regarding what is right/true and wrong/false, nothing else. Nations rise and fall upon their beliefs.

It is crystal clear that interest is a major sin that can doom a person to hell. God curses the one who consumes interest, the one who gives interest and the one who writes down the transaction. God even declares war upon those who are involved in interest and when they are resurrected they will be given weapons and told to go fight God. Of course God will obliterate all who fight against him and there is no weapon that can harm him. Therefore it is not in your best interest to have God declare war on you by getting involved with interest transactions. Even from a purely economic point of view, interest creates inflation, which is an increase in the supply of money that often causes the subsequent value of each monetary unit to decrease. Inflation tends to be destructive to wealth and society. In fact economists admit that the lower the interest rates are the better it is for the economy because less debt is created and loans given tend to have less chance of a default because high risk or unnecessary loans are unlikely since the reward for the risk being taken is so low. Typically high interest rates = high risk, low interest rates= low risk, but in the modern economy there is artificial manipulation and regulation of interest rates so true risk levels are not being reflected at the present time. The reason interest rates are forced so low by governments and/or private banking institutions around the world today is to encourage productivity. Low interest rates encourage borrowing, high interest rates discourage borrowing. It encourages businesses to borrow in order to grow and expand, thereby stimulating what they hope to be an economic boom, so they can steal those businesses' profits via taxation and then pay off their debts that keep growing with interest being continuously added. With productivity increasing as interest rates decrease, a 0% interest rate would result in the highest productivity possible. There would be no hidden inflation. People would only loan money if they had good reasons to do so and there would be little to no waste of resources. Obviously no one would lend money taking the risk of not getting repaid unless it was for a truly good reason which they believed would benefit society in some way, or as a favor to someone. In an Islamic economic system there would be no interest and if a person didn't pay back a loan on time then the lender could either forgive the debt and would be rewarded by God as if it were charity, or the lender could give more time for payment, or have the Shariah courts facilitate payment through a lien with a guardian being put in charge of the bankrupt person's financial affairs to ensure prompt repayment if no one could be found to pay the person's debt for them. There wouldn't be any loan sharks breaking legs, harassment, murders as a result of unpaid debts, or people filing bankruptcy when they still have significant assets which they could survive without thereby leaving the debtor never getting their capital back. Islam utilizes equity financing instead of debt financing. In Islamic finance there are no contracts with "fine print" at the bottom, a Muslim calls such deceptive text "sly print" which is potentially forbidden. An Islamic economy is a truly just and fair economic system which many countries with non-Muslim majority populations have recently considered adopting. This hasn't happened because the interest system benefits the rich who have money to lend, with the result being that the rich get richer and the poor get poorer with those in the middle getting poorer as well, due to the hidden inflation caused by interest which makes the cost of living go up and the value of savings go down. While indebted governments like inflation, because then they can pay off their debts more easily since the value of what they owe is less than the value of the amount they borrowed. For example, $100 a hundred years ago could get you a lot more than $100 today, so governments borrow today planning to pay in the distant future with money that's worth much less. This is exactly what the Bond and Treasury markets are. Those who buy bonds and such are really just stupid idiots who forget inflation and think they will beat it or their country won't have it. The bonds were made by governments to pay for wars they couldn't afford, so people initially bought bonds solely for patriotic reasons. Yet because so few did because it was known to be a government scam, governments promised to buy back the bond in full at the expiry date and make annual interest payments. Stupid citizens thought that was a great investment not realizing the government basically admitted they were going to inflate the hell out of their currency in order to pay it back. Thus all governments who sell bonds are forced to inflate their currency or else they can't pay it back. To fiscally stay afloat they gotta inflate their currency boat even if doing so causes it to pop like a bubble. To deflate means to sink the ship and to not inflate is to get eaten by the loan sharks. This policy stems from keynsian economics. Usually nations intentionally weaken their currencies trying to promote exports and generate export related jobs. Such inflation/devaluation is designed to import inflation in the form of higher import prices. (What this means is when you hear politicians saying they want to increase exports and domestic jobs, they are saying they will inflate/devalue the currency making prices go up. Idiots tend to cheer such politicians and seemingly patriotic policies because they are economically illiterate.) Typically most people benefit from deflation which encourages saving because money increases in value as prices go down. However governments hate deflation because it makes the value of debts increase and destroys their tax collection intake. The American Director of the National Taxpayer's Union, James Davidson explained the US bond market in detail: "*A Federal Reserve Note [is] merely an IOU. Here's how it works. When the politicians want more money, they dispatch a request to the Federal Reserve for whatever sum they desire. The Bureau of Printing and Engraving then prints up bonds indenturing taxpayers to redeem their debts. The bonds are then 'sold' to the Federal Reserve. But note this unusual twist=the bonds are paid for with a check backed by nothing! It is just as if you were to look into your account and see a balance of $412 and then, hearing that government bonds were for sale, write a draft for $1 billion. Of course, if you did that, you would go to jail. The bankers do not. In effect, they print the money that enables their checks to clear.*" In case you still don't get the full picture: governments want X,000 money to spend. So banks tell governments they will lend them X,000 money with interest by adding some zeroes to their accounts, except the banks don't have that money in reality but invent it via accounting because of patriotic duty to help the government or for a desire of revenue and influence over governments. Then the government uses that digital money, or paper if it's printed on the spot, while at the

213

end of the year taxpayers pay the government to pay back the banks for the money they invented to lend them. When the government gets a loan they use taxpayers as the collateral, or basically the ones whom the banks are told to go after if the government doesn't pay it's debts. Oh and governments don't ask taxpayers if they can take out loans the politicians just agree to do it and don't bother to inform the taxpayers, or if they do they say it in a elaborate language most taxpayers cannot decode. However this game can break if those whom the government buys stuff from try to cash the checks, usually when that happens banks print more money to cover the balance sheet. The local branches don't print money, that's the national bank's job. They retain the exclusive right in order to make sure inflation doesn't get too out of hand with all the banks playing the same game, the central national or international banks then ship the paper money to the local branches when they need it; for a fee of course since even money costs money. Seriously all the banks actually pay money to have paper money sent to their institution. If someone happens to try to cash a check at a bank and the bank has yet to receive it's shipment of money then they just take the money out of someone else's account at the bank hoping that person doesn't ask for their money until the shipment comes in. If the shipment doesn't come in then the banks just don't cash checks and go out of business, or they just steal money from some accounts to stay in business; which is illegal but the governments can't really shut down the ones giving them money to buy stuff because to shut down such banks would mean that they would need to find a new lender or stop buying stuff, which they can't do because they buy stuff for the benefit of it's citizenry(sometimes). Thus they say banks are "too big to fail" because if the banks go down then the government's money supplier goes down and they have no way to get stuff to give it's employees or citizens. Therefore the printing of money or digitally inventing it continues so the game can be played. While governments help their banks reduce the cash flow out of banks by restricing the amounts that can be withdrawn or transferred to other countries. Yet all this printing causes inflation and the problem is that many local banks are lending money they don't have playing the same game with everybody, but expecting everyone to pay them. The game is that people are simply trusting the banks at their words thinking they actually have money in a vault or that because your online statement says you have X money then you can go and get X money out of your account when in reality you can only do that if the central bank prints more money and ships it to your local bank before they run out. Digital currencies are being invented to solve this paper risk to the scam. At the end of the game people are not going to give governments goods and services for digital or paper money perpetually. The point of trade is to get something you want and can utilize. At the fundamental level you cannot eat, burn or use digital money to help you biologically, so for biological purposes digital currency has no value and paper currency isn't worth much to that effect either. Gold and Silver was traditionally valued as a medium of exchange because you could turn them into weapons, armor, jewelry or religious items. Whereas while in theory the inflation game could be played for a long time, eventually people producing things governments buy will need to be recompensed with real raw materials that are biologically beneficial or with things they can exchange for such real goods. Basically you only care about money because of what you can buy with money and there is a limited supply of things you want and there is a limited supply of real things that money can buy. Due to the inflation of this interest/printing game the purchasing power decreases for those getting paid with paper or digital currencies and naturally the real supply of real goods decreases too as time goes by. So the reason the game of printing money can't continue forever is because there is a limit to what can be bought and what governments can have sold to them, regardless of money supply there is a limited supply of raw materials. For example if a government needed X apples to feed its poor citizens and there are only 1/2 X apples available to sell at the market it doesn't matter if the government can afford to buy X apples by printing money the apples they need just won't exist to be bought and the apple seller won't sell them any apples anyways because they might want water, and the water seller won't sell water to the apple seller for the government's paper money because they want wood to burn for heat and the wood seller wants animals to eat for food. Therefore the apple seller won't want the government's money in exchange for apples because those he wants things from don't want that money but something else instead. So for the government to get any apples it would need to give the apple seller animals or wood in exchange but the government can't print animals or wood to trade with and they might not be able to buy what they need to get the animals or wood they need to get the apples. So the government despite being able to print all the money it wants might not be able to get the apples it's humans need to eat due to not having the resources to trade for apples nor having the resources to get something to obtain what is needed to trade. It all comes down to the apple seller wanting a piece of paper that X government printed in fancy colors. Yet what is the difference between paper money printed by X government and money printed by you or me? There is no difference, it's just paper at the end of the day. The paper is only worth something to you if you can trade it for something you want, if those who have what you want don't want the particular pieces of paper you have and prefer a different color or maybe something that's not paper then you can't buy stuff. Which when you really think about it makes the whole fiat money system quite fragile, if many people agreed to not accept X paper in trades then the world would change overnight. That's why it's ironic that lots of the fiat money says "In God we Trust", because despite the fact of God being trustworthy, for us to trust in an intrinsically worthless currency takes a great deal more than faith. To think your money is worth something requires a religious financial belief. Therefore it's odd whenever you see kids destroy paper money and a parent scolds them, because such scenes look as those the parent is scolding the child for desecrating pages of sacred scripture. Yet despite treating paper money as if it were holy they say they don't worship money. Also many claim they value knowledge more than money but if a book of knowledge is on the ground and some money is on the ground, which one gets picked up first with more zeal and posessiveness? Likewise regarding knowledge and money, examine the time people spend learning knowledge versus the time they spend earning money and you will know which one they value more. In fact don't people learn in colleges just so that they can earn more money later? The time they spend tells you more truths about them than their tongue. If you could choose between being rich, healthy and dumb versus being poor, unhealthy and wise, which would you choose? However as bad and valueless as paper money is, at least you can hold it and it's anonymous and can be earned/spent without the government knowing it. Yet as society degrades/advances into a cashless economy as digital currencies become the norm, this will give the governments greater power to inflate, confiscate and track/control economic transactions. Meaning you won't be able to earn a cent, spend a cent or even store a cent without the government knowing it and giving you the permission to do so. With paper money at least the government has to physically take it out of your hand to get it, but with digital currency it's much easier for them to rob you without you even getting a punch in for self-defense. They can even digitally tax you without you even knowing it. It's much easier for the government to delete a digital trail and/or manufacture a digital trail than it is for the subjects. Governments could easily rob you digitally and then blame it on "hackers" and there would be nothing you could do about it even if you knew those "hackers" were the government. People also forget that the internet and electronics are not immortal, a single solar flare can destroy the entire internet and all the electronics on earth, as can a man-made EMP. Thus digital currencies always have fundamental risks especially since they are inherently not tangible or stand-alone commodities. So as much as I hate paper fiat money, digital fiat money is even worse and digital currency is technologically perishable aka deletable or inaccessable. Fiat money is a major problem but some types of fiat money are better than others even though they might be less convenient in some ways. The problem is people are smart enough to earn money, corrupt enough to love money but too lazy or stupid to understand money. People love, live, lie, steal, cheat, fight and die for something they don't understand. Many worship a fiat deity called money without even realizing it is worthless and can't benefit or harm them and has no power even over itself. Fiat money is the religious equivalent of a man-made deity, they just made it up themselves and it is intrinsically worthless. Nontheless many people value a "good dollar" more than a good deed even though the good deed pays dividends in this life and the next. That in our time paper money is printed and exchanged for real goods is a historical anomaly many think is done to make it easier for the apple seller to buy water without trading animals to the wood seller for wood to trade that wood to the water seller for water. The sellers of stuff governments want simply need to consume real things in their life to exist and inflation makes it harder for them to use that money, which governments pay them in trading, to get those real things they need to live. This difficulty of using fiat money to buy stuff increases as a result of the printing game to the point that those who have real materials will only want to exchange their stuff for other real things, and people go back to crude bartering because they know if they trade their real materials or services for paper or digital currencies of X government then they won't be able to get what they want/ need by exchanging such monetary instruments because the inflation made them worthless. The paper money will be worthless as a medium of exchange because the inflation caused by continuous printing will happen so fast, due to ever increasing interest payments, that the government's money no longer retains value over time long enough to use it for trading purposes because the money supply is being increased too rapidly in order to pay off debt and supply bank demand for money. Essentially if you sold 10 knives for Z paper money thinking that you could then buy food with Z paper money and in the meantime the money supply increased so that you needed 3Z paper money then you would be stuck without knives or food and as such get pissed off and stop using that paper money since it was dropping in value too fast. Thereupon since government's paper money would be no good when someone tried to buy stuff then whatever goods/services they would've bought will not be bought and the citizenry will suffer due to a lack of trade as a result of the inflation of their medium of exchange. To obtain that paper money would be to starve oneself and waste one's wealth via trading for paper. Meaning by having fiat money in your pocket you would be losing purchasing power by the second, depending on how fast the government prints more money. That's what printing money means, it means a loss of purchasing power. So while in theory governments can always print more money, in practice they can't because there is a limit as to how low the purchasing power of a currency can go before everyone decides to stop using it because it can't be used to purchase things since it doesn't retain value due to excessive and rapid printing. Essentially the value of fiat money has an expiration date where it has to be used before it becomes worthless, the expiration date of fiat money is determined by how much fiat money exists and how fast more of it is created. The higher the supply of fiat money, the lower the demand and the value of money lies in the demand. Hence governments can print all they want but printing money reduces demand which reduces the value. So contrary to what the financially illiterate thinks, printing more money makes everyone who uses/has that money poor. Governments can do that, but if they want to improve their financial health they wouldn't. The trouble is that for governments fiat money is like an addicting drug that gives them a fake feeling of wealth due to credit and faith in fiat which eventually leads them to making more fiat money to keep themselves alive even though making more fiat money reduces the standard of living for everyone who uses fiat money. Fiat money is a financial drug which exploitative governments/banks are dealing to the people, but eventually the buzz will wear off and withdrawal systems will set in until the governments/banks overdose on fiat money causing the death of an economy/country. Economies which use fiat currencies are financial fiat junkies and as with any addiction the junkie's addiction hurts everyone they interact/transact with, especially since the fiat junkie supports their addiction to fiat by getting others to use fiat. To put this in a real perspective imagine selling something valueable for some fake play money from a board game and then going to the store trying to buy something. The same applies in many countries if you shop with foreign currency, they will all admit that the currency is real but they don't just want it; so for you it doesn't serve it's purpose due to the other party's trading preference. Simply having money doesn't in itself mean you can use that money to buy something. It's possible someone might want to sell you something for paper money but there is no guarrantee, so by having your wealth in paper you are at risk to some extent, especially since paper is flammable. While in theory the money printing game could still go on if a government were self-sufficient but one must remember that the banks who do the lending still get paid the interest or else the bankers fire their employees and they starve, or the bankers declare war on the governments and hire an army to get their money that is owed to them. And that's the caveat with the idea of government's just choosing to "not buy foreign goods" in that they have to pay interest on their debts which already exist. Yet who pays these governments to pay the banks? The taxpayer does, and taxpayers cannot continue to pay more and more and more forever. Taxpayers cannot keep up with the money printer. There is an amount that taxpayers cannot pay even at gunpoint. Also taxpayers don't like to pay anything at all to governments because they want to keep their own resources and money for themselves. Thus despite theory indicating that possibly every government could play this game with banks perpetually loaning them invented money, that can only happen if the taxpayers pay for the government's desires + the interest bankers added. But the only way taxpayers could pay for everything a government desires to buy is if they had their own resource printing press, and they don't because resources are in a limited supply. Therefore at some point government's must stop the printing game and bankers must not get paid, however government's don't just buy luxuries but necessities too such as food and raw materials and that's why this debt game is so dangerous. By inventing money to buy things in the present, governments are increasing the prices for everyone else while paying extra in the future to cover present day expenses due to interest. To pay the interest they must increase the money supply or get more money in taxes, but since they have a limit to taxation and increasing taxation causes poverty and unrest then they must invent money to play this game. Yet doing that decreases the value of said money making the prices of real goods increase to the extent that eventually all goods become impossible for non-government parties to afford thereby causing widespread poverty and unrest for the citizens. In summary the governments can in theory play this interest/inflation/money invention game forever, but the citizens of such a government and most of the people who uses that government's money will starve to death in the process. This is because they won't be able to buy anything with the money and only governments and banks will be left as buyers and sellers, which since they tend not to produce anything real or valuable that causes big problems in the productivity department leading to mass poverty and death. Therefore this game governments are playing with inventing money is designed to cause massive poverty that will lead to death or abolishment of said governments. Historically every nation who has ever played with fiat money suffers for it to the point of destruction, unless other nations start to play an even bigger game of fiat money so that way they can keep playing but eventually the fiat game ends badly. Unless the aliens from every planet start playing the same fiat money game, the game can't continue on earth for much longer, severe sudden abject poverty for the masses is the end result of the game. Therefore any government who begins to play this game of printing money has started a financial war against it's citizenry that will end with either the enslavement and extinction of its citizenry or the end of that government. Some in government know this game results in war with their citizens and that's why they buy materials like weapons with their imaginary money so it will help them enslave the citizens when the breaking point of revolt against taxation and inflation or starve occurs. In symbolic terms the inflation caused by the money printing game is like inflating a balloon, eventually the air supply pops the container as the supply increases beyond the volume the population can safely handle. When that happens the balloon that was once big and rich is reduced in size and damaged, which means that the continuous increase in the money supply via artificial unnatural infaltionary methods leads to the decrease in population due to poverty as the bubble of invented wealth pops and everyone becomes poor. The one who says *"The government has a printer and they can just keep printing money forever so there will never be problems."* is akin to the one who is inflating a balloon and says *"I can inflate this balloon forever and it will never pop because I have a machine to keep inflating it."* The ability to print or inflate has little to do with the feasilbility of it being done without problems. Currently the governments playing the currency printing game are like people who try to inflate a balloon enough so that it stays afloat in the air, when it starts to deflate and fall to the ground they inflate again. The governments think they can do this forever, without the balloon ever hitting the ground due to deflation or popping due to overinflation, however everytime they inflate they have to inflate with a larger amount of air than before. The balloon size is the size of the population that uses their particular fiat currency. No balloon can sustain perpetual inflation and likewise no population can survive a constant game of monetary inflation or an ever increasing monetary supply that is disproportionate to the increase in population. Whereas population cannot perpetually increase either because there is a limited amount of space on the planet and in the Universe at this moment, and God is not going to help government's play this game perpetually on a universal scale. God will not expand the Universe so governments can keep oppressing people. It's also far more likely for governments to fight each other for extra land and mutually destroy each other before chasing the "empty land" in space to settle their citizens on in order to continue the money printing game. Governments would rather fight wars over land on earth than quit the fiat money game. An example of this is WWII, Germany had to conquer Europe in order to keep printing money to survive, it was either win the world via war or starve. While since the Jewish bankers got Germany into the money printing game, Germans didn't respond too kindly. Wars are caused by inflation. While the death of people during wars cause inflation as well, since to decrease the population is to decrease the balloon size. Since interest causes this deadly destructive inflation then interest causes that deadly destruction of nations/people when the money supply pops after the governments taxation no longer pays the banker's bills and they have to resort to inflation to pay their debt. In such a scenario either governments fight the banks, or their citizens, or other nations, or they cease to exist. Who do you think wins in such wars? Governments vs. Banks(who control most governments) vs. everyone else. Typically citizens are the group that pays the price in the pocket and population size. There is a term for planned inflationary policies enacted by governments and banks. John Maynard Keynes, who is credited with inventing "modern economics" and inspiring fractional reserve banking aka the modern money printing game, explained inflation as follows: "*Inflation is a method of taxation which the government uses to secure command over real resources; resources just as real as those obtained by ordinary taxation.* **What is raised by printing notes is just as much taken from the public, as is an income tax**. *A government can live by this means, when it can live by no other. It is the form of taxation that the public finds hardest to evade, and even the weakest government can enforce it when it can enforce no other.* **By a continuous process of inflation, government can confiscate secretly and unobserved an important part of the wealth of their citizens.** *By this method, they not only confiscate, they confiscate arbitrarily, and while the confiscation impoverishes many, it enriches some. Lenin was certainly right, 'there is no surer way of overturning a society, than to debauch the currency.' The process engages all the hidden forces of economic law on the side of destruction, and does so in such a manner that only one man in a million is able to diagnose it.*" So when most governments claim they "don't want inflation or higher prices" they are lying through their teeth. For a government to say they "don't want inflation" is equal to saying they don't want more tax revenue even though they could get it by popular demand. In a financial religious context inflation is like sin, many governments denounce it while preaching and practicing it. Also remember increases in the minimum wage causes inflation, as does interest. So to protest for increased "minimum wages" is to protest for increased taxation and higher prices. The reason politicians can publicly preach policies that cause inflation and get cheered by the masses is that the masses learned the government curriculum in school so they don't understand economics correctly. They will take a course on economics and be taught nonsense thinking interest is good or necessary for "market liquidity". Personally much of what I learned in high school in the allegedly elitist "Academy of Finance" was backwards destructive economic doctrines. I wouldn't say what they teach is useless but I did have to unlearn what they taught me because what they taught me in school about how economics works or is supposed to work was wrong, it's not useless what they teach is destructive. Basically most modern economics teachers teach nations how to collectively commit financial suicide in the name of self-interest and prosperity. If I went back to school today I'd probably challenge the economics curriculum and refute it and refuse to answer their questions on tests because their "right answers" are the wrong answers. It's sad when I think of or interact with bankers because I know from personal experience that many really don't understand what unislamic banking does to the world and they actually believe the crazy destructive economic theories they preach and practice and think they provide a good service to the world. Economics is actually a subcategory of religion and as such the theories of economics are in reality religious tenets that can be good or bad, from God or from man. Yet despite seperating Church and State the western governments have not been able to seperate Bank and State because a state needs authority over banking to function just as it needs religion to function. Although since people pretend religion can be seperated from a state they ignore the unbreakable connection between economics and state which leads to Bank's abuses and manipulating of states to oppress people just as the Church did centuries before. Although rather than using banks to rob their people (or being used by the banks) sometimes the governments fight the banks on behalf of their people and the banks lose. Other times banks fight the governments and the governments lose. But it is extremely rare for citizens to win these wars against banks and/or governments, and even when they do win they tend to bring back one or the other sooner or later because governments are a necessity and then governments want to buy more than they can afford as do the citizens. The problem now is that most of the usurious governments are playing the fiat money game but they can't all inflate their currencies at the same time because then in practical finance there would be no inflationary effects for anybody; except for the poor who would just die off or turn to crime. Thus the bankers are in a type of conundrum where if everyone pays them then they don't really get paid by anybody because the inflation would be universal. Yet not only would such universal inflation be bad business for them, but it would be bad for everyone and give governments an edge over citizens and banks in the final showdown; which as partial citizens banks would prefer to not be enslaved by governments in case of government winning the 3-party war. Therefore to prevent the collusion of governments in creating a global government to enslave citizens and banks, the banks have to have some governments lose the game and suffer inflation to the point of nonexistance. Although no government wants to be "that government" that ceases to exist, they all hope it will never be their turn to vanish as long as other governments are playing. The global fiat monetary system today is like a game of musical chairs. Except the chairs are underwater with oxygen masks attached to them and instead of a player being eliminated at the end of every song when a chair is removed, everyone keeps playing and a chair with an oxygen mask gets removed. Oh and it is always raining while they are playing, so as time goes by the participants are inevitably getting deeper and deeper underwater as there is less and less oxygen to go around. Eventually all who are playing will lose, one way or the other, it's just a matter of who will be the last one still alive swimming underwater in debt, having yet to pay the price for going underwater via the fiat money adventure. At this point in time many governments who are playing cannot get to the surface even if they tried, so they think their "best choice" is to keep playing in order to keep playing. Sadly though the few governments who have the ever decreasing quantity of oxygen masks that themselves are decreasing in oxygen levels call the time they are on the oxygen mask "prosperity" or "growth/development", oblivious to the fact that "a breath of fresh air" when you are underwater in debt playing the fiat money game is not indicative of financial health. Each government hopes to be the last one standing after the banks take down all the rest, or hope that because so many others are playing the game then somehow it will all turn out okay. Banks know this and use this to their advantage playing governments against each other while governments play banks against each other. Banks are the music makers who are also "making it rain" so to say on the governments playing the game, who to protect themselves from player retaliation offer oxygen to any who protect the banks from other governments/citizens. The citizens/residents/users of fiat money are the cells of the governmental players playing the game, we can let other cells or even the government know they are in danger but our influence is minimal especially when we aren't the "brain cells" of governments nor banks. Yet still some of us foolishly give our money or energy to these banks so they can make more music/rain or give our money or energy to the governments so they can keep playing competing with others. Hopefully when the game ends we will be part of one of the few organs that survives the "endgame" and gets transplanted to a new body(government) that doesn't play the fiat money game. Other "cells"(people) just figure they have a short lifespan anyways so as long as they die before their government loses the game then they don't care. Meanwhile to keep all the cells subordinate the governments stress we should help them play and enjoy the competitive sport called "life" where to preserve our own wellbeing they say we must unite and work hard to outdo the competition from other nations lest we perish or fall behind. The cells that object to the game or don't want to help the government or banks keep playing get punished, or told they can go to some other government/body if they don't like their system. Which while it's possible for cells that are living on the extremities of their nation's institutional system to transplant themselves via a skingraft on another body/nation, it isn't always easy. Yet even if one does manage to change their economic environment the banks have gotten nearly everybody involved and if a nation isn't involved in the fiat money game the constant rain the bankers manufacture harms those living ashore on a firm non-fiat non-interest foundation causing flooding and wetness or civilized "market liquidity". Most of the transactions which involve interest are justified on the basis of "market liquidity". However what bankers don't understand is that naturally God has created economic environments with the correct amount of liquidity, if there are unnatural shortages in liquidity it's most likely due to somebody somewhere doing something sinful or satanic desires where we desire more liquidity than we need or should get. To solve the real or imaginary liquidity problem caused by the existance of sinful non-interest transactions, like stealing, gambling, taxation, exploitation, institutional impoverishment etc the usurious create artificial rain with interest based liquidity. They do this with the mistaken belief that interest based liquidity will fix economic problems ignorant of or in denial/rejection of the fact that such sinful liquidity due to interest is just as good for economic growth as acid rain is for crops and sealife. Acid Rain doesn't help and neither does interest, unfortunately interest hurts people in the afterlife as well as this life. Earning lawful money is like drinking fresh water, earning sinful money is like drinking contaminated salt water, while earning interest money is like drinking acid rain out of the sewer. It's hard to find clean natural fresh water today but it's what we need to sustain ourselves in both the short term life and the long term afterlife. Hence we have the modern currency wars that resulted in artificial booms and busts designed to cover up government and bank attempts to intentionally devalue the money of their citizens and/or clients.   Furthermore every speculative economic bubble that I'm aware of has been directly caused by interest or fueled by interest-caused liquidity. All the currency wars in world history as well as those currently taking place today use interest policies as weapons. Thus this game continues and the balloons fill until eventually they will pop. When they pop, power will be up for grabs for whoever can pick up the pieces. Bankers and governments prepare ahead of time to pick up the pieces after the bubbles/balloons burst. To be the best prepared takes time so to delay the inevitable pop and power grab they creatively try to maintain the status quo, but in doing so are only making the trouble balloon bigger so more people get hurt in the end. This is desired because the bigger and more painful the pop is then the smaller the pieces to pick up will be and the easier it will be for the surviving parties to assert authority over the rest of the surviving pieces. You see the one strength citizens have in this fight is their numbers surpassing that of the bankers and governments combined. Their weakness is disunity, stupidity, self-interest and lack of preparation. Since poor people are less likely to be prepared for a power grab and disunited, the means in which the staus quo is to be temporarily maintained are also designed to impoverish and disunite the masses of citizenry so they kill each other for survival and accept either banks or governments to be their saviors rather than seizing power for themselves. Typically the poor are led and don't lead, because they are concerned with the hardship of poverty and too self-centered to care whether they are oppressed or not. They are too busy trying to survive than to care about power. The poor tend to trade power in exchange for a plate of food. Oppressors know this and try to keep their populace too poor to revolt, because while poverty can cause revolutions it can also prevent and defeat them if the people are too poor to push for political change. People need a minimum level of nutrition and stability to realize they are oppressed and hope for a better future after sacrifice. For people to make the sacrifices necessary for political change they need to have enough to be able to survive the sacrifices. If they are too poor to survive the revolution then it will never occur because most prefer life to strife, and if it does occur despite the survival instinct then it will likely fail unless God intercedes. So to "win the game" in the end banks and governments creatively impoverish while delaying the end of the money printing game. For example at the time of this writing Europe, Switzerland, Sweden and Japan have negative interest rates in order to intentionally devalue their currencies claiming that doing so will encourage exports and pay off their debts. Seriously if you go to banks in those nations today and put your money in the bank they will tell you "*Ok come back in X time and we will give you less than what you gave us, and it will buy less stuff than it can today.*" And people deposit money anyway. People are literally paying banks to hold their money, and the banks don't even do that but use it to make speculative investments or interest loans. The reason people do this is because they've been brainwashed to think having your money in the bank is safe, and the governments encourage this myth by claiming to insure bank deposits and not stopping crime. You see the banks and governments are in cahoots on many levels, conspiracy theorists don't distinguish between their cooperation and opposition but I try to. I think banksters plan to betray governments and that they are just friendly enemies using each other while both plan to dominate the other, eventually. Regardless banks are the riskiest place to put your money in and this has been demonstrated recently in Cyprus and Greece where the banks told their depositors that they won't be getting their money back because the government is in debt and the government decided to confiscate their deposits in taxation for the good of the nation. The citizens couldn't do anything at all, they just lost their funds or had them "converted into bank shares" which they can't sell or withdraw. Fortunately though their deposits were insured by the very governments who robbed them, the loophole was that the citizens were not insured against government confiscation. Meaning when it comes down to giving your money to you or giving it to the government so it can pay it's debts to banks, the banks will always give your money to the government because they know you legally can't do nothing when the governments and banks work together to take your money. One can't call the government to have the banks return your money, because they took it and if you try to use force against the banks then they call the government on you and you go to jail. So if you give your money to banks the government decides if you get it back when you want or if they get it to pay their debts. This myth of banks being a safe place to put money in isn't just false today, it was false 200 years ago and it has always been false ever since the beginning of banks. The modern banking system which stems from the Templar knights was built on a lie about Muslims robbing non-Muslim pilgrims traveling to the Holy Land. Templars told Europeans to deposit their money with them and then they could travel without money and after their journey they could withdraw money at another Templar bank minus a fee, which in reality was a negative interest rate. Today modern nations are actually going back to the medieval Templar banking system, but they pretend it's modern and not medieval or evil. But what's even worse is that the claim of Muslims robbing the non-Muslim pilgrims was a lie! The roads were safe for pilgrims, just not for crusaders. The Templars were attacked by Muslims because they were openly at war with Muslims, the pilgrims were safe until they started traveling with the Templars in caravans thinking Templars were needed to protect them. Yet it was because Templars were with caravans that they got attacked, but once a few caravans experienced the Templars get attacked they mistakenly thought they'd be in more danger without the Templars with them. Thus Templars endangered pilgrims by accompanying them and then tricked the pilgrims into paying them to endanger them. Historians repeat the Templar salespitch because without it they would have to admit that the entire modern interest banking system was built on a lie about Muslims who coincidentally say interest is forbidden by God. Which makes one wonder how many other bad things, systems or policies in the world today exist solely because of lies that were told to non-Muslims about Muslims? Basically inflation exists because of interest and interest exists because of the Crusader's lying about Muslims, so inflation exists in part due to non-Muslims hating Islam and Muslims. So one reason why prices keep going up is because hundreds of years ago people hated Muslims and thought they posed a violent threat. Everyone has been paying the price for that belief ever since. Hence religious beliefs are the reason why prices keep rising. To change the economic trend the religious beliefs must be changed. Any sane unselfish financially literate person would realize how crazy and unjust negative as well as positive interest is, but most don't because interest-based economics is part of the religious doctrine of hedonistic consumerism. People say you can't have your cake and eat it too, well you can't have interest without injustice. So if anyone wants world peace, or the end of poverty and injustice you will have to eliminate interest first. Some economically informed people may disagree and say the problem is fiat money. They are only partially correct, it is technically impossible to have economic justice if people are paid for doing work with money that is constantly fluctuating in value. This is actually what led the father of Socialism, Robert Owen, to experiment with a currency of labor notes which represented hours of labor. For example instead of bills worth $1, $5, $10 etc he made bills worth 1 hour of labor and such. Which of course this didn't work because there are many different types of labor. Also this didn't work because labor cannot be notarized if nobody has the same definition of what exactly "1 hour of labor" is worth. Yet the whole money problem is that everything is actually fiat money, including gold and silver because their values fluctuate just like everything else. While contrary to conventional belief even things people value like life, health and family fluctuates. For instance on a person's wedding day they value their spouse a certain amount. 5 years later, 15 years later and 50 years later that value is going to be different. The same goes for parents valuing their children. The only currency that is guaranteed to maintain and increase its value over time and always be exchangeable for what you truly need and want is good deeds combined with the correct religious belief. Yet for worldly matters since a temporary medium of exchange is necessary and nobody can accurately trade their good deeds since their true value is still unknown, gold and silver are good as alternative currencies. The reason being is that those metals were used as money by prophets. So that's a monetary currency endorsed by prophets of God. Honestly that's the only good reason to accept a gold and silver monetary standard, is because prophets used it. We could use something else that is commonly considered "non-perishable" but if we are to use something then we would be better off with the prophetic monetary standard. Although even with the prophetic monetary standard, interest can still mess up such an economy. Fiat money only exacerbates the effects of interest, it is interest transactions that are the root cause of economic turmoil. Economics is inherently anti-interest, interest exists in the world due to ignorance, greed and religious reasons. Whose interests does interest serve? Interest is certainly not in the borrower's best interest and interest goes against what is in the best interest of society.

While the negative interest rates recently are entirely uncharted waters which will result in unknown economic ripples. It is only the rich lenders who have an interest in the institution of interest, to the loss of everyone else. Many of the governments worldwide are obnoxiously in debt, this causes them to be manipulated and controlled by their debtors. One would think those burdened by interest would be in favor of Islam, at least from an economic point of view. However when governments are in debt they are often forced to choose between retaining power or getting out of debt. Hence the American President James Garfield said, "*Whoever controls the money in any country is master of all its legislation and commerce.*" and the Jewish Banker Baron M.A. Rothschild said "*Give me control of a nation's currency and I care not who makes its laws.*" Therefore it should not be surprising that the country's most indebted, with billions-trillions to pay in interest, happen to be against an Islamic state being established which would be interest and stagflation free. Because those they owe interest to, who control government policy are opposed to the Islamic principal prohibiting interest and do not want the world to see it put into practice. As US president Woodrow Wilson stated in 1916 CE, 3 years after the creation of the Federal Reserve Bank by the Jew Paul Warburg, "*Our system of credit is concentrated. The growth of the nation, therefore, and all our activities are in the hands of a few men. We have come to be one of the ruled, one of the most completely controlled and dominated governments in the civilized world - no longer a government by free opinion, no longer a government by conviction and the vote of the majority, but a government by the opinion and duress of small groups of dominant men.*" Ironically many financial institutions today have Jewish origins and/or owners, causing many conspiracies to arise. They must not yet have learned the lesson Jesus pbuh intended to teach them when attacking the money lenders who consumed interest despite its clear prohibition. I'm not anti-Jew but interest is a big problem, it's slightly odd that historically Jews tend to be deeply involved with interest. Which because of the Jewish Proverb, "*People come to poverty in two ways: accumulating debts and paying them off.*" many who learn of economic oppression suspect Jews must want a type of global gentile poverty to enslave non-Jews and incorrectly conclude the problem is the Jews. But the problem is NOT Jews. The problem is interest whether it's paid or received by Jews or non-Jews, the poision is not Jewry but usury. It is also interesting to note that according to the bible, the gospel of Luke, if you lend money to your enemies without interest or expecting it to be repaid then "*you will be children of the Most High*". Basically the Christian bible that says a "son of God" is someone who voluntarily lends money to their enemies without interest or expectation of repayment. Thus it follows that a "Son of Satan" is one who pays or earns interest.

If one was reasonably ignorant of interest money being sinful, then one may be allowed to use the interest money they previously acquired as long as they stop involving themselves with interest transactions once they know that it's sinful. But if someone read this and learned interest is sinful, then they would become accountable for any interest they consumed after knowing interest money is spiritually illegal. If one has obtained interest from a bank after they knew it was sinful and then repents, they shouldn't return or consume the interest money. The way to dispose of such illegal wealth is to spend it on charitable causes such as giving to the poor, but one should make it clear to the organization it's donated to that it is interest money so that they don't use it on things which require uncontaminated funding. There is no reward for donating this interest money, that's how bad it is. It is because interest is so sinful that Jesus pbuh went berserk in the holy temple. That extra % in interest is not worth the consequences that are attached to it. It is not in a person's eternal interest to be involved with interest transactions in this temporary life. This is not an exclusively Islamic ruling. Interest is forbidden in the religions of all Muslims, Jews and Christians. The prevalence of interest institutions around the world doesn't mean that it's permissible, it only shows that few people are practicing their religion. The problem which I didn't realize as a Christian was that some Christian groups don't practice what they preach, but what's even worse than that, is how they don't even preach what they're supposed to. This is a serious problem I draw attention to out of concern for those people who are intentionally left ignorant of sins that they will be held accountable for, which may ultimately affect where their final destination is. Therein lies the danger of Churchianity.

Going back to the second part of the fig tree story it says, *"when you are standing in prayer"* meaning they had a specific way to pray. You couldn't just do anything you wanted and call it a prayer there is a certain method in which it was to be done. It also says, *"so that the Father in heaven may forgive you your sins"* meaning according to this bible verse in the words of Jesus pbuh, Jesus pbuh does not have the authority to forgive sins and he advises his companions to ask forgiveness from something other than him. It is also important to note Jesus pbuh is said to have said "**the** Father". Jesus pbuh did not have a father, and if God was his father as some people claim when referring to God he would have said "**MY** father" every time without any slip ups. This is not what the bible has him saying, consider the famous "Our Father" prayer most Christians recite. Its first two words are "**OUR** Father" the bible says Jesus pbuh taught this prayer, if that's the case and if God was the father of Jesus pbuh in any sense whatsoever he would have said to say "Jesus' Father" or "Father of Jesus" or "His Father". The word "our" is inclusive and plural meaning that you have the same relationship to the subject of the sentence as everyone included in "our". If the bible verse that says Jesus pbuh said the "Our Father" is authentic, then Jesus pbuh is openly teaching he has the same relationship to this "Father" as his companions and anyone else who recites this prayer. In other words in his own words he is not the exclusive son of God. Biblically the term "Father" was akin to leader or lord and isn't meant in a literal sense. Two examples from an English New International Version of the Bible illustrate this. The first is Psalm 2:7, *"I will proclaim the LORD's decree: He said to me, "You are my son; today I have become your father."* This verse is from psalms in the Old Testament, thought to be revealed to the prophet David pbuh. Whether you believe the Psalms we have today are the same as what was revealed to David pbuh makes no difference concerning this. This verse says that God has become the "father" of David pbuh. David pbuh had a biological father and mother so the word "father" here cannot possibly mean that David pbuh was literally a son of God. There are many other places and references of other prophets being called sons of God, such as Abraham pbuh, but in every instance the term "son of God" always means that they are a very pious person whom God is pleased with. If you think otherwise then practically all the prophets are the sons of God, and many of those prophets had parents and children. This common misunderstanding of the terms "Father" and "son of God" if applied whenever the bible says it, and not just when it says it about Jesus pbuh, would open up a whole can of confusion with people today claiming they are the grandsons and granddaughters of God despite being completely corrupt irreligious individuals. John 8:37-46 has Jesus pbuh saying to the Pharisees: *37 I know that you are Abraham's descendants. Yet you are looking for a way to kill me, because you have no room for my word. 38 I am telling you what I have seen in the Father's presence, and you are doing what you have heard from your father." 39 "Abraham is our father," they answered.* **"If you were Abraham's children," said Jesus, "then you would do what Abraham did.** *40 As it is, you are looking for a way to kill me, a man who has told you the truth that I heard from God. Abraham did not do such things. 41* **You are doing the works of your own father."** *"We are not illegitimate children," they protested. "The only Father we have is God himself."* **42 Jesus said to them, "If God were your Father, you would love me, for I have come here from God. I have not come on my own; God sent me.** *43 Why is my language not clear to you? Because you are unable to hear what I say. 44 You belong to your father, the devil, and you want to carry out your father's desires. He was a murderer from the beginning, not holding to the truth, for there is no truth in him. When he lies, he speaks his native language, for he is a liar and the father of lies. 45 Yet because I tell the truth, you do not believe me! 46 Can any of you prove me guilty of sin? If I am telling the truth, why don't you believe me?"* These verses involve the Pharisees being told by Jesus pbuh" *You belong to your father, the devil*". Before that it's written that he said, " *I know that you are Abraham's descendants*" so clearly Jesus pbuh didn't use the word "father" in a literal biological sense accusing them of having been born of the devil. He knew their human lineage, "father" was a matter of speech to refer to who you followed and obeyed. Also when Jesus pbuh calls the devil "*the father of lies*" he doesn't mean the devil gave birth to children called lies, the word father is used in the sense of being the originator or founder. The Pharisees reply, "*The only Father we have is God himself."* Obviously the Pharisees didn't mean they were divine, or biologically sons of God, had they meant that since this dispute was public people would have cited them for being blasphemous liars, because the people would've known who the parents of the Pharisees were. These are a few examples of how the word "Father" in biblical context is very different from how we understand the word father today, many people are led astray because they don't understand the meaning the speakers had. It can be confusing if you don't know what the speaker's definitions of words are, communication can become impossible; especially if the words are being translated. Even today people call young kids "son" when they aren't the parent of the child they are talking to, but it is understood as a term of endearment from an older authority figure. It's important to understand what the speaker meant by what was said, instead of drawing our own conclusions based on what we think such words might have meant. When we are contemplating dialogue thousands of years old, it must be understood that the vocabulary then was different and our understanding must be based on the meaning the words had in that time period when they were originally spoken or written.

    During this time I was filling out applications to enter a seminarian program. One part of the application required the applicant to describe their relationship with family and to write some essays about the family members that most influenced your life. If I wrote honestly I feared they might have rejected my application. If rejected then one can't re-apply until 4 years have gone by. With all the drama and probation I decided it was best to not apply at that time deciding to wait until later when I was out of high school, until then my focus would turn to my Christian rap career. Ironically all the trouble happened with the police before I had even released one song. However now that I think about it perhaps telling them my plans to rap had some affect on the way they treated me. Unfortunately their unfriendly behavior only served to motivate me. It wasn't all bad though, because some of the fights would result in my parents trying to buy my love and the price was becoming increasingly more expensive with jewelry being my new addiction. Initially the extravagance made me feel proud, inflating my self-esteem, however it soon became a crutch and then a necessity. When one wears expensive jewelry the intention is typically to create envy in the hearts of others, to show off or gain attention and stick out from the crowd via fashion. Although if people have seen it before then it doesn't have the same shock value quickly losing affect and becomes old, thus new jewelry is required more and more, bigger and better, more exclusive and expensive. It became a burden that escalated to the point where I felt naked if I wasn't wearing flashy jewelry in public. This ended up having the exact opposite effect it initially had on my self-esteem, because I couldn't go out without being "iced out" while everyone else seemed happy without the jewelry. It was similar to how some women feel with makeup. At this beginning stage it wasn't obnoxiously excessive, but it got to the point where I would be wearing a minimum of 4 chains, a rosary, a bracelet (sometimes 2), a watch, metal teeth with jewels and 8 of my fingers would have rings on them. I had specially made custom hats, custom watch, custom ring, custom chains and even custom shoes that had my rap name on them. It was a very extravagant and expensive appearance. Some of these pieces cost thousands of dollars. Honestly it's a depressed lifestyle. I even had a custom made life-sized heart completely covered in black precious stones that took months to have made, I wore it on a black chain which itself had black stones encrusted in it. The "black iced out heart" was to symbolize my emptyness while looking cool and romantic from a thug point of view. I got it hoping some girl would see me wearing it, get the hint and fix my life via romance. Inside my real heart was so black that I literally had a black heart of jewelry I wore around my neck. Yet I had so much jewelry, with pressure to stay "fresh" and fashionable, that I only wore it a few times, probably less than 10 times in my life. When I was wearing those rings it hindered my typing, at home I would take them off and would often take off the rest of the jewelry inside the house because it was so inconvenient to have on the body, it was a burden to carry physically, emotionally and mentally. On top of that most of it was fake, but you should note that fake does not mean cheap. One of my jewelers happened to be the same one a very famous rapper uses who has sold millions of records and starred in movies. I'm not going to go into details that could cause others to fall into the same trap, but this famous rapper every rap fan knows of buys jewelry that is made using materials that are made not mined. They are not real diamonds and they don't cost as much, but they are shinier than diamonds to such an extent that it is nearly impossible to tell the difference even when brought to a professional jeweler. My stuff fooled a pro in a jewelry store when they examined it. Once when getting a watch fitted in a professional high-class jewelry store, I even had to insist to them my jewelry was a "gift"(I wasn't going to say it was fake after they got fooled) because they were concerned about a teenager having jewelery like I had and didn't think I could legally have obtained such stuff; and of course I looked like a gangster too. While the metal tends to be real the "diamonds" are often synthetic and made to pass diamond testers. All that glitters isn't gold and even gold isn't always good. Don't idolize these celebrities thinking that things are as they appear, because when I was living this fake lifestyle wearing exactly the same things the famous wealthy celebrities are wearing, it didn't make me happy. Even in their music videos usually the cars and luxury items are loaned or borrowed from someone else, the only time the artist has access to them is in the video, it really isn't theirs they just want you to think it is. No amount of jewelry was enough to give me confidence in my appearance, on top of that the envy inspired by the jewelry caused others to hate, creating enemies rather than friends. I would go to school, act cool come home and feel like killing myself, coming dangerously close to doing so. All thanks and praises be to God that I don't wear any jewelry anymore, I feel much better without the bling.

    Even with my favorite football team, the New Orleans Saints, winning the super bowl that year there was no true happiness or contentment. Although not only did my favorite football team win the championship during my senior year in high school, but my favorite hockey team the Pittsburgh Penguins also won the championship in 2010 CE against the very team that beat them the year before in the 2009 CE championship. So my two favorite sports teams, that I was a fan of for years, both became champions in 2010 CE. After they won life was even worse because the dream became a reality and was found to be empty. Whenever "your team" wins it all and is on top of the world there is nothing left but for them to go down. You realize that you truly got nothing out of their championship, all your efforts being wasted without benefit and the temporary bragging rights turning against you when they fail to keep winning the championship year after year. Reflecting back I still have the raw emotions the championships initially inspired in me but they seem so foolish and illogical for me to have about other people winning a sporting event. To be a passionate or casual fan of a sports team means to have foolish unhealthy feelings of affection for a business franchise that employs athletic strangers to play games. The fun a fan has when their team wins is due to them fantasizing that they are part of the team and share the victory, or that the team represents them in some way. Being a sports fan is simply a diluted form of tribalism in which the teams are the modern form of tribes, where instead of winning violent wars to rule the world the teams play games to win the league with the fan feeling they are part of the tribe/team despite not participating in the game itself. The tribal wars turned into professional sports, which while less violent and deadly are perhaps more psychologically and emotionally unhealthy. Plus being a sports team's fan is addicting and many modern fan bases are more like cults. Yet as with any cult, it's difficult for the sports fan to free themselves from the fun fantasy of fandom. Being a fan supplements their spiritual emptiness from having a lack of faith and distracts them from the misery of their real life. The very word "fan" comes from the word "fanatic" which describes a type of worship wherein servants to rulers who claimed to be gods would "fan a tick". Ticks are deadly insects that upon landing on the skin of a human can burrow inside it, and if they do so they cause harmful diseases and death. So when royal kings who claimed divinity would go outside they had servants who loved them so much they would fan away the ticks so the ruler didn't have to fan the bugs away themselves. Of course such zealous entusiasm the servant had for their job fanning away the ticks led them to have the ticks burrow in their own skin since they had no "fan-a-tick" followers. Yet the servant loved their ruler/god so much they didn't care about themselves, their master's success was more important to them than their own. These insane people were called fanatics because of their fanatical unhealthy devotional compulsive fanning. Later the term was shortened to fan and the sports team cults refer to their fanatics as fans and the stupid fans are endeared to the term and "proud to be a fan" not realizing that being "a fan" is a type of religious category of cultic insanity. By definition a fan is a zealous fanatic worshipping whatever they are being a fan to/of. Yet as I know from experience the fans can rarely see their own fanaticism because being a fan of a team is to belong to a cult. Why else do you think the fans have/get/display so much team memorabilia? Sadly the fanatics enjoy their fandom not realizing it's an addiction of religious proportions. Honestly think of how a sports fan reacts when their team scores or wins a close game, and how they react when worshipping God. Or how does the sports fan react when a big error is committed by their team, the rival team scores, or their team loses a close game versus how they react when they sin and disobey God. Truly the team a fan follows gets more love and affection from them than does the Creator of everything. For a sports fan their team winning the championship is equated with attaining eternal salvation and their religion's domination of the world. Professional sports today have achieved the status of sacred. As such with my 2 favorite teams from 2 different sports winning the championships in the same year, I experienced what was essentially a "professional sports fans paradise". From an outsider's view I'd appear to have every reason to live and probably seemed like the happiest most popular kid in school, but inside there was such darkness and emptiness that I felt there was no reason to live despite all the materials, fame and goals I had. At that time, unbeknownst to perhaps everybody, suicide or death seemed to be the answer to all my problems.

    It is a well known belief in most religions that committing suicide results in going to hell. Firstly because you are showing the ultimate ungratefulness for the life God has given you and are going against his command. God did not create you to kill yourself. Secondly because there is no way to repent or ask for forgiveness for the sin, because when you do it you're dead. The third reason why I didn't kill myself was because if I did and went to hell, hell would definitely be worse than whatever trouble I was going through and it would be permanent without the option to commit suicide as a means to escape. To the many people who have and are contemplating suicide they should know that we have an enemy Satan, who has promised God to lead the bulk of humanity to hell getting the majority to prove themselves ungrateful. Satan wants you to kill yourself. Common logic dictates that throwing your life away is not going to end up with God rewarding you. Remembering the prophets pbut helps, because they went through much worse than anyone of us ever can, especially concerning family relationships and social problems with rejection, slander and abuse. Truly if you are reading this and haven't ever felt suicidal, you are either over indulging in vices, intoxicated by earthly pleasures, or are ignoring what is happening in the world due to youth or constant distractions. It's my opinion that if you honestly haven't thought of killing yourself in this day and age, you are crazy, how could you not? The amount of pain and suffering you go through in this world far outweighs the pleasure, so if death was just like sleep or nothingness everyone would kill themselves to save themselves from the hardships. However people don't because they know deep down that death is not nothingness and that there is an afterlife that is affected by our actions in this life. Rather than an end, death is a journey that we all take, voluntarily or involuntarily. Like every journey provisions are needed or it will be a miserable trip, it is good deeds that will be our provision while we are in the grave.

Not to digress but the grave is important to elaborate upon, especially what will happen to a person there. Knowledge about life in the grave is something many people live their lives entirely ignorant of and are in for a terrible surprise once they're there. For whoever is saved in the grave, what comes after will be easier and whoever is not saved in the grave, what comes after will be worse. I will skip over the details on what happens when the angel of death comes to take the soul out of the body, because that experience differs based on whether the individual is a believer or a disbeliever. Instead I will focus on the shared test which both believers and disbelievers must face in the grave. Imagine the moment after the angel of death returns your soul to the body whilst in the grave, you hear the last person walk away and their footsteps fade, you are all alone, underground, cramped into a small dark dirty space there to stay till the day of resurrection. Suddenly the ultimate test begins! Did you study? This test cannot be postponed or retaken, if you fail the first time then your whole existence after it will be the miserable existence of a failure. The two black and blue angels named Munkar and Nakir come to you, with a hammer. The hammer is so big that two nations could not lift it. They quickly force you to sit up and they ask you 3 questions. **"WHO IS YOUR LORD?", "WHAT RELIGION DO YOU PRACTICE?", "WHO WAS THE MAN SENT TO YOU?"** All 3 must be answered correctly or else you will have failed. Every dead person will be asked this, now is the time for us to prepare to answer these questions before we are asked. There will be people who are speechless and cannot answer, there will be others who say *"uh I don't know"*, and there will be others who will say that *"I heard people say it was such and such so I'll say him"*. All those who answer in such a fashion will have answered incorrectly and failed. You cannot memorize the correct answers and manage to say them without having believed and acted upon it in life. The angels will be given knowledge to know whether you are telling the truth and if you're lying they will say so. Even if you do manage to answer honestly these questions are not multiple choice, each question has only one acceptable answer. What if you don't say the correct answers? Everyone who fails to answer correctly with sincerity and a life that was a proof to match their answers, will then be smashed with that huge hammer right in the face. They will scream in pain so loud that all of creation will hear them except for humans and jinn, who are unable to hear that frequency. Then the Creator of everything in the universe announces the test result of failure from the heavens proclaiming: "***MY SERVANT LIES!!!!!*** *so provide for them from hellfire, clothe them with hellfire, and open for them a door from hellfire*". After which the heat of hell will be felt in the grave and it will become tight, crushingly small until the ribs interlock. Then such a person will have all of their bad deeds come to them, in the form of a hideous ugly foul smelling person who stinks worse than the smelliest cadaver and will reside with them in the grave. This person will dread the Day of Judgment and hope it never comes. Every day their place in hellfire will be displayed before their eyes letting them know that things will only get worse. Then depending on the sins of the person there are different punishments they will experience before the Day of Terror, but I will refrain from mentioning them because to do so would turn this into a horror book. This is no fairytale, this is the realest reality there is and something we should keep in our mind on a daily basis because it is happening every day. Soon it will be your day in the grave and you will be asked the 3 questions just like all the rest. What will your answer be when the angels ask you?

Back then I didn't quite realize that suicidal thoughts were whispered by the devils who actively seek our destruction. Since my path to the priesthood was put on hold, I mistakenly believed that the solution to my personal problems could be solved by having a girlfriend. It should come as no surprise that the first time this girl and I met was during square-dancing in 10th grade. In 11th grade we were in the same english class and our teacher knew I wanted to be a priest, since I made it known, and probably could see as I could see that this girl kind of subtly flirted with me. Or at least that's what I thought/felt which made life awkward because I wasn't sure if it was just me and I was crazy and hoping it or if it was just as much as the girl dared to do in public since I was publicly adament on becoming a priest and girls tend not to want to be identified with flirting with those types of guys. Suffice it to say I did not make flirting with me easy, because publicly I didn't want anything to do with girls. So for me to think she was flirtatious means she either really obviously was, or I was extremely delusional. Yet after the initial seating arrangements changed, the teacher, who could see the friction or at least could see what I thought was friction, would sit me and this girl in close proximity to each other and I think such seating was done on purpose because the teacher thought it'd be interesting to see how things played out. Although to be fair, I would politely challenge the authority/intelligence/morals of the female teacher in class on occasion, though I was the best student, so maybe that was their way of getting revenge on me or entertainment. Or maybe since the teacher was a girl she could see the girl's obvious flirtation and my awkward uncharacteristic lack of averison/condemnation of it and tried to "match-make". If I was delusional and the girl wasn't interested in me at all or even if she was, I still don't see why the teacher would sit us in close proximity so often. Out of all the girls in the school she was one of the few that made me question training for the priesthood, yet the teacher routinely sat her near me. I don't think such seating was random coincidence, nor was it due to alphabetical seating either because the teacher assigned seats non-alphabetically. I can't blame the teacher 100%, but for the record I think the teacher is partially responsible for any feelings that resulted between this girl and I. At the very least the teacher knew we were teenagers with hormones, so seating the same teens of opposite genders close together is sure to have certain results. Boy-girl seating in school results in baby boys and baby girls being born, or the activity of baby-making being done without the baby being made. Say what you will about integration, but all-boy schools and all girl-schools tend to not have their students dating each other. Whereas even if in integrated schools some students don't date, I guarantee they will have their education stunted due to the possibilities and ideas about dating schoolmates. At the very least I must admit that I found it difficult to concentrate in school and classes because fantasies and possibilities of dating occupied some of my thoughts. However the main problem was that, before and after putting my plans for the priesthood on hold, I saw this fellow human being as my door to emotional happiness and stability. While she was attractive my intentions were not sexual, yet selfish nonetheless. Also being in 12th grade there was significant pressure to go to the traditional prom dance. By my logic if I had to suffer the hassle that prom entails then it was foolish to go through the ordeal without having some stable relationship as a result. Plus I was publicly known to most people for years as "that guy who wants to be a priest", so for "that guy" to be having any type of relationship with a female definately risked my social reputation. I had no interest in a one night relationship, especially if I was going to have to "break character". Afterall for almost 3 years I was telling people I was going to be a priest, so for me to go to the prom would cause social shockwaves that would not be worth enduring for a one-night relationship. Anyways what kind of person only wants have an intimate/romantic short-term relationship? It's not real affection if it has a rapid expiration. Thus if I were to get involved with someone, it couldn't be just any-body. I've always been a serious type of person and as such tend to only be interested in serious relationships. Coincidentally I thought this girl was interested in the past and would have been interested myself had I not committed myself to celibacy for the priesthood. Her friend asked me what I would do/say if someone wanted to date me, and me thinking it was a hypothetical question since it was asked in a hypothetical way responded how I'd gently explain how I can't because of the priesthood. Yet while publicly saying that to her friend I wondered if I'd actually say that if she were to ask. I didn't know the girl was a friend with the questioner, and only found out later on the day of my 11th grade english exam when she sat behind me and I overheard her loudly talking to that same questioner on how she wants a boyfriend and dumped her other one because he was bad, while her friend (who didn't like me), gave me a weird hinting type of look while loudly telling her she was messing up her life making a mistake by being single. In hindsight I'm guessing that was some type of signal, but I was interacting with the police hours before so I was too frazzled to pay heed and was busy telling the guy ahead of me about my police problems. Thus my parents calling the police on me may have prevented a dating relationship. Anyways I was in 12th grade and had high hopes about a relationship with this girl so I "broke character" and "directly expressed my interest". Immediately after expressing my interest she told me she already had a boyfriend. Ironically her boyfriend lived on the same street as me and we knew each other. We had even frequently played with each other as kids since his older brother was friends with my older step-cousin(adopted but not related) and we rode the same bus to school, but we were never close or liked each other much due to having regularly competed with each other(even when we played on the same teams) and having different personalities and interests. I was a little stunned to say the least, that the only 2 times where I asked out a girl who seemed genuinely interested in me who I was genuinely interested in, they both had other boyfriends. Both times there were "other guys". What's even more ironic about this 2nd love triangle of mine is that 8 years later my family told me the very same guy is now engaged to my cousin, who as fate would have it has the same first name as the girl I asked out who turned me down because she was dating him. Such irony proves God exists and has a great sense of humor. Surely my experiences with "relationships" couldn't have been coincidental randomized chaotic chance, only God could plan such emotionally riveting comedic brilliance in advance. Now it seems obvious that God was cleverly preventing me from dating people, in many different ways at many different times. I'm not bitter over it rather I'm thankful this guy was dating who he was in 2010 CE because through him God prevented me from dating. In the past I was a little bitter towards all the "other guys", but now I'm grateful to God I wasn't able to date when I wanted to date, because based on my emotional state and narcissism any relationship would have been a very unhealthy relationship. At the least any type of romanticish relationship probably would have made me more depressed than I was before it began. The amount of time dating would have consumed from this critical formative period in my life would have set my own personal development back by years. I think many married people would agree that if you've got problems while being single having a partner only adds to the stress level, quantity and complexity of the problems in your life. Still this realization hadn't fully materialized until later and the few peers who I told about my rejection would try to console me by saying I haven't met the "right person" yet. While terrible advice, this is true in a sense because with me having something wrong with my person there is no way I could even recognize who the right person would be. How can you expect to find what is right if you're wrong? Even if you find romance and "feel the butterflies", any love given to you by another human being will be conditional. When someone says "*I love you*" there is a condition to that love, there is a limit where if you hurt them so severely they will stop loving you. (Whether it's if you cheat, slander them, rob them, cripple them, kill their family, etc.) That type of "love" is only temporary and insincere. The "butterflies" have a very short lifespan. You will find the people who say "*I love you*" to everyone use the word so frequently it applies to everything and in reality they may love food or sleep most of all, with you not even being in the top ten. By believing someone "*loves you*" at face value one day it may shock you to discover they love the television more and if they had to choose between the two, you would be the one kicked out the door to the curb. Fundamentally there are 3 types of love: "Baby love", which is akin to someone thinking "*Love ME! Love ME! Love ME!*" just like they were a baby. Many people desire this narcissistic "Baby love". Next is "Reciprocal love" where one thinks "*I'll love you and in return you will love me. We'll love each other more and more.*" Most think this is true love and it's sad because this is not love, but animalistic self-interest just like monkeys picking bugs off each others backs, it's mutual back scratching for emotions not love. Yet many actually think this is how love is supposed to be, in that the more you give the more you will get back. However Reciprocal love doesn't work just as reciprocal sex doesn't work. For example the way a male feels sexual pleasure is very different than the way a female does. So if a male were to try having reciprocal sex where he let the female penetrate him, it's not going to work since that is unnatural and not how females receive true sexual pleasure. Now is it possible some crazy people might enjoy such a thing? It's possible but that's not true sexual pleasure it's a perverse ugly and unhealthy thing which shouldn't be pleasureable at all. Yet sadly this is the only type of love the majority of people will give or receive in life. Lastly there is "Mature love" this is to "*Give love unconditionally in the right love language. In the way the loved being wants/needs to receive the love.*" In regards to men and women this "Mature love" is rare because it involves giving and not receiving love back, while the giving of love isn't in the way the giver deems fit but is in the way the receiver desires it. For example the way a man feels love is very different than a woman does, the same applies to sexual pleasure. Thus this mature love is for one to give love to another in the way the other expects or desires to receive it and NOT in the way the giver wants to or finds easy to. It's a type of one-way sacrificial love with a risk that one will not get any love back. With humans this "mature love" is high risk and high reward, but if two mature lovers are together they can have high levels of love for each other. However with us humans mature love still will never last forever as it requires a daily effort and conditions always change where some days the mature lover just has an off day where the love doesn't get given correctly or in sufficient quantity so their lover gets dismayed and feels unloved. Deep down humans want that "Baby love", don't hide it, you would love it if everybody loved you just because it's you. Yet that's not healthy nor realistic, but even with mature love other humans will disappoint us and never be able to give us love the way we want/need it on a consistent basis. So should we just accept humans are flawed creatures and take whatever type of love we can get and try to be happy with it? No you deserve better than "mature love" from somebody. You deserve true love. What is true love? True love is the type where you have mature love as does the one you love have it towards you. But this is not something humans can provide, no human can ever give this to you, sorry. The only true love that will ever fill us up completely with satisfaction, security and contentment is the love of our Creator. God can give you the love you want the way you want it for eternity. However the love of God is true love, it ain't Baby love nor reciprocal love, nor mature love because you can't benefit God in any way and God doesn't need your love the way you need his and you would have to be a God to truly have a reciprocal relationship with God. Although if you have mature love for God then God will have true love for you that will be much better than any love anything else could provide and the timeframe is on our side. For instance unlike with a marriage where you have to give love everyday, with God you only have to give mature love during your life, if you do so God will love you if you give him love the way he wants while you are alive and then when you die God will keep on giving love to you for eternity as a reward for your mature love which you gave God during life. That's true divine love. If the one who made you loves you then it won't matter if the whole of humanity hates you, it won't faze you. Whereas if the whole of humanity loves you and your Creator doesn't then you really have nothing of value and are a true loser despite what people think. Unfortunately some people think that the Creator loves everybody by default. This is not the case. God doesn't give adults "Baby love", that's only for babies who don't have the capacity to know what God loves and hates so as to have a mature relationship with God. Yet how do you know what God loves and hates so you can give him true mature love? Well God has to tell you through divine revelation or prophets. God did and gave us criteria so we know how to get on the special list of those whom who God loves and who love God. For God to be all-loving he would have to wish that no evil would exist and if he is all-powerful then he must be able to abolish all evil. Since evil exists then God cannot be both all-loving and all-powerful. Now we know for certain that God is all-powerful but God has never said he was or is all-loving, people have said that but they were not prophets. Christians have taught that "For God so loved the world he gave us Jesus to die for our sins." and thus many people have wrongly concluded that God must be all-loving because of the Christian description of God. Sadly this Christian definition/expectation of an all-loving God has caused many people to become atheists. In fact I'd estimate that the number 1 reason people become atheists is because they learn about God as being "all-loving" from Christian theology and then they deduce from life experience that the "all-loving" doctrine doesn't make sense with reality. Yet rather than conclude God is not all-loving they just disbelieve in the existance of God altogether. Thus because Christians preach a false doctrine about an "all-loving" God whether explicitly or implicitly they create the causes for many people to become atheists. Hence wherever Christianity goes atheism soon follows and this is traceable country by country. In Pagan Polytheistic Greece and Rome nearly nobody disbelieved in the notion of gods existing, nobody. Yet after Christianity dominated public thought then atheism spread in the Christian world. Likewise there were no atheists in the Americas until after Christianity spread there, and the same goes for Africa and Asia. Wherever Christianity goes, Atheism follows because of this "Baby love" concept of God that Christians have taught which is irreconcilable with reality. Yet no prophet ever taught that God had "Baby love" for the world, this is the New Testament of the bible but for the record no prophet ever penned one letter of the New Testament. The notion of a "all-loving God" is not a prophetic doctrine. The prophets were basically delivering an invitation from God to us saying how God wants to have a special semi-mature loving relationship and if we follow the instructions God gave them for us to follow then we would display our love for God and God would love us. First God created us, but God didn't force us to love him, that'd be like spiritual rape if he did. God gives us the choice to love him, while if we don't God takes it personally since he created us and love is not too much to ask. For us to not love God is to hate God. Yet keep in mind to love God and be loved by God is not to just say "I love you God!", that doesn't even work with spouses. God doesn't fall for empty phrases, God knows what's in our heart better than we do. Thus when loving God that love must be expressed the way God wants it to be expressed. The divine revelations we've received from the prophets pbut have stated that the Creator does not love the oppressors, the arrogant, those who don't love their Creator (i.e. worship others instead of God or as partners alongside God), the treacherous, the disobedient, the ungrateful, or those who break their ties of kinship. The Hellfire of eternal displeasure was not created for those whom God loves, it was created for those God does not love. Ironically the very reason we want God to love us is because God is not all-loving, since if God loved everyone or everything then that type of love is worthless. But if God only loves certain things and beings then that's a very special type of love. God's love is not for free nor cheaply attained. God's love is worth it because you have to work hard for it. If as Christians have taught that God loves everyone by default then that would be a foolish and faulty type of love. That type of love would be like a whore's love, but even whores have standards so to think/say God is "all-loving" is to reduce God's standards to being lower than a whore's. But God is far from being comparable to a whore and that's why this "all-loving" deity doctrine is so horrible, even if it didn't contribute to atheism. Unfortunately rather than reject the doctrine atheists reject the deity due to some religious folk spreading a false doctrine about God which they deduce as false but then fail to reconfigure their concept that God could be other than what Christians have told them or other than what they believe at that time. Fortunately though God handles rejection with more patience than most people do and gives people time to learn and change before he gets retribution. Unlike us, God only ever has a binary attitude, God either loves you or hates you there is no neutral indifferent attitude which God can have for someone. The Creator can never have a neutral indifferent disposition towards his creation and he hates them if they have such a disposition towards him. God gives us life for free, but to get his love we must do something extra than just live. This is the love we should strive for and concern ourselves with rather than some member of the opposite gender who will end up dead and decomposing. Ironically that love is possible between married spouses is a proof God exists because animals don't have that love for their mates that humans can potentially have for spouses. Thus we aren't "just advanced animals" because our capacity to love our spouses transcends logic and scientific explanation. Only God can put mature love for a spouse into someone's heart. Sadly though we tend to treat our spouses better than the one who created our spouse and the love that exists between us. Yet regardless mature love for a spouse is a sign God exists. Some may even believe or say that mature love is miraculous. Yet marriage itself while a requirement for such a "miraculous" mature love does not guarrantee it because only God is capable of blessing his creatures with that. Creatures can try, and they do with all types of means such as makup, lies, money and magic, but only God can ever make someone truly "love you" and make you feel it. Marriage is not a guarrantee for that love but it allows the opportunity for it to exist, grow and develop. Just as miracles have recipes so does a healthy loving marriage. One indicator to tell that someone is lying when they say they *"love you"* is their relationship with their Creator. If this is a person who doesn't believe in the one who made them and shows no gratitude for the countless gifts God has bestowed upon them, then how can they possibly love you? How can God bless them with love for you when God hasn't even blessed them with love for God? Not to be cruel but God loves himself more than God loves you, and having someone love God is God's number 1 priority before the priority of them loving you. You can't even come close to giving them what God has given them and they don't even acknowledge the existence of their Creator! Let alone show any appreciation that is due to the divinity. Honestly a disbeliever is incapable of loving their spouse to the full capacity which human love can reach. Disbelieving spouses might have some fun and romance but never ever can they experience "pure true love". Which means they can't give it nor receive it and thus a disbeliever is incapable of "mature love" due to their sore inexperience regarding love and the lack of their loving relationship with God. If they can't or don't love God they can't and won't love anything and technically speaking they aren't even qualified to use the word "love" when talking about their feelings. They still use the word "love" but they don't have the license to use that word nor do they know or do justice to what it means when they use it. Even amongst those who do believe in and worship God, you can be the best to them 99.999% of the time, if you say one word they don't like they'll become your enemy the next minute with all that love you showed them meaning nothing, no matter how many times you say sorry. The bottom line is that people will never be able to make you happy and you will never make people happy. This is because we don't know what makes us happy nor what makes others happy. So even if we believe we can't ever truly have "mature love" fully for another human because we don't know how to best love them and neither do they even if they try to tell us, because they don't know themselves that well to tell us how best to love them. But there is someone who does know other humans and ourself well enough to tell people how to best express love for each other, that is their Creator. Whereas even if you get the information on how to love someone correctly from the Creator, which God will only give you if you believe in, love him and learn from him and his prophets, then still it won't work unless the person is willing to receive the love. Sometimes even if they want to receive it and you want to deliver it the other person won't get the love, just as how someone throwing a ball doesn't always complete the pass to the one trying to receive it. Satan and many other things are waiting to intercept or deflect love transfers between spouses. How does one connect with a mature love for someone else? God has to help and God won't help you or your human lover if God don't love you. God might let you have other types of love with people even if he hates you, but if you ever want that true love with another person then God has to make that connection work. But that connection with a person will only work if you put God first and anyways the other person only can love you a limited time and in a limited manner. Really consider who will be able to give you more and better love, the Creator of the Universe or some human? Nobody knows how to love like God does. So that potential for true love from a human, is just a tiny gift of God's love. Yet why do we have such a desire for it? Because it's a gift God wants us to be given from him. You see God started the love relationship with us, before we did with him, but now that we are mature in order to go from "Baby love" to "Mature Adult love" we need to believe certain things and live a certain lifestyle. Now God wants our love for him to be 100%, it doesn't mean we can't love a human but that love for a human is only because God would want us to have that. Not because they make your private parts feel special, or say things you like to hear. If God doesn't love X human then we shouldn't either and if God does love X human then we should because God does and we love God and who God loves because we love God. Loving who God loves for no other reason than that God loves them makes God love us more, if we love people for personal reasons then God doesn't really like that type of love and won't love us for having that type of love. Thus such petty love is wasted love in a sense because it doesn't help God love us and that is our top priority. So the only reason you should ever enter into a relationship with another person is if it will have a positive impact on your relationship with your Creator. If having a relationship with them damages the relationship with your Creator you'd be better off alone. There are even some relationships where people have had to make the choice of going to paradise alone or going to hell together. Every relationship and interaction we have is a test, marriage is an opportunity to do extra good deeds and to have a person remind you to do good and stay away from evil. Spouses are supposed to rectify each others flaws while combining their efforts to do more good deeds than they could possibly do independently. A spouse does not exist to make you happy, they don't and won't, a spouse only exists to worship God and pass the test of life God has given them. Consider every person you interact with as a fellow test taker, God will grade your tests separately but it's possible to get extra points if you both work together in the right way for the right reason. Also remember that no lover or spouse will keep you company in the grave, thus you should love good deeds more than them since they'll join you in the grave. The successful long-term love relationship is the one you have with God and good deeds(deeds God loves). The reality is that the more attached and invested you get with people the more vulnerable you become and susceptible you are to getting hurt by them, but the more attached and invested you become in your relationship with God the less likely you are to get hurt by or disappointed with God. God is the only one who will reward your love by doing more for you than you've done for God. God treats his friends well and his better friends better, with God friendship just gets better and better forever; as long as you do your part correctly. God is not only your Creator but also the best friend ever, that is if you want him to be your friend and make an effort to be his. Instead of a girlfriend or a boyfriend, get a Godfriend.

      Marriage, or the delay/lack thereof, is intertwined with the issues of sinful sexual activities. Parents must realize that worldwide girls now have the least amount of supervision in their relations with boys than at any other time in history. Also worldwide nearly every single obstacle to sexual relationships between young unmarried persons has disappeared and such relationships are routine as well as expected. What I'm saying is that historically it has never been easier for a boy and girl to have premarital sex, a lot. Likewise generally there has never been as much incentive to have premarital sex as there is today, while boys and girls today know more about sex than any generations before them ever did. So sex is happening make no mistake about it, in fact when I went to high school it was naturally assumed that if people were dating then they were having sex together. This was because so many are having sex with people they aren't dating that if you were dating and you weren't having sex then it was thought that either you or the partner must be crazy. Of course the parents and family typically ignore such things and pretend it's not happening to their descendants who are dating because they imagine themselves to be such great parents who "instilled morals in their kid". Yet in reality that just means the kids will be secret about it and unfortunately the taboo/secrecy makes the sinful sex more exhilarating. I don't care what kind of "morals" a kid has, they have hormones that will make them act like a whore too. Ask the scientists which 1 wins when morals fight hormones. So if the youth are going to have sex why don't they just get married? Many people today don't get married because of fairytales and family. If a person's parents have divorced, such a person suffers psychologically and emotionally and their whole perspective on marriage and life is distorted. Intellectually and spiritually such persons are handicapped because they are less likely to look into the meaning of their lives or to discard their opinions. Typically they have desperate platitudes of self-determination, respecting the "rights", opinions and decisions of others and have unnatural aversion to emotional risks and commitments; while psychologists train people to think having guilt is sinful. The children of divorced parents tend to lack intellectual courage because of a lack of confidence in their future due to a heightened aversion to risk and interpersonal rejections. They simultaneously fear isolation as well as attachment, so they don't want to be alone and they don't want to be dependent. Their enthusiasm gets replaced with self-survival and they fear guilt and regret more than they should. Therefore as a result of their parents' divorce they tend to have a childhood aversion to marriage because they know firsthand what can go wrong and fear the same result happening to them. Even if a divorce were on friendly terms such children can not escape the fact that their mommy (whom they love) doesn't love their daddy for some reasons they may or may not know of, while their daddy (whom they love) doesn't love their mommy for some reasons they may or may not know of. Thus such people will always have a nagging issue in their mind/heart where they try to love 2 different people who they know dislike each other so much they separated. What makes this worse is that the parents will always say they never regret having sex to conceive their child, but they just regret getting/being married. Therefore such children will internalize that with sex there are never regrets or mistakes but with marriage there are, and then Satan will push them to have sex prior to and without marriage. Yet this whole issue of divorces makes no sense. When people date and separate it's understood that in the majority of cases it just didn't work out, yet with marriage the institution itself is bashed because of the individuals incompatibility or bad experiences. Since more dating relationships end than marriages do, then dating should be less popular with a worse reputation. Why isn't it? This is because of Catholicism. The Catholic Church teaches that God/Jesus gave Peter, and by extension all the popes to follow, the ability to bind things together on earth and in heaven. Many Christians believe a similar doctrine but they use their hierarchy as the binding force instead of the Catholic hierarchy or their interpretation of the bible as the binding force. This distorted doctrine was applied to marriage based on misunderstood New Testament bible passages which people thought meant Jesus pbuh prohibited divorce. Religiously speaking divorce is a big deal, but it's not a sin. The Catholic Church taught and many Christians still believe that divorce is a sin. This is because when a priest married two people to each other it was thought that to break that binding done by the church was to oppose the church itself and combat it's authority. Divorce used to be considered akin to apostasy, in that if you divorced then you disbelieved. Thus they taught people to vow at the marriage ceremony they'd stay together "for better or worse" and death would be the only way out no matter how "worse" things got, and they still do this today but they think it's romantic to say "til death do us part". Later on the loophole of papal annulment was invented to allow Catholics a way to separate without getting a divorce if the Pope allowed them to. However this mentality towards divorce has made marriage seem to be the ultimate never ending commitment, that's more serious than even picking a religion itself. Foolishly some actually view getting married or divorced as a bigger decision than changing religions. This is why many people will change/compromise their religion to get married but few will get divorced/change their marital status because of religious reasons. This irrational fear of divorce has become an obstacle to marriage and a reason people choose many of the sinful alternatives to marriage. Fortunately despite such fears many still do want to get married. So why don't they? The fairytales, culture and family have brainwashed girls to expect a supergenius handsome prince with super strength in shining armor, who will fight their way through hell just to sweep them off their feet at first glance in order to marry them, then take them away from their family problems to live happily ever after in their castle. Thus women have unrealistic expectations of husband material. I've yet to meet one guy who fits a single fairytale's criteria of husband material. While the adults expectations tend to be less fantastical and "armor" is not seen as a requirement, many of the princely expectations still remain in a diluted form. Yet parents today don't think their standards fit the princely mold. Most will think a guy should be wealthy, healthy, handsome, smart, funny, kind, with a good reputation and the ability to give their daughters a life of luxury oh and did I mention perfect? Religion is hardly a concern and neither is their emotional or psychological states. In practice the minimum standards tend to be, be old enough, have a "good job" and house or plan to get a house. Yet this "old enough" standard has nothing at all to due with their maturity it is literally just a number. I know people younger than me who I think are ready for marriage who aren't married and I know many who are much older than me who've been married for a long time who I don't think are qualified for it. Instead this "old enough" cliche is just a way to say "marry someone rich". Of course they won't say that but they will say *"Wait until after school, then after they get a safe well-paying job, settle down in their own place and can afford a family etc."* This is the basic model today. However this is NOT the prophetic model or prophetic standard at all. This is the capitalist pseudo fairytale standard. In the past people would marry in order to make it easier to survive because they couldn't survive on their own. Today people think they have to be self-sufficient before they ever get married. This is because of the fairytales and poor family relationships that has led the western mentality to think it's improper or bad for a husband or wife to live with their parents. Moses pbuh was a poor homeless fugitive wanted for manslaughter by the world's superpower when a man offered him his daughter in marriage, simply because he was strong, modest and trustworthy containing sound religious beliefs with upright behavior. How many parents today would marry their daughter off to a homeless fugitive who had a severe stutter, but was also religious with morals? If not then I guess Moses pbuh himself wouldn't be good enough and they would refuse to marry their daughter to Moses pbuh. On the other hand if Pharaoh proposed to their daughter how many would refuse? Just look at Pharaoh's qualifications and credentials, 1. Well educated. 2. Rich 3. Steady job 4. Famous with political power 5. Handsome 6. Respected in society with noble lineage too. Honestly the only thing unappealing about Pharaoh would be his religious beliefs and religious character. This is why so many people today get married to Pharaohs, because their marriage criteria is designed to find them a Pharaoh to marry and reject those like Moses pbuh. Outside the West in many places around the world families live in one household. In North America this is considered strange because, they can't stand their families and historically the colonists tended to be expansionary and new families were granted new uncleared farmland to encourage further territorial expansion. Yet this has become a foolish superstition in that once 2 people get married then they are expected to live together in their own place. Economically this is no longer a realistic notion and is unfeasible for the majority of people. The older generation thinks *"First comes school, then comes job, then a house, then comes marriage happy ever after."* Whereas post-secondary school itself will likely put a person in debt and most people shouldn't even go because it's a useless economic scam, since the universities know people treat diplomas as a qualification for a happy life and a qualification for marriage. Secondly many who graduate will not get a job or an education and will not get a well-paying job which will allow them to pay off their debt. So if you make college a standard for your prince then don't expect to live in a castle. Thirdly those castles/houses are overpriced because of this superstition that a house is needed for the happily ever after marriage/life. Thus debt is used to get that too and with all this debt from college and a house then a big salary will be needed, so people take a job they will not enjoy doing simply because they need to pay off an astronomical debt with interest. Well that makes for one miserable prince. So from the guy's perspective, typically the only thing the princess brings to the marriage is sex appeal, wealth and status. Thus many guys think that if they have to be a prince to get married then they better be getting a queen and since there are no queens willing to marry "non-royalty" they settle for a drag-queen, or a beauty queen, or a sleeping beauty since no good female role models are ever depicted in the fairytales for guys to view as a realistic template. Just look at the fairytales from a male perspective and think what a little boy will look for in a potential spouse. All the "good girls" in fairytales are either magical, mythical or supergenius hardworking supermodels that are somehow desperate for a man. While the girl is taught they need magic/glamour or to change their biological nature to get a man or just settle for a beast with a castle and hope he magically turns into a prince or that kissing a frog will turn him into a prince. Yet for the guy once the beauty goes that "happy ever after" tends to just be "ever after" aka "for worse" and for the girl they learn that prince charming ain't so princely and ain't too charming after marriage/sex. Many such people are miserable because they ended up marrying a myth. Tragically those who marry a myth have their marriage turn into a monstrous nightmare. It all starts off with false expectations on the wedding day for most. Think of how even before the wedding a guy and girl have their "wedding day" visualized and fantasize about how great it will be. By default reality disappoints because they planned the first day and moments of their marriage in the realm of fantasy. What do they dress like? They dress better than they've ever dressed before and better than they'll ever dress again. Now if this were the case with any other thing we'd say we got scammed and misled by false advertising. Therefore by trying to look great on one's wedding day people make themselves look bad for their entire marriage. Since both spouses remember what the other looked like on their "*special day*", they'll always subconsiously think on every later day, "*that's not what you looked like when I married you*". Then Satan will say you got defrauded and thereby you will not have those same feelings as you did on the wedding day because your partner wasn't dressing the way they normally would. Whereas if they didn't try to make a fantasy wedding hyping themselves up prior to the marriage to put on a great show for both families, then the husband and wife might actually find their spouse more beautiful for the rest of their marriage. This is because if they didn't dress up fancy then each will remember the other looking much the same as they did on their first day married, and since they cared about them then they will care about them now and tomorrow because they will feel as though it's the same person, except they know them even better and care about them more. If you want to have a really good marriage then be real at your wedding and don't hype yourself up dressing fancy for the day, because marriage is a long-term commitment, which deserves the same commitment from you each day. If you try making the first day "extra special" then none of the other days will be. By acting and dressing normal on your wedding day, it can make every day of your marriage a "special day". If you take the care to dress up special on day one and don't for all the rest, then it shows you don't really care on the other days as much and you really only dressed up for all the wedding guests. It's because the wedding day is portrayed as "the special day" that everyday of marriage isn't considered special. A wedding is only the beginning, the joy is supposed to be a result of the marriage's potential. Some view weddings as the final accomplishment when it's really just the start.

Unfortunately some who get married put more effort into the wedding day than they do the whole marriage. This is because of how we think of the entire concept of marriage. For instance everyone hears good things about "getting married" but how many times do we hear good things about "staying married"? As a result of this mentality the wedding becomes the best part of marriage and few would think to disagree, while marriage becomes the burdensome baggage one gets stuck with after their happy "special day". Since deep inside all know that marriage comes after the wedding, because it doesn't get the good publicity this leads people to neglect or dislike getting married because of the consequences which are seen as consequences instead of rewards. How did this mental aversion take root? Because of the jokes and fairytales. Rarely do people joke about how bad weddings are in general, but everybody always hears jokes about how bad marriage is and how difficult life with a spouse is. While the fairytales and romantic stories tend to end at the wedding, teaching marriage is not romantic nor is it a "happy ending". Thus if you watch enough of them or get exposed to "love-stories" too much, you will involuntarily internalize the idea that the wedding is the pinnacle of romantic happiness and then the story ends. Therefore people get to the point where their hearts and minds are so used to the wedding being portrayed as the happy ending, they actually subconsciously don't want their own story to go on past the wedding into marriage. Then people get the "post-honeymoon effect" where they become disillusioned because their idea of marriage didn't go past the fun and easy orientation stage. Psychologically they viewed marriage as a fun short-term contract instead of an arduous long term commitment that involves ups and downs, they thought the highs of marriage would be better and that the lows would be less low and more fun. For all intents and purposes the proliferation of "love stories" and such have caused this heinous problem of humans thinking that marriage just ruins the happy ending from the wedding. Therefore you will have some people who will say they'd like to have a wedding but don't want to get married. Hence due to the romantic fairytales some people fear getting married. Sadly it gets worse because the fantastical royal wedding requires a royal feast called a wedding party. This is where the tribalistic family customs make people fear the wedding. Ever since the tribal days a wedding meant expansion of the tribe. This is why family members who hate each other will come together and enjoy weddings because of family pride at gaining a new member. The problem is these wedding parties are blown out of proportion and everybody who's anybody gets invited, even if those people will never ever see the married couple again. It gets crazy too in that people will get mad if they don't get invited and they'll get mad if their invitation arrives later than someone else's invitation and they get mad if it arrives the same time as everyone else's invitation too. So they're mad if they don't get invited and they're mad if they do and then they criticize the invitation too. Then at the expensive party which neither the groom nor bride really wants to be at or have, but only do so people don't get mad at them for breaking sacred tribal customs, the families complain about the seating arrangements, the food, the lighting, the heat, the colors, the theme, the place, the parking, the timing, the weather and everything imaginable and they'll never let it go and will compare it to every other royal feast they've ever been to. Whereas from the bride and groom's perspective they have just spent much much more than they wanted to or could afford to in order to try to please fickle family who they don't even know yet. Thus they try to meet everyone in the other person's family but they don't know who is who and who they'll be meeting with in the future. Frequently the distant relatives who barely made the list will then exploit this spotlight for all it's worth and the new member of the clan then ends up spending more time than the clan thinks is appropriate talking to such a distant member while the bride/groom thought they were doing the right thing trying to get to know family, yet in reality they're making the family they'll be spending the most time with upset by not giving them the attention they feel entitled to. In short wedding parties tend to be disasters and can completely ruin a marriage because of the financial strain alone. Personally I dread the wedding party and see it to be the worst and most stressful part of getting married. Now the prophets have instructed us to have wedding feasts but the prophetic method is a lot different than the modern princely method. My problem isn't with the wedding party in principle but with the way it's commonly practiced. Therefore with all this garbage that goes into getting married, it's no wonder why people put it off or avoid it and just date/live together/have sinful sex casually. Marriage is a big thing, but society has made it into a scary and dreadful thing without us even realizing why our generation has more aversions to marriage than the generations who came before. That is not how it is supposed to be. I went over some of what families do and now I'll share what I think they should do and why. As for the fairytale problems, the solution for fantasy is reality. Fantasy and reality are mortal enemies, the more a person invests in one realm the less successful they will be in the other. A healthy balance between the two can not exist, one must choose fantasy or reality or they will develop a split-personality. I suggest everyone chooses reality, since the road to paradise only exists in the realm of reality. The realm of fantasy is Satan's dungeon for humans where he tricks his prisoners into thinking it's an amusement park. May God guide us to and keep us in the realm of reality, far from the realm of fantasy which is a gateway to insanity and a relative of lunacy. Unfortunately Satan's trapdoor to the dungeon of fantasy gets called imagination. Imagination is not needed for creativity. Some may think they can enjoy both reality and fantasy/fiction or "imagination", but imagination and fiction only hurts marriages and God is not a fan of fantasy. God made the realm of reality so why wouldn't we be pleased with it and satisfied? The easiest way to tell someone is depressed is that they enjoy fiction. Fiction is used by people to escape reality while giving themselves the illusion of social interactions, thereby stunting their developement by replcaing true interpersonal development with imaginary interpersonal skills. Sadly such an addiction to fiction can happen very soon after birth in the form of stuffed animals who act as imaginary friends or as I refer to them "love objects". Psychologists refer to these as "comfort objects" because when a person is psychologically weak they seek such objects to provide comfort, such as a blanket, animal or toy. Frequently emergency responders carry such "comfort objects" in their vehicles, not for kids as you'd expect, but for adults. This is because after a traumatic incident rather than deal with an adult victim's damaged psychological state, which most are unable to do, they give them a "comfort object" to fix them up enough so they can survive the situation. A kid with a stuffed animal which they love and pretend is a real character is emotionally unhealthy. Any such "love object" denotes a difficulty coping with reality and the object is merely an unhealthy anchor. Initially "love objects" are the substitute for the mother once the child learns they cannot have motherly love 100% of the time as they felt they did when in the womb. Hence their "love object" is a fantasized bond with the mother which is dependant upon them instead of being dependant upon their mother for emotional support and love. The first such "love object" is typically our mother's breast, which not only provides a deep intimate connection but nutrition as well. When we lose that original intimate connection with our mother many of us suck our thumbs as a replacement breast because it feels like the intimacy which we lost. The primary reason kids have "love objects" is because they don't feel loved by the people in their life don't have intimate connections with people and they don't know how to love people yet, or love themselves, get more love, or to handle life with less love or less intimacy. "Love objects" are also used by the kid to help them in going to sleep and in times of anxiety, which are typically times when intimacy is desired. Therefore to get the love they need and want their childish mind creates a "love object" or many "love objects" which they name and treat as friends/lovers, unfortunately with many adults playing along not realizing how dangerous that is. A child will then give their love to their "love object" and in return it will makeup for the love it isn't getting from people. The "imaginary friend" prevents the child from developing intimate relationships with people. But don't kids grow out of "love objects" and imaginary friends? No. Instead they realize they need more love than their "love object" can provide so they begin to love toys or "heroes". Others get pets to be their new "love object" which in the short term is better for kids, but in the long term it's worse because they never develop past having emotional intimacy with animals and society thinks pet owners are normal despite the phenomenon being psychologically insane and emotionally abnormal. Whereas many parents rejoice when their kid gives up their "love object" not realizing that they didn't give it up, their addiction tolerance just increased. Most kids don't give up their imaginary friend they just replace them with another substance or behavior that fulfills their emotional needs. Real friends don't fulfill the same emotional needs as the imaginary friends did. After the toys fail to fulfill the individual's emotional needs they turn to bigger and better toys. Eventually if they can no longer afford or obtain bigger and better toys to make them emotionally satisfied this returns them to fiction, and/or they turn to an addictive substance. Most addicts in the world today are simply "self-sucking" their thumbs in a different way than kids are. Then when adults get married many see the spouse as their final "love object" who will fulfill all their emotional and intimacy needs/desires. However not only is this job impossible for another person to do but "self-suckers" don't even know how to be emotionally or mentally intimate and communicate because of a lifetime of "love objects". They think they will go from being self-suckers to spouse-suckers and the spouse gets suckered into marrying a self-sucker who would suck their very life force out of them trying to fulfill their emotional needs and still not be happy. They've never had to develop intimate interpersonal skills with their "love objects" and many don't know how, so when the spouse doesn't fulfill all their emotional needs as they expected then they move on to other "love objects"; such as addictions or fiction or a combination of many alternatives. Essentially many addictions and bad marriages are directly caused by "love objects" being used as a child. Sadly parents don't know the long-term effects such things have but suffice it to say a stuffed animal can destroy your child's marriage. Most addictions are caused by a suppression of feelings. If we could learn how to feel our emotions and express them in a healthy way rather than judging, suppressing or fearing them, many addictions and recovery programs would cease to exist. What complicates this is that letting go of a substance or behavior that's helped us "change the channel" when we've had awkward or painful feelings, is like saying goodbye to an old friend who's been the only truly reliable source of connection or comfort we've ever known. Addicts feel/think it's always been there for them when they've had a need for relief so even just the thought of letting go of that relationship triggers sensations of loss, grief and anxiety which causes a desire to indulge again. This is why addictions are so difficult to give up, because the addiction is simply an advanced version of the "love object" we adopted after we stopped breast feeding. The imaginary friend and/or "love object" was the beginning of the addiction. Hence the true culprit of addiction, aside from Satan and oneself, is fiction. We began by seeking emotional satisfaction in things that can't supply it, thereby piling up an emotional debt or love scarcity due to low supply of love and increasingly higher demand. Fiction is what created the relationship with our first love object. It was fiction that got us married to a doll, blanket, stuffed animal or our thumbs. Fiction is literally the way to emotionally and mentally "change the channel" of our real life when we don't like how it's going and want to see/experience something other than the reality which we are having a difficult time living with. Fiction is for quitters and therefore the enemy of marriage is fiction. I've yet to meet someone who is capable of a successful marriage who indulges in fiction. Fiction disqualifies you for living in real life. Addictions are caused by fiction and fiction also destroys/prevents marriages. No spouse can replace our mother's breast and the time for suckling is over. Self-sucking our thumbs/toys/drugs is not the way to achieve happiness or comfortable intimacy and our spouse is not a "love object". Our "love objects" were essentially "love idols" because we didn't worship God correctly as we were supposed to; probably because our parents didn't do so or teach us to do so. Yet God was always there to help and comfort us, we just failed to turn to God when we were a child so we developed emotions for objects or behaviors as a replacement. Yet since those objects and behaviors were never enough we replaced them with others continuously until we needed a spouse, then kids, then grandkids, money, health, fame, legacies and so on but none of them were ever sought for the correct healthy purposes which God intended us to have them for. God didn't create money to make us happy. God didn't create kids to make us happy. God didn't create marriage to make us happy either, Satan told us that our spouse would make us happy deliberately trying to make us cause each other misery when we failed to live up to the other's expectations. Consider Adam pbuh and Eve were married in paradise yet Satan still got them to sin via a "comfort object". How could that happen if marriage equals happiness? It doesn't and that's why Adam pbuh and Eve sinned because marriage is not equivalent to happiness, it is a relationship. Who knows maybe Satan even told them the food would be an aphrodisiac and spice up their marriage. Yet the lesson is that marriage itself did not make Adam pbuh or Eve sufficiently happy to be able to avoid sin, even though they were both literally married to the best man/woman in the world. Eve was married to the very first man ever made, who God personally physically made. People talk about a "match made in heaven", well Adam pbuh and Eve were literally a match not only made in heaven but each one of them was physically created by God's own hand. Today people don't get made by hand but back then God made people by hand, so you know they looked super sexy. Yet still Adam pbuh and Eve weren't happy having a spouse made by God himself because they still gave in to sin. Therefore the way to be happy does not come through your spouse, if it did then surely Adam pbuh and Eve would be too happy to sin. So always remember that even if God handcrafted your spouse they still would not be able to make you emotionally satisfied or happy. A spouse is not an emotional superhero to save us from depression, lonliness, sadness, self-esteem issues or our fears. I repeat, a spouse is not an emotional superhero. If you go into marriage thinking your spouse is a emotional superhero then you are an emotional supervillain. This is why the age of marriage is not as big a deal as many think because the emotional development plays a larger role in marriage than the physical development. Emotionally many people who get married are no different than the child sucking their thumb, they just use something more pleasurable to replace sucking their thumb. A young person who has no "love objects" in their life is emotionally qualified for marriage, while an adult with "love objects" is emotionally unqualified; while if an adult has a fondness for fiction then they are mentally unqualified as well. As regards solving the issues of modern marriages in the realm of reality, the whole idea of a minimum age limit for marriage is phoney idiocy. If someone is old enough to date then they're old enough to get married, and if they aren't then they shouldn't be dating. The dating age is the same as the marriage age. Ideally marriage should occur after puberty, the attainment of responsibility and spiritual, mental and emotional maturity. Unfortunately many today never attain spiritual, mental or emotional maturity. Of course personal finances play a factor in whether someone should get married or not, moreso for the guy than for the girl, although God has promised to provide sustenance for those poor people who get married seeking chastity. So while wealth isn't a requirement for marriage, poverty shouldn't be a deal breaker either. There is absolutely nothing wrong with people getting married and living separately with their own parents. In fact that actually serves as motivation for such youths to move out because they will want to live together more and more and will be forced to develop good saving habits to attain that goal. On the other hand there is nothing wrong with young people getting married and then having one live with the other while living with their parents. Such a practice would actually strengthen the family ties, as well as make sure prospective spouses are really sincere in their intentions for marriage. Just think about it, if someone is willing to live with you AND your family then they must really be committed and care about you and making the marriage work. In such a situation they could even rotate with the young couple living a week with the wife's parents then a week with the husband's parents and then maybe some time separately as a break or whatever type of situation is best. Such a routine would greatly strengthen the family ties and prevent family problems. Sadly many can't accept this because they can't tolerate their families and see marriage/dating as an escape from their family, which they think will give them the emotional and psychological comfort their families don't. Ironically parents tend to be more opposed to this idea than the youth do because they see marriage as a way to get free time away from their kids and as a way to stop financially supporting their kids. Yet in such a scenario as I described it would give both sets of parents free-time and help their finances as both families would be helping the young couple as well as deepening their relationships together. For this idea to work parents must accept reality. Financially this whole notion of each house belonging to one couple is unsustainable and unfeasible. In the modern economy most people cannot afford to live alone or by their own means, nor can most young people (and by "young people" I mean those under 40) afford to live as a couple together, even if both are working. Economically it's unrealistic. Don't be mad at me, it's just the economic reality. We have to be real to get real solutions and not optimistically idealistic or "old-fashioned". What about the school requirement? Well schooling has only existed for a few hundred years so finishing school has nothing to do with marriage ability. I know people my age who got married while in college and it actually helped them be a better student because it takes stress off and gives them motivation to succeed. In fact I'd say it's probably better for people to be married when attending post-secondary school because it is such a sexualized environment in which sex is basically an extracurricular activity. At the end of the day the youth have 4 options. They will either get married, fornicate, masturbate or severely and painfully struggle not to masturbate. From personal experience with many different people who attended college while single, while dating and while married, those who are married (without kids) tend to be the best students because they don't have the sexual distractions and they have more motivation to excel, whereas those pitiful people who date tend to be the worst performing students. Parents who think their kid won't do good in college if they're married are fools. Just think of the difference between having a parent read your college report card versus having your spouse read your college report card, who do you think will have a better report card? Likewise if you don't want your kid to go to college and party, get STDs, or do drugs then if they get married they won't be going to no frat parties, picking up STDS, or trying drugs. They're going to be at home with their spouse studying. Remember the primary reason for the whole sexual dilemma with pornography, dating, fornication and masturbation is because people don't get married. People have to deal with the sexual reality and the spiritual consequences. Most of the youth who aren't married will either be fornicating or masturbating, both of which are grave sins. It's just a plain fact. So marriage is the solution, dating is not; dating is the gateway to fornication and it always has been. It's really simple, if young people are interested in someone they should just go to that person's parents and say they're interested in marriage and think that person's son or daughter may be a potential spouse and would like to discuss such a possibility with them and their son or daughter. Then the parent/guardian should monitor and be present for all such discussions, while present they should be making sure the meetings are only about discussing compatibility for potential marriage. It's not dating, it's just genuinely getting to know someone through repeated interviews for marriage. If they are compatible and willing to get married then they should get married. So what if they are young and can't afford a royal wedding feast? So what if they can't afford to live together in their own place? Would you rather they fornicate? Would you rather they masturbate and suffer all the spiritual, emotional, mental and physical harms such a sin will cause that may well destroy them and prevent them from ever getting married or ruin any marriage they have in the future as well as cause them punishment in the next life? Getting married doesn't mean automatically having kids, at the earliest a kid will be delayed by about 9 months, but even then it can be much longer especially if the youth know they aren't ready for kids yet. It's possible to select the mother or father of your future child well before you are ready to raise one. Waiting until one is absolutely ready for kids before getting married is wrong, it's something to consider but it's not a requirement. Being ready for kids isn't even a prerequisite for sex, although it should be considered as an outcome just in case, but that's another point in that getting married doesn't automatically mean having sex. I know people who got married and they didn't consummate their marriage until a long time had passed. I even know of people who got married and didn't have sex until years later. So that's where people must understand that marriage and sex are different things, marriage simply allows for a lawful sexual outlet, it's not a compulsory aspect of marriage in that if you're married then you have to do it immediately or at all. If the youth don't get married they will get married without permission at best, elope, or do many other types of sinful things. To stop the sex industry parents have to get their kids married and stop creating obstacles and hurdles to marriage. The educational and financial obstacles aren't even valid. Of course marriage is a life-changing decision that shouldn't be taken lightly, but the youth know this. Most won't jump into marriage without serious considerations, but if they date then they will because they will fall in lust and think it's love. So that's where personally if I had kids I'd never let them date. My policy would be they either get engaged, or get married, or stay single. Whereas the engagement itself would just be a countdown for being single and wouldn't be dating. Engagement would be just like waiting for your first day of work after accepting the job offer. If kids aren't prepared to get married by the time they are in their twenties then maybe that's because the parents did a bad job raising their kids and let them develop life-wasting habits that stunted their spiritual, mental and emotional growth. The worst that could happen is a youth marries someone they're incompatible with and they get divorced. Yet even if that happens it's better for them. Firstly a divorce when you are young is a lot easier than when old, especially if it's before kids and finances enter the picture. Secondly that would prepare them for marriage in the future and give them great life experience that would help them in school and in the workplace. Imagine a 25 year old who graduated college and has been divorced, they would actually be a more valuable employee because they have all those life lessons of marriage and divorce which the other kids leaving college don't have. So marriage and divorce would actually help young people on their resume and make it easier to find employment, especially if they're married. From an employer's perspective if someone was willing to marry their child to such a young person then they must be something special and they definitely have responsibility and motivation to work well, also single employees are likely to cause trouble in the workplace via romance with coworkers. Thus parents thinking that getting their young kids married will hurt their prospects in life are wrong and damaging their child's life in more ways than they know or will ever know. Just reflect upon Moses pbuh and when he got married. The father in-law of Moses pbuh decided to get him married to one of his daughters on the very first day he met him. He didn't say *"Well let me give this Moses a job first and after getting to know him well then if I like him I'll let him date one of my daughters, and if they end up falling in love and like each other then later maybe months or years down the road perhaps he could become my son in-law."* That's not at all what the father in-law of Moses pbuh did, he got him married on the first day he met him BEFORE employing him. Many forget what it means that

Moses pbuh worked for his father in-law and got employed after getting engaged/married. Realistically most people today would offer a job to a guy before they offer their daughter, but that's not how the father in-law of Moses pbuh did it because he realized how important marriage is. Few would fault the father in-law of Moses pbuh if he offered Moses pbuh a job first and then got to know Moses pbuh well before giving him his daughter to marry. The father didn't do this because he knew what he needed to know about Moses pbuh and his religious character to be completely happy with having him as a son in-law, despite him being a homeless unemployed fugitive. Hence the father in-law of Moses pbuh taught us that dating is useless and sinful, because if it was useful and lawful then he would have offered Moses pbuh a job and let him date his daughter, but he didn't because he'd prefer she get married the first day he/she met the guy than let her date him. Another lesson society as a whole fails to learn from this is that the father in-law of Moses pbuh thought it was more important to get married than it was to get a job. That's why the marriage arrangements were made before the job offer. Of course I'm not saying this is the best for everyone, however to think employment is a requirement for a good spouse and a prerequisite for marriage is wrong and that was one of the lessons the father in-law of Moses pbuh taught us. Today many parents have a mentality that is opposite the one which the father in-law of Moses pbuh had. That's why their kids date a bunch of Pharaohs before getting married to a Pharaoh, if they even get married at all. Notice I say "if they even get married", I didn't say "if they have kids" because most people are going to have the kids, marriage unfortunately is less likely. In this era you are more likely to have a grandkid than to have a son or daughter in-law. If trends continue, the numbers of kids born out of wedlock will be higher than the number of divorces. If not for abortions, the number would already be higher. In the modern world parents must know their kids are faced with a different reality than they were, for the overwhelming majority it really is marry, fornicate or masturbate. Parents really have no clue at all of the sexual temptations their children go through because they are different and more severe temptations. The younger generations have had more exposure to sexification than the older generations, so grandparents and parents honestly don't know what their kids go through; it just isn't the same. The experiences are different, the technology is different, the society is different, the opportunities are different so for a parent to think that because they may have handled their temptations then their kids can do it too is completely wrong. Their kids are different people facing an entirely different test. Sadly many youth today are afflicted with what some have called "hornyosis" or "lustitis" and rather than being repulsed by such terms they'd actually have a sexileptic arousal because of their chronic sexilepsy. Some may even laugh at such terms thinking they are erotic jokes despite them being severely debilitating conditions. So if parents want the best for their kids they'd get them married, like the father in-law of Moses pbuh did. People don't need to date and shouldn't. It's easy to determine if people are compatible for marriage beforehand if people know how to, the problem is most don't so they date; until they fall in lust that leads to marriage if not fornication beforehand. Then you end up with some people who will have sex, have kids, live together, although maybe not all in that order, and yet they still don't get married. It astounds me, because I can't understand why they don't get married too when they're doing all the rest. I even know of several people who have kids with people and say, "*I know we got kids together but we're not ready for marriage"* How can they handle kids together yet not be "ready for marriage"? God has made marriage a prerequisite for kids! Meaning it's illegal to have kids without getting married first. It's frustrating because if they only got married it would prevent so many sins, yet because of taboo and being indoctrinated with unrealistic/incorrect expectations and qualifications for marriage they don't, so they get the sins instead. Divorce is not a sin! Getting married too soon is not a sin! Most all the other stuff that people are doing is. It'd be better for a young person to get married and divorced 100 times before they're 30 than for them to fornicate or masturbate even once. That's the reality, people gotta wakeup and get married instead of dating. Of course don't misunderstand this if you're single or a parent and think today's the day and one must rush to get married before it's too late. That's one of Satan's tricks to make people pick someone too soon or the wrong person because they think/fear *"it's now or never, the sooner the better"*. Know there is a difference between being lonely and ready. If a person is going to harm their spouse in any way, including verbally, emotionally, mentally or spiritually, then it may be less sinful for them if they stayed single. However sometimes the sins done being single can only be prevented through marriage and this is evidenced by Lot pbuh offering the sodomites his daughters and the women of Sodom in lawful marriage. Lot pbuh didn't think they were great husband material but he recognized that it would be better for them and society if the sodomites had gotten married to females so they would be less likely to commit the sin of sodomy. Lot pbuh, a prophet of God, cared so much about stopping the sin of sodomy that he was willing to get his own daughters married to sodomites and offered them to any/every sodomite in the city. Now I'm not saying parents should let anybody marry their child but Lot's example shows how important marriage is and how grievous sexual sins are. To prevent sexual sins from occuring Lot pbuh was prepared to let any guy, of the same religion, to marry his daughters. Again that is another example of marriage being proposed based on religion and morality, without regard for education, wealth, fame, looks, lineage etc. Lot pbuh just wanted a guy who wasn't gay and was willing to accept/practice the true religion. Lot pbuh didn't care about the superficial critera. However Lot pbuh, despite being their prophet, wasn't forcing marriage upon his daughters in order to stop sin, his daughters consented to have Lot pbuh offer them in marriage to any qualified candidates he deemed worthy in the entire region because they were ready to marry as well. So being ready for marriage is a valid prerequisite which most families neglect to cultivate in their youth or help their youth with. (Notice I said families, it's not just the parents' job to prepare children for marriage.) Simply having a will to marry is different than being ready, it's a start but willingness is 1 a part of being prepared/qualified. Marriage is a major decision and most times that I've felt "in the mood for marriage", I just read a list of 100 questions I found online to ask a potential spouse before marriage and realized I wasn't ready for marriage nor ready to discuss it, let alone qualified because I hadn't yet learned the rights of a wife and child which a man must know before becoming a husband. The same applies for women needing to know a husband's and child's rights before becoming a wife. Yet some people are ready for marriage but they don't know it because they don't know how to determine if they are ready, or who is a good person for them to marry(which is different than finding a good person or enjoyable person to spend time with) or their parents/society are preventing them from marrying due to having a false set of requirements for marriage and it is causing major problems. One important overlooked aspect is that it's one thing to know you aren't ready for marriage, but most people don't know how to get ready so they perpetually stay "not ready" failing to learn the steps they can take to become ready spiritually, mentally and emotionally. Dating is not a method to find the correct spouse, it's just a romantic/sexual tense friendship. That's not just my personal religious opinion either, that's the scientific secular opinion as well. Science is supposed by most to be based on theory and observations. Scientifically it is impossible to know someone through observation and experiences prior to marriage, because while dating people are always on their best behavior and don't feel comfortable to show their true private self. Dating is a controlled experiment without the variables of reality or genuine authenticity. A girlfriend or boyfriend is a completely different person than a wife or husband. The same goes for those who try "living together", because without the marriage there is no commitment so even when "living together" people will never truly be themselves because they will view the other person as a roommate and not a true legal spiritual partner they can fully trust and depend on. So if anybody ever slyly tells you "*I can't get married until after I date them for awhile or live together to see if we're compatible*" they are delusional, scientifically wrong and spiritually wrong. Whereas dating does nothing to determine compatibility and I've seen the real life outcomes of people who date, then get married and then they are miserable. The problem is they dated and fell in love with their desires(it's impossible to fall in love with a person before marriage) and their date died once they got married. You marry a husband or a wife, nobody has ever married a boyfriend or girlfriend so if you are in love with the one you date then it's a guarantee that you won't enjoy being married to that person. Guys fall in lust with their girlfriend and then hate their wife, while girls fall in lust with their boyfriend and hate their husband. One way to tell that spouses are going through hell together is if they criticize or make fun of each other in public. They usually do this in a friendly comedic socially acceptable way. If someone ever criticizes their spouse in public, especially in front of their spouse, then you know that inside the home they have a terrible marriage. They might think or say their marriage is happy or ok but that's because they don't know what a good or happy marriage is. The solution is to accept the fact that love doesn't come until after marriage. Even in the movies love doesn't exist before marriage! The movies have actors and actresses that lie about what they really think and feel towards their coworkers. Movies and TV shows are actually a good proof that it's so easy to fool people into thinking they love someone. Everyone who watches a romance knows the actors don't really love each other, are just paid to act that way and in reality might even hate each other. Yet after a few minutes the audience has been fooled so thoroughly that they actually believe X character loves Y character and they'd be "happy ever after" together and they will passionately cry if they aren't. So if those people can fool so many into thinking they really "love" someone, it's too easy for Satan to fool girlfriends/boyfriends and their families. The reason dating is disastrous is because it's a romantic friendship and people can be great friends, even best friends but it would be hell if they lived together. Whereas even if people "live together", roommates can get along enjoyably but they could never handle being married or raising kids together. Marriage causes a psychological, spiritual and emotional difference, dating and living together only distort marriage and limit it's potential. Dating itself has only been socially practiced since 1896 CE, it's a very new phenomenon that resulted from the freedom movement and the alleged decline of misogynism in western societies, then as with many European/American ideas it was exported to the rest of the world. As a result of dating people think marriage is a legal friendship with benefits and that's not what marriage is. The real solution for the sexual issues of the day are for children to be raised properly without the entertaining distractions that waste their life and stunt them and then get married while they're younger than the current average marriage age. Within the Roman Empire the age for marriage without parental consent was 12 for girls and 14 for boys. Although for a girl's first marriage she needed her father's consent if she was under 24. After the fall of the Roman Empire the Catholic Church initially kept the ages for marriagability without parental consent but removed the clause requiring a first-time bride needing her father's permission. By the 12th century the founder of Catholic Canon law, Gratian, stated that anyone older than 7 could get married without parental consent. However if any kids under the age of 7 got married then it would only be valid if they stayed together until they both turned 7. Believe it or not some people as young as 2 years old are recorded to have gotten married, however for all those who were under the age of 7 when they got married they needed to have parental consent. Keep in mind how during the 1100s CE the Catholic Church would marry boys and girls to each other without parental consent as long as they were over 7 years old and they said there was nothing wrong with that and God was fine with it. Although currently the Catholic Church states boys must be 16 and girls must be 14 to get married. So either they lied about the marriage age for hundreds of years, or they are lying today, and/or just making it up as they go along without any definitive divine instruction regarding the age of marriage. During the Renaissance era in Europe girls could and did get betrothed at the age of 3, though marriage itself would be delayed until they were 12. So when the little girls in Europe were kids dreaming about their future wedding, most were already engaged and weren't "thinking about it" it was being planned and they were counting down the days. In the past little kids didn't think about their future weddings until after they were already engaged. In Europe during the 1400s CE if a girl wasn't married before she turned 15 it was a disgrace for the whole family and they'd consider sending her to a convent to become a nun, since obviously if she wasn't married by the age of 15 she would probably never get married; it was common sense. 600 years ago there was no conceivably justifiable reason for a girl not to be married by the age of 15. In the 1500s CE due to families valuing girls spending extra time in school to get a college education the new disgrace age for unmarried daugthers was 17. That's including college, girls were expected to be married by the age of 17, if they weren't married by the age of 17 then everyone knew something was wrong and it embarrassed the whole family. Yet today most governments say getting married before the age of 18 is illegal. 500 years ago common knowledge was that if a girl wasn't married by the age of 17 then she was unmarryable, but today many think the exact opposite in that those 17 and under are unmarryable and they must be older. Past generations of humans say we get married too old and many today think they got married too young, yet are not both generations human beings? Who is to say what age is right? Consider all the difficulties kids go through with sexual temptations during puberty in our modern "civilized" era and then consider how in the past kids would be married before they went through puberty. Which society is really smarter and "cares about the kids"? In America during the 1700s CE it was considered a shameful disgrace to have not yet married at the age of 21. Such a rare occurance was scandalous. Regarding marriage during his era the 17th century English jurist Edward Coke stated, "*the marriage of girls under 12 was normal, and the age at which a girl who was a wife was eligible for a dower from her husband's estate was 9 even though her husband be only four years old.*" In case you don't understand this, the English Judge during the 1600s CE stated that legally according to Christian English law it was fine for girls to get married at the age of 9 and boys to get married at the age of 4. Needless to say Christian and English legal standards have changed. Prior to the French Revolution in France girls would be married at 12 and boys at 14, but in 1792 CE the law was changed so girls had to be 13 and boys 15. Napolean changed French law again in 1804 CE stipulating girls had to be 15 and boys 18, and that standard lasted until 2006 CE when 18 was made the minimum age for all genders in France. Meaning in 2005 CE it was perfectly legal for 15 year old girls in France to get married even though the minimum age for driving was 18. In the future maybe the age for marriage will be 40 and up, and they'll say 39 year olds are "too young" to get married and it's "just not right". What's ironic is how if you consider the ages at which people got married in the past and the ages people get married today, many in the past would be celebrating 20+ years of marriage by the time they were the age most people are when they get married for the first time in our era. Our idea regarding the ages of a "young newlywed couple" would be the age of "old long-married grandparents" in the past. So one of the main reasons why pre-marital sex wasn't rampant in the past is because people got married and had marital sex sooner, much sooner than we do. Also you'll notice that repeatedly I mentioned it was a "family disgrace" for people not to be married. That means in the past families actually cared about their young people getting married and played an active role in facilitating marriage. Today many families don't consider late marriages a disgrace because they don't view any individual family member getting married or not as reflecting on them having to do with their responsibilities as a family member. While the reason there is a rising divorce rate is because now people date, and believe it or not scientifically dating someone harms any resultant marriage with that person or any other. Dating is destructive to marriage, anyone who says it's beneficial or a precursor to marriage is just plain ignorant. Also don't think "*well maybe if he ever dated he wouldn't write this stuff because he'd know*", I don't need to have dated to know the effects of dating just like I don't need to take drugs to know the harmful effects of drugs. Actually those who have dated may be less qualified to voice an opinion on it because they are prejudiced just as a drug user would be who has a penchant for drugs. Just as with those who use drugs, those who date are damaged and can never fully recognize the total extent of the damage dating does to them because they're damaged. Honestly at first I didn't date because I tried and found no willing participants, I'll admit that, I'm prouder to say I tried and didn't date because dating makes one a loser and by "failing to date" I was saved from a big mistake. Now I choose not to date because I know what dating is and plan to get married someday and be a good husband when married Godwilling, and dating makes that harder and less likely. When people tell me they are dating I actually console them like it's bad news because it is, I treat them as if by them telling me they are dating they told me they got a disease. I tell them that's terrible news to hear and hope they can extract themselves from such a awful relationship, as every dating relationship is and cannot be anything but awful, by either getting married or becoming single. This type of conversation is easier with people who are married and mention they used to date than with people currently dating although sometimes they have even bigger problems in their life than dating, such as disbelief, so I try to focus on what's more important because there is greater benefit in saving someone from disbelief than from dating even though both are deceptions of the devil, both of which amount to dating the devil if one is involved with either affliction.   Though as fun as it can be to say "Oh, so you're dating the devil." when someone tells you they are dating, it can be socially dangerous and unwise to do so; trust me people can get super pissed off if you tell them that especially if you say that in front of their date and they may never ever talk to you again and end their relationship with you on the spot. It's fun to think of saying that though and important to think when you hear such news because otherwise the devil will make you think dating isn't that bad and you might end up dating the devil yourself, or even worse and end up married to him/her/it. But isn't marriage such a big step to take from being single, especially if you don't date before getting married? Not as big as the devil would have you think. Parents must play an active role in facilitating marriage, they should look for quality candidates taking into consideration their child's criteria. Religious beliefs and religious character should be most important, followed by personality compatibility, intellectual compatibility, lifestyle compatibiliy, goals and a genuine attraction then being considered, with finances and lineage being even less important. Unfortunately many parents denigrate their kids with false/backwards requirements for marriage and abuse them by saying things like: *"No spouse will ever put up with X behavior"*, or *"How will you ever get married if you don't XYZ?"*, or *"The way you are I' don't know how you'll ever find someone to get married to. I don't think anyone could handle being married to you the way you are/act."* Parents say these things when they are mad or trying to motivate their children, but they are actually the worst things a parent can say. Satan leads people to interpret such statements internally as *"I'm defective and undesirable."*, *"Everyone will reject me."*, *"Noone will ever love me because I'm so inferior."*, *"I'm just too messed up to ever get married or have kids."* and *"I don't deserve to get married to anybody. Not even my own parents think I'm worthy or capable so how could anyone else ever think I was."* thus their self-esteem suffers and they lower their standards for a potential spouse because of their parents unintentionally teaching them they aren't good enough for anybody. Then if anybody at all is interested they tend to latch on and never let go, or despair and develop addictions or destructive habits to cope with negative feelings and emotions, or they are never comfortable in their marriage always feeling that if only their spouse knew who they really were they'd have no spouse so whatever love their spouse claims/displays must be do to ignorance or a performance that tricks them into loving you for someone you aren't. They fall in love with the idea that someone could possibly love them while simultaneously thinking such a thing to be impossible even if it's obtained, they become love addicts. Such people will fall in love with someone simply if they hear that person likes them, while if that person says they "love" them too then that love addict becomes a full blown slave but thinks it's "true love". Sadly it's common for a sexual predator or manipulator to come along and take advantage of this type of person who's been verbally abused and assaulted into desperation concerning potential spousal relationships. It is truly tragic for love addicts because you can ask them if they are ready to get married they will truly believe and tell everyone they aren't interested in it at all and it might be decades before they even think of such a prospect, BUT then 1 minute later if they even suspect for the flimsiest of reasons that a member of the opposite gender is interested in them they instantly flip-flop and seriously consider if tomorrow they should marry that person they don't even know. It sounds hilarious, but for them it's not because it's painfully emotional and they think if they don't take advantage of the possible long-shot theoretical opportunity then it will never come along again and they'll be doomed to eternal depression and loneliness. Thus they trick themselves into incorrectly thinking it's either choose to marry the one who is slightly or maybe even truly interested, or celibacy; even though minutes before they knew with 100% certainty they weren't ready or interested in marriage at that time. It's just because of their low self-esteem they think they must seize the possibility lest it slip away because Satan tricked them into thinking it will be impossible for them to get married, thus they literally think someone possibly being interested is like a miracle. Whereas to them it isn't funny but is extremely depressing. Of course if they then try to propose or date and fail to achieve the object of their infatuation they could get so depressed they commit suicide. Then of course some idiot trying to be funny, or mean, being completely oblivious to the person's fragile inner emotionality only reenforces their satanic disposition explictly telling them it'd be a miracle if they ever found someone to marry. So all that comedy and teasing causes global depression, suicides and terrible marriages. Many people have actually killed themselves due to rejection from romantic targets, not because of the rejection itself but because of their fragility due to "innocent jokes" or off the cuff remarks said by people meant to tease or vent frustration at another person. While if the love addict survives and does get married they usually expect their spouse to be some type of personal angelic slave, instead of their spouse being a flawed human sinner who makes mistakes. When people think their spouse is perfect then their marriage is bound to be a disaster. Also such a love addict is typically entirely unprepared for the real eventuality that their spouse will die and when it happens it can severely cripple them, especially if it happens early in the marriage. Afterall the fairytale "happy ever after" stories never include the fact that one of them dies before the other and then they live without being together, no the fairytales pretend that couples die at exactly the same second. Forgetting death will occur and failing to be ready for it is actually a serious problem in society. As a result many elderly couples fearing the emotional loss either will suffer in the likely event that one will die before the other frequently decide to commit suicide together so that neither has to live without the other. While those who don't and become widows frequently commit suicide due to being unable to cope with the loss of a spouse plus all the other hardships of old age. Elderly people are actually the most likely age group to kill themselves and it's largely because they don't know how to handle the death of a spouse. Many either remarry, commit suicide or get depressed and hide their depression from others. Some even disbelieve in God when they hear someone they cared about died saying "Why God?" (disbelieving in predestination) or "God is no good"(insulting God and disbelieving in his goodness) etc. I've even witnessed this where upon learning of someone else's physical death people spiritually die, and that's the danger of "loving" people too much, that your very spirituality is determined by their life or quality of life. Whereas for those people who will disbelieve in God upon the end of their romantic relationship, it truly would be better if they never had that romantic relationship. Meaning if you love your spouse so much that if they die you end up disbelieving in God then you should not married to them nor in a relationship with them, or you better fix it so it's appropriate since having such an extreme love for a created being is sinful regardless of how fun it may momentarily feel. Sometimes a person doesn't even have to die, if they just get hurt or break up with you people will stop believing in God because their planned partnership didn't go as long or as smoothly as hoped for. Many due to an unpleasant change in their relationship status voluntarily damage or discard their relationship with God due to their emotions for other humans. The death of a spouse is something most never actually prepare to handle beforehand and if it happens unexpectedly it devastates them, and even if they prepare many still don't have the faith to be able to keep any faith or keep enough faith to survive the test of the loss of a relative, spouse or friend. However it's common for people to die while engaged to be married, on the wedding day itself, or soon after the wedding. Thus whoever one marries you must keep in mind they will die, and they may die very soon after the marriage. Don't think you are special and your spouse is going to live a long time and that you will likely die first, your spouse will die sooner than you think. Less than 10% of people actually live to become elderly, and 90% of people die when they are considered to be young. It's important to remember death as a part of marriage so one can survive the death of a spouse, especially if it is unexpected or traumatic. I'm not saying to avoid marriage because spouses die, that's a Satanic trap, but keep it in mind so you don't expect eternal happiness from a spouse who will die. If you go into marriage expecting your spouse to die first and soon then you will enjoy whatever time you have and have a better marriage overall when both spouses remember the mortality and fast approaching death of each other. If you don't think about your spouse dying every day then you don't really care about them, of course some people think about their spouse dying every day for the wrong reasons and that type of thinking is not okay, but to remember death as a part of your marriage on a daily basis is important and crucial for a healthy wonderful successful marriage. Part of your test of life is dealing with the end of the lives of other people, many fail this test terribly, and in my experience some of the biggest sins a person ever commits in their life is due to how they react to the deaths of other people. Especially the death of their family, particularly the death of a parent or child. With children you should be expecting the death of your child even before you get engaged to get married. Death is just one of many things that can effect a marriage, your spouse could be imprisoned, lose some limbs, go into a coma, get blinded, lose 100% of their memory, become mentally ill or brain dead and many other things happen everyday to ordinary people who never thought it would happen to their spouse. The love addicts never think that could happen to them though, which shows they aren't ready for marriage but are just lovesick. A male love addict will even forget that women menstruate once a month, of which menstruation can normally occur for 3-7 days. While pre-menstrual tension can occur up to 7 days earlier. So normally menstruation and pre-menstruation can effect 14 days of every month of marriage. Menstruation doesn't factor into male love addict fantasies because it's a fantasy they are in love with and the reality of marriage is much much different. Afterall they don't show the female menstruation in all those romantic movies and love songs. You ever see the pretty girls menstruate in the fairytales? No, because reality doesn't work in the genre of fictional romance. So all these cultural and social influences allegedly promoting marriage are selling a false fantasy that will make marriage harder for those who desire it. Others who avoid marriage fear commitment and/or rejection so they become pathological daters or "live together", because they fear the risk of getting hurt in any way via a divorce if they wholeheartedly commit in marriage. They cannot fully open up their heart to another person fearing to be emotionally vulnerable and at risk of theoretical rejection. Some consider divorce worse than death because they mistake divorce as a rejection of them as a person, thus to avoid the possibility of such misplaced notions of rejection they avoid marriage altogether. Of course all that negative verbal abuse about people not being able to handle marriage to you due to personal defects only reinforces this fear of divorce which leads to fear of marriage and thus depression because globally to not be married gets depicted as rejection in itself. Similar to how satanic idiots think virginity does. Wheras just because someone isn't married or hasn't had sex before doesn't mean they aren't desireable or good people, it just means they aren't married or had sex, but Satan frequently makes people feel otherwise oftentimes by using other people to make unmarried or sexually pure people feel that way about themselves. Sometimes those people don't even mean to be mean, but their friendly "jokes" hurt more than the worst insults. For example sometimes a person may ask another "*When are you getting married?*" or comically ask them how their spouse and kids are when the person isn't even married. Then when the single person gets serious explaining why they aren't married, or don't feel prepared for it, or why they don't have a wife or kids, the questioner quickly and cooly replies "It was a joke." and that just tears the person's heart out; especially if the person knows the one joking with them and/or respects them. The "joke" hurts even more in the future because Satan will always utilize that person's "joke" as a means to trick the single person into thinking the very idea of them ever getting married is "a joke" which is too laughable to even consider as a possibility and they will depress themselves into misery. Yet the joker never even meant that at all, but this is what Satan does with their "joke" and uses it to prevent people from getting married because they heard so many "jokes" from people who were "just having fun" and "kidding" about marriage and offspring. Marriage and children are two things to never joke about, ever; and such jokes are some of the most psychologically damaging things one can ever hear. Honestly I consider jokes about marriage to be nearly sinful, because they can cause so much damage. The prophets never joked about marriage. Really what the hell is wrong with the world that we tell jokes about marriage or raising children? Those things are not matters to joke about! Satan loves when people think or act like marriage or raising children is a joke, because such jokes destroy families before they can be made and prevents marriage from taking place. So that's where someone should never ever tell another person things that could ever possibly dash their hopes or criticize their potential for marriage. Many do this, even kids do it to each other and it has terrible consequences for all of society. Seriously I'm even afraid to tell you how damaging such statements are because you might use them intentionally to hurt someone, don't do that. I only included this so those who do it know not to do it and that those who have had it done to them know that such stuff isn't true and not to be desperate with relationships as a result of such verbal abuse. Satan just makes some people say very nasty things to hurt your feelings and lead you into sin and sorrow. There are billions of people and God specifically creates spouses for those he decreed will have spouses, so never think the problem will be finding someone to marry, finding a person willing to marry you is the easy part. Narrowing it down to the best person for you is the hard part. Actually so many would be willing to marry you that you will have to ask God for help to narrow down all the potential spouses for you and set you up with the best one for you and bring you together. And guess what? If you want God to help you to get the best spouse, one must have a good relationship with God and get married using the procedure God has legislated. God didn't tell anyone at anytime to go on a date. Satan wants the dating. Dating happens primarily because kids don't think their parents will help them to get married to a good person, especially after parents make nasty statements or jokes about them and their marriage prospects. Many kids simply think their parents only want them to get married because they want grandkids, or want their kids to get out of the house, leave them alone or to have family pride/prestige such as the royal wedding feast. Dating is what led to the problems of fornication which were facilitated by kids thinking they can't or aren't good enough for marriage, yet because they wanted sex they decided to just do it regardless of the consequences. That's actually how dating started. It used to be people would simply get married without dating, but parents stopped this because they knew or thought their kids weren't ready for marriage, but parents didn't want to admit it was because of their bad parenting job. Therefore they allowed dating as an alternative to placate the kids' demands for interaction with the other gender without giving into their demands for marriage that would lead to their exposure as a bad parent. In the "old days" fornication took place between dating couples as well, the kids just didn't dare to admit it lest it destroy the whole dating system. Besides since parents and kids alike were pretending it was harmless romance nobody wanted to ruin their reputation and seem scandalous. It's much the same today how people dating have sex and will brag about it to their friends and peers but then when they're with family they pretend they're very virtuous and would never ever do such stuff while dating. So the reason dating started had nothing to do with "finding out if X is the right person for me to marry" it began because kids wanted to have sex but their parents didn't want them to get married because they feared getting embarrassed should the marriage expose them as not having raised their kids well. Dating was the alternative to marriage, it wasn't considered a precursor at all. People would date, everyone would pretend they weren't having sex and then when the person matured their parents would help them to get married to somebody else when they finally grew up into an adult. Dating was, is and always will be a form of erotic foreplay. The only reason people came up with the excuse that dating led to marriage was because parents became such bad parents that they no longer bothered getting their kids married at all because their kids never really became fit for marriage. Yet since no parent wanted to admit this, they collectively decided to tell the kids it's up to them to find someone through dating so that way when their marriages are terrible nobody can blame the parents for being bad parents or for being married to someone who isn't fit for marriage. The governments directly promoted the dating game too, this is why women were integrated into the workforce. World governments partially advocated female labor in order to encourage dating since work was a way to get people together, when at the time there were very few opportunities for the opposite genders to casually intermingle. But the government's dating games didn't end with an integrated workforce, the economies were designed to make women earn much less than men and sometimes even less than one needed to survive. Many think this was solely because of sexism or legitimate economic valuation on the differences between male and female labor, but no economic statutes encouraged this gender wage disparity even among children laborers because of the social revolution that such a disparity would cause. This is how the tradition of men paying for their female date's dinner came to be. Some women could not afford to eat, despite working. For many females in the Western world during the early 20th century they had to go on dates in order to live, because if men weren't taking them on dates buying stuff for them then they would've starved to death. However economically guys saw this as a bad deal to be financially paying for their female co-workers who had no familial relation to them, thus sex after a date became customary. As dates became known for sexual encounters, prostitutes upgraded the dating game. In fact one could actually say prostitutes originally invented dating with clients becoming boyfriends. Regardless dating became known as prostitution, especially since it was mainly done by poor women who needed a man to pay for their food on a routine basis since their families weren't taking care of them and they weren't married. In the early 1900s CE laws were passed in the Western world prohibiting dates because it was considered to be nothing but illegal prostitution and women would get arrested if they went on a date. However as with less romantic more clandestine forms of prostitution, the law enforcers did not thoroughly enforce the ban. This has been one of the anomalies with prostitution throughout time. In the past prostitution was created by governments as a way for poor women to make money and create revenue for the state and provide a means for politicians to get some cheap sinful sex on the side without the other sinful sex criminals rebelling for politicians having unfair priviliges while they get punished for committing the same sexual crimes. For example in the 7th Century BCE the Chinese philosopher-king Kuang Chung openly taxed prostitutes and is rumored to have even issued prostitute licenses. While in the 5th century BCE the Athenian legislator Solon used the taxdollars of Greeks to create state owned and operated brothels of which the government's prostitutes paid a tax on their earnings. Under Greek democracy during the " golden age of enlightenment" prostitutes were official government employees. Whereas during 180 BCE the Roman Emperor Caligula issued a special tax on prostitutes, throughout the Roman empire brothels had to be inspected and prostitutes registered themselves with the government. Prostitutes who didn't register with Rome were scourged and fined, prostiution was only legal if one registered with the government so they could get a piece of the monetary action and be "intimately familiar with the industy". Essentially prostitutes being registered with the government helped the government know who to go to if they ever needed specialized services such as the type which prostitutes provide. Needless to say within such states business tended to always be booming, audibly booming one could say. The industry was booming so much you could hear it. In 525 CE the Christian Byzantine Emperor Justinian "the Great" married an alleged prostitute. In 1161 CE King Henry II required brothels to have weekly inspections by the english government, forbid prostitutes from getting married since that would be bad for business and he told prostitutes they should avoid working a "short shift"(I'm not explaining what that means, but I think married couples know and most can correctly guess). In 1358 CE Venice declared prostitution to be "absolutely indispensible" and opened a state-run brothel in 1360 CE, as did Florence in 1403 CE, followed by Sienna's state brothel in 1421 CE. In 1490 CE out of a population 90,000 papal Rome had 6,800 prostitutes, which is 7.5% of the population. (the "holy city" sure had a whole lot of whores) Prostitutes were so popular in Renaissance Rome that when the prostitute Faustina Mancina died, half the city mourned for her and the famous Michelangelo wrote a sonnet in her memory. Prostitutes were beloved celebrities during the Renaissance. The artist Raphael even reportedly used the prostitute Imperia as the model for Sappho in his "Parnassus", Imperia was so well-liked that 50 poets lamented her death when she was buried inside the church of San Gregorio in 1511 CE with a engraved marble tomb. I repeat she was a prostitute, not a prophet or prophetess, a prostitute. Although since Rome was the papal city center such a place isn't really a good generic example of the average Population-Prostitute ratio of the past. The 1509 CE census of Venice is probably a better example of European whoredom as a whole, where out of a population of 300,000 the prostitutes numbered 11,654 (3.9%). Yet even still I think 4 out of every 100 people being professional prostitutes is a bad thing, they might not have but I think that's too many for God to be happy. Afterall economically prostitution isn't a trade that produces wealth in the world, the world as a whole does not benefit due to a prostitute working whereas other professions can greatly benefit the world. Basically prostitution is wasteful along with being sinful, but sadly governments see it as something beneficial which they can tax and even occasionally utilize for purposes of political advantage or "personal pleasure to patriotically give jobs to the people"(What else did you think politicians meant when they said they were going to give their citizens more jobs? They meant they were going to screw their people, literally. Wasn't that obvious by the way the people cheered when they hear such promises from politicians? Clearly they know the deal. Why else would they react that way to the news/claims/promises?). Prostitutes have influenced history in major ways via espionage, assassination and blackmail just to name a few. Civil wars have been fought because of the sons of prostitutes claiming the throne of their real or alleged King fathers, so never diminish the political impact prostitutes had on history. Who knows maybe prostitutes even played a role in telling historian clients how to write the history books? Surely prostitutes must have left a mark on the publishing world and the material it contains via means and methods unrelated to publishing. In 1617 CE the city of Edo, Japan created a specialized district for prostitutes called "the red light district", in 1656 CE the city of Edo was renamed Tokyo. Officially France banned prostitution in 1560 CE but for some reason the police continued to unofficially issue licenses to prostitutes in contravention of the ban, so in 1778 CE France stated prostitutes, which technically didn't and weren't supposed to exist, have to prostitute in certain areas specifically designated by the state; that is *"If any do prostitute in France, which they don't because it's illegal, then they should prostitute in X areas but they won't because prostitution is illegal as we said and everyone already knows and is glad about because nobody ever uses or wants such filthy stuff in our nation. It's just in case such a thing ever occurs, which we know it won't, we are letting police know they are not allowed to stop prostitution in X areas., but they won't have to nor even think of doing so because nobody would ever prostitute in France even though we have those special areas where we don't want police to ban it and we are publicly informing the nation about these places and their special theoretical hypothetical utterly irreleveant unique legal status that is technically mythical despite us being so serious, morally upright and professional in our public service announcement."* But that pristine legal conundrum was resolved after the French Revolution when France created a official state department of prostituion in 1802 CE that flourished until it was disbanded during the German invasion of World War I. WWI ended the French government's prostitute agency but prostitution remains legal in France to this day. Napolean also exported prostitution to the Netherlands in 1810, but it left with the French withdrawal in 1813 only to return in 1851 CE when the Netherlands regulated prostitution allegedly to "prevent sexual diseases". Although in 2000 CE Netherlands officially sanctioned prostitution as "just another business" that must be licensed and now being a prostitute at a brothel is considered the same as being a regular employee. Britain followed suit during the 1860s saying prostitution was only allowed in towns and bases used by the military. The "prostitutes" would be brought in for "health checkups" by the British military but a lot of the women inspected were upset by this practice and claimed they weren't prostitutes. This "issue" of prostitute "misidentification" was later solved in Britain when they made prostitution legal in 1959 CE. In 1870 CE the state of Missouri required prostitutes to register and get licensed by the state. In 1874 CE America passed a law banning foreign prostitutes from immigrating to America because they hurt the American prostitution industry and didn't pay the taxes that American prostitutes paid. In 1857 CE the city of New Orleans passed a law saying prostitution was illegal if it was done on the first floor of a building, however the Supreme Court ruled this ban on prostitution was unconstitutional. Yes the US Constitution enshrines prostitution and to ban prostitution from occuring on the first floor of buildings is "unconstitutional". The US constitution allows prostitution on every floor in America. To ban prostitution would be to go against the US Constitution. Americans fought for the rights of prostitutes to prostitute, what else did you think the "pursuit of happiness" in the declaration of independence referred to? This is why in 1909 CE the case of Keller vs. US decided that for America to deport a foreigner who became a prostitute on US soil would violate the 10th Amendment. Meaning it's illegal for America to deport prostitutes who aren't American, because being a prostitute is such an important part of the economy that it is more important to the government than citizenship. In 1911 CE the US Supreme Court further ruled that it is illegal for the US federal government to ban or regulate prostitution. As long as the US Constitution exists prostitution is legal in America. In 1927 CE Germany decided to decriminalize prostitution making it legal and unregulated, but the Churches disagreed therefore to get the Christians of Germany to agree to legalize prostitution they passed a law making it illegal for prostitutes to solicit next to churches and schools. German churches basically said *"Prostitution is okay as long as you don't do it in church."* but then in 1933 CE the Nazis made prostitution illegal. However even the Nazis gave in to prostitute money and sanctioned prostitution making Nazi brothels in 1939 CE in order to use prostitution to procreate Aryans. Thus under the Nazi regime Aryan prostitution was made legal and supported by the state, while non-Aryan prostitution was illegal. The Nazis essentially customized their prostitutes so they met a certain visual criteria/fetish. Practically the Nazi's perpetrated a "Prostitute Holocaust", but what has ever been done for these "victims" who were unemployed or employed depending on your view of this type of Holocaust? Should the prostitutes, or non-aryan wannabe prostitutes, be given Palestine? No? What about the Jewish prostitutes? In the 1940s CE Hawaii would charge prostitutes $1 a year for their "prostitute license" and they were required to report every transaction filing and paying taxes to the IRS on their income for each service. At Hawaii Pearl Harbor was the prime prostitution market because officially prostitution was illegal in Hawaii, the prostitute licenses were issued so that Hawaiins could service the American military units stationed there. Hawaii was not yet an American state at the time, but the American government required prostitutes for it's military which decided to base itself at the island. So despite Hawaii not being an American state it was forced to create prostitutes and issue them licenses even though prostitution was illegal because the US troops wanted them and when American soldiers want prostitutes they get prostitutes, even if the land they are stationed in says prostitution is against the law of the land. Oh and the Hawaiins paid taxes to the US for the profits gained from this prostitution service which was technically illegal but allowed due to US soldiers' demand. Of course after Hawaii became a state then prostitution was made legal, because it's unconstitutional to ban it in America. And then the IRS tax revenue would go towards paying for more US soldiers to be stationed in Pearl Harbor, Hawaii so more Hawaiins had to become prostitutes and pay taxes on it to the US. So technically speaking the IRS was a pimp and they still operate the same way, except now US soldiers are stationed in more places and have more perverse fetishes so the prostitutes have a harder job servicing a larger more demanding market. But as they say in America "Support the Troops! Or you're a bad crazy traitor who has something wrong with them for not loving and supporting our soldiers." (that 2nd part is usually left unsaid or unwritten) In 2002 CE Germany declared that prostitution is not immoral and pimping is legal as long as a written formal contract is used with each transaction, prostitues can even sue clients in German courts for non-payment and the brothel employees are provided with health insurance paid for by the German government. Yet despite such policies on prostitution, some people mistakenly imagine Germany is being Islamized even though Islam outlaws prostitution and everything leading to it. Many fear/believe Muslims in Germany pose a threat to the prostitute market and the German government's revenue from that market, which is true but few ever get informed of how "Muslims are a threat to Germany". In 2003 CE New Zealand legalized prostitution. In 2009 CE Taiwan legalized prostitution. While in 2010 CE Canada declared that to ban prostitution, brothels or restrict the solicitation of sex is unconstitutional. Why are all these nations legalizing prostitution? Because they are perverted? Maybe, but with prostitution legalized governments get paid for each transaction. To governments prostitution is a way to create jobs and make money off of sex which they can't profit from when sex is done within marriage. Any threat to prostitution is therefore a threat to the job market of those nations and the government budgets of those nations. As a result of the profitability of legal prostitution when people began dating the governments around the world legally banned dating at the same time they sanctioned prostitution. This was because prostitutes lost business when people dated and governments lost money since dating was a type of untaxed sexual encounter. Thus prostitution was patriotic and dating was criminal and unpatriotic. The theory was if you loved your country then you would pay people for sex instead of dating them and having sex without paying and paying taxes on the profits of such transacitions. Prostitutes adapted though and realized they personally could make more money by dating than by prostituting, and they preferred untaxed sex with the benefits of a date more than taxed income from prostitution without the benefits of a date. So many prostitutes became criminals and started having sex for free with expenses paid for in the form of a date and governments didn't know how to stop it because it was a hard financial crime to prevent. It was akin to stopping adultery, many governments just don't know how to stop it no matter how much they want to do so, or in our era "if" they want to. The food and entertainment or gifts given on the date would be the price of sex and it could be unreported income since it was an "unofficial" transaction. Governments quickly responded by banning dating because they felt screwed by the prostitutes who found a loophole to legally prostitute without having to pay the governments but the punishments implemented for dating were not a deterrent and it was unfeasible to identify dating couples and non-dating couples since they could date in public since most of the dating activities aside from the sex was considered perfectly legal to do. Then the rich and middle classes adopted this new way of untaxed prostitution called dating and the music and movie industries made it romantic and popular. Then the kids followed the lead of the rich and famous daters and started dating in schools but most weren't doing the sex but just doing it because it was a type of "cool crime that isn't illegal" so they could feel rebellious. Plus hormones made it titulating to try and the popularity of the dating couple would soar, especially if parents were uncool and banned it in addition to governments banning it. Kids thought it was cool but didn't quite have the means to do the sex part, which was the illegal part but they liked other kids to think they were and most still do even though the sex part is no longer illegal yet they don't know why it "seems cool to have had sex while dating" because they haven't studied the history of dating and they don't teach that in schools, though ironically they teach kids how to have sex in schools. Anyways governments had a problem in that they realized dating was a more glorified form of prostitution they couldn't tax. However they noticed a pattern in that those who dated tended to not get married which meant they paid more in taxes as long as they were unmarried and then if they did get married those who dated tended to get divorced. So there was a silver lining to the prostitute tax evasion that might in the long-term prove more financially profitable for governments, yet data at that time couldn't indicate whether it would or wouldn't since dating was a new phenomenon. Meanwhile as the trend of dating continued covertly the government learned that dating caused money to circulate in the economy more rapidly, and since they taxed transactions and the incomes of business that profited from dating then it resulted in government tax revenue totals being larger than they were without dating. As a result of the increased tax revenue in other sectors outweighing the loss in prostitution tax revenue governments changed their mind when they saw they earned more money from people dating than when they didn't. Governments learned that the whole time thay had been trying to profit from prostitution they could've been making so much more money if they didn't tax prostitutes and larger numbers of people dated. The key to profitability was more people having sex via dating than people having sex with only prostitutes and no dating. As a result governments gambled and declared dating was no longer to be categorized as illegal prostitution but would be classified as a legal form of prostitution that need not require a license as long as no official sexual transaction took place. The sex could happen but as long as it wasn't pre-arranged or a business service that was paid for then it wouldn't be taxed directly. This new type of prostitution became legal and widespread because people called it dating, it was new and it seemed more dignified as whores no longer needed to advertise themselves or be publicly known as whores to people they weren't servicing. It was a way for prostitutes to engage in a economically advantageous excursion in public without the public being aware of the sexual permiscuity of the prostitute or the client. Originally dating was just a legal loophole for prostitutes to escape taxation of which other women who wanted to prostitute themselves but didn't want to register, pay the prostitute tax, or feel the shame of the industry would "date" to survive instead of getting married or being prostitutes. Dating wasn't done by people who desired to prepare for marriage, it was done by people who wanted to have sex but didn't want to or couldn't get married. Dating is just a innovated version of untaxed prostitution which is difficult to publicly identify in the process of it taking place, since people dating can always make easy excuses that they aren't dating; in most countries that is the actions and interactions that occur publicly on a date are legalized. The only way for governments to have been able to stop the dating loopholes invented by prostitutes would be to criminalize, discourage and prevent the inter-gender mixing in public between people who aren't married or related. Over time kids dating began to fall in lust thinking it was love and were afraid of losing their sexual outlets by marrying someone else they weren't as "familiar with". Although after generations of parents who weren't raised properly themselves and didn't raise their own kids properly, dating relationships themselves (sinful as they are) are starting to become too sophisticated for the underdeveloped youth. The prostitutes handled it well but they stopped considering themselves prostitutes because so many non-prostitutes exploited the dating loophole that the prostitutes using it to evade taxation became a minority and history was not publicized because it made daters have a social stigma that deterred dating when people learned dating was invented by prostitutes to escape taxation. Yet this is why so many people date person after person or for date after date after date without getting married, because dating was never ever meant to lead to marriage. Governments knew this and that's why they legalized it because if it lead to marriage they would've lost tax revenue since married people are taxed at lower rates due to historical and religious precedents designed to encourage marriage and families. Unfortunately not only does dating not lead to marriage but it makes it harder to have a successful marriage and this is why those who date the most tend to get married the least, or take the longest time to get married while those who barely date get married faster once they decide they are ready and willing to marry somebody who they may or may not already know. The extent of dating deterring people from marriage and psychologically depreparing them combined with poor parenting and stunted maturity levels has reached the point where now people say *"I'm not ready for dating, let's just fornicate."* So dating is now turning back into classical prostitution except now the prostitutes don't get paid and don't even get the economic advantages of a date. One would think this would decrease govenment revenue but it doesn't because instead of dating, the people work more and finance more productive industries than the industries that facilitate the dating game. So governments actually make more money than before and prostitutes are seriously endangered of going extinct because now there are whores who do it for free, literally for free on demand without even requiring a dinner or a dance. Technology made this type of whore become widespread with ease as before societies could not function with too many free whores because communication methods and natural human shyness prevented the connections from being made. Therefore it's ironic in that prostitutes created dating to avoid paying taxes and now dating is going out of style and sex has become nearly free thereby eliminating the prostitution industry. Which might sound good but it's bad. Essentially so many people are having sex outside of marriage now that few are willing to pay for it. The supply of sex is getting to be almost higher than the demand. Sinful sex no longer sells, now people do it for free. Prostitutes invented dating and the dating industry screwed the prostitutes out of their jobs and income stream and then got screwed itself by technology that was adopted by daters to enhance the dating experience. So Satan seems the likely culprit behind the trend, he started with paid sex, then free sex + socialization/care/economic bonuses to the fornicators, until now it's just plain free sex with 100% sin and no pleasure/benefit aside from that gleaned from sinful sexual activity. Which since sinful sex became cheaper in worldly terms it has become more common, more widespread and more grotesque/perverse as the sexual tolerance of society builds it becomes more extreme since normal sex is no longer exciting enough of a dose and sex can be such an addictive drug. Governments on the other hand don't miss the extra revenue from dating because since sex is now free for all, people get married even less than when they dated and therefore there are more unmarried people who pay a higher income tax since they aren't married which results in more revenue for the government than if people dated and married. At the root cause behind dating, governments make the least money off of married people, more off of single people, then they make more off of widowers/divorcees, making more money off of daters and make the most money off of people who have sex without dating. So the government would rather you date than get married and rather you be widowed or divorced rather than single and never married, and they'd rather you just have spontaneous sex with strangers rather than sex with people you date. So far the dating industry is striving to survive and retain market share but the economic trend is against it, governments make more money if people don't date and have sex spontaneously because the industries that facilitate dating are less desired and less useful to a government/nation than the industries that would exist/profit if the pro-dating industries died. So in the long-term because governments will make more in tax revenue if people have sex without dating or marrying then they will consciously or subconsciously enact policies that hurt the dating industry and promote the free quick sex industry. For now though dating is a bridge for the religious and moral folk to transition to that animalistic sexual lifestyle. Of course no industry/institution that deals in sex is likely to go extinct as evidence by the existance of prostitution still, but the market share of marriage, the market share of prostitution, and the market share of dating will decrease as the market share of animalistic sex rises with governmental support which will be given by all governments who are greedy for more money. And the greediest governments in regards to money tend to be those that owe money and have debt. So those nations with lots of debt tend to have the lowest morals. Currently the Aemrican government is #1 in debt beating/losing to every other country in the world. But why are the individual people today turning away from the dating games? This is because they have been verbally abused so much by people telling them they'll never be able to get a girlfriend or boyfriend(since marriage is already out of the question) that they believe it. Others have had so many dates and dating relationships go bad that they publicly state that they don't want to date anymore but just want sex. I even know of girls who started dating thinking that it leads to marriage then they went through several relationships and built up their sexual cravings through sexual experiences in those relationships to the point where now they only want casual sexual relationships without emotional attachments or commitments. It's really sad too because they start out intending to find someone to get married to and they end up as a dirty whore addicted to the male genitalia. As bad as prostitutes are known to be, they are worse than prostitutes, because a prostitute will get some money for throwing their body at somebody but many youth today who whore themselves out don't even get paid. Today many youth are on a lower level of respectability than prostitutes but they think they're "smart" and figured out how to live life right, some even pay others to pimp themselves online and hook them up with free fornication. Dating sites are basically virtual pimps except both parties pay the pimp and it's completely legal because the government taxes the dating sites (pimps) as well as contraceptive making companies. Today both guys and girls pay companies to get them in contact with each other so they can have sex. I ask what is the difference between a guy paying a prostitute's pimp and a guy paying a dating or fornication website? The websites are legal and both parties pay but they don't call it "prostitution" anymore because now the pimps get paid and keep 200% minus the government's share. Dating and subsequent dating sites and apps have simply put prostitutes out of business and expanded the fornicition business making it popular and legal. So porn stars and prostitutes as despicable as they are, actually have more dignity than many of the youth today and are better in the sight of God. Dating was a way for the governments to undercut prostitutes, increase tax revenue and expand the sex industry while creating a love and fashion industry. Then people wonder why rappers use such foul words for women calling them "hoes" and such. To be honest it is out of disrespect but economically speaking dating is simply prostitution the difference is that the dating games generate more tax revenue. Governments are practically the pimp of everyone who dates in their country. Dating was first practiced by prostitutes so they could earn untaxed incomes, and to their clients a date was just a cheaper type of prostitute. Instead of a guy saying he had a history with a prostitute he could simply say he had a "girlfriend". Originally for guys the term "girlfriend" meant "unofficial classy prostitute" who worked a "longer shift" for a cheaper price. Then today girls who date wonder why most boyfriends treat them as they do. While for prostitutes their "boyfriend" was an untaxed income source whom they could publicly associate with so as to feel better about their filthy profession. Dating was the innovation that made prostitution legally untaxed and publicly acceptable among the masses. A girlfriend or boyfriend is simply the things prostitutes evolved into. So any girlfriend or boyfriend is nothing but an evolved prostitute who may or may not solicit sex in exchange for an emotional connection or experience. Anyone who thinks otherwise is a damn fool who doesn't know anything about dating just like someone can own and drive a car yet still "be clueless when it comes to cars" according to their own testimony despite the fact of their personal experience with cars. Dating was adopted by prostitutes for them to get money potentially without even having sex where they could just get paid for providing an experience which non-married people desired. Because parents did a bad job parenting and kids didn't get married, and governments taxed prostitutes they invented dating taking advantage of unmarried people and because dating prevented marriage and increased government tax revenues this sinful interaction became popular. Dating was never meant to help people get ready for marriage. So anyone thinking dating will lead to marriage is wrong, dating will turn a good girl into a whore before it turns her into a wife and that's a guarantee. Even if a girl does date and get married then she'll still be messed up and will be pressured to commit adultery because her husband won't be the same as her boyfriends were, some wives do this today and just want a sexual partner on the side to compensate for their husband's difference. However if people never experienced pre-marital sex to begin with then they wouldn't have had anyone to compare their spouse to and would be totally satisfied. It is a proven fact that virgins are more sexually passionate with their spouses than non-virgins because they have exclusive experience with their spouse and the "first-time" creates a permanent special mental, emotional and spiritual bond. Just take the "first kiss" as an example, if your special "first kiss" is with your spouse then that will lead to some very happy marital experiences and special feelings. But is kissing really that big of a deal? Yes. Kissing is a method of sexual foreplay. It's actually unhealthy for humans to kiss lots of different people. The disease mononucleosis, known more popularly as "mono" is contracted solely by kissing. If you kiss multiple people you are highly exposed and susceptible to getting this disease which attacks the liver and requires several weeks of bedrest to recuperate from. I've even had classmates of mine who would kiss their dates get this disease and miss weeks of school as a result. Scientifically dating is a health risk because if you are kissing then you are exposing yourself to serious life-threatening diseases. Dating may lead you to get a kiss of death or to give a kiss of death to someone. While if you just don't partake in dating, you won't be kissing any other than your spouse, so you won't have to worry. If your "first kiss" is with your spouse, then by default your spouse will be the best kisser you've ever experienced and ideally this will be mutual so you will be giving them the best kisses of their life by default as well. It makes one get fuzzy feelings inside just thinking about it, but dating kills those fuzzy feelings and ruins all your kisses with your spouse and all of their kisses with you. So dating destroys future marriages and ruins the person's sexual life, while risking one's health. Realistically just ask yourself how many romantic dates you would want your future spouse and the parent of your children to go on with another person or other people? My number is zero. Isn't yours zero too? If not then you aren't a human being. Even animals don't want their mates interacting with other animals. So since nobody wants their spouse to date anybody then you shouldn't date anybody either. Whereas if that's not "fair" for you, then just remember God has made the spouses and the rules for how to find and get good ones. Seriously marriage is not very easy, you will definitely need God's help in your marriage so it's best if you get God's help through the whole process by doing it the prophetic way. The prophets got engaged and married, they never dated anybody. Prostitutes started dating. So you either choose the prophetic way to have a relationship with a member of the opposite gender or the propstitutes way. Which do you think will lead to success in both this life and the next? Following the example of the prophets via engagement and marriage or the example of the prostitutes via dating? Do you think God wants you to follow in the footsteps of prostitutes by dating? Religiously, dating is sinful and divorce is not. Anyone dating is actually sinning. Dating is worse than divorce. God hates dating and would rather you get divorced 900 times than go on 1 date. I actually have much more respect for people who get divorced than I do for those who date. I even refuse to be friends with guys who have girlfriends because people who date are not good people. When people date the devil joins them for every single interaction. Thus when someone goes on a date with their girlfriend or boyfriend they are also dating Satan at the same time. That's why its sad when people have girlfriends and boyfriends because by having those "friends" they have a devilfriend. If you are dating right now, just end the relationship or get married, or end it until you are ready for marriage. There is no good in dating, if there was the prophets would've done it and I would encourage it but I'm saying it's bad because it really is bad for all involved. People can be punished in hell for dating, the dating game equals pain in this life and the next for those who don't repent. Whereas if you just want frivolous sex without marriage or to "live together" then I guess you must be interested in animals because that's not how civilized humans do things. However what is the proper age for marriage? Religions give different ages, but generally after puberty and maturity. Although I will share with you what the best scientific age for having sex and giving birth is. Puberty in girls can start between the ages of 6-14. Yes some girls begin puberty at age 6. While boys can start puberty between the ages of 7-14. Now when the signs of puberty take place or the age it finishes differs with each individual. However anatomically women are best suited to give birth to children while they are teenagers. That's science, you might not like to hear it but anatomically women are designed to give birth as teenagers and it is the easiest time for them to do so. While physically men have the most sexual desires while they are teenagers too. So males have the most desire for sex they will ever have in their life while they are teenagers and females will have the easiest time giving birth while they are teenagers. Scientifically speaking the human species is designed to produce offspring while they are teenagers. Does that mean they should be? Well if one says marriage is a spiritual prerequisite for children then that means spiritually God has no issue with teenagers getting married, if they are mature, consent and are spiritually fit for it. Unfortunately for the human species most teenagers today are intellectual, emotional and spiritual toddlers. With most adults also being intellectual, emotional and spiritual toddlers. Men are hard to find today and most males are simply over-grown boys with most females being over-grown girls instead of women or ladies. However the fact remains the human species is designed to reproduce kids as teenagers, if our teens aren't ready for marriage at that age then maybe our "civilization" is not as civilized as we'd like to believe it is, because the ancient humans in the past were mature enough to do it. So why aren't we? Could it be too much entertainment and not enough religion and childhood responsibility? Will freedom make us infertile? Only a few centuries ago, teenagers were competent rulers of nations and leading armies into battle. While our "civilized" teenagers can't even be trusted to be safe if they are left at home all alone unsupervised. Seriously the people we consider as barbarians would laugh at our world if they knew people weren't ready for marriage until such a late age. They would likely conquer us in a day if our technologies were the same. Yet now many "people" are getting so mean they're even saying to others that they'll never have sex even if they tried to do it sinfully. This is what kids say in school to each other to be mean and it's what people say on the internet, in advertisements and the real world too. I've heard such awful things get told to people. Such statements can destroy a person's entire self-esteem and sexual identity. Psychologically people interpret such statements to mean they are so defective they can't even sin if they wanted to and Satan himself helped them. Surely that's one of the most Satanic statements a person can be told and it's actually a form of Satanic deception to lure one into evil sinful sex. Some get so insulted in such a way so much on a routine basis that they eventually change their sexuality or gender because of constant verbal abuse. That freedom of speech allows for such social abuse results in abnormal and abominable sexualities. Unfortunatley some members of our species can be so cruel to other members that they get them to believe that nobody of the other gender would ever interact with them, romantically or sexually. Some teach this explicitly some teach this implicitly. For instance some will say, *"Beauty is in the eye of the beholder"*. Do you know what that means? That statement tells everyone that your beauty is determined by the eyeballs of those who look at you, if their eye doesn't think you're beautiful then you aren't. This statement is abusive and completely false, your beauty is not about the opinion of an eyeball! God defines true beauty and causes appreciation for it. Whereas Satan beautifies what God has defined as ugly, such as sin. Spiritually there are 2 different ad campaigns being run, God says A is beautiful and Satan says Z is beautiful, the hearts will control whether the eye is pleased by something or not. To the virtuous believer a believing righteous spouse is beautiful beyond measure while the stripper is hideous. To the corrupted heart the stripper and anyone but the spouse is beautiful. So the eyeball ain't nothing but a tool to absorb light, how that light is interpreted varies but beauty has nothing to do with the opinion of people. The prophet Joseph pbuh was the most beautiful person to have existed. Why is that, because he was the sexiest man alive? No, it was because he was close to God and had special qualities and traits which no other human has ever had, because of that God made him beautiful to people because God thought he was beautiful. God makes his creatures love who/what he loves, yet our word for "love" isn't the same as God's definition of love. Likewise God's definition of beauty is different than ours. To state beauty is a personal visual opinion is bullying and a sales pitch by the cosmetics and fashion industry to make you think you can buy beauty and therein buy a good spouse or buy happiness. These examples of verbal abuse and bullying which I've mentioned causes sodomites, lesbians, transgenders and rapists as well as the general decline in the quality of the human species. Whereas in the future humans may degenerate so much that they'll say *"Oh I'm not ready to fornicate, I'll just masturbate"*; Why else do you think there's such a push for advanced robots? These types of regressed animalistic sexualities are actually exactly what governments want, because most opposition to government has always come as a result of a threat to the family.

Governments will use this state of affairs to institute breeding programs where people fornicate and instead of aborting the babies they get paid to deliver by the government and then the government raises the children in their own facilities. Therein the government will become the family of it's citizens and the spouse of it's citizens and God only knows how wicked such a government would be and how much oppression such citizens would suffer as a result. Pornography was actually developed and promoted by governments for those not yet ready to date/fornicate or not capable of dating/fornicating because of parents not raising their kids correctly. Dating was the first step towards the government becoming the practical parents of it's citizens and making citizens love their government as they used to love parents. Should that stage succeed then the government will then take the steps to publicly become the gods of their citizens. This is what governments tried to do in the past, but they didn't have the ideological, societal and cultural infrastructures for it to last. Instead of having a "family", governments plan on people being a "selfie". While God doesn't like "selfies" of any kind. Governments want people to "live together" without marriage because non-married people get taxed at higher rates, so the government makes more money if you aren't married and they make the most money if you are dating. The main reason people delay marriage due to not being ready is primarily a result of self-centeredness. This self-centerdness isn't selfishness but is more like narcissism. Basically single people can't stop thinking about themselves and they are the center of their world. While because of constantly thinking of themselves they develop a low self-esteem thinking it's humility when it's usually a lack of pride. Now arrogance is sinful, but a certain level of pride is needed to have confidence and be mentally/emotionally healthy. Single people thinking about themself most of the time develop negative thoughts about themself and Satan exarcerbates those thoughts to decrease their confidence. Then Satan combines their fear of rejection for being seen as ignorant, bad or incapable with weak confidence leading them to inaction so they are "not ready for marriage" forever. This is part of the Imposter Syndrome. The Imposter Syndrome is of 2 types, one is the person who is unaware of their own incompetance and thinks they are better than everyone, while the other has good qualities but thinks they are worse than everyone and thus "not ready for marriage". Everyone has flaws, the key is to recognize one's flaws and try to work at them AND recognize one's strengths and be proud of your virtues so you can become confident. Afterall nobody is 100% flawed, everyone has good qualities that a spouse would desire, and I mean everyone; even you. Everyone also has some bad qualities that everyone would find unappealing, even prophets. So one must have a healthy doubt in one's abilities to be a spouse but not let it reach the level of insecurity or despair. To help one get "ready for marriage" they can make a list of their good qualities and bad qualities so they can see what they are doing right and wrong in order to feel better about doing good stuff and become aware of weaknesses to work on. Family and friends are great to ask for help in listing one's good qualities and bad qualities so you can get a better picture of how good and how bad you are. Our self-image is nearly always 100% inaccurate but others can see things in us, both good and bad that we don't. So to better learn about if you are ready for marriage you have to learn more about yourself instead of thinking you know yourself better than anybody else. Who knows maybe you are ready but because it was you personal bias blinded your analysis of yourself. Try to become a person you would want to marry and learn how to grow day by day into a better more complete person who knows how good/bad they are, and is at peace with who they are despite wishing and trying to be better. Don't be complacent but just accept that you are human, being human means you have a lot of problems. It's normal to have a lot of flaws, any person you marry will have a lot of flaws too. The key is to learn to love oneself despite the flaws and to be able to love and receive love from another person of the opposite gender who has lots of flaws. To love yourself means to make an investment in your spiritual development and to love your spouse means to invest in their spiritual development. The only way you would need to be perfect to get married is if you were going to marry a perfect person, but since you aren't going to marry a perfect person then relax about not being perfect. Remember you are supposed to be a good spouse not a perfect spouse. But this works both ways, meaning your spouse will not be perfect either, though they should be good individually and good/compatible for you. God wants us to get married because he knows that being married can help us become a better person. Likewise being a parent can help one become a better person, because of the extra pressure good spouses or good kids will put on us to be a better person. God wants us to have a partner to struggle besides us on the road to paradise following the footsteps of the prophets away from Satan. Also your spouse can sometimes tell you when Satan is tricking you, so spouses can be useful security alarms to warn you when you are going astay and help you repent. Or you could end up dating and wakeup married to a devil, since the devil called cupid shot you with a poisionous arrow making you marry someone who will harm your relationship with God. Although if you focus on your relationship with God and only seek marriage to please God then even though your spouse won't be angelic the marriage could be a match that leads you both to heaven. That's the end goal, one gets married to make God happy. If you want to get married for any other reason then it's wrong and you are NOT ready for marriage. I myself know this because personally I thought and felt that I wasn't ready for marriage and would never be able to get married, except for the occasional instances when someone seemed to be interested in me, but that was a love addict's or rather a love cripple's reaction, not a genuine desire for marriage even though it felt strong. However that changed one day when I analyzed my life and plans, afterwhich I could clearly see that God would be pleased if I got married since monasticsm is a sinful innovation, but the problem was that I was "not ready for marriage". Although my analysis told me that God would be happy if I got married. Since that moment when I realized marriage would please God, I forced myself to find out how I could get ready and then I got ready because I had to marry to please God. It wasn't a matter of do I want to or not, or am I ready or not, it was just that I knew it would please God so I signed up; and hope/pray God helps. I did not have any individual person in mind when I became ready, you have to be ready before you search for someone. Also you should read a lot of books about marriage and child rearing before your search begins, to not read about marriage before engagement shows you may not be dedicated enough to marry nor prepared for the reality of it. Would you want to get married to someone who didn't read books about marriage? People read books before driving vehicles so the least they should do is read about marriage before becoming a couple. People study for years and read volumes about their possible career choices, but rarely study how to pick a husband or wife which will also be the father or mother of their child. And that's what irks me about those who date. They'll date and date and date until they take the bait and then end up getting married without ever reading a single book about marriage their whole lives. I call such couples maritally illiterate. They say marital partners should be like an open book with each other yet many don't even bother to read a book about marriage before choosing their life partner. I think such people should read before they breed, if they can't commit to reading some pages they probably shouldn't be making marital engagements. The bookworms will help your marriage more than butterflies. Although there is a limit to being "ready" because technically you can never be 100% ready to get married just as you can never be 100% ready for a kid, since you never know 100% what a marriage to X person will be like until you are in it and you will never know 100% what being a parent of X kid will be like until you are it's parent. However despite not being able to be 100% ready it is possible to be ready to be ready. Whereas that is a transition most should make well in advance. Many who are "not ready" don't know how to get ready or get ready to get ready. Many want to get married but they are smart enough to know or they feel they aren't ready so they say they aren't but they don't know how to transition and nobody recongnizes that they don't know and are hoping for advice when they say they aren't ready. When someone says they aren't ready for marriage that usually means they want advice on how to get ready, because all they know is they aren't ready for it and don't know how to make the next step towards marital preparedness. So you can ask them when they plan on getting ready to get ready, or how they plan to get ready when they want to get ready and what areas they think they should improve to become ready. Then inform them part of being prepared for marriage is being willing to be a partner instead of an independent individual. A spouse is not someone to depend on but is going to be a partner. Partnerships have difficulties that require both sides to sacrifice their ego and desires on a regular basis in order for the partnership to survive. Just as a individual requires hard work to be healthy a partnership requires hard work to be healthy. Thus during the marriage process when people learn about husband rights and wife rights they get excited and nervous but few are aware that when one gets married they don't just get rights but lose rights as well. Individuals have certain rights which partners don't have while partners have rights individuals don't have. Many of the problems in marriages happen because people are ignorant of the fact that they lose some of their individual rights when getting married because for marriage to work successfully the two individuals must become partners and give up the rights they had as individuals. So marriage requires a sacrifice of one's rights just as any type of commitment or position results in a sacrifice of one thing or the other. One loses some rights and gains other rights, but if one doesn't let go of the individual rights and the individual oriented mentality they will not be a partner in the marriage but an individual. Thus marriage is like joining a team, both lose individuality but gain as a team. One key to becoming ready is learning how be a team member for the game of life. Your life becomes "our life". Your "Me" becomes "We". Which means that you no longer are concerned with just your own needs and wants, whether physical, mental, emotional, financial or spiritual but are concerned with the team's needs and wants. During marriage your needs and wants sometimes may not be in the best interest of the team and in such an event the team takes precedent, which can be difficult but good clear communication can make such individual sacrifices for the team easier so that the team members don't resent each other or drift apart. Team unity and team satisfaction are important so as to prevent the team members from competing against each other as if they played for opposing teams. Always remember you and your spouse are on the same team, so you gotta act like it even when it's hard. Rarely do teams who fight and argue with each other achieve success, unless they learn how to successfully resolve their issues. Fortunately the prophets of God taught people in detail how to resolve arguments with people step by step, including when you should stand and when you should sit and many other minute details which if we don't follow those prophetic guidelines for arguing then our arguments would turn into sinful disasters every time, even if the team doesn't know it. You submit to God and commit to your spouse and kid(s). If you disbelieve you'll dwell in eternal hellfire while divorce is a last resort to escape hell on earth. If you commit 100% then your marriage could be like a paradise yet if you submit to the right being 100% you get to live in eternal paradise. When married the goal is no longer for you alone to go to paradise but for both your spouse and kid(s) to get there too. So the team's goal must be to sincerely follow the prophets. Which since the prophets didn't date and forbid dating then if you married someone you dated then you didn't marry into a winning team. Of course you are marrying a person and not their potential but anyone who dates before marrying is known to have lower religious potential as a spouse, parent and individual. They might become a better team player over time but if the foundation of the team is not based on prophetic guidelines then the chances of team success are zero until the team rebrands itself and commits to a prophetic gameplan for their life. This is because no matter how good a team may be at working together and communicating if they don't follow the divine gameplan they aren't going to win in life. Being part of a winning team is always more difficult than being part of a losing team and there are more losing teams than there are winning teams but doing what it takes to win as a team results in great things and great experiences. Just as championship calibre teams have different methods for selecting their members than the terrible teams do the teams following the prophetic programs are built in a different manner than the way teams following other programs are built. For example prophets taught kids come after marriage, as does sexual activity. Most will agree to this, but the prophetic team-building program also taught that you don't date. Now that's one filter wherein the higher calibre of team members become more easily distinguished from the lower quality prospects and the search for the best person for your team begins to have a lower number of candidates. Yet since many will only ever marry 1 person you don't need a long list of potential candidates to marry. The less who are on the list the better because the more on your list of potential spouses the more likely you will pick the wrong spouse or miss the best person available. So that's where you should never worry if "not many people fit your criteria for marriage" because you aren't looking to marry many people. Regardless of each individual's areas which they think they need to improve on, the way to become "ready for marriage" or fit for being a spouse or parent is to cultivate a desire to please God. Once your #1 goal is pleasing God then after you determine if/when God would be pleased with you getting married, which might take awhile, it will become easy to make the shift from "not ready" to ready. Unfortunately many never have that #1 goal but get married anyways thinking they're ready, yet if your reason(s) for getting married is anything other than pleasing God then you are NOT ready for marriage even if you're already married and have been married for years. Whether someone is married or not has nothing to do with whether they are ready/qualified for it. Marriage is a realtionship with another human being, if your relationship with God isn't good then you cannot have a good relationship with anything on the planet. Especially with marriage and all the sacrifices it requires, you will never be able to make the necessary sacrifices if you aren't getting married to make God happy. If you get married for love, then you will not make the sacrifices to have a good marriage. Love is not strong enough to make you a good spouse. Only God and marriage done sincerly for God's sake can do that. So if you become a friend of God then you will be better able to be a spouse. And if you aren't a friend of God then why would someone want to marry you? Simply put no good person would and you might end up married to an enemy of God. Although if you become a friend of God then it's likely that God will match you up with another one of his friends to marry, if that is what pleases God and will help both of you become better worshippers of him. While for those already married, if you become a friend of God then maybe God will turn your spouse into a friend of God too. If we are to marry then we can't go wrong with a friend of God, but a friend of God deserves to be with a friend of God. Therefore become a friend of God yourself and God will help you out in every aspect of life, just like a good friend does. The first step to a great marriage is friendship with God. Then if you do eventually get married to a friend of God, after doing so for God's pleasure in the manner the prophets taught us to seek, meet and wed a spouse, perhaps God will test you with parenthood to see if you raise a friend of God. However always remember as fun or enjoyble marriage and parenthood can be, those things are part of the test of life. But how can one become a great husband/father or great wife/mother? It's simple. A man should ask God to make them a better husband and a better father/grandfather, with sincerity, on a daily basis. While a woman should ask God to make them a better wife and a better mother/grandmother, with sincerity, on a daily basis. Sadly though most people never ask God to make them a better spouse or parent and if they do they don't do it daily nor do they do it with sincerity. Yet for those who don't they are all bad spouses and bad parents, though they may think otherwise. But if you happen to be married to such a person, don't despair just remember the goal of marriage. The goal is to please God. Whether your spouse is good or bad has nothing to do with you and whether you are good or bad. You are supposed to be a good spouse to make God happy, what they are doing is between them and God and you won't be judged based on what they do but you will be judged according to how you treat them. For example never ever do something just to "make your spouse happy" because of care for your spouse or the hopes of reciprocated happiness. I'm not saying don't do things to make your spouse happy but when doing those things the reason you should do them should not be for yourself nor even for your spouse, but to make God happy. The reason one does something to make their spouse happy is to make God happy. There is a big difference between something done to make the spouse happy versus something done to make the spouse happy because you want God to be happy that you made your spouse happy. With one the goal is the pleasure of the person with the other the goal is the pleasure of God and the pleasure of the person is a byproduct that has nothing to do with you doing the deed or not nor your enjoyment in doing the deed. <u>If doing something to make your spouse happy does not make God happy then don't do it. While if doing something with/to/for your spouse will make God happy then you do it and are happy to do it even if the spouse doesn't appreciate it or get happy as a result because your treatment of your spouse is based on making God happy</u>. God likes spouses to be happy but in a way he likes, spouses can be happy as a result of sinful things as well as good things. God is only happy when one makes their spouse happy by doing lawful good things and God hates it when one makes their spouse happy doing sinful things. It's more important to be a good spouse and parent yourself than to have your partner be a good spouse and parent. It's better for you to have a bad spouse while being a good one yourself, than to have a good spouse while you are a bad one. The reason you ask God to be a better spouse every day is not so your spouse treats you better or likes you more, it is so that God can be more and more pleased with you as time goes by. Every spouse will be questioned and judged on how they treated their spouse and every parent will be questioned and judged on how they raised their child. Thus it's a big risky responsibility to marry or have kids, but it can be very rewarding in this life and the next if we do it for the right reasons and follow the prophetic teachings when doing it. A good marriage is the one that makes God happy and leads you to paradise. This is what many fail to understand. For example you do not have to love your spouse in order to have a successful marriage, nor does your spouse have to love you for the marriage to be successful. As a matter of fact many married couples who are deeply in love with each other have extremely unsuccessful marriages. So while mutual, or even singular, marital love can be greatly beneficial for a couple, it is not an absolute requirement for a great marriage. Unfortunately though many people think love is the only ingredient for a successful marriage when the cold hard truth is that love is not even a key ingredient. Is it great to have? Yes, but love is NOT a key ingredient within a successful marriage, it's just a additive for extra savory flavor. The marriages that use love as a foundational building block are like the cakes where frosting is the core component instead of flour, they are very sweet but they have no substance or nutrition and if consumed are extremely unhealthy. Again the good successful marriage is the one that makes God happy and leads you to better spot in paradise as a result of it. Yet the saddest paradox is how most third party people who claim to care about us care a lot to ask about our love lives and our kids, and they focus on learning about our relationship with our spouse or children and how we are getting along, but they should be focused more on our special relationship with our personal Creator and how that's going. Too many times people ask how our relationships with others are when our relationship with God is the important one that determines how all the other relationships we have turn out. If you really want a "happy ever after" relationship, the only one who you can ever have that with is the Creator of Paradise. No human will ever make you "happy ever after", but God can.

      As 2010 CE began I was preparing my first musical cd, planning to release it around Easter time. For help I asked my drug-dealing friend who had graduated the year before to review my material and maybe make some of his own beats for me to rap to. I also wanted him to help me record. Well he wasn't going to just help me for free you know, he wanted to get something out of it. He didn't want money for helping me, no nothing like that at all. Instead he wanted me to get him a gun. Yes a gun, a hand gun, specifically a gloc which is the type of gun police officers and gang members carry. Now I was 17 years old and he was 18 years old and it would be illegal for me to get him a unregistered, unlicensed gun. Also since I was the one with desires to be the Pope I didn't really "feel comfortable" with this transaction especially since he was a drug dealer who I personally witnessed selling alcohol to minors in school when he was 17 years old. On top of that the guy already had a gun, because the first time I went to his house he came out with a shotgun pointed at me, mad that I of all people had come to his house when he never gave me the address and I got it from a mutual drug-using friend. Honestly I thought he was joking with me when he asked me to get a gun for him. He himself even admitted it was kind of a funny request to ask me, but that's why it would work because I'd be such an unlikely candidate for the job. Nobody would ever suspect someone like me getting someone like him a gun, illegally. However I did not know how to get a gun illegally and I didn't want to get a gun illegally anyways and I was on probation at the time! Now obviously I did not tell my parents or my probation officer about this gun proposal. But I did tell some nerd and athlete friends in school, because it was just too funny and surprising. Although I must clarify what I mean when I use the word "friends", afterall when someone answers the door with a shotgun and says they won't help you or review your music unless you get them a gun illegally, most people would not consider such a person to be their friend. Yet I considered this person to be my best friend, even though he was a drug dealer. Which is rather ironic since I completetly detested him as a drug dealer and never took any of the drugs he sold. I took the approach of "Hate the sin, but not the sinner" therefore my best friend was a drug dealer who pointed guns at me when I visited him to ask for help. Because that's how "Hate the sin, but not the sinner" works, you end up being friends with drug dealers and married to abusive spouses. After 10th grade I never had anyone from school come over the house to play with me and I never went to anyone else's houses to play. In the summers I'd play sports and games with my cousins who lived 2 houses away. But in school I wasn't a social outcast persay, just different. Since I was so religious and wanted to be a priest and convert the school to strict Catholicism, nobody was really a "close friend". I was social friends with athletes, nerds, gamers, drug-users and drug dealers. Each group tended to have some overlapping members but there was no "religious group" and the Church I went to and had religious education in was only attended by one other kid from my school, who was not religious. This was because there were Catholic churches in my city but I didn't go to them because I lived on the edge of the city and the Church in another city was closer, or at least that's where my parents went; there actually was another closer Catholic church but my uncle's ex-wife would go there so my parents and I didn't. Yet at the religious education classes I went to, since I didn't go to the same schools as those kids, they didn't really socialze much with me. Whereas in my school I was smart enough and studious enough to associate with the geniuses and geeks but I was also athletic, was a rap enthusiast, was ultra-religious and had a very "in your face" personality. Basically I had a big loud mouth and wasn't very "respectful" when talking to people all the time. If I wasn't preaching, then I was probably trash-talking. Essentially I was friends with most guys in my grade but nobody was really my "close friend" and none of them would ever do anything with me outside of school.

Everyone must've just thought I was popular and had other friends to do stuff with outside of school, but I didn't and I didn't really want any either because I had lots of homework and in my free time I'd play videogames(they were very hard to give up and despite attempts I didn't attain sobriety from the addiction until 2012) and/or work on my rap career. Of which my rap career was still a secret I hadn't shared with most people. Anyways I told my nerd friends who'd also get high grades about my other friend wanting me to get him a gun and most didn't believe me, neither did the athlete friends. This was because I was so popular that nobody really knew the full story of what was going on with me except maybe 2 or 3 people who I'd vent stuff to, and those guys just thought I was a hilarious guy to talk to but not one of their friends. Yet those were the same ones I considered my closest friends. But are they really friends if they refuse to help you unless you get them a gun illegally? Those were my friends, what could I do? Make new ones? Get a girlfriend? (I tried) I already knew everybody and didn't want other friends or "close friends". I had lots of friends, I was popular, it was just that my home/non-school life and my friends were kept separate. As you should've guessed, I did not get my friend the gun he desired and decided to make my music by myself.

   After discovering that my "friends" weren't as supportive or helpful as I anticipated, I released my first rap song via the internet. With hopes that being a rapper would make me happy, rectify my affairs, gain me new friends and spread Christianity. Within the week word of mouth spread, more classmates than I ever imagined knew about my rap and everyone had an opinion. Suddenly most people in the school knew who I was and my popularity was the highest it had ever been. More people in school knew who I was than I knew people. Even teachers who I didn't know the names of and kids in other grades who I never met knew who I was. Teachers I never had would talk about me in their classes and kids would write about me on their homework assignments and tests. Whereas while I walked the halls some teachers who I had in the past would make a point to communicate with me in front of their students, so they could seem cool because they knew me personally and thereby gained respect from their students. Other teachers pretended that they knew me in order to get respect from their students and seem cool. While those teachers I currently had noticeably treated me different than all the other students, they would talk to me differently than they talked to other students and I could tell that I made some of them uneasy, while others teachers were open fans. Not one teacher of mine in the 2nd Semester was able to fully ignore my rap career, some tried to and some tried to pretend to but they couldn't because other students wouldn't let them. I was able to use this to my advantage sometimes and sometimes it resulted in disadvantages. When you are that popular you can get teachers to allow you to break certain school rules and have them treat you as more of an equal, not because of the popularity but because of the confidence one acquires. Yet some teachers feel threatened by that confidence or are jealous that you get more respect than they do, those use scholastic ways to get revenge on you. One time a kid I hardly knew asked for my autograph on behalf of someone else. I just took a page out and wrote my rap name down and the person was overjoyed remarking that it will make the other person very happy. It seemed stupid that my signature would be worth so much to someone, I'm just a human being like everyone else. How my scribbling or the scribbles of another can be considered valuable is a laughable notion. I never intend on giving any autographs ever again fueling someone's unhealthy obsession. So don't ask me to sign a copy of this book. It goes without saying that the first time you do something the lack of experience affects the outcome, with one ideally becoming better with every subsequent attempt. Apparently not everyone is privy to this information and overnight my entire high school turned into critic central, or "Hater School". I quickly realized the downside of fame. For example I would go to a restaurant and people would come up to me, say my rap name and say they knew me. Although I had never seen these people before in my life! I would wonder how many songs did they listen to, how much do they know about me and what do they think? Are they a friend or a foe and how do I know? This is the downside of fame that people who haven't experienced it don't know about. To go out in public and not know who knows you and whether the people looking at you know your life story or not is a terrible feeling that deprives you of the ability to relax. To have a complete stranger call out your name unexpectedly and not know who they are or what they think about you is torture. Even if they tell you what they think, you don't know if they're honest or trustworthy and are trying to make fun of you, or what angle they are playing. Being famous means you have zero privacy and can never relax in public. If you have ever bumped into someone who knew you but you couldn't remember who they were, or how well they knew you, that is semi-comparable to being famous; except that anxious uneasiness with the estranged forgotten acquaintance is felt with everybody; however when famous you actually don't know them. Fame turns every stranger into a critic and potential enemy. Having celebrity status means having critics. Unfortunately not all critics have good intentions, some are just jealous and envious viewing you as a platform to step on in order to get their own spotlight. Others have motives that even they don't understand. Within a month of releasing my first song I received my first death threat at the age of 17. This can make a person paranoid if they aren't prepared for death and it had that effect on me. When people leave anonymous voicemails saying they're going to kill you if you don't stop rapping, it makes you reconsider your career choice; but it had the effect of increasing my dedication. At the time I was still suicidal so you would've thought that death threats would be well received, but they weren't. Even kids in school would publicly come up to me and in front of both students and teachers ask me if I wanted them to kill me. To which I'd reply, *"It would be suicide if I let you do so without putting up any resistance, I'm not going to let you have a free shot but you're welcome to try any time"*. This is the tough guy way of asking for euthanasia. You might be wondering, why didn't I tell the police? Well seeing as how they put me on probation it led me to think they didn't value my life as much as I did. Although because some death threats were left on my parents' home phone answering machine, they informed the police themselves. The police said there was nothing they could do because of freedom of speech and didn't even bother trying to trace the calls. The police instructed me to inform them if/when I get attacked. At this time I still didn't understand what their badges meant by *"to serve and protect"*, they seemed to have more of a cleanup crew attitude. The day I turned 18 I received legal papers officially releasing me from probation, then I bought a bullet proof vest. At that time it was perfectly legal for people 18 and older. A bullet proof vest isn't a weapon that needs a license or registration, it's just a piece of personal protection like knee pads or a helmet, its purpose was for safety. Instead of "friends" showing concern over my insecurity, they thought it was funny and wanted to test the vest with a knife or gun; which increased my paranoia. What kind of friends are those? One day, that I wasn't wearing the vest, about a half hour before the end of school one of the police security guards took me away from my classmates escorting me to the office without letting me know what it was about. After getting searched and questioned, I finally learned that my mother had found the vest in my closet and called the police. So I explained my reasons for having a bullet proof vest in front of the police, principal, social workers and my mother. In the end my vest was confiscated by the police. Since I spent money on the vest and still had reasons to wear it, I wanted my vest back. Yet it was taken and they don't tell you nothing else. So I didn't know how I was going to get my vest back or where it was. Of course my "friends" who knew I had a vest thought it was hilarious the police took my vest. Then one day in a class about the U.S. Government which I was taking for college credit, my teacher who was also a politician had his friend the Mayor visit our class to talk. So during the question and answer session I explained to Mayor Robert G. Ortt that the police confiscated my bulletproof vest and nobody told me how I can get it back, so I told him I thought if anybody knew how I could get it back then it would be him. The Mayor's response was something like, "*You see kids, these are the types of dumb questions you get asked when you're the mayor.*" The class laughed loudly and he went on to the next question. Currently he is the New York State Senator as I write this. Eventually after asking around I think someone at the police station told me I had to ask the officer who confiscated it, so I asked for his contact information to contact him and I was told that they can't give that information to me because he filed his application to retire. So I asked how am I supposed to get my vest then and they said you have to ask the officer who confiscated it. Yet they refused to give me his contact information. Fortunately I remembered that officer's face from the day of confiscation and it turned out that he simultaneously worked as a security guard in the high school. One day I saw him in school so I explained my quest to get my vest back and he told me I could get it after graduation by getting permission from the city judge. I also learned that my vest was never confiscated but had been turned in to the police by my mother. So in the summer I went to the city judge and gave a letter to the clerk explaining my reasons for the purchase and the desire to have my private property returned, or have the cost refunded. When I returned to ask if the judge read my request the clerk simply said "*He read it*". When I asked what the response was she said, "*the answer is no*" without giving me any reasons why. So I asked her why and she said, "*the answer is no*". Therefore I never saw the vest again. However in 2017 CE I found a copy of the letter I gave the judge and got more upset thinking there was no reason for them to keep it, until I noticed a typo wherein I said 2009 instead of 2010. Then I realized how my typo could have resulted in jailtime and the judge was actually being nice to me. I turned 18 in 2010 then bought the vest because it was illegal for minors to have them, if I recall correctly. But in my letter dated 2010 I wrote my vest was turned in/confiscated in April 2009 by mistake even though it was really usurped in April 2010 as I hadn't even gotten a debit card until October 2009 and couldn't have possibly bought my vest the time I said I had it taken in the letter and if I had it might have been illegal. Thus in my eagerness to regain my vest I mistakenly described myself suspiciously as waiting over a year before asking, or implying that I failed a grade and potentially implying I had illegally purchased it even though all those deductions my typo could cause were false because it was 2010 instead of 2009 which I mistakenly typed. Thus after 7 years of anger I was relieved to learn that I could've potentially been charged as a criminal because of a typo I wrote when trying to get my legally obtained vest back. Also since my typo displayed the wrong year there probably was no record of it at the time I said there should have been thus I couldn't get it even if they tried because of my typo. Tis a frustrating story that I now find funny since I thought I was a victim for so many years only to realize I was in reality of victim of my own typographical error and the judge by ignoring me actually protected me from myself and my own stupidity. I also realized it's possible to mistakenly frame yourself for a crime you are innocent of without knowing it or intending to do so. Whereas you might be frustrated and feel screwed but in reality God is protecting you from harms you don't expect. Anyways now I realize how stupid a purchase my vest was, not because of the money lost, or the confiscation, but because death cannot be prevented or delayed. Everyone shall have the taste of death, we all have an appointed time and place of death already predetermined by our Creator that cannot be hastened or postponed, no matter how much you try. There is a true story about a group of 4 friends who used to go out together. One night 1 of the 4 decided not to go out with the rest, it turned out that his friends all died that night in a car crash that he might have been in if he went with them. His mother was shocked and overjoyed that her son had stayed home that night, quickly going to his room to tell him the bad news and how much she loved him. When she entered she found him dead in his bed with no medical reason or explanation as to why. It was just his time and God sent the angel of death to take his soul, it didn't matter if he was in the car crash or not he was still meant to die that night and he died in exactly the way God intended. In Egypt there was a man doing construction work on a tall building, he fell off the building from what should've been a fatal height, amazingly he was unharmed. Overjoyed he decided to celebrate with the people there and crossed the street to buy some treats to eat and got hit by a car and died; just minutes after surviving what should have been a fatal fall. These deaths can be a lesson to us. Some people think medicine will advance to the degree where all you will need is to take a pill once a day in order to live forever. What's going to happen to such a person when God destroys the universe and nothing is left? What good will the pill do them then without oxygen, sunlight, water or matter? Death is inevitable, there's no escape, it can happen any time so we must be ready constantly. Do you know why we must always be ready to die? There is no deathproof vest to stop the Angel of death. When the Angel of death comes to you, there is no delay or rescheduling, he's got a list of people to go to next, you will not get special treatment in the slightest, he's heard all the excuses you could ever think of and he never accepted one. The Angel of death is on his way to meet you right now, he's been waiting to take your soul since before you were born. When he comes, you go, no questions asked; until you are in the grave and meet Munkar and Nakir. Are you ready now? Seriously, are you ready right now? When you see the angel of death that means it's the end of your test of life.

    As my music career progressed more publicity was needed to advance. In other words, I needed to get more attention. At that time in 2010 CE, facebook was the place to get it, I reluctantly joined with the sole purpose being to promote my music and get more attention. Initially it seemed foolish with idiotic functions like a "poke" button, which I thought was kind of sodomous since I only "poked" guys, and a newsfeed full of people posting stupid stuff that I didn't want or need to know about. It seemed others used it as a "flirtbook" or a perverted "lookbook". Gradually as my number of facebook friends grew it became apparent that some of these facebook friends seemed more like enemies. I wondered if those who had thousands of "friends" also had facebook enemies they were friends with. Another important thing I learned on facebook was how fast gossip spread and how easily a reputation can be destroyed or distorted. What was especially frustrating was when I'd make several comments on someone else's profile in a conversation only to have some of my comments deleted, so that I appeared to have different opinions than those which I posted, because my posts were taken out of context. If someone deletes half of what you said, then people get a different message than what you intended. One popular saying in the music industry is that *"any publicity is good publicity"*. Although on social networks everyone is a celebrity, fame is easy to gain, but to maintain it requires bigger and larger spotlights, not necessarily brighter. In short I became a facebook addict. Once again I had escaped my real life via a virtual life. All thanks and praises be to the Creator of reality who has given us real life.

    In real life I was getting more attention but it wasn't the good kind. After the bullet proof vest incident, my locker would be unexpectedly searched and I would find it disheveled on days police and school personnel rifled through it. When I chastised the vice principal publicly in the hall he denied anything of the sort was going on. So I taped an insulting note in my locker addressed to those searching, then one day it was gone without a trace. Another time a folder for my psychology class went missing and I was certain it had been in my locker. I told the psychology teacher my suspicions but because I had no proof was graded as though I had lost it. Maybe I did lose it, but if these locker searchers took a note that I taped to the inside of my locker then it makes sense that they would take a psychology folder full of notes and self-analysis. While they might've felt in the right rifling through my things, I felt violated and couldn't understand why they didn't just ask for my permission and/or notify me. They still would have gotten their information and I would've had some peace of mind. Then after releasing a certain rap specifically addressing my critics, I had another chat with the principal who was concerned I was inciting violence or threatening students. This was hilarious because the person they said I had threatened in the song was one of the few people on relatively good terms with me. When they took him to the office to interview him, he was actually sitting at the same lunch table as me and we were talking and joking with each other. This was an experience that taught me how people take things out of context and don't listen to the entire message. Had they listened to the entire song or even the verse or sentence the person's name was mentioned in, they would have realized there was no problem at all. Sometimes people have selective hearing. I hope you don't have selective reading. It demonstrated how people often jump to the worst of conclusions and will misuse fragments to support their misunderstood baseless biased hypothesis. They get the wrong first impression and all interactions after it are tainted by the false initial perception. It would be funny if it didn't happen so frequently and their suspicions weren't so serious. During the last half of my senior year I was in a rough spot where I felt stuck being abused at both home and school. I didn't know which was worse, so the suicidal thoughts continued.

Soon after finishing high school and getting my Advanced Regents Honors diploma my family relationships were visibly disintegrating, especially with my parents. At this time I realized that all these "friends" in high school suddenly disappeared and stopped returning calls and messages, leaving me disenchanted, feeling increasingly isolated without support. Almost every day resulted in a fight with my parents before nighttime that would end with me leaving the house, sometimes out of rage and sometimes out of fear, some nights I was right and some nights I was wrong; regardless Satan was winning all along. By now I had a driver's license and car, which I had extorted my parents to give me in order for me to continue living with them. Our relationship was so bitter that I nearly signed up to live at a half-way house to get away from them, the only reason I didn't was in exchange for a car. This was a family with a bad foundation quickly turning into ruin. The 4th of July 2010 CE was the first night I spent sleeping outside on a playground, which unfortunately had rowdy drunks playing nearby it at night. Filled with self-pity I assumed they would offer some assistance, or at least a kind word, but that was not within their capacity. After a night on the playground, I spent the majority of summer nights out of the house sleeping in my car at various locations. It can be extremely uncomfortable, but the body has an extraordinary ability to adjust. When bitterness and hatred consume a person they do stupid things, like give up their bed out of pride for not apologizing. One such night parked in a park, which also had rowdy people partying in another part, the sound of knocking on the window and a flashlight in my face wakes me up. It was the police, thinking I was associated with the other park people because my windows were fogged up from sleeping. After explaining my situation that I was sleeping out of the home to avoid further confrontation, the police said it was illegal to park there (despite me not seeing any sign) and actually advised me to park in a business plaza at any store. Shockingly that is illegal, with numerous warning signs saying it's against the law. Instead I decided to park in the parking lot of the church I attended and in the early morning I'd participate in the daily mass. As a result of serving communion to people as a Eucharistic minister I had started going to church at a different time than my parents, but their friends would go the same time as I went. When you hate someone, you hate their friends by default, so I started going to a different church than my parents.

Off topic let me explain the hate relationship, because some claim Islam teaches hate. Let's say you "love" your spouse, they tell you they hate so and so because of such and such. Now if you say anything that's not in agreement with them you'd be in big trouble. If you said "*oh but I love so and so*" you might be left without a spouse or kicked out of the house. It's impossible for a person to love something and simultaneously love what their beloved hates. The heart cannot have conflicting loves. Even on a personal level, many times spouses eating together in a restaurant tell the server, "*I'll have the same thing they're having*" because they love what that person loves and hate what that person hates, so they automatically trust they will be satisfied eating whatever that person chooses to eat. The same goes for nationalism, when one has "love for one's country" that also means hating who that country hates, which is typically determined by who the government says to hate. Yet when it comes to God frequently people have a delusion that God doesn't hate anything ignoring all the evidence to the contrary. As it relates to Islam, a Muslim loves God; therefore a

Muslim loves what God loves. However there are things God hates, so if a Muslim really loves God they must also hate what God hates. Some examples of what God hates include: Satan, the friends of Satan, corruption, sin, idolatry, falsehood, tyranny, oppressors, injustice, greed, liars. Who in their right mind wouldn't hate these things? You cannot truly love God until you hate what God hates. If God makes clear his hatred for ____ and you say "*oh but I love ____*" do you think God will love you while you love what he hates? Loving what God hates may make God hate you and is tantamount to you hating God. A person cannot love God and the prophets of God while loving the enemies of God and the enemies of the prophets. If you were to love an "enemy of the state" the state would consider you an enemy and punish you, so what do you think God will think of and do to someone who loves his enemies? Examples of enemies would be: the Pharaoh who rejected Moses pbuh or the Goliath who fought David pbuh. The same goes for hating the prophets, someone who hates or slanders even one prophet would be hating God simultaneously; whether they know it or not. A true friend wouldn't be a friend with your enemy, if they were no sane person would keep them as a friend. This is a leveraged relationship, in that the more you love God the more you hate Satan, and the more you love the friends of God (the prophets and believers) the more you hate the enemies of God (the friends of Satan and the disbelievers).   Examples of specific people whom we are obligated to hate today would be the antichrist and the peoples of Gog and Magog. Some think one should just hate the sin but love the sinner. This notion is wrong. For instance no believer would say: "*I love Pharaoh, but I hate what he did to Moses pbuh*" , or "*I love Goliath but I just hate what he did to David pbuh*" or "*I love the antichrist but I just hate the sins that he commits.*" One cannot separate the sins from the sinner who did them. Now of course this doesn't mean if someone on God's team sins then they should be hated as enemies of God. Different sins result in different amounts of hate. Think of it like 2 rival sports teams. A sports fan loves everyone on their team and hates everyone on the rival team by default. No matter what a player on the rival team does that's good the true fan will always hate them because of their team. Likewise the sports fan will always love their team's players even if they do bad things, in such cases they will hate the bad things their team's players do but their love for the players supersedes the hate for their team members mistakes. Whereas their hate for the rival team overpowers any good that the rival team member may do. Thus believers love all believers and hate all disbelievers, while they may have some hate for believers but such hate is due to their sins only. Therefore one is to love the believer, and hate the disbeliever, love the good deed and hate the sin. Whereas religion is the heaviest weight that determines the main attitude one will have, so whether someone is a believer or a disbeliever accounts for over 99% of a believer's attitude towards that person. So it's similar to how a sports fan hates their team when they make a foolish mistake and or lose the game, but that hate is very minuscule whereas the hatred for the rival team(s) is always strong even if they were to beat another rival team and in doing so ended up benefiting the fan's team some way. Regarding religions take Mother Teresa and Mahatma Gandhi, currently these are revered by many as having been pious virtuous people, yet one was a Christian and the other a Hindu. Now in God's view there is no way both could ever be loved by God if they were on different teams. They both could be hated if those 2 teams were rivals to the believing team but it's impossible for God to have loved both and thus a believer can never love both regardless of how many good things they may have done; a believer would have to hate one or the other or both. Those people in the highest ranks of paradise are the prophets because they are the best friends of God who hate Satan and disbelief and disbelievers the most. While those in the lowest level of hellfire are the best friends of Satan who hate God and belief the most. May we be registered amongst the friends of God and not the friends of Satan. The English translation of the New International Version of the Bible also teaches this:

> **Proverbs 6:16-19** "16 *There are six things <u>the LORD hates</u>, seven that are detestable to him:*17 *haughty eyes, a lying tongue, hands that shed innocent blood,* 18 *a heart that devises wicked schemes, feet that are quick to rush into evil,* 19 *a false witness who pours out lies and a person who stirs up conflict in the community.*"
>
> **Psalms 139:21-22** "<u>Do I not hate those who hate you, LORD</u>, and abhor <u>those who are in rebellion against you</u>?22 **<u>I have nothing but hatred for them; I count them my enemies</u>**."
>
> **Luke 14:25-26** "25 *Large crowds were traveling with <u>Jesus,</u> and turning to them he <u>said</u>:* 26 "**<u>If anyone comes to me and does not hate father and mother, wife and children, brothers and sisters</u>** *– yes, even their own life –* **<u>such a person cannot be my disciple.</u>**"

The verses in Proverbs list some things that put a person on God's hated list. The verses in Psalm 139 denote hatred for those who hate God and "abhorrence" for those who rebel against God are not only virtuous qualities, but obligatory for a believer to have. In context one actually wouldn't be a believer if they didn't have these attitudes or feelings of hatred towards such people. Also know that being "*in rebellion*" against God meant rejecting God's laws or religion. In fact the Psalms actually teach the believer is to have "nothing but hatred for them", meaning it would be forbidden according to the bible to have even an ounce of love for someone of a different religion. In Luke the bible says Jesus pbuh made it obligatory to hate one's family in order to be his disciple is not a general rule for everybody's family. The people he would've been addressing were specifically Jews whose family members didn't believe in his prophethood. So hating one's family depends on whether they are believers or not. The bible further explains how Jesus pbuh taught believers to treat family in Matthew 8:18-22, 18 *When Jesus saw the crowd around him, he gave orders to cross to the other side of the lake.* 19 *Then a teacher of the law came to him and said, "Teacher, I will follow you wherever you go."* 20 *Jesus replied, "Foxes have dens and birds have nests, but the Son of Man has no place to lay his head."* 21 <u>*Another disciple said to him, "Lord, first let me go and bury my father."*</u> 22 *But* **Jesus told him, "Follow me, and let the dead bury their own dead."**

This excerpt begins with "*a teacher of the law*" telling Jesus pbuh he will follow him to wherever. Jesus pbuh basically told him that he as the "Son of Man" referring to Adam pbuh, his and our forefather, has no place to sleep and that he's a homeless man and following him is not going to be comfortable. This is because the believers are not well liked by the majority of humans and they get boycotted, exiled and blacklisted since they don't care for this life. Next "*Another disciple*" of Jesus pbuh asks Jesus pbuh to let him bury his father before following Jesus pbuh. That the text says "*Another*" lets us know the previously mentioned "*teacher of the law*" became a disciple and had no qualms with poverty and didn't cite any religious law saying that homelessness or poverty is anti-religious. Jesus pbuh tells the other disciple to follow him and "*let the dead bury their own dead*". Jesus pbuh told his "*disciple*" not to bury his own father. Why? Jesus pbuh said the dead should bury their own. This doesn't mean corpses bury corpses, but Jesus pbuh was referring to the father as being spiritually dead because he was a disbeliever and teaches us that disbelievers should bury their own and believers shouldn't attend the funerals of disbelievers nor bury them. The bible clearly and explicitly teaches that people should hate people of different religions.

Unfortunately at that time my hate wasn't hate for the right reasons. When a person hates for the wrong reasons it leaves a bad taste in the mouth and is like carrying a huge weight around affecting everything you do. Satan can lead a person to become a slave to hatred, which will lead to the hater having distorted thinking and trying to justify unjust behavior they do because of their hatred. Whereas in Islam no matter how unjustly someone may treat you it doesn't give you the right to transgress and/or treat them unjustly violating their rights. When Satan stirs enmity between family members he patiently cultivates the hate letting it stew for years, without either side forgiving the other, often unbeknownst to those not directly involved (unless it's a gossipy family), ultimately culminating in a blowup that might forever change the family dynamic; destroying the unity which may take years to repair if it's at all possible. Oftentimes Satan can cause some tiny thing to get stuck in a person's mind, whereas their object of hate doesn't even remember doing what the hater feels so strongly about, which only enrages the hater further. The first different Catholic church I went to, in order to escape my family and their friends, ostracized me based on my rapper appearance. I decided to find a 3rd Catholic church that was less hypocritical. Churches claim to be welcoming to everyone, but one rarely finds diversity there of any kind. I brought a "friend" along on Sundays to the 3rd Catholic church I went to. They still treated me like a thug at this church too, but by the time my "friend" stopped tagging along the people had grown on me and the habit of attending there developed. I was also interested in one of the girls who used to sit a few pews away, so that provided me with lots of motivation to go on every single Sunday. First it was money that brought me to church and then it was women. All thanks and praises be to God for guiding me and may we all have the correct sincere motivation when it comes to religion.

By the end of summer my parents and I came to the conclusion that our differences were irreconcilable and we decided to live in separate places, so we didn't end up killing each other. Remember the first murder done to mankind involved the brothers Cain and Abel, the sons of Adam pbuh, with Satan exploiting envy turning it to hate, then teaching Cain how to kill. When families fight amongst each other things can get more dangerous than they would amongst strangers. They moved and I stayed. My behavior was so bad that it drove my parents away. Technically I was living by myself although my parents were financially supporting me. When someone is living alone it can go two different ways. Either they indulge in their addictions losing all discipline and self-control, or they mature and develop becoming responsible. Usually it is a mix between the two with the balance fluctuating from one side to the other. While it wasn't ideal, at least I wasn't fighting with my parents as much. However the paranoia one has increases drastically since you're "home alone". Years of movies and TV viewing made me think every noise was an intruder about to attack or rob me. Especially since I owned an exorbitant amount of jewelry and boasted to everyone I could, the death threats also made me anxious. This led to mental and emotional insecurity and I decided to get my own protection. A rapper's worst fear is getting robbed because it damages their reputation, and a celebrity's reputation is everything to them. Therefore I purchased a dangerous weapon and carried it around with me wherever I went, college, church, you name a place and I had it with me.(except government buildings) The trouble with carrying a weapon is that you have to be ready to use it at all times, or else it's useless. When you are always on edge ready to harm someone else it causes a mental and emotional disassociation, which only serves to increase the paranoia and imagined dangers. Carrying a weapon requires that you be ready to potentially use it on everyone around you before they cause you harm. It makes you view everyone as a potential threat whom you are about to use your weapon on should they act a certain way. The more "protection" you have, the more you think you need and the more you think you need the less safe you feel. It is a very dangerous cycle that results in you feeling less safe the more dangerous you become.

   In the fall, my first year of college began and by summertime I was to graduate with an Associate's degree in "Audio recording and production". As a commuter who lived off campus I never went to any college parties or experienced any of the horrors campus life entails. Although compared with high school, college is a much more dangerous and sinful environment. American colleges have booths to call security every 89 steps because there is such a serious danger of getting raped. In America 25% of women will be raped at least once in their life, over 1 million females are raped every year in America. Although many don't even report it. In 1999 CE American male college freshman were surveyed and 25% of them stated if they were on a date, paid for a dinner and the girl doesn't have sex with them then they have the "*right to force her to have sex*". Yet older people think I'm mistaken when I say dating is prostitution and that most who date have pre-marital sex, the younger ones don't refute my claims because they know and probably already had sex after going on dates themselves. So whether that is reflective of dating culture and sex or the rape culture, lots of sex is happening and there are too many rapes. In Japan women are so frequently raped that they invented vending machine disguises that can be put on in a few seconds so that a woman can hide next to vending machines in costume as a way to escape rapists. It's gotten so bad they've even made special divisions of female police who purposely try to lure rapists to rape them so they can try to catch and stop rapists; seriously that's what they do in several countries as well as major cities. They "stop rape" by trying to trap rapists by tricking them to try to rape police instead of civilians. Obviously it hasn't been working too well, and the taxpayers feel the cost, but they have expanded the program to molesters as well. So many women get molested, especially in crowded areas, that tax-dollars get spent on having police simply try to get groped or observe gropers in the act because there is a groping pandemic and democratic countries just don't know how to stop it. I've even been groped many times, even in public places like restaurants, stores and schools. It goes without saying that groping occurs in colleges,(I know firsthand) sadly though much of it is consensual or considered "innocent flirting". Once some of my collegiate classmates were loudly discussing a drug deal in class. I was completely shocked when they asked if I wanted to purchase something with them, to which I politely refused hiding my disapproval in an attempt to maintain my rapper image and to seem "cool". I was very surprised how easy it was to get drugs in college, and my best friends in high school were drug dealers so for me to think it was easy to get drugs in college meant the typical college kid must think it's extremely easy; or I'm wrong to say think there because they already know its easy. It's a lot easier for kids to get illegal drugs in college than it is for them to get enrolled at a college. In college sin is "in" and encouraging morality is asking for a social fatality. Yet on top of that college is practically useless. Practically no job at all in the world today requires 4 years of training, except for the hardest of the hardest careers involved in natural sciences. Most college degrees today should and can be attained within 2 years but alas colleges are corporate business who want to milk their business model for all they can get whether they have a justifiable reason to teach something or not. Today colleges are the churches of the religion of Careerism. Most students realize that you just gotta study and do the work to pass the test to get the paper to get the job to get the paper to pay off the debt you got when studying for the test to get the paper that helped you get the paper to pay off the debt you got. While some are too dim to understand that previous sentence because of their lousy education so they take a few years longer in college and get more debt on their plate, thinking the crumbs they'll get to eat as a result of their diploma are worth it. Whereas because the religion of hedonism goes hand in hand with careerism, the colleges have created a debt bubble so big it can't even be paid for. Therefore the governments kindly step in and offer to get the colleges to forgive the students' loans in exchange for free labor from the students. Thus colleges have become a way for governments to get free employees who work for nearly nothing because they have no choice due to their debts they incurred while getting a piece of paper. Of course the governments don't tell parents or students that they'll end up working for the government for free, either temporarily or permanently, because of their debts that can't be paid and because their "knowledge" they "learned" in college isn't useful or desired in the real world. This is even known subconsciously by everyone in America. For example every student whether they are in college or any level of schooling is always and always and always asked by people "So how is school?" or "How is School going?" or when will they finish school. It is the de facto standard conversation when talking to someone who is in school. It's boring and annoying and repetitive and typically unenjoyable by all who have it, yet have it they do, to "show they care". Whereas nearly nobody, and I'm saying nearly only because it's possible that somebody somewhere might, ever asks a student in school "What did you learn in school?" and a parent never seriously asks their kid "What did you learn in school today?" because everyone knows deep down that you don't really learn anything good or useful in school. So all the questions are just about when the student gets let out or how they are emotionally handling it, or the workload. Yet nothing at all is ever asked about what is learned, and the students never say what they learn either. Because they don't even know they are supposed to learn. This is because public schools and colleges are not places one goes to learn but they go to get trained/certified. It is done as a job orientation, that job being a happy stupid hard-working tax-paying patriotic citizen. You can test this out to see how little students actually learn by asking them "What did you learn this year?" and then last month, last week, yesterday, today and in the last class. Finally asking what will they learn in the future semesters and the next class they go to, and you will discover most don't even plan on learning anything when they go to school. Most just want a diploma or at best information on how to do the job they desire to have in the future. They don't want to learn anything important spiritually or even politically, nor do most care to learn how to improve themselves or the world. Most just want to learn to party and have a good time so they go to school to learn what they need to know to pay for future "good times" and a pathetic life of mindless entertainment. But at the end of it all they get a *"prestigious college diploma"*. That's very useful, people can use it as toilet paper someday. Yet the same applies even with adults asking "How are you doing?" our whole society is trained to only care about feelings, nobody cares about what people are doing or learning because we don't think those things are important. Seriously when was the last time an adult asked another adult "What have you learned recently?" and have it be a serious question that isn't about sports, or the news but out of a genuine desire to gain beneficial knowledge? That's what I try to do and it's great because you actually learn a lot just by saying "What have you learned?" instead of "How are you doing?". Even when it comes to books, even books like this, if you tell someone you are reading or read this book they will likely ask "Is it good?" or "Do/did you like it?". Very few would ask "What did you learn from it?" or "Has it helped you and if so then how?" because as a society we are so stupid and wrong that our species can't even ask the right questions. Just based on the page count alone most wouldn't even want to read this and think it's crazy to read a book with so many pages. Yet they'd be willing to read a hundred useless fiction novels or "good short books" which in total have many more pages and teach them literally nothing, but bad morals while promoting false religions and sin all the while wasting their time and money on the realm of fantasy, aka Satan's playground. Or if they aren't sophisticated enough to read then they'd spend millions of hours on fictional movies, videogames, music or TV shows because they think long books are boring, no fun and would make them a loser somehow; unless of course such a "long book" were a textbook for college or school. While others would read a "long book" just to brag about it and/or see how long it takes thinking the page count is important, not realizing pages mean nothing but it's the information conveyed that can be valueable. More pages just means more information so a long book may possibly have more valueable text simply based on mathematical probability, however that's not always the case and many times shorter books can be more valueable than longer books. Not because they are shorter or less expensive but it's all about the knowledge depth, quantity and usefulness the text written has. Every book is simply a tool for your brain and life, some are bad some are good and some are useless wastes of paper. Each book is different and every collection is different and can be used differently by people who may or may not use such tools(books) fully or properly in a way that pleases the Creator of everything. The author (tool maker) can only do so much, but the reader has to be qualified, willing and able to use the book to it's maximum potential for a book to benefit themselves and the world as much as it can. Thus every reader of a book has a responsibility regarding what they choose to read and what they do with the information they learn from all the books which they read. Yet most book sellers never bother to tell people that because they don't know or care to tell people just what exactly a book is, and most authors don't know or care to tell people what books are either. But as you can tell, this book ain't like other books. That doesn't mean it's good or pleasing to God, but it is a bit different. Thus as a reader you can't be reading this book like other readers read other books. As the author I can dictate that reading this book requires you to have personal sincerity, dedication and responsibility. What? Did you think I'd let you read my book however you wanted to and then use it's info however you wanted? Think again, that's not how this book works. What kind of author would I be then and what kind of reader would you be? More importantly what kind of reader will you be? Don't stop reading. I'm just telling you, "Read better". Reading a book is not a game to be done for fun. Every book you read should help you become a better person, fiction doesn't help you become a better person. How can you possibly gain a good moral lesson from characters that never existed in a setting that never existed doing things that never really happened? You can't get a lesson from something that didn't happen, learn your morality from reality. If your morality comes from fantasy then your morals are fictitious. By pretending and concerning oneself with an imaginary universe that doesn't exist one forgets the reality of Heaven and Hell and that in a few moments they will be taken from this world into one of those places to reside therein forever. God created us to be in this world for a specific reason. When you read you are making an investment of time and energy in that book, so that investment in reading a book better help you in this life and the next. Basically if the book won't aid your journey to paradise in any way then you should not read it. Whenever you read a book you have to have a goal. That goal must be religious in some aspect and it is religious even if the reader isn't. This is because every book is a work of religious propagation aka propaganda. Whenever someone writes a book they have a reason for it. Trust me with the amount of work involved in writing a book and then editing and editing and editing nobody writes books for the fun of it. While it is exhilarating to write, if there is no specific reason for someone to write then they won't have the motivation to finish. So why in the world would someone spend so much time and effort to write about things which never happened? It could be for money, fame, credentials, egotism or any other base selfish reason. However there are many other potential motivations. People could write for religious reasons, romantic reasons, political reasons, psychotic reasons or for self-esteem reasons. Although primarily an author will write because they want to have a social impact and influence on individuals who read their book which then leads to having an influence on society. Many authors want to change the way people think and act, for better or worse. I'm no different. I could keep this information about books to myself and try to "brainwash" or whatever, but that's not how the prophets taught people. I'm not playing mind games with you, I'm just letting you know how authors can have big influences and am warning you not to let me be too influential because I'm just another human being much like you. I would like to hope I'm writing to please my Creator and doing a deed which will benefit me while I'm in the grave but as a secondary reason I also desire to influence society by enjoining what is good and forbidding what is evil so that the world I live in can be a better place in the present and future. At least I'm straightforward about it. I'm honest enough to tell you that I write with an intention to persuade/influence. Most authors just play the game trying to manipulate the author effect to get maximum influence over their readers without their readers knowing it. However a non-fiction writer has a much more difficult task for influencing society than a fiction writer does. This is because when you read a non-fiction book such as this, you know that I'm a human being who is communicating some information directly to you, so you have a certain level of social awareness making you less likely to be persuaded by what you read. Especially if an author does something like I've done and admit that authors have influence and agendas. With fiction on the other hand, most oftentimes the author veils themselves and their message behind imaginary characters so you completely forget about the author and thus forget they have motives. At the end of the fictional tale there may be a certain lesson that is easy to identify, but from cover to cover there are many more lessons and doctrines being propagated that are not easily identified because they are disguised as plot details or character dialogue. The best way to determine why a book has been written is to look at the effects the book has had after its publication. Did the author get rich and famous as a result? Then it might have been written for money or fame. Even if that is the case every author still conveys messages to their audience even if they do so unintentionally. But usually fiction is an intentional means to teach someone something without them knowing that you were teaching them, thus an entertaining distraction is concocted to make the reader emotionally attached to the book so their intellectual guard goes down. To easily identify what messages the author of fiction has conveyed just examine the effect the story has upon the reader. Ask the reader what they thought about the book and what it was about. Then as they share their opinion, ignore the plot of the book and focus on the actions of its characters and view the fictional characters as though the author just told the reader this is how you should act in real life. With such an approach you will be able to see what the effect such characters had upon the reader. This is because humans tend to be imitative beings who imitate characters they are presented with due to emotional conformity. This is why God has sent us prophets so we can follow them rather than make every single person a prophet. This is a common problem people have with fiction. They automatically assume that the lesson is good and that the author is a good person who if obeyed will lead you to heaven, even if they know the author is not a good person. Many people think a bad person is capable of writing a good book. They aren't, yes a bad person could write an entertaining book, but if there is no goodness in the author then how can they possibly put goodness down on the pages? They could be good while writing and turn bad after putting their goodness on the pages but there must be some good in an author for them to share something good. The sad reality is that authors of fiction are liars who will lead you to hell. The very definition of fiction is falsehood. It is impossible to teach something good by means of doing something bad. For example beating one's spouse so they apologize for insulting you in front of your kids is not going to teach your kids that it is wrong to insult people, it will teach them it's right to assault people. Doing bad things teaches bad things even if good lessons are intended. Just like stealing or gambling in order to get money to give for charity will not teach someone to give charity nor will it be a good deed. Likewise lying about things by making up a fictional story cannot possibly teach a good lesson overall. Because before any lesson can be learned it requires one to agree that it is ok to lie and make stuff up in the first place. So you have to do a bad deed before you can even write/film or read/watch the work of fiction. To accept the existance of a work of fiction is to accept lying as being okay. By reading a work of fiction one is making lying a legitimate form of communicating so there is guranteed harm that outweighs any alleged benefit. Seriously a creator of fiction is saying "*I'm going to tell lots of lies to tell a story, but there's a good reason for me to make all this stuff up. Just listen to my lies and enjoy learning.*" Whereas personally I'd just stop the fiction fabricator right there and say "*No. Don't lie. Tell me what you want without telling me any lies. If you have to tell a lie to tell me what you want then don't because to tell the lies is sinful. So I'm not interested in your fiction because I want the truth and hate lies.*" Personally I wouldn't even read fiction if it were assigned in school unless it were to analyze and expose the religious doctrines and lessons taught by the author both plainly and subliminally. But is that what teachers and students do in school when they read works of fiction? Do they treat it as a detective would trying to identify the lies and evil doctrines spewed by the fiction maker? Typically not. Instead the teachers foolishly tend to try to make the student think about the psychology of the fictional characters and their motivations as if they were real people, thereby the teachers try to make the students identify with the characters thinking it will better help them with interpersonal and communication skills in life or gain new perspectives. Yet the characters aren't real and were just made up by the fiction maker to teach people certain things without them knowing it and identifying/sympathizing with the characters is exactly how the things intending to be subliminally taught are taught. Thus most who "study a work of fiction" are imbibing its hidden doctrines even moreso than the one just enjoying it for fun without studying. For example when was the last time a teacher teaching a work of fiction ever told their student, "*Why do you think X author would just lie and make up this character and portray them in such a way doing these things which they never did? What do you think the author wants you to believe and do after learning about this character?*" Sadly nearly zero teachers do this because they simply don't know how to teach, they are simply professional indoctrinators without knowing it because they've been indoctrinated themselves to teach a doctrine they don't even know they are teaching when they teach things. Hence I say most kids who go to most schools exit as a fool that has been trained to be a tool to be used to serve the desires of those they won't even know are benefitting by their labor and play when they labor and play. Thus fiction is a subgenre of religion in which every author of fiction teaches their own faith. Also a creator of fiction is imitating God because God has created everything. Yet in the fictional world the author is the creator of characters and much more. Essentially a creator of fiction becomes the God of their own fantasy land. Because that fantasy land is inevitably different from the real world the real God made, they are putting forth the idea that they can make something better than God has. Why else would they try to teach a lesson using imaginary characters? We have the prophets as role models, we don't need imaginary characters to learn from. The imaginary characters are not going to paradise so they cannot possibly help you to go to paradise. So if they cannot teach you or motivate you to go to paradise then imaginary characters can only teach you and lead you to hell. Fiction is the genre of Satan and it leads to toleration of false religions and lies and all other sorts of ills and evils that plague our species. While I have focused mainly on written works of fiction the same applies to fictional movies, songs, news broadcasts, plays, operas, tv shows, videos, games, skits etc. All these are works of fiction that have the same result and negative immoral influences on those that are affected by them or interact with those affected by them. What is the proof that all works of fiction are satanic productions, aside from the fact that fiction is a entre of lies? Well look at the fundamental lesson taught by every work of fiction. What lesson is that? The fundamental lesson in fiction is so obvious you should be ashamed to not have seen it and if you haven't it shows that you have been thoroughly brainwashed by the genre of fiction. Do you really not know the overarching theme of fiction? The fictional worlds take God and the prophetic religion out of the picture entirely. Consider the role the prophetic religion plays in fictional tales. How many times does the main character pray every day? How often do the characters mention the prophets and cite them as examples to help them know what the best course of action is? By and large the overwhelming majority of fictional stories don't even contain the word God let alone give any significant importance to God in their fictional universe. Therein lies the fundamental goal of fiction, to make people believe in a world free from God and the prophetic religion. Consider the heroes of the fictional tales, typically their religion is self-made and they act as though they are their own prophet making their own rules to life as if somehow that's okay. Whereas if you use God's criteria, if you were to take all the fictional characters that have ever existed, more than 99.9% of them would burn in hell forever. Yet at the end of a thrilling fictional story how often are you left thinking all the characters will burn in hell forever and are wicked people hated by God? Never, instead one is left sympathetic to these fictional devils and will most likely apply more lessons learned from that fictional story than they will lessons the prophets of God taught. In sum the fiction genre portrays people God labels bad as good so that by being exposed to fiction you begin to believe that those God would hate are good people to learn from or imitate. Basically fiction causes people to sympathize with the forces of Satan and acclimate to a world without God or the prophetic religion. The effect of most fiction being that you waste X hours of your life to get less religious while watching/reading something wherein you don't think of God for a single second. Which if you recall is exactly what Satan wants you to do with your life. So some might claim fiction is just fun, but in reality fiction interrupts one's relationship with God and makes you forget your Creator despite your Creator never forgetting you. While even the rare religiously themed fiction is poision because it justifies the genre and makes people think it's okay to lie which is the exact opposite of what the prophetic religion teaches. The prophetic religion forbids fiction and lying so how then can one possibly teach X religion by doing something X religion says is forbidden? Simply put one can't even if one intended to, and that's why the prophets never promoted fiction. Another reason fiction is destructive is because it is a closed circuit. Learning information from a fictional story will not benefit you in any aspect of life outside of that fictional fantasy. If you read one fictional book from one author and another fictional book from another the previous book does not help you or enhance the 2nd book you read. In comparison every non-fiction book improves your future experiences reading non-fiction books because the information carries over. For example I may read about a certain historical event in a non-fiction book in depth. Next I read another non-fiction book that makes a comment referring to that historical event I read about in the other book. Because I read the first non-fiction book and know about the event the second book mentioned, my understanding of the second book is greatly enhanced and improved as a result. What is even more amazing is that the author of the second book had no idea that I would have such knowledge to be able to benefit in such a way from their brief comment. So by me reading non-fiction books it makes non-fiction books I read in the future more informative and beneficial than they would have been if I had not read the other non-fiction books in the past. Therein lies innumerable benefits that carry over from one book to the next in a never-ending series of non-fiction books. Essentially all non-fiction books belong to the same series and you can read the series in any order you want without being out of the loop. Non-fiction also keeps you in the realm of the real world. Therefore the person is not using books as an escape outlet into a virtual world. The non-fiction consumer is better able to develop mentally, emotionally and spiritually because they are consistently dealing with reality. They are never deluded into pretending life is different than what it is. Thus they can improve themselves and their society because they are familiar with reality and problem solving in the real world. The most powerful people in the world today are readers of non-fiction. Napolean Bonaparte testified to this when he said: "*Show me a family of readers, and I will show you the people who move the world.*" The solutions in fictional stories do not work in the real world, else you would find them in non-fiction. Every book you read should help you become a better person, fiction doesn't help you become a better person no matter what type of fiction it is. As with any investment the reason people read a book is to get some sort of return out of it, or profit. Ideally the return should be beneficial knowledge which helps you achieve your life goals or better equips you towards such achievement. However fiction is usually treated as an escape from reality, or something popular to consume or "study". Although in reality it is much more sinister because every piece of literature is promoting a certain code of morality which influences its reader's thought process and subsequently the morality of society. At best you do not get any reward for spending time on fiction. Yet because that is a waste of the body parts God has given you as well as the time God has given you, spending time on frivolous fiction is actually a bad deed and sin, regardless of what the fiction is about. Whereas most fiction is sinful in subject and content as well. Although as a disclaimer some fiction can be "studied" to see it's effects on the world but this is not for average people to do "for fun", nor for students to do. Whereas that's the problem with schools and most "book clubs", in that they "study fiction" trying to analyze it not realizing it's just something somebody made up that is all a bunch of lies. It doesn't matter if it was Shakespeare, if it's fiction it's filthy garbage no matter how famous it is. Shakespeare is a scoundrel because he is a liar who made things up thus teaching people it was okay and fun to lie. That is the principle lesson of all works of fiction in that they all teach lying is permissible, and at that point they are wrong so one shouldn't even bother listening to anything else they have to say after that. Although Shakespeare is even worse in this regard because he was a plaigarist. The "Romeo and Juliet" story appeared in Arthur Brooke's "*Tragical History of Romeus and Juliet*" in 1562 CE and William Painter's 1567 CE "*Palace of Pleasure*" long before Shakespeare stole the story and published his "*Romeo and Juliet*" play in 1597 CE. Yet Arthur Brooke also stole the story from Masuccio Salernito's "*Mariotto and Ganozza*" published in 1476 CE which Luigi Da Porto published as "Giuletta e Romeo" in 1531 CE and Matteo Bandello, who Shakespeare stole 4 stories from, published an english version before he died in 1562 CE coincidentally the very same year Arthur Brooke published his version of the tale. In summary Shakespeare's Romeo and Juliet tale was published 121 years earlier and by 5 different people before Shakespeare. Shakespeare also stole from others when getting material for his other famous plays. So Shakespeare plaigarized plaigarists and then they say he's the greatest. Do the prestigious english or history teachers even tell students that Shakespeare was a story thief who stole his stories from plaigiarists? No because they don't know the material they teach because they teach a religious government curriculum and not a legitimate academic subject. Seriously most of these teachers with degrees haven't the slightest clue about what they are teaching, when they do they knowingly teach falsehood. They have "Masters degrees in teaching" but they don't know anything worth teaching. So they are a "Master at teaching" but they simply teach whatever they get told. Outside of the "Educational world" they call such people actors and actresses. Regardless, whether it's Shakespeare or someone with more literary dignity it is the epitome of stupidity to discuss fiction in a manner of "What do you think will happen next?" or "What do you think they did/happened to them after that?". I don't even tolerate people seriously discussing fiction around me, because it's too stupid to ignore. I'll interrupt and say *"Are you discussing what fictional characters will do in a nonexistant realm/timeline? Do you realize that those characters do not exist and their stories never happened? Why are you spending your time talking and thinking about characters who don't exist and possible activities that will never ever and could never ever occur? Do you realize none of that movie/tv show/book was real and that stuff did not happen? Why are you talking about nonsense that non-existant characters never did in real life? If you want to discuss fiction why don't you do it in the fictional world? Go back to fantasy land if you want to talk about fantasy, right now you are in reality so please act and think accordingly. Please change the setting on your brain and tongue to "real-life mode". Do you realize that in the real world all those fictional characters are villains trying to suck you out of reality to the poisionous realm of fantasy? Be a real-life hero and fight fiction so the fictional characters don't take over reality. The more attention you pay to fiction the more powerful they become. Those fictional fiends have enslaved you and taken real time from your real life. They feed on your time, thoughts and feelings, it is time to be liberated from them once and for all lest they destroy you and us all. Fight your fiction addiction and conquer it before it conquers you. They aren't real, the stories didn't happen, don't waste your life."* Comedy tends to be an ally of fiction since so much comedy is based upon or involves fiction, so I give comedy a similar treatment as fiction in that if it's not real it's not funny and most comedy today is vulgar or sinful anyways. Now don't mistake this to mean one can't have fun reading, listening or watching things but fiction and most comedy genres are wasteful and destructive to the intellect and morality of it's consumers. The only reason any scholar could ever justify studying fiction is to discern what false religious messages were disseminated by popular fictional tales so that people can be informed where they got their false ideas about religion, life and bad morals from. Fiction is highly influential as well, for example the famous fictional "Christmas Carol" story published by Charles Dickens in 1834 CE described the villain "Scrooge" forcing his employee to work on Christmas. Many today think that's cruel, yet when Dickens wrote that story Christmas was an illegal holiday in America due to Puritan Christians banning it, so everybody worked on Christmas; even the politicians and in some states

Americans would get fined if they celebrated it. However as a result of the popularity of Dickens' fable in the state of Alabama in 1836 CE declared Christmas a legal holiday and other states followed until Oklahoma was the final state to legalize Christmas in 1907 CE. (The Federal Government made it a legal civil holiday in 1870 CE) Thus a fictional story ended up changing Christmas from an illegal holiday to a legal popular one. Now some might think that's good but, whether it's good or bad is irrelevant the point is fiction changes the world and it does so based on lies. It's because of our society tolerating peaceful fiction that we end up killing each other in wars waged due to lies. If the world is to change for the better it has to be changed via telling the truth not by popular fictional falsehood. The ends accomplished by fiction do not justify the means. Falsehood is what made the world a mess in the first place. Fairytales turned the real world into a nightmarish hellhole. Thus while the fiction itself should be ignored, the effects of fiction can be studied so as to learn from the ways fiction influenced us so as to diminish the effects fiction has on the world in the present and future. Consider fiction like drugs, you study the drugs to learn how to rid the world of them but you don't ingest the drugs yourself. Like drugs frequently the fiction addiction blinds the junkie to the negative side effects of fiction, while those who know of the dangers of fiction abstain from it. Whereas studying comedy is a joke because most of the jokes are only funny if you have corrupt morals, so comedy has less of a role on society but is more of a supplement to other things that influence society. Laypeople should ignore fiction so the wicked cycle of lies can stop and scholars can focus of fixing real-world problems. Comedy can be useful to employ if it is done naturally for a good purpose but it's not a hobby or a valid interest. Comedy itself teaches many religious messages more easily because it makes things funny when they could be sinful or not funny. Prophets weren't comedians and not a single companion of a prophet was known to be a funny joker. Prophets didn't hang around people who told lots of jokes because life isn't that funny, making things in life funny all the time is a type of fiction. Comedy can be a gateway to fiction. That's why Satan usually starts with a joke to make you comfortable in life before teaching you to sin and disbelieve. Satan starts with comedy and gets the last laugh when you die as a sinful disbeliever due to laughing through life as if God created you to giggle. God lets you giggle once in awhile when it's appropriate but we are in the middle of a spiritual war against Satan so laughter can't cause us to leave our guard down. Both Fiction and Comedy teach religious doctrines. As an author I hope that through this book you will learn that every book and work teaches a religious message even if they don't claim or intend to do so. Thus any message that comes to you through any way messages are conveyed, fictional or otherwise, virtually or through reality, it is a type of religious propaganda. <u>There is no such thing as a non-religious message.</u> Because even the choice of priority of information to be conveyed and the way it is conveyed involves religious lessons. Morals are a part of religion and religion cannot be removed from communication methods. So whatever it is you are doing or communicating it becomes a religious act teaching a religious message to the world, and any type of entertainment you choose to entertain yourself with is also teaching religious messages to you whether you want them to or not. Hence every joke is religious and has to do with religion, there is no such thing as a non-religious joke. Religion is a integral unavoidable part of life that plays a dominant role in everything at every moment in every person's life. Now you know. Without knowing this one is at risk of the false religions and their evil messages. So as you proceed with life be aware of how religion is in everything and be aware of the fiction that something can be "unreligious" or "just for fun". Thinking everything has to do with religion, is not fanatical, it's factual. Those who think there is something that has nothing to do with religion are simply spiritually unaware and ignorant. The peddlers of fiction are false prophets in disguise. I'm not a prophet but I do teach a religion just the same, it's impossible not to. I'm just letting you know that you reading anything is a religious activity that should help you become a better person. When reading this book your goal should be to be better after reading what I wrote. If you are reading and don't plan to be better after reading, then I strongly suggest you become a better reader who reads better with the goal of getting better as a result of reading what I've written. It can be fun to read, but this is not to be read for entertainment. This book is a form of direct communication from me to you. Consider every book or type of media/entertainment as a type of direct communication and take whatever is true and good and reject whatever is false and bad. Never fall in love with an author. The only books that are flawless are those of divine revelation and the only people who you can trust to be right 100% of the time are legitimate prophets of God. Any book written by anyone else will never be perfect. My book isn't perfect but it might have some good stuff in it that can help you. Books are tools, that can help or harm you, therefore read this book as the prophets would want you to. My goal in writing should be to please our Creator and your goal in reading should be to please our Creator and be a better person after reading my words than you were before reading. Therefore if anything I write in this book is right and good you should read it the right way and react to it the right way. Your intentions reading anything should be to please your Creator. I could try to influence you without telling you "for the greater good" but that's not how the prophets of God operated. The prophets preached to please God, that was their #1 goal. They never pretended they had no motives to influence people to think and act different/better, they all publicly admitted they wanted people to be different after hearing their religious messages of propaganda. Likewise I want you to be different/better after reading. Yet the prophets' #1 goal was NOT to convert people to their faith, they just wanted to please their Creator. When they spoke, wrote, listened or read it was to please the Creator. Why do you speak, write, listen or read?

  In September 2010 CE, while in a college class a person called Terry Jones was being discussed. At the time this person was a Christian Pastor gaining notoriety for his Islamophobic attitude and threats to burn the Quran on September 11th of that year. At the time as a staunch Catholic who hated Islam and Muslims I was in complete agreement with this person and his planned arson. The teacher of the class I was in mentioned how the Pope said the Catholic Church didn't approve of this activity whatsoever and that the Vatican encourages tolerance. This caused a temporary inner conflict. I knew the official Church teachings were entirely intolerant, but publicly because the modern Church is weak and doesn't have the authority to launch any more crusades or inquisitions, the Vatican can't express its true feelings for fear that it could negatively impact the Church or the image of Christianity. They preach tolerance when weak, intolerance when strong. With my rap career giving me a platform, I decided to devote some time to researching Islam in order to expose it as being evil so nobody would be Muslims and would be ready to kill Muslims in the future. I went to a bookstore and bought an English translation of the Quran and would read it in full view of others before class after having visibly prayed the rosary. This would make it appear to people that I was an expert on Islam and since I was praying the rosary (Catholic prayer beads) it would imply that I came to the conclusion that Catholicism was correct after studious analysis. By being seen while reading a translation of the Quran no one could say I was a bigot whose intolerance was unjustified. I would only read it in front of others, so it gave off the appearance of reading a lot but in reality I read very little. My first impression was that the style it was written in was very authoritative as if the author thought they knew it all. Hopefully I don't come across that way. I couldn't tell whether the information inside it was from many scholars or just one super genius. There were some places where it mentioned statements of disbelief people say attempting to justify atheism and the responses that should be given proving the reality of God. Some of these statements were word for word what I had heard from atheist classmates in high school trying to refute me. The verses were so short yet profound that I even shared some of these verses of the Quran translation with "friends" on facebook, even though I was Catholic and hated Muslims. Then I read one of those "violent verses" of the Quran translation and even though I hated Muslims couldn't find anything wrong with it. It had been blatantly taken out of context every time I heard of it before. The same could be done with the Bible to make it look aggressively violent with Luke 19:27 which says Jesus pbuh said: "*27 But those enemies of mine who did not want me to be king over them – bring them here and kill them in front of me.*" Yet how many people are saying to burn the bible claiming it teaches people to kill others? If that was the only verse a non-Christian had ever heard from the bible they might believe the bible promotes forced conversions not realizing it's taken out of context. I had to admit, my prior beliefs about the Quran were unfounded. Another thing that surprised me was that the Quran mentions prophets such as Noah, Abraham, and Moses pbut as prophets and narrates what they did in their lives. Prior to reading that translation I didn't know Muslims believed in those prophets and that they were positively mentioned in the Quran as role models. All I really knew about Islam and Muslims aside from general vaguities and common school teachings was that Muslims thought they believed in "the religion of Abraham" and that was how they identified Muslims from non-Muslims. Thus my plan if I was ever captured by Muslims during a crusade was to tell them that "I believe in the religion of Abraham." so they would think I was one of them and wouldn't kill me for not being Muslim, while secretly I would still remain a Christian in my heart meaning Abraham Lincoln and not whatever Abraham their religion was from, which was definitely not Judaism or Christianity. By reading the little that I did of the Quran translation it equipped me with Islamic vocabulary that could be included in my raps allowing me to say, "*the Quran says such and such*" so that the listener would be under the impression I had read the whole thing and choose Christianity because it had solid evidences in comparison, whereas in actuality all I had read was a few paragraphs. This is a tactic opponents of Islam use to fool people into thinking they are truthful and justified in their intolerance and attacks when in fact they don't really know what they're talking or writing about. News reporters are a perfect example of people sounding like experts who know what they're talking about despite only learning a few sentences about their subject matter. Yet if you listen to them they sound so convincing you'd think they knew intricate details of the events they are reading about from a teleprompter. In reality many of the statements presented during news broadcastings are theoretical with genuine honesty getting discarded in exchange for efforts to appear objective. You can't even trust the mainstream media to tell you the truth about the weather! Sadly most media reports more fiction than fact. This is because the purpose of most media is to excite and inflame passions so people can be manipulated by them or to serve the selfish ends of controlling parties. The illusion of a free press is given by governments seeming to permit criticism by the media but in reality the media is only allowed to critique specific points or positions the government has already predetermined that it would alter. Thus governments use the illusion of a free media to make people think they change according to public opinion when in reality the public opinion is only permitted regarding things the government wants to change anyways. Whereas while the media might not control exactly what we think, they're very successful at determining what we think about, as well as what we talk about. Regarding American news, Tom Fenton who famously worked as a CBS newscaster for 34 years, said: "*Americans are too broadly underinformed to digest nuggets of information that seem to contradict what they know of the world. Instead, news channels prefer to feed Americans a constant stream of simplified information, all of which fits what they already know. That way they don't have to devote more air time or newsprint space to explanations or further investigations... Politicians and the media have conspired to infantilize, to dumb down, the American public. At heart, politicians don't believe that Americans can handle complex truths, and the news media, especially television news, basically agrees.*" While the columnist Brian Reade said "*Americans are wonderfully courteous to strangers, yet indiscriminately shoot kids in schools. They believe they are masters of the world, yet know nothing about what goes on outside their shores. They are people who believe the world stretches from California to Boston and everything outside is the bit they have to bomb to keep the price of oil down. Only one in five Americans hold a passport and the only foreign stories that make their news are floods, famine, and wars, because it makes them feel good to be an American. Feeling good to be American is what they live for.*" But I like Thomas Jefferson's quote about American media the best when he said, "*The advertisements are the most truthful part of a newspaper.*" Jefferson also said, "*The man who reads nothing at all is better educated than the man who reads nothing but newspapers.*" Anyways finding my anti-Islamic distortion successful I put the english translation of the Quran back on the bookshelf. Others distort and destroy, I just distorted.

By the end of 2010 CE I had finished my 3rd album and it was released. It was about the Gregorian calendar year with 12 of the songs being about each month in the year, with some bonus songs about birthdays and my Christian beliefs regarding the end of the world. I tried to put each song about each month into a Christian religious context. For this project I researched the history behind the celebrations that take place each month and learned some very interesting information that the vast majority of people are unaware of. For example I learned why there is a Easter bunny and why it is associated with eggs, as well as the origins of such holidays as Mother's day, Halloween, April Fools and all the rest. The traditions involved with these celebrations were fascinating as well considering their roots and evolution throughout time. It turns out many of these holidays have pagan origins and the modern celebrations that take place on those days have numerous traditions that stem from pagan rituals and beliefs that are rich in symbolism. Some of these I mentioned in my raps, but others that concerned Christian holidays like Valentine's Day, St. Patrick's Day and Christmas I purposely ignored, preferring not to reveal the dark truth behind them. This was yet again another instance of the hypocrisy that plagued my Christian rap career. I would ignore and reject anything I didn't like to learn whether it was true or not. I dismissed information solely on the basis that it didn't agree with what I already believed. May God help us to be humble enough to accept the truth wherever we may find it and whatever it may be, even if it means admitting we had been wrong our entire lives. This is important because God does not love those who deny the truth, and we don't want to be in the category of those God doesn't love.

While in 12th grade in order to become more religious I had started fasting. Fasting is a form of sacrifice done by the prophets pbut which increases one's appreciation for food and develops self-control. It also helps concentration abilities and memory, as well as having numerous health benefits. The way a Christian fasts is by abstaining from all food and all drink for however many days they fast. However a more modern opinion holds that Christians are allowed to drink water and that fasting means to only abstain from food. That's the easier version. Some Christian groups don't practice this at all and others practice it frequently with some reportedly surviving on water alone for 40 days straight. In the past Christians used to fast and abstain from food and drink the entire month of Lent, except for Sundays. Most don't know this but Christians actually used to go without eating from Monday-Saturday for the month of Lent which is 44 days, from Ash Wednesday to Good Friday. So minus 6 Sundays which Christians would eat on, that's 38 days of the year where Christians used to not eat or drink anything; and that's not counting the fasts for "Holy Days". However some classical Christians, there are still a few left, fast the whole 44 days of Lent without taking Sundays off. Wednesdays and Fridays were also days Christians traditionally abstained from eating or drinking anything for a full 24 hours and in the 18th century Methodists even made it a requirement for ordination that all ministers had to fast every Wednesday and Friday. Anyways since I was trying to practice Christianity and reach that level where I could go 44 days without eating or drinking as all Christians allegedly used to do, and which a extreme minority still do and survive, (because the bible says Jesus pbuh did it, and "the power of Christ compels thee to succeed" thus proving Christianity as true) I had to practice fasting for a lot longer than most Christians consider normal, healthy or possible. Whereas it isn't impossible to do because Christians used to fast for that long on a routine basis,(and of course Christian doctrine states through Jesus all things are possible) but they got lazy and started saying *"Well Jesus was Jesus and since we aren't God/son of God we don't really have to fast anymore like he did. He fasted so we don't have to, and while we used to fast that was hard so it was probably wrong to do."* Fundamentally Christians had no legitimate religious excuse to abandon fasting, but most did so just because it was difficult and they stopped practicing their faith. Then they changed it because they didn't want to be known for not fasting as the religion requires. Anyways if Christians tell you they practice Christianity and follow Jesus pbuh then they should be fasting 40+ days without food or drink the way the bible says Jesus pbuh did and the way Christians in the past used to do. It takes practice and I was able to go a few days at a time sometimes and other times less than a day, before giving in and gorging. I'd set tiny goals like 24 hours without food, or from X day to Z day without food and sometimes I could do it and reach my goal while other times my parents would buy me some really tasty food that I couldn't resist or I'd just get too hungry and quit. After 3 days without food the digestive system stops working and the stomach pains are less frequent, with fatigue and hunger becoming the main challenges. I started practicing to fast by fasting from food only and would drink throughout the day. Which technically that is not the "biblical way" another Christian opinion says liquids are permissible and I decided to take the easy opinion when fasting. Although someday I thought I'd try going fully biblical in my fasts, but I was at a beginner level so I figured abstaining from just food was good enough even though it wasn't really the biblical or classical Christian method of fasting. When fasting I'd still go for communion in church but I would just drink the wine and not eat the bread. Which I knew it was dangerous to be drinking wine on a literally empty stomach but I didn't consider the wine to be wine, I believed it to be the "blood of Jesus/God". To not drink the wine thinking it to be unhealthy to drink while fasting because of it being wine would be tantamount to disbelief in Catholicism as well as other types of Christianity. The doctrine of transubstantiation states that the wine is not wine and you aren't a Christian if you think it is wine after the priest says the words which allegedly change it into the blood of Jesus pbuh. So there was never a doubt in my mind the blood would be bad to drink on an empty stomach, in fact I thought it was better to drink the blood of Jesus pbuh when fasting because then you got nothing but Jesus pbuh in you. That belief of mine also led me to eat the bread during communion too because I didn't see the wafer as bread but as the body of Jesus pbuh. It was a spiritual food, not a real piece of food, or while it was a real tangible food I considered the communion bread/wine to be special exceptions to the rule when fasting so I'd eat those when fasting to enhance their spiritual effect on my soul. But you only get a tiny circle of wafer and a few sips of wine per church service, so it wasn't like I was gluttonously gorging myself in church or anything. Anyways the only stuff I'd eat/drink when fasting besides water, juices, soup broth or coffee/hot chocolate was the "body and blood of Christ". For the Gregorian year ending 2010 CE I went without food for 7 consecutive days (not counting the "Body of Christ") from December 24th 2010 CE to January 1st 2011 CE foolishly believing in the superstitions surrounding the Gregorian New Year's celebrations. I thought that fasting from Christmas to New Year's would cause some positive things to happen in my life during the year 2011 CE. Afterwards I became ill and had difficulty digesting food once I reintroduced my body to it. You see that is the trick to fasting in such a manner for such a long period of time, in that you can't just start eating agian, you have to slowly transition to complex solid foods. If one stuffs their face after not eating for a long period of time you can destroy your intestines due to shock and digestive trauma. That's why if you actually give food to starving people, they can die as a result of eating it if it's too complex for them to digest. It has even occurred where stupid philanthropists go to Africa and feed starving children fast-food burgers and they die because the food is not natural and has too many complex artificial ingredients for them to digest or get nutrients from so the starving kids die by eating food because they ate the wrong type of food. Thus if one is starving they have to eat real natural healthy foods, that aren't complex or too acidic or else eating could kill them. You have to feed starving people almost as if they were a baby until their body can recover. I knew that but it was hard to not eat all your favorite extra tasty foods after not eating for 7 days. So while I tried to "eat slow and simple" when my fast ended, I ate too much, too fancy, too fast and got really sick for about a week and ended up getting pills to help me digest food once again. I figured next time I'd just have to control my appetite better so as to not get sick. Now it is clear to me that the Christian way of fasting is unnatural and unhealthy. Yet I wasn't even fasting the way the majority of Christians use to fast in the past. To me I found the "easy loophole" method of Christian fasting to be extremely difficult to do consistently. However to this day I still believe it's possible, it's very hard and probably a little unhealthy but Christians could do it if they tried. Obviously most will never try, much less succeed, but going without food/drink for many days at a time consistently throughout the year is what the bible and Christianity teaches. Just don't expect the preachers to tell you that or practice it. The majority of Christians won't even skip a single meal in their life. They'll complain and pretend to be pious because they abstain from eating meat on Fridays, during Lent only, and it's "really hard to do". Or maybe they "tried" giving up Chocolate or Candy during Lent. Such fasts are jokes. Such "piety" is pitiful. The fasting days of Christians were replaced with feast days. Rather than "go without" they give thanks by getting gluttonous.

Christmas 2010 CE was also the year that proved to me beyond a doubt that Santa Claus was not real. On Christmas Eve there were no presents when I went to sleep and there were no presents after waking up on the 25th of December. Finally after over 18 years I could confidently proclaim to the world that: "*Santa Claus does not exist.*" When I posted my proof on facebook I was shocked to discover people older than me making excuses saying how I must have been bad or whatever, even though according to the myth bad boys get coal from Santa. This revealed that no matter how much proof one may present on behalf of the truth, there will be people who still reject it and willingly choose to believe a lie whilst they know the truth inside. May God protect us from being like such creatures. I say creatures instead of people because a person accepts the truth when they learn it whereas a creature doesn't. Everyone is a creature by default but some of us are more like animals than we are like people while some animals are more like people than they are like creatures. Afterall this is why Noah pbuh brought some animals into the ark with him to survive the flood while some humans were left outside to drown. The flood demonstrates that people who reject the truth when it comes to them are worse than animals and that's why God instructed Noah pbuh to rescue the animals from the flood and let those who rejected the truth drown in their disbelief figuratively and literally. While Noah pbuh didn't openly tell them they were worse than animals, as far as I know, they found out what their status was with God eventually; as we all will. Maybe you think me writing this is harsh or extreme but consider there are humans who believe in Santa Claus, however there is not one animal on the planet who believes in Santa Claus; not even reindeers. Both humans and animals have rights, yet some of these humans who are worse than animals violate the rights of animals whereas the animals never violate the rights of humans. Yet what's even worse than this humanistic behavior that's worse than animalistic behavior is how some humans treat animals in comparison to humans. For instance there are millions of humans who are ill, poor, starving, homeless and in dire need of material assistance. What does the splendid human species do to help their own kind? Why they get pets of course and decide to welcome animals into their homes and care for cats, dogs, fish, rodents, insects, reptiles, birds and other kinds of beasts while the humans in need are left neglected. Consider that we have a world where there are homeless humans while simultaneously we have animal shelters and animal furniture. We have animal hospitals and animal medicines yet deny to give dignity to our own species. We spend millions to build zoos to look at animals we stole from their natural habitats, meanwhile humans have no place to take cover from the rain, shelter from the sun nor can they find a safe place to sleep much less something edible to eat. Us humans are stealing animals by force locking them up in prisons just to satisfy our curiosity, while we are forcing humans to go try surviving amongst the animals in the wild because nobody cares about them. People die because they have no clothes to wear, while other "people" buy clothes for their animals to wear. We have animal shows performed in aquariums, theme parks, at circuses, in movies, on tv and in plays yet when someone presents statistics on the amount of needy humans in the world the animal lovers say, *"Don't show me. Don't tell me."* Consider the animal industry with all the pet shops and the accessories, or even the sinful animal games such as horse racing , dog racing or the cruel animal fights that take place. Oh and don't forget the hunters and all the money they spend seeking out animals to kill, for fun, or food because they like the taste of what they kill. There are people who will live with a filthy dog, the saliva of which is one of the most unhealthy germ-ridden things a human can encounter, so much so that human sperm is actually cleaner for a human to come in contact with than a dog's saliva. But how many in the world would prefer to have a bunch of strangers' sperm touch them instead of 1 dog's saliva? Of course some perverts might, but a dog's saliva is actually dirtier than human ejaculate. Dog urine is even cleaner than dog saliva. While despite the health risk of just living with a canine, this human is willing to get up early in the morning to walk their dog an hour every day rain, snow or sleet picking up its feces whenever and wherever it poops and clean up its urine stains when it pees in their house, while giving their dog bathes, playing with it and keeping it fed with the most nutritious food, even letting it's filthy tongue slobber all over them and their stuff. Yet those same people won't give even an hour a month to help a human in need, or to give them bathing supplies or scraps of food or clothing; or even pay them 5 minutes of attention so that they could vent their problems and worries. People say they love their pets but at what price? What are the benefits of owning a animal when compared with helping a human? Tell me what do you think the prophets would do and advise people in the animal industry as well as pet owners to do? People love to say they follow the prophets and take them as role models in their life. Well what would those prophets tell pet owners and animal lovers to do when there are millions of people in need? I'm not against all types of pet ownership, just certain pets, but in principle which is more important helping humans or having a pet? Why do humans let humans suffer while they pay to take care of animals? If even less than a quarter of the pet owners were to live without pets and spend their budget for pet money to rectify the affairs of needy humans then we wouldn't have needy humans. It's actually disgusting when you consider the time, effort and money people spend to see, touch and interact with animals while at the same time members of our own species are begging and praying for anyone to help them in any way they can. Which do you think will benefit you more on the Day of Judgment, the animal you pampered or the needy human you helped? We have people adopting pets and abandoning orphans. Instead of humanitarians we have animaltarians, and what's worse is that they're proud of it. Some of them even publicly boast of themselves being a dog person or a cat person, but in reality they don't even deserve to be called a person. No animal would abandon it's own species in order to entertain itself with a human companion. As dirty as the dog may be, it's a very honorable beast when compared to many humans I see. That's including some of the humans I see whom a dog has on a leash leading them around for everyone to see the dog forcing the human to follow them and pick up their feces which they then carry with them for the rest of the time the dog walks the human around the block. The sad thing is that such members of the human species take pride in this walk of subordinate shame that reveals their complete lack of concern for their own species and their devotion to a mere animal who doesn't even have freewill. To be fair I will admit that the dog is probably innocent of leashing the human and is likely embarrassed by its human slave, but for many such dog walkers who follow their leashed dog they themselves have a leash on their neck with Satan leading them in front of their dog. Satan is walking many of these dog walkers, along with most dog owners and all the dog co-habitors. I've even seen some walking dogs through snow in winter, before the sun rises. Seriously before it is even time for the "early morning" Islamic prayer, I've seen people walking their dogs through the snow in the dark. People say it's a dog eat dog world, but dogs don't eat dogs. It's really just some humans who treat animals, like dogs, better than their fellow humans and knowing that they don't deserve the title of "human" such people labeled the society as a dog eat dog society thereby slandering the noble yet dirty dog. Or they'll say they're stuck in the "rat race" thereby insulting rats by implying rats live how they live and desire what they desire. I must issue a disclaimer and make it clear that owning a dog is not sinful, but living with a dog is. If you have a dog, get them a dog house they don't belong in a human house! I say this because it is known that the angels of mercy don't enter houses which have dogs or pictures of animate beings. So if the angels of mercy don't enter your house then how can you expect mercy from God? Who will deliver the mercy and blessings to your household? The dog? The pictures? Thus dog co-habitors and picture collectors end up choosing those things as companions rather than the angels of mercy. Yet it doesn't stop there some "humans" even stop having sex the human way and do it "doggy style" or even love animals so much they have sex with animals. In 2005 CE a man in Washington even died in a hospital because of a ruptured colon after being sodomized by a horse at an "animal brothel". Oh yes, in America bestiality is legal and a right according to the U.S. Constitution. It's only recently that some states, 37 out of 50 or 74%, have limited how far one can legally sexually go with an animal. Prior to that people and animals were having sex in America, with 8.3 % of men admitting to having sexual relations with animals as of 1948 CE and 3.6% of women having done the same as of 1953 CE. Yet now that sodomy has become legal, beastiality is soon to follow. Afterall many american states also banned sodomite marriage and all those laws were overturned because they were unconstitutional as are the laws banning bestiality/zoophilia. That's crazy! (or freedom) I mean Sodom was destroyed for doing it "doggy style" with humans of the same gender, so what do you think

God thinks about those who do that with their wives, or people they aren't married to, or God forbid do it "animal style" with the animals themselves? Even with it against the law people still do it, like the Green Beret special forces American soldier from Fort Bragg who filmed pornographic videos showing himself and his wife having sex with their dogs and cats. Another guy in Cambodia has so much passion for his dog that he prefers sleeping in bed with his dog over his human wife, so she divorced him because he preferred to sleep with his dog instead of her and it wasn't even sexual. The guy loved to sleep with his dog so much he chose to get divorced from his human wife so he could sleep next to his dog. Whereas while most of us would say that guy is crazy, pet owners prefer to spend money on their pets rather than spend it on needy humans so what is the difference? Just the way some humans act is enough to disprove the false theory that humans evolved from animals because many are acting much worse than the beasts. It's not just pet owners either. As a species we have starving people while at the same time we spend millions to create, promote and consume pills designed to extend the time penile erections last. We spend billions on researching sleep, making pills to induce sleep or products to prevent sleep, meanwhile millions of humans have no place to sleep. What kind of species is this? Would you sell your infant's crib and kick them out into the gutter in order to buy a sleeping pill? Well humanity has done this, but since they don't hear those babies cry and die they don't care and think they are good people who God loves. Maybe all these health issues exist because the bodies of extravagant humans know they are bad people and are trying to punish them into doing what's right, yet unfortunately it tends to make such beings more selfish and miserly. In conclusion regarding human rights and "civilized behavior" many people could learn a lot from animals. Animals may lie in filth but they don't tell filthy lies. Some animals may be classified as shellfish but none are classified as selfish. If we reject the truth when we know it then we are worse than the dung beetles, skunks, maggots, flies and swine. Some of the animals may naturally be too loud but none of the animals are intellectually or spiritually too proud. It makes perfect since that no gnats are arrogant but it doesn't make any sense for humans not to be humble. Worms are sincere and humble to accept the facts of life above and below the ground, as human life forms we should accept the facts before we join the worms underground in our afterlife. Afterall our afterlife is longer than our present life. If you don't believe me just check the dates on the graves of dead people. Most of them have been dead for longer than they've been alive. How much time did they spend preparing to live in their grave? Since you are going to the same destination then you deserve to be asked the same question, since you will indeed be asked the same 3 questions as they were. How much time have you spent preparing for your life in the grave and afterlife? Is that enough?

TIME

Nearly all who believe in a God agree that it's important to thank God for what he has given you but what does it mean to thank God? Let's consider a real life example. A child is given a gift by an adult. In scenario A the child responds by saying *"Oh...everyone has one of these, it's about time I got one. What took you so long in getting me one?"* Now would we consider this an expression of gratitude? Yet many people treat the gifts God gives them in this way. In scenario B the child responds by saying "thank you" but this gift is a one of the kind gift that is extremely expensive to the extent that a simple "thanks" is actually offensive and the adult asks the child *"I went through all that trouble to get you this and all you say is "thanks"? Do you know how valuable that is? Do you know how millions of others would've reacted if I gave it to them instead of you? All you have to say is "thanks"?!"* In scenario C the child reacts by completely ignoring the gift after opening it and asking *"What else are you giving me?"* Would we consider this gratitude? Yet how many of us act this way with God's gifts he's already given to us, such as life itself. In scenario D the child opens a gift which was extremely expensive custom made and custom wrapped with care and love taking hours and hours of time to perfect, so the child would thoroughly enjoy everything about it and it would benefit them all throughout their life, every single day. What does the child do? They open it up, spray graffiti on it, pour acid on it, light it on fire, urinate and defecate on it, then smash it to bits with a hammer and throw it in the garbage. Would we consider this gratitude? What do you think the adult would do to that kid after they see them react to their gift like that? Do you think they'll be getting a gift next year? Yet this is what people do when they alter their body, take drugs, fill it with junk or sinful food/drink, abuse it in destructive manners intentionally or through sinful lifestyles/habits and then some even kill themselves. Even one of such sins which harm oneself would be tantamount to doing this to a gift one has given you. So why don't we value our life or our time or any of the other things God has given us as we do a gift given by a lesser being that is worth much less? In scenario E the child loves the gift and thinks it's the best thing ever. So do you know what they do? They immediately run past the adult who gave them the gift, go outside and give a big hug to the stray street dog and say: *"Oh you're best doG ever! I love you doG, I'll do whatever you want doG, for the rest of my life I will love you will all my heart mind and soul thank you so much doG! You know what doG, I can tell you love me too, because you gave me such a great gift and everything in my life I owe to you doG. Not only am I going to love you and thank you forever, I'm going to tell everyone on the planet that they should thank you too for the gifts you gave them and tell them how you will give them the same gift you gave me and more if they thank you the way I am. Oh doG no matter what anyone says I'll never stop giving you my love and thanks or trying to get others to thank you for the gifts you gave me and them because I know that's what you want and will please you and after having received such a great gift it's the least I could do in return."* Now what do you think the adult who gave the kid this great gift will think of this kid and feel towards them? Clearly this is the worst type of reaction the kid could have and it will result in the most anger towards the child as possible by the true giftgiver, especially since they use the gift given to them to help them in thanking the doG. Such a child would be hated by the giftgiver and the giftgiver would be severely offended until the kid were to apologize and then give the giftgiver the appropriate thanks due to him and renounce that undeserving doG they had attached themselves so devotedly to. This scenario is exactly like what a human does when they pick the wrong religion. They think they are thanking God and doing what God wants and pleases God but they basically confused God with a severely inferior doG. The doG is a false God. Whereas some might go and thank many doGs instead of just one. Or some may say "*I know that God is the giftgiver but this doG is his only begotten son and I know he wants me to thank this doG just as much if not more.*" Some even will say "*I know God is the giftgiver but God turned into a doG so thanking the doG is the same thing as thanking God, especially since people told me the doG said to worship God only.*" Then we have scenario F where after getting told by their parents "*What do you say when someone gives you a gift?*" the child says "THANK YOU" then the parents say "*Now go give them a hug*" and the child slowly walks over and gives the giftgiver a feeble hug. Would we consider this gratitude? Yet isn't this the same attitude we take with religion, in waiting for religious people to tell us how to thank God and then begrudgingly giving a lazy half-hearted effort? So you see even if we give thanks for the gift the sincerity and enthusiasm plays a big role in whether it is truly gratitude or not. Yet in all these scenarios one mistake is common throughout them all. The mistake is that the kid doesn't know what an appropriate amount of thanks is due for the gift that they've been given. Therefore how can one ever thank God if you don't know how God expects you to thank him? This is why God sent books and prophets to instruct us on how to thank God for the gifts God has already given us in order for us to display proper gratitude and so that we will receive future gifts in the future. That is the other thing common to all the scenarios, in that no matter what the one given gifts does they will either earn more favor in the view of the gift giver, which will result in future gifts being given, or they will incur anger or hurt feelings which may result in less gifts in the future, or it may even result in punitive measures being taken against the very party who was given the gift of life in the first place. Thus saying "thank you" may not be enough gratitude, likewise giving a hug may not be enough gratitude. The human's personal opinion of what is grateful enough has nothing to do with the reality of what truly is grateful enough. The giftgiver, God is the one who tells us how, when, in what way and how often to thank God for the gifts we have received already and those given to us every single second that passes, of which the very seconds themselves are gifts which deserve a show of appreciation. So if you want to thank God properly you have to follow the protocol God gave you through the prophets. You don't compare yourself with everyone else who got a gift and say, well I'm more thankful than the other kids who got a gift. Other folks don't matter, your gratitude is between you and God. You don't have the authority to say whether you've thanked God properly or enough. The one who receives the gifts doesn't make the rules for giving thanks. Just imagine if some kid came up to you and said, "*I want you to know I like the gift you gave me, but this is how I show appreciation and I say how I show gratitude is good enough so if you don't think it is then that's too bad because that's all the thanks your getting. I'm busy with the gift of life you know. I'm too busy enjoying it and using it to say thanks any more or in a better way. Afterall if I was supposed to or expected to thank you differently than I am then you wouldn't have given me the gift that you gave me, surely you understand that me using this gift you gave me prevents me from thanking you any more than I already have. In fact I'm actually expecting better gifts from you in the short term and long term and can't understand what's taking so long for you to give them to me."* Obviously nobody would consider this to be gratitude, in fact we'd probably say that kid is looking for trouble and should expect punishment instead of gifts. Yet sadly many people have this attitude towards God and religion, thinking that they are too busy with the gift of life to pray the way God says to, where God says to, the times God says to and that it just doesn't seem realistic that they'd have to use their gift of life in a different manner than they have been in order to properly thank God. Just think from a logical point of view if you gave someone a free cellphone and paid for all they use it for and then they said they are too busy using their phone for business or entertainment to talk to you X times a day. They say: *"Thanks for the cellphone and all, it's great I really love it, I don't know how I'd live without it. But I'm just too busy using it to survive and thrive and enjoy myself to use it to communicate with you X times a day. I mean I have friends, co-workers, employees, bosses, customers and family which I use it to talk to. So obviously using the phone you gave me for free, and still pay for me to use, to communicate X times a day with you is too hard and unrealistic for you to expect of me. I mean seriously who do you think you are to tell me what to do with MY cellphone? Also who do you think you are to tell me what I can do with MY phone such as what I can look at, who I can talk to, when I can use it and what I can do with it? Who are you to tell ME and restrict what I can and can't do with MY cellphone?!"* We could draw the same lesson with any other product whether it's a computer, vehicle or whatever. If someone gave us a mansion and a trillion dollars for free and said *"I just want you to stop by my house to communicate with me for a few minutes a few times each day"*. Who in their right mind would say they're too busy and that demand is unreasonable? Although God hasn't given us just one thing for free, God has given us everything in our life for free and the stuff God has given you is priceless and worth much more than trillions of dollars and anything else imaginable. Literally God has given you so much that it's impossible to even make a list of 1% of the stuff God has given you. Forget about getting a cellphone from God, you got every single cell in your body from God and every single cell in the Universe! God not only gave us this life for free but he maintains our life and is the reason we are able to use it and everything we've ever experienced or can experience in this universe. Therefore when God sends a book and a prophet to tell us *"This is what God expects from you to show gratitude for your life and these are the rules to follow. Whereas if you follow these rules you will get upgrades and a better eternal life and if you don't you will get downgraded and punished, possibly for eternity."* Nobody and I mean nobody at all has the right to complain or say anything in rebuttal. You like life that's good, there are rules and consequences with associated rewards and punishments. You don't like life, well that's too bad because you got it, because it's best for you to have it, and there are rules and consequences with associated rewards and punishment. You can either complain/refuse to follow the rules and eventually get punished, or submit and utilize life within the appropriate limits that have been set and get rewarded for it with a reward you are guaranteed to enjoy beyond your wildest dreams. So if you don't like life as it is then you have incentive to obey because it'll only get worse if you don't and if you obey you will like it. Whereas if you do like life then you have even more incentive to submit because you already are enjoying yourself and don't want it to get worse, nor do you want to miss out on the opportunity of eternal paradise. It's about time we got serious in showing gratitude to God the way he deserves, not as we think he deserves but in the way that he has informed us to do so. To "thank God" in any way he hasn't legislated for us isn't showing gratitude but is actually insulting. Just as certain gifts require a certain minimum amount of time and enthusiasm devoted to expressing gratitude, our God-given life deserves at the minimum for us to show gratitude wholeheartedly for the rest of our life. Although just how much time is enough to show gratitude to God? The Creator has given us countless gifts and there is nothing we can truly give back to the Creator as a way to reciprocate because he provided everything there is for us, from our wealth to our body even the time we use. If we didn't have time none of the other gifts would be of any use to us. Some say time is money, because Benjamin Franklin said that in 1748 CE, thinking it to be true because many are paid according to how much time they spend working. Although if that were true then money would be exchangeable with time and people would be able to "buy time" and increase the time they have to live, extend the time they have with family or get more time before a deadline. Time is not money. Time is much more valuable than money. To this day it is difficult for people to define time without saying how to measure the passage of time or the word time itself. But it's simple to define what time is. Time is a creature created by God and like all creatures it will die. This is what is meant by the "*end of time*" it is essentially the death of time. One purpose the creature known as time has is to be a measure of life, we were born in time, we live in time and we will die in time. There is no such thing as "free time", but there is such a thing as wasting time. If we are wasting our time then we are wasting our life. With every second that passes our lifespan is reduced brining us closer to the day we will be brought to account for every second. If you waste time then you are committing suicide. Now that the importance of time is established let's examine the most important thing we can do with our time, worshipping God thus expressing our gratitude. How much time do we devote to the Creator of time?

    Many people who consider themselves righteous may go to their place of worship once a week. Anyone who goes more than this tends to be either the spiritual leader, a person with lots of time to spare, or they're considered to be extremely religious. However, many people only go once or twice on holidays, unless there is a wedding, funeral or some other social event that obliges them to enter a place of worship. Let's break this down, there are 24 hours in a day, with 7 days in a week and in the Gregorian calendar 365 days a year with roughly 52 weeks. We'll be generous and credit the weekly worshippers with 55 hours, even though once a week only equals 52 hours. 24 hours a day X 7 days in a week = 168 hours in a week. Let's say our weekly worshipper went twice this week for 2 hours, because it was a holiday or there was a special reason to go, divided by 168 hours a week means they would've spent 1.19% of the week "worshipping". Maybe next week they only go to worship for 1 hour, that would mean they spent 0.59% of the week "worshipping". That is if they weren't sleeping through the service, thinking of the people around them, the sports game, financial worries or whatever else they might have been distracted by. Over the course of the year maybe they go to a few funerals, weddings, religious ceremonies, when a relative gets sick, or before a job interview and somehow get 55 hours. Again we're being generous with this number because these types are more likely to go less than 52 hours a year than more. 52 weeks of 168 hours = 8736 hours in one Gregorian calendar year, divided by 55 hours would mean they spent 0.6% of the year "worshipping" and realistically very few spend 55 hours in a place of worship a year. Now let's compare this with another activity everyone does, urinating and defecating. Again we'll be generous, let's say you spend an average of 15 minutes a day relieving yourself on the toilet, it would equal 91 hours or 1.04% of the Gregorian calendar year. So that means people who go to worship an hour every week and then some extra hours throughout the year are spending more time peeing and pooping than they are "worshipping". We could extend these projections to last a person's lifetime but I think you get the point. Even if that person is following the true religion correctly do you really think a person who spends less than 1% of their time in life on religion is going to be rewarded with unimaginable bliss in paradise getting happier and happier and happier without end? Without end is incomprehensible to us, we know what one million means or one trillion, but even those numbers we can't imagine in year form. Paradise is not just for one million or trillion years it is for infinity, we cannot comprehend infinity time. Some people think they can devote 0.6% of their time towards the afterlife with 99.4% for this worldly life and expect that when this worldly life, that took so much of their time to get so little, ends they will be rewarded for infinity because they gave 0.6% of their time for the afterlife. Such an idea is preposterous! What would an employer say to an employee who only worked less than 1% of the time they were on the clock? Maybe the employer would say something like "YOU'RE FIRED!" so why would God reward such a person who cares so little about worshipping him with eternal paradise? There are angels who spend their entire existence worshipping God until the end of time and at the end they will say how they didn't worship God enough. They're spending 100% of their time perfectly worshipping with sinless lives much longer than our own and we expect them to be our servants in paradise after spending less than 1% of our life "worshipping"? Do you really want to be someone who spends more time pooping than praying and be judged by God having that as your reputation? Do you think because you're spending more time than everyone else you know that it is some kind of excuse or that there is a big difference between 0% and 0.6%? This is like being in a sinking ship and then seeing another sinking ship and saying, "*Well at least that ship is sinking faster than mine*". If you got a problem, you got a problem; everyone else's problems have nothing to do with your problems and will not make your problem any less severe or bad. Less than 1% is less than 1% any way you look at it. Imagine if your wife or husband gave you less than 1% of their time, how would that make you feel? What is even more boggling than the false sense of security people have is that weekly worshippers oftentimes think they are qualified to speak about religion as if they're an expert on the subject. If such people are experts on religion then they must be masters of the toilet. How can they be so sure what the true religion is when they invest so little time into studying the matter? Although there is another calculation for the sports fan. Since I'm American and the American NFL has the least amount of games in a season out of the other popular professional sports we will examine how much time a "non-fanatic fan" watches their NFL. In the regular season there are 16 games and each game lasts about 3 hours. So if someone only watches their favorite team or the local team play all their games then that's 48 hours of time spent watching, just 1 team play 1 game a week. Then if say the person watches 1 game in each playoff round, either because it's their team or they pick a team for the playoffs or "just for fun to watch 1 game on the weekend", that adds 4 games or 12 hours. So watching 1 American football game a week, ending after the championship amounts to 51 hours a year, and that doesn't count the 3 hour pro-bowl or watching anything in preseason. Nor does that count watching any seconds of any other games throughout the season. Keep in mind NFL games are played and can be watched live on sundays for about 11 hours straight, then there is a 3 hour game on mondays, and sometimes thursdays (2 Thursday games on thanksgiving) and some games are on Saturdays. But I'm just counting watching 1 game a week on sunday adds up to 51 hours, remember the weekly churchgoer spends 52 hours a year in church. So if a christian is religious for going to church every sunday then what can we say of the one who watches just 1 game of football a week from September to the end of January? Also keep in mind such a 51 hour investment is not considered to make someone a real fan in the eyes of most fans. Because the real fan discusses the games, watches pre-game and post-game analysis, watches highlights, reads articles, follows off-season news, follows injuries and rival teams and keeps track of the rest of the league and commonly thinks about the team/sport and of course it takes time to travel to watch the games in question or prepare for the rituals of watching. Note those 51 hours are solely just the act of watching on TV, and don't include time spent outside of the duration of a game whether that is traveling to a stadium or talking/thinking about the sports with others. The amount of hours sports fans actually spend on sports is incalculable, this calculation is just for the one who "occassionally watches 1 game a week" and only 1 game; nothing else. Clearly when compared with time spent on religion the "non-fanatical fan" who is considered normal and moderate is spending more time on sports than God and religion. Yet how many people only watch/discuss 1 sport? Also keep in mind these 51 hours is just with the NFL, the NHL, NBA, MLB, MLS, PGA, WWE, NASCAR, Bowling, Boxing, Tennis, Hunting, Fishing, Horse racing, Dog racing, Bullfighting and other sports all have longer seasons, longer matches and more matches in a year. And that is just a sample of the "professional sports", not counting college sports, kids sports or worst of all the olympics. To go along with that, they got sport videogames and movies too. There are even 24 hour sports tv stations where all the shows are about sports related topics. When one really does the math it's easy to classify sports fans as belonging to religions because they are truly spending more time on sports than religion and that's if they are a "very religious type" who worships 1 hour a week. Sadly these sports teams have become the idols of many and they consume so much of the time which God has given us. Such sports entusiasts will claim to be religious and they're right, they watch, play, discuss and think about sports religiously. Watching sports "occasionally" is not healthy physically or spiritually and is a gregarious waste of your time, mind and life. Most of the time invested in sports amounts to points being scored by Satan as the precious time left before our test of life ends decreases. On the test of life there are no breaks or "time outs" every second counts. The average man will spend 3 years of their life on the toilet. In comparison to the toilet the average person will spend 10 years of their life watching Television. Now lets break down the 24 hour day. Lets say you work 8 hours a day(everyday of the week), then transportation takes up 1 hour, then eating/cleaning etc takes up 1 hour, then lets say sleeping takes 8 hours, that person still has 6 hours of free time every single work day. What are they doing with it? That 6 hours a day, amounts to 42 hours a week, or 2,184 hours every Gregorian year; and keep in mind that's if they are working 8 hours every day and sleeping 8 hours every day which most likely is not the case. So for those who say they're too busy working to spend time on religion, it's just plain false, they do have the time they just don't want to be grateful to God for all that he has given them in their life and use lack of time as a pathetic excuse. Well God knows the time people really have and how much time they waste so while people may try to fool other people and may even succeed in convincing people they "don't have the time", that excuse doesn't work on God. In fact God will specifically ask people what they did with their time on the Day of Judgement so for those who think time will be an excuse their time will actually be used as evidence against them. Someone who works 8 hours every single day and sleeps 8 hours every single day will still have well over 2000+ hours of free time every year where they aren't working, eating or sleeping. So what are they doing with that time? What are they doing with their life? What will they have on their time sheet when they are called by God to account for every second they were given in life? Will they come with a lifetime of TV, Music, Movies, Games, Sports, Chatting, Day-Dreaming, Entertainment, "Relaxation", Internet, Emails, News, Masturbation and any other kind of nonsense people waste their life with? How will such a person who works, sleeps and plays their whole life even be able to face God almighty? Imagine if God told them: *"You slept X hours a day so you could work X hours a day so you could play X hours a day. Sadly you didn't think it was too important to spend time for religion on earth. You had the time and choose not to care about me to please me with it. So likewise now for eternity I have the time and ability to please you but I will choose not to, so you can see how it feels, for eternity. I gave you all the time you ever had. All the rest of these people in paradise were given time just as I gave you, in fact I gave many of them far less time than I gave you and they all made great use of it pleasing me and even enjoyed doing so. Thus I love them and give them much much more forever and ever and ever beyond imagination. Whereas you couldn't even appropriately use the gift of time I gave you. So since you "didn't have time" to use my gift of time then I'm not going to waste any more gifts on you. But what's even worse is that you read a book which told you how valuable time was and what you should do with it, so you really have none to blame but yourself. You can't even pretend to be surprised by this wretched outcome. If you thought time was money then financially you blew your life savings before the afterlife even started. But you didn't just waste your lifetime, you malinvested your time doing bad deeds and avoiding good deeds. So now it's time to pay the price for malinvesting the time I generously gave you. Whereas since the time I gave you was priceless, you will never finish paying the price in hell."* Surely Satan has misled many distracting us from our purpose, may God guide us to the straight path and help us to make religion our top priority in life. Some have a mentality of *"Work hard, Play harder, Pray hardly"*; they are called losers and hated by God. Afterall Satan isn't trying to get us to disobey and disbelieve in God only once a year, or once a month, or once a week, or once a day, or 0.6% of the time. Satan is working against us 100% of the time to make us misuse our time. If we only devote 0.6% of our time to God then Satan has nearly achieved a total victory. The least we can do is to spend more of our time on religion than we do on the toilet or the visual recycling toilet, known as television. Whereas the internet or "web" are traps which Satan can utilize to snare us in nets and webs to consume our precious commodity of time. For instance some people get a dream from Satan telling them they don't have to pray and God will still love them and they believe it. When you then tell them all the prophets prayed and told everyone else to pray daily, they say they got a dream so they don't have to, and God is okay with it because they got a dream. Now you and me can probably agree such people are stupid idiots being misled by Satan. However such vivid demonic dreams wherein Satan sells sin and negligence to us are not always nocturnal, one is called "The American Dream". Always remember God gave you every single second of your life and expects you to do something important with every second, there are no free seconds God gave you to waste or to do sins with. Any hardship you face doing good deeds will pass. Any temptation you face to do bad deeds will pass. The time will pass but the deeds will remain. Time has rights and if you abuse time then time itself will label you as an oppressive tyrant who used it for evil/wasteful things and time the creature will demand that God punishes you for abusing it, and justice will be served. Your time will either testify for you or against you on the Day of Judgment, but it will testify as to every second of it you used/abused. So fulfill the rights of time. Trade your time for good deeds and you will be successful for eternity. If God judged you based solely on what you were doing for the next 10 seconds would you be willing to stake your eternal destination on it? There are only 2 destinations, paradise and hellfire. If you don't want to spend any seconds in the second place then invest all the seconds you have to please God and you will have an infinite amount of time in paradise. The time you have now will either be invested for a share in paradise, expire and be wasted in this life, or mal-invested for a debt that will have to be paid off in the afterlife. Thousands of people will have had their souls extracted by the angel of death by the time you finish reading this. It's almost time for your appointment with God. Prepare for it every second because in a few seconds God, the Creator of time, will ask what you did with the seconds God gave you.

AGES 19-20

      Most of the people I went to high school with had little contact with me by this time aside from an occasional facebook interaction. The few "friends" I had were kept for the purpose of anticipated usefulness in assisting my rap career. In a similar manner to how I witnessed people change before when placed in new environments, after they went to college I noticed a change within my "friends". Once I was over a "friend's" house watching sports. All 4 of the people there had been on good terms with me in high school, it was supposed to be a nice reunion. Suddenly one of them poured some white cocaine powder on a glass table and snorted it up his nose directly in front of me. I had never been so close to cocaine before in my life and was mentally freaking out that everyone was so casual about it. I'm thinking *"That's cocaine! RUN!"* as if a ticking time bomb had been placed on the table, but everyone else was calm and collective as if the cocaine was chip dip. The person sitting on my left said he had never tried cocaine and asked how to do it, then snorted it up his nose just like the first guy. At the time, this second person was attending an Ivy League school with his tuition paid for in full by the university. He always had grades much higher than mine so I was surprised he'd be so stupid as to do cocaine. When offered to try I declined and advised them they shouldn't do that because it wasn't their house and it might mess up the glass table, but that was not a sufficient deterrent for them and they didn't care if it was a sin. Then we started debating morality, just like in high school, with the first cocaine consumer bragging to me about how he had sex with his girlfriend over 100 times without her getting pregnant. I had experience talking to him about sex before so I knew saying it was sinful was futile. I told him that he might have some kind of health defect with his reproductive system because I don't think it's normal to have sex over 100 times without a pregnancy, there might be something wrong. I advised him to get his reproductive organ medically examined because he might be sterile or infertile since he had a 0% pregnancy rate. He was speechless and didn't know what to say, then he went in the other room telling someone what I said, finally coming back and saying that it's actually not a failure because he doesn't want to have a pregnancy so he is successful in his attempts of prevention. I asked him why he was having sex then if he's so afraid of a pregnancy, isn't that something to be expected when having intercourse? Even the sexification programs in school taught us that's how babies were made. Why would he plant the seed so many times if he didn't want it to grow? If having excessive sex made him happy why did he need to do cocaine? The "High Life" didn't seem to be anything at all like what it was cracked up to be.

      That night my "friends" left the house at halftime wanting to go buy cigarettes taking me in the car with them while smoking on the way, ignoring my complaints about the difficulty I had breathing as a result of their smoking. Instead of returning to watch the game as I wanted, they were interested in buying marijuana and took me along to meet the dealer. They didn't care about my protests or endangering my reputation, possibly disqualifying me from the priesthood or causing a scandal when I became Pope. Fortunately that dealer was out of stock and they finally went back to the house. Yet they still had the craving to get high(er) and still wanted to buy marijuana from someone else. The guy with over 100 nights of sex asked me to take him and the other who had done cocaine to the meeting place in my own car. I refused explaining my reluctance to help someone to do something I believe to be wrong, he said he understood. Then I decided to go home and missed watching the game.

    This wasn't an isolated incident, even the friends who weren't "bad" in high school had degenerated afterwards. I knew blue collar drug dealers and white collar drug dealers. It seemed like everyone I knew from high school was involving themselves in some serious wrongdoing, with the best amongst them being fornicators, or at the least unashamed masturbators who dreamed of being fornicators. It became apparent that the removal of parental and high school discipline resulted with them revealing their true immoral character since they thought they were finally old enough to do what they wanted without reprisal. The only thing stopping them from acting immorally before was constant adult supervision, now they were drowning in sin and I didn't want to get wet. For the first time in their life they were able to fully enjoy the freedom which Americans cherish and they gladly took full advantage of it. They didn't realize God is constantly aware of what we do and how there are angels assigned to every individual writing down all their deeds keeping a record. We will be brought to account for everything written in our book of deeds and will have to review each and every action before our Creator with the rest of humanity being privy to our most secret sins. What happens in Vegas doesn't stay in Vegas, both our good deeds and our bad deeds will factor into our final result on the test of life affecting our eternal abode in the afterlife. May God make us one of the few who are given a private audience on the Day of Judgment and treated with mercy and not wrath.

    The events of that night made me reexamine what my life had become and the crowd I was involved with. Here I was, someone who wanted to become a priest doing Christian rap on the side with aspirations to become the Pope, spending the nights with fornicators watching them do cocaine and riding along for drug deals. The people I was "friends" with were not on the same path I wanted to be on and it seemed as though there were irreconcilable differences between our lifestyles. It dawned on me that these people didn't really offer me anything beneficial other than being able to brag that "*I have friends*". It became clear to me that it was better to have no friends than to have bad friends. Not bad friends in the sense of "*they never call me*" or "*I always have to pay when we go out*" I mean friends that have a bad influence or character. For instance if someone insults you or makes fun of you then they are not your friend, even if they do it jokingly or teasingly, that is a bully not your friend. Sadly many people today only have bullies which they consider to be friends. Bad friends are those who are gossipy, back-biting, dishonest, materialistic, foul-mouthed, over-indulgent whose main concern is this life and having as much fun as possible whether God has made it legal or not. Such people might not even believe in God or discuss religion with you at all, these are what bad friends are. Imagine you are with such a person when God decides to take their life and you die in the same "accident" with them. How do you expect God to treat you if you were the friend of such a person, keeping in mind there are people who are friends of Satan and enemies of God? How are you going to say, "*I wasn't like them, I would just hang out*"? What will your answer be if God asks, "*If you weren't one of them then why were you with them? Why would you hang out with such a wicked evildoer who had no respect for me and sinned without regret? Why didn't you tell them what they were doing was wrong? Why should I grant you paradise when you hung out with the inhabitants of hellfire? Why did you spend more time befriending these people than you did worshipping me?*" At that moment one will realize how wrong they were in taking such a person for a friend and that Satan fooled them through threats of loneliness. There is a term called "tacit consent" which means each person who lives in a community and accepts its benefits is tacitly agreeing to the rules by which the community is governed. Pertaining to friends it means that if you consider a person to be a friend and benefit from that friendship then that means you agree with what that person does and are culpable since you benefit from what they are doing. For example if you are friends with a thief who gets their money from stealing and this thief gives you gifts, takes you to dinner and drives you around then that means you endorse their thievery and are actually responsible for their theft since you benefit from it. Any food they feed you with stolen money makes that stolen food, which if you consume makes you a thief just the same, even though "technically speaking" you're "just friends" and didn't personally take part in the original crime. There is a famous saying, "*when in Rome do as the Romans do*" consider that Jesus pbuh lived in the Roman Empire and distinctly did not do as the pagan Romans did. I think this saying was inspired by the devil because it is easily transfigured into being, "*when among pagans do as the pagans do*" and "*when among sinners do as the sinners do*" or "*when you're the minority then follow the majority*", if you're doing what they're doing you will be going where they're going. Living in a bad environment doesn't give you an excuse to do bad. Granted the majority of the world is not inhabited by righteous people, but if you can't escape the bad environment you're in then try to change it, or at the least don't let it influence you as much. Please don't fall for the trap of "*if you can't beat em join em*" this is another one of Satan's slogans, which if we actually take literally would mean that you cannot beat God so you better join God's team. Unfortunately people seem to use these sayings as a reason to join bad organizations, forgetting who is truly powerful. There is only one way to stop an injustice, it should be obvious what it is but for some reason it has become a secret. No matter what injustice it is, the only way for one to stop an injustice is to……… stop the injustice. A person cannot destroy the prison system by getting sent to prison and becoming a prisoner or by being a prison guard. Likewise joining the "bad guys" will only make you into a bad guy too. A bad system cannot be reformed, the only hope is to reform ourselves and for the people that are part of that bad system to reform themselves and abandon/abolish it. Personally I even know people who thought they could fix a bad system and got elected to be presidents of said associations. One of them I even talked to before they got elected, we both agreed the current president of the association was a problem, but I said the problem is the democratic system that elected the problematic president so by you becoming president you can't fix it as you think because even if you did then when the next president takes your place they will change it right back, unless of course you abolished elections and the system itself. They disagreed and got elected as president. About 7 months later I overheard them ardently complaining to their advisors about how they can't change anything, can't rely on people to do simple tasks, can barely do anything because of internal politics, were disgusted with the whole association and just planned to finish their term trying to keep the association united as one. I didn't say "I told you so" but every single elected leader of every single organization has this same problem, except some just like the position and pride that come from the title so they desire it longer than others. So I don't care what organization or system it is, if it has fundamental flaws or is corrupted then joining it will not fix it. No system is designed to destroy itself, yet that's what people think they'll make it do by utilizing a bad system. It doesn't work, that's what Satan wants people to do. Satan wants people to be his friend thinking they can change him and they are the ones who end up getting changed by Satan; every single time. If you hate a satanic or bad system as you should, and you join that system trying to change it, then by joining that system and being a part of it you must hate yourself too. Thus if you join a bad system or group, you will either end up hating yourself or changing your attitude about the system or group. You'd be surprised how often the system changes those who joined it with the intention of changing it. The people change, the systems don't. So to change the system the people must change and collectively starve the system. I repeat nobody can "change the system". Many people think they are different or that X system is different and can be changed for the better, this can't be done. To illustrate how impossible it is to change a bad system one can examine criminal gangs. Now what if somebody told you, *"I'm going to join a criminal gang in order to gain influence over them and/or become the leader of the gang. Once I have influence over the gang or if I'm the leader of the gang then I'll be able to change the gang and get them to stop doing crimes."* Everyone would agree such a person is crazy and will fail. There are only 3 ways to fix a fundamentally flawed system. Either you kill all the members, imprison all the members or they all quit and abolish the system themselves. Option 1 is not feasible, nor safe, nor wise, nor desireable. Option 2 is illogical and impractical. Option 3 is unlikely but possible. However the point is that joining a bad organization built on flawed principles never purifies it. So I don't care whether it's a peaceful democratic society or a violent criminal gang, you don't fix it by joining them. They have to quit the system and join you not the other way around. One doesn't get influence over others by joining them, that's how they get influence over you. These are basic political facts that few understand. A change in membership quality or quantity does nothing to improve a system built on a flawed foundation. The premise and principles of the organization/system must be fixed at the fundamental level with a new foundation and organization/system being born in order to replace the broken system. Basically when political systems or organizations are broken, you can't fix them without rebuilding from scratch. The worst flaw of broken and/or flawed systems is that they give people the false impression that they can be fixed. Wherever there is a bad organization there are bad principles and ideas at the root of the problem. The systems are built on ideas, when you change your ideas your ideas don't change, you just replaced your old ideas with new ideas. Thus systems can only be replaced they can never change, those who try to change them get changed themselves. Everyone who has ever become a member of a bad system or organization did so with the intentions of improving it and they failed. So the key to success in fixing the system is to not join in it but create an alternative system. It's best to have God in your group than abandon God and join another group intending to fix it for the sake of God. People will go in groups on the Day of Judgment with the groups they were with during this world. That means the backbiters will get together, the adulterers will get together, the alcoholics will get together, the gamblers will get together, but on that day they won't be getting together to backbite, commit adultery, drink alcohol or gamble. On that day they will all get together to go to hell. Comparing the % of time one spends with good people and the % of time one spends with bad people can indicate whether one is more likely to be good or bad themselves. Be careful who you spend time with, you might be spending eternity with them. A good friend is one who encourages you to do good deeds God likes AND forbids you from doing bad deeds God hates, they will support you only when you are correct and they won't support you when you are wrong; rather they will actually oppose/refute you when you are wrong. That's a true friend. Most people just want a person who will support them no matter what, but that's a bad friend and that's why most people have bad friends. Whether they are "fun" or not has nothing to do with whether they are good or bad, afterall Satan can be quite an entertaining companion. Likewise being "friendly" doesn't make someone friend worthy, since Satan is friendly too; just as being "righteous" doesn't mean someone is right. That's why I dislike the word "friendly" because your worst enemies can be the most "friendly" to you of all. Friendship of the sinful is an avenue to the hellfire, while friendship of the righteous is an avenue to paradise. The lesson of Jonah pbuh is that the people who were in the boat with Jonah pbuh were endangered because of being with someone who disobeyed God. Therefore choose your road trip companions wisely because it's a one way trip and whether you are the driver or the passenger, both end up at the same destination. Don't carpool with bad companions, you don't want to go where they're going.

  The classes I took in college were mostly about music, some taught musical history and development, some taught music as an art and some taught music as a science. However the more important and technical training courses plainly taught that music is a drug. At first it sounded ludicrous, but there was no way to deny the scientific proof the professors presented to prove their thesis about music being an auditory drug. They taught us the way the ear is structured and how sound is processed and the effects music has on the brain, emotions, mentality and body. At first it seemed as though they had exposed a big secret, but inside we all knew music was a drug all along. Nevertheless I decided to employ this drug in my Christian rap, attempting to convert people to Catholicism creating crusaders, fully aware of the brainwashing capabilities music has. Think about how when you hear a professionally manufactured song, your head starts nodding, your finger and foot starts tapping then your lips start mouthing the lyrics. All that is done automatically without your conscious exertion. A force strong enough to control your body and make you move without thinking about it is strong enough to make you murder, rape and rob. How often has a song gotten stuck in your head and you cannot get it out no matter what you try? That is not something that happens with normal consumer products. That is what happens with drug addictions. Music is so powerful that you can go decades without hearing a song, then you overhear it for 5 seconds by accident and the entire song comes back to your mind with you knowing all the lyrics by heart while your emotions go back to how you felt when you used to listen to it. This type of experience is unparalleled and very dangerous. Imagine someone made a song you liked the sound of but it had some bad advice. By having your brain remember that song against your will that bad advice will be stuck in your head for the rest of your life, and who knows when your brain might act upon it without telling you where it got that idea from. Music is a drug according to the elite of the music industry and professors who train people how to create music professionally. The little kids like pop stars because the pop music is the gateway drug, everyone enjoys it their first time but when they develop a taste for a more refined composite intoxicant then pop music doesn't have that same buzz. The pop music is still intoxicating but those with more musical experience don't get the same high from the generic gateway drug of music as they do with the more dangerous compound varieties. People having different tastes in music is the same as people having different tastes regarding drugs. All forms of the drug type known as music are dangerous and intoxicating, they just have different flavors and side effects with some being more damaging or addictive than others. As a former music junkie, trust me when I say it's not something you want to get hooked on, it will damage your ears, poison your mind, corrupt your heart and take control over your life without you even realizing it. If you do listen to music there is a 99% chance you will be enslaved to melodious rhythm and brainwashed by the musicians. Second-hand smoke is actually less likely to effect you than music. All thanks and praises be to God for liberating me from such a toxic drug.

In order to graduate from the college program I was in I was required to do an internship related to my field of study. Audio recording and production is a specialized field with few entry level openings. Eventually I ended up as a intern sound engineer working at a famous club in Buffalo, New York. Underneath the club I worked at, on the first floor was a Gay/Lesbian club. Another intern and I would frequently joke *"always remember we work on the second floor, you don't want to go on the first floor by mistake"* in order to avoid interacting with the sodomous drag queens and transgenders; but more on that later. A sound engineer pretty much does all the setup for a concert and keeps the sound going during the event. This is a very stressful job. Every night there is a different group of people you have to work with, there is a constant race against the clock to get everything set up before the show starts and people come in. Of course you get blamed for anything that goes wrong with the equipment, or if the act gets booed through no fault of your own. Meeting these musicians in the flesh and working with them off-stage made me realize these "superstars" really aren't super at all. Most of them tend to think they are the best to have ever come there, and others are so focused on the money they plan to get from ticket sales and merchandise that it even hinders their performance and equipment set-up, because they are always asking, *"What % of the ticket sales do I get again?"* and/or *"Who do I see to get paid?"*. Nobody on the sound crew knew these answers, but we were always repeatedly asked over and over again. At first I thought they were such bad people because of their musical genre, because no rappers had ever been there when I was working. Then one day there was a Christian rapper who I helped set up for, he also had other Christian rappers as guests for the performance. While he had Christian themes in his songs, if I hadn't heard him prior to the show during the sound check I wouldn't have known he or his friends were even Christian because they acted like all the rest if not worse.

At this club many people would consume alcohol and get drunk. Shockingly one of the bar tenders at this club was the librarian at the public library, who worked at the club part time. Being a regular visitor at the library she knew me and it was awkward ever after, at both the library and club whenever she was working. I never would've guessed she would be in such a place serving booze late at night. It made we wonder what other "plain people" have such wild lives.

Speaking of wild, some nights that club seemed like a jungle combined with an insane asylum, making it difficult to distinguish between mammals and humans. One unforgettable night there was an international electronic music group, they only played instrumentals that were nearly hypnotic and seizure inducing. For that show all the tables were removed and a makeshift dance floor was prepared. When they first started playing everyone was just standing still and it was really awkward. Suddenly one guy started having spasms as though he were possessed, I almost laughed at him thinking he was completely crazy for being the only one "busting moves". Then like a chain reaction another person started pulsating and then another and another, within minutes everyone was dancing with such fervor as I had never seen before or since. I don't know if it was a mosh pit or what, but I was actually frightened because I couldn't feel what compelled them and had no inclination to dance whatsoever. For the most part I think they were all strangers. Nevertheless many approaches and sexual provocations were attempted and rejected, with other attempts being visibly welcomed. It was mesmerizing to witness for hours people moving so strenuously without fatigue, finally there was a break for intermission and it became eerily quiet as soon as the dancing and music ceased. It was so quiet and calm that I doubted they would even dance for the second half of the performance imagining they were all out of energy. The second half was even crazier, not in reference to the music, but the people dancing seemed to have lost control of their bodies; some even got hurt in the fray. It was unbelievable the things this music could make those people do, I have not seen a more powerful man-made force since capable of having such an effect on people, it gives me chills just remembering. That night I witnessed firsthand the influence music can have on a group of people and it was terrifying to see. It was definitely unnatural and I could find no explanation for their extreme exuberance at that time. The victims of the musicians were no match for their audio weaponry. It's said that the pen is more powerful than the sword, similarly music overpowers the keyboard.

I think it might've been the very same night when a transvestite from the club below started a fire in the bathroom setting off the fire alarms. With the alarms activated the 2nd floor elevator which we used to transport musicians gear stopped working. It was late at night and the musicians couldn't wait to leave so we ended up hauling all their gear down the stairs. Fortunately I didn't have to carry too much and mostly held the door open for others. While doing this I had close encounters with some of the drag queens and drag kings coming and going. It was repulsive, with most of them it was hard to tell whether they were guys or girls or something else entirely. There is a famous popular saying "*they only come out at night*", well it was night time and I was at the place where "*they*" go to when they come out. In their natural habitat "*they*" left me speechless with their complete disregard in approaching me with sexual innuendo and flirting. When these transvestites were hitting on me it felt like they were from another planet as though they actually expected to fornicate with me right there and then on the spot in public, without any shame or formality in the slightest. It was disgusting and I imagine many women can relate if they have ever received undesired sexual solicitations. There is a time and a place with a proper way to copulate. That experience shined a light on the putrid filth which unnatural sinful sexuality is. Prior to that night of terror, my attitude was purely theoretical without having any real world experience with transvestites. I even repressed this memory for a good portion of time because it was so sickening.

On the 1st floor there were the transvestites who were slaves to sex of any kind. On the 2nd floor there were musicians manipulating masses of people, making them move against their will. Night after night these things could be witnessed taking place with people from all walks of life dancing away to the satanic symphonies, whilst creatures with unknown sexualities and genders were committing unknown abominations below. But the crazy thing is how the other workers at the club didn't see anything wrong with what was going on. Every night their main concern was the money and how much their cut was, others were focused on the next big promotion, but it made me wonder what exactly it was this building was promoting. It was one of the most immoral environments I have ever been in and all thanks and praises be to God that I'm no longer amongst them. Worst of all is how this is happening to people each and every night with the angel of death always prepared waiting anxiously to extinguish their life and take their soul. Humans were not created for such a vain corrupted purpose.

Gradually I would get more and more responsibilities placed upon me increasing my culpability in the events. One thing I was personally responsible for was interpreting the secret symbols used, which are not detected by the public. For example if a musician can't hear a certain track in their monitor, or they want less of it or more, they communicate their desires in the middle of the show often during the middle of a song with gestures because it is impossible to talk without disrupting the event to make the changes. Everyone tends to have different signs for different things, which can make it confusing and frustrating for all involved hindering communication. Sometimes it's something as simple as wanting water and other times they could be wanting some kind of special audio alteration or effect. All this is communicated from the musicians non-verbally during the performance in front of everybody. Although those not responsible for keeping the show going have no idea what is going on because they haven't been trained to recognize the signs and symbols. This is a common phenomenon in the performing industries so I presume it is just as prevalent in other areas of life as well. Perhaps politicians are conveying secret meanings to certain people during their public appearances? Celebrities or the financial elite could easily be suspected of this type of communication as well. These are just thoughts, not accusations however it was important for me to learn firsthand how the public is typically ignorant of the messages being conveyed, even when they are paying close attention to the messengers. A person could publicly be saying one thing while secretly gesturing the opposite meaning to those who they wish to communicate with. Criminal gangs are notorious for special hand signals the meaning of which are known primarily throughout gangdom, gang culture or law enforcement. Yet with petty thugs they foolishly take pride in "Gang signs" forgetting the very purpose of "gang signals" was to communicate undetected. Today gang culture makes the signs popular thus allowing many posers to signal their way to street status to "be cool". So with most "secret gestures" the very purpose of them is defeated if the masses learn the meanings of them or can identify them as having some type of meaning. The classification of "secret gestures" is called semiotics. The study of Semiotics is a very fascinating field but sadly conspiracy theorists ruin it by going overboard thinking every little hand gesture is automatically a secret sign of cult membership or something. Sometimes people can make cult signs by accident, because there are so many cult signs that are natural gestures normal people can routinely make. Plus one must remember that just as fake gangsters make gang signs to be cool or the police make the signs to entrap people, many can be making "cult hand signals" because they want people to think they are in X cult for whatever reason. Politicians or celebrities can make semiotic signals to "be cool" or be funny and get attention from the conspiratorial minded. Honestly if some world leader learned that X gesture means you are satanic, some of them might purposely make the symbol for fun as a joke to see if people start calling them the anti-christ. Although to totally ignore the art and existance of semiotics is dangerous. The danger of semiotics isn't in secret occult communication, or membership identifications, but the subliminal semiotics that can be used to program one's subconscious mind due to repetitive signals being seen or heard in entertainment mediums. Whether public figures are sending secret signals to each other is irrelevant to us. However as there is subliminal imagery there is also subliminal audio messages, both of which are hard to detect or avoid. So the problem is that a typical person can be getting signals without knowing it and eventually could influence them. Basically semiotics can be used as a type of brainwashing via repeated exposure to subliminal imagery or subliminal audio. While I'm not fluent in semiotics and consider most of semiotics to be nonsense, coincidental, or innocent, I found it very exciting to be on "the inside" of undetectable semiotic communication methods. Hopefully this doesn't make you paranoid to the extent that you start analyzing this very book looking for some kind of secret message hidden in these pages, I'm telling you directly that there are no intentionally secret messages in these pages or paragraphs. Too many waste their time trying to find something that's not there which can cause them to miss the clear truth that's right in front of them. Yet many more are clueless as to what is really going on and only see what they are shown, remaining oblivious to the reality. May God help us to see things clearly for what they truly are. The problem we have is that we search for the signs of conspirators and evil satanists and ignore the signs of God. Rarely do people think *"What signs will God be sending me today?"* instead they try to learn how the devils are communicating. Most of the knowledge we seek is of no benefit and can only waste our time/mind or expose us to harm/temptations. We look for the wrong signals for the wrong reasons and ignore the right signals failing to benefit from them due to our sins and ignorance. God gives us big STOP signs so we stop sinning but when do we ever stop?

Working as an intern at the club meant having to come the earliest and leave the latest, usually being forced to stay until everyone else had left including the musicians. Frequently I stayed there until 3 or 4 am after having arrived at 2pm, many nights I did shifts longer than 12 hours, this was an unpaid internship. On one such occasion while driving home, there was a police car in front of me at the red light. There was no traffic, the police car put on its lights without sound went through the red light and turned off its lights after crossing the intersection. I waited till the light turned green, drove through the intersection and stopped behind the same police car at the next red light. They did it again turning on their lights to go through the red light and turning them off afterwards. I waited for the green light and again caught up to the police, but they turned left at the next light and I went straight. If the police had been behind me and I went through the red light without traffic it would have been a crime, but I saw them do it twice without need and get away with it. What could I do, call the police and say "*I saw the police run a red light without a reason!*"? It displays the injustice and hypocrisy of the "justice system". Who will police the police? Who will police the police watchers? How did such people who break the laws they hold others to get to be in such positions of legal authority? Years later I witnessed the same thing happen with another police car running a light without reason at 7:04 pm with numerous witnesses. It's not just police, civilians go through red lights on purpose at night as well and the same civilians often complain when others do it during daylight by mistake. Another time I saw a police car simply turn on its lights and illegally pass a slower car driving in front of it by crossing a double yellow line, then turning off it's lights after it passed. The police used their lights, paid for by taxpayers, so they could pass another car on a road where it's illegal to pass on. The problem is that humans are corrupt. This is actually why the prohibition of alcohol failed in America. It wasn't because the criminal underground couldn't be stopped from bootlegging and police were powerless to prevent people from drinking alcohol. It was because the police were corrupt and took bribes, even personally participating in the smuggling and consumption of illegal alcohol. The police let their personal beliefs about alcohol and freedom affect their implementation of the law. Prohibiting alcohol in America was completely feasible, the problem was the police just didn't want to prohibit it and preferred to get rich for letting the law get broken. As a result drinking alcohol wasn't seen as a crime but became a patriotic activity done for the sake of freedom and to be cool for "technically breaking the law". Eventually such views promoted by the police to paint corrupt police as patriotic also depicted gangsters as patriotic heroes. Ultimately the prohibition was repealed because the American ideocracy got different ideas about alcohol and the majority opinion made it popular and said legalizing it would bring tax revenue to the federal and state governments and make alcohol safer/less potent. But the tax revenue was what really made the government repeal prohibition in 1932 CE during the midst of the economic depression. However money only became a motivation after the non-corrupt police proved how much money could be made by taxing alcohol citing the corrupt police as an example. Prohibition didn't work in America, because the police liked to drink alcohol. It's really that simple. Even today American police are notorious for being the most alcoholic profession, reasearch indicates that 90% of American police officers drink alcohol and 25% of American police officers are addicted to alcohol and need it to cope with the stress of being a US police officer. Obviously this indicates that the police must have a severe moral dilemma when "serving and protecting" all "the people" and implementing the unjust man-made laws. So this is further evidence that a bad system makes good people bad and does not change from the inside out. During the alcohol prohibition police effectively made the law what they wanted it to be and if they didn't like the laws then they didn't obey them if they could get away with it. This still happens today. In fact remember the drug-dealing friend I told you about who wanted me to get him a gun illegally? Well he changed careers, sort of. To my surprise he told me he was going to become a police officer. I flipped out on him thinking he is the last person in the world who I could picture as a police officer and I thought our dislike for police was mutually agreed upon. He explained to me that he was going to be a "cool police officer", the type that when they see people doing drugs would just look the other way and be cool about it. I explained to him that he sells illegal drugs and he can not do that and be a cop at the same time. So I asked if this meant he was going to stop selling drugs and he told me no, but he was still going to be a cop too. Basically my drug-dealing friend told me he was planning on becoming a corrupt drug-dealing cop. So if people think cops only get corrupted on the job, they are wrong, I know someone who deliberately planned to be a corrupt cop before they even signed up for training. Many people are like this and will break the law if they think they won't get caught or reprimanded. Whereas God is a witness to all we do. True justice will be served based on what we did in our public lives and private lives. We will be held accountable for what we did when no one else was looking. There wouldn't be a need for so much law enforcement or surveillance if the population were aware of this simple truth. Satan has deceived many people and often makes us forget temporarily if not entirely of how we should be conducting ourselves publicly and privately. I'm not saying you're going to hell for running a red light, but there are things that God has made illegal for us to do. Although because the governments and societies we live in say it's ok, people think it's not a crime since they aren't immediately punished for doing it. We take advantage of the mercy of God when we do this. If we disobey the government, our parents or employers, immediately we get punished and have our privileges taken away. God could treat us the same way, where if we eat something we shouldn't God could take away our teeth. Or if we say something we shouldn't God could take away our tongue and the ability to speak. It's the same with eyesight, if we see something we shouldn't then God would be entirely just if he were to immediately take our eyesight away because we broke the rules. Realistically God doesn't even have to tell us about heaven or hell as a motivation for us to obey. God is God, if God makes a law it is to be obeyed. We shouldn't need to know what the punishment is if we disobey or what the reward is for obedience. Yet God is so merciful that he allows us time to repent and will forgive us without punishment if we repent before it's too late. God deserves to be obeyed regardless, but the mercy of God is so great that we have been informed somewhat of the rewards and consequences for obeying or not. God did not have to tell mankind about Hell, it could have been kept as a surprise, just like heaven could have been kept a secret. Although since we do know what will happen if we violate the law and die as unrepentant unforgiven criminals, there is absolutely no reason at all for someone to disobey. That we are not immediately punished further displays the mercy of God because it allows us to make mistakes without instantly suffering in full because of them. Unfortunately Satan has deceived us into thinking that because we are not immediately punished when we commit a sin then that means we will never be punished, but this is a false notion. This falsity could be comparable to jumping off a cliff, you won't immediately hit the ground below and die, it will take a few seconds. Likewise when we sin we won't immediately go to hell, but if we don't sincerely repent to the lawmaker alone then hell is guaranteed just as hitting the ground would be for someone who jumps off a cliff; it's just a short matter of time. It is important to remember the <u>gravity of sin</u> so that we <u>don't fall</u> into it.

If you have no shame to do wrong in the sight of God then you will likely be one of those ashamed of themselves when in the presence of God being judged for all the wrong you did unashamedly. For example no one would want to be caught stealing things or looking at pornography (stealing a glance at what you shouldn't be seeing) by their parents, spouse, kids or the police. Yet many don't even think twice about being caught doing such dirty deeds by their Creator. When people are being filmed doing something they know is wrong or would look bad to others then they quickly try to stop themselves from getting filmed and recorded, sometimes even using violence rather than just changing their behavior so it's proper and correct. Yet God is recording everything we do at all times and so are the angels he has appointed to record our deeds who cannot be prevented from recording us. So since we are being recorded in a manner that cannot be stopped and will soon be brought to account by our Creator, why don't we act like we are being observed and recorded? God has informed us he is recording us, so we should live a life God enjoys to observe and reward us for and not something God will hate to observe and punish us for. Because the U.S. government is monitoring everything you say on the phone or type in emails, you might not express yourself in a way they may not like. Why don't we use such restraint out of respect for God? God has incalculably more power to punish us for a much longer time frame in many more severe ways than the U.S. government. Do you fear the government more than God?

Just as the ungodly powers on earth have little power to punish, they have very little with which to reward us for obedience. The lowest ranking person in paradise, who is the last to enter, will have the like of 10 kingdoms of earth and everything they desire forever. This would be more than enough to satisfy any one of us, yet this is the lowest of the people in paradise. We cannot even contemplate this person's reward because it is so far beyond anything possible on earth, no one can even think of what it would be like to have this. Yet that is just the minimum of the rewards awaiting those who worship God alone, are obedient, grateful, patient and repentant. We cannot contemplate either the rewards of God or the divine punishment. Knowing that we cannot even know the severity of the torture should be enough not to disobey, but we are weak fallible humans who make mistakes. Although when there is some other force, with very finite ability to reward or punish we strictly never ever consider disobeying them. If there is a paper to sign and it says *"don't write in the margins"* there are people who will follow these rules so strictly they won't even come close to writing in the margins and will write everything in the center of the page, 5 inches away from both margins. In this instance there isn't even any real reason to obey the instructions, other than because it's written, logically a stray line or two doesn't even make a difference and the paper is accepted regardless, yet people are still terrified to disobey. Especially students writing papers being told by teachers "don't write in the margins". Most people don't even know why the "don't write in the margins" rule ever began. The empty margins rule is for authors having manuscripts published. Authors have a policy keeping the margins of papers empty because of the printing process. But if you aren't an author writing a book worried the printer might chop off text if you write it in the margin, then there is no good reason not to write in the margins. In fact you should write in the margins because it saves paper to do so. Still how many today dare to write in the margins? The rule only applies to those having their material photocopied or printed, yet people follow these margin rules because of fear for those who told them the rules, despite such rules not even applying to them. We should take the rules and instructions of the Creator even more seriously. God should be the last one we disobey, but all too often he is the first and only one we are heedless of and disrespectful to. Our priorities must be rearranged, changed and improved with God having more influence and importance in our lives, now before we die.

      Having met no good friends in college, I devoted more time to religion and went to church for daily mass, beginning to pray the rosary and read the bible almost every day. When you go to church every day the first thing you notice is how empty it is and how old the few who go to church daily are. Few teenagers or young adults attend church on weekdays, even in the summer. The Monday-Friday services offer a very different experience than on Sunday or Saturday. There is no music and no collections of money (that I can remember giving to unless it was a "holy day") while the sermons are of a different tone and quality. During a typical church service a few passages are read from different parts of the bible and then a homily (sermon) is given trying to relate the passages together attempting to teach a common moral lesson that oftentimes has no practical relevance to modern life. Theoretically rumor has it that if you go to church every day for 4 years you are supposed to hear them read the whole bible during church. On Sunday it flows smoothly, on weekdays not so much. The priests oftentimes connect gospels on the flimsiest of reasoning's with the sermons tending to be more of a re-interpretation of the passages, as though the bible were a history book that doesn't need to be followed today. Most sermons stress that the bible is symbolic and doesn't really mean what it says, unless of course it's a symbolic passage. Ironically the symbolic stuff is taken literally and the literal stuff is taken symbolically. Some days it was disheartening to attend because the priests seemed unprepared and made their speeches up on the spot. However there was a rotation, so that made it interesting and entertaining when the priests would contradict the one from the day before not knowing that they are teaching the opposite of what we had previously been taught, despite the daily readings having come from the same chapter. It left the impression that for the most part the bible means whatever you want it to mean, it's open to any interpretation as long as you call yourself Christian and say what the group says agreeing with the declaration of faith. Once at an early morning mass, during the communion ritual the Eucharistic minister tripped and fell, dropping the wafers after they were supposed to have changed into God and/or Jesus pbuh. Most everyone remained seated, speechless, and then tried not to laugh when the old guy couldn't get up.

Eventually people helped him up and the service finished with no one ever discussing what happened. I didn't realize it at the time but this is another proof that the Eucharist is not what it's widely believed to be. This man dropped what we thought was the body of God and/or Jesus pbuh, imagine what he was thinking *"OOPS, I just dropped God!"* This is abhorrent blasphemy thinking that God could possibly be dropped in any way shape or form. God would not permit humiliation at the hands of some human. Even if you say that the bread isn't God but the "son of God" this still wouldn't be allowed to occur at any time or place in the universe. The fact that it happened shows that the Eucharist is not some divine food, it's plain old bread. If anyone says otherwise you are saying that God got dropped and couldn't help it, that's an insult. Amazingly what this fumble implied didn't register in my mind until recently, long after the fact. All thanks and praises be to God I was given the ability to see things for what they were, eventually.

Previously I mentioned the Catholic Sacrament of Confession, in the modern Catholic religion it's the only way to receive forgiveness for your sins aside from a deathbed blessing. This sacrament has no biblical basis and many Christian groups have abandoned the practice, but the Catholic Church continues it. To the Catholic this means the priest has a monopoly on salvation seeing as how you can't tell just anyone your sins to get forgiven, but it has to be a priest who claims to act on behalf of God. This will make things interesting as there are fewer and fewer priests to go around making it impossible for every Catholic to go to confession, thereby making it impossible for them to receive salvation according to their own religion. When the priest has sins to confess he tells another priest, thereby keeping the sins within the organization secret to the public, while all the sins of the Catholic public are privy to the clergy. In the past the knowledge gained in the confessional was used by the Church as leverage manipulated for political purposes. Prior to the Protestant Reformation there was a practice in which the Catholic Church would sell salvation, or "real estate in paradise" on pieces of paper for money, calling them indulgences. As one might expect the price of paradise wasn't cheap, but one Jew saw the high supply and low demand for the hellfire so he decided to buy 100% of the hellfire from the Catholic Church for a paltry sum. Stupid right? After receiving his receipt for the hellfire this Jew told everyone to stop buying pieces of paradise from the Church, because he had bought Hell, owned it all 100%, and wasn't going to let anybody else in. This silly logic led to a drop in business for the Church and they quickly bought back the hellfire from the Jew paying him multiples of what they sold the piece of paper for. Pretty clever Jew to get the Vatican to buy the very Hellfire that they originally sold to him. Imagine the dialogue that took place during these business transactions, first the Pope asks the Jew, *"So I hear you're interested in buying the hellfire? Just how much did you want to buy from us?"* Then when the Vatican buys it back the Jew says, *"Well well well, here comes the Pope trying to pay for his place in hell. Now just how much are you willing to pay in exchange for Hell?"* Every Catholic today agrees this was a bad business without biblical basis. Unfortunately many people assume that because this one sinful blasphemous practice eventually stopped during the Counter-Reformation, then everything else the Church currently does is up to code. Assumptions are dangerous and there is a famous well-known saying that discourages making assumptions. Indulgences are a great example of this, in that while some types stopped, others continued and new types developed.

Such as when in 1857 CE Pope Pius IX granted a fifty day indulgence to anybody who kissed the foot of a bronze statue of St. Peter after going to confession in St. Peter's Basilica in Vatican City. Seriously he taught that if you kissed the foot of X statue after confessing your sins in X place then you would get a spiritual pass of forgiveness for 50 days worth of sins. Now if that type of thing is not idolatry I don't know what is.

As a human being frequently I make mistakes and sin, regrettably. As a Catholic I confessed these sins as soon as possible in order to be forgiven quickly in case of unexpected death. Also because the Church teaches that if you have un-confessed "mortal sins" then you're not allowed to participate in communion. Most Catholics are ignorant of this and get communion regardless, and most have no clue just how many things are considered to be "mortal sins" (there's quite a lot, and you probably did some). But I actually believed in this religion and followed the rules I knew of, which meant the embarrassment of having people wonder what evil deed I did which disqualified me from communion. Not going to communion as a result of having un-confessed mortal sin(s) was especially noticeable on Sunday when I sat in the front row. Since I was such a sinful person this meant I was going to confession once, twice or sometimes three times a week. There is a short window of time during the week confessions are held, most churches only offer it once a week for no more than an hour. If there is a long line and time runs out before you get to confess, which frequently happens, then you have to wait for another day to get heard and forgiven, hoping not to die before then or else you'd be going to hell. Since I couldn't wait a week, I'd go to multiple churches on different days to confess. It sounds ridiculous to me now, but I had been raised thinking this was how the forgiveness of God was obtained. Usually when people go to confession there is a screen in between the priest and the sinner, to give the impression that the priest won't know who you are. An option of going face to face is available for those who are handicapped, or foolish enough to tell their sins face to face. Sometimes face to face is the only option, after doing it a few times I got comfortable with it and preferred confessing face to face because it felt better, also the priest tended to give better advice since he knew you knew that he knew who it was, so he could be upfront. Different priests would give different advice on how to stop doing certain sins, but none of them ever provided a long term solution. Which was odd because they were supposed to be abstaining from the same sins as me. I expected them to have advice that worked, never thinking they were doing the same sins I was confessing to. Depending on the priest you would get a different penance, a penance is what the priest tells you to do after confession in order to get forgiven. If you don't do the penance you don't get forgiven. When reflecting on it all it seems contradictory to the allegation Christians postulate of Jesus pbuh dying for people's sins. If that happened then why tell the priest your sins to be forgiven? They say *"in order to prove you are sorry"*. Even if that's the case, if Jesus pbuh paid the price why do I have to do the penance the priest gives? They say *"in order to prove you are sorry"*, which is the same answer as for why one is confessing to the priest. A person can go to confession yet not regret their sins, so doing confession in itself doesn't actually prove you're sorry at all. God knows whether we are sorry or not and loves to forgive those who repent. Why does the priest have to know what we did wrong? Who are we really trying to prove we are sorry to? God knows everything, the priest on the other hand wouldn't know you were sorry for your sins, or even know that you did a sin unless you went to confession and told him. What's difficult to understand is how I could do the same exact sin and get two different penances from two different priests. One priest would say to do X amount of "Hail Mary" prayers to be forgiven, and another would tell me to do Y amount. How they came up with different numbers for the same exact sin is unexplainable to me, unless they were just making it up as they went along. Sometimes it was even the same priest giving me different numbers or prayers as a penance for the same sin(s). There seems to be no standard. Since in the past people had less access to commit sins they must have sinned less, this causes one to wonder how little they must have had as a penance. Yet it's widely known that previous generations of Catholics were given lengthy penances that took hours to do, if not days. This leads one to conclude that forgiveness has gotten cheaper in recent years. Clearly there couldn't have been deflation in the spiritual economy. Maybe the technology has changed making the cost of forgiveness decrease? To this day I don't know what type of valuation they use to decide what someone must do in order to be forgiven. Some would say God gives them a different number every time, but that seems too random, one would think the penance should fit the crime. As I went week after week time after time a relationship began to develop between me and the ones who knew all my bad deeds. During the confessions the priests would chat and ask me to tell them any dreams I had or if there were any questions of mine they could answer. It was hard to tell when they were speaking on God's behalf and when it was just guy to guy. All thanks and praises be to God who guided me to the path of direct repentance to the one whom I offend when I sin.

Another time when confessing my sins face to face one after the other on a hot summer day, the priest fell asleep. There I was saying how sorry I am for this and for that, when the person who is supposed to forgive me on God's behalf has his eyes closed taking a snooze! I didn't realize until I had finished confessing, I waited just to make sure he wasn't deep in thought and then woke him up in order to be told what my penance would be. How he could give me a penance for all my sins when he didn't hear them because he was sleeping is another thing I couldn't understand. God doesn't sleep under any circumstances. When I am asking God for forgiveness via a priest who is supposed to be acting with God's authority and he falls asleep it's hard not to think something is wrong with this method of asking God for forgiveness. I encourage every Catholic to seriously reconsider the legitimacy of confession and ask yourself if it was what the followers of previous prophets did to be forgiven. Biblically John the Baptist pbuh would do baptism for those who needed expiation of sins. Many people would get baptized over and over again every time they sinned. According to the bible baptism had nothing to do with an "original sin" it was just a way for people to get their own sins metaphorically washed away and get physically purified. Did Jesus pbuh or his companions ever do anything even remotely resembling confession? Where did this practice come from, St. ___ (blank) or Satan? Adam pbuh and Eve didn't go to confession when they first sinned, neither did Moses pbuh when he killed a man, how were they forgiven? Jesus pbuh hadn't yet been born so it couldn't have been through him. Later I was to discover that the sacrament of Confession was introduced by Pope Gregory I in the sixth century CE, over 500 years after Jesus pbuh! Pope Gregory cited as evidence James 5:15-16 which the English New

International Version of the Bible translates as: "*And the prayer offered in faith will make the sick person well; the Lord will raise them up. If they have sinned, they will be forgiven. 16 Therefore confess your sins to each other and pray for each other so that you may be healed. The prayer of a righteous person is powerful and effective.*" But if this verse was known to Christians for over 500 years then why didn't the earliest Christians closest to Jesus pbuh practice confession? Yet not only did early Christians not practice confession but even after Pope Gregory I started it few Catholics went to it. It wasn't until November 1st, 1215 CE that confession became popular when the Lateran Council made it so that all Catholic adults were obligated to make confession to their parish priest and recieving communion at least once a year on Easter. This rule is still in effect today and despite few Catholics making confession or accepting communion on a yearly basis, according to Catholicism if they don't then technically they are not Catholic. The bottom line is that not one person ever went to Jesus pbuh and confessed their sins in order to be forgiven. Recently Pope Francis went to Israel and wrote prayers on a piece of paper and put them in the wailing wall, which is a Jewish shrine originally owned by Muslims who called it the Buraq wall. Jews believe it is a part of the original Jewish temple, but during the reign of Herod it was actually part of a shopping centre, it wasn't until 1520 CE that Jews thought it was religiously important. Pope Francis claims to be the representative of God on earth who thinks he is in direct communication with God. If that is true then why did he write down his prayers on a piece of paper and put it in a wall crack where his paper will later be taken out by Jewish Israelis and recycled, likely into toilet paper? This same person writing notes to God putting them in a Jewish shrine claims to have the authority to forgive people's sins and that when he is hearing people confess he is hearing them as God and giving them a penance not from himself but from God. Clearly something isn't right with this picture. Either the Pope can forgive sins and really is the representative of God or he is a fraud. If the Pope really is the representative of God who can grant absolution in the confessional then there is absolutely no reason a person with such a connection to the divine would write their prayers on paper and stick them in a wall of a Jewish shrine. It's stupid regardless but the Pope's not even Jewish! He's writing letters to God similar to how little kids write letters to Santa Claus. No prophet ever taught people to write letters to God and it is foolish. Aside from creating the sacrament of Confession Pope Gregory the first also introduced the idea of purgatory which has absolutely zero biblical basis; he also was the first to say that "*Satan has horns and hooves and powers to control the weather*" basically turning the evil pagan "Horned god" also known as Pan or Faunus into Satan. Essentially the "saint" Pope Gregory I (that's a "the first symbol" not an i) created the popular modern symbol of Satan. This information particularly shocked me because this innovative Pope Gregory and I shared the same first name. I'm ashamed to have the same name as someone who invented religious doctrines that weren't biblically sanctioned and never taught by Jesus pbuh.

    Meanwhile I was still pursuing rap, but it became less Christian and more gangster. The effects of listening to gangster rap all day, watching gangster movies, playing violent videogames, watching bad TV shows and being harassed by police with estranged family relations makes one have a criminal mentality, or a thug outlook on life. My materialism was at its highest and my self-esteem was at its lowest. Suicidal thoughts were constantly on my mind, with over the counter "medications" intended to stop depression having no effect. Anyways pills are not a true long-term solution, people don't just get sad for no reason, they might not know why they are sad but that doesn't mean there is no reason. Sadness isn't just some bodily chemical imbalance. A pill will not solve your problems permanently. When you see the bill for that depression pill you will be sadder than you were before, now having side effects to pay for as well. Anti-depressants actually rewire the brain and cause permanent damage. Yet let's pretend such a pill did work and you became happy despite all the side effects. (Which can include suicidal thoughts and more depression, even though that's why people take the pill to begin with.) What happens if they stop making that pill? How will you live without it? What is the difference between someone using pills for depression and someone using alcohol, or someone using sex, or someone using drugs, or someone using music? They are all addicts suppressing their problem delaying its solution, making its inevitable confrontation even more difficult by exponentially increasing the problems on their plate. It became clear to me something was seriously wrong with my lifestyle. If I was going to church everyday then why was I miserable? No amount of music, food, movies, games, jewelry or anything else would make me whole. There was some fundamental problem that was at the root cause of all the others. At that time I still didn't know what it was, because everyone else on facebook seemed to have the same problem. Like everyone else on facebook I thought I needed "love". But the girlfriend never appeared, nobody was good enough, or interested. Even if there had been a girl it would have been a parasitic relationship on my part, if not on the other persons part as well. The love that I needed and craved was not from any person or group, but the only love that is important and vital to daily existence. The love of the one who made me, the Creator of everything.

  Throughout my life I had been convinced of my good fortune to have been raised upon the true religion. Then while reading the Hip Hop Gospel (yes hip hop is a religion, it is not just a music style or culture) something struck me and cast a shadow of doubt on my theory of being right since birth. The author asked whether all of humanity would accept the truth if it was proven to everyone beyond a doubt. He asked: Would everyone in the world become a Hindu if they came across indisputable proof supporting Hinduism's beliefs about the caste system, reincarnation and the sanctity of cows? Or if Osama bin Laden's version of Islam were proven to be true would all the Americans give up their current religions and admit they had all been wrong and apologize making Osama their leader?(By the way Osama bin Laden's version of Islam is not correct. He espoused deviant khawarij doctrines and had been labeled a dangerous deviant by Muslim scholars in the 1990s CE.) Would all the Jews and Muslims become Christian if there was evidence that it was the only true religion and they were following falsehood? Would the whole world become atheist if it was proven that God didn't exist and every religion was false? If it was proven to all that only Buddhism was correct would every other doctrine be abandoned? Or would people continue to cling on to their false religions and ideologies even after it became clear that they and their ancestors had been wrong all along?

I had to admit that it seemed unlikely everyone on earth would accept the truth even if there was a way to prove it 100% to everyone without a doubt. Some people would be too arrogant to admit they were wrong, some wouldn't want to change their ways, the propagators of falsehood would be afraid of losing all they had gained. Then again, there are many people raised by Hindu parents who stay Hindu there whole life thinking it to be the only true religion. There are Buddhists raised by Buddhist parents who live life thinking their religion is the only truth. There are Christians raised by Christians who live life thinking Christianity is true, and so on and so forth for all the other groups. Not all of these people could be correct. However just because something is different than what you personally believe does not mean that it is automatically false. Everyone believes they are right, yet we can all agree that not everyone is right, therefore some religions must be wrong and personal opinion cannot be used when determining which. Some people must live their whole life following the wrong religion because their whole family is that religion and raise their children upon that religion thinking they were right, only to find out after death that they had been wrong the whole time. So just because I was raised Catholic didn't necessarily make it the true religion, I could be just as wrong as the others. This made me honestly wonder what if I wasn't raised to follow the correct religion? Would I be able to admit I had been wrong for so many years and be willing to change my life in order to follow the true religion no matter what it was? Would you?

Would we follow the example and instruction of Joshua pbuh in the verses of the English translation of the bible in Joshua 24:14-15?

"Now fear the LORD and serve him with all faithfulness. **Throw away the gods your ancestors worshiped** *beyond the Euphrates River and in Egypt,* **and serve the LORD.** *¹⁵ But if serving the LORD seems undesirable to you, then choose for yourselves this day whom you will serve, whether the gods your ancestors served beyond the Euphrates, or the gods of the Amorites, in whose land you are living. But as for me and my household, we will serve the LORD."*

The true religion is not a family heirloom to be passed down to future generations, it is guidance from the Creator to be cherished and practiced. Just because your parents, family, friends, country, community or ancestors believe/believed or practice/practiced something has nothing to do with whether that is true, right and good or false, wrong and bad. My ancestors and family members were human and made many mistakes in life, they were not angelic or infallible. If they made a mistake concerning religion would I follow their mistake? Would I obey the Creator or my family and/or society?

These important questions began to circulate in my mind, but I had rhymes to make and music to produce. By now it had become manifest that the quality of music has nothing to do with success in the business; marketing is the most important factor. I devoted more attention to the promotional aspect while trying to prevent the business mentality from interfering with artistic creativity. It was impossible to do everything on my own so I reached out to others to help produce an animated music video for a song that was anti-police, intellectually mocking, ridiculing and exposing their hypocrisy and corruption. This song and video was supposed to be released in June/July 2011 CE. However when other people are working on your projects they tend to take a longer time than anticipated and I ended up waiting until October before I finally decided to get someone else to do the project for me, since my "friend" wasn't helping as fast as I wanted. In August I had another encounter with the police after this song had been made, prior to it being released. I was in my car "iced out" blasting profane rap music so loud that I had earplugs in my ears (I wanted the world to hear but didn't want to hurt my ears) when seemingly out of nowhere a state trooper or sheriff pulled up alongside me at the red light on a six lane road telling me to pull over into the left turn lane. I pulled over, turned off the music and took out my earplugs. The officer came up and asked me if it was my car registered to my name and asked for information. I answered that it was my car, registered to me and gave him all the id and paperwork he asked for, then asked him why he pulled me over. The officer said it was because my license plate showed up in the system as being reported stolen. I had no idea and asked who reported it and when, also asking him why wasn't I informed about this report. The officer said he didn't know and told me to ask the DMV returning my paperwork and letting me go. The next day I went to the DMV (Department of Motor Vehicles) and they had absolutely no record of any such reports concerning me or my vehicle. The DMV said they didn't know where the officer got his information from but my car had never been reported stolen. This made me feel as though the officer had profiled me wanting to harass me because of my hip hop appearance. It's ironic that I had already recorded an anti-police song based on my prior frustrations and observations of them, then this incident occurred before I could release it. Many might've thought I made the song in response to this incident. In the music industry most music is made long before it is ever heard by the public, sometimes years before, with the few exceptions being songs that cite current events that allow one to pinpoint a timeframe that it could've been made in. Frequently songs are made prior to events happening that accidentally tie directly into the song which were unintentionally alluded to when the song was first made. For example one time I made a song advising that a certain actor should not be a role model for people. Shortly after releasing the song this same actor had a mental breakdown and gained international notoriety for claiming they did cocaine and were abnormally intoxicated having blood that wasn't human. Subsequently this person's career went into a downward spiral and any who heard my reference of that person in the song would've thought it had been made as a result of those events. The song was actually released before that and I had no idea the person had such a terrible drug problem. Many times musicians and authors seem more clever than they really are.

    In regards to music videos, what the viewer sees isn't real. All those cars, women, clothing and glamorous accessories are all rented or borrowed from others and get returned after the filming is completed. While filming there is actually no singing or speaking involved because it would mess up the video. The musicians are actually miming the words and the scenes are filmed with the musicians awkwardly moving their lips without sound coming out. Later on the videos are edited and made to synchronize with the song lyrics to make it seem to be naturally flowing. There is so much deception in the music industry that its almost embarrassing to be a part of. If people knew what a fraud the musician's lifestyle was like they wouldn't put them on a pedestal or even respect them. Unfortunately the listeners will often believe whatever they hear and only see what the musician desires them to see. Many musicians actually think this deception of people is funny. It is sickening to know that some musicians secretly laugh at their fans in private because the fans have been fooled into thinking the artist is what they pretend to be. In summary, the music industry was just like middle school, everyone in the industry is a poser but they don't want others to know. Now you know. Don't be fooled by the publicity stunts, smoke and mirrors or by what you hear. Don't fall for the expensive optical and auditory illusions they create. All musicians are actors.

    Difference in music quality is like graphic design, if two people have an idea for a picture their ideas don't really make much difference as to which picture will be better it depends on the technology. For instance the one who draws their picture on a cave wall is going to have a lower quality product than the one using the latest graphic design computer software, regardless of what their ideas and talents were. The technology trumps everything when manufacturing music. Therefore the more money that is spent on making music the higher the quality regardless of whether the artist is talented or not. So when people say X artist is bad, many times it simply means they have a low budget and the listener isn't used to listening to music made with that type of budget. Money can make terrible artists sound great and lack of money can make elite artists sound terrible. High quality music is not priceless, it's just out of the price range of most people. Thus the artist is marketed as a brand. As part of increasing business they must spend on their public image, namely give the impression they're getting rich off of music because then the public will psychologically think their music is good because they seem and claim to get so much money for it. The richer they appear the more people will think they make, and the better a musician they become in the public's eyes the better they will sound to the public's ears. Therefore the musicians spend lavishly on jewelry and such stuff to boost their image in order to gain more customers in order to spend money on their brand. Thus creating a cycle of spending money on music and promotion to make money on music to spend money on music and promotion without ever really making any genuine money unless they get to an extremely high level where they can use that celebrity status as a source of revenue through other means outside of music. Most all of the money an artist makes goes into promoting themselves, thus in order to cut costs they will wear fake jewelry and rent things for music videos. Those who do spend lavishly on themselves aren't getting that money exclusively from selling music and if they are then they risk their musical product falling behind the quality of the other competitors; which is why you have one hit wonders. The "one hit wonder" is the person who didn't spend enough money on their next song and promotion but spent it on other things. Hit songs are easy to make, songs are "hits" simply because of familiarity and people listen to a song because it's what they routinely expect to hear. Music junkies will listen to a song they "don't like" or even one they "hate" because it's familiar and they can sing along. A "hit" is just a formulaic song which a music junkie can't resist. New songs can be purposefully made into popular hit songs by radio stations if they just play the new song after and before other popular songs, thereby making a "hit sandwich" where the middle meat of a new song placed between two loaves of hit songs causes the new song to be considered as a bread and butter hit. It's really that easy, in reality people do not even have a choice whether a song becomes a hit song or not. The musical industry is purely a financial business. Anyone can be a star with enough money spent on their music and promotion, the only thing is whether that particular brand name can turn a profit for the corporate record labels who decide to sell them as a product. The music industry is basically like prostitution, some prostitutes have a pimp and some don't. The product rendered from both is the same, the only difference is the amount of money spent on the promotion and healthcare as well as customers having different tastes. Just as the sex addict has more expensive tastes than those less experienced, the music addict doesn't find the same pleasure from the less expensive music so they will oftentimes supplement their addiction with quantity once their taste in quality has plateued. Although unlike with prostitution the musical technology continues to advance in sophistication much faster than typical drug potency increases. So music is a special type of drug in which there is no "rock bottom" possible because the music industry continues to increase the potency of it's drug along with the rapid technological advancements. The only catch is that the musical technology upgrades so fast, the musical junkies can't keep up with the increased potency which is why many old folks who love music don't care for the new music because in audio terms it's too complex and potent for their system to handle. Thus older folk get a musical overload which triggers an audio effect similar to a drug overdose which is why they will say "That ain't music!" just like a drug user will say about a drug they can't handle "That ain't no drug!" Whereas the young music junkies who grew up on the more complex musical drug will hardly get a buzz from the old music, unless a particular song was specifically associated with an emotional feeling or timeframe so that it triggers nostalgia for them. This is because whether a person likes or dislikes a particular song is based on the amount of mental effort it takes for them to listen to it. The less resistance the brain has to a song then the greater the tolerance for that song will be and the more it can be enjoyed or used to get a buzz. Yet because of the personal nature of music, it's not quite the same as a mere drug, because drugs typically don't have much to do with their manufacturers or dealers, whereas music is intimately related to their manufacturers and dealers. Music has the elements of emotional drugs as well as the elements of physical drugs while being a mental drug with a unique auditory injection system that can in theory never be blocked by attempts to detox since the ears cannot be turned off, nor can the ears be shut down via an overdose. As long as volume is kept within safe ranges then there is no limit to how much one can indulge in music, they could even be taking it while they are sleeping. Thus all these qualities make music the ultimate drug. However because unlike other drugs music can be laced with ideas and messages, it can be used as a special category of propaganda that is extremely unique and influential beyond measure. For those with experience and training it's very easy to compose a melismatic rhythm with both conjunct and/or disjunct motion accompanied by various pitches to create a harmony or chord of consonance and/or dissonance that overwhelms the senses filling the body and brain with dopamine rendering the listener mindless and thereby susceptible to believe and act upon any suggestions they hear. Those suggestions tend to be called lyrics with the instrumentals being the main compound which facilitates the lyrical dose of propaganda. Although the vocals can either be an integral layer of texture or in strophic format making them easily interchangeable and replaceable regardless of the tempo, dynamics, genre or form of music. Meaning the lyrics can be intoxicating by themselves without any accompanying instrumentals or they can have nothing to do with the musical composition and be 100% constructed without any attention as to how they will fit in with the music since the way some music is made can allow for literally any type of lyrics to be inserted and sound compatible, or the lyrics to a song can be both; or neither if the music is of poor quality. And by poor quality music here I mean it has less intoxicating effect, similar to how an alcoholic will say "X is a good brew and Y is a bad brew" even though it's still alcohol the quality is linked to intoxication ability and not necessarily the pleasure derived from flavor. Monophonic, Polyphonic, Imitative Polyphonic and Homophonic music all intoxicate the listener but on different unique levels. Think of those terms as Class A drug of music, Class B drug of music, Class C drug of music and Class D drug of music, the genre itself has minimal effect on intoxication and the different classes don't necessarily denote higher ability to intoxicate but they are just different classifications regarding the complexity of the compounds that generally are more intoxicating to those who use their ears to experiment or indulge with such sounds. No music can ever have its total impact measured or analysed by humans. All types of music will "get you high" but in different ways and to different levels of intoxication. Some just get higher off some musical drug classes more than others. The record labels are pimps and the artists are prostitutes, some musicians become their own pimps with varying results. The prostitute(musician) with a pimp(record label) will appeal to more people while the independent prostitute(musician) will usually have a smaller consumer base, yet their consumers will be more devoted because of the lack of the intermediary. Although with advances in social networking now those artists with pimps can easily attain the same close connection with their consumers as unsigned artists did in the past. The music industry is pure prostitution and those in the industry know it, the main difference is that it's legalized and primarily sells an auditory product or performance instead of a sexual encounter. Any who are in the industry and think they're different is just like the prostitute who doesn't want to face the fact they are a prostitute but claims to be an "artist". Many fans will think their favorite artist is the exception in the business, but I assure you there are no exceptions. Musicians are as fond of their fans as prostitutes or strippers are of their clientele. Just as the prostitute claims to really love their patron the musicians will say the same about their fans. Do some prostitues genuinely fall in love with their clients? Yes, but it's a delusional narcissism based off the lust of the clients. Musicians love fans because the fans love their music. Also when making the drug of music, you get exposed to your own material during the creation process thereby getting high off of your own product, and it is even more powerful because you are making it so it's like tasting your own cooking; even if it has bad flavor it tastes good because of you making it. As a result musicians can frequently become addicted to their own music and start to believe it. Meaning, they've smelled their own poop so much that they think it's tasty nutritious food which they eat and market to others. When that happens, and it is a when not an if, they have their music take over their life to the point where they are no longer creating the music but the music is creating the musician and they're addicted to it. Thus a music junkie musician becomes their own drug dealer. While fans then become enablers to a music junkie encouraging them to make more of the drug they all use and glorify a musical drug dealer that gets high off his own supply. Which will either push the musician to make more and more of higher potency, using their musical drug to help them make stronger musical drugs or they get so high off their own music they crash and burn since they can't perform and maintain or increase their level of drug creativity nor quality. Yet just like the drug dealers on the street corners, all the musicians say they got the best supply on the market, except for those who are deeply addicted to other musicians since most of them are consumers before they are producers. Whereas the dream of the junkie musician then is typically to get rich and famous making your own auditory drugs for your own consumption while getting a bunch of fans to cheer you on for doing it and love you for it; taking your own drugs like some type of hero. Some musicians even get called kings but they are drug kingpins, and for those called gods they are really druglords. It's an industry unlike any other ever known to mankind.

 Before releasing my music video, I received my first offer from a record label who wanted me to sign with their company. I declined because they were a small company without much experience in the hip hop genre, being more of a rock and roll brand. Later on I received a second offer from a different record label that was hip hop oriented. The owner of this record label said he would make me famous and rich if I signed with his organization, but there was a catch. The major condition was that I had to sell him my soul. No joke. The guy actually made me selling my soul to him a condition of the contract. It was unbelievable. You hear things about musicians selling their soul for wealth and fame to the devil, but I never took such things that seriously. I never thought I would ever get such an opportunity. Of course all the talk of getting rich and famous is probably used in every record label executive's sales pitch, but the soul selling cliché was something I couldn't sign up for, especially considering I was propagating religion through rap; it would be hypocritical. This executive said he had plans for me, I told him God has plans too and declined his offer. After rejecting his bad deal the executive proceeded to defame me, spreading lies about me while still communicating to me in secret saying he would stop slandering me if I signed on with his group. This is the reality of the music industry which the fans don't know about. All thanks and praises be to God for saving me from it and I hope God forgives me for all I did whilst a part of it.

 Despite the increasing fame I was still depressed and no amount of attention was enough to satisfy me. I realized religion was necessary in order to fill the emotional void in my heart. In order to practice my religion I needed to understand the religious texts. To better understand the bible I enrolled in the bible study at the church I had been attending. One thing that struck me right away was how when following along with the teacher while she was reading I noticed my bible had different words than the bible she was reading from. Sometimes the verses in mine were so different from hers that I found our bibles were saying different things in the same places. This was troubling because if we had two bibles that say different things when they are supposed to have the same verses, then clearly our bibles could not be from the same sources. They couldn't both be the word of God. Yet these were both Catholic bibles, just different editions. If two Catholic bibles were so different then what about the other versions from different denominations? There are easily over 50 different versions of the bible in English, hundreds of versions if you count all the different languages, thousands if you count the different editions. On top of that they are not just different translations, some of the different bibles have completely different gospels and chapters. Some of these bibles say something is a sin while other bibles say it's not. This led me to ask the important question *"Which one is right?"* Eternal Salvation and Eternal Damnation was hanging in the balance so this was a very serious matter to consider. I had to go to the source and origins researching the time of Jesus pbuh and the creation of the bible. It turns out there were many different gospels written by many different people and each early church had their own collection of scripture. Every church practiced Christianity differently because they didn't all have access to the same scriptures. Ebionites kept all the Jewish laws requiring circumcision, kosher food, keeping the Sabbath and believed that only a Jew could become Christian. Ebionites also believed Jesus pbuh was completely human with a human father and not divine in any way, thinking he was an "adopted son of God" in a figurative sense. Ebionites also abstained from all meat and milk while teaching that the law of Moses wasn't just for Jews and Christians but that everyone had to follow the law of Moses, even pagans. However Ebionites rejected the entire Old Testament and only followed a gospel of Matthew and a gospel according to the Hebrews. The Marcionites were nearly complete opposites. Marcionites didn't keep any of the Jewish laws and said the God of Jesus pbuh was a different god altogether than the God of Israel because the God of Jesus was merciful and the God of Israel was full of wrath. Marcionites only accepted gentiles (non Jews) into their form of Christianity, no Jews were allowed. They thought Jesus pbuh wasn't human at all but only pretended to be human in order to pay a ransom for mankind to the God of the Jews, tricking the God of Israel into thinking a human paid the price for all sins, which he was forced to accept. Many other Christian denominations existed too, there were the Adoptionists, Agnoites, Alogians, Apellaeans, Apocarites, Apollinarianists, Aquarians, Archonticks, Artemonites, Artotytrites, Asclepidoteans, Ascodrogites, Ascodrutes, Bardesanistes, Basilidians, Beryllians, Bonosians, Cainians, Carpocratians, Cerdonians, Cerinthians, Chiliasts, Colluthians, Collylyridians, Docetists, Donatists, Elcesaites, Encratites, Eudoxians, Eusebians, Eustathians, Eutuchites, Eutychians, Florinians, Gacianitae, Gnostics, Helsaites, Heracleonites, Hermogenians, Heterousians, Hieracites, Lucianists, Luciferians, Macedonians, Manicheans, Marcellians, Marcosians, Maronites, Massalians, Melecians, Melchizedichians, Menanderians, Monarchianists, Monophysites, Montanists, Nazareans, Neonomians, Nestorians, Nicolaitians, Noetians, Novations, Ophites, Originists, Ossenians, Patricians, Paulianists, Pelagianists, Photinians, Priscillianists, Proclianites, Psaytrians, Ptolemattes, Proto-Coptics, Quartodecimani, Quintillians, Sabellians, Sachophori, Satanians, Saturnians, Secundians, Seleucians, Semi-Arians, Semi-Pelagians, Serverians, Sethians, Simonians, Soldins, Stilites, Subordinationists, Tatianites, Theopaschites, Trisormiani, Tritheists, Valentinians, Universalists, Zacheans, and that's just to name a few. I'm not being sarcastic either, that is only a few of the many which existed. All the diverse early Christian groups each had their own gospels supporting their views. This is biblically evident with Paul's numerous letters to the different churches that were practicing different forms of Christianity. It is important to note that Paul himself founded all those churches he wrote to. Paul wrote many letters because there were so many different forms of Christianity being practiced and so many different "scriptures" were being used to justify the drastically different ancient Christian denominations.

First of all who was Paul? Paul was originally known as Saul. Saul was a Pharisee of a certain Jewish sect that both John and Jesus pbut referred to as vipers advising believers to stay far away from them (including Saul). Saul was actually killing the people who followed Jesus pbuh, systematically eliminating every Christian community he came across, one by one. A little know fact about Saul was that he had proposed to a woman with amber hair named Poppaea Sabina asking her to marry him, she turned him down went to Rome and ended up marrying the Roman emperor Nero. It's not every day someone's pagan girlfriend says no to marriage and then runs off to marry the most powerful, famous and wealthy man on the planet. Saul must have been bitterly devastated and in desperate need for emotional validation, who wouldn't be in that situation? On the way to Damascus to kill more Christians, Saul allegedly had a vision which blinded him and was told he was called to a special mission by Jesus pbuh. There are different versions of this vision, some say he was alone, another says a certain number of people were with him with other contradictions over the number of people that were with him (if any) and whether they also heard what Saul was told or not. Then there is a great deal of controversy over what the vision actually was, whether it was Jesus pbuh, or if it was light, or what, but whatever happened on the road to Damascus Saul/Paul decided to change his approach to Christianity. Saul went into Damascus proclaiming that he converted to Christianity. In Damascus the Christians there said he was a liar, saying that he was planning to kill them before and now he was trying to corrupt their religion by following the strategy of joining them because he couldn't beat them in an attempt to distort and destroy Christianity from the inside. Saul/Paul was chased out of town, forced to leave the city at night in a basket-case, most likely as an emotional and spiritual basketcase as well. The biblical book of Acts says the Jews caused him to leave but this is spurious, because the whole reason Saul was going to Damascus was to kill Christians because no Jews were there who could kill them. Thus for Acts to then say that Jews caused the Christian Saul to leave contradicts the very reason Jewish Saul was going there. If Jews were there Saul wouldn't have went, if Saul went then it means if there were Jews in Damascus they couldn't harm anybody, especially not a killing machine like Saul. After Damascus Saul/Paul spent 3 years in Arabia with no record of what he was doing. Perhaps he went there searching for someone as part of his bounty hunter job, or maybe went to visit the Jews of Madinah who taught that the Torah said a prophet would be coming to that city. Next Saul/Paul resurfaced in Jerusalem and began teaching his theology to the actual companions of Jesus pbuh such as Peter, Barnabas, James and Thomas. The companions of Jesus pbuh rebuked Saul/Paul saying he was spreading heresy. Peter, considered to be the leading companion and "rock of the Church", wanted to kill Saul/Paul. Before they were able to kill Saul, who changed his name to Paul so as not to be associated with his past slaughtering of Christians, Barnabas (the 2nd closest companion of Jesus pbuh) convinced Peter and the others to spare Saul/Paul and teach him the truth about Jesus pbuh. Barnabas was the only companion of Jesus pbuh who thought Saul/Paul was sincere, but just confused. Up until this time the close companions only preached to Jews as per the instructions of Jesus pbuh:

Matthew 10:5-6 "*⁵ These twelve Jesus sent out with the following instructions: "<u>Do not go among the Gentiles or enter any town of the Samaritans.⁶ Go rather to the lost sheep of Israel.</u>""*

Matthew 15:22-26 "*²² A Canaanite woman from that vicinity came to him, crying out, "<u>Lord, Son of David</u>, have mercy on me! My daughter is demon-possessed and suffering terribly." ²³ <u>Jesus did not answer a word. So his disciples came to him and urged him</u>, "Send her away, for she keeps crying out after us." ²⁴* **He answered, "I was sent <u>only</u> to the lost sheep of Israel."***²⁵ The woman came and knelt before him. "<u>Lord, help me!" she said.</u> ²⁶ He replied, <u>"It is not right to take the children's bread and toss it to the dogs.</u>""*

  Saul/Paul accompanied Barnabas in his journeys. However Barnabas still strictly limited his teaching to Jews because the Pagans weren't fit to understand the message of Jesus pbuh, as evidenced by the account in the English translation of the New International Version of the Bible where the pagans mistakenly think Paul and Barnabas are gods and want to worship them in Acts 14:11-13,"*¹¹ When the crowd saw what Paul had done, <u>they shouted in the Lycaonian language,</u> **"The gods have come down to us in human form!"** ¹² **Barnabas they called Zeus, and Paul they called Hermes** because he was the chief speaker. ¹³ The priest of Zeus, whose temple was just outside the city, brought bulls and wreaths to the city gates because he and <u>the crowd wanted to offer sacrifices to them.</u>"* Paul eventually built up a name for himself using the credibility of the disciple Barnabas. In old age Barnabas retired to what is modern day Cyprus giving up on correcting Paul's heretical views, primarily because Paul refused to travel with John Mark who was Barnabas' Greek translator. Paul basically made Barnabas choose between using Paul as a translator or not traveling with Paul at all. Barnabas chose to retire rather than trust Paul to translate for him correctly. Paul then went out on his own to preach, using the contacts and credentials he obtained when traveling with the disciple Barnabas. Paul had never met Jesus pbuh during his time on earth. Luke acted as Paul's physician and likewise had never actually met or heard Jesus pbuh during his time on earth. Mark was the scribe of Peter and also never actually saw or heard Jesus pbuh while he was on earth. When Paul first began preaching, no Jews or Christians would listen to him and maintained he was a heretic of both religions. After having no success, he began preaching his Pauline version of Christianity to pagans who hadn't heard the teachings of Jesus pbuh before and were also unfamiliar with the teachings of Judaism. In the English translation of the New International Version of the bible Romans 15:20 Paul cites his reasons why: "*²⁰ **It has always been my ambition** to preach the gospel where Christ was not known, so that I would not be building on someone else's foundation.*" It is rather suspicious that a "follower of Jesus"(pbuh) would not want to build on his foundation but would want to preach to people who didn't know Christ pbuh. This implies that Paul did not see Jesus pbuh in a vision nor change his religion, because if that were the case he would be obligated to teach those who heard of Christ pbuh the new updates he had learned from Jesus pbuh, but as he unequivocally states he "always" wanted to preach "*where Christ was not known*" (pbuh). That Paul says "*it has always been my ambition*" is clearly a lie. It certainly was not Paul's ambition to preach the message of Jesus pbuh when he was killing Christians under the name of Saul. So what does Paul mean when he says, "*It has always been my ambition to preach the gospel where Christ was not known*"? Did Paul always intend to preach a religion to gentiles? What "gospel" is Paul referring to since the biblical gospels weren't written at that time? Was it just a slip of the tongue? But this sentence is in the bible, surely the bible doesn't contain any "slips of the tongue" or errors, does it? Paul's brand of Christianity was distinctly different from the others. The previously mentioned Marcionites, who believed the God of Moses pbuh was different than the God of Jesus pbuh, were actually descendants of Paul's ideology and they considered him to be a Saint. Paul later claimed that God personally revealed to him (technically this means he claims to be a prophet) that no Jewish laws had to be observed and that Jesus pbuh had replaced it all with a "new covenant", abrogating everything that came before him including the 10 commandments. When Paul told this to Jews and Christians he was laughed out of town, because they knew Jesus pbuh was circumcised, kept Kosher and stressed keeping all of the Law given to Moses pbuh in spirit and practice to the letter. As Matthew 5:17-18 says Jesus pbuh said " *Do not think that I have come to abolish the Law or the Prophets; I have not come to abolish them but to fulfill them. 18 For truly I tell you, until heaven and earth disappear, not the smallest letter, not the least stroke of a pen, will by any means disappear from the Law* " The real flesh and blood Jesus pbuh publicly accused the Rabbi's of ignoring the major principles and focusing too much on the minute specifics while breaking the Law of Moses pbuh themselves. Jesus pbuh never said the laws weren't to be followed, or anything about a "new covenant" rather he exposed the hypocrisy of the Jewish leaders who didn't follow the laws of Moses pbuh as they were supposed to be followed and corrupted the laws to suit their desires, following that which they pleased and/or ignoring the stuff they didn't like. The problem according to Jesus pbuh was not with the law at all, the problem was with the way people weren't following the law. May God protect us from falling into hypocrisy like the Pharisees. Paul said the unrealistic law of God was the problem and that God himself knew the law was too hard to follow. So therefore the body/blood of Jesus pbuh allegedly liberated everyone from having to follow any of God's laws. Jesus pbuh was not on earth to comment on Paul's claims.

    The conversion of Saul/Paul would be comparable to a conversion of Adolf Hitler to Judaism during WWII. Saul had the same reputation to early Christians as Hitler does to Jews today. Imagine if on the road to Auschwitz Hitler claimed to have had a vision, which only he saw and heard, that was from Moses pbuh who had given him special instructions to teach the Jews "the truth" about their religion. Imagine if Adolf Hitler then made a new Hebrew Bible and included 14 of his own books in it making Hitler's writings equal to 52% of the new Jewish Scripture, which they were expected to follow as though Hitler were inspired by the God of the Jews. Also Hitler being so moved by his newfound Judaism decides to change his name and writes all these new "Jewish holy scriptures" in his new name so that the reader wouldn't know his prior name or past history. Would it be reasonable to expect Jews to follow Adolf Hitler as an authority figure in their religion and label him as a saint? Perhaps if 100% of International Jewry confirmed him as genuine and his message to be true it would be acceptable to believe this. Although if 100% of Jews rejected the teachings of Hitler and said he wasn't teaching the truth about their religion, it would be a crime to consider Hitler an authority on Judaism, or even Jewish at all. If Hitler then taught gentiles his new version of Judaism and his converts called themselves Jews, it would still be unjust to consider Hitler a follower of Judaism or any of those who followed his teachings, regardless of whatever they claimed about themselves. This scenario is similar to how drastic the conversion of Saul/Paul was to Christianity. Because Saul was such a staunch enemy of the followers of Jesus pbuh it is important to scrutinize what exactly he taught in order to verify his sincerity. This way we can discover whether his intentions were pure or whether he had an ulterior motive. Strangely those who personally met and heard Jesus pbuh in the flesh all said that Paul was lying about the prophet Jesus pbuh. Those whom Paul was formerly persecuting rejected him and his new interpretation of the person of Jesus pbuh. Without success preaching to Jews or Christians, Paul went to pagan gentiles. With the pagans Paul had tons of success in spreading his religious views, with his followers calling themselves Christians even though they were technically Paulians. Like Paul they never actually met Jesus pbuh while he was on earth.

Before we discuss what Saul/Paul taught to the pagans who didn't know Christ pbuh about Christ pbuh, it is important to know what these pagans believed about God and religion. We must learn what their pagan rituals were so we can be aware of the circumstances and settings Paul was walking into. Thereby we can appreciate the difficulty he would encounter in having his teachings accepted by people who had never heard of Jesus pbuh.

The Ankh cross was adored in Egypt thousands of years before Jesus pbuh was born. Not by Jews or Christians, but by pagans. The Catholic Church adopted the cross symbol approximately 600 years after Jesus pbuh was believed to have been crucified. The early Christians of North Africa even rejected the pagan wooden cross after Tertullian condemned it. One of the famous fathers of the Church Tertullian conceded that the pagans worshiped crucified saviors who would be hanging on a cross. Tertullian considered it blasphemy for Christians to have anything to do with crosses because they were a pagan symbol frequently glorified in rituals of idolatry, *"Crosses, moreover, we Christians neither venerate nor wish for. You indeed who consecrate gods of wood venerate wooden crosses, perhaps as parts of your gods. For your very standards, as well as your banners, and flags of your camps, what are they but crosses gilded and adorned? Your victorious trophies not only imitate the appearance of a simple cross, but also that of a man affixed to it."* The bishop Tertullian believed Jesus pbuh was crucified, even still he rejected the cross as a pagan object and un-Christian. Despite being a Christian, Tertullian said that Christianity borrowed the cross and the atonement concept of *"dying for the sins of mankind"* from pagans.

The original form of the first cross was the initial letter T of the pagan Babylonian god Tammuz, written like "†". During Babylonian baptism ceremonies, the pagan priests of Tammuz would make the sign of the cross on the forehead of the baptized. When praying the worshippers of Tammuz would make the sign of the "†" over their heart. The Babylonian virgins would also wear this symbol of Tammuz around their necks as a sign of their faith. During March and April for 40 days the pagans would mourn the death of Tammuz who was thought to be the only begotten son of the sun-god and moon goddess. The bible refers specifically to this 40-day period of mourning for the pagan god Tammuz, when it took place in Jerusalem with the pagan idol Tammuz in the temple during the Babylonian occupation.

Ezekiel 8:14-20 *"14 Then he brought me to the entrance of the north gate of the house of the LORD, and <u>I saw women sitting there, mourning the god Tammuz.</u> 15 <u>He said to me, "Do you see this, **son of man**? You will see things that are</u>*

even more detestable than this." ¹⁶ *He then brought me into the inner court of the house of the* LORD, *and there at the entrance to the temple, between the portico and the altar, were about twenty-five men. With their backs toward the temple of the* LORD *and their faces toward the east,* they were bowing down to the sun *in the east.* ¹⁷ *He said to me, "Have you seen this, son of man?* Is it a trivial matter for the people of Judah to do the detestable things they are doing here? *Must they also fill the land with violence and continually arouse my anger?* **Look at them putting the branch to their nose!** ¹⁸ *Therefore I will deal with them in anger; I will not look on them with pity or spare them. Although they shout in my ears, I will not listen to them."* Verses from an English translation of the New International Version of the Bible.

Ezekiel says, "*I saw women sitting there, mourning the god Tammuz*" this indicates that he didn't hear what they were saying but was able to visibly identify them. Most probably because they were wearing the cross of Tammuz around their neck. The verses also repeatedly stress how Ezekiel saw, seen and will see; indicating that the witnessing of detestable things was entirely visual. That verse 15 refers to Ezekiel as "son of man" is also important because many Christians think "son of man" means "son of God" whenever Jesus pbuh is referred to by such a title but clearly Ezekiel was not a son of God; thus we can deduce that the phrase "son of man" does not mean "son of God". It continues to explain how the people were bowing (in some translations worshipping) the Sun. God didn't think it was trivial and when they "put the branch to their nose" it caused God to cut ties with them so that he wouldn't answer their prayers because of them worshipping falsehood. But what does it mean that they "put the branch to their nose"? It's simple really, whenever believers worshiped they put their nose on the ground in prostration to pray, thus "*putting the branch to their nose*" means they worshiped the branch. Since Tammuz and Sun worship is also mentioned, in context it literally means these people worshiped the cross. In actual meaning they worshiped the idea that the Sun or Son of the Sun God "Tammuz" died for the forgiveness of their sins. As a result the bible tells us that God said: "*Therefore I will deal with them in anger; I will not look on them with pity or spare them. Although they shout in my ears, I will not listen to them."*

Some pagans believed that the "sun of God" was their savior instead of a son of God. They thought the sun was visibly hung on a cross or "crossified" when it passed through the equinoxes. People in northern climates were "*saved*" by the "crossification" of the sun when it crossed over the equatorial line into the season of spring, at the vernal equinox. Coincidentally Easter is always the first Sunday after the full moon of vernal equinox. The sun gave out a saving heat and light to the world stimulating the generative organs of animal and vegetable life. They believed the sun was the light of the world for which all life on earth was eternally dependent upon.

In Rome the mythical founder Romulus was allegedly born of a virgin priestess of Vesta who had sworn herself to celibacy before claiming to be impregnated by the divine. The king didn't believe it and tossed Romulus and his twin Remus into the river to die. Romulus is believed to have been saved by a heavenly wind and proclaimed to be the "son of god". After "post-death" appearances he became known as

Quirinus who is a part of the Archaic Trinity which was worshiped by the Romans. The sun was also thought to have grown dark on the day of the death of Romulus.

In Greece Dionysus was believed to have been born in a manger on December 25th. Allegedly crucified after a final supper with his 12 companions, he told his enemies "*You know not what you are doing.*" Dionysius was thought to have risen from the dead on March 25th. He was also symbolically eaten in a Eucharistic ceremony as a means of purification. He was called "*King of Kings*", "*God of Gods*", "*Redeemer*", "*Savior*", "*Sin-Bearer*", "*Anointed One*", "*Only begotten Son*" and the "*Alpha and Omega*"(the first and last letters of the Greek alphabet). Dionysus is also thought to have turned water into wine. He was represented by the letters "IHS" and sometimes "IES".

The Celtic Druids and Gauls worshiped a person they called Esus or sometimes Hesus. He was believed to have been born on December 25th to a virgin as the son of the sun god and was the third person of the Celtic trinity. Hesus/Esus was believed to have been crucified with an elephant on one side and a lamb on the other. The elephant symbolizing the sins of the world and the lamb representing the innocence of Hesus/Esus. In some sense they believed "*the lamb of God took away the sins of the world*". The Celtic/Druid cross of Esus/Hesus which they worshiped remains popular to this day. The cross of Esus/Hesus was represented as an artistic cross made of interwoven branches on top of a circle, which symbolized the crucified son of the sun deity. Unfortunately many Christians mistake this Celtic/Druid cross as a Irish Christian cross and unknowingly wear them not knowing it's a cross of Esus/Hesus and not one of Jesus pbuh. When Julius Caesar conquered Gaul many Druids became roman slaves eventually gaining roman citizenship and their religion spread throughout the Roman Empire and is still practiced by some people today.

In Persia Zoroaster was called the "*Word made flesh*" and had a sacred cup teaching a religion that performed the Eucharist ritual. Allegedly born of a virgin, baptized in a river by "water, fire and holy wind", at 30 years of age he began his teaching, was tempted in the wilderness by the devil, cast demons out and reportedly gave sight to a blind man. While he is often depicted as one man it is more likely that there were many Zoroasters and they all conflated into one persona. The next Zoroaster is believed to come in 2341 CE and again be born to a virgin and begin his ministry at the age of 30.

Another deity of pagan Greece, Prometheus was called the "Logos"(Word) and had a fisherman friend known as "Petraeus"(Peter) who had deserted him. Prometheus was believed to have descended from heaven as God incarnated, he was thought to have been crucified and then risen from the dead in order to save mankind. When the pagan greeks performed their rituals they based their actions on the trinity. For instance they would sprinkle "holy water" on the altar 3 times and then sprinkle the people with it as well 3 times. Next they'd take some frankincense with three fingers and toss it upon the altar 3 times. This was done in accordance with what their oracle told them about all sacred things being done in threes.

In MesoAmerica the deity Quetzacoatl and his father Tezcatlipoca were believed to have killed the demon deity Cipatcli by pulling him apart in 4 directions, after distracting him by getting Cipatcli to eat the foot of Tezcatlipoca. The heaven was then made from the head of Cipatcli, earth made from his body and the underworld made from his tail. Then after the sacrifce of Tezcatlipoca's foot, Father and Son, created the Universe then Quetzacoatl came to earth as a human to be sacrificed for the salvation of all mankind. The Aztec and Mayan god Quetzalcoatl was believed to have been born of a virgin, tempted and fasted 40 days. Archaeological evidence suggests he had been crucified with nails driven through his hands and feet. Quetzalcoatl is sometimes represented as having been crucified between two thieves. Or with 3 crosses, a large cross in between two smaller crosses. After being crucified Quetzalcoatl is thought to have went to hell and rose from the dead on the third day before heading east. Mexican scriptures also depict Quetzalcoatl as having healed people, baptized, forgiven sins and been anointed with oil. A Eucharistic tradition also existed among Aztecs. Aztecs believed they ate the body of Quetzalcoatl in the form of a proxy, Aztecs were expecting his second coming when the Christian Spaniards invaded. One can imagine them arguing over religion, with the Christian shouting Jesus (pbuh) and the Aztec shouting Quetzalcoatl, both shoving crosses in each other's faces. Hernando Cortes, the Spanish conquistador who conquered the Aztecs, commented: "*the Devil had positively taught to the Mexicans the same things God had taught to Christendom.*" Incas and Aztecs also worshiped the "sun of God" thinking it would die if they didn't sacrifice people to it. Aztecs and Mayans who weren't killed by Spanish diseases or weapons eventually ended up converting to Christianity under the presumption that Quetzalcoatl and Christ were the same persons and that Christian rituals were just a different version of their pagan rites, some Aztecs even thought Cortez was Quetzalcoatl. The Spaniard's swords also provided them with extra motivation to become Christian too. After the Christianization process took place many books, monuments, artifacts and temples demonstrating the similarities between the mesoamerican religions and Christianity were destroyed or defaced. Although not all the evidence was destroyed and we are able to know of the eerie similarities between Aztec and Christian beliefs. It is amazing how they held such similar beliefs despite Aztecs and early Christians not having contact with each other. It is a real shame that they don't teach the similarities between Aztec and Christian beliefs to kids in school when they teach children about the Aztecs. Although it's easy to guess why they don't, Aztec parents would probably complain.

Attis of Phrygia was believed to have been born on December 25th. On "Black Friday" Attis was allegedly mutilated and bled to death under a pine tree. Believers in Attis thought he was the savior slain for the salvation of mankind who had his holy blood spilt for the redemption of the earth, who then descended into the underworld and rose again three days later. His festival took place during March 22-25th, a pine tree was cut on the 22nd and an image of Attis tied to the trunk, then the effigy was burned in a tomb. At night on March 24th priests opened the tomb and would conveniently find it empty to the astonishment of the crowd. On the 25th they celebrated the resurrection of Attis baptizing his followers in blood which caused their sins to be washed away, they were told they had been "born again" through Attis. Usually this would happen under a platform with the candidate standing in a pit where the blood of a bull would flow over them. The poor baptism candidates who couldn't afford to sacrifice a bull would use a sheep instead believing their sins were literally washed away by *"the blood of the lamb"*. The symbol of Astoria is the egg, which is part of the Easter egg tradition that people practice today. Thought of as being both the divine son and the father, the body of Attis was symbolically eaten in a ritual by his worshippers in the form of bread.

The birthday of Jesus Christ pbuh was first celebrated by some churches in the spring and other churches celebrated it on January 6th. Orthodox Christians still celebrate it on January 6th to this day. There was significant confusion concerning the actual date of the birth of Jesus pbuh, even today no one knows the true date which the birth took place. Probably because Jesus pbuh never celebrated his own birthday anniversaries. In 345 CE Pope Julius decreed that the birthday should thenceforth be held on December 25th, three days after the winter solstice, the same day on which the births of Mithras, Dionysus, Sol Invictus, Apollo, Attis, Dusares and several other pagan gods were celebrated. It was the most pagan day of the year and Pope Julius knew it. This means December 25th was the worst possible day he could have picked, unless he considered Christianity to be another pagan religion thinking that by celebrating the birth of Jesus pbuh on the same day as the pagans' celebrations it would make pagans more likely to convert to the Christian faith. But what's even worse than picking a pagan day to celebrate the birthday was that most Christians at the time condemned birthday celebrations in total and didn't celebrate anybody's birthday, including their own, because they knew them to be a pagan religious ritual based on astrology, horoscopes, superstitions and the belief that a person had a special protector spirit/god since the day they were born and would throw a party for that god on the anniversary of their birthdate. Which of course since this spirit/god didn't exist the gifts were consumed by the pagan individual themselves. The popular Church father Origen even wrote that not only should Christians refrain from birthday celebrations but they should look upon their own birthdays with disgust. Although as baptism candles were given(and still are) which are meant to be lit on the anniversary of one's baptism, since pagans also used birthday candles for their superstitions and Christians considered baptism to be their "rebirth" eventually the Christians incorporated the pagan tradition of birthday candles with their baptismal candles. Doing this helped pagans who celebrated their birthdays convert to Christianity thinking they could still do their birthday parties, but could just call it a baptism party instead using the candle they got when baptised. Yet over time the baptismal candle tradition has been practically abandoned and now most Christians just do birthday celebrations exactly how the pagans did theirs. While Christians justify this by saying Jesus pbuh celebrated his birthday, which he didn't but even if they are referring to the Christmas story that's very different than the celebrations that get held today with entirely different rituals. Yet more importantly at best any celebration that may have took place when Jesus pbuh was born was a one day thing, they didn't do it every year. So doing it on the anniversary of your birth actually means such people think they are more important than Jesus pbuh since they claim he had one party in his life and they celebrate themselves once a year. The exception for Jesus pbuh is that his birth was divine miracle so that's actually something worth celebrating, once. Ours is not. Plus you know who's really special? Adam pbuh and Eve, they didn't have a "birthday" they had a "God created me" day, which they never celebrated annually because it's not an accomplishment of theirs and it doesn't please God.

Not only would Paul be preaching something to sun cults, but also vegetation cults which were even older. Originally the king or leader of the tribe would be the sacrificial victim. Ancient man believed the prosperity of the tribe was dependent on the ruler's wellbeing. When the king became old or feeble, it was expected the tribe would suffer a similar decline. So the king, which they regarded as a god in human form, was sacrificed and then replaced. As their ideologies evolved instead of killing the king of the tribe they would substitute the son of the king to take his place in the sacrificial rite. The son being believed to be the offspring of divinity was called the "*son of god*". He was generally slain while tied to a sacred tree with arms outstretched in the shape of a cross. After that the body would be entombed and was thought to rise from the dead after three days, specifically three days because of the interval between the old and new moons. The moon was believed to have a direct correlation with the growth of crops. With the crop of wheat being made into bread which sustained the life of the world population. The English translation of the New International Version of the bible references pagan Moabites killing the firstborn son of their king in a battle with Israelites thinking the sacrifice would grant them salvation from defeat in 2 Kings 3:26-27, "*When the king of Moab saw that the battle had gone against him, he took with him seven hundred swordsmen to break through to the king of Edom, but they failed.* ²⁷ **Then he took his firstborn son, who was to succeed him as king, and offered him as a sacrifice on the city wall.** *The fury against Israel was great; they withdrew and returned to their own land.*"

The English translation of the New International Version of the bible also says God hates sons being sacrificed and it's a practice of disbelievers to kill their kids in 2 Kings 16:2-4, "*Ahaz was twenty years old when he became king, and he reigned in Jerusalem sixteen years.* **Unlike David his father, he did not do what was right** *in the eyes of the* L{ORD} *his God.* ³ *He followed the ways of the kings of Israel and* **even sacrificed his son in the fire, engaging in the detestable practices of the nations the** L{ORD} **had driven out before the Israelites.** ⁴ *He offered sacrifices and burned incense at the high places, on the hilltops and under every spreading tree.*" These verses also indicate that David pbuh did what was right in the view of God thereby clearing him of the slander other parts of the bible contain accusing him of adultery. They also inform us that burning incense as an act of worship is another thing God detests. Yet today many Christians burn incense in church as part of their worship services. While the English translation of the New International Version of the bible continues to tell another instance of what Jews did that caused God to hate them in 2 Kings 21:1-16,"*Manasseh was twelve years old when he became king, and he reigned in Jerusalem fifty-five years. His mother's name was Hephzibah.* ² **He did evil in the eyes of the** L{ORD}**, following the detestable practices of the nations the** L{ORD} **had driven out before the Israelites.** ³ **He rebuilt the high places his father Hezekiah had destroyed; he also erected altars to Baal and made an Asherah pole**, as Ahab king of Israel had done. **He bowed down to all the starry hosts and worshiped them.** ⁴ **He built altars in the temple of the** L{ORD}, of which the L{ORD} had said, "In Jerusalem I will put my Name." ⁵ **In the two courts of the temple of the** L{ORD}**, he built altars to all the starry hosts.** ⁶ **He sacrificed his own son in the fire, practiced divination, sought omens, and consulted mediums and spiritists. He did much evil in the eyes of the** L{ORD}**, arousing his anger.** ⁷ *He took the carved*

Asherah pole he had made and put it in the temple, of which the LORD had said to David and to his son Solomon, "In this temple and in Jerusalem, which I have chosen out of all the tribes of Israel, I will put my Name forever. ⁸ I will not again make the feet of the Israelites wander from the land I gave their ancestors, if only they will be careful to do everything I commanded them and will keep the whole Law that my servant Moses gave them." ⁹ But the people did not listen. Manasseh led them astray, so that **they did more evil than the nations the LORD had destroyed** before the Israelites. ¹⁰ **The LORD said through his servants the prophets:** ¹¹ "Manasseh king of Judah has committed **these detestable sins.** He has done more evil than the Amorites who preceded him and has led Judah into sin with his idols." ¹² Therefore this is what the LORD, the God of Israel, says: I am going to bring such disaster on Jerusalem and Judah that the ears of everyone who hears of it will tingle. ¹³ I will stretch out over Jerusalem the measuring line used against Samaria and the plumb line used against the house of Ahab. I will wipe out Jerusalem as one wipes a dish, wiping it and turning it upside down. ¹⁴ I will forsake the remnant of my inheritance and give them into the hands of enemies. They will be looted and plundered by all their enemies; ¹⁵ *they have done evil in my eyes and have aroused my anger from the day their ancestors came out of Egypt until this day.*" ¹⁶ *Moreover, Manasseh also shed so much innocent blood* that he filled Jerusalem from end to end – besides the sin that he had caused Judah to commit, so that they did evil in the eyes of the LORD."

    This passage highlights specific acts of pagan worship the Israelites copied which God hates with a passion. Rebuilding pagan places was detested. Making altars to Baal and an Asherah pole was also detestable. As was building altars in temples in general. Yet Christians are famous for altars in churches, and christian scholars even say that the altars started out being built as tombs over martyrs. Thus the graves of Christian martyrs were made into places of worship, as the Vatican is believed to be built on the graves of Peter and Paul. Regarding Baal many pagans used the word "Baal", which means "Lord", to describe their god but there is a specific type of Baal which is referenced here that God detests, verse 3 tells us Manasseh erected altars to the same Baal that Ahab had done. According to the bible Ahab had married a famous disbeliever called Jezebel who worshiped a Baal who was considered the son of El and had been killed and resurrected from the dead. The word El was short for Elohim, which was a name for the Creator of everything, so the Baal Jezebel worshiped was an alleged son of the true God who they thought was killed and rose from the dead. While the Asherah pole was a phallic pole or obelisk; similar to the phallic Washington Monument and the obelisk outside the Vatican in St. Peter's Square. The key difference between Asherah poles and regular phallic obelisks was that pagans put sunbursts on top of the Asherah poles. They were essentially sun pillars where people gathered to worship the Sun of God likely combining it with the phallic pagan obelisks to emphasize how just as when an erect penis "dies" or loses it's erection after intercourse thereby giving life as a result, the Sun of God also died at the vernal equinox so that they could have eternal life and they would rejoice everyday when the Sun of God rose again over the phallic pillar stirring them to daily exuberance and excitement akin to the excitement an erect penis causes. Since the penis didn't stay erect forever it meant humans wouldn't live forever as life given by man was temporary, but because the sun pillar or Asherah pole stayed erect 24/7 and the sun would always shine it's light on the pole and those around it, they likely took it to mean that the "Sun of God" provides eternal life only to those who worship it around the Asherah pole.

God is said to have immensely detested the Israelites' worshipping the numerous "Baals" of the polytheistic pagans in the English translation of the New International Version of the Bible in Judges 2:11-13,

"Then <u>the Israelites did evil in the eyes of the LORD and served the Baals.</u> 12 They forsook the LORD, the God of their ancestors, who had brought them out of Egypt. They followed and worshiped various gods of the peoples around them. They aroused the LORD's anger 13 because they forsook him and served Baal and the Ashtoreths."

And in Judges 3:1-7, *"These are the nations the LORD left to test all those Israelites who had not experienced any of the wars in Canaan 2 (he did this only to teach warfare to the descendants of the Israelites who had not had previous battle experience): 3 the five rulers of the Philistines, all the Canaanites, the Sidonians, and the Hivites living in the Lebanon mountains from Mount Baal Hermon to Lebo Hamath. 4 <u>They were left to test the Israelites to see whether they would obey the LORD's commands, which he had given their ancestors through Moses.</u> 5 The Israelites lived among the Canaanites, Hittites, Amorites, Perizzites, Hivites and Jebusites. 6 They took their daughters in marriage and gave their own daughters to their sons, and served their gods. 7 <u>**The Israelites did evil in the eyes of the LORD; they forgot the LORD their God and served the Baals and the Asherahs.**</u>"*

Keep in mind those who worshiped Baal still believed that God had created everything. The problem was they attributed a son to God which he never had and claimed their Baal was the Lord instead of God. The way God uses the word "Baals" in the bible indicates that he didn't distinguish between one Baal and the other, they were all false deities that were alleged to be his sons. A misconception is that all pagan idolatry involved worshipping statues. While it is idolatrous to have statues, most pagans who worshiped these Baals considered the statue to be a powerless representation of the alleged son of God whom they were praying to. So when the bible says serving Baals was evil idolatry, it's not simply because the pagans had statues of Baals. The idolatry was the fact that they falsely attributed sons to God and prayed to them instead of God alone. The bible explains that Israelites fell into this polytheism by marrying disbelievers which led them and their children to believe in alleged sons of God which God never had. Thus they forgot that they should only pray to God and no others besides him, as the first commandment instructed. The Israelites didn't forget the commandment itself, they just distorted it's meaning and didn't follow it as Moses pbuh taught them to. Some likely just used Baal as an intercessor, thinking he wasn't God but that Baal would pray to God on their behalf if they prayed to Baal. To God this was disbelief. But it gets even worse as verse 7 indicates they also served Asherahs. This is not to be confused with Asherah poles which have already been explained. Asherah herself was thought of as a consort to El or Elohim/Yahweh/God. Also referred to as the "Queen of Heaven". Which ironically enough is the same exact title which Catholics and some Eastern Orthodox Christians give for Mary the mother of Jesus pbuh. They also claim that Mary is the "Mother of God", since they consider her son Jesus pbuh to be God their Lord and Savior. Whereas Asherah was considered the mother of Baal. When the bible condemns people serving Baals and Asherahs, it is a condemnation of all the false religions that teach God has kids or consorts. The prophets Elijah and Elisha pbut condemned these evil beliefs and practices as idolatry and the bible says they killed those guilty of such crimes. This is alluded to in Jeremiah 44:1-23 and Israelites are told of the punishment that will come because of adopting such polytheistic practices:"*This word came to Jeremiah concerning all the Jews living in Lower Egypt – in Migdol, Tahpanhes and Memphis – and in Upper Egypt:* ² *"This is what the L*ORD *Almighty, the God of Israel, says: You saw the great disaster I brought on Jerusalem and on all the towns of Judah. Today they lie deserted and in ruins* ³ *because of the evil they have done. They aroused my anger by burning incense to and worshipping other gods that neither they nor you nor your ancestors ever knew.* ⁴ **Again and again I sent my servants the prophets, who said, 'Do not do this detestable thing that I hate!'** ⁵ *But they did not listen or pay attention; they did not turn from their wickedness or stop burning incense to other gods.* ⁶ *Therefore, my fierce anger was poured out; it raged against the towns of Judah and the streets of Jerusalem and made them the desolate ruins they are today.* ⁷ *"Now this is what the L*ORD *God Almighty, the God of Israel, says: Why bring such great disaster on yourselves by cutting off from Judah the men and women, the children and infants, and so leave yourselves without a remnant?* ⁸ *Why arouse my anger with what your hands have made, burning incense to other gods in Egypt, where you have come to live? You will destroy yourselves and make yourselves a curse and an object of reproach among all the nations on earth.* ⁹ *Have you forgotten the wickedness committed by your ancestors and by the kings and queens of Judah and the wickedness committed by you and your wives in the land of Judah and the streets of Jerusalem?* ¹⁰ *To this day they have not humbled themselves or shown reverence, nor have they followed my law and the decrees I set before you and your ancestors.* ¹¹ *"Therefore this is what the L*ORD *Almighty, the God of Israel, says: I am determined to bring disaster on you and to destroy all Judah.* ¹² *I will take away the remnant of Judah who were determined to go to Egypt to settle there. They will all perish in Egypt; they will fall by the sword or die from famine. From the least to the greatest, they will die by sword or famine. They will become a curse and an object of horror, a curse and an object of reproach.* ¹³ *I will punish those who live in Egypt with the sword, famine and plague, as I punished Jerusalem.* ¹⁴ *None of the remnant of Judah who have gone to live in Egypt will escape or survive to return to the land of Judah, to which they long to return and live; none will return except a few fugitives."* ¹⁵ *Then all the men who knew that their wives were burning incense to other gods, along with all the women who were present – a large assembly – and all the people living in Lower and Upper Egypt, said to Jeremiah,* ¹⁶ *"We will not listen to the message you have spoken to us in the name of the L*ORD*!* ¹⁷ *We will certainly do everything we said we would: We will burn incense to the Queen of Heaven and will pour out drink offerings to her just as we and our ancestors, our kings and our officials did in the towns of Judah and in the streets of Jerusalem. At that time we had plenty of food and were well off and suffered no harm.* ¹⁸ *But ever since we stopped burning incense to the Queen of Heaven and pouring out drink offerings to her, we have had nothing and have been perishing by sword and famine."* ¹⁹ *The women added, "When we burned incense to the Queen of Heaven and poured out drink offerings to her, did not our husbands know that we were* **making cakes impressed with her image** *and pouring out drink offerings to her?"* ²⁰ *Then Jeremiah said to all the people, both men and women, who were answering him,* ²¹ *"Did not the L*ORD *remember and call to mind the incense burned in the towns of Judah and the streets of Jerusalem by you and your ancestors, your kings and your officials and the people of the land?* ²² *When the L*ORD *could no longer endure your wicked actions and the detestable things you did, your land became a curse and a desolate waste without inhabitants, as it is today.* ²³ *Because* **you have burned incense and have sinned against the L**ORD **and have not obeyed him or followed his law or his decrees or his stipulations**, *this disaster has come upon you, as you now see."*

These bible verses inform us of the warning Jeremiah pbuh gave to the Jews who chose to live amongst disbelievers in Egypt and as a result adopted the pagan customs and practices which resulted in their disbelief although they didn't realize it. This is similar to the status of many people today living in communities of disbelievers where they celebrate pagan holidays and practices not knowing that by doing so they become disbelievers. The ancient Jews when told they would be punished scoffed the warning, illogically reasoning that if God didn't like what they were doing then he wouldn't let them have gotten rich when they were doing it. This is a common excuse people use today. They will think that God must not hate them because they have money and an easy life, thinking that if they had disbelieved God would automatically have harmed them as a result. The Jews who were hated by God thought the same thing. Then the bible says how they burned incense to other than God and made cakes and offerings of drink as a part of these innovated rituals. Thus the bible describes the disbelieving Jews as having participated in some type of Eucharist ceremony. With historical knowledge and biblical cross referencing we are able to better understand the detestable practices in 2 Kings 21 about Manasseh erecting altars to Baal and making an Asherah pole. Thus we can continue with the verses from 2 Kings 21 that were shown on previous pages which you may want to check again and reread in order to experience the difference of reading bible verses with contextual knowledge. By rereading the verses earlier mentioned and then rereading the verses from Jeremiah we can see how the verses from Jeremiah relate to the verses in 2 Kings 21 showing how the biblical promise to destroy Judah and Jerusalem because of these sins came true, according to the bible, but instead of stopping the sins as a result the Jews just migrated to pagan Egypt, becoming even bigger sinners.

Manasseh *"bowing down to the starry hosts"* can have 2 meanings. One is that he could've worshiped the sun which is a star, and the other is that he could've practiced astrology believing in zodiac signs foretelling the future, both equal disbelief. On top of that Manasseh is said to have sacrificed his own son to the fire, which God hated. Yet some Christians claim God sacrificed Jesus pbuh and sent him to hellfire so that he would suffer for everyone else and that when he was let out of hellfire by the devil (who realistically isn't in charge of hell) for being unjustly put there since he was innocent, then allegedly the doors wouldn't close and all the prophets and previous dead people in hell allegedly followed Jesus pbuh out. Which according to some Christians was done out of God's love for all even though there is no biblical basis for this fringe Christian theory, it's a fringe theory today but used to be the mainstream doctrine. On the contrary the biblical God says someone sacrificing their son to the fire was evil. Other evils were divination, seeking omens, consulting mediums and spiritists (aka fortune tellers and those who claim to speak to dead people) as well as putting an Asherah pole in the temple. Which could be meant literally or that he figuratively made the Sun of God the object of worship in the temple. The bible says these things were more evil than the evil done by those pagan nations God had destroyed and that the prophets proclaimed that these were detestable sins, idolatry and worse than what the pagans who will burn in hell forever had done. As if it couldn't get any worse then we are informed he shed innocent blood, which was evil. This shows us how important it is for a country not to shed innocent blood. Any countries today who kill innocents are evil according to the bible, that includes innocents who get killed while killing the guilty. God instructs us to either only kill guilty people or don't kill anybody. There is never any room for mistakes when blood is shed. Yet despite God expressing his hatred for the shedding of innocent blood, Christians fervently believe that the shedding of the innocent blood of Jesus pbuh is a requirement for salvation and that God did what he said he hated being done, out of love. This is a contradictory belief to say God hates the shedding of innocent blood but loves the shedding of the innocent blood of Jesus pbuh. In the bible itself God made no exception to the rule, God hates the shedding of all innocent blood. How could salvation and paradise be gained through something God hates and forbid?

So that is a short explanation of the sun cults which existed and historically contaminated the Israelites' beliefs causing God to hate them, but there were also other religions practiced at the time Paul started preaching his message.

The Buddhist priests of Tibet are called Lamas. The Grand Lama (Dalai Lama) is believed to be the direct successor to the Saint La having the actual soul of Saint La within him and acts as Supreme Pontiff, who is thought to be immaculate and infallible just as Roman Catholics believe the Pope is. The Dalai Lama is thought to have the power to bless people and is considered the vicegerent of God whose interpretation of sacred books is thought to be divine inspiration, once more just like what Roman Catholics believe about the Pope. When a French Jesuit missionary named Father Evariste Régis Huc visited the Lamas in Tibet he saw their religion included: "Holy water", prayers for the dead, singing in their services, relics of their saints, the burning of incense, monasteries and convents, monks who chant, fasting and prayer beads as well. Vajra Buddhism even has a baptismal rite of initiation! Then the Jesuit missionary tried to persuade the Buddhists to become Roman Catholic. After the Catholic missionary finished his lengthy explanation of Catholicism, the Tibetan lama famously replied: "*Your religion is the same as ours.*" Now what people typically don't know is that Buddha is a title referring to "one who is awake" and is a state of mind, not a name. The title of Buddha doesn't necessarily refer to the most famous Buddha Siddhārtha Gautama. Buddhists believe in 28 confirmed Buddhas, Gautama being the most recent, although more than 28 are believed to have existed. There are many different Buddhas and forms of Buddhism. Some Buddhists even believe in one Buddha who was crucified, died and resurrected who had been nailed through his hands and feet. Of course not all denominations of Buddhism believe this, but there are Sanskrit texts which teach that this other Buddha had 12 disciples, was thought to be divine and taught baptism in the name of Buddha, the Dharma and the Samgha. Another little known fact about Buddhism is that Buddhists believe in a trinity, but it is difficult to explain and understand since the many different Buddhist branches have different names for the parts of it and exactly what/who it is. One narration of a Buddha has him say, "*Enough, Vakkali. Why do you want to see this filthy body? Whoever sees the Dhamma sees me; whoever sees me sees the Dhamma.*" Some Buddhists think this statement confirms that particular Buddha's divinity in that he and the Dhamma are one and the Buddha is part of the trinity. Coincidentally this is nearly identical to the bible verse which claims Jesus pbuh said whoever sees him has seen the father although the Buddhist record predates the gospel verse. Professor Soothill has even recorded that he heard Buddhist children in India singing *"Buddha loves me, this I know. For the Sutras tell me so."* which is nearly identical to the Christian lyrics to a popular hymn/song except Christian's replace the word Buddha with Jesus and Sutras with Bible. On most key points concerning morality, Buddhism and Christianity are nearly identical and in complete agreement. Therefore when we look deep into Catholicism and Buddhism it makes total sense for the Tibetan Lama to have told the Jesuit missionary that *"Your religion is the same as ours."* Since Buddhism is much older than Christianity some have claimed Christianity is a copycat, but personally I don't think Paul or early Christians came into contact with Buddhism or were directly influenced by Buddhist doctrines. Although Buddhism was purportedly studied and practiced in Egypt during the time of Jesus pbuh. The cultural center of Alexandria, which was an interfaith melting pot, may have been a learning center for many early Christian leaders. If as I believe there was no influence on Christianity by Buddhism, then it makes the coincidences and similarities between these religions that much more remarkable but then again it might not be coincidence. Yet since writing developed in China, Central America, Egypt and Mesopotamia all independently and simultaneously around 3,000 BCE, it could all be coincidental.

In India Krishna is said to have had his birth heralded by a bright star, descending from royal lineage he was humbly born in a cave and visited by wise men and shepherds as an infant; thousands of years before Jesus pbuh. King Kansa ordered the killing of all male children born on the same night as Krishna in an attempt to kill the boy, but his parents were warned by angels to flee to safety. Krishna was believed to be "without sin" who was both a human and divine son of God, as well as God incarnated who came to earth to cleanse human beings of all sins. Titles for Krishna included: *"Redeemer"*, *"Son of God"*, *"Firstborn"*, *"Universal Word"*, *"Sin-Bearer"* and *"Our Lord and Saviour"*. Hindus also burn incense in their temples. Those who wash with sacred water before entering the Hindu temple are thought to have all their sins washed away and are "born again". A Hindu Brahmin who did the half-month sacrifices regularly was thought to become a god for that time-frame. To transition from being mortal to being immortal they were sprinkled with water to symbolize a seed. Then they pretended to be an embryo by being shut up in a special hut symbolizing the womb. Under their robe would be a belt and black antelope skin to represent the inner and outer membranes an embryo is wrapped in. While pretending to be an embryo they couldn't scratch themselves with nails or sticks, because if an embryo were scratched with such things it would die. If they moved in the hut it was because embryos move in the womb, if the fists were clenched it was because embryo's fists are clenched in the womb as well. If while bathing they took off the antelope skin but kept the robe on it was because the child is born with the inner membrane but not the outer. After this embryo stage the Brahmin was "born again" as a god on earth. In modern India these "born again" ceremonies are for sinners who become a new person after expiation, no longer thinking themselves to be responsible for the sins they committed in their earlier state. Aborigines of India punish criminals with a "born-again" ceremony where the guilty is put in a sealed earthen pot, buried in the sand and comes out as a fresh incarnation of earth. However then they are put in a grass hut that is burned and they run out as it burns to get immersed in water, afterward they get their hair cut and pay a fee. Thereby they are "born-again" as a new person and free from all responsibility for the previous crimes they committed. There are other hindu "born again" ceremonies as well that involve rituals similar to baptism, and those who do them have a similar attitude as "born again" Christians. The Hindu deity Krishna was known as "the lion of the tribe of Saki" in contrast to Jesus pbuh being known as "the lion of the tribe of Judah". While by a tree, Krishna is said to have been pierced by an arrow the force of which nailed him to it causing him to die, although some statues show both his hands and feet having been pierced and other statues show actual nails in his hands and feet with his side being pierced too. The light of the sun is said to have been blotted out at noon on the day Krishna died while the sky rained fire and ashes. Then Krishna is believed to have risen from the dead as he had prophesied and many allegedly witnessed him ascend to heaven. If one doesn't believe in the divinity of Krishna, his resurrection and status as the savior of the world, then it is thought that person will be in hell forever whereas those who believe Krishna died for their sins will be forgiven and enjoy paradise forever. The second person in the Hindu trinity is Krishna. Their trinity consists of Brahma, Vishnu and Siva Krishna with Krishna being considered as the human incarnation of Vishnu. Hindus believe in the concept of purgatory just like Catholics. Hinduism is well known as a polytheist religion, yet the Catholics believe in a trinity just like Hindus and have many other striking similarities.

    The mystery of the trinity is solved when its origins are examined. The word trinity itself does not occur in the entire bible one time, so belief in it has no basis from the bible at all. The Greek pagan philosopher Plato promoted belief in a trinity in his Phaedon written in 400 BCE. Plato taught the trinity was "*Agathon, Logos and Psyche*" which translated from Greek means "*The Father, the Word and the Spirit* ". "St." Augustine had said he found the beginning of John's Gospel in Plato's Phaedon, which is an admission of the similarities between pagan doctrine and Christian doctrine and a potential admission of copying. An ancient pagan obelisk at Rome had a Greek inscription which said, "*1. The Mighty God. 2. The Begotten God. 3. Apollo the Spirit.*" The famous Christian authority St. Jerome himself even stated, "*All the ancient nations believed in the trinity.*" Which is rather self-condemning because most of the ancient nations are considered to be polytheistic pagans with Jews being the only monotheists known of from ancient times. If polytheist pagans of old believed in a trinity, wouldn't that mean belief in a trinity is a form of polytheism? Pagan trinities also depicted the second part of the trinity as being begotten by the first part. Surely the belief in a trinity cannot be a divinely revealed doctrine if heathens were practicing it long beforehand. If so then it would mean the pagans had the right idea about God all along and their pagan faith was based on divine revelation. Either the pagans were divinely inspired long before Trinitarian Christians or neither of these groups were. If pagans were wrong to believe in a trinity before the coming of Jesus pbuh, then it would necessarily mean Trinitarian Christians are wrong to believe in a trinity after Jesus pbuh. If Trinitarian Christians are right to believe in a trinity, then it would mean that the disbelieving pagans living before Jesus pbuh were right to believe in a trinity. I did not like that my faith was so directly connected and similar to pagan polytheism.

    I had been taught since birth that nobody believed in a trinity before Christians did and it was an original divinely revealed doctrine, to learn that ancient pagans believed in the trinity was startling to say the least. Evidently I was taught incorrect information and history had been covered up. It was a very emotional experience to realize that I had been lied to about religious history. Whether the Christian trinity is true or false, I was still lied to when I was told it was an original doctrine. I took it personally thinking everyone had intentionally deceived me. Although considering that I had also taught the same thing to others while in a state of ignorance, most people probably just don't know they're teaching false information and do so with good intentions thinking what they are teaching is true. Whether it's done intentionally or unintentionally, a lie is still a lie. If I had been lied to about one thing regarding my religious beliefs then how many other lies had I been told and believed? Most Christians consider themselves monotheistic despite the many ancient polytheistic religions essentially believing the same thing. Both Christians and pagans believed in one god who had a son who is both divine and human simultaneously. However each pagan religion thinks their object of worship is the "*only son*" of God and the savior who died for their sins, their primary reason for believing their exclusivity to the truth being "*because their scriptures say so*". It is significant that most of the titles and beliefs of what we consider pagan and polytheistic gods are exactly the same as what many Christians call and believe about Jesus pbuh. Although the pagans and polytheists believed these things about their false gods long before Jesus pbuh was born. The similarities between all these different faiths leads one to wonder whether they are all the same religion that originated from the same source. What's ironic is that they all think their religion is unique in its beliefs because they never bother to research what the "disbelievers" believe, even though their beliefs are so much alike they think they are completely different from each other.

The few Christians who learn of the similarities Christianity has with pagan religions that predated Christianity often either try to completely reject all similarities outright, ignoring historical and archaeological facts, or the other response is to say that the devil created all these religions to be similar to Christianity in order to make people doubt it. Others say the pagan religions were prophecies foretelling the coming of Christ pbuh. I find the latter two explanations to be very weak arguments. Although unfortunately some people do make false claims about the similarities between Christianity and other religions that are not true; Christians rightly expose those similarities as false. However striking similarities still remain which are true that unfortunately also get labeled false during Christian counter responses. I have tried to only write those similarities that are genuine and have not mentioned those which I have found to be dubious and unsubstantiated. Nevertheless the similarities do arouse suspicions as to the originality of the Christian faith, especially since some of these pagan religions would have been known by early Christians, such as the Roman, Greek and Egyptian pagan religions. Other religions are similar, like the Aztec faith, but in no way could have had any influence on Christianity; their parallels are still interesting nonetheless. Keep in mind I'm not saying that any of those ancient religious beliefs are true, or that the events pagans believed in actually took place, historically it isn't proven aside from what their scriptures say, believing in it depends solely on believing pagan scriptures to be true as they did; which I don't. Many of the pagan deities were actually real people who existed as humans, who walked the earth just like Jesus pbuh, but the later generations that arose afterwards distorted their teachings and the people were deified without permission.

The early Church father Justin Martyr remarked on the similarities between Pagan and Christian doctrines in his "First Apology", which was an apologetic evangelical work in which he wrote: "*And when we say also that the Word, who is the first-birth of God, was produced without sexual union, and that He, Jesus Christ, our Teacher, was crucified and died, and rose again, and ascended into heaven, we propound nothing different from what you believe regarding those whom you esteem sons of Jupiter...*" According to Justin Martyr, Christianity was "*nothing different*" from what the pagan polytheists believed. In the sight of this famous early Christian scholar of antiquity the Christian doctrine wasn't strange, new, or unheard of. This is the religious environment Paul set about preaching his message to. What Paul taught would have been seen as common to what was already widely believed and practiced amongst the pagan polytheist gentiles.

However ethnic Jews who believed in God, such as the followers of Jesus pbuh, would have known from their history and the religious texts which they had that God prohibited practicing similarly to pagans and adopting their innovations; as Deuteronomy 12:28-32 warn:

*"Be careful to **obey all these regulations** I am giving you, so that it may always go well with you and your children after you, because you will be doing what is good and right in the eyes of the LORD your God.²⁹ The LORD your God will cut off before you the nations you are about to invade and dispossess. But when you have driven them out and settled in their land,³⁰ and after they have been destroyed before you, be careful not to be ensnared by inquiring about their gods, saying, "How do these nations serve their gods? We will do the same."³¹ **You must not worship the LORD your God in their way**, because **in worshipping their gods, they do all kinds of detestable things the LORD hates**. They even burn their sons and daughters in the fire as sacrifices to their gods. ³² See that you **do all I command** you; **do not add to it or take away from it.**"*

Another pagan god Mithra/Mithras was alleged to have been born to a virgin named Anahita in a cave on December 25th. Believed to be the second person of a holy trinity both human and divine, his human mother was titled "*the Mother of God*". On January 6th there would be a reenactment of the magi who came to worship the baby Mithras while he was still in the cradle, the magi brought frankincense, gold and myrrh as gifts to the newborn god in keeping with the pagan tradition that these three things are to be used when worshipping a god. Other denominations of this religion depict him as being born out of a rock as a god in human form, without mother or father making him the "*son of God*". This was probably a misunderstanding taken out of context by misinterpretations of Mithraic scriptures which say he was born in a cave, interpreters and translators could have easily made "born in a cave" into "born of a rock" by mistake. His earliest worshippers were shepherds, it is thought he had 12 companions who would accompany him learning what he taught. He was known as: "*the Light of the World*", "*the Way, the Truth, the Light*", "*the Life*", "*the Word*", "*the Son of God*", "*the Redeemer*", "*the Savior*", "*the Logos*" and "*the Good Shepherd*". He was considered to be a mediator between heaven and earth, and his worshippers were called "soldiers of Mithra". Mithras was believed to have healed the sick and raised the dead. Mithras is believed to have said: "*He who will not eat of my body and drink of my blood, so that he will be made one with me and I with him, the same shall not know salvation.*"

Mithraists did this by drinking wine and eating bread which represented the body and blood of Mithras, doing this gave them a reputation for being cannibals. The followers of Mithras were baptized in water naked and would then put on a white gown thinking their sins had been washed away. The rituals of the worshippers of Mithras took place on Sunday, which since Mithras was considered "the Lord" the worshippers of Mithras called Sunday "the Lord's day". Ancient sites of Mithraic worship have been found in many places of the world including: Britain, Italy, Romania, Germany, Hungary, Bulgaria, Turkey, Persia, Armenia, Syria, Israel, India, China and North Africa. The Christian "St." Augustine went so far as to say that Mithraists worshiped the same God he did, citing how both Mithraists and Catholics had 7 sacraments which were basically the same. The early Church father Tertullian commented on the popular Mithraic faith by saying, "*The priests of Mithras promised absolution from sin on confession and baptism.*" Mithraic priests would even lay hands on confirmation candidates in the same manner as I had experienced when I was confirmed as a Catholic. As a former Catholic, while not having as much authority as Tertullian or "St." Augustine, I can personally testify that there are very few differences between Mithraic and Catholic doctrines and practices. The major difference is that Mithras isn't believed to have been crucified. Instead Mithra/Mithras is believed to have slaughtered a large bull whose blood was accepted as atonement for the sins of the world. Any Mithraist who believed Mithra/Mithras had made the sacrifice and worshiped him as the son of God thinking Mithra/Mithras obtained the salvation of man, by spilling the blood of a mighty bull, thought eternal paradise awaited them with eternal hellfire awaiting the non-Mithraists. The depiction of this event includes many other animals in the scene and rich imagery too detailed to describe here, but each thing represented has symbolic correlation with the zodiac or some other thing of pagan spiritual significance. Some even believe the depiction of the bull being slaughtered by Mithra/Mithras is representative of him sacrificing himself as an atonement for sins, since he was also known as "*the great bull of the Sun*". The sacrifice was followed by a Last Supper that Mithras had with his companions where they dined before Mithras ascended to heaven having accomplished his sacrificial mission, later to return to combat the forces of evil. Since this sacrifice includes extensive symbolism I doubt it is an accurate portrayal of any historical event, it was probably specifically depicted because of its symbolism without any basis from an actual sacrifice. It is noteworthy that the depiction of the sacrifice is always in a cave, which was symbolic of the world and the victory of Mithras. The success of his sacrifice is depicted with him leaving the cave surrounded by light. The religion of Mithras was practiced by many people throughout the Roman Empire long before Jesus pbuh was born. Learning how similar the pagan religion of Mithraists was to Roman Catholicism deeply disturbed me. Especially when learning that in Rome more than a hundred inscriptions dedicated to Mithras have been discovered, along with 75 sculpture fragments, and a series of Mithraic temples situated in all parts of the city. Of course it was well known that Rome wasn't always Catholic, but I didn't know it use to be a spiritual center of the pagan Mithraic religion. The Mithraists also had a "*pope who always lived at Rome*" and called him "Papa" or "Pontifus Maximus", while ordinary worship leaders were called "*fathers*". I didn't know how these similarities between Catholicism and Christianity to pagan religions could be explained, especially when the leaders of the early

Catholic Church were aware of these pagan religions and their striking similarities. If Catholicism was divinely inspired then how come so many of the "divinely inspired" rituals originated in a pagan religion? Does that mean the worshippers of Mithras were also divinely inspired? What is even more disturbing is that the Mithraic scholars traced the origin of their pagan religion of Mithras to have first started in the city of Tarsus in Cilicia. This Tarsus is the same city Saul/Paul was born in. Saul/Paul would've known about this pagan religion since birth and had been at the epicenter of the Mithraic world. Therefore Saul needed to change his name to Paul because being known as "Saul of Tarsus" would have led people to think he was just preaching the religion of his hometown. This information left me speechless. Particularly after learning that some people still practice this pagan religion today, openly saying they worship Mithras claiming that Catholics and Christians stole their religious practices and ideas. Mithraism was so popular in ancient Rome that in 307 CE the roman emperor proclaimed Mithra to be the "protector of the empire". In the fourth century the roman emperor Julian, who was raised Christian, left Christianity and adopted Mithraism establishing temples devoted to Mithras at Constantinople. In 362 CE Julian proclaimed the Roman Empire would have freedom of religion and Mithraism remained a serious contender and rival to Christianity. Considering that the Jewish and Christian people knew of this pagan religion and rejected Paul's teachings casts extreme doubt on his claims of divine inspiration. Saul/Paul himself even admits that no Christians or Jews followed him, so he taught gentile pagans the "truth about Jesus" pbuh and it was accepted by them. Many pagans already practiced most of what Saul/Paul was teaching anyways, a transition from pagan Mithraism to Paul's religion would have been very easy to make.

Undoubtedly Saul/Paul had access to and inspiration from ancient pagan beliefs when formulating his doctrine. Paul's teachings were nearly a carbon copy of combined pagan religions, with the only difference being the name of the "crucified savior/ divine son". The idea of a divine son of God who was part of a trinity being crucified for the sins of mankind was already a common belief held throughout the pagan roman empire. The Jews witnessed this and would have known not to believe in anything like it, because of the previously mentioned verses from Deuteronomy. When qualities of one set of beliefs are absorbed under another religious code it is called Syncretism, and this is not how the religion of the prophets pbut developed. Prophets received inspiration, syncretism is how man-made religions developed. Owing to the syncretism of the Pauline doctrine it is unlikely he was inspired as he claimed to be. Many pagans were already doing what Saul/Paul would later say were divinely inspired rituals taught exclusively to him by God and/or Jesus pbuh. It actually seems that the pagans taught Paul instead of Paul teaching the pagans. After all it is easier to take something from another religion and absorb it into your own rather than having people give it up, this strategy makes it much easier to gain converts. That's not how the prophets pbut worked, but it does seem like that was Saul/Paul's method of operating. Not everyone believed Saul/Paul was genuine, nor did they accept his new doctrine because they had their own gospels, alleged to have been written by Thomas, James, Peter, Barnabas and many others. They taught a very different version of Jesus pbuh than the one preached by Paul; who never met Jesus pbuh while he was on earth. Although not all of these gospels were actually written by the one whom the texts claim, often they were written pseudonymously. Some were forgeries and others were changed after being written by the copiers, intentionally and unintentionally. Essentially every church had a different understanding of Jesus pbuh based on different scriptures and there was little uniformity among early Christians. This continued for some time with different denominations denouncing the others as heretics. Everyone was claiming to be followers of Jesus pbuh, frequently their arguments would turn violent and blood would be shed. This continued until Constantine became the emperor of Rome and wanted the chaos to stop in order to rule over a unified empire. Constantine called for the Council of Nicea in 325 CE inviting the leaders of different denominations to end the bickering and agree, hoping that one day Christianity could potentially unify the expansive Roman empire and be used as a political tool for control. Many bishops from all over the world with different theologies attended this council. The various bishops all brought their own scriptures with them in order to support their religious beliefs. Some bishops had all their expenses paid for by Constantine before they were "convinced" they should attend. Some church laws that were made official at the council of Nicaea include:

- The prohibition of usury among the clergy.
- The declaration of the invalidity of the baptism ritual done by Paulian heretics.
- The prohibition of kneeling on Sundays and during the Pentecost. (Standing was the normal posture for prayer at that time. Kneeling was for penitential prayer, not to be done at Sunday services which were of a festive nature in remembrance of Easter.)

The canon was thus designed to ensure uniformity. Other things Constantine declared at the council of Nicaea, which early Christians continued to disagree over, included:

- His declaration that the Roman Sun-day was to be the Christian Sabbath.
- He borrowed the emblem of the Sun-god (the cross of light) to be the emblem of Christianity.
- He adopted the traditional birthday of the Sun-god, and established the twenty-fifth of December, as the birthday of Jesus (pbuh).
- He ordered for a statue of Jesus (pbuh) to replace the idol of the Sun-god, and decided to incorporate the ceremonies and rituals which were performed at the Sun-god's birthday celebrations into Christian ceremonies and rituals.
- He ruled that Christian clergymen shouldn't have intercourse with their wives after being ordained as priests. (At that time priests were still allowed to get married and have kids.)

These changes would make non-Christian pagans more comfortable on Christian holidays since all citizens would be celebrating the same way, on the same day, but just in different places using different phrases. The Roman Empire essentially became what we today call interfaith and the idea began to spread that everyone was all worshipping the same god, but just in different ways. The differences between religions were minimized to promote a common culture and it was difficult to tell who was worshipping Jesus pbuh, who was worshipping Mithras and who was worshipping Osiris because all the different places of worship were doing many things the same. This fusion of one or more gods combining to become one god is called theocrasia. It took a learned theologian to tell the difference between a pagan and a Christian. Sometimes today it still takes a theologian to tell the difference between a Christian and a non-Christian if the Christian isn't wearing a cross, even Christians have a hard time identifying fellow Christians.

Not everyone who called themselves followers of Jesus pbuh accepted these later to be adopted propositions. The bishop Arius denounced these aberrations and resisted, maintaining that Jesus pbuh was not equal to God nor the "son of God", but a miraculously created man who taught us to worship our Creator alone. It is said that after hearing this at the council of Nicaea the real "St." Nicholas went over to Arius and slapped/punched him in the face. As happens today the different religious denominations continuously bickered refusing to agree, with each sticking to their own scriptures as the only "true proof", or using their fists as proof as "St." Nicholas allegedly did. That's what usually happens when a religious person can't win a debate because what they believe is wrong but they refuse to lose and want the other party to change their religious opinon, they resort to violence. A pagan at the time, Constantine was no theologian, he was a politician who had no patience for further arguing. The bishops adjourned for the day and were ordered to leave all their gospels behind them in a big pile in the center of the room. The doors were locked and the bishops were told to pray that God would sort it all out. There were between 270-4,000 different gospels in there such as the Gospel of Phillip, the Gospel of Peter, the Gospel of Thomas, the Gospel of Judas, the Gospel of Truth, the Gospel of Mary, the Gospel of Mary Magdalene, the Gospel of the Nazarites and many others we don't know the titles of. When they opened the doors the next day, under the impression that no one had been inside since the day before, it was discovered that all but 4 books were thrown about and scattered across the room making it completely disorganized while the 4 gospels of Matthew, Mark, Luke and John were neatly placed on the long meeting table. The bishops were told it was a sign from God that no one could doubt, even though there were no witnesses and it is unknown who had the keys to the doors on that night. Irenaeus says there had to be exactly 4 gospels no more and no less, because there are 4 winds of the earth and 4 corners of the earth.(thus people thought the world was flat) Why did they think there were 4 corners of earth? Because in the bible Isaiah 11:12 says, *"He will set up a banner for the nations, And will assemble the outcasts of Israel, And gather together the dispersed of Judah From the four corners of the earth."* Likewise the verses of Job 38:13, Jeremiah 16:19, Daniel 4:11 and Isaiah 40:22 mentioning the "ends of the earth" and God sitting upon the "circle of the earth" was interpreted to mean that "the earth" is flat on the bottom with 4 corners but in the middle it has a half-dome shape giving it some vertical depth as though it were a 3-d object resting on a flat surface with the whole model being called earth instead of just the half-dome part. Earth was thought by those who believed in the bible to have a flat bottom with land only being on the top parts of the dome and the water filling in the rest of the flat earth structure so that way instead of just falling off the dome to the bottom of the map water levels rose in order to be even with the land in all places. Think of it as though you had a half slice of apple in a tank filled with water just high enough so that some parts of the dome part of the apple were visible. Those dry parts were called land, the whole tank and it's contents were called "earth". Of course it sounds crazy, but if you actually look at early Christian maps of the world you will see how they depicted a flat circular 4-cornered world, from the bird's eye view that doesn't show the dome outdentation. Jerusalem was thought to be at the center of earth on top of the dome, hence the middle east was logically the driest since it was furthest from the water of the tank. Anyways since the bible taught the world had 4 corners then there were to be 4 gospels, no more no less. At that time instead of being called Sacred Scripture the 4 chosen books were called *"Memoirs of the apostles"*. Thereafter the 4 gospels of Matthew, Mark, Luke, and John became popular. Although these versions of Matthew, Mark, Luke and John are not the same as we have today, none of them were in English. They consisted of gospels written in Hebrew, Aramaic and Syriac with the oldest versions being written in Greek. It was ordered that all the other gospels, which people still considered authentic scriptures, were to be burned and banned throughout the Roman Empire and those found with such gospels were killed on the spot. Millions were killed. Thus many of these gospels have been lost to us forever, with only a few surviving the mass-burnings. People risked their lives hiding second hand copies of the originals of these banned gospels that were to be found by later generations. Many were rediscovered at Nag Hammadi. Some gospels have been excavated from graves like the Gospel of Barnabas found in Barnabas' grave in 478 CE. Although modern Christians claim Barnabas' grave had a gospel of Matthew in it, but that makes no sense. Think about it, why would Barnabas who wrote his own gospel which was later banned be buried with Matthew's gospel when Matthew's gospel was written after Barnabas had died? You can't get buried with a book that's not written yet! If not for such grave excavations we wouldn't have any information about the contents of these early Christian gospels aside from what heresiologists of the Trinitarian Church said they contained. Since these gospels have been rediscovered it has become evident that the early Church fathers didn't always tell the truth about what these other gospels said. Despite the ban, Arius continued teaching what he thought was the truth about Jesus pbuh, his motto was *"Follow Jesus as he preached"*. Arius was branded heretical because his motto meant rejecting Paul and Trinitarianism. Those who believed as Arius did were persecuted in Northern Africa, the Middle East and Eastern Europe for many years but then the truth of their doctrine spread and Arius was made bishop of Constantinople. Interestingly arians didn't persecute the trinitarians where they were the majority but the trinitarians persecuted arians where arians were the minority. After Arius was murdered in 336 CE, the emperor Constantine reflected and recanted his previous religious beliefs becoming an Arian.(not to be confused with Aryan) Constantine then believed that the brand of Christianity he had previously helped to create and promote was a heresy and proclaimed that Paul was a false teacher, Constantine died the next year in 337 CE. The next emperor, Constantine's son Constantius II, was enthusiastically Arian and rejected the idea that Jesus pbuh was divine, even exiling the Trinitarian Roman Pope Liberius to Thrace. During the reign of Constantinus II it was commonly held that the Arian Christian faith was true and that the Pauline Trinitarian belief was false, the majority of Christians in the Roman Empire were Arians believing that Jesus pbuh was a 100% human prophet sent by the One God who created everything. Things changed when Theodosius I became the roman emperor, he didn't believe in the doctrine promoted by Arius. Theodosius decreed the Pauline version of Christianity that was practiced in the city of Rome was to become the official religion of the Roman Empire in 380 CE. This was 18 years after the emperor Julian had proclaimed freedom of religion throughout the Roman Empire. Pauline Christianity ended religious freedom in the Roman Empire. It then became a crime to believe anything about Jesus pbuh that was different than the Trinitarian church of Rome, or to believe in any other religion; with the exception being Judaism. All other versions of Christianity that were not Roman Catholic were declared heretical, eventually made extinct through force. The law courts of Rome, called Basilicas, were turned into Catholic places of worship/preaching. Many people were killed because they didn't believe in what the church of Rome believed in. Ironically 30 years after the Roman Empire became Catholic, the Germanic Arians sacked Rome in 410, 455 and 546 CE destroying the Roman Empire. It's ironic because the early Catholic Church leaders preached that God would cause the Roman empire to prosper and expand since it had made what they considered "*the truth*" the official religion. I had always been taught the word Catholic meant universal Christian. However since the religion is called Roman Catholicism and its adherents Roman Catholics, the name reveals that Catholicism was just the form of Christianity practiced in the city of Rome. Roman Catholicism was not globally recognized, let alone universally thought to be true and it never has been. If we believe the word Catholicus in Latin means universal Christian, and Roman means Roman, then the term "*Roman Catholic*" would mean "*Roman Universal Christian*". It is impossible to be Roman and Universal at the same time, just like a business cannot be local and intergalatic at the same time. Also that Latin has a specific word for universal called "universalis" indicates Catholic does not mean universal no matter how many Catholics or Christians of whatever time period say otherwise. The word universalis came first and Catholicus has no linguistic connection to it. These words cannot be related, nor can they have similar meanings.

    In the end, might decided what was right and which books were to be put in the yet to be completed Bible, that would gradually become accepted as scripture. Unfortunately none of the original versions of Matthew, Mark, Luke and John exist today. Time has caused them to decompose destroying them. Instead of the originals, translations were used when creating what we today know of as the New Testament. One can only hope they were translated honestly with integrity having as few mistakes as possible without the translator intentionally changing the texts, as ancient translators had a tendency to do. It's not as though copyists or translators always intentionally made errors, but keep in mind every letter was copied and/or translated by hand. You can try this yourself to see how difficult it is to copy a gospel by hand accurately. Try writing on a separate piece of paper an entire gospel from the bible, letter by letter making sure what you write is exactly the same as what is written. Even though you are far more literate and your source of copying is easier to read than what the ancient copyists and translators would have used, you will still make many mistakes. If the 1st copyist of the gospel were to make a mistake, then the 2nd copyist copying the 1st's copy of the gospel would copy the mistake, unless they corrected it realizing it was a mistake. Although the 2nd copyist could also "correct" something that is not a mistake, making a new mistake while not correcting the real mistakes, thereby adding more mistakes. The 3rd copyist would have an even greater dilemma and harder job to do than the previous copyists. Since all were handwritten, every single copy would have been unique, different from the rest in different handwriting. Everyone knows that different types of handwriting can be interpreted in different ways. Depending on who is reading the words they will think different words were written, solely because of the handwriting style. A copyist could also make a mistake by thinking a note in the margins by an earlier copyist was actually a part of the text, so in their copy they would mistakenly add the previous copyist's notes into the scripture. Sometimes alterations were intentionally made to make the texts say what people wanted them to say. It also doesn't help that we don't know who copied and translated these documents, which casts doubt on the reliability of the translations. For all we know it could've been some 5 year old who copied or translated the original gospels, or a pagan priestess or Jew; we simply don't know. Let's assume that they were translated from accurate copies without malicious intentions as best as is humanely possible. A translation, no matter how good it is, can never mean the same as the text did in its original form. This is because rhythm, double meaning, idioms, informalization, rhetoric and puns are not translatable. Take "William Shakespeare" for example, who is regarded to be the best English playwright of his time if not all time; according to the popular belief of the majority. If you translate Shakespeare's works into Swahili the translated works will not have the same effect nor the same meaning. Some words simply can't be translated so the character dialogues in his translated stories will be of a different quality, making any plays performed in Swahili have a different plot than the same play would have had it been done in English. But the English bible we have today was not translated from the original texts, because the originals didn't exist by the time Christianity came to English speaking people. Even if the originals still existed there is another problem because the gospels and epistles were first written in Greek. Jesus pbuh and his apostles didn't speak Greek. This means the original New Testament was translated before it was ever written down, so the originals were actually translations, but for the sake of argument let's assume the oral tradition the Greek texts came from were translated correctly, even though when translating from a semitic languages such as Hebrew or Aramaic into non-semitic languages like Greek 80% of the meaning is automatically lost. Next they were translated from Greek into Latin, then translated from Latin into German, then translated from German into French, then translated from French into English. Now those early Church fathers Tertullian and Augustine which I mentioned earlier did not know Greek, they relied on Jerome's Latin translation. Which means the leading scholars of the early Christian Church were relying on texts that were translated a minimum of 2 times. Meaning it would be like you reading Shakespere for the first time ever in a Chinese translation, but not a direct Chinese translation from english rather a Chinese translation of the Swahili Shakespeare. Do you think you'd get the same meaning as you would by reading the original English? Today nobody denies that the English bibles are translations. Yet they rarely admit the Bible to be a translation of a translation of a translation of a translation of a translated oral tradition. If you were to translate Shakespeare into French, then take the French Shakespeare and translate it into German, then take the German Shakespeare twice translated and translate it to Latin, then the Latin Shakespeare thrice translated and translate it into

Greek, then take the Greek Shakespeare 4 times translated and translate it back into English, you would find that the English Shakespeare that went through so many translations would be very different than the original writings of Shakespeare. Therefore the Shakespeare that was translated many times would no longer be considered to be the actual words of Shakespeare. The translated Shakespeare compared to the actual words of Shakespeare would be obviously different. You can try this yourself with basic free internet translation tools, or try with an expensive professional translation service. A translation can never be the actual words of the original. Which is why if you are reading this book in a language other than English as the author I can assure you that you are not getting the same meaning as you would if you were reading it in its original English. I tried this in Google translate myself with Romans 12:2. Originally the English of the New International Version of the bible said:

> "Do not conform any longer to the pattern of this world, but be transformed by the renewing of your mind. Then you will be able to test and approve what God's will is – his good, pleasing and perfect will."

I translated it from English, to French, to German, to Latin, to Greek, also translating the Greek into Hebrew since that is what the original oral tradition the Greek author wrote was supposedly spoken in. After translating the Hebrew into English it read:

> "Not suited to this world, but be transformed by the renewal of your mind. So you will be able to test and approve what is the will of God, what is good and acceptable and perfect."

Clearly the text had changed somewhere in the translation process despite it originally being the same verse. That was just one verse; imagine translating verses, paragraphs or books? It wasn't even possible to have one verse survive the translation process, a whole gospel would be impossible. I had always been taught that the English bible was the word of God, or at least inspired by God. Although if it's too hard to translate Shakespeare without having the text change, then it is impossible to translate God. English could not be considered the word of God because it had been translated by humans. One would hope they knew what they were doing, but I had physical evidence that showed my Catholic bible had been translated into different words than the other Catholic bibles at the bible study. God knows which language to use to best communicate his message to us. God intentionally gave revelation in certain languages because the message intended to be transmitted was best expressed in that language. The full meaning of scripture can only be completely understood in the original language in which it was revealed. We simply don't have access to the original gospels in order to know what they really said so they could be compared with our translations. It is equivalent to not having access to the original english Shakespeare and in order to get any Shakespeare in english one would have to translate from the Chinese Shakespeare translation that was translated from the Swahili Shakespeare translation. Everyone knows that if we had no original english Shakespeare then we don't have any legitimate Shakespeare. Yet most Christians tend not to accept this simple fact when they learn that the biblical books of the New Testament were translated before they were ever written down. Not only were they translated before they were written, but there are more differences between the few Greek manuscripts we do have than there are words in the New Testament itself. Out of the 5,700 Greek New Testament manuscripts we have today, there are over 400,000 variations and scholars are still counting. Computers cannot even calculate all the differences between the manuscripts. Since there are no copies of the original gospels in their original language then it means there is absolutely zero proof that they have been correctly translated or transmitted through time. Not only do we not have the original gospels or the original translations, we don't even have the original copies! Today we don't have first copies, second copies (copy of first copy), or even third copies (copy of second copy). Many of the earliest copies available are hundreds of years older than what was originally written and keep in mind what was originally written was already passed down and translated from an oral tradition. The original writings are translations, yet we don't even have those. The earliest fragment P52 is a papyrus fragment dated from the early 2nd century. Meaning there is not one shred of "scripture" that we know of which exists that was written in the century Jesus pbuh walked the earth. On top of that there is no complete manuscript available that dates from before the Council of Nicaea in 325 CE. Most manuscripts of the New Testament in different versions date from the middle ages. So basically the Council of Nicaea told Christians what to believe and then the books were printed in order to support that belief, while earlier books were forbidden and destroyed. If a person doesn't have access to the divinely inspired words of God in their original form, then how will that person ever be able to know what God wants them to know? Essentially it's a matter of faith to believe that the bible(s) is divine or divinely inspired. Yet if there is no proof and we just have to take someone's word that the bible is accurate, despite the literary impossibilities, then that argument is no different than the belief in Santa Claus. Santa Claus is a matter of faith too. If you believe in the bible just because someone said to, then why not believe in the Hindu scriptures, or Buddhist scriptures based on the same principle? Why not believe in the Quran just because Muslims say to? Do you think your parents or the priest would never lie, but that everyone else does? Didn't your parents and the priest also tell you to believe in Santa Claus as a matter of faith too? It's not as though everyone intentionally lies, most of the time when it comes to religion it's unintentional, people are just repeating what they've been told and believe. Feelings don't make things facts, someone having a "feeling" the bible is true doesn't make it true. People frequently feel like sinning, but just because they feel like it doesn't mean it's right. If you don't have proof, then it's probably not the truth. Why would God punish a person for eternity for not believing in something for which there was no proof? Surely that would be unjust and God is not unjust, so somewhere somehow God must have left us proof. It also surprised me to read the preface of Luke 1:1-4 which the English translation of the New International Version of the Bible has the author stating:

"<u>Many have undertaken to draw up an account</u> of the things that have been fulfilled among us, ² <u>just as they were handed down to us</u> by those who from the first were eyewitnesses and servants of the word.³ **<u>With this in mind</u>**, since I myself have carefully investigated everything from the beginning, <u>I too decided to write</u> an orderly account for you, most excellent **Theophilus**,⁴ <u>so that you may know the certainty of the things you have been taught</u>."

The problem is that the "Theophilus" whom Luke addressed this to was bishop of Antioch from 169-177 CE. This means the earliest this gospel could've been written was 169 CE. It could not possibly have been Luke who actually wrote it unless he lived to be over 150 years old. But then why wait over 130 years before writing down the life of Jesus pbuh? Was he waiting for a special type of ink to be invented or what? The Catholic Encyclopedia says that the gospel of Luke was not written until 200 years after the events it describes. According to the Catholic Encyclopedia, at the time he allegedly wrote the gospel Luke was over 200 years old! Don't you think he would have been a little more famous had that been the case? After all how many authors can claim to have been over 200 years old before they started writing? Also the very author of the gospel writes that he wasn't eyewitness to the events he is writing about and that he has read the writings of other people. What he was writing was not the word of God, or inspired by God in his eyes. The author wrote stuff based on what others wrote in order to support what has already been taught and believed in. The "scripture" was written after the belief was taught, so the belief created the writings instead of the writings creating the belief. That's definitely not what I had been told by the priest in the pulpit. The bible plainly says it's not the word of God, but the priest says it is. If the priest is right then it means the bible is lying when it's written inside that it is not divinely inspired. This led to that same dilemma, do I believe what I'm reading in the Bible or do I believe the priest? Christianity or Churchianity? Do I follow Christ pbuh or the Christians? How could I follow Jesus pbuh if the bible was unreliable? If the bible is the word of God and Jesus pbuh is God, or the son of God, then why didn't Jesus pbuh write the bible? Why doesn't the bible have a "Gospel of Jesus"?

After extensive research I came to one conclusion, the Church has repeatedly changed over the years and they don't practice what Jesus pbuh used to. Even if one believes the Bible to be entirely true and accurate, the Catholic Church isn't practicing it or preaching it fully. This actually became official Vatican policy in 1959 CE. Pope John XXIII called the second Vatican council insisting the principle of aggiornamento was to be followed. Aggiornamento means that the Church should change and develop along with society and history. Basically it means that Catholicism is to be a religion that changes with the times, regardless of what the teachings of Jesus pbuh were. So I thought *"Has God kept changing the religion over and over again?"* That seemed unlikely since all the prophets were always sent to bring people back to the message of the previous prophet after it had been changed beyond repair. The prophets did not change the religion of God to suit the attitudes and cultures of their time. Despite all the doubts I had about the Catholic Church I still believed in God and wanted to follow Jesus pbuh. I knew in my heart that he was a prophet and a good example to be followed, just like all the other prophets and I didn't think I could get to heaven by ignoring him. Although I didn't know how to live the way Jesus pbuh would want me to. The Church had changed the rules so many times throughout the years that I couldn't find out what the original rules Jesus pbuh said to live by were. For instance the early Christians prayed 3 times a day and fasted Wednesdays and Fridays. But there is no record today that tells us how early Christians prayed or what they said during their 3 daily prayers, let alone if Jesus pbuh actually taught them to do those things. So not only was it impossible to learn how to live like Jesus pbuh did and taught, but it was also impossible to learn how to live like the followers of

Jesus pbuh. I was forced to contemplate the likelihood that modern Christianity might be a man-made religion that has been corrupted beyond repair.

During October in a Saturday confession, I told the priest my thoughts and mentioned that it seemed Christianity was extreme in its portrayal of God. I cited how the bible mentions numerous times God destroyed entire societies for doing one sin, like the people of Noah pbuh with the flood, the people of Lot pbuh for sodomy, those who followed Pharaoh and even the same people who followed Moses pbuh out of Egypt had been punished and left to wander the desert for 40 years for not fighting for the promised land when commanded to do so. It seemed that God took sins and disobedience seriously, it didn't seem fair that those people would be so severely punished for their sins while I wouldn't be because Jesus pbuh allegedly took the blame for me and paid the price. It seemed as though I was taking advantage of God's mercy by doing the same sins over and over and then just going to confession for forgiveness, doing this was keeping the sin cycle going on and on never stopping. I had to get serious about not sinning. In the past God didn't play around when it came to disobedience. Being eternal means God doesn't change. I don't think there was a change in the attitude of God deciding he had been too tuff on humans and would just forgive them all for everything just like that, never punishing people again as a result of their sins. God knows what we can do, he couldn't make a rule and expect us to abide by it if it were impossible for us. Even though it may be difficult God knows we are capable. I told the priest it seems like the Church focuses too much on God's mercy and forgets that God can be wrathful if we aren't doing what we're supposed to. He didn't answer any of my questions and just nodded saying to say X amount of prayers as my penance to be forgiven. Then he asked what books I had been reading and I said the Bible, the Gospel of Hip Hop and the Quran, although I had only read a little of the Quran I didn't say I only read a little. As soon as I said "the Quran" it was as though the priest was frozen and unable to speak. The priest's mouth closed and he was deep in thought, but it was as though he couldn't say anything negative. The priest had just shut his mouth and sat there not moving, never saying I was wrong in anything that I said. It got awkward waiting for a response so I said goodbye to him and left. The next day on Sunday the same priest I had talked to in confession, whom I respected, was giving the homily. As usual I was sitting in the front row on the right side. The priest said something like: *"There are some people who say we only focus on the mercy of God and never pay attention to God's wrath. That's not true. We have the bible and we believe in it all and live accordingly"*. At first I was glad thinking that he was going to answer all my doubts and make me see why Catholicism was the only true religion. I felt he was specially addressing me, but he didn't answer one point that I made and his whole speech could be summed up as, *"People say this but it's not true"*. He never offered any proof or examples to support his case. I felt betrayed as though the priest had played a dirty trick trying to use empty buzzwords in order to drive my doubts away. Also I felt he had broken my trust because what is said in confession is supposed to stay in confession and it is sinful if the priest tells people what was said inside, but he was practically quoting what I told him the day before. It was like somebody picking their nose and the whole time they're picking their nose they are saying over and over again, *"people say I pick my nose but it's not true"* all the while picking their nose while verbally saying they don't. In such a situation if one were to believe what they hear it would require them to ignore what they see. Not only had I been ignoring what I saw as a Catholic, but I had ignored what I saw, smelt, felt, heard and tasted during the Catholic ritual of communion. When participating in communion I was denying all 5 senses before swallowing the story the priest told me about what I was eating. God gave us all 5 senses, it doesn't make sense the true religion would require us to deny all of them at once. If a person was deaf so they couldn't be told and blind so they couldn't see, how would they be able to tell the difference between regular wine and the alleged blood being drunken at communion? No Catholic I know of has ever said that the liquid at communion tastes like blood. If something looks like poison, smells like poison, tastes like poison, feels like poison and sounds like poison I would think it was poison. But when it comes to the liquid at communion the priest tells people to use a different method of thinking, basically just believing what he says. To believe the bread and wine actually transfigures means to ignore your God given senses of sight, touch, taste, hearing and smell. How could God's religion require us to disbelieve in what the very senses God gave us are telling us? God gave us these senses to make it easier to worship him not harder. No prophet ever taught people to deny all 5 senses in order to believe in God and practice the true religion. Furthermore the communion doesn't have any genuine beneficial effect, it is more of a placebo. For example a famous cartoon sailor gets super strength when he eats spinach, but no Christian gets super anything when they eat the communion products. So don't you think if you were eating God or God's son, you would get super powers? If eating Garlic gives you bad breath then what would eating God do to you? Really, eating God isn't like eating regular food there has to be some type of physical side effect. What are the nutritional values of God per serving? Is it healthy to eat God? Is anybody allergic? Should pregnant women eat God? What does drinking the blood of Jesus do to one's blood pressure and cholesterol? For diabetics how much insulin should they take when they eat God or drink Jesus pbuh? At the very least communion should have some serious genetic or health effects identifiable by modern science. Even the bible says that when a woman touched Jesus pbuh all her physical ailments were healed just by touching his body, but no Christian gets healed when they eat what is allegedly Jesus' body in bread form nor drink his alleged blood in wine or juice form. So biblically speaking if the body of Jesus pbuh heals people then that piece of bread Christians eat must do the same, but in reality it doesn't because it ain't Jesus pbuh. Why would God want you to eat his kid? I don't think the 11th commandment given to Moses pbuh would've been "*And thou shalt eat my kid.*" All praises and thanks be to the Creator (not dinner) that I don't follow the priest's dietary instructions anymore and use a different menu, that doesn't include God or Jesus pbuh. His rebuttal in response to the questions I asked was basically: "*Just believe what I'm telling you and don't ask any questions.*" Even though earlier when I had started confessing to him he specifically told me to ask him any questions I might have. He didn't say he didn't know the answers to the questions, he just refused to answer and tried to change my attention to focus on something else. The priest basically used the tactic of pointing in the distance and saying, "*Look quick there's something behind you!*" and then running away when the person turns to look. But this was my religion we were talking about, I wasn't just going to drop the issue and believe without knowing the correct answers. It's important to distinguish the difference between answers and the correct answers. In response to my questions the priest repeated my questions and then proceeded to something else never satisfactorily answering. One could say that was his answer, but there is a big difference between answering a question correctly and just giving an answer to a question. Anybody can answer a question, but not everybody can or will tell you the correct answer. A response is not an explanation and explaning something is not the same as proving it.

I decided to calm down and think things through, not wanting to make any hasty decisions based on emotions. So what if the priest betrayed my trust and the confessional confidentiality? He's human I wasn't a Catholic in order to make friends, I was Catholic because I thought it was the true religion. If I was going to leave the Church it wasn't going to be a result of personal problems, because every church will have some problem. This was a matter of religion and I couldn't let anger cloud my judgment or affect my decision. I decided to remain Catholic and still go to church on Monday. The next day I went to confession again, but to a different priest. In that confession I told this priest the same doubts and to my astonishment he said that the flood during the time of Noah might not even be true. It was shocking to learn that the priests don't even believe what they preach. I don't remember if it was that confession, or the Saturday one, or the Saturday before, but while leaving the confessional the female bible study teacher was in a pew praying with her eyes closed as I walked by and I remember her mouth smiled while I passed even though her eyes were closed. It looked like a smile of pure evil and terrified me. I asked God for guidance and realized that God wanted me to worship him. With that being the case God would never allow the true religion to become so corrupted that it were impossible for someone to worship God in the way he wanted. God wouldn't create us if we couldn't worship him the way he wanted us to. If you exist then you can worship God correctly. If the true religion were corrupted or lost, God would send a new prophet, otherwise everyone would have a valid excuse for not worshipping God correctly. There was no doubt in my mind that the true religion was still being practiced somewhere in the world, my doubt was whether Catholicism, or even Christianity, were true. I say Christianity as well because if the Catholic bible was unreliable, because of its dependence on translations due to the nonexistence of the originals, then any group that used the bible would have to be unreliable too because they had no way to access the original gospels either. I didn't know what I was going to do. My entire life up until that point had revolved around Catholicism and Christianity.

Tuesday was the next day and the priest giving the mass was the one who heard my confession the night before, he was young in his 20s or 30s and I respected him very much. It was also a Catholic holy day so all the kids from the Catholic school were in church wearing their uniforms. The homily was about telling the truth no matter what. The priest said if you see a crime then you should report it, or if you see someone cheat you should tell the teacher(telling the kids not to cheat and to tattletale on cheaters) he stressed that Jesus pbuh(he didn't say peace be upon him) taught us and wanted us to tell the truth even if it puts our life in danger, he said the truth is the most important thing no matter what others might think or what kind of effect telling the truth might have on your life. Just trust in God and follow the truth wherever it leads. I felt it was a sign that was sent from God through a deceitful institution unaware of the irony. Sometimes even a liar can tell the truth unwittingly. After the service I usually would pray the rosary before leaving, but there was a girl in a nearby pew who had been hard to ignore the whole time and I thought she was flirting with me. At that moment in my life I knew that the last thing I needed at that time was a girlfriend and that there were much more important things which needed my attention. So I quickly left to get away from the temptation fearing that she was just about to ask me for my contact information. That day I decided that I had to follow the truth even if it meant not being Catholic and changing my religion.

This was the most distressing time of my life. I had suddenly become what one would consider to be an agnostic, which means one without knowledge. I believed in God and I believed in Heaven and Hell, however I had no idea how God wanted me to worship and I had no idea how I was going to get to paradise. This was frightening because I knew that if I died in that state, then there was zero chance I would be going to paradise, because I didn't know how to get there. You cannot take a trip and expect to arrive at the intended destination if you don't have directions or know which way to go. I wanted some directions! I was lost and if I died I knew I'd be going to hell. Remember I had also received death threats so dying wasn't some abstract long off notion, it was an everyday possibility and it still is. People on the web who had learned my real name even said they were going to come by my house. I know others who say they are agnostic and that they believe in God but just don't know which religion is correct, I was once one of them and it was the most stressful experience of my life. I can't understand how a person can call themselves an agnostic and live life without being in a constant state of worry and distress. When I was agnostic I dropped everything that was going on in my life and focused solely on religions trying to find out which one was true. I put my music career entirely on hold even though I had just released a music video and was supposed to release my 4th album in less than 2 months. If you are agnostic I suggest you fix that, and take the time necessary for you to find out the truth with certainty. There is no time to waste, no one should ever be "*killing time*" because you will die long before time does. God has given us time so we shouldn't be ungrateful and "kill" such a precious gift. Realistically it is impossible to be "*killing time*" at anytime, rather we are simply wasting our time but don't like to say so, even though God knows it and punishes that crime. Verily Satan has deceived us concerning our relationship with time and God.

I decided to research other religions to see if maybe one of them was correct or could clarify some things. Beforehand I had bought a book on Buddhist mythology and the Buddhist teachings on evil. I read that and it seemed too transcendental and metaphysical, involving living with a spiritual world mentality, meditating into different planes by going into trances attaining new levels of consciousness and secret knowledge. To me it seemed too difficult and wasn't practical for the whole world so not everyone would even have a chance at salvation in this doctrine, only the special spiritual elite. The Buddhist concept of 89 different levels of consciousness was also difficult to subscribe to. Also Tibetan Buddhism teaches a belief in "tulpas" which are allegedly physical beings created as a result of human thought and imagination. Which is actually the same thing people teach kids about Santa Claus, in that he's real if you believe he is. Religiously speaking those who promote Santa Claus as being real are actually promoting Buddhism and those who believe Santa is real have Buddhist beliefs. Which makes it doubly distressing to witness people tell kids Santa Claus is real because it makes such kids not only polytheists but also partially Buddhist. Of course "tulpas" are not real, those who claim to have "proof" of tuplas were simply tricked by Jinn as a result of them doing magic, illusions and colluding with other Jinns in order to get people to disbelieve in the Creator of the Universe being the only Creator. I simply cannot believe in a religion like Tibetan Buddhism because in principle it teaches that Santa Claus is real. I still believed in the prophets of the bible and wanted to follow them, but they play no role in Buddhism so I kept searching for the truth.

In the Hip Hop industry there is a 5%er movement, it's more of an influence, also known as "the nation of Gods and earths" which is an offshoot of the "Nation of Islam", which is a black supremacist cult made by Wallace Fard Muhammed in the 1930s CE. The 5%er movement is an offshoot of the "Nation of Islam" and was made by Elijah Muhammed who claimed to be a prophet in the 1960s CE. None of these Muhammeds practice Islam or follow the prophet Muhammad bin Abdullah of Arabia pbuh. The 5%er name comes from their belief that 85% of the world's population is ignorant of "the truth". 10% knows "the truth" but intentionally lie such as priests, politicians and rabbis. 5% know "the truth" and live according to it, with them claiming to be the 5% even though their numbers don't agree with the math. They use many acronyms making words mean different things to their members than what they do to the outside world. They call themselves muslims and say they worship A.L.L.A.H. and claim to believe in I.S.L.A.M. To them I.S.L.A.M. means **I S**elf **L**ord **A**nd **M**aster. When 5%er's or the Nation of Islam claims to worship A.L.L.A.H. to them it means **A**rm **L**eg **L**eg **A**rm **H**ead. It is a form of humanism in which they worship themselves. They do not believe in the Quran or the prophethood of the Muhammad from the Quaraysh tribe of Mecca pbuh. Although because of the names of their cult leaders and the acronyms they use there is much confusion for those who are unfamiliar. The same word can mean different things to different people if you don't know what people mean when they use those words. Sometimes people speak with words they don't know the meaning of thereby sending the wrong message than what they intended. The 5%ers actually use the Quran and Bible to support their foolish self-worship. They will cite verses from the Quran as evidence that God created man. Then 5%ers will cite the infamous Bible verse which says something like, "God created man in his own image". Using the biblical verse they say that it means God made the first man in the image of God. Following that they say that since there is no such thing as God the first man and all his descendants are gods. (This is a blatant contradiction saying God made man and then saying God doesn't exist.) Then they say the first man must have been black, so therefore all black men are gods, with black women being earths since gods use them to reproduce continuing creation and giving life to the earth. Then 5%ers and the self-proclaimed "Nation of Islam" say that the white man was made via a scientific skin graphing experiment by the black man, but something went wrong. Since white people have a history of oppressing black people on earth and in their minds the black man is god, then the whites who were made by them must be devils. The 5%ers believe in a form of reincarnation. They are afro centric and honor pagan African religions. They have different ranks in order to distinguish their members.

The religion of Hip Hop as practiced by the Hip Hop Temple is an offshoot of the 5%ers which is open to people of all ethnicities. Hip Hop Kulture is the unifying bond and they essentially worship hip hop kulture, although they may not say so, with the laws of Hip Hop being the code of conduct to live by. Most would be surprised to learn Hip Hop is a religion, but so is Rock and Roll and other things which most people consider hobbies or interests; such as yoga. The thing with such minor religions is that only those who get deeply involved into them learn that they aren't hobbies or interests at all but are actually religions. So I guess instead of minor religions they should be called religions incognito, because people don't learn they are religions until they are already practicing them and these religions actually have a major unrecognized influence on society with widespread membership among the masses; albeit most members don't know they are members of a religion and consider what they are doing as a hobby instead of religious rituals. Anyways the Hip Hop Temple uses anachronisms just like the 5% do, and have many ranks based on what one knows and how much they have done for Hip Hop Kulture. Because cult is the root of the word culture, the Hip Hop Temple uses the word kulture instead as a way to disassociate their various Hip Hop philosophies and traditions from the cult-like characteristics of cultures. Yet the Hip Hop Temple only scratches the surface. The idea of "culture" was established in an attempt to find the dignity of humans within the context of modern science. Basically the concept of "culture" was invented to make people feel special and superior to animals without using religion or religious factors as the reason. This is because psychology teaches humans are nothing but brutes, yet everyone wanted to respect the dignity of man and still be "scientific" at the same time. Since religion had a bad reputation in Euro-merica they began to call it culture instead in order to replace religion with religiosity. That's why today if you change your religion many families will have little to no problem, but if you criticize or abandon your family's "cultural traditions" you might just get boiled alive. Some family's will say *"Oh your ancestors would be turning over in their graves if they knew you didn't keep their traditions going"*. Most "cultural traditions" are the modern religious rituals. People will even say that "*If you want to marry someone of a different religion that's ok, but just make sure they have the same culture as you or else you'll have problems and difficulties.*" Religious tribalism has re-emerged under the name of "culture". However to have a culture means to think it's superior to all other cultures and hence every culture must advocate war against chaos AND all other cultures. That's why today they say it's a "clash of cultures" and not a clash of faiths, because secularists think a religious war is silly and wrong but cultural wars are ok and moral. Instead of "*converting the heathens*" they "*civilize the barbarians*". Yet since cultures got confused with ethnicities and nationalities, today what was once known as "faith" that later became "culture" is now called "values". In the West the word "values" replaced the phrase "religious doctrines". Although because false and incorrect "values" are not rational and not grounded in the natures of those subject to them they must be imposed by force in order to defeat opposing "values". Rational persuasion cannot make "values" be believed if they are false. Thus false "values" are never objectively debated because they'd get exposed as false which would cause embarrassment to those who hold them, and lead to cultural and political turmoil. Which is why you will find military force used to defend "values" and spread "values" because these "values" are false and incorrect. Essentially the Spanish Inquisitors were simply promoting and defending their "values" they just didn't have an issue with calling it religion. Since many today think religious violence is wrong they wage war for "values" instead. It's the same exact game, but nobody likes the stigma of the old name. Also this is because there is no concept of a "bad value", people say you either have "good values" or "no values". This makes a war waged to protect or promote "our values" automatically good and righteous to do, regardless of what those values actually are. There is no such thing as an "unjust war" waged for the sake of "values". However producing false or incorrect "values" and believing in them are acts of will. The reason people don't adopt false or incorrect "values" is not because of a lack of understanding it's because of their lack of will to have those false or incorrect "values". Basically they see those "values" as false and don't want them. That's why false and incorrect "values" are only spread through ideological war, economic warfare, military warfare and "cultural warfare". Or rather than call it "cultural warfare" today the term they use is "cultural diffusion". Many just come right out and advocate "total war" without any prospective hope for negotiation because to negotiate in a war fought because of your "values" would mean to negotiate and change those "values". Always remember that "values" is the modern english equivalent of "religious doctrines". This is why you can tell most people you think they have a bad or satanic religion without them getting too offended at your opinion, because it's "just your opinion" but if you tell them you think they have bad/false/incorrect or satanic values they feel very offended. In the past when wars were admitted to be waged over religious doctrines there was always a chance peace could come by one side changing their religious doctrines, but thus far no people or nation has ever rejected their "values" and accepted the "values" of their enemy. So these wars for the sake of "values" might be the warhawk rhetoric for quite a few centuries, until all the bloodshed makes those with false and incorrect "values" see their "values" as less valueable. Therefore commitment is the equivalent of faith when God is replaced with self-provided "values". Which is why people started saying *"where there's a will there's a way"* because their faith is no longer in God but in themself and their goals. They become their God and those who teach them their "culture" or "values" are their prophets. Globally religion has not declined in popularity, the vocabulary and terminology used when talking about religion just changed. Religion and Culture/Values switched roles in society. Hence a "Hip Hop Culture" is actually a "Hip Hop religion" the same applies to most cultures and sub-cultures whether it's sports culture, family culture, political culture etc. All cultures teach their own type of religious creeds, some can be combined to overlap and complement each other while others will always contradict and conflict with each other. In short any theoretical "melting pot" can only have either pure sea water or salt sea water. This is because pure sea water and salt sea water don't mix together in the same pot despite both types of water being able to contain the same demographic ingredients when cooking various recipes for civilization. Likewise most of the creatures from salt water can't survive in non-salt water nor can most fresh water creatures survive in salt water. There are some creatures who can live in both, but most people cannot survive with 1 religion in a cultural "melting pot" with many various religions posing as "values". All values a person has comes from their religion, zero values come from a nation, culture, family, school, business, etc. If a person has values coming from multiple sources then either they have a religion which allows multiple values (but if they conflict/contradict that faith is false) or they have many religious influences shaping their individual custom religion. Every environment on earth is a religious environment, in our modern era we enter many poly-religious environments. Basically you might actually believe in more than 1 religion. Most people today do, unfortunately few of us ever realize it. So in some regards ancient polytheists were smarter than us because they knew when they believed in multiple religions. We tend not to know, but still live, fight and die for religions. While the fighting and dying may never end, our true religions and religious reasons should be recognized because if we don't know our religions then our religion is ignorance. It is unanimously agreed that ignorance is not the true faith leading to paradise and true prophets didn't teach ignorance. We should have a faith that views human ignorance as sinful. Truly ignorance is the primary theological enemy of us all. Sadly for the majority of people religious ignorance is a value.

All three of these supremacist groups (the 5%ers, the Nation of Islam and the Hip Hop Temple) espouse the famous pagan slogan "*know thyself*" and cite "*knowledge of self*" as the key to truth, as do metaphysicians, New Agers and transcendentalists. While it may sound nice, they mean that one must gain the "knowledge" of your own godhood and that you should worship yourself. Seriously at the end of the journey of "self-discovery" they tell you that you are a god. I don't consider this to be knowledge at all, to me it's insanity. How silly can it be to worship a human being? Especially if it's yourself! Yet this is exactly what Pharaoh did when he rejected Moses pbuh. Pharaoh was so arrogant that he called himself a god and the Egyptians were foolish enough to believe their leader was a deity despite seeing all the miracles Moses pbuh was sent with as proof. The Pharaoh told people that he was only guiding his people to what he thought was right. Pharaoh told the Egyptians that following Moses pbuh would mean that their forefathers and ancestors were wrong, which he considered impossible and disrespectful. As we know the Pharaoh who called himself god was drowned and his ancestors were indeed wrong and shouldn't have been followed but denounced. May God help us to accept proof when it is presented to us and not be blinded by arrogance, or foolishness, or ancestral loyalty when it conflicts with what is right. Also we essentially do worship ourselves when we believe democracy is a legitimate institution capable of creating laws. The Egyptians worshiped Pharaoh giving him the right to make the laws and denied the laws of God. Therefore if a country makes legal what God has made illegal then by accepting that law as legitimate we are saying the man-made laws are more important than the laws of the one who made man. Vice Versa if man-made legal systems make illegal what God has commanded a person to do. If we accept these types of laws as legitimate then we are essentially demoting God and obeying others, which would constitute our worshipping governments instead of God when their laws conflict with divine laws. While it's easy to dismiss the self-worship of the racist 5%ers, it is easy to fall into the same trap of worshipping humans when we give them more authority over us than they deserve. God is the Creator of the land and is the only one who has the authority to make the laws which govern it. It's actually very simple: God's land, God's laws.

As a white man, there was no possible way I could sign up for a religion which considered white people to be devils. I knew my desires had to be controlled, not blindly indulged in, because one gains satisfaction through abstinence and overcoming temptations. If we were meant to indulge there would be no inner satisfaction when we resist desires, therefore it must have been hardwired by the Creator not to indulge. I knew myself too well to worship myself, and while I liked hip hop very much I didn't really think the prophets of the bible pbut would have been down with hip hop kulture as a way of life (religion).

One part of the 5%er falsehood that I feel I must address is their interpretation of the bibles which say "God created man in his own image." Many misunderstand this to mean man is in the image of God, this is blasphemous and incorrect. There actually used to be a heretical Christian sect called the Melatoni whose leader Mileto taught the body of man was made after God's image. Other bible verses contextually may claim such a thing but those verses aren't authentic and no Jew believes they mean what they literally say anyways. Ironically people say Moses pbuh wrote these verses, yet Moses pbuh and all the other Jewish prophets taught that Israel was God's "chosen people" exclusively special and superior to the rest of Adam's descendents pbuh. While Jews could never have taught nor believed that if they read those verses, or those verses meant Adam pbuh was literally God's image or perfect as Christian's claim in order to say everyone is equal and their religion is for everyone. Other Christians use New Testament verses in conjunction with this Old Testament interpolation trying to say that all humans are "children of God". Yet the problem with this is that people know that they aren't. Whereas you can't be a child of God and not know it. For one person to claim that they are not a child of God would mean that God's kids don't even know they are God's kids and that's impossible. The same thing applies to the "godhood" of the humanists. All of these self-proclaimed "gods" used to not know they were "gods". So you can't be a god if you don't know you're a god. Because that would be a contradiction since a god must always know it's a god or else it's not a god. Likewise for other humans to say they aren't gods, as humanists claim, then it would mean there are gods who are wrong to say they aren't gods. Thus either the "gods" and "children of God" are wrong or people aren't "gods" or "children of God" at all. If you meet one of these types who claim to be a "child of God" or a god then just ask to see their birth certificate, talk to their mother and the doctor who delivered them at birth. Those who think they are gods or children of God because "God made man in his own image" are just confused and misinterpret texts the authenticity of which is dubious at best. This type of problem comes from having different verses and a different interpretation of verses than the ones the prophets taught us. The verse means that God made man, Adam pbuh, in man's own image. The "His" refers to Adam pbuh, not to God. People misunderstand semitic grammar when it's translated into english, grammar rules aren't translated, to fully understand a translation you need to know the grammar rules of the language the text was translated from. Translators don't always make things clear. Meaning the first man was made as a full grown man in his own image and never had to go through infancy, childhood, puberty or teenage years. He never lost his baby teeth, or had his body get bigger and bigger changing in size or shape, he was born with his beard. Adam pbuh was made in his own image as a full grown man, which was the special image which God selected for Adam pbuh to look like. It's as simple as that. Remember Moses pbuh was not allowed to see God, no one has. If God made Adam pbuh in the image of God then the children of Adam pbuh or his wife might have gotten confused as to who is God and who was man. Some might even say that compared to some animals man is less beautiful. Under no circumstances whatsoever did God make man as a literal duplicate twin image of God. God doesn't clone himself. Anyone who believes such a notion is considered a disbeliever by God, regardless of what else they may believe. Nevertheless some stubborn Christians may still insist that Adam pbuh was made in God's image and that it means God's image. Well do you know what that means? That means it was God's design, meaning God was the artist and he didn't copy anyone else's design but formed man especially by himself and as such the image of mankind is the intellectual property of God. Now one could say that all creatures are designed by God so being made in the image of God made isn't all that special, but it is just because it's God making our image and because our image isn't like the other creatures are. For instance many animals like fish, reptiles, insects and even mammals look identical and are not visually distinct. However all humans have visual distinction to make every one of us unique, even the "identical twins" are not really identical. So each human has their own custom made look that's different from every other human that ever existed and ever will. Thus Islam forbids Muslims from insulting how a human naturally looks, because that's God's design/image. God was/is the artist, it doesn't mean the image(us) is God or of Godly comparison/substance. Being "made in the image of God" means we were made with astute attention being paid by God as to how he made each of us. It doesn't mean we are the image of God, but that the image was made by the brand called God; or is trademarked so to say by God. Meaning it's an original image God made you and me in. Instead of the image of mankind being "Made in China" it was made by God, but since one can't say "Made in Godland" the phrase in the "image of God" was used to show nothing else was really there except God when the blueprint for the image of every human was first recorded before creation. Basically God knew what image we would be prior to creating our image, thus the image originated of Godly design and not through a design of experimentation, trial and error, spontanaity or "evolution". Therefore rather than feel arrogant and special for being/looking as we do it should make us feel humble and fearful of not fulfilling the duties that come with such a exclusive individual image privilege.

  If you are a white person you might think it's obvious that the 5%ers who teach black people are gods and white people are devils are crazy, but there is a white version as well. A white supremacist group exists that manipulates verses of the bible to try and make them mean that 10 out of the 12 tribes of Israel were white, instead of just one. They then postulate that rather than the white Israelites returning to Jerusalem after being in Babylon, that these 10 tribes went to Europe instead and became known as the *"lost tribes of Israel"*. When reading bible verses of Jesus pbuh saying he was only sent to the *"lost sheep of Israel"* they interpret this as Jesus pbuh meaning *"I'm only sent to white people"*. These white supremacist Christians take this idea and run with it.

They state that since human blood is red for everyone, then skin color must have nothing to do with blood or genetics. In their minds white skin is pure and good while black skin is indicative of sin and evil. Their idea is that the darker you are the more sinful you are. Mormons also taught this with their 2nd prophet Brigham Young(also a freemason) stating that ,"*The Lord has cursed Cain's seed with blackness*", "*Shall I tell you the law of God in regard to the African race? If the white man who belongs to the chosen seed mixes his blood with the seed of Cain, the penalty, under the law of God, is death on the spot. This will always be so.*" Although to be fair in 1978 CE the Mormons officially changed their position on black people, but then the Mormon faith fractured into the LDS and FLDS churches. LDS stands for Church of Latter Day Saints and the FLDS is the Fundamentalist one, which is still racist. Although the LDS is pretty racist too if you ask me despite their multi-skin tone advertisements. This is because a light brown skinned Muslim once interacted with 3 white LDS Mormons specifically talking to them about Mormon views regarding skin color, exposing how they were racist and had changed their views. In response they flip flopped over a bit and one of them even said that the skin color is just a temporary thing and that when a black or brown person becomes a Mormon their skin color changes to white. So the Muslim asked if he went to a Mormon church whether he would see any black or brown people there or are they all white? And rather than change his view the Mormon said that the skin color change isn't instanteous but takes time and that over time the skin color of black Mormons turns lighter and lighter until they are white, and that personally he can't even tell the difference between most Mormons as to whether they used to be black or not. Except of course those Mormons in Africa, for some reason they don't turn completely white, but according to the Mormon guy they visibly get a lighter skin color over time. The sad thing is there are black Mormons who tend to have no idea what Mormon doctrines taught and teach about black skin. In fact Mormons don't like to tell anybody much of anything about their doctrines at all until after they become a Mormon. I've even asked 2 white Mormon missionaries what their Mormon doctrines teach about black people and they just said "*We heard some things, but we aren't really sure*" then they refused to tell me what they had heard or what Mormon doctrines say. But aside from Mormons, there are other types of Christian faiths with a white supremacist type of Jesus. In this form of Christianity Jesus pbuh did not die for the sins of the world, they think that Jesus pbuh only died for the sins of white people and that only white people can enter paradise through Jesus Christ pbuh. When they say Jesus pbuh died for the sins of the world they take it to mean the white world. Now before you start thinking white is right pause for a moment, because not all white people are really white people according to them. Pinkish white and ultra white are not really white according to this form of Christianity. The way to tell if a person is a white Israeli according to them is based on a number of skin reactions. When a "true white" gets mad their face turns red, whereas a "fake white" has their face turn black when they are mad. Also a "true white" gets sunburn when exposed to the sun, whereas a "fake white" gets tanned. According to these Christians if a white person can get a tan then they aren't really a white person and are ineligible for paradise because they aren't of pure white Israeli blood. Which is funny when you consider they believe "*the son of God only came to save whites whose skin gets burned by the sun of God*". Learning such a white supremacist Christian doctrine exists puts the notion of a white Jesus in perspective and it becomes a major point of contention integral to the faith of the racist white Christian. If Jesus pbuh wasn't white then no white Christian could be racist, so all racist white Christians have a substantial interest in making all depictions of Jesus pbuh white whether he was or not. Their real religion is racism, but they claim to be Christians following the instructions of Jesus pbuh. They are just another example of people who exist today that truly believe they are good people following the example and teachings of Jesus pbuh, whom they love, but they are completely wrong and are actually directly opposing the teachings of Jesus pbuh without realizing it. May God help us to realize the true teachings of Jesus pbuh and follow them, no matter what others say about Jesus pbuh or what they say he taught.

  In the late summer and early fall I had read a book analyzing different cults and their beliefs. When I read it I was still in my crusader mentality so it shocked me to find out that Islam was not listed as one of the cults. According to cult definitions, structures, methods and policies there were actually some Christian denominations that qualified as cults, like the Jehovah's Witnesses or Mormons. I had been taught to hate Islam and heard so many bad things about it that reading a professional unbiased research book written by a non-Muslim on cults that expressly gave reasons why Islam is not considered a cult caused a slight change in my attitude, because the author definitely knew what they were writing about. With this new mentality that Islam is not a cult, since I had no idea what religion was true and didn't feel like researching Hinduism with the caste system and the sanctity of bovines. I dusted off the English translation of the Quran I had bought the year before and decided to read it. Immediately I began to feel better and more stable while reading, thinking that at least I was trying, it wasn't as though I didn't care about religion. I was actively trying to find out what God wanted from me. It was just that everything seemed to have been corrupted making it confusing to know which religion was true, but at least I was trying to find out what God wanted from me. By sincerley trying every second with all my heart to learn the true religion then there was a chance God would guide me to it, or forgive me if I died before then. The Quran is unlike any other book in the world because it's not in chronological order like other books. In one chapter it could be mentioning Moses pbuh and then a few paragraphs later it focuses on Abraham pbuh and then it's commenting about the Day of Judgment before mentioning the creation of everything when it changes topics again relating it all to the present continuing to move on to another subject in a continuous train of thought. It was full of surprises in every chapter but at the same time it was entirely coherent and made sense when reading. It was sporadic yet organized. Whenever a question popped into my head it would soon mention the very same question word for word and answer the question. I was wondering, am I reading this book or is this book reading me? Everything was simple and easy to understand but at the same time it was extremely profound and complex in its meanings. Something that took me years of studying to learn on my own, I'd find covered and expanded upon in one sentence of the Quran. I had considered myself a genius for figuring something out and this book explains the concept better than I ever could in only a few words. It included the past prophets and the laws and explained the future and the present, yet this had been around on earth for over 1400 years. It was really disturbing when it addressed me and referred to things I would say, think or do that no one could have known. Reading such specific information about the creation and myself made me seriously question what this Quran really was, the information contained inside it could come from no other but the Creator. It was scary and intriguing at the same time. These experiences reading it made me excited and I wanted to rush and finish reading it. Then I came across the 114th verse in the 20th Chapter of the Quran which says:

$$\text{فَتَعَٰلَى ٱللَّهُ ٱلْمَلِكُ ٱلْحَقُّ ۗ وَلَا تَعْجَلْ بِٱلْقُرْءَانِ مِن قَبْلِ أَن يُقْضَىٰٓ إِلَيْكَ وَحْيُهُۥ ۖ وَقُل رَّبِّ زِدْنِى عِلْمًا ۝١١٤}$$

Although I was reading an all English translation of the meanings of the Quran, which had translated 20:114 as: *"High above all is Allah, the King, the Truth! Be not in haste with the Qur´an before its revelation to thee is completed, but say, "O my Lord! advance me in knowledge."*

I realized this was a miracle. No man-made book can have such information, or present it in such a fashion and it even gave a challenge for those who doubt that the Quran is from God. It gave a burden of proof! On top of that it said what the result would be for any who dared to try. To this day, the challenge has stood for 1440 years and counting with many who have tried and failed. It had answered all my questions and the questions others had asked me. Another thing that was amazing was how despite it seeming to be completely disorganized constantly changing the subjects throughout and returning to them, nothing contradicted. On top of that it even mentioned contradictions as another challenge to prove its authenticity. The Quran says in 4:82,

$$\text{أَفَلَا يَتَدَبَّرُونَ ٱلْقُرْءَانَ ۚ وَلَوْ كَانَ مِنْ عِندِ غَيْرِ ٱللَّهِ لَوَجَدُوا۟ فِيهِ ٱخْتِلَـٰفًا كَثِيرًا ۝٨٢}$$

Which in my all English translation was:

"Do they not consider the Qur´an (with care)? Had it been from other Than Allah, they would surely have found therein Much discrepancy."

Lastly some people ignorantly and malignantly spread a myth that Allah is a pagan moon deity and that if you worship Allah and prostrate in prayer facing the Kaba as the Quran says to do then you are worshipping some moon god. Nothing could be further from the truth and in context the Quran itself refutes such falsehood in 41:33-37 which says what in english means:

"And who is better in speech than he who says: "My Lord is Allâh (believes in His Oneness)," and then stands firm (acts upon His Order), and invites (men) to Allâh's (Islâmic Monotheism), and does righteous deeds, and says: "I am one of the Muslims." The good deed and the evil deed cannot be equal. Repel (the evil) with one which is better (i.e. Allâh orders the faithful believers to be patient at the time of anger, and to excuse those who treat them badly), then verily! he, between whom and you there was enmity, (will become) as though he was a close friend. But none is granted it (the above quality) except those who are patient - and none is granted it except the owner of the great

*portion (of happiness in the Hereafter i.e. Paradise and of a high moral character) in this world. And if an evil whisper from Shaitân (Satan) tries to turn you away (O Muhammad) (from doing good), then **seek refuge in Allâh**. Verily, **He is the All-Hearer, the All-Knower**. And from among His Signs are the night and the day, and the sun and the moon. **Prostrate yourselves not to the sun nor to the moon, but prostrate yourselves to Allâh Who created them, if you (really) worship Him.***"

As you can see the Quran explictly says Allah is not the moon and forbids people from prostrating to or worshipping the moon or anything else except the "All-Hearer and All-Knower, who created the sun and the moon" which would be God. Thus when people say Allah is a moon god, they either have no clue about Islam or the Quran, are evil people deliberately telling lies they know are false, or they are just repeating lies they heard or read that were spewed by people who deliberately told lies and fooled people into spreading such lies to others. For someone to claim Allah is a pagan moon deity is equivalent to someone claiming that Moses pbuh and the Torah taught people to worship a Golden Calf. So I learned that Allah is not some moon god like I had been told, it's the same God Adam, Abraham, Moses and Jesus pbut had worshiped. Linguistically "Allah" is an Arabic word that roughly translates to mean: "*the one who is worshiped*" referring to the Creator of all. Jesus pbuh spoke Aramaic, which is a language related to Arabic, in Aramaic the word for the Creator is also "Allah". Whenever Jesus pbuh said "God" in Aramaic he would've said "Allah". Even today in the Arabic bible on the first page of the book of Genesis it has the word "Allah" 17 times, in place of "God", while the word "Allah" is used 6 times in the first paragraph. Over 20 million Arab Christians and Arab Jews say that Allah is the Creator and the one the prophets worshiped. If you go to the middle east and visit the Arab churches the Christians there say Allah is God. Even Arab Jehovah's Witnesses say the name of God is Allah, but the non-Arab Jehovah's Witnesses are ignorant of this and insist Jehovah is the name to use and won't believe you if you tell them otherwise despite there not even being a "v" in the arabic language; making it impossible for Arab Jehovah's Witnesses to even say the word "Jehovah". The word Allah is used by so many Jews and Christians that in Malaysia the courts legally imposed a ban on non-Muslims using the word Allah because it causes confusion. In response the Christians and Jews took to the street protesting the government for the "right to use the word Allah as God". That's what actually happened, they rallied in protest because the Muslim court told non-Muslims to stop using the word Allah for who they worship because they aren't Muslims. Thus any Christian who foolishly claims "Allah is the devil" should go tell that to the millions of Christians who claim to worship Allah in churches before telling it to Western peoples or Muslims, because Christians in the holy land say they worship Allah. As a word "Allah" is neither masculine nor feminine, it is a more accurate term because one cannot make "Allah" plural by adding an "s" as you can with the English word "God". There are no uppercases or lowercases in Arabic so you cannot alter the meaning as you can with "God" by making the g lowercase. The word "God" can mean different things to people with different beliefs, but it's impossible to be confused when using the word "Allah"; unless you're one of those 5%ers who deceitfully uses an acronym. But it's an Arabic word and there are no acronyms in classical Arabic.

The only problem was that I thought I was possessed. Because I had been brainwashed and was training to be an exorcist a mechanism existed in my mind to doubt anything disagreeing with Catholicism, automatically assuming that anything non-Catholic was satanic. I felt certain Islam was true but could not proceed with haste unless it was a mistake. Thus I did more research hoping to be guided. I was still going to the bible study class, although I didn't go to church. At first not going to church felt strange and weird because it was a habit that developed for many years over the course of my life. Yet no matter how it felt skipping church and wondering what people would think, I couldn't go and pretend to believe because it'd make me a hypocrite. Something said to go if only just for the girls, but I knew that wasn't God. Life is about pleasing God, and going to church was not how to do it. I went back to bible study and asked God to send a sign making things clear. That day there was a guy who had never come to class before and he said what I was thinking almost to the word. He asked the bible teacher what to do when people read the bible and find it to be contradicting and that it teaches different things than what the Church does. She said that we shouldn't let people read the bible on their own because they'll get confused, they should be brought to church so we can tell them what the bible means according to the Church. That way before they read it they will already know what to think and how to interpret the verses. She said it's better for them to be told what the bible means rather than have people learn from it themselves. I was stunned and remained silent finally realizing how the Catholic Church had misguided millions. No one else reacted and seemed not to understand the gravity of what she said. Suddenly it became clear that I had been brainwashed since baptism. Literally, at baptism a priest washed my head with water contaminating my brain and telling me what to believe then I grew up thinking my beliefs came from the bible because he told me they were. Hence whenever I read the bible I had been using it as a tool to support my beliefs rather than see what it said or get my beliefs from the text itself. I thought my beliefs were right and because I read the bible then that made me think my beliefs were biblical, because I believed in the bible and my beliefs simultaneously even though my beliefs came before my belief in the bible and my belief in the bible came from my beliefs and not as a result of reading the bible itself. Basically I believed in the bible before I ever read it, and I read it because I believed in it and thus I believed that whatever it was that I read in the bible then somehow it supported my beliefs, even if in reality it taught something else contradictory to my beliefs or the book itself. This is what happens whenever the bible is read. Most get confused seeing the bible teaches different things than what their preachers said, but then they recognize a verse they had heard many times before which causes them to relax thinking it's all related because they remembered the story, sometimes even considering themselves to be a genius for only remembering what was important. Although the content of the bible is usually taken out of context and had they never been pre-programmed they would've interpreted it differently. Furthermore many who read the bible deliberately read it out of context due to selective quotations chosen by religious leaders, excessively lenghty bible studies or by themselves with one of those "Read the bible in 1 year" scams. The scam says if you buy their book or follow their instructions of reading certain passages everyday then you will read the whole bible by the end of 1 year. However the catch is you don't read it cover to cover, but skip around and read several bits of multiple chapters in different biblical books each day. Meaning someone might read the first sentence of Book 1 chapter 3, then read the last paragraph of Book 34 chapter 18, then read some verses from Book 15 chapter 6, followed by a paragraph from Book 45 chapter 30 and concluding with a passage from Book 3 chapter 2. Then after reading in such a convuluted fashion every day for 1 year, they get told they read the whole bible and know what it teaches. Obviously that's insanity and not how to read a book to understand a book, but they don't even end up reading the whole book as advertised. On top of that the concept is faulty. Just consider which is the faster way to read a book, from beginning to end or by constantly flipping through the pages reading different selections in a completely different order than they were written or organized in? In the time it takes to flip back and forth and back and forth you'd probably be able to read half the book if you just read from the beginning onward. How are you reading this book? Beginning to end? That's the correct and quickest way to read a book and that's how to read if you want to understand what you are reading. But this is not how Christians tend to read the bible. Even in church they pick three unconnected readings and try to relate them rather than reading 3 consecutive passages. This is done because the only way one can believe in the Christian faiths is by reading the bible out of context picking certain verses and relating them to others which don't even relate unless one never read the bible in context cover to cover first. Essentially to believe in Christianity one must believe in it before reading the bible, and to believe in the bibe one must believe in Christianity first. But most Christians think it's the other way around. Another peculiarity with the bible is how it compared to the Quran. I read the english translation of the Quran in a few days, but there are some who read the full Quran twice a day. Yet nobody is reading the bible as quickly because it's such a long book that nearly nobody even finishes reading it once in a lifetime. Thus they have the "Read the bible in 1 year" scams, because to Christians reading their religious text in 1 year is considered a short time to have read it in. However realistically if God gave mankind a book by which all people are supposed to read and follow what it teaches, then doesn't it make more sense that the book should be short? Really if God sent the bible to guide all of mankind then why is it such a long book that takes such a long time to read? Wouldn't God want every person to be able to read his book lots of times throughout their life? The Quran can be read in a very short time, even twice a day. So practically speaking the Quran is of a more appropriate length for a book of daily divine guidance. Why does the bible take so long to read? Why did the Christian bible study teacher say people shouldn't read the bible on their own? Why did the bible study teacher say people should be taught in church first and told what to think before they ever read the bible? It was amazing to hear the bible study teacher say that people shouldn't read what she said was the word of God. Who would have thought a Christian bible study teacher would be saying that people shouldn't read the bible? Why would she be afraid of people reading the bible? What did she know that I didn't and if it's a book of God wouldn't God want all to read it? How can people follow something they don't read?

    Further research revealed this was actually official Vatican policy for centuries. At the outset during 382 CE soon after Roman Catholicism was declared the official religion of the Empire, Pope Damascus forbid those who weren't priests from reading the bible and priests were not allowed to teach the bible either. Bible translations were expressly prohibited and considered sinful. In 860 CE Pope Nicholas I banned the bible from being used in public by any who weren't Catholic priests. Another Pope Gregory renewed and supported the ban in 1073 CE. My former role model, Pope Innocent III in 1198 CE ruled that anyone caught reading a bible who wasn't a Catholic priest would be stoned to death by "soldiers of the Church". In 1229 CE it was prohibited for laymen to even possess the Old or New Testament. Eventually by the 14th century CE if you were found with a bible and were not a Catholic priest you would be whipped, have all your property confiscated and then would be burned to death at the stake. Now why would the Christian leaders go to such an extreme extent and mete out such severe punishment to those who possessed what they say is *"the word of God"*? Keep in mind being burned at the stake was for possession of the bible, one cannot even imagine what they would have done if a person was caught committing the crime of reading the bible. In fact the first man to translate the full bible into english was William Tyndale and because of committing such a "heretical blasphemous deed" he was burned to death in 1536 CE. Isn't this suspicious? What was in the bible that they didn't want the world to know? Is that dangerous information still in the bibles we know of today? Have you ever heard of anything more hypocritical than Christian religious leaders prohibiting people from possessing a bible? This period where the bible was prohibited throughout Europe is known as the golden age of Christianity. How could that be if Christianity is based on the bible? This isn't ancient history either, because of a law passed by King Henry VIII it was illegal for women in England to read the bible until 1850 CE. Now this Henry VIII died in 1547. However in 1535 CE, 12 years before his death, he commissioned the Church of England, which he created, to translate the bible into english in order to have a bible that agreed with his personal theology. This bible became what is known as "The Great Bible" and was published in 1539 CE. Then Queen Elizabeth reigned and created the state-sponsored Angelican church in 1559 CE. Since the bible of King Henry VIII was rather anti-clerical, in 1568 CE the Angelican Church of England published the "Bishop's Bible" and this bible gave more authority to clergy than King Henry's version. Although King James I decided this Bishop's bible was too favorable and didn't give the King as much authority as he'd like. You see King James I had a very specific view about government which he announced to the English Parliament in 1609 CE saying,

> *"The state of monarchy is the supremest thing on earth. For Kings are not only God's lieutenants on earth, and sit upon God's throne, but even by God Himself are called gods...Kings are justly called gods, for that they excercise a manner or resemblance of divine power on earth; for if you will consider the attributes of God, you shall se how they agree in the person of a king. God hath power to create or destroy, make or unmake at His pleasure, to give life or send death, to judge all and be judged nor accountable to none...And the like power have kings; they make and unmake their subjects, they have power of raising and casting down, of life and death; judges over all their subjects and in all causes, and yet accountable to none but God only. They have power to...make of their subjects like men at the chess-a pawn to take a bishop or a knight- and to cry up or down any of their subjects, as they do their money."*

Many don't know this side of King James. Prior to this speech by James, not since the Roman Empire had a European ruler claimed to be the viceroy of God. Only the popes had dared to make such a claim in Europe. There are a few other details about King James you may not have been aware of. King James I of England was the Protestant son of the Scottish Catholic Queen Mary Stuart. At 8 months old his father Darnley was killed, at 10 months of age his mother had to flee the country due to revolt against her as a Catholic and he never saw her again. James became the King of Scotland officially when he was 13 months old, but only began to rule at the age of 17. As King of Scotland his name was James VI. For political reasons he promised to believe in, defend and promote Calvinism as long as he was King. At the age of 20, King James VI told Queen Elizabeth of England that he would be fine with her beheading his mother Mary Stuart, whom she held in captivity for the last 19 years, if Elizabeth gave him a larger monthly pension. Yes King James told Queen Elizabeth to kill his mother, so as requested she executed his mother and predecessor Mary Stuart in 1587 CE and increased his pension. King James VI later acquired a reputation for being the "hardest drinker in all of Europe". James was famous for drinking alcohol, and he could drink much more than anyone else in Europe; one could say he was "King Alcoholic". The Scottish people being religious Calvinists didn't like the King and believed in a democratic clerical government. Scottish preachers riled the crowds saying kings were the children of devils and that James was Satan himself. Thus by 1596 CE the Scots came for James while he was in the Holyrood Palace in Edinburgh. James fled and said Edinburgh was not fit to be the capital of Scotland and he would only come back to kill rebels. So nearly everyone left the city and James returned in 1597 CE. Later in 1597 CE James wrote his book on "*Demonologie*" which was all the stuff he knew about demons and how to detect witches, wizards, demons, devils and combat evil. In 1598 CE James VI wrote 2 more books "*Kingly Gift*" and "*The True Law of Free Monarchies*" promoting absolute monarchy saying that Kings were chosen by God and their divine appointment was a mystery as holy and ineffable as any sacrament therefore any resistance to absolute monarchy was a sin that was bound to cause greater harm than any tyranny. According to King James to oppose a King's decree was possibly the worst sin a Christian could ever commit. Then since Queen Elizabeth had no heirs and James VI was loosely related and one of the better claims to the English crown the English government asked if King James VI of Scotland wanted to also be King of England after Elizabeth died in 1603 CE. If James was King of both England and Scotland then they could become united as one country under 1 king. King James VI agreed, but there was a catch, England was Angelican and Calvinists were a persecuted minority so if James VI were to be King of England he would have to change his religion to Angelicanism. He didn't hesitate to agree to be the Angelican King of England. So on May 6th, 1603 CE the Scottish King James VI was crowned in London as King James I of England and Scotland. At that time he was 37 years old, known for swearing, stammering and having a habit of fondling young boys at his court. King James hated water and as a result rarely bathed. On January 14, 1604 CE King James called a Council at Hampton Court because he wanted the Angelicans, Calvinists(who in England were called Puritans as a derogatory term since 1564 CE), Catholics and Protestants to all agree and combine into one religion. It was like an English version of the Council of Nicea Constantine had assembled in 325 CE. Episcopacy (the King's divine authority to legislate) was indispensible to the State and not up for discussion, but aside from that King James wanted all the Christian denominations to agree on "*one doctrine, and one discipline, one religion in substance and ceremony*". The Angelican Bishop of London said James was divinely inspired, "*the like of which has not been seen since the time of Christ*". The rest of the Christian representatives thought James was a corrupt fool playing a game with religious differences as if they were politicians. They agreed with each other that they were not going to be able to agree on religion like how King James wanted. At the end of the conference King James decreed "All Christians will be Angelican." and he promised to publish a bible for all of England to use which was to be the only legal bible. Any clergy who refused to convert to Angelicanism were imprisoned until they either quit, or choose to move to Holland or America. King James put the Catholic priests to death, forbid Catholics from practicing medicine or law, serving as executors or guardians and made it illegal for any Catholic to travel more than 5 miles from their house. King James also decreed that sporting events would take place on Sundays, which continues to this day, despite many Christians complaining it was sacreligious. Forks also became popular during the reign of King James. The Catholic Guy Fawkes tried to assassinate King James by blowing up Parliament on 11/5/1605 CE, but he got caught on the 4th. Ironically November 5th, became a popular public holiday in England called "Guy Fawkes Day". This famous King James was the man who started or restarted in Europe the belief in the "Divine Right of Kings". It was a very bold move and as the head of the Angelican Church, having claimed he is the representative of God on earth he had to write his own bible; especially since the "Bishop's bible" had limited the power of Kings that King Henry's bible had previously endorsed at the expense of the clergy. Therefore in 1611 CE the King James bible was printed. The King James bible was supposed to end the biblical tug of war where Protestant episcopalians altered the bible to fit their theology, but in fact the tug of war got worse. The Calvinists/Puritans were outraged at this King James bible and left England to go to America, leaving the King James bible behind taking their Geneva Bible with them. Nobody outside of England believed in King James' bible because it was an Angelican bible and only England was Angelican because the state invented Angelicanism and said English people had to be Angelican officially making it a legal requirement in 1628 CE. Plus the rest of Europe didn't really speak English so they didn't use the Angelican English King's bible printed in English. However other Kings took note of this process where Kings were writing their own bible to suit themselves and make their desires become doctrines believed to have come from God. Therefore many kings wrote their own bible that promoted their state policies. In England, they didn't want to cause religious instability or doubt by having every king make his own bible since that would make the bible be seen as the King's book instead of sacred scripture. So in England future Kings and Christian clergy members decided they would simply change the biblical text but keep the same general name as "King James' bible" so the public would be none the wiser. Unfortunately this ruse has worked and many today think the King James Bibles they have are old books when they are very modern. The trick is they have "The Authorized King James Version", "The King James Version", "The King James Bible", "The New King James Bible", "The Revised King James Bible", "The New Revised King James Bible", "The standard King James Bible" and many other completely different bibles, but because of their names being so similar all saying "King James" the average person is unaware that each of those bibles say very different things with different theological teachings. There are more bibles associated with King James than there have been Kings who were named James. To further complicate the situation, rather than changing the name everytime they changed the bible, they started simply changing the date of publication. For instance "X bible" published in 1953 is a very different book than "X bible" published in 1961, yet on the bookshelf they have the same exact name and extremely similar covers. So these various "King James bibles" that exist were never read by King James nor have anything to do with him. Honestly if you get someone a copy of the original 1611 CE text published by King James I, which wasn't even called the King James bible until 1715 CE, an english person today can't even read it or understand what it says because it's written in 17th century olde olde english. Most who do manage to actually think they've seen the infamous real King James bible ask what language it is when they read it, because they don't even consider the true "King James Bible" to be english since by modern english standards it's not. However nobody even knows which bible published by King James in 1611 CE is "the original" because even in 1611 CE they had different versions right off the presses. As an example there are the "He" and "She" bibles of 1611 CE, where for Ruth 3:15 some King James bibles printed say "he went into the city" and others say that "she went into the city". I guess it's possible that the biblical character might have been a transvestite and that could explain some bibles saying he and others saying she, but that excuse is even more scandalous than saying that errors always existed in the english bibles. This He/She error isn't even thought to have been a translator's error but an error due to bibles being printed in different locations. Meaning that depending on the address your bible was printed at, it will say different things. Note that I say the address it was printed at, because since a bookseller gets their books from multiple places IF bibles were sold in stores, instead of to clergymen and churches directly, then on one bookshelf at a store you could easily have found that every single bible on the bookshelf which was printed in the same year based off of the same manuscript all would've said different things because of the various locations they were printed at. To put this chaos in a modern perspective, imagine if every single book you've ever seen whether it be in a library, in a school or at a store, was a one of a kind which said things no other book did even if it was supposed to be the same book. For instance imagine if every student in a classroom had their textbook teach different things. That's what happened when the bibles were printed throughout Europe, except ordinary folk weren't allowed to read them, only clergymen were. Thus it's no wonder they denounced each other for not following the bible, their bibles literally said different things but rather than blame the publishers they blamed the preachers. Even with one standard text being used by certain Christian denominations, differences still existed among the bibles of the very same version and edition because of the European process of printing a book itself, whereby every machine churned out a book with different words because of the mechanical differences of machines which existed even after machines became standarized having the same parts because not everybody kept their book machines in factory conditions or kept them at factory settings. Afterall as a book printer if you were printing on the same machine as your competition then in order to make your products stand out you had to do some tinkering, and even if you didn't because other people did then your books would still be different because of your competition tinkering with their printing press. Also because of the manual labor involed in typesetting, humans still deeply effected the printing process of each individual book. Because of human involvement, up until the 1800s you could've in theory had everyone using the same script, printing on identical machines with identical settings but because the machines were operated by different people they would produce different results. Although it used to be even worse in that the same person wouldn't have been able to copy themselves from book to book because each book used to be done all at once, so it was similar to copying books by hand except they were printed by hand set type. Fortunately for Europeans and Americans the photostat was invented in 1907 CE which was a type of printing that utilized a camera to take a photo of the script, books printed this way were basically picture books of pages of a book's manuscript. Unfortunately however the moveable type remained popular until the 1960s CE and it wasn't until the late 1960s CE that universal standards in book publishing were set throughout the industry; so that every copy of a book would actually be the same regardless of where it was printed at, what machine was used and who used the machine and when they used it. I even remember seeing a manual typesetting printer at the local library when I was a kid. Yet perhaps the funniest part about all these King James advocates who passionately stress "the King James bible is the best" is that when King James was King and published his olde olde english version, women were forbidden to read it. King James actually said women were not allowed to read his bible. Thus it's humorous when people have the notion King James was inspired by God to write a bible, even though he didn't even write the book or translate it, when this very same King would punish women if they read his bible. Realistically if one says God inspired King James to put out a reliable bible then one would also have to say that God must not want women to read the bible, because the guy he allegedly inspired forbid women from reading it and punished any who did. King James even said that God told him that God doesn't want women to read his King James bible and that it was sinful for them to do. King James taught that a Christian woman would burn in hell if she read the King James Bible. I repeat that King James would physically harm women if they read his bible, or any bible, even more if they read other bibles because those bibles were forbidden by James. So that's where modern Christians would say, *"Well clearly King James made some big mistakes in his life. Like asking Elizabeth to kill his mother, being an alcoholic, changing religions for kingship, fondling boys, claiming God appoints all Kings and that they are infallible gods among men. I also think King James was wrong to say God said women are forbidden to read the bible and it's sinful for them to do."* Yet then they turn around and say their fake modern version and edition of the "King James Bible" is the word of God and that King James was inspired by God to publish it. Yet sadly the majority of Christians don't have a clue who King James was, but most Protestant denominations love the bibles printed in his namesake, which they think are the same as his, even though in his own lifetime only Angelicans accepted it. The reason the King James biblical namesake became popular was only because the British Empire made lots of colonies and that was "The English bible". King James was not a champion of Christianity, he was a tyrannical English King. Ironically now that it is no longer a death sentence to read a bible, very few Christians bother to read it. After all those laws that have been overturned to give people the opportunity to safely read what they believe is sacred scripture, the vast majority still don't. The whole history of bibles are a publishers worst nightmare, except for those getting paid to publish bibles. Needless to say this is not the type of information people get taught while attending Christian "bible studies".

More questions had been asked and the new guy at bible study raised his hand again. He asked about Muslims and what they believed about Jesus (pbuh), I was very eager to hear what the teacher would say to that. She sounded unprepared and didn't know what to say seemingly frightened and reluctant to answer. Finally she generalized saying Muslims believe in Jesus (pbuh) but don't think that he was God. Then she spoke further and lies came out of her mouth, she said all the Muslims were converting becoming Christians and some had even seen Jesus (pbuh) come. She said many had received visions supporting Catholicism and converted because Jesus pbuh told them to in a vision. At that, I knew she was a liar and I rudely laughed. Beforehand I researched looking to see if there were any Muslim conversions to Christianity. I searched everywhere and couldn't find any at all. I had never searched for something harder in my life, training for the priesthood I knew that Catholic numbers had been dropping, without a doubt she was lying about Muslims becoming Catholic due to visions of Jesus pbuh appearing. It sure sounded nice and reassuring, but it was a blatant lie and I knew it. I only found 2 convert stories and they were both beyond belief. The first was a woman who said she was inspired by Jesus pbuh. She had been a Christian Episcopalian Minister, but what was so surprising was that she said Jesus (pbuh) led her to become a Muslim. This female Christian preacher started teaching this to her congregation in the church and got defrocked for telling Christians Jesus pbuh led her to Islam. The other was an alleged ex-Muslim and I just couldn't believe him because he was an obvious liar. I knew very little about Islam, but even I could tell he was lying. To become a Muslim is easy, no ceremony is necessary, you just have to believe in certain things and then say a certain phrase. On a TV show he said the phrase and gave an incorrect translation. So he could never have been a Muslim because he didn't even know what to say to become one. He said the correct phrase in Arabic and said the wrong meaning for it in English. And that's the only catch in taking the shahada, which is the declaration of faith said to become a Muslim, you have to know and believe the meaning of what you are saying and be sincere or else the shahada isn't valid. Non-Arabic speakers usually repeat it in their native language to confirm they know what they are saying. Even still there is a difference between knowing the translation of those words and knowing the meaning of those words. This bible teacher said that many Muslims were converting, I had looked all over the internet so then why couldn't I find any? I seriously could not find even one that seemed remotely genuine and I was trying very hard. The only story I found of Jesus pbuh inspiring a conversion was of the Christian woman saying Jesus pbuh led her to Islam. Recently I learned about a Spanish American who entered a masjid and saw Muslims praying the morning prayer, then he told them he wanted to be a follower of Muhammad pbuh, embrace Islam and be informed what to do to become a Muslim. The Muslims wanted to know his story and why he wanted to become a Muslim and he said they should just guide him and not ask. He did ghusl and said the shahada becoming a Muslim, then asked to stay in the Islamic center for a few days to learn Islam. He stayed 3 days and would cry a lot, prostrate in prayer very long and was keen to listen to the Quran. After the Sunset prayer he came to one of the Muslims and asked him to listen to him recite Quran to check his pronunciation. The Muslim wanted to know the guy's story so he told him. The guy said that as a Christian he had cried every night for 4 years asking God to guide him to the true religion. Then one night he had a dream where he saw Jesus the son of Mary pbuh who told him to become a follower of Muhammad pbuh and that Jesus and Muhammad pbut are two prophets who's religion is one; Islam. When he awoke that morning he went inside the first masjid he passed by. While talking it became time for the nighttime prayer so the guy stopped his story and in the first prostration he didn't get up but stayed prostrating. The Muslims called him to get up, but he didn't, then one nudged him and his body fell over and they realized he was dead. He had died prostrating in prayer as a Muslim. Who would've thought that Jesus pbuh would appear to a Christian in their dream telling them to become a Muslim? Although it doesn't even matter what the numbers of conversions are, just because more people might believe something doesn't make it true. And if the numbers of adherents of a certain religious group decreases, that doesn't mean it's false. The common misconception people have when it comes to religion is that some think it's like democracy or Santa Claus.

Then as I was leaving a lady offered me a book. I said I didn't want it, knowing I wouldn't be coming back to return it. The lady offered it to the bible study teacher saying it was really good. The bible study teacher then said something very ignorant. She said, *"I only read the Bible because it's the best book, I don't read anything else because the bible is the best"*. This statement is ridiculous and also contradicted her prior statement that people shouldn't read the bible. Ok, she only reads the bible because she says that it's the best, but if that's the only thing she's ever read then how does she know that it's the best? There is nothing she's ever compared it to and has never put her theory to the test. If all you have known is lies and have never experienced the truth then you would never know you'd been lied to. A person is guaranteed to be deceived if they intellectually isolate themselves. If it's the only thing she's ever read, then that means for her the bible is also the worst book she's ever read. I realized at that moment that the brainwashers themselves are brainwashed, it's sad that they continue brainwashing themselves. Especially because they don't know what they're doing, or that they're making God so mad.

At last I had felt certain, however I still did one last test. Having been a deeply devout Catholic I had obtained and held in my possession what was supposed to be a relic of the true cross. This was a very expensive pendant with verified authentic seals from long dead christian bishops as certification. Allegedly it contained two splinters in the shape of a cross from the alleged cross Jesus pbuh was said to have been crucified on. The splinters are believed to have special powers that have been active since first discovered, allegedly. The story goes that Constantine's Trinitarian mother Helena searched for Christian relics. She found 3 wooden crosses after demolishing a pagan temple devoted to either Venus or Jupiter, scholars differ as to which, then a sick person touched one of the crosses and they later recovered from their illness, so people started thinking the cross that she touched had powers and that it was "the one" Jesus pbuh was allegedly crucified on. This discovery is thought to have happened between 326-328 CE, about 300 years after Christ pbuh. It is important to note that the cross was only found AFTER the council of Nicaea when Christianity became a legal religion of the Roman Empire by decree. As pilgrims went to visit the relic they would kiss the cross and take splinters home between their teeth. At other times pieces would be broken off of it and given to prestigious people as gifts. During the crusades Christian armies would take this cross into battle with them thinking it gave them victory. Prior to the 3rd crusade the Muslim leader Yusuf ibn Ayubi known as "Salah Ad-Deen" and his army defeated the army of the crusader kingdom of Jerusalem at the battle of hattin on July 4th, 1187 CE. The Christians lost the cross and it went into Muslim possession and has disappeared from history ever since. When the news of this battle came to Pope Urban III he instantly died from shock. This used to make me very angry every 4th of July, especially when American Christians are typically ignorant of such history. I couldn't figure out why God would let the "true cross" fall into Muslim hands allowing it to be forever lost. If Christianity were true and we all had to believe in it to be saved, surely God could have prevented it and the cross could've been used today to revitalize the Christian faith. It also made me suspicious of the American government, why would they make the fourth of July the day to party when the "birth of the nation" according to the declaration of independence and President John Adams was on July 2nd, 1776 CE? It seemed as though they distinctly wanted to avoid the embarrassment of Christianity having lost the "true cross" in a "holy war" to Muslims. I thought if people knew the history it would anger Christians and they could then be manipulated to start another crusade, hoping to re-capture the cross after all these years. Having learned America's founding fathers were not Christian they couldn't have wanted to spare Christians any embarrassment. Rather they likely changed the date to make the memory of the Muslim victory fade away. However after researching I learned why "Independence day" was changed from the 2nd to the 4th. Three of America's first five presidents died on July 4th. Americans partied as a result of their presidents' deaths because they became independent from the presidents. Also on July 4th, 1863 CE the Confederate States surrendered at Vicksburg, Mississippi. Making it a cruel twist of irony for southerners to celebrate the 4th as "Independence day" when it was the day their Confederacy surrendered to the Union. In 1998 CE the U.S. Congress passed a bill which declared the 21 days between Flag Day and the fourth of July as "Honor America Days". Apparently the government thinks all American subjects should "*Honor America*" for 3 weeks straight, whether congress means the land, the symbols, the politicians or the tax system is anybody's guess. Also since their secular policies are intended to ignore religion, hoping it fades away from the public sphere, it would make sense to create a political nationalistic holiday on that day. Hypocritically they encourage people to get drunk and blow stuff up on that day despite fireworks being against the law in most states. The government makes an excuse that it's legal on the 4th of July because it's being done for patriotic reasons. It's almost as though blowing up fireworks on the 4th of July were some form of religious sacrifice to the government, which it technically is since they tax the sales of those illegal fireworks and levy income taxes on the fireworks manufacturers. This was done by pagan governments as well in that sacrificing people was illegal unless it was done in support of the government. If you can only use fireworks when the government says then what kind of "freedom" is that? Yet many cities in America don't even allow the 4th of July fireworks and arrest anyone who uses them sending such people to jail for celebrating their "freedom". But what's even more ironic is that many Americans celebrate patriotic holidays such as Memorial Day and the 4th of July in Canada. What does it say about a nation who's citizens choose to celebrate their most patriotic holiday in another country? If America is so great then why do so many Americans celebrate their patriotic American holidays in Canada?

Anyways I had what the Roman Catholic authorities said were splinters of the cross Jesus pbuh was alleged to have been crucified on. When studying to become an exorcist I had learned that if someone is possessed, which I thought I was, then if any cross at all is placed on their forehead then it will burn an imprint on it. So I put the relic of what was the alleged "true cross" on my forehead and contrary to Vatican teachings nothing happened. With it still pressed against my head I said that, "Jesus is not God or the son of God" and nothing happened. Then it was clear that this was foolish and Christianity was a false religion. Next I disposed of the "true cross" so no one else worships it through delusion. I had tried as much as possible not to come to that conclusion, but falsehood is falsehood even if you've believed in it your whole life. On my own initiative I unintentionally learned Christianity was lies upon lies upon lies upon modern lies. An example of this is the "true cross" and famous "Church of the Holy Sepulchre" in Jerusalem. The official history of the "Church of the Holy Sepulchre" states that it is both the place Jesus pbuh was biblically crucified and the same spot he was buried in a sepulchre to later rise from the dead 3 days later. Officially both events are said to have occured at this spot and that's what they tell tourists. Yet the bible itself refutes this and says both locations were miles apart from each other. The Christian tourists who flock there don't care, even though they should know better. Most figure if it wasn't true then they wouldn't say it was, because they can't fathom such a blatant big time public lie. But it gets worse. This Church of the "Holy Sepulchre" did not exist until 325 CE. If you remember 325 CE is the same year the Council of Nicaea took place, during that year Constantine also established this "Church of the Holy Sepulchre in Jerusalem". What was there before? It was an ancient pagan temple devoted to the greek goddess Aphrodite. Yet in 325 CE it became a holy church. But it gets worse still. The famous event of Helena finding the true cross Jesus pbuh was alleged to have died on took place between 326-328 CE in a former temple devoted to Jupiter or Venus; as has already been mentioned. What does that have to do with the Church of the Holy Sepulchre? Absolutely nothing, right? Well the Christians say that the place Helena found the true cross is the same place where the Church of the Holy Sepulchre is and that's why it was built there. However it is impossible for Helena in 326-328 CE to find the legendary "true cross" in a temple devoted to Jupiter or Venus in the same place a church was built the year earlier in 325 CE on a site formerly dedicated to Aphrodite. The legend of the true cross basically says Helena found the crosses in a church after the church was built but when she found these crosses in that church it wasn't a church, then she went back in time and built the church on the same spot years earlier; except Christians ignore the implied time traveling bit that is necessary for their stories of the Church being the site of the Sepulchre and the Crucifiction and the place the "True Cross" was found be true. Typically they only tell one story at a time, frequently without citing dates, names, or history so the contradictions are left unknown. Another such "holy site" Christian tourists visit is the "Church of the Nativity" in Bethlehem, which is alleged to be the spot Jesus pbuh was born. Who built this church? Constantine's mother Helena did in 327 CE, again 2 years after the Council of Nicaea. This church in Bethlehem was formerly a temple devoted to the god Adonis, who was the greek god of beauty/desire, prior to being a temple to adonis it was a temple dedicated to Tammuz. So by claiming that is the site Jesus pbuh was born Christians are unwittingly saying that Jesus pbuh was born inside of a pagan temple wherein a pagan son of god/man-god crucified savior idol was worshipped, except since Christians don't know the architectural history they insist it was a cave at the time ignoring the archaelogical facts. Even the famous Jerome who was a priest at the Church of the Nativity said that prior to it becoming the Church of the Nativity it was a consecrated heathen temple. Yet tourists today insist it's the birthplace of Jesus pbuh despite the priest who said mass there on a regular basis in the 400s CE saying it is not the birthplace of Jesus pbuh but the site of a pagan temple converted into a church. Anyone looking at the official stories of such Christian "holy sites" can see they are logistically and historically impossible folktales. Christian tourists are being lied to and scammed out of their money. Constantine's mother invented the Christian tourism and relic industries. While the famous Constantine and Helena Cathedral built in 326 CE, was previously a temple where Baal was worshippped. Simply put the Christian "holy sites" have no real connection to Jesus pbuh but are simply tourist traps created because Christians will pay to visit places to get told they are seeing spots Jesus pbuh once was. Millions of Christians flock to such "sacred sites" each year to get spiritually charged claiming such former pagan sites are proofs of Christian doctrine being true. The worst part about it is the Crusades were started because Christians were told these sacred tourist sites were endangered. Well I had been the most practicing Catholic I knew of, who wasn't an ordained priest, but there was no way I could twist and turn to try and pretend Christianity was a true religion. The facts say Christian beliefs were thoroughly contaminated with pagan fiction. All praises and thanks be to Allah for having guided me away from a man-made religion.

    After reading a translation of the Quran I was amazed because Muhammad pbuh was rarely mentioned. It said he was a prophet and a Messenger, but the whole revelation remains in the same form as it had been given to him. I had read a translation of the exact revelation in the first person. Muhammad pbuh didn't insert any commentary or interpretation, in fact in some places it advised him on what to do concerning personal situations. Since it was revealed to him, it didn't really contain much information about him because he didn't have to be told much about who he was, since he knew who he was. Therefore it would be silly for God's revelation to Muhammad pbuh to include a biography of Muhammad pbuh. The Quran couldn't have been written by Muhammad pbuh, because it bluntly corrected him telling him specific things he should or shouldn't do, chastising his mistakes. If it wasn't divine revelation someone would not have left that type of information in. I had read an English translation of the exact revelation he had heard. Being a non-Muslim I didn't know much about Muhammad pbuh and the Quran doesn't tell much about what he did with his life's duration. The Quran said there was only 1 God to be worshiped and that Muhammad pbuh was his final messenger and prophet. I believed that it was true, but felt I needed to know what his life was like before I could adopt Islam as my religion. This is because joining a religion is like signing a contract, spiritually it is legally a big deal and every religion has consequences if you don't fulfill your part of the contract or decide to nullify the agreement. For instance according to the bible I should've been killed for leaving Christianity. In fact even the New Testament has extremely inhumane rules for how Christians must treat non-Christians, who were never even Christian to begin with. I even feel like putting in the intolerant post-Jesus teachings because one really has to see them to believe how badly the bible says Christians should be treating non-Christians. The reason I'm not is because I don't want my Christian relatives to read such verses and then start treating other family members who leave Christianity the way the bible says they should. The verses are so bad, it's dangerous for me to share them. So it's a big deal to leave a religion and it's a big deal to join one too. Unlike with business contracts in all religions if one decides to leave it's akin to committing treason. Your religion is like spiritual citizenship, now do you need to know every single detail about a country before you choose to become a citizen? No, but it's best to know a few things about it before you do. Then I learned something beautiful about Islam that distinguishes it from other religions, Muhammad's life story pbuh is in another narration. The Quran is the word of God it's not a series of biographies or history. Outside of the Quran I read the different biographies of Muhammad pbuh and learned a great deal about him. For instance I never learned in school that Muhammad's parents died when he was young and he grew up an orphan pbuh. Now some people might say, *"there's no way it can actually be proven what was actually said or happened in the past, so you'll never really know."* Actually the past can be proven, but it takes a lot of work and that's where the hadith come in.

In Islam there are collections of hadith. A hadith is a report relating something Muhammad pbuh either said, did or witnessed without commenting on, which would mean that thing isn't wrong or else he would have commented and corrected. There are volumes of hadith collections. The scholarly attention to detail in hadiths is unmatched and the scholars are honest and realistic. For example one cannot say Muhammad pbuh said "____" and have it accepted at face value. First of all he spoke Arabic, so if it's not Arabic it's not accurate. Second of all he died before we were born so how do we know this information if we didn't personally hear him say it? This is where it gets scholarly with the chain of narration of the transmitters. In order to know what Muhammad pbuh had said there had to be witnesses, and since we were not witnesses we must have heard it from someone a witness told. A hadith's chain of narrators may be like this: "***Person E heard from Person D who heard from Person C who was told by Person B that Person A said***: *When I was eating dinner with the prophet pbuh, after he had finished eating a piece of gourd he had selected with his right hand, of which gourd was his favorite food, I saw Muhammad pbuh smile so much his molar teeth were visible and heard him say:"_____"*. This chain of narrators is called the isnad. Imaam Bukhari, a Scholar from what is modern day Russia who memorized millions of hadiths including their isnads, said regarding the isnad:***"The isnad is part of the religion: had it not been for the isnad, whoever wished to would have said whatever he liked."*** While the Scholar Imam Ash'Shafi'i said in regards to the isnad: *"Whoever attempts to seek and learn hadith without an isnad he is like one who gathers wood at night in the darkness. He picks up wood, not knowing there is a serpant inside."* Now the bible does not have any isnads at all, not for even 1 biblical verse. So the isnad is a special proof of authentic information Islam has, which all other faiths and texts of other religions do not have. No other religion can prove that the information they teach today attributing it to X person is the exact same material that was actually taught by X person in the past many years ago. Others faiths say to "trust in God and their texts", Muslims trust in God but prove their religious texts are trustworthy. You trust the material that's from God or his prophets only after its been proven to really come from God or his prophets. If it's not proven you can't treat it as though it's prophetic, even if it is, because the prophets taught us to follow only what was proven to have truly come from God.

      Some collectors of hadith would not be comfortable classifying a hadith as 100% sound unless they heard two different *isnads* regarding the same occurrence. This was before the internet, phones, cars or planes. They would go to a place and study under a teacher learning hadith from those who knew them firsthand and then would travel by foot, camel, boat or horse all the way to the other part of the world just to hear 1 hadith before accepting the hadith they had already learned. They traveled all that distance just to confirm what they already knew, to double check its authenticity and reliability because they were that scrupulous in being certain what they heard was true. Who amongst us takes the truth so seriously today? One example is that of Imaam Bukhari who often survived on just 1 or 2 almonds a day because he couldn't afford to both travel and eat so he chose to travel seeking knowledge over eating. One time Bukhari spent 3 days eating leaves in Syria because he ran out of money when traveling to study hadith from a specific teacher in person. He was also blind until when at the age of 8 years old his mother asked Allah to give him sight to see so he could be better able to help the cause of Islam. After having his blindness cured Bukhari went on to learn from more than 1,080 scholars and traveled extensively spending 1/4 of his life compiling a book of sahih(authentic) hadith. Bukhari had a phenomenal photogenic memory and published his first scholastic book when he was 18 years old. May Allah be pleased with him. As great as this man was Muslims don't pray to him, celebrate his birthday, say he's guaranteed paradise or call him a saint. We don't know everything the man did, we only know what he did publicly. On the Day of Judgment his private life will also be factored in, so that's why we say, *"May Allah be pleased with him"* because we don't know for certain. We just hope for the best and acknowledge all the good he has done for the religion and hope Allah rewards him with what is good. May Allah be pleased with you and me as well.

      There is a methodology for authentication and it is historically scientific. Because of the intellectual honesty of Muslim scholars, the hadiths have various classifications. Islamic scholars admit that not everything people say about Muhammad pbuh is true. There are hadiths which have been forged and fabricated, or are doubtful. Muslim scholars have preserved them, as well as those which are true. There are even books by Muslim scholars devoted to lies people said about Muhammad pbuh detailing who started the lie and why it is a lie. There are also books by Muslim scholars who say: it appears this hadith is true and seems like something Muhammad pbuh would do but we cannot prove it. Then there are classes of hadith which have been proven to be 100% true. No other religion has such intellectual honesty where they say what's true and what's false and what can't be verified; every other religion just says, *"everything we're telling you is true, just trust us"*. A Muslim scholar will tell you if what he is saying has not been proven as well as how strong a religious opinion is. Even non-Muslim scholars have said that Muslims should be proud of their hadith tradition because it is beyond scholastic comparison and no other religion has anything comparable to it. A legal or religious ruling can only be based upon authentic information. Weak(da'eef) or doubtful hadiths by themselves cannot be used to justify doing or not doing something. For a hadith to be classified as sahih or authentic it has to meet a high level of criteria. Usually there must be two separate chains of narration confirming the same tradition. Meaning there must have been more than one witness to the event in question unless it were something specific, such as something that only his wife could witness, but then that has to be mentioned if there is only one chain. The chain must be entirely reliable throughout, meaning all the narrators must have been able to have actually learned from each other and been in the same place at the same time in their lives. Sometimes you will find that person E will say they heard from person D but person D died before person E was born, so it would have been impossible for person E to have learned from person D, or perhaps persons D and E while both alive at the same time and in the same city they may never have actually been able to communicate with each other and share information, these details must be made known and those types of things affect the grade of a hadith. Those in the chain of narration and the scholars must know the biographies of every single person in the chain of each narration, knowing what they did with their life, who they learned from and who they taught, what their morals were like, if they were honest or forgetful and must make sure they are all of reputable character. You cannot just accept a narration at face value, you have to know exactly who these narrators actually were and what they and their memories were like. You cannot just say "I heard from so and so who heard from so and so", when discussing something the prophet Muhammad pbuh said or did, you have to know if "so and so #1" is trustworthy and reliable and you have to know if "so and so #2" is trustworthy and reliable and so on and so forth for the whole chain of narrators for each and every hadith. This is a serious scientific intellectual processing method which is actually inconvenient, however it's the only way to be certain that information is authentic. The authentically proven sound hadith are scholastically more reliable than the bible. The science of hadith is so precise that it even requires critical thinking talents just to contemplate and it overwhelmed me when I first learned about it. I felt like a total fool when I first learned about hadith and realized I could not really prove most of what I thought I knew and considered true. May Allah help us to have correct comprehension, give us understanding, guide us to the truth and make us of those who accept and follow it.

Different scholars have slightly different criteria for grading hadith but some basic principles are:

1. The chain of narration, from Muhammad pbuh to the final narrator, must be connected in such a way that every single person in the chain has himself heard or received this narration from the person he is narrating from.

2. All the narrators in the chain must be upright, meaning that they must be:

a) Muslim
   b) Of the age of puberty
   c) Sane
   d) Not an open sinner
   e) Free from bad habits

3. All the narrators must possess the ability to preserve the hadith precisely.

4. The hadith should not contradict other hadiths which have come from more reliable narrators.

5. There are no other hidden weaknesses in the hadith or isnad – such as a hidden gap in the chain of narration.

6. Upon the absence of any one of the above 5 conditions, the hadith immediately is classed as Weak (*da'if*). But if all of the conditions are met with the third (preservation) being of a lower degree, then it is classed as Sound/Good (*hasan*). A hadith is classed as rigorously verified to be 100% true and Authentic (*sahih*) if it meets the above 5 conditions and has a high degree of preservation.

In regards to Imam Bukhari's criteria for a hadith he was one of many who strictly would refuse to accept something as being authentic unless he knew of 2 separate isnads for a hadith. So his criteria was even stricter than they needed to be. Basically he required 2 authentic hadiths before he'd consider what either one of them taught as being true. However Imam Bukhari lived a few generations after Muhammad pbuh, were Muslims always so strict about verifying whether something someone said about Muhammad pbuh was true or false? The answer to this is evident in the incident which occurred between Abu Musa Al-Ash'ari and Umar bin Khattab. The background context of this incident is important, this took place only a few years after the death of Muhammad pbuh. At most within 13 years of his death because Umar was the Khalifh at the time this took place. Umar became Khalifh 2 years after Muhammad pbuh died and ruled for 10 years, before dying about 13 years after Muhammad pbuh died. The incident was reported by Abu Musa Al-Ash'ari himself who says what in english means:

"*I sought permission to see Umar and I did not have permission after three times. Hence, I left. He called me and said: 'Abdullah, have you found it hard to wait at my door? You better know that people may find it hard to wait at your door.' I said: 'No. I have sought permission three times and I did not obtain it; so I returned, as we have been ordered to do so.'* **He said: 'Whom have you heard this from?' I said: 'From the Prophet.' He then said to me: 'Have you heard from the Prophet what we have not heard? You will either support your statement with further evidence or I will certainly punish you.'** *I left him and went to the masjid where I found a member of the Ansar.* <u>I asked them about the case, and they said: 'Is this to be doubted?' I told them what Umar said to me.</u> *They said: 'Then the best way is that the youngest among us should go with you as witness.' Thus, Abu Saeed al-Khudri came with me to*

Umar and told him: 'We accompanied the Prophet when he went to Saad ibn Ubadah. When he arrived, he offered the greeting of peace, 'Assalam alaikum', but no permission was given to him. He repeated his greeting a second time and a third, but no permission was given. He then said: 'We have done what we can.' Then he left. Saad came fast after him, and said: 'Messenger of God! By Him who has sent you with the message of the truth, every time you said the greeting I heard it and replied. But I only wanted that you offer more greetings to me and to my household.' **Abu Musa then said (to Umar): 'By God I am worthy of trust** *when it comes to reporting the Prophet's Hadith.'* **Umar said: 'Certainly. I only wanted to ascertain the matter.'**"

This incident occured between the companions of Muhammad pbuh shortly after he had died. None of them ever lied about Muhammad pbuh, since they became Muslims, to suspect a Muslim of lying about Muhammad pbuh at that time was to accuse them of disbelief because Muhammad pbuh himself taught that those who lie about him should prepare for their place in the hellfire. Whereas Abu Musa (which was his nickname, Abdullah was his real name) was a well known trustworthy person. Yet Umar the ruler of the Muslims threatened to physically harm him with punishment for acting upon what he said he heard Muhammad pbuh teach him with his own two ears. Umar himself never even actually doubted Abu Musa but he did not want Muslims to think they could just say "Muhammad pbuh said X" and have it get believed without corroborating evidence as would be legally required in a court of law when giving testimony about what somebody had said. Legally Muslims who had lived with Muhammad pbuh were not allowed to even say what he taught them unless they could prove that he actually taught them what they claimed Muhammad pbuh taught them. Amongst the companions of Muhammad pbuh it was legally a punishable offense to just say "*Muhammad pbuh told me so*" the early generations of Muslims had to prove it, and this was even though they all knew that they had seen and heard Muhammad pbuh in the flesh. Obviously this is a very serious process of information verification that is the legal standard used throughout the world in courts today. Today many even sarcastically say "*Gee you don't have to make it a federal case*" when you ask for proof about to back up they say. Well for Muslims when it comes to saying that Muhammad pbuh said or taught something, it was always a federal case; literally. For someone known to have met Muhammad pbuh, for them to say something about Muhammad pbuh without proving what they said was true was considered to be a crime. If they couldn't prove what they claimed was true they would be convicted as criminals. The early Muslims took it as a matter of law to prove what they said about Muhammad pbuh was true because to have false information about a prophet of Allah circulate was too great a risk. To not have such strict requirements would imperil the entire religion. Is it a pain in the butt to do? Yes. But it must be done or else people will be able to change the religion with ease and without even being detected. Scholastically speaking there is no other way than this way. So this is "*the way to know what really happened in the past*", it has to have been a legal crime to not prove the past true from now all the way up to the past event one is referencing. One can only be able to prove the past if those past generations took this precaution in the past, unfortunately not every community has cared to diligently preserve the truth of their present while they were alive knowing that one day it would be the past. However this was the Muslim practice and standard for the first 3 generations of Muslims after the prophet Muhammad pbuh. Umar actually declared the first principles for hadith to be:

1. The report should be literally faithful.
2. Every Hadith narrated should carry with it the name of the narrator and the chain of narrators.
3. The narrators must be of proven faith and integrity.
4. In judging the veracity of a report the occasion and circumstances involved should be taken into consideration.
5. The report cannot be repugnant/contradictory to Quran.
6. The report should be rational.

It still remains the legal religious standard but over time some Muslims became lax and then people said stuff without fully proving it and some made stuff up. This is when hadith qualities began to differ. For the first 3 generations there were only authentic hadiths and the isnads or chains of narrators were short. Such as Abu Musa's chain was a direct personal connection to Muhammad pbuh and he would be person A with Umar being person B. Yet when time passes and people get added on to that chain later then it can cause problems if those later people aren't considered trustworthy or reliable. This is because an unreliable person can relate something that's proven to be true and is 100% authentic, however because of their personal lack of credibility it tarnishes the trustworthiness of the information itself. A good example of this is the internet. If you say "*I learned on the internet....*"it's only natural that people are skeptical about such information just because of the source you learned it from even though the information may be completely trustworthy. Thus as a result of more links in the chains of narrators being added through time and the criteria that each chain in the link of narration has to be known as a reliable source, some hadith which were and are 100% true and authentic cannot in our modern day be labeled or classified as 100% authentic because our chain of information may not be 100% reliable or preserved to a high degree of precision. This is also because the principles of the science of hadith have evolved to be more strict to ensure authenticity, today the criteria is stricter because there is more information in the chain and the liers have evolved their lies as well. Anyone who sees a physical chain can understand this, in that 2 links are hard to separate from each other yet a chain with many links can easily be broken. As a result, today some hadith which are not classified as 100% true could be true, but legally we cannot say that they are because of the strict criteria of proving the truth. But don't get the wrong idea. There are thousands of authentic hadith who's chain is rock-solid 100% reliable and true who have been precisely preserved to a high degree. I'm just saying this because some people may incorrectly think that a "Good" or "Weak" hadith is automatically false because it's not labeled as Sahih or authentic. It is incorrect to think this. However legally from a religious perspective, even though a "Good" or "Weak" hadith may contain true information, such information alone cannot be used to justify a religious belief or action. What this means is that if someone says "*in X hadith it says.....*" and X hadith is classified as weak then the hadith could be true but you can't use that to justify believing or doing what it teaches. The hadith's grade would not be high enough to pass the test of usability. It's interesting information to ponder, or speculate about, but it's not very useful, in a practical sense. Unfortunately some Muslims don't understand this legal standard and they do things thinking it's okay to do because they learned it from a hadith of Muhammad pbuh. Whereas they forget that a "Weak" hadith means "It might NOT be true", so it's for safety reasons that one only follows 100% authentic information. It's a foolproof system, where if you can't prove it to be true then you can't legally use it as a religious proof, or else you'd be a fool. Such a method may seem strict but it's safe and legally necessary, because God will ask us why we believed what we believed and why we did what we did and you don't want to be basing your religion on something that "might be true". If it was that important to know or practice then God would've preserved such information with 100% authenticity. There is so much authentic information that one can live an entire lifetime without learning it all, so in general it is dangerous and needless to look into weak hadith. Also what is the point of reading something is attributed to Muhammad pbuh if you can't legally act upon it? Very little point indeed and there's no point at all for those who haven't learned the authentic information to begin with. When it comes to fabricated hadith those are classified as 100% false. Yet unfortunately some of the Muslims and non-Muslims don't check the authenticity but just read "*Muhammad pbuh said....*" and they believe it and act upon it. Sometimes even Muslims will just say "Muhammad pbuh said..." and they don't say whether it is an authentic report or not and it can occasionally be a fabricated report which they don't know is fabricated, yet by sharing that information others think it is authentic and believe/act accordingly. That's what causes huge problems. Not that people following weak hadith doesn't cause problems, both things cause problems but with a weak hadith at least on a technical basis they could be possibly correct, even though they are legally wrong. However with fabricated hadith one would be guaranteed to be 100% wrong to believe or act upon it. I hope that wasn't too much information, but in this case it can take a lot of information to explain the abundant amount of information about Muhammad pbuh, and how to determine what is true and what is false and how to view such information if at all. Since at the end of the day whatever the available information is, what you believe about and do with that information is the important part. During the first 3 generations of Muslims after Muhammad pbuh, most every hadith available was authentic. It was only later that some of those authentic hadith were graded as weak, solely because of later persons in the chain of narration. Basically it was for technical reasons of strictness. While others then fabricated hadith making them appear to be weak because they sought to corrupt Islam and saw some Muslims would act upon hadith graded as weak. Which is why one cannot act upon weak hadith today, because they might just be good fabrications and not authentic at all. Fortunately to deal with this problem, which arose the 4th generation and later Muslim scholars composed collections of books which contain only authentic hadith. Thereby making it much easier for the layperson to navigate the information and get straight to the 100% true useable information. The older the book of authentic hadith the better and more authentic the hadiths in it are because it has less links in the chain of narration. Imam Bukhari's collection of authentic is an old one, not the oldest hadith book ever, but it is the first to contain only authentic sahih hadith which are still graded as sahih to this date. No books after Bukhari's hadith sahih collection have ever been more authentic, because they are newer with more links in the isnads. Through the various compilation of authentic hadiths it ensured that the religion of Islam remained uncorrupted and furthermore it can be proven Islam remains uncorrupted. How many "authentic hadith" reports are there? Well it depends on how you count. For example if say Muhammad pbuh said "It's bad to yawn." to person X when they were all alone then person X would be the only one who knew so we would count that as 1 hadith. However if person X then tells his hadith to person A, B and C then for the next generation you'd have 3 different yet identical hadith. You'd have "Person A heard from Person X that Muhammad pbuh said "It's bad to yawn."", as well as "Person B heard from Person X that Muhammad pbuh said "It's bad to yawn."", and "Person C heard from Person X that Muhammad pbuh said "It's bad to yawn."" Whereas if Person A, B and C then told 3 people their hadith which they learned directly from person X then by the third generation that 1 hadith of person X would have 9 different authentic chains. Thus you could learn about the same one-time event in 9 different reports. Yet despite there being 9 reports if Muhammad pbuh only said it once would that be considered 1 hadith or 9? It depends on how you count. As time goes by this phenomena of 1 hadith having many chains of narration multiplies as teachers tend to teach more and more people. So that's where today the number of hadith seems bigger because of the repetition of reports commonly found in books. Why would authors of authentic hadith collections repeat the same hadith with different narrations or isnads? Because it shows who else considered the hadith authentic so that way in case somebody considered a certain person in a hadith's isnad to be untrustworthy or unreliable or a liar then there are still other chains which teach the same exact hadith. This way it makes it much harder for someone to reject a hadith which is authentic because of it's narrartors, since it's one thing to say a hadith you heard is incorrect because of Person Z but if there are many reports of that hadith which don't include person Z then that makes it much harder for the hadith to be dismissed since the reliability of person Z is not needed to know whether the hadith is authentic or not.

For example there is a common claim that if you get a row of twenty people and whisper one thing in the ear of one person on the end and tell them to pass it on then by the time it gets to the person on the other end it will be different than what you said as it gets changed through transmission. People try this and see it work out so they think it's impossible to ever know the truth of the past through oral transmission. However this argument is baseless and incorrect despite the real-world test seeming to match the hypothesis. First of all regarding the hadith or anything for that matter, nobody is whsipering as they do in the chain game transmission test. Regarding the transmission of things in real life people speak aloud and clarify what they heard multiple times to ensure they remember it 100% correctly before passing it on. This isn't done during the chain game transmission test so of course you will get different results if people are whispering and can't repeat themselves or write it down or take their time when transmitting information. Also the chain game test uses the general populace which makes the test invalid because the general populace is never used for oral transmission. Typically only those with impeccable character and prodigious memory are given such a responsibility. Whereas if you were to play the chain game with people who have great memories, speak clearly and seriously think that if they mess up the transmission they will be attributing a falsehood to God or a prophet of God and thus go to hell forever then you will get different results. For example teachers sometimes play the chain game in classes for fun with the original saying getting distorted. But imagine if the teacher told the kids that if the original saying gets distorted then every kid in the chain will fail the class. Would they get the same results? No. Likewise if the teacher made sure that they had each transmitter also whisper in their ear what they heard and what they said so the teacher could monitor each link in the chain and stipulated that only those who mess up the transmission of what they heard and said would fail would the same results be had? No. However some may ignorantly argue that no matter what there will always be a weak link in the chain preventing accurate transmission. This is the claim some may make with authentic hadith by saying Person C is a weak link in the isnad so it can't be trusted or graded as authentic. But Muhammad pbuh was no fool to only transmit his teachings to 1 person, he told many. So while one could say that person C in a chain is weak, what if you have 5 different chains which all say the same exact thing? Person C being weak would only discount 1 chain so then there would still be 4 chains free of person C that would require refuting in order to reject a teaching of the prophet. Hence the more reports there are the less likely they are unreliable if they all agree especially if the narrators in each chain never met together and conspiracy would be impossible. For instance lets say every class in the school gets told by the principal a special phrase to transmit via the chain game and are told that if they correctly transmit it they will get rewarded. Each class gets told the same thing for oral transmission and are not allowed to speak to other students. Now is it possible that every class will correctly transmit the phrase 100% intact? Yes, it is. Is it possible that some classes will mess up while others will succeed? Yes. Now is it possible for every class to fail to correctly transmit? Yes, in theory but it is highly unlikely and it is even more unlikely if the students at this school are intellectual elites with great memories and skills in oral transmission and truly care about correctly transmitting. Now to make it more like real life oral transmission one could do the following experiment. In his office a principal tells all the teachers in the school the message XYZ is to be orally transmitted via isnad. In class A Teacher #1 empties the classroom and has Student A1 come in and out loud tells the the hadith XYZ from the principal until the student learns it. After Student A1 learns it then Student A2 comes in and Student A1 reports "Teacher #1 told me the principal told her: "XYZ" pass it on along with the isnad. Then Teacher #1 leaves the room (simulating death) and Student A3 enters while it is Student A2's job to transmit. Student A2 says "Student A1 told me the teacher was told by the principal: XYZ" pass it on with the isnad. Then Student A1 leaves the room symbolizing death while Student A4 comes in to learn from Student A3 and on and on with the incoming student being able to confirm with the previous 2 students since the previous 2 generations are typically still alive to be consulted as confirmation for their part in the isnad. Now if every Teacher #1-26 used this method and every class did this it is entirely feasible to expect that every student would learn that the Principal said XYZ even though the Principal only told the Teachers XYZ and the majority of students would have learned it only from students and not the teachers much less the principal. This is how we are able to learn from God or a prophet without ever directly learning from God or a prophet. However isn't is possible for some students to mess up the transmission? Yes. It is because of this possibility for the narrarators to theoretically mess up that there are multiple isnads for hadith. Imagine the Principal as Muhammad pbuh and the teachers of classes are his companions. None of the teachers (companions), would lie about what the principal said to pass on but the students(later Muslims) could make mistakes. However due to the large number and care taken the probabilty for accurate transmission becomes a near certainty and by having so many chains of transmission it eliminates the ability for someone to reject something the principal/prophet said simply because they have a problem with a student(narrator) or a particular chain of transmission (class). Some chains/isnads could be faulty but as a whole this method of oral transmission is reliable if done with care by intellectuals. Thus the claim *"It's impossible to ever know what someone in the past said through oral transmission."* is invalid if oral transmission is done in a methodologically correct manner by trustworthy individuals. Islam uses this method as well as the method of writing, other religions have not used this method since the times of their prophet, but Muslims have. Is it the ideal best manner? Maybe not but at the end of the day is there any better way for people in the 600s to have accurately conveyed information from Muhammad pbuh to us? Really lets consider those people met someone they believed was a prophet and believed they had to accurately convey his teachings to us today living thousands of years later. With the technology available to them what else could they have done which they didn't do? Every honest person must accept the fact that the scientific method of hadith is sound and the most realistic way for teachings to be accurately conveyed throughout history to the modern day and that to merely dismiss hadith as impossible to be true simply because Muhammad pbuh has been dead for so long is academically bigoted. It is 100% possible that Muslims have accurately preserved 100% of the teachings of Muhammad pbuh via oral transmission and writing. Any who claim otherwise are simply arrogant, ingnorant bigots. Hence for the sake of resolving arguments about isnads and those who would reject a hadith due to a particular isnad, the multiple reports allow the authentic information to be known even if people have personal problems with some of the previous people who taught that authentic information. This makes it so that in order to reject an authentic hadith, one is not just forced to reject 1 isnad but many many isnads. To put it in a Christian perspective imagine if there were 1 million gospels in the bible which all said the same exact thing. It'd be harder for people to reject that than if there were just 4 which contradict each other. Of course gospels don't even have an isnad, I'm just using this as an example to show how multiple reports of the same thing are useful from an academic perspective. This is why a single hadith would be reported multiple times so that more chains would be made so as to reduce the possibility of a weak link in any particular chain making the information itself be lost or rejected even though it's authentic. This leads us back to the question of how many authentic hadith are there? The short answer is a lot if you count all the repeated hadith reports, but not too many if you only count the teachings of the hadith. For example there may be hundreds of authentic hadith today which say Muhammad pbuh said X but technically Muhammad pbuh saying X is just 1 hadith. So if you take the short method of counting the teachings there are only a few thousand authentic hadith. If you take the long method of counting every authentic hadith report to date with every isnad, then you may get millions due to repeats. However to give you a perspective of how many authentic hadith there could possibly be, keeping in mind some hadith considered "weak" today due to their isnads could in theory be authentic there were only 1,060 companions of Muhammad pbuh who reported hadith. Of which 500 of those 1,060 only reported 1 hadith. So 47% of the people who met Muhammad pbuh and reported hadith from him only adds up to 500 hadith, however the total number of authentic hadith is more because the other 560 sahabah who reported hadith reported more than just 1 hadith. Whereas you don't need to have a photogenic memory to accurately remember and report 1 hadith from Muhammad pbuh, so it's not as though every Sahabah who reported hadith was a genius master at memorization. 500 Sahabis only reported a single hadith. Some reported 2, some reported more than 2, some reported more than 10, while 120 companions of Muhammad pbuh reported 20+ hadith and seven noteworthy individuals reported more than a thousand each, although to be fair even these companions have some repeats amongst them where they both reported the same incident from their perspective. The 7 companions in the thousand + reported club are Abu Hurairah, Abdullah bin Umar, Anas bin Malik, Aisha bint Abi Bakr, Abdullah ibn Abbas, Jabir bin Abdullah and Abu Said Al Khudri. The vast majority of the hadith were written down by the Sahabah during the lifetime of Muhammad pbuh. The individual man who reported the most hadith was Abu Hurairah. The woman who reported the most was Aisha (Muhammad's wife). All the hadith reported by the companions were authentic as the credibility of the companions is attested to in the Quran and was testified to by Muhammad pbuh but some of the hadith which they reported are repeats. For example the hadith total reported by Aishah and Abu Hurairah doesn't equal 7,384 as one might think, and many will say after basic research, because some of the hadith they reported are the same but they are just person A in their respective report and some of the hadiths which only they reported are counted more than once in most calculations due to them reporting it to multiple people. For example if 2 people report a car crash they've seen to the police even though there are 2 reports only 1 crash occured, if those 2 people then report to a judge and/or the news outlets telling their report 50 times each at the end of the day even though they gave 100 total reports there was only 1 car crash which all those reports are about. Those reports should all be identical but even if they are one would still count them as 100 reports even though it's the same report repeated 100 times simply because there were 100 reports of the same event. So just because there are thousands of authentic reports of hadith does not necessarily mean the number of authentic individual lessons/hadith reported number in the thousands, they do but the individual incidents reliably reported are less than the total number of authentic reports. For example Muhammad pbuh may have said something once but if 5 people heard him say it and each one reported it then you would have 5 authentic hadith even though technically it is just 1 thing which all the 5 hadith are about. So depending on how you count in such a scenario there could be 1 hadith or 5, both are correct but depending on the understanding of those taught the incorrect meaning could be unintentionally conveyed. The # of reports then compounds when those who hear the report report to others and they report to others as time goes by and the number of reports grows as the number of students and teachers grows. In the past Muslim scholars of the generation after the companions of the companions of Muhammad pbuh, known as the Tabi-Tabieen would count every single report narrated by a person as a hadith even if that same hadith was reported multiple times to different people. So that's where since the companions reported their hadith to more than 1 person, many of the hadith were counted multiple times in the tallies of some because they counted the # of reports from Sahabah rather than the # of unique hadiths relayed by that Sahabah. Many counted the number of reports instead of the number of hadith because to them each was seperate since it had a seperate chain/isnad, others counted both the chains/reports and the hadiths individually but some don't know which number is which when they look at the lists of numbers of hadith. One must know whether "X # of hadith" refers to # of reports of hadith or # of hadith. Many people today just look at the numbers of hadith reported and assume they refer to the number of individual hadith without checking the hadith to make sure their assumption is correct. Thus you have someone like Abu Hurairah being commonly said to have reported 5000+ hadith when in reality he only reported around 1,236 but those hadith got counted multiple times by people tallying the count because they counted it from their perspective of how many reports of hadith came to them from Abu Hurairah rather than Abu Hurairah's perspective of how many hadith he got from Muhammad pbuh. How many unique authentic hadith reports are in total reported to and by the companions of Muhammad pbuh without counting repeats or re-reports? Between 4,000 and 5,000. More than half are contained in the 2 famous sahih collections known as Sahih Bukhari and Sahih Mulim which contain 2,500-2,900 unique reports of authentic hadith, in total those books both have more than that number of hadith but they report the same hadith with multiple chains/isnads and both books also report some of the same hadiths with the same isnads. Why do they report the same hadith with the same isnad more than once in their books? Because their books are organized according to subject matter so if a hadith talks about multiple subjects they would put it in their book multiple times. Other books were written based on different categorization methods. Some were categorized according to the sahabah who reported them, those books would report every hadith reported by every sahabah and repeated hadith because some sahabah would relate the same hadith to people. Every author has their own style they choose to write their book in. Although this is why some will say there are many more authentic hadith, or hadith in general, because of how they count hadith, regarding whether they count the hadith's or the isnad's of the hadiths or the number of hadiths in a book. Unfortunately there are 2 extremes with some thinking there are so many different authentic hadith reports that it's too much to learn or too much to be authentic and others think it's too few to be true or all-encompassing for everything one needs to know for life. Whereas it's neither too much nor too little and the hadith explain what sources to use if anything is not found in the hadith directly. Basically the Quran teaches that it has the answers and any answer not in the Quran can be found in the authentic hadith. The authentic hadith have the answers the Quran doesn't elaborate/enumerate and refers people to the companions of the prophet known as Sahabah, the Sahabah's companions known as the Tabieen and the companions of the Tabieen known as theTabi-Tabieen, for any extra information and for the correct explanation of the Quran and Sunnah. Those 3 generations are known as the Salaf. Both the Quran and authentic hadith also establish rules for deriving the correct analysis and rules from the Quran, authentic hadith, and the Salaf. Such principles include Ijma (consensus of the companions, the Salaf, the scholars, or the

Muslims as a whole) as well as Qiyas (analogy). However Ijma and Qiyas are 4th and 5th regarding the sources of Shariah. #1 is the Quran, #2 is the Sunnah of Muhammad pbuh(found in the authentic hadith), #3 is the Salaf, #4 Ijma, #5 Qiyas. Sadly some mistakenly take Qiyas and put it in a higher rank than it is allowed to go in. Or they will mistake something as Ijma when it is not or think that the Ijma of the past is the same as the Ijma at the particular masjid they go to in the modern era, or mistakenly think that the Ijma of the past is the same as the Ijma of the Salaf. Others foolishly and blasphemously go out of order thinking Qiyas is #1 then Quran is #2 or any other kind of mixed up order contrary to the order Allah and Muhammad pbuh taught us. Others incorrectly limit the numbers of sources and will ignorantly say things like Qiyas is all I need or the Quran is all one needs, not realizing that the Quran itself says one needs to follow/know #2-5 too. Though fundamentally if you follow the Quran and Sunnah that's all you need but technically and in reality the 3rd, 4th and 5th components of Islam are subcategories of the Quran and Sunnah. Technically the Sunnah is a subcategory of the Quran too but because there is a deviant heretical sect that takes only the Quran and rejects the Sunnah thinking the Quran is all they need then I'm not going to say that because they would mistake it without understanding that followng the Quran involves following the Sunnah which involves following the Companions and Salaf which involves following Ijma and occasionally using Qiyas when appropriate. Such people are called Quranites and are as foolish as a Jew saying all they need is "the Law of Moses" and to stick to the book so any hadith/statement of Moses pbuh they reject it since they only follow "the Law of Moses". Whereas anyone can see such a methodology is preposterous and silly but perhaps they might not because there are no authentic hadith of Moses pbuh which have survived transmission to this day. So to summarize the 2 components of the Quran + Sunnah teach Islam while the Shariah is derived from the Quran + Sunnah which consist of 5 things (Quran+Sunnah+Way of Salaf+Ijma+Qiyas). Thus Muslims say if you follow the Quran and Sunnah then that's Islam, the reason extremists go astray is because of inappropriately defining or following the Quran+Sunnah incompletely by either missing one of the 5 components of it or neglecting/misunderstanding the texts in full context. Hence definitions are important because every Muslim claims to follow the Quran+Sunnah but they may not all mean the 5 components of it or know the 5 components even if they are trying to follow them completely and correctly. The point is that the religion of Islam is preserved completely and amounts to a complete way of life in every aspect with built in principles to apply to every age and situation. Islam does have something to say about everything even if there isn't a specific word for word text on X scenario. Basically Muhammad pbuh taught *"This is all you need to know and all you need to know about how to know the right and wrong thing in the future as technology and cultures change after I die."* Fortunately most stuff regarding how a Muslim should live life in the modern era is actually covered by the texts of the Quran and the authentic hadith, since fundamentally life as a human is not all that different today as it was in the past. Hence Islam today is identical to what it was during the prophet's time, the only difference is the people, culture, and technology; the prophetic religion is 100% exactly the same. Muslims base their entire lifestyle around trying to imitate him, while using the technology of our own time for good as he used the technology of his time. That's one thing that separates Muslims and groups like the

Amish and Hutterites. Muslims use modern technology, there's nothing wrong with it as long as it's not used sinfully. Islam is a religion for all places, all peoples and all time periods. Learning this stunned me because after having learned on my own that so many religions had changed over time to find out individually how Islam has never changed and is for practical reasons unchangeable, that made Islam very unique + special. Now some people might not believe in Islam, however it is 100% proven that the teachings of Muhammad pbuh are available today in exactly the same language as he originally taught in. Thus there is no question about what Muhammad pbuh really said, did or taught. It is legally and scientifically proven what he said and what he did, the only question is whether he was sent by God and was a prophet of God as he claimed. What better way to determine if he was than by examining his authentic teachings? Of course if you don't know arabic, translations are available, but since even with the arabic things can be misunderstood or misinterpreted or taken out of context, with a translation such potential for misunderstanding can be multiplied. However the information is remarkably available, the main thing is being knowledgeable enough to understand it. How does one get to be that knowledgeable? First by being sincere in wanting to get that knowledge for the right reasons and then doing what it takes to get that knoweldge with patience. You have to start somewhere, for many a translation is a good starting point. There are no limitations on who can access the information or understand it. The only limitations to learning are from God and oneself.

   It's important to comprehend the level Islamic knowledge is at. Muslim Scholars don't just make stuff up out of thin air, if they don't know something they say so; nobody can know everything. When reading about Muhammad pbuh I learned he was an honest man, an exemplary husband, a role model father, righteous leader, noble warrior, patient teacher, generous philanthropist, and humble prophet. No other person in the history of the world has had their life more thoroughly documented than him. It is known how he ate, how he slept, how he walked, how he talked, how he smiled, how he prayed, what he wore and even how he went to the bathroom. It's even known when Muhammad pbuh had 10 white hairs, then when he had 14, then when he had 17 and then when he had 20. That's what you call people really paying attention to details. Most women today wouldn't even know the number of white hairs their own sons or husbands have at any time in their lives, let alone keep a timeline of them. This type of information is not available for anyone else, because nobody else really cares about anyone else that much to report in detail who they really were. We know more about Muhammad pbuh than we can possibly know about any other person today because he was so closely observed and his life was so meticulously recorded. Abdullah ibn Amr used to write down all he said, then he stopped when teased about it by non-Muslims, but then he continued to write what Muhammad pbuh said after being instructed by Muhammad pbuh to record the things he said lest the knowledge be lost. This is important regarding the hadith in that people who wrote hadith wrote it during the lifetime of Muhammad pbuh and he interacted with his contemporaries. Whereas with other people like Moses or Jesus pbuh they were never known to have instructed people to write down what they taught nor do we have contemporary reports about them. For example nobody has Pharaoh's version of what Moses pbuh was like, or the Pharisees version of what Jesus pbuh was like but we do have the reports of the anti-

Muhammad contemporaries of Muhammad pbuh which for scholastic documentation purposes is very important. Because when you only have one side of the story, as the Christians do with the Christian side of the story of Jesus pbuh, then you never know if you got the enemies' side of the story or not since you only got one story. Likewise regarding documentation nowhere in the bible do you have a prophet being recorded as saying "Make sure you write down what I'm saying." which might seem like a small thing but it's really not. Really consider if Moses pbuh and Jesus pbuh had something to do with the bible then why doesn't the bible say they told people to write stuff down? A realistic book would have that information. For example I started writing this book in 2013 CE, stopped writing in 2017 CE and published a condensed version of this book in 2019 CE and this further condensed 2nd edition in 2021 CE. I'm saying that in this book because that's what a real person writing a real book about their real life would do. It's how to tell it's real. So that Muhammad pbuh himself is recorded as having told specific individuals to write down what he said, when they stopped doing it because non-Muslims teased them for doing it, shows the realism of Islamic texts and the Islamic religion which no other religion has. No other religion has a realistic prophet acting the way you'd expect a real human to act if they were a real prophet from God. All other religions are simply unrealistic with unrealistic depictions of their role models/prophets. Islam is realistically the true religion. Really forget all the claims, partisanship and bigotry and consider all the religions. You will find that all the others aren't realistically genuine in how they are depicted/reported. The rest of the religions are all taught in the same exact format in which myths are taught in and for those who don't believe in them they feel like myths too. Take miracles for example, other religions act like miracles are ordinary and almost depict the companions of prophets as being unfazed by miracles or theatrically effected. Yet Islam treats miracles like miracles, like *"Wow that's not normal stuff. That stuff is amazing! This must be a miracle because it's so awesomely impossible and unnaturally inexplicable."* Islam doesn't require belief in mysterious feel-good fairytales, it only expects realistic beliefs in a realistic prophetic religion. Blind following of modern non-prophet people is forbidden. The difference between Islamic knowledge and the rest is not just top-tier scholarship, the difference is genuine sincerity. A disbeliever can never be sincere since if they were they'd have to accept the truth once it comes to them and abandon errors. Are you sincere regarding your acquisition of knowledge?

When non-Muslims slander the prophet saying nasty things, every single time they are either lying or taking things out of context trying to misrepresent him. For example Muslim Scholars have been saying for centuries that X hadith is fabricated and such and such person in the chain of narrations was a liar for a specific reason. Then some non-Muslim comes and uses it saying, *"According to hadith X Muhammad said _____"*(peace be upon him) whereas the Muslims that preserved the information have said that hadith is not true. It is dishonest for people to take these things and try to make them seem like they are true. They wouldn't even be able to try to pass off their false statement if it wasn't for the integrity of Muslim Scholars preserving the false hadith and saying why it is false. Many enemies of Islam aren't even making up their own lies, they are using lies that Muslim Scholars have classified as lies. Although that may be precisely why those lies are used, because an old lie is less scrutinized than a lie that hasn't been heard before. Yet no matter how many centuries a lie has been told that doesn't change the fact that it's a lie, the passage of time does not turn a lie into the truth. Unfortunately many people think lies are a modern invention as if every lie being told today is new. Sadly many well-intentioned Muslims also tell lies about Muhammad pbuh thinking they're telling the truth because they don't research whether a hadith is authentic, especially if it's popular and well-known. For example there is a popular story that goes something like this: "*The Prophet Muhammad pbuh had a jewish neighbor who used to throw trash at his door every day. The Prophet pbuh was patient and did not retaliate or get upset. One day, the Prophet noticed that there was no trash at his door, so he went to check on his neighbor who turned out to be sick. She asked him how did he know she was sick and he said because there was no trash at his door that day. Thus the woman was so moved by his kindness despite her animosity and abuse that she accepted Islam.*" Some say it was a Jewish man some say it was a Jewish woman, most Muslims have probably heard this story and I myself read it in the first book I read about Muhammad pbuh, but this story is a fabrication. There is no mention of it in any authentic books of hadith. It is true that people would throw garbage on the prophet Muhammad pbuh on a routine basis and he was patient with them, but this famous conversion story has no evidence to support it. Muhammad's two neighbors were Abu Lahab and Uqba bin Abi Mu'eet; both pagans not Jews. In fact for centuries Jews and Christians were not even allowed to enter or live in Mecca because the pagan idolaters didn't want them preaching against idolatry in Mecca, so Jews and Christians were only allowed in Mecca as slaves. This "conversion story" could never have possibly happened. Unfortunately many Muslims use this story to say how Muslims living among non-Muslims should be extra kind to non-Muslims and live in loving harmony celebrating their holidays and joining them in sin. But this is wrong. Muslims are kind, but we cannot join the disbelievers in sin and disbelief or pretend that they aren't on the road to hellfire. Islam teaches Muslims to hate all those who hate their Creator and don't worship him exclusively and accept all the prophets including Muhammad pbuh. That doesn't mean Muslims aren't kind and polite to disbelievers. Just as a Christian can never possibly love a Jew because they reject the prophethood of Jesus pbuh, a Muslim can never love someone who doesn't accept the prophet Muhammad pbuh. It is obligatory for us to hate, but hate does not mean harm, in most instances it's actually forbidden to harm non-Muslims. Unfortunately some Muslims that have been westernized are reluctant to publicly teach or even privately think that Islam teaches hate for all non-Muslims is obligatory, based on the kind treatment the prophet Muhammad pbuh displayed and they use this famous false story as a reason for their unislamic position. That's an example of how some Muslims dilute the hate while other Muslims dilute the kindness. In short Islam is more hateful than some Muslims think and it's less hateful than some non-Muslims think. The confusion stems from the satanic idea that it's wrong to hate people who God hates. One should hate for God's sake but also treat those whom God hates the way God says to. God doesn't allow people to kill or harm everyone whom he hates, because those people may change and become people he loves. Islam is balanced, it is not interfaith nor is it a cut-throat faith.

    The enemies of Islam and violent extremists take things out of context distorting the reality. Some will say "*the Quran says this*" and then lie about how Muhammad pbuh understood or implemented that verse. I hope that the Creator guides them and that they study Islam objectively with sincerity. Disbelievers attacking

Muhammad pbuh with such passion only proves that he's important and deserves our attention. All the prophets are slandered by those who disbelieve in their prophethood. The more attention brought to Muhammad pbuh the more people embrace Islam after seeing the truth of Islam which is Muhammad's religion pbuh. After all I bought my first translation of the Quran after an Islamophobic Christian declared he was burning Qurans. I think Allah may have used this enemy of Islam as a tool to guide me. This is a prime example of how the plan of God cannot be defeated.

Finally I was certain that Islam was the true religion. There was just one problem, I didn't know how to practice it. I figured I better know what I'm doing before I join because becoming a Muslim is a life-changing decision that requires daily commitment. However I was wrong to hesitate because all humans should already be following the correct religion, so delaying my embrace of Islam until I learned the exact rituals put me at risk and led me to miss out on the rewards I could've gained. When you are sure of the true religion you should submit in case you die. You don't need to know the full playbook for God's team before you join, you should know what will be expected of you and your responsibilities, but you don't have to know everything about Islam before joining because it's impossible for one to ever know everything about it. Likewise the prophets didn't have such a policy either and those who believed in the prophets didn't require them to tell them everything they ever taught before they believed in their religion. Anyways until then I hadn't thought I'd ever met a Muslim in person, so there was no one available to personally teach me the religion. The Quran is the book of Allah, but it doesn't have all the necessary information for daily implementation. For example it says when to pray, but few details are given explaining how to pray. In order to learn the complete way one had to learn it from the prophet. The way of the prophet Muhammad pbuh is called the Sunnah. Today the Sunnah can be learned from the authentic hadith. To practice Islam a Muslim follows the Quran and Sunnah according to the understanding of the righteous companions of Muhammad pbuh, because those are the people who knew Muhammad pbuh best. Not knowing any Muslims to learn how to pray from directly, I got instructions on prayer from Sheikh Google.

Before prayer a Muslim has to be in a state of purity having washed their body, since Muslims pray 5 times a day I thought that meant one needed to wash before every prayer. Washing involves using clean water to wash the hands, rinse the mouth, rinse the nose, wash the face, wash the forearms, wiping the head, cleaning the ears, washing the feet and ankles. That's a heck of a lot of steps to remember for someone who had never done it before. Therefore I had a paper printed out showing the order and how to do it, by the end of my first try I had given up and said, *"this religion's too hard I can't do it, I'm too old to learn all this stuff"*. It was especially difficult putting my foot in the sink since my muscles were unaccustomed to it. A little while later I reconsidered, there was no doubt that Islam was the true religion and if that's what you got to do to get to heaven then that's what you got to do. Don't they always say *"the road to paradise is traveled one foot at a time"*? I didn't want to go to hell for being too lazy to wash my feet. Then I remembered in church near Easter time the priests would wash the feet of the altar servers saying how Jesus pbuh used to do that and taught us to wash our feet, as well as to teach others as he taught us and to follow his example. This is also another instance where if Jesus pbuh were God then that means God washed the feet of several people, and that's ungodly. It suddenly made sense, Jesus pbuh was teaching how to do wudu, which is the ablution done by Muslims to purify the body. Jesus pbuh washed his feet and the bible says other prophets washed before praying too. I also remembered that 1.7 billion Muslims do this every day so it can't be that hard. I decided to wash my feet in the shower until I was flexible enough to get them up to the sink. Many Muslim houses have a special foot sink low on the ground to make wudu convenient, but I was not living in a Muslim house. In hindsight I could've used a spray nozzle instead and just put a bucket under my feet to keep the floor from getting wet. If water isn't available or usable a Muslim can purify themselves by doing tayammum, which is dry ablution done without water. You might initially think wudu is excessive or merely ritualistic but it really does make a physical difference in many ways. For instance prior to becoming a Muslim I would not wash my hands after using the toilet, but since urinating or defecating breaks wudu then since becoming a Muslim I make wudu and wash my hands after expelling waste. Furthermore during wudu the Muslim rinses their mouth out with water 3 times. This has an effect on the tongue because it makes one far less likely to backbite or swear because of the consistent spiritual purification of the mouth. So as a result of becoming a Muslim I was washing my hands so that way poop and pee germs didn't get on my food which would then get in my mouth, also I wasn't eating filthy foods and with the additional measure of washing my mouth several times a day my foul language which included numerous swear words disappeared. Now I know swearing is the favorite language of Satan. The funny thing is how many parents when frustrated with their children swearing will threaten to or actually wash their kid's mouth out with soap, to no avail. While with doing wudu the tongue itself starts to hate the taste of filthy words and evil speech. So wudu is really what people should do to clean up their act.

    Finally I was ready to pray, except I didn't know Arabic and Muhammad pbuh was taught by Allah to pray in Arabic. In order to pray the way God taught the prophet to one must pronounce the prayers in Arabic. Otherwise it's not legitimate, when it comes to performing a prayer it must be done in the language God originally taught it in. Jews today also pray in Hebrew knowing that you can't translate prayer for convenience. The Catholic Church used to do all their services in Latin in every country, but as with most of their traditions they changed that too and in the 1960s CE allowed the native tongue to be used instead and largely abandoned Latin mass. Yet Catholics now tell me the Church changed back to Latin services after I left in 2011 CE, saying they had been wrong for over 40 years. This means Pope John Paul II, who was Pope during that time and canonized as a "saint", was not infalliable or else he didn't bother telling Catholics they weren't worshipping correctly. How can it be a true religion if its members admit to have been worshipping the wrong way for 40+ years? If God said to say "____" you have to say that exactly as God said to, you cannot translate it and think you are praying how God instructed mankind to pray. God never said prayer could be translated or that it was valid if done in a different language than what was taught by the prophets, humans have no right to translate it without divine permission. It frustrates me when people say Jesus pbuh taught people to pray the "Our Father" because he didn't speak English, those words are being put in his mouth. To avoid confusion you should know that prayer in Islam is different than in Christianity. Most Christians tend to define prayer as *"talking to God anytime, anyplace, as a private conversation"* whereas in Islam that would be called a supplication. A supplication is done asking God alone for something and can be done in your native language. Whereas the Islamic prayer would be comparable to a church service, except it only takes about 5-10 minutes and can be done nearly anywhere, alone or with others. Although unlike church, praying as a Muslim was actually fun, every time I did it I eagerly anticipated the next one and still enjoy praying the Islamic way to this very day. The more I worshiped Allah the correct way the more I wanted to do it and the more enjoyable it was. It frequently seems to end too soon and it has no comparable experience. Even while typing this I'm counting down the minutes until the next prayer as are billions of other Muslims. Nothing makes one happier than worshipping the Creator correctly.

Since I didn't know the steps of the prayer, I would look at a prayer sheet and read the English transliterations of Arabic in order to know what to say when. An Arabic transliteration is the phonetic spelling of Arabic using English letters. When praying a good portion is silent and the lips move without sound coming out, but because I was learning off the internet I didn't know that. I was incorrectly saying everything out loud instead of saying the silent parts silently. Later I'd realize Sheikh Google is not the best to learn from.

Sometimes non-Muslims ask me to pray for them not realizing that asking a Muslim to do that "for you" is like asking a Christian to go to church for you. Everybody has to do their own prayers, I can make a supplication to Allah asking him something for someone else, but I can't do someone else's prayers for them. The way to tell the difference between a prayer and supplication is that prayer is called *"Salat"* and a supplication is called *"Dua"*. Salat is done 5 times a day minimum in Arabic, with prayer being forbidden during some times. Dua can be done in any language, at any time without being in a purified condition. Generally it is blameworthy to ask others to supplicate for you for personal benefit, because if Allah won't answer your supplications then someone else supplicating for you won't be of much benefit. That's like one person who's drowning asking another person who's drowning to help them stop drowning. It can also make the one asked to supplicate for someone else arrogant thinking they are more righteous than others and have some special relationship with Allah. Furthermore asking others to make supplications for you makes one rely on others, similar to how Christians rely on others and dead righteous people to pray for them, when Allah has given us a direct connection to ask him directly. Besides, others might ask the Creator to give you something that you don't want. I do deliberately do that sometimes, people will come up to you and say *"Can you ask God to help me with my visa or help me with X or pass a test or bla bla bla or to recover from an illness?"* So I deliberately do the opposite and make dua for what I think is best saying things like *"O God make them be happy to get deported away from this sinful place. Forgive their sins through their sickness and help them enjoy it for as long as you decree it to afflict them, if being sick helps them avoid sins then help them avoid sins. Or help them to enjoy being poor."* Really it pisses me off when people tell me what to pray for X on their behalf. How arrogant can they be to dictate your dua? You're the one they want to pray yet they don't even want you to pray for them the way you want to. Who are they to tell you how, what, when and for who to pray for? Are they a prophet of God? If not then you can say no, you probably shouldn't refuse but you can say no whether you actually refuse to comply entirely is not advisable but it's not sinful to tell them no and then do it in secret. Sometimes it can be fun to do, just to get a reaction and to teach them. Other times it's obligatory to say no because people can ask you to pray God helps them to do something sinful like steal, gamble, murder, get intoxicated or have illicit sexual relations. In reality they just want X from God and they want you to pray and get it for them. They may say they don't really think you can get what they want from God, but if that's the case then why do they ask? If they really didn't think you making dua would improve the odds of them getting what they want then they wouldn't have asked you to make dua for them or for a specific things(s). So they really do think you can get them what they what in a very real sense. Because they have a weak relationship with God they ask you to be a middleman, but of course they'll deny you are their middleman because they also say their own prayers and know such a concept can be sinful disbelief, yet at the very least they are making you their sidekick, cheerleader or wingman. While the energy used to ask another to supplicate for you could've been more wisely used in supplicating to the Creator yourself. If someone asks me to make dua for them I respond by saying "*I know someone even better than me who has every dua they make answered immediately. He's nearby, do you want me to introduce you right now so you can ask them to ask Allah to make dua on your behalf?*" Then I say "*The one who you should ask to make dua to Allah for you is, Allah.*" When they get frustrated or confused then say, "*Well if you think it's silly for you to ask God to ask God for something then it's even sillier for you to ask me to ask God. Whereas if you asked God to ask God for you then surely the outcome is not going to be any worse than if I ask for you, because God has a much better relationship with God than I do. If you want to get God's attention then God is the only one to ask, not me.*" Yet sometimes they still persist and ask me to make a dua. In such a case right then on the spot make dua in front of them so they can hear you saying "*O Allah please help this person to trust entirely in you with certainty. O Allah make them such that they never ever ask another person to make dua or pray for them again in their life and that they encourage others to ask you directly for everything and anything they want and need. Make them satisfied with what you decree so they never ever ask anyone to make dua for them again. And if they never ask anyone except for you then grant them the easy entry into paradise and forgive all their sins without account.*" Then you can tell them that is your dua which you just made for them, and it'd be dumb to make any others because if God doesn't accept that one then you got your own big problems with God to deal with. Tell them it is a conditional dua that is linked to them never asking anyone else to make dua for them again, if they ask for dua then your dua can't come true, so to ever ask for another dua is to reject the dua you made for them and that even applies to if they ask you ever again. Some Muslims think it's good to ask dua from others but this is due to weak ahadith and customs, the companions of Muhammad pbuh only asked specific individuals to make dua for them because Muhammad pbuh told them ask X person from X city to make dua for you because God will answer it. It was not a promotion of asking others, it was a specific case only applicable to them. Other hadith mention how duas of certain people are accepted but it doesn't mean to ask, and most hadith of such incidents are people responding to others asking them to make dua by saying rather you should make it for me rather than asking me to do it for you. So in reality they weren't asking for others to make dua for them but discouraging people asking them by saying they should make a dua rather than asking a dua be made. Rather than ask someone to ask God for you, just ask God yourself. Seriously if you are not in paradise and are not safe from the hellfire then what business do you have asking God to do something for someone else? Worry about yourself! After you are in paradise safe from the hellfire then you can start asking God to help out others, but truly it's a better use of your time to ask God directly yourself for your own stuff. You are taking the test of life, you don't have time to be asking God to help others out on their test of life you need God to help you yourself. If people ask you to pray for them then tell them you are too busy asking God for your own stuff to have time to ask on behalf of others and they should likewise be talking to God instead of you. Seriously ask them if they think you can help them better than God can. Don't you know there will be people burning in hell forever and while alive they used to pray to God on behalf of others? Imagine how much regret they'll feel hating themselves wishing they had asked God to forgive them 1 extra time rather than *"praying for others"* or *"keeping others in their duas"*. Never ask somebody to ask God on your behalf. God is not some friend of a friend, God is your personal Creator and personal provider. Do you ask others for oxygen? No God gives it to you. Do you ask others to give you sunshine or rain? No God provides everything. So why ask other people for stuff when God is already giving you what you want and need without even asking, if you ask the only way he'd not grant your request is if you were a disbeliever or if you didn't fulfill the conditions to get your dua accepted or if it what you asked for wasn't in the best interest of the world. Never be shy to use the abilities God gave you to ask God directly for things, that's precisely why God gives you the abilities. The prophets where sent with the specific mission to tell people to only ask God alone for everything. God sent prophets and books to us simply to let us know that God wants us all to ask him only and him alone for all we want and need. So today we shouldn't ask others to ask God on our behalf. We have a direct connection with the divine, there are no middlemen, middlewomen, middlechildren or any created intermediate intermediaries between us and the Creator of the entire Universe, the All-Hearing All-Seeing. Just consider that God actually hears and sees people when they go and ask others "Can you pray for me or ask God for me?" How stupid is that? Don't they know God can hear them and see them when they are asking others instead of God directly? Really how do you think that makes God feel? Ask God yourself directly, in all of history God hasn't bitten anybody so you got no reason to be shy. Satan has made it his lifelong job merely to break up your relationship with God by inserting incapable intermediaries so you and God don't talk. God created you specifically to ask him for stuff. A single dua you make to God is better than asking everyone in the world to supplicate for you. Instead of asking people to supplicate for you, just ask God to have those creatures whose supplications are answered by him to supplicate for you. Then those you want to supplicate for you, like angels, will supplicate for you, or you could always do specific good deeds that make the angels supplicate for you. Or better yet just ask God to be satisfied with whatever he wills for you. If you become a friend of God then you won't ask others to supplicate for you because you will supplicate to God directly. God destined for you to read this paragraph so that you would supplicate to him directly for all you need/want. It'd be insulting to God to ask anyone to supplicate for you after you read this about asking only God for everything. In a Sahih hadith in Al-Tirmidhi's collection of Sahih Al-Jami 2418 Muhammad pbuh said what means: "*Verily the person who does not ask Allah, Allah gets angry at him.*" From this I understand it to be almost sinful to ask people to ask Allah on your behalf, because in the moment you are asking people to make dua then you are not asking Allah and Allah gets angry at sins. God commands you to ask him directly, there is no proof to say God wants you to ask so-so to ask God for you. (In the past there were some people God wanted some people to ask to supplicate for them, but nobody on earth today is known to be on such a list and there is no order to ask others to ask. Likewise even when people asked prophet Muhammad pbuh to supplicate for them there is not a single report saying they asked him to ask God to help them in worldy matters.) It is both obligatory to ask God directly and obligatory to avoid God's anger. It might not be sinful to ask others but it's best to ask only God. The odds of you getting what you want are better if you only ask God because God answers and aids those who rely only upon him more often and more readily than those who ask others to ask for God for them. That is what all the prophets taught. Satan told people to ask others to ask, then ask dead people to ask, then ask statues dead people to ask, then ask idols to ask God. That's what idolatry is and how it originally started, most idol worshippers didn't/don't think idols were/are gods but just intercessors with God. Just ask your Creator, leave the other creatures alone.

In my mind since I didn't publicly say the "shahada", which is the Islamic declaration of faith, I didn't think I was Muslim, but technically I was because a Muslim says it during the prayer. At first I thought praying 5 times a day would be a hassle, but the 5 prayers actually took a lot less time than 1 church service. Also repeating it 5 times a day really helps one to learn it quickly. At this point I hadn't yet told anyone in my family that I had left the Catholic Church, which made it tricky when my parents visited. I remembered earlier when my mom saw the English translation of the Quran she said: "*You better not be becoming no Muslim, or you can get the **** out of this house and live somewhere else!*" Given our bad relationship I took that threat seriously and tried practicing Islam secretly. May Allah help us all to worship him correctly without fear of what others might think or do. Nothing can ever happen to us without the Creator's permission and we will never suffer persecution as severe as what the prophets endured, God never places a burden on someone that is greater than they can bear.

I was still a Christian rapper and my 4th album was coming out in December, the music was already made and I was working on my 7th album at the time. Musicians tend to work far in advance and by the time the fans hear a "new" song, it's actually old from the musician's viewpoint. All those songs you hear by the "new sensation" where they're describing what their newly obtained wealth and fame is like were in all probability made long before they became popular. At the time they made the song their reality was different than what they claimed in the song, even after the song is released the reality is still different than what they claim. Being a deeply religious person, changing my religion had a drastic effect on my life and personality. I essentially went from training to be a priest who went to church everyday to trying to be a Muslim who practiced Islam like Muhammad pbuh, understandably my lifestyle was drastically affected by that. I stopped wearing crosses and necklaces of Jesus pbuh because I didn't want people getting the wrong idea, later on learning about the 2nd commandment and the reasons depictions of prophets are false, sinful and insulting. Yet a major decision loomed in front of me, should I keep rapping?

     After becoming a Muslim, music felt different when I listened to it and songs would be stuck in my head while praying. I realized Satan would bring the songs to my thoughts at that specific time to distract me. I paid more attention to the lyrics of the songs and found all of them to be filthy and sacrilegious. I felt like a celebrity and it was hard to not have vanity. It became evident that my raps really wouldn't help anybody. No matter how good the morals preached in a song are, the listener will get addicted to the sound. Then when they tire of the moral song they'll go to some other artist for their fix being attracted to the best sound. The songs which sound the best have the worst messages, because the lyrics are so immoral that they need the most hypnotic sounds in order to compensate. It occurred to me that none of the prophets ever used music to influence others or spread their message. If music could've been useful in spreading religion then the prophets would have used it. Having fans and haters pay attention to me made me feel very important, they cared about me more than what was healthy and it made me feel like somebody special. It's difficult to be humble when it is your job to be famous. The lifestyle of a musician is actually anti-religious and they are given far too much undeserved influence. Music itself creates false desires and emotions also causing one to reminisce. Every song prevented me from letting go of the past. If I was mad or sad when I first heard the song it put me back in that condition. For example a "wedding song" takes one back to that memory and emotional state, every song has that same effect to various degrees. With every different song I heard it made me feel like a different person. Then I remembered music is a tool for brainwashing. Music is such an effective brainwashing tool that a U.S. Senate Committee admitted that the CIA conducted experiments on animals using radio transmissions for mind control in the 1950s CE. If the government officially admits that, then it's easy to imagine them unofficially using radio for mind control on humans. A former CIA agent turned journalist Edward Hunter actually invented the English term "brainwashing". If you honestly look at someone when a radio is turned on and register their initial reaction and how they change the more music or radio broadcasting they hear, it's perfectly plain for the person with earmuffs on to see that the audio waves are manipulating the listener. If you were to watch a video of a concert with the audio muted, you would see the craziness music causes. Most dances actually look like religious or magical rituals if you can't hear the music the dancers are dancing to. Taking one look at "American Idol" is enough to see people are worshipping musicians, people watch that musical show religiously. The lyrics by themselves contain idolatrous verses, obviously some songs promote worshipping money, but others are more subtle. As an example love songs say things like, "*I can't live without you*", "*I can't breathe without you*", "*I need you in my life*", "*I'm nothing without you*" anyone of those four you've probably heard before in a love song, but when you look at the words themselves these are things you should only say to God.

Many songs are technically prayers and can make their listeners disbelievers if they recite the lyrics. If you hear them over and over again subconsciously you'll start thinking like the singers. People even say things like music is their life, and I've heard people call hip hop their wife. These types of statements are made by drug addicts, scientifically music is a drug. I came to the conclusion that music is a drug too dangerous to be using which is impossible not to abuse, or come under the influence of, if it is heard. Why do you think movie production companies spend millions of dollars to include just a couple of songs in a movie? They do this because the music is more important than the plot and the acting. A movie can have a bad story or acting performance, but well placed music can turn it into a classic. For example I have never seen the movie "Jaws", which is about a killer shark, yet the music from that movie has had such an effect on the planet that I still know the "Da dum, Da dum" sound is the sound of Jaws coming to eat somebody. If you study every box office hit, you will see they all feature expensive prolific music that changes the moviegoer's mood on impact. Music is added to movies to hypnotize and mezmerize people making them susceptible to brainwashing. The actual origins of mesmerization and hypnotism started with music, long before the pendulum and swirling figures. Hypnotists admit that music is a strong tool used by them to induce trances of suggestibility. While scientists have concluded that 10-15% of adults are highly susceptible to hypnotism, with 80-85% of children under the age of 12 being highly susceptible to hypnosis. Although keep in mind those figures are just about those classified as "highly hypnotizable", everyone is capable of being hypnotized, some are just more easily hypnotized than others. It is because music is such an effective tool for hypnosis that many kids shows/movies involve music and "sing-alongs"? All of those sing-alongs are methods of hypnosis, and that's how "nursery rhymes" were invented, the rhymes are typically nonsense but they were used by teachers to inculcate post-hypnotic doctrines into students. If you still doubt children are hypnotized by TV, movies, games and musical programs examine the famous words of a purple dinosaur I used to watch as a child, whose song said, "*I love you, you love me. We're a happy family.*" Whenever this lyric was uttered all the kids would sing along with the purple dinosaur. However you have to be majorly hypnotized to say something like that to a stranger and mean it. If any adult said that to someone's kid and their kid repeatedly enthusiastically sang along, most parents would see how that adult is brainwashing their kid to love/trust them which will eventually lead them to believe and do whatever that singer tells them to do. But when it's some corporate tv show with a singer in a costume somehow that type of indoctrination is "innocent fun" and just a "silly catchy kids song"? Unfortunately this type of indoctrination isn't exclusive to kids sing-along songs, adults also sing-along to songs and whether they sing along or not is irrelevant as to whether post-hypnotic beliefs are retained by the brain after listening to a song. Just as kids songs have many actions the kids perform as part of the song, such as with the "Teapot song" where kids act like a teapot, songs for adults cause them to act like the songs say to act. The teapot song makes kids act like a teapot, the gangster songs make people act like a gangster, love songs make people act like they're in love and frequently feel as such too and songs about sex and drugs lead people to be inclined towards having sex and doing drugs. Music doesn't just alter behavior though, but the minds, personalities and spiritualities are also changed by music and that's why movies include so much music. How often have you heard people say, "*that movie changed the way I think*" or that it was "*life-changing*"? This is the power of music, it will change and consume your life taking control while you get lost in the rhythm. Hence Plato taught that music is the barbarous expression of the soul. While Vladimir Lenin said "*I can't listen to music too often. It affects your nerves, makes you want to say stupid, nice things, and stroke the heads of people who could create such beauty while living in this vile hell. And now you mustn't stroke anyone's head-you might get your hand bitten off.*" NASA spent obscene amounts of money sending the space shuttle "Voyager" into space with a specially made golden record containing the music of earth. Why? Because they want any aliens who hear the music to get brainwashed before coming into contact with humans. NASA says that the music made by humans can brainwash aliens. So what do you think music made by humans does to human listeners? Music is powerful enough to brainwash multiple species, it has been used as a weapon of war in the past and present. Music isn't for entertaining, it's used for enslaving. Music is not art! It is a dangerous drug. Patriotic songs are made to stupefy the citizens into becoming obedient taxpayers who love to serve their nation and don't complain. Now why do you think they play music in churches?

    Christians who are addicted to music will say: "*Well doesn't the bible say how Solomon played and listened to music with the Songs of Solomon? How can it be sinful if it's in the bible?*" Yet those same Christians have no clue what else the bible says about Solomon pbuh. In 1 Kings 11 the bible teaches that Solomon pbuh had hundreds of pagan wives and concubines whom the bible says he loved and that he ended up worshipping pagan gods and building pagan shrines. It doesn't stop there, the biblical chapter continues to say God even appeared to him 2 times to tell him to stop but he continued and as a result God himself allegedly raised up enemies against Solomon pbuh to take his kingdom away such as Hadad the Edomite, Rezon bin Eliada and Jeroboam. The bible teaches that the prophet of God, Solomon pbuh, died as a disbelieving pagan! While at the same time they claim Solomon pbuh also wrote the biblical books of Proverbs, Ecclesiastes and the Songs of Solomon. So the bible says Solomon pbuh was a disbeliever and then Christians say he wrote 3 books of their bible. How does that work out? Because frankly Christians don't know what the bible teaches. Deep down they know that the slander of Solomon pbuh in the bible is false, and it is most certainly false as are many other biblical slanders. Yet ignorant Christians will use the bible saying this very same false pagan biblical Solomon listened to and promoted music so that must mean it's good and not sinful. Whereas anyone who actually knew the bible would know that biblically Solomon pbuh is depicted as evil and someone not to follow. So that the bible falsely teaches Solomon pbuh used or promoted music, which he didn't, is actually a biblical proof against music because the bible says Solomon pbuh was an evil pagan who God fought against. Indirectly the bible teaches that "If you listen to music then God will fight you." Furthermore the Jews and their Talmud and traditions say Solomon pbuh performed magic. So would that mean magic is ok too because the Jews say he did it? Of course not! Also the bible teaches Lot pbuh, who never disbelieved according to the bible had incest with his daughters. So does that mean incest is good to do and ok because the bible says a prophet did it? The bible also says Noah pbuh got drunk so much he took of all his clothes and passed out, so it that ok to do to since the bible says a prophet did it? Of course we are supposed to follow the prophets and do what they did but did any prophet ever say the whole bible was accurate? Which prophet said to follow the bible or that it was true? The Christian dilemma is that if the bible is false when it says Solomon pbuh lived as and died a pagan then that means the bible is false and they can't use it to justify their religion, much less music. Whereas if the bible is true about Solomon pbuh allegedly being a pagan then that means music is bad since the bible says Solomon pbuh promoted it. In reality the information about Solomon pbuh in the bible is false and unreliable, but even if it were true then it means one shouldn't listen to music regardless. For a Christian to say the bible says music is ok and/or good is like saying that killing babies is good because the bible says Pharaoh used to do it. Furthermore if you actually read the "Songs of Solomon" in the bible, you will not find the word God mentioned once. Do you know what these songs are about? They are erotic songs about people having sex with each other. Seriously they are sexual songs, right in the middle of the bible. No respectable person would ever dare sing these songs in public because they are so lewd, even by today's standards. Even today the biblical "Songs of Solomon" would not be allowed on public radio because they are so promiscuous. Even Christian radio stations won't play them because they are so immoral, but then Christians use these immoral sex songs to say music is okay to listen to if "it's good". In response now Christians falsely brand the biblical Psalms as "songs" when they aren't and never where considered to be songs until recently, after they found out they couldn't justify music at all and the "Songs of Solomon" were too pornographic. Of which the bible says in 1 Kings 4:2 that Solomon pbuh wrote thousands of songs but oddly enough the bible only has 2 which get attributed to him. Thus if these songs were so good and written by a prophet then why don't they exist today and why weren't they put in the bible? As a last resort to protect their pro-music position Christians will say the bible says David pbuh played a harp/lyre, to which I say that the bible also says that David pbuh committed adultery, murdered his own soldier (the husband of who he allegedly did adultery with) and allowed his son Ammon to rape David's daughter Tammar (who was Ammon's half-sister). So the bible says a whole lot of stuff and that if Christians want to say Solomon and David pbut did something then they better follow all the laws that David and Solomon pbut followed as well. But no they don't want to grow a beard, get circumcised, keep kosher, keep the sabbath, observe the new-moons, make daily ablutions and follow all the rules. They just like music and want to listen to it, so they try to pull it out of the bible to justify what they were doing before they read the bible. No Christians were living a life without music and then read a bible verse and decided to start listening to music because of their reading of the bible. All of them were already listening to music and just want to keep on doing it and feel the buzz of the rhythm of the beat. However what does the bible really say about David pbuh playing a harp/lyre making music? This alleged event is depicted in 1 Samuel 18:10-11, "**<u>The next day an evil spirit from God came forcefully on Saul</u>**. *He was prophesying in his house,* **<u>while David was playing the lyre</u>**, *as he usually did. Saul had a spear in his hand* [11] *and he hurled it, saying to himself, "I'll pin David to the wall." But David eluded him twice.*" So what is the lesson of this example? Christians would say "as he usually did" is the lesson that proves music is good and okay. Yet in context evil spirits appear when music is played and while playing a musical instrument David pbuh was almost killed because of his playing the instrument and the incitement of the "evil spirit" which came when the music was played. Thus the true lesson of David pbuh allegedly playing music in the bible is that it causes devils to come around and influence the listeners. Likewise it also shows how sometimes Jews attributed evil spirits as coming from God since they were occasionally dualistic equating the devil with God as his villanous alter-ego. For all the evil the bible attributes to Saul, music is a main culprit to blame. So if Saul was evil it would be partially due to David's evil playing of music but then again only the bible says Saul was evil which I remind you Jews wrote that part of the bible and it is known from before Saul was officially crowned they hated him and didn't want Saul to be king. So since the beginning of Saul's reign as King Jews thought he was evil even when he wasn't. Thus when Jews write about Saul as evil and David pbuh "their idolized hero" as playing music, their motives must be considered. Eventually though the Jews even attacked David pbuh in their literature accusing him of evil deeds as well. So in short Jewish texts are trivial when it concerns them writing about prophets and as such Jewish narrations are not admissible in a theological court of jurisprudence when establishing prophetic precedents because Jewish testimony is not credible concerning kings nor prophets, of which David and Solomon pbut were both. Yet even if one believes Jewish writings, written long after the fact by people who never actually met David pbuh then still the biblical text condemns the music played by David pbuh since it caused evil spirits to posess people. That is the lesson of the "biblical prophetic music" in that music can cause the demonic posession of religious people. So the claim that "Well the bible says David pbuh played music" is a proof for music being sinful. Whereas it doesn't even matter if the case were otherwise because Christians claim to be followers of Jesus pbuh, so if they claim that then bring something where Jesus pbuh allowed music or promoted it. Not Paul, but Jesus pbuh and there's nothing except the alleged wedding which is only mentioned in "John". To which I say fine if you want music at a wedding then whatever, but outside of weddings there is no biblical justification. Note that in Islam a specific type of "music" is allowed at weddings and on eids based on what Muhammad pbuh taught. Yet music in general is prohibited and even then music at weddings is an exception and restricted to special types of instruments which personally due to my past history and knowledge of music I don't think I'd risk having music at my theoretical wedding. Whereas again that biblical wedding where there was music is highly doubtful as to whether it even took place at all, since the other gospels say Jesus was fasting in the wilderness on the day this wedding allegedly took place. So was Jesus pbuh fasting with piety or jamming at a party? The prophet J.C. pbuh was not an MC or a DJ. Remember I'm not saying that every single song is a magical spell, but I know that some of them are and that it's impossible for anyone to know whether a song has been produced with magic or not even if they were personally involved in the production of the song itself. Just think of certain things about music. For instance there is "Soul music". Do you really think "Soul music" has no effect on the soul? They say "it comes from the soul", but what exactly are the souls of those artists' like? Likewise many artists will say their stuff "comes from the heart", well just what kind of hearts are these? If soul music comes from and effects the soul then what makes it so different that it causes an effect on the soul but the other types of music don't? There is no difference. Why is it that all the musicians that reach the highest levels of music are on drugs? It's because you can't humanely get to the highest levels of music naturally. In addition to that, artists are the most likely category of people to become addicts because the personality of an addict helps creativity, at a steep price. That's why if you study famous artists of the various art forms, you will learn how despite being great artists psychologically most were messed up and half-crazy with deep inner problems or "demons". It's just that mentally and emotionally healthy people are too normal to make great art, advanced art requires psychological abnormality sometimes to the extent of insanity. Truly you will not find a mentally healthy elite musician in all of history, do the research. Seriously not a single "great musician" has ever been sane. Musicians are basically crazy people who don't get locked up because they can function just enough to seem semi-stable and safe in society and people are addicted to the sounds they make. Whereas such psychological abnormalities and addiction increase one's risk of possession, especially when you add a drug like music to the mix. Drugs lead one to be vulnerable to possession by Jinn, so those musical "geniuses" might just be getting used by Jinn to influence us. Elite artists know that elite art is not entirely human and this applies outside of the world of music as well. Thus when I present the case that music can be magical having magical effects on it's listeners and Jinn can play a role in it's creation, it's really not farfetched at all to anyone who has experience with the entertainment arts. It's no crazy conspiracy, the entertainment and arts industries are really into some wicked stuff behind the scenes. The celebrities don't tell you what's going on and most don't even know what's really going on with them themselves. They just want money, glory and influence. There is no exception to these 3 motivations, if they don't want the money or glory or influence then they'd keep their "art" private. The reason music, movies, art etc is made public is because the artists want to influence what people think and believe. Now if you have influential people who are good at getting the attention of the masses then don't you think they'd be prime targets for the Jinn? Those are not only the best targets but frequently the most vulnerable. I can't speak on all types of art but I can speak on music and how it's not a normal healthy product and it's not even just a dangerous drug. I was approached by a guy who wanted me to sell him my soul as part of a record label deal, so this stuff isn't a joke to play around with. Although I've recently learned my music career was even worse than I ever thought. It'd actually be more surprising if music didn't have anything to do with magic than to learn that it did. While writing this book I was horrified to learn of a magical symbol called the Chaos Star. This is because in 2010 CE I made a song titled "Where will I go?" for my second album. It was a lyrically advanced and very creative pity song about me feeling homeless without family support, getting harassed by police and not being on the road to the priesthood having absolutely no clue about where I would go in life, or literally the next night. Truly it was a song about chaos in my personal life. Since it was a leading single I made a custom art design to advertise the song and it was a very intricate logo that was extraordinarily -appealing and pleasurable to look at. I even made shirts of the logo which I invented all by myself and people who didn't even like my music told me they wanted to buy the shirts because the logo/symbol I made was so cool. I planned to get a custom pendant of my fancy logo which I made for the song. Yet "my design" was not really mine at all, but it was really a neo-pagan magical chaos star of sorts. It's one thing for me to say others might be doing magic intentionally or ignorantly but I learned that I myself was doing this stuff promoting magical symbols and had no clue. It's a shock that I can't express with words, it's like living a crazy horror movie finding out that you were the monster all along. It just makes one speechlessly wonder "*How could this be possible?*". It's a traumatic soul shaking feeling because there is no way I could have accidentally made such a wicked magical symbol that was so detailed and precise without having been influenced by evil or demonic forces. It's impossible for it to have been a coincidence, especially since the song itself was about my own personal chaotic life. There's no coincidence about it, I was getting screwed around by some demons influencing me to make music and images promoting magic without knowing it and personally intending the exact opposite.   Lyrically the song promoted resisting temptations, doing the right thing no matter what, focusing on the afterlife since you will go to either heaven or hell and wherever you go in this world doesn't change the fact that you either will go to heaven or hell in the end for eternity. Yet despite the moral religious lyrics, the song promoted magic and I didn't know it.   So the lesson is it doesn't matter what the words of a song say, music is bad even when people try to make it good. Trust me I tried my hardest to make " religious music" that taught good things that I thought God would love. But God has forbidden music and thus it is impossible to make "good music" because it's sinful. There is no good in disobeying God. Even if you try and believe that what you are doing is good, if God or a prophet says it's not then it's not and it doesn't matter if you realize how or why it's bad, it's bad; God doesn't need to prove it. It feels like I just found out that I was getting raped for years and didn't know it, and enjoyed it while stupidly participating. Yet now I know more of the reality of music, I say "more" because the more I learn about it the worse it turns out to be. So as long as I know, it doesn't matter if you believe me or not. It'd be good for you if you did but I'm just glad and amazed that I found out myself and hope you can benefit from it and God rewards me for writing this. Since this happened to me it can happen to any disbeliever or even a believer if they aren't practicing their religion fully, consistently and sincerely with knowledge. You could be the worst of people and not even know it until you get judged and sentenced by God for what you really were. So whether or not you want to accept insider information from artists and musicians exposing how supernatural beings are influencing their works, just be careful. If I'm wrong about some music being magical then I'm wrong, but music is just not worth the risk. If you listen to music you are literally risking your soul, and Satan will make you groove all the way to the grave.   Don't forget about those dancing plagues that killed Europeans. Personally I even use noise cancelling earplugs, earmuffs and/or have headphones on when I enter places that play music because listening to public music is like getting second-hand smoke; since music is an intoxicating drug that can be magical as well.

Many Christian denominations like Primitive Baptists, Greek Orthodox and reformed Presbytarians reject instrumental music used in worship services citing biblical reasons and Martin Luther (invented Protestantism and Lutheranism) John Wesley (invented Methodism) and John Calvin (invented Presbyterianism) all rejected instrumental music in worship as well. Following are some quotes of what the non-Muslim Scholars and Christians themselves have said regarding Christians and music, in case any Christian reader needs more evidence to accept the religious ruling on music being forbidden:

"*In view of the controversies over the use of instrumental music in worship, which have been so violent in the British and American Protestant churches, it is an interesting question whether instruments were employed by the primitive Christians. We know that instruments performed an important function in the Hebrew temple service and in the ceremonies of the Greeks. At this point, however, a break was made with all previous practice, and although the lyre and flute were sometimes employed by the Greek converts, as a general rule the use of instruments in worship was condemned.*" … "*<u>Many of the fathers, speaking of religious songs, made no mention of instruments; others, like Clement of Alexandria and St. Chrysostom, refer to them only to denounce them.</u> Clement says, "Only one instrument do we use, viz. the cord of peace wherewith we honor God, no longer the old psaltery, trumpet, drum, and flute." Chrysostom exclaims: "David formerly sang in psalms, also we sing today with him; he had a lyre with lifeless strings, the church has a lyre with living strings. **<u>Our tongues are the strings of the lyre</u>**, with a different tone, indeed, but with a more accordant piety." St. Ambrose expresses his scorn for those who would play the lyre and psaltery instead of singing hymns and psalms; and St. Augustine adjures believers not to turn their hearts to theatrical instruments. The religious guides of the early Christian felt that there would be an incongruity, and even profanity, in the use of the sensuous nerve-exciting effects of instrumental sound in their mystical, spiritual worship. Their high religious and moral enthusiasm needed no aid from external strings; the **<u>pure vocal utterance</u>** as the more proper expression of their faith. While the Greek and Roman songs were metrical, the **<u>Christian psalms were anitphons, prayers, responses, etc., were unmetrical</u>**; and while the pagan melodies were always sung to an instrumental accompaniment, **<u>the church chant was exclusively vocal</u>**"- Edward Dickinson (Musical Scholar)

Unmetrical means that they didn't have a "beat" or rhythmic tempo. Today we'd say it's not music but some type of lame poetry. Don't think that being purely vocal means they would sing because singing is metrical whereas the early Christians' definition of singing was completely unlike what Christians today think is singing, even without music.

"*This species. which is the most natural, is to be considered to have existed before any other... **<u>Instrumental music is also of very ancient date, its invention being ascribed to Tubal, the sixth descendant from Cain.</u>** The instrumental music was not practiced by the primitive Christians, but was an aid to devotion of later times, is evident from church history.*" Fessenden's Encyclopedia of Art & Music

Muslims have been saying the descendants of Cain were the first to have been introduced to music by Satan for years and Christians say that we're crazy and wouldn't know. Well there is a non-Muslim musical scholar and historian who agrees. It's a fact that's where music came from, humans didn't invent it.

"*The early Christians refused to have anything to do with the instrumental music which they might have inherited from the ancient world.*" Theodore Finney(A History of Music, p. 43)

"*There is no command in the New Testament, Greek or English, commanding the use of the instrument. Such a command would be entirely out of harmony with the New Testament.*" J.H. Garrison, of "Christian Church"

"*The church, although lapsing more and more into deflection from the truth and into a corrupting of apostolic practice, had not instrumental music for 1200 years (that is, it was not in general use before this time); The*

Calvinistic Reform Church ejected it from its service as an element of popery, even the church of England having come very nigh its extrusion from her worship. It is heresy in the sphere of worship." John Giradeau, (Presbyterian professor in Columbia Theological Seminary, Instrumental Music, p. 179)

"Instrumental music is permissible for a church under the following conditions: 1. When a church never had or has lost the Spirit of Christ. 2. If a church has a preacher who never had or has lost the Spirit of Christ, who has become a dry, prosing and lifeless preacher. 3. If a church only intends being a fashionable society, a mere place of amusements and secular entertainment and abandoning the idea of religion and worship. 4. If a church has within it a large number of dishonest and corrupt men. 5. If a church has given up all idea of trying to convert the world." -Ben Franklin (editor of American Christian Review, 1860.)

*"<u>**Neither he [Paul] nor any other apostle, nor the Lord Jesus, nor any of the disciples for five hundred years, used instruments.** This too, in the face of the fact that the Jews had used instruments in the days of their prosperity and that the Greeks and heathen nations all used them in their worship.</u> They were dropped out with such emphasis that they were not taken up till the middle of the Dark Ages, and came in as part of the order of the Roman Catholic Church. <u>It seems there cannot be doubt but that the use of instrumental music in connection with the worship of God, whether used as a part of the worship or as an attraction accompaniment, is unauthorized by God and violates the oft-repeated prohibition to add nothing to, take nothing from, the commandments of the Lord.</u> It destroys the difference between the clean and the unclean, the holy and unholy, counts the blood of the Son of God unclean, and tramples under foot the authority of the Son of God. They have not been authorized by God or sanctified with the blood of his Son."* -David Lipscomb

"And if any man who is a preacher believes that the apostle teaches the use of instrumental music in the church by enjoining the singing of psalms, he is one of those smatters in Greek who can believe anything that he wishes to believe. When the wish is father to the thought, correct exegesis is like water on a duck's back" J. W. McGarvey (Biblical Criticism, p. 116)

*"We cannot, therefore, by any possibility, know that a certain element of worship is acceptable to God in the Christian dispensation, when the Scriptures which speak of that dispensation are silent in reference to it. To introduce **<u>any such element is unscriptural and presumptuous</u>**. It is will worship, if any such thing as will worship can exist. <u>On this ground **we condemn the burning of incense, the lighting of candles, the wearing of priestly robes, and the reading of printed prayers.**</u> On the same ground <u>**we condemn instrumental music**</u>."* J.W. McGarvey

*"<u>**We have no real knowledge of the exact character of the music** which formed a part of the religious devotion of the first Christian congregations. It was, however purely vocal.</u>"* Frederic Louis Ritter (History of Music from the Christian Era to the Present Time, p. 28)

I cannot stress enough that music is a drug, this is not my opinion, it is a scientific fact that music is an intoxicant. Music activates the hormone melatonin in the pineal gland. This gland when activated by music also affects the reproductive cycle and sexual mood. Music is proven to cause unnatural and unhealthy sex drives. One reason why people today have less control over their lust and much more of it, is because they listen to a lot more music today than people in the past used to listen to. Music is also thought to trigger puberty, so listening to music can actually cause puberty to occur before it would normally occur. So the mental chemical hormones which music activates and reacts with cause a type of auditory orgasm, or "Braingasm" if you will. Essentially if one considers the extreme effect that pornography has on the eyes, music has a similar effect on the ears and both drastically alter and change the structure of your brain. Music actually causes brain damage. People say a picture is worth a thousand words, but a single musical note conveys a thousand pictures worth of messages to your brain and your ears can't decode or filter it, the brain absorbs it all and the musical pollution takes it toll. If you get exposed and become a music junkie you can lose your soul. If you critically analyze musical lyrics (don't listen to the music) you will see the same exact pattern and satanic messages throughout them all, even the purportedly religious ones. Even if there were religious songs they'd be hooking people on the musical drug, but there is no such thing as a religious song; at least not one that calls to the true religion of God. I know this because I myself wrote songs that were "religious" and when re-reading the lyrics I see them as satanic now. All of my rhymes were actually crimes. Although when I wrote them I originally thought they were calling people to goodness and God. I wrote these Satanic lyrics without even knowing the Satanic messages they contained and had good intentions at the time. Ironically Frederich Nietzche taught that all music was religious in the service of gods and was primitive without reason. He also taught that music was a mixture of cruelty and coarse sensuality that is hostile to reason. Whearas since the truth and the religion of God is incompatible with music, as Nietzche classified it, then it's easy to see why the prophets pbut never used music. If you research the origins of how music was introduced to mankind you will learn that Adam pbuh and Eve never experienced music, even though they experienced paradise. The origin of music doesn't stem from man. The first time man heard music was when Satan himself brought it and taught it to the people descended from Cain. The same Cain who killed his brother Abel, both of which were the sons of Adam pbuh. Originally Satan was the one who introduced mankind to music. May Allah forgive me and all others who were involved with music and give us correct understanding and protection from Satanic productions. May Allah help us all to stop doing drugs that are bad for us and increase me in gratitude for guiding me away from the drug of music.

    Initially it was difficult to give up music and I would use songs as a pick me up. It quickly became apparent that music had always been a crutch I used to distract myself from real life. I listened in order to escape from emotions I didn't like. My mood swings started to leave and my thinking became clearer the less I listened to music. Perhaps as a result of not being in a continuous musical daze, I became interested in nature. The sounds of the rain, wind, birds and others all seemed to be amazing, whereas the musical sounds seemed fake and cheap in comparison. As I detoxed and achieved sobriety from music, my productivity shot through the roof and my focus gained precision. These lines might rhyme a little but by not listening to music I was liberated from the need for rhythm. Before I thought that music was my life, after I learned to live without it I see how it has destroyed people's lives. Subliminally suggested messages are implanted by the artists and the listener ends up getting played as though they were an instrument.

      Sadly not only have some wasted their lives dancing away, some have died dancing. Most famously in the Dancing Plague of 1518 CE in France. In July 1518 CE in Strasbourg, France a woman known as Frau Troffea started dancing in the middle of a narrow street and continued for 4-6 days without eating, drinking or sleeping. By the end of the week at least 34 others had joined in and by the end of the month 400 people were there dancing in the street without ceasing. Medically Frau should've died after 3 days from dehydration, but she was still dancing and didn't drop dead until later, as did many who joined her. By the end of that summer dozens had died there having just kept dancing continuously without eating, drinking or sleeping and this is an undisputed well documented historical fact. The authorities even built a wooden stage and hired musicians thinking it was just "hot blood" and that people would dance it out of their system. The spooky thing wasn't just that these people died dancing but that so many witnessed them dance in such a manner even though then and now medical science says it's impossible and unnatural. Unfortunately many who watched them dance would also get infected with the contagion and be unable to stop themselves from joining in and dancing til their death. This deadly phenomenon has occurred more than once throughout history, in Italy, England, Prussia, Belgium, the Netherlands, and much of Europe also afflicting Hungarians, Polish, Austrians, Bohemians, and even occurring in America as well. There are many famously documented cases of mass breakouts of Dancing Plagues taking place. One being in 1840 CE in Madagascar, with another in Aix-la-Chapelle, Germany during 1374 CE where the afflicted claimed they saw the heavens open and show Christ upon a throne. In fact the word "Dancers" comes from a German sect of Christians who as their main ritual would get together and dance until they suffocated and dropped breathless on the ground, they claimed to receive visions and revelations during these dancing experiences and hence were called "Dancers". Although even before them the Eicetes where a Christian sect in 680 CE who said in order to pray to God one had to do it through dancing. Dancing was the Eicete way of praying and it was a heretical form of Christianity, that happened to have it's heretical ritual of dancing become massively popular inside and outside of Christianity. Likewise dancing was the main religious ritual of animistic Native American religions. So dancing has always been a religious ritual and form of worship. The first documented occurrence of dancing mania was on December 24th in 1027 CE, which took place during a Christmas Eve church service in Bernburg, Germany. In the 14th century this epidemic was labeled the dance of St. John's, with people thinking it had something to do with the Germans having incorporated the pagan ritual dance of "Nodfyr", done by pagans during the summer solstice, into the Christian celebrations of St. John's Day which takes place on the formerly pagan holiday. Others called it the St. Vitus dance because it was thought that going to the chapels of St. Vitus could get one healed from this dancing disease. Although the only recorded instances of these pandemics took place in Christian regions, which makes it ironic that Christians continue to use music in their worship services despite the dangers involved with it. Now perhaps you may be thinking how can these dance plagues possibly have been true historical occurences, wouldn't people eventually fall asleep? No. This has recently been proven in Bakersfield, California during the events which occured from July 11th to July 17th, 2015 CE. During those 6 days, a 38 year old woman Carrie Swidecki played the dancing videogame "*Just Dance 4*". She danced for 138 hours straight during which she had posted a live video stream of the event where she was observed dancing for 138 hours. It broke many world records. This is a modern scientifically verified and recorded occurence of someone unnaturally dancing without stopping for days on end. She seriously danced for 138 hours, it's a fact. It's not a fluke either, during previous years she danced for periods of 15 hours in 2010, 16 hours in 2011, 22 hours in 2012 and also 24 hours in 2012 and 49 hours in 2013 and 76 hours in 2014. These dancing spells are not natural, without a doubt music and dance have unnatural ingredients. All these documented occurrences prove how powerful music and dance can be to humanity, they really have supernatural effects on a human being which none of our species can control or prevent. May the Almighty All-Hearing God protect all of us from these deadly plagues and diseases caused by dancing and music.

After the album came out I quit music and shortly after that I said the shahada, which is the declaration of faith that makes one a Muslim. Unlike Christianity you don't need to take a bunch of classes, have sponsors or go through numerous sacraments to become a Muslim. The minimum requirements are that one believes in the 5 pillars of Islam and the 6 articles of Faith. The 5 pillars of Islam are:

1. <u>**Shahada**</u>: Testifying in Arabic and a language you understand (if you don't know Arabic) that "*I testify that there is no deity worthy of being worshiped except Allah, and I testify that Muhammad (pbuh) is the final messenger of Allah and his servant*".

The Shahada is the password to Islam. It expresses a person's total acceptance of and commitment to Islam, which will be applied and practiced to the best of one's abilities according to what they know. One doesn't have to know everything, but whatever one learns they accept and try to practice while continuously trying to learn more so they can better please Allah. The shahada is both a negative statement rejecting the worship(in any way) of anything but Allah and rejecting any claims of people claiming to be prophets after Muhammad pbuh, and an affirmative statement affirming that Allah alone is the only being/entity to be worshipped (in any way) and that Muhammad pbuh is his final messenger and thus his teachings take precedent over the teachings/statements/opinions of all who come after him.

2. <u>**Salat**</u>: The five daily prayers at dawn, noon, mid-afternoon, sunset and night. To be prayed in the way which the prophet Muhammad pbuh prayed. Prayed while facing toward the Kabah in Mecca whether praying alone or in congregation, indoors or outdoors.

Muslims don't worship the Kabah. They face that direction because Allah said to do so in the Quran in order to distinguish the Muslims from the Jews who face towards Jerusalem, as well as the Christians who are supposed to face Jerusalem when they pray. The Kabah in Mecca was built by the prophet Abraham pbuh. It is the first building to have ever been dedicated to worshipping God. People can even go inside of it, it is not an idol. The Kabah in Mecca is a focal point that creates uniformity so all Muslims in the world are facing the same direction when they pray. A bird's eye view of Mecca would show the world forming rings around the Kaba with all the Muslims praying together towards the same place, hoping we all eventually get to the same place called paradise.

3. **Zakat:** A annual charity paid by every Muslim eligible to pay it, which equals 1/40th or 2.5% of a Muslim's total net worth. Zakat goes to support the neediest members of the Muslim society.

   A Muslim is eligible to pay zakat if the amount of wealth one possesses is greater than the value of 85 grams of gold/ 595 grams of silver, and is owned for a lunar year, then it is obligatory for a Muslim to pay zakat on it. The zakat is paid to those who own less than the value of 85 grams of gold/ 595 grams of silver and other special persons. Most who receive it are too poor to pay it. This ensures the social inequality gap among Muslims doesn't become extreme and the poor are not abandoned. This pillar legally forces Muslims to take care of each other.

4. **Sawm:** Fasting during the holy month of Ramadan every day from dawn to sunset.

   Fasting is a form of worship that increases one's gratitude to Allah, makes one humble, develop self-control and simulates what the poor endure every day. The heightened spiritual sensitivity from temporarily abstaining helps one to strengthen their faith and give up any sinful habits. Every able bodied Muslim goes without food or drink and sex from dawn to sunset in order to please Allah. Everyday at sunset the Muslims break their fast, eat and drink; ideally spending the night in worship. At the end of Ramadan a large communal feast is held and it is a time for Muslims to get together. Gifts are frequently given to children on the first day after Ramadan.

5. **Hajj:** For Muslims who are physically and financially able to travel to Mecca, it is a duty to perform the pilgrimage once in their lifetime.

   Hajj began with the prophet Abraham pbuh and the sacred ritual continues to this day, drawing millions of people every year from all corners of the world who come to do the pilgrimage in the same manner as Muhammad pbuh did it. Old, young, rich, poor, black, white, yellow, brown; all men wear the same outfit without social distinctions between them. Both men and women come as pilgrims and do the same ritual together all hoping to please their Maker. It is a deeply humbling religious experience which makes one realize just how insignificant we are and how on the Day of Judgment everyone who ever existed will be gathered together all at the same place hoping for Allah's mercy while fearing his punishment. Nothing other than the religion of Islam is capable of gathering such a diverse crowd of people to all do the same thing at the same time for the same reason in the same way as it has been done for thousands of years. The Hajj has been going on for thousands of years, when people claim America to be a melting pot of blended cultures and ethnicities they are ignorant of the history of Mecca.

These 5 pillars are the fundamental foundations of the religion of Islam. Although a strong building needs more than just 5 pillars in order to be complete, the whole building must have all its parts perfectly put together. If one part is neglected, or not fixed, the whole house could be damaged despite all the other parts being in perfect condition working properly. Yet without these 5 pillars supporting the foundation, the building can never be built to begin with. The most important pillar is the shahada. Think of it as though the 5 pillars are 5 tent posts with the 1st pillar being in the middle holding up the tent in it's entirety, without belief in and the maintainence of the integrity of the central pillar the other 4 are useless, yet without the other 4 the shahada itself won't serve much of a purpose though it would still be a key foundation.. All the pillars are important to the maintenance of the faith but everything else in Islam is meant primarily to supplement and aid in the raising of the #1 pillar. In addition there are 6 main principles or articles of the Islamic faith:

1. **Oneness of God:** A Muslim believes in **1 God**, who is Supreme and Eternal, Infinite and Mighty, Merciful and Compassionate, the Creator of all and Provider for all. God has no father or mother, no son or daughter. None are equal or similar to God. He is the God of all humankind and jinnkind, not the exclusive god of a special tribe, country or race.

2. **Messengers and Prophets of God:** The Quran mentions 25 prophets by name, but there were many others, some mentioned in other scriptures, some whose stories are not known to us. All the messengers were mortal human beings, endowed with Divine revelations and appointed by God to teach mankind. The same core message was brought by all Prophets: to believe in One God and not to associate partners with Him, to stay away from sins and to lead a life devoted to seeking God's pleasure. Some of the Prophets are: Adam pbuh, Noah pbuh, Abraham pbuh, Lot pbuh, Moses pbuh, David pbuh, Jesus pbuh, and Muhammad pbuh. Muslims follow and accept all of them, none are rejected, denied or slandered.

3. **The Divine Revelations of God:** A Muslim must believe in <u>all scriptures and revelations of God</u>, as they were complete <u>in their original versions</u>. Some of these scriptures include the Suhuf given to Abraham pbuh, the Torah given to Moses pbuh, the Zabur given to David pbuh, and the Injeel given to Jesus pbuh. But none of these remain today 100% complete in their original forms as they were when initially revealed. The Quran is the final revelation and is the only one available that remains entirely uncorrupted today and is in the same Arabic as it was revealed to the Messenger Muhammad pbuh. Every Arabic Quran in the world from all time periods is exactly the same letter for letter, there is only 1 version. It is the Uncreated Speech of God, not made by man, nor Jinn.

4. **The Unseen:** Muslims believe in things of the unseen such as Angels and Jinn. Angels are creatures made of light created by God. They worship God devoutly and do not have freewill, it is impossible for

an angel to disobey God. They do not eat, drink, or sleep. Each angel has a special duty and purpose for which God created them. Gabriel is one of them. Jinn are made of smokeless fire. They have freewill and can choose to obey or disobey God. Jinn eat, drink, sleep and reproduce. Satan is one of them. Neither Angels nor Jinn are typically seen by humans so they are part of the Unseen. God is also part of the Unseen since nobody has seen God.

5. **The Day of Judgment:** A Muslim believes in a life after death when all of mankind will be raised from the dead and brought to account for all that they have done. People who believe, do good and are forgiven by God will go to Paradise. People who do not believe, do bad and are not forgiven by God will go to Hell. Only God knows when the Day of Judgment will be.

6. **Predestination:** A Muslim believes that God knows all that will and will not happen, as well as how what will not happen would've happened if it did. The plans of God are beyond our ability to comprehend, but we trust that they are good even if we cannot understand how. God knows best why things happen and is never unjust to anyone. A Muslim doesn't get mad at the decree of God but accepts it regardless of what it is. All that happens occurs with the permission of God. In fact without predestination we couldn't have divine revelation, prophesies or prophets because God can't send us a book nor a prophet that tells us future events unless God knows everything before it happens. Likewise God couldn't make someone a prophet, help them perform miracles or entrust a prophet with his revelation unless God knew they would act how he wanted before they did. God knew everything that will happen and every possibility that doesn't come to reality before he created anything, that's one thing that makes him God and deserving of exclusive worship. Another proof that everything is already decreed and known before it happens is the phenomena commonly called "Deja Vu", in which one has a dream of the future and then they forget about having that dream until they witness it come true and they remember they had dreamed up exactly word for word down to every detail the event(s) they just experienced. These events frequently involve many freewill decisions that could never be planned, even if the person had remembered the dream and tried to make it come true they couldn't have done so. Yet they know with 100% certainty they dreamed of what they experienced, long before they experienced it, sometimes days, weeks or months in advance. I used to experience this before becoming Muslim, but moreso after becoming a Muslim. It is also a sign of the end ot time that believers will have more and more "true dreams" where they accurately dream of future events. This can only happen due to God's predestination and this is an irrefutable proof for it.

Believing in the 5 pillars and the 6 principles of faith, I became a Muslim Fundamentalist. A Fundamentalist by definition is someone who believes in and follows the basics, or "fundamentals". Therefore a Muslim Fundamentalist is someone who believes in and practices the basics of Islam. Unfortunately a common mistake many people make is to confuse a fundamentalist for an extremist. A comparison between the two is like a child riding a bicycle with training wheels, a helmet, horn, reflectors, protective gear and a first aid kit. The child may not use the bicycle completely utilizing its full potential, but they're safely following the fundamentals, so they are a bicycling fundamentalist. Whereas a bicycling extremist, not only rides without the training wheels and restrictive saftey measures, but they go overboard and may have specially customized bicycles which are barely classifiable as bikes which they use in extreme competitions doing extreme stunts without any protective gear at all. Now the fundamentalist is pretty safe and there isn't much that can go wrong, but the extremist can be dangerous and lots of things could go wrong. The fundamentalist is unlikely to get hurt or make a mistake, whereas the extremist is likely to make mistakes and get hurt. The fundamentalist tends to play things safe and err on the side of caution. The extremist tends to be high-risk and is liable to make an error with dangerous consequences. When it comes to religion you want to be a fundamentalist because an extremist is astray and not following the religion as it is supposed to be followed. May Allah help us to be fundamentalists and not extremists.

   If I remember correctly, Sunday December 11th, 2011 CE is the first day I publicly proclaimed myself to be a Muslim. It is not required for witnesses to hear you say the words because Allah is a witness, as are the Angels which record all the deeds we do. Although it is preferred that the Shahada be said in front of at least 2 people, it will still count if one does it alone. Some people I know were afraid to do it publicly so instead they just said the Arabic version of the shahada in front of two people who didn't understand what it meant; doing this would still count as long as the speaker knew the meaning of what they were saying. Shortly after saying the Shahada alone I decided to post the English meaning of the Shahada to facebook so that people knew I became a Muslim. My account was listed in my Christian rap name and I planned to change the name on the account shortly after the post. I took a picture of the newsfeed post and was going to make it my profile picture so people would realize that it was still me but that I had a different profile name and became a Muslim. I took the picture very quickly but before I could even update the profile people started commenting. Within 3 seconds after I had first posted "*I testify that there is no god but Allah and that Muhammad is his servant and his messenger*" a person I went to elementary school with, who was always on good terms with me whom I played with at his house when we were kids, posted "*I testify that you are an idiot.*" I think that person's insulting post got more "likes" than any other post that had ever been on my profile. Internet bullying was a frequent occurrence I was accustomed to from people who didn't like my music. Although now the minority who liked my Christian rap had turned against me, while the haters of the Christian rap ironically hated me even more. It was also surprising that some of the people who never cared about religion were suddenly religious fanatics saying how I'm making a big mistake and that I'm stupid for not believing in Christianity. If they weren't so mean it would've been funny because I had been telling these same people for years to stop sinning and embrace Christianity. I never would've thought that by becoming a Muslim it would cause them to become zealous Christians. Then again it was December, even atheists become Christians until the 26th in order to get Christmas gifts. The few who didn't insult me couldn't believe that I of all people would become a Muslim. People even posted comments asking if my account had been hacked because they couldn't come to terms with the fact that the most devout Christian they knew would become a Muslim. Since I had decided to stop rapping I changed the name on my account, however my real name was Gregory which is distinctly Christian. Gregory was the name of many popes, including the one they call "Gregory the Great" who did some pretty bad things, such as adopting Ash Wednesday from the pagan Norse who would put ashes on their forehead on Wednesday, or Odin's day, thinking it would cause Odin to protect them. Although in the bible Jesus pbuh forbid people to put ashes on their faces when fasting, which Christians are supposed to be doing on Ash Wednesday except today most Christians don't fast that day at all and it's basically just a "*look at me I'm a pious Christian who got ashes on their forehead today*" event where Christians can publicly identify each other and feel devout for not washing the ashes off. Yet the english translation of the New International Version of the bible says Jesus pbuh said in Matthew 6:16-18, ¹⁶ "**When you fast, do not look somber as the hypocrites do, for they disfigure their faces to show others they are fasting**. *Truly I tell you, they have received their reward in full.* ¹⁷ *But <u>when you fast, put oil on your head and wash your face,</u>* ¹⁸ <u>*so that it will not be obvious to others that you are fasting, but only* **to your Father, who is unseen**</u>; *and* **your Father**, *who sees what is done in secret, will reward you.*" While Pope Gregory XIII invented the solar based Gregorian calendar system in 1582 CE. Muslims use the lunar calendar which is more accurate. The lunar calendar is 10-11 days shorter than the Gregorian and doesn't have any "leap years". 235 lunar months = 19 years in the Gregorian calendar, which is 6,940 days. According to the Gregorian calendar I was 19 years old when I embraced Islam and Gregory was my name. What you are called affects how you identify yourself. When I adopted a rap name my personality changed, when people called me by it an alter-ego developed. Even before using a rap name, in high school my personality changed when classmates would call me names like "*Father Heary*", "*Reverend Greg*" or "*Papa G*" because of my ambitions to be a priest and obnoxious evangelizing. Also when getting confirmed into the Catholic Church I got a new name. When becoming a Muslim one does not necessarily have to change their name, however mine was distinctly Christian from a distinctly bad pope. I'd compare it to having the name of Goliath, whereas that name is almost anti-religious in a sense because the famous Goliath was an enemy of the prophet David pbuh. Another important point relating to names concerns the prison system. In prison they call inmates by numbers so that they stop associating with their street names, in the hopes that by identifying as a number the inmate will start to act differently, because it's hard to change if you're always being called the same thing. Likewise when you're in trouble a teacher, parent or government official might call you Mr. (or Ms.) ___ (insert your last name) in order to get your attention, intimidate, or control your reaction and attitude. As a new Muslim I was going to be living differently trying to be a better person. If I retained my Christian name I thought it would be more difficult to make the transition from a Christian lifestyle to a Muslim lifestyle. After changing my name on facebook the negative comments multiplied and people would post insulting things with foul language saying how they don't remember becoming friends with a_____ (expletives). One person who made such a comment, saying he didn't remember becoming "friends" with me, had actually friend requested me to begin with. The profile picture showed it was me and that my rapper name posted the Islamic declaration of faith, but it was almost as though they didn't want to come to grips with the Christian rapper/priest in training leaving Christianity and embracing Islam. Every time I logged on I'd have less and less "friends" because they really didn't want to be "friends" with me now that I was Muslim. I had anticipated some blowback, but the excessive amount of antagonism I received made me realize that Islam really is the correct religion. If I had changed to any other religion in the world it would not have resulted in such a negative reaction. Now it became manifest that they were living their life according to Satan's dictations, even from a Christian point of view most of them were entirely corrupted sinners. The fact that they all simultaneously banded together against Islam was amazing to see, because there was no other thing that could have unified them, none of these people had much in common except for their anti-Muslim sentiment. It became clear that none of these people were ever really "friends" and that I never intended to be on facebook for "friends", I wanted fans. Since I was no longer rapping and my "friend count" was declining by the hour, after a week I decided to close my account. I posted a message announcing the decision to close my account in 7 days and said that if anyone wanted to stay in touch then they could message me before then in order to get my contact information. Out of all those hundreds of "friends" only 1 person wanted to stay in touch. On facebook "friend" is just a word that means nothing more than another number to boost the "friend" count. If they are only your "friend" on facebook, your phonebook or at any other strictly social environment/network, then that means they probably aren't really your friend. After closing my facebook account, my life immediately improved. I was no longer inundated with the drama of other people and distracted by their useless updates and posts. Neither did I feel pressured to post about myself having to always think of something clever or interesting to share publicly. By not having everything I said or did be rated and commented on by people, I stopped caring whether people "liked" what I said or did and was able to focus on getting "likes" from the Creator of the universe. Without being on a social network I had privacy once more. By deleting my virtual life my real life became enjoyable. Sadly people treat facebook as if it were a book of divine revelation.

  Another book people treat as though it were divine revelation is "the dictionary", of which there are many. You might have noticed in this book that I have invented a few words, authors can do that you know, that's what the authors of the dictionaries do. They put out a book saying X is a word and this is how you spell it and this what it means. Yet they are human beings just writing a book about words based on human opinions. Many didn't agree with the first dictionary and decided to make their own to tell the world what the words really were, how they're really spelled and what they really mean. The funny thing is that when people get into a dispute over words they'll say "*Ok let's look it up in the dictionary!*" Which again is ignoring the fact that there are many dictionaries all of which have different words and different meaning and spellings for the same words. Regardless typically whenever a word is "*looked up in the dictionary*" there's nothing left to say. I mean that's "*the dictionary!*" Do you know who wrote the dictionary? Was it God? Was it a prophet? Was it the devil? No, it was just some person or some people. Furthermore the dictionary is based on democracy. Do you know what happens if you don't believe in the dictionary? Seriously, what happens if someone says "*I do not believe in the dictionary!*" Will they burn in hell forever? Will they be prohibited from paradise? If not then why do people care so much about the dictionary? Shamefully some give the dictionaries more esteem than they do divine revelation. You can write your own dictionary and it's exactly the same as "the dictionary", it would just happen to be the dictionary you wrote. You can even do this on the spot, just write a word, define it and then show and explain what you just wrote is what "the dictionary says" and insist that you have the same amount of authority to write a dictionary as the authors of other dictionaries. If someone complains just tell them that your dictionary is just as valid, even if it has less words or eloquence or fame. Why should you accept their dictionary as being true or authoritative when they don't accept the dictionary you wrote? Dictionaries can be racist and dictionaries can be sexist. Most importantly the dictionary not only can be but sometimes is blatantly wrong. Books known as dictionaries are just one opinion of what words mean and the dictionaries are published as a means of mental control. To control a language of a people is to control that people and the dictionaries are used as tools to control what is and isn't a word and what those words do and do not mean. For example if you look up a word of disbelief in the dictionary and a "swear word" which is worse according to the dictionary? God will say a word of disbelief can put you in eternal hellfire while a vulgarity is just sinful. Yet the dictionary doesn't teach us that but trains us to view words in a different manner than God desires. All dictionaries are religious books. Just look up the word God in a dictionary, they define God, that's theology not objectivity. Likewise if you look up Muslim, Hindu, Jew, Christian nobody gets defined as a disbeliever and if you live life based on a dictionary's definition of belief in God or a dictionary's definition of sin, good, piety, honesty, truth, success etc. you will be a evil person doomed to eternal hellfire. The dictionaries definition of heaven and hell isn't right either. While only a fool would believe in the dictionary's definition of wisdom, wealth, health, religion, history, friendshp, prophet or success. Dictionaries certainly don't do justice to the word justice. No dictionary has the right to list and define words, unless God published it. There is no separation between religion and words, every dictionary is a theological treatise. So the next time someone tells you, "*The dictionary says...*" or "*according to the dictionary...*" just say, "*Who cares? It's the dictionary! It's not divine revelation or the words of a prophet.*" Tell them you don't believe in the religion the dictionary teaches and think it's a blasphemous book which no prophets would approve of. Most dictionaries are illegitimate books of theology disguised as unbiased language books, teaching a religion via definitions. Words are too important and meaningful to be defined by men. The dictionaries linguistically enslave literate people by definition. If you believe what a dictionary says then you'll believe in any type of nonsense you read in a book. Perhaps the worst definition in any dictionary is for the word dictionary.

     At that time I hadn't attended or celebrated any family functions for years, because I was estranged. It was already routinely expected by my family not to celebrate Christmas with me, so Christmas came and went and still no one in my family knew I was Muslim. In the back of my mind Shaitan was still threatening me with homelessness if I told my parents. Therefore I continued to keep my religion a secret because I was still too materialistic, and while they didn't really follow the bible or Catholicism since both teach that death is the penalty for those who quit I figured there was a real possibility that I could become homeless if my family learned I was Muslim. Then one day outside a grocery store two women dressed like Muslims passed by. I was so surprised because I had never thought I'd seen a Muslim before, and now that I was one I felt a strong connection as though I wasn't the only one, but I didn't say anything to them. I was still dressing like a gangster and based on my appearance they probably wouldn't have believed I was a Muslim. While checking out, I heard two people who I thought knew me from school having a conversation. I think I heard one say "*I heard he became a ......*" and the other said "*well then why is he dressing like a ...*" I didn't hear exactly what they said, but I felt it applied directly to me and the way I dressed. Then it became evident that clothing has psychological power. I remembered when I began to dress in hip hop attire at the onset of 12th grade, many people stereotyped me and treated me like a gangster; eventually their treatment sunk in. I began to think like a gangster, talk like a gangster, walk like a gangster and act like a gangster. The way people treated me based upon my clothing directly influenced my attitude and behavior. Thus the thought occured to me that if I were to dress like the prophets then perhaps I would start to act like the prophets. Therefore since as a Muslim my attitude towards life changed it was only logical that my attitude towards clothing would change as well. One thing that caused this change in my view towards clothing was a joke.

Once a comedian made an observation about women wearing revealing clothes which I found insightful. The comedian explained how women say, "*just because I'm dressed this way DOES NOT make me a whore*" which he said was true and that just because women dress a certain way doesn't mean they are a certain way, but that for guys it was very confusing. He compared it to himself walking around the streets in a cop uniform, then somebody runs up and begs him to come help and protect them from criminals. The comedian said he'd reply, "*just because I'm dressed this way it DOES NOT make me a police officer*". He concluded by saying he understands that a woman dressed provocatively is not a whore, but because she is wearing the uniform of a whore misunderstandings can happen. This helped me see that it made no sense to be dressed like a thug if I was a Muslim, it would give a bad image to Islam and people might think I was still a Christian or a non-Muslim, I didn't want anyone to have any misunderstanding about who/what I was.

The rapper 2pac has become an idol in the world of hip hop, some people even believe that he isn't dead and faked his death, or will rise from the dead because of how they misinterpret his sayings out of their extreme devotion to him. One interesting thing 2pac said in an interview was, "*you understand me? and thought I was going to choose a career before I choose my ******* principles, my manhood, so I said ok cool fire me from this $100,000 movie because I ain't gonna play no gangbanger who's a Muslim. There ain't no such thang. I refuse to play parts that don't exist.*" 2pac made that statement before his death in 1996 CE, back when $100,000 was a lot of money to walk away from. Even though he wasn't a Muslim he was honest enough not to portray a Muslim gangbanger, because a gangster and a Muslim are complete opposites. Linguistically a Muslim is one who submits and surrenders themselves entirely to Allah. The phrase "Muslim gangster" is an oxymoron that has been invented by morons. It is impossible for a Muslim who submits to Allah to be a gangster. It's like saying someone is a vegetarian carnivore, a virgin adulterer or a youth elder. Someone simply cannot simultaneously be both things, such a person would be a walking contradiction. Gangster activities are contrary to how Islam teaches a human being to live. This goes back to the same principle of loving what Allah loves and hating what Allah hates. Allah hates the sins gangsters participate in and the murdering of innocents, if you don't hate those as well then you are not a complete Muslim. This principle of hating what and who Allah hates also means that Muslims must hate all gangsters too. So how could a practicing Muslim choose to be someone who they and Allah hates? It is hypocritical and difficult to be both good and bad at the same time. A "Muslim gangster" at the best would have one foot going toward heaven and one foot going towards hell, having each foot on a different road would only result in wasted time, energy and groin pain. Allah did not create time for us to waste. There are 3 types of people: one who does more good deeds today than they did yesterday, one who does more bad deeds today than they did yesterday and the one who does the same amount of good and bad deeds today as they did yesterday. The one who does more good has learned from the prior day and improved. The one who does the same hasn't learned anything from the day before and is wasting their days by not reflecting and improving. The one who does more bad today than yesterday is only digging themselves into a deeper hole and erasing their good deeds, which if they continue down that path will end up having all their good deeds erased. May Allah make us one of those who do less bad deeds and more good deeds with each day that passes. An important factor to remember regarding this Gangster vs. Muslim controversy is that Gangsterism is a religion. Yes indeed, gangsters follow the faith of Gangsterism. In the religion of Gangsterism their man-made laws are referred to as the "G-code". The "G-code" does not mean "God's code" it stands for the Gangster code of conduct and it involves such gangster themed laws of *"No snitching.", "Bros before Hoes, Gangsters over Girls, Get Riches **** *******"* and *"Life for Life"*(in perpetuity with Killers of Killers Getting Killed For Killing Killers (KKGKFKK)). I actually just made up that KKGKFKK acronym code for the killing cycle, but that's how the G-code goes; every gangster has their own unique unwritten code. Yet they all pretend it's the same for all and all the "true G's" really know what it really is. In reality the "G-code" is a myth of gangster folklore. Just as there is no honor amongst thieves there is no code amongst G's. Whereas then there is always the ignorant idiot who says *"You may have book smarts, but you don't have street smarts. I got street smarts, you wouldn't survive out there on the streets like I do/would. Because you only got book smarts."* While those people don't even know english because "smarts" is not a word and more importantly they don't have street smarts either. If they had some "book smarts" (intelligence from reading non-fiction books like this) they would learn that there is no such thing as "street smarts". This is because the G-code is a fantasy and the rules of the streets aren't written down nor agreed upon. Every single literal street has its own rules because the people on those streets have their own custom G-codes. Nobody writes their G-code down because that's a violation of most G-codes. So if by some miracle you learned one person's G-code who ruled one street, as soon as you go to another street or across the street, you got different people with different rules. Sometimes even 1 street has multiple unwritten unknown rules. Plus even if you learn the imaginary rules then they change according to circumstances and over time as different people take charge who got their own special codes too. So anyone who ever claims they got "street smarts" is certifiably street stupid and book stupid and are the most likely candidate to get harmed on the streets because their confidence makes them think they know something when they don't know nothing. In comparison the "book smart" person knows what they know and has a slight grasp on what they don't know and are smart enough to know they don't know the many G-codes the various thugs follow. Thereby because they know they are ignorant they are cautious and safe because of their caution, while the "street smart" sassmouth becomes a victim real quick because gangsters love targeting "street smart" people and have respect for "book smart" people so they leave the "book smart" people alone unless they present themselves as unrespectable wannabe book smart people. Whereas if any gangster breaks a tenant of the "G-code" they get punished accordingly depending on the infraction they commit and the interpretation of "G-code" by the gangsters who are to enforce it. All too frequently the punishments for a gangster who breaks the "G-code" of the religion of Gangsterism can be fatal. However the "G-code" is NOT Shariah nor is it compliant with Allah's code of conduct which he ordained for mankind and Muslims alike. This "G-code" is in direct opposition and conflict with the code of conduct Muhammad pbuh taught Muslims to believe in, live by and preach to others. So any gangster or wannabe gangster who believes in, lives by, preaches and dies by the "G-code" is going to be in the hellfire forever because they would have died upon the false man-made (or rather Gangster made, because gangsters aren't even men) religion of Gangsterism. On top of that the religion of Gangsterism ain't even fun or enjoyable. (Yeah gangsters use the word ain't as part of their dialect, but dialects don't make one a gangster according to most G-codes. Although according to religions that are not Gangsterism, an individual's linguistic mannerism, vocabulary and etiquette is a strong indication of one's religion.) I even made a song called the "G-code Curse" describing how it felt while following what I thought was "THE G-code" when I thought "MY G-code" was the true and only G-code, as all gangsters and gangster wannabes believe and claim. I wasn't even a legitimate gangster though, I was a wannabe gangster and it sucked. So for the real gangsters it really sucks. Everyone involved with the religion of Gangsterism knows this, but the rules of most "G-codes" of Gangsterism dictates members never show it. Or at least the "real gangsters" never show or tell it, unless they are a musician then it's allowed to admit the pain. The only "real gangster" is the devil, everyone else is faking. "Gangsters" are the greatest actors in the world and they know it. Then when/if you call them out, most G-codes dictate that they have to do a violent action in retaliation to keep up the performance for the public and themselves. Thus most gangster violence is actually religious violence so that the gangster is not seen as tolerant of blasphemers, since most G-codes say that controlling one's anger when insulted is "not gangster" unless it's only done momentarily as part of a gangsterish revenge plot. Most of the G-codes do not permit the gangster to ever forgive another for any offense, real or imagined, or perceived as such by the public. Obviously all the G-codes have commandments that the prophets of God would not approve of. Why then are most "gangsters" religious? For the same reason most of the religious people are religious. All the false religions have commandments and teach things which the prophets of God hate which they would refute and denounce. So why do people think the gangsters of Gangsterism shouldn't be religious when other members of false faiths are? Is it because it's less popular and less easy to refute and denounce the other false faiths? Fundamentally the man-made religion of Gangsterism is exactly the same as all false religions in that they have man-made beliefs and rules. The main difference is that adherents of Gangsterism admit that their religion and G-code doesn't come from God, they are frequenty unashamed to be sinful and they do many things which governments may decree to be illegal. So essentially the special feature of Gangsterism is that it admits it's a false faith that has a negative impact on its practitioners and society at large. Now if only the rest of the false religions would do the same the world would be a better place. The redeeming quality of Gangsterism is it's honesty. Gangsters are basically an evolved more glorified version of pirates. Nevertheless the famous self-proclaimed gangster 2pac himself told the world that there are no Muslim gangbangers. In summary Islam says Muslims can't be gangsters and the "gangsters" say that gangsters can't be Muslim. In plain terms, Islam is a religion and Gangsterism is a different religion, and Muslims and Gangsters are enemies to each other who vehemently hate each other. There has never been a truce between the two groups and there never will be. Thus I learned that if I want to be a Muslim it would not befit me to dress like a gangster. Whereas even the "gangsters" know that your religious code determines your dress code and people on the same team dress the same so as to clearly distinguish oneself apart from one's enemies who follow a different code of conduct. The Islamic dresscode not only teaches the Muslim to be modest but also to distinguish themselves from non-Muslims so that everyone can tell they are a Muslim just by looking at them. Islamically if someone (Muslim or non-Muslim) can't tell you are a Muslim just by looking at you then that Muslim isn't fulfilling the Islamic dress code. Also your behavior is influenced by the way you dress because people treat you according to your clothes. The woman who dresses promiscuously is more likely to do promiscuous deeds because of the reaction her clothes will cause others to have and people will treat her based on how she dresses, thereby creating more opportunities for promiscuity and a flirtatious environment. Allah has differentiated humans from every type of animal by giving them fur, feathers, scales, hair, wool, shells etc while giving us clothing and the innate shame so that we desire clothing to cover ourselves. Modesty and shame is what separates us from the animals who wear no clothes. Clothing is a test to see if we will be grateful and whether we will wear the appropriate clothes when we are given so many various types to choose from. Unfortunately many people fail this test and wear clothing which is so revealing that even animals would be embarrassed to wear it. What does it say about a person if an animal with no clothes is better able to cover their body from predatory eyes than humans? It means such people are extremely poor, either financially or morally. People say not to judge a book by its cover but it's impossible not to, just take a dictionary, a diary, a Bible or a Quran as an example. If you see covers of books with those titles, those are just covers, inside the covers there could be an entirely different thing than what's advertised on the cover. The same applies to pornographic magazines, if someone picked up such a magazine in public and started reading it and was asked "*What in the world are you doing?*" Couldn't they just say, "*Hey don't judge a book by its cover. Don't be so shallow, it's what's on the inside that counts. It doesn't matter what cover the stuff on the inside covers itself with. Does it?*" Incidentally you judged this book by its cover despite the popularity of the saying. Thus generally speaking everyone knows it's a good policy to judge a book by its cover. There are exceptions to the rule, but typically bad people have bad covers, or as the case is today immodest or arrogant covers. At the very least the cover or apparant appearance indicates what is on the inside, it's extremely rare for it to be the complete opposite. The saintly woman doesn't dress like a stripper on the outside. While the pious man doesn't dress like a pimp on the outside. One dresses for the occasion. When hunters go outside to hunt, they wear their hunting gear. When you go outside you must consider what exactly are you hunting after dressed the way you are? Are you hunting for heaven or something else? Also remember many other creatures are hunting you. When they approach you they might be trying to poach you. Watch out because Satan will whisper to people while they watch you. Don't help Satan use you as a temptation to get someone to sin and disobey your God. If you want to be God's friend then you should dress the part. If you are a believer then people should know it just by looking at you. This too is another point many misunderstand, they'll think if their religion is X they should dress how their coreligionists dress, hence some Muslims will look at Arabs see a red and white checkered scarf and think that's Islamic. Yet where do we get religious fashions from? From prophets and no prophet ever wore a red/white checkered scarf or turban. Do you know the origin of the red/white scarf? A Saudi from Saudi Arabia told me how when the British oil drillers came to drill oil they would eat lunch on a red/white checkered picnic cloth. The Saudis saw that, thought it looked unique and exotic so they tied it around their head and started a trend that spread throughout the middle east. Yet this silly red/white checkered scarf is in reality a British picnic cloth. The British sarcastically assured the Saudis they looked cool wearing their picnic cloth, thinking it was hilarious, since those Saudis who started wearing it got rich from the oil drilling it became fashionable amongst Arabs because *"that's what the rich wear"*. Such a pattern is disgraceful to wear when you think about it, and it's ironic when you consider the history of the crusaders in the middle east using red and white as their color scheme. Some Muslims today may wear this British Picnic cloth color using such fabrics for headwear but it is a very silly unislamic garb. Some Muslims even dress in both the red/white scarf and a necktie but just because some Muslims wear that crazy costume it is not the uniform of a slave of God. So that's where when I'm stressing you follow a religious dresscode that God likes, don't look at the modern religious folk, look to the prophets and their companions for fashion advice. Remember God gives you credit for doing good deeds if you dress modestly the way God likes to see. Since you have to wear clothes anyways, you might as well get good deeds for doing so. By now you should know that your Creator is watching you closely at all times. So how would you answer your God if he asked, **"What are you wearing? Why?"**

| Which one of these two women is oppressed? ||
Eve	Mary
Not allowed to work and forced to be poor.	Allowed to work and can become wealthy.
Cannot live with family and has limits placed on when she can visit them and for how long.	Lives with family as long as she wants, if she moves out she can return to live with them whenever and stay as long as she wants and can never get evicted.
Cannot inherit anything from any family members.	Automatically inherits from family including her offspring and siblings.
Is forbidden to get married or have children.	Is encouraged to get married and have a family. If she does get married she is entitled to pick the price of her dowry.
Forced to live off of charity and spend the little she gets from donations on others.	Husband or guardian is obligated to pay for all her expenses and she doesn't have to pay for any of her expenses or her children's.
No choice in where she lives, she is assigned. She lives with other women in similar poverty, whether she likes or hates them. Her family cannot live with her under any circumstances. Can be reassigned against her will.	Lives with her family or husband and children. Her family can move in and live with her. When she is old her children are obligated to take care of her and let her live with them if she so desires.
Dresses modestly like Mary everywhere she is, in public and private. She cannot dress fashionably or display her beauty for anyone at anytime at any place. Only has 1 look. Has a fictional husband which she shares with millions of others like her.	Dresses modestly in public, but at home with family she dresses fashionably. To her husband she is literally the most beautiful woman he's ever seen and he is protective that others may pester, or see her.

In the Left hand Column is a Catholic nun named Eve, in the right hand column is a Muslim woman named Mary. Now honestly which one of these two religious women sounds oppressed to you? When Muhammad pbuh taught Islam in 7th century Arabia the pagan, Jew and Christian male society freaked out because of all the rights Islam gave women and many men still freak out and say Islam gives women too many rights. Sadly some "Muslim" men even purposely move to countries in the West because they can legally get away with financially oppressing women in the West. What western non-Muslims don't understand is that many women basically run the show in Islamic countries behind the scenes, except that their bodies aren't for show. While in the West the women aren't running any shows and their bodies are on show at all times whether they like it or not. That's why the Niqab and Hijab are such a threat to Western countries because visually Muslim women are saying: "*I don't want any of you perverts looking at my body! You can't look at my body even if you try to, I won't let you! You can't see me and you can't touch me!*" Seriously in countries like France where they banned the niqab, the Muslim men sat at home like cowards while Muslim women went out in the streets in France to protest that according to Islam legally men have absolutely no right to see their bodies and they are going to cover themselves whether the perverted Frenchmen or French government likes it or not. Today despite the so-called "freedoms of the West" the Muslim women in France have to pay a hefty fine to cover their bodies in public, principally France tells the Muslim women we give you the freedom to dress like a slut and show us your body parts but if you don't want us to ogle you and desire modesty then you have to pay a fine. This was made a law in France during 2010 CE and in 2014 CE it was disputed in the European Court for Human Rights as being a violation of human rights, but it was upheld because apparently France can legally force women to undress themselves and show their bodies against their will in order to have a common communal culture. This fee is currently "up to" 150 Euros. Meaning everytime a Muslim woman in France leaves her home she is likely going to pay 150 Euros if a police or government official sees her or she gets reported, because of how she chooses to dress. Yet people have the nerve to say women in the West are liberated and Muslim women are oppressed in Islamic countries? Tell me if everytime you left your house you had to pay 150 Euros to the government would you feel liberated or oppressed? But hey that's democracy, what else can be expected? It's just the hypocrisy of Western false advertising and the ignorantly arrogant superiority complex. Whereas Islamic countries don't say people can dress as they like, there is a minimum amount of clothing to be worn in public for the sake of modesty. Surely everyone would agree a country has a right to make a legal minimum amount of clothing to be required in public. However in Democratic countries like France, because democracy gives power to the perverts they say there is a maximum amount one can wear and if you wear too much or dress "too modestly" you are breaking the law. Islamic countries make immodesty illegal, while the unislamic countries make modesty illegal. Yet Muslim women in France voluntarily choose to pay this fine for Islamic modesty with their own money because their Muslim male family members pay for all their needs. Just think that if pornstars are the worst of women because they show the most in public then what would that make Muslim women who show the least in public? Certainly perverts have been telling B-rated lies, lying about the definition of "liberation". One difference between the Muslim view towards women and the non-Muslim view is that non-Muslims view women as stones which are common and can be seen and touched by anybody. Muslims view women like precious gemstones that are priceless and rare which should be cherished, treasured and protected; not flaunted in public because the stuff that is truly beautiful and valued in life is that which is kept private. No one shows their treasures to the world if they really think they are treasures. It's a true shame that many non-Muslims think only a woman's private parts are worth keeping private. Islam teaches that a woman's beauty and value is in more than her private parts, it is because of this priceless value a Muslim woman has that more of her is kept private. Whereas the Western woman thinks of herself as a free woman, not realizing that free means cheap and free is not priceless. To be a free woman means she's not precious. For instance there's lots of free stones laying around, but I've yet to find a "free diamond". Likewise a free wife is not a loyal wife and a "free mother" is irresponsible and neglectful. The worst things in life are free, such as disease, insanity, sorrow, injury and poverty. To be a free woman means that they don't think they are of value, that's why "free women" no longer get a dowry paid to them as women used to get. Do you know why the niqab is really banned in some Western countries? It's because when a Muslim woman covers her face in public she is telling everyone that she is not equal to other women. The perverts in parliaments want to place their peepers on all people and the Muslim woman by dressing modestly is saying, "*No, you can't look at me like you do other women because all women are NOT equal.*" So based on the principle there is opposition because if you can't see all the women then clearly it means Muslim women are different. This is why it will not stop at banning niqab, the hijab will be banned next and it's already getting banned in schools and workplaces throughout the world. Meanwhile the ban on the burqa has expanded to other nations such as Belgium in 2011, Chad in 2015 as well as some places in Cameroon, Niger, the Congo, and Switzerland. Recently France banned the "burkini" which is a female swimsuit Muslim women wore at beaches that covers all but the face, hands and feet. Basically the Burkini is a one piece swimsuit that reaches the ankles and covers the hair. Yet France was outraged that women choose to wear such a modest bathing suit on public beaches. The former french president Nicolas Sarkosy called it a "provocation". The French then made the burkini one piece female swimsuit illegal to wear on beaches. They essentially stated how if women are swimming then they have to show lots of skin if they want to swim in French waters or be on French beaches. A female commentator supporting a similar ban on the burkini in Britain even wrote, "*I'm afraid the fact that a woman may "choose" to wear a burkini doesn't mean that her "choice" must always be respected. Not if it ends up intimidating other Muslim women into feeling ashamed for exposing their own flesh, making integration harder. It's not what the burkini is, but the poisionous ideaology it represents.*" Then after bashing the Islamic teachings of female modesty they ended their article saying "*Burkinis? We shall fight them on the beaches. We shall defend our bikinis. We shall never surrender the rights men and women died for.*" Which if you actually analyze it, the female is saying they will fight peaceful modest Muslim women who want to wear a 1-piece swimsuit because allegedly "*men and women <u>died for</u>*" the "<u>*rights*</u>" to wear a bikini. However if you notice the way she links "defend our bikinis", with " *never surrender the rights men and women died for*" they actually mean that the bikini is obligatory and that by Muslim women not wearing a bikini on beaches, but a burkini, that somehow violates the "rights" people "died for". The anti-burkini female actually implies people died so that bikinis could be obligatory. And she's a "*free liberated educated journalist*"? All I'll say is that with intelligence like that it's no wonder she is willing to "*fight*" to "*defend our bikinis*" since they are obviously very important in her life. Personally I don't like the idea of the burkini and think it is too tight and that modern beaches aren't really family friendly places with the way most people on public beaches dress. Yet why would non-Muslims be so offended and provoked by a burkini which if you actually get technical violates the female islamic dress code, because it is too tight and reveals too much of the shape of the body. So the burkini isn't even something Muslim women can wear in public yet non-Muslims are willing to literally fight over this unislamic less revealing alternative swimwear? Why? Well they explicitly explained the reason why, it's because of "*the poisonous ideaology it represents*". What is that ideology? Women being modest, oh no not that, they'll say it's the "oppression of women" but how are women oppressed if they are the ones choosing it and islam even prohibits the thing? How does Islam get blamed for sinful unislamic swimwear that some Muslim women wear? It is because all these issues people have with the Muslim dresscode is due to it's conflict with the religious freemason/humanist doctrine of equality. Muslim women say that strange men don't have the right to look at them nor do non-Muslim women and by dressing differently they are saying to the world they are different, and people know that Muslim women are different and are not equal to non-Muslim women because they can visually see there is a difference between them. If one woman's hair, face and body can be drooled over and another woman's hair, face and body can't then perverts do not have equal opportunity to drool and sexually fantasize. Thus perverts want to see all women equally and immodest females don't like that other women get spared from the perverts gazes because it exposes them as immodest in comparison. Thus Muslim women make non-Muslim women feel subconsciously shameful about dressing immodestly since the modesty level of the Muslim women is not equal to their own, but higher. Essentially the nudists are offended that other people wear clothes so they want the clothes wearers to wear less clothes so the nudists don't feel weird or shameful for being nudists. Rather than put more clothes on themselves they want others to take off their clothes and they demand this declothing in the name of "women's rights" and "freedom of choice" telling lies saying that Muslim women are brainwashed. Yet truly consider the conflict. One woman wants to cover herself in public and the other wants to wear a bikini in public and wants all other women to wear a bikini as well. Of the two which do you honestly think is brainwashed, the one choosing a bikini or the one choosing a burka? Since they claim the brainwashed women are brainwashed by male sexists, lets consider which female choice is more likely to be due to male brainwashing? Is the woman who doesn't let any guys see what she looks like brainwashed by men? Or is the woman who wears bikinis, will fight on behalf of bikinis, thinks people died so she could wear a bikini and wants all woman to be forced to wear bikinis possibly brainwashed by perverted guys? Personally I think the bikini girl is brainwashed by the guys rather than the burka girl. I almost think a girl has to be brainwashed to be comfortable wearing a bikini in public. I sure wouldn't feel comfortable wearing such an outfit in public. Of the two I think I could handle a burka without getting brainwashed, but never a bikini. At the very least such females are not equal in their beliefs, esteem or appearance. Kids recognize this in school too and internalize the idea that everyone is not equal because Muslim women have privacy from perverts eyes, modesty and genuine respect from people that's not based on sex appeal while all of the other non-Muslim females don't. So banning the niqab and hijab actually violates the personal privacy of Muslim women and is a severe form of oppression. Just imagine if a government made a law saying that you have to wear less clothes than you feel comfortable wearing and you have to let everyone see parts of you that you don't want them to see. Because that is what the "liberal laws" of western countries actually say and some even say *"it's a sacred right paid for with blood that you must wear less than you want to or feel comfortable wearing"*. And they confidently say that if you disagree with such idiocy then you are the one who is "an extremely evil sexist". Then they get it legally declared as a fact because of democracy where the majority opinion can proclaim that the stupid anti-modest insanity is a "self-evident truth" and "right". Aside from Western religious principles, economics also plays a major role in this oppression. Just ask a western non-Muslim girl how much money she spends on make-up. She might even get insulted, because if she says how much then the large amount might make her sound or feel ugly. Now if women are covering up in public they aren't buying or using as much makeup, so the entire makeup industry suffers. Even the shampoo and hair stylist industries suffer since women who don't wear hijab tend to spend thousands of dollars on their hair every year, even though people pretend hair has nothing to do with sexual appeal. As a result all those taxes the governments collect from cosmetics being made and sold also evaporate. So for a Muslim woman to cover her face it actually costs western governments tax revenue they would've gotten from makeup and shampoo sales, the same concept applies if they wear hijab to only cover their hair without covering their face. This is why it will not stop at banning the burqa or the niqab or even the liberal hijab. Nicolas Sarkosy, president of France from 2007-2012 CE, made it clear after he left office the plans which the French government has for Muslim women in the future saying: *"We don't want any women with headscarves in France"*. So even though today they may play games and say *"it's only the face-veil we banned for security reasons"* those are words of liars, they don't want Muslim women dressing Islamically and they will eventually try to make it illegal for any to dress in a way that is modest or appears to be Islamic. Governments want to collect the income taxes and sales taxes from females buying immodest accessories. Because let's face it, if a Muslim woman were to take off her burka and show her face and hair then what? She didn't wear makeup under the burka and all the other women wear makeup in public so is the Muslim woman just supposed to take off her burka or niqab and then be the only woman in the city who doesn't spend exorbitant amounts of time and money to look pretty in public? How would that Muslim woman feel if she was forced to go about in public and be the only girl without makeup and cosmetics plastered over herself? Do you think she will feel proud and confident or do you think she will be disrespected for looking "real" as compared to all the fake females made up with fictional appearances due to makeup? What is she to do? Deal with looking real in a society of fake female looks, or give in to the sex appeal trend and spend spend spend to look sexy? That is what non-Muslim girls do right? Spend Spend Spend to look sexy. Or am I missing a few "spends" because it never ends? Which is really oppression, the Muslim woman covering herself or being disrespected for looking real unless she pays to look fake? In western countries women don't have the right to respect for looking real in public. Yet even if all women abandoned the fashion industry and looked real in public, still all women don't look equal so the sex appeal of real will still cause biased unfair treatment by men and other women. Thus the burka, niqab and hijab when you really analyze it is the true way for all women to be treated equal in the public setting. The problem is some women don't want to be equal in public but wanted to be treated special for looking pretty and for faking their looks to look "pretty". Women who's only attractive quality is their body don't want to live in a world where physical appearance doesn't influence treatment. Thus they preach equality but really mean inequality. Afterall how can women be considered equal in unislamic socities without wearing islamic dress if all the cosmetics can not be used by all women? If a rich woman can buy better makeup than a poor woman then that is not equality because then looks are determined by money, so instead of it being random favoritism based on real looks we get favoritism based on rich girls paying more to look pretty than other girls. So this whole fashion industry and immodest fashion sense is really just a way for rich girls to become viewed as physically prettier than poor girls even though they aren't. That's why the fashion revolution is truthful when it claims to be fueled by females, it was fueled by rich ugly females who wanted to be known as prettier than all the poor pretty girls. It's like all those famous fantasy stories where a rich queen or a witch wants to destroy and harm the pretty poor girl out of envy for her looks. In the folktales they use magic, while in the real world they use makeup and made the fashion industry to suck pretty girls into a game they will lose to the ugly rich girls since magic could've always been used by the poor girls too, but money is the one area where rich girls knew they couldn't lose the beauty contest. That's the real reason why the cosmetics and female fashion industry exist, to make rich girls feel and get treated better than poor girls. True modesty means that you don't spend money to look pretty, unislamic governments and unislamic economies hate such a fashion policy. Selling beauty is a booming business but Islam teaches that beauty and attraction isn't sold or something that can be allowed to influence public interactions/reputations. God has made all women beautiful by nature, some people simply try to profit by getting other people to disobey the prophets and make-up a satanic self-esteem that God didn't make all women beautiful. If you believe God made a woman then she don't need any upgrades, you will find her beautiful because God himself made her to look like that. If you love God then you love his work, make-up just messes it up. There is no such thing as a girl putting make-up on her face, in reality she just puts stuff on to mess-up her face God made. Some people lie to your face, while females who wear makeup lie about their face to their own face as well as everyone else's eyes. You can easily spot a female liar today because her face is a lie that she made-up with makeup. At least with most guys you have to wait for them to speak to get hit with their lies, but with immodest females their very face is falsehood. Such girls are literally the face of falsehood and falsehood is never pretty. Also you can't trust a female who puts make-up on her face, because she doesn't want you to see the truth and puts on a disguise to fool you via cosmetics. If a girl lies about what her face looks like then for certain she will lie about her thoughts and feelings. Girls who wear makeup are lying to every single person who sees them, that's a lot of lies and a lot of sins for lying for the sake of what? Good guys don't like liars so such girls only attract guys who lie and love lies. Such females build their relationships on visible lies and maintain them with lies and then call that "love" if the lies of both sides are believed. For females who use makeup, every day is like Halloween for them because every day they have to wear a mask of fashion in order to get a certain treatment which they are tricked into desiring. I don't even refer to such females as women because women don't makeup lies about their face. Whereas it's a scientific fact that those chemicals actually cause pre-mature aging and damage the face as well as contributing to deteriorating health in old age. So the modern "make-up" isn't even safe to use in the long term big picture. The cosmetics are synthetically designed to make one uglier, so people buy more in the future just like a drug addict needs more and more to try to get back to normal. If you put on $50 worth of make-up today then tomorrow you will likely need $100 worth of make-up to look half as good as you did yesterday without any make-up. Cosmetics are like drugs for the appearance of the body, they have similar side-effects on a person's personality and body too. Even if one uses "organic" makeup, just because it's organic doesn't mean it belongs on your face; feces is organic too. Whether a human's makeup and cosmetics are organic or synthetic they are a big nasty slap in God's face and a blatant criticism and rejection of the face which God made for you. Instead of using makeup or being fashionable, the truly beautiful woman is she who spends her wealth in charity for God's sake, even pawning her jewelry to help the needy. Honestly there is nothing more beautiful than a woman who spends in charity instead of on cosmetics. While the one who spends on cosmetics instead of in charity is a very ugly woman indeed, and is stupid and selfish as well; realistically such a vain woman is not even wife material let alone mother material. The woman who puts on make-up is the type you keep away from your kids telling them she puts on a mask of makeup to attract the devils and perverts. Personally I would not even marry a woman who wears makeup, and if my theoretical wife were to ever wear makeup, even just to beautify herself for her husband, I'd consider that as a potential reason for divorce. Whereas any man in this day and age who lets their wife wear makeup, even if it's just for their own viewing in private, then I don't even consider them to be a man. Since it would seem preposterous if a man were to put on makeup to beautify themselves for their wife, especially if a wife asked their husband to do so, then to me it seems equally ridiculous for a woman to wear make-up; unless there were some type of physical harm that disfigured her face which she wanted to disguise. Yet personally I don't consider a woman and makeup to be compatible in this day and age when people are starving and in dire need, a true pious believing woman wouldn't dare to spend on beauty when there is such a need for charity. Real women always choose charity over beauty. Whereas because they are such good people their husband's love their mannerisms, character and morals. Yet because other girls are such bad people they really need to look pretty, because most everything about their manners, character, lifestyle, attitude(bratittude) and morals is putrid and repulsing. Beauty comes from the inside and shines out, if you think you aren't beautiful then fix your spiritual condition and the external condition will follow naturally automatically. But if you try improving the external then you may end up harming the internal spirit which is eternal. Telling a female she looks pretty or beautiful with makeup on is akin to telling someone wearing a mask that they look beautiful, it's truly an insult not a compliment. You can't compliment somebody who wears makeup because to do so is to compliment their mask that hides their true beauty. While even IF you don't find your spouse "beautiful" or "sexy" then do you know what the solution is to fix that? Do you drink lots of alcohol and do drugs like the musicians say to do? No that stuff is sinful and poisonous. Yet most know that poison can make ugly people attractive. So if sinful poisons can make evil ugly people physically and emotionally attractive enough to motivate people to have sinful illegal sex with them, then God can make lawful good spouses much more attractive so spouses are better able to enjoy the good deed of marital intimacy. Think about it. There are sinful things to do to make illegal sinful sex easier or more enjoyable, so there surely must be good deeds to do to make lawful good sex easier and more enjoyable. But what can you do and how much does it cost? First you must be sincere. Next you ask God to help you find your spouse to be more attractive, and then God makes them more attractive to you without even changing their appearance; God will just change and increase your attraction you don't need to buy something from Satan that harms the body and decrease one's esteem. Just ask God to make your spouse view you with attraction or to make your spouse look better in your sight, it's free and God does a much better job than makeup AND you get rewarding for asking God since that is a type of worship. Yes God will reward you for asking him to make your spouse seem more pretty to you, but what eternal divine reward will cosmetics bring you? In regards to every other human's body, God has made it so you better get his permission before you look at it, touch it or talk to it. All of God's creatures get a dresscode, all those who obey it are truly beautiful and all who violate it are ugly by default.

  Near Christmas time I noticed nativity scenes in people's yards. One thing that I hadn't noticed as a Christian was how Mary the mother of Jesus pbuh would be depicted wearing hijab dressed like a Muslim woman. This is further proof that Jesus pbuh was Muslim and Islam was the religion of all the prophets pbut. No Christian is intentionally dressing their statue of Mary up as a Muslim; they know that the hijab is what she wore. No matter what people say they cannot hide the fact that Mary was a Muslim and dressed like a Muslim, they can say whatever they want but actions speak louder than words. In the time of Mary very few women dressed as modestly as she did. The women of the roman empire were known to wear less clothes than some women do today. In Palestine it can get awfully hot and there was no air conditioning back then to cool off. It was unfashionable and uncomfortable to dress as Mary did, but the fires of hell are much hotter and knowing this she dressed for success in the hereafter. One can easily imagine someone asking Mary why she wore so much clothing and covered her hair when the majority of women living then and there didn't, but she wasn't dressing to please people or even herself, she dressed to please her Creator. When the angel Gabriel announced to Mary she was to give birth to the prophet Jesus pbuh she replied: *"How shall I have a son, seeing that no man has touched me, and I am not unchaste?"* In comparison many women living today would say "How when I use contraceptives?" or "But I haven't had sex!" Mary(may Allah be pleased with her) had not even had a man so much as touch her, she was that concerned with maintaining her chastity. How many women can say the same today? Mary's father had died before she was born and her mother died shortly after giving birth, Mary had been placed under the guardianship of the prophet Zachariah pbuh. It is entirely plausible that literally no man had ever laid a finger on her body. She wasn't giving hugs or kisses, shaking hands with guys, or getting spanked on the butt. Imagine a woman so pious that no male had ever touched her; that was Mary. Many people today would quickly call her an extremist, radical, fanatic or her behavior "crazy". But God blessed and honored her because of it. The level of piety Mary had is beyond comparison. According to Islam, Mary is the best woman of all time. Not only did she give birth to Jesus pbuh miraculously but her birth itself was miraculous. The 19th chapter of the Quran is titled after Mary the mother of Jesus pbuh. A whole chapter named after her! No bible gives her such an honor. While Mary's father Imran (Jesus' grandfather) has the 3rd chapter of the Quran named after him. Mary is even mentioned more in the Quran than she is in the bible, in the bible she is mentioned 18 times total (17 times total in Matthew, Mark, and Luke only once in the next 24 books) in the Quran she is mentioned 31 times. The mother of Muhammad pbuh is not mentioned once in the Quran, so any claims that Muhammad pbuh made the Quran make no sense in light of this. Many people today says it's what's on the inside that counts and as long as their heart is good it doesn't matter what they wear. Well Mary had the best heart of all females and she wore modest clothing and didn't fraternize with unrelated men. Women who dress less modest and say that it's what's on the inside that counts are insinuating that they are better than Mary the mother of Jesus pbuh, claiming that their hearts are better than Mary's. Subconsciously that is the case they make, that because they think they have such good hearts they don't have to dress modest, but because Mary the mother of Jesus pbuh didn't have as good a heart as they do she had to dress modest. This is clearly a slander by women against Mary who simply want to wear what Satan wants them to wear and will make any excuse they can to justify wearing less and less in a more provocative fashion. Sadly many non-Muslim women are naked while being clothed and from a guy's perspective they are showing their private parts despite having cloth on them, in that you can see their figures and basically know what they look like naked except you just don't know the skin color of their parts under their clothes. Sadly when it comes to most non-Muslim women the only thing a guy need imagine is the skin color, but in reality they already know the skin color. So her clothes aren't really doing the job, just wearing cloth on your skin doesn't mean you are wearing clothing. Clothing is to conceal your figure, not highlight it or show it's shapes off. Sometimes as a concerned human I feel like telling girls that they should go home and put some clothes on, then if one were to say she has clothes on covering her body I'd say, *"Well your clothes need some clothing."* Realistically if women looked at themselves in the mirror every morning and said that: *"God created me like this and I am very beautiful so much so that Satan tempts men with my beauty in ways I can't imagine."* they might think twice before putting chemicals on their face, nails, lips, hair and so forth. Guys and girls don't understand the effect they can have on the other gender, some guy can be pious thinking about God and have a great relationship with God then all of a sudden he sees some pretty girl and he can't stop thinking about her for the rest of his life and it ruins his relationship with God, his family, friends, work, marriage and afterlife as a result. Especially in regards to Muslim sisters who follow the weak modern Western opinion, that hijab doesn't require their face to be covered. This is a new idea and rather than debate it I will just speak from personal experience as a Muslim man. To a Muslim man the most beautiful part of a Muslim woman is her forehead because that is the part she prostrates with for the sake of God a minimum of 34 times a day (in the 5 daily prayers). So when the Muslim women go around covering the hair and most else but leaving the face exposed lots of Muslim men are still seeing the most attractive part of that Muslim woman. Meanwhile faces are unforgettable, you can forget what a girls butt or breasts look like, but from personal experience it's much harder to forget a girl's face. So that's where the modern hijab that shows the face can still result in lust or infatuation should a man see the girl. Maybe other guys don't find the Muslim woman's forehead or nose that touches the ground in prostration to God to be the most attractive parts, but for those who do it is torturous to see the Muslim girls in "hijab" and not niqab or burqa; because automatically Muslim men are more attracted to Muslim women because they believe/practice Islam. Thus the Muslim girl may think she is covering herself out of modesty but all the Muslim guys just see she is Muslim by her garb and they see the most beautiful parts on her. Now I'm not saying a Muslim girl should take off the hijab, because some hijab is better than none but I'm just trying to tell those sisters that while the perverted non-Muslim guys eyes might not see their beauty the Muslim guys eyes still do if her forehead and nose show. Thus Muslim girls who don't want to cover their face run the risk of ruining a Muslim guys life should he see her face. The same applies to guys that can mess up a girl's life without ever talking to her or even knowing she existed. Imagine what God would say to such people who's beauty ended up distracting people from God? Imagine if God said to you " *I used to have a great relationship with so and so but they saw you one day and ever since they haven't been able to think about me the same and our relationship has deteriorated? Why did you harm my relationship with so and so with the very beauty that I gave you?*" Satan wants people to use their God-given beauty to lead people away from God even if it's just for a second's thought. Therefore both men and women should ask themselves this question when they get dressed and before they leave the house, "*If I go out dressed like this will I be pleasing God or pleasing Satan?*" Those are the two options and if you are dressing to please people or gain attention then it is Satan who is pleased by that outfit, whether the wearer is cognizant of it or not. People dress to impress, your clothing either impresses God or disgusts him. Seriously why would anyone want to dress to impress Satan? The clothes we wear now can determine what we wear in the afterlife. The people in the hellfire will be wearing garments made of hellfire. I'd rather be sweating, or get insulted, because of my clothes in this life, than be burning because of my clothes in the next.   Likewise as a white guy if I don't dress like a Muslim most non-Muslims won't think I'm a Muslim and won't treat me like one. Whereas I'd rather be treated like a Muslim even if it results in persecution than be treated like a non-Muslim without persecution. This is because being treated like a Muslim helps me act like one and since I want to be treated like a Muslim in the afterlife then to get that treatment then I should get treated like a Muslim now as well. I may not live the part all the time but at least I can look the part. Plus Islam is something to be proud of, dressing like a Muslim on earth is a spiritual honor in both this life and moreso in the next. So dress for success, success in the afterlife.

    From a man's perspective I could not reconcile my wardrobe with the way the prophets pbut would've dressed. I decided to abandon the gangster gear and all the jewelry that contributed to my extravagant arrogance. All thanks and praises be to Allah for guiding me. By dressing less flashy my self-esteem actually improved contrary to what all the songs, advertisements and movies would have one think. Wearing modest islamic clothing increased my confidence and helped me focus on my character rather than my costume. At first I felt ridiculous but that is the whole point, it prevents you from being arrogant and makes you humble. Dressing in a fashion that pleases God brings so much more happiness to life than if everyone were to compliment the way I looked in clothes God didn't like. God does care about what we wear, he cares about everything we do and clothing is one thing that God will judge us by. Ever since the beginning clothing was a status symbol, when according to the scholar Wahb Ibn Munabah Adam pbuh and Eve had clothes made of light. Loss of their clothes signified a loss in their status/change in their relationship with God. When Adam pbuh and Eve put on clothes after their nakedness became known to them they weren't putting on clothes to "look good" they did it to please Allah. Whereas our ancestors first experience of nakedness is also a sign in that Satan ain't satisfied with having us out of paradise, he wants us to lose our clothes as well. Today you see people taking off clothes and dressing in order to please others or themselves, in a sense they are worshipping themselves or social norms/tastes instead of the Creator. Fashion determines their wardrobe instead of faith because modern fashion is important to them than their faith. Yet not only are many modern fashions distasteful, immodest and in violation of human dignity, but they are also deadly. For instance in unislamic societies the rate of malignant melanoma cancer amongst women has skyrocketed. Scientists wondered why women and why unislamic societies? After numerous studies they concluded that because unislamic women reveal more of their skin in public it means more UV rays from the sun shine on their skin which in turn causes this cancer to develop, of which women are more at risk of contracting than men because men biologically have thicker skin than women. They found that the percentage of women with this cancer has increased proportionately to the decreased amount of clothing which women wear. Meaning the less clothing women wear in public the more likely they are to get cancer and die. For instance women showing cleavage risk breast cancer and wearing a bikini is a complete medical disaster. Scientifically it's been proven that dressing sexy in public is a health hazard. So when a woman dresses like a whore horrible things happen to her. Females dressing sexy or showing skin in public is a sign of medical insanity and reveals a woman who scientifically doesn't respect her body. Dressing sexy just ain't safe for females, clothes are healthy. It was also discovered that men who grow beards are protected from skin cancer because the beard shades the man from 33% of the Sun's UV rays with a protection factor of 90-95%. Since pollution is weakening the ozone layer everyday, allowing the UV rays which shine through to be even stronger and more dangerous, the scientific medical community has concluded that the cheapest, easiest and safest solution to prevent cancer would be for women to show as little skin in public as possible and for men to grow and keep beards. On top of that, many of the medical scientists who have publicly supported this conclusion aren't even Muslims, they simply used science looking for the best solution to stop skin cancer and proved that the Islamic dresscode is the best solution. So this is where following God's dresscode and dressing the way God likes has many worldly benefits aside from the spiritual benefits, both of which we are unable to fully appreciate. May Allah help us to dress in a way that is blessed which we get rewarded for and not in attire that will be a reason for us to be punished or cursed. In the Quran Allah compares a spouse as being like a garment in intimacy and importance, thereby not only teaching us how important and close a spouse is to us but also stressing how important it is to dress correctly just as it is important to have the correct type of spouse. Always remember there are two influences designing your wardrobe, Allah and Satan. Are you dressing in preparation for paradise or are you dressing in preparation for hell? Would you want to die in the clothes you are wearing, get buried in those clothes and then be asked those three questions by the Angels in the grave wearing what you are currently wearing? If not then you are not dressed for death. If you are not even dressed for death then you are definitely not prepared for it. If you fail to plan for the afterlife then you're planning to fail.

After embracing Islam and becoming a Muslim I stopped carrying weapons with me everywhere I went. It no longer mattered what I had, if I got robbed, or killed. The only thing that is important in life is whether the Creator loves you or not, if you will go to paradise or hell, if your sins will be forgiven and how many good deeds you have to your name. Death is inevitable and cannot come any sooner or later than when Allah has decreed. Of course you can defend yourself, but it's more important to defend oneself from Satan and his minions' influences than fellow human beings. Physical weapons are useless during spiritual warfare. Rather if we're in a state where Allah loves us and wants to meet us we would not be afraid to die. Loving this worldly life and hating death is a disease possessed by the inhabitants of the hellfire, may the Creator of heaven and hell protect us from that disease and where it leads to. Instead of protecting one's life and possessions the top priority should be to please the one who made everything, regardless of what others think. Sooner or later I will die and you will die, so the time to get ready for the day we are judged is now. Today is the day to get ready, because we will be judged for what we do today, every day will be factored in, not one day in our life has been given to us to waste. The days we have to live are few and the stakes are high. Contrary to the widespread misconception being propagated throughout the world, after becoming a Muslim I no longer wanted to commit suicide. Who would have thought that Islam was the solution for stopping suicidal thoughts? A life without Islam is not worth living and that is why I was suicidal before, because if you are not worshipping the Creator correctly on a daily basis then your life is pointless. I'm a living testimony to that, I had the fame, I had the jewelry, I had the games, the music, the career and I went to church more than many Christians will ever go to church in their lives, yet all of that was joyless and worthless because it isn't what God created us for. Even though I didn't know the reason why, as a non-Muslim I knew deep inside that my life was pointless, that is why I wanted to end it because I wasn't fulfilling my purpose. I was living the Christian American Dream, but that's the point it's a dream. No matter how pleasant a dream may seem the only way someone will enjoy it is if they are unconscious. Some people may be unconscious their whole life enjoying every moment indulging in every vice, but sooner or later every one of us will be woken up by the angels Munkar and Nakir asking us those 3 questions in the grave. At the moment the angels awaken those people, who were unconscious all their life, they won't even remember one second of the pleasure they had while they were "living the Dream". Those non-Muslims who are living life thinking and feeling they don't have deep problems, have bigger problems than those who are addicts, suicidal and depressed, because their problems are so big and large they can't see them for what they are. At least the non-Muslim with "big problems" knows they have problems and can try to alleviate them with some half-measures even if they don't know Islam is the cure or accept the Islamic solutions. The non-Muslims who are "happy" living "without psychological problems" have the biggest problem of all, in that they don't know the problems they have and risk not knowing until it's too late. Honestly when I meet non-Muslims who "have problems" I respect them more and think better of them than those who "are happy and doing good" because they are either liars, insane or ignorant people going through life spiritually unconscious. From a materialistic perspective, as a Muslim I had no reason to even wake up in the morning, I had stopped listening to music, had no career, no friends of either gender, absolutely nothing on my schedule that needed to be done on any given day, except for Islamic prayers. Although because it's the correct prayers that our Creator wants from us, I had never felt better mentally, emotionally, or physically and never felt more complete in my life. Forget all the advertisements and forget what you've been told, the only thing that will make you truly happy is following the prophets of old.   The true religion is the solution to all problems, that's actually the definition of the true religion which God wants us to follow. With God's true religion, if you follow it correctly and understand God's instructions you won't have any problems, but if you are religiously blind you can't identify problems nor the true religion or most of the false faiths that cause problems. Remember problems only started happening to humans when they followed Satanic "advice" and "solutions". Meaning that when there are no sins there are no problems. Sins are the cause of all problems, having elements of faith helps you identify problems, following the true faith solves those problems and prevents problems from occuring and helps one succeed with the test of life and any/all problems that you aren't personally responsible for. The believer isn't necessarily living a life free from facing problems, because sin causes problems even if it is the sins of others or the sins of Satan. Yet the problems that are caused by Satan or other sinners never cause problems for the believer because the prophetic religion is the "problem solver". For example Satan causes problems for the angels but everyone knows that angels truly don't have problems because they don't sin. All humans sin so we all have problems but those who believe in the prophetic solution have half-solved all of their problems and need to only implement the prophetic solutions to solve them fully and prevent any and all problems from harming them in this life and the next. The fundamental problem of humanity is we don't follow the prophetic problem solvers and think we don't have problems or that something other than God or prophets can provide solutions to problems we have or face. The test of life is full of "problems" but for those who pass their test most of the "problems" are seen as opportunities to please God. Everyone in the world can agree that people having problems is a problem. God knows that and provided the cure for all problems anyone can ever possibly have, by giving us the prophetic religion. The prophet's weren't "just preachers" they were problem solvers. Their greatest miracle was being able to teach us the tools to use and how to use them for solving all of humanity's problems. Our problem is in failing to follow them. God told us what our problems are and how to solve them, we just tend to listen to Satan's "advice" or let him tutor us or get answers from Satan instead of God when taking the test of life. The common problem our species has in life is that when it comes to God we usually don't hear God or obey his advice, so we don't know the problems or implement the right solutions. God has stated and solved our problems, we just must hear and obey when we are told by God what is wrong and what is right. <u>Only God defines what problems are and what the solutions are</u>. Our problems are what God says they are and our solutions are what God says they are and we use the means God says to solve all problems on the test of life. Then God gives eternal paradise to those who pass the test of life and eternal problems for those who failed to accept God's ruling on problems and solutions.

    My family still didn't know I had become a Muslim, but my parents could definitely notice a change. In Islam parents have rights over their children and children have a duty to obey them and treat them with kindness, even if they are not Muslim. The only time a Muslim can disobey their parents is if they ask them to disobey Allah or do something that's against the religion. Some would argue that Christianity teaches the same, however if you disrespect your parents in Christianity Jesus pbuh pays the price. Whereas in Islam Jesus pbuh is not going to get me off the hook if I sinfully treat my parents badly, I will be brought to account for every wrong I do to them and under Islam you can potentially burn in hell if you treat your parents inappropriately. So Islam is very different than Christianity because no Christians think they will burn in hell if they are rude or mean to their parents so Islam really doesn't mess around when it comes to parental rights. At first this was very difficult because before Islam I scorned my parents, yet Islam is teaching me to be nice to them and obey, so it came down to choosing between continuing to spurn my parents and family or following Islam. From a personal standpoint I had sore feelings and didn't want to treat them properly, regardless of all the past sacrifices they made to raise me. Knowing that Islam is true and what happens to those who don't fulfill their duty to their parents who raised them from infancy, I wasn't going to risk the hellfire and continue rebuffing my parents. I forgave them and gradually began to show kindness and reconnect. I didn't do it because it was right, or because it was time, or because I wanted to. If I had it my way I'd probably still be vilifying my parents and family to this day and they wouldn't know me at all or my whereabouts. But Allah commanded to forgive and to treat one's parents kindly, so it didn't matter how I felt or whatever wrong things they had done to me, when Allah says to be kind to one's parents there are no "buts, ifs or unless" conditions; Muslim means one who submits to the will of God unconditionally. If the one who made all things gives orders for someone to do something, nobody should ever think twice or hesitate. The prophet Yusuf (Joseph) pbuh is a prime example of family forgiveness. Yusuf's brothers developed sore feelings towards him because they thought their father loved him more than them even though he didn't work and they did. Thus Joseph pbuh was thrown into a well by his brothers. Now pause, you might know the rest of the story, but just consider being in the well itself. Joseph pbuh was a young boy, when all of a sudden 10 of his brothers decide to throw him down a well intentionally and leave him there. He doesn't know why and he has no clue what will happen to him. He's wet, scared, in the dark, has no food and is all alone knowing that his beloved brothers physically put him there and don't intend on coming back and his father doesn't know where he is, he may well die there in that well and he doesn't even know why. But that was just the beginning of Yusuf's hardships in life. Next his rescuers from the well sold him into slavery in a foreign country. Then Yusuf pbuh gets a chance to have sex with a beautiful, smart, rich women and resists despite her chasing him down and ripping his shirt. What happens as a result? The woman gets the rest of the women of the city together and after they see him they all want to have sex with him. Then he gets put in prison unjustly because he didn't want to have sex with any or all those women. In prison he correctly predicts the dreams of his fellow inmates and tells them to help him get out, but the guy forgets once he is free himself. Then after all those years Yusuf pbuh finally becomes the second most powerful man in Egypt when lo and behold those same brothers come to him asking for food during the famine. His brothers didn't even recognize him, since he was a boy when they betrayed him. As a result when one gets framed for stealing something they tell Yusuf to his face that "their other brother Yusuf must've been an even bigger thief and that's where the thievery must've come from in their family". They say this right to Yusuf's face pbuh not realizing he is Yusuf pbuh, the very same they threw down the well and have the audacity to lie about and slander to a man in his position. Yet instead of blaming them for all the suffering he went through in life and accusing him of a crime right to his face, Yusuf pbuh forgave without venting and told them to never bring it up again. Then Yusuf pbuh invited his family to live in Egypt with him and shared his wealth with them. That is true forgiveness, where you not only never bring it up again, but you don't let it affect your future interactions either. The prophets are the best of examples and our role models for how to live life. I had to forgive my family just as they did theirs. It didn't matter what they did to me, it didn't matter if they were wrong and I was right, it didn't even matter if they refused to apologize and thought I should apologize I had to forgive them in order to live like a Muslim. Also how can I ever expect mercy from God for my sins if I don't show mercy to others and forgive? That is hypocritical and hypocrites are the worst of people. Christians say biblical Jesus pbuh said to forgive people 70 X 7 times, which equals 490 times. Well Muhammad pbuh taught Muslims to forgive people as many times as they want God to forgive them. May Allah protect us from the disease of hypocrisy in all its manifestations. May Allah help us to forgive everyone who ever wrongs us and may Allah also forgive us for any wrong we ever do. Forgiveness is a generous gift of charity, which we all beg for at one time or another. Miserliness is to be unmerciful. Whatever someone else ever does to you I gurantee that what you have done to yourself is worse. This is because you sin and your sins can put you in hell forever and nothing someone else does can have that type of effect on you. Thus you treat yourself worse than anyone else ever has, will or is capable of doing, so since you forgive yourself for doing sins that hurt yourself in this life and the next and damage your relationship with God then logically you should forgive those who hurt you when they are hurting you much less than you hurt yourself. If you can't forgive others for hurting you, then you can't forgive yourself for hurting you and if you can't forgive yourself you can't help yourself to grow and develop. Also God loves those who forgive, so if you want God to love you then you must forgive. Is it easy? Hell no! That's why God loves when you do it because honestly there is no logically justifiable reason for you to forgive someone who hurts you, trust me I can prove it, logically human reason dictates you should never forgive. The only reason you should forgive is because it makes God happy for you to do so, since it makes you realize how amazing God is to be able to forgive all your sins. Truly imagine how hard it is to forgive 1 person for a tiny thing they did to hurt you, it's hard stuff. Yet God can forgive everything for everyone, if they just believe, regret, apologize to the Creator alone and repent. But does God just forgive people for their sins and that's it? No God forgives and then gives them eternal paradise as a reward. Surely a glorious being that can forgive and give to such great extents cannot be human and deserves our worship. Hence if such a being asks us to forgive then how can we refuse when God also promises us large rewards if we forgive those who hurt us? Just consider that Satan does not want you to forgive others. To forgive another person pisses off Satan and to hold a grudge is to obey him, so rather than hate for personal reasons redirect all that hatred towards Satan and his allies/soldiers. Forgive for the sake of God so you are given forgiveness + gifts by God.

However still I had no intention of telling my parents that I became a Muslim because they explicitly told me I'd be homeless if I became a Muslim and I didn't really want to be kicked out onto the street, especially as a brand new Musim, and considering how facebook responded to the news I was not too optimistic about how my parents would react. Although in January 2012 CE one day my mom was very very upset at me. As soon as she came in the door I was in big time trouble and I didn't know why. After I answered her questions befuddled as to their oddity and suspicious as to her reasons for asking such odd uncharacteristic questions I asked why she was asking for such information and corrected her that the info she found on the internet about a Greg Heary having a girlfriend and a job in Oregon at some place were false and whoever it was that she was talking about it was not me. She said she found it on google and so I asked why she was googling me, again, and explained how there are other Gregory Hearys besides me in the world so she probably got another one's info. I was actually semi-relieved at that because I had tried to delete my info online specifically because I didn't want anyone to find me online. But my relief vanished as I learned why she was doing research on me. It turned out that an FBI agent had harassed her trying to get information about me from her scaring her by saying that he was "afraid I was under the influence of bad individuals" and was changing my name. My mom then told me that the FBI agent thought I was a terrorist. Obviously she wanted an explanation from me and wanted to know what the hell I was doing that the FBI was calling her with such ideas about me. She blamed my rap career saying that I should've never made the anti-police song because now they are harassing her and then she wanted to know why is the FBI saying they think I'm being influenced by bad people and where did they learn about my intentions to change my name?(My parents already knew for awhile that I wanted to change my name because I told them years earlier, although back when I first told them the change was for different non-islamic reasons.) Therefore I was in a bind because what could I say to explain a potential reason for why the FBI would be harassing her in such a way other than by telling her that I became a Muslim and that might be why she is getting harassed. However I didn't think that was the best time or way to say *"Hey Mom I'm not a Christian anymore, I became a Muslim."* So I told her how the FBI harassment has nothing to do with my rap because I had quit rapping weeks before. Although then she wanted to know why I quit rapping. Which of course I then had to explain why I quit rapping because of Islam. As to the "negative influences" I explained how I didn't even know a single Muslim so nobody influenced me into Islam and my bad non-Muslim associates had dumped me after they found out I was Muslim or I dumped them beforehand because they were bad. So honestly I could say the FBI was wrong and stupid to fear I was "being influenced by bad people" because I had cut ties with the baddest people months earlier and didn't at that time have any friends. So I couldn't have negative influences if I didn't have any influences on me to begin with. How could they dare tell my mom they are worried I have "bad friends" when I had no friends? What friends were they talking about? My facebook was already deleted so I didn't even have virtual friends so what friends did the FBI say I had? Thus I had to tell my mom how the FBI was lying when they said I have bad friends because I didn't have any and didn't even know any Muslims, male or female. So even if they said Muslims were evil terrorists then still they couldn't say I had bad friends because I didn't have any at all of any type, not even imaginary friends. Thus truly the FBI was lying about me when they said I had friends. Plain and simple the FBI blatantly lied about me when talking to others about me and "building a case" on me. Regarding the name change I said how the FBI guy probably saw me change my name on my facebook weeks before, after I changed my name on there prior to having the account deleted before Christmas. Thus I concluded saying the FBI probably saw on facebook that I became a Muslim and went crazy because they hate me and Muslims, so as a result they probably hate me twice as much now. Also since I kind of have a nearly criminal record because of my history with police, having been on "unofficial" probabtion, and having a bullet proof vest confiscated, to their stereotypical mindset learning that a zealous religious gangsteresque anti-government white rapper with my history became a Muslim was likely interpreted as apocalyptic news and set off their mental alarms. So it kind of makes sense that the FBI would harass her if they were paranoid and thought I was becoming a terrorist or something but it is still wrong for them to do and they could've just talked to me if they wanted information. Although I probably would've refused to talk to them anyways if I had the choice, which most of the time you do despite them pretending you don't. So there it was in the open, I had finally told my parents that I was Muslim; after the FBI sort of told them first and forced me to tell them. They said they had wondered why I didn't use foul language, blast rap music, dress like a thug or disrespect them anymore. So I told them that was because I became a Muslim and Islam says not to do that type of stuff or you can go to hell. Then I expected they would tell me to pack my bags and leave and/or go to hell. Yet that wasn't how they reacted and they weren't too upset that I was no longer Catholic. Whereas since they knew the FBI was already causing trouble because of my new religion and I was open about my life with them they were actually glad that I was communicating now when I had been cutting them off so harshly for so long beforehand. Also because they witnessed my improved behavior, they knew that the Islamic code of conduct was superior, and they actually liked how I treated them as a Muslim more than how I treated them as a Catholic/Christian and since my kindness was due to Islam then it was hard for them to be mad and upset at the reason for our recovering relationship. They never really liked the rap career much either so learning that Islam made me quit rap was another benefit for them that Islam had on me. My parents told me that they would've preferred I told them earlier myself about embracing Islam before the FBI had harassed them about me. However they were happy that at least we were on the same side of the government this time, instead of our previous rounds where the government would be against either me or them depending on the situation and stories we told. My mom said it was just a slip of the tongue when she said the anti-Muslim statements before and actually didn't even remember saying them, and that even still it was different saying it when I wasn't a Muslim and that by being a Muslim myself then that makes it different even though they knew they didn't give off that type of impression. Thus it became evident that

Satan can trick us into saying things that we do not mean. Satan also makes us remember the bad things that others say attempting to create enmity amongst humanity. Satan plots to disunite mankind so they can be attacked one by one. Unfortunately there are many ways to disunite mankind, governments being just one of them. Satan has been practicing ways to disunite us for as long as our species has existed. All thanks and praises be to Allah for having guided me to Islam and healing my relationship with my parents. May we all be united upon the truth so we can be united together in paradise to dwell therein for infinity.

FIRST TIME AT A MASJID

After embracing Islam, I learned about the Friday prayer in congregation. A Muslim can pray nearly everywhere, but on Friday men should pray together in the masjid. On Fridays at the masjids there is a short sermon followed by a short prayer that is a special prayer only done on Friday during congregational prayer; it substitutes the regular noon prayer. If you miss the congregational prayer then you do the regular noon prayer instead, if you make the congregational prayer then you don't have to do the regular noon prayer because the congregational prayer suffices. I learned that it was mandatory for men to attend on Friday and if one missed 3 weeks straight then Allah would place a seal upon their heart. Women do not have to attend if they don't want to, but men need to learn a weekly lesson; as all married women can attest to. Fortunately in Islam if you didn't know then you're not liable, but once I learned this information I had 3 weeks until I'd be religiously accountable. Ignorance is excusable when it's reasonable, but your intentional ignorance becomes sinful. There is a difference between not knowing and not wanting to know. I had never been to a masjid before and didn't know what to expect. There are numerous reasons Friday is singled out for the day of mandatory congregational prayer, Adam pbuh was created on a Friday, Adam pbuh entered Earth on a Friday, many of the miracles performed by the prophets occurred on Friday, the Day of Judgment will be on a Friday and most importantly the Quran instructs the believers to pray the Juma prayer together on Friday. It also distinguishes Muslims from the Jews and Christians who hold their major congregational prayer on Saturday and Sunday. As a Christian once a year I would attend a "Good Friday" church service. Now as a Muslim every Friday I hear the Khutbah and pray in congregation is a good Friday. The phrase T.G.I.F. (Thank God it's Friday), may have originated with Muslims because every Friday is a Muslim holiday wherein extra rewards can be earned. Although Muslims thank God and pray every day, since God deserves to be worshiped more than once a week. Instead of having weekly *"Happy Hour"*, Muslims have a *"Happy Life"*.

So I knew I had to go to a masjid for the Friday prayer but I had a little bit of anxiety for several reasons. In January 2012 CE the FBI had harassed my family and forced me to tell my parents I became a Muslim but nearly nobody else knew and I didn't really want anyone to know either because I had been threatened with death as a Christian rapper so becoming a Muslim probably didn't do too much to take the target off my back. I figured people would have more motivation to kill me as a Muslim than they did when I was a Christian. Then in February 2012 CE all the news outlets were reporting something that shook me to my core. It concerned the still ongoing occupation of Afghanistan that started in 2001 CE. American soldiers guarding prisons were burning the Quran claiming it was being used by inmates to pass messages to each other. It seems that claim was baseless, because if that were true they'd just take the book away, they wouldn't burn it. Also the soldiers left all the other books in the prison library for inmates to keep using so if they were using the Quran to pass notes, burning the Qurans would not stop the note passing if the other books were still left to their disposal too. Later the official explanation given for why the U.S. soldiers burned the Qurans was "because they had extremist inscriptions in them". Thus officialy the US military burned the Quran in a Muslim country because it was an extremist book according to their definition of extremism. It was a religious book burning of the Quran which I had recently come to believe was the divine revelation of God. So I thought since my government says it's an extremist book, what would they consider someone like me to be and what would they do to me if they knew I was Muslim? Truly it is rather shocking to see your government's soldiers burning books of what you consider to be divine revelation only a few months after having joined a new religion. This was also just a month after the FBI harassed my mom and I realized that America does not have a tolerant government. I got their message loud and clear. The anger and betrayal that one feels knowing that "your country" is burning divine revelation cannot be expressed with words. There is no way to describe what that feels like, it is a clear signal that you are not on the same side as your government is. What do you do when God sends a book of guidance to you and all mankind and then your government burns it to ashes. It definitely makes you reconsider your relationship between you and your government and you and your country. Suffering genuine religious persecution was a very new thing, Christians in America really don't know what it's like. It's a worse feeling than racism and racism itself can't even be known or described. Not only were they burning the arabic versions which are sacred, but stolen money(tax dollars) was spent to fund these unjust fires which burned a still existing miracle. To better illustrate how this made me feel imagine if you were Catholic and your nation's soldiers were burning bibles in the Vatican. Do you think such an act might change the relationship between Catholics and the American government? People were rioting all across Afghanistan clamoring for justice but because they were American soldiers they were legally protected from Afghanistan authorities. It didn't matter they had committed the crime in Afghanistan because they were American soldiers, so only the US military could punish them. Eventually the riots died down and the burnings faded from public memory, it was months before any punishment would be meted out. Yet March 2012 CE brought further clarification to my new position as a Muslim living in America. In March 2012 CE my parents told me how it's in all the newspapers and on TV that the NYPD and FBI has undercover cops in the masjids in New York State and the Western New York region to do secret surveillance on the Muslims so they can be put into the system, monitored and arrested and imprisoned should the need arise. That news really got me because this is unknown and unthinkable for a non-Muslim to imagine being illegally monitored secretly by the government pretending to belong to their religion at their religious places of worship. First of all I was thinking I don't really want to go to a masjid where the people might be undercover FBI agents or NYPD members because I didn't know any Muslims or much about Islam so I would be the last one to know and I did not want to be registered in the system as a new Muslim by the government. Also I had never been to a masjid, was a new Muslim, didn't know a single Muslim in the country and I'm white too. So as a white native born American who just became a Muslim, I deduced that if I went to a masjid then the Muslims would most likely think I was an undercover agent because I'm so obviously different and how convenient it'd be for an undercover to sneak in as a "new Muslim" right after the papers and TV expose how the government has planted undercover spies in masjids. It's scary enough going for the first time when you don't know anybody and just joined a new religion, but when you add the element of "undercover government spies" looking to lock people who go there up in Guantanomo Bay forever I was not prepared to walk into such a situation. Satan was also giving me many reasons not to go as well and I hadn't learned I had to go to the Friday prayer until April or May, so I just figured I didn't have to go and it'd be fine with God. Yet once I learned I had to go within 3 weeks or a seal would be placed on my heart I was so worried I decided I would not go to an American masjid at all. I actually decided to go to a masjid in Canada instead because I was too afraid to go to an American masjid due to all of the anti-islamic policies of the U.S. government. I didn't live that far from the border, I had a passport and a car so it was inconvenient but personally I felt I could not go to an American masjid because I thought I'd get arrested or killed if I did by the U.S. government. At the time I was still pretending to myself that the FBI didn't know I was a Muslim yet and maybe they thought it was just a joke or excuse to quit rap as others might have. I actually thought that if they knew I was really a Muslim then I would be in jail or dead. So to Canada I went, with my parents coming to help me across the border for my first time and then I went to a masjid by myself after dropping them off at the place I told the border people we were going since I didn't want the Canadian government to know I was Muslim either. Of course I didn't dress islamically since I was pretending I wasn't a Muslim at all and it worked without getting caught, arrested or killed.

    I did a little research before going to the masjid, so I knew what to expect. After going inside I took off my shoes and put them in the shoe rack. Typically Muslims take off their shoes whenever they go inside a home, out of respect to the owner because shoes get dirty and would cause a mess if worn inside. At a masjid people prostrate on the carpet, wearing shoes inside would cause everyone's faces to get dirty and people wouldn't like it. It's not a mandatory part of the religion to take your shoes off when entering a masjid, but wearing shoes in a masjid nowadays is inconsiderate. Although in the time of Muhammad pbuh the floor of the masjids were dirt and people kept their shoes on. It was empty when I arrived so I wondered if I made a mistake removing my shoes, thinking I'd be the only fool in the room without their shoes on. The bathrooms were very clean and there was a separate area to make wudu, which is the washing for purification before prayer if it's needed. In the wudu area there were little blocks to sit on and a special trough to wash one's feet over. Inside the prayer area the floor was carpeted and colorful books of many different languages lined the shelves with many arabic Qurans and translations of it as well as books of hadith. Whereas churches don't have bibles available for people to read, typically a church only has one bible in it and access is restricted to those quoting from it during the service. The books available in church pews only tell people what to do during church, because attendance is so irregular people read them to know what to do during the service. Having known nothing but churches, the masjid was very refreshing in that not only did it have the scriptures available to everyone, it also had beginning, intermediate and advanced books on Islam. The masjid was almost like going to a religious library, except they also had a library outside of the prayer area that anyone could use. There were only a few chairs to sit on in the masjid and I had read online that people sat on the floor, but wasn't sure if it were true. I noticed it was calm and peaceful with no statues. The floor was a pattern of prayer mats lined in rows all pointing towards Mecca. Each floor prayer space was about 2 feet wide by 4 feet long. I wondered how many people would come. I read online that there were separate sections for both women and men, but since no one was there I didn't know which section I was in.

Having separate prayer areas for men and women might seem strange to non-Muslims. First it should be understood that having separate areas does not mean they are unequal, both the men and women have the same amenities. One reason why they have separate areas is because when Muslims pray they prostrate with their forehead on the ground. Now if a man were praying behind a woman the temptation to look up early and sneak a peek would be overwhelming, the man wouldn't be able to concentrate while praying. A woman may also be tempted to sneak a peek if she were behind a man, but since I'm a guy I wouldn't know if women would have such a temptation. Even if women weren't tempted to look at the guys they would feel different praying with guys behind them and it could corrupt their intention of praying solely to worship Allah. A Muslim prays as a duty to Allah, strictly to please the Creator. The main reason a person goes to a masjid is to pray, not to socialize, socializing does happen and social events do take place but when a Muslim goes to pray their purpose should be to pray. Separating the men from the women into separate prayer areas helps both to have sincerity and concentration during the prayer. In comparison to Christianity, in church it is practically part of the religion to look at the butts of the people sitting in front of you. Don't misunderstand my dramatization thinking it is officially part of the doctrine. But when a Christian is kneeling at a pew they are supposed to be looking down, if they do so they'd be looking at the backside of whoever is in front of them. At best they'd be looking at the legs of the one ahead of them, one could close their eyes but the eyes are supposed to remain open. That's one of the reasons why I sat in front when I went to church on Sunday, because I didn't want to be looking at other people's butts. As a male, going to church oftentimes inspired strong sexual thoughts because of all the women around in close proximity dressing scantily, especially when they try to dress special on Sunday. Some women wear their sexiest outfit of the week to show off at Church, thinking they are inspiring the men to pray, or causing them to thank God for such a sight. Some women intentionally or unintentionally by the way they dress, give a whole different meaning to the church phrases spoken by men such as: "*Amen*", "*Halleluyah*" or "*Thanks be to God*". In Church men have an easy ability to look at women from behind, or shake their hands if they're sitting nearby since shaking hands is a part of the church service. Then at communion all the women go up to the front strutting their stuff and return to their seats. The guys take this opportunity to freely look at the women as they go to the front and back to their seat, and the males gaze intensely as one female after another passes him by, with both girl and guy feeling the effects of the wine if they drank it. Lots of people meet their girlfriends and boyfriends in church. Since it is the same environment Christian marriages take place naturally it is a romantic environment, especially with the music playing, the talk about eternity, eternal bliss, virginity, childbirth and getting told how much you are loved. Any guy who says they've never sexually fantasized in church is a liar, don't believe them. The Catholic Church use to have priests perform masses with priests having their backs towards the people the entire time. Do you know why? It was because if the priests were looking at the people and seen the women they would have sexual thoughts and be unable to concentrate. It was not until after the second Vatican council in 1965 CE that the Catholic Church changed their own rules and started having the priest face the congregation when saying mass, some say it was to discourage people from leaving early while the priest wasn't looking. When people say *"oh nobody has sexual thoughts in church"* for over 1,900 years the Vatican said priests, altar servers and all the other men would have sexual thoughts and be unable to concentrate if they saw women in church. But let us forget what the Church said for a moment, lets see what science says. You believe in science don't you? Christians like to say they do. Well scientific studies have proven that males cannot look at females who they are not related to for more than 3 seconds without subconsciously fantasizing about having sex with them. It is a scientific fact that has nothing to do with whether a guy has morals or self-control or not, it's just a biological mechanism in the male brain that's vital for the reproduction of the human species. Guys can't turn it off, they might not even know it's there if they get desensitzed but if their eyes see the visual stimulus of a female for 3 seconds, sometimes less, no matter what she looks like the brain will create a sexual scenario in the man's subconscious mind. It might be in his conscious mind too sometimes, but it's guaranteed to be in the subconsicous mind for every guy who sees a female non-relative for more than a few seconds; no matter how they are dressed whether the guy is single or not. Sorry guys, that's science, it doesn't mean we're all perverts. The perverts are the one's who pretend they don't have a weakness for women and deny the scientific facts of what happens to their brains when their eyes see a female for more than 3 seconds. If they look for more than a few seconds then those guys are the perverts, intentionally or unintentionally. It's just how God made men to be attracted to women. Yet if God made men with such a weakness for women then we must have been taught safety measures too. We have, through God's prophets and revelation. Thus the Quran teaches men to lower their gaze and limit their interactions to absolute necessities with women they aren't related to. While also telling women to dress modestly, not to draw attention to themselves or speak in tones that will pulverize a man's heart. Yes the female voice has the potential to destroy a man. Although many guys will probably hate me for sharing the secret. While in the 600s CE Muhammad pbuh said the first glance a man has accidentally is innocent, but for them to stare a few seconds more is sinful. Whereas science concurs and has specified that 3 seconds is the exact amount of time after which sexual thoughts automatically occur in the male mind. So if ever a guy tells you *"I don't get sexual thoughts after looking at girls."* then urgently advise them to go to the laboratory for testing because they must have some mutated DNA that means they are not a real man, or they must have a sexual identity crisis. Scientists have proven that there is actually something wrong with a man's brain or sexuality if he doesn't get subconscious sexual thoughts after 3 seconds of looking at a non-related female. Scientists have also agreed that the type of system suggested by Islam fixes the problem of subconscious lust that happens after 3 seconds of staring because Islamic people keep their eyes and ears free from over-exposure and the Islamic dresscode for females can provide some extra mili-seconds of safety regarding accidental gazes. Anyone who says or thinks a "less strict" alternative will work is wrong both according to Islam and according to science. Now if you are a non-Muslim and want to say that Islam is wrong then ok, but are you going to say science is wrong too? Although don't men and women have to work together and interact in our modern society? Well according to scientific research our species would be more productive if men and women didn't interact in the workforce together. It's not sexism it's science. Many experiments have been done and it is proven that the cognitive ability of men is reduced if they merely anticipate working with a female, and it doesn't matter if the female is single or married or what the potential for a sexual encounter actually is in reality. Yet that's just with males anticipating interaction with a female, the cognitive ability of males while they were actually interacting with females were "under the charts" so to say. The male brain is biologicially not capable of stopping itself from devoting mental resources to the thought of mating with females when they intereact with females. Guys don't work well with girls, they are too pretty. It doesn't matter what the social conditions are, the brain don't care, it is programmed to trigger the mating attempt. So it is a scientific fact that women can and do make men stupid when they interact because of them simply being females. That's likely why Eve got blamed by Jews and Christians for influencing Adam pbuh to make the mistake he made, it's not neccessarily that she ate first and persuaded Adam pbuh to eat second, it's that because Adam pbuh was attracted to Eve his mental faculties weren't 100% focused. It's not Eve's fault and women shouldn't be ostracized as they were when Christians decided celibacy was the cure for distractions, marriage is the cure but spouses should spend a certain amount of time apart for their psychological health. The problem with Adam pbuh and Eve was that they didn't spend a healthy amount of time apart from each other when in paradise, their pre-earth life was like a perpetual first day of marriage. Which not to bash weddings but everyone who has every been married knows that mentally they were preoccupied with thoughts about their spouse on that day. Adam pbuh and Eve had those feelings for a long time and then Satan came to tempt them with immortality, which was like selling love to lovebirds. Satan basically told the first couple that by obeying him they could have an eternal wedding night. So while we can sympathize with them, we must learn from that lesson in how men and women are still just as vulnerable to subconsious mental distractions about sex due to sight, hearing, smell, and touch. The male brain devotes energy to the potential of mating even if the guy himself doesn't consciously want or desire to mate. Girls don't have this mating brain drain mechanism but guys do, and it's a good thing we do or else our species likely would not have reproduced in extreme survival conditions when resources were scarce. So we can be mature about this, or be unscientific bigots who insist men and women are equal and can work together and interact without any special restrictions or measures being taken. Yet if we want society to materially advance and be as productive as possible, then the women will have to change their dress code and the interactions must be limited deliberately to avoid and reduce feminine attractiveness in public. Will society take this important step for the sake of worldly advancement? Well Islam teaches that it's necessary for spritual safety and God's pleasure, so we probably should even if it's hard or socially unpopular at this crazy time when everything is sexualized but we get told there is no such thing as natural sexual tension between the genders. Will the human race please grow up? Men and Women have sexual tension with each other. The little kids recognize the clear differences between genders and place better limitations on interactions than the "civilized adults" do. Even car insurance companies admit the guys are at risk when driving because their brains are wired to be on the search for mates. Thus because the scientists who work for car insurance companies have determined that when a male driver sees a female it causes his brain to devote mental energy and resources to the mating process, they have labeled men as higher risks to insure than women. As a result car insurance companies make guys pay more than girls pay, by default, because the male brain loses focus when a guy's eye sees a female. Especially in the West they charge guys extra to insure because the way western women dress can and has caused some guys to get into car accidents because they saw a girl while they were driving and could not control their thoughts sufficiently to maintain control of their vehicle. Guys aren't perverted, that is just how the male brain is, girls distract guys whether they try to or not. Girls today are simply too sexy in public and it is hindering the development of society and even threatening our daily lives. The proof is overwhelming. As female fashions change to be more and more attractive, the male brain becomes less and less effective which causes them to pay more for everything in life while the females pay more to get guys to pay attention to them more than other females. Hence many industries have large financial interests in female clothing and integrating the genders more and more in society. To these industries the more attractive women are in public and the more guys and girls interact in public then the more money they make. One cannot even count the industries that benefit from an increase in male/female interaction and increased sexualization of female fashion. Just with advertising alone, hundreds of trillions of dollars are to be made if men and women interact in public. If they were to reduce that interaction just a tiny bit, trillions of dollars would be lost. Or the dollars wouldn't be lost per say, they would just be spent on other things that might be more beneficial to or desired by humans. That's the thing with economic "losses", many times the "losses" are just a redirecting of funds from one avenue to another. For example instead of spending millions on a new clothing line, those millions get spend on medical research or ending poverty. So a loss for one industry means a gain for another. Do people lose jobs? Yes, but they get rehired in the industries that take over. If there is no unemployment at all, then no industry can ever grow and no new companies can be made or increase it's workforce. So unemployment is actually necessary for development, but too much unemployment can stall and/or prevent growth. However some people care more about themselves and their own job security and maintaining the status quo than they do about progress and growth. Thus our world will soon find itself at a point where in order to advance, the fashion and advertising industries must suffer and lose their importance, influence and revenues. Economically and intellectually for the human species to progress we must become more modest and more restrained in our interactions with the opposite gender. Whereas girls themselves cannot judge whether they are "too sexy" in public or not, the guys themselves know the girls can't tell how attractive they are. If girls only knew and collaborated they'd enslave the male gender. The number one reason women get raped is because they are visually attractive in the eyes of a rapist. Now many women think if they aren't showing cleavage or their legs then they must be "modest". This is not modesty, honestly sometimes the women who don't show cleavage and/or their legs can be more attractive than those who do. Visual attractiveness increases the odds of rape and it is proven that the female garb does play a major role in rape rates. For example if you compare the % of non-Muslim women who are nuns and those who aren't you will find that statistically nuns are raped at a lower rate than the non-nuns are which is disproportionate to their correlative membership in the female population. In plainspeak *"Something about nuns is peculiar and it causes them to get raped much less than the data projects they would be."* What is it that's different about nuns in comparison to other non-Muslim women? They cover their hair. So that's where what women wear really does effect the odds of rape and the women who don't cover their hair are statistically proven to have a higher probability of being raped. When we weigh the pros and cons of women covering their hair and not covering it, can we really say that it's better for women to be "free" to show their hair in public? Do you want women to be raped? Relgion aside, the rate of rape has increased as female fashion has become more "liberated". Peacefully and cheaply we can prevent most rapes simply if women covered their hair in public, and it's not about if X women gets raped or not then she should cover her hair. As with vaccinations where they say "herd immunity" is important, "herd modesty" is needed to stop the plague of rape. However girls don't know and are incapable of knowing how attractive they look to guys, no matter what they are wearing and sadly some can think they are dressing modestly when they are actually increasing their sexual appeal. So females are incapable of defining modesty, when it comes to how they dress, or even speech. All too often girls get approached by guys who thought they were being flirted with and the girl had no intention to send such a message at all. Thus just as guys can be clueless as to how they tempt girls, many girls are likewise on how she can unwittingly be tempting guys. Yet because guys are guys we cannot be trusted to make the female dress code either, because Mr. penis creates a conflict of interest. Nor can guys or girls correctly determine how much interaction is too much or what type of interactions are inappropriate. Many have tried for centuries but they still can't get it right, because it's biologically impossible to know through human sources of information. We are too biased, because we are designed to desire to create a mating environment. Our private parts will not permit our brains to figure out the best way to discipline, thwart and restrain our sexual desires. The body is built to mate and modesty prevents/disrupts mating, so nobody is capable of discovering what modesty really is. Especially when Satan is taken into account and adds his comments to our ideas. Thus we need God to tell us how to dress and interact through divine revelation. If God doesn't tell us then we will never get the right answer to this dilemma and never be the best we can be. Islam claims to have God's instructions, those who disagree with the Islamic dress code tend to say humans can choose their own clothes or make a dress code via democracy. Yet that's what led to the fashion mess we are in today. The problem is guys are embarassed to let women know the truth lest they use it against them, as some have, while other guys think if they make the truth known then they'll get labeled as perverts. While most females just don't know how they affect males, so they believe the nonsense excuse of men just controlling their thoughts no matter what/who they see/hear. I'm sorry ladies but guys just can't control their brains or other organs that way, we'd like to but we can't. So you either accept the scientific reality or reject it, but it is what it is and that's how male brains function. A possible explanation all women can easily understand is an analogy with food. When someone looks at food their brain lets them know that is a source of nourishment and is edible, so many different body parts immediately send signals to the brain telling it to try to get that food eaten so the cells of the body can benefit, especially if the person is hungry or their tongure really likes the taste of that food. However if the person sees food and they aren't hungry, or they can't legally eat the food because they don't own it and can't afford it, or if it's a religiously prohibited food to eat, or it's a religiously prohibited time to eat, or even if they just don't like the taste of that food the brain still automatically devotes mental energy towards developing and executing a plan to consume that food even if consciously the person doesn't want to ever eat that food. Even if someone else is eating that food, every person who sees/smells that food has their brain working by default to figure out how it can get that food in it's own body, there will always be a tiny desire to have that person's food in one's own mouth on a subconscious level. That's similar to how the male brain reacts to the visual, physical, scentual and audible stimului of female. Even if the man is married or the woman they experience is married the male body still reacts to females in the same subconscious manner as it was designed to react, just as food is still desireable even if the viewer is not hungry and is watching that food item being consumed by someone else. Just consider most pornography, the viewer is literally watching someone else with the "object of desire" yet their body/mind/heart still desires what they already know is being taken/used by someone else. Some may say it's just a "make-believe fantasy" but tell me what is the difference between sexual arousal or ejaculation due to fantastical desires and one due to legitimate desires? The sexual parts don't distinguish between real and fake, it's all real to them. So just as all types of food are biologically desired by all humans at all times even if they aren't hungry, for males all types of females are biologically desired at all times even if they aren't horny. If society wants to pretend males are different and chooses to act like guys brains are different than they really are it will cause many problems. Sadly Christians have fallen into this modern self-control trap even though they used preach the male attraction/weakness. Yet because they blamed women for it they went to extremes and didn't really have rules from God for how to solve the issue. The bible says Jesus pbuh said a guy should take out his eye if he looks at a girl with lust. So since scientifically that happens after a few seconds, Christians were in trouble and had to either reject/misinterpret the bible, or pretend lust is only voluntary and doesn't automatically subconsciously happen after a few seconds of looking as science proves it does, or the Christians would have to admit they don't follow the bible or Jesus pbuh and they've never admitted that in all of history. Christians mainly gave up when their extremist unnatural sexual repression triggered the sexual revolution and they picked the easiest thing to change and that was the definition of lust and modesty and "what the bible means". Whereas Islam teaches that men shouldn't look and if they get an accidental split-second peek then they look away, fortunately unlike the bible there is no eyeball taking clause if one's gaze strays. But that's just between men and the females they aren't related to. Jews and Christians used to have nearly identical rules, except they had much stricter punishments. Previously Christians used to segregate the genders in church. Some Christian groups still segregate in church such as Greek Orthodox, Coptic Orthodox,

Anabaptists, Amish as well as Orthodox Jews; although the extent of segregation varies from place to place. In the past Christian women were required to cover their hair while they were in church, just like Muslim women cover their hair in public. Today some Christian women continue this practice, but think they only need to have something on their head not realizing the reason for it or all the stuff that is supposed to be covered. Some Catholic women today foolishly put tissues on their head in church trying to keep it on top the entire time. I'm not joking. I've seen elderly women in church trying to balance a tissue on their head for nearly an hour thinking they'd be sinful if they didn't, other women wear hats in church instead. Considering modern Christian female wardrobes, it's far more likely a priest or man would sexually fantasize in Church today than hundreds of years ago, yet Christians insist that men are more virtuous in the modern age. Thereby implying that the penis has evolved and become "civilized" or now Christian penises have more morals than past penises had. And the women believe it, as do some of the men because they don't preach their penis philosophy in plain terms. Anyways it was a nice surprise to learn Muslim men and women have separate prayer areas in masjids, so both can concentrate without sexual tension, or be under pressure to impress the other gender. Both guys and girls can discuss specific gender-related issues amongst themselves without embarrassment. Having the men separate from the women allows both to act naturally. When it comes to kids scientists have demonstrated that in school because of the sexual cognitive drain on the male brain that is activated by female presence, or anticipated female presence, it causes boys to do worse in schools that are mixed. It's been proven that a male student will perform better on tests if there are no females in the room, and they will get better grades if they are in an all-boys school. So for any parent who has a male child, if they want them to get the best grades they are capable of and do the very best they can in school, they would not let them be schooled in an enviroment where they'd have females around. Mixed schools actually cheat males from getting the education they deserve and expose girls to perverts and scoundrels. Coincidentally girls are also proven to do better in all-girl schools than they do in mixed schools. So if the West wants smart kids, they would segregate the schools. But they don't because of a satanic religion called feminism, and governments don't really want their population to be thinking at full capacity. Gender segregation in public really is natural, it's undeniable. Even in schools when given the choice to sit wherever they want, boys and girls will always segregate themselves no matter what age they are; even in college. It is the school teachers who assign boy-girl seating and mixing because of school/government/international policies to encourage sexualization and eliminate our natural modesty and shyness towards the other gender. It's proper to be shy around the opposite gender, that's how God designed us to be. That way our shyness helps us to be devoted spouses and stay far away from promiscuity and infidelity. Those who say they only have eyes for their spouses are lying if they look at other non-related members of the opposite gender. If you aren't married yet then save your eyes now just as you'd want your spouse to save their eyes for you. Don't be visually cheating on your spouse before you meet. Truly the less people you see the prettier your spouse looks, and the more you look at others of the opposite gender then the uglier your spouse will appear to you. Thus the beauty of your spouse has more to do with you than it does with them. It really isn't about how they look it's about what you look at. If you don't see them as beautiful its because of visual sins. If guys simply didn't look at other girls their wives wouldn't need to wear makeup or stylize in order to appear attractive. Many are abusing their spouses by looking at others. Most times viewing the other gender results in blinding yourself. Don't let 2 eyeballs cause your whole body to burn eternally. To not commit visual sins, when able, is to do a good deed. In this age, our eyes alone can determine our eternal prizes. God looks at us while we look at things, as do the angels who are assigned to us to record all of our visual deeds. Every look of yours will be recorded in your book of deeds. Don't cause others to sin if/when they look at you.

    After a few minutes of waiting at the masjid with nobody else there, I really wanted to leave and just go home because I had no clue what was going to happen, I was in a foreign country all alone, I had to pretend I wasn't a Muslim when crossing the border and what if they found out on the way back and I'm a new Muslim and don't really know what people do at a masjid and on top of it all I've never even talked to another Muslim before. Plus the place is empty and I don't even know what time they start or if I was in the guys section or the girls section, plus I took my shoes off and I didn't really know if Muslims actually do that or if it was just a rumor on the internet that's going to make me look like a gigantic fool and get mightily embarassed. Also I'm an American so these Canadian Muslims might probably think I'm an undercover American spy and they have a bunch of security cameras so I've already been caught on tape. Yet the friday prayer in congregation is a very important part of Islam and I would get in big trouble with Allah if I didn't stay, so I stayed for a few more seconds because that's Islam, to be a Muslim that's what I had to do. Finally a older guy came in to the masjid, which let me know I was in the guy's section, and I immediately said I was a new Muslim and it's my first time and I don't know what to do. The guy also took off his shoes and was quite friendly, or at least he seemed that way to me because I was so scared and wasn't even used to saying I was a Muslim in public. Inside we prayed together and I noticed he did some things differently, it soon became obvious that Sheikh Google hadn't taught me to pray correctly. Then the old guy intoduced me to someone else who helped me to memorize the first chapter of the Quran so I could recite it properly during prayers, it's only 7 verses long. I thought I already kind of knew it but my pronunciation was incorrect and needed a lot of practice. Other men continued coming in while I practiced and I started getting nervous since I had never been around so many Muslims before in my life. I wasn't afraid because I knew we were all brothers, but I had no idea how many people would come, they just kept coming and coming. Never having met another Muslim man since becoming one, to see all these Muslim men was amazing. Soon there were hundreds of Muslim men of all ages, colors and nationalities. Most everyone who was physically able sat down on the ground, very close to each other practically touching, it was that crowded. I sat leaning against a wall not knowing the proper etiquette of how to sit or act during Juma. Juma is the name for the Friday congregational prayer. Then a person beautifully made the Athan, the call to prayer. Soon after a man stood up and gave a speech beginning immediately. The person was an intelligent man who spoke in both Arabic and English. Immediately after the lecture we all got up to pray, every 2x4 prayer space had about two people in each with nearly 700 men in total I'd guess. I barely fit in the row I prayed in and another guy kindly moved over making extra space. We prayed shoulder to shoulder and foot to foot with all of us making the same gestures and motions at the same time. In a few minutes the prayer was over and announcements were made and people began to leave, it was perhaps 40 minutes in total. A 30 minute speech and then a few minutes of prayer, it was actually exciting the whole time. The speech was extremely informative and practical giving us advice we could use daily in our personal lives. After the prayer I decided to strike up a conversation making small talk with the guy who made extra room for me. It was hard to understand him and I didn't think he could understand me, after I motioned with my finger signaling 1, saying it was my first time he said "no English" and told me he was from Libya. I thought that was amazing, we didn't know each other's language, we were from different countries, different ethnicities and couldn't even converse, yet we prayed right next to each other in the exact same way at the same time. Then he went to get some English speaking people for me to meet. Everyone was friendly and I felt like it was true family. When I left and saw my parents they told me I was beaming and never looked happier. Crossing back into Canada was fine and in the future weeks I went to Canada alone and just said I was going to meet people I had met on previous trips and it worked without having to say I was Muslim or going to an Islamic place of worship.

One thing I learned at the masjid was how to do wudu, or ablution done when in a minor state of impurity such as after anything comes out of your private parts (including gas) after excessive bleeding, or after unconsciousness. It turns out that one can just wipe over the tops of the Khuffs and it will suffice for washing the feet, if you had washed your feet before putting on the Khuffs and 24 hours hasn't passed. (a khuff is a type of leather sock) When traveling one can go 72 hours washing the feet only once as long as the Khuff is kept on. Knowing that made doing wudu so much easier because prior to knowing that I was washing my bare feet every time. I also learned about ghusl at the masjid, which is the full body ablution done when in a state of major impurity, such as after having a sexual discharge, having one's private parts touch another's private parts, menstruation, post-natal bleeding or after becoming a Muslim since a new Muslim most likely never did ghusl before so they would be in need of it. Although the good thing about Islam is that since I didn't know I was supposed to do ghusl after becoming a Muslim I wasn't held accountable for not having done it when I needed it, since I had a legit excuse.

Every week the masjid would have a different speaker give a speech because they didn't have a permanent imam at that time. An imam is the community's spiritual leader who is most knowledgeable regarding Islam. The imams can get married and they are hired by the community directly, not appointed by a global hierarchy. This way if an imam were to hypothetically do something like molest a child, then that imam would have their reputation shattered, get replaced and would probably never be given such a position of authority again. Also since the imams marry and have children they actually have personal experience they can relate to when giving advice to married couples or parents. Whereas in the Catholic Church a priest is celibate and forbidden to marry, last time I checked. If a Catholic priest were to molest a child then the standard practice is to move him to another parish, once the congregation finds out and complains. The new parish the sexually abusive priest gets assigned to is not informed that their new priest is a child molester. This happens a lot more than gets publicized, as evidenced by a statement read by Archbishop Silvano Maria Tomasi in September 2009 CE, the Holy See stated:"*We know now that in the last 50 years somewhere between 1.5% and 5% of the Catholic clergy has been involved in sexual abuse cases*". There were 410,593 Catholic priests in the world in 2009 CE, according to official Vatican statistics. If we are generous and use the round number of 400,000 in our calculations then we would discover that according to the Vatican between the years 1959-2009 CE there were between 6,000 and 20,000 cases of sexual abuse perpetrated by Catholic priests that the Vatican publicly admits knowledge of. In my opinion a person who sexually abuses another person, should not be given a position of religious leadership. Although the Vatican disagrees and keeps such priests on the payroll.

    One thing that struck me was how Muslims greet each other with the arabic way of saying "*Peace be upon you*" just as the Old and New Testament say believers are told to do in Genesis 43:23, Judges 6:23, 1 Samuel 25:6, Numbers 6:26, 1 Samuel 1:17, Luke 24:36, John 20:19 and John 20:26. Christians will do it once in church all at the same time to those they are sitting nearby, but Muslims greet each other this way everytime they see each other even if they don't know each other or speak to each other after that. Muslims don't greet each other with "hello" they say in arabic "*Peace be upon you*" no matter where it is they meet. Whereas Christians say "*Peace be with you*" only once in church and mainly because it's socially expected for them to do it at a specific time of the service. Furthermore Luke 10:5 commands *"When you enter a house, first say, 'Peace to this house.'"* whereas no Christians I know of ever say this when they enter a house. After the Friday prayer in the masjid people would sit around and talk, go back to work, or sometimes go out to lunch, with many returning when it was time to pray again in the afternoon. In all my life I had never been in a more diverse place, there were whites, blacks, browns, Arabs, Africans, Europeans, Canadians, Asians, Americans and people from all kinds of ethnic backgrounds and nations. I don't mean this ancestrally, I mean this literally, almost every other person had a passport and citizenship from a different country. There were many different languages represented, yet we all prayed the same way. Despite all the cultural differences we were all so much the same, we all lived according to the same routine, we all went to the bathroom the same way, prayed at the same times each day facing the same direction, abstained from the same things, and had the same prophet as a role model. Everyone there used the same manual for life as I did. Honestly if it weren't for skin colors and accents one would easily guess everyone was from the same country. Another thing I noticed was how many Muslims were named after prophets. I know Muslims with the names of Moses, David, Muhammad, Solomon, Joseph, Jonah, Elijah and more Abrahams than I can remember. I've even met several Muslims named Jesus! When praying we would be shoulder to shoulder, foot to foot all across the rows. One row could have citizens of Canada, America, Sudan, Algeria, Morocco, Tanzania, Palestine, Libya, Somalia, Eritrea, Saudi Arabia, Egypt, Yemen, Jordan, Tunisia, Pakistan, Oman, U.A.E., South Africa, Syria, France, Qatar, Afghanistan, Iraq, Belgium, Turkey all standing shoulder to shoulder in one row! The masjid was the most diverse place I've ever been on earth. There are a lot less Muslim Arabs than one would think, Arabs actually make up less than 18% of the Muslim demographic. Meaning 82% of Muslims are not of Arab ethnicities. In Islam there is no racism because everyone is a descendant from Adam pbuh. Adam pbuh was made of many different shades of clay, the different skin colors exist today because he had those colors' genetic makeup in his DNA. In Islam the only distinction between people that is made is that of piety, ethnic differences are put aside. What's amazing is that all these different people of different colors, countries and languages all came to the same place at the same time to worship the Creator of everything. From every corner of the world people came together to the same spot, we might not even be able to talk to each other, but we're worshipping Allah the same way. With any other thing we'd probably have different ways of doing them, but when it comes to religion it unites Muslims of all nations and generations. Compared to Christianity every single church has a different way of worshipping. They tend to have congregations that are from only one cultural background and ethnicity. Also most of the Christian ceremonies end up being empty lip service that's insincere.

     One major benefit from being around such diversity is that I was able to learn about different countries firsthand from actual citizens who have lived there. Also the funny cultural confusions that frequently take place make us realize how ethnocentrism is stupid. The reality of what is happening in faraway countries is very different than what gets depicted on the local, regional and national news. It helps one to really understand the world when you learn firsthand from actual citizens, because a tourist gets a different perspective on visits. I have heard eyewitness accounts of the things that were done by American troops in Afghanistan, by Israelis to Palestinians and by Gaddafi to Libyans. The citizens usually experience the good and the bad and can tell you what the reality is, which is sometimes the exact opposite of what gets printed in the newsstand. Muslims who spent time in Africa told me about what Christian missionaries do to the Muslims when they evangelize. The African Muslims are starving and dying in poverty, the Christian missionaries come offering food to them with a condition. In order to get food from a Christian mission they must be wearing a cross and be a Christian. Any Muslim who refuses to convert gets no food or assistance. Some Africans who do convert to Christianity out of hunger are even forced to change their names from Muhammad to Bob, or else the Christian missionaries let them starve. Then the Christians build schools too and have the same policy in that the kid has to practice Christianity and say the Christian prayers, even confess their sins to a priest if it's a Catholic mission, in order to get an education. Learning this from people who've lived there gave me a new perspective. I remembered many times in church an African missionary would come asking for donations and saying how there are so many new Christians, but if they don't get more money the Christians will leave the religion. It's just another instance of Christianity being spread through force. Since they can't use the sword as much today, they try to exploit the non-Christian starvation and poverty. This is why the Christian missions are always in the poor countries, they can't get away with this stuff in the rich non-Christian countries. When they try they get deported and then the Christians say those countries are anti-Christian and should be bombed. Why else do you think the Christian charities in Africa usually always show the people frowning? Very rarely do you ever see African "Christian" charity cases smiling. It's a sad reality that reveals Christian hypocrisy.

Crossing the border between Canada and America every Friday eventually led me to get pulled over by the Canadian government. They took me into a station after searching my car and wanted more information. I said how I was just going to meet a person, using the least islamic sounding name I knew of the people who went to the masjid, but they thought it was sketchy so they took me into a room and a lady was there to interview me alone. Now immediately I'm thinking I can't be alone with this woman because Muhammad pbuh taught that when a man and woman who aren't married or related are alone then the third is Satan, BUT if I say I don't want to be alone with her for that reason then they will learn that I'm Muslim and kill me or hand me over to the Americans to kill me. Thus I was determined to not let them know I was Muslim because if they found out I didn't know what they'd do. The tricky part though was getting across the border to go to a masjid to pray with Muslims without the Canadian government knowing any of that, without telling any lies even though they are directly asking questions about why you are going to Canada and what you plan to do there. After a few minutes of questions she said they think I'm buying drugs and are not going to let me cross the border ever again unless I tell them exactly what I'm doing and give them more information. So then I figured I might as well just go home and let them think what they want rather than risk telling them I'm a Muslim and have the Canadian government put me in their system as a Muslim on record. I actually thought it would be better if they ban me thinking I'm a drug dealer than tell them I'm a Muslim coming to Canada to pray, but then I thought that if I can't go to Canada to pray in the masjid then where would I go? Mexico was too far. To me I thought it was Canada or nothing so I started crying because I realized I can't practice Islam unless I tell them I'm coming to Canada to pray but if I tell them then they may kill me or imprison me or at the very least I'd be labeled a Muslim by the Canadian government and the U.S. government would find out and kill me. So with tears coming down my cheeks I told the Canadian border patrol that I'm a new Muslim and I was coming to Canada to pray at the masjid because in America they hate Muslims and have undercover government agents acting as spies in the masjids so I couldn't go pray there and I didn't want to tell them specific information when they asked because I didn't want them to know I was Muslim and I can't lie because if I lied it would be a sin and that I didn't want to tell them I was Muslim because then the U.S. government might find out and never let me back into the country and I don't know what I'd do if they don't let me back in since all my stuff is there. To my shock and surprise they let me live and said they aren't like the American government and you can just tell them when crossing the border that you are going to pray at the masjid and it will be fine. She also told me that the Americans legally according to International law can't stop me from coming back to America because I'm a citizen, so I don't have to worry about telling them I'm Muslim and can just tell them I went to the masjid. So the Canadian government let me go and that was that, for awhile. From time to time I'd get stopped again by the Canadians but it would just typically be a car search and they'd let me go until they got more paranoid and I ended up being interrogated by a CSIS agent, then the DHS and FBI. By 2014 CE interrogations were routine because of increasing anti-Muslim prejudices. It's just their job, they could be less prejudiced but it is their job to be prejudiced and oppressive because the governments they serve are. One can't complain about officials *"doing their job"*. Bad people take bad jobs and do bad things while doing them. It does indeed make them bad people for doing the job, but it is to be expected. One can just patiently try to make them be better people by sharing Islam with them when/if pestered by them. The flawed system they are a part of cannot be changed, but people can. So change the people and build new systems, eradicating the old ones that cause the oppression and corruption.

The first Sunni masjid I went to in America was in Boston, Massachusetts in September 2012 CE just days after the US ambassador to Libya got killed by Muslims. My parents took me there on vacation and it was my first time on vacation as a Muslim and as a Muslim I still had to pray 5 times every day. Fortunately there are certain concessions for Muslim travelers in that the noon, afternoon and nighttime prayer is 2 units instead of 4 but inevitably I still had to pray in public in America just days after a big "Islamic attack". Needless to say I was a little nervous, particularly since there were no other Muslims with me and I had to pray in some pretty public areas not remote locations. If I were to be attacked only Allah could've protected me but to my surprise I wasn't attacked while praying in public and didn't really get any verbal abuse as far as I could tell. Although my parents said while I was praying outside an aquarium some lady angrily shouted "Go back to your own country!" However I never heard her and thought they were joking, but they were afraid every time I tried to pray thinking they'd have to save me from a lynch mob. Yet I found praying in public to be no big deal as I thought it would be. Other Muslims had previously told me they prayed on planes, boats and many other things and while sometimes it can be awkward or people laugh or make remarks, the prayers are obligatory to do, please Allah and frequently aid in starting discussions about Islam with strangers. Yet despite praying in public in multiple states and going to a Sunni masjid in Boston, I didn't want to risk going to any New York masjids. I didn't want the US government to ever learn I was a Muslim and I was pretending/hoping the FBI guy and US border patrol just didn't report me and that was why I was still alive. I figured if the US government knew and believed I was Muslim I would not be free to live in society or be breathing. So I kept telling myself that they must not know I'm Muslim. I didn't want them to find out by going to a NY masjid and having their undercover agents put me on the "Muslim list". In November 2012 CE, 11 months after I thought I officially became a Muslim, my mom told me I had to try out the local American Sunni masjid too to see how/if it was different. I protested and planned to just keep going to Canada to pray in the masjid on Fridays until I left America and could practice Islam safely. However my mother persuaded me, despite my claims it would endanger my life to go to a masjid in New York state because of the FBI and NYPD. Thus I went with her to the masjid, against my will, to pray the noon prayer and nobody was there. My mother asked where everyone was, since she had been to see the Canadian masjid and was used to seeing hundreds of people come for prayer and I just said I didn't know it's my first time. Just because I'm a Muslim doesn't mean I know where the Muslims are. However at that moment I realized that contrary to what I had read and heard on the news, there were no undercover government agents in the masjid because I was the only guy there and I knew I wasn't undercover. So I prayed and left, my mom met some Muslim women on the way out and I thought it wasn't as bad as I had feared. The next week I came back and Muslim guys were there and I talked to some and my previous optimism was crushed. I was still very paranoid about undercover agents, so despite regularly dressing Islamically in public around non-Muslims when I went the the masjid I would dress in jeans and fashionable attire (non-gangsterish, but still "fashionable"). Believe it or not I was afraid to dress like a Muslim in the masjid when praying with other Muslims even though I felt perfectly fine dressing Islamically amongst non-Muslims and in public. It might seem paradoxical but I was afraid the people at the US masjid might think I was extreme if I dressed like a Muslim they would report me and I'd get sent to Guantanomo Bay, tortured and killed if I dressed Islamically in the US masjid amongst Muslims. If I recall correctly the first Sunni Muslim guy I met at a masjid in America was the "President of the Islamic School" at that masjid. One of the first things he told me was "Your beard is too long, you should trim it." I was immediately shocked. Now Islamically men are commanded by God to let their beards grow and it is considered sinful mutilation to shave them, unless there is a special medical necessity to shave their beard or it's for military espionage reasons so as to infiltrate the enemy. It's not obligatory for men to have one, because not all men can grow one but whatever does grow should stay. Some scholars say if it's longer than a fist length then they are permitted to trim the amount that's longer but it's better to let it grow as men get a reward for each hair and the longer each beard hair the more the reward. Whereas if you never shave, the beard will naturally grow very slowly. The point being is my "beard" at that point, which had only been attempted for less than one year was much shorter than fist length and thus Islamically it would be sinful for me to trim my beard since it wasn't long enough to trim it even if one thought trimming were permissible. So one of the first pieces of "advice" I was given by American Muslims was to commit a sin. In fact my beard was so short in November 2012 CE, when the American Muslim told me it was "too long" that 6 months later in April 2013 CE in Canada some of my Muslim companions were teasing me about it. They shouldn't have done that but I will mention what they said to show the difference between Canadian Muslims and American ones. In November 2012 CE an American Muslim "President of the Islamic School" told me "Your beard is too long, you should trim it.", I didn't and let it grow longer. In April 2013 CE, another Christian turned Muslim jokingly told me "*You remind me of the comapanion of Muhammad pbuh who only had 1 hair for his beard.*" Before I could reply another companion said "*What do you mean 1 hair? He has like 7.*" I laughed because they had no clue what I had been told in America 6 months earlier about my beard being "too long" and here they were debating on whether I had 1 hair or 7. My guess was I had maybe 15 to 25 hairs in total but by the American Muslim standard that was "too long", yet according to the normal Muslim standard it was almost laughable. I say almost because it is disbelief to joke or mock Islamic practices but they weren't mocking the beard itself though their joking was close to being sinful; however contextually it was just a loving remark on how it was unusual to see such a small beard. Anyways by all accounts I learned very quickly that the rumors I had heard online and in Canada about "American Islam" not really being Islam was confirmed, on my 2nd visit to a Sunni masjid in NY state. I was also told to do other sinful things that were unislamic that deeply distressed me. Therefore I decided to not go the American Sunni masjids because I was afraid the US Muslims would think I was extreme since they seemed extremely unislamic and seemed to think I was already extreme even when I was a brand new Muslim just practicing a few basic parts of Islam and even hiding my Islamic identity by purposely dressing unislamically only in the masjid so as not to get reported as Muslim. I was afraid of the government's spies learning I was a Muslim, so for the US Muslims to be making me feel extreme I figured if any government spies were around they'd be practically signing my death warrant by the way they talked to me about how I dressed even though I was in mostly unislamic fashion except for a kufi, beard and pants above my ankles(as Muhammad pbuh told Muslim men to wear their pants, since dragging the pants below the ankles is sinful arrogance that prevents male humility and modesty). Therefore I continued going to Canada to pray on Fridays and never wanted to go back to a Sunni US masjid again, lest the government spies find out I was Muslim or even worse think I was an extremist; which I hadn't even considered as a possibility until I met the American Muslims at the local Sunni masjid. There were also other concerns I had in that I thought if I dressed Islamically in American masjids since I was a new white Muslim appearing months after reports about government spies in masjids, then the other Muslims might suspect me as a likely undercover non-Muslim FBI agent. So I didn't want to dress Islamicly around US Muslims lest they think I wasn't a Muslim but was faking it and given the initial experience I had getting told my "1 hair beard" was "too long/much" I genuinely feared that if I dressed Islamically then the Muslims in America would probably report me as a terrorist. In Canada I felt I could be Islamic, but in America I was most afraid of being Islamic around other Muslims in the masjid. I had discovered American Muslims were a different kind of unreligious extremist that I had never expected to encounter. It's really sad because after all I had been through to become a Muslim and end up in a masjid in America, 11 months after becoming a Muslim, the Muslims in America made me more afraid to practice Islam among them than I was to practice Islam among non-Muslims when I didn't know any Muslims. Meeting American Sunni Muslims was disheartening. Prior to that I thought all Muslims practiced Islam since it was so clear on what was right, wrong, recomended and disliked and everything had so much proof to back up every individual practice down to the tiniest of details. It was sad. Many Muslims in America had no clue how beautiful and full the religion of Islam is. They didn't value or know their faith. I had vastly overestimated the religiosity of the US Muslims and became disillusioned with the extreme ignorance I saw. As someone who was Muslim less than a year it was depressing to discover I knew more about Islam than many American Muslims I met, they were even more scared to practice Islam than I was despite being from Muslim families/countries. I was afraid of their unislamic ignorance, after having started to become Islamic and good they were telling me to be unislamic and sinful like I was before Islam. They would tell me to do the opposite of what Islam teaches and I didn't understand why they would advise that because the whole point of me becoming Muslim was to practice Islam. Thus if I followed their advice and didn't practice what Islam taught I figured there was no point in becoming a Muslim if I acted the same as I was before I embraced Islam. To me religion is something you commit to wholeheartedly, if you believe in a religion you should practice what it teaches. I believed accepting the true religion would mean changing my lifestyle accordingly but they insisted I could just keep doing the same sinful stuff as before I became Muslim just like they did and that I only had to make a few tiny tweaks regarding what I believe, praying and other obvious neccesities and didn't have to be "so strict about things". I didn't think I was being too strict, I just believed if Islam teaches you should do X and that doing Y is a sin then you should do X and avoid Y but the Americans Muslims said that was "strict", I thought it was called practicing Islam. Yet the worst part was they told me that was what Islam taught. So it was almost like I had come out of prison after having been amongst evil and evildoers for 20 years, only to learn that all the "good non-criminals" preached crime was what God taught us to do in his book, via his prophets and that by trying to be Islamic/good it was unislamic/bad/extreme. If I met American Muslims before becoming a Muslim I might have never become a Muslim because most of them compromise/dilute Islam thinking it's extreme or too strict for American tastes. While the ignorance makes them believe themselves. So I had found Islam while in America but I didn't find knowledgeable confident practicing Muslims despite meeting people in the masjid claiming to teach Islam. I felt like a minority before going to the American masjids to meet Muslims and felt like a bigger minority afterwards. I feared telling them how wrong and unislamic they were because I didn't want them to accuse me of being extreme. Eventually I found proper American masjids where they practiced and taught Islam correctly. Unfortunately the sad truth is that not every masjid in America teaches/practices Islam right.

    My first Ramadan as a Muslim began in July 2012 CE. Since the Lunar year is about 10 or 11 days shorter than the Gregorian year, in the Gregorian/Christian calendar the month of Ramadan starts and ends on different days each year. It begins when the new crescent of the moon of the month of Ramadan is visually seen by the naked eye, it's extreme and potentially sinful to fast before the moon of Ramadan is actually seen. If it is cloudy and the moon cannot be seen by anyone in the local community/country then the preceding month of Shaban is counted as 30 days. Although Shaban could be 28 or 29 days depending on the lunar cycle. This makes it exciting to go out at night and/or check on the internet to see if anyone has seen the moon in anticipation of Ramadan. It would be comparable to the Gregorian new years eve countdown's final ten seconds stretched out over a period of several days. Anyways I was excited to experience a whole month of fasting. Compared to the Christian way of fasting, fasting as a Muslim was easy, just from sun up to sundown, some days you don't even get hungry. It's mostly the thirst that is hardest, but sacrificing helps one focus. Surprisingly you can get a lot more done with more efficiency on an empty stomach. Although fasting isn't just about abstaining from food and drink. In Islam when a person fasts they fast from sinful speech, hearing sinful things, using the eyes for sinful purposes and ideally fasting from all sinful deeds. When 1.8 billion people on the planet do this every year for an entire month it has an effect on the world, causing it to be a better place during Ramadan. Spiritually the soul takes priority and flourishes. Fasting also cleans out bad toxins from the body. There are so many benefits of fasting the list would be endless, but the number one reason to do it is because Allah says. Allah made all the food, drink, mouths, teeth and tongue with which we eat. If our Creator instructs us not to eat and drink at a certain time, who are we to disagree? If Allah gives us dietary restrictions on what we can eat, with so many other alternatives what kind of lunatic would disobey? Some tips I learned to make fasting easier is to drink a bottle of water in the morning before dawn so one isn't as thirsty, then try not to exert oneself too excessively physically during the day. Contrary to what people might think, voluntarily going without is very rewarding, not only personally but eternally. It also makes one humble and helps one to appreciate things. Muslims also make extra effort to fast from egotism, fast with their eyes by abstaining from sinful sights and fast with their ears by abstaining from hearing sinful or useless things during Ramadan, but we should be fasting from such things all the time anyways. During the nights in Ramadan there is a special voluntary prayer called "Taraweeh". Taraweeh is just like a regular prayer, except it's only done during Ramadan every night. When a Muslim prays they recite verses from the Quran. If one attends every Taraweeh prayer for the month of Ramadan they will have heard the entire Quran recited by the imam while praying. The one who leads the Taraweeh prayer is usually someone who has memorized the entire Quran, known as a Hafiz. If the Hafiz makes any mistakes then the other people who have memorized that verse correct him during the prayer, reciting the verse correctly to him so he repeats it and recites it perfectly with proper pronunciation. Every masjid in the world does Taraweeh every year during Ramadan. The end of Ramadan is when the first crescent of the moon of Shawwal is visually seen and if it is too cloudy for anyone to see then Ramadan is counted as 30 days. It is important to make sure it is really the month of Shawwal and wait for the moon to be seen or 30 days, because if one stops fasting during the days thinking it's Shawwal when it's really Ramadan they wouldn't have fasted the full month. Thus if someone were to accidentally start Ramadan a day early based on calculations instead of visually sighting the moon then they may accidentally skip fasting the last day of Ramadan and not know it. So Ramadan is exciting and unpredictable when it starts each year and Ramadan is also exciting and unpredictable when it ends, similar to how our life is exciting and unpredictable when we are born and when we die. On the first day of the month of Shawwal Muslims can eat and drink again when the sun is out. To celebrate there is a special communal prayer and a big feast. It's usually done outside if the weather is permitting, as that is how Muhammad pbuh did it. Since Ramadan ended in August that year the feast "*eid-al-fitr*" was done outside. A park was rented out and filled to maximum occupancy, almost everyone there was a Muslim and we numbered in the thousands. Again everyone was all so similar yet we had never met before. On eid there is a special speech after the special eid prayer before we eat. It's such a fun day Muslims look forward to it every year. Experiencing a holiday for the first time as an adult was weird; I didn't know what to expect my first holiday memory would be like. It was a great holiday and genuine, there was no pretend fantasy or deceiving of children. Children were given gifts out of kindness and everyone ate together solely because they wanted to, there was no social obligation. At the same time, eating on eid is a form of worshipping because we were celebrating the same thing in the same way as the Prophet Muhammad pbuh. I've celebrated all the nationalist, personal and Christian holidays that are observed in America. All praises and thanks be to Allah that I've been guided away from them and experience the Muslim holidays. Fasting one day in Ramadan is better than Christmas, Halloween, Easter, Valentines and one's birthday combined. I apologize for being unable to express the excitement and pleasure experienced on a Muslim holiday; it's something which only a Muslim can understand. Also know that every holiday is a religious commemoration, hence the word "holiday" which comes from "holy day". Only God has the right to establish a specific day of the year to be celebrated annually as a holiday, because every single holiday is a religious event with religious rituals. A secular holiday cannot exist, because a holiday observed on a annual basis can only be ordained by the one who made time. People cannot invent holidays to thank God. It's God who tells us how and when to celebrate, not governments, family, friends or cultural traditions. Basically if God didn't teach you about that holiday then you know that it's not something God is pleased with. Realistically all the holidays that God hasn't decreed aren't really holidays at all, but are pay days for the economy and ways for governments to control when and what people do, literally dictating when and how families are supposed to get together whether they want to or not. Haven't you wondered why so many family's dread "getting through the holidays"? It's because those holidays are unnatural and not something we were created to do. This is how people end up worshiping governments because by celebrating when governments allow/order them to, they end up thinking celebrations can be dictated by the government and give God's authority to others. Also most of those holidays when folks are partying is when governments do their dirty work passing oppressive laws, because they know people are too busy to notice. Frequent and diverse holidays also make populations emotionally unstable as their emotions change according to the calendar and social pressure controls their behavior. Therefore Muslims don't participate in any of the unislamic holidays. We don't even take off from work on them, or at least Muslims aren't supposed to, sometimes we get forced to do so against our will because places get closed.

  While learning more about Islam, in 2012, I noticed the importance of the ties of kinship was often stressed. At that time all my family, except my parents, had virtually no communication with me. Maintaining kinship ties is a duty for every Muslim, even if it isn't easy. After learning that it was not enough to forgive my family in my heart and that I had to reconnect, I was in an awkward situation. How do you break the news to Christian family members that you shunned and haven't communicated to in years that you are sorry, want to reconnect and also became a Muslim? Very carefully. It was a stressful situation and Satan presented all kinds of negative potential reactions. Eventually I decided writing a letter would be the best way to communicate my intentions to reconnect and my embracing of Islam. Writing a letter allowed me to clear up any misconceptions that I thought my family was likely to have without having to react on the spot, which would have been especially difficult if talking to more than one family member at a time if they kept interrupting, as people tend to do. Writing messages also helps to prevent emotions from taking over and leading us to say things we later regret. To my surprise most all the responses were positive and only one response tried to tell me Christianity was the truth. I responded to that response asking for clarification on Christian doctrines and asked for evidence as to why Christianity was true hoping it would be provided, but never received a response. I'm not upset about it because everyone takes time. Although some family members informed me to never comminicate with them and others just move without telling me their new contact information. Had I learned a family member became a Muslim while I was Catholic I'd have treated them terribly. I was actually surprised nobody in my family harassed me about being Muslim or embracing Islam, because I studied the bible and Vatican policy while training to be a priest and knew that Christianity is intolerant. On the one hand I was relieved that all my worries were for nothing, but on the other hand I was sad that so few of my family cared about religion. Of course they had initial questions that I tried to answer with the limited knowledge that I had. Although after the initial questions and telling a rough story of "how/why I became a Muslim" they tended to drop the topic of religion altogether ignoring the fact that Muslims and Christians believe different things and cannot both be going to paradise. It shows that my family really doesn't care about what happens to me in the afterlife. According to their Christian religions Muslims go to hell. Yet aside from the one response I already mentioned, another Christian letter originally sent by a church that family remailed to me and occasional talks with my parents, none of my family tries to tell me why they believe Christianity is a true religion. This may be because they know I'm intimately familiar with Christianity. Although if they really believed Christianity is the way to heaven, then they would try to persuade me. Yet at the time of this writing, most of my family nearly never discusses religion unless I bring it up, which frequently seems like a laborious chore to do as if it causes them pain to talk about or hear. They tell me they "love me" while at the same time believing that if I die as a Muslim I'll go to hell forever. If they really cared about me they would want to discuss religion with me at every opportunity fearing my fate if I were to die, as I fear their fate if they die in the state they are currently in. Since they don't discuss religion with me often, it shows that they don't truly care about my final destination. So that's where most people only "love you" on their own terms and conditions, they define what "love" is and the one whom they "love" has no authority over defining "love" or criticizing their "love" and proving it to be fake. They want to use the word but don't want to live up to it. Then they'll say they want me to be with them in paradise yet they're okay with me belonging to a different religion. Furthermore no family member of mine has ever tried to make the case that Islam is false. This shows that subconsciously they know it is true even if they won't admit it, or else they just don't care about me or God. That is the main reason why people are non-Muslims, because they don't know about Islam or care about God or Muslims. Although the main reason people become Christian is because their parents raised them as Christians. But how did their parents become Christian? Typically because their parents were Christian too. Yet who was the first member of my family to become Christian and why? My family members have no answer for me and don't know when we became Christian but just assume it was because it was true. However I looked into it, my mother's family traces their ancestry to Poland and my father's traces to Ireland and Germany.

Regarding my mother's family of Polish lineage, Poland did not exist as a nation until Miesko I of the Piast Dynasty created it in the 10th century, at the time most people in the region were pagans. Although Miesko I ran into trouble when the Catholic Germans became militarily superior and the pagan priest class of Poland prevented him from centralizing state power. So in 965 CE Miesko I married a Catholic Bohemian princess in order to seal the Polish-Bohemian alliance and became Catholic on the spot. Now safe from the threat of a German invasion, in 966 CE Miesko I made Catholicism the state sponsored religion and eliminated the pagan priest class that caused him so much trouble, the civilians were thus "motivated" to become Catholic. Yet most didn't and in 1030 CE the pagans rebelled in Poland to fight back against the

Christianization program instigated by the rulers who were supported by the Popes in Rome. It led to civil wars between pagans and Catholics to the extent that history says Poland had no ruler between 1034-1040 CE. In the end the pagans lost. Yet still many Polish people refused to be Catholic, so the Church sent in the military order of the Teutonic Knights to convert them and kill those who refused. Since many Polish were Christian by force, when the Protestant reformation broke out the Polish saw it as an opportunity to be neutral and agnostic so to say. That was until Fausto Paolo Sozini came to Poland after an invitation and spread his teaching about Jesus pbuh being completely human. He used the bible to say how the trinity and son of god theory is false and was invented by Greek pagan philosophers. He taught that Jesus couldn't offer an infinite atonement for sin because according to the Gospels he only suffered for a short time. Whereas the most intense suffering possible on earth cannot compare with the eternal suffering of hell which man is liable to receive, and if one said Christ was infinite then his ability to endure suffering would be infinite but even if a being with an infinite pain threshold were to suffer, which is impossible, that cannot atone for eternal suffering. Because the level of suffering could only atone for that level, it cannot account for an eternal time. So if Jesus endured maximum pain equivalent enough for all to be saved from hell for X hours, then they'd only get saved for X hours from hell, and only those who sinned before the event could be saved since he couldn't atone for sins not yet committed. Whereas if one argued Jesus could atone for future sins then that means there is no repentence or even such a thing as God's forgiveness because baptism would be a stamped ticket to paradise which no sin could revoke. All sins would be atoned for before they were committed and before God could forgive them. Thus if Trinitarianism and the doctrine of Atonement were true, a Christian could do anything they wanted and didn't need any rules at all. But this would apply to everyone, because if Jesus had atoned for sins and could offer infinite payment then people didn't even need baptism because if Jesus could save anyone and everyone then he would. Thus Sozini said Jesus could not and can not be God, nor a son of God nor could he have atoned for any sins. Catholics and Protestants called his Unitarian faith Socianism or New Arianism and tried to kill him, but he survived and his faith spread throughout Poland. However in 1638 CE Socianists started being hunted down and killed for their faith, until in 1658 CE the people of Poland were given an ultimatum to either become Catholic or leave the country. Thus many dispersed throughout Europe and only Catholics were left in Poland.

However the real kicker about my "Polish" maternal family is that they aren't Polish at all. Both of my maternal grandparents were born in America around the years 1919-1920 CE, so without dispute they, their kids and grandkids are all American, none of whom have ever been to Poland; as far as I know. Now my Grandmother's parents and her grandparents were also born in America and she can't remember when they originally came from Poland to America, but it was at least 3-4 generations before she was born; in the 1800s or earlier. While my Grandfather said how his uncle fought in WWI as an American so his family was definitely in America before WWI, which started in 1914 CE. So why do I say my family isn't Polish if they came from Poland to America in the 1800s or before WWI? Well Poland ceased to exist as a nation in 1795 CE. America is actually older than Poland. From 1795 all the way until 1918 CE Poland did not exist, and it's various regions belonged to Russia, Prussia and Germany. Then again from 1939-1952 Poland also did not exist, as during that time it was Germany and then Russia. So when my ancestors first came to America they did not come from Poland and were not Polish citizens. Where did they come from? My family doesn't know but it certainly wasn't a place called Poland. Yet most of my maternal family members think they have Polish heritage and Polish traditions when in reality all these alleged Polish customs aren't Polish customs at all and they aren't even practiced in Poland today. Thus at holidays when they make certain foods and do silly things saying "It's our Polish custom", it's not Polish today and it's not Polish then and we aren't Polish at all, even if our ancestors who came to America were which they weren't. That's another key point, because even if my ancestors came to America from Poland, I and my family still would not be Polish because we are born and raised American citizens with absolutely no link to Poland at all. If any of my family went to Poland they'd say we are stupid Americans. If you weren't born there and aren't a citizen then you aren't one of them, your ancestry is irrelevant. To use an American example, starting in 1822 CE the American Colonization society began colonizing a piece of west Africa having black Americans go and live there. In 1847 CE this colony declared independence from America and called itself Liberia. America finally recognized this independence in 1862 CE, 15 years later. Which is funny when you consider Britain only took 7 years to recognize America's declared independence. But what's even funnier is that when I saw it only takes 2 years of residence to qualify for Liberian citizenship I was shocked to see they have a condition for citizenship based on their 1847 CE constitution still in effect today that says: "*No person shall be naturalized unless he is a Negro or of Negro descent.*" Meaning Liberia, founded by former black Americans to this day still do not allow anyone except a "Negro" to be a citizen. As a "white", briefly interested in Liberian citizenship, it was funny to learn "*No you can't be a citizen of this country because you are white and don't have brown skin.*" Now if today some black Liberian who was born and raised in Liberia since his family moved there in the 1800s and only speaks Liberian Kreyol told some posh white American that they were an American what would happen? The American would probably say "*You wish! You're a lying Liberian you ain't American even a little bit! You're a thoroughbred African.*" Which is true, he's not American but Liberian, but how stupid would Americans consider him to be if every holiday he told everyone he was joyfully practicing his longstanding American family traditions? Even the Liberians would say he was crazy. Yet Americans do this same thing claiming their silly traditions are from another country and think it's different because they believe their family at one time came to America from somewhere else. Whereas even if they did, that has nothing to do with them today and the traditions they are doing are just plain stupid and pointless and that's why people in those countries don't do those stupid things anymore. Realistically it makes just as much sense for someone to paint on a wall and say they are following their caveman family traditions. Seriously why did the caveman painting traditions stop? Because God did not like those traditions. The funny part about this is that many would think such comments would be very offensive to my elders, yet my maternal grandparents agree with me in that we aren't Polish and that the holiday traditions are sinful and stupid. Today they tell me they wish they didn't pass those family traditions on to the next generation. The problem is my maternal family members like my aunts, uncles and some cousins take pride in feeling special and having sinful stupid traditions for holidays. When I point out these stupid sinful family holiday traditions are also Pagan they tend to think that our family has always been Christian just like how they think they're Polish. The point is that if you aren't Polish, or never thought you were of Polish ancestry, you and your family might still be in the same boat thinking your family was Christian when they were really pagans who fought against Christianity. Yet the point is that your family is not you, they believed and did what they did and you will not be held accountable for anyone's beliefs and actions except for your own. However if you choose to believe and do what your family or what you think your family did, God will hold you accountable 100%. Saying "*It's a family tradition*" doesn't make a sin a good deed.

Regarding Germany during the Christian Reformation and Thirty Years war as well as with the public policy of the "Holy Roman Empire" religious persuasion was political persuasion. Politics was what determined whether you were Catholic or Protestant. But prior to Christianity, Germans were pagans who worshipped trees, as many others did. In fact in pagan Ireland oak trees were so sacred that it was illegal to cut one down. The saying "knock on wood" even comes from the Celts of Ireland who would knock on an oak tree to start a conversation with the tree spirit. Both Greeks and Celts thought touching oak tees could bring good fortune, in a sense believing that money grows or comes from oak trees. The pagan Germans would put evergreens in their houses during winter because they stayed green all year long and so they thought by putting them inside during winter it would give them life inside the home while all else died outside. They thought having a tree inside during winter would help them survive the winter, if they tenderly tended to it and treated it properly of course. The evergreen trees were considered lucky magical mysterious survival charms. When Arian Christians came to Germany, some pagans became Arian Christians and some didn't. Although when the Catholics conquered Germany they forced Germany to convert by the sword. They killed the Arians and absorbed the pagan religions into Catholicism turning the German pine trees into Christmas trees, then just brainwashed the kids to think differently about the tree and become Catholics. Prior to that until the 3rd century CE Christians vehemently prohibited having trees in the house, or decorating them, because of the following bible verses in Jeremiah 10:1-4, "*Hear what the* LORD *says to you, people of Israel.* ² *This is what* **the** **LORD** **says**: *"Do not learn the ways of the nations or be terrified by signs in the heavens, though the nations are terrified by them.* ³ *For* **the practices of the peoples are worthless; they cut a tree out of the forest, and a craftsman shapes it with his chisel.** ⁴ **They adorn it with silver and gold; they fasten it with hammer and nails so it will not totter.**" Those verses of the bible clearly indisputably explain down to the trimmings the pagan tree tradition known today as the Christmas tree. Before Jesus pbuh was even born "The Lord" said it was a sinful wicked pagan practice. Do you remember the Asherah poles condemned in the bible verses I mentioned earlier? Those were wooden and some biblical scholars have explicitly said they were trees kept in the house as part of a pagan's personal home shrine. As the bible mentions pagan trees were not left undecorated, just as people do today glass balls/ornaments were hung on the trees. But why did they do that? Well for some the ornaments were symbolic testicles. The tree was a phallic symbol of the penis and the ornaments were testicles making it an extremely sexual object of fertility in the midst of winter, but it didn't stop there. There is also a winter wreath, which is a woven circle symbolizing the sun disc, a female womb and the ouroborus. They'd put this wreath on top of their tree to simulate intercourse but since that was too sexually graphic for developing Christian tastes a tradition of putting a star or angel or other figue on the top of the tree's symbolic phallus tip substituted the pornographic wreath/womb topping. Yet still people get the winter wreaths regardless not knowing they were originally for putting on the fertility tree to depict intercourse. But what about the tinsel? (traditionally gold and sliver stringy lace put on the trees) The tinsel was to symbolize ejaculate, one color was the ejaculate of the male deity and the other color of tinsel was the ejaculate of the female deity. The proto-Christmas tree was basically how pagans taught their kids about sex. From it kids learned how some time after the fertility ritual occurs "gifts appear out of nowhere" under the tree just as how a baby appears some time after sex. However the sex cults weren't the only ones with decorated trees during winter, the magicians did this too for fertility rituals as well as magical spells. To them the ornaments on the trees were "witch balls" magically enchanted designed to ward off evil spirits and magic by the magical balls and the tree creating a magical winter spell of protection for the household. However other witch balls would contain things inside them like string or figures or any number of objects/materials. Those witch balls were made to entice demons to come to the house/tree mesmerized by the colorful ball and then once they entered the ball the magic was supposed to trap the devils inside the ornaments so they could become the slave of the magician. So ornaments on Christmas trees is actually a type of witchcraft designed to bring demons to your house and trap them inside, which of course since most today aren't doing the magical spells for their ornaments the demons don't get trapped inside their ornaments with Christmas trees but they still come to visit the household which has Christmas trees nonetheless. It's just that now the bait that used to be fertility trees no longer contains intentional magical traps, except for those made by magicians and cursed with magical incantations/rituals. It's like cheese being left out for mice without any mousetraps, except it's not cheese but Christmas trees and instead of mice it's demons. Other superstitions held that the ornaments were magical orbs designed to bewitch the eyes of visiting onlookers so they wouldn't notice or desire the family's gifts stored under the fertility tree. Sadly many today are ignorant about these satanic dangerous "Christmas traditions", which actually endanger our species. Hanging ornaments on a tree was a type of magic designed to harm people and invite devils. Christmas trees are practically demon magnets designed to harm people by causing evil or inviting evil. The bible actually forbids Christmas Trees, but that doesn't stop Christians from putting them up in houses, squares, stores and churches. Yet these same Christians have the nerve to claim that they follow the bible? Have they not read the bible? Why don't they read these verses from the bible in church? They are doing exactly word for word what the bible explicitly says God said "Do not do". One way to tell a Christian hasn't read the bible is if they have Christmas trees, and that includes priests and pastors who put Christmas trees in their churches. People just assume that if someone's a priest then they must have read the bible. I was training to be a priest, reading the bible is not a requirement to become a priest. You can become a Catholic priest, or a minister for non-Catholic denominations, without ever reading the bible. For the Christians who have Christmas trees and maintain they read the bible, then it proves that they either don't understand what they're reading or they are misinterpreting it, because if they read these bible verses they wouldn't have Christmas trees. Christmas trees are sinful every way you look at it, the problem is Christians don't think they have sinful family traditions. If they do accept that it's a sin then most will say Jesus pbuh paid the price for it so it's ok. Yet the Christmas tree sin is a sin because it's an idol, so with Christian logic one might as well have a golden cow in the house like the Israelites had in the desert, or statues of Zeus, Baal, Buddha or Krishna. Most Christians would take offense to Sozini's teaching that the doctrine of atonement lets Christians do any sin they want, but in reality Christians will have Christmas trees using the very reason Sozini says they would use to justify the sin even when their own bible says it's a sin. Just see for yourself what happens when you try to tell a Christian during the month of December their bible says Christmas trees are sinful and God said not to have them.

That's the history regarding how Poland and Germany became Christian countries. Ireland has a similar story which has unfortunately been glossed over and romanticized with St. Patrick's Day. The historical Patrick was British, brought to Ireland as a slave, escaped after 6 years and later went back to spread Catholicism and kill all the Celts, Druids and pagans who didn't convert during the 5th century CE. When people say that St. Patrick rid Ireland of all snakes they misunderstand what that means. First of all to rid a place of snakes meant to kill them all, but there never were snakes in Ireland and there are no snake fossils there. The legend goes Patrick chased all snakes into the sea, but what modern Christians forget is that the snakes were a symbolic representation of non-Catholics. So the policy of "St." Patrick was either you become Catholic or live in the ocean. Thus you can see why Patrick is known for having had so much success in spreading Catholicism in Ireland. Although there were many Catholic missionaries in Ireland forcing people to convert. Patrick is the one who gets the most credit because he wrote 2 letters, one was an autobiographical confession and the other was a letter to the soldiers of Coroticus. Thus with documented evidence of his existence Patrick could be turned into a hero for Catholics to idolize. Because for Church propagada it's not about if a person did what is attributed to them, it's about if they can prove a person with that name existed at that time, then they can say whatever they want and get away with it. Many have such a belief about historical people, they think if you can prove a person with that name existed at that time then everything they believe about them is true. Jesus pbuh is another example. Many think that if you agree a man named Jesus pbuh existed then you are forced to believe that everything else they say about him is true. Allegedly Patrick used the green shamrock having 3 leaves on 1 plant as an explanation of the trinity, but historically Patrick never used it as an explanation for the trinity. Not one time did he write about a shamrock nor did any Christian missionaries in Ireland write about it. Not until 1571 CE was the shamrock ever written about in Ireland in english and it wasn't written about in Gaelic until 1707 CE, but even then it still wasn't believed to be a symbol of the trinity. The now popular Christian myth that the shamrock was St. Patrick's explanation of the trinity began in 1726 CE. The Catholic Church made up that explanation as an excuse for why the Irish converted to Catholicism long after the fact, because admitting that it was do or die wasn't a very good story anymore. Prior to that the pagan holiday Ostra was turned into St. Patrick's Day in order to replace it and

Christianize it. The Irish were celebrating "St. Patrick's Day" long before anyone claimed he used the shamrock to explain the trinity. The Irish had a custom of eating the shamrock on Ostra day or "St. Patrick's day" after dousing it in liquor. This alcoholic recipe was known as "drowning the Shamrock" which later became known as "St. Patrick's Pot" and in modern times the drunks dye their alcohol green instead of adding the leaf. Hundreds of years ago no Christians used a shamrock to "convince someone" of the trinity doctrine, they used a sword. The shamrock story is a recent fiction, to replace historical facts of the gory sword. St. Patrick used the sword and the ocean, he did not use the shamrock, the shamrock was the symbol of Druid deity he was denouncing. The ancient Druids also believed that the 4-leaf shamrock/clover caused good luck, since there is only about 1 for every 10,000 that grow. Every Christian nation in Europe and the Americas has the same story of forced conversion via violence. The reason historians don't tell people about the pagan religions and myths of Europe isn't because they didn't exist, it is because Christians either killed all the pagans or incorporated their be<u>lie</u>fs into Christianity turning the pagan gods into saints as is the case with St. Anthony, St. Blaise, St. Valentine and countless others. Pagan temples in Europe became churches and the idols became saints so that the first generation of pagans turned Christians could worship their pagan gods under the guise of Christianity, whilst the Church would brainwash their kids to be Catholics. Basically the pagans forced to convert were told: *"If you want to worship X that's ok but we will call it Saint XYZ and so must you. However you must also agree to let us make your kids Christians, but don't worry because they can pray to Saint XYZ all they want. Oh and your temple is now a Church and your religious holidays are still the same days as before but now they are Christian holidays."* Thus since the Church allowed saints to be prayed to and kept the holidays, the brainwashed kids didn't anathemise their parents for praying to saints and the secretly pagan parents just hoped their kids would continue praying to their pagan god as a Saint. Pagan parents were unable to denounce Christianity for fear of death, yet because the saints and holidays left an opening for their religion to survive to some extent they didn't resist the Christianization process as much as they would have otherwise. The Myths became Legends and the Legends became Christianized Saints and as the population became Christian those stories were accepted as uncontested facts because they were so popular. Just as a little kid believes in Santa Claus because all the other little kids believe in Santa Claus and their parents don't have the guts to tell their kids they were lied to because they think there is a benefit from the falsehood and fear social difficulties if they tell the truth. The pagan converts were comparable to someone being put into a position where they would be killed if they told their kids Santa Claus wasn't real. This is how and why most Christians today were raised by Christians who were raised by Christians who were raised by Christians for as long as they can remember without any of them knowing who the first Christian in their family was. You get the same response if you ask who was the first person in the family to teach kids about Santa Claus. Seriously ask someone who's family teaches kids about Santa Claus who the first liar in their family was who began the tradition of lying to kids about Santa Claus and why. On the other hand many Muslims know their entire family tree dating back thousands of years. For instance I personally know someone who knows their entire paternal lineage and history name by name from him all the way back to Ibn Abbas, who is a famous companion of the prophet Muhammad pbuh. The mother of Ibn Abbas became a Muslim before he was born and was the second woman to enter Islam becoming a Muslim after Khadijah did on the very first day Muhammad pbuh became a prophet. So that is the first Muslim in his family he knows of. Of course this person is an Arab and Arabs are known for their genealogical records, but the fact remains that many Muslims can trace their family history back to the first Muslim and know why, when and how their ancestors became Muslims. I've also met a guy who descends from Muhammad pbuh through Ali ibn abi Talib(the guy who married the Muhammad's daughter Fatima) is his 42nd Grandparent. While again he was able to confirm that his family had been Muslim for 42 generations and it is well known exactly how Ali became a Muslim to start with. Whereas if you ask a non-Muslim who their 42nd grandparent is and what the religion of every ancestor in between was then you likely won't get answers. Most families with Christian histories either cannot or will not be able to tell you who the first Christian in their family history was, because their ancestors were originally converted by force or did so to get married; hence it was never a matter of pride to be recorded and regaled through the generations but a matter of shame to be hidden and forgotten.

    Obviously my family doesn't want to hear this stuff from the first Muslim of their family, so we have a very awkward relationship since I don't join them in any of the traditional holiday celebrations because they all have evil origins and rituals which my family thinks are innocent or beneficial and don't want to know about, or care to act differently even if I tell them. Thus I stay away on their holidays, but unfortunately my family doesn't really get together unless it's for a holiday. The problem is that I think Satan makes them think I stay away from them because of personal reasons or laziness. Although it's not personal at all, the reason I stay away is because I hate their religions, their beliefs, their holidays and their sinful behaviour. Everyone is supposed to hate what God hates and God hates disbelievers. Unfortunately they are disbelievers at this time, but they don't have to be. So while I hate them it's solely for religious reasons. Yet most of them don't have a clue and would be totally surprised to learn that I hate them, because I'm kind and polite as Islam teaches me to be. Ironically I'm kinder to them as a Muslim while hating them than I was as a Christian when I liked and possibly "loved" them. Most of them probably think I feel the complete opposite about them than I really do. They don't seem to understand why I'm distant and when I'm with them they don't want to have lengthy religious dialogues. Instead they just want use whatever time they have with me to "have fun", not realizing that if we had lengthy religious dialogues they would learn that I don't spend much time with them because many of their "fun" activities involve sin. What makes it even worse is that they don't even know what's sinful, so on the rare occasions we do interact they may think they are being accommodating when at the same time they ask me to participate in sins or involve me in sinful behaviour by force against my will. Gossip/Backbiting is an example. To talk about someone without them knowing it is gossip, even if you are saying good things. To talk about someone mentioning things they would dislike you to say about them is backbiting. While saying things that aren't true about someone unbeknownst to them which they don't like being said is slander. The one who hears gossip, backbiting or slander is guilty of the same sin being committed unless they stop and forbid the evil. Yet it's not easy to politely and effectively prevent someone from talking about people who aren't present. I hope my mentioning this isn't backbiting in itself, and I ask that they and any I backbite forgive me for all of my transgressions, but I mention it because so many people talk about people to others without those being talked about being present. This is a huge issue that's so evil that the person who backbites another actually transfers their good deeds to that person. So the backbiter gains sins and loses their good deeds. Yet it causes even bigger problems because if I hear someone talk about someone else without them present to hear all that is said about them, then I know that same person will talk about me when I'm not around to hear what they say as well. Personally I try to get away from such people, when they mention others. Really if they want to talk about that person then they should go talk to that person and not me, you or anyone else. Although some are arrogant enough to do just that and insult someone to their face. Whereas that's sinful too and it's called "face-biting". The tongue is one of the main reasons people spend time in the hellfire and all of these various sins of the tongue are major sins. Heed these words: "*It's better for you to bite your own tongue off than to backbite or facebite someone else.*" It's such a serious issue I'm even afraid and reluctant to get married, because I don't want to expose another human being to a gossipy/backbiting family. Backbiting/facebiting is a form of cannibalism, which Muslims can't do during Ramadan or at any other time. There is a simple rule to stay safe: If they can't hear what you are saying while you say it then don't talk about them, unless you are genuinely praising them for noble reasons. If you hear someone else backbiting somebody, then go up to them, turn around and ask them to sink their teeth into your back because you would rather they literally bite your back than listen to them backbite and be guilty of participating by hearing it. Gossip, backbiting, slander and all the sins done by any means of communication are not just abuse to the frequently defenseless victims but to all who hear or see it. Such deeds don't lead to paradise and we must all be extra careful regarding what we say and write, especially about parents and even about our enemies. Satan is our enemy and he uses our own tongues to destroy ourselves and each other. Rather than say more prayers we should say less curses. The main source of pollution on this planet is our tongues. Our contagious verbal vomit contaminates so many that we are now experiencing a plauge of poisonous communication. Truly our tongues have destroyed any claim we have of being peaceful people. Our words cause wounds which do damage forever and hurt us more than anyone else. Being pious is impossible if we don't learn how to keep quiet. Of course this is easy to say but it's harder to remain silent. Our tongues are not our friends, they are the things that hurt our friends and family and everyone it takes as a target. We frequently consider our tongues a gift from God but we use them as though they were given to us by Satan. Humans have the most dangerous type of tongue out of all the other creatures on the planet. I apologize to my family for writing about this and being guilty of the very same verbal venom and written wickedness which I condemn but hopefully you can learn a lesson that I and so many others consistently forget to practice. Our families must not help our tongues to commit crimes nor should we defame our familes with them. Maybe our families don't control their tongues but that gives us no excuse to support their verbal vandalization with our ears. Our tongue must denounce all tongues that torture things. It's surprising dentists even dare to come near our tongues when our tongues are much more of a threat than our teeth.

Truly the way most of us use our mouths it's a disgrace we use that same monster to kiss with. If you ever hear your spouse, kids or family backbite, gossip, swear or slander then you shouldn't kiss them for at least a week after they've had a clean mouth. Honestly tell them you don't want to contract their disease of foul speech which is more foul to God than foul breath is to us. Teach them a lesson by refusing to kiss criminal lips. You don't want such a dangerous mouth touching your own, spritually it's just not safe. Kissing the one who speaks or writes evil is almost like kissing Satan. Sadly our tongues can be more filthy than overflowing toilets. If someone ever backbites near toilets then quickly get the plunger to stop their mouth from spewing verbal sewage. The thing with family is that unlike with bad friends whom one is supposed to sever ties with if they are a negative influence and refuse to reform, God commanded mankind to maintain ties with family even if they're bad. You should know by now that religion is very important to me and that religion is my top priority. Unfortunately at the time I wrote this, it seems none of my family has religion as their number 1 priority in life. Generally most people are distracted by this deceptively glittering world and its amusements. I think this has to do with the anti-religious secularist nature of American culture combined with Christianity. Most Christians are taught and believe that salvation is practically guaranteed, thinking Jesus pbuh died for their sins. Many Christians consider salvation a foregone conclusion not worth much attention or effort. Realistically Christianity is the easiest religion in the world that requires the least from its adherents. Typically the easiest way to do something is not the right way, but Christians tend to ignore this reality of life when it comes to their religion. Throughout history people have shifted the blame and refused to accept responsibility and accountability for their actions, Jews have a scape-goat, Egyptians had a scape-ox, Hindus had a scape-horse, Chaldeans a scape-ram, Brahmans a scape-bull, Aztecs a scape-lamb, Tamalese a scape-hen and Christians have a scape-God/son of God. This is why the average Christian is typically the least religious person if they're grouped together with average adherents of other religions. The vast majority of Christians think that all they have to do is go to church once in awhile, believe what they're told, give money to church and it makes them a "good person" who is certain to enter paradise. I don't mean to stereotype or create strawmen, but as a former Christian evangelist I know that this is the reality of what the average Christian believes. The reality of the afterlife is that paradise is not that easy to attain. The road to paradise is surrounded by hardship and tribulation while the roads to hell are surrounded by desires and entertainment. A ticket to paradise is the most expensive type of ticket there is! If religion is not a daily thing then how can a person expect to spend infinity in heaven? Religion may not be a daily thing to most people, but for Satan religion is a daily concern and he goes to war with us relentlessly every second without ceasing. This irresponsibility of humans towards religion is heartbreaking. However I think my family's lesser religiosity is more about their failure to give religion proper importance than their lack of care for me. Regardless it can be difficult sometimes to be with family when religion is such a small part of their life. They might think it's a major part, but for most of them it's not a daily thing. While for Muslims religion is pertinent every second. Perhaps my family will read this book and learn just how important religion is and that Muslims and non-Muslims do not both go to paradise. Now I consider that reality to be the biggest type of family emergency one can have. Yet they haven't had any type of intervention or even thought it was that big of a deal that I chose to travel a different road to the afterlife than they are which leads to a very different eternal destination. Some claim they want to spend time with me, but they don't care about us never spending any time together for eternity which is what will happen if we die upon different faiths and one of them is true. Maybe by learning that they will care to discuss religion more with me so that we can discover the true religion, practice it faithfully and all spend eternity together in paradise, God-willing. Or at least maybe some of my family in humanity (you) will learn this lesson so you can prioritize better and we can meet each other in paradise, God-willing. Unfortunately people exist in the world today who will get this book and stop reading it before even getting this far out of anger at something they might have read which they disliked or disagreed with. Maybe they will use the arrogant excuse and misconception that religion isn't worth the time. God is the reason we even have time, or the ability to do anything with time. Religion and worshipping God is the reason for which we were created. The reason God is giving you oxygen this very second is because the Creator wants you to use it to worship him. The reason you haven't died yet is because God wants you to worship him more than you have, better than you have, and is generously giving you more time to get points on the test of life. Think about that fact of life carefully and consistently before you answer the final 3 questions in the grave. In a factory the final product is created for a specific reason to do a specific thing. Imagine if that product then decided that the purpose for which it was created for wasn't something it had much time for and decided to focus on other things instead. We would agree that this product is useless because it doesn't do what it was made to do. As we are creations made by God then what does it say about the humans who treat religion as something they don't have much time for? Just as we would call the unproductive factory product defective what do you think God will do to the human that is recalled who didn't make worshipping God their top priority? All praises and thanks be to God that we have the time and opportunity to become better creatures that God is more and more pleased with, before we get recalled and judged based on our performance in fulfilling our chief purpose. From the moment you and I read this sentence may God help us to make worshipping him and pleasing him our top priority at all times.

In January 2013 CE at a public library I met with some family members for the first time since being Muslim. It went pretty well I thought, although I think one might've stayed in the car because he hates Muslims. He was training to be a police officer at the time, and to this day I haven't seen him or heard from him. Anyways after the meeting it was time to pray so I was just going to pray in front of the library. Although my parents were afraid my family would videotape me on their phones, laugh at me and then post the video on the internet or something. I didn't think that would happen and didn't care if it did, it was time to pray I had to pray. I was dressed Islamically so even though the US Sunni masjid was minutes away I was afraid to go there dressed Islamically because of what the Muslims might think or what the spies might think or report if they saw me dressed Islamically when the other US Muslim guys dressed like non-Muslims. If they were dressing like Muslims in the masjid I would've felt fine but I didn't want to be the only Muslim in the masjid dressed Islamically like a Muslim. Ironically the Muslims made me afraid to be dressed Islamically around them even though I had just finished meeting non-Muslim relatives for the first time as a Muslim after not having seen them in years. Anyways my parents begged me not to pray in front of the library lest I get made fun of and they get embarassed. So I was stuck in a dilemma in that I had to pray but my parents wanted me to pray in another location than the one I had chosen. Since their request wasn't a violation of Islamic commandments or a sin then I figured I could pray in another location so my parents would feel better about me praying in public. In the parking lot there was a nursing home nearby but I noticed you couldn't park there unless you had business being there. I noticed the only other nearby place was the police station. There were some trees and a hill about 60 yards away from it so I figured I'd just pray there and that would a safe spot where I wouldn't get beat up by anyone who saw me pray. While praying there something very unexpected happened. Many police cars started filling the parking lot and I noticed I was being surrounded by lots of police carrying guns wearing bullet proof vests. The police came closer and closer. Near the end of my prayer an officer said "*Excuse me? Excuse me! What are you doing here sire? Can you hear me? What are you doing here?*" I wonderd what I should do, should I finish my prayer and ignore them or stop praying and reply? I was sooo close to finishing, just a few seconds away. But then I considered that there was a real possibility they might shoot me dead on the spot if I try to finish my prayer. So I said something like "Hi. I'm praying." Then they told me that I was on private property and I wasn't allowed to pray in front of the police station without permission. So I asked for permission and they did not give me permission. I told them I thought I was on public property and that given the fear my parents had just expressed about me praying in public I thought it would be best to pray in front of a police station without anybody potentially harassing me. They asked more questions about how, why and when I became a Muslim and why I was praying there at that time and I told them I was praying there because I had met with family nearby in the same parking lot complex and it was time to pray so I was praying as Islam says to pray on time and my parents didn't want me to pray by the library and I thought this was the best spot to pray in. They took my ID, scanned my license plate, searched my car and I concluded they were terrified of me, and being dressed Islamically they probably thought I was some terrorist praying before trying to blow up the station or something. At that moment I realized it might not have been the best idea to pray in front of an American police station unannounced. Initially I thought it was a great backup to my plan of praying in front of the Library, I never thought the police would raise the alarm and surround me. Then I wondered what my parents would think and say if they found out where I prayed when they told me they didn't want me to cause a scene by praying by the Library. I didn't tell them for 9 months, lest I get in trouble with them who might not be as "polite" as the police were. Anyways regarding my police station incident, they let me go without further hindrance and I redid my prayer at home. Then it hit me. If the government didn't know I was Muslim before, they probably know now after I prayed in front of a police station and gave them all my ID and verbally told them and saw them put me in the system as a Muslim and took pictures of my car with islamic bumperstickers on it. I could no longer pretend that the government didn't know I was Muslim because I essentially unintentionally announced it by doing what I did, at my parents request. Yet I still lived despite me knowing the government knew I was Muslim, and probably thought I was a "little different" than every other Muslim they knew of. In hindsight I think the correct thing to do was probably finish the prayer and risk the bullets, but I was a fool then and I've regretted not finishing my prayer due to police. However that event certainly made me much more comfortable praying in public. No other times have ever been so confrontational or stressful as that time praying in public. Later I'd pray in the outdoors detainment cage at the US border and outside the detainment station at the Canadian border, when/if I was detained and it was time to pray. In outdoor weather the Americans have a cage-like structure for detainees, Canadians let you pray on the sidewalk outside, when you ask of course. Although Canadians asked me if I had to pray, with Americans you have to tell them it's time to pray and you want to know where you should pray and which way Mecca(or it's direction is) is if you don't know. Whenever praying on private property, or public property with restricted usage allowances, Islam says Muslims should ask first, all property owners have rights. While in America tax-funded public government buildings are legally private property. After my realization and acceptance that the US government knew I was Muslim I gradually started going to the local US Sunni masjid and being Islamic there. First it would be just for 1 prayer a day, months later that became 2 or 3 a day, months later 4 a day and eventually I got to the point where I try to go 5 times a day Godwilling. Sadly though I think many other Muslim guys who don't come as frequently to the masjid are as foolish and/or afraid as I was. That's the only reason I can think of them having. Although I don't know if it's just me or just America, but in America it's easy to get caught in a satanic trap of thinking other Muslims are undercover while they think you are undercover and then neither of you ever talk to each other. I used to have such fears more than anyone else but all such fear is foolish and even sinful for Muslims to have regarding masjids or other Muslims. In conclusion surviving persecution and confrontation was what made me finally become comfortable being a Muslim and known as a Muslim. Had I never experienced the confrontations and persecution I had feared then I never would have been able to Islamically develop. So the persecution of Muslims helped me practice Islam. I really really didn't want it, but I'm really really really happy that I got it a lot. Today I see past persecution as a true blessing. The enemies of Islam are only scary when you don't confront them and avoid confrontation or potential persecution. Yet as much as one might try to avoid confrontation or persecution, and I really tried hard to do just that, it makes no difference because what God wills to happen will happen. All you can do is prepare to be pleased with God's decree and unafraid of anything and everything except for God and upsetting God. As long as a Muslim is doing what is right Islamically they have nothing to fear even if Islam were to become illegal. It was none other but Satan who made me afraid of persecution. The FBI, Canadian and American governments helped me, by the will of Allah, to become more Islamic as a result of them trying to intimidate and literally prevent me from praying. Fear is a type of enslavement and the Muslim is only the slave of God. Fear for other than God cannot exist within the heart of a true Muslim. If a Muslim fears some worldy thing other than God then something is deficient in their faith and spirituality; as well as their intellect and heart. I had said the Shahada in 2011 CE but it was only much later that I became a true Muslim or at least closer to being a true Muslim, there is always improvement to be made until no time is left in life. When I first went to a masjid in America unislamic Muslims scared me away but then the police persecuted me back to it. God frequently guides us in the most unexpected of ways. The important time is not the first time I went to a masjid, but the next time that I go to one Godwilling for the next prayer. How was your first time?

BIG BUSINESS RELIGION

The prophet Muhammad pbuh taught that you must not make your religion a source of income. Many Christian ministries don't follow this teaching, priests, preachers, nuns, monks, bishops, cardinals and popes survive off of the charitable donations of hard working people. Televangelists are making millions of dollars a year from their popular evangelical sermons they televise. Many Christian institutions are structured like pyramid schemes and their hierarchies operate the same as corporate franchises. Pope Leo X is reported to have remarked "*What profit has not that fable of Christ brought us!*" The Catholic Church is estimated to make $850 million a week through church donations. That equals $42.5 billion dollars for 50 weeks out of the year, not counting "holy days", Christmas and Easter. A popular joke among Catholic priests is that they have to exercise much more than other people, because with all the free food that is given to them it is difficult for a priest not to become fat. I've never heard of any other prestigious career in which it is "*difficult not to become fat*" because of the job. This is as good an indication as any that such people are less inclined to tell the truth because their livelihood is endangered if people don't like what they say. This is why a priest will not tell you that getting 0.05% interest from the bank will cause you to be punished in hell, even though the Scriptures and Pope say so, because people would be able to respond to him and say, "*Well we pay your salary so why do you accept our money if it's so sinful?*" The priest is afraid his customers (congregation) may go to a different church that says what they like to hear. He is afraid of his "flock" leaving before he fleeces them. This preaching for pay isn't restricted to Catholics or even Christianity, however while Catholics are perhaps the most famous for simony other Christians have beat them at this game. Personally the richest pastor in the world today is "non-denominational" (get more money that way) and has a networth of over $150 million. I'm not even going to bother listing a who's who of the richest preachers in the world because they compete so fiercely just last year the number 1 guy today was worth only $18 million dollars and was number 6. Overall many popular public preachers are paid as if they were MVP professional athletes winning the championship every year. Movie stars and Musicians actually get paid less to act and perform than preachers do. The point is that if you have to pay someone money for them to advise you on how to enter paradise, then they are running a business of salvation and don't really care if you suffer eternal damnation. They're not doing it for God if they're doing it for money. Don't let the uniform of the messenger fool you, even if it's a modest costume, examine the content of their message. Such people claim that their devotion to religion doesn't give them time to obtain sustenance like everyone else, the prophets pbut were much more devoted to religion than them and had much more to teach, they did it for free without one prophet ever profiting because of their religious guidance or advisement. None of the companions of the prophets ever turned their religious propagation into a racket either and it was their duty to preserve all that the prophet pbuh said and did while spreading his message. The companions of the prophets followed the prophets, many religious leaders today are following the profits. A true ascetic is not someone who lives off the charity of others. Many religious teachers have sold their religion. If they're getting paid for their religious work in this life then how can they expect any profit in the next? Not only do they sell themselves like prostitutes, but they will make you purchase what they claim to be the scriptures of God. Making what they say is divine revelation inaccessible to the poor, who are more likely to desire knowledge of the afterlife because they realize how this life does not offer contentment. Profiteering religious teachers do not care about your salvation, they're mostly concerned with how much they can get from you. Most of them don't even realize that this is their true intention, because the brainwashers have been brainwashed themselves. When doing Christian rap and planning to be a priest, I myself didn't realize how the money played a factor in what I was doing. If they had told me I'd be in tattered rags after becoming a priest I might never have begun training, but they told me I'd have all my expenses paid for as long as I lived and served the Church. They also said they'd cover college tuition, campus expenses and Seminary tuition and expenses too, with a catch. The catch was they'd pay for it as long as I was pursuing the priesthood, but if for any reason I were to stop pursuing the priesthood or say get ordained as a priest and then quit then I would have to pay back all the expenses they paid for since, *"It wouldn't be right for the Church to pay for your schooling so you benefit and then for the Church to not benefit from the schooling they paid for."* When I first heard that I thought that's only fair, but now I realize this traps people into the priesthood because they will have to pay a huge astronomical bill if they drop out or quit. Whereas especially if one is already ordained, they may not be able to pay such a debt if they ever quit, thus many must just not quit for financial reasons. This is why even when they know their religion is false they will keep on preaching it to others. Really lets say someone is an elderly priest who finds out their faith is false, what are they going to do? Of course most people assume they'll just quit their job but do you know what happens to them if they do that? They aren't allowed to live in the rectory they had been living at, so they become homeless and unemployed and they become indebted for the educational services they were given as a priest. How many do you think are willing to be homeless, unemployed and in debt for the sake of abandoning a religion they learned was false. Keeping in mind many may not know which one is true at the same time they learn their faith is false. Consider what is a priest, monk, minister or nun who apostates from Christianity to do for money? What company hires a priest or preacher who apostated? What references and skills will they have to put on their resume? Their former parishioners, their former supervisor, all of whom consider them an evil heretic? It's easier for an ex-convict to get a job than for a former preacher of a religion they abandoned, because if people can't stick with their faith then that's not a desireable type of employee and preaching a religion isn't exactly considered "great work experience". The ex-convict is seen as a reformed criminal with a bad past, but most look at a preacher who changed their religion as a former outstanding citizen who has become a religious criminal. Just imagine if the head of your religious organization apostated and then asked you if you could give them a positive referral for employment somewhere else despite them thinking your religion is evil/wrong. Would you help an apostate get a more comfortable life as an apostate? That'd be like Pharaoh building a house for Moses pbuh, or the

Jewish Rabbis trying to help get Jesus a job, or the Pope helping Martin Luther open a business. Also what about their retirement package? Any preacher who changes their religion also loses their pension. So that's where the older a preacher gets the less likely they are to change their faith, especially if they've persisted in knowingly preaching falsehood for awhile. What I mean to say is that people may not just be preaching for greed, but may delusionally think they are preaching due to their needs. Both the needy and greedy preach false faiths for money. The messages are the same, their intentions differ, both are sinful. Religious preachers who change their faith are faced with significant social and economic stress moreso than non-preachers. It's not that being more religious than others means they are less likely to change their religion, in fact you need to be more religious than most to be willing to change your religion, however those who are more religious tend to have greater worldly consequences for changing their faith. Thus despite being more religious sometimes the more religious someone is the harder it will be for them to change their religion, not for religious reasons but for worldly reasons. People never really know how attached they are to the worldly life until they have an option to voluntarily make worldly sacrifices or not. Being patient under hardship is not patience, patience is choosing hardship and being patient when you could have chosen an easier way less pleasing to God. For example we wouldn't say Jonah pbuh was patient in the belly of the whale, because if he was patient he wouldn't have ended up in the belly of the whale to begin with. This shows the trial of preachers, a prophet was willing to disobey God in order to avoid preaching the hard way opting to preach what would be easier to preach and God punished him for it. God punished Jonah pbuh just for wanting to preach the true faith but in a different setting than the one God wanted, Jonah pbuh did this because it's not easy to preach what God wants, where God wants, to who God wants, the way God wants it preached. So imagine how hard then it is to stop preaching the false faith and begin preaching the truth faith instead? Jonah pbuh had difficulty due to a location/population, yet a false preacher who realizes they've been preaching falsehood has to change a lot more of their preaching than just the location/population they are preaching to. Many simply won't preach what/how God wants, not only that but they aren't even strong enough to stop preaching what God hates. There are many different levels of preaching and each level is harder the closer you get to preaching the right religion perfectly. It's so hard to preach anything that the preachers actually tend to think that because it's hard for them to preach then their false religion must be true because it's so hard and is met with such opposition. Preaching is harder than any other profession in the world, and to change industries within the preaching profession is the hardest of all types of changes to make. It's not like changing your sports team, or even your citizenship, it's literally akin to changing your species. It's probably easier to get a sex change than it is to change the way a preacher preaches or the message which one preaches. Yet that difficulty in changing methods or messages doesn't even account for the worldly difficulties such a theological change entails. Likewise preachers have family and friends too, so how do you think the family and friends of a preacher who turns apostate will react to the news? How many would treat a professional preacher changing their religion as a good thing or something to be proud of? Some may even be married, and if a preacher were married then their spouse is likely religious enough to want to divorce them for changing their religion. I'm not saying that's wrong to do, sometimes it's even obligatory to divorce if one spouse changes their religion, yet this is just one thing out of the many things people consider when they find out the religion which they are upon is false. Sadly some are so attached to their spouse that they are willing to burn in hell forever rather than risk a potential divorce or get a divorce if need be. Some aren't even willing to risk losing a boyfriend or girlfriend, or any other type of friend, for the sake of religion. They value human friendships more than their friendship with God. Others change their faith just to get married. So if people are changing their faith to get married, how many do you think are willing to risk their marriage by changing their faith? Religious leaders have the most to lose out of any other category of people if they convert to another faith or apostate, even Kings have less to lose for changing their religion and it's known that political leaders rarely change religions. This causes many preachers to preach even after they learn what they are preaching is wrong because they are tricked into thinking the consequences of abandoning falsehood are too great for them to bear, not knowing the price of paradise is worth it. Some religious leaders are well aware their faith which they zealously promote is false and do their jobs for fame/fortune or other reasons, as demonstrated when in 1999 CE the Dalai Lama told reporter John Perkins: *"Don't become a buddhist. The world doesn't need more buddhists. Do practice compassion. The world needs more compassion."* Now if Buddhism were a genuinely good or correct religion then why would the Dalai Lama ever publicly tell someone else *"Don't become a buddhist."*? Because he knows deep down that Buddhism is false and wicked. He might not denounce it and continue to promote it but he knows. Yet what is the Dalai Lama to do? Quit and try to get a job? What is the Pope to do? Really where is the "Preacher hotline" for preachers who realize their religion is false but they have responsibilities to preach X religion as being true? Many preachers feel that they cannot stop preaching X regardless of what is right and wrong. Once one starts preaching something it's psychological, mentally, and emotionally difficult to ever stop doing so. God-willing the esteemed leaders of false religions will publicly come clean and stop laundering money through their brainwashing machines. Peer pressure, as well as economic, political and social pressure keeps the preachers of falsehood persistant even after they know better. Which may be why it has been said that: *"The ignorance of the laity is the revenue of the clergy."* It's because of fools believing the preachers of falsehood and paying them to preach to them that they keep on preaching falsehood despite knowing it's blatantly false. Preachers rarely admit it but their audience influences them and their message a lot. Few preachers actually say what they want, believe or feel. All preachers are slaves, some are slaves of God, other to themselves or their religion and others are enslaved to those they preach to because preaching is their job which they are remunerated for in more ways than one. With preaching such financial and religious crimes have almost always been the case with the leaders of Christian religions, clerical or not. Hence Francesco Guicciardi remarked on his desire to be a leader of Christianity, but for atypical reasons when he wrote: *"To no man is it more displeasing than to me to see the ambition, covetousness, and excesses of priests, not only because all wickedness is hateful in itself, but because...such wickedness should find no place in men whose state of life implies a special relationship with God. My relations with several popes have made me desire their greatness at the expense of my own interest. Had it not been for this consideration, I would have loved Martin Luther as myself, not that I might set myself free from the laws imposed upon us by Christianity, but that I might see this swarm of scoundrels confined within due limits, so that they might be forced to choose between a life of crime or a life without power."*

Christians complain that Christmas has become too commercialized, it has always been a commercial sales event; it's just that now people who aren't preachers decided to get their share of the market. At least corporate companies are honest that they're main interest is the money. It's no secret why Christian preachers complain about the commercialization of Christmas, they miss the extra profit. Those golden chalices, illustrious statues and jewel encrusted crosses don't come cheap. The website www.barbiconi.it is a site where clerical vestments and church accessories are sold directly to priests. You can go to the website yourself to see their catalogue and just how expensive the clothes of the Priests, Bishops, Cardinals and Pope are. The outfit a priest wears at mass can easily cost more than $20,000 after everything is added up. The stole alone, which is the fancy scarf clerics where around their neck, can cost over $450 before taxes and shipping, although to be fair some can cost as low as $35. Even when dressing plainly for regular stuff something as miniscule as the clerical collar which many clerics of multiple Christian denominations wear can cost $11. Those collars clerics cost more than ties worn by presidents. The clergy may claim to take a vow of poverty, but the price of the clothes they wear cannot be afforded by poor men. In other words no poor man can dress like they do, so are they really "in poverty"? As someone who was training to be a Catholic Priest and a former rapper, I can say that the outfit and accessories a Catholic Priest wears during church costs more than the outfits most rappers wear while performing at a concert. All thanks and praises be to God that I'm no longer pursuing such careers, the wardrobes of both are astronomically expensive. The "*Pulpit Pimp*", "*Reverend Grift*", "*Saint Salesman*", "*Minister Moneybags*", "*Famous Father Fortune*" and the "*Billion Dollar Bible-Thumper*" are not just fabled characterizations, they are popular professions. It's actually become a part of the Christian religion to pass around a collection plate during the services, so everyone can pay. Parishoners are given personalized envelopes with their names printed on them and the dates so it can be recorded who paid what on which days, they are supposed to drop their envelope in the basket/plate every week on the day the envelope is dated. Why does the church need to know how much is paid by who and when? If it was about keeping track of church attendance, as they claim, they could just make a sign-in sheet, which would be harder to forge than giving someone else your envelope to turn in. In actuality God is witness to who comes to the service and what they pay, so it makes one suspect that the large donators are treated differently. I can attest that the priests treated me differently than others when I started wearing jewelry and their eyes would often sparkle while gazing at it. Of course churches have a long tradition of passing around the collection plate, but did Jesus pbuh pass around a collection plate when he was giving sermons? If it's not something Jesus pbuh did even though he could have, then by Christians doing it today it shows they think they know better than Jesus pbuh. Christians even pay for tickets to enter certain churches, like the Sistine Chapel. Seriously, Christians pay just to enter special churches to pray. But have you ever wondered how much money those churches cost to build?

The Muslims during Muhammad's time built their masjids by hand and the Prophet's masjid in Medinah had dirt floors, no electricity, no plumbing, no heating, air conditioning or fans, no sound system, it didn't even have a full roof either, whenever it rained the masjid floor in some parts turned to mud. Yet that was good enough. The Muslims would prostrate on dirt in the masjid for decades. Nobody thought it was shameful or a "cheap building". Muhammad pbuh never prayed in masjids with carpets, chandeliers, fancy designs, pictures etc. It wasn't like he had a carpet and everyone praying behind him didn't, all the Muslims prostrated on the same surface, dirt. Prophets were economical when they built places of worship because they knew the important thing was if you frequently prayed perfectly in it or not, it didn't matter how much the people paid for it. Today "religious people" pay more for religious buildings and pray in them less. In general and across the planet, you'll find countries like America the prices to build a masjid or church are exorbitant compared to the prices to build masjids or churches in poor countries, yet in those poor countries many more people pray in their places of worship a lot more. I personally know of someone who built a modern masjid in the Caribean for $15,000 yet religious buildings of other faiths in other locales and even on the same island the masjid was built on cost millions to make. In the "civilized" nations there is a extravagently higher prayer unit price than in "impoverished" nations. Basically it's more expensive to pray in "civilized" nations than it is in "impoverished" regions. Typically the more religious people are the less they pay for their place of worship, the less religious they are the more they pay. Although "civilized religious folk" insist they aren't hypocrites despite paying more to pray less. The few who admit their hypocrisy, even do so hypocritically. They'll just lament their lack of relilgiosity and don't change as if God doesn't know that they admitted they lack religiosity or that God will forget them intending to be better and then not improving. The biggest hypocrites of all are those seemingly religious people who say they are hypocrites and then keep on being hypocrites, such types are bigger hypocrites than those who don't consider themselves hypocrites. The latter are just idiots, you have to be semi-intelligent to be a hypocrite. On average the cheapest prices as of 2016 CE (when $1 could buy 0.027 grams of gold) which I found for church furnishings for various items are as follows:

A single pew, long bench, costs between $3660 and $7510. depending on many details such as if it's all wooden, if it has upholstery on the seat or the backing or both, and even tiny details like the shape of the pew ends and the miniscule engravings on those ends effect the prices. You can even mix and match the top designs of pew ends with different pew end bottom designs. Every single ity bitty detail has a different price with many different options. The very angle of the seats cost different prices as well. With the price of the pew kneelers varying depending on whether they are wooden or metal, but generally they cost about $54 a foot. So when one considers how typically one person takes up 2 feet worth of kneeler then it costs over $100 for every person in the church to use a kneeler. Also if you want things on the back of the pews that costs extra. Having a book or hymnal holder on the back of pews costs between $39-55 for each holder. A pencil and Envelope holder on the back of pews costs $19. While a communion cup holder costs $17. A church can easily spend over $1 million on just pews. Pews can be rather expensive and this is why some churches rent their pews instead of buying them. In the past churches would buy/build the pews and then allow people to rent a bench/pew in church at a certain location or with a certain cushion so they would have a reserved spot to sit in every time they came. It used to be that if you wanted to sit in the front during church you had to pre-order the pew and pay to have your seat in church reserved. Of course there is always the type who wants to sit in the back as well so the Churches would sell the back row seating too. Hence if you wanted to sit in the front or back you had to pay extra and pre-order your seat for church services. Although it's not like every seat was up for sale to just anybody, you had to be from a certain class and naturally a certain skin color was necessary. Black folk weren't allowed to buy certain seats, or even pay the price of admission to pray in certain churches. This is why today you have "all-black churches" because they couldn't afford to pay the pew prices in the past and/or if they could they weren't allowed to, some churches wouldn't even let black folk stand in their churches during services. That's why they made their own with similar anti-white policies. Wealthy and arrogant families took advantage of the ancient pew rental practice and would sponsor pews or "donate them" if they had their names credited on the pew. Old movie theaters used to do this too, as do parks with bench sponsorships or other organizations which put the name of the financer on the thing they financed. Whenever Christmas and Easter or special holi-days came around, then Christians could/would bid on the pew they wanted to sit in for that special service. These pew auctions used to be very popular and were seen as a way to raise funds for churches and honor those who were most generous by giving them the preferred seating. This is why there used to be ushers in churches, to take people to their seats according to their ranks and pre-orders. Other perks would come with the first pew as well, such as having communion delivered to the first row so they didn't have to get out of their seats and come to the altar like everyone else. Politicians loved this because if they got out of the pew, then they were seen as extra pious because they didn't have to but did it anyways. In modern times this privilege of serving the front row continues but the handicapped tend to take advantage of it as the pew auctions/rentals are rarely done anymore. Usually most modern churches either buy or rent their pews from companies. A few churches require their parishioners to explicitly pay the rental price the company sets for the pews without any perks in exchange. Other services that have been and are still for sale include liturgical positions, whether it's seating in the choir, alter server positions or special spots during special services like the foot washing candidates. During Easter-time Christians tend to publicly have the ministers wash the feet of 12 or so people since Jesus pbuh taught his companions to wash feet (for wudu). Some churches actually sell these spots, or give them to special community members, but in the past people could pay money to be one of the few who got their feet washed by the minister near Easter in front of everybody else, the auctions for these spots were not typically held publicly since the ministers were rather picky over who the 12 would be each year. Honestly though this "washing of the feet" is a joke the way Christians symbolically do it before Easter each year in services. Yet the bigger joke is perhaps the "Holy Water" they'll dip their hands into when entering a church. Jesus pbuh never did this dip your hand in holy water and make the sign of the cross routine and it's extremely unhygienic, since the whole church uses the same holy water hand dishes putting all their germs in 1 tiny water bowl which everyone uses to wet themselves upon entering or leaving the church. For fun somebody should put some dye in them to make the water look black, blue, green or yellow to see how people will react if their "holy water" were a different color than normal "unholy" water. Maybe someone could put a dark brown piece of bread with brown dye in these holy water containers. Regarding the distribution of "holy water" the fonts people dip their fingers in cost $80-$100 for cheap ones. Why so expensive? Because it holds the "holy water". So when people dip their fingers into water when entering or leaving church they are dipping into a very expensive tiny dish. In addition to that in some churches the minister sprinkles holy water on the people. The pot this water is carried in costs $130-$160, while the device used to sprinkle can cost $20-$40. Yet again Jesus pbuh didn't do this stuff. The monstrances, which hold the communion wafer carried by ministers, can cost $30-thousands. While all the storage facilities for the church tools and props also cost extra because it's for sacred stuff. Everything a church uses costs extra just because it's a religious organization. It's almost like a anti-religion discount where religious organizations pay more than non-religious customers or organizations. Even the toilets for religious buildings cost extra but it seems that no price is considered too high for religious folk to pay for since they think it's all for God's sake so the more they pay they think they get more reward. Most religious organizations forget that the more they save the more they can give to others in charitable causes and the less they have to ask for when asking people to donate. This is why religious organizations get charged extra by companies, because they aren't spending their own money but the money of people who donate to them. Hence they spend as wastefully as most governments do because they feel the community's money is free for them to spend as they see fit and that they can always get more and people always have to give. If the people don't give what they budget for and the income from gambling events like bingo, dinners or sales to cover the shortfall doesn't add up then things like pews get rented or auctioned. Yet the worst thing about the practice of renting/auctioning pews is that sometimes some "Charitable Christians" will buy out the front seats and then "donate them to the homeless" so that instead of a homeless person being outside they get a free 1-hour seat in the front row during church, whether they wanted it or not. During Christmas this happens a lot and homeless folk are forced to accept it just to get out of the snow and cold even though many don't want to be in the church. The shelters, who are closely related to and are interdependent with the Christian evangelical organizations, (if not covert or outright Christian Evangelists) tell them to go to church services if they want to sleep at the shelter that night. Christians call this charity, I call it coercive economic manipulation to promote their religion.

Upholstered Chairs cost between $104 (if you buy more than 100) to $173. And then one can pay extra if they want accessories like kneelers that attach to the back of the chairs or underseat book racks or back bookracks. If you want armrests on the chairs it costs over $30 extra per chair. Meaning that each armrest for a chair costs about $15 per arm. So that's $30 just for armrests and that doesn't pay for the chair's seat, back or legs. It also costs extra money per chairs if you want them to be stackable. While if you want metal chairs they cost over $50 each while nonupholstered wooden chairs cost over $100 up to $223 each. Church chairs are very expensive, although to be nice companies do offer slight discounts if more than one thousand chairs are bought at a time.

Steeples put on top of churches, symbolizing a phallus, can weigh hundreds or thousands of pounds and cost between $1,144 -$21,780. While to put a cross on top of them costs a few hundred dollars extra. Cuppolas cost $1,285-$23,485 and weigh hundreds to thousands of pounds.

Flower Stands cost $230-$1,125 and they're just a fancy wooden pillar to put a bouquet of flowers on.

Offering tables cost $505-$1,040, with inscriptions costing about $34 if you want it to say "Offering table". Prayer desks cost $700 -$1,955. Communion tables cost $815-$3,585

Wall crosses can weigh hundreds of pounds and cost thousands of dollars.

Altars cost $2,700 to $5,590 if you want them to look simple and cheap. Theoretically the limit on the cost of an altar is based on imagination and financial abilities, some can cost over a million dollars. The napkin/towel that covers the altar costs $25-$440.

The advent wreathes displayed in churches cost $595 if cheap and designed to sit on a table, or around $3,150 if self-standing.

The candle lighters which altar servers use to light candles cost $55-$270 depending on their length and the material they are made out of. The rack/stand to hold the candlelighters costs $180-$540. While the candlestick holders themselves which you put the candles in cost between $150 and $2,000. Seriously you can pay $2,000 for a stand to hold a single candle and churches do it, and typically have a lot more than just 1 candle in the building. While candelabras (devices that hold more than 1 candle) can cost even more than single candle holders. The candles themselves can cost hundreds of dollars or thousands if it's a extremely special candle because they can't just use any type of candle for church. Although despite paying so much for candles, they use electric lights to see. Why then do they pay so much for candles? Because Christians used to do magic with the candles and that's why so many tiny details regarding them are paid attention to as well as the reason they have a baptismal candle, a communion candle, a confirmation candle and a wedding candle they give to people. There are really important religious reasons for the Christian Churches having such an extreme candle fetish but it is beyond the scope of this book and chapter to elaborate upon. Furthermore church candles aren't just blown out by altar servers but extinguished with special candle extinguishers so the smoke doesn't dissipate randomly. Yet remember that these candles are not used for visibility purposes, they use electric light for that; usually. Although sometimes there are nightime candle light services or vigils where everyone gets their own candle for lighting. Those types of candles cost about $1 each. Meaning each person at such a service must give a dollar each just to cover the cost of the candles they use, although some churches reuse the candles.

Pulpits cost $1,030-$6,280 and if one wants a railing with it they cost hundreds of dollars per foot.

Portable Baptistries cost $5,440 -$8,825 each, but that doesn't include the $1,100 heater which is needed so the water is warm. Other expensive accessories include, underwater lights, steps, drains, filters, matching colors and blister resistant coating. With the Baptismal fonts costing between $690 and $1,115. The baptismal bowls cost between $140 and $440. The tiny "Baptismal towels" the little babies wear when baptized cost about $20-$40. Many Christian babies are wearing a $40 outfit to get baptized in, it's likely the most expensive outfit the baby will ever wear. While a child's baptismal gown costs $80 and the adult's costs $90. The outfit worn by the cleric performing the baptism costs $140, despite the prophet John the Baptist's outfit used when allegedly baptizing people being much less expensive. A portable holy water sprinkler, used in last rites or for blessing sick people, costs about $20.

Wooden circular collection plates are also purchasable, these are passed around in church at collection time for people to donate. It costs $95 dollars if it's all wood, but to have the extra green felt inside will raise its price to $120 per collection plate. If it's an "offering bag" that can cost $40-120. While a tithe box, which is just a stationary wooden donation box, costs $220 -$905.

The hymn boards, which are the lists the chorus uses to show which songs will be sung and the order they'll sing them in, costs $275-$366. Musical Instruments are bought at higher than normal prices as well, once the instrument sellers learn they are being bought to make "holy music". Yet neither Adam, Noah, Abraham, Lot Isaac, Jacob, Joseph, Moses, Aaron, Job, Zachariah, Jesus or John pbut are even alleged to have ever made "holy music" with instruments; particularly during a religious service. Altar bells, the ringing sound at communion when the bread/wine allegedly change into body/blood, cost anywhere from $50-$150. I guess it'd be worth it if Jesus pbuh taught Christians to ring a bell when the communion food products get held up, but as far as I know Jesus pbuh didn't use any bells. The large noisy church bells can cost thousands of dollars. When you hear them do they sound expensive or worth it?

Pulpit chairs cost $730 -$885. While the Clergy seats cost from $650 to $845. The celebrant chairs can cost $220-$1,500 and that price applies to side chairs for assistants to sit on. Clergy and Christian ministers have the most expensive chairs to sit in on the job out of any other job but they don't even look fancy. They don't even vibrate or give massages it's just felt or comfortable. Individual prayer kneelers cost between $273-$1,100, and that's not including the chair. Now altar servers sit in front during church in the chairs that can cost $1,500 and get kneelers that can be $1,100. Just to have 1 kid as an altar server be able to sit and kneel costs between $495-$2,600 per kid/server. I did that job a couple of times without any formal training or certification or anything just because the other kids wouldn't show up. Now I don't know whether the seat and kneeler I used cost more towards the $495 range or the $2,600 range but I can say that whatever they paid it was definitely not worth it. As expensive as these things are and as sacred or pretty they may seem, they aren't comfortable to use. But as long as Christians keep donating then these expensive furnishings will still be bought and used. What else would churches be spending all that money on? Don't you think Jesus pbuh would pay $1,100 for a cushioned kneeler to use in prayer? Or $2,600 for a cushioned seat to use during a church service?

The censers, things that hold the incense as it burns, cost between $20-$90. (Incense costs extra.)

"*Holy oils*" for anointing stuff are more expensive than perfume.

The holding place for the bible to be placed in while its read during church services costs $40-$400.

Wall pedestals, for putting statues on elevated platforms next to walls, cost $98-$400.

Being a church, they can't just let the fire extinguisher lay out there for people to see, that would look cheap, unsanctified and unprofessional so the specially made fire extinguisher cabinets cost $52-$65 and if you ask the average Christian churchgoer where the fire extinguisher is none of them know. Which makes sense if you consider how the average Christian doesn't know how to save themselves from the hellfire either but just expect Jesus pbuh to save them by dying. Maybe they expect Jesus to use the fire extinguisher too. Although I think they are gravely mistaken to have such expectations for Jesus pbuh.

The famous ashes used during "Ash Wednesday" cost about $20 in order to get enough for 500 people, while the dish the special ashes get held in cost about $15-$140.

The cloth or pall they drape coffins with cost between $995 and $1,365, the cloth for urns is $185-$275. While those sign-in registries used at wakes to prove attendance at a wake or funeral cost about $65.

The confessional screens that flimsily disguise the faces of those confessing their sins from their confessor cost between $510-$865. It's just a tiny screen but it's very expensive to purchase.

Now I'm sure you are wondering how much those communion wafers/hosts cost, which is allegedly the "body of Christ". Well first of all it depends if you get the white kind of wheat wafer or the brown kind of whole wheat. Most churches get the cheap communion host made of wheat flour, shortening, salt and water that has a little cross on it. Those cost about $20 for 1,000 making each individual host worth exactly 2 cents. So in an economic sense the "body of Christ" costs 2 cents, plus shipping, handling and distribution costs. The brown whole wheat pieces can cost $50 for 1,700 serving pieces costing about 3 cents each and only contain whole wheat and water, without the salt or shortening. I guess that's like a "*Diet Christ*" or "*Healthy Host*". However there is also the "double thick" variety which costs about $10 for 250 pieces which cost 4 cents per piece. But it doesn't stop there because a gluten free communion wafer also exists, which costs $16 for 25 pieces or 64 cents per piece. So a single serving of the "body of Christ" in church can cost anywhere from 2 cents for the cheap stuff and 64 cents for the expensive gluten-free "body". Sometimes Jesus is gluten-free and sometimes not, sometimes he's brown and sometimes he's white, sometimes he thin sometimes he's thick, it depends on which "body of Christ" the church decides to order and serve people. Currently eating the gluten-free body of god costs a lot more than the non-gluten free edible god does. Surely though it must be a very special type of job to make income from selling the body of God or Jesus pbuh so people can eat God or Jesus pbuh. But you don't need any special religious training or certification to sell this stuff. Anyone could sell it, but only trained certified Christians can serve it to people. Theologically anyone can be the chef but you need special training and permits to be the waiter or waitress. The portable communion sets taken to hospitals and house visits cost between $20 and $310. The bowl or cup used to hold the communion wafers in while being distributed costs between $40 and $1,040. While the cup or chalice used to hold the blood/wine can cost anywhere from $35 to millions of dollars. A cloth cover for the chalice or communion bowl costs $4-$95.

Do you know how much the first church built by Jesus pbuh cost? Nothing because he never built one. Neither the prophet Jesus nor the prophet John pbut ever set foot in a church or wanted one. For the first three centuries after Jesus pbuh left earth Christians didn't have churches but met in houses or in public places like markets or streets, except for a few prison churches or Christian worship buildings on travel routes. Pagans actually criticized Christians because Christianity was the only religion known to have no sanctified places of worship. After Constantine that changed and pagan temples got Christined. This may be partially because all these church making/furnishing industries keep people employed and helps the governments collect tax revenue by taxing the incomes of those involved, materials used and transactions for every step in the economic process. Christianity was an economic threat to many wasteful corrupt industries until some Christians agreed to start making expensive buildings to pray in. Without making/selling/installing all the props for religious buildings people would actually have to do something economically productive that improves the well-being of the world, just as the prophets taught us to do as part of worshipping God. But this way religious preachers have expensive theatrical stages. In fact the word "pulpit" which most Christians have in some form originates from the Latin word "pulpitum" which means stage. While the word "pew" comes from the word "podium" which originally referred to a balcony. Linguistically churches are religious theaters with the rituals designed to be observed by spectators as if they were watching a sporting event, play or movie. Church buildings were and still are designed in a concert style and most Christian services are practically fancy musical concerts. While it may be hard to imagine today, in the ancient past Pagans considered going to their temple to be a form of entertainment. Likewise Christians used to consider churches as forums to be entertained in because of how the buildings were designed. This design is not conducive to sincere or solemn individual participation in worshipping God but facilitates a sit and soak-in style of indoctrination. Basically if one were to intentionally design a place to brainwash multitudes at a time the arena or church format would be the theatrical style best suited for the task. Hence churches spend money where it counts, to keep Christians in their seats bedazzled by beauty so as to be brainwashed due to the spectacle of a "holy environment". Spending on the churches ensures more is donated and the donaters continue to believe their faith is right. Sometimes might is seen as right other times beauty/wealth is. The more a ritual costs to perform the more attention is paid to it by the insincere and easily impressionable ignorant commoners. An expensive pen keeps the sheep happy when they get fleeced. Some religious buildings spend so much that they can't even afford their extravagent theatrical stage and need to have supplementary income streams to stay in business. So they will put advertisements in their newsletters, advertising nearly anything and everything people are willing to pay for and some even put digital or television advertisments in their places of worship. As a kid I remember a cartoon once mockingly had a church which "sold-out" advertising in pews and installed TVs in the place of worship to make money with advertisement space but of course such ludicrous fundraising methods were only possible in a cartoon, or so I thought. Yet unfortunately I have personally witnessed with my own eyes allegedly religious "houses of God" that have TV sets worth thousands of dollars located on the premises that show business advertisments 24 hours a day 7 days a week. It's sounds too crazy to be true but I've seen it with my own eyes. Tragically though the religious organizations who sell such advertising space are too blinded by the dollar signs to see how sacreligious they have become. And they think those who condemn such practices are the crazy ones. The Jewish Pharisees in Jesus' time were amateurs compared to many religious leaders today who claim they follow Jesus pbuh..

    It goes back to big business religions following the profits, instead of the prophets. Many don't realize the situation for what it is, but then again it's not uncommon to find people buying poison, even if it's clearly labeled. Some even justify their purchase of poison by saying they like the flavor. Think twice before giving money to a religious charity. Are you doing it because it will please God or are you doing it because it's customary? Are you doing it publicly or privately? Anonymously or not?

    The same principle applies to any religious teacher, if money is involved eventually it will influence the content of what is being taught; it is inevitable. Ask any public school teacher if they would teach the same stuff in the same way if they received more or less money and it is evident that the teaching experience of the students would not remain the same. The teacher who gets paid money can never possibly teach their students morality effectively with sincerity. I don't mean to offend anybody who is in the religious field, I'm just trying to explain why religion should not be treated as a commodity or industry. Because wherever that is the case more often than not you will discover that such a person's true object of worship is money, even if they claim otherwise. Those who worship wealth or desire worldly ranking and prestige are not guides to paradise, they are manipulating religion for their own satanically inspired purposes. The majority of people find it difficult to receive honest helpful religious advice that tells them what they are doing is wrong, or that they should do more good deeds. So if it is hard to accept religious advice when they get it for free, then how could it be that people are paying someone for sincere religious advice? Yet what's even worse is that if a religious leader is paid a salary then if they ever make any mistake or misguide someone by accidental ignorance or misunderstandings then that can make their whole income sinful because they'd be getting paid to misguide people. Sadly oftentimes the case is that a cohort committee, board, or society of people with reputation/wealth in the community end up calling the shots and exerting influence upon the community regardless of whether their decisions/policies agree with their religion or not. In practice usually such committees violate their religion in attempts to promote various community activities. Then they make membership of their pseudo-religious community a club which requires payment for you and your opinion to count. Whereas none of the prophets had a policy where you had to pay membership dues each year to be considered a member of the religious community. And they had religious communities at that time since the religious places of worship needed community leaders just as they do today. Of all the companions of prophets who went out and built places of worship not a single one of them ever instituded democratic systems where people voted for positions, had treasurers, vice presidents, boards, committes and constitutions or charters. For thousands of years places of worship operated without elections or political circusry. No companion of any prophet of God ever instituted such a scheme for a place of worship nor it's community and they most certainly didn't have paid membership dues either . If you believed in the religion and prayed there just once, then such a person was automatically a full fledged member with a valid opinion as long as their opinion was legitimate according to the religion. You didn't need to pay to pray the way places make you do today. It's unbelievable such organizations exist where people pay to be a "member" of a place they are supposed to pray in. You can actually be attending a place of worship to pray on a daily basis but if you don't pay the "membership fees" they'll say you aren't a member. Ironically those who do pay the price to pray tend to barely pray at the place so they don't even get their money's worth, yet because they "pay their dues" they are an honorary member with political influence over the governing body of the religious building. It's truly funny for me because I don't pay membership fees and I pray at places more than the ones who pay to pray there. You'd think they'd be praying there more than me since they are paying more than me. Sadly though it seems those who are paying from home tend to have more authority at places of worship than those who are consistently praying there. What lesson does that teach? If it's a "religious organiztion" why does paying give one more political points and credentials than praying? Of course actions speak louder than words but sometimes silent payments of money seem to talk louder than actions. No such organization of a place of worship with paid membership is rightly guided. If you are paying to be a member at a place of worship then you should know that club will cause problems and not follow the religion as it is supposed to be followed. That's a guarantee, if they have paid membership then they will cause problems. You are literally paying them to cause problems and that they require payment for membership is a problem in itself, thus they have caused a problem even before they got paid to cause problems with that money they pilfer. They basically hold a religion ransom claiming you have to pay to belong. In reality they take the power away from the religious and give it to the rich, thus they want membership to be paid so they can pay for power they wouldn't get otherwise if leadership and influence were determined by religious criteria. They don't want the poor to have any influence thus they exclude them with the fee and they know the religious intellectuals won't pay to join a sacreligious organization when the very principle of paying to be a member contradicts their religion. With such "religious organizations" the best policy you can have with them is to not join even if they pay you to join. I won't even join such organizations even if they tried to pay me. But most won't ever offer to pay you instead they want you to pay them. Instead stay far away from them if you want to enter heaven. As much as they may try to trick you into thinking paying for membership will get you a better seat in paradise, it won't so don't. God does not want you to pay to belong to such shameful religious rackets. Also don't be mistaken by the false slogan of "joining in order to reform". Institutions don't get fixed by you joining them, by you joining them all that means is that they have corrupted you. Rather than you join them, they should change and join you. If any such religious organization ever asks you why you don't join them or get involved, then tell them you were wondering the same as to why they don't abolish their religious racket and hypocritical sacreligious political tyranny to join you in practicing the religion correctly. Some of these religious rackets are so filthy that they will even rent the place out for people to have religious celebrations. For example if there is a celebration for a religious ceremony for a baby or a wedding they will actually charge people a fee to use the space owned by the religious organization in order to celebrate something the religion proscribes they celebrate. Basically the religion says you should do X as part of your religion and the organzation says *"Well if you want to do X on our premises, as our religion says you should/must do, then you're going to have to pay us to reserve or use the space."* It's pathetic that people pay for the "privilege" to practice their religion and celebrate a religious event at a religious place which is supposedly created to serve the communities religious needs. Why do they even have the space if they won't let people use it without paying for it? Another scam includes the bribery of a religious leader to perform a marriage ceremony. I think they prefer to call it a fee but in reality it's bribery, fundamentally marriage is a religious ceremony the preachers preach and encourage people to perform so as to legally create a family. So this is something they tell us God wants to happen, yet the leaders charge money for marrying people. Why? Does God say to pay someone money to perform a marriage? If so how much does God say to pay? Or did the religious person just add that fee to the faith themselves? When Adam pbuh and Eve got married they didn't pay to have it done and they didn't charge their kids a fee when getting them married either. People have to get married to create families the right way so how can religious leaders then make money off of matrimony? Either they are greedy for the money, or they have to be paid to marry those specific individuals because they don't think they should get married. So when a couple pays a religious person to marry them then either it's a bad couple that needs to bribe a religious person to unite them since nobody would dare do so for free, or it's a fake religious person who is making money by making families. Either case is indicative of a difficult marriage and incompatible couple since they in actuality bought their marriage and a marriage that is bought is guranteed to be a cheap one. If any religious person requires payment to perform your marriage then just tell them that you won't get married by them because your marriage is too valueable to put a pricetag on it's beginning. If they can put a price on them performing your marriage then you'd prefer a more religious person who values marriage more than that. Personally I don't consider someone qualified to perform a marriage if they charge a fee for doing it. Secondly I don't think such a person is qualified to get married themselves. Those couples who do pay someone to marry them will always have their first experience together being getting scammed by paying someone to do their marriage. Getting scammed is not the best way to start a marriage nor one's religious education. Sadly I've seen places of worship where they charge a few hundred dollars for parents to enroll their kid in the children's weekend education program and then if you are a "registered member of the society" you enjoy a 10% discount on the price you pay them to teach your child their religion. Yet they claim to be a religious organization when they won't even teach their religion at their place worship to children without getting paid to do so. That's really religious aye? You have to pay them to preach to you and teach your kids. Sometimes it's hard to wonder whether you are practicing a religion or paying for a product at a store. It's truly scandalous that many places dare to charge their members who already paid for membership another fee to have their kids get taught religion. Being a paying member doesn't even entitle you or your kids to get taught religion. To me it sounds exactly like a business where you get a discount on what they are selling if you have a membership card. Except unlike the stores these places and organizations frequently require an oath of allegiance and subservience to them and all their decisions, which is sinful to make in their religion anyways because of the way the organization is designed in a sacreligious way let alone with how it's run and what it does and/or doesn't do. One must ask if that is how God desires religious societies to operate? Did God send prophets who taught people to teach kids religion for a price. Did prophets ask people for a salary for being their prophet? Did any prophet of God ever accept a salary from his people? Yet simultaneously kids classes for religion at places of worship occur where the nations boast about religious freedom. How is it religious freedom if a kid can't be taught their religion at their place of worship unless their parents pay money? That doesn't seem free to me. Neither a cost nor a discount for such clasees should exist. While if the teachers are getting paid, they shouldn't be teaching religion since that they agree to work for such organizations indicates they don't really know their religion to begin with. Yet what's worse is that the teachers typically don't even get paid, it's purely a religious education racket by the religious organization, and they don't even properly teach the kids. Instead the money the organizations get paid fills their pockets and is not invested in the kids' religious miseducation. Tragically one will typically discover that the most prominent and influential board/society/commitee members tend to be the least religious. I honestly don't know how it happens but it does, must be proof that democracy results in stupidity. Usually these corrupt modern boards/committees have their leadership determined by elections wherein each paying member gets an equal vote for candidates, who obviously must have paid the membership fee to be eligible as a candidate in the election. Islamic organizations don't operate this way, because of Shariah but also for logistical and integrity reasons which are justification enough even if one were ignorant of the Islamic Shariah. For example typically Muslim women don't pray much in the masjid since it's more rewarding for them to pray at home, the logistics of segregated areas, and spiritually safe traveling to/fro without unneccessary temptation, etc. So imagine if in theory a hypothetical masjid were to hold elections to determine who the administrative leaders were to be. If the paying male members and paying female members get a vote then those votes cannot under any circumstances be equal. Why? Because the women don't come to the masjid much to know which guys are religious and go to the masjid, while the segregation and lack of female masjid attedance means the men don't know who the religious women are either. Therefore because the Muslim women are guranteed to be unaware of the religious qualifications/qualities of the men and the Muslim men are guranteed to be unaware of the religious qualifications/character of the women then the men cannot legitimately choose the best woman via election nor can the women choose the best man via election due to their lack of knowledge regarding the religiosity of the members of the opposite gender. So in any hypothetical election a man's vote for a man must neccessarily be worth more than a woman's vote for a male candidate, and a woman's vote for a woman must neccessarily be worth more than a man's vote for a female candidate. Hence male and female voters cannot be counted equally. That's one reason Islamic administration cannot be established democratically. The other is that even if one were to have seperate administrations for men and women voting would still be unjust because not every member's opinion on who should be the leader is equal. For example a brand new convert who doesn't know anything about the religion cannot possibly have the same amount of influence in their vote as a scholar or person who spent years practicing the religion. Similarily the guy who only comes once a week to pray cannot possibly have an equal vote as someone who comes 5 times a day to pray. Why? Because the one who barely comes to pray won't know who comes 5 times a day and the one who does will know and thus is better informed to cast a vote for a religious candidate due to the differences in the level of religiosity amongst the voters of the same gender. Therefore the knowledge and religiosity of male voters means no two Muslim men can possibly have an equal say in who should be the leader of an administration because no two Muslim men are equal in knowledge or religiosity or familiarity with the knowledge and religiosity of the candidates who can be elected. This is why it is utterly impossible and sheer criminality for any organization to determine it's leadership/administrators via elections or voting. I swear to God every single organization who does this is getting their leader in a unjust unintelligent matter and guarantee they will not have the best possible candidate for the job, it is utterly impossible for elections where all votes are equal to be just. Every election wherein every vote counts equally is a crime guaranteed to result in illegitimate leaders. This is why never in the history of Islam has there ever been an election for Islamic leadership wherein every person got an equal vote for various qualified candidates. It has never happened and never will. Now does that mean absolutely no "Muslim organizations" determine their leadershiip via elections? Sadly no. Some ignorant Muslims do this because they don't know about Islamic Shariah nor can they see how democratic elections are insanely unjust and illegitimate. However every single Muslim group which operates democratically has a plethora of problems, sometimes even to the extent that some of the members are heretical and not even considered Muslims according to Islam. Most heretical organizations, within non-Muslim democratic nations, which claim to be Muslim operate according to democratic methods but no Islamic organizations within Muslim or non-Muslim organizations do. Not a single one. Yet do understand I'm not saying any/every organization that operates democratically is inherently staffed or participated in by heretics falsely claiming or ignorantly claiming to be Muslims. Many democratic groups are, but generally speaking "democratic Muslim organizations" have membership lists composed of people who are idiots that misunderstand Islam and democracy. So while democratically organized groups may have Muslim members, those Muslim members by virtue and definition of their membership in such an organization are fools who know little about Islam. The hard part is they may not know that because of their ignorance and arrogance, while it can be extremely hard to make them understand that without them thinking you are extreme or ignorant yourself. However hypocrites know democratic methods are designed to be unjust and result in religiously lacksadaisacl leadership and this is why they use and promote those methods. That's because hypocrites, idiots and people who don't practice Islam too much can't become leaders via legitimate Islamic procedures for determining leadership as stipulated by the Islamic Shariah. Fortunately Muslims have Shariah so they know explictly how religious organizations should determine who the leaders and administrative positions should be held by, but religions other than Islam tend not to specify how to get the best most qualified people for such positions so non-Muslims tend to have even worse leaders than the rare ignorant Muslim groups that may use democratic means to get their leaders. I won't go into the lengthy explanation of how exactly Shariah selects Muslim leadership here or in this book, but an example from the Catholic Church is a useful analogy. To determine the Pope, Catholics have the theoretically most knowledgable, pious people (alleged to be the Cardinals, who were appointed by the allegedly most knoledgable and pious Catholic (the previous Pope)) choose the leader by voting. Of course this is unjust for the reasons stated above but the point is that not every member of the Catholic Church has an equal say in who their leader will be. Everyone can see how it would be chaotic and disastrous if the Poper were determined by a global elections where every Catholic or self-proclaimed Catholic aged zero-oldest got an equal vote. Since to get a religious leader you can't just let general laypeople, have too much influence because of the very fact they are laypeople who are less knowledgable and less practicing than the religious and clerical (who are not always more religious or knowledgeable than the laypeople). Yet although Catholics get this point to some extent when it comes to picking their Pope as leader, commonly they too have general elections for lesser leadership positions, despite all the top positions in the Church being appointed positions by the hierarchy. This is pure hypocrisy since if religious hierarchy were the best method to pick a leader then every leader at every level should be chosen via the same method, instead of just the top positions. Of course if the hierarchy were corrupt then naturally such a method wouldn't be the best, nor would any hierarchy of a false faith be anything but corrupt since a false faith cannot have anything but corrupt adherants. Yet the point is that the best method of selecting a leader should be employed at every level no matter what that method is. I believe that method is Shariah because I'm Muslim, but if there were a better method then it must be used at every level. For example if Catholics pick the Pope one way then every leader in the institution should be picked in the same manner. While if say a government chooses their President via election where every registered voter has an equal vote, then for that method to be the best method to pick the president then it must also by definition be the best method for picking every position in that government and every government employee would have to be appointed via a general election where every registered voter's vote counts equally. If this is not practical or deemed the best way for lesser positions then it cannot be deemed practical nor the best method for higher positions. By virtue of disproportionate application, without a consistent method applied at every level in every situation one cannot but be stuck using a method different than the best. Basically by definition if you don't use X method for determining who gets positions #1-infinity then you should not use X method for determining who gets any position at all. If you don't use the same method for everything then you shouldn't use that method for anything. The reason people do not have the best leaders possible nor are positions filled by the best people for the job is because the best method is not being applied or utilized. And where do you learn what the best method for determining leadership is? From God. How do you learn stuff from God? From God via God's book, or by learning it from God's prophet(s). Thus if a community really wanted to follow their prophet, they wouldn't have these committees, societies, board elections, presidents, chairpersons, membership fees, educational fees, etc. Instead of such "religious committees" following the prophetic policies when making communal decisions, thes religious rackets are designed to make the popular decisions. Whreas religious leadership is supposed to make the correct unpopular decisions, but the committee members can't even get influence or power unless they attain popularity. Those who gain their position via popularity will have popularity as their priority so as to keep their position, since once they have power they don't want to lose it and thus in reality they have little power because they are afraid to use it lest using it the right way causes them to lose it. Regardless usually organized religious rackets tend to be popular within religious communities, but where do they meet when they make decisions effecting the community? Is it in the public prayer area of the place of worship itself? Of course not they wouldn't dare concoct their sacreligious plots in the "house of God" publicly where semi-religious and religious people pray and could observe their diabolical decision making process possibly refuting it or making them anxious due to their sacreligious audacity. Instead it's all done behind closed doors in secret offices or "meeting rooms". Their chosen setting for their meetings proves how unreligious they are, because if they were religious they would have their religious meetings that decide the affairs of "God's house" and place of prayer at God's house itself, especially when it's known the devils avoid such locations. How in the world can "religious leaders" determine the correct decisions for the religious community, who worships at a house of God, to take when they aren't even having the meetings take place in God's house? Clearly that shows they don't want God to help them making the decisions which inevitably effect God's house and his worshippers. Muhammad pbuh would have his religious meetings with his advisor and the members of the community in the same exact spot where he led the public prayers. Literally the same spot he led the prayers in the masjid was the same exact spot where he would make decisions regarding the masjid or Muslim community or state. Which especially regarding politics is highly signifiacant. What political leader today has their office in the "house of God" and their "political seat of power" where they make decisions is the same place they publicly go to pray? Why don't people see these leaders for the types of people they truly are? Really how can you consider a person to be religious if the biggest and more important decisions they make in their life is made at locations other than the house of God? How can God be guiding your decision-making process if you aren't making those decisions in God's house? God could still guide one's decisions outside of his house, and frequently does but logistically you are more likely to be guided if you are inside of God's house at the time rather than outside of it. Why? Because God said so, his prophets said so and nearly every religion teaches that the devil's don't enter God's houses much or in as much force as they posess outside of them. So while some may think it unusual for one to spend lots of time in a place of worship, truly it's the smart thing to do. Personally I doubt the legitimacy of a religious organization's decisions if the decisions are made in secret and/or not in the public prayer areas of places of worship. Religious clubs are supposed to make religious decisions, not make decisions about religion. Thus if they are making good religious decisions they would be meeting in a religious place, not some classroom, office, cafeteria or board room. If they can't even pick the best religious place to meet in when making decisions thus how can they make the best decisions? Simply put they can't, don't and won't, that was obvious when they created a religious club with paid membership built on sacreligious political doctrines with positions obtained/determined via illegitimate unjust sacreligious methods. When you actually think about it, their secret meetings in non-religious places/rooms almost implicate them as conspirators who prefer devils to be present at their decision making meetings rather than angels. In comparison prophets would have their meetings in public with the people in the prayer areas of the houses of worship. Although just because someone frequents a place of worship in itself doesn't mean they are good people or even religious, since hypocrites frequented Muhammad's masjid in Medinah and they were the worst of all people and least religious. Similarily if one was in a house of idolatry or one where false religions are taught and other than God is worshipped in then that would be one of the worst places to be in as those places despite being advertised as "houses of God" would literally be the houses/temples of devils and you will find the worst types of people in them. Trust me, I used to spend lots of time in churches, you find the worst types of people there though most Christians consider those types to be the best but they think that because those people are great actors/actresses and both the thinkers and those thought of are ignorant regarding religious realities and truths. Yet if even the hypocrites in the prophet's time who didn't even believe in his religion frequented the prophetic places of worship then what does that say about modern religious leaders who come to the places of worship even less than hypocrites used to do? Hypocrites in the past were more religious than most of the modern religious leaders/organizations who "lead us" today. Truly those who faked it with the prophets were more religious than those who actually believe in those prophets and practice their religion today. Yet somehow the religious leaders today portray themselves as pious and religious. It's hard to know who is more ignorant regarding religion, our religious leaders who don't know, can't/won't preach and don't practice or us for thinking such leaders are religious or respectable. Honestly I find the religious leaders of the modern era funnier than the professional comedians and clowns. But then again I try not to look in the mirror too much, so that could be why. With the calibre of religious leaders we have today, we don't even need to have Satan and his soldiers as spiritual enemies. Then for the occassional staged events(discussions/meetings) where the public(by which I mean only members who pay) get invited to attend to roleplay and give the illusion of legitimacy to religious organizations, the events still aren't held in the "house of God" or prayer areas but some other nearby location like a banquet hall or something. Customarily such "religious societies" have annual meetings or public events at a eating area where they partake in gluttonous activity all the while thinking they are religious being "involved with religion" doing something God likes. Let's face it those people are coming for food and the opportunity to fraternize not because of their faith. Think otherwise? See what happens when the food isn't free and it gets turned into a fundraising event, which of course the "religious organizations" hold fundraising events to get even more money out of people than they ordinarily do because "*somehow or for some important unexpected reason they need more, a lot more, and soon, from you, and remember our religion says you should give charity to us*" (perpetually). Whereas I don't mean to mock fundraisers done for legitimate reasons by sincere organizations, but it's just extremely easy for "religious organizations" to have habitual fundraisers and exploit the religion for finacial salespitches. For instance both Jesus pbuh and the Jewish Pharisees encouraged people to give in charity to religious organizations for religious reasons, but they did so for very different reasons in slightly different ways. And keep in mind I said that Jesus pbuh and the Pharisees both did it "in slightly different ways", so that shows how easy it is to be fooled thinking a group is prophetically motivated when they are in reality profetically motivated, or sincerely motivated versus satanically motivated. Some groups are even sincerely motivated but for satanic reasons due to stupidity. Some of the religious rackets even have paid positions! I'm not joking either!!!! Hopefully you aren't so desentisized by spiritual scam artists that you find the news of religious groups having paid positions to be normal or unshocking. If you aren't shocked by such news then you're probably familiar with a lot of bad phony religious organizations and don't know the reality about them or have a prophetic disposition yourself. So even if there are those organizations with paid positions, the way you feel about those organizations and positions can also indicate quite a few things about yourself and your religiosity. If you think it's perfectly fine and normal to get paid for having a position within a religiously motivated organization then you actually have an abnormal religious disposition at odds with the prophetic perspective. I mean that'd be comparable to thinking it's fine and normal to sell a religious book to somebody. Could you even imagine such religious insincerity? Such authors, publishers and readers don't know the value of the religious information they are buying and selling. Course in the case of religious falsehood or error you'd be wise to pay people to dispose of and get dangerous religious books away from you and others. Hence one who sells a religious book must either be selling you something religiously dangerous to get rid of it asap, be on the brink of starvation in desperate need of money, be insincere or they are extremely stupid and ignorant as to the value of the information they part with for a price. In that case buying a good beneficial book is comparable to stealing, though while it's not sinful as stealing is you should feel a little pity at getting such a great bargain that you wouldn't have gotten had the book seller been smart. Thus if you want to know who is foolish, those who sell religious books are some of the dumbest people in the world, but not for the reasons the anti-religious would think and mockingly say. In fact it's actually a good idea to tell someone who sells you a good religious book with prohetic information in it after you buy the book, "*You just made one of the dumbest decisions of your life. I actually feel sorry you are so stupid and don't understand this transaction. Are you sure you want to sell me this book? Really? You won't be mad that I'm buying it from you? Are you sure? Seriously you aren't going to be cursing me later for buying this from you are you? Please don't, I feel bad enough already but it's just too good of a deal to pass on. May God forgive you for your foollishness and make your income from this transaction lawful."* Anyways regarding paid religious positions, those whose position comes with a salary will usually be treated as a person bought with a price tag, that will be replaced and exchanged for someone else if they make unpopular decisions that contravene the majority, their employer or the organization. Ironically both the paid religious leader and the boards/committees tend to blame each other when people complain to them, yet sometimes they both agree and are wrong at the same time. In those instances it's really sad for members of a community who want to practice their religion correctly because those who want to practice correctly frequently tend to be the non-influential minority, at least in the West. The prophets pbut were rebuked for telling people about religion for free. The fact that our society today makes religious leadership a paid position implies several things. First of all it implies nobody wants the job, because it is very difficult and carries an enormous responsibility. Secondly it implies that people are buying religious advice and it is not being freely given. This means that most of the religious advice given today is tainted and not entirely sincere. If it's not sincere then it's probably not sound or correct advice. Let's say a person had a large income from immoral means and then they gave a large donation to a charitable religious organization. If that religious organization was sincere in their religion they would advise the person while returning their donation by saying that they didn't want that person's illicit contaminated money and that the person should quit gaining sinful wealth. How many religious organizations would do that today? Well that's what happened when a Muslim won the lottery in England, he tried to give money to a masjid and they gave it back refusing to accept it saying his money was sinful. The guy figured that masjid was just extreme so he went to others and unanimously every single masjid in England refused to accept the money won from the lottery and the guy was embarrassed that every single Islamic place of worship shunned and rejected his donations because his money was sinful according to Islam. Thus he was made into an example for people all over the world that money gained from gambling is very bad and forbidden to have. However just because a religious organization may not be sincere doesn't necessarily mean their religion is wrong, they could just be hypocritical. A hypocrite doesn't have your best interests for salvation in their heart and being around them might contaminate you with the disease of hypocrisy. Whereas the religious leader who is paid can never make the difficult unpopular right decisions because their financial interest conflicts with the interests of their religion. To illustrate this one time a religious leader told me that a reason my parents don't listen to my advice to them regarding religion is because I live in their house and get paid by them for doing work in and around their house, and that if I really wanted them to respect and listen to my religious advice then I had to move out of their house and be financially independent. Now perhaps you agree with such a sentiment. However the religious leader who told me this at the time was living in a house owned by the religious organization who paid to maintain/repair it and they also paid his salary. Thus when he criticized me saying my parents won't listen to my religious advice or instruction because I live in their house and financially get paid by them, he was in the exact same boat except the religious organization he is supposedly the leader of had the role with him which my parents had with me. So if he is correct in his analysis of my situation, as most would agree, then he must also been in a position without influence over the religious organization even though he is publicly portrayed as the community's leader. And that is why religious communities pay their leaders, because the organizations know that if they pay the leader then they will watch what they say and be flexible due to the financial risk. But the religious leader who isn't getting a single penny from the people, he will fearlessly tell them exactly what they need to hear even if they don't want to hear it and apply pressure to stop his preaching the religion as the prophets taught it. That's why most places won't accept some religiously qualified person who offers to lead the community for free because they know that the free preachers plan on making them into good religious people who don't live the sinful lifestyles they currently enjoy and want to maintain. Some religious organizations go so far to maintain the status quo of their power over people that they will reject a free offer by a qualified leader in order to pay someone else who is less qualified to lead the community in religious worship. Regarding religious leadership you get what you pay for. If you want someone cheap in morals, knowledge and religiosity then pay them money and if you want someone who is religiously knowledgeable, upright and beneficial then the only payment they will accept is sincere attention and religious actions when they advise people to practice their religion in the correct prophetic way completely. As some say there should be seperation between church and state, I say religious leadership must be financially independent of the people they are leading. Religious leaders don't get paid by those they lead, followers get paid by those they follow. A good religious leader can't be hired because their services aren't for sale. The services of a good religious leader are given for free because their advice it's priceless. The more they are paid monetarily then the less their advice is worth. Instead of religious leaders, most places of worship have religious employees wearing the uniform and title of a leader without the authority or influence. While you are more likely to find the leaders sinful than sincere. It's easy to tell who is in charge at a place of worship, you look at who is paying everyone else and who doesn't get paid anything. That's the price of religious leadership. Although frequently people don't even get what they pay for because these "religious leaders" take days off. Can you believe it? Their job is getting paid to help people do what God wants and they take days off? Did God tell them to not guide the people on X day of the week? Did prophets take a day off from preaching and teaching? True religious leaders don't take days off because their religion is too important and being a religious leader is a 24/7 job where the boss is God. There is no "day off" when God gives you a job. God's definition of a religious leader's workweek means you work all week, every week, even when you're weak. When they take a "day off" it's not a day off, it's just a day that they aren't doing their job that's what it is. Oh but these "leaders" don't just take days off, they take vacations to exotic places leaving the sinners who paid them to guide them behind. Could there be a worse example? I don't care what somebody preaches, if they are a religious leader and take days off or vacations then by taking days off they are teaching people it's okay to take a vacation from their religion. Of course they may not intend to teach that but that is what they are teaching. They are what I call "sacreligious religious folk". Some who are explicitly paid to lead others in prayer don't even show up to the prayers. What does that teach people when the religious leader who literally is getting paid to pray doesn't show up? Why would anybody else come to the place of worship to pray? Why even have a religious leader if they aren't going to come and lead you daily in religious prayers? If they aren't there then they clearly aren't a religious leader because if they were they'd be there leading all of the prayers. These are just some of the lessons these allegedly religious pseudo-leaders teach via their actions, but what they preach via their speech is sometimes even worse. Seriously as much as I detest religious leaders who take "days off", sometimes when you hear what they say you pray that they take more days off. The problem is that originally our religious leaders were the prophets but today our leaders are profiteers. Many see religion as a business and this is not what the true religion is. Religion is a way of life, the true religion is the way of life our Creator wants us to live by. Religion involves both belief and actions, but religious businesses would have us neglect one or the other, or both. I'm not advocating you shouldn't give charity, but consider who your religious teacher(s) is and why. Why would they require your money if the Creator was paying them and their main focus was teaching you to get rewarded in the afterlife? Unfortunately today many "religious people" are really business people and they cannot sell you the ticket to paradise as they claim. Whenever you talk to a religious person, listen to them, or read their materials, always consider the following: Are they advising you or are they advertising to you? Sadly, myself included can seem to be sincerely sharing religious advice when they are simply arrogant promoting a righteous knowledgeable self-image. Sometimes people may not preach for money, fame, or power but neither is it for God's sake, they can be addicted to preaching. Though Satan can and does make sincere people think they are addicted to get them to stop, some people preach because doing so makes them feel superior and better than others or it just helps them improve their self-esteem and ego. So even if someone is preaching the truth 100% there can always be underlying motives within that makes them insincere, arrogant and corrupt. A sound preacher is like finding a pure freshwater raindrop in a saltwater ocean and finding a sincere sound preacher is like finding a microscopic molecule inside the atom of that fresh raindrop that's in the ocean of saltwater. And then what happens if God blesses you with coming across such a preacher or their message? Most us fail to implement the good they teach us to do. Who is worse, corrupt preachers or those who are too corrupt to be effected and change when exposed to prophetic teachings?

   Take the following incident as a perfect example of the absurdity of religious organizations today and how these boards, committes and places of worship are frequently run. One time I was at a nearly empty religious place of worship with only a few others with me. Then some guy came in and explained his dire situation. He explained how he was driving to the hospital from a distant city to visit his father who was on life support and it was unknown whether he would survive the night. Unfortunately the guy was so distraught he missed his exit on the highway and then shortly after that he was extremely low on gas. Thus the state police trooper got involved with his vehicle trouble and the guy just told him how if he can just get to a place of worship of the same faith as him then he'll be fine since they would help him out, so the trooper gave him a car ride. Thus was how he came to me and the others who were with me, explaining his story and how he had no fuel and no money to buy gas. I didn't have my wallet with me at the time but I figured I'd just explain the situation to the religious leader and presto everything would get solved via financial charity. Yet it turns out that didn't solve anything. The religious leader informed the guy that the "board's policy" or "the institution's policy" says they can only write checks. So the religious organization could give the guy a check but no cash or coin. It was a weekend, so a check couldn't be cashed and the guy's dad was in the hospital on his deathbed, so he didn't have time to wait days for banks to open and even if he did he had no transportation except to drive to a gas station to get more gas. He didn't have the gas to go cash any check. I was stunned to learn this and strongly confronted the religious leader about it. I asked why he didn't help and if there was something he could do. The religious leader simply told me how they have a policy and procedure to follow that says they only write checks. I criticized the policy exposing it's flaws and inadequacies finally saying how this policy even goes against our religion(the religion I had at that time). Thus I said we can't follow this policy and we have to help as part of our religion. Also the guy in need of help was a new member of our religion too and a traveler, both of whom are categories religiously entitled to charity. Yet I was told "there's a procedure". By that time a small crowd had gathered around and I said to break the procedure, ignore the policy, do the right thing and that we don't have to follow the procedure in these circumstances. Then I said how our prophet would not have such a policy of writing checks, he would just give and help. I got told, *"Well the prophet didn't live in America either."* Of course I was furious with that rebuttal because it didn't even have anything at all to do with the matter at hand, but was more of a personal jab at me because of my sentiments about America which the leader knew about. I also had issues before with this organization, this leader and this "board/committee/presidents" and their policies with which I strongly disagreed with their whole structure, methodology and ideology. So I appealed to the leader as an individual person trying to pressure him to help the guy from his own pocket since I knew he lived right next to the place of worship, thus he could've helped the guy outside of his official capacity if procedures prevented immediate aid. I figured maybe the leader just didn't want to officially break policy because of his contract with the religious organization who pays his annual salary, which also owns and maintains the house he lives in; which him getting paid to be the leader was another thing I disagreed with as well. Yet since I knew the leader had a salary and I knew he had access to his personal funds on the spot, I knew he had the money to help if he personally wanted to. So it was no longer a matter of organizational policy it was a matter of his personal choice. Thus I informed him that he could help the guy personally himself outside of the official capacity so he's not breaking policy. Surprisingly he didn't want to do that but wanted to stick to the policy, saying he/we can't go against the policy that's been setup. I asked the others who were crowded around to help the guy and they didn't say nothing to me but looked at me like I was rebellious and silly for not accepting the policy and complaining for the sake of giving a fellow co-religionist in dire need some charitable assistance as our religion obligates us all to do. Thus I left in frustration and disgust. But the situation was even worse. The worst part is that this occured the day after the weekly money collection and the location where all the financial donations get kept was right behind the religious leader whilst I had this conversation with him. So all the money was literally right behind this religious leader, you could smell it if you tried, yet he adamantly refused to help someone of his own faith in dire need because of the organization's policy which is set by the board or committe. The cash was directly behind him but he stubbornly insisted the organization can only give a check and the guy's timeframe didn't allow for a check so he didn't want the check. The guy needed cash and they had the cash but they would only give a check which wouldn't help the guy out of his trouble. Whereas even personally the "religious leader" didn't want to dip into his own pocket to help another person, but since he didn't want to say he didn't want to help he blamed "*the board procedures*". Which was only 1 part of the problem, of which both those in power and the policies were blameworthy for multiple reasons. To this day it's saddens me that I witnessed this scandal, where they had the cash as an organization and as a private individual but refused to give it to someone in need because of "policy" and "procedures". Some religious organizations even have policies where they set a limit on how much they can give to needy people and how many times! Could you imagine a prophet of God saying "*Sorry, but I already gave you the maximum amount that I'm allowed to give you.*" Imagine if the religious people who give donations at houses of worship set such maximum limits on the amount of or the quantity of the donations they give to religious societies? All the societies would say such policies are wrong, yet they dare to make such policies themselves regarding them distributing those very same funds which people donated to them to be distributed and used for religious reasons. On top of it all the "religious leader" who obstinately refused to give charity to a fellow co-religionist in need, either from the community funds or his personal funds, had the legal name of "Khalilullah" which is a non-english name that when translated into english means "friend of God". As if the irony/hypocrisy of such a name weren't tragic enough that name in itself was forbidden to have according to the very prophet he claimed to follow since that prophet pbuh told people who were named "Bara" which means "Pious" that such a name is sinful/forbidden because only God knows who is truly pious and to ascribe piety to oneself by one's name is arrogance/forbidden. So the "religious leader" not only was sinful in nature but also sinful by name according to the very religion he allegedly preaches. How did such a person ever attain a position of religious leadership? That's what is called the "American Dream" and why America is called the "land of opportunity, where anybody can become anything they wish and strive to be" even if they are unqualifed. Thus one must keep in mind that since most who don't follow the prophets won't admit to following profits, we should remember to follow the prophets instead of procedures. The prophets set the procedures we are to follow. There is no religious "board" who is to be treated as though they are the Lord. Committee members can be hypocritical sinners. An "elected president" is not heaven sent. Any Society's constitution or charter should not be thought of as a sacred doctrine paid for with the blood of martyrs. Not every form of prostitution involves sexual activity, some include clandestine miserliness by religious "non-profit" corporation's. For sure most religious organizations are truthful when they claim to be "not-for-profit", but they are misspelling the word "profit" using the letters "f-i-t" instead of "p-h-e-t" and lack sincerity when it comes to giving charity. Of course they believe in the signs God has sent to them. Although it is the dollar signs of profits they believe in rather than the divine signs of God's prophets. It's almost funny the money in America says "In God we trust" whereas the religious organizations say "In money we trust". Businesses are becoming more like popular religious cults and religions are transforming into special business corporations.

These verses from the English translation of the New International Version of the Bible need no explanation.

Hosea 4:7-12 "<u>The more priests there were, the more they sinned</u> against me; they exchanged their glorious God for something disgraceful.⁸ <u>They feed on the sins of my people and relish their wickedness.</u> ⁹ And it will be: <u>Like people, like priests. I will punish both of them for their ways</u> and repay them for their deeds. ¹⁰ "<u>They will eat but not have enough</u>; they will engage in prostitution but not flourish, because they have deserted the LORD to give themselves ¹¹ to prostitution; <u>old wine and new wine take away their understanding.</u> ¹² <u>My people consult a wooden idol, and a diviner's rod speaks to them.</u> A spirit of prostitution leads them astray; <u>they are unfaithful to their God.</u>"

The Quran informs believers of the situation and instructed Muhammad pbuh what to say to such rich "religious leaders" and informs us exactly what will happen to them in 9:34-35,

﷽ يَـٰٓأَيُّهَا ٱلَّذِينَ ءَامَنُوٓا۟ إِنَّ كَثِيرًا مِّنَ ٱلْأَحْبَارِ وَٱلرُّهْبَانِ لَيَأْكُلُونَ أَمْوَٰلَ ٱلنَّاسِ بِٱلْبَـٰطِلِ وَيَصُدُّونَ عَن سَبِيلِ ٱللَّهِ ۗ وَٱلَّذِينَ يَكْنِزُونَ ٱلذَّهَبَ وَٱلْفِضَّةَ وَلَا يُنفِقُونَهَا فِى سَبِيلِ ٱللَّهِ فَبَشِّرْهُم بِعَذَابٍ أَلِيمٍ ۝٣٤ يَوْمَ يُحْمَىٰ عَلَيْهَا فِى نَارِ جَهَنَّمَ فَتُكْوَىٰ بِهَا جِبَاهُهُمْ وَجُنُوبُهُمْ وَظُهُورُهُمْ ۖ هَـٰذَا مَا كَنَزْتُمْ لِأَنفُسِكُمْ فَذُوقُوا۟ مَا كُنتُمْ تَكْنِزُونَ ۝٣٥

"O you who believe! Verily, there are many of the (Jewish) rabbis and the (Christian) monks who devour the wealth of mankind in falsehood, and hinder (them) from the Way of Allah (i.e. Allah's Religion of Islamic Monotheism). And those who hoard up gold and silver [Al-Kanz: the money, the Zakat of which has not been paid], and spend it not in the Way of Allah, -announce unto them a painful torment. On the Day when that (Al-Kanz: money, gold and silver, etc., the Zakat of which has not been paid) will be heated in the Fire of Hell and with it will be branded their foreheads, their flanks, and their backs, (and it will be said unto them):-"This is the treasure which you hoarded for yourselves. Now taste of what you used to hoard.""

Another chapter of the Quran #107 Al-Maun (Small things) is also relevant for all Big Business Religions to reflect upon.

أَرَءَيْتَ ٱلَّذِى يُكَذِّبُ بِٱلدِّينِ (١) فَذَٰلِكَ ٱلَّذِى يَدُعُّ ٱلْيَتِيمَ (٢) وَلَا يَحُضُّ عَلَىٰ طَعَامِ ٱلْمِسْكِينِ (٣) فَوَيْلٌ لِّلْمُصَلِّينَ (٤) ٱلَّذِينَ هُمْ عَن صَلَاتِهِمْ سَاهُونَ (٥) ٱلَّذِينَ هُمْ يُرَاءُونَ (٦) وَيَمْنَعُونَ ٱلْمَاعُونَ

"Have you observed the one who belies the religion? Who repulses the orphan, and who does not encourage the feeding of the poor? So woe to those who pray, but are neglectful of (and/or insincere in) their prayer. Those who do things only to be seen by others. And are uncharitable even over small things."

SHIA

One of the few things I was taught in school about Islam was about the Sunni and Shia distinction. My non-Muslim teachers told me the difference between them is that Sunni's think leadership of the Muslims after the Prophet Muhammad pbuh should have passed to the best and most qualified person, which it did. Whereas the Shia believe leadership should be hereditary and only be held by those of the bloodline of Muhammad pbuh, regardless of how moral or qualified those people may be. Obviously leadership should go to those best suited for the job rather than the descendants of Muhammad pbuh by default. Therefore I didn't look into the differences between the Sunni and Shia and figured it was just politics.

A member of my immediate family knew a Shia. As a result, after learning I was Muslim many family members suggested I go to the Shia masjid to see how it is. I did not want to go because I wasn't a Shia, wasn't going to go there regularly and didn't want to go there to get misguided. By this time I had heard the differences were more than just political, but I didn't know many details. Having non-Muslim family members they didn't quite understand how at best Shia could be considered a different denomination, they just thought Muslim is Muslim and everyone who claims to be one is the same. It would appear to be bigotry if I continually refused to go to visit the Shia masjid. One day I decided to go in order to see for myself firsthand what they are really all about. I got lost on the way and it was time to pray while I was still driving. I'm thinking *"Great, the first time I go to the place and I'm going show up late in the middle of prayer, that's a terrible first impression to make"*. Panicking over the embarrassment and awkwardness I'm expecting to walk into, I was surprised at what I found. When I walked in, I saw half the building was a basketball court and the other half was a prayer area, split into different male and female sections. I had never been in a masjid with an indoor basketball court, which was only separated from the prayer area by a thin glass door. It would be comparable to finding a swimming pool behind the last pew in a church. I thought *"What the heck is going on here?"* it was quite shocking. Even more shocking was that the kids were still playing basketball and the few adults that were there weren't praying. I entered the prayer area and asked if they already prayed and found out that they hadn't even started. That was confusing because I was late to the prayer, they should have been praying before I arrived. Then I prayed some voluntary prayers, known as Sunnah prayers because the prophet pbuh prayed them even though they aren't required, before the noon prayer while waiting for prayer to start any minute. Finally a person called to prayer, but it sounded very different than what the call to prayer is supposed to be and I think they mentioned the name of Ali, which shouldn't be mentioned in that manner or at that time. Anyways I line up with the rest and we are just about to pray, when I look down to where I'm going to prostrate and notice something very strange. Everyone in the entire row has a stone in the place where the Muslim is supposed to put their forehead. I was the only one who didn't have a stone in front of him. I was worried that someone would give me a stone, thinking I had forgotten one, because I wouldn't know what to do with it since Muslims don't use stones to pray. It was appalling and scary. When prostrating

I had to peek to see if they were doing what I thought they were doing. Scandalously I saw them putting their foreheads on the stone when prostrating and it freaked me out. After the prayer I remained sitting, counting the zikr that's done after prayer on my fingers. Zikr or Dhikr or Tasbeeh is quietly saying things like "Allahu Akbar", loosely translated as God is greater, and other phrases that glorify God or ask for forgiveness. From a Christian perspective zikr would be comparable to repeating phrases like "Hallelujah", or for a Catholic like saying the rosary. Whereas prayer for a Muslim would be comparable to a service for a Christian except it only takes a few minutes, is done multiple times a day, can be done anywhere on earth and isn't restricted to a specific building. Zikr can be done at any time, but there are certain times one should say certain zikr for extra reward, such as after the prayer. So I'm keeping count on my fingers and I notice everyone else is using beads. When I was a brand new Muslim I researched whether Muslims use prayer beads or not, because I didn't know. I discovered that Muhammad pbuh never used prayer beads but counted on his fingers when doing zikr and commanded others to do the same because the fingers will bear witness as to our deeds, whereas beads won't. Since prayer beads were easily available he could've used them if he wanted to, but he intentionally didn't. This means prayer beads are a bida, or an innovation in the religion. When it comes to religion only a prophet with direct guidance from God can introduce something when it comes to worship. Also before it was decided how to publicly call Muslims to prayer, some suggested using a horn like the Jews use, or a bell like the Christians, but the prophet explictly forbid calling people to pray the way they do because Muslims are different with a different religion and we don't imitate those of other faiths. Thus since nearly all the faiths other than Islam use prayer beads this precedent applies to forbid the beads as well. All innovated matters concerning religion that are not taught by prophets are misguidance. Therefore all religious innovations are dangerous and detestable. The prophets were taught the religion by God, to teach the people so that people can please the Creator and live how Allah wants us to. The beads were never used by prophets, so anyone today who prays with beads is actually saying that they know better than the prophets and are better worshippers than they were, even though the prophets were taught by God how to worship. This is why the classical Muslim Scholar Imam Malik said what in arabic means:"*Whoever introduces something new to this religion, which those who came before him did not observe, must contend that theMessenger of Allah has betrayed the faith, since Allah has said:* **(Today I have completed for you your religion)** *(5:3). Whatever was not part of religion on that day, is no part of it today.*" Another Muslim scholar and prominent companion of Muhammad pbuh, Abdullah Ibn Masood warned: ""*You will find people calling you to the Book of Allah(the Quran), though they themselves have rejected it completely. You must seek knowledge, beware of the innovator, the intransigent and the entrenched. Always go back to the very beginning.*" Who today can say God personally taught them to use prayer beads? Who today can say X prophet used prayer beads? How much money and economic resources are wasted on prayer beads? Some Muslims may say that the prophet didn't use beads but there are narrations about his companions who used pebbles, date pits, or knots in a rope to help keep count. First of all those aren't beads and beads are distinctly something non-Muslims use which again the prophet pbuh didn't use and forbid us to imitate non-Muslims, especially in religious matters. Secondly some of the narrations used refering to an extreme minority of companions counting on other things were classified as fabricated according to the hadith scholar Sheikh Nasir ud-Deen al-Albani. Thirdly there are narrations of the companions of Muhammad pbuh and the salaf such as Ibn Masood expressly and angrily forbidding people inside of a masjid from doing zikr on pebbles anyways, saying it was a detestable bida and grave sin. However even IF the narrations about the salaf counting on other than their fingers were authentic and the narrations saying the salaf forbid counting on pebbles and such weren't, there is nothing at all to prove beads were used. Beads were widely available and could've been used but they weren't. The argument of bead users is to claim pebbles, date pits and ropes are the same as beads but they aren't because no disbelievers count zikr on pebbles, date pits or ropes yet most all disbelievers use beads. Plus Muhammad pbuh said to count on our fingers. So when the prophet pbuh says count on your fingers, that's what one does. Also the Quran instructs Muslims that when they differ amongst themselves to refer it to Allah(via the Quran) and the Messenger(via the Sunnah) and the Messenger pbuh said to count zikr on our fingers. It doesn't say refer to companion so and so, it says refer to Allah and his Messenger first and foremost. Some Muslims mistakenly think that having good intentions makes something good, even if it's not a part of the Sunnah or opposing the Sunnah of Muhammad pbuh. For example, Muslims know the Sunnah is to count zikr on the fingers but will use the beads anyways saying their intentions are good. Imām Sa'īd bin Al-Musayyib once saw a guy with such a mentality praying after dawn more than the 2 units of the 1 voluntary Sunnah prayer which Muhammad pbuh would do before the obligatory prayer. The guy was praying a lot of extra prayers when Muhammad pbuh only used to do 1 voluntary prayer at that time of the day. So Imam Sa'id forbade the guy from praying. The guy said, *"Is Allāh going to punish me for praying?"* Sa'īd told him, *"No, but He will punish you for contradicting the Sunnah."* Unfortunately Satan manipulates the good intentions of people and makes them think that it's ok to make things up in regards to worship. Satan loves this even more than when people sin, because a sin is easy to recognize as wrong and when a person sincerely repents they are forgiven. Although people rarely repent for practicing a religious innovation, because they don't ever consider that what they are doing is wrong. This amounts to people following their own desires and ideas instead of the divinely inspired instructions revealed to prophets. Essentially God told humans to pray like this, and then they say, *"well it's easier or more convenient to do it like this"*. Doing something the prophets pbut didn't teach and opposing them for something else implies that you know better than God who taught the prophets. When it comes to worship if you cannot prove that the prophet pbuh did it or his companions, then it can't be accepted as a valid way to worship. Despite good intentions it's impossible to get closer to God doing something that God has not legislated or instructed you to do.

- Good intention + Good action = Good deed
- Bad intention + Bad action = Bad deed
- Bad intention + Good action = Bad deed
- Good intention + Bad action = Bad deed

While the prayer beads might at first seem innocent or pious they are actually very bad and should be eliminated. Even outside of the religious legal ruling, socially speaking the prayer beads are bad because they draw attention to the bead counter leading to arrogance or worse. For instance in a masjid where they have a flimsy divider between men and women one can hear girls counting on beads and vice versa. Now when guys can hear girls they can't see counting on prayer beads, it's quite a distraction even if they aren't religious, moreso if they are regardless of their position on whether prayer beads are permitted or forbidden. I have seen with my own eyes a Muslim guy in a masjid hear a girl counting on prayer beads clicking them and he turns his head and just stares at the divider not being able to focus on praying because of the audible distraction/temptation. Whereas all the other guys just wish the girl would stop clicking her prayer beads and distracting everybody, especially since the beads are a bida. Yet the whole time and every time these girls probably think they are pleasing God or something by counting prayer beads not realizing they are tormenting every single guy in the masjid coming in between them and Allah with their prayer bead clickery. Then even if they silently click/count them one can still hear them put the beads back in whatever container they got them from and then when the guys hear that they all get tense because now they know there is a girl on the other side of the divider and they didn't know that before. Of course I'm sure the bead clickery issue goes both ways, I'm just giving the male perspective which shows how the beads have a bad effect which the sunnah way of counting on one's fingers does not have. Regarding prayer beads Imam al-Ghazali commented: "*People count with self-satisfaction the number of times they have recited the name of God on their prayer beads, but they keep no beads for reckoning the number of idle words they speak.*" Unfortunately many use prayer beads both non-Muslim and Muslim alike out of ignorance, cultural tradition and habit, but that still doesn't make it right. So while counting on my fingers I heard the Shia say "*What's he doing?*" which made me realize the jig is up and now they know that I'm not one of them, if they hadn't already figured it out when I did the "Sunnah" prayers. I had decided to leave immediately after finishing, before they confronted me. Suddenly everyone stood up and began to pray again. I was completely surprised since the next prayer wasn't for a few hours. Since there was a row of people behind me I couldn't just leave. I prayed again not knowing what was going on, how long they would pray for or what they were praying. After that I was wondering "*How am I going to get out of here?*" Then Satan started whispering things to me such as: "*What were you thinking? You should've known not to come. Why did you listen to your family who don't even know anything about Islam? Don't ever listen to anything they ever say again! You better give them an earful and let them have it if you ever get out of here!*" Of course Shaitan whispered this to me using my own voice and mental thoughts trying to deceive me into being mean or having sore feelings for my family, he is very tricky and constantly trying to exploit every opportunity. After the second prayer the person on the right got up shook the imam's hand, then turned around facing everyone else standing beside the imam. Then the next person in the row shook the imam's hand and the other guy's hand, then stood next to him forming a line facing the rest. This continued happening like a sports team tunnel with everyone going down the line shaking hands before getting in line themselves. I went through the line and faced the rest like everyone else. One thing I noticed was that all the people had black marks on their forehead, which I guessed was from prostrating on stones. I didn't see whether the people picked up their stones or left them on the ground. However I decided that I wasn't going to leave until I got some answers as to what the heck was going on. I asked a Shia guy what the reason was behind the stones. I learned that they use the stones so "*they don't forget that they are on earth*". On the face of it this reasoning is ludicrous. When in their life has a person not been on earth? How could anybody ever forget they are on earth if they always have been on earth and don't know what it's like not to be there? I asked him, "*Did the prophet Muhammad pbuh ever use stones when he was praying?*" The guy didn't respond, but I already knew the answer was no. That means it is an innovation to prostrate on stones and is not part of the religion of Islam. Later I learned they use stones from a specific place, called Karbala in Iraq, from the site of the grave of Husayn the son of Ali. Then I asked a Shia guy what they think about Ali, so I could hear what a Shia thinks with my own two ears. What I heard was inappropriate and incorrect, I'm not even going to mention it lest it spread their extremely deviant opinion. Then I asked what the second prayer was and why they didn't pray the noon prayer on time. They said because it was the weekend they combine the noon and afternoon prayers to make it more convenient. Now combining those two prayers is allowed if there is a legitimate reason, such as if you are traveling, or if there is very bad weather that would make it dangerous for people to go to the masjid repeatedly. But to combine the prayers just because it's the weekend is not a legitimate reason. A Muslim adapts their life to the religion, a Muslim doesn't adapt the religion to suit their life. Later I'd learn that Shia also do wudu incorrectly too. After that the Shia asked me to join them later that week for their holiday. It was a Shia holiday and I didn't even know it existed or that a holiday was coming up. I said "*What holiday?*" learning it was a holiday dedicated to a descendant of Ali. I declined their invitation because none of the companions of the prophet or the prophet celebrated it. This holiday is another innovation there is no basis for in Islam. Then I left the Shia masjid never to return again. Later I decided to research what Shias actually believe and how big and numerous the differences between Sunni and Shia are.

    First some background information is required on the subject of the Muslim leadership succession itself before the Shia can be properly discussed. On the orders of Muhammad pbuh, his best friend, close companion and father in-law Abu Bakr became the leader of the Muslims after the death of the Prophet pbuh. While Muhammad pbuh was sick on his deathbed unable to lead the prayers Abu Bakr led the prayers, which reveals the community had no qualms with his leadership. In Islam there is no specific position for those who lead the prayers as there is in other religions. Any Muslim can lead the prayer, but there is a rank of who gets preference depending on who is at the prayer. Out of those present the Muslim who has memorized the most Quran and has the best Tajweed(pronunciation of the Quran) is the one who leads, if some know equal amounts of the Quran then the one who knows the most about the rulings and specifics regarding prayer leads, if more than one are equal in this type of knowledge as well then the one who knows more about the Sunnah leads. If they both know the same amount of Islam then the Muslim who emigrated from the land of dar al-kufr to dar al-islam earlier leads the prayer. If they both emigrated at the same time then the one who became a Muslim first leads the prayer. If they are still equal in all these categories then the elder of the knowledgeable is the one who leads. Lastly all other things being equal the one whose domain it is should lead, meaning the last distinction to determine the prayer leader after age is whoever lives closest to the masjid should lead. The prayer leader changes for every prayer depending on who is there, nobody is ever declared to be the permanent prayer leader, because they may decrease in knowledge and forget, or others could become more knowledgeable. Also if that person didn't show up to prayer on time for whatever reason then the prayer must be prayed regardless and is not delayed. Using this system of leadership is just and nobody ever has sore feelings that they aren't leading the prayer, it's actually a huge responsibility that people tend to shy away from, the prayers only take a few minutes so it's not a long term leadership. Wealth, ethnicity or nationality has nothing to do with who is considered to lead the prayers. There are no extra benefits for leading the prayer except for the extra reward one would get from Allah. Even when Muhammad pbuh was healthy and in charge, if someone had a question for Muhammad pbuh and he wasn't in the city Muhammad pbuh had instructed people to consult Abu Bakr in such a situation. Abu Bakr was the first man to embrace Islam and accept Muhammad pbuh as a prophet and he was the first man to be the leader of the Muslims after the death of Muhammad pbuh. Abu Bakr al-Siddiq died after being the leader of the Muslims for 2 years, 2 months and 14 days. When Abu Bakr became the Khalifah he gave the following speech, which in english means:

> *"O people, I have been appointed over you, though I am not the best among you. If I do well, then help me; and if I act wrongly, then correct me. Truthfulness is synonymous with fulfilling the trust, and lying is equivalent to treachery. The weak among you is deemed strong by me, until I return to them that which is rightfully theirs, if Allah wills. And the strong among you is deemed weak by me, until I take from them what is rightfully (someone else's), if Allah wills. No group of people abandons military/armed struggle in the path of Allah, except that Allah makes them suffer humiliation. And evil / mischief does not become widespread among a people, except that Allah inflicts them with widespread calamity. Obey me so long as I obey Allah and His Messenger. And if I disobey Allah and His Messenger, then I have no right to your obedience. Stand up now to pray, may Allah have mercy on you."*

For his first 3 days as Khalifah Abu Bakr would publicly plead with the Muslims that they make someone else the leader instead of him. They refused and said he was the best. Abu Bakr refused to be refused and did not want to be leader so he kept begging and begging that someone else be put in charge. Yet the Muslims persistantly refused to let anyone else be in charge except Abu Bakr, because he really was the best even though he said he wasn't and asked for 3 days to be replaced. Some famous statements of Abu Bakr are:

- *He who is not impressed by sound advice lacks faith.*
- *When a noble man learns knowledge he becomes humble; when an ignoble person gains knowledge he gets conceited.*
- *When knowledge is limited, it leads to folly; when knowledge exceeds a certain limit, it leads to exploitation.*

- *When you advise any person you should be guided by the fear of Allah.*
- *Solitude is better than a society of evil people.*
- *If you expect the blessings of God, be good to His people.*
- *To be safe from trial and thankful is more beloved to me than to be tested and patient.*
- *I wish I were a hair in the side of a believing servant.*
- *If an ignorant person is attracted by the things of the world that is bad. But if a learned person is thus attracted, it is worse.*
- *A man who is shy and modest, is an amazing character, but a woman who is shy and modest is beyond amazing.*
- *We used to leave seventy doors to the lawful, out of fear that we might enter one of the doors to the unlawful.*
- *Cry and if you can't, try hard to.*
- *The people who abandon Jihad fall a victim to humility and degradation.*
- *Jihad is obligatory for the Muslims.*
- *It is bad for a young man to sin, but it is worse for an old man to sin.*
- *If you want to control other people, first control yourself.*
- *Cursed is the man who dies, but the evil done by him survives.*
- *Run away from greatness, and greatness will follow you.*
- *Every day, nay every moment, try to do some good deed.*

After Abu Bakr, Umar bin Khattab was Muhammad's 2nd favorite companion. Abu Bakr and Umar use to compete with each other in doing good deeds seeking the pleasure of the Creator, and there is a famous incident that took place between them that illustrates just what kind of men they were. Once Umar went to Muhammad pbuh to donate charity for the cause of Islam and to help the Muslims, it was a large amount of money and when asked by the prophet how much he left for his family he replied "*the same amount*", meaning he gave 50% of all he had away in charity all at one time. Then Abu Bakr came and gave a donation, the prophet pbuh also asked him what he left for his family. Abu Bakr replied how he left them Allah and the message of Islam, meaning that he gave 100% of his wealth in charity all at once and completely trusted that Allah would provide for his family just as Allah provides for everything. That Abu Bakr left them with Islam shows that religion is more important than anything else in this world. Another lesson to learn from this is that it's not the amount of wealth one gives that is important because Umar actually gave a larger amount than

Abu Bakr, rather it is about the amount you don't give that determines how good the deed is. Abu Bakr was better in this instance because he held 0% back. Thus when we give our wealth or time for the sake of God it isn't about how much we give, the important factor is how much we don't give, the less we hold back the better. Unlike the ascetics of other religions, Abu Bakr and Umar didn't just give their wealth away in charity and live in poverty, they went back to work the very next day and continued earning a living and giving more in charity until they died. When these men became leaders, they were fairly well-off having re-earned more than what they gave, which shows that charity will never decrease a person's wealth. Both Abu Bakr and Umar gave all their wealth in charity to the treasury of the Islamic State after assuming leadership and did not use their position as a means of gaining riches, but saw leadership as a burden and heavy responsibility. Today the opposite is the case where leaders enter office poor and leave rich, but Muslim leaders were wealthy when they became leaders and poor when they left. When Abu Bakr was sick and felt he was nearing his death he gave up his position of leadership. Abu Bakr said he was no longer healthy enough to fulfill his duties so he was returning the authority entrusted to him back to the Muslims and told them to choose a new leader before he died so there wouldn't be chaos and disputes after his death. The Muslims couldn't unanimously agree on who to pick so they asked Abu Bakr who he thought would be best. After a while Abu Bakr asked Abdur Rahman bin Auf what he thought of Umar and he told Abu Bakr that however good he(Abu Bakr) thinks Umar is then Umar is better than what he thinks. Abu Bakr asked another and was told that Umar is unlike all the other Muslims and his private deeds are better than his public deeds. On it went with Abu Bakr asking Muslim after Muslim what they thought of Umar with Umar getting recomended by all who were asked, until people began to guess Umar would be chosen because Abu Bakr kept asking about him. However a few people were afraid of Umar becoming the leader because he was a very strict and strong willed man. So they asked Abu Bakr what he would say to his Lord after he dies as an explanation for having appointed Umar bin Khattab to be the leader of the Muslims to which he replied, *"Have you come to frighten me? I swear that when I meet my Lord, I will gladly tell Him that I appointed as ruler over His people, the man who was the best of them all."* Shortly after this Abu Bakr ordered that his last will be written with his appointment of Umar bin Khattab as the next Khalifah. After the will was sealed Abu Bakr asked the Muslim population whether they will give the pledge of allegiance to whomever he had chosen to be the next leader in his will. When asked nearly every Muslim replied they would accept Abu Bakr's choice for the next leader except for Ali bin abi Talib. Ali did not say yes and did not say he would accept whoever Abu Baker chose. Do you know what Ali bin Abi Talib said instead? Ali said that he would never accept anyone being the next leader unless it is Umar. Ali publicly said he will only accept Umar as the next leader and nobody else, then it was revealed that Umar was the very man whom Abu Bakr had already chosen. So Ali comically agreed that was a good choice and he has no problem with Abu Bakr's choice afterall. Upon hearing the news that he had been selected to be the leader of the Muslim Empire, Umar bin al-Khattab cried and got extremely depressed thinking about how Allah would hold him accountable for every discomfort of every creature in the empire and that even plants would complain to Allah on the Day of Judgement saying Umar bin Khattab didn't fulfill their rights despite being the leader of the Muslim nation and owing them just treatment. On his deathbed Abu Bakr told Umar bin Khattab the following: *"Fear Allah, O 'Umar, and know that Allah has deeds to be done for Him in the day which He will not accept if done at night, and He has deeds to be done for Him at night which He will not accept if done during the day. He will not accept extra (nâfilah) deeds unless you fulfill the obligatory deeds. The scales of those whose scales will be weighty on the Day of Resurrection will only be weighty because they followed the truth in this life and it was weighty to them. And scales in which the truth will be placed tomorrow truly deserve to be heavy. And the scales of those whose scales will be light on the Day of Resurrection will only be light because they followed falsehood in this life and it was a light matter to them. And scales in which falsehood will be placed tomorrow truly deserve to be light. Allah the Exalted has mentioned the people of Paradise and mentioned them in the context of their best deeds, and overlooked their evil deeds, so when I remember them I say to myself: I fear that I will not be included with them. And Allah the Exalted has mentioned the people of Hell and mentioned them in the context of their worst deeds and rejected their best deeds, so when I remember them I say: I hope I won't be amongst them. Allah's worshippers should always be in a state of hope and fear, they shouldn't wish flimsy wishes about Allah and neither should they despair of Allah's mercy. If you keep to this advice of mine, no one who is not with you now should be more beloved to you than death – and it is sure to come to you. But if you disregard this advice, no one who is not with you now should be more hated to you than death – and you cannot escape it."*

Upon becoming the political Successor to the political Successor of Muhammad pbuh, Umar bin Khattab made the following inaugural speech which in english means:

"O ye faithful! Abu Bakr is no more amongst us. After having led us for about two years, he has returned to His Maker. He has the satisfaction that he has successfully piloted the ship of the Muslim state to safety after negotiating the stormy sea. He successfully waged the apostasy wars, and thanks to him, Islam is now supreme in Arabia. Islam is now on the move and we are carrying Jihad in the name of Allah against the mighty empires of Byzantine and Persia.

After Abu Bakr, the mantle of Khilafat has fallen on my shoulders. I swear it before God that I never coveted this office. I wished that it would have devolved on some other person more worthy than me. But now that in national interest, the responsibility for leading the Muslims has come to vest in me, I assure you that I will not run away from my post, and will make an earnest effort to discharge the onerous duties of the office to the best of my capacity in accordance with the injunctions of Islam.

In the performance of my duties, I will seek guidance from the Blessed Book(the Quran), and will follow the examples set by the Blessed Prophet (Muhammad) and Abu Bakr. In this task I seek your assistance. If I follow the right path, follow me. If I deviate from the right path, correct me so that we are not led astray.

Now brothers I offer a few prayers and you say Ameen to them.

O Allah I am hard, make me soft to promote the Truth, to comply with your injunctions and to aspire to a better life in the world hereafter.

O Allah make me hard for the enemies of Islam and for those who create mischief so that their designs against Allah come to naught.

O Allah I am miser; make me generous in the promotion of the good.

O Allah save me from hypocrisy. Strengthen my resolves so that whatever I do, I do for the sake of winning Your approbation.

O Allah soften my heart for the faithful so that I attend to their needs with a sense of dedication.

O Allah, I am careless, make me responsible enough so that I do not lose sight of You.

O Allah I am weak in offering my obedience to You; make me active and fortify my faith.

O Allah bestow on me faith, and the power to do good.

O Allah give me the power of self-criticism and self- assessment.

O Allah bestow on me the insight into the meaning of the Quran and the strength to act in accordance with what the Quran says.

O Allah You are capable of doing anything: bless us with Your favour. Ameen."

Later when Umar bin Khattab was asked about his son being a potential successor he replied that he wouldn't want two members of his family to be held accountable on the Day of Resurrection for the heavy responsibility of being leader of the Muslims. Umar had 2 black lines that ran down his face because he used to cry so much for the sake of Allah. For his diet Umar ate the cheapest and harshest food available because he felt that he would not be able to truly care for the poorest unless he ate what they ate. When Umar's friends or governors serving under him would come to visit he would offer them food to eat, but they couldn't eat his food because it was hard to chew and not very tasty. His political subordinates were used to finer foods and embarassingly admitted to him that they can't eat like he eats. Upon hearing this Umar would scold them for being so extravegant and threaten to dismiss them from governorship for having such luxurious tastes because such oppulence and enjoyment of worldy things does not befit anyone who is a leader, according to Umar. In times of famine Umar would vow not to eat until he was certain everyone else in the city had something to eat, because he figured he cannot possibly care for the hungry and keep their interests in mind if he wasn't hungry himself. His idea was that leaders are servants of the people and their interests come last after everyone elses, even if that "interest" is eating. Umar's policy was that if someone in his country had nothing to eat then he as a leader would/could eat nothing until they did. Otherwise he felt he'd be an oppressive ruler who was not fulfilling his duties as leader. However not only did Umar apply this rule to himself but he decreed as law that if anyone in the entire country ever died due to starvation, he would require the entire community they died in to pay blood money to the heirs because the community had a certain level of culpability in the death since they failed to feed the person and starvation was the reason for the death. Umar felt that for a community to let one of their members to starve to death was a type of communal murder that he was not going to let occur without punishing those who dared to let humans in their community starve. Regarding Jizya paid by Jews and Christians, Umar decreed that those who were unable to pay it due to poverty would receive payment themselves so they didn't live in poverty. Needless to say, Umar was the type of man you wanted to be leader during the middle of a famine or any other time for that matter. After a caravan came supplying food for the city during the famine, people brought food to Umar so he could break his vow and eat. Umar asked how much the food cost. When Umar heard the price he refused to eat saying it was too expensive, even though the price was only inflated because it was a famine and food was in high demand with low supply. Yet still Umar refused to eat expensive food because he didn't think leaders should eat better or more expensive food than those they serve. Umar's belief was that the leader should be the poorest person in the nation and have the hardest life. Once Umar met with one of his governors named Muawwiya. When Muawwiya came in to meet with Umar, without saying a word Umar grabbed a stick and started beating Muawwiya with it causing him to cry and complain saying such a beating was unjustified, demanding an immediate explanation. Umar replied that when he saw Muawwiya walk in, he noticed a tiny bit of arrogance in him, so as a good friend and ruler he wanted to beat the arrogance out of his governor so that he didn't rule unjustly or go to hellfire for having a mustard seed's worth of arrogance in his heart. Some may see such actions as extreme but as the leader of a nation Umar was keen to purify the nation and did not want arrogance having any part in any person which he appointed to administrative or leadership positions. To Umar arrogance disqualified one from having any type of power, administrative job or influence. As the Khalifah Umar would only eat something if everyone in the country could afford to buy/ eat it. He didn't limit this policy to food alone, but applied this to his clothes and house too. Umar lived in a rustic mud hut despite conquering/ruling Persia, Palestine, Syria, Egypt, Arabia and Libya. Umar would even sew patches on his clothes rather than buy new ones and had dozens of patches on his outfit when he entered Jerusalem to accept it's surrender, of which his servant was riding the donkey while Umar was walking. This was because it was the servant's turn to ride and Umar's turn to walk when they reached Jerusalem, since Umar only owned 1 riding animal for official government travel and shared turns riding it with his servant since it was too weak to carry 2 people at once. Umar refused to take his servant's riding turn even though they were entering Jerusalam on a diplomatic mission to accept it's surrender from the Christians and he was the leader of all Muslims. Umar's servant even told him he should get on the donkey because it will look bad if the leader of all Muslims is walking while his servant rides, but Umar rebuked him and said he was afraid he'd go to hell for oppression if he arrogantly took part of his servant's riding turn. The bishops of Jerusalem came out thinking the guy on the donkey was Umar and that Umar was just a servant, until they got corrected by the Christian Patriarch Sophronious. This frequently happened to Umar where people wouldn't recognize him to be the leader because of his lifestyle. It was even reported that one time while he was the Khalifah Umar came late to the Friday prayer when he was supposed to lead it. It was extremely scandalous and unimaginable that a Khalifah or that Umar would be late to the most important prayer of the week especially when he was supposed to lead it and give a sermon. So Umar was asked why he was late and he didn't want to say why. Yet the Muslims refused to let Umar keep his reason a secret. The reason that the Khalifah Umar came late to the prayer was because he only had 1 outfit to wear. Umar handwashed it, but it didn't dry fast enough so he waited for his clothes to dry since he didn't want to come outside soaking wet or naked. That was the type of leader of the Muslim empire that Umar bin Khattab was, he only owned a single outfit (1 for winter and 1 for summer) and he didn't have a closet. Muhammad pbuh had set a similar example and there are incidents where bedouins asked Muhammad pbuh for charity while he was the leader of the Muslim state and took his only shirt off of him causing Muhammad pbuh to ask them to give him his shirt back, since at that time he only owned that one and if he had anything he could've given them in charity then he would've, but he literally didn't and that they were actually more wealthy than him despite asking him for charity. I mention the bit about Umar only owning 1 outfit not to excessively praise him but to demonstrate how he was not a prophet yet he was that ascetic as the leader of the Muslim empire. Leaders of countries, businesses, masjids, commitees, associations and households could learn a valuable lesson from such examples. Really how many clothes do we need when others have none? Do they need to be as fancy and expensive as they are when globally throughout history most people have worn much more rustic attire? Do we dress richly or righteously? Why do we live the lifestyles we live? Is it because our lifestyles are based on the prophetic piety and asecticism, or is it based on our society and love for this worldly life? Where did our definition of "poor" and "comfortable" come from? I'm not saying it's bad to be rich or comfortable, I'm just saying we might be too comfortable. Our modern lives are probably better than what people in the past thought paradise would be like. Just consider God as a miracle/sign would provide Mary with fruits that only grew in summer to eat while it was winter and would provide wintertime fruits for her in summer. That was a sign from God, yet today we can get that just by going to the grocery store or even buying them online. Thus the lifestyle we consider as something normal to which we are entitled would be classified as miraculous in the not to distant past. As another example Pineapple is called the "King's fruit" for the reason that only a King could afford to eat it because the shipping costs and preservation methods were so expensive you had to literally be a King of a nation just to eat 1 piece of pineapple. Yet we don't consider ourselves to be "living like Kings" do we? No, we tend to think we aren't that rich. If we use the prophetic lifestyles as examples, in many "civilized" countries if you wanted to live in a house like the houses the prophets lived in and live with their type of piety, despite using modern technology, some governments would lock you up for insanity and unsanitarily violating housing codes and such. Many modern governments actually make it illegal to try to live in the minimalistic type of lifestyle the prophets choose to have. Homlessness they permit, but prophetic austerity and minimalism is made illegal. Of course David and Solomon pbut are examples of wealthy prophets, but most prophets lived by choice in what most today would consider abject squalid unhealthy life-threatening poverty. Yet they and all of their companions were better than us because of such "non-luxurious lifestyles". So when making our financial goals we might be better off choosing prophets who lived in poverty as our role models of "success" rather than rich folk. Wealth isn't bad but neither is poverty or ascetism, the important thing is our priorities and motivations. For some comfortable lives are best spiritually, while for others austere lives are best. Muhammad pbuh stated that a single dirham(coin) given in charity can be worth 700 in reward in the next life but a single dirham spent on yourself is only worth 1 in reward in this life. When adding up the wealth of people in the next life, those who gave charity will be in a much better material position than if they had spent on themselves. So the real financial genius is the one who gives more in charity than they spend on themselves in this life. Basically you have 2 lives you can spend your money on, the present life at a ratio of 1:1 or you can spend on the next life via charity at a ratio of 1:700 x paradise money x eternity. It's this mentality towards wealth that the best followers of prophets have. They regret spending on themselves in this life because they'd rather invest it in the next life, but alas one has to live on this earth for awhile; prior to our life in the grave until finally moving into our eternal home. Thus we must spend something on ourself/family because we are currently travelers en route and must spend to arrive at our final destination. Regardless the successful prefer charity to themselves, those who follow Satan prefer themselves to charity. Sadly we tend to lean more towards the latter financial category. Yet it is nearly always better to give than to receive/keep. Muhammad pbuh taught Muslims to have this attitude towards wealth, so Umar had it and lived accordingly despite being able to live otherwise if he chose to have opulence. Also it's important to note that Umar had multiple outfits before becoming the Khalifh, but when he became a leader he became more austere since austerity befits leaders and the wealthy. Basically the more powerful you get the more poor and austere you should be since it is the worldy life that causes the powerful to abuse their power, thus worldy comfort is the enemy of those in leadership. The higher Umar rose in material/communal standing the lower his "standard of living" went, the more he got the larger a percentage of his wealth he gave in charity. Many cannot strictly live according to such an attitude or outlook even if they have it, so out of ignorance they brand those who try as extreme, crazy or miserly rather than admire and intend to imitate as much as possible. Even Umar's contemporary the Christian Byzantine emperor Heraclius was astounded by how austere Umar was in comparison to himself. At Antioch during the Muslim conquest of Syria, Heraclius asked a captive Muslim named Rifa'ah bin Zuhayr bin Ziyad bin Abid bin Sariyah al-Juruhumi these questions and received the following responses:

Emperor Heraclius: *"We have heard that your Khalifah wears patched rags when he has indescribable things from our wealth. Why does he not dress like a king?"*

Rifa'ah (Muslim, prisoner of war): *"His desire is for the Hereafter and his fear of the King of Kings prevents him from that."*

Emperor Heraclius: *"What does his court look like?"*

Rifa'ah : *"It is built of mud and has no chamberlains. Instead, it is filled with the poor."*

Emperor Heraclius: *"What is his carpet like?"*

Rifa'ah : *"It is justice and helping others."*

Emperor Heraclius: *"What is his throne like?"*

Rifa'ah: *"It is intelligence and conviction."*

Emperor Heraclius: *"What is his royal dress like?"*

Rifa'ah: *"It is asceticism and piety."*

Emperor Heraclius: *"What is his treasure-house like?"*

Rifa'ah: *"It is reliance upon the Lord of all the worlds."*

Emperor Heraclius: *"Who are his soldiers?"*

Rifa'ah: *"Those who take Allah to be One. O Caesar! Do you not know that his men said to him, "O Umar, you now have the wealth of the Caesars, the patricians and the emperors of Persia, so why do you not wear good clothing?" He replied, "You are desirous of apparent worldy beauty while I desire the Lord of this world and the next.""*

Some famous statements of Umar bin Khattab include:

- *Do not be misled by hearing of anyone's reputation.*
- *I have never regretted my silence. As for my speech, I have regretted it over and over again.*
- *No amount of guilt can change the past and no amount of worrying can change the futue.*
- *To stop sinning is easier than to bear the burden of seeking repentance.*
- *I am not worried about whether my du'a will be responded to, but rather I am worried about whether I will be able to make du'a or not. So if I have been guided (by Allah) to make du'a, then (I know) that the response will come with it.*
- *Everyday it is said: so and so has died. And there must come a day when it will be said: `Umar has died.*
- *After Faith, there is no greater gift than a pious wife.*
- *No man can have anything better after faith than a woman of righteous character, loving and child-bearing. And no man can have anything worse after disbelief than a sharp-tongued woman of bad character.*
- *I will not allow anyone to oppress or transgress the rights of others, but I will put his cheek on the ground and place my foot on his other cheek until he submits to the truth. But I will lay my own cheek on the ground before those who are humble and modest.*
- *To side with the oppressor is oppression on the oppressed.*
- *To laugh excessively is a sign of no remorse for death.*

- Whoever increases his sayings increases his punishment, and whoever increases his punishment decreases modesty, and whoever decreases his modesty decreases al-Wara' (Fear), and whoever decreases al-Wara' deadens the heart.

- When you see that any scholar loves the world, then his scholarship is in doubt.

- The person who calls himself learned, indeed he is ignorant, and whoever says he is a believer then he is a disbeliever, and the one who calls himself from the dwellers of Paradise surely he is from the dwellers of Hell.

- May Allah bless the man who says less and does more.

- God forbid, men should be desirous of knowledge as they are desirous of women.

- Do not put off today's work for tomorrow.

- Be careful from remembering people for it is an illness, and be in the remembrance of Allah for it is a medicine.

- Faith is not achieved until one gives up lying in jest.

- Woe to he to whom this life represents his hope and sins are his deeds, whose appetite is tremendous, whose wisdom is minute, who has knowledge in this life but is ignorant in/of the Hereafter.

- I do not like this world except for three things: the place where my forehead touches the ground in prostration, the places where people gather for knowledge seeking good words as they would choose the best dates from the dish, and Jihad for Allah's sake.

- Whosoever shows you your faults, he is your friend. Those that pay you lip service in praise are your executioners.

- The person who constantly discloses my faults to me is dearest to me.

- May Allah have mercy on him who sends me my faults as a present.

- The judge should always uphold the principle of equality before law.

- He, who pretends to be what he is not, is a hypocrite.

- Do not be mislead by a person's prayers and fasting; look to his sincerity and wisdom.

- The efficacy of a prayer depends not on the words but on the sincerity of intention.

- I am surprised at 3 things. Man runs from death while it is inevitable. One sees minor faults of others, but overlooks his major faults. When there is any defect to one's cattle he tries to cure it, but does not cure his own defects.

- *A man should be like a child with his wives, but if they need him, he should act like a man.*
- *Do not depend upon the morality of a person until you have seen him behave while in anger.*
- *The ruler whose intention is good will have the help of Allah in the administration of his affairs; he whose intention is bad will come to disgrace.*
- *He who has public responsibility should perform his duties without caring for criticism.*
- *Prefer for the people what you prefer for yourself. What you do not wish for yourself, do not impose on others.*
- *That ruler is most accursed whose misconduct leads to distress of the people.*
- *Every ruler should keep his door open to the people.*
- *Without consultation, the Khilafah is unlawful.*
- *Acquire knowledge before you become leaders and pride prevents you from learning and you live in ignorance.*
- *The death of a thousand worshipers is easier to bear than the death of a scholar who has knowledge of what Allah has permitted and forbidden.*
- *If a man comes out of his house carrying a burden of sins like the mountains of Tihamah, then when he hears some knowledge he fears Allah and repents, he will go back home with no sins on him. So do not forsake the gatherings of the scholars.*
- *Verily, the followers of opinion are the enemies of the Sunan (the teachings of Allâh's Messenger as passed down in hadith): they were unable to preserve them and their meanings escaped them, and when asked [questions] they were too embarrassed to say 'We don't know,' so they opposed the Sunan with their opinions.*
- *Islam will be destroyed by the mistakes of scholars, the arguments of hypocrites who misinterpret the Quran to support their views and misleading rulers.*
- *I fear the day when the Kuffar are proud of their falsehood, and the Muslims are shy of their faith.*
- *Trust is that there should be no difference between what you do and say and what you think.*
- *If a person's parents are opponents of Allah and His messenger, it does not behoove a believer to be friendly with them.*
- *He who does not live in the way of his beliefs starts to believe in the way he lives.*
- *If Allah wants for a people ill, he gives them debates and takes away from them actions.*

- *There is no goodness in people who don't give advice, and there is no goodness in people who don't like to be advised.*

These Khalifahs were humble men not after fame, fortune or power. They were leaders who truly did not want to be leaders and tried to have others be leaders instead of them when they were appointed, but nobody would let them give the leadership to anyone else. The Khalifahs were solely focused on pleasing their Creator by being great Muslims. They were certainly not like the world "leaders" of our time. Even some enemies would become their friends. For example as soon as the Christian Byzantine Emperor Heraclius heard that Umar bin Khattab became the Khalifah he sent a Christian Arab named Tali'ah bin Maran to assassinate Umar. Yet after observing Umar from a tree, which he planned to assassinate Umar from, Tali'ah came down embraced Umar and became a Muslim because he could see the difference between the Christian Byzantine emperor Heraclius and the Muslim Khalifah and knew with certainty that Umar was better and had a better faith. Then again, when the Muslim army besieged Antioch, Heraclius sent another Christian assasin, Wathiq bin Musafir al-Ghassani, to Madinah to kill Umar. A similar incident occured as before where the assassin hid in a tree and was going to kill Umar when he slept under it but after observing Umar the Christian assassin changed their mind, revealed themself and embraced Islam. This type of thing also happened to Muhammad pbuh too as illustrated by the miraculous case of Umayr bin Wahb after the Battle of Badr, or the miraculous case of Fadaalah bin Umair when Muhammad pbuh was making tawaf after the Fath Al-Makkah, but more famously in the case of Umar bin Khattab. Now you might have the impression that Umar was some kind of super-Muslim and he was. But Umar used to be a great enemy of Islam who tortured Muslims on a daily basis in Mecca. One day Umar got so fed up with Islam and Muslims that he decided he was going to go kill Muhammad pbuh and he didn't care what happened as a result, it was to be a suicide mission. Yet because the way Umar became a Muslim during his suicidal assassination mission is so well-known among Muslims, I will not repeat it here. The point is that just as 2 of Umar's would-be assassins became Muslims many of Muhammad's would be assassins also became Muslims including Umar bin Khattab. So just because someone may try to assassinate you for religious reasons, they can also end up becoming one of your best friends. Later during the Khilafah of Umar, a non-Muslim Persian slave named Firuz (enslaved because he was captured as a Persian soldier in the Battle of Qadisiyyah) complained that the fee his master al-Mughira placed on what he earned was too high and appealed to Umar. Firuz was a carpenter, painter, ironsmith and windmill maker, as well as a former soldier. His Muslim master, in exchange for letting Firuz freely do contracting work, required him to pay 2 dirhams a day. At the time in 644-645 CE a single dirham was about 3 grams of silver. So the non-Muslim slave Firuz would be paying approximately $1.38 a day to his master, based on the valuation of silver at the time of this writing. Umar bin Khattab said because Firuz was highly skilled and making lots of money that 2 dirhams a day was not too much and told him to be patient. Firuz wasn't satisfied and appealed again, this time his master brought facts and paperwork to prove that the 2 dirhams a day was easily affordable and fair for his slave to pay him. Again Umar maintained that no reduction was to be made in what the slave Firuz would give of his earnings to his master. Firuz was enraged and hatred for Umar developed within his heart. Yet unbeknownst to Firuz, Umar bin Khattab had secretly told his master to be extra nice and kind to Firuz so he isn't dissatisfied. Given the dissatisfaction of Firuz, al-Mughira promised Firuz that if he worked and paid the 2 dirhams a day for 100 days then he would give Firuz his freedom. So Firuz would soon be free in 100 days, if he could simply be patient in paying 2 dirhams to his master for every day he worked. But alas, Firuz Nahavandi was not a patient man nor a Muslim, but a proud Persian POW Zoroastrian/Magian; although some Muslim scholars like Al-Tabari have said Firuz was a Christian. Impatience would not profit Firuz.

It may be confusing to an American reader that a disbelieving slave would repeatedly publicly complain to the Commander of the believers about sharing his earnings with the Muslim man who owned him. When Americans tend to think of slavery they typically imagine the white racist southerner abusing a black African, with inhumane treatment and torture. The notion that slavery is somehow inherently immoral is a reaction to the way slavery was promoted and practiced in America where the U.S. constitution declares black slaves are to be counted as 3/5th of a person. American slavery was and is, since you can still be turned into a slave in America if you break the government's laws or illegally fail to pay your "fair share of taxes", totally unjust and oppressive. In the 7th century CE slavery was widespread in Arabia and the rest of the world. Slaves were property and considered nothing more. When Islam came to Arabia it gave slaves rights that nothing before or after has ever given to them. For example in Islam it is forbidden to force a slave into prostitution. In Islam slavery is not based on race, nationality or religion, rather one either voluntarily becomes a slave in order to pay off a debt or because they are a prisoner of war. Rather than endorse slavery, Islam actually limited the ways people could become slaves at a time when anyone could be enslaved for nearly any reason at all at any time in any place. Hence Islam abolished many different types of slavery and permits only 2 types, both of which are the result of voluntary deeds. Basically if you never want to become a slave then Islam says you won't, but if your nation/leaders voluntarily do something like fight Muslims then they are risking the enslavement of the entire population should they lose. Slavery is the consequence of losing a war with Muslims. Therefore it's an absolute lie for non-Muslims to claim they are fighting Muslims for the sake of liberty because if they just surrendered they would have liberty, but if they lose their fight against Muslims they lose the liberty they would've had if they surrendered. However if one is ever enslaved, under Islam one is not always a slave for life. The Quran mentions in many places the rewards for freeing a slave and sometimes it is commanded to free a slave if one commits a certain sin. In those same verses the Quran also says what to do as an alternative expiation instead of freeing a slave if one cannot find any slaves. At the time these verses were revealed, it was inconceivable that one would be unable to find a slave that could be bought and set free because slavery was everywhere and thought to be perfectly normal. Yet the Quran had these verses explaining a time when slaves will not be easily found. No man in that time would have guessed slavery would become uncommon, but these verses were in the Quran over 1400 years ago. Furthermore Islamic law legislated "Slave rights". Islam entitles the slave to have quality food, clothing, shelter and medical treatment if needed. If the master cannot afford to provide properly for the slave they should sell the slave or free them. Muslims are even supposed to clothe slaves with the same clothing they wear, eat their meals together with their slave eating the same food as them and the owner must help the slave to do stuff if it's hard for them. Muhammad pbuh actually commanded Muslims that whenever a slave brings a meal to their owner then if for some reason they don't let their slave share their meal with them then the owner is at least required to give the slave a mouthful or two mouthfuls of the meal they prepared. Otherwise it wouldn't be fair for the slave to cook and not get to eat the food they labored over cooking. If your slave cooks food for you, Islam gives them the right to eat a bite or two. Umar bin Khattab even said, "*May Allah curse the people who hesitate to dine with the slaves.*" Likewise Muslims were forbidden to call their slave "slave", but were to call them "My lad", "My lass" or "My boy". While a slave owner could never be called "Lord" by their slave but the most formal title they could be called was "Master" or "Guardian", nobody in Islamic society could ever have the title of "Lord" because God is the only one deserving of the title "Lord". Across the board, in Islam slaves are treated better than modern people treat maids or butlers. Some slaves in Islamic history even ruled entire nations such as the Mamluk dynasty or the Turkish Janissaries. The part about Islamic slavery that I found surprising was how the Quran teaches that if a slave asks their master for a contract so they can earn their freedom then the master is instructed to give them the opportunity to have freedom and when they earn their freedom their master should give them some wealth too after setting them free. However many Muslims seeking the reward from Allah for freeing slaves would free them just to do a good deed. For example Abu ala Maududi reports that in his lifetime Muhammad pbuh personally freed 63 slaves. While the historians have recorded that the total number of slaves freed by Muhammad pbuh + his household + his friends equals 39,237. The point is that the non-Muslim slave Firuz was not suffering under oppression because Islam prohibits oppression of all types. Even regarding slavery, oppression is forbidden. For instance in Riyad-us Saliheen in Book 18 hadith #1605 Ibn Umar narrates a hadith where he heard prophet Muhammad pbuh say: "من ضرب غلامًا له حدًّا لم يأتِهِ، أو لطمه، فإن كفارته أن يعتقه" Which in english means: "*The expiation for beating or slapping a slave on the face, for no fault of his is that he should be set free.*" The bible also sanctions slavery, but gives different rules for slave-owners than the Quran and Sunnah does. For example in the Old Testament:

Exodus 21:20-21,"<u>Anyone who beats their male or female slave with a rod must be punished if the slave dies</u> as a direct result, 21 but <u>**they are not to be punished if the slave recovers after a day or two**</u>, since <u>the slave is their property.</u>"

Leviticus 25:44-46,"*Your male and female slaves are to come from the nations around you; from them <u>**you may buy slaves**</u>. 45 You may also buy some of the temporary residents living among you and members of their clans born in your country, and <u>**they will become your property**</u>. 46 <u>**You can bequeath them to your children as inherited property and can make them slaves for life**</u>, but you must not rule over your fellow Israelites ruthlessly.*"

In response Christians may say the Old Testament was different and doesn't apply today or Jesus pbuh changed the rules. But on the contrary the New Testament actually promotes Christians owning other Christians as slaves.

Ephesians 6:5, "*Slaves, obey your earthly masters with respect and fear, and with sincerity of heart, just as you would obey Christ.*"

1 Timothy 6:1-2, "*All who are under the yoke of slavery should consider their masters worthy of full respect, so that God's name and our teaching may not be slandered. ² Those **who have believing masters should not show them disrespect** just because they are fellow believers. Instead, they should serve them even better because their masters are dear to them as fellow believers and are devoted to the welfare of their slaves. These are the things you are to teach and insist on.*"

These bible verses promoting slavery are excerpts from an English translation of the New International Version of the bible. If a person believes in the bible then they also have to believe in slavery because the bible has specific rules for how to practice slavery, which the bible says God instituted and that Christians must "*teach and insist on*". Meaning in order to be a Christian it is obligatory to teach the world and insist they practice slavery in the way the bible says to in the Old and New testament, or at the least the way the New Testament says to if Christians want to reject the Old. The Catholic Church even profited from slaves they oppressed until "Magdalene Laundries" was shut down in 1996 CE and the slaves were freed. As with anything in life, there is a way to do it right which God has legislated and a way to do it wrong which God has prohibited. In Islam slavery is permitted but it's not promoted, although it cannot be prohibited since God has legalized it. Whereas in Christianity it is a requirement to promote slavery or else one isn't a Christian. The other reason people are averse to the idea of slavery is because of the Satanic notion that humans are free and can do anything we want. In reality we are the property of God, who is our master. But God isn't like any master. God provides everything for us, asking for little in return for us to get further reward. God made certain things obligatory for us, yet if we do them we will get forgiven for all our mistakes. If we choose to disobey our Master/Creator then punishment rightfully awaits. God sends people to hell because they don't want his forgiveness because they don't do what God made obligatory for us to do in order to attain his forgiveness. God literally says "*Do X or else you go to hell, and if you do X then I'll forgive you and give you paradise. So if you don't let me forgive you by doing X then I'm going to be really upset and hate you.*" A believer is a slave of God, while a disbeliever is a slave of Satan and/or their desires. There is no such thing as a free human, you are either a slave of God or a slave to something else. Technically we're all slaves of God, some are just disobedient and rebellious, too proud to admit that the one who created them owns them and can dictate their lifestyle; so they choose to become slaves of Satan. An obedient slave of God is the best thing a human can be, it's the definition of a Muslim. The frustrating thing is that people afflicted with the freedom faith syndrome incorrectly think God promotes freedom because they want freedom for themselves. Usually such people have a Santa Claus type belief in God, where they think if they like something then God also likes it and if they don't like something then God doesn't either. This is especially the case with atheists, philosophers or agnostics/deists but also Christians. You expect it from philosophers, but when Christians tell me "*I don't think God wants me to be his slave.*" it's ironic because even in the New Testatment of the bible in Romans 6:12-22 it says,

"Therefore do not let sin reign in your mortal body so that you obey its evil desires. ¹³ *Do not offer any part of yourself to sin as an instrument of wickedness, but rather* **offer yourselves to God** *as those who have been brought from death to life; and offer every part of yourself to him as an instrument of righteousness.* ¹⁴ *For* sin shall no longer be your master, *because you are not under the law, but under grace.*¹⁵ *What then? Shall we sin because we are not under the law but under grace? By no means!* ¹⁶ Don't you know that when you offer yourselves to someone as obedient slaves, **you are slaves of the one you obey** *— whether you are slaves to sin, which leads to death, or to obedience, which leads to righteousness?* ¹⁷ *But thanks be to God that, though* you used to be slaves to sin, *you have come to obey from your heart the pattern of teaching that has now claimed your allegiance.* ¹⁸ *You have been set free from sin and have* become slaves to righteousness. ¹⁹ *I am using an example from everyday life because of your human limitations. Just as you used to offer yourselves as slaves to impurity and to ever-increasing wickedness, so now* offer yourselves as slaves to righteousness *leading to holiness.* ²⁰ *When you were slaves to sin, you were free from the control of righteousness.* ²¹ *What benefit did you reap at that time from the things you are now ashamed of? Those things result in death!* ²² *But now that you have been set free from sin and have* **become slaves of God**, *the benefit you reap leads to holiness, and the result is eternal life."*

As you can see it's explicit the bible teaches people they must become "slaves of God". In fact biblically it's an obligation, or else one isn't a believer and will never go to paradise but burn in hell. Christians tend not to like this idea about being slaves of God because of what they believe about Jesus pbuh. For example if they think Jesus pbuh is God incarnate then being a "slave of God" would mean being a "slave of Jesus" pbuh, but everyone knows that Jesus pbuh did not go around telling people to be his slave, thus he can't be God or part of a trinity. Also the idea of God loving people so much he kills Jesus his alleged son on a cross for our sins contradicts the notion that such a God would then require slavery for those he loves so much. Thus there is a fundamental issue in that Christianity tends to be all about love and no fear for God exists because of the Christian beliefs about the crucfixtion of Jesus pbuh. While since Mary the mother of Jesus pbuh was a believer, if believers are slaves of God then that would mean she was a slave of God. Yet how could Jesus pbuh be a son of God if his mother is a slave of God? Does God make a virgin slave of his give birth to his son? Without even a kiss, hug or a dinner? Also if Jesus pbuh were God and Mary the "mother of God", how could she be the slave of her son? And at what stage would Mary have become the slave of her son, while he was still in the womb? Before the placenta was cut? Plus everyone knows that the cross could not be a key to free us from sins and a shackle for divine slavery. God either wants to save us or enslave us, it's one or the other. Now that slavery can be good and lead to salvation, but the cross cannot perform a dual function. So did Jesus pbuh teach God wanted to save us or enslave us? Jesus pbuh taught we should be slaves of God, although frequently in english it gets translated into "servants". But back then there were no "day-job servants", every servant was a slave so when Jesus pbuh teaches people to be a "servant of God" in our modern english tongue that's supposed to be translated as "slave of God". Then when Christians finally see that Jesus pbuh was a slave of God and all believers are slaves of God, they then claim they are slaves of God too just as the Muslims are even though minutes before they were debating and ridiculing the idea of being a slave of

God. I've witnessed them go from saying nobody is and nobody should be a slave of God to saying that everybody who believes in a God is a slave of God, in mere minutes. Therefore I have to clarify that Christians and Muslims cannot both be slaves of God when we believe in different prophets, follow different laws, have different doctrines and live drastically different lifestyles. So who is the real slave of God? Since Christians don't even know or claim to be slaves of God, and ridicule the idea, I don't think it's them because when it comes to being a slave of God you must actively know you're trying to be a slave. It's a conscious struggle.

Anyways the slave Firuz was angry with Umar bin Khattab because he didn't reduce the fee Firuz was required to pay his master. As a result, Firuz would go around slandering Umar in public claiming him to be corrupt in his treatment of Firuz and nobody else and that there was some huge conspiracy against him. Umar saw and heard him doing this so to be kind Umar asked Firuz to build him a windmill and he would pay him for it out of his own pocket since Firuz was such a skilled builder. Firuz replied that he will build him a windmill which the earth will speak about. At this Umar asked his companions if they knew that Firuz meant he was going to try to assassinate him. They said no and told Umar that if that's the case they should arrest/punish/kill him before he tries. However Umar told them that "Pre-emptive action is not justified due to suspicion." Meaning just because Umar, as head of state, suspected Firuz of plotting to assassinate him it would be unjust to punish Firuz, even though he was a disbeliever, due to mere suspicion of intent and the verbalization of a threat. Unfortunately most leaders today have yet to learn this and commonly harm people with pre-emptive actions for no valid reason at all. Some nations even go to war with entire nations due to mere suspicions, yet Umar wasn't even willing to punish or indict someone who he heard with his own mouth imply he would try to kill him. Shortly after this while Umar was leading the early morning prayer, Firuz came to the prayer with a special double bladed weapon he crafted covered with poison. There was no electricity at that time and it was relatively dark in the masjid as the sun hadn't yet risen. Firuz hid in one of the corners of the masjid at the front. While Umar was leading the prayer Firuz rushed towards Umar and attacked, stabbing him six times. He then stabbed thirteen other Muslims, 7 of which died. After Firuz saw there would be no escape from the scene of the crime he killed himself. This is how foolish anger can cause a person to be. Firuz killed Umar because he didn't want to pay his master and as a result ends up killing himself. This is a prime example of how Satan can use anger and hatred to lead a person to their destruction. Umar died as a result of the wounds a few days later ending his 10 year rule. Ibn Abbas narrated, *"When (the dead body of) `Umar was put on his deathbed, the people gathered around him and invoked (Allah) and prayed for him before the body was taken away, and I was amongst them. Suddenly I felt somebody taking hold of my shoulder and found out that he was `Ali bin AbiTalib. `Ali invoked Allah's Mercy for `Umar and said, "O `Umar! You have not left behind you a person whose deeds I like to imitate and meet Allah with more than I like your deeds. By Allah! I always thought that Allah would keep you with your two companions, for very often I used to hear the Prophet saying, 'I, Abu Bakr and `Umar went (somewhere); I, Abu Bakr and `Umar entered (somewhere); and I, Abu Bakr and `Umar went out."*-That hadith is from Sahih al-Bukhari hadith #3685. Umar was also the husband of Umm Kulthum bint Ali who was the daughter of Ali bin Abi Talib and the granddaughter of the prophet Muhammad pbuh. Before his death Umar created a committee of six people to choose the next leader from amongst them, one of the six withdrew himself from consideration, eventually the choice was narrowed down to two people: Uthman bin Affan and Ali bin Abi Talib. They were both asked: *"If you are elected as the Khalif do you undertake to follow the Quran and the Sunnah, and the traditions set by your predecessors?"* The response of Ali was that he would follow the Quran and the Sunnah, but in the matter of the traditions of his predecessors he would follow them as far as possible and would exercise his own judgment in each case. The response of Uthman was an unconditional yes. Uthman was then appointed as leader of the Muslims and Ali was the first one to pledge allegiance to him. One of the many noticeable virtues of the character of Uthman is that since becoming a Muslim every friday he used to buy a slave just so he could immediately set them free after buying them. Uthman became a Muslim in 610 CE and died in 656 CE. If you do the math Uthman personally liberated over 2,300 slaves in his life. Uthman also gave over 900 camels in charity to assist the Muslims in the Tabook expedition. As a literate Arab Uthman was also the first Muslim to write down some verses of the Quran after they started being revealed in 610 CE. Also while Ali had married Muhammad's daughter Fatima, Uthman had married 2 of Muhammad's daughters, Ruqayya and then Umm Kulthoom bint Muhammad after Ruqayya had died. Both Ruqayya and Umm Kulthoom had children with Uthman, making Uthman a parent of some of Muhammad's grandkids, though Uthman's kids would grow up to be much less famous than Ali's. After Uthman bin Affan was selected to be the Khilafah he got up to give a inaugural speech but broke down in tears and couldn't stop crying, so he simply said the following which in english means:

"O people, it is not easy to manage a new horse. If God willing I live, there will be several other occasions to talk to you. Right now I cannot address you. You know that I am not good at making public speeches."

Some famous statements of Uthman bin Affan include:

- *Under all circumstances, a person should be patient, otherwise disgrace would be his lot.*

- *The world is proud. Leave it alone lest it entraps by its guises, and teaches you pride which will keep you away from Allah.*

- *Concern for the world is a darkness for the heart, and concern for the Hereafter is a light for it.*

- *The highest degree in Iman (faith) is that you always regard yourself in the presence of Allah.*

- *Were your hearts purified, you would never be satiated by the words of your Lord.* (never "have enough" of the Quran)

- *No man accomplishes an action but that God, Most High, clothes whim with its mantle- if good, then with good and if evil, with evil.*

- *When the Muslims are disunited they would falter in their faith, and would be bereft of their inherent strength.*

- *Son of Adam! Know that the angel of death who has been assigned to you has not ceased to pass you and move on to others, ever since you have been in this world. But it is as if he is about to pass someone else and move on to target you, so be careful and prepare for him (by correcting your deeds). And do not forget him, for he does not forget you. And know, oh son of Adam, if you are heedless about yourself and do not prepare, no one else will prepare for you. You must meet Allah the Mighty and Majestic, so take for yourself and do not leave it to someone else. Peace be on you.*

- *If I were to stand between Paradise and Hell, not knowing where I would be taken, I would rather choose to be ashes before I should know my final destination.*

- *You will not be conscious of the reality of faith till love for Allah is held dearer than the passion to acquire wealth.*

- *Enjoin what is good and forbid what is evil before the worst among you are given authority over you and then when even the best of you make dua against them, their duas will not be accepted.*

While Uthman was leader, a Jew named Abdullah ibn Saba tried to destroy the Islamic State from within; he outwardly embraced Islam and appeared to be a pious Muslim. However he instigated rebellion in the wealthy cities and split the community into separate factions, also instituting new practices, or bidas, into the religion that were not taught by the Prophet pbuh. Abdullah bin Saba went to Basra, Iraq and told the people to replace Uthman with Zubair ibn Al-Awwam. Next Abdullah bin Saba went to Kufa, Iraq and told them to replace Uthman with Talha ibn Udaidullah. Abdullah bin Saba also went to Egypt and told the people to replace Uthman with Ali ibn abi Talib. Basically his plan was to get rid of Uthman and for the Muslims to fight each other afterwards over political leadership so that Muslims would become weak, disunited and that Islam could stop spreading. Soon revolt broke out in the regions of Iraq and Egypt resulting in insurgents coming to the capital in Madinah, Arabia. Ali was on the side of Uthman and after a few days of tension the insurgents declared they were satisfied with Uthman's promise of political reform and left. Every issue they presented with Uthman was due to their ignorance about Islam and the reasons for his actions because they were the new generation of Muslims who never met the prophet pbuh and didn't really know the companions of Muhammad pbuh well or their history/character. However with patience Uthman explained the islamic justifications for all their complaints against his actions and then he even acceded to their request for him to replace the governor of Egypt. So the insurgents left Medinah happy. Yet they suddenly returned after a couple of days claiming to have intercepted a letter from Uthman that instructed the Egyptian governor to imprison the insurgents when they returned. Ali was suspicious of their claim and the letter was discovered to be a forgery that Uthman had no knowledge of. Ali admitted the signature seal was Uthman's but the handwriting was not Uthman's but another person's who Ali then brought to Uthman and told Uthman to kill him for such a deception. Yet when Uthman asked the guy charged with the forgery if he did it, he said no. So since Uthman had no proof he decided to let the man go free despite Ali insisting he be killed for fomenting rebellion. Yet then the rebels got mad at Uthman for not killing the guy accused of forging the letter. So they said either Uthman gets killed or the man accused of forgery, or both and Uthman said that nobody is getting killed for anything. Regardless the rebels gave Uthman an ultimatum to immediately resign, which he declined. The reason for their problem with Uthman now was that because he replaced their governor when they asked him to they feared he will give in to everyone and do anything anyone asks. So essentially they just didn't like what Uthman did whether he did what they wanted or not. There was no way to please them, even when he tried. Thus the rebels threatened to kill Uthman and surrounded his house trapping him inside. They wanted Uthman to be publicly reprimanded, even though in Islam advising the leader is done in private so that the leader is not shamed, these are parts of the etiquettes of advice. The Muslims in the capital vowed to defend him till the death, but Uthman instructed them not to fight because he didn't want anyone to be harmed because of him. The companions of Muhammad pbuh told Uthman to order the soldiers to come into the city and protect him but Uthman refused. Uthman said if the soldiers come into the city to protect him then they will eat the food and the poor people will not have access to food or it would cause the price of food to increase to be more than they can afford, so Uthman didn't want any of them to suffer as a result of his actions. Uthman reasoned that it'd be better for him to suffer, even if he is killed than to do something as a leader that would cause anyone else to suffer even minutely. So Uthman sat in his house and read Quran trusting in Allah trying to please him and be patient. An insurgent entered the house with his sword drawn intending to kill Uthman, Uthman said to him that between you and me is the book of Allah, the man lost his nerve and didn't dare to attack while the Quran was in between them so he left. A second man came with the intention to murder and Uthman again said that between you and me is the book of Allah, this man didn't care and swung his sword fatally wounding Uthman who died with his blood stopping on select verses of the Quran. These people who killed Uthman were the Khawarijj, which is a type of Muslim extremist sect. The Khawarijj/Takfiris tend to go overboard in Islam and condemn Muslims who commit major sins as disbelievers and tend to label those who disagree with them as apostates by default without establishing proper proof. After Uthman was assassinated then Ali became the leader. Ali had been raised by the prophet Muhammad pbuh when he was a kid, because Ali's biological father had financial troubles so Muhammad pbuh offered to let Ali live in his house. Ali later married Muhammad's daughter Fatima and was a great warrior on the battlefield. When Ali was offered the Khilafah he was hesitant because the Muslims were no longer as they had been when Muhammad pbuh was alive and he was worried about disobedience and possibly civil war since afterall Uthman had just been murdered the methaphorical seat of power was not too safe to sit in. Thus prior to becoming the Khalifah Ali made conditions upon his acceptance, so this was technically his inaugural speech pre-nomination which in english means:

"I have perfect knowledge and understanding of the Book of God, and of the practices and precedents of His Messenger. In ruling the Muslim nation, I shall put their commandments and prohibitions before everything else. I shall not show any flexibility in this matter. I shall take charge of the government only if this condition is acceptable to you. If it is, and the Muslims are willing to take the oath of allegiance to me, then tell them to assemble in the Masjid of the Prophet."

Not everyone pledged allegiance under these conditions, but many did, and therefore after accepting the Khilafah Ali made the following speech considered to be inaugural which means:

"O Muslims! You have given me your pledge of loyalty, and I know that you have not done so without forethought. Yet, your aims and my aims in the tasks lying ahead of us, may not necessarily be the same. I want to mobilize you for obedience and service to God; but many among you are hoping that I will give them rich estates or high ranks in the government. This is something that will not happen.

Remember that there are two ways of life; the right and the wrong. Some of you will adopt the right way and others the wrong. You are free to choose. But if you see that a majority has adopted the wrong way, do not be dismayed or surprised by it. It has often been like that, and the world is full of paradoxes. But Justice and Truth will triumph in the end even if at a given moment they may appear to be on the defensive.

Verily, when God sent Muhammad as His Messenger to this world, there was not a single soul in all Arabia who knew anything about guidance and rectitude. He led the Arabs out of the wilderness of sin and iniquity until they saw the light of guidance, and found the road to eternal salvation. I was by his side from the beginning of his mission to its end, and I fought against disobedience to God all my life. I never felt weary of the struggle nor was I ever dismayed by the opposition of the guardians and champions of the pre-Islamic order, no matter how formidable it was.

O Muslims! I call upon you to assist me in my program of reconstruction. God is a Witness to my statement that my paramount objective is to restore justice in Dar-ul-Islam, just as it is His wish that I do so. I shall not rest until I have destroyed injustice. Listen to this with attention: I shall not transgress the bounds of the Book of God for anything. I will not be partial to anyone whoever he may be. In my sight, all of you are equal. I shall promulgate the Laws of God which are enshrined in His Book, and I shall do so in the light of the precedents only of His Messenger, Muhammad, the blessed one.

My mission today is the same as it was in the times of the Messenger of God, Muhammad; may God bless him and his family, and it's to establish or to reestablish the Kingdom of God on this earth."

Some famous statements of Ali are:

- *To fight against one's desires is the greatest of all fights.*
- *The strongest amongst you is he who subdues his self.*
- *Knowledge and practice are twins, and both go toghether. There is no knowledge without practice, and no practice without knowledge.*
- *The most helpless person is the one who is helpless in reforming himself.*
- *Greed is permanent slavery.*
- *Wealth and greed are the roots of all evils.*
- *Riches without faith are the greatest poverty.*
- *The most happy is he to whom God has given a good wife.*

- *Of all the follies the greatest is to love the World.*
- *A true friend is one who sees a fault, gives you advice and who defends you in your absence.*
- *The one who has no control over his desires has no control over his mind.*
- *Silence is the best reply to a fool.*
- *Do not take someone's silence as his pride, perhaps he is busy fighting with his self.*
- *Knowledge is of 2 kinds: that which is absorbed and that which is heard. And that which is heard does not profit if it is not absorbed.*
- *The worst of our faults is our interest in other people's faults.*
- *Man comes from a drop of semen and leaves as a piece of dust. He doesn't know when he came and he doesn't know when he's leaving, yet he walks on the earth thinking he knows everything.*
- *He who trusts the world, the world betrays him.*
- *Fear Allah and you will have no cause to fear anyone.*
- *The (true) value of every person is weighed according to the good that he does.*
- *It is better to listen to a wise enemy than to seek counsel from a foolish friend.*
- *A person of riyaa (showing off) has 3 characteristics: He is lazy when alone, energetic when with others, and increases in his actions when he is praised while decreasing in them when he is criticized.*
- *Fear the sins that you commit in secret, because the witness of those sins is the Judge himself!*
- *Do not use the sharpness of your speech on your mother who taught you how to speak.*
- *The best revenge is to improve yourself.*
- *How strange and foolish is man. He loses his health in gaining wealth. Then to regain health he wastes his wealth. He ruins his present while worrying about his future, but weeps in the future by recalling his past. He lives as though death shall never come to him, but dies in a way as if he were never born.*
- *What I fear for you is following your desires and hoping for a long life, for following one's desires makes a man ignore the truth, and hoping for a long life makes him forget the Hereafter.*
- *When proven wrong, the wise man will correct himself and the ignorant will keep arguing.*
- *It is enough an honor for knowledge that even those who are not proficient in it claim it and are happy whenever they are addressed as knowledgeable. And it is enough a condemnation for ignorance that even an ignorant person despises being called ignorant.*

- *Having unfading hope makes one forget the Hereafter, while following one's desires deviates from the truth. This world is retreating and the Hereafter is coming, so be among the sons of the Hereafter, but do not be among the followers of this world; because today there is action without reckoning, whereas tomorrow, there is reckoning without (any more) action.*

- *Everyone who is taken by death asks for more time, while everyone who still has time makes excuses for procrastination.*

- *Truly, if you remain, the Qur'an will be recited by three groups of people: one group for Allah, one group for the world, and one group for argumentation. He who seeks by it will attain.*

- *He who fights against the truth, the truth will defeat him.*

- *Do not sell your conscience for anything but heaven.*

Years after becoming the Khalifah Ali was murdered by the same extremist group that killed Uthman, which still exists today. Although because they don't call themselves the Khawarijj, but pose and claim to be Muslims, many are mistakenly lead astray without realizing. Yet as bad as the Khawarij are the Shia are even worse, throughout history these two groups always tend to arise around the same time. Unfortunately all the different deviant sects pose and claim to be Muslims even when some of their beliefs or actions take them outside the fold of Islam. But if Islam is true and there is only one Quran and the authentic hadith are available then why are there so many different sects? This is actually a fulfillment of a statement in a well-known authentic hadith wherein Muhammad pbuh said what in english means, "*The jews split up into seventy-one sects, the christians split up into seventy-two sects and this ummah(nation) will split up into seventy-three sects; all of them are in the Fire except one." Someone asked: "Which is that one O Messenger of Allah? salalahu alayhi wa salam. He replied: "Whoever is upon that which I am upon today and my companions."* All 73 of these sects will claim to be Muslims but some are actually disbelievers and others are just misguided, sinful or deviant. The route to complete safety from hell and the bliss of paradise is to follow the prophet pbuh the way he said to and practice Islam the way he and his companions did. It is important to note that no rightly guided Emir al-Mumineen was ever self-appointed, the leader of all the Muslims was always chosen by the most righteous and knowledgable of Islam. Soon after these 4 rightly guided leaders were gone, the Muslim community and State fractured, disuniting the Muslim world. This is where the Shia entered the picture.

The Shia religion was started by that same Jew named Abdullah ibn Saba who set in motion the events that led to the murder of Uthman bin Affan. After Ali's death, he taught the Shia to believe that Ali should have been the first leader after Muhammad pbuh because of his family relationship. Sadly some ignorant new Muslims fell for this lie because they did not know that Islam eliminates tribalism and nationalism. In Islam having an upright and religious ancestor doesn't entitle a person to any special position if they are not qualified for it, or they are a bad person. It is the same in the afterlife, there are many instances of relatives of prophets who were evil and disbelieved, such as the father of Abraham pbuh, or the son of Noah pbuh, despite being related to prophets these people will be judged according to their disbelief and actions; their prophetic family members will not be able to save them from the punishment of the Creator. Ali himself never held any enmity towards his friends and predecessors. Ali never believed in leadership being inherited based on kinship ties, he never once disputed the leadership of Abu Bakr, Umar or Uthman. They were his dear friends and he pledged allegiance to all three of them. During the Khilafah of Ali, he heard that some people were saying he was better than Abu Bakr and Umar. As a result Ali gave a speech prohibiting people from saying such a thing and ruled that any who said such a thing after he gave his speech would be punished as a slanderer and given 80 lashes. Which means despite the Shia's alleged love for him, Ali himself would give a member of the Shia 80 lashes for proclaiming their slanderous false belief. Not only do Shia reject the leadership of Abu Bakr, Umar and Uthman but they curse them thinking they were evil men. For a Muslim these men were among the best companions of the Prophet Muhammad pbuh. The greatest enemy of a Muslim is Satan. For the Shia their number 1 enemy is Abu Bakr, their number 2 enemy is Umar and their 3rd greatest enemy is Satan. They think these righteous men who have been buried in their graves for 1400+ years are more of a danger to them than Satan. These Muslim leaders were praised by the prophet Muhammad pbuh and the very Ali whom they practically deify. Ali himself even married his daughter to the very Umar whom Shia curse. That Shia think and say the long buried rightly guided Muslim leaders are more dangerous than Satan is delusional and shows extremist hate, lunacy and deviance. Unfortunately the Shia take their belief a step further and think divine guidance and revelation is genetically inherited as well, although never in two people at the same time. When one dies then Shia believe the revelation goes to their living heirs, but not until death. The Shia foolishly consider Ali to be a prophet after Muhammad pbuh and they believe in 12 people after Ali whom they think would talk directly to God, basing this belief on their family tree. Why do they reject the Uthmanic line of Muhammad's grandkids? Because they are fanatical for Ali but then reject the descendants of Ali whom he had with his wives besides Fatimah, after she died. Hence the Shia chain of prophethood is fatimid only and doesn't follow the chain of Ali, nor of Ruqqaya nor Umm Kulthoom all 3 of whom were related to Muhammad pbuh 2 of which were his daughters from Khadijah who was the mother of Fatima. The Shiite belief Ali's descendants are supposed to be followed or the leaders of Muslims has no basis whatsoever but Shia don't even believe that, that is the common misconception, Shia actually only believe Ali's kids with Fatima count as real because some of the others were named after the 3 Khalifhs who preceded Ali thus preventing Shia from saying Ali was usurped by Abu Bakr, Umar and Uthman but Ali then named his rightful heirs after those very same people Shia slanderously say he hated. Anyways the Shia don't follow Ali's descendants only Fatima's, those who think otherwise (particularly non-Muslims) are mistaken and teaching falsehood as phony pseudo-experts. These 12 Shia Fatimidi Imams(alleged to be nearly prophets by the Shia) were not all righteous and didn't practice Islam correctly, or even follow some of the basics. Yet Shia frequently invoke them in prayer similar to how Catholics pray to people they think are saints. In Islam this is known as shirk, or associating partners with God, and is a form of idolatry because only the Creator can answer prayers and only the Creator deserves prayers. We have a direct connection with the one who created us, we don't need a middle man and it is offensive to use one because God has commanded us to pray to him directly and him alone. Likewise no prophet ever told people to pray to them so they would intercede after death. When a person is dead they are dead, no dead person can help a living person in any way and the living cannot communicate with them either, but jinn play tricks misleading people to think otherwise. Jinn commonly come to people in dreams pretending to be their dead relatives or appear as ghosts to deceive people. Nobody ever prays to Moses pbuh, why people of lesser stature are prayed to boggles the mind. The 12 Imams are believed to be infallible, just like how Roman Catholics believe the Pope to be infallible, except the idea of infallibility began with the Shia first. The Pope and the Shia Imam's don't have "advisors" because they are considered the most knowledgeable people on earth in every subject and are above receiving advice, even though the prophets received advice. They have "interpreters" who don't advise them, but just "interpret" what God allegedly inspires them to say or write. The Pope is referred to as "His Holiness" although no prophet including Jesus pbuh was called by this title, I do not know if Shia call their Imams by the same title. Also if a Catholic is walking down the street and gets a call on the phone from the Pope, the Catholic is not allowed to keep walking and talking, the Catholic would have to get down on their knees in the middle of the street for the duration of their conversation with the man who is Pope. This is another thing Catholics do in their treatment of the Pope that I don't know if Shia do with their Imams. Either way Shia or Catholic no person deserves to be treated so royally, especially when considering the prophets pbut never required these protocols. Despite this simple truth, Buddhists kiss a shoe of the Dalai Lama when they meet him and think he can choose whether he reincarnates or not. Shia don't just believe their Imams are infallible, in some aspects they take it a step further than the Catholic does with the Pope and the Buddhists do with their Dalai Lama. Some Shia actually believe their Imams know their time of death and can only die if and when they choose to die. These are impossible abilities for humans to have which Shia attribute to their leaders. You might be wondering why is there only twelve Imams if the Shia have been around for over a thousand years? In 874 CE the 11th Imamate, or spiritual and political leader whom the Shia follow, died. The 12th Imamate was only 5 years old at the time, but they believed him to be the wisest of all people in the world, who received divine revelation. The Shia believed he was the Mahdi. Sunnis believe in the Mahdi, but consider him to be a good Muslim leader that will rule the Islamic State during the time of the antichrist and fight the antichrist before the second coming of Jesus pbuh. Sunni Muslims do not believe the Mahdi will have any special revelation or powers, but just that he will be a good Muslim ruler who was prophesied as opposing the antichrist during that time. The Shia problem is that this little boy they thought was the Mahdi ran away from the people and disappeared never to be seen again. Despite this happening in 874 CE the Shia do not think this human being died, they think he is just hiding in a cave waiting until the right time to come out and lead them. By the Shiites own calculations he would be 1,146 years old at the time of this writing and nobody has ever seen him during that time. Realistically the little boy who ran away is probably dead by now, not in secret hiding biding his time. Although this is what the Shia believe. Every year many Shia go to the last place the boy was seen near a cave in Samarra, Iraq and call for him to come out and lead them, every year they go away disappointed to repeat the process the next year. It never occurs to them the little boy is likely dead because their religious leaders tell them otherwise. Islam does not say the Mahdi will live this long, be divine, infallible or anything like what the Shia say, so don't be confused and think Muslims believe in this missing little boy leader who is in hiding. The crazy thing is despite all these years which have passed, Shia still think he is a little 5 year old boy and hasn't aged. Where Shia came up with this idea of the boy being ageless I do not know. Although the crazy Shia beliefs about their Mahdi are not peaceful and are actually anti-Islamic and anti-Muslim.

    To be a Sunni basically just means one is "not Shia". That is generally all that Sunni means, it is a term made to exclude Shia. Just because someone calls themselves a Shia doesn't necessarily mean they aren't Muslim. In Islam if you label a specific individual as a disbeliever and they aren't then you will become a disbeliever yourself, because of calling someone who believes a disbeliever. It's a very serious matter to label someone a disbeliever which can backfire and give you the label you were incorrectly giving others. This is because once someone is publicly known to have believed in Islam and become a Muslim then they cannot be considered a disbeliever until solid proof is established to such an effect. Now this doesn't apply to people who have never been known to publicly embrace Islam, such as Christians or Jews, since they are known to be non-Muslims one needs proof that they've become Muslims before they can be considered as anything other than disbelievers in Islam. There is no middle where one can be half-Muslim and half-non-Muslim. There are Muslims, Non-Muslims and hypocrites of which depending on the level of hypocrisy it can make a Muslim into a disbeliever but there are hypocrites amongst disbelievers as well. So hypocrisy itself isn't really a category of religion it can exist in both Islam and Kufr and put a Muslim into Kufr but it cannot put someone into Islam, however not all types of hypocrisy expel one from Islam. Proof is needed to establish someone as a Muslim, such as their shahada and once someone becomes a Muslim then proof is needed if they are ever to be declared disbelievers. Muslims accept what is publicly apparent unless there is proof to prove otherwise. Therefore in order to tell whether a individual Shia is considered a non-Muslim, according to the Islamic religion, someone of knowledge would have to personally go to that individual and have conversations with them, asking them specific questions in order to find out from that individual what they actually believe. The person could have been lied about, or maybe they are just confused and don't know any better. It could well be the case that they are ignorant of Islam and didn't know the beliefs they held were incorrect and un-Islamic. We cannot make overgeneralizations in general, especially when it concerns matters of belief and disbelief. Although if a individual person believes what Shia books and Scholars teach, then according to Islam those people are not Muslims. They may look like a Muslim, act like a Muslim, dress like a Muslim and say they are Muslim, but according to the religion of Islam they wouldn't be. Overall the masses of Shia are generally heretical disbelievers according to Islamic criteria with rare exceptions usually where the people mistakenly identify as Shia. This confuses many people, but the differences unfortunately are not restrained to theology. Shia celebrate different holidays than Muslims and celebrate in different ways. For example during the month of Muharram some Shia cut their foreheads open with swords and flagellate themselves with knives until bloody on an annual basis, commemorating one of the grandsons of Muhammad pbuh being slain. Shia children as young as 2 years of age participate in this gory ritual. Islam forbids Muslims to hurt themselves, but the Shia perform this bloody spectacle every year. The Shia claim Ali, who was the cousin and son in law of Muhammad pbuh, was a prophet and some call on Ali for help when praying, elevating him to godlike status. Some Shia deify the descendants of Muhammad pbuh even if they are immoral people. Shia scholars teach that Sunni Muslims are not Muslims and that it is not a sin to steal from or kill them, they encourage Shia to do both to Muslims whenever possible. In the Shia book called "manhaj sadikeen", which ironically means "methodology of the truthful", in volume 2 page 495 Shia scholars teach a tradition called "Muta". "Muta" is said to be a part of the religion that if you don't believe in it you do not follow the same religion as the Shia. Muta is to have a short temporary marriage, usually with a prostitute, without witnesses or a wedding, for a short predetermined amount of time. Typically the Muta marriage is set to expire after they've had sex. If a child is born from that sexual relationship it is believed that they are more honorable because of it and should boast about the nature of their conception. Shia scholars teach that every child born from this type of intercourse is better than any child who is born in wedlock. Since the prostitute mother has this type of sex often, it means the child doesn't even know who their father is. Whereas in Islam every child must know who their father is for lineage and naming purposes. Yet Shia kids are told that it's a privilege to be born from Muta, despite the high probability of being born with STDs or genetic defects. Shia scholars teach having sex in this way is the most pleasing thing to God. According to Shia if you don't believe in Muta then you are not a Muslim. According to the Quran and the teachings of Muhammad pbuh this "Muta" is illegal, sinful and an abomination; Muhammad pbuh forbid it from being practiced after the battle of Khaibar. This alone is evidence that those who believe in what the Shia scholars teach are upon a different faith than the religion of Islam. They themselves say if you don't believe in Muta then you are of a different religion. Well Muhammad pbuh specifically forbid it, so according to Shia scholars the prophet Muhammad pbuh is of a different religion than the Shia. On top of that do you know who said Muhammad pbuh forbade Muta after Khaibar? Ali ibn Abi Talib according to authentic Sahih hadith narrations, the same Ali Shia deify. Ali himself taught the opposite of what the Shia believe/teach/do, similar to how Christians believe/teach/do the opposite of what Jesus pbuh taught. To be fair not all who claim to be Shia do these blasphemous sinful things, but this is what the Shia scholars actually teach, preach and instruct Shia to believe and do.

Throughout history the Shia have not only taught a different religion than Islam in the guise of Islam but they have ruthlessly oppressed Muslims and suppressed Islam. Notable is the tyranny of the Shia Fatimid Empire which began in 909 CE. It was started by an Ismaili Shiite who changed his name to Ubayd-Allah, made it government policy to slander the companions of Muhammad pbuh and claimed to be the Mahdi. Later some claimed he was the son of the prophet Muhammad pbuh (which was impossible) and then some claimed he was Allah in human form. Some Shia would even pray towards wherever this ruler was, instead of praying towards the Kabah in Mecca as Allah says to do in the Quran. All these things meant disbelief in Islam, but the Fatimids also persecuted the Muslims. For example they changed the wording of the call to prayer and abolished the taraweeh prayer, with the result being that Muslims stopped going to the masjids for prayer. So the Fatimids would bring their horses into the masjids using them as stables. One time a Muslim dared to give the Islamic call to prayer correctly, as a result he had his tongue cut out and placed between his eyes, afterwhich he was paraded through the streets and killed. Thus Muslim scholars said it was permissible to say the Shia extra additions to the athan vocally but not meaning it in the heart, for the harm of not doing so outweighed the benefit. Now this is an important point concerning the harm of doing something sinful outweighing the benefit of not doing it. In Islam we don't voluntarily "choose the lesser evil", because if you have a choice to not to choose any evil then you don't; such as in the examples provided in the section about voting which is a false dilemma. However sometimes one simply is faced with 2 evils, one of which will take place if the other doesn't. For example if you are on an island starving to death and only a pig is available to eat then in order to survive a Muslim would be allowed to eat pig despite it being sinful because choosing to starve to death instead would be the only alternative and an even greater evil, and Allah explains this in the Quran. Although clearly the conditions in America are not ideal or very islamic, neither were the conditions the prophets lived in. The lives of the prophets provide the example to follow in taking the least evil course available. Tacit consent does not necessarily apply in all cases. For instance Abraham's father was an idolater who made money selling idols who then used that money to raise Abraham pbuh until he became an adult. Now Abraham pbuh knew this was an evil source of income, yet his only alternative would've been to leave and possibly starve to death or stay getting supported by his idol making dad and teach his people about Islam. Abraham pbuh stayed teaching Islam until his father told him to get out of the house or he'd kill him. A similar case of benefiting from sinful things or supporting an evil country's economy while teaching Islam took place with Moses pbuh and the believers in Egypt. Now Jihad against Pharaoh was justified since he called himself God, was oppressing believers and killing babies on a routine basis. However God sent Moses pbuh to preach, not to fight. This took some time, during which the believing slaves remained working for the Egyptian government contributing to their economy and one could imagine Moses pbuh as well traded with the Egyptians in order to buy supplies thereby contributing to their economy, which in turn bought weapons for Pharaoh's military which killed innocents and Muslims. Yet Moses pbuh remained preaching Islam until all the proofs were established and the truth was made clear beyond a doubt. Then instead of waging Jihad against Pharaoh, the believers simply left Egypt. Why is that? Because that generation was not prepared to wage Jihad, thereby showing us we have to work with what we have. These prophets could have refrained from benefiting in any way from the evil systems of their day but doing so would have hindered their duty and mission to teach people God's religion. I mention this so you are aware that failing to do good deeds because sin is involved can sometimes result in bigger evil occurring as a result. Satan can manipulate a sincere person who doesn't have knowledge to neglect doing good deeds because they fear doing sins. However others take the extreme opposite side and say good deeds should be done regardless of the sin so then they go take an interest loan to go for Hajj, or participate in unislamic holidays or sinful activities, or do blasphemous interfaith gatherings to be able to "spread Islam" to non-Muslims, all of which is not permissible. The point is knowing information about Islam is different than having knowledge, a sincere good person with information but lacking knowledge can easily be led astray without knowing it thinking they are right. This is what leads to groups like the Khawarrij who ended up killing Uthman and Ali with good intentions simply because they lacked knowledge. Therefore the role of Muslim scholars is to derive the correct ruling on an issue by using the knowledge and massive amount of information which they've learned. Sometimes Muslim scholars make mistakes because there is absolutely no single scholar who knows everything or every proof, which is why one must follow the strongest most correct opinion with the strongest proofs regardless of whether it's from their favorite scholar or not. Limiting oneself to only one specific individual scholar or madhhab means you will be guaranteed to make the mistakes made by that single scholar or madhhab. Muslim Scholars are like doctors, they are qualified to give you sound advice but even the best sometimes make a mistake and misdiagnose or give an incorrect prescription, thus by referring to other scholars as well to see who has the strongest proof is like getting multiple opinions from doctors. Sometimes the doctors can all be right but some doctors are more right and offer a better regiment to follow that result in a more healthy spiritual relationship with God that is more rewarding. While sometimes some doctors can be wrong simply because of lack of data or miscommunication on behalf of the patient. The thing is that many factors come into making an Islamic legal ruling, and different circumstances can cause different rulings. A doctor may give the same, different or even contradicting health advice to everyone in the world but that doesn't mean he/she isn't giving everyone the correct advice to each individual. This is because different people in different environments have different rules to follow to live a healthy lifestyle, even though they are all humans, external factors affect them differently. Unfortunately in the West some Muslims use this as an excuse and say that because they aren't in an Islamic country then they can do all kinds of sins, like buy a house with interest; which is something they can't do because they have lawful alternatives such as renting. Now if they already have a mortgage and didn't know it was forbidden, or they're a new Muslim and got the house beforehand then different legal rulings apply based on those individual situations. So Islam does have some flexibility that you should be aware of. The religion doesn't change with the times, nor does it adapt to the times, but Islam has built in principles within "Usool ul-Fiqh" which are used to apply Islam the correct way throughout all time in every circumstance for every individual. So while Islam strictly stays the same, some flexibility exists regarding some things. Allah makes Islam easy, but remember it's Allah who facilitates the ease, not the people themselves, scholars don't change the religion they just extract the correct Islamic ruling for each particular individual situation. Sometimes it even happens where two different people can ask the same exact question and receive 2 different answers/rulings because the individuals and their circumstances are different. So every legal ruling does not always apply to every person, some do some don't. A sick person won't have the same responsibilities as a healthy person because they don't have equal abilities, likewise for men and women, or new Muslims and old Muslims. The problem is some play games with this and look up fatwas from scholars on the internet or keep asking the same question to every scholar until they get the answer they want so they can exploit every loophole that can possibly exist, purposely following the minority opinions, easiest opinions, or the rare mistakes which a scholar made so they can live however they want to doing every sin they like and then they claim they are Muslims who submit as slaves to God. That is not Islam. That's like going to every doctor you can and they all tell you you're unhealthy foolishly endangering your life and must stop doing certain things or you will die, until one doctor is finally found who says it's ok to do what you're doing and then you go around telling everyone that all the stuff you're doing is perfectly fine, and even healthy because a doctor told you so. This is what happens with bead users who will find a scholar that tells them it's okay to use prayer beads and there are scholars who will say this even though it's wrong. Likewise there are some scholars who say suicide bombing is permissible too, even though that's wrong, I'm not joking it's possible to find Muslim Scholars who say such things. So just because someone finds a scholar who gives them an answer doesn't mean it's the right answer. Even though the flexibility exists where extreme circumstances can allow for actions that wouldn't be allowed under ideal circumstances, sometimes the correct course of action is to practice Islam fully without utilizing the concessions or flexibility that Islam allows for. This requires sincerity and knowledge. Both are required to practice Islam correctly, having only one without the other leads to doubts, extremism, sin, hypocrisy and potentially disbelief. You also need to know how to get knowledge and be aware of what you don't know. Some people even need scholars' opinions on the opinions of other scholars to understand correctly. I'm not a scholar so don't take what I write as official legal rulings, I'm just trying to share some fundamental principles and teachings of Islam. Don't think my way of living is the only valid Islamic way to live. Yet being "valid" is like being "alive" whereas being alive is different than being healthy. Yet different people are at different levels with different responsibilities since we all get a slightly different test of life. There are different levels of practicing Islam because there are different levels of paradise. You won't reach the level the prophets reached, but by striving you could end up as their neighbor in paradise. It's not good to make things unnecessarily hard when you don't need to if you can't handle it, doing extra doesn't always mean extra reward and sometimes doing extra can be bad, or sinful, or even disbelief. Please keep in mind <u>it takes practice to become a practicing Muslim</u> and practice Islam. One has be mindful of the level they are on and strive to make improvements at a rate they can religiously handle without doing to much too soon. A Muslim struggling for the sake of struggling is not Jihad. Taking the best and most correct course of action in Islam is not always the easiest, or the only available option, nor is it always the strictest, but it is always the most rewarding. Which leads us back to how Muslims lived, or struggled to live, under Shia rule in the Fatimid Empire.

    The Shia Fatimids abolished Shariah law making major sins permissible and good deeds illegal, banning anyone from following the teachings of Sunni Scholars and they burned the libraries and books of the Muslims, hypocritically doing so in the name of Islam. The Shia in Egypt even began the religious unislamic innovation of celebrating Muhammad's birthday pbuh because they wanted to imitate and copy the Christians who were celebrating Christmas. Although just like the prayer beads celebrating the prophets birthdays are not allowed because the prophets didn't do it themselves and neither did the companions of the prophets who loved them much more than we do. Thus if birthdays of prophets were good to do the companions of the prophets would've done it, they didn't do it because it is a bad deed to do even if it is done with a good intention. Believers show respect for the prophets by obeying their instructions on how to live life on a daily basis, not by throwing an annual party that the prophets don't even come to. In reality these parties and celebrations are for themselves and not the prophets at all. These types use the prophets as an excuse to party just as others use the prophets to gain financial profits. It was also the Fatimid policy to force people to follow calculations for Ramadan instead of starting Ramadan when the moon was seen and ending when the moon of Shawwal was seen. What happened to Muhammad ibn al-Hubula, the Imam and Qadi of Barqah (a Qadi is a Judge), shows how important it is in Islam to fast Ramadan according to the moon sightings as well as how anti-Islamic the Shia Fatimids were. The Emir of Barqah came and told him, "*Tomorrow is Eid.*" The Qadi said, "*We should see the new moon (first); I will not tell the people to break the fast, and bear their sins.*" (The emir) said, "*Instructions to that effect came in a letter from al-Mansoor.*" The Fatimid view was that they should break the fast based on calculations, and should not pay any attention to the sighting of the moon. The moon was not sighted, but the next day the emir ordered that there be drums, banners and preparations for Eid. The Imam/Qadi said, "*I will not go out or pray (the Eid prayer).*" So the emir ordered another man to deliver the khutbah and he wrote to al-Mansoor telling him what happened. Al-Mansoor ordered that the Qadi be brought to him, He went to him and (Al-Mansoor) said, "*Change your mind and I will pardon you*," but he refused. So he ordered that the Qadi be hung out in the sun until he died. The Qadi kept asking for water because he was thirsty but wasn't given any. Know that he was asking to drink water in Ramadan, which would be a sin but because he would die as a result of the torture if he didn't drink water then it wouldn't be a sin for him to break the fast in that situation but would rather be compulsory to try to break the fast so as to prevent his own death. Yet publicly telling the whole city to break the fast meant approving of changing the religion and telling the masses to commit a major sin and eat/drink on an obligatory day of fasting when he knew they shouldn't. The Qadi didn't want to do that and the Shia couldn't kill all those who kept the fast, thus this endangering of his life was different than fasting while being dried out by the sun to die. Thus he decided to risk his life so the city would correctly fast all of Ramadan as Allah commanded, as a result of his decision and steadfastness the Shia crucified him. After the first Crusade the Shia Fatimids made alliances with the Crusader states and would fight with them against the Muslims. Until finally after 262 years of Shia injustice, Allah facilitated the Sunni Revival in Egypt that had been spearheaded by Muslim scholars, which then led to the Fatimid Empire being reformed and destroyed in 1171 CE by a Muslim Scholar whom the Fatimids had appointed as a Vizier. That Muslim's name was Yusuf ibn Ayubi, who later became known by the moniker Salah Ad-Deen. This is also a lesson for the Khawarrij of today, because they would say everyone in a Shia country or non-Muslim country that is fighting Muslims should either fight back inside that country or leave since by supporting them or living under them they are automatically disbelievers since their leaders are enemies of Islam. (Note not everyone who says this is a Khariji but this is what Kharijis say regarding each and every non-Muslim majority country as well as nearly every unislamic Muslim majority country.) They say "*Either emigrate to us or fight there where you are!*" This is not what Muhammad pbuh told every Muslim to do who lived in Mecca under pagan rule while he was in Madinah and the pagans were fighting Muslims, even though the Quran commanded the believers to emigrate to the prophet. Some special cases existed of Muslims with exceptions who neither fought the pagans nor emigrated from Mecca despite the Quran commanding Muslims to join the prophet in Madinah. Also during the Crusades Muslim Fundamentalist Scholars didn't teach this *"emigrate to us or fight there where you are"* slogan either. Of course they didn't go to Rome or England to preach Islam, but they did go to Egypt and preached Islam in Shia territory despite them being there indirectly contributing to the Shia economy taxed by the government which fought against Muslims and allied with the Crusaders. Although eventually in the long term their efforts and patience reversed and improved the situation. However keep in mind, it was Muslim SCHOLARS who went to live in the non-Muslim lands to preach Islam to the Shiites, regular Sunni Muslims didn't migrate to preach Islam, it was Scholars who did this. Similarily Moses pbuh paved the way for the warrior prophet Joshua pbuh. Likewise David pbuh didn't fight Goliath until the message of Islam had been conveyed. Offensive Jihad against any country cannot be waged until the message is conveyed. Now defensive Jihad is a different matter and doesn't always have to be waged perfectly according to Islamic guidelines because a defensive military struggle is do or die with you literally fighting for your life. This is where the harm of those ignorant Muslims in not fighting back at all would outweigh the benefits of fighting in a sinful unislamic fashion. In such a dire situation Muslims defending themselves unislamically doesn't mean it's not Jihad, ideally every single Muslim would only fight in islamic manners following every rule of Islam, but nobody's perfect. A Muslim Mujahid fighting sinfully doesn't necessarily negate the virtue of their Jihad or delegitimize it, people can and do make mistakes, even the companions of Muhammad pbuh would occasionally make mistakes when fighting in Jihad. Yet again this doesn't mean any type of fighting method is permissible just because it is a survival situation or because it was a legitimate Jihad and the intentions were in the right place. Islam teaches Muslims to distinguish between a military and it's subjects. What this means is that a country and it's people can have different rulings apply. Groups can be categorized in one manner and treated in one manner, while the individuals in that group can be categorized in another matter though they may be treated in the manner the group is treated in because they belong to that group. The problem is people lack knowledge and don't distinguish because of the false religions of nationalism, tribalism, emotionalism, democracy, ignorance, arrogance, etc. Sound knowledge is needed to determine the correct course of action, generalizing is dangerous and emotionalism leads to sinful errors. Then we run into trouble between the difference of what something says and what something means, which is why we have to look at how did the prophet Muhammad pbuh and his companions interpret the verses, and to do that you need full comprehensive knowledge. Now if you don't have full comprehensive knowledge then you ask Muslim scholars to clarify the correct opinion and even if one is a scholar, the scholars are smart enough to know that they should ask other scholars as well to concur. Thus the same Islamic principles used to learn what is the correct thing to do, which some may think "goes too deep", is actually the very thing that eliminates and prevents extremism. The reason innocents get killed in the name of Islam is because some people don't follow these principles of knowledge but place their hopes in good intentions and sincerity. If you recall this is the same principle that let us know prayer beads are bad. Whereas some may think me saying prayer beads are not allowed is extreme, but in actuality the extremist methodology is the one used by the bead user. The only difference is one uses it to justify beads and the other uses it to justify suicide bombings of civilians, but they use the same exact principle. That is why these "little things" are fundamentally very important. The problem is that the Islamic doctrine is rarely presented to people completely and many just want a one word answer when a one word answer is not correct regardless of what it is. Before you can accept the correct answer you have to know how the correct answer can be found. Such as in math in order to do addition you not only need to know the numbers you are adding, but you need to know addition as well or else you may come up with the wrong answer even though you are using the correct information. 1+2 can equal many different things if someone doesn't correctly apply the fundamental principle of addition, even though they'd be correct when they discuss what 1 and 2 mean. Likewise 2+1 or 4-1 could be used to arrive at the same answer. But to have the correct Islamic answer one must use the correct authentic information according to the correct methodology with the correct principles and the correct intention. Basically it's Fundamental. Those who don't take a fundamentalist approach are guaranteed to be fundamentally wrong even if against all odds they happen to randomly get the correct answer somehow. The fundamentalist may not always be right since they are human, but they will be right fundamentally and that is why Muslim scholars can have different and even conflicting opinions yet both can be considered right. It does not literally mean all answers from Muslim scholars are right, it means they used the right methodology the right way with authentic information correctly and have the qualifications and apparently sincere pure intentions. Although sometimes the differences amongst Muslim scholars can all be right and one answer is just "more right or more correct" or as I'd say "they're all valid but some are healthier than others". Yet sometimes scholars are fundamentally right whilst being wrong and that is why it's dangerous to be a blind follower of just one scholar or madhhab, a blind follower is one who doesn't even look at the proofs or reasons scholars give for their answers. Likewise sometimes the majority opinion can be wrong too. Blind following is forbidden in Islam. Muslims don't follow scholars we follow the Quran and the prophet, a scholar's job is to organize the abundant amount of information available to present the correct proof to determine the best decision. Yet if one isn't a scholar themselves they may not understand scholastic principles or the level of authenticity of the proof, similar to how a patient visiting many doctors might not understand which doctor's opinion is best. So they'd ask a doctor to explain which doctor's opinion is best and why, the problem some have regarding religion is that they don't bother to learn why a certain opinion is best or most correct and thereby can fall into errors unknowingly. Prophets were sent to explain the fundamental and specific principles, give us authentic information and be living examples because there are some issues that arise where people simply don't naturally know what God wants them to do in a specific situation. The prophets told us what to follow and that is what we are to follow. Today scholars exist simply to pass along the best correct legal ruling in our present time based on the proof and evidence already relayed to us by God and his prophet(s), so that those who don't yet know the best correct thing to do and why it's best can benefit from their knowledge when the matters are unknown or confusing. Scholars aren't followed, one follows the proof the scholars present which comes from the Quran and Sunnah. One famous Muslim scholar Imam Abu Hanifa even said what means: "*it is prohibited for a Muslim to say what we say until he knows from where we took.*" Meaning a Muslim must know the "why" and the reasons why a scholar gave such a ruling and the proof from which that ruling was based on before they repeat such a ruling to someone else. This is a fundamental principle related to the addition analogy, in that you can't share the correct answer with someone unless you know the full equation that resulted in that answer. Otherwise you wouldn't know if it's correct. So in Islam there is the short answers of "*yes, no*"and "*it depends*" as well as the long answer, however all of these answers require proof and if an answer/ruling is ever given without a proof then one is to say "Godwilling that is correct" or "And God knows best" but it's safest to say that stuff anyways just in case. Another famous scholar Imam ash-Shafi'i used to say: "*if a hadith is authentic then that is my madhhab.*" A madhhab is a "school of thought", this statement of his reveals that his "school of thought" or methodology was what is called Ahl-hadith. Which means Imam Ash-Shafi'i would base his religion upon the Quran and Sunnah and the early generations of Muslims (the salaf). He didn't base his religion upon what scholars said but the authentic proof. To illustrate what this means once a man came to Imam Ash-Shafi'i and said: "*O Imam! The prophet pbuh said in a hadith such and such about such and such, so what do you say?*" In reply Imam Ash-Shafi'i got angry and said: "*What is this?! Does it look like I have come out of a Church!? You say to me that the Prophet has said such and such and then you ask me what my view is on the matter?! I have no view except that view of the Prophet pbuh!*" Thereby he revealed that the prophetic guidance is the religion of Islam. His response also reveals how he'd answer the issue of counting zikr on prayer beads or the fingers. The rightly guided Muslim scholars didn't follow scholars, as some people do today, they followed the Quran first and foremost since that is the book of Allah. However the book without the teacher is not sufficient. The prophet Muhammad pbuh was the teacher of Allah's book. So if scholars couldn't find an answer directly in the Quran they followed the Prophet Muhammad's Sunnah pbuh. Hence Imâm Mâlik said, "*I am but a man. I make mistakes sometimes and I am correct sometimes, so examine my opinions and accept anything that agrees with the Book(Quran) and Sunnah; and leave anything that does not agree with the Book(Quran) and Sunnah.*" Yet the prophet(teacher) is no longer alive today. So what do you do if you can't ask the teacher for the answer to your specific question directly? You ask your classmates who are taking the same class from the same teacher using the same book. Thus if scholars still didn't find a direct answer from the Quran and Sunnah they would get the answer from the statements of the companions of the prophet Muhammad pbuh. The statements of the companions regarding belief were given more importance than their statements on jurisprudence. If there were a rare instance when the companions differed on a certain matter of jurisprudence then the scholars would simply say what all the various opinons that existed were. If you recall Muhammad pbuh made it clear that the saved sect is, "*Whoever is upon that which I am upon today and my companions.*" Therefore regardless of which opinion of the companions one followed then such a person would qualify to belong to this group who will enter paradise. Whatever scholars found in the Quran they used the Sunnah to judge it and anything found within the Sunnah they would judge according to the understanding of the salaf (the first 3 generations of Muslims after the prophet pbuh). This is the pure religion of Islam. Why is it just the first 3 generations of Muslims who are considered the "salaf"? Because in authentic hadiths in both Sahih Bukhari and Sahih Muslim it is reported that Muhammad pbuh said what means: *"The best of my Ummah(nation) is my generation, then those who follow them, then those who follow them."* So Muhammad pbuh himself gave his stamp of approval for the first 3 generations of practicing Muslims. The problem which occured later is that after the early scholars died some people misunderstood their Ahl-hadith or Salafi methodology and instead just followed the scholars' opinions which the scholars got from the Quran, Sunnah, or Companions, but the later followers of the scholars followed those opinions without knowing the proofs and determined that the scholar's opinion in itself was a proof since they knew the scholar's wouldn't make an opinion if there wasn't proof for it. Yet there is a huge difference between agreeing with a scholar because of their proof vs. agreeing with a scholar because you know they wouldn't say something unless they had proof. The latter is blind following. As a result "Madhhabs" later developed that were schools of thought based upon the opinons of such scholars and/or their students and then madhhabs developed based on the students of these madhhabs so that today there are madhhabs within madhhabs. Tragically these same salafi scholars such as Imam Abu Hanifa, Imam Malik, Imam Hanbal and Imam Shafi'i who based their opinons on proofs and told people not to blindly follow scholars, or to accept a scholar's statement as a proof, ended up being blindly followed themselves. It'd almost be funny if it weren't so tragic. For example there is the Hanafi madhhab which purportedly teaches according to the methodology of Imam Hanifa, then the Maliki madhhab purportedly teaching the methodology of Imam Malik, then the Shafi madhhab purportedly teaching the methodology of Imam Shafi then the Hanbali madhhab purportedly teaching the methodology of Imam Hanbali. All these schools of thought give different jurisprudential rulings. However all these Imams had the same exact methodology in reality and actually taught each other. For example Imam Abu Hanifa's students taught Imam Malik and Imam Malik was a teacher of Imam Shafi and Imam Shafi was also a student of the same students of Imam Hanifa who taught Imam Malik. While Imam Shafi was a teacher of Imam Hanbal. What this proves is that none of these illustrious scholars believed in blindly following the opinions of their sheikhs. If Imam Hanbal believed in taqlid he'd have been a Shafii. If Imam Shafi believed in taqlid he'd have been a Malikki. If Imam Malikki had believed in taqlid he'd have been a Hanafi. While if Imam Abu Hanifa had believed in taqlid he'd have been a Massoodi since one of his teachers was Abdullah ibn Masood. Of the 4 most popular madhhabs the Hanbali is technically the most refined and accurate because Imam Malik refined Imam Abu Hanifa's fiqh, while Imam Shafi refined both of their fiqh, while Imam Hanbal refined all their respective fiqhs but the chain of jurisprudence doesn't stop there. Scholars today still refine fiqh correcting any errors scholars in the past may have made due to lack of information or errors. The madhhabs themselves claim to refine themselves as well. Although fundamentally none of their madhhab methodologies teach taqlid, some Muslims who belong to these madhhabs mistakenly believe in taqlid and teach it. To be clear people today who claim to belong to such madhhabs based on certain scholars' teachings aren't all blind followers of scholars, most of them will research the proofs their scholars base their rulings on but then some don't bother checking the counter arguments of the other scholars who may have better proofs. While if they do check the other opinions, sadly some tend to just follow their own madhhab's opinion out of prejudice, which is incorrect to do. Yet this very practice of not checking the opinions of rival madhhabs is contrary to the alleged founders of the madhhabs. For example Imam Shafi as a student of Imam Malik agreed with some things he taught, then he moved to learn form Imam Malik's Hanafi teachers and changed his opinions on some things he previously agreed with from Imam Malik, then later in life he changed opinions again on some things based on proof he found that indicated the correct position on certain matters where different than what both his Maliki and Hanafi teachers had taught. So the Imams always followed what they believed was the strongest proof, using the Quran, Sunnah and statements/practices of the salaf as their sources for authentic information. For example once Imam Malik was told by someone how the amount of water that Muhammad pbuh used for wudu was X amount and not the amount which Imam Malik was teaching people based on a certain hadith the person had heard. So Imam Malik, who lived in Medinah, told the man to wait while he got the cup which Muhammad pbuh used to use so they could see if the guy's hadith was true or not. That was the type of proof scholars would use, one guy comes and basically says *"My teacher told me Muhammad pbuh used X amount of water and you are wrong to say it was Y amount because my teacher said so!"* and Imam Malik basically replies *"Well you brought me an alleged statement of Muhammad pbuh about how much water he used and I brought you the actual cup he used. So look at the cup yourself and see if your teacher's statement is true when you fill the cup with water. It doesn't matter what your teacher told you, we have the cup to prove the truth. Which do you think is more likely to be accurate about the amount of water Muhammad pbuh used for wudu? His cup or your teacher? Can the cup make a mistake or be wrong? If the cup implies your scholarly teacher is wrong then which opinion will you believe to be correct?"* It's a funny story but sad at the same time because some people have such a devotion to blindly following their teachers that it is spiritually unhealthy and leads them to have incorrect beliefs which leads to incorrect practices based on following teachers/scholars instead of following the proofs provided by teachers/scholars. This doctrine is also commonly found in non-Muslim schools where they teach you "the teacher is always right" and "to pass the test you have to give the answer the teacher wants" but the test of life doesn't work that way. God gave us proof and prophets with proofs to know the right answers for the test of life and God and the prophets also told us how to find the answers to any issues that may arise after the prophets depart. Neither God nor the prophets taught to "Just follow what your scholars teach you." That's exactly how the Jews and Christians were led astray. Furthermore during Imam Hanbal's life the Islamic religion was almost corrupted by an oppressive Muatazila regime who tried to get Muslim scholars to say the Quran was not the word of God but was manufactured/created. The Mu'tazilas used force and intimidation to coerce the scholars into saying what they were told. 700 Muslim scholars around Baghdad were tested by the Mu'tazila inquisitors and of the 700 only 4 resisted changing their Islamic beliefs, Imam Ahmed Hanbal was one of those 4. So in the area around Baghdad only about 0.05% of Muslim scholars resisted the inquistion and remained firm upon the correct belief. The important point about this well documented dark era in Islam is that those who blindly followed the Hanafi, Malikki, and Shafi madhhabs succumbed to the Mu'tazila error in that era entirely due to their blind following of the scholars. Imam Hanbal knew the danger of Islam itself vanishing if he too gave in to the anti-Islamic inquisition. After being whipped 1,000 times, he was told by the other Muslim scholars that it was "islamically permissible" for him to say words of disbelief and agree with the Mu'tazila in order to save his life. Imam Hanbal replied, "*If I remained silent and you remained silent, then who will teach the ignorant?*" The reason Imam Hanbal didn't remain silent and opposed the unislamic doctrine insisting the Quran was the word of God was because the proof said his position was right and that the "scholars" were wrong even though they were a majority of 99.05%. Hence not only does Imam Hanbal's stand for Islam prove how blind following is wrong but it also proves that the majority opinion can be wrong too, thus meaning democracy and voting is wrong. This raises another issue in that some mistakenly think that if the majority of people are doing something then it's part of Islam or if the majority of Muslims aren't doing something then it's not part of Islam. On such a poisonous philosophy there was an incident that occured amongst an ignorant person, a scholar and the scholar's student that reveals how foolish the "But all the other people" doctrine is. Abdullah bin Al-Hasan used to sit with the scholar Rabî'ah bin Abdul Al-Rahman. One day they were revising and studying various practices from the Sunnah when a man in the gathering said, "*[But] this is not what is practiced [by the people].*" 'Abdullah said, "*So if the ignorant become so numerous that they become the rulers and judges, will they then be a proof over the Sunnah?*" Rabî'ah said, "*I bear witness that these are the words of the sons of the Prophets.*" Meaning the prophets and their sons refuted this doctrine of "people power" because it is satanic/democratic. Yet despite Imam Hanbal's lesson in following the proofs instead of the majority or the scholars today some Muslims incorrectly blindly follow Imam Ahmed Hanbal himself despite him teaching to only follow the proofs his entire life. Some will even say "*Oh Imam Hanbal said to do X, okay I'll do that because he said so. All I need to know is what Imam Hanbal said to do or what X madhhab says to do. I don't need to know why they say to do X, I trust that they are right because they are smart scholars and know more than me.*" Hopefully you can see how foolish this type of methodology is. For such people who insist this is somehow Islamic or prophetic, Imam Hanbal himself wrote "*Do not follow my opinion, neither follow the opinion of Malik or Ash-Shafi, nor Awzai, nor ath-Thari, but take from where they took (authentic hadith).*" So those who blindly follow Imam Hanbal or any scholar is explicitly disobeying these very same scholars despite claiming to be following them they are not because the scholars all said "*Do not follow me, follow the authentic information taught by the prophet Muhammad pbuh.*" Although at least the Sunni madhhabs today aren't as bad as they used to be. It used to be that in many masjids all 4 madhhabs would pray at different times because they disagreed with each other and each madhhab only wanted to follow what their scholars taught so they wouldn't pray with other Muslims. This even happened in Mecca of all places! During the era of peak Madhhabism instead of Muslims performing 5 prayers a day if a bird were to observe them they would see 20 prayers a day because the 4 main madhhabs were so stubborn upon blindly following their scholars that they refused to pray together. It wasn't until 1925 CE when the descendants of Ibn Saud and the students of the students of Muhammad ibn abdul Wahhab took over Mecca that they put a stop to this deviant practice of all 4 madhhabs praying separately in Mecca. At the time the Muslim world was outraged that the "Wahhabis" (as they were derogatorily called) told the Muslims they were all supposed to be praying together even if they had different madhhabs and demolished the various Makhtabas(places for prayer leader from each Madhhab to stand) making it so there was just one establishing prayer as it was supposed to be done. Today though nearly every Muslim in the world agrees the "Wahhabis" were right and that mere differences in maddhhab don't justify Sunnis praying seperately. Yet some taqleedis, who tend not to even know the history of the deviant taqleed of madhhabism that led Muslims to pray apart as recently as 1924, still resent the Muslims who correctly brought Muslims back to praying correctly and deride those Muslims with the label of "Wahhabi" trying to insinuate they make taqleed of a particular personality Muhammad ibn abdu-Wahhab rather than Islam. Which is rather ironic because if you ask taqleedis they say "Wahhabis" are extremists for making taqleed of Muslims who say it's forbidden to make taqleed. The Taqleedis hypocritically contradict themselves by saying people sinfully blindly follow those who say it's sinful to blindly follow non-prophets. The Taqleedis say one should only blindly follow those who say it's not sinful to blindly follow, whereas true Muslims don't do taqleed of anyone but Muhammad pbuh. Notice I said true Muslims, I did not say the majority. Needless to say taqleed is not what Islam teaches nor what Muhammad pbuh taught Muslims. And when did this concept of Taqlid creep into the Muslim nation? After the Shia started saying their Imams and Scholars were infalliable. <u>No Muslims did Taqlid before the Shia existed</u>. Then to justify taqlid fabrications hadith were invented such as the most famous one where they say "If you have no sheikh/Imam then Satan is your sheikh/Imam." This is the calling card of taqleedis but Muhammad pbuh never said this, it's a purely unislamic fabricated statement of falsehood, invented to promote the falsehood of blindly following Imams. Taqlid is the core methodology of Shi'ism but to be explictly clear not everybody who does Taqlid is a Shia. Due to this matter of Madhhabs and the blind following of Madhhabs some Muslim scholars like Sheikh Muhammad Sultan Al-Ma'soomi Al-Khajnadee have said that following a Madhhab is a bida or forbidden innovation. Note that one can follow one of the Sunni Madhhabs if they don't have adequate knowledge, but if/when they learn that the correct opinion on something is different than that Madhhab's opinion then they must follow what is correct instead of that Madhhab's opinion on that matter. Unfortunately some Madhhab followers are blind followers who follow scholars without knowing their reasons or evidences used for saying things in matters of jurisprudence. The trouble is that some today forget that these prestigious scholars in the past taught to follow the proof and not the scholar themself and that the only human one should blindly follow is the most recent/final prophet. Fortunately, unlike in other religions, the Quran today is exactly the same as it was during the time of Muhammad pbuh, the prophetic Sunnah is preserved as well as the information about the companions and salaf. So the problem has nothing to do with lack of information or the authenticity of infomation, but is simply that some Muslims have fundamental issues regarding their methodology on how to find out or how to acquire and determine an islamic legal ruling. It doesn't mean they aren't Muslims, it just means they aren't a fundamentalist because their methodology has some fundamental issues. Keep in mind that doesn't mean what they believe or do is wrong, because as has been explained one can still get the correct answer even though they are fundamentally wrong. Many times such Muslims' beliefs and practices are correct and based on authentic correct information, so the thing that causes an occasional issue is usually just a difference in methodology. Such differences in methodology are what cause differences among Muslims, most are valid differences that are perfectly fine to have and many Muslims exist who do the same exact things I do for the same exact reasons even though we're using different methodologies. There is no hierarchy in Islam, so regardless of one's methodology every Sunni attends the same masjids. Don't misunderstand it thinking there are special masjids depending on one's methodology, there aren't; except for the Shia and some extremist Sufis and sects that are outside the fold of Islam but claim to be within the fold of Islam like Ahmadiyya. This causes a slight amount of chaos at masjids because not only do the multiple masjids of Sunnis pray in the same masjids but the various Sunni sects do as well and sometimes the masjid can be composed of many different "Muslims" who have very different theologies. I mean just imagine if all the different denominations of Christians prayed together in the same church. Sects believe in different theologies, creeds and doctrines while madhhabs believe in different methodologies and scholastic approaches to/rulings of jurisprudence. Muslims can have different madhhabs and still believe in the same religion, but the different sects of Muslims can have theological differences which result in them believing in different religions yet they all say they believe in Islam and follow it correctly and go to the same masjids. Christians generally have sepaerate churches for each sect/denomination, Muslims generally don't. Hence I say masjids can be slightly chaotic from a theological aspect if it is theologically diverse, which is dangerous for Muslims who don't know the prophetic theology and can be misled by those who belong to deviant sects without knowing it. However it's very important to remember the distinction between madhhabs and sects. You could be part of the same sect as someone who belongs to a different madhhab and/or you could be part of the same madhhab as someone while belonging to a different sect than them. Surface similarities may be all that exist or on the surface people could seem very different while being theologically the same, in theory. To put it in Catholic terms the Sunni Madhhabs would be like different religious orders, in that within Catholicism there are Jesuits, Franciscans, Benedictines, Dominicans and others. Now technically all people who belong to and follow those various Catholic orders are all considered Catholics even though they all pray slightly differently, however Jesus pbuh didn't belong to any of those orders and didn't teach any of those orders. Thus those various Catholic orders are not really based on the prophet Jesus pbuh or his teachings but on the teachings of specific Catholic individuals. Catholicism isn't based on Jesus' teachings either, but for the sake of argument/example we'll say the religion of Jesus pbuh predates those Catholic orders. So a follower or adherant of those various Catholic orders cannot really say they are fundamentally or fully following the religion of Jesus pbuh; even if Catholicism were theoretically taught by Jesus pbuh which it wasn't. So since all the modern madhhabs of today, arose long after the prophet Muhammad pbuh, those madhhabs while they may be within the fold of Islam are not the pure 100% fundamental methodology taught by Muhammad pbuh. There used to be many Sunni madhhabs, but over time most went extinct and today the number of famous mainstream Sunni madhhabs has been reduced to 4. Maybe there will be less in the future or more, but the Ahl-Hadith (Salafi) methodology has always existed and will until the end. Sadly those who tend to follow one of the 4 famous madhhabs tend to not know or believe there are other methodologies and they incorrectly ignorantly assume that Ahl-Hadith or Salafi is something new or innovated when it's actually the original prophetic methodology. Sometimes it is heartbreaking because of the arroagant passionate ignorance some Muslims have not knowing that the Salafi methodology is the prophetic methodology. Such aversion to the way of the salaf is theologically a type of aversion to the way of Muhammad pbuh and his companions and their students and those students' students. As a result of their confusion some of non-salafi Muslims then treat the rightly guided Muslims like they are innovators or extremists or even non-Muslims because they mistakenly think they are wrong about a certain practice being recomended, permissible or forbidden. Case in point being the prayer beads, telling people their prayer beads are sinful to use can result in negative reactions even if you warn them with kind compassion. As an example there are many ways to "forbid the beads", I've learned some ways are better than others. Now you could give all the reasons why they are bad or you can take a different approach more suited to the individual and the situation. For instance once I saw a stranger using the beads sitting next to me and there were only a few minutes until the prayer time. Being harsh and rude likely wouldn't work but I didn't want to just be quiet about it, I had to say something to "forbid the evil of the beads". But what? I just told him how I read the prophet Muhammad pbuh said to count zikr with your fingers because they will testify for you on the day of Judgement. He said yes, and continued using the beads. However Islamically I did essentially forbid him and tell him to use his fingers and not the beads by telling him Muhammad pbuh said to use the fingers, know he might mistakenly think the beads count as the fingers, but in the sight of God I did tell him and conveyed the message so maybe it will sink in some day. Then I started counting on my fingers so he could see me counting so perhaps he would subtly learn that I was telling him the beads were incorrect without explicitly saying that or maybe he will choose the fingers voluntarily. However though he may have still continued using the beads me saying what I said was better than being silent letting him continue the sin, plus he had no negative reaction to that. Although then I figured if in another situation like that I could also make an audible dua after that asking God to guide the Muslims away from the bida of prayer beads and to the Sunnah of counting zikr on their fingers. That might have gotten a more unpleasant reaction but also may be more effective. I use this as an example for how to "kindly forbid", many unfortunately know why something is wrong but don't know how to "forbid evil" effectively. In fact with every bida, and God knows best, I think it's a good idea to audibly ask God in dua to "Guide the Muslims away from the bida of X" so that although you aren't confrontationally telling them about it being bida they may hear it is bida due to hearing your dua and reconsider, change and repent. In the end you have to ask God to guide them anyways since you cannot guide/correct them unless God decrees guidance for them. Yet some ignorant or arrogant people will react negatively to corrections/advice no matter how it's done. Regarding such negative reactions from people, acquiring/implementing knowledge and following the way of the salaf regarding proofs and forsaking taqlid many Muslim Scholars have commented:

Abu Darda (a companion of Muhammad pbuh) said,

Woe one time, to he who does not know and acts! If Allah wants, He will teach him. And Woe seven times to he who knows and does not act upon his knowledge!

The Scholar Al-Fudayl bin Iyad who died in 803 said,

Abandoning deeds because of people is riyaa' (showing off)! And doing deeds because of people is shirk (polytheism)! And ikhlaas (sincerity) is that Allah protects you from both of that. Seventy sins are forgiven for an ignorant man, before one sin is forgiven for a scholar.

The bearer of the Qur'an is the bearer of the banner of Islam. It does not befit him to indulge in idle talk or activity with those who do so, or to be heedless with those who are so, or to indulge in frivolity with those who do so.

The believer speaks little, but does much. And the hypocrite talks a lot, but does little. The believer's speech is wisdom, his silence is contemplation, his gaze is pondering, his actions are righteous. So if this is your state, you shall perpetually be in worship.

Allah 'azza wa jalla accepts only those deeds which are both correct and sincere (pure). If the deed is done correctly but not sincerely, it will not be accepted. And if it is sincere but not correct, it will not be accepted." He was asked, "Abû 'Alî! What is the sincere and correct deed?" He replied, "The sincere deed is one that is done only for Allah 'azza wa jall. And the correct deed is one done according to the Sunnah."

"When backbiting appears, brotherhood for Allâh will disappear; and at that time you will be like things plated with gold and silver: wooden on the inside, [merely] looking good on the outside."

As long as people are doing fine, their true nature is concealed, but when calamity strikes, their true natures are revealed, so the believer resorts to his faith and the hypocrite resorts to his hypocrisy."

"Whenever someone asks you, "Do you love Allah?" Remain silent, because if you say no, then you are a disbeliever. If you say yes, then your actions contradict your words."

"A believer in this life is worried and sad. His worry is the objective of preparing himself. So whoever's condition in this life is such, then he has no concern other than taking provisions from what will benefit him during the return to his homeland. So he does not compete with the people of the land, among whom he is merely a stranger, in what they consider honorable. And he does not become worried if he seems insignificant among them."

"Stick to the path of guidance, and do not be hurt by the small number of people who take this path, and beware of the path of misguidance, and do not be fooled by the large number of people who destroy themselves on this path."

"Whosoever is saddened by loneliness and feels tranquil around the people, is not safe from Riyaa."

Whoever sits with a person if innovation, then beware of him and whoever sits with a person of innovation has not ben given wisdom. I (would) love that there was a fort of iron between me and a person of innovation. That I eat with a Jew and a Christian is more beloved to me than that I should eat with a person of Innovation."

I met the best of people, all of them people of the sunnah and they used to forbid from accompanying the people of Innovation."

Follow the path of guidance, and do not worry about how few are the people who follow it. Beware of the paths of misguidance, and do not be deceived by the large numbers of those who doomed.

Whoever marries his beloved daughter to an innovator has cut off the ties of relationship with her."

The Scholar Al-Awza'i who died in 774 CE said,

> "Hold fast to the narrations of the Salaf, even if people abandon you. Beware of the opinions of men, no matter how much they beautify it with their speech, for indeed the matter will become manifest whilst you will be upon the correct straight path concerning it."

The scholar Abdullah Ibn Abi Zayd al Qairawani who died in 996 CE said,

> "Salvation lies in seeking protection in the Book of Allah Almighty and the Sunnah of His Prophet and following the path of the believers and that of the best of generations of the best community produced for mankind. Reliance on that is protection. Salvation lies in following the righteous Salaf."

The scholar Abu Al-Qasim Al-Lalikai who died in 1013 CE said,

> "From the greatests of statements, and the clearest of proofs and reasoning, is Allah's Book, the clear truth, then the saying of the Messenger of Allah –Sallallahu Alayhi wa Sallam- and his pious companions, then what was agreed upon by the Righteous Salaf, then holding on to it until the day of judgement, and avoiding innovations and listening to it from what was innovated by the misguided."

The scholar Al-Hasan Al-Basri who died in 728 CE said,

> " If a man from amongst the Salaf were to be sent forth today, he would not recognize anything from Islam." He put his hand on his cheek and added, "Except this prayer (<u>s</u>alâh)." Then he said, "But by Allâh, this does not apply to the person who lives in this unfamiliar time, never having seen the Righteous Predecessors, but who sees [instead] the innovator calling to his bid'ah, and the follower of worldly wealth calling to his materialism, but Allâh protects him from all this and makes his heart love and aspire to those Righteous Predecessors, asking about their way, searching and trying to follow in their footsteps, and adhering to their path. Such is a person who will be recompensed with an immense and great reward. So be you all like this, by Allâh's permission"

The scholar Al-Khateeb Al-Baghdadi who died in 1071 CE said,

Allaah has made these people – Ahl al-Hadith (salafis)– the pillars of sharee'ah, and He has destroyed through them all abhorrent innovations (bidas). They are the trustees of Allaah among His creation, the intermediaries between the Prophet (peace and blessings of Allaah be upon him) and his ummah. They are the ones who are striving hard to protect his religion; their light is shining, their virtues are well known, the signs of their sincerity are obvious, their way is prevailing, and their evidence is supreme. Every group has its own focal point which is based on whims and desires, apart from the people of hadeeth, whose reference point is the Qur'aan, whose evidence is the Sunnah and whose leader is the Messenger to whom they belong; they do not pay any attention to whims and desires, and they do not care about personal opinions. They are content with what is narrated from the Messenger, and they are the ones who are entrusted with it and they take care of it. They are the guardians and keepers of the faith, the vessels and bearers of knowledge. If there is a difference of opinion concerning a hadeeth, people refer to them, and what they rule is what is accepted and listened to. Among them are prominent faqeehs, great imams, ascetics who are well-known among their tribes, men who are known for their virtue, skilled reciters of Qur'aan and good speakers. They are the majority and their way is the right way. Every innovator pretends to be following their path, and cannot dare to claim any other way. Whoever opposes them, Allaah will destroy him, and whoever goes against them, Allaah will humiliate him. They are not harmed by those who forsake them, and those who stay away from them will not prosper. The one who cares for his religion needs their help, the one who looks down on them is a loser, and Allaah is able to support them.

The scholar Ibn Taymiyya who died in 1328 CE said,

Hence it is clear that the people who most deserve to be called the victorious group are "Ahl al-Hadeeth wa'l-Sunnah", who have no leader to follow blindly apart from the Messenger of Allaah peace and blessings of Allah be upon him. (They only do taqlid to/of God's prophet and no one else no matter who it is.) They are the most knowledgeable of people concerning his words and deeds, the most able to distinguish between what is sound and what is not. Their imams have deep knowledge of that, they are the ones who understand its meanings and are the most sincere in following it. They accept it and believe in it, and act upon it. They show love to those who adopt it and they show enmity to those who oppose it. They are the ones who measure any idea against that which is proven in the Qur'aan and Sunnah, so they never adopt any idea and make it one of the basic principles of their religion unless it is proven in that which the Messenger brought. Rather they make that which the Messenger brought, the Qur'aan and Sunnah, the foundation and basis of their beliefs. With regard to the issues concerning which people dispute, such as the attributes of Allaah, the divine decree, the threat of Hell, the names of Allaah and the principle of enjoining what is good and forbidding what is evil, etc., they refer that to Allaah and His Messenger. They examine the general ideas concerning which the different groups dispute, and whatever of these ideas is in accordance with the Qur'aan and Sunnah, they approve of it, and whatever goes against the Qur'aan and Sunnah, they reject it. They do not follow conjecture or whims and desires. For following conjecture is ignorance and following whims and desires without any guidance from Allaah is wrongdoing." He also said in another statement that: *"There is no shame in declaring oneself to be a follower of the salaf, belonging to it and feeling proud of it; rather that must be accepted from him,* *according to scholarly consensus. <u>The madhhab of the salaf cannot be anything but true.</u> If a person adheres to it inwardly and outwardly, then he is like the believer who is following truth inwardly and outwardly. If he adheres to it outwardly only, and not inwardly, then he is like the hypocrite; he is to be accepted as he appears to be, and what is hidden in his heart is left to Allah."*

Unfortunately some differences that result from having an improper methodology can lead to innovations, extremism, or even disbelief in Islam. Cases in point being the Shia or the Khawarij. In a nutshell this is why differences exist among people claiming to practice Islam and be Muslims. Yet despite methodological differences there are generally only two types of masjids, Sunni and Shia. Scholars are not supposed to be blindly followed but are thought of as fellow classmates or tutors. For instance the road to paradise has been traveled by many people before us. So lets say you're planning to drive to the finish line on the road to paradise, you have your car manual, instructions and map. You get onto the highway and you realize you are the only one on the road driving. Naturally you would wonder if you made a wrong turn or something since it's unusal to be the only one on the road, while it's historical impossible to be the first to drive on the road to paradise. Referring to scholarly opinions is to ensure that you are correctly understanding and applying the manual and instructions and didn't take a road to hell or deviate from the road to paradise by mistake. Yet remember they are travelers too, so make sure you know the proof and follow the proof, not the scholar; because when trying to drive to paradise anybody could get lost. The Muslim book is the Quran, our teacher is Muhammad pbuh, his students were the sahabah who were and taught the salaf. Later and modern Muslim scholars are students and tutors of Islam. Our goal is one, to pass the test of life successfully completing our journey on the road to paradise. Blind following is forbidden, however a convoy is the safest way to travel. Thus Muslims follow in the footsteps of the prophets which have also been followed by earlier generations. The prophet Muhammad pbuh also said what means: *"There will not cease to be a group from this Ummah who are clearly apparent on the truth until the Hour is established."* The Ummah is the Muslim nation, so the prophet pbuh taught there will be some Muslims who are more rightly guided than others. It doesn't mean people who aren't of the Ahl-Hadith or Salafi methodology aren't Muslims, many of them are. In fact theologically the majority of Muslims are Salafi and everyone pays lipservice to "following the way of the salaf", it's just that methodologically some Muslims incorrectly follow other ways. However there are different types of Muslims and the goal is to be the best of the best so that we get rewarded with the best in paradise as well as in this life. Ahlus Sunnah wa Jamah is another term for Salafi, although this has recently become a more generic term that encompasses and is used by most all Sunni sects even if they aren't really following Islam fully or correctly. Many misunderstand the word "Jamah" thinking it means the majority opinion of Sunni Muslims however it actually refers to the majority opinion of the rightly guided; meaning the first 3 generations of Muslims known as the Salaf and those who follow the way of the Salaf. In some places and times one person has been the Jamah even though they were the minority. Thus personally I don't use the label Ahlus Sunnah wa Jamah much because everybody tends to think it means them and everyone says they are upon that methodology just like how everyone says they follow the Quran and the Sunnah too; even the Shia. Whereas the term Salafi is also a term used by people who may be trying to be or thinking they are Salafi, but they really aren't due to ignorance or for other reasons. So Ahl-Hadith is the classic term for what is popularly called Salafiyyah or Salafi. Which is pure unadulterated Islam as taught by the prophet Muhammad pbuh. In other words it is Islam in it's pure fundamental prophetic format. It's the safest and most rewarding lane on the Islamic road to paradise whereas all the other lanes have potholes which if one drives in those lanes they may or may not hit and if they do it could stop them from continuing, damage them, or cause them to veer off the road without knowing it. Following a madhhab with Taqlid or "blind following" is not the way to travel the road to paradise, just imagine putting a blindfold on and then trying to walk in a perfectly straight line for the rest of your life. It's impossible to even walk across a continent via blind following, so you are definately not going to successfully travel the road to paradise being blindfolded. Taqlid is a spiritual blindfold, it's better than nothing because by following directions without seeing the proofs there is a tiny possibilty you could walk in the right direction for a few steps, but Satan is sure to trip you up eventually; that is if you don't fall or go astray all by yourself. Although since people who practice taqlid tend to blindly follow people who practice taqlid, then those guilty of taqlid are tantamount to the blind being led by the blind being led by the blind and only God knows the length of the blind chain of taqlid. Satan doesn't even need to try to trip people who do taqlid. Such a calamity isn't guaranteed to happen if one doesn't take the Ahl- Hadith lane, but personallyI'm not going to take such risks, because I don't want to take any detours to the hellfire before entering paradise. This is because when the prophet pbuh taught how all the other sects the Muslims will split into will be in the hellfire that didn't mean permanently for all of them. Some sects of Muslims are outside the fold of Islam and will be eternally punished, others aren't and will just be temporarily punished prior to entering paradise, while for some people on those stray Islamic paths it will depend on the specific individual if Allah enters them into paradise without a detour to the hellfire. Also there is a difference between a Muslim being punished in hellfire and a non-Muslim, because for disbelievers their torment is doubled and it's eternal. Although if you are cautious like me and never want to enter hellfire then the safe path is salafi. Now does a Muslim have to identify themselves as "Salafi"? No, but they are supposed to have that methodology and believe/live accordingly. Usually I refer to myself as a Muslim or a Muslim Fundamentalist Godwilling unless I'm having a technical scholastic conversation with someone who will understand what I mean when I say Salafi or Ahl-Hadith. Yet it is dangerous to mislabel oneself and thereby misrepresent an entire movement, that's why the Scholar Salih Al-Fawzan said, *"Calling oneself Salafi, if it is true, is fine and there is nothing wrong with it. But if it is a mere claim, then it is not permissible to call oneself a Salafi when one is not following the way of the salaf."* So because I'm smart enough to know that I'm not really following the way of the salaf 100%, as any salafi who reads this book will know, then I feel I should clarify that I'm trying to be salafi and that's the goal but officially I don't think I make the cut or rightly deserve to claim such a noble title for myself. I may forget and use the label from time to time but while I may be salafi according to the modern definition, the salaf themselves likely would not consider me to be a salafi despite my intentions, efforts and claims to be trying. This is because I give my own opinions and speculations much more authority than a salafi is supposed to. I say/write things they didn't say/write based on my own research so technically that's not quite the salafi way. Although sometimes with certain people it's better to identify oneself methodologically since one shouldn't be ashamed of trying to follow the correct pure Islamic methodology and to distinguish oneself from those upon other methodologies. So while some may dispute whether one should call themself salafi or not, there is consensus that it's the pure prophetic methodology and that even though everyone might not be one all the the Muslims should strive to be one. So any can say they are trying to be one, if they actually are /intend to do so and aren't just faking it to bring ill repute upon the methodology. The label dilemma is similar to how Sunni Muslims typically don't call themselves Sunni unless it's to distinguish themselves from the Shia. You don't have to call yourself a Sunni but sometimes circumstances dictate that you should. The trouble is we don't know what path or lane we will be on when our time on the test of life is up and we die, thus we say Godwilling. Muslims even say "I'm a Muslim, Godwilling" because many think they are Muslims but in the sight of God they aren't. Plus we recognize that the guidance comes from Allah alone, if God doesn't bless us with the guidance of Islam then we have no chance. This is because guidance is not a constant thing in that once you are guided then you will always be guided. It's similar to being healthy, being healthy once doesn't mean you will always be healthy nor does it mean that you are currently healthy. Just ask anyone who has gone to a doctor feeling fine thinking they are healthy only to learn they have a deadly disease and didn't know it. Or ask anyone who has ever gotten lost while traveling even though they had the correct instructions and were trying to follow them. So when Muslims pray we not only ask God for guidance to the straight path of those whom he's blessed(the prophets) but also for him to help us to worship him alone. We actually admit we need God to help us to worship him. While we also ask God to protect us from being or becoming like those who were misguided and earned God's anger (ie. the Jews) or of those who have gone astray (ie. the Christians). This is because the Jews and Christians at one time had the truth and were on the path to paradise, but despite historically receiving guidance they rejected it, distorted it, and chose a different path than that which the prophets were sent to teach us. Thus the prophet Muhammad pbuh was sent to guide them and all mankind. In every unit of every prayer Muslims ask God for this because it's so important and Allah himself instructed us to ask him for this. When God specifically says "*ask me for this frequently every day*" then you know it is definitely a vital, precious and valuable gift. Sometimes in life the long answer is necessary in order to get the correct answer, because by shortening it or blindly following then some may come to the wrong conclusions. Also sometimes the long answer isn't fit for everyone to know because they aren't capable of understanding it and too much information will confuse them and lead them astray. Thus I'm in a predicament of trying not to give more information than you can handle while at the same time not leaving too much information out so that you get the wrong idea or come to incorrect conclusions. Please forgive me if I share too much or too little information. I don't know what level you are at, I just presume you want to be the best and most knowledgeable person you can be, if this is too advanced right now don't worry about it, you can always re-read this book in the future if God wills. Sometimes being too honest can be a bad thing. That's how Satan can turn a good deed into an overdone good deed that becomes a bad deed or sin.

While Satan will also use the confusion to torment a person and cause them to hasten or delay so they make the wrong decision. Thus we need God's help to worship him/live correctly because it's very easy to go astray, especially if religion is not our top priority. If we care more about anything other than living how God wants, then we're guaranteed to go astray. If you make pleasing God and entering paradise your top priority then God will make it his top priority to help you succeed in that, if money, family or health is your priority then don't think God will make you going to paradise his top priority. Don't tell God you try your best, prove it to God and be the best. God's definition of "your best" is different than your definition. Your personal opinion of "trying your best" doesn't count. Only God knows what "our best" is, we don't know.

Iran is a Shia country which incorrectly calls itself an Islamic republic. In Iran the men and women dress like Muslims also claiming to believe in and follow Islam. But like the 5%ers, their concept of Islam is not really Islam. Many non-Muslims and Muslims alike are deceived and actually think Iran is a Muslim country. In the "Islamic Republic" of Iran it is a crime to memorize the Quran, this "crime" of memorizing what Islam teaches is the book of Allah is punishable with a death sentence. Muslims have been put to death in Iran because they memorized the Quran. Shia Iran also allows "Muta" for as short a time frame as 1 hour. Legally in Iran they let people have marriages that are designed to last for 1 hour. That's not Islamic! Furthermore in Iran the Shia constructed a shrine dedicated to Firuz, the assassin of Umar bin Khattab. They refer to Firuz, the Persian Zoroastrian who killed the 2nd Khilafah and father in-law of Muhammad pbuh, as Baba Shuajuddin which means "the honored brave defender of the religion". The Shia even annually celebrate the assasination of Umar bin Khattab and make pilgrimages to circumambulate the shrine of Firuz where he is allegedly buried glorifying him to this very day. The Shiite Iranian regime is both anti-Islamic and anti-Muslim. Israel and Iran are actually allies who both want Muslims to be killed, but they pretend to be enemies to divert international attention from the reality of their designs. Israel capitalizes on Zionist, Jewish and Christian support while Iran pretends to be a Muslim country intentionally trying to portray a bad image of Islam and Muslims to the world. Thus when Iranian Shias start killing Muslims the non-Muslim world doesn't notice because they think Iran is a Muslim country, which they hate. The hate people have for Iran is then transferred to Muslims making people feel no pity when Iranian Shias start killing Muslims. Unfortunately this ruse works and people start to think Iran is a representative of Islam and Muslims even though the Iranian government is actively exterminating Muslims and trying to eliminate Islam. Then when any negativity is directed towards Iran they direct it towards Islam and use the opportunity to kill more Muslims. It's a bloody repetitive cycle with one goal in mind, namely to destroy Islam and Muslims. Unfortunately the majority of people just believe what they hear on the local TV from people reading from a teleprompter and think the evil state of Iran is actually an Islamic land. If Iran were an islamic state I would go live there if God willed and helped me to go there, but I don't because it's not! The Shia are enemies of Muslims. Similar to the Iranian confusion, is the Shia in Iraq, Syria, Yemen and Lebanon. When the Shia blow themselves up killing Muslims in marketplaces and at masjids Muslims are being attacked by a foreign enemy of a different religion and we are getting told we are killing ourselves. The Quran clearly prohibits killing oneself! The Shia were the first to use suicide bombers in the middle east, continuing to use the tactic to kill Muslims and tarnish Islam ever since and the Khawarij adopted this practice as well. In Lebanon the group Hezbollah publicly portrays itself as an avowed enemy of Israel, but privately Hezbollah collaborates with Israel and provokes Israeli retaliation intentionally to kill Muslims, while at the same time killing Muslims as well. Shia want people to think they are Muslims so that they can get away with killing Muslims, while destroying the reputation of Islam. The very books of the Shia scholars advise Shia to lie about their religion so they can achieve their aims. Some Shia will lie right to your face and lie about lying. You can take a book from a Shia scholar to a Shia and ask if they believe in it. After they say yes if you open the book and show them where their book plainly says Shia should lie then they will say they don't believe in that book. If you call them out for having lied the first time they will maintain they never lie and always held the same position. So the Shia don't even tell the truth about their religious beliefs in lying, even if you catch them in the act!

    Unfortunately opponents of Islam will use these Shia books and claim that Islam teaches Muslims they can lie about Islam, which is an entirely false notion. I really hate when they do that too, because it's a lie about Islam and Muslims where they lie to people telling them that Muslims are liars and you can't believe anything we say. Sadly some people get so thoroughly brainwashed through this fearmongering that you can't even have a civil conversation with them or say anything about Islam because they just insist that Muslims always lie and lie and lie and lie. Why is that and how would they know? Because a non-Muslim person who hates Muslims and says that non-Muslims should kill all the Muslims told them so. Then when if you ask them if they considered that person was lying when they said Muslims tell nothing but lies, because they want you to join their army and kill Muslims, they refuse to consider it because such enemies of Islam are patriotic defenders of freedom. This happens frequently where the opponents of Islam will cite a Shia belief, like the Shia belief in lying, or a statement from a Shia Ayatollah and use it as a reason to reject Islam or hate/kill Muslims. Sometimes they'll even get real fancy and quote 26 translated words of the Quran. But those words aren't complete sentences and they are taken from different verses. I even read such a report and saw they quoted 8 words from chapter 8 of the Quran, 4 words from chapter 33, 3 words from a different part of chapter 8, 7 words from chapter 98, then they list a verse from chapter 3 but don't offer any text, then list a verse from chapter 4 and don't offer any text, finally finishing up with 4 words from chapter 3 which most of the report being their own words of slander and hatred. Afterwhich they concluded that everyone should fight the Muslims before it's too late, and not to trust anything Muslims say because the reader knows all they need to know to justify killing based on the 26 translated out of context words they were shown and told distorted meanings of. You might think I'm joking but this pathetic ploy actually works on people, especially if they get a alleged "ex-Muslim" born in the middle east to be their mouthpiece because surely such an Arab could never ever tell such a big lie against billions of people calling for their death if they weren't really on the good guys side, right? Those advocating the mass-murder of Muslims saying we are all liars somehow get believed and seen as good guys, simply if they promote Christianity, Democracy, Secularism or Freedom. It's always one of those 4 religions they are promoting against Islam, sometimes it's all. Yet Islam and Muslims themselves reject the Shia doctines and these evil Ayatollah's claims. It would be comparable to a Muslim saying Protestantism is false because of something Catholics believe or what the Pope said, whereas Protestants themselves have rejected Catholicism and the Pope so such an argument is baseless. Imagine what people would think, say and do if someone said all the Protestants should be killed because of what Catholics believe. Such a person would be sent to a crazy house or jail, yet people can say Muslims should be killed because of what Shia believe? Although what's worse is that much of the stuff people claim Muslims do and plot is the actual stuff which Shia plot, do and teach Shia to do to Muslims. The enemies of Islam just take out the word Shia and replace it with Muslim, while taking the word Muslim out and inserting the word non-Muslim. So enemies of Islam trick people into hating Muslims wanting them dead because they get taught Shia doctrines about Muslims and get told that they are Islamic doctrines regarding non-Muslims and that Shia are just a political flavor of Muslims. This blatant lie is so big that's it's unbelievable it works so effectively when used against Muslims and Islam. It works mainly because of freedom of speech and those lying about Islam are promoting freedom while Islam opposes freedom. Then such opponents will say "See I told ya they were against freedom of speech, everything I said about them being liars was true. Kill em quickly!" Whereas a major reason why Islam is against freedom of speech is because Islam prohibits lying. So how can we oppose freedom of speech because it supports lies if our religion teaches us to lie to people? We couldn't. On the other hand if someone's career is based on bashing Islam and lying about Muslims, they would need freedom of speech to keep their business in operation. Since liars have the most to lose if freedom of speech is abolished, then rationally the Muslims should be considered the least dishonest because they want lies to become illegal. Whereas those who love freedom of speech should be those that are suspected of lying because they want lies to stay legal. If Muslims were liars then they wouldn't oppose freedom of speech. Therefore being publicly against freedom of speech is a proof that we aren't liars and that our opponents saying we are liars trying to defend the Western lie machines are the true liars who lie about Islam and Muslims. In the afterlife such liars are exposed as liars and burn in hell eternally wearing pants which are made of the hellfire.

In conclusion if someone is going to attack Islam then attack Islam for what it is, don't attack Shia doctrines and say that it's Islam. The reason Islamophobes consistently denounce Shia doctrine yet label it as Islamic doctrine is because there is nothing about Islam that can be attacked on theological, scientific, intellectual, logical, rational, economic or moral grounds. Thus the only tactic enemies of Islam can use is to attack something other than Islam and mislabel it in order to deceive their audience. Next time you see something on the news Iran is doing, or the Shia in Iraq, Yemen, Lebanon, Syria or elsewhere please don't consider it a representation of Muslims, or be tricked into thinking their actions are something that is taught by Islam. Remember according to both all the Sunni and Shia scholars, the Islamic prophet Muhammad bin Abdullah pbuh, to whom the Quran was revealed, practiced and taught a different religion than the one which the Shia's teach, practice and believe in. So if you remember anything at all from this chapter then it should be these 2 things:

1. The Shia religion is not Islam.

2. The pure Islamic methodology or madhhab that was taught by the prophet Muhammad pbuh is known as Ahl-hadith, or Salafiyyah/Salafi, also known as Ahlus Sunnah wa Jamah.

LIFE AS A MUSLIM

Nobody, including myself would have ever guessed that I would ever become a Muslim in their wildest dreams. When I reunite with people who knew me from high school some refuse to believe that I'm Muslim because it's so surprising and many are left speechless at the implications of the most Christian person they knew leaving Christianity for Islam. In their minds I would've been the last person on earth to embrace Islam. Prior to Islam I would never have believed I would voluntarily choose to spend time with my parents, or get closer to them and had even started to take legal steps to permanently distance myself from them. My parents themselves cannot believe how much Islam has improved my character and admit how Islam teaches people better morals than Christianity, despite them still being Christian at the time of this writing.

I don't mention these things to boast, just as an example of how no matter who you are, or what evil things you have done, it is possible to change for the better no matter how bad you may be or have been. As long as you are alive Allah can forgive all your sins if you are sincerely sorry, repent to him alone, promise not to do them again and try your best to keep that promise. All the prophets pbut taught that this was how to be forgiven and attain salvation. There is no need for a baptism, confession or crucifixion in order for God to forgive us, God loves to forgive those who sincerely repent to him alone, it actually makes God happy to forgive people who regret their sins. When a person becomes a Muslim all the sins they committed before Islam are forgiven and any good deeds they did are carried over. A new Muslim doesn't just get their slate wiped clean, but it gets polished as well.

Islam is a way of life which places importance on how you live as well as what you believe. Actions without the correct belief are futile and having the correct belief without actions is lacking. If someone were to tell me 3 years ago that I would be living the way I am today I would have sincerely thought they were insane. Coincidentally many prophets pbut were labeled insane by those who rejected them and many who disbelieve in their prophethood call those same prophets insane today. Although it is the deniers of the truth who are crazy, rather than the prophets and their followers who get accused. Before long it will become clear to all who was right and who was wrong and what was true and what was false and who was good and who was bad. May we be of those who are Good, Truthful and Righteous and not of those who are evil, false and in error or arrogant.

Islam also caused me to begin communicating with my extended family again despite our previously strained relationship and the antipathy for them Satan had instilled within me. Unfortunately I fear some family relationships may have been permanently damaged and will take a long time to repair in order for us to become as close as we were before, or closer. While I was changing from bad to worse prior to becoming Muslim in the interim they were also changing and it seems there is too much to catch up on and that we now have little in common. I think Satan exploits these differences between us by making us feel it isn't worth the effort to reconnect which results in us getting isolated from each other making my family as a whole more susceptible to Satan attacking us in smaller groups. However sometimes when families get together in big groups Satan uses that to cause trouble between a few members who then make the family choose sides in the argument, not realizing it was all a plot by our predator Satan to disunite the family in order to make them more susceptible to his attacks. Just like practicing Islam, strengthening family relations is a day by day process that cannot be expected to happen overnight. Human babies begin walking in steps one at a time falling many times before being able to walk and take years before they can survive without constant parental assistance. Whereas many animals are able to survive on their own only days after being born. There is a great lesson in this. It takes humans time to develop and grow so in order to grow closer to Allah and develop our relationship with our Creator it will take time and effort, but the harder it is the more reward one gets. Fortunately Allah makes it easy for us once we submit ourselves to our Maker wholeheartedly. Spiritually most of us are infants and Islam initially seems too hard just as life would seem hard for a baby, yet if a baby told us that they will never be able to run or live life as adults do we would say they were wrong. Likewise if you think Islam is too hard for you then you are wrong. Allah created the whole universe so he can easily help you to do what he wants you to do, the only catch is that you have to want to do it before he helps you and makes it easy. If you want to worship God he'll make it easy and fun, if you don't want to then Satan will give you a pathetic excuse to use on yourself to ensure you fail the test of life. If you're unsure, ask the one who made your brain to help you know, ask the one who made your heart for the courage to follow the truth once you know and ask the one who made your body for the ability to do what it was created to do. You might think you don't have the time to learn or practice Islam and you're right, you don't have the time to do anything. It is the Creator who gives you time, so you can be certain that when you have the will then God will provide the opportunity. God just wants you to struggle before he makes it easy so that you become grateful and cognizant that doing what he wants results in happiness and ease, while God also wants to have an excuse to reward you in this life and the next. God has already given and given and given you everything you've ever had or experienced, you just gotta give a little effort for him in return and in exchange you get so much more. All you need to do is travel the road to paradise for a few seconds, after those seconds pass just travel it a few seconds more. Allah just wants a few seconds of the time he's given you. So if you don't have the time to learn or practice Islam then you don't have time to be alive, because the only reason you are alive is because the Creator of time wants you to worship him and has created you and given you time specifically for that reason so you can feel the pleasure of fulfilling your purpose and get rewarded with paradise for having the fun of doing what you were designed to do. Pretty sweet deal eh? The only trouble is Satan telling us it's sour.

      Of course it'd be cliché to say that after becoming Muslim I lived happy ever after, but that's not realistic. Without a doubt I have been happier as a Muslim than I ever was before, however the only time one will be able to say they were "*happy ever after*" is after they enter paradise. This world is not the place for everlasting happiness, if it were there would be no point in paradise. If you consider yourself to be happy all the time in this life then it's an indication that you will not be happy at all in the next life. This is because humans sin and you shouldn't be happy when you sin. For the disbeliever this world is a temporary paradise and the next life is an eternal prison. While for the believer this world is a temporary prison and the next one is an eternal paradise. When in prison, you are not allowed to do whatever you want, you can't go wherever you want, you can't sleep whenever you want, you can't say whatever you want, you can't eat whatever you want, you can't dress however you want, a prisoner is restricted in what they can and cannot do. Likewise a believer has restrictions on what they can and cannot do. If you live your life with complete freedom without any restrictions whatsoever on your conduct then that is the very definition of a disbeliever who disregards the Creator. You can choose today whether you want total freedom in this life or total freedom in the next life, but you cannot have both. The path to paradise requires sacrifice, personal sacrifice. It's like climbing a mountain, it's not easy, it requires discipline, self-control, guidance and concentration in order to reach the top. Whereas the path to the hellfire is like descending a slippery slope, it's easy to give in to your desires, the more you give in the faster and farther down you go, you don't even have to pay attention and gravity will take you down without any effort on your part, not only is no effort required but Satan is pulling and pushing you down the slope as much as he can so directions aren't even necessary. Although don't get the wrong idea that being a believer isn't fun, there are many fun things a believer can do that Allah has permitted and prophets have encouraged. The permissible things are much more numerous than the impermissible. Take food for instance, you don't need to eat every single food in the world in order to satisfy your hunger and there is plenty to eat that isn't forbidden. Likewise you don't need to eat all the time to satisfy your hunger either, so fasting while the sun is out during Ramadan is only a temporary sacrifice which billions of people do every year, they just eat and drink once the sun goes down and before it rises. It's similar to the test Adam pbuh was given when instructed not to eat from a specific fruit, for us there are just a couple of other things that's not on the menu Allah gave us. Personally I would never have believed myself capable of making the lifestyle changes I have since becoming Muslim, but Allah makes it easy and following his instructions satisfies in a way that nothing else can. There is nothing that will make one happier than doing that which pleases the Creator and avoiding that which displeases the Creator.

  There is a famous saying that one can never live morally and appreciate it unless they have lived immorally before. Although I do not recommend one tries living immorally because this is what Satan wants, yet sometimes Satan leads humans astray and the detour ends up taking them to the straight path which Satan was trying to make them avoid thereby making his plan backfire. So regardless of how many times Satan has fooled you and led you into error, you can turn the tables on him, choose the right path and be forgiven by Allah to Satan's consternation. For instance I was once deceived into following a false Satanic religion, but by the will of Allah I was guided and able to use my experience and knowledge from my time of misguidance to write this book hopefully exposing the false religion(s) and immorality Satan has spread, God-willing. Every time Satan misleads us we should use it as an opportunity to come closer to Allah. If Satan leads us to do a sin, then we repent and start doing extra good deeds hoping to be forgiven for the sin. Even though we messed up and did wrong, we end up doing more good because our mistakes put pressure on us to reform and improve.

This is one reason why Allah has created Satan. However we should never regard any sin as being small because all it took was one sin for Adam pbuh to be ejected from paradise, thus by us doing one sin it could also prevent us from entering paradise. Rather than think of how small or trivial a sin we do is, we should contemplate on the power and greatness of Allah whom we offend when we sin. The small sins which are consistently committed eventually add up into a mountain of sin. Persistance in sinning causes minor sins to become major sins. Many of the deeds we view as harmless our Creator considers to be felonious. Yet Allah is so great that we could be potentially forgiven for all our major and minor sins as long as we don't commit the ultimate sin. The ultimate sin would be to worship other than Allah, or associate partners with Allah, or to lie about Allah by claiming he has children, parents or relatives, or to reject any of the Prophets and Messengers whom Allah has sent.

      You might think I'm some special case with a remarkable life story, but I've heard and read many which are better. There are billions of people who became Muslims who were not raised as Muslims and every one of them has an amazing story of how they realized Islam was the true religion. For example Michael DeCero studied at a Catholic Monastary for 8.5 years learning Latin and Greek until he was guided to the straight path of Islam, became a Muslim and he's written books as well. Salman Farsi's story is even more amazing. One secondhand story I heard from the person who heard directly from the revert himself involves a card. One day a guy met a Muslim and was asked if he was a Muslim, the guy said no, so the Muslim gave him a card with the information of a masjid on it and said *"When you're thinking about becoming a Muslim you can get more information here."* The guy had no interest in becoming a Muslim at all. So he just put the card on a shelf in his residence somewhere and there it sat. For 20 years, it sat there and the guy never felt like learning more about Islam or Muslims, but as unislamic life goes the guy eventually decided to commit suicide. He went out to his balcony and decided to jump off and end it all, then he asked God to guide him and show him a sign if he should keep living, if God didn't do so in 1 minute then he would jump. (Don't test God like this, it's sinful.) However before his final minute was up the wind came and blew that card he got from the Muslim 20 years ago outside, he saw and realizing it was the sign he asked for, so shortly after that he became a Muslim, told his story to another person who then told it to me and I'm telling it to you. Perhaps the best story I know of is that of the brothers Yuqanna and Yuhanna of which Yuqanna was the political leader of Aleppo and Yuhanna was its religious leader when the Muslims came to conquer it, their story is so good I really wanted to include it in this book but it would be unjust to summarize it. The point is my story isn't special and anyways it's the end of the story that matters. Personally I have met so many reverts to Islam that I've lost count of how many I've met. I use the word revert because Islam is not a con, nobody is conned into Islam. Becoming a Muslim is to revert to the original state of submission to the Creator we were in when in the womb. There might even be more Muslims in the world today who weren't raised Muslims than there are Muslims who have been Muslim throughout their life. For instance one day I struck up a random conversation with an elderly stranger sitting next to me in a Canadian masjid. It turns out before becoming a Muslim he was a Catholic priest. I was speechless, after all I had been through Allah preordained that I would end up in a masjid as a Muslim American sitting next to an elderly Muslim Belgian who used to be a Catholic priest, in Canada. It turns out he was a Catholic priest in Belgium and first met Muslims helping elderly people in France. He said at the time there probably weren't any Muslims in Belgium, although currently there are nearly 1 million. He is a prime example of how no matter who you are or how deep into sin you've fallen you can still change and become a Muslim whom God loves and raises to a high rank in paradise. Terry Holdbrooks used to be a prison guard at Guantanomo bay before he became a Muslim while still serving as a prison guard there, before he stopped. Even if you are a Pope, King or Convict, Allah will make it easy for you and greatly reward any who repent/reform. It doesn't matter how young or old you are either. There was one Jehovah Witness female who was 119 years old, she discovered Islam, became a Muslim and then started telling people about Islam for 7 years until she died at 126 years of age. So whoever you are, wherever you are, Allah will help you to worship him and follow the true religion, you are capable don't let Satan discourage you. You may have a feeling that *"I'm so sinful and have done so many bad things I don't think Allah will ever forgive me and let me into paradise. I just know I'm going to hell no matter how hard I try."* That feeling is directly from Satan. I have heard this statement so many times from so many different people who didn't know the other people said it with each thinking the feeling was something new and that they were the first to ever speak such a phrase that I've lost count. Most of the times I hear this idea the people utter this with exactly the same words as others do. I have heard people say this very statement word for word only to me and they all think it's an original unique statement. None of them heard the others say it, they all think it's coming from themselves. This is an example of one of Satan's whispers, it is a satanic statement of despair; it's a catchphrase of his. Really think about it, take that italicized text and imagine having a serious conversation with Satan asking him how he feels and this is exactly what Satan would say and it is exactly what he wants us to feel and say. We make mistakes, the biggest mistake one can make is to think Allah cannot easily forgive all their mistakes. This is because only disbelievers despair of the mercy of Allah. If you are alive reading this sentence right now, then you can potentially enter paradise. One of the worst sins one can commit is to think that Allah cannot forgive your sins because it constitutes disbelief in the mercy of Allah. Don't be tricked by the popular Satanic slogan of "Sorry doesn't cut it" that leads you to hoplessness, despair, depression, more sins and false pagan polytheistic idolatrous religions in which a "savior" gets punished in your place and you pray to them hoping for them to intercede with your Creator to obtain paradise and safety from the hellfire.

Sorry does cut it. When mankind was created to be established on the earth the angels asked Allah why he was making us when we would cause mischief and bloodshed on earth while they(the angels) were devout worshippers who never disobeyed him or sinned. Allah said because he knows what they do not know. Elsewhere Allah said that had you, I or humans been sinless he would have destroyed us all and replaced us with people who would sin. Do you know why? Because Allah is the Most Merciful and loves to forgive. Allah enjoys when a person repents. That is all you and I need to do, no matter what we've done with our lives. If we acknowledge we did wrong, sincerely regret it, tearfully apologize to Allah only, desperately asking for forgiveness and promise and try our very best to never do it again, then Allah has promised to forgive such a person. If we then mess up again and do the same sin or even worse sins and then repent again then again Allah will forgive us, every single time. Allah will continue to forgive us again and again and again and again more times than is possible to calculate, as long as we are sincere and alive. Even when we die Allah may still forgive us because he is that merciful and loves to forgive. However there is one sin so great so abhorrent so ugly filthy rotten disgusting and evil that if you die upon it then Allah will never ever ever forgive you for all eternity. That sin is to associate something with Allah or to elevate something above Allah in your heart or disbelieve/reject the way of life God has ordained for us. This is what all the false religions do. They associate with Allah other beings that have no power to Create the universe, to give life or death, who have no authority on the Day of Judgement and don't even know what or when it is and are themselves created who are either creatures themselves or figments of a satanic imagination. One may do this by saying there is more than 1 God, or that God has children, or by denying some of the attributes of God. Maybe instead they take their desires to be their God. Whereas if God says to do or not to do something they do what they want in opposition to God's command thereby elevating their own cravings above Allah obeying themselves instead of their Creator. Maybe they make other people their god by obeying a priest, rabbi, politician, employer, friend, spouse, child, parent, or imam, instead of Allah when they conflict. Maybe they reject God's prophets because other people told them to or they don't like what the prophets say or where they're from or think they know better than a prophet even though God has said the prophets know better and should be followed. Maybe they even worship the prophet unintentionally thinking they are doing what the prophet wanted or honoring the prophet out of respect despite the prophets setting clear limits to the love they deserve and warning not to exceed those limits. This sin of worshipping people or other than Allah is the one which will cause eternal damnation for those who die without repenting from it. Anything else may be forgiven. However we must remember that Allah is the most severe in punishment as well as the most forgiving. Thus if any sins we haven't repented from aren't forgiven on the Day of Judgement we may have to temporarily suffer for them a severe punishment much more than we would like and much more painful than we would like. But a person who submits to the will of Allah (Muslim) and worships him alone dying in a state of such submission (Islam) will eventually go to paradise and be taken out of hell. Yet we are so blessed to be alive we could be forgiven for everything before we die if we repent and go into paradise without any suffering at all if Allah wills. All we have to do is repent, believe and do good deeds. If you are alive to read this then that means you still got a chance. Even if you make such a foolish mistake as to knowingly commit a major sin, utter a statement of disbelief or temporarily start worshipping your desires, even after all that you could still be forgiven if you repent like you've never repented before and have a life-changing moment becoming a better person then Allah may forgive you, but not only may Allah forgive you he may actually LOVE you. That is what we need. Allah doesn't need us to love him, rather you and I absolutely must obtain the love of our Creator. What are we waiting for? Soon we will die, be resurrected and meet him. If he loves us then we will experience unimaginable _____. There is no way to finish the previous sentence of how glorious and amazing being loved by the Creator for all eternity will feel. Words and emotions cannot simulate it for us. Yet remember if Allah hates us when we return to him then likewise we will experience unimaginable_____ the terror and sorrow of which words and emotions cannot simulate for us, it would be a depression worse than the kind that makes people kill themselves and those they love. Today may be our last. I may not even be alive when you are reading this. We want Allah to love us for eternity, then the least we could do is demonstrate to Allah in public and private that we love him with all our heart, mind, soul and body by following the true religion he has ordained for us and created us to follow.

Earlier in this book I wrote about "addictions" of various types: Drug, Alcohol, Cigarrette, Music, Luxury, Videogame, Sexual, Food, Fiction, Fortune and there are many more things and behaviors which one can have "addictions" with such as the internet or the phone and every addict has their own. However in reality there is no such thing as an addict or an addiction, this is a satanic deception. No prophet ever told someone they were an addict or addicted to something to which they couldn't control themselves. When we were born nobody was an addict, this means one voluntarily chooses to oppress oneself and become an addict. Therefore everyone can voluntarily choose to stop being "addicted" regardless of how long it's been or how much damage has been done. Neuroplasticity in particular proves this. The 12 step recovery programs that involve people admitting they are addicted and will just have to try to manage their addiction for life are setting themselves up for excuses, despair and failure despite possibly achieving abstinence from whatever vice they have. The inventor of Alcoholics Anonymous, Bill Wilson, actually founded A.A. after being pumped full of hallucinogens at a detox facility which made him "feel a white light". He came up with 12 steps in a rush one night while sitting in bed based on the idea that Jesus pbuh had 12 apostles. A.A. wasn't based on science or addiction therapy at all, he just made his social habit of drinking alcohol into a social habit of confessions about drinking alcohol. In 2014 CE A.A. came under the microscope and it was discovered only 5-10% of their members actually stop drinking alcohol. So the famous 12-step alcholol addiction recovery program has a 90-95% rate of failure. Why then is it so popular and well-respected? Could it be due to government funding and sponsorship? Maybe. Such 12-step programs tend to offer resignation, shame and excuses neglecting to tell their members that some things can only be cured by the Creator and as a policy most are agnostic in order to increase membership. Those who think they are addicts incapable of change just haven't learned of the cure. Such people with problems would be better off using a Pavlok shock wristband than exposing their sins at a social pity party for similar sinners. Or safely lighting something on fire whenever tempted to sin can greatly help one get through difficult tempting seconds. Even if one had to singe themself a little to avoid indulgence sometimes that's better and can help addicts avoid relapses. The burning of a fire is more potent than the burning from withdrawal symptoms. Every addict prefers withdrawal. Ideally one shouldn't hurt oneself but fire can be a great reminder and motivator when Satan tempts us to do something that leads to the hellfire. It's rare for Satan's false promises about sin to make a stronger argument than fire. Yet Satan frequently makes addicts forget how great a friend fire can be. Fire can give someone a better incentive to not sin than almost any "sponsor". That's why these addict support groups didn't come into existance until after fire became rare amongst the masses and it's also why communities who still frequently use fire on a daily basis typically don't have any of these addict support groups. Most addiction groups turn "your problem" into a club membership pairing you with a "sponsor" making you rely on them instead of God. Many religiously believe/teach that people "need people" to recover from addiction. Whereas while people can be very helpful, if an addict were the only person on an island or on earth they could still fully recover if God helped them. Most of the addict clubs/programs always stress that one must rely on God and "surrender" but then rely on healthy social networking more than God or alongside God it seems. Not to nock healthy relationships with people but there is a way to recover from addiction without people, and while that may not be the way for every sinner/addict God really will help people be his friend and recover from addictions, with or without using people to do so. People can help a bit but God helps more when relied upon alone, it may take a long time but the help of God is always near, God may help people with people but God should be the one relied upon 100%. Many addiction recovery groups unknowingly teach a religion and a method of repentance not proscribed by prophets, and that's why they tend to perpetually fail to rehabilitate their members. Since the addict club is like a social cult in many many ways subconsciously to stay in the club part of the addicts ensure that "their problem" persists. Which is why addict cults say you're in for life with such clubs aiming for sobriety and not recovery. A recovered addict quits going to addict groups just like a recovered patient leaves the hospital and surrounds themselves with healthy people now that they are no longer sick. Addiction clubs say that sick people have to stick with sick people or they'll never get healthy. They become addicted to confessing their flaws and troubles because it is a way to dump their guilt. They become addicted to addiction recovery and addiction therapy. Most of the addict recovery programs are cults. Useful cults, beneficial to many in many ways but still cultlike in their methodology and unprophetic in doctrine. Imagine a hospital that said everyone who enters it is in for life, we would know that such a hospital must not be helping anybody. Rather these "addictions" are diseases. All diseases can be cured completely as there is no disease which Allah has sent down except that Allah has also sent down the cure. We may not know the cure for everything, but Allah does and will provide the cure. Reading the Quran can and is a cure for many things, especially ignorance and arrogance which are the two fundamental causes of sin. The cure may even be just sincerley asking Allah to cure oneself. So many times we ask God to help us stop sinning but we should also ask God to protect us from having sinful desires to begin with. If you have a consistent problem with X desires that lead you to do X sin then sincerely and consistently ask God to protect you from having X desires as well. Even if you keep sinning always keep asking, God wants you to ask and Satan wants you to stop asking. In fact asking God alone for a cure itself is a type of medicine for spiritual diseases. Yet asking God is not enough it is upon us to take the medicine that Allah proscribes to heal from the diseases completely as well as to prevent future infections from satanic diseases. Allah can and will cure us of any "addiction" or disease if we ask, but we have to take the steps to develop a spiritual immune system by getting proper spiritual nutrition and exercising the correct spiritual hygiene, which can only be done by following the examples of the prophets. Could God cure us upon request? Yes but God knows how best to heal us and it may sometimes take many attempts at healing/repenting to be fully cured because God is the best doctor and wants us to appreciate spiritual health and develop healthy habits. Many doctors know that for some people getting sick and not getting better is/was better in the long run for their health than if they never got sick or got cured quickly because of the person seeking the cure for a prolonged difficult journey led them to become. For some cases the medicine could be as simple as staying away from other diseased people so you can develop an immune system without exposure to the virus. Some diseases we may never get and some we may contract repeatedly. While things like addictions are special diseases which are symptoms of diseases as well. Addiction is a side effect of another disease. Fixing an addiction can only be done by fixing the lifestyle that led one to pick up that addiction, addiction is just a symptom and side-effect of an unislamic mentality, personality and lifestyle. The cure can only be found with the true prophetic guidance for life. A disbeliever can never be free from addiction, they might attain sobriety from certain substances or behaviors but they will always have the mentality, personality and lifestyle which causes destructive addictions. I repeat every disbeliever is an addict of something and most have the personality of an addict; or at the very least the personality of a disbeliever which is very similar and only slightly different than that of an addict. Unfortunately not every Muslim has a 100% Islamic personality and this leads them to have unislamic behavior. Hence prophets were sent by God to humanity to guide us all, if the guidance they brought to humanity can't cure an addiction nothing can. Addictions have always existed and so has the cure for them, the cure is the prophetic faith. A "modern approach" is not the solution, God understands humans better than modern scientists so his solutions work, we don't need to know and may never know the precise science behind it because science can't explain it all. Science doesn't account for Satan and Satan plays a role in addiction. Yes science can add useful insight but Islam is the cure. The problem is with the way people today and historically failed to correctly accept and use the prophetic medicine of Islam for all the spiritual diseases they ever contract. Muslims still have the faith but they fail to use it correctly, the prophetic medicine is available most just don't know how to use it or fail to use it appropriately with consistency. When many try they fail and then fail to try again improving with sincerity, knowledge and patience until they die in the process. Every patient always dies in the process of seeking good health, so too does the believer die in the process of seeking good spiritual health. To stop sinning one needs patience because it usually takes many attempts to be successful and true success in in the struggle for the success in the afterlife. God doesn't tell mankind "Struggle to stop sinning." God tells us to struggle to enter paradise so truly success does not exist in this life. The only "successful person" is the one in paradise. If you are still alive on earth and never died then you are not "successful" because you are still taking the test of life. So accept that "success" does not exist on earth "striving" is the best you can experience. Be patient, be patient. Death and success or failure comes sooner than you think, don't rush it. Typically we are enslaved to our own impatience, of which impatience is a root cause of all types of sins. We tend to think that "One day I'll wakeup and never feel like sinning." Such a day will never exist because Satan exists, other sins may replace your current ones but everyday Satan will try something. So while one can recover from addiction, Satan will always be around to mislead us. It's not that "once an addict, always an addict" it's just that Satan works 24/7. But Satan's work in a sense is worthless as he is simply a slaver trying to enslave us, whom we strive to defeat. Slavery is unenforceable, all slaves choose slavery. "Addiction" is another form of slavery, every addict is a slave to a certain vice. In Islam the Muslim is the slave of Allah, nothing else. Yet never does a Muslim or non-Muslim ever get forced into slavery of any type. Satan likes us to think we are powerless slaves to sin but our freewill is stronger than all Satan can use. No Satanic slavery is too much for us to get out of and keep away from. Only Allah has authority, Satan has none unless we delusionally choose to obey him when he pesters. Our patience must be greater than Satan's to be successful. Satan might lay a billion traps for us but it's never too many, even if we fall into every trap he sets we can still travel the road to paradise and achieve forgiveness and success. If we fail it's because we choose to fail and let Satan lead us to lose. Just as Satan had no power over Adam pbuh Satan has no power over us. Satan is a creature and is thus powerless since all might and power belongs to Allah alone and Allah has refused to allow Satan to have any power over his true slaves. God just wants us to sincerely with knowledge and patience seek refuge with him from Satan, not just once but everytime. How do we seek refuge with God from Satan? Not through words alone but with our beliefs, intentions and deeds too.

Allah says in his Quran 14:22

وَقَالَ ٱلشَّيْطَٰنُ لَمَّا قُضِيَ ٱلْأَمْرُ إِنَّ ٱللَّهَ وَعَدَكُمْ وَعْدَ ٱلْحَقِّ وَوَعَدتُّكُمْ فَأَخْلَفْتُكُمْ ۖ وَمَا كَانَ لِىَ عَلَيْكُم مِّن سُلْطَٰنٍ إِلَّآ أَن دَعَوْتُكُمْ فَٱسْتَجَبْتُمْ لِى ۖ فَلَا تَلُومُونِى وَلُومُوٓا۟ أَنفُسَكُم ۖ مَّآ أَنَا۠ بِمُصْرِخِكُمْ وَمَآ أَنتُم بِمُصْرِخِىَّ ۖ إِنِّى كَفَرْتُ بِمَآ أَشْرَكْتُمُونِ مِن قَبْلُ ۗ إِنَّ ٱلظَّٰلِمِينَ لَهُمْ عَذَابٌ أَلِيمٌ ﴿٢٢﴾

"And <u>Shaitan (Satan) will say when the matter has been decided</u>: "Verily, Allah promised you a promise of truth. And I too promised you, but I betrayed you. <u>I had no authority over you except that I called you, so you responded to me. So blame me not, but blame yourselves.</u> I cannot help you, nor can you help me. I deny your former act in associating me (Satan) as a partner with Allah (by obeying me in the life of the world). Verily, there is a painful torment for the Zalimun (polytheists and wrong-doers, etc.)"-Verses from an attempted English translation of the meanings of the Quran by Muhshin Khan and Taqi-ud-Deen Hilaali.

     This means that in the end when Satan and those he misled are thrown into hell, Satan will then admit he had no power or control over us and that all he had done was call upon us and we listened and obeyed him. But we don't have to. God would never punish a person for doing something they couldn't stop themselves from doing. This means at all times a person is in total control of their actions and will be held accountable for them all. Satan wants us to think that we've sinned so much that now we can't stop ourselves from sinning no matter how hard we try, but this is false and Allah tells us the truth of it. Allah is not lying to us when he reveals that Satan has no control over us. It is Satan who lies and tricks us into thinking we are hopeless sinners that can never reform and be cured. Whatever your disease is it can be cured this instant 100% so that you never fall into that sin or vice again, just ask Allah to cure it and to protect you; by being his slave as a Muslim it protects you from all other forms of slavery. Humans don't need recovery programs, we need Islam. Satan has the same power over us as a fisherman has over fish. Satan just presents some sinful opportunities baiting us with a plan to hook us after we take the bait, so that we end up getting damaged, taken out of our natural state (or fitra) and then suffer for the rest of our life in sin until we are grilled over the hellfire for eternity. Why else do you think they use the name masturbate for satanic solo sex? Since the satanic bait becomes ur master, doing such a sinful action is to masturbate. Those are Satan's main moves, he casts bait and calls us just as a fisherman says "Here fishy fishy fishy". We don't have to obey Satan or take the bait no matter how tempting it may be or how pleasurable it may be to take a nibble or a bite. Even if we do make a mistake or many and get hooked many times we must fight back and not get taken off the path. How do you fight Satan? You seek refuge in God and follow the prophets. Obviously it's best not to get hooked at all, but Satan uses as many lines and nets as possible to catch us, so if we get hooked that doesn't mean it's game over, it just means we have to work harder when we're hooked. Satan is just a skilled fisherman who will be trying to catch us all our life. He has no authority over us, we can take his hooks out or sever his lines, nets or any other trap we fall into. Even if we swallow a sinful satanic hook and it hooks into our heart that doesn't mean we're done for, because the line can always be cut by God and the hook surgically/spiritually removed, but it does mean we might suffer some damage and hardship for a while as a result of swallowing Satan's hook or having bitten into it. Yet clever as he is Satan tries to make us think when caught that in order to get out of his net we should nibble then bite then swallow a baited hook or bigger hooks. Of course Satan never comes out and says to swallow he just tells us to look at the bait or listen to it or touch it or think about it, then a while later he persuades us to nibble and nibble and nibble until before we know it we swallowed the whole hook and it's inside us allowing Satan to pull our heart with great force. At that point some of us can feel something is wrong and we sincerely want to change lest we get barbequed in hell. Then Satan will pretend to tell us how to get his hook(s) out but in reality he simply offers painkillers which have bigger hooks in them as well to weaken our resistance and make his job easier, or he tells us to go into an electrified net which will numb us so we feel better, or that we're already hooked so we might as well keep eating the bait and have fun before we're grilled in hell. Therefore to repent we need both sincerity to change and knowledge from God as to how to correctly fix ourselves which we can learn only through God's divine revelation and prophets, with only the prophet of our time giving us the specific solutions we need in our lives. If we commit a sin, instead of repeating, or despairing, Godwilling we can turn that sin into sincere repentance and gain forgiveness so we aren't seared in the hellfire for that sinfulness. So we are going to have the sin and the cere or the searing one way or the other. It's just a matter of whether we will have the pious repentful sincerity, or the sinful searing in the hellfire suffering severely for eternity. Thus we must repent as soon as possible, because to delay repentance is a sin itself.

Adam pbuh the first man was made by Allah from clay. He became the worst man alive and then became the best man alive. Adam pbuh was the worst man alive because he committed the first sin and was the most sinful man for a period of time. Yet then Adam pbuh repented, was forgiven and subsequently was the best man alive since he was the only man to have repented for a period of time. Throughout both his worst moment and his best he was still of clay. This shows you, me and everyone else that humans can indeed be reformed and reformed and reformed just as clay changes forms. Some can be good forms and some can be bad forms. Some forms can look good but be bad and some forms can look bad but be good. Outside foreign forces may influence and shape us, but we can change and be molded into what Allah desires. Sure we may be in a bad state or even in the worse state we have ever been before in our lives but because we are human we can reform ourselves and our ways and our Creator will help us to be who he wants us to be and to do what he created us to do. As humans are made from clay it means worshipping prophets, governments, family, culture, any human system or even worshipping ourselves by being slaves to our desires is tantamount to worshipping an idol of clay. As clay we want what is good for us this is why Allah promises righteous believers Gardens in Paradise, because Gardens are great for clay to be in. While Allah threatens the disobedient and disbelievers with Hellfire because fire is terrible for clay. As clay our hearts can grow hard and hard clay is bad without much worth. The solution to hard clay is water, meaning sincere tears for the sake of Allah and the sweat of doing good deeds for the sake of our Maker alone. Also using water to perform wudu(ablution) removes one's sins and protects one from shaitan. Islam is the perfect mold for us, all we have to do is enter it wholeheartedly, stick to it and let Allah guide us while we are patient and grateful. Yet it goes both ways, as long as we are alive we can be misinformed, disfigured and transformed by Satan and our own flaws and lose our good form Allah has guided us to and suffer the tragedy of dying in a bad form. The bottom line is that as long as we are alive we can change for better or worse just as clay can. God-willing we will die in a better condition than we are currently in today. It's not about the past, what's done is done; what's important is what you do next. The test of life isn't over yet.

I didn't become a fully practicing Muslim on day 1 and I'm constantly learning new things about Islam on a daily basis that help me to better worship Allah and live correctly. Perfection in every aspect may be impossible, but my definition of perfection is to strive for perfection. As with the roads in this life the road to paradise has a speed limit, if you travel on it faster than you can handle you may crash and burn. Also if Satan persuades you to go too slow out of fear, or laziness, you will run out of fuel before you reach your destination and also crash and burn for a different reason. The most important thing is to be on the road to paradise and not on one of the many roads to hell. If you can't travel on it at the same speed as me, that's okay you don't have to, but you do have to get on the road to paradise. Just try to practice Islam as much as you can, that's all God wants you to do. God will never punish you for not doing something which God knows you can't do.

Don't mistake my high standards as the minimum standards for being a practicing Muslim, each individual has different minimums set by God based on their knowledge, ability, circumstances and many other variables. Sadly sometimes because I set the bar so high it can cause non-Muslims to misunderstand Islam thinking they have to reach a high level when being a Muslim is easy. I wrote this book so it could improve everybody, both elite Muslims and non-Muslims, whether they are the top Muslim scholar of all time or the worst kafir of all. So if you are a non-Muslim thinking Islam is super hard or too hard for you, then don't, please understand I've tried to write a book that will turn it's readers into Muslim heroes. You could become one, try making them, do both, or do otherwise. To become a Muslim though you just need a sincere shahada knowing what it means in word and the signficance of it's meaning with an intention to fulfill it as best you can. A shahada is the minimum criteria needed to pass the test of life and enter paradise. To be a Muslim hero you need extra stuff the "practicing Muslim" doesn't have/do. You don't have to be a Muslim hero if you don't want to, but why not try? Truly if you sincerely ask God to help you and put in some effort then God can help you become a Muslim hero. Again God defines Muslim heroes, not people, there might be some super-Muslim doing all kinds of great deeds but another person who struggles to do a few mandatory deeds could well be vastly superior to the Muslim who everyone else thinks is the hero of the Muslim world. There are many different types of people who are Muslim heroes. Based on my knowledge of myself I don't think I'm one of them, but I hope you or someone who reads this or is indirectly influenced by it can become one so I may benefit for whatever role I played in aiding their theological victories Godwilling. Yet even then aid only comes from Allah, I just hope to be a slave that Allah uses to improve his other slaves. Doctors get ill too, but just because they may be sick doesn't mean that they quit advising others because of being unhealthy themselves. Sometimes after committing a sin I end up condemning that sin or sins to someone else, which is hypocritical but in reality I may not have done so if I wasn't trying to condemn the sins I was guilty of in order to help myself repent. Whereas by me hypocritically remorsefully condemning what I'm guilty of to others might just be exactly what they needed to hear and God may have used my speech at that moment to stop someone else from sinning. Likewise it may be that when I get good advice, the other person may have only done that to recompense for their sins. Hence while God hates our sins, the effects of our sins or rather our repentance can lead us to help each other stop doing sins. This doesn't mean you should sin thinking it's okay, because Satan will try to tell people that, but it does mean that even if you are sinful and hypocritical one still must talk the talk because God wants us to, even though we may not practice what we preach. Though God knows all our sins before we do them we are still fully responsible for them, and ours sins displease God despite his foreknowledge of them. God simply knows the mistakes we will make before they happen, they are still mistakes. Those who think God knowing our sins before we do them somehow means they aren't sinful or that God is responsible are believing exactly what Satan believed and said when Satan blamed God for his sins. It's not God's fault we sin, it's our fault and all our sins are wrong, however sometimes the long-term consequences of our sins can result in great things such as life-changing improvements so this is why God allows some sins to occur. God hates our sins but can love the way we repent from sins. What I'm saying is don't do any sins but if/when you do then don't despair or stop doing good deeds just because you messed up a little (or a lot). Never think you gotta be perfect to preach prophetically. Don't think for a second that I'm some perfect Muslim hero who doesn't do anything wrong. Allah knows my sins, you don't. Trust me you can't write a book like this without having done many dastardly sins in your lifetime. The sins didn't help me to write at all, they made it harder, it's only the attempts at repentance that help and motivate one to do good; just to make up for all the evil which one does. If you think this book is long, my personal book of sins which I've committed is much longer. While the list of good sincere deeds I've done may not even exist and frequently gets shorter and shorter. I've read this book many times before you did and should read it many times after you do because I need to be advised and reminded continuously. The reader me wishes I could be half as good as how the author me seems to be. I know I condemned fiction before but in reality my autobiography gives off a fictional impression, this isn't my "full story" and its highly polished. Nobody ever shares the full truth of who they really are, because we even fool ourselves for self-esteem reasons. The only non-fictional autobiography is our book of deeds. You and I will never be 100% perfect, but that's no reason not to try. The goal isn't for us to be perfect, the goal God set for us is to be like the prophets. In order for you to obtain the love of Allah, his friendship and paradise you have to die trying. If you don't even try to obey the divine law, then it's disrespectful to the Creator of us all. Never stop doing good deeds no matter how sinful you are. <u>It is sinful to have no fear when doing sins and then have such fear doing good actions that you fail to do them. How dare you be fearless when doing sins and then have fear when doing something good that God commands/wants?</u> Such a satanic fear is something to fear afflicting us. The more good deeds you do the less you will fear doing them and the more sins you do the less you will fear doing those. While the more sins you do the more you will fear doing good deeds, and the more good deeds you do the more you will fear doing sins. Thus stop your sins and increase your good deeds, but even if you struggle to stop sinning always try to do more good deeds because eventually they will cure you Godwilling. We may be hypocrites but a sinful hypocrite who does good deeds is far better than the one who doesn't. A single good deed can give God an excuse to forgive all sins. Good deeds are more precious than time itself, always do good. Even if you have to die to do a good deed it's worth it. Whereas if you have to die in the effort of avoiding sin, that is worth dying for. Live/Die doing good sincerely for God's sake, without fear.

  A Muslim does not have "bad days" because for the Muslim everyday is a good day. Every day we have a chance to worship, repent and please our Creator is a good day because we can still do good deeds. Every day is a good opportunity we shouldn't waste, especially when so many have already died who wish they could have the opportunities we now have. Also by not doing bad deeds we get good credit as well. When a difficulty or hardship comes their way, the Muslim is patient, praises Allah and is grateful, never bitter or in despair. The prophets pbut were tested with the hardest tests mankind has ever faced and Allah loves them the most. Being tested is a sign that Allah loves you. On the other hand it could also be preemptory punishment for disbelievers when hardships come their way, or an opportunity sent for them to change, or a way for them to be guided. Getting a flat tire when traveling on the road to hell is a good thing because it stops your sinful progression. We are tested so it can be made clear who is wicked and who is good, so that no one will be able to make excuses and think Allah has treated people unjustly on the Day of Judgment. The harder the test the greater the reward for passing. The more tests one passes the higher the level in paradise one will have, just like climbing a steep mountain, it's easy at the bottom. The road to paradise is steep, not cheap. If you become Muslim don't expect life to be easy ever after, do not think you will simply say, "*I believe*" and then will be left alone without being tested. Allah has promised mankind that they will be tested, so whether we want it or not we are going to get it. You might as well get rewarded for the suffering by enduring it as a patient grateful believer. While our purpose in life is to be constantly tested, there is Satan who has made it his goal to try to make us fail. Although Allah has promised that we will never be burdened with something greater than we can bear, that includes addictions. So if you got a burden, whatever it is, you can handle it. Maybe you can't handle it too well at this minute, but that's why Allah allows you to be burdened because Allah wants to help you out. You see the reason Allah says people are never given a burden that's greater than they can bear is because they always have Allah to help them out and lighten the burden for them. If we would just ask as a devout slave and do what's needed for Allah's friendship we will get that help. Asking isn't enough, action is commanded as well because Allah doesn't want to pamper us and turn into our slave. We are the slave and Allah is the master, as the slave we don't ask and wait for help from the master because that's not how a master operates. A master gives the slave the tools first then the advice then maybe more tools and then after the slave does all they can possibly do the master helps them finish. The means we take to get a cure are not the cure themselves, because 2 people can have identical conditions, make identical requests and take identical actions but one gets cured and the other doesn't. The cure is with Allah alone. Our battles are not won by our worldly weapons, strategy, support, efforts or experience. The outcome rests with God. To trust in the means is to not trust in God. The only reason we use means to an end is because God commands it, it's not because they can actually help us achieve our goal. It might appear that way to the ignorant but that's not the reality. The means we take are just another test to see that when God helps us after taking actions are we going to think our actions had something to do with success? Or will we give our Creator 100% of the credit? This applies to all actions, even prayer. Prayer itself is not a means to success, it can only lead to success if our Creator makes it be successful. Many people pray to no avail, many do good deeds but go to hell. So it's important to remember your goal is to play a role as a slave, your action doesn't truly effect the outcome Allah just wants you to do good deeds and live a certain way to prove your commitment. Basically the Creator wants to know if you will work hard as he commands even when you know it won't determine the outcome, or will you work hard as he commands and then think your efforts had something to do with your results. If you do the good deeds and avoid the evil God will cause results and even may give you success, but that degree of success will be different depending on why you did what you did. Thus it comes down to true sincerity. When you do something, whatever it is whether it's eating, sleeping etc, are you doing it to please God, or come closer to God, or for yourself? If for yourself then that's selfish and wrong to do. Yet in the Quran Allah says to save yourself from the hellfire? But why should we save ourself from the hellfire? Because it hurts? NO. Because Allah said so that's why. Why do we do good deeds and strive for paradise? For eternal pleasure? Because Allah says we'll enjoy it? NO. Because Allah said to do that and he's knows what's best for us. We are supposed to just enjoy doing what our Creator wants us to do. That's how we were designed. We shouldn't enjoy paradise because it's fun, we should enjoy it because it makes God happy if we enjoy it. Thus even if God wanted us to be in hellfire, we should enjoy that, if it's what God wanted. However God doesn't want anyone to be in hellfire, yet he is just, so people will be there forever and it will make God even more upset with them that they are there because it displeases God to punish his creation. But rules are rules so God will do so if we don't follow the rules which have been given to us. The rules are there, what's truth and falsehood are made clear, we've been taught right from wrong by the prophets and given our one time try on the test of life. A main part of that test is living it correctly, avoiding errors and fixing our mistakes before we die. However when living this test the reason why we try to pass and do our best is part of that test. Some get good grades to please their parents, some to please themselves, some because good grades are better than bad grades, some because they want the reward whereas some simply try to get good grades to please the one who gave them the test. We should be of those who pass our test of life with this singular purpose of passing because the test giver wants us to. What is done with us after that we just hope it is what pleases our Creator. God will keep his promise of paradise to those who pass but even if theoretically he didn't we shouldn't care because we should want what God wants. Hate and Fear to be in hell because God wants you to feel that way. Love and Desire Paradise because God wants you to. Live for God and Die for God as a slave, the only reason we should try to be God's friend is because God tells us to do so.

Try to always be aware that every second of every day you are being tested and that Satan is there trying to make you fail every single test. Satan is patient too and has short term, mid-term and long term plots and has more plans than there are letters in all the alphabets. Satan uses sneakier strategies and more dangerous weapons as we develop so we can never let our guard down. Time is running out, soon we will no longer be tested and will receive the results of whether we passed or failed. Remember we are in a lifelong competition and Satan won't quit. God-willing we shall pass and our enemy Satan will fail. God-willing I will be someone who follows my own advice. May Allah protect us all from disbelief, hypocrisy and every type of sin. God tells us that Satan is our enemy and commands us to take him as our enemy. Satan will disavow us in the afterlife so why wait? Let's disavow him in this life and reject his offer of friendship so that we can be God's friend instead. God wants you to be his friend. It's the toughest type friendship of all to maintain and billions will try to break it up, ourselves included, but it's the best type of friendship to live with and die with. We're just trying our best, it's all we can do. Every time a Muslim prays we ask Allah to: "*guide us to the straight path, the path of those who are blessed, not the path of those who have earned your wrath nor of those who have gone astray*". Everyone of us needs constant guidance more and more, should that guidance leave us then surely we would go astray and become evildoers. I can't guide anyone, trust me I've tried and tried and tried and tried and tried, I need guidance myself. It's easy to preach, it's harder to practice, God-willing preaching will help me practice. If Allah doesn't guide me I'd be demonic. Truly if Allah doesn't protect me every second from my evil intentions and evil actions I'd be the most evil hypocritical person of all time. Just take the people of Moses pbuh as an example, Moses pbuh left them for only 40 days and they ended up worshipping a golden calf despite all their prior guidance, good deeds and struggles to believe in the face of severe persecution. They believed through years of hardship but disbelieved in less than 40 days after their prophet left them to go get more guidance from God for them. Many books exist where those who read it are better than the one who wrote it. Even if theoretically someone writes a good book that does not mean they're a good person, writing a good book doesn't even mean they got credit for doing a good deed. Our good deeds will be weighed, not counted. One sincere great deed can easily outweigh a lifetime's worth of good deeds. While one bad deed can destroy a lifetime of great deeds. Whereas I know for a fact that every letter written in this book is not sincerely written for the sake of God, some letters are written to be funny, or vent emotions, promote my personal views, out of arrogance and other reasons. It's even a plausible possibility that I might not have even written this book if I had a therapist, as some of what I've written seems more appropriate to tell a therapist than a reader, but God is the best therapist of all. Likewise since addicts tend to crave attention and be egotistical, as someone previously afflicted with addictions (or currently since most addicts hide and deny their addictions or are addicted to being addicticted) this entire book could realistically be an unhealthy cry for attention to fuel an extravagant ego. That prior sentence itself isn't sincere, even though that's the type of stuff a sincere person would say or think that doesn't mean it's sincerely for God's sake. Neither is that last sentance nor this one 100% sincere either. <u>Do not confuse honesty for sincerity or piety</u>. Many arrogant egotistical people know how to sound and speak humbly and sincerely and I know how to make you think I'm sincere even if I'm not. Which is exactly what someone who wants people to think they are sincere would say, just as they'd write this sentence as well. All you have to do is tell people you aren't sincere and they think you are and then if you say "No really I'm not." they think "Now I know he really is." so if I were really good at being insincere I'd try to make you think I was by writing the stuff I've just written, including this because "What kind of insincere person would go this deep into sincerity unless they were sincere?" My kind would and does all the time, it's part of the whole act. In summary it is impossible to tell whether someone is sincere for the sake of God in this life. The more I try to explain this or cite my own insincerity the more sincere you'd think I was, the same applies if I were to simply drop the debate over it. Someone talking the talk doesn't mean God is giving them points for it. Likewise walking the walk doesn't mean God will necessarily reward the walker. Sometimes the mute and lame can get more rewards from God than the talker/walker. At the end of the day, I either publish the book or I don't. I'm not 100% sincere throughout this with every letter that was written, but does that mean I shouldn't publish the book at all because it's not 100% sincerely for God's sake? What would God prefer and what would Satan prefer? Some of the things I've written are sinful insincere and hypocritical but the reason to inform others about Islam is to fulfill the duty of conveying the message so one isn't blameworthy and to get rewarded for doing so God-willing, it's Allah who determines the results. The prophets finished their jobs and taught us the message from God. Our job is to implement what they taught us and to pass it on. Even if we don't implement the prophetic religion, we still are obligated to teach it to others, personal level of practice aside. Concealing knowledge is a sinful crime which many knowledgable people are guilty of. Whether I'm sincere or do what I say others should do, has nothing to do with whether I write what I write or publish it. Hypocrites should actually preach more than sincere people because it will help them be less hypocritical, God-willing. Honestly I don't follow all the stuff I enjoin in this book, I have lots of flaws and my real self wishes I could be like the author but currently I'm not. Publishing can motivate me to take the advice therein more sincerely and implement it by putting extra pressure to do what I know and say I should do. My book hopefully makes me a better person by writing and reading it. If I don't get better from writing or reading this then what is the point? Why write for the sake of someone other than God or for improving your relationship with God? My personal book of deeds may suck but if this one is good or beneficial then my personal book of deeds may improve. Likewise God uses hypocrites to do his will and guides many people through the words and deeds of wicked hypocrites. Sometimes God will use a sinful insincere hypocrite whom he will punish eternally in hellfire as a sign for someone else to believe in and practice Islam whom he will reward forever. Muhammad pbuh said Allah will spread Islam to many via the efforts of wicked hypocritical Muslim preachers who will burn in the hellfire forever while those they preach to will go to paradise forever if they follow the advice. I may or may not be the former but Godwilling you will be the latter. Whoever Allah guides no one can lead astray and whoever Allah allows to go astray no one can guide. Truly only Allah can guide someone, not even Abraham, Moses, Jesus or Muhammad pbut could guide people they cared about and they were prophets with miracles and revelation. If they couldn't guide someone then I definitely can't, if you are guided then the guidance is from Allah and Allah alone. Truly it has nothing to do with what I wrote, other people have read what I wrote and heard what I say and they turn away in arrogance and bigotry. Yet the words they've heard and read are the same as what you've read, the difference is Allah didn't choose to guide them because they were not sincere at that time. Unfortunately sincerity is not constant, you may be sincere one second and an arrogant hypocrite the next. Sincere deeds can become insincere deeds long after they are done. Those who can be consistently sincere are those who are truly blessed beyond measure. Being guided yesterday doesn't mean you will be upon guidance tomorrow, and being sincere one minute doesn't mean your sincerity will last for even a full 60 seconds. Thus sincerity in life is one of the best gifts God can give you and without having it one can not enter paradise. Thus always ask God for sincerity, knowledge to go with it and distinguish right from wrong and the ability to do what is right and avoid all that is wrong. But do you know what the best thing to ask God for is? It is to sincerely ask God alone for God to help you to worship God. While most importantly ask God for the gift of dying in such a state. To die in such a state one needs the knowledge along with the sincere desire. But what is "knowledge"? Knowledge is applied wisdom, not just useful important information. Information only gives you the possibility of action. Knowing things is just potential. Knowledge is only static information if it's not put to use. But applied knowledge turns that potential possibility into your reality. Knowledge does not exist to be merely learned but applied to oneself and spread to others. And which people have that knowledge if you seek it? The scholars, but who is a scholar? The ones with degrees, certificates and titles? No. In Islam the scholar is not the one who knows lots of information. The Muslim scholar is the one who knows Islam and acts upon what they know with sincerity, and is classified as a scholar by the other scholars. How do we get knowledge? First we make dua for the sincerity and ability. Then Allah will test us with knowledge and in the afterlife Allah will ask us what we did with the gift of knowledge we asked for once Allah bestowed it upon us. All knowledge is either for you or against you. So when we consistently ask for guidance and knowledge, we must ask for the sincerity and ability or else that knowledge could count against us. Also don't forget to be patient, Sabr(patience) is mentioned 90 times in the Quran because it is so important. Although if asking for patience one should ask for safety along with it because patience can only be a reaction to difficulties, gratitude is a reaction to bounties, but to be patient with the bounties and grateful for the difficulties is an elite type of faith. Likewise one shouldn't be selfish, one could be charitable by asking that everyone is given these gifts. Since ignorance is dangerous the risky responsibility of knowledge must be born. May Allah help us with it. You can't pass the test of life without knowledge. Yet knowledge without sincerity makes a sinner more sinful. Being smart filled with extensive religious knowledge doesn't mean you will go to paradise. You could, or you could end up like the ones mentioned in the famous hadith found in Sahih Bukhari, Sahih Muslim and elsewhere wherein Usama bin Zaid reported that he heard Muhammad pbuh say: "*A man will be brought on the Day of Resurrection and thrown into the Fire. His intestines will be hanging out, spilling onto the ground, and he will go around like a donkey goes around a millstone. The inhabitants of the Fire will gather around him and say:* "O so and so! What is your affair? Didn't you used to order us to do good deeds and forbid us from doing bad deeds?" He will reply, "Yes I used to order you to do good deeds, but I did not do them myself, and I used to forbid you from doing bad deeds, yet I used to do them myself". Great preachers of the true prophetic religion go to hell too, if they don't sincerely practice, and none will ever know who is sincere until God announces it to all of us.

    Unlike all other religions, when accepting Islam and becoming a Muslim you only become qualified to enter paradise. It's not as if one becomes Muslim then they are done, get a ticket to paradise and don't have to worry about the hellfire anymore. Because all of us sin we also qualify to be punished if Allah doesn't forgive us. Being a Muslim qualifies one to be forgiven if you repent, while dying upon any other religion besides Islam disqualifies one from forgiveness no matter how much they repent or how many good deeds they may do. Becoming a Muslim is not a guarrantee of paradise because one could become a Muslim and then die upon a religion other than Islam, which would make them worse than those disbelievers who never became Muslim. Or a Muslim could die as a hypocrite, whereas the Muslim hypocrites are in a lower position in the hellfire than the disbelievers, for faking it and not sincerely acting upon the knowledge which Allah blessed them with. Becoming a Muslim only qualifies one for paradise, but if a person is sincere and practices Islam in the right prophetic manner wholeheartedly to the best of their abilities and dies in such a state as a Muslim, then paradise will await them guaranteed. However if someone learns about Islam and rejects it after knowing what it is about and they die in that condition, then there is absolutely no way they will ever be taken out of the hellfire, they will never have the privilege of seeing their Creator and such a person will remain in miserable torment forever without end, despite their wishes and pleas to be ended and obliterated. May Allah help us to die as sincere grateful obedient believers and grant us the worldly benefits and eternal rewards they are entitled to and protect us from disbelief, hypocrisy, despair, sin, religious innovations, ignorance, arrogance and the consequences thereof.

Sincere repentance means you don't do that sin again. Repentance is not something where you just cry your eyes out and profusely apologize to God and promise and promise and promise not to do X sin ever again. True sincere repentance is a lifelong struggle, and this is why one typically only knows whether they are forgiven by God when they die. Repentance is a form of Jihad. True repentance doesn't only mean you don't do that sin anymore, it means you don't even want to do that sin anymore and no longer desire to do it. Acknowlegment of the sin, Regret of the sin, Apologizing to God and asking forgiveness for the sin is just 3/4 parts of repentance. Now there is no such thing as 75% forgiveness. Eventually when all is settled you are either forgiven 100% or 0%. Even if you are a believer, if you only do those 3 things when you repent then you will not be forgiven for your sins. The 4th part of promising never to do those sins again is a major determining factor as to whether one will be forgiven. The Quran teaches that those who believe AND do good deeds will be forgiven. It doesn't say those who believe and say sorry will be forgiven. It teaches those who <u>believe</u>, <u>repent</u> <u>and do good deeds</u> will be forgiven. So the key to repentance is keeping your promise as best as possible to not do those sins again. Since if you really do know X is wrong, why would you do it? If you really regret doing X in the past would you do it again? If you really regret a sin then how could you ever desire to do it again? This is why an addict is not someone who has fully repented, an addict could be forgiven but for an addict to still desire the sin indicates their repentance is not fully completed. If you told God you were sincerely sorry for X sin why would you do it again? The reason is because we are humans and as such we are not always sincere. Many think repentance just means not doing the sin again but true repentance involves not even having that sinful desire. We might be sincerely sorry and sincerely repent soon after committing the sin yet some minutes, days, weeks, months, years or decades later we might lose that sincerity and do X sin again or desire to do X sin again. Simply to have a desire to do a particular sin again after repenting is a sign of an insincere repentance. Thus we should repent not just from our deeds but our sinful desires and our lack of repenance as well as our laxity in repenting after sinning. For example if you commit X sin and then an hour later you repent, that is 2 sins there. First you did X sin and then you did another sin by waiting a whole hour to repent. Yet how many of us repent for laziness in repenting? This is how Satan traps many people, because while we can get forgiven for sins we commit if we repent we have to repent from doing them. To delay repentance is a sin which many of us rarely consider major, regret, apologize for or avoid and truly repent from. If you are doing X sin then repent immediately, even if you do X repent do X again and repent and do X over and over in a very short period of time, you'd be half as sinful if you repented for X sin immediately after doing it rather than repenting later. Hence sinful as you may be you can be 50% less sinful just by repenting sooner than you currently do. If you mess up and do a sin then do the repentance as soon as possible, don't mess up the repentance as well because the sin in delaying repentance could result in a punishment greater than the punishment you'd get for X sin you are repenting from doing.

These are the games Satan plays where people think they're doing good but remain sinful and unrepentant by not repenting for their flaws, insincerity and delay in repenting. Thus when many repent from X sin they should really do 2 types of repentance, one for X sin and another for their poor repentance. Those who "repent" rarely do it enough or sincerely and this is why we persist in committing the same sins consistently, because our "repentance" has lots of problems with it. We must ask forgiveness for the faults we have in our laxity in asking for forgiveness. We might be forgiven for the sins we repent from but end up getting punished for making a lousy delayed repentance. Satan not only tries to get us to sin, but also wants to make our repentance insincere, delayed, deficient and incomplete. Such is the test of life, just as a test taker can always change their answers until the test is over, we can always have our bad deeds turn into good deeds or vice versa. We don't just want to give the correct answers to our test of life but want complete credit for our correct answers and to correct our mistakes fully in the best manner. Sincere repentance consists of a lifelong attitude and lifelong action. This is why God commands us to not just believe but to do good deeds as well in abundance, because God knows that the only way for us to stop doing bad sins is if we use our time, energy etc to do the good deeds instead. The point is our test is not over yet, God has deliberately given us this moment to continue taking the test. We have this moment to do better before our time is gone and our test score becomes permanent for all eternity. Whatever your score on the test of life is at this moment, it is not your final score. The stakes are high, the time is nearly over. What are you currently doing to do better on your test? What will you do tomorrow to do better on your test of life? Always remember that one day you will plan to do better tomorrow and time will be up and you will die with whatever score you have at that moment. Soon your current score on the test of life and your current relationship with God will be your eternal score and your eternal relationship with God. Are you satisfied to die this second and have your current relationship with God be the same for all eternity? If you get another second to live then it means God wants you to have a better score on the test of life and a better relationship than the one you have now. It doesn't matter whether you think you are doing good or if you are doing so bad you just wish it were over, you don't know what your score is at this moment and you don't know whether it will improve or get worse should your life be extended. Yet whoever you are, God wants you to be better. So believe, repent and do good deeds, repeatedly until death. Fear the worst, hope for the best, follow the prophets and ask God for true success. At one time or another we've both been sinners, but Godwilling we can both die as sincere believers. Every time you've sinned that is a sign from God that you have something that you should fix in your life and change, where if you do so then you've learned and improved. Being a human is a very unique experience, humans are special creatures who are made to live a life where they never stop improving their relationship with their Creator and Master. Your whole life amounts to answering 3 questions in the grave. If you don't answer correctly you lose the test of life. God has told us the answers and told us why to answer and how we will be able to answer the way God desires us to. The key is to live the right answers for the right reasons in this test of life. Of all who are asked the 3 questions in the grave, the few who pass are those whom when the questions are asked they are only asked because God has promised they'd be asked. In reality the 3 questions are rhetorical. Even though the questions will be verbally responded to, our lifetime of actions will speak a far louder answer than our words. The believer is also asked the 3 questions in their grave by the angels Munkar and Nakir, "***Who is your Lord? What religion did you practice? Who is the man that was sent to you?***" After the believer correctly answers each question correctly they will be asked a 4th, "***How do you know this?***" This 4th question will only be asked to a believer and only true believers will be able to answer it correctly and honestly with confidence saying: "*I read Allah's book, believed in it, obeyed it and applied it.*" Then Allah will call out: "***My slave has spoken the truth, so prepare for him a bed from Paradise and clothe him from Paradise, and open for him a gate to Paradise.***" Then the believer will smell a sweet fragrance better than anything they ever smelled before, their grave will be filled with light and made wide as far as they can see. The good deeds of the believer will come to them in the grave in the form of a beautiful person with fine clothes and a sweet smell. Then they will ask Allah to hasten the Day of Resurrection/Judgement with anticipation for the rewards awaiting them. Will you be able to answer the questions in the grave correctly and quickly with confidence and sincerity? You could be asked these questions in the grave today. Perhaps within the hour. Will you pass the test?

WHY DOESN'T GOD HELP EVERYONE TO BELIEVE IN ALL THE RIGHT THINGS?

Many people are befuddled with the reason why everyone doesn't believe in the same religion if they were all made by the same God if God wants everyone to believe the same thing and follow the same religion. Those who are religiously astute will note that one reason why people don't all agree upon the same true religion is because of freewill. Which when combined with Satan, human desires and stupidity/arrogance can explain why some people don't believe in the true religion. They will answer that God allows disbelief because if God forced everyone to believe in the truth then it wouldn't be voluntary or sincere. This is true but it doesn't satisfy the skeptic disbeliever who thinks that the existance of a different opinion means there is no absolute truth of which all the other opinions are inferior and hateworthy in comparison to. They are the types who struggle to accept the idea that only 1 religion can be true because they believe in the religion of equality and that everyone is equally cared about by God because all of us were created by God. Yet that notion is false because God created other things too, but none would say God cares as much about trees, water, worms, rocks, birds, and fish equally as he cares about humans. So all creatures have individual relationships with God that determines how God views and feels towards them. Sometimes God can love animals more than humans as in the case of Noah pbuh or God can care more about humans than animals by the fact that we can eat animals while few animals eat us. The same applies to us eating plants with few plants eating us as a sign of God caring more for some creatures than others in some respects. Yet eating in itself doesn't prove God's love or care as being greater because if it did then microbes would be the most loved creatures since they eat us and most dead things. Also since worms eat humans, then based on the doctrine of "food chain love" we'd assume God loved worms more than us, but the food chain doesn't indicate who or what God cares most about. Of course some may claim that worms only eat humans after they are dead, but the same can be said of most animals which humans eat. While worms do indeed eat live humans too, as in the case of intestinal worms and many other types that can eat one's brain or cause blindness. So being the top of the food chain doesn't mean that God values you more than the food you eat. God could love what one eats more than he does the one doing the eating. Afterall what sin have the plants and animals who get eaten ever done? In comparison what sins have the ones eating the plants and animals done? Although this doesn't mean plants and animals are by default better than sinners, because God loves and forgives those sinners who repent sincerely in the prophetic manner. So being a sinner doesn't mean God cares more about what you are eating for dinner than he does you, but it could depending on the sinner and the circumstances. Thus all humans who eat things are not equal, some eaters are valued less by God than the food which they eat. Afterall no animals or plants will burn in hell, yet in this world they will get eaten by people who will dwell in hell forever. However despite this reality humans have rights that allow them a priority over animals and plants in many aspects, contrary to what misanthropists satanically suppose. Yet the disbeliever who doesn't believe in the notion of disbelievers, unless they count atheists, may then think that God loves all humans equally since we are the same species. This is disproven by the example of Noah's people and the natural feelings we ourselves have for other humans in that we don't all think of or love each other the same when we are the same species. This is because our dispositions towards people tend to be based on what those people believe, say and do, then in response to their beliefs, statements and actions we rate them accordingly in comparison with everyone else we know of. Even amongst ourselves there are no 2 people whom we care about with exactly identical amounts of love or hate whatever the case may be. There is someone you love more than all the rest and someone you hate more than all the rest, even though both are humans. Thus God is no different and does not love all equally nor hate all equally because humans are not equal. The idea of human equality is simply a false religion. As is human superiority, lets not forget there are the species of creatures called Jinn and the species called Angels. The religious belief of human equality leads those who believe in it to disbelieve in the very idea of there being such a thing as a false religion, since they want God to care about everyone equally; mainly because they hate the idea that God could care about someone else more than them. Particularly someone alive today, especially someone they think is inferior to themselves. They don't like the fact that God has favoritism based on every individual's faith and piety. So to avoid saying *"God doesn't like anyone on earth more than me."* they just say God loves everybody equally. But what they really mean and believe and feel is that nobody else is closer to God than they are because they think they are the greatest person on earth today. Yet the idea of human equality as regards what God thinks and feels about humans is too easy of an idea to refute since it is illogical. Plus we must remember the main reason they have this attitude is because they don't want to change their religion and abandon the false faith they are upon. So their end goal is to be left alone upon whatever wrong religion they are upon living the sinful life they are living and to have you shutup and stop making them feel wrong or bad due to their religion or sinful lifestyle. Basically they feel insecure that God might not like them or hate them for who they are. However insecurity about your relationship with God is necessary to have the correct healthy relationship with God as befits him as God and you as his creation. If you don't feel your relationship with God is vulnerable and there is a chance of rejection due to your beliefs or actions then you can never truly feel love from God. Since to feel true love there must be the possibility of there being no love. This is the problem with Christianity and Judaism, they have no sense of vulnerability with their relationship with God. Jews think God loves them due to their race and Christians think God loves them so much automatically that he died for them or sent a son of his to die for them. Thus both the Jews and Christians are spiritually immature and have a "Baby Love" selfish attitude with God where they expect God to love them and only wonder about how much God loves them rather than if. Truly Judaism and Christianity fundamentally teach that God loves you and everyone by default and it's only a question of how much do you want God to love you, thus they do good and avoid evil only to get more love never to avoid/decrease God's hatred. It is because of this doctrine of special unconditional love as taught by Judaism and Christianity combining with the doctrines of freedom of belief and human equality along with arrogance and Satanic influences that cause people to think that God doesn't love only the people of 1 religion while hating all the rest and that if God did then everyone would agree. This belief is also similar to what ancient pagans believed about religion. Today people took this notion and mixed it with freedom and equality, so they think God has to distribute his love for people equally and that excercising freedom cannot cause God to stop loving or start hating them. This is because the American drafters of the "Declaration of Independence" taught: *"God created mankind equal and all have the God-given right to life, liberty and the pursuit of happiness (freedom)"* and people believe what these prophets of Americanism said about God making everyone equal and giving them these rights such as *"the right to do what makes you happy and believe what you want"*. Therefore when confronted with the prophetic doctrine that God only loves Muslims and hates all non-Muslims they postulate an emergency Satanic response saying *"If God wanted everyone to believe the same thing then why don't we?"* To which the standard refutation is because of freewill, which means people can choose to disbelieve and be wrong because they are stupid and influenced by Satan or prefer falsehood and evil to truth and good. However they tend not to like this response and they have a good reason to reject the freewill refutation. Because even though God can't force people to believe, he could help everyone to all agree if he wanted to. They are correct on that point and freewill alone cannot refute that point. So this doctrine of multiple religions meaning God must like them all is totally nonsense, that exists because people feel entitled to be loved by God just because they were created. Arrogance of humans leads them to think we are equal and that God should treat us all equal as well. However the mere existance of different opinions does not mean a single one of those opinions has any validity whatsoever, especially when it comes to religion. Nor does a difference of opinion mean all are invalid either, which is the 2nd emergency excuse in that they'll say *"Either all of the religions are right and acceptable to God or everybody on earth is wrong."* Yet to think that is to be an intellectual absolutist of the extremist variety, which again is due to a "pro-equality complex" where either everyone is right or everyone is wrong because they can't comprehend that people are not equal to each other or that God has favoritistic traits. It's very simple to understand that only 1 religion is correct, that's what every prophet taught. So then why doesn't God help people so that everyone chooses to believe in and practice the correct religion? Afterall Satan is our enemy so what chance do we have if God doesn't guide everybody? Is it not unfair for God not to guide everyone if God also created Satan too? First of all God does help everyone to see Islam is true and all the other faiths are false, but some don't recongnize the help and/or ignore the signs they get. They think if religious diversity is confusing to them and the majority are all on different religions, then God must not have a special policy towards 1 faith and it's adherents over others, or else he'd help everyone to join the right religion. Essentially they have a democratic attitude in that only a majority opinion can declare something to be right. They think this because they think God loves everyone or at least the majority, but they do have a point even though their notion of God loving all or all equally or the majority is false. The correct question people who doubt 1 faith having a "monopoly on salvation" should ask is, *"Why doesn't God help everyone believe in and practice the right religion?"* That is the correct question to ask. If they want to really know they have to ask the right question first if they really want to learn answers. Most don't ask this question though because they don't really want an answer but are asking sacarstically thinking they already know and have the answer. The freewill refutation doesn't work if they ask the correct question because its a question of God giving direct guidance so it becomes extremely easy for all to believe, to the point that all do believe because God makes everyone know how evil and wrong all the false religions are and how true and right the one correct religion is. Afterall doesn't God want everyone to believe in the true religion? Well the answer is simply no. God doesn't want everyone to believe in the correct religion because if he did then we all would. So you really do have to honest and admit that, *"Yes God could guide everybody to believe in the 1 true religion, but God just doesn't want to."* That's right, it's true, God does not want every human to be sinless and worship him. Do you know why? Because God already has creatures who do 100% what God wants them to do. They are called angels. Every angel believes in the right thing, does the right thing and never sins. So those who insist God could make everyone believe and stop us from doing evil if he wanted to are right, God could, but he doesn't want to because he already has angels to be like that so why create a repeat species of angels? Is there some rule that says God can only create angels and no other type of creature? Why do humans think God can only create angels or it's unfair? God is creative and doesn't want to only create angels, God wants plants, animals, humans, devils, etc because it displays his immense power and to truly understand why you would need the knowledge of God anyways. Yet lets consider some attributes of God such as being forgiving and merciful. Now if nobody ever disobeyed God then how could God be forgiving if he never forgave anybody for doing wrong? God could not be forgiving if nobody ever sinned so God could forgive them. God is also the most severe in punishment, but if God never punished anybody how could he be the most severe in punishment? Basically for God to be God as God has defined himself then God has to act accordingly and since God is merciful there must be opportunities to display that mercy, so by us humans existing and repenting it allows God to be merciful and forgive, likewise humans existing and not repenting from disbelief or sins shows God as forbearing and then as just when God finally does punish the guilty ones. So the existance of human freewill shows the depth and complexity of God, because if only angels existed that would be a very bland boring one dimensional under-developed God. Such a "god" would have an ungodly personality/character that would be emotionally inferior to us. For such a "god" to exist would be impossible because by definition the Creator must be more complex than its creation, so God could never give us such a wide range of attributes or characteristics if God was such a undeveloped entity that was less complex than its creatures. Emotionally God must be more complex than us, but God couldn't be if everyone believed and obeyed. If God created only angels or 100% obedient beings and nothing else then that would be an uncreative and nearly insecure God rather than the full God we have which can create such a diverse universe and have such a wide range of various treatments for the things within it. God allows falsehood to exist so God can prove he and his truth destroys all falsehood, God could say it but to prove it is a different matter. God proves all that he lets us know about himself, God isn't "just talk". Similarily since God is the one who guides, some creatures need to be misguided in order for God to guide them. Also if all were guided by God then that guidance wouldn't be anything special since it would be generic and guidance would practically be expected as if we "deserve to be guided". Whereas that's basically the issue with the confused people who can't understand religious diversity failing to undermine the fact that one religion has exclusivity of the truth. These types of people expect that all humans "deserve" to know what is true and false, right and wrong, before they die. They think we "*deserve to go to paradise, just because we are human*" and that "*nobody can ever deserve to go to hell because we are human and can never be that bad*". If you ask them point-blank this is what they believe, that everyone deserves to go to paradise and they think it's unfair for God to not guide those he chooses not to guide. Or they try to blame their badness on God and say it's God's fault they are bad so therefore it's unfair for them to be punished because of their decisions. Basically they think freewill is unfair, but many also think "freedom" is a "right", so they actually just believe that it's unfair for God to give them freewill and expect responsibility. They think God shouldn't let them be evil if he doesn't want them to be evil, but that's like a child telling a parent that they shouldn't ever allow any possibility for them to break any rules if they really don't want them to break the rules. Such an argument is crazy because only an irresponsible person would make such a claim. Responsibility is a fact of life, just because people don't like the consequences of their beliefs/actions doesn't mean there is anything wrong with responsibility. Without responsibility one cannot succeed or get rewarded. If there is no possibility of failure no success or reward can ever exist. Hence for Heaven to exist as a possibility then Hell must exist or else that would not be just. It's not like God doesn't help us at all, that would be unfair. God actively tries to guide everybody as much as he can without making the test of life invalid. For you to get the reward for passing the test of life, God can't take it for you or make it impossible for you to fail because then it wouldn't be a true test and there would be no justifiable reason/excuse to give you any rewards at all. God chooses to guide or allows people to go astray based on them and whether they truly want guidance to submit or not. All have an equal opportunity, but God gives extra help only to those who truly want it and appreciate it. God won't go out of the way to guide people who don't sincerely want God's help on the test of life. On a personal and general level God wants every individual to believe correctly but legally God doesn't want 100% believers. Since if everyone passed the test of life then that would be an unfair test that in effect means it's impossible to fail since nobody failed it. Another reason for the existance of false religions is because if 100% of people believed then lots of the benefits of disbelief and disbelievers would not exist. Yes, false religions and disbelievers actually do have a positive effect on the world and God desires this positive effect of disbelief and disbelievers even though God hates disbelief and disbelievers. An example is Satan. God hates Satan but he allows him to exist despite that hatred because he is more pleased with the long-term effects that Satan's actions bring about than God would be if Satan didn't exist at all. The benefit of Satan existing is greater than his harm, the same applies to false religions. Yet some think if they use some religious terms then their doctrine about multiple religions being valid will somehow count. Thus I've met people who say "*If God wanted everyone to believe in just 1 particular religion then why were there 12 tribes of Israel?*" This type of question infuriates me. 1. Israel is the name of the prophet Jacob who had 12 kids, including the prophet Joseph pbuh. They all had the same religious beliefs. They were just called the 12 tribes because those 12 kids of Jacob had lots of descendants to the point that 12 large tribes came about, with each tribe being the progeny of 1 of Jacob's 12 sons. This is why sometimes the members of those 12 tribes are called the "Children of Israel" or the "Nation of Israel". To say that God allows for multiple religions and doesn't want everyone to believe in just 1 religion because there are 12 tribes of Israel instead of 1 is equivalent to saying that *"If God wanted everyone to believe the same religion then in the beginning why did he make 2 people, 1 man and 1 woman? If only 1 religion is true then why were there two genders of people and not 1? And why did Adam and Eve have more than one child if there is only 1 true religion? If there is only 1 way the 1 God wants us to worship him then why does more than 1 person exist?"* Whereas anyone who understands religion will realize how stupid and invalid such questions are. Such questions are so foolish they are dangerous and that's how you know such questions come from Satan and not the idiot themselves. Thus don't call them an idiot because they are really just parroting what Satan tells them to say so you get mad and stop trying to guide the person. Yet some people persist in giving me such responses when I invite them to become Muslims insisting they either join Islam or tell me why they think it's wrong so I can quit because only 1 religion counts and I want us both to go to paradise and can't stand the two of us not being on the same path to paradise. Of course this is not the prophetic way nor the salafi way so I don't suggest most people do this, since it can be dangerous if you enter into debates you are unqualifed to be in, Satan could make you disbelieve simply because your opponent had better arguing abilities and won despite being upon a false religion. Winning a debate is not a valid proof of being right or upon the truth. However I use this tactic occasionally because a disbeliever will usually accept it as reasonable. I must say though the proof should be followed never the stronger arguement, debates are rarely won by those who have the best proofs, arguments are a type of warfare and the winner of an argument is not always the one who was right. I've even been in situations where I've won arguments but knew and later admitted that I was wrong and the other party was right despite me winning the argument. So don't take arguments as proofs in themselves, only accept proofs. Just because you lose an argument doesn't necessarily mean you were wrong, you could be, but losing an argument just means you lost an argument. Anyways I offer such challenges to kafirs because truly they have no good reason to reject Islam and if/when they realize this then many of them try to attack the idea that only 1 religion is true so they can end the conversation without having to change their life or tell me to change mine(which usually they can't effectively try to do). I only give an ultimateum seeming to risk my faith because Allah says to give some ultimateums, such as brining a chapter like the Quran if one thinks it's not from God. So I'm not technically putting my faith on the line because the proofs that would be needed for me to reject Islam are impossible to bring if Allah really chose Islam as his religion and the Quran is true. So putting the faith on the line, isn't really putting it on the line because Allah says it's not really on the line, although if it were false it would be but since it's true then technically it never is. Issuing a challenge God said cannot be met is not really risking one's faith, it's simply obedience. I clarify this so people don't misunderstand "My challenge" in that it's not mine, it's God's. I don't make my own challenge, I just repeat the challenge Allah said to give. The challenged who reply with something like the 12 tribes question is simply their emergency excuse for them to try to maintain the religious status quo and get back to "having fun with their life doing whatever they want to do". However the Quran mentions such people and such excuses in 2:122-141,

يَـٰبَنِىٓ إِسْرَٰٓءِيلَ ٱذْكُرُوا۟ نِعْمَتِىَ ٱلَّتِىٓ أَنْعَمْتُ عَلَيْكُمْ وَأَنِّى فَضَّلْتُكُمْ عَلَى ٱلْعَـٰلَمِينَ (١٢٢) وَٱتَّقُوا۟ يَوْمًا لَّا تَجْزِى نَفْسٌ عَن نَّفْسٍ شَيْـًٔا وَلَا يُقْبَلُ مِنْهَا عَدْلٌ وَلَا تَنفَعُهَا شَفَـٰعَةٌ وَلَا هُمْ يُنصَرُونَ (١٢٣) ۞ وَإِذِ ٱبْتَلَىٰٓ إِبْرَٰهِـۧمَ رَبُّهُۥ بِكَلِمَـٰتٍ فَأَتَمَّهُنَّ ۖ قَالَ إِنِّى جَاعِلُكَ لِلنَّاسِ إِمَامًا ۖ قَالَ وَمِن ذُرِّيَّتِى ۖ قَالَ لَا يَنَالُ عَهْدِى ٱلظَّـٰلِمِينَ (١٢٤) وَإِذْ جَعَلْنَا ٱلْبَيْتَ مَثَابَةً لِّلنَّاسِ وَأَمْنًا وَٱتَّخِذُوا۟ مِن مَّقَامِ إِبْرَٰهِـۧمَ مُصَلًّى ۖ وَعَهِدْنَآ إِلَىٰٓ إِبْرَٰهِـۧمَ وَإِسْمَـٰعِيلَ أَن طَهِّرَا بَيْتِىَ لِلطَّآئِفِينَ وَٱلْعَـٰكِفِينَ وَٱلرُّكَّعِ ٱلسُّجُودِ (١٢٥) وَإِذْ قَالَ إِبْرَٰهِـۧمُ رَبِّ ٱجْعَلْ هَـٰذَا بَلَدًا ءَامِنًا وَٱرْزُقْ أَهْلَهُۥ مِنَ ٱلثَّمَرَٰتِ مَنْ ءَامَنَ مِنْهُم بِٱللَّهِ وَٱلْيَوْمِ ٱلْـَٔاخِرِ ۖ قَالَ وَمَن كَفَرَ فَأُمَتِّعُهُۥ قَلِيلًا ثُمَّ أَضْطَرُّهُۥٓ إِلَىٰ عَذَابِ ٱلنَّارِ ۖ وَبِئْسَ ٱلْمَصِيرُ (١٢٦) وَإِذْ يَرْفَعُ إِبْرَٰهِـۧمُ ٱلْقَوَاعِدَ مِنَ ٱلْبَيْتِ وَإِسْمَـٰعِيلُ رَبَّنَا تَقَبَّلْ مِنَّآ ۖ إِنَّكَ أَنتَ ٱلسَّمِيعُ ٱلْعَلِيمُ (١٢٧) رَبَّنَا وَٱجْعَلْنَا مُسْلِمَيْنِ لَكَ وَمِن ذُرِّيَّتِنَآ أُمَّةً مُّسْلِمَةً لَّكَ وَأَرِنَا مَنَاسِكَنَا وَتُبْ عَلَيْنَآ ۖ إِنَّكَ أَنتَ ٱلتَّوَّابُ ٱلرَّحِيمُ (١٢٨) رَبَّنَا وَٱبْعَثْ فِيهِمْ رَسُولًا مِّنْهُمْ يَتْلُوا۟ عَلَيْهِمْ ءَايَـٰتِكَ وَيُعَلِّمُهُمُ ٱلْكِتَـٰبَ وَٱلْحِكْمَةَ وَيُزَكِّيهِمْ ۚ إِنَّكَ أَنتَ ٱلْعَزِيزُ ٱلْحَكِيمُ (١٢٩) وَمَن يَرْغَبُ عَن مِّلَّةِ إِبْرَٰهِـۧمَ إِلَّا مَن سَفِهَ نَفْسَهُۥ ۚ وَلَقَدِ ٱصْطَفَيْنَـٰهُ فِى ٱلدُّنْيَا ۖ وَإِنَّهُۥ فِى ٱلْـَٔاخِرَةِ لَمِنَ ٱلصَّـٰلِحِينَ (١٣٠) إِذْ قَالَ لَهُۥ رَبُّهُۥٓ أَسْلِمْ ۖ قَالَ أَسْلَمْتُ لِرَبِّ ٱلْعَـٰلَمِينَ (١٣١) وَوَصَّىٰ بِهَآ إِبْرَٰهِـۧمُ بَنِيهِ وَيَعْقُوبُ يَـٰبَنِىَّ إِنَّ ٱللَّهَ ٱصْطَفَىٰ لَكُمُ ٱلدِّينَ فَلَا تَمُوتُنَّ إِلَّا وَأَنتُم مُّسْلِمُونَ (١٣٢) أَمْ كُنتُمْ شُهَدَآءَ إِذْ حَضَرَ يَعْقُوبَ ٱلْمَوْتُ إِذْ قَالَ لِبَنِيهِ مَا تَعْبُدُونَ مِنۢ بَعْدِى قَالُوا۟ نَعْبُدُ إِلَـٰهَكَ وَإِلَـٰهَ ءَابَآئِكَ إِبْرَٰهِـۧمَ وَإِسْمَـٰعِيلَ وَإِسْحَـٰقَ إِلَـٰهًا وَٰحِدًا وَنَحْنُ لَهُۥ مُسْلِمُونَ (١٣٣) تِلْكَ أُمَّةٌ قَدْ خَلَتْ ۖ لَهَا مَا كَسَبَتْ وَلَكُم مَّا كَسَبْتُمْ ۖ وَلَا تُسْـَٔلُونَ عَمَّا كَانُوا۟ يَعْمَلُونَ (١٣٤) وَقَالُوا۟ كُونُوا۟ هُودًا أَوْ نَصَـٰرَىٰ تَهْتَدُوا۟ ۗ قُلْ بَلْ مِلَّةَ إِبْرَٰهِـۧمَ حَنِيفًا ۖ وَمَا كَانَ مِنَ ٱلْمُشْرِكِينَ (١٣٥) قُولُوٓا۟ ءَامَنَّا بِٱللَّهِ وَمَآ أُنزِلَ إِلَيْنَا وَمَآ أُنزِلَ إِلَىٰٓ إِبْرَٰهِـۧمَ وَإِسْمَـٰعِيلَ وَإِسْحَـٰقَ وَيَعْقُوبَ وَٱلْأَسْبَاطِ وَمَآ أُوتِىَ مُوسَىٰ وَعِيسَىٰ وَمَآ أُوتِىَ ٱلنَّبِيُّونَ مِن رَّبِّهِمْ لَا نُفَرِّقُ بَيْنَ أَحَدٍ مِّنْهُمْ وَنَحْنُ لَهُۥ مُسْلِمُونَ (١٣٦) فَإِنْ ءَامَنُوا۟ بِمِثْلِ مَآ ءَامَنتُم بِهِۦ فَقَدِ ٱهْتَدَوا۟ ۖ وَّإِن تَوَلَّوْا۟ فَإِنَّمَا هُمْ فِى شِقَاقٍ ۖ فَسَيَكْفِيكَهُمُ ٱللَّهُ ۚ وَهُوَ ٱلسَّمِيعُ ٱلْعَلِيمُ (١٣٧) صِبْغَةَ ٱللَّهِ ۖ وَمَنْ أَحْسَنُ مِنَ ٱللَّهِ صِبْغَةً ۖ وَنَحْنُ لَهُۥ عَـٰبِدُونَ (١٣٨) قُلْ أَتُحَآجُّونَنَا فِى ٱللَّهِ وَهُوَ رَبُّنَا وَرَبُّكُمْ وَلَنَآ أَعْمَـٰلُنَا وَلَكُمْ أَعْمَـٰلُكُمْ وَنَحْنُ لَهُۥ مُخْلِصُونَ (١٣٩) أَمْ تَقُولُونَ إِنَّ إِبْرَٰهِـۧمَ وَإِسْمَـٰعِيلَ وَإِسْحَـٰقَ وَيَعْقُوبَ وَٱلْأَسْبَاطَ كَانُوا۟ هُودًا أَوْ نَصَـٰرَىٰ ۗ قُلْ ءَأَنتُمْ أَعْلَمُ أَمِ ٱللَّهُ ۗ وَمَنْ أَظْلَمُ مِمَّن كَتَمَ شَهَـٰدَةً عِندَهُۥ مِنَ ٱللَّهِ ۗ وَمَا ٱللَّهُ بِغَـٰفِلٍ عَمَّا تَعْمَلُونَ (١٤٠) تِلْكَ أُمَّةٌ قَدْ خَلَتْ ۖ لَهَا مَا كَسَبَتْ وَلَكُم مَّا كَسَبْتُمْ ۖ وَلَا تُسْـَٔلُونَ عَمَّا كَانُوا۟ يَعْمَلُونَ (١٤١)

"O Children of Israel! Remember My favour wherewith I favoured you and how I preferred you to (all) creatures. And guard (yourselves) against a day when no soul will in aught avail another, nor will compensation be accepted from it, nor will intercession be of use to it; nor will they be helped. And (remember) when his Lord tried Abraham with (His) commands, and he fulfilled them, He said: Lo! I have appointed thee a leader for mankind. (Abraham) said: And of my offspring (will there be leaders)? He said: My covenant includeth not the disbelievers and wrong-doers. And when We made the House (at Mecca) a resort for mankind and sanctuary, (saying): Take as your place of worship the place where

*Abraham stood (to pray). And We imposed a duty upon Abraham and Ishmael, (saying): Purify My house for those who go around and those who meditate therein and those who bow down and prostrate themselves (in worship). And when Abraham prayed: My Lord! Make this city a place of security and bestow upon its people fruits, such of them as believe in Allah and the Last Day, He answered: As for him who disbelieveth, I shall leave him in contentment for a while, then I shall compel him to the doom of Fire - a hapless journey's end! And when Abraham and Ishmael were raising the foundations of the House, (Abraham prayed): Our Lord! Accept from us (this duty). Verily You, only You, art the All-Hearer, the All-Knower. Our Lord! And make us submissive unto Thee and of our offspring a nation submissive unto Thee, and show us our ways of worship, and relent toward us. Truly You are the one who accepts repentance the most merciful. Our Lord! And raise up in their midst a messenger from among them (the people of Mecca, of the offspring of Ishmael) who shall recite unto them Your Verses and instruct them in the Book (this Qur'ân) and Al-Hikmah (full knowledge of the Islâmic laws and jurisprudence or wisdom or Prophethood), and purify them. Verily! You are the All-Mighty, the All-Wise." <u>And who turns away from the religion of Abraham (Islâmic Monotheism) except him who befools himself?</u> Truly, We chose him in this world and verily, in the Hereafter he will be among the righteous. When his Lord said to him, "Submit (be a Muslim)!" He said, "I have submitted myself (as a Muslim) to the Lord of the 'Alamîn (mankind, jinn and all that exists)." And this (submission to Allâh, Islâm) was enjoined by Abraham upon his sons and by Jacob, (saying), "O my sons! Allâh has chosen for you the true religion, then die not except in the Faith of Islâm." <u>Or were you witnesses when death approached Jacob? When he said unto his sons, "What will you worship after me?" They said, "We shall worship your Ilâh (God - Allâh), the Ilâh (God) of your fathers, Abraham, Ishmael, Isaac, One Ilâh (God), and to Him we submit (in Islâm)."</u> Those are a people who have passed away. They shall receive the reward of what they earned and you of what you earn. And you will not be asked of what they used to do. And they say, "Be Jews or Christians, then you will be guided." Say (to them), "Nay, <u>**(We follow) only the religion of Ibrâhim (Abraham), Hanifa** [Islâmic Monotheism, i.e. to worship none but Allâh (Alone)], and he was not of Al-Mushrikûn (those who worshipped others along with Allâh)."</u> Say, <u>"We believe in Allâh and that which has been sent down to us and that which has been sent down to Abraham, Ishmael, Isaac, Jacob, and to Al-Asbât [the offspring twelve sons of Jacob], and that which has been given to Mûsa (Moses) and Isâ (Jesus), and that which has been given to the Prophets from their Lord. We make no distinction between any of them, and to Him we have submitted (in Islâm)."</u> So if they believe in the like of that which you believe, then they are rightly guided, but if they turn away, then they are only in opposition. So Allâh will suffice for you against them. And He is the All-Hearer, the All-Knower. [Our Sibghah (religion) is] the Sibghah (Religion) of Allâh (Islâm) and which Sibghah (religion) can be better than Allâh's? And we are His worshippers. Say "**Dispute you with us about Allâh while He is our Lord and your Lord? And we are to be rewarded for our deeds and you for your deeds. And we are sincere to Him [in worship and obedience (we worship Him Alone and none else, and we obey His Orders).]**" Or say you that Abraham, Ishmael, Isaac, Jacob and Al-Asbât [the offspring twelve sons of Jacob] were Jews or Christians? Say, "Do you know better or does Allâh (know better that they all were Muslims)? **And <u>who is more unjust than he who conceals the testimony he has from Allâh?</u>** And Allâh is not unaware of what you do." Those are a people who have passed away. They shall receive the reward of what they earned, and you of what you earn. And you will not be asked of what they used to do."*

I once read a paper concerning this very topic of why do disbelievers exist if there is only 1 true religion and God wants everyone to follow it. This paper had points listing some benefits of the existance of non-Muslims; aka "kuffar". To conclude I will include some points they made:

- By the existence of the Kuffar it shows Allah has total control and cannot be harmed in the least.
- By the existence of the Kuffar we learn that Allah does not force anyone to believe or obey him.
- By the existence of the Kuffar we are given the opportunity to get rewarded for doing Dawah.
- By the existence of the Kuffar we are given a living example of how NOT to live life.
- By the existence of the Kuffar we learn to appreciate the special gift Allah has given us in Islam.
- By the existence of the Kuffar we know that Allah loves us more than he does others and that instead of being friends with everyone Allah has given us an honor to be his friend when we could have been cursed as one of Allah's enemies.
- By the existence of the Kuffar we have an opportunity to do Jihad and achieve martyrdom.
- By the existence of the Kuffar we learn that this worldly life doesn't matter to Allah at all because if Allah valued this world as much as the wing of a mosquito a kaffir wouldn't even get a drop of water to drink. Since the Kuffar get so much bounty from Allah despite their ingratitude and evilness it shows that this world is of nearly zero value.
- By the existence of the Kuffar we benefit from the lessons of the numerous prophets Allah sent to warn the Kuffar.
- By the existence of the Kuffar many verses of the Quran were revealed saying what they say, do and think and instructing us what to say to, do to and think of them. For surah fatiha would not be the same without the final verses which we say 17 times a day, asking Allah not to let us be one of those whom he is angry with or has led astray.
- By the existence of the Kuffar paradise is much more enjoyable because not only will the Muslims in paradise rejoice in their domain, but they will be rejoice they aren't in the hellfire with the Kuffar and Munafiqeen.
- By the existance of the Kuffar the believers benefit in ways which they would not be able to had everyone been a believer.

I'd also add that if there were no disbelievers then I may not have been able to write what I wrote in this book. Therefore rather than use the existance of disbelievers as a means of doubt, or an excuse to reject the one true religion of Islam, we should thank and praise God for having given us all these lessons, blessings and opportunities for reward as a result of his wise creation of the accursed disbelievers. While at the same time avoiding complacency or arrogance and striving to be true Muslims protected from all forms of Kufr, Shirk, Bida, Hypocrisy and Sins that are predominant in all of the unislamic societies, the unislamic households and the unislamic hearts. Until we die in such a protected state of guidance and enter paradise to live there forever Godwilling.

LAST WORDS

      The Quran is the direct message from your Creator which guides you to the truth and paradise, which remains in the same form as revealed to God's prophet Muhammad pbuh in the first person. It is the final revelation that completes and perfects mankind's religion. I have researched every major religion practiced in the world today and many of the minor religions and found Islam to be the only true religion. But do not take my word for it, I simply ask you to do your own genuine research about Islam yourself, with an open mind. You have nothing to lose, absolutely nothing. If Islam is false then you will be able to tell and will be more confident in whatever religion you have right now, or at least one step closer to the truth whatever it is. If Islam is true then you will have the opportunity to obtain eternal bliss in the afterlife with inner peace and purpose in this life. At the minimum you would have a better understanding of nearly 2 billion people on the planet and be less likely to believe a lie when it is told to you. What if Muhammad pbuh really is the final messenger of our Creator? Would you follow him and the rest of the prophets to paradise? Or would you reject it even if it was proven without a doubt to be the truth to you? What if the Quran is a direct message from your Creator and after me informing you about this fact you scoff at it and never bother to look into it, how do you think your Creator will treat you on the Day of judgment if you die in that condition? On that day you won't be able to say you didn't have time, or that no one ever warned you. You have time now. If you had time to read this book you definitely have time to read a translation of the meanings of the Quran more than once. Type "*Free Quran*" into any internet search engine and you can get a free Quran or a translation or the Arabic with a translation in electronic, audio or physical form. People often ask me the question "*Why did you become a Muslim?*" it's easy to answer. I became a Muslim because Islam is the only true religion that is monotheistic and hasn't become corrupted; all the previous prophets before Muhammad pbuh such as Adam, Noah, Abraham, Moses and Jesus pbut were all Muslims and taught Islam, so I'm just following their wonderful example. With full confidence I can say that the religion of Islam is perfect. But Muslims are not. Muslim imperfections tend to make people think our religion is imperfect when we slip up and act contrary to what Islam teaches. Remember human Muslims are humans, we're not angels. You shouldn't base your opinion of Islam on the actions of Muslims, or the allegations of non-Muslims. Instead study Islam itself on your own from its own sources. Muslims are like fireflys who shine with the God-given light of Islam once in a while to help other creatures see the way in the darkness, while Satan is the bug zapper constantly and loudly giving off deadly artificial light that destroys. We can choose which kind of guidance we follow and the results will be different. Whereas whenever Muslims ask me when I became a Muslim, I reply "I don't know, I'm still trying." If they ask how long I've been Muslim I reply, "It's about how you die not how long you try." If they repeatedly try to learn a date I say "Allah knows best. It's about finishing the race to paradise, the details of how or when I started don't matter unless I finish." If they still persist asking "When did you first say the shahada?", or if they are non-Muslims asking me, I simply say "*Not soon enough.*" The more important question that should be asked is "*When will you become a Muslim?*" For "Muslims" I tell them "*I don't care when you became Muslim, my question is when are you going to start practicing Islam?*" In the end it's your choice to make, but choices have consequences and since this is a big choice it has big consequences with eternal results. Everyone who goes to hell chooses to, by choosing to reject the truth and the prophet(s) that were sent to them. Whether that's by choosing to disbelieve in the prophetic religion or by choosing not to practice it makes no difference. We all get the choice to follow the path of the prophets or the path of Satan. I hope you make the right choice, but on the day you are raised and judged based on the choice you made please don't say that no one ever conveyed the message of Islam to you. Today you have been given the choice to accept or reject Islam, you could delay making that decision, but you have been given the choice so there is no way you can say you had no chance. The biggest fools in the world aside from those who disbelieve are those who delay believing in Islam and becoming a Muslim. Some people might have even chosen not to finish reading this book and put it away, as soon as they read something they disliked or disagreed with. Maybe some people will just skip to the back and only read this chapter or the last page and still reject it as they do to the Quran without reading it all. That's their choice, Allah does not force mankind to worship him and go to paradise. You were destined to read this book, it is no random coincidence or accident. I hope Allah will forgive me for all the mistakes I make and reward me for my efforts in a good way. While as much as I may and should fret over the things I've written in this book, of which God will question me about the intentions and the effects of each letter, there is another book that is even more dangerous that can displease God and doom one for eternity. That book is your book of deeds. I stress over this book and the mistakes therein but your book of deeds is of a far greater length with many more mistakes. Make sure that you correct your book of deeds before you die and be very careful what you write with the short time that is left of your lifetime of intentions/deeds. Your afterlife depends on it. The time for editing is almost done and God will publish your book of deeds for all to see God publicly critique. I end this book with the shahada in Arabic, English transliteration and English. May you and I also end our lives with the shahada as well, and have it count; God-willing.

أشهد أن لا إله إلاَّ الله و أشهد أن محمد رسول الله

ASH-HADU ANLA ELAHA ILLA-ALLAH, WA ASH-HADU ANNA MOHAMMADAN RASUL-ALLAH

I bear witness that there is nothing worthy of worship but Allah, and I bear witness that Muhammad is the messenger of Allah.

Will you?

www.ingramcontent.com/pod-product-compliance
Lightning Source LLC
Chambersburg PA
CBHW060406010526
44107CB00005B/605